Financial Management

A Strategic Perspective

Financial Management

A Strategic Perspective

Nikhil Chandra Shil
Bhagaban Das

ATLANTIC
PUBLISHERS & DISTRIBUTORS (P) LTD

ATLANTIC
PUBLISHERS & DISTRIBUTORS (P) LTD

7/22, Ansari Road, Darya Ganj, New Delhi
Tel.: +91-11-4077 5252, 2327 3880
E-mail: orders@atlanticbooks.com
Web: www.atlanticbooks.com

Published by Atlantic Publishers & Distributors (P) Ltd 2024

Previously Published by SAGE Publications in 2017

Printed & bound in India by Atlantic Print Services

Brief Contents

Detailed Contents

List of Tables

List of Figures

List of Exhibits

Preface

In the last few decades, countries around the world have become more financially integrated, driven by the potential benefits of financial globalization. One of the main benefits of financial globalization is the development of the financial sector. Today's financial world is changing dramatically, and this is reflected in the regional financial management practices in a rapid evolutionary curve conceptualized by numerous environmental influences; first, a rapidly increasing organizational scale, geographical scope of operations and business diversity; second, an emergence of financial markets with opportunities to access a wider set of innovative financing options with the need of increased reporting and transparency; third, an increased merger and buyout activities capitalized by private equity and a need to enhance corporate valuations and, finally, an increasingly globalized competitive business environment with associated risks and uncertainties.

In order to improve firms' ability in the above context, finance professionals need to make a wise linkage between financial policy and corporate strategies at different levels. Complexity in financial analysis along with the volatile global financial market adds extra momentum to this bridging process. Mere knowledge on financial jargons will not provide any competitive edge at this level. The integration of business strategy and policy with financial management has brought a whole new dimension in business practices, which mandates the financial criterion for all management decision-making. Considering this in mind, this book makes a proper blend of financial management issues with that of corporate strategies to attain the long-run vision of the business by taking right financial decisions. It covers the topics starting from the strategy formulation till strategy implementation and attainment.

The book has been divided into four parts, consisting of 20 chapters. Part A starts with a simple introduction of strategic financial management with its peripheral role in strategic cost and value based management. Part B covers some matured topics of financial management, like capital budgeting and investing decisions, risk in capital budgeting, capital structure theory and dividend policy. Part C puts special emphasis on corporate restructuring through different management and financial avenues. It covers different forms of corporate expansion through financial restructuring in the form of merger, acquisitions, takeovers, joint ventures, demerger, leveraged buyouts, employee stock ownership plans and so on within regulatory framework as applicable to India. Finally, the book ends up with some advanced topics of strategic finance, like financial engineering, options pricing, forwards and futures, swaps and formation of stock market index in Part D. In appropriate cases, some real-life case studies have been incorporated to give the learners a critical look on the application of theories discussed in the book, which make the book special of its kind. Another specialty of the book is that it incorporates three additional chapters titled Corporate Sickness (Chapter 21), Corporate Restructuring: A Strategic Perspective (Chapter 22) and Benchmarking (Chapter 23) with numerous case studies and solutions to some chapter-end exercises in the companion website of the book (https://study.sagepub.in/shil_FMSP) for easy and free downloads, which extends the scope of the book further.

The book is useful for the students of BBA, MBA, PGDBM, MCom, CA, cost and management accountancy (CMA), Master of Finance and Control (MFC) and other management courses of all universities across India and abroad. The book adapts some mathematical problems from different professional examinations that will give the students some professional insight into the area of strategic finance. Throughout this book, students can explore a range of issues relating to organizational strategic direction and fit internal and external analyses. They can also examine various financial management tools in light of the strategic choices and strategic issues that impact upon organizations' success. Besides students, experts in the corporate sector, like chief executive officers (CEOs), chief financial officers (CFOs), corporate strategists and other senior executives, investment analysts and professors will also find the book quite useful.

Nikhil Chandra Shil
Bhagaban Das

Acknowledgements

Throughout the process of writing this book, many individuals from the community have extended their support within their capacities. A thousand miles' journey starts with a single step. Similarly, this book is the outcome of thousands of peoples' efforts; we two simply codified it. My family, friends, colleagues and, most importantly, my students are my main inspiration. My wife, Shuvra, daughter Archita and son Durgo always provide full support to my works. Archita and Durgo feel proud to find their father as a university professor. Although they are very tender in age, but they hold their temptation to disturb me while they come to know that I am busy with academic writing. I really deprived them to steal time from their right. On the other hand, my life partner also extends her full support managing all household chores without taking much time from me. I would like to dedicate my effort to all three of them. My friends and colleagues also take care of my work and allow me to manage time by freeing me from different social gathering. I am really thankful to them. My students' community always encourage me to involve in such initiative, and they always acknowledge my contribution whenever any opportunity comes. I must not forget to express my sincere gratitude to my brotherly Dr Das who is my mentor. I am blessed with his knowledge and wisdom, which purifies me in my profession. I believe he is a gift of God to me. He has taken the initiative to write the book, and I have only supported this noble cause. I feel honoured to have a relation with him and expect to have it forever.

Nikhil Chandra Shil

In line with the acknowledgement of Nikhil above, I would like to thank my wife, Minali, for standing beside me throughout my career and writing this book. She has been my inspiration and motivation for continuing to improve my knowledge and move my career forward. She is my rock, and I dedicate this book to her. I also thank my younger daughter Flora for always making me smile, bearing the entire domestic burden. Further, I would like to mention the name of my elder wonderful daughter Twinkle, son Sujit and new addition Neel for understanding on those weekend mornings when I was writing this book instead of chatting with them. I hope that one day they can read this book and understand why I spent so much time in front of my computer. I would like to thank my mother, Anita Devi, for allowing me to follow my ambitions throughout my childhood. My family, including my in-laws, has always supported me throughout my career and authoring this book, and I really appreciate it. I look forward to discussing this book with my family at future gatherings as I am sure they will all read it soon. My co-workers, Sathya, Artaa, Debadutta, Biswajit and others, deserve special thanks for their encouragement and support with the manuscript preparation. I would really like to thank Nikhil for providing me with the opportunity to become the co-author for this book. I appreciate that he believed in me to provide the leadership and knowledge to make this book a reality. Nikhil is a great a scholar; without him, this book may not have been written. Nikhil and I collaborated to write this book. In the end, I believe that he has provided the best of his ability and expertise in authoring this book. I thank him for devoting his time and effort towards this book; I think that it will be a great asset to the community! Thanks for everything. I look forward to writing the second edition soon! We owe a huge thanks to Indrani Dutta and Amit Kumar for providing excellent support and advice.

Bhagaban Das

About the Authors

Nikhil Chandra Shil is working as a Professor of Accounting in the Department of Business Administration of East West University, Dhaka, Bangladesh. He holds BBA and MBA degrees with concentration in Accounting and Information Systems from the University of Dhaka. He has been awarded the degree of Doctor of Philosophy in management accounting practices from the University of Dhaka. He is a fellow member (FCMA) of the Institute of Cost and Management Accountants of Bangladesh. He is also an associate member of the Chartered Institute of Management Accountants (CIMA) UK, a Chartered Global Management Accountant (CGMA) and a member (CPFA) of Chartered Institute of Public Finance and Accountancy (CIPFA) UK. He has vast experience of working in corporates, professional bodies and most importantly in universities at various capacities. In his research career, he published more than 100 research papers in reputed international and local journals. He has also authored several textbooks, research monographs, working papers, conference papers, book chapters and edited books. He serves as reviewers and editorial board members of a few reputed journals. His research area covers management accounting practices, management control, emerging issues in accounting, public finance management, and behavioral research in accounting.

Bhagaban Das is Former Professor and Head in PG Department of Business Management in Fakir Mohan University, Balasore, a state university established by the Government of Odisha. A national scholarship awardee throughout his career, Professor Das stood second in MCom Examination in Utkal University (1982). As a luminous teacher, he has more than three decades of teaching experience both at undergraduate and postgraduate levels. In addition to authoring 21 books, which are widely appreciated by readers, he has published more than 50 research papers both in national and international journals. Fifteen scholars have already been awarded PhD under his guidance, and 8 more are still working at present for the purpose. He is as an active member of the Indian Accounting Association, the Indian Commerce Association as well as the All Odisha Commerce Association. His current areas of interest include environmental accounting and financial literacy. Currently, he is the director of Distance and Continuing Education and a member of the syndicate.

Part A

Introduction

Chapter 1

Introduction

Chapter Objectives

On completion of this chapter, you will be able to understand:

- Strategy: The concept and nature
- Importance of strategy and strategic management
- Financial planning in business's development
- Interface between financial strategy and strategic management
- Concept and components of financial strategy
- Role of financial strategy in organizations
- The role of strategic financial management
- Definition of strategic financial management
- Characteristics of strategic financial management
- Scope of strategic financial management
- Functions of strategic financial management
- Problems in strategic financial management
- Causes of the problems in strategic financial management

The Ministry of Defence is in a better position now than it was in 2010 to manage its future spending plans effectively. It has taken substantial steps to lay the foundations for future stability. There are, however, some significant risks that the Department must manage, including delivering the savings already removed from budget allocations. Good financial management alone will not achieve all the necessary changes. This will also be dependent on changing the behavior necessary for the system to work, and improving the skills within DE&S and DIO. As with any long-term strategy, it is inevitable the Department will face challenges sustaining progress.

Source: Amyas Morse, Head of the National Audit Office, 17 July 2015.[1]

1.1 Introduction

Nowadays, no enterprise can achieve its goals without planning and having a strategy. Due to liberalization and globalization, there has been an unprecedented growth of various industries, leading to cut-throat competition. The surge in the competitiveness within

[1] https://www.nao.org.uk/report/strategic-financial-management-in-the-ministry-of-defence/

the industries has made it imperative for the enterprises to keep themselves abreast of the emerging strategies. To maintain competitive strength, a determined strategy is needed and, in between, financial strategy plays an important and determining role. However, the role and importance of strategy in today's turbulent world is no secret and the role of financial strategies due to financial status and financial management of the company has doubled the importance. Besides, the demanding dynamic environment has called for the top managers, especially finance managers, to be proactive and constantly evolving for a perfect blending of financial management techniques with strategic management concepts. In this context, strategic financial management, which is the integration of strategic management and business policy with financial management, has brought a whole new dimension in business practices.

The prefix 'strategic', to financial management, means that decisions to accept or reject proposals have to be based on strategic factors. Capital investment decisions are typical examples of these decisions. An investment proposal may add value to the business based on the application of the discounted cash flow techniques which takes into account only the quantifiable cash flows. However, the decision might be to reject the proposal if some highly uncertain but very beneficial inputs are not considered. On the other hand, a proposal might be accepted on strategic bases even if, based on quantifiable cash flows alone, it subtracts value from the business.

In order to understand what 'strategic financial management' is about, it is necessary to know the meaning of the word 'strategy'.

1.2 Strategy: The Concept and Nature

The word 'strategy' is derived from the Greek word *strategtia*, which was used first around 400 BC. This connotes the art and science of directing military forces. In business parlance, there is no definite meaning assigned to strategy. A few definitions stated below may clarify the concept of corporate strategy.

According to Kenneth Andrews (1955), 'The pattern of objectives, purpose, goals and the major policies and plans for achieving these goals stated in such a way so as to define what business the company is in or is to be and the kind of company it is or is to be'.

This definition refers to the business definition.

Igor Ansoff (1965) explained the concept of strategy as 'the common thread among the organizations, activities and product markets that defines the essential nature of business that the organization was or planned to be in future'.

The definition stressed on the commonality of approach that exists in diverse organizational activities.

Henry Mintzberg (1987) explains that 'strategies are not always the outcome of rational planning. ... a pattern in a stream of decisions and actions'.

The definition makes a distinction between intended strategies and emergent strategies.

According to Ansoff (1984), 'Basically a strategy is a set of decision-making rules for the guidance of organizational behavior'.

This definition has changed drastically since what Ansoff had said earlier in 1965.

William Glueck (1976) defines the term strategy as 'the unified, comprehensive and integrated plan that relates the strategic advantage of the firm to the challenges of the environment and is designed to ensure that basic objectives of the enterprise are achieved through implementation process'.

The definition lays stress on the following:

- It is a unified, comprehensive and integrated plan.
- Challenges of the environment are seen in the context of strategic advantage.
- Strategy ensures achievement of basic objectives through proper implementation process.

The term 'strategy' has been defined in a variety of ways, but almost always with a common theme, that of a deliberate conscious set of guidelines that determines decisions into the future. In game theory, strategy represents the set of rules that is to govern the moves of the players. In military theory, strategy is 'the utilization during both peace and war, of all of the nation's forces, through large-scale, long-range planning and development, to ensure security and victory'. And in management theory, the *Chandler* definition is typical: '...the determination of the basic long-term goals and objectives of an enterprise and the adoption of courses of action and the allocation of resources necessary for carrying out these goals'.

In common terminology, a strategy is a 'plan' (Mintzberg 1978).

From the definitions discussed above, we may identify the following elements of strategy:

1. It is a plan or course of action or a set of decision rules.
2. It is derived from its policies, objectives and goals.
3. It is related to pursue those activities that move an organization from its current position to a desired future state.
4. It is concerned with the requisite resources to implement a plan.

The term 'corporate strategy' is gaining importance in the era of privatization, globalization and liberalization. A few aspects regarding the nature of strategy are as follows:

1. Corporate strategy is related mostly to external environment.
2. Corporate strategy is being formulated at the higher level of management. At the operational level, operational strategies are also formulated.
3. Corporate strategy integrates three distinct and closely related activities in strategy making. The activities are strategic planning, strategic implementation and strategic evaluation and control.
4. Corporate strategy is related to long term.
5. It requires systems and norms for its efficient adoption in any organization.
6. It provides an overall framework for guiding enterprise thinking and action.
7. It is concerned with a unified direction and efficient allocation of organizational resources.
8. Corporate strategy provides an integrated approach for the organization and aids in meeting the challenges posed by environment.

1.3 Importance of Strategy and Strategic Management

In the present-day competitive environment, organizations are constantly facing turbulent situation and environmental threats are endangering their existence and survival from every direction (Figure 1.1). Organizations must understand their current position and analyse their strengths and weaknesses exactly and avail environmental opportunity by focusing on strengths and prepare themselves to confront the threats. Corporate strategy has an important role to play in coping with environment. It has great utility in planning, coordination, control and direction. Thus, it is said that no business organization can dream of survival without formulating appropriate corporate strategy.

The following areas clearly show the importance of corporate strategy:

1. Corporate strategy rationalizes allocation of scarce resources.
2. Corporate strategy motivates employees to shape their work in the context of shared corporate goals.
3. Strategy assists management to meet unanticipated future changes.

Figure 1.1 Strategy

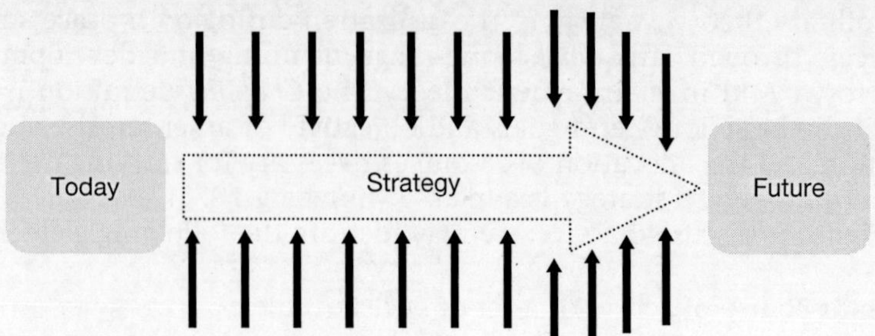

Source: Mintzberg and Waters (1985: 258).

4. Organizational effectiveness is ensured through implementing and evaluating the strategy.
5. Corporate strategy is a powerful tool to management to deal with the future which is uncertain and hazy in all respects.
6. Corporate strategy improves the capability of management in coping with the volatile external environmental forces.
7. Corporate strategy encourages the management to choose the best course of action to realize the objectives.
8. Strategy planning system provides an objective basis for measuring performance.

Now, the question 'Why should an organization engage in strategic management?' must be answered by looking at the relationship between strategic management and performance. Many researchers have been of the opinion that formalized strategic management results in superior performance by organizations. Each of these studies was able to provide convincing evidence of the profitability of strategy formulation and implementation. The formalized strategic management process makes a difference in the recorded measurements of profits, sales and return on assets. Organizations that adopt a strategic management approach can expect that the new system will lead to improved financial performance. Regardless of the profitability of strategic management, several behavioural effects can be expected to improve the welfare of the firm. Again, strategic management is needed to cope with and manage uncertainty in decision making.

1.4 Financial Planning in Business Development

In the 21st century business landscape in a complex competitive situation and influenced by multiple factors, such as globalization, technological development and diffusion of new technologies have been growing rapidly. In the framework of this new perspective, the company is to survive and thrive to be different from their previous work. In particular, companies should be looking for new sources of competitive advantage and new forms of competition to operate, which requires a clear understanding of the nature and dynamics of competition. One of the most important factors and tool in helping companies to develop and competition in business is having managed funds and sources management that requires empowered financial managers to control the fund inflows and outflows. All these are nothing but require strategic financial planning.

Financial planning is the backbone of the business planning. It helps in defining the feasible area of operation for all types of activities and thereby defines the overall planning framework. Outcomes of the financial planning are the financial objectives, financial decision making and financial measures for the evaluation of the corporate performance.

Profit Maximization vs. Wealth Maximization: Profit may be an important consideration for businesses but not its maximization because profit maximization as a financial objective suffers from multiple limitations. Wealth maximization, on the other hand, is measured in terms of its net present value (NPV) to take care of both risk and time factors. Wealth ensures financial strength of the firm, long-term solvency and viability. It can be used as a decision criterion in a precisely defined manner and can reflect the business efficiency without any scope for ambiguity.

Cash Flow: It deals with the movement of cash and, as a matter of conventions, refers to surplus of internally generated funds over expenditures.

Credit Position: It describes its strength in mobilizing borrowed money. In case the internal generation of cash position is weak, the firm may exploit its strong credit position to go ahead in the expansion of its activities.

Liquidity Position of the Business: It describes the extent of idle working capital. It measures the ability of the firm in handling unforeseen contingencies.

1.5 Interface Between Financial Planning and Strategic Management

The interface of strategic management and financial policy will be clearly understood if we appreciate the fact that the starting point of an organization is money and the end point of that organization is also money. No organization can run an existing business and promote a new expansion project without a suitable internally mobilized financial base or both internally and externally mobilized financial base.

Financing Decisions: Sources of finance and capital structure are the most important dimensions of a strategic plan. The generation of funds may arise out of ownership capital and/or borrowed capital. A company may issue equity shares and/or preference shares for mobilizing ownership capital. Along with the mobilization of funds, policymakers should decide on the capital structure to indicate the desired mix of equity capital and debt capital. There are some norms for debt equity ratio. However, this ratio in its ideal form varies from industry to industry. It also depends on the planning mode of the organization under study.

Investment and Fund Allocation Decisions: Another important dimension of strategic management and financial policy interface is the investment and fund allocation decisions. A planner has to frame policies for regulating investments in fixed assets and for restraining of current assets. Investment proposals mooted by different business units may be addition of a new product, increasing the level of operation of an existing product and cost reduction and efficient utilization of resources through a new approach and/or closer monitoring of the different critical activities.

Dividend Decisions: Dividend policy is yet another area for making financial policy decisions affecting the strategic performance of the company. A close interface is needed to frame the policy to be beneficial to all. A dividend policy decision deals with the extent of earnings to be distributed as dividend and the extent of earnings to be retained for the future expansion scheme of the firm.

It may be noted from the above discussions that the financial policy of a company cannot be worked out in isolation from other functional policies. It has a wider appeal and closer link with the overall organizational performance and direction of growth. These policies are related to external awareness about the firm, especially the awareness of the investors about the firm, in respect of its internal performance. There is always a process of evaluation active in the minds of the current and future stakeholders of the company. As a result, the preference and patronage for the company depends significantly on the financial policy framework. And, hence, attention of the corporate planners must be drawn while framing financial policies not at a later stage but during the stage of corporate planning itself.

1.6 Financial Strategy: The Concept and Components

A financial strategy is integral to an organization's strategic plan. It sets out how the organization plans to finance its overall operations to meet its objectives now and in the future. A financial strategy summarizes targets, and the actions to be taken over a three- to five-year period to achieve the targets. It also clearly states key policies which will guide those actions. The following few definitions suggest the structure and contents for a financial strategy.

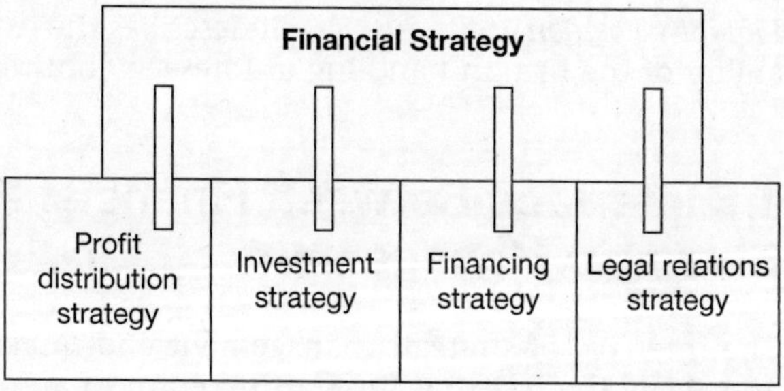

Financial strategy can broadly be defined as 'an interdisciplinary methodology to more efficiently allocate scarce resources within a firm to better or more economically satisfy customer preferences over time'. (Calandro and Flynn 2007)

Financial strategy, as a functional strategy, is subject to overall corporate strategy. Therefore, financial strategy includes profit distribution strategy, investment strategy, financing strategy and legal relations strategy. (Pavlicek, 2009)

A Financial Strategy shows how to finance and invest company's resources in order to achieve the company's goals, that is shareholder wealth increase. The period of a financial strategy is equal to the period of a company overall plan. (Thompson, 2003)

A financial strategy has four components as follows:

Start-up Costs: A new business venture, even those started by existing companies, has start-up costs. An existing manufacturer looking to release a new line of product has costs that may include new fabricating equipment, new packaging and a marketing plan. Start-up costs are to be included in financial strategy.

Competitive Analysis: Competition affects how we make money and how we spend money. The products and marketing activities of our competition should be included in the financial strategy. An analysis of how the competition will affect revenue needs to be included in financial planning.

Ongoing Costs: These include labour, materials, equipment maintenance, shipping and facilities costs, such as lease and utilities. Ongoing cost projections should also be included as part of the financial strategy.

Revenue: In order to create an effective financial strategy, there is a need to forecast revenue over the length of the project. A comprehensive revenue forecast is necessary when determining how much will be available to pay for ongoing costs, and how much will remain as profit.

1.7 Role of Financial Strategy in Organizations

Today, most organizations use a set of related strategies instead of adopting a comprehensive strategy that each are designed for a certain level in the organization and called 'chain strategy' or 'strategy hierarchy' (Figure 1.2). Hierarchies of strategies include: (a) corporate strategy, (b) business strategy and (c) functional strategy (such as financial strategy, marketing strategy, manufacturing and operations strategy, human resources (HR) strategy, research and development (R&D) strategy, information systems strategy). This hierarchy or chain strategy is a set of interrelated strategies that complement and support each other like a puzzle. Therefore, task strategy supports the business strategy, and this also supports the corporate strategy.

Each functional strategy, in addition to response to environmental conditions as well as strengths and competitive competences of the business unit and the level of organization as a whole, should be matched with strategies of other levels. Thus, in the strategic management

Figure 1.2 Relationship Between Financial Strategy with Corporate and Other Strategies

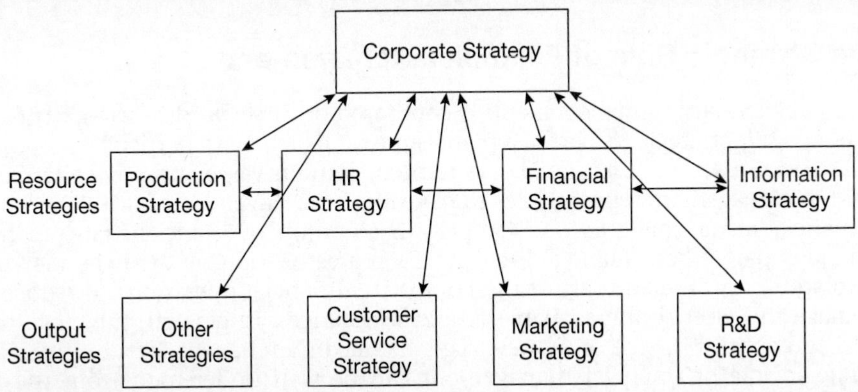

Source: Baghaei and Mousavi (2009: 132).

Figure 1.3 Interaction of Different Types of Strategy in an Organization

Source: Baghaei and Mousavi (2009: 133).

literature, there is great emphasis on coordinating strategies at different levels (Figure 1.3) and coordination of those levels to changing external environment.

Financial strategy is the most basic strategy that is considered by managers of leading companies, and therefore the need for interaction of this strategy with other strategies in organization is very important (Baghaei and Mousavi 2009: 133).

1.8 Strategic Financial Management

1.8.1 The Strategic Role of Financial Management

The term 'strategic financial management' is composed of three words: strategic, financial and management. While strategic, as part of a plan, is meant to achieve a particular purpose, finance relates to financial resources that are always limited, contain value and have alternative usage and, lastly, the management aspect relates to planning, sourcing, allocating and controlling. So, strategic financial management involves employing a number of financial strategies designed to operate in a company's best financial interests. Each area of strategic financial management is designed to address a different part of the company's financial operations to reduce financial risks and make the most of the available financial resources. In general, this practice seeks to understand and control the use of money to get its maximum benefit for a business.

The strategic role of financial management can be well understood from the following discussion.

Financial management plays a strategic role in the survival and development of any business. Managing finances is necessary to increase profits, manage debt, pay overhead and secure investments. These components are used to steer a company towards growth and achieve its goal of earning as much money as possible for the owners, investors and employees.

Increase Profits: Financial management entails looking at profit margins with regard to a company's line of products and looking to maximize them. There are two ways for a company to increase a product's profitability: either increase the price of the finished goods or decrease its cost of manufacturing. A company that has a strategic plan with regard to finances will be able to determine if cutting costs is a viable option. If not, the company needs to raise the price in order to become more profitable.

Manage Debt: Debt management is a critical part of finances. The amount of money a company owes plays a vital role in being able to obtain loans for improvements. It is also used in the valuation of stock for publicly traded companies. Businesses that owe great sums of money have to display the ability to pay off their debts in order to attract investors. Being able to manage debt effectively is an important business strategy for companies that want to become industry leaders.

Pay Overhead: An organization needs to be able to manage its finances in order to pay employees and utilities. This basic fundamental of financial management is used to keep a business moving forward and continue production or delivery of service. Paying salary is a primary objective for any company. Employment is a legal contract wherein employees are compensated for their work. Beyond salary, businesses have other expenses that need to be taken care of. Raw material suppliers and transportation companies expect to be paid in a timely fashion.

Secure Investments: Companies need to evolve and make improvements over time. With strategic financial planning, they can secure investments that will help future business. Property is generally a solid investment for businesses, as it allows for potential expansion of existing structures or the construction of new facilities. Technology is another area of investment that requires capital. Discovering more efficient methods and developing better products help make a company more competitive in an economic environment. Corporate investments are also made by spending money to recruit talented employees.

1.8.2 Definition of Strategic Financial Management

Many academicians and Internet resources have defined this contemporary discipline, strategic financial management, as follows:

> Strategic financial management refers to study of finance with a long-term view considering the strategic goals of the enterprise. Financial management is nowadays increasingly referred to as 'Strategic Financial Management' so as to give it an increased frame of reference.[2]
>
> Strategic financial management is managing an organization's financial resources so as to achieve its business objectives and maximize its value.[3]

[2] https://en.wikipedia.org/wiki/Strategic_financial_management
[3] http://www.investopedia.com/terms/s/strategic-financial-management.asp

> Strategic financial management consists of 'financial strategies which are goals, patterns or alternatives designed to improve and optimize financial management in order to achieve corporate results'. (Liu 2010)
>
> Strategic Financial Management refers to both, the financial implications or aspects of various business strategies, and the strategic management of finances. (Jakhotiya 2001)
>
> Strategic financial management is 'the application to strategic decisions of financial techniques in order to help achieve the objectives of the decision makers'.[4]
>
> Strategic financial management is both, financial implications or aspects of various business strategies, and strategic management of finance. (Varghese 2011)

Thus, strategic financial management can be defined as the application of financial techniques to strategic decisions in order to achieve the decision-makers' objectives. It is an approach to management that applies financial techniques to strategic decision making.

1.8.3 Characteristics of Strategic Financial Management

Strategic financial management as a contemporary discipline has incorporated the practices, methodologies and perspectives of strategic management and financial management. So, the salient features and characteristics contain the contributions of both these fields of study to promote sustenance and growth of enterprises. Various prominent features identified are as follows:

Holistic View of the Organization

Strategic financial management involves a defined sequence of steps that encompasses the full range of a company's finances, from setting out objectives and identifying resources, analysing data and making financial decisions to tracking the variance between actual and budgeted results and identifying the reasons for this variance.

Long-term Management of Funds

The term 'strategic' means that this approach that takes a long-term view of financial performance of the business enterprise. It incorporates management with a strategic perspective on finances, as to how they are to be accumulated, allocated, invested and reaped back in multiples.

Focus on Wealth Maximization

The strategic financial management has come a long way by shifting its focus from traditional approach to modern approach. The modern approach focuses on wealth maximization rather than on profit maximization. This gives a longer term horizon for assessment, making way for sustainable performance by businesses.

A myopic business is mostly concerned about short-term benefits. A short-term horizon can fulfil objective of earning profit but may not help in creating wealth. It is because wealth creation needs a longer term horizon. Therefore, strategic financial management emphasizes

[4] www.icaiknowledgegateway.org/littledms/download.php?id=2833

on wealth maximization rather than on profit maximization. For a business, it is not necessary that profit should be the only objective; it may concentrate on various other aspects like increasing sales, capturing more market share and so on, which will take care of profitability. So, we can say that profit maximization is a subset of wealth, and being a subset, it will facilitate wealth creation.

Convergence of Corporate Resources

The world has many resources. There are 'haves' and 'have-nots'. There are people who desire change for betterment. Similarly, enterprises also want change for their development. The mantra for the change is 'resource convergence'. The desired results can be achieved when there is a convergence of resources that is, right project selection, right people, right resources and, most important, an open mindset.

Human activities are happening all around. It is human to develop and change for betterment. A holistic approach for change and convergence of resources can do wonders. As strategic financial management considers a holistic view of the organization, it helps in resource convergence for the betterment of the organization. Resources are directed towards the visionary pursuits and objectives of the organization.

Coherence Between Long-term Objectives and Financial Ability

A strategic plan with key long-term objectives serves as a framework for making decisions and provides a basis for planning. Putting together a strategic plan can provide the insight needed to keep a company on track by setting goals and measuring accomplishments. By analysing the information in the long-term plan, executives can make necessary changes and set the stage for further planning.

Balancing Financial Goals vis-à-vis Sustainable Growth

Sustainable growth is important to enterprise long-term development. A too fast or too slow growth will go against enterprise growth and development, so strategic financial plays an important role in enterprise development, adopting suitable financial policy initiative to make sure enterprise grows at a speed close to sustainable growth ratio and have sustainable healthy development. To take an illustration, let us refer to the fuel industry, where resources are limited in quantity and a judicious use of resources is needed to cater to the need of the future customers along with the need of the present customers. One may have noticed the save-fuel campaign, a demarketing campaign that deviates from the usual approach of sales growth strategy and preaches for conservation of fuel for its use across generation. This is an example of stable growth strategy adopted by the oil industry as a whole under resource constraints and the long-run objective of survival over the years.

Managing and Acquiring Assets as per the Objectives of the Firm

Decisions regarding the management of assets are made in accordance with the underlying objective of the firm: to maximize shareholder wealth. Investment in cash, marketable securities, accounts receivables and inventories are properly examined. In the past, the management of working capital (current assets and their supporting financing) dominated the role of financial managers. Although this traditional function continues to be vital, expanded attention is now being paid to the management of longer term assets and liabilities by the strategic finance.

Emphasis on Interests of All Stakeholders

Strategic financial management aims to provide the shareholders with consistent, stable and progressive benefits over time for being associated with the business enterprise. It may focus on wealth creation and capital appreciation through a strategic approach to dividend policy. It strives to cater to the interests of all the stakeholders.

Flexible in Nature

Strategic financial management is flexible in nature. Though some methodologies for analysis are structured, but decisions are taken in a flexible manner like exercising one out of many feasible options. Flexibility here refers to a company's ability to react to unexpected expenses and investment opportunities. Companies with superior financial flexibility are able to both survive tough economic times and take advantage of unexpected investment opportunities. Companies that are unable to respond adequately to unforeseen setbacks may lack the resources to survive longer term economic downturns.

Perpetual Process

Strategic financial management is in the developing stage. To achieve the strategic financial objectives, especially enhancing the value of the firm, it engages in constant and continuous renovation of strategies.

Proactive in Nature

Strategic financial management is the field of study that is proactive in nature. It adopts a strategic approach to the efficient management of funds to help companies survive competition in business and sustain in the long run. It is a multi-faceted field and can include a number of decisions in its scope.

Thus, strategic financial management is basically about the identification of the possible strategies capable of maximizing an organization's market value. It involves the allocation of scarce capital resources among competing opportunities. It also encompasses the implementation and monitoring of the chosen strategy so as to achieve agreed objectives.

1.8.4 Scope of Strategic Financial Management

Strategic financial management is of recent origin. Challenges have necessitated the requirement to adopt a multi-dimensional approach to the management of resources. The all-pervasive management function is becoming comprehensive to include various combinations of aspects spread across in the organization. Strategic financial management has a wide scope and includes various management discipline inputs to provide for profitability and sustenance to strengthen the financial status of the firm. Broadly, the scope of strategic financial management extends to five main areas:

Strategic Investment Management

Investment decision relates to the selection of assets in which funds will be invested by a firm. The assets that can be acquired fall into two broad groups: (a) long-term assets (capital budgeting) and (b) short-term or current assets (working capital/liquidity management).

Capital budgeting is probably the most crucial financial decision of a firm. It relates to the selection of an asset or investment proposal or course of action, such as investing in R&D, opening a new branch, replacing a machine and so on, whose benefits are likely to be available in the future over the lifetime of the project. A project is worth pursuing if it increases the value of the company. A project typically adds value to the company if it earns a rate of return that exceeds the cost of capital. The opportunity cost of capital is the expected return that is foregone by investing in the project rather than in comparable financial securities, such as shares, with the same risk as the project under consideration.

While capital budgeting is a fairly straightforward process from a conceptual viewpoint, it can be very challenging in practice. Not only it is difficult to determine the group's appropriate cost of capital, it is often even trickier to accurately forecast the incremental cash flows that result from taking on the project. Strategic investments are made if the returns are adequate in the long run.

Strategic Financing Management

Financial decision is the second major important function that a financial manger must perform. It is important to make wise decisions about when, where and how should a business acquire funds. Funds can be acquired through many ways and channels. Broadly speaking, a correct ratio of an equity and debt has to be maintained. This mix of equity capital and debt is known as a firm's capital structure.

A firm tends to benefit most when the market value of a company's share maximizes. This not only is a sign of growth for the firm but also maximizes shareholders wealth. On the other hand, the use of debt affects the risk and return of a shareholder. It is more risky, although it may increase the return on equity (ROE) funds.

A sound financial structure is said to be one that aims at maximizing shareholders return with minimum risk. In such a scenario, the market value of the firm will maximize and hence an optimum capital structure would be achieved. Other than equity and debt, there are several other tools that are used in deciding a firm's capital structure. A firm cannot anytime raise any amount of funds as it has to maintain a balance between the costs to pay for raising these funds like interest payments for raising debt or payment of dividends to shareholders and so on over the long run.

Strategic Liquidity Management

It is very important to maintain a liquidity position of a firm to avoid insolvency. A firm's profitability, liquidity and risk all are associated with the investment in current assets. In order to maintain a trade-off between profitability and liquidity, it is important to invest sufficient funds in current assets. But since current assets do not earn anything for business, a proper calculation must be done before investing in current assets. Current assets should be properly valued and disposed of from time to time once they become nonprofitable. Currents assets must be used in times of liquidity problems and times of insolvency.

Strategic Dividend Decision

Dividend decision is another major strategic financial decision. The financial manager must decide whether the firm should distribute all profits, or retain them, or distribute a portion and retain the balance. Like the debt policy, the dividend policy should be determined strategically in terms of its impact on the shareholders' value. The optimum dividend policy is one that maximizes the market value of the firm's shares. Thus, if shareholders are not indifferent to the firm's dividend policy, the financial manager must determine the optimum dividend payout ratio. The payout ratio is equal to the percentage of dividends to earnings available to shareholders. The financial manager should also consider the questions of dividend stability, bonus shares and cash dividends in practice. Most profitable companies pay cash dividends regularly. Periodically, additional shares, called 'bonus shares' (stock dividend), are also issued to the existing shareholders in addition to the cash dividend.

Along with the areas discussed above, other interrelated areas in the purview of strategic financial management are as follows.

Strategic Risk Management

One of the lessons many organizations learnt from the global financial crisis is that they need to clearly link strategy and risk management and be able to identify and manage risk in a highly uncertain environment. Another lesson is that they must focus risk management on creating value as well as protecting value.

Strategic risk management is a process for identifying, assessing and managing risks and uncertainties, created by internal and external events or scenarios, that could inhibit an organization's ability to achieve its strategy and strategic objectives with the ultimate goal of creating and protecting shareholder and stakeholder value. For instance, for market risks in capital markets, companies need to make provisions for expected dividends by the shareholders to consistently cater to their interest over a long period to build a good image.

Strategic Capital Restructuring

Capital restructuring is a type of business operational strategy that is employed to make changes to the capital structure of a company. Usually it is used to rearrange capital assets in order to position the business so that the company's owners can take advantage of a growth opportunity. Essentially, this type of process seeks to make changes to company finances and holdings so that the business is able to operate more efficiently and move towards its stated goals.

There is no single process for engaging in capital restructuring. Typically, company owners and managers may perceive a need to make some changes in order to improve the overall prospects of the company. At times, the effort is triggered by a change in the economy such as the onset of a recession. In this scenario, the restructuring may focus on protecting the core business and keeping it intact during the economic downturn, possibly by using certain capital assets to offset operating expenses in the interim. The restructuring may also come about due to positive events in the economy that create growth opportunities for the business, prompting owners to rearrange assets in order to take advantage of those possibilities and increase both the reputation and the bottom line of the business.

However, while considering a capital restructuring, it is important to assess the capital structure and understand the need to change anything. Identifying the reasons for the change will often make it easier to determine what changes should be made in order to generate the most benefits.

Corporate Restructuring

Restructuring a corporate entity is often a necessity when the company has grown to the point that the original structure can no longer efficiently manage the output and general interests of the company. For example, a corporate restructuring may call for spinning off some departments into its subsidiaries as a means of creating a more effective management model as well as taking advantage of tax breaks that would allow the corporation to divert more revenue to the production process. In this scenario, the restructuring is seen as a positive sign of growth of the company and is often welcomed by those who desire to see the corporation gain a larger market share.

Corporate restructuring may take place as a result of the acquisition of the company by new owners. The acquisition may be in the form of a leveraged buyout, a hostile takeover, or a merger of some type that keeps the company intact as a subsidiary of the controlling corporation. When the restructuring is due to a hostile takeover, corporate raiders often implement a dismantling of the company, selling off properties and other assets in order to make a profit from the buyout. What remains after this restructuring may be a smaller entity that can continue to function, albeit not at the level possible before the takeover took place. In general, the idea of restructuring is to allow the company to continue functioning in some manner. Even when corporate raiders break up the company and leave behind a shell of the original structure, there is still a hope that residual unit can function well enough for a new buyer to purchase the diminished corporation and return it to profitability.

Strategic Financial Engineering

Strategic financial management helps to devise innovative financial tools, techniques and securities to combat the evolving dynamics of business environment. Over the last two decades, the financial risk faced by companies has increased tremendously and the payoffs of managing risk successfully are very high. In response to this increased risk and the incentive to manage it, older instruments of risk management such as forwards and futures have been expanded in scope and many new instruments devised. The process of adaptation of existing financial instruments and processes to develop new ones to cope with the changing situation by the financial market participants effectively is known as financial engineering (Marshall 1992).

Strategic Cost Management

In today's era, organizations are trying their hard to reduce their costs. Ascertaining cost and finding out the ways to reduce it have become the main issue for the organizations stepping into the uncertain environment of the 21st century. By following certain steps and framework of cost management, an organization can effectively and efficiently implement some good strategies related to the reduction of costs and that in turn will decide the future competitive advantage of the companies trying to maintain their market share and brand image in the tough competitive markets.

Strategic cost management has become an essential area nowadays. While formulating the strategy for the accomplishment of overall organizational objectives, a different cost driver should be clearly identified. The identification of key cost drivers helps companies to focus on key activities that will constitute almost 90% of the total costs. In view of this, the importance of strategic cost management should not be underestimated. This implies that the organization should be installing an appropriate framework of strategic cost management to reduce its costs in key areas on which its success is heavily dependent.

1.8.5 Functions of Strategic Cost Management

Strategic financial management is the portfolio constituent of the corporate strategic plan that embraces the optimum investment and financing decisions required to attain the overall specified objectives. In this connection, it is necessary to distinguish between strategic, tactical and operational financial planning. While strategy is a long-term course of action, tactics are intermediate plans, while operations are short-term functions. Senior management decides strategy, middle level decides tactics and operations are looked after by the line management. Irrespective of the time horizon, the investment and financial decisions functions involve the following:

Proactive Planning

A little planning goes a long way. Strategic financial management ensures availability of funds whenever these are required and ensures that firm does not raise resources unnecessarily. It plans not only for the availability of sufficient funds in the company for different purposes, such as for purchase of long-term assets to meet day-to-day expenses and so on, but it also ensures timely availability of finance. Again, excess funding is as bad like inadequate or shortage of funds. If there is surplus money, strategic financial management invests it in the best possible manner because keeping financial resources idle is a great loss to an organization.

Strategic financial planning includes both short-term as well as long-term planning. Long-term planning focuses on capital expenditure plan, whereas short-term financial plans are called budgets, which include a detailed plan of action for a period of one year or less.

Investment Planning

Strategic financial management advocates that the projects must generate expected value to the firm that is more than the amount invested in the projects. The plans are evaluated on the perspective of time value of money, returns are brought to the real value and analysed for the feasibility of financial inputs. This ensures better profitability in the future.

Profit Planning

Profit earning is one of the prime functions of strategic financial management. Profit earning is important for the survival and sustenance of any organization. Profit planning refers to proper usage of the profit generated by the firm. Profit arises due to many factors, such as pricing, industry competition, state of the economy, mechanism of demand and supply, cost and output. A healthy mix of variable and fixed factors of production can lead to an increase in the profitability of the firm. Fixed costs are incurred by the use of fixed factors of production, such as land and machinery. In order to maintain a tandem, it is important to continuously value the depreciation cost of fixed cost of production. An opportunity cost must be calculated in order to replace those factors of production that have gone through wear and tear. If this is not noted, then these fixed costs can cause huge fluctuations in profit.

Collection of Optimum Funds and Its Optimal Utilization

The strategic financial management, by the help of various tools and techniques, estimates the precise requirement of funds to avoid wastage and the overcapitalization situation. The return on investment (ROI) helps analyse the productivity of financial decisions and a parameter to judge the real worth of returns over a long period of time through technique such as NPV, which discounts future cash flows to reveal the intrinsic worth of returns received over a long period of time.

Protecting Interest of the Stakeholder

Traditional financial management enabled companies to embark on the 'shareholder value-oriented approach,' the main focus being on the owners of equity. In terms of this shareholder value approach, the interests of the shareholders are paramount and interests of other stakeholders are considered only if their advancement will lead to shareholder value maximization, that is, 'through the prism of shareholder profit maximization'. Strategic financial management, however, gives recognition to a variety of interests that should be considered wider than only those of the shareholders. The wider variety of interests includes environmental concerns and the interests of stakeholders, such as employees, suppliers, consumers and the community.

Understanding Capital Markets

Shares of a company are traded on stock exchange and there is a continuous sale and purchase of securities. Hence, a clear understanding of the capital market is an important function of strategic financial management. When securities are traded on the stock market, there involves a huge amount of risk involved. Therefore, a strategic financial manger understands and calculates the risk involved in this trading of shares and debentures. It is the discretion of a financial manager how to distribute the profits. Many investors do not like the firm to distribute the profits amongst shareholders as dividend and instead invest in the business itself to enhance growth. The practices of a financial manager directly impact the operation in the capital market.

Perspective beyond Working Capital Requirements

Strategic financial management pushes the strategist to have a multi-dimensional perspective on the business and its future. It no longer stays restricted to catering to short-term fund needs. It facilitates foresight and concrete analysis of financial information.

Risk Hedging

Strategic financial management provides for risk analysis and handling techniques. There can be various risks, such as business risks, exchange rate risks in currencies, uncertainty of expected returns from projects, economic downturns and so on. Strategic financial management provides techniques to understand environment and possible overtures to counter these challenges through foresight.

These factors are not comprehensive or exhaustive. There are many emergent benefits of strategic financial management, which may be qualitative as well as situational.

Cost Containment

A key responsibility of a financial manager is to control the company's expenses. This requires more than simply setting spending levels and cutting costs. Cost containment includes creating requests for proposals, bidding processes and purchasing policies for contractors, vendors and suppliers to ensure the company gets the best combination of quality and price. The financial manager sets benchmarks that determine when it is most cost-effective to perform activities using in-house staff and when it is better to use contractors. Cost-containment efforts include managing debt to ensure interest payments do not wipe out company profits. Financial managers also create strategies that help reduce a company's tax liability, such as depreciating assets.

Cash Flow Management

One of the most important functions of a strategic financial manager is to project and manage the company's cash flow. Cash flow refers to the actual receipt of money and payment of bills, as opposed to the company's budgeted income and expenses. Assuming that a business has more income than expenses it can pay its bills can lead to disaster. For example, if the company does not negotiate customer credit terms and vendor and supplier payment terms correctly, the business might be waiting to collect sales invoices long after bills have become due. Cash flow management includes monitoring receivables turnover and keeping enough credit and cash reserves available to keep the company financially stable.

Legal Compliance

The strategic financial manager ensures that the business meets all of its legal obligations, such as sales and income tax payments, employee benefits contributions, state and federal labour wage requirements and Securities and Exchange Board of India (SEBI) reporting, if the company is a public company.

1.9 Problems in Strategic Financial Management

Strategic financial management has certain problems that come into picture when strategists have to make crucial decisions with. Currently, some common problems include the following.

1.9.1 Lacking in Scientific and Standardized Financial Strategies

Quite a few enterprises have no financial strategies at all, not to mention their implementation. As for some others, the effect of their strategic financial management is greatly affected due to their unscientific and irregular strategies, which are characterized by the following features: first, their strategic financial aims depart from their enterprises' overall ones; second, financial strategies are regarded equal to financial plans, hence neglecting the comprehensiveness of financial strategies; third, financial strategies are not made based on their enterprises' long-term goals and therefore have great randomness.

1.9.2 Neglecting Strategic Environment Analysis and Having Unreasonable Strategic Financial Goals

Strategic environment analysis is both the foundation of financial strategies and the guarantee for its implementation. It includes internal and external environment analysis, with the former being the internal foundation and implementation basis for the establishment of financial strategies. At present, quite a lot of enterprises have not realized the importance of strategic environment for the establishment and implementation of financial strategies and accordingly failed to have proper analysis on their strategic financial environment, especially its internal environment. As a result, their unpractical and unreasonable strategies have restricted the effective implementation of their financial strategies.

1.9.3 Lessening the Role of Budgeting in Strategic Financial Implementation

Budgeting mainly exerts its role in strategic financial implementation in two aspects. First, it clarifies and specifies strategic financial ideas so as to be understood and conducted by all the staff. Budgeting can help to divide strategic goals into every section of an enterprise and even every employee. In addition, when implementing a task jointly, all sections and all employees will have better cooperation and communication with each other. Second, budgeting also provides a standard for an enterprise's daily operation and performance. With a quantitative financial goal set in budget, the actual implementation can be compared with the budget to reveal the disparity between the goal and the reality and take effective countermeasures. Now, most of the enterprises in India have no systematic and complete budget system made up of sales budget, production cost budget, general indirect cost budget, loss and expense budget and cash budget and so on. Even if some enterprises have such a system, its shortage of careful budgeting and strict implementation also lessens the role of budgeting as well as the implementation of financial strategies.

1.9.4 Problems in Enterprises' Financial Management

Some problems in enterprises' financial management have also restricted the establishment and implementation of their financial strategies. A few problems are as follows:

1. Enterprises have 'no idea that corporate management' should be based on financial management and financial management should centre on capital management. Again, entrepreneurs and financial staff lack scientific and advanced financial ideas, including time value, risk value, marginal cost, opportunity cost and have insufficient knowledge about financial management theories and methods. All these have resulted in unclear duty division, disordered management, ineffective monitoring, false accounting information and so on.
2. 'Difficult financing' mainly manifested in insufficient channels and scales of financing channels as well as disordered financing orders. Currently, most enterprises are faced with great difficulty in gaining short-term loans, not to mention long-term ones.
3. *Poor financial control*. First, loose cash management tends to cause inactive or insufficient capital. For some enterprises, the more cash, the better. Therefore, a large sum of cash is not allocated to operation, failing to exert its role; for some others, their cash is overspent on real properties, hence failing to tackle some emergent uses. Second, slow turnover of accounts receivable causes great difficulty in recovering capital or even bad debts. Third, the control over stock is poor. Many enterprises have a stock over twice its turnover, leading to failures in capital turnover. Fourth, too much emphasis is put on money instead of properties, causing serious waste of assets. Actually, quite a few enterprises are lacking in effective management of their raw materials, semi-manufactured goods, fixed assets and so on, as a result of which asset wastes are quite serious.

1.10 Causes of the Problems in Strategic Financial Management

The causes of the problems in strategic financial management are due to the following reasons.

1.10.1 Rigid Management Pattern/Laggard Management Idea

At present, most enterprises, especially private ones, employ high unification of ownership and management rights, in which the investor is the manager whose power cannot be restricted in any case. Having no clear division of duties and strict regulations, these managers do not embody financial management into an effective corporate management system, not to mention financial strategies as a significant part of the enterprise's overall strategies, hence lessening their significance and function. These managers do not believe in strategy but good luck, not system but ties of blood, not procedures but tackling key points, not management but technology and market.

1.10.2 Managers' Poor Quality

Especially for those enterprises venturing out of niches, an unfavourable environment is the chief offender. In addition, managers' poor quality is also an important cause for the failure of financial strategies. It is well known that most managers in enterprises have poor comprehension quality, insufficient management experience and low efficiency because they have not gone through any systematic learning of management theories and special professional training. Therefore, they are not able to have reasonable predictions, decisions, budgets, control, analysis and evaluation based on their own characteristics and the market, to have an understanding of the financial environment and lay down applicable and feasible strategies for financing, investment as well as profit distribution or to fully realize the importance of financial budgeting and therefore to have effective control over its implementation in order to serve the overall goals of their enterprises' development strategies in a better way.

1.10.3 Lacking Independent Financing System with Diversified Channels

With a changeable market, operational risks are greater, so are financial ones caused by a large amount of debt and high financing cost, hence resulting in enterprises' low credit. Besides, their credit is also affected by their non-transparent operation process, non-standardized financial reports as well as asymmetrical information, hence leading to difficulty in achieving financing goals.

Seen from the perspective of the financing system, enterprises' lack of independent financing system with diversified channels has greatly restricted their financing strategies. First, there is no national institution or preferential policies to assist enterprises with their management, causing their unfavourable financing situation. Second, some banks set rigid requirements for loans because of some traditional ideas and administrative interferences. Third, there are not enough financial agencies and loan-guarantee institutions specially serving for enterprises. Fourth, most enterprises have no direct financing rights and cannot issue stocks or bonds. The main bond market is inaccessible and the second bond market is too risky.

1.10.4 Poor Investment Ability and Lacking Feasibility Research

Many enterprises suffer from insufficient registered capital and limited operational capital; hence they have poor investment ability. Focusing on short-term goals to recover investment, they have to rely on simple reproduction instead of an expanded one. In addition, without any special institution for market analysis, their investment activities tend to be based on their perception and therefore blindness. These decision makers usually fail to have an overall grasp of the characteristics or principles of market economy or to pursue reasonable economic profits with their proper operation at the capital market. Their poor abilities are also reflected in the shortage of some feasibility research on their shrink and expansion strategies, how to choose financing channels and structures, how to establish new investment directions and so on. All these greatly affect the establishment and implementation of an enterprise's strategic financial goals.

1.10.5 Personal Biasness of Strategists

Improving strategic decision-making requires limiting own biases of the decision maker or strategist, limiting others' biases and limiting group biases. It is easier said than done, because biases are hardwired in our nature and we cannot overcome them by simply trying harder. Instead, we need a new approach to our daily leadership activities that impact decisions (such as managing meetings, gathering and analysing data and stimulating debate) that will minimize the impact of cognitive biases on critical decisions. To clarify where the problem lies, let us take a look at the decision-making process. Any basic decision-making process pretty much looks like this:

Research/Analysis + Insight/Judgment = Decision

Thus, the mindset of the decision maker or strategist determines the quality of decisions and the vision for the organization to be followed. Their incapability may affect the overall development of the organization, which may be detrimental. Preconceived biases must be dislodged.

1.10.6 Incomplete Internal Control System Leading to Ineffective Control

An incomplete internal control system commonly exists in enterprises, which is profoundly manifested in having no or just incomplete internal control system, hence failing to effectively restrain their own economic behaviour institutionally. A lot of enterprises have no department for internal audit to guarantee the strict implementation of their financial system. Even if some establish such a department, its lack of independence may lead to ineffective internal control. As a result, financial management as well as financial strategies will be greatly affected.

Multiple Choice Questions

1. In common terminology, a strategy is a ________
   a. Mission b. Vision c. Plan d. Objectives
2. No business organization can dream of survival without formulating appropriate ________
   a. Corporate strategy b. Functional strategy c. Goals d. None
3. 'Shareholder wealth' in a firm is represented by
   a. The number of people employed in the firm
   b. The book value of the firm's assets less the book value of its liabilities
   c. The amount of salary paid to its employees
   d. The market price per share of the firm's common stock

4. The long-run objective of financial management is to
   a. Maximize earnings per share
   b. Maximize the value of the firm's common stock
   c. Maximize ROI
   d. Maximize market share
5. A(n) _______ would be an example of a 'principal', while a(n) _______ would be an example of an 'agent'.
   a. Shareholder; manager
   b. Manager; owner
   c. Accountant; bondholder
   d. Shareholder; bondholder
6. The focal point of financial management in a firm is
   a. The number and types of products or services provided by the firm
   b. The minimization of the amount of taxes paid by the firm
   c. The creation of value for shareholders
   d. The dollars profits earned by the firm
7. The decision function of financial management can be broken down into which of the following decisions?
   a. Financing and investment
   b. Investment, financing, and asset management
   c. Financing and dividend
   d. Capital budgeting, cash management, and credit management
8. Financial strategy of a firm includes which one of the following?
   a. Profit distribution strategy c. Financing strategy
   b. Investment strategy d. All
9. Which one of the following category of strategy forms the lowest category of strategy in terms of hierarchy?
   a. Corporate b. Business c. Functional d. None
10. A financial strategy should not include which one of the following components?
   a. Competitive analysis b. Start-up costs c. Ongoing costs d. Sunk costs

Review Questions

1. What do you mean by strategy? Discuss its nature and importance.
2. Elaborate the interface between financial strategy and strategic management.
3. Discuss the meaning of strategic financial management. How does it help in planning for the organization, especially financial resources?
4. Throw some light on the role of financial strategy in organizations.
5. Define strategic financial management. What are the salient features of this field of management studies?
6. 'Strategic financial management has a multidimensional purview'. Discuss the statement and provide details on the scope of strategic financial management.
7. What are the functions and constraints to strategic financial management?
8. Discuss the problems faced in strategic financial management and what are its causes?

References

Ali, Baghaei, and Mohammad Reza Mousavi. 2009. 'Reliable Ear, Financial Strategy for Risk Management During the Financial Downturn'. *Management Thought*, Winter: 129–48.

Andrews, Kenneth R. 1980. *The Concept of Corporate Strategy*. Homewood, IL: Richard D. Irwin.

Ansoff, H. Igor. 1984. *Implanting Strategic Management*. Englewood Cliffs, NJ: Prentice Hall.

Calandro, Joseph Jr., and Flynn Robert. 2007. 'On Financial Strategy'. *Business Strategy Series*, 8(6): 409–17.

Glueck, William F. 1976. *Business Policy, Strategy Formation, and Management Action,* 2nd ed. New York: McGraw Hill.

Jakhotiya, G.P. 2001. *Strategic Financial Management*. New Delhi: Vikas Publications.

Liu, Z. 2010. 'Strategic Financial Management in Small- and Medium-Sized Enterprises'. *International Journal of Business & Management*, 5(2): 887–94.

Marshall, John F. 1992. *Financial Engineering: A Complete Guide to Financial Innovation*. New York: New York Institute of Finance.

Mintzberg, Henry. 1978. 'Patterns in Strategy Formation'. *Management Science*, 24(9): 934–94.

Mintzberg, Henry. 1987. 'Of Strategy Delivered and Emergent'. *Strategic Management Journal*, 6(3): 257–72.

Mintzberg, Henry and Hames A. Water. 1985. 'Of Strategy Delivered and Emergent'. *Strategic Management Journal*, 6(3): 258.

Pavlíček, Jaroslav. 2009. 'Corporate Financial Strategy in SMEs'. In *Proceedings of the World Congress on Engineering*, Vol. II WCE 2009, 1–3 July, London, UK.

Thompson, Arthur A. 2003. *Strategic Management: Concepts and Cases*. New York: McGraw-Hill/Irwin.

Varghese, B.J. 2011. *International Student Barometer Project 2010*. Canberra: Universities Australia.

Further Readings

Kleinová, J., and E. Mainzová. 2006. 'Target Costing Methodology'. In *Management, Economics and Business Development in the New European Conditions*, Akademickénakladatelství CERM, Brno, pp. 1–10.

Newman, William A., and J.P. Logan. 1971. *Strategy, Policy, and Central Management*. Cincinnati, OH: Southwestern Pub.

Chapter 2

Strategic Cost Management

Chapter Objectives

On completion of this chapter, you will be able to understand:

- Meaning of strategic cost management
- Objectives of strategic cost management
- Framework of strategic cost management
- Guiding principles of strategic cost management
- Cost drivers of strategic cost management
- Concepts of strategic cost management
- Value chain analysis
- Target costing
- Activity-based costing and management
- Porter's competitive strategies
- Value engineering
- Business process re-engineering (BPR)
- Balanced scorecard
- Just in time (JIT)
- Six Sigma and lean manufacturing

JetBlue's Success Model

JetBlue succeeded because of its cost advantages and no-nonsense approach to business. The company adopted aggressive cost cutting by doing away with most of the frills other airlines provided (which only increased their cost and did not improve customer value) without compromising on quality or comfort.

Neeleman said, 'You can be efficient and effective and deliver a great experience at the same time'. JetBlue's aim was to create a cost structure that would support low fares, without lowering service standards. The fares charged by JetBlue for a round trip averaged between $98 to $498, which was more than 50 per cent less than those charged by the majors in the industry. (For instance, a round trip from New York to Florida cost about $500 on the major airlines; JetBlue charged about $140 for the same trip with a seven-day advance purchase.) To support its decision to become a cost leader, JetBlue adopted a number of innovative measures on its flights. JetBlue decided not to serve meals on its flights, no matter what the distance or duration. Neeleman identified food as an area in which major cost cutting was possible....

Looking Ahead

JetBlue succeeded where a number of other airlines failed. The primary reason for this success was that the airline tried to be different. It built its success on low cost and high standards, which attracted and kept passengers, and at the same time helped the airline remain solvent in times when the majors were crumbling to dust.

However, analysts wonder whether this magnitude of success can be sustained for a longer period. JetBlue's cost leader approach succeeded because the airline was in its growing stage and could yet exercise close control over the business. There were no labor problems because the airline was small enough for all the employees to feel involved and for the management to look after its employees well. Things cannot be the same forever. With JetBlue growing at a very rapid pace, its real success would be in replicating the same model successfully on a larger scale. An important factor in JetBlue's success was that it operated in a niche market, where it had no competition. It adopted the Southwest model, but did not operate in the same markets. However, competitors were catching up with JetBlue....

Source: Excerpts of a case titled 'Jetblue Airlines' Success Story'. Available at http://www.icmrindia.org/casestudies/catalogue/Business%20Strategy1/BSTR045.htm

2.1 Introduction

The case on JetBlue's success put special focus on strategic cost management. Strategic cost management is a consequence of mutations that occur in the current environment and requires a permanent adaptation of tools and techniques so as to improve the strategic position of organizations. In today's highly competitive environment, cost management has become critical survival skill for many firms, but it is not sufficient to simply reduce costs; instead, costs must be managed strategically. Strategic cost management is the application of cost management techniques so that they simultaneously improve the strategic position of a firm and reduce costs.

Many of the terms are not new: cost reduction, target costing, total cost management or cost avoidance. These efforts have been targeted in several organizations. But how many purchasing and supply organizations have adopted these tactics for the short-term gain and how many have taken a strategic approach that spans several links in the supply chain? More and more organizations will be taking the strategic approach, focusing on strategic cost management. It has become a buzzword in the street of corporate houses. Corporate houses are now searching out for ways to manage their huge conglomerates.

The downsizing and reengineering initiatives so prevalent in the early 1990s have largely proved financially short-sighted. With hindsight, we now know that almost half of downsizing companies reported lower profits the year following their cutbacks. Cost-cutters' stock prices grew more slowly than those of companies that successfully grew both their top and bottom lines. Fewer than one in five cost-cutters were subsequently able to put their companies back on a profitable growth track. Pressures on costs come from many external quarters, including shifting customer priorities, the emergence of new competitors and channels and increasingly inquisitive financial market.

2.2 Meaning of Strategic Cost Management

Strategic cost management describes the methods and activities used by managers in planning and control decisions on the short and long term that allow increased commercial value of products and services to an organization and reduced costs. Managers may, for example, take decisions on the amount and type of materials used and on changes in production processes and product design. Information provided by current accounting information systems help managers to take such decisions, but this information and accounting information system is not a strategic cost management. Strategic cost management has a wide application; it includes (but not limited to), for example, the objective of reducing ongoing costs.

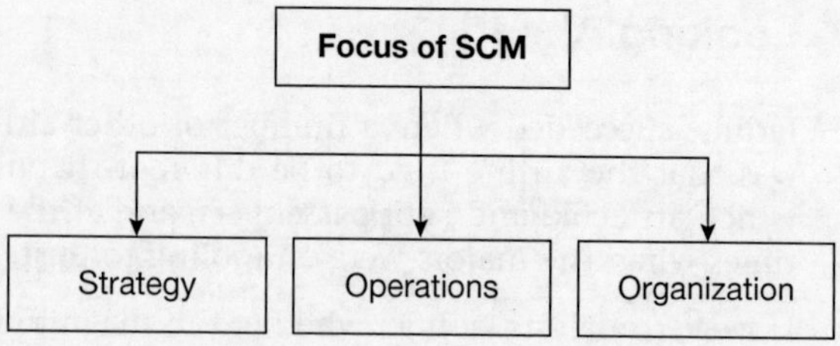

Strategic cost management is the use of cost data to develop and identify superior strategies that will produce a sustainable competitive advantage. The strategic cost management has a broad focus, it is not confined to the continuous reduction of costs and controlling of costs and it is far more concerned with management's use of cost information for decision making. Strategic cost management is also not confined to use cost management techniques that reduce costs and improve the strategic position of a firm at the same time. There are three basic business areas where strategic cost management can be applied.

2.2.1 Strategy

A strategy in general terms refers to a plan of action that will shape the direction of organization's success. Companies of late have realized the importance of clear articulation of strategy and its effective implementation. Before formulating any strategy, the management should think about whether the business model it is still relevant or needs to be changed? Or, whether the objectives of the business are going to be accomplished through a laid-out strategy. It is the art of winning the war. It applies to the company in so far as it fights against competitors when its survival is threatened.

2.2.2 Operations

By setting the priorities according to their significance, we can operate the tasks effectively and efficiently.

2.2.3 Organization

A company should time and again check whether it is allocating its limited resources in the businesses that generate more value for the entire organization. Resources as such are the liming factors for any organization and that is why the company should focus on the structure of the business and it should decide well in advance whether it should own all resources.

2.3 Objectives of Strategic Cost Management

Strategic cost management philosophy reciprocates the changing environment. The traditional cost management system mostly relied on the cost reduction effort, which serves only a part of total strategic management goals. Due to trends and changes in the business environment, such as increase of global competition, increasingly demanding customers and shareholders

Figure 2.1 Forces of Change and Strategic Cost Management

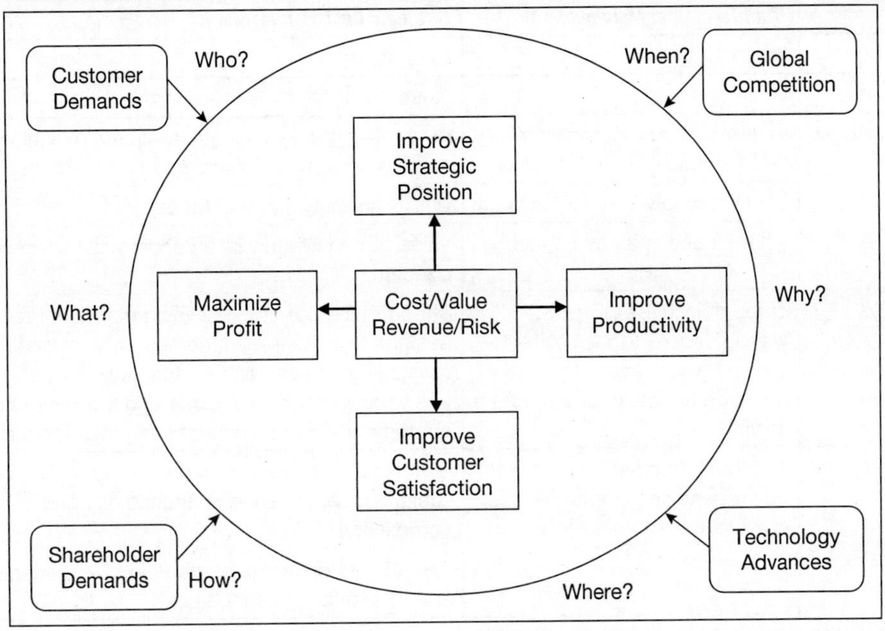

Source: Adapted from McNair (2000).

and rapid advances in information and manufacturing technology, traditional cost management may be not adaptable to these events. Strategic cost management must bridge the gap between cost and value as well as between the language of the market and the language of the business. Cost and revenue management is the present role of strategic cost management; the primary concern of strategic cost management will be not only to manage costs but also to increase revenues, improve productivity and customer satisfaction and, at the same time, improve the strategic position of the company as shown in Figure 2.1.

The key is that costs must be viewed by looking simultaneously at the value they provide. Strategic cost management must recognize that cost/value and revenue are complementary, not competing terms—both must be understood if an organization is to intelligently choose its customers and markets. Traditional cost management during the 20th century faced many criticisms because it took a narrower scope. However, strategic cost management during the 21st century faces a future that will be unique and rewarding compared to its current realities. The key features and shifts that define this transition are detailed in Table 2.1.

In the 21st century, the primary concerns and objectives of strategic cost management will not only be cost management but also revenue management. Therefore, strategic cost management, as a philosophy of improving cost and revenue, takes a proactive attitude and a set of techniques can enable the company to improve costs, increase revenues, improve productivity and customer satisfaction and at the same time improve the strategic position of the company. A wider picture of the concept and objectives of strategic cost management is presented in Figure 2.2, combining cost management and revenue enhancement efforts of organizations for ensuring success through integrating attitudes, philosophies and set of techniques in the field of strategic cost management.

Table 2.1 Comparison of Traditional Cost Management and Strategic Cost Management

	Traditional Cost Management	*Strategic Cost Management*
Focus	Internal	External
Perspective	Value added	Value chain
Cost analysis—way	In terms of: product, customer and function	In terms of the various stages of the overall value chain of which the firm is a part
	With a strongly internal focus	With a strongly external focus
	Value added is a key concept	Value added is seen as a dangerously narrow concept
Cost analysis—objective	Three objectives all apply, without regard to the strategic context: score keeping, attention directing, and problem solving.	Although the three objectives are always present, the design of the cost management system changes dramatically depending on the basic strategic positioning of the firm: either under a cost-leadership strategy or under a product differentiation strategy.
Cost driver concept	A single fundamental cost driver pervades literature—cost is a function of volume.	Multiple cost drivers such as structural drivers (e.g., scale, scope, experience, technology and complexity). Executional drivers (e.g., participative management and total quality management)
	Applied too often only at the overall firm level.	Each value activity has a set of unique cost drivers.
Cost containment philosophy	Cost reduction approached via responsibility centres or product cost issues	Cost containment is a function of the cost driver(s) regulating each value activity.
Primary concern	Cost impact	Cost/value/revenue relationship
Key disciplines	Finance/accounting	Marketing/economies
Primary role	Scorekeeper	Analyst and consultant
Management responsibility	Follower/reactive	Leader/proactive
	Risk averse	Comfortable with ambiguity

Source: Adapted from Fischer (1993), Shank and Govindarajan (1993) and McNair (2000).

2.4 Framework for Strategic Cost Management

The strategic cost management framework provides a clear plan of attack for addressing costs and decisions that affect them. The following are the three core components of this framework.

2.4.1 Core Functions

Core functions elaborate on the nature of the business. These answer the very obvious question, what type of business are we in? At this stage, the company has to clearly identify its courses of actions with respect to strategy planning, R&D and product development.

Figure 2.2 Strategic Cost Management Concept and Objectives

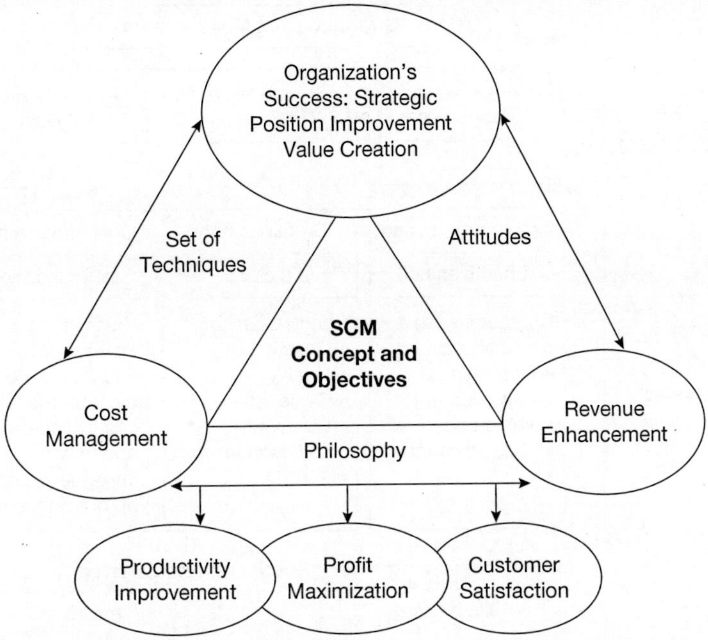

Source: Adapted from Hilton et al. (2001).

2.4.2 Customer Delivery Functions

This step emphasizes more on value addition with various activities, such as marketing, sales, manufacturing, quality assurance and control, sourcing, procurement and logistics, engineering and maintenance, customer service and technical support and so on. Excellence in those activities can create a sort of competitive advantage for the company if it could harness its resources intelligently than its competitors.

2.4.3 Support Functions

As the name suggests, supporting the core activities of the business, some secondary activities are to be carried out, which include information technology (IT), finance and accounting, HR management and general administration. These activities will facilitate the performance of the core activities in a way that goals of the business can be accomplished successfully without wasting limited resources. They will also help in synchronizing the different tasks that are to be carried out simultaneously.

On completion of these three core components, strategic cost management will enhance productivity and thus ensure customer value as shown in Figure 2.3.

Strategic cost management is the understanding of costs and the causes of costs as well as how to drive the greatest possible productivity through the firm. Many studies generally focus on the equation that productivity is defined as the quantity of output produced divided by the quantity of input. Other authors have a broader view of productivity and understand it as

Figure 2.3 Strategic Cost Management, Productivity Improvement and Customer Value

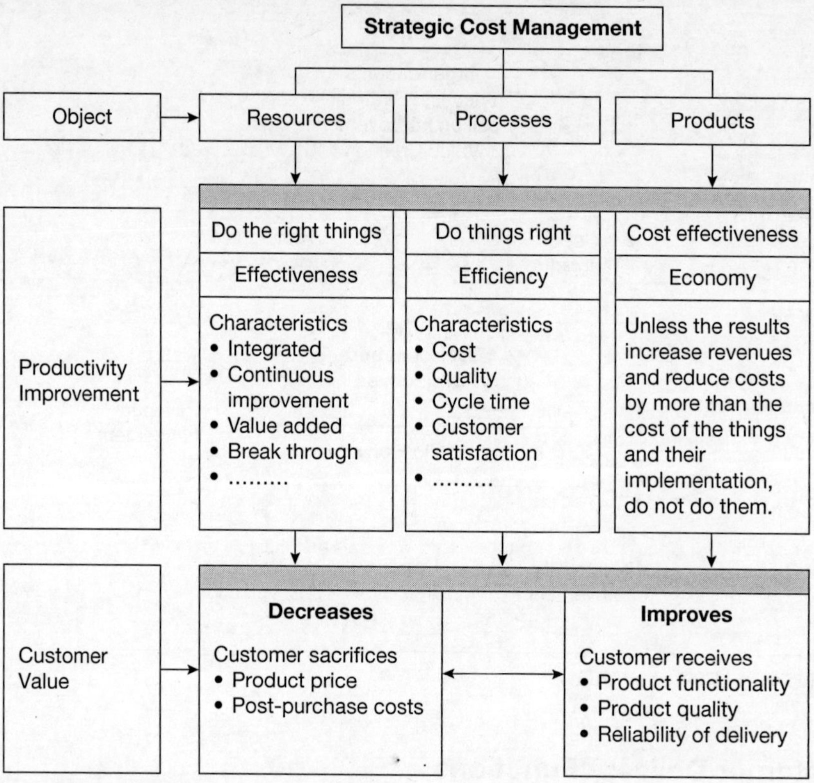

Source: Authors' own compilation based on Bryce (1992) and Ansari et al. (1997).

three (Es): effectiveness, efficiency and economy. This is more simply stated as follows: 'Do the right job, do it right and do it cost-effectively'. Furthermore, successful strategic cost management must help a company to develop and identify superior strategies that will produce a sustainable competitive advantage. Competitive advantage is creating better customer value for the same or lower cost than offered by competitors or creating equivalent value for lower cost than offered by competitors. Customer value is the difference between what a customer receives and what the customer gives up. Strategic cost management should influence the attributes associated with the dimensions of customer value (decrease the customer sacrifice and improve the customer receivables) in order to help a company increase customer value and thereby improve strategic positioning.

2.5 Guiding Principles of Strategic Cost Management

Adoption and implementation of strategic cost management in an organizational context largely depends on the adherence to some guiding principles. These principles are the core to the strategic cost management framework. Berliner and Brimson (1988) have identified several guiding principles to assist in improved and effective cost management. To reach the desired objectives of strategic cost management, the following principles should be considered when implementing strategic cost management:

1. Understanding cost and revenue causality: Understanding the causal relationship between an activity and its cost enables management to focus improvement efforts on the areas that will produce the best results in the form of revenue enhancement and cost rationalization.
2. Identify and promote activities to gain competitive advantage: Strategic cost management efforts are focused on improving the strategic activities of the company, trace costs to value chain activities, and use the activity–cost information to manage the strategic value chain activities better than other companies in the industry.
3. Understand and reduce complexity: Complexity factors are the biggest single driver of cost. They also are the single biggest inhibitors of throughput. The complex cause-and-effect relationships must be sorted out with the purpose of reducing it through proper planning. Reducing complexity means constantly questioning why work is done, and how it can be done more efficiently. The costs associated with this complexity fall as manufacturing processes are simplified and standardized and as companies offer fewer product options.
4. Increase effectiveness and continuously improve costs: A company should redefine its cost structure to select the costs that generate profit by eliminating non–value-added costs. Management and employees must be constantly identifying opportunities for eliminating or reducing unprofitable work.
5. Use strategy to manage costs: In tough times, a company may rush to cut costs without thinking carefully about its long-term impact. Strategic cost management techniques may be used to screen costs initially for further decision.
6. Build skills: Strategic cost management cannot be implemented without a competitive and dedicated team. In an organization that practices cost management, employees must know that they are responsible for managing costs, have the skills to do so, receive positive reinforcement for cost management and get timely feedback on the results.
7. Encouraging participative decisions: Organization should instil a culture of mutual discussion before taking any decision that will impact the whole organization. It is a type of indirect consent taken from them who will implement it. Soliciting input from the employees will not only give management a better understanding, but it will give employees more incentive to become involved.

2.6 Strategic Cost Management: Cost Drivers

It is important to note that cost driver analysis occupies a very important position in strategic cost management. Some companies, especially those following the cost-leadership strategy, use cost management to maintain or improve their competitive position. Cost management requires a good understanding of how the total cost of an object changes as the cost driver changes. Cost drivers are those that cause costs to incur. Thus, cost management is not possible without knowing the cost driver. From the late 1920s to the 1970s, identifying cost drivers was directly related to the production area. Rummel (1949) used a functional approach to identify the relationship between cost drivers and costs; he assumed that costs can be split up into partial costs for each cost driver and this assumption depends on planning and carrying out the cost calculation. Figure 2.4 shows the functional approach of cost driver analysis as used by Rummel (1949).

Over the last three decades of the 20th century, there were considerable changes in the cost structures of companies caused by new conditions of the business environment. These

Figure 2.4 The Functional Approach of Cost Drivers

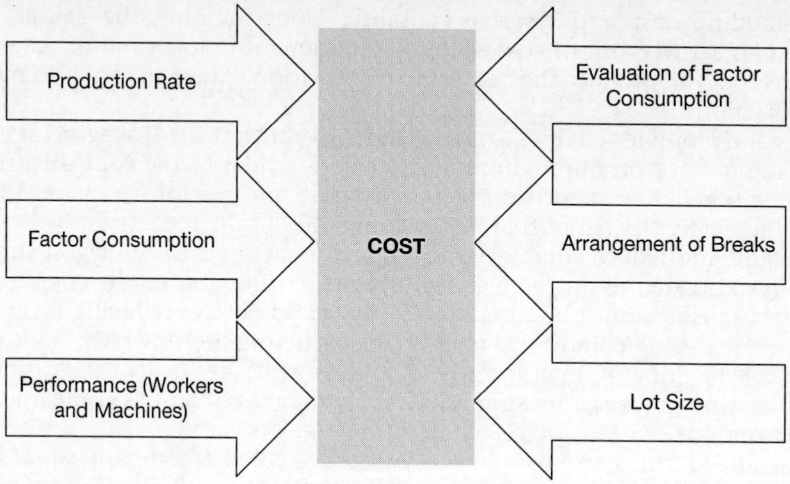

Source: Adapted from Rummel (1949).

changes have resulted in higher overhead rates; investment in machinery and services has reduced direct labour costs and simultaneously increased overhead costs. Thus, Miller and Vollman (1985), in their study 'The hidden factory' argued that most production managers understand what drives direct labour and materials costs, but they are much less aware of what drives overhead costs. Miller and Vollman explained that the real driving force of overhead costs comes from different transactions, not physical products. Shank and Govindarajan (1993) argued that the basic concept of strategic cost drivers is to get away from the notion that volume drives cost. In strategic cost management, cost is caused by a multitude of factors that are related to each other in complex ways. Identifying and analysing these factors mean best explaining the changing relationship between these factors and costs over time and therefore understanding the cost behaviour and cost structure of a company. They broke the list of cost drivers into two categories (Table 2.2).

Table 2.2 Structural and Executional Cost Drivers

Structural Cost Drivers	***Executional Cost Drivers***
• Scale of investment in capacity	• Workforce involvement
• Degree of vertical integration	• Total quality management
• Experience	• Utilization of capacity
• Technology: process technology employed	• Product design
• Complexity: breadth of product line	• Exploitation of external linkages
	• Plant layout efficiency

Source: Shank and Govindarajan (1993).

The first category is called 'structural' cost drivers and deals with the following strategic choices:

1. Economies of scale: How big an investment to make in facilities for R&D, manufacturing and marketing?
2. Scope: Degree of vertical integration. Horizontal integration is related to scale.
3. Experience: How many times in the past, the firm has already done what it is doing now?
4. Technology: What process technologies are used at each step of the firm value chain (state of the art)?
5. Complexity: How wide a line of products or services to offer to the customers?

The second category of cost drivers is called 'executional' cost drivers that constitute determinants of a successful cost position. The most important executional cost drivers include the following:

1. Workforce involvement (participation): workforce commitment to continuous improvement.
2. Total quality management (TQM): beliefs and achievement regarding product and process quality.
3. Capacity utilization (given the scale choice on plant location).
4. Plant layout efficiency. (How efficient against current norms, is the plant layout?)
5. Product configuration. (Is the design or formulation effective?)
6. Exploiting linkages with suppliers and/or customers in the firm's value chain.

2.7 Value Chain Analysis

The idea of the value chain is based on the process view of companies, the idea of seeing a manufacturing (or service) company as a system, made up of subsystems each with inputs, transformation processes and outputs. Examining all activities a company performs and how they interact is necessary for improving cost position and customer value and the value chain is a systematic way of doing so. Porter (1998) argued that the value chain approach, which involves disaggregating a company's operations into its strategically relevant activities, can be an important managerial tool to understand how value chain activities are performed, to identify what cost drivers of value chain activities are and the existing and potential opportunities for improving cost position and customer value. While one can define or group the activities a company performs at different levels of detail, Figure 2.5 represents a common approach (Porter's value chain) to categorize such activities.

Porter divided activities into the primary and support categories (Exhibit 2.1). Primary activities are directly involved in creating and bringing value to the customer. They deal with physical products. They can be grouped into five main areas: inbound logistics, operations, outbound logistics, marketing and sales and service. Each of these primary activities is linked to support activities, which help to improve their effectiveness or efficiency. There are four main areas of support activities: procurement, technology development (including R&D), HR management and infrastructure (systems for planning, finance, quality, information management and so on). As shown in Figure 2.5, the value chain contains the element of margin. The term 'margin' implies that a company realizes a profit margin that depends on

Figure 2.5 Porter's Value Chain

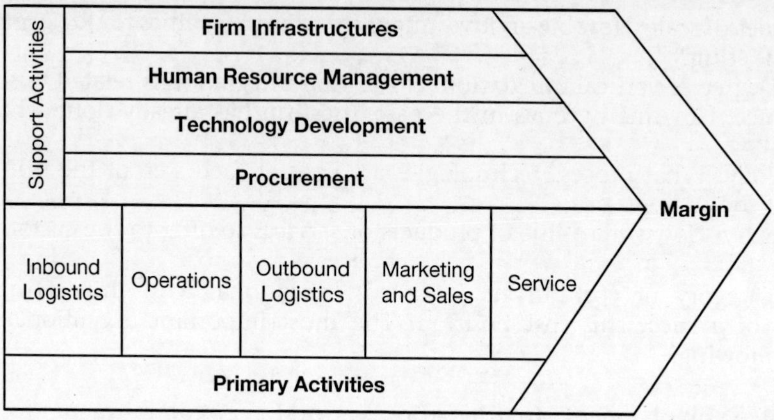

Source: Porter (1998).

Exhibit 2.1 Primary Versus Secondary Activities in Porter's Value Chain

Primary activities

1. Inbound logistics: This deals with the delivery, movement and handling of raw materials from suppliers.
2. Operations: Transformational activities that create end products from raw materials and inputs.
3. Outbound logistics: This refers to the processes that transfer products to distribution channels.
4. Marketing/sales: This includes such activities as advertising, promotion, product mix, pricing, working with buyers and wholesalers and sales force issues.
5. Service: Customer service issues include warranty, repair, installation, customer support, product adjustment and modification.

Support activities

1. Procurement: Firm's purchase of material and supplies for its activities.
2. Technology development: This focuses on improving the processes in primary value-adding activity.
3. HR management: Hiring, training, compensating, developing and relation with the firm's people.
4. Infrastructure: This is a broad term for such activities as finance, accounting, legal, government relations.

A company's value chain is a system of interdependent activities that are connected by linkages. Linkages exist when the way in which one activity is performed affects the cost or effectiveness of other activity.

its ability to manage the linkages between all activities in the value chain. In other words, the company is able to deliver a product/service for which the customer is willing to pay more than the sum of the costs of all activities in the value chain.

2.8 Target Costing

Target costing is an important technique for managing product costs during the design stage.

It is essentially concerned with setting a target cost to be achieved in the product development process, such that a sufficient profit margin is realized when the product is introduced into the market. Traditional product development starts with a basic product design developed in the R&D branch of the firm and the initial idea for the product may have come from the market. After the basic product design has been developed, the price is typically found by adding all costs and desired profit margin. If this price is acceptable in the market, the product is actually introduced and offered to potential customers. If it is more than the attainable market price for the product, the product has to be redesigned until the market price can be met. Under this traditional method, selling price is calculated as follows:

$$\text{Selling price} = \text{cost of product} + \text{target profit margin}$$

On the other hand, the target costing approach brings the management accountant into the process at the early planning stage. The management accountant is contributing to the early decisions, such as should the company be making this kind of product? What constraints need to be applied in the design stage? Is the market demand consistent with our projections? Can we achieve the determined return in this competitive market? Here, the target cost is computed as follows:

$$\text{Target cost} = \text{target price} - \text{desired profit}$$

Target costing is more of an engineering approach where a cost is targeted to remain competitive in the market. Here, the target is mainly to remain cost competitive within the provision of supplying demanded quality. It is a market-oriented approach focused on achievement of low costs that are regarded as the basis for gaining competitive advantage. For a successful implementation of target costing approach, a cross-functional product development team should work together leaving sub-optimal decisions. Value engineering process is applied severely to attain goal congruence of low-cost and high-profit target keeping contentment of customers.

2.9 Activity-based Costing and Management

Activity-based costing (ABC) and activity-based management (ABM) are important tools in continuous improvement effort of companies. ABC is not a method of costing, but a technique for managing the organization better. It is a one-off exercise that measures the cost and performance of activities, resources and the objects that consume them in order to generate more accurate and meaningful information for decision-making. ABC assigns manufacturing overhead costs to products in a more logical manner than the traditional approach of simply allocating costs on the basis of machine hours or labour hours. ABC first assigns costs to the activities that are the real cause of the overhead. It then assigns the cost of those activities only to the products that are actually demanding the activities.

ABM is a system-wide, integrated approach that focuses management's attention on activities with the objectives of improving customer value and the profit achieved by providing this value. The management gains a thorough understanding of its business processes and cost behaviour during the ABC analysis process and the management also

Figure 2.6 Cost Dimension and a Process Dimension

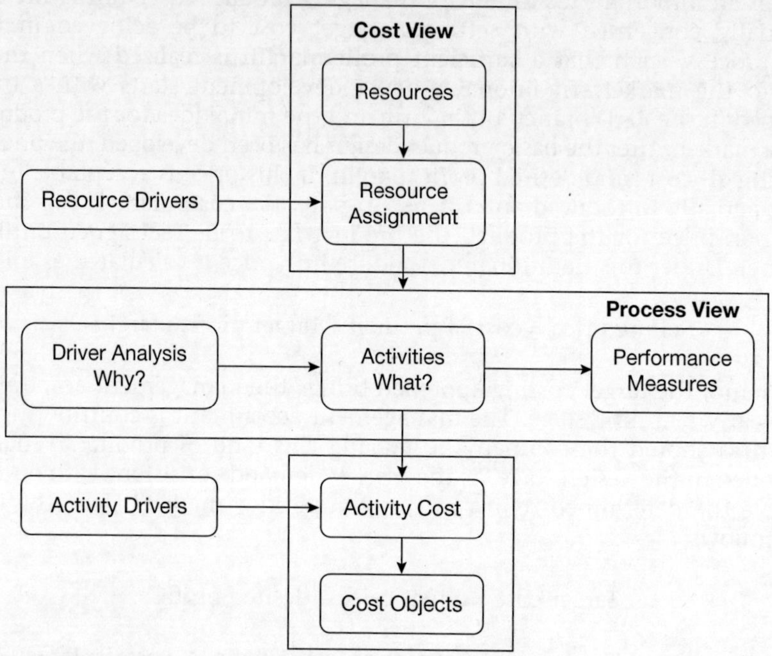

Source: Hasen and Mowen (2006).

applies the insights gained during ABC fact gathering and analysis to improve decision-making at both operating and strategic levels. This is the essence of ABM. ABM has two dimensions: a cost dimension and a process dimension. The cost dimension provides cost information about resources, activities and cost objects of interests such as products, customers, suppliers and distribution channels. The objective of the cost dimension is improving the accuracy of cost assignments. As the model in Figure 2.6 suggests, the cost of resources is traced to activities and then the cost of activities is assigned to cost objects. This ABC dimension is useful for product costing, strategic cost management and tactical analysis. The second dimension, the process dimension, provides information about what activities are performed, why they are performed and how well they are performed. This dimension's objective is cost reduction. It is this dimension that provides the ability to engage in and measure continuous improvement.

2.10 Porter's Competitive Strategies

Competitive strategy is the choice of how an organization or business unit is going to compete in its particular industry or market. By far, the best known and most used set of competitive strategies are Michael Porter's generic strategies. Michael Porter sees three ways in which a firm can gain a competitive advantage: cost leadership, differentiation and focus.

Table 2.3 Generic Competitive Business Strategies

	Strategic Advantage	
Target Scope	***Low-cost Position***	***Uniqueness Perceived by the Customer***
Broad (industry wide)	Cost-leadership strategy	Differentiation strategy
Narrow (market segment)	Focus strategy (low cost)	Focus strategy (differentiation)

Source: Porter (1998).

He calls these generic strategies because they can be applied to a firm in any industry. Table 2.3 illustrates Porter's generic strategies.

2.10.1 Cost-leadership Strategy

This category of strategy seeks to improve efficiency and control costs throughout the organization's supply chain. It is pursued by organizations that strive to be the lowest-cost producers in an industry, through approaches such as economics of scale of production, learning curve effects, tight cost control and cost minimization in areas, for example R&D, services, sales force or advertising. They compete with each other in areas such as process technology, raw material input costs and capacity utilization. Organizations that operate in this category usually sell a standard product. Examples of organizations following this strategy include Walmart, Texas Instruments, Timex and Hyundai. While cost leaders may be the cheapest producers in their market, they cannot ignore the basis of differentiation. If the consumer perceives that the leader's product is not comparable to its competitors, then a cost leader may be forced to discount its price even further to ensure the sale. For example, when Texas Instruments entered the 'affordable' watch market, but were forced to reduce the sale price of their product in the short term and carry out a major product redevelopment. This was due to the customer perception that their product was inferior to their main competitors, namely Casio. The main risk for organizations that decide to compete in this category is that there can only be one cost leader and competition can intensify, leading to a price war where no one wins.

2.10.2 Differentiation Strategy

According to this strategy, the company seeks to differentiate itself from its rivals by achieving a degree of uniqueness that is valued by many customer segments. The company can charge a price premium, where the premium achieved is more than the costs incurred, leading to higher-than-average margins. Organizations that pursue this strategy design their products to possess one or a number of the attributes that are of value to the customer and that make their products 'stand out' from those of their competitors. Characteristics that are common for organizations operating in this category are that they have higher-than-average profit margin due to being unique in the market and will continuously be updating their products to ensure that they are in touch with the needs of their customers.

This category differs from the cost-leader category, since there can be more than one successful differentiation strategy within a market if there are a number of attributes that are widely valued by the buyer. Organizations have succeeded in differentiating their products through improving quality, better after-sales services and more reliable delivery as well as through increasing the functionality. The majority of organizations choose to operate within this category. Examples of companies following this strategy and their approaches to product differentiation include brand loyalty (Coca Cola in soft drinks), superior customer service (IBM in computer), dealer network (Caterpillar Tractors in construction equipment), product design and product features (Hewlett Packard in electronics) and/or product technology (Coleman in camping equipment). The main risk for organizations operating with strategies from this category is that the consumer may sacrifice some of the uniqueness of the differentiated product in order to avail large cost savings. This is what happened in the US in the late 1980s, when Kawasaki succeeded in taking a significant portion of Harley-Davidson's market share due to much lower sales price for their motorcycles. Another risk associated with this category is that imitation by competitors will narrow the perceived differentiation between the products (e.g., IBM PC and IMB clone PCs).

2.10.3 Niche Market Strategy

The focus strategy concentrates on a narrowly defined segment of the market (market niche) and attempts to make its organization the market leader within this niche. The segment may be a particular group of customers, a specific geographic area or a certain part of the product or service line. The rationale is that by specialization, the organization can serve the market segment more effectively than competitors can who attempt to cover the entire market. The focus strategy still relies on a cost leadership or a differentiation strategy, or perhaps both, to establish a strong position within the particular market segment or niche.

The differentiation within a focus strategy can occur by exploiting differences in the special needs or wants of a buyer in a specific market segment and tailoring products to the specialized needs of the market segment. In the cost-focus strategy, the organization strives to exploit differences in the cost behaviour of specific market segments. It can be based on finding a distinct group of customers whose needs are slightly below average. Costs are saved by meeting their needs specifically and avoiding unnecessary additional costs. Organizations in this category have adopted the opinion that 'It is better to be a big fish in a small pond, rather than a minor swimming with whales'. Some risks of focus strategies include imitation and changes in the target segments. Furthermore, the success will encourage other organizations into the market niche. This increases competition and tightens margins since the market available is not large enough to be financially viable. Finally, other focusers may be able to carve out sub-segments that they can serve even better. Examples of companies that have successfully adopted a niche strategy are Toyota's Lexis car market or Rolex in the 'expensive' time-piece market.

2.10.4 A Combination of Generic Strategies: Stuck in the Middle

Porter asserted that the three strategies were distinct and mutually exclusive alternatives. He argued that firms may be able to successfully pursue more than one of these strategies simultaneously, but 'this is rarely possible'. A firm that failed to follow one of the strategies was 'stuck in the middle', which guaranteed the firm low profitability, as shown in Figure 2.7. An organization that is stuck in the middle is not able to sustain a competitive advantage. This often happens when a successfully differentiated organization attempts to diversify outside its area of expertise, the area where it can not compete effectively.

Figure 2.7 Stuck-in-the-middle Strategy

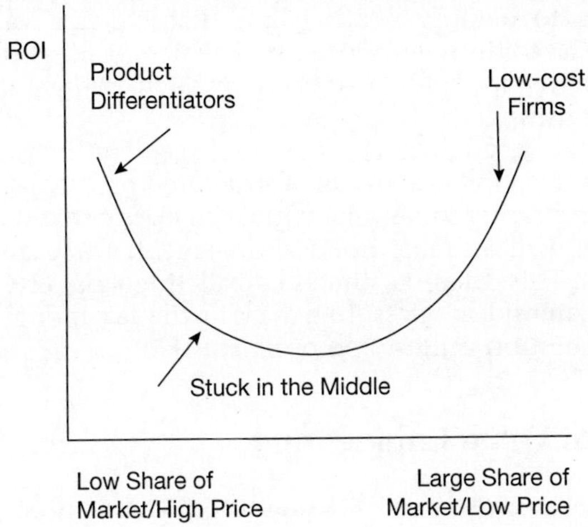

Source: Porter (1998).

Also, focus organizations have failed by moving outside their area of focus. For example, People Express airline lost its successful geographic niche when it began to expand to a national market, where it could not compete successfully.

2.11 Value Engineering

Value engineering is a systematic method to improve the 'value' of goods or products and services by using an examination of function. Value, as defined, is the ratio of function to cost. Value can, therefore, be increased by either improving the function or reducing the cost. It is a primary tenet of value engineering that basic functions be preserved and not be reduced as a consequence of pursuing value improvements.

In the United States, value engineering is specifically spelled out in Public Law 104-106, which states, 'Each executive agency shall establish and maintain cost-effective value engineering procedures and processes'. Value engineering is sometimes taught within the project management or industrial engineering body of knowledge as a technique in which the value of a system's outputs is optimized by crafting a mix of performance (function) and costs. In most cases, this practice identifies and removes unnecessary expenditures, thereby increasing the value for the manufacturer and/or their customers.

Value engineering follows a structured thought process that is based exclusively on 'function', that is, what something 'does' not what it is. For example, a screw driver that is being used to stir a can of paint has a 'function' of mixing the contents of paint can and not the original connotation of securing a screw into a screw hole. In value engineering, 'functions' are always described in a two-word abridgment of an active verb and measurable noun (what is being done—the verb—and what it is being done to—the noun), and to do so in the most non-prescriptive way possible. In the screw driver and can of paint example, the most basic function would be 'blend liquid', which is less prescriptive than 'stir paint', which can be seen to limit the action (by stirring) and to limit the application (only considers paint). This is the basis of what value engineering refers to as 'function analysis'.

Value engineering uses rational logic (a unique 'how'–'why' questioning technique) and the analysis of function to identify relationships that increase value. It is considered a quantitative method similar to the scientific method, which focuses on hypothesis–conclusion approaches to test relationships and operations research, which uses model building to identify predictive relationships.

Value engineering is also referred to as 'value management' or 'value methodology', and 'value analysis'. Value engineering is above all a structured problem-solving process based on function analysis—understanding something with such clarity that it can be described in two words, the active verb and measurable noun abridgement. For example, the function of a pencil is to 'make marks'. This, then, facilitates considering what else can make marks. From a spray can, lipstick, a diamond on glass, to a stick in the sand, one can then clearly decide upon which alternative solution is most appropriate.

2.11.1 The Origins of Value Engineering

Value engineering began at General Electric Co. during the Second World War. Because of the war, there were shortage of skilled labour, raw materials and component parts. Lawrence Miles, Jerry Leftow, and Harry Erlicher at G.E. looked for acceptable substitutes. They noticed that these substitutions often reduced costs, improved the product or both. What started out as an accident of necessity was turned into a systematic process. They called their technique 'value analysis'.

2.11.2 The Job Plan

Value engineering is often done by systematically following a multi-stage job plan. Larry Miles' original system was a six-step procedure that he called the 'value analysis job plan'. Others have varied the job plan to fit their constraints. Depending on the application, there may be four, five, six or more stages. One modern version has the following eight steps:

1. Preparation
2. Information
3. Analysis
4. Creation
5. Evaluation
6. Development
7. Presentation
8. Follow-up

2.11.3 Five Phases of Value Engineering Process during Design Phase

Information Phase: During this phase, the value engineering team gathers as much information as possible about the programme requirements, project design, background, constraints and estimated/projected costs. The team performs functional analysis of systems and sub-systems to identify high cost areas. The project designer provides additional design data and participates in the initial value engineering team conference.

Speculative/Creative Phase: The team uses a group interaction process to identify alternative ideas for accomplishing the function of a system or sub-system.

Evaluation/Analytical Phase: The ideas generated during the speculative/creative phase are screened and evaluated by the team. The ideas showing the greatest potential for cost savings and project improvement are selected for further study.

Development/Recommendation Phase: The team researches the selected ideas and prepares descriptions, sketches and life-cycle cost estimates to support the value engineering proposal (VEP) recommendations.

Report Phase: The team presents the VEPs to the government during an oral presentation at the conclusion of the workshop. Shortly after the completion of the value engineering workshop, a preliminary value engineering report encompassing the entire value engineering effort is prepared by the value engineering team leader and submitted to the government.

2.11.4 Examples of Value Engineering

Limehouse Link Tunnel London

This is a major relief road that provides access to Canary Wharf. The contract comprised a 1.1 mile stretch of road and tunnel, employing cut and cover. Value engineering was employed to good effect. One example relates to the omission of 150,000 square metres of roof waterproofing and substituting concrete crack control that prevents the moisture from reaching the rebar. The diameter of the rebar was also reduced to eliminate the need for a crane. Both of these changes produced a significant saving in both cost and time.

City Place Chicago

This is an example of value engineering that was successfully carried out when the work on site was well advanced. The work comprised a 40-story reinforced concrete tower. Work was well underway when a redesign took place. However, a $475k saving was effected by replacing a steel arch roof with a space-frame assembly. The mechanical penthouse was also replaced by a pre-fabricated metal building.

Commercial Building in the City of London

This example is included in *Value Engineering: The Search for Unnecessary Cost,*[1] where the value engineering took place after the initial cost estimate produced from the initial design made the project barely financially feasible. The facility was a commercial office development on a congested site that was intended to be let on completion. A major construction company was requested to provide a team to value engineer the design down to an acceptable level. The team comprised a chair, two structural engineers, a project manager, a cost engineer and a quantity surveyor. Several design changes were suggested, which increased the lettable area from 75% to 80% and concentrated the location of the main plant items in the basement. The team met for 70 hours, costing £30,000, and resulted in the design producing a more financially viable scheme.

[1] Available at www.theqsi.co.uk/cpdmod/value%20engineering.doc (last accessed on 18 July 2015).

Residential Premises Peoria, Illinois, United States

This case serves to illustrate that not all value engineering exercises prove to be successful. It became necessary to reduce cost and the insulation was identified as a possible source of saving. The domestic and hydronic systems were insulated with fibreglass and it was decided that a rubberized closed cellular type of insulation would achieve the required reduction in cost. Unfortunately, the heat trace hot water maintenance system in the domestic system was incompatible with the rubberized insulation and extensive cost was incurred in correcting the fault. It was obvious in hindsight that when undertaking the value engineering the whole process should have been considered and not just the component. This perhaps is a good example of a cost-cutting process masquerading as value engineering.

2.12 Business Process Re-engineering

BPR began as a private sector technique to help organizations fundamentally rethink how they do their work in order to dramatically improve customer service, cut operational costs and become world-class competitors. A key stimulus for re-engineering has been the continuing development and deployment of sophisticated information systems and networks. Leading organizations are becoming bolder in using this technology to support innovative business processes, rather than refining current ways of doing work. Some commonly referred definitions of BPR are as follows:

> '...the fundamental rethinking and radical redesign of business processes to achieve dramatic improvements in critical contemporary measures of performance, such as cost, quality, service, and speed'.
>
> 'encompasses the envisioning of new work strategies, the actual process design activity, and the implementation of the change in all its complex technological, human, and organizational dimensions'. (Hammer and Champy 1993)

Additionally, Davenport (1993) points out the major difference between BPR and other approaches to organization development, especially the continuous improvement or TQM movement, when he states: 'Today firms must seek not fractional, but multiplicative levels of improvement, 10× rather than 10%'. Finally, Johansson et al. (1993) provides a description of BPR relative to other process-oriented views, such as TQM and JIT and states:

> Business Process Reengineering, although a close relative, seeks radical rather than merely continuous improvement. It escalates the efforts of JIT and TQM to make process orientation a strategic tool and a core competence of the organization. BPR concentrates on core business processes, and uses the specific techniques within the JIT and TQM 'toolboxes' as enablers, while broadening the process vision.

In order to achieve the major improvements BPR is seeking, the change of structural organizational variables and other ways of managing and performing work are often considered as being insufficient. For being able to reap the achievable benefits fully, the use of IT is conceived as a major contributing factor. While IT traditionally has been used for supporting the existing business functions, that is, it was used for increasing organizational efficiency, it now plays a role as enabler of new organizational forms and patterns of collaboration within and between organizations.

Figure 2.8 The Business System Diamond

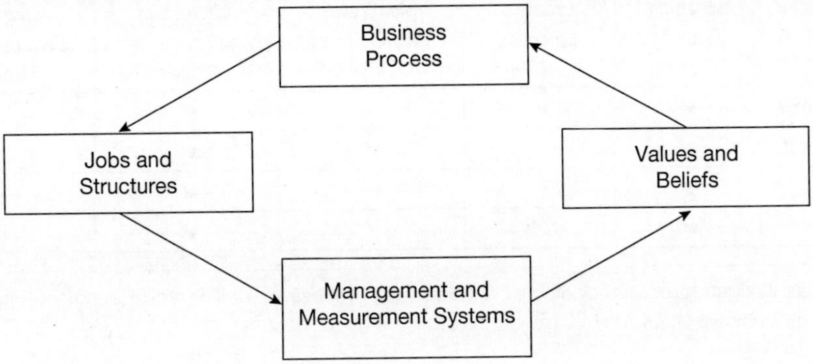

Source: Hammer and Champy (1993).

BPR derives its existence from different disciplines and four major areas can be identified as being subjected to change in BPR—organization, technology, strategy and people—where a process view is used as common framework for considering these dimensions. The approach can be graphically depicted by a modification of 'Leavitt's diamond'. Hammer and Champy (1993) call these aspects the four points of the business system diamond, which is depicted in Figure 2.8.

Business strategy is the primary driver of BPR initiatives and other dimensions are governed by a strategy's encompassing role. The organization dimension reflects the structural elements of the company, such as hierarchical levels, the composition of organizational units and the distribution of work between them. Technology is concerned with the use of computer systems and other forms of communication technology in the business. In BPR, IT is generally considered as playing a role as enabler of new forms of organizing and collaborating, rather than supporting existing business functions. The people/HR dimension deals with aspects such as education, training, motivation and reward systems. The concept of business processes—interrelated activities aiming at creating a value-added output to a customer—is the basic underlying idea of BPR. These processes are characterized by a number of attributes: Process ownership, customer focus, value adding and cross-functionality. Different types of BPR methodologies having some common traits are developed and applied. A summary presentation is given in Table 2.4, leaving details, as it is outside the scope of this book.

2.13 Balanced Scorecard

The balanced scorecard is a management system (not only a measurement system) that enables organizations to clarify their vision and strategy and translate them into action. It provides feedback around both the internal business processes and external outcomes in order to continuously improve strategic performance and results. When fully deployed, the balanced scorecard transforms strategic planning from an academic exercise into the nerve centre of an enterprise.

The balance scorecard advocates a top-down approach to business performance management, starting with business strategic intent expressed through the organization down to operationally

Table 2.4 Comparison of BPR Methodology

Methodology	*Learning Process Phase*	*Create a Business Vision*	*Model and Analyse Current Process*	*Model and Analyse 'to-be' Process*	*Transition to Continuous Process Improvement*
Hammer/Champy	✔	✔	–	✔	–
Davenport/Short	–	✔	✔	✔	–
PADM	–	–	✔	✔	✔
Jacobson	✔	✔	✔	✔	–

Source: Aphrodite Tsalgatidou. 'Methodologies for Business Process Modelling and Reengineering'. Available at cgi.di.uoa.gr (last accessed on 14 May 2015).

relevant targets. The focus of the balance scorecard approach is on the link and/or influences between its various components, which include business strategy, perspectives, objectives, measures, initiatives and milestones as well as softer contextual information.

In other words, it is a concept that ensures what managers should do to overlap the problems by providing a current view of the organizations and necessary actions of strategy.

Robert Kaplan (Harvard Business School) and David Norton proposed the approach in the early 1990s, recognizing some of the weaknesses and vagueness of previous management approaches. The balanced scorecard approach provides a clear prescription as to what companies should measure in order to 'balance' the financial perspective. Kaplan and Norton describe the innovation of the balanced scorecard as follows:

> The balanced scorecard retains traditional financial measures. But financial measures tell the story of past events, an adequate story for industrial age companies for which investments in long-term capabilities and customer relationships were not critical for success. These financial measures are inadequate, however, for guiding and evaluating the journey that information age companies must make to create future value through investment in customers, suppliers, employees, processes, technology, and innovation. (Kaplan and Norton 1992)

A balanced scorecard defines what management means by 'performance' and measures whether management is achieving desired results. The balanced scorecard translates mission and vision statements into a comprehensive set of objectives and performance measures that can be quantified and appraised. These measures typically include the following categories of performance (Figure 2.9):

- Financial performance (revenues, earnings, return on capital, cash flow);
- Customer value performance (market share, customer satisfaction measures, customer loyalty);
- Internal business process performance (productivity rates, quality measures, timeliness);
- Innovation performance (percentage of revenue from new products, employee suggestions, rate of improvement index);
- Employee performance (confidence, knowledge, turnover, use of best demonstrated practices).

It is a continuous cyclical process, which means it has neither beginning nor end. Its task is not directly linked with the mission.

Figure 2.9 Four Perspectives of the Balanced Scorecard (BSC)

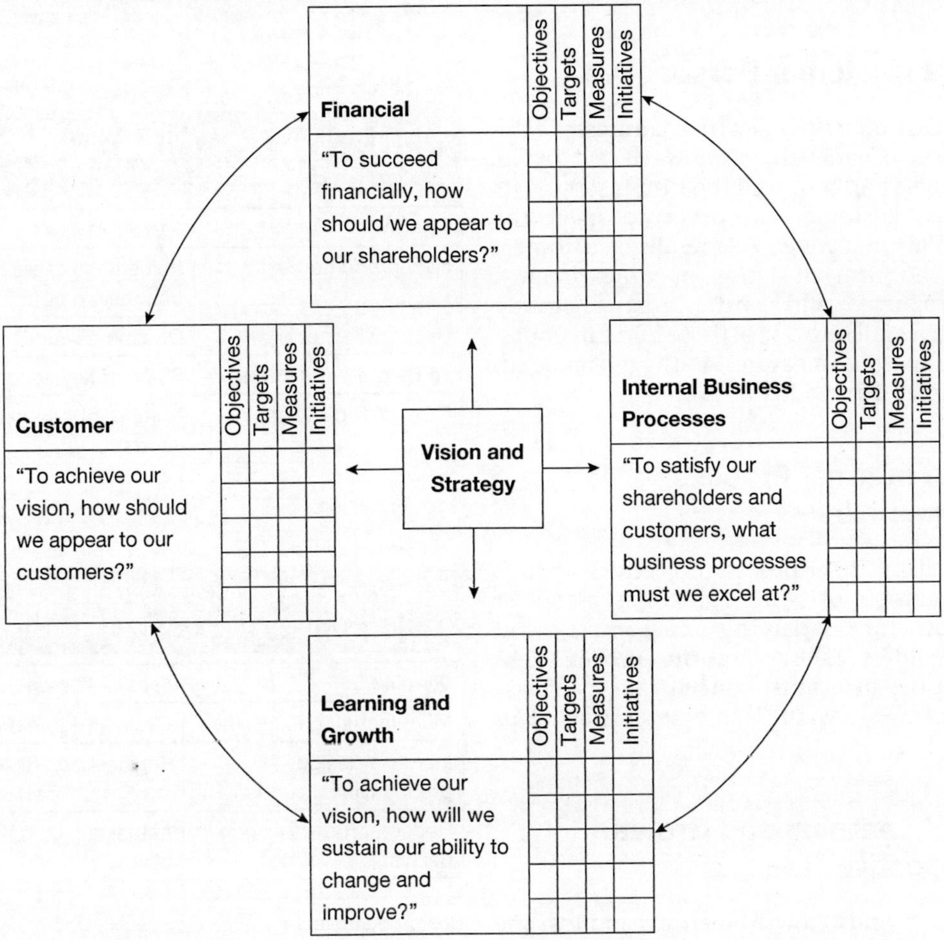

Source: Kaplan and Norton (1992).

2.13.1 Financial Perspective

The financial perspective addresses the question of how shareholders view the firm and which financial goals are desired from the shareholder's perspective.

The specific goals depend on the company's stage in the business life cycle (Table 2.5). For example:

- Growth stage—goal is growth, such as revenue growth rate

Table 2.5 Objectives and Specific Measures of Financial Perspective

Objective	***Specific Measure***
Growth	Revenue growth
Profitability	ROE
Cost leadership	Unit cost

Source: Authors.

- Sustain stage—goal is profitability, such ROE, return on common equity (ROCE), and economic value added (EVA)
- Harvest stage—goal is cash flow and reduction in capital requirements

2.13.2 Customer Perspective

The customer perspective addresses the question of how the firm is viewed by its customers and how well the firm is serving its targeted customers in order to meet the financial objectives. Generally, customers view the firm in terms of time, quality, performance, and cost. Most customer objectives fall into one of these four categories. Some specific measures with reference to objectives is provided in Table 2.6.

Table 2.6 Objectives and Specific Measures of Customer Perspective

Objective	*Specific Measure*
New products	Percentage of sales from new products
Responsive supply	On time delivery
To be preferred supplier	Share of key accounts
Customer partnerships	Number of cooperative efforts

Source: Authors.

2.13.3 Internal Process Perspective

Internal business process objectives address the question of which processes are most critical for satisfying customers and shareholders. These are the processes in which the firm must concentrate its efforts to excel. Follow the examples provided in Table 2.7.

Table 2.7 Objectives and Specific Measures of Internal Process Perspective

Objective	*Specific Measure*
Manufacturing excellence	Cycle time, yield
Increase design productivity	Engineering efficiency
Reduce product launch delays	Actual launch date vs. plan

Source: Authors.

2.13.4 Learning and Growth Perspective

Learning and growth metrics address the question of how the firm must learn, improve and innovate in order to meet its objectives. Much of this perspective is employee-centered, which is reflected Table 2.8.

Table 2.8 Objectives and Specific Measures of Learning and Growth Perspective

Objective	*Specific Measure*
Manufacturing learning	Time to new process maturity
Product focus	Percentage of products representing 80% of sales
Time to market	Time compared to that of competitors

Source: Authors.

2.13.5 The Process of Building a Balanced Scorecard

While there are many ways to develop a balanced scorecard, Kaplan and Norton (1992) defined a four-step process that has been used across a wide range of organizations.

1. Define the measurement architecture: When a company initially introduces the balanced scorecard, it is more manageable to apply it at the strategic business unit (SBU) level rather than at the corporate level. However, interactions must be considered in order to avoid optimizing the results of one business unit at the expense of others.
2. Specify strategic objectives: The top three or four objectives for each perspective are agreed upon. Potential measures are identified for each objective.
3. Selection of strategic measures: Measures that are closely related to the actual performance drivers are selected for evaluating the progress made towards achieving the objectives.
4. Develop the implementation plan: Target values are assigned to the measures. An information system is developed to link the top-level metrics to lower level operational measures. The scorecard is integrated into the management system.

2.14 Just in Time

What is the just-in-time (JIT) concept? Since the emergence of this term it was difficult for sciences and business people to define it. Even today, many companies think that they are using the JIT concept but, actually, they are not realizing that JIT must be integrated in company philosophy and not just dead letters. JIT production is a manufacturing philosophy that eliminates waste associated with time, labour and storage space. Basics of the concept are that the company produces only what is needed, when it is needed and in the quantity that is needed. The company produces only what the customer requests, to actual orders, not to forecast. JIT can also be defined as producing the necessary units, with the required quality, in the necessary quantities, at the last safe moment. It means that the company can manage with their own resources and allocate them very easily. Figure 2.10 shows a drawing of the JIT concept.

Figure 2.10 The JIT Concept

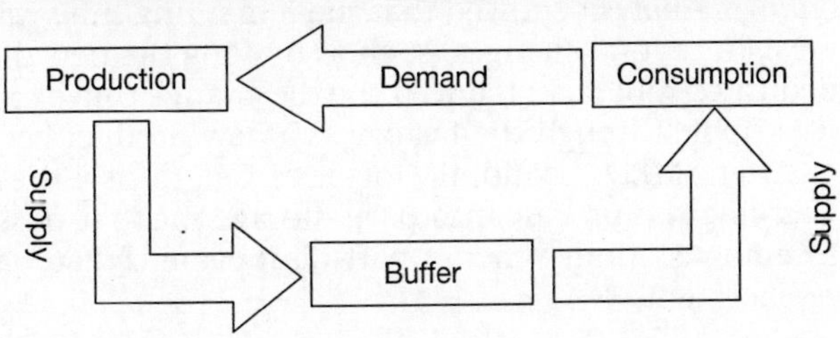

Source: Authors.

2.14.1 History of JIT

The technique was first used by the Ford Motor Company, which describes the concept of 'dock to factory floor' in which incoming materials are not even stored or warehoused before going into production. The concept needed an effective freight management system; Ford's *Today and Tomorrow* (1988) describes one. The technique was subsequently adopted and publicized by Toyota Motor Corporation of Japan as part of its Toyota Production System (TPS).

Japanese corporations cannot afford large amounts of land to warehouse finished products and parts. Before the 1950s, this was thought to be a disadvantage because it reduced the economic lot size (an economic lot size is the number of identical products that should be produced, given the cost of changing the production process over to another product). The undesirable result was poor ROI for a factory.

The chief engineer at Toyota in the 1950s, Taiichi Ohno, examined accounting assumptions and realized that another method was possible. The factory could be made more flexible, reducing the overhead costs of retooling and reducing the economic lot size to the available warehouse space. Over a period of several years, Toyota engineers re-designed car models for commonality of tooling for such production processes as paint spraying and welding. Toyota was one of the first to apply flexible robotic systems for these tasks. Some of the changes were as simple as standardizing the hole sizes used to hang parts on hooks. The number and types of fasteners were reduced in order to standardize assembly steps and tools. In some cases, identical sub-assemblies could be used in several models.

Toyota engineers then determined that the remaining critical bottleneck in the retooling process was the time required to change the stamping dies used for body parts. These were adjusted by hand, using crowbars and wrenches. It sometimes took as long as several days to install a large (multi-ton) die set and adjust it for acceptable quality. Further, these were usually installed one at a time by a team of experts so that the line was down for several weeks.

Toyota implemented a strategy called Single Minute Exchange of Die (SMED), developed by Shigeo Shingo. With very simple fixtures, measurements were substituted for adjustments. Almost immediately, die change times fell to about half an hour. At the same time, quality of the stampings became controlled by a written recipe, reducing the skill required for the change. Analysis showed that the remaining time was used to search for hand tools and move dies. Procedural changes (such as moving the new die in place with the line in operation) and dedicated tool racks reduced the die change times to as little as 40 seconds. Dies were changed in a ripple through the factory as a new product began flowing.

After SMED, economic lot sizes fell to as little as one vehicle in some Toyota plants. Carrying the process into parts-storage made it possible to store as little as one part in each assembly station. When a part disappeared, that was used as a signal to produce or order a replacement.

2.14.2 Philosophy of JIT

The JIT inventory system is not just a simple method that a company has to buy in to, it has a whole philosophy that the company must follow. The ideas in this philosophy come from many different disciplines, including statistics, industrial engineering, production management and behavioural science. In the JIT inventory philosophy, there are views with respect to how inventory is looked upon, what it says about the management within the company and the main principle behind JIT.

Inventory is seen as incurring costs instead of adding value, contrary to traditional thinking. Under this philosophy, businesses are encouraged to eliminate inventory that does not add value to the product. Second, it sees inventory as a sign of sub-par management as it is simply there to hide problems within the production system. These problems include backups at work centres, lack of flexibility for employees and equipment and inadequate capacity, among other things.

In short, the JIT inventory system is all about having 'the right material, at the right time, at the right place, and in the exact amount'. An example of using JIT in GM is given in Exhibit 2.2.

Exhibit 2.2 General Motors: An Application of JIT

General Motors (GM) in the United States has (approximately) 1,700 suppliers who ship to 31 assembly plants scattered throughout the continental United States. These shipments total about 30 million metric tons per day and GM spends about $1,000 million a year in transport costs on these shipments (1990 figures).

JIT implies frequent but small shipments. When GM moved to JIT, there were simply too many (lightly loaded) trucks attempting to deliver to each assembly plant. GM's solution to this problem was to introduce 'consolidation centres' at which full truckloads were consolidated from supplier deliveries.

This obviously involved deciding how many consolidation centres to have, where they should be, what should be their size (capacity) and which suppliers should ship to which consolidation centres (suppliers can also still ship direct to assembly plants).

As of 1990, some 20% by weight of shipments go through consolidation centres and about 98% of suppliers ship at least one item through a consolidation centre.

2.14.3 Some Key Elements of JIT

1. *Stabilize and level the Master Production Schedule (MPS) with uniform plant loading* (heijunka *in Japanese*): Create a uniform load on all work centres through constant daily production (establish freeze windows to prevent changes in the production plan for some period of time) and mixed model assembly (produce roughly the same mix of products each day, using a repeating sequence if several products are produced on the same line). Meet demand fluctuations through end-item inventory rather than through fluctuations in the production level. Use of a stable production schedule also permits the use of back-flushing to manage inventory: an end-item's bill of materials is periodically exploded to calculate the usage quantities of the various components that were used to make the item, eliminating the need to collect detailed usage information on the shop floor.
2. *Reduce or eliminate set-up times: aim for single-digit setup times (less than 10 minutes) or 'one-touch' set-up*: This can be done through better planning, process redesign and product redesign. A good example of the potential for improved set-up times can be found in auto racing, where a National Association for Stock Car Auto Racing (NASCAR) pit crew can change all four tires and put gas in the tank in under 20 seconds. (How long would it take you to change just one tire on your car?) The pit crew's efficiency is the result of a team effort using specialized equipment and a coordinated, well-rehearsed process.
3. *Reduce lot sizes (manufacturing and purchase)*: Reducing set-up times allows economical production of smaller lots, and close cooperation with suppliers is necessary to achieve reductions in lot sizes for purchased items, since this will require more frequent deliveries.
4. *Reduce lead times (production and delivery)*: Production lead times can be reduced by moving work stations closer together, applying group technology and cellular manufacturing concepts, reducing queue length (reducing the number of jobs waiting to be processed at a given machine), and improving the coordination and cooperation between successive processes. Delivery lead times can be reduced through close cooperation with suppliers, possibly by inducing suppliers to locate closer to the factory.
5. *Preventive maintenance*: Use machine and worker idle time to maintain equipment and prevent breakdowns.

6. *Flexible workforce*: Workers should be trained to operate several machines, to perform maintenance tasks and to perform quality inspections. In general, JIT requires teams of competent, empowered employees who have more responsibility for their own work. The TPS concept of 'respect for people' contributes to building a good relationship between workers and management.
7. *Require supplier quality assurance and implement a zero-defects quality programme*: Errors leading to defective items must be eliminated, since there are no buffers of excess parts. A quality at the source (*jidoka*) programme must be implemented to give workers the personal responsibility for the quality of the work they do, and the authority to stop production when something goes wrong. Techniques such as 'JIT lights' (to indicate line slowdowns or stoppages) and 'tally boards' (to record and analyse causes of production stoppages and slowdowns to facilitate correcting them later) may be used.
8. *Small-lot (single unit) conveyance*: Use a control system such as a *kanban* (card) system (or other signalling system) to convey parts between work stations in small quantities (ideally, one unit at a time). In its largest sense, JIT is not the same thing as a *kanban* system, and a *kanban* system is not required to implement JIT (some companies have instituted a JIT programme along with a material requirement planning system), although JIT is required to implement a *kanban* system and the two concepts are frequently equated with one another.

2.15 Six Sigma and Lean Manufacturing

Six sigma and lean manufacturing are toolkits to reduce waste in business processes. Both are proven concepts and have saved clients millions of dollars without capital investment.

2.15.1 What Is Six Sigma?

Six sigma is a philosophy of doing business with a focus on eliminating defects through fundamental process knowledge. Six sigma methods integrate principles of business, statistics and engineering to achieve tangible results. Six sigma tools are used to improve the processes and products of a company. They are applicable across every discipline, including production, sales, marketing, design, administration and service. Six sigma offers a wealth of tangible benefits. When skilfully applied, six sigma:

- reduces costs by 50% or more through a self-funded approach to improvement,
- reduces the waste chain,
- affords a better understanding of customer requirements,
- improves delivery and quality performance,
- provides critical process inputs needed to respond to changing customer requirements and
- develops robust products and processes.

2.15.2 What Is Lean Manufacturing?

Lean manufacturing is a proven approach to reduce waste and streamline operations. Lean manufacturing embraces a philosophy of continually increasing the proportion of value added activity of their business through ongoing waste elimination. A lean manufacturing approach provides companies with tools to survive in a global market that demands higher quality, faster delivery and lower prices. Specifically, lean manufacturing:

- dramatically reduces the waste chain,
- reduces inventory and floor space requirements,
- creates more robust production systems,
- develops appropriate material delivery systems and
- improves layouts for increased flexibility.

2.15.3 Increasing Firm Value Using Six Sigma

Successful executives are highly focused on one fundamental goal: Increasing the value of the firm while simultaneously honouring the social responsibility of the firm. Increasing the value of the firm typically involves three important steps. First, executives determine a strategy that will increase the value of the firm. Second, they identify a methodology or infrastructure to best support the strategy. Finally, the methodology or infrastructure aligns the organizational activities and resources. To this end, a number of strategies can be employed. The common strategies address profitable revenue growth and lowering business cost structure. Examples of strategies address decreasing operating costs, increasing key customer retention, increasing customer value through product enhancement, reducing cycle time of manufacturing or service delivery, leveraging economies of scale and so on. The methodologies to accomplish these goals have been plentiful in the past 30 years. Most recently, we have seen a wave of industry consolidation primarily through mergers and acquisitions to capture the benefits of economies of scale. Financial engineering has reached new levels of sophistication, and the arrival of financial derivatives has brought new opportunities to many organizations and their trading partners. Prior to that, re-engineering was used extensively to capture the opportunities with regard to organizational structure and agency costs.

Figure 2.11 Six Sigma and Business Processes

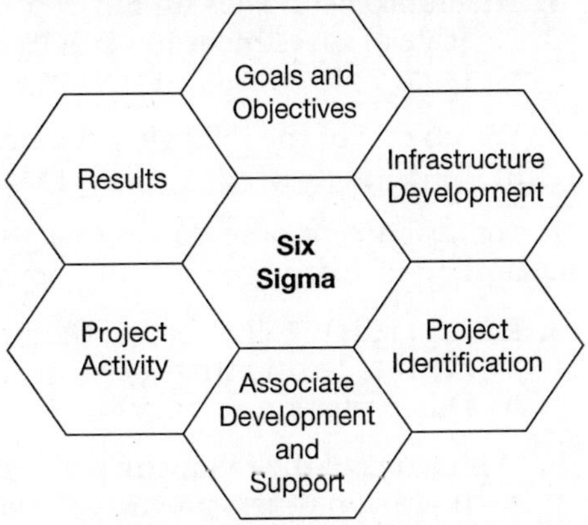

Source: Authors.

In the past 10 years, a fundamental methodology has emerged and rewarded business leaders with measurable results to the bottom line while simultaneously improving organizational culture. The methodology, six sigma, improves the processes that constitute the business engine (Figure 2.11). The approach has been so successful that companies like Motorola, AlliedSignal and General Electric have used it to substantially improve stockholder value. It has been recognized at Wall Street as a sound business initiative. Six sigma eliminates cost and increases value, like few other process improvement methodologies, in part because it forces quantitative measurements on the results of organizational activities. It has been utilized in manufacturing as well as in service and other non-manufacturing environments. It is successful because non-value-added expenses often represent up to 50% of an organization's cost structure, thus providing savvy leadership a veritable goldmine of quantifiable opportunity.

Multiple Choice Questions

1. Strategic cost management focuses on ________
   a. Strategy b. Operations c. Organizations d. All
2. Which one of the following does not impose any forces for change in strategic cost management?
   a. Shareholders b. Competition c. Customer d. Strategy
3. The focus of traditional cost management is mostly________
   a. Internal b. External c. Both d. None
4. Which one of the following function is not considered in framework for strategic cost management?
   a. Customer delivery b. Core c. Non-value added d. Support
5. Structural cost drivers do not depend on ________
   a. Scale of investment in capacity
   b. Degree of vertical integration
   c. Utilization of capacity
   d. Complexity
6. Which one of the following activity is not primary activity in Porter's value chain?
   a. Inbound logistics b. Procurement c. Operations d. Service
7. For assignment of resources to activities, what type of driver is used?
   a. Resource driver b. Activity driver c. Anyone d. None
8. If a firm fails to follow one of the strategies independently, it is actually following ________
   a. Cost-leadership strategy
   b. Differentiation strategy
   c. Focus strategy
   d. Stuck-in-the-middle strategy
9. Which one of the following perspective is the first step in designing a balanced scorecard?
   a. Internal business process
   b. Financial
   c. Learning and growth
   d. Customer
10. Which one of the following strategic cost management tools targets to eliminate defects through fundamental process knowledge?
    a. Lean manufacturing
    b. Six sigma
    c. JIT
    d. ABM

Review Questions

1. Critically explain strategic cost management with its focus.
2. Clearly identify the objectives of strategic cost management.
3. Differentiate between traditional and strategic cost management.
4. Explain the framework for strategic cost management. How strategic cost management ensures customer value through productivity improvement?
5. Explain the guiding principles of strategic cost management.
6. Write a critical note on cost driver. Differentiate between structural and executional cost drivers.
7. Critically evaluate the use of value chain analysis in strategic cost management.
8. Target costing is more an engineering approach—critically evaluate.
9. What are the differences between ABC and ABM?

10. Evaluate Porter's competitive strategies. In which market, cost leadership is considered a suitable competitive strategy?
11. Explain value engineering concept with some examples.
12. How does BPR add values to the process?
13. Explain balanced scorecard as a strategic cost management tool.
14. How JIT can bring cost competitiveness in the market?
15. Differentiate between six sigma and lean manufacturing.

References

Ansari, S., J. Bell, T. Klammer, and C. Lawrence. 1997. *Strategy and Management Accounting: Version 1.1.* Homewood, IL: Richard D. Irwin.

Berliner, C., and J. Brimson. 1988. *Cost Management for Today's Advanced Manufacturing: The CAM-I Conceptual Design*. Boston, MA: Harvard Business School Press.

Bryce, M. 1992. 'Focus on Effectiveness'. *Information Systems Management*, 9(4): 70–72.

Davenport, T.H. 1993. *Process Innovation: Reengineering Work through Information Technology*. Boston MA: Harvard Business School Press.

Fischer, T. 1993. *Kosten management strategischer Erfolgsfaktoren*. München: Verlag Vahlen.

Ford, Henry. 1988. *Today and Tomorrow*–Special Edition of Ford's 1926 Classic. Productivity Press.

Hammer, M., and J. Champy. 1993. *Reengineering the Corporation: A Manifesto for Business Revolution*. New York: Harper Business Press.

Hansen, D., and M. Mowen. 2006. *Cost Management: Accounting and Control*. Mason, OH/London: Thomson/South-Western.

Hilton, R., Maher, Selto, F.M., and B. Sainty. 2001. *Cost Management: Strategies for Business Decisions* (1st ed.). New York: The McGraw-Hill Ryerson.

Johansson, Henry J. et al. 1993. *Business Process Reengineering: Break Point Strategies for Market Dominance*. Chichester: John Wiley & Sons.

Kaplan, R.S., and D.P. Norton. 1992. 'The Balanced Scorecard: Measures that Drive Performance', *Harvard Business Review*. (January–February): 71–79.

McNair, C. 2000. 'Defining and Shaping the Future of Cost Management'. *Journal of Cost Management*, 14(5): 28–32.

Miller, J.G., and Vollman, T. 1985. 'The Hidden Factory'. *Harvard Business Review*, 63(5): 142–50.

Porter, M. 1998. *Competitive Strategy: Techniques for Analyzing Industries and Competitors: With a New Introduction*. New York: The Free Press.

Rummel, K. 1949. Einheitliche Kostenrechnung auf der Grundlageeinervorausgesetzten Proportionalität der KostenzubetrieblichenGrößen, Düsseldorf.

Shank, J., and V. Govindarajan. 1993. *Strategic Cost Management: The New Tool for Competitive Advantage*. New York: The Free Press.

Chapter

3

Value-based Management

Chapter Objectives

On completion of this chapter, you will be able to understand:

- Basics of value-based management (VBM)
- Brief history of VBM
- Shareholder value and VBM
- Criticisms of traditional accounting measures and shareholder value concept
- Corporate objective function
- Measurement of value
- Return on investment
- Residual income
- Return on equity
- Return on capital employed
- Return on net assets
- Economic value added (EVA)
- Cash-flow return on investment
- Residual cash flow
- Cash value added (CVA)

The Value of Corporate Values

Corporate values are in vogue, but what does the fashion tell us about enduring corporate practice, as it is and as it could be?

Increasingly, companies around the world have adopted formal statements of corporate values, and senior executives now routinely identify ethical behaviour, honesty, integrity and social concerns as top issues on their companies' agendas.

The meaning of this new emphasis on values, however, is less obvious than the trend itself. So to explore how deeply these values are embedded in organizations and to examine the role that values are playing, in 2004 Booz Allen Hamilton and the Aspen Institute, a non-profit and non-partisan forum focused on values-based leadership and public policy and conducted a global study of corporations in 30 countries and five regions. Senior executives of 365 companies were polled, almost one-third of whom were CEOs or board members. The purpose of the survey was to examine the way companies define corporate values, to expand on research about the relationship of values to business performance and to identify best practices for managing corporate values.

Source: Illustration by Red Nose Studio.

The survey's most significant finding was that a large number of companies are making their values explicit. That is a change, quite a significant change, from corporate practices 10 years ago. The ramifications of this shift are just beginning to be understood.

At Xerox, CEO Anne Mulcahy says that corporate values 'helped save Xerox during the worst crisis in our history,' and that 'living our values' has been one of Xerox's five performance objectives for the past several years. These values—which include customer satisfaction, quality and excellence, premium return on assets, use of technology for market leadership, valuing employees and corporate citizenship—are 'far from words on a piece of paper. They are accompanied by specific objectives and hard measures,' adds Ms. Mulcahy.

According to market and social trend analyst Daniel Yankelovich, the public's widespread cynicism toward businesses today is the third wave of public mistrust about corporations in the past 90 years. The first, set off by the Great Depression, continued until the Second World War; the second, caused in part by economic stagflation and the Vietnam War, lasted from the early 1960s until the early 1980s. In each of these periods, Dr Yankelovich wrote in the May 2003 report 'Making Trust a Competitive Asset: Breaking Out of Narrow Frameworks', companies tended to be reactive, blaming 'a few bad apples', dismissing values as 'not central to what we do' or ignoring opportunities to improve because 'we don't have to make major changes'.

The current wave of disapproval began in 2001 with the bursting of the dot-com bubble, the ensuing bear market and the financial scandals involving Enron, WorldCom, Tyco and others. But this time, according to the survey, the response appears to be different. More and more companies are looking inward to see what has gone wrong and looking outward for answers. They are questioning the quality of their management systems and their ability to inculcate and reinforce values that benefit the firm, its various constituencies and the wider world. Rather than wall themselves off from critics, more companies are listening to them and looking for new ideas. And more firms are taking action to turn their corporation's values into a competitive asset.

If the new attention to values were simply a transitory reaction to the business scandals of recent years or merely a public relations device to direct or deflect media and investor attention, it would be worth little note. But more companies are going well beyond simply displaying values statements: They are engaging in values-driven management improvement efforts. Among those efforts are training staff in values, appraising executives and staff on their adherence to values and hiring organizational experts to help address how values affect corporate performance.

Source: Lee, Fabish and McGaw (2005).

3.1 What Is VBM?

Management philosophy in recent days has observed a dramatic shift from profit based to VBM. VBM is the alignment of key organizational processes such as strategic planning, budgeting, compensation, performance measurement, training and communication around value creation. The organization needs this alignment and consistency to develop a culture whereby individuals, at all levels, will make decisions focused on sustainable long-term value creation. Value is created when owners receive a return that more than compensates them for the perceived risk of the investment. For example, if I offered you an investment opportunity that would pay $100 in one year, would you accept? Maybe, but you would first want to know at least two other pieces of information: required investment and estimated project risk. Then, if you deemed that the potential reward compensated you for the perceived risk, you would accept the investment opportunity. With VBM, employees need to engage in the same thought process when considering investment/allocation of the firm's resources and ultimately when considering how to allocate their own time. The basic questions that need to be answered are as follows:

1. How much do I have to invest in this project/activity?
2. What will my returns be for the project/activity?
3. Do the returns from the project/activity compensate me for the perceived risk?

A few key events have shaped VBM into a financial management framework. The seminal event was the movement from accounting-based measures of performance, such as net income, to value-based metrics such as economic profit. Traditional accounting-based measures such as net income provide information on a company's book returns but do not address how much economic capital was invested, or amount of risk exposed to, to generate the returns on the investment. Economic profit addresses these shortcomings by including a capital charge. Look at the comparative picture of income statement as given in Table 3.1, where the differences between the two incomes are clearly observed. A capital charge is in essence a rental charge for the capital used to generate the firm's profits. To calculate the capital charge, you multiply the investment in the business by the investors' expected percentage returns. If your profits are more than the capital charge, then value is being created since investor expectations were exceeded. Alternatively, if the profits do not cover the capital charge, then value is destroyed since the profits did not cover the capital charge.

Table 3.1 Accounting and Value-based Income Statement

	Accounting Income Statement		***Value-Based Income Statement***
	Revenues		Revenues
less:	Cost of goods sold	less:	Cost of goods sold
equals:	Gross profit	equals:	Gross profit
less:	Depreciation, sales and administration, and other	less:	Depreciation, sales and administration, and other
equals:	Profit before interest and taxes (PBIT)	equals:	PBIT
less:	Interest	less:	Adjusted taxes
equals:	Profit before taxes	equals:	Net operating profit after taxes (NOPAT)
less:	Taxes	less:	Capital charge
equals:	Net income	equals:	EVA

Source: Authors.

Let us take a quick look at a simple example to gain some insight into the benefits of economic profit. We will build on the example from above, where we had the opportunity to earn $100. Let us assume that instead of one opportunity, we actually have two opportunities to earn $100. Should we pursue one, both, or neither? If we are just concerned with growing net income, then our decision is easy. We would pursue both projects if each had positive net income. However, if we are concerned with value creation, we must find out how much we have to invest in each project and the expected return. Suppose the first project requires an investment of $500 while the second project requires an investment of $1,500. We also find out that both investments are of similar risk and require a 10% return. Let us now look at the analysis and make a decision.

Project 1		***Project 2***	
Profit	$100	Profit	$100
Capital charge ($500 × 10%)	50	Capital charge ($1,500 × 10%)	150
Economic profit	$50	Economic profit	($50)

Since economic profit is positive in case of project 1, we should accept it. For the same reason, we should not pursue project 2. If we put importance on accounting profit, in that case both of the projects make profit; however, both of the projects do not add value to the stakeholders. VBM takes care of value creation in every decision.

It did not take long for practitioners to realize that on its own, a performance-based metric was interesting, but for it to truly take hold, incentive programmes would need to be re-designed. Thus, incentive plans were re-designed to pay people for value creation represented by improvement in economic profit. Initially, companies thought that implementing a new metric, tying incentive to the metric and providing some initial training was all that was necessary for a successful VBM programme. These are all necessary but not sufficient conditions for VBM to be successful. Rather, they represent the price of admission to developing a VBM culture. The true gains are made when companies integrate VBM into their culture. The Harvard Business Review study[1] highlights this importance: 62% of the successful VBM companies report training more than 75% of their managers in VBM concepts, whereas only 27% of the unsuccessful companies trained a great proportion of their management staff. Realizing that VBM is a cultural change is the key to a lasting change that will create sustainable improvements in shareholder value. Some definitions of VBM have been presented in Exhibit 3.1 to understand the area of VBM in a very brief manner.

3.2 Brief History of VBM

From profit maximization to wealth maximization to value maximization—it is a long journey in today's value creation drive. By the end of the 1970s, authors in the auditing field started questioning whether traditional measures, for instance profit per share, were actually reliable as indicators of the market value of a share. Instead, companies should use discounted cash flows to evaluate the future values of their shares. US investment banks, which started

[1] Steve Chopp and John K. Paglia, PhD, 2002, Build a Culture of Value Creation, Three essential steps for value-based management, *Graziado Business Review, A Peer Reviewed Journal of Relevant Information and Analysis*, Vol. 5, Issue 1, available at https://gbr.pepperdine.edu/2010/08/build-a-culture-of-value-creation/ retrieved on February 3, 2014.

Exhibit 3.1 Definitions of VBM

'Value-based Management is essentially a management approach whereby Companies' driving philosophy is to maximize shareholder value by producing returns in excess of the cost of capital.' (Simms 2001)

'Value-based Management says, in a nutshell, the key to increased shareholder value lies in the integration of strategic planning, performance measurement and compensation'. (Leahy 2000)

'Value-based Management is a holistic management approach that encompasses redefined goals, redesigned structures and systems, rejuvenated strategic and operational processes, and revamped human-resources practices. Value-based Management is not a quick fix but a path requiring persistence and commitment'. (Boulos et al. 2001).

using methods based on cash flows in order to identify companies whose shares were undervalued on the markets initially accepted this approach. The undervalued companies were acquired and restructured in order to visualize hidden assets, and thereafter sold off gainfully. Moreover, these ideas for more consideration about shareholder value occurred coincided with an increasing level of institutional ownership. The threat of being acquired by big players became an additional incentive for executive managers to seriously consider the market values of their companies. Large US companies, such as Coca Cola and Procter & Gamble (the latter Svenska Cellulosa Aktiebolaget [SCA's] main competitor and benchmark in the hygiene area), were the first to turn to VBM.

In 1986, Alfred Rappaport published his book *Creating Shareholder Value,* which became a source of inspiration for research into VBM (Rappaport 1986). In the book's preface, he states that a company's objective to increase shareholder value is hardly controversial. However, 'there is great uncertainty about how to evaluate strategies and subsequent performance with measures that are reliably linked to the objective of providing maximum returns to shareholders', which is the book's overall theme. Anyway, Rappaport seriously advocated value creation from shareholders' perspective without considering the broader stakeholder perspective.

VBM receives extra attention from industrial revolution due to added complexity in corporate management. It seems that the internal and external complexity is highly correlated with the philosophy of VBM, which has been observed in stakeholders' value maximization theory. Before the industrial revolution, value creation was very much straightforward as the companies were small in every respect without complexity. Gradually, it became commonplace, as shown in Figure 3.1. However, an evolution of VBM is presented below to give an idea of how the concept got momentum in different time periods.

3.2.1 Implicit Value Management (±1800–1890)

This is the beginning of value management where economies of scale are achieved through improved production management driven by the Industrial Revolution. The value creation concept was not explicitly advocated; however, value creation was targeted through investment in machineries, hiring skilled manpower, implementing smart production scheduling methods and so on. During the 19th century, these methods gradually improved using transportation and communication mechanisms that became available. Behind the scene, value creation was made for the shareholders, that is, shareholders' value maximization got its birth.

3.2.2 Explicit Value-(Based) Management (±1890–2000)

This period witnessed significant development in the field of VBM, which is explicit. Some advocators sold the concept of VBM through different books, articles and models. Some notable initiatives are identified as follows:

1. 1911: Frederick Taylor developed scientific management.
2. 1938: Grant uses time value of money in investment projects.
3. 1954: Dean uses the discounted cash flow method in investment and other decisions.
4. 1964: Sharpe introduces capital asset pricing model (CAPM).
5. 1964: Peter Drucker writes *Managing for Results*.
6. 1973: Black and Scholes introduce the formula to value financial options
7. 1986: Alfred Rappaport writes *Creating Shareholder Value*.
8. 1994: Jim Mc Taggart uses the term 'value-based management' in his book *The Value Imperative: Managing for Superior Shareholders Return*.

Figure 3.1 Complexity and Need for VBM

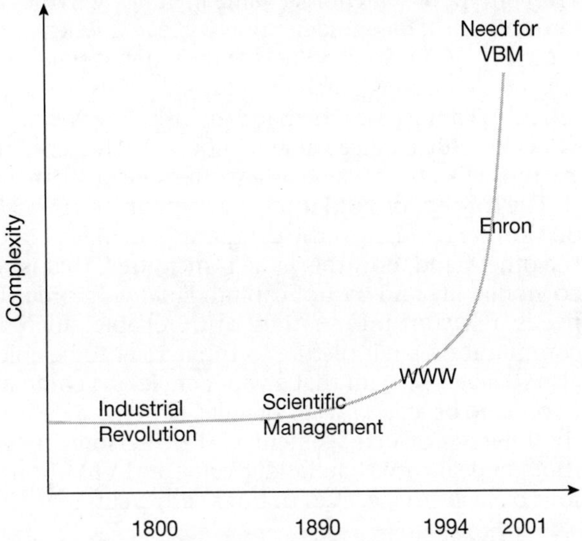

Source: http://www.valuebasedmanagement.net/faq_history_value_based_management.html (last accessed on 5 December 2014).

3.2.3 Holistic VBM (2000–Now)

The beginning of the dot-com crisis and Enron scandals brought new dimension in VBM due to the depreciation of shareholders' wealth as exposed in those crises. Among the most prominent ideas to prevent further disasters in the future are:

1. Strict accounting practices and rules
2. Improved corporate governance
3. Separation of analysts from other banking activities
4. More attention for business ethics and corporate social responsibility
5. Rules for executive remuneration
6. Protection of shareholders' interest
7. Attention for stakeholders' interest
8. A long-term view towards value creation

Despite good intentions and belief, such drive brings further complexities in corporate management, which warrants a holistic approach in VBM theory.

3.3 Shareholder Value and VBM

The concept of shareholder value includes activities aimed at maximizing the shareholders' long-term returns. Shareholder value is created when the ROE exceeds the weighted average cost of capital (WACC). Shareholders expect management to generate value over and above the costs of resources consumed, including the cost of using capital. If suppliers of capital do not receive a fair return to compensate them for the risk they are taking, they will withdraw their capital in search of better returns since value will be lost. The term 'value' has many meanings but when market analysts talk about 'value', they often mean what the market is willing to pay for the shares.

The concept of VBM links the companies' strategies with its behaviour. The concept includes, on the one hand, how the company is managed to create value, that is, its value drivers and, on the other hand, how the value is measured, that is, a focus on investments, operating cash flow, economic life and cost of capital. Finally, in order to make correct decisions, a decision maker needs relevant information and reliable analytical tools. Moreover, it is important to communicate a fair picture to the market to be able to realize a company's intrinsic value. It is also received wisdom that a wider circle of a company's decision makers should be remunerated in order to be able to act as owners, which is a basic idea of VBM. That is the way to link together the interests of management and ownership in order to avoid conflicts. Different schools of thought deal with shareholder value and VBM from different perspectives. This section presents four of such perspectives in brief with a summary in Table 3.2.

3.3.1 Concept of Rappaport

Alfred Rappaport (1986) contends that accounting-based performance measures such as net profit, ROI and ROE are inadequate measures to assess the achievement of the proclaimed goal of value creation for shareholders. Instead, Rappaport advocates the use of the shareholder value (SV) as a key performance indicator. Shareholder value is the difference between the company value and the market value of debt. Company value can be calculated as the net present value (NPV) of cash flows from operations plus a residual value and the market value of tradeable securities. Three main items have to be determined for this calculation: the free cash flows (FCF) available to compensate debt holders and shareholders, the residual value after the planning horizon and the cost of capital. The cost of capital is calculated as the WACC,

Table 3.2 Comparison of Valuation Methods of VBM Concepts

		Performance Measure per Period		***Present Value over***
Proponents	***Cost of Capital***	***Residual***	***Return***	***Life Cycle***
Rappaport	WACC, cost of equity according to CAPM	SVA	Return on sales	Shareholder value
Copeland et al.	WACC, cost of equity according to CAPM	Economic profit	ROIC	Equity Value
Lewis	Empirically determined average cost of capital	CVA	CFROI	Market value of equity
Stern and Stewart	WACC, cost of equity according to CAPM	EVA	ROCE	MVA

Source: Hahn and Hintze (2006).

using the aspired (market value-based) capital structure to weigh the after-tax cost of debt and the cost of equity. The latter is determined in accordance with the capital asset pricing model (CAPM). In addition to SV, Rappaport (1999) introduces the shareholder value added (SVA). It is a measure for residual firm performance within one period and reflects a change in shareholder value.

3.3.2 Concept of Copeland, Koller and Murrin

Copeland, Koller and Murrin (2002) distinguish between two ways of calculating SV: the 'entity model' and the 'economic profit model'. The entity model follows the aforementioned approach of Rappaport (1986) with only minor adaptations. In the economic profit model, the sum of the currently invested capital and the present value of all future economic profits constitute company value. The authors define economic profit as the residual rent of the invested capital, that is, the difference between return on invested capital (ROIC) and WACC. To discount future economic profits, the WACC is applied.

3.3.3 Concept of Lewis

Thomas G. Lewis (1995) suggests total shareholder return (TSR) on the basis of stock price changes and dividend payments as a key performance indicator (Figure 3.2). Lewis identifies three drivers that increase future FCF and thus TSR: increasing returns, growth in activities whose returns exceed their cost of capital and dividend payments whenever an investment in activities whose returns are above their cost of capital is impossible. To measure the return on an activity, Lewis propagates the cash flow return on investment (CFROI), because, in his view, traditional accounting-based performance measures are not sufficiently correlated with company value. The CFROI is a ratio of the cash flow a company has generated to the cash invested in the company's assets in a given period. It represents an internal rate of return (IRR). The cash value added (CVA) as a residual profit measure of an investment for a specific period depends on the difference between the investment's CFROI and its cost of capital. The latter is calculated on the basis of a broad portfolio of companies listed in the most important national economies. This implies a standardized cost of capital without firm-specific adjustments. Lewis explicitly rejects the WACC with the cost of equity according to the CAPM as empirical substantiation for it is lacking.

Figure 3.2 Total Shareholder Return

Total Shareholder Return (TSR)	Capital Gains	Profitability (ROI)
		Growth (Investment)
	Dividends	Free Cash Flow

Source: Adapted from Thomas G. Lewis (1995).

3.3.4 Concept of Stern and Stewart

The concept of Joel M. Stern and G. Bennett Stewart builds on the EVA. Its starting point is a firm's net operating profit after taxes (NOPAT). From the NOPAT, a charge for the capital employed (CE), which is used to generate the NOPAT, is subtracted to yield the EVA. The capital charge is calculated by applying the standard WACC to the CE. The EVA is a measure of residual profits from an entity perspective for one period. The analogue multiperiodical measure is the market value added (MVA). It is a cumulative measure of a firm's performance, which illustrates the assessment of the NPV of all current and planned investment projects of a company. From an external point of view, MVA is the difference between the market value of a company and its book value. From an internal perspective, MVA is equal to the NPV of all future EVAs. The EVAs are discounted with the WACC. Maximizing MVA should be on a firm's top priorities and EVA should be used to measure periodical performance.

3.4 Criticism of Traditional Accounting Measures and the Shareholder Value Concept

The VBM approach starts out from analyses of cash flows instead of traditional historical key variables, based on accounting records, as a basis for decision-making relating to strategies and investments. Accounting-based standards such as earnings, earnings per share and growth in earnings have long been used, and still are, to measure a company's performance. Advocates of VBM (for instance, Society of Management 1997) are, however, critical of the usage of accounting-based standards as guidelines for the governance of companies. Their arguments are as follows:

1. Accounting measures such as earnings per share and profit or growth in earnings do not take into account the cost of the investment required to run the business.
2. Return-based measures such as return on assets often motivate managers to make short-term dysfunctional decisions that encourage under-investment.
3. Neither earnings nor return measures appear to correlate well with actual market values of companies.

James Knight (1998), for instance, claims that these standards, used as management tools, lend themselves to abuses because of misleading signals resulting in incorrect managerial behaviour. In the end, the shareholders have to pay for these incorrect decisions in the form of unsatisfactory returns on their investments. The linkage of managers' bonuses to the growth of the share's value was the first step in trying to affect a company's shareholder value. This incentive implied that managers began to make only those decisions that would boost the price of the share in order to increase their own capital worth. Allan Kennedy (2000), for instance, suggests that 'the short-term maximising shareholder value thinking' should be replaced by 'the idea of long-term building and sharing wealth'. However, the increased attention on management performance is positive. Companies that do not perform well enough risk being taken over, which in turn increases the incentive for managers to perform well.

3.4.1 A Model for Interpreting the VBM Process

The model in Figure 3.3 describes how VBM leads to increased market value through three different sub-processes in a company.

Improved internal dialogue increases the focus in the company on what is relevant when creating value. Improved numerical analysis refers to the measuring of the company's performance in a fair way. These two sub-processes contribute to mobilizing the whole company to work at creating value through improved decision-making, which in turn leads to increased intrinsic value. This will hopefully imply increased market value if the company succeeds in communicating its real intrinsic value to the market.

Figure 3.3 The VBM Process

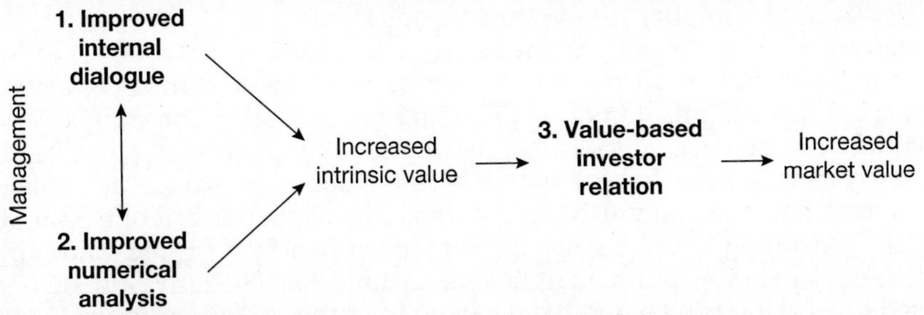

Source: Weissenrieder (1997: 35–36).

3.4.2 A Chart for Value Creation

Many suggestions have been put forward as framework for creating shareholder value. Black et al. (1998) produce a chart of five core value processes to describe a value creation process (Figure 3.4). The five steps in the chart, to some extent, overlap the six general steps presented in Christopher Ittner and David Larcker's framework (2001). However, the fifth step in the chart of Black et al. (1998), value communication and reporting, is not included as a general step in Ittner and Larcker's model. Black et al.'s model is illuminated further as follows:

1. *Corporate value strategies and goals*: The first step is to answer basic questions such as: What are the success criteria in the markets? How do we achieve the results needed for

Figure 3.4 Five Core Value Processes

Source: Black et al. (1998).

value creation? It is important that there is a direct linkage between strategies and value creation. In essence, the value drivers at the strategic level are growth, return and risk. The management has to consider these three factors when formulating the company's strategies by giving priority to investment for growth.

2. *Resource allocation and planning*: If the management has decided to focus on shareholder value, the allocation of all resources must be implemented in accordance with that policy. If the investments do not yield enough in relation to the company's objectives, the capital must be released for other, more profitable projects.
3. *Performance management*: To be able to increase shareholder value, the management has to perceive what is actually driving the value, in Rappaport's terms 'The Shareholder Network'. Operating decisions are impounded primarily in three value drivers: sales growth rate, operating profit margin and income tax rate. Investment decisions are reflected in working capital and fixed capital investment. Proportions of debt to equity govern the cost of capital value driver. The final driver, value growth duration, concerns the number of years that investments can yield returns in excess of the cost of capital.
4. *Compensation*: The company's remuneration system is regarded as being an important component in engaging employees and making them take personal responsibility for enabling changes. According to the Society of Management, a well-functioning performance measure:

    - must be tied to shareholder value creation;
    - should be unambiguous and objectively measurable;
    - must be a measure that can be directly affected by managerial decisions;
    - be transparent and understandable; managers need to understand what they are being measured against;
    - must not be possible to manipulate.

    The reasons why it is not very wise to link the system to the development of the stock price are that on a bull market the management is remunerated whether they have done well or not, and the stock price can be forced upwards by a general upswing. It can also increase the executives' exposure to risk. This may make them more conservative than the shareholders want. Thus, remuneration systems linked to value creation based on a company's cash flow achievements are considered appropriate if the executive management applies a long-term perspective, 'while people in middle management or on the shop floor will view value through a short-term lens'.
5. *Value communication and reporting*: To make sure that the company will be valued at its intrinsic value on the markets, the management has to strictly communicate its objectives, strategies and action plans. It is supposed that without an effective communication plan, investors will not be able to pay attention to the company's efforts to create shareholder value. Moreover, everybody is supposed to work to achieve objectives and strategies. In other words, there must be an education process of teaching everyone to think and communicate in the same terms: 'aligning goals with actions'.

3.5 Corporate Objective Function

It is useful to think of managers as agents, that is, they are the agents for the owners of the firm. Agents make decisions for principals. Managers specialize in decision-making. Correspondingly, think of stockholders as principals, that is, they are the 'owners' of the firm. Stockholders specialize in risk bearing through their ownership of the 'residual claims' of the cash flows of the firm or the common stock. Stockholders are 'residual owners' in that they get paid last, that is, after the other claims against the firm's cash flows are paid off, for example suppliers, bank loans, bondholders and the preferred stockholders. Keep in mind that the shareholders 'own' the firm. Without their equity capital, the firm would not exist. You do not borrow money without an equity base. Accordingly, the managers 'work for' the stockholders. The shareholders elect the board of directors. The board of directors hires, compensates, promotes and, far too infrequently, fires the managers.

Given the above discussion, what do you think the managers should have as their objective? A long list of objectives is possible. Here is a list of fatally flawed objectives:

1. Maximize profits? (Problems? Not cash flow oriented. No time horizon. No incorporation of risk)
2. Maximize earnings per share? (Same problems as above)
3. Size maximization, either book value of assets or sales? (Size may not be in shareholders' best interest; size does not equal value! Size does not incorporate future cash flows or risk)
4. Market share maximization? (Market share at what price? Cash flows? Risk? This objective may not be in shareholders' best interest)
5. Compensation (manager) maximization? (Obviously a flawed objective from the shareholders' perspective.)

We choose the appropriate objective function for the financial manager as shareholder wealth maximization. Can you discuss and defend (or refute) this objective? Think about maximizing shareholder wealth, that is, share price maximization. Shareholders are, after all, the owners of the firm. Is shareholder wealth maximization what shareholders want managers to do? Yes. This objective is logical. If managers make decisions that maximize shareholder wealth, shareholders can make their own optimal investment and consumption decisions. If they choose to give to charities, they can have a bigger impact if they have more wealth. By wealth maximization, we maximize shareholders' wherewithal.

Is shareholder wealth maximization socially irresponsible? No! Why? What will happen to share price if managers 'rip off'

1. Employees?
2. Suppliers?
3. Customers?
4. Government?
5. Society?

In the long run, shareholder wealth maximization must consider these other stakeholders in the firm. Share price will suffer when the penalties associated with corporate 'rip offs' of other stakeholders are assessed. Future cash flows and risk will be damaged if the firm is not a responsible citizen. This argument, however, assumes that these 'markets' are well functioning, which may not always be the case; consider pollution as an example. Figure 3.5 explains the corporate objectives along with the value drivers for those objectives. The figure clearly specifies how shareholders' value has been created by the management decisions in four important areas with the relevant value drivers.

From a broader perspective, corporate objective not only covers the shareholders' value rather it also covers value creation for other related parties, such as bondholders, financial markets and society at large. Thus, the classic objective function may also be considered from a different perspective where managers serve all the stakeholder groups as shown in Figure 3.6.

However, traditional corporate financial theory breaks down when the interests/objectives of the decision makers in the firm conflict with the interests of stockholders, which may take the following forms:

Figure 3.5 Corporate Objective and Value Drivers

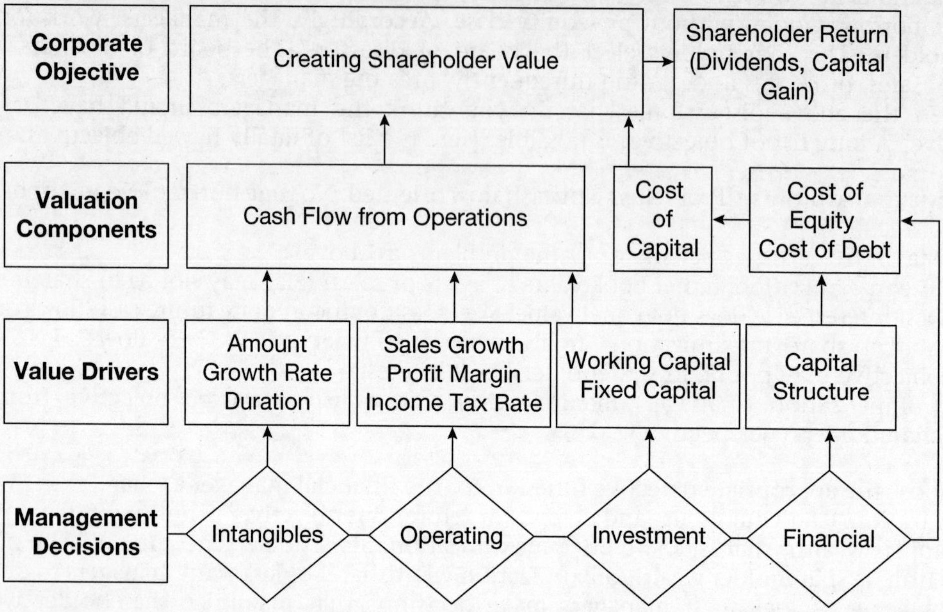

Source: Adapted from Rappaport (1986).

Figure 3.6 The Classical Objective Function

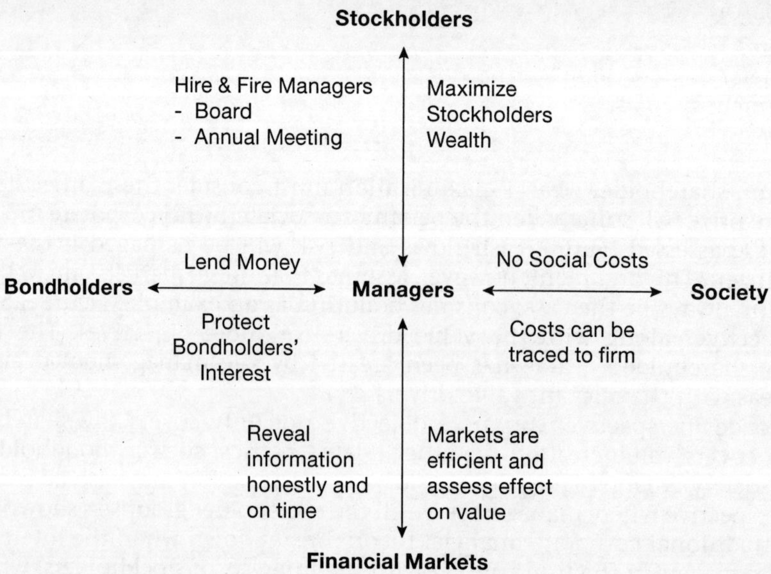

Source: Authors.

1. Bondholders (lenders) are not protected against expropriation by stockholders.
2. Financial markets do not operate efficiently and stock prices do not reflect the underlying value of the firm.
3. Significant social costs can be created as a by-product of stock price maximization.

3.6 Measurement of Value

Both companies and consultants have developed a number of different models to measure value, for instance, FCF model, EVA, CFROI and CVA. The purpose of finding a relevant model is to obtain a management tool for value creating decisions, which could guide employees of the company towards value creation. Before starting discussion on different methods for measuring value, we should reckon the following two points:

1. Traditional accounting and financial functions need to spend a lot more time on real financial management. This can encompass many things that are value-driven. For example, using a new decision model programme for capital investment decisions can help ensure that investments end up creating value.
2. The financial function should be prepared to lead the way on value creation by becoming a strategic centre on how to increase values. This can lead to VBM, a formal programme for managing the organization in terms of economic performance.

Fortunately, in recent years there has been a proliferation of measurement programmes for VBM. This section focuses on some of those methods considering the importance and focus of the book. It is important to note that since value-based metrics is a relatively new field, new conclusions and ideas are still forthcoming. Also, since this is an evolving field, it is important for all organizations to not place their entire emphasis on one measurement system. The most prudent approach to measuring value (like capital budgeting) is to use a combination of metrics when evaluating value creation. An overview of value-based performance measures is summarized in Exhibit 3.2.

Exhibit 3.2 Value-based Performance Measures: An Overview

Measures	Formula
Absolute measures, based on accounting numbers: ✓ EVA: Economic Value Added (Stern Stewart & Co.) ✓ Economic Earnings (A.T. Kearney) ✓ Economic Profit (McKinsey) ✓ ERIC: Earnings less Risk-free Interest Charges (KPMG)	Economic Profit = Income − r × invested capital
Absolute measures, based on cash flows: ✓ CVA: Cash Value Added (BCG)	CVA = Gross Cash Flow (GCF) − Economic Depreciation (ED) − r × invested capital
Rate-of-return measures, based on accounting numbers: ✓ ROI, ROCE, RONA, ROE etc.	$\frac{\text{Income}}{\text{(Invested Capital)}}$
Rate-of-return measures, based on cash flows: ✓ CFROI (BCG, PriceWaterhouseCoopers, Deloitte & Touche)	$\text{CFROI} = \frac{\text{(GCF − ED)}}{\text{(Invested Capital)}}$

3.6.1 Return on Investment

ROI is a performance measure used to evaluate the efficiency of an investment or to compare the efficiency of a number of different investments. ROI measures the amount of return on an investment relative to the investment's cost. To calculate ROI, the benefit (or return) of an investment is divided by the cost of the investment and the result is expressed as a percentage or a ratio. An ROI calculation can be illustrated by the purchase and subsequent sale of a house. Let us assume a cash purchase of a residence for $100,000. The house is held for 10 years and is then sold for $150,000; during its 10 years of ownership, maintenance costs have been $1,000 per year, so the net sales value is $140,000. This sum, less the purchase price, nets out to $40,000. That is, $40,000 divided by the purchase price produces 0.4 or 40%. The ROI of this transaction has therefore been 40%. This elaborate example is presented with a purpose. ROIs are typically calculated in different ways. In this example, for instance, the owner may have rented the house for $200 per month and realized a 10-year income stream of $24,000 as well. If that income is factored in, the net benefit will be $64,000, rather than $40,000, and the ROI will be 64%. Thus, the basic formula of ROI can be written as follows:

$$\text{ROI} = \frac{\text{Net profit}}{\text{Total investment}} \times 100$$

Example: You are a house flipper. You purchased a house at the courthouse auction for $75,000 and spent $35,000 in renovations. After sales, expenses and commission, you netted $160,000 on the sale of the renovated house. What is the ROI? Your net profit is going to be what you netted ($160,000) minus what you spent ($75,000 + $35,000), so it is $50,000. Your total investment is also what you spent ($75,000 + $35,000), which is $110,000. Thus, ROI become 45% ($50,000 ÷ $110,000).

3.6.2 Residual Income

The concept of residual income dates back to Alfred Marshall in the late 1880s. In the 1920s, General Motors used the concept to evaluate its business segments. Residual income was called EVA as copyrighted by Stern Stewart & Co, a consulting firm, in 1994, which has been discussed in detail in a separate section. Here, the very basic form of residual income is presented, which is based on accounting calculations. Residual income is a company's or division's performance measure. It can also be used to evaluate investment alternatives. The basic formula for computing residual income is as follows:

$$\text{Residual income} = \text{Income} - \text{Minimum acceptable income}$$

Companies can use the 'income values' in the formula as income from operations (IFO) or earnings before interest and taxes (EBIT), NOPAT, net income and so on. The 'minimum acceptable income' is usually determined by multiplying average operating assets by a minimum rate of return (i.e., WACC). For example, if division A has $200,000 of average operating assets and the top management established 10% as the minimum acceptable rate of return (i.e., based on the cost of financing the business operations), then the minimum acceptable income for division A is $20,000 (i.e., $200,000 × 10%). When a positive residual income takes place, a company (division, segment, investment) is creating wealth. When a negative residual income takes place, a company (division, segment, investment) is consuming capital.

Example: CP Inc. is a company engaged in the production and distribution of computers and printers. It has two main operating departments: department C specializes in design, production and marketing of computers and department P deals in printers. The following information is produced with reference to both the departments:

	Department C	*Department P*
Net operating profit	$300 million	$130 million
Operating assets: opening	$1 billion	$1.1 billion
Operating assets: ending	$0.5 billion	$0.7 billion

The company's WACC is 12% and it can use all the assets on a new project that earns a return of 15%.

Since the company can earn 15% on alternate projects, it is treated as the minimum required return. Department C's average operating assets are $1.05 billion, on which the minimum required return is $157.5 million. Its residual income, hence, is $142.5 million ($300 – $157.5 million). Department P's average operating assets are $0.6 billion, on which the minimum required return is $90 million. Its residual income, hence, is $40 million ($130 – $90 million). Department C has earned $142.5 million residual income as compared to $40 million earned by department P. Residual income allows us to compare the dollar amount of residual income earned by different departments. Since the residual income in both cases is positive, we conclude that both have met the minimum return requirements. However, with residual income it is not easy to compare performance.

ROI calculates total return in percentage terms and is a better measure of relative performance. In this example, department C has an ROI of 28.6% ($300 million/$1,050 million), while department P has an ROI of 18.6% ($130 million/$700 million).

3.6.3 Return on Equity

The ROE ratio, or ROE, is a profitability ratio that measures the ability of a firm to generate profits from its shareholders' investments in the company. It measures a corporation's profitability by revealing how much profit a company generates with the money shareholders have invested. The ROE is useful for comparing the profitability of a company to that of other firms in the same industry. The ROE ratio formula is calculated by dividing net income by shareholder's equity.

$$\text{ROE ratio} = \frac{\text{Net income}}{\text{Shareholders' equity}}$$

There are several variations on the formula that investors may use:

1. Investors wishing to see the return on common equity (ROCE) may modify the above formula by subtracting preferred dividends from net income and subtracting preferred equity from shareholders' equity, giving the following: ROCE = net income – preferred dividends/common equity.
2. ROE may also be calculated by dividing net income by 'average' shareholders' equity. Average shareholders' equity is calculated by adding the shareholders' equity at the beginning of a period to the shareholders' equity at period's end and dividing the result by two.

3. Investors may also calculate the change in ROE for a period by first using the shareholders' equity figure from the beginning of a period as a denominator to determine the beginning ROE. Then, the end-of-period shareholders' equity can be used as the denominator to determine the ending ROE. Calculating both beginning and ending ROEs allows an investor to determine the change in profitability over the period.

Example: Smith Company is a retail store that sells tools to construction companies across the country. Smith reported a net income of $100,000 and issued preferred dividends of $10,000 during the year. Smith also had 10,000, $5 par common shares outstanding during the year. Smith would calculate his ROCE as $1.80 ($90,000 ÷ $50,000).

As you can see, after preferred dividends are removed from the net income, Smith's ROE is 1.8. This means that every dollar of common shareholders' equity earned about $1.80 this year. In other words, shareholders saw a 180% return on their investment. Smith's ratio is most likely considered high for his industry. This could indicate that Smith's is a growing company. An average of 5 to 10 years of ROE ratios will give investors a better picture of the growth of this company. Company growth or a higher ROE does not necessarily get passed onto the investors however. If the company retains these profits, the common shareholders will only realize this gain by having an appreciated stock.

DuPont Analysis

The Dupont analysis, also called the Dupont model, is a financial ratio based on the ROE ratio that is used to analyse a company's ability to increase its ROE. DuPont analysis examines the ROE, by analysing profit margin, total asset turnover and financial leverage. It was created by the DuPont Corporation in the 1920s. It results in a composite ratio giving a more meaning to ROE with three different matrices. The formula as per the model is as follows:

$$\text{ROE} = \frac{\text{Net income}}{\text{Sales}} \times \frac{\text{Net sales}}{\text{Average total assets}} \times \frac{\text{Total assets}}{\text{Total equity}}$$

In simplified form,

$$\text{ROE} = \text{Profit margin} \times \text{argin asset turnovert turn ed fleverage}$$

Thus, the model helps to analyse the ROE in a more focused way. The formula also helps to find out the ways of maximizing ROE via improving all the three parameters.

Example: Let us take a look at Tommy's Retailers and Sammy's Retailers. Both of these companies operate in the same apparel industry and have the same ROE ratio of 45%. This model can be used to show the strengths and weaknesses of each company. Each company has the following ratios:

Ratio	***Tommy***	***Sammy***
Profit margin	30%	15%
Total asset turnover	0.50	6.00
Financial leverage	3.00	0.50
ROE	45%	45%

As you can see, both companies have the same overall ROE, but the companies' operations are completely different. Tommy is generating sales while maintaining a lower cost of goods as evidenced by its higher profit margin. Sammy is having a difficult time turning over large amounts of sales.

Sammy's business, on the other hand, is selling products at a smaller margin, but it is turning over a lot of products. You can see this from its low profit margin and extremely high asset turnover. This model helps investors compare similar companies like these with similar ratios. Investors can then apply perceived risks with regard to each company's business model.

3.6.4 Return on Capital Employed

Return on capital employed, or ROCE, is a profitability ratio that measures how efficiently a company can generate profits from its capital employed by comparing net operating profit to capital employed. In other words, ROCE shows investors how many dollars in profits each dollar of capital employed generates. ROCE is a long-term profitability ratio because it shows how effectively assets are performing while taking into consideration long-term financing. This is why ROCE is a more useful ratio than ROE to evaluate the longevity of a company. This ratio measures how efficiently and effectively management has deployed the resources available to it. A change in the ROCE may be due to changes in profit margins, asset utilization, sales mix or errors in inventory counting. It is a composite measure, as shown in Figure 3.7, which considers two important parameters of performance together.

Figure 3.7 ROCE Determinants and Operational Value Drivers

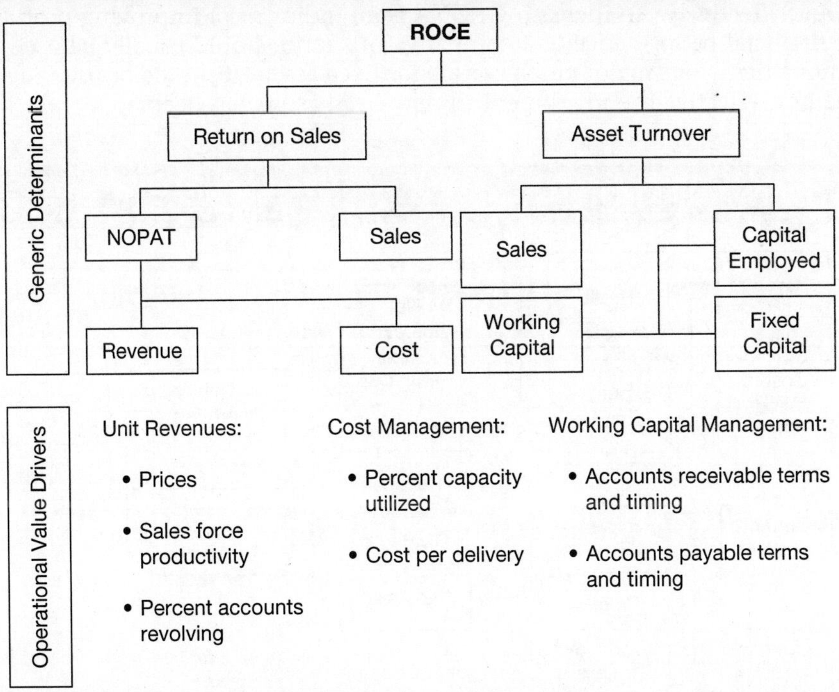

Source: Koller (1994).

Example: Scott's Auto Body Shop customizes cars for celebrities and movie sets. During the year, Scott had a net operating profit of $100,000. Scott reported $100,000 of total assets and $25,000 of current liabilities on his balance sheet for the year. Accordingly, Scott's ROCE would be calculated like this:

$$\text{ROCE} = \frac{\text{Net operating profit}}{\text{Total assets} - \text{Total liabilities}} = \frac{\$100{,}000}{\$100{,}000 - \$25{,}000} = 1.33$$

As you can see, Scott has a return of 1.33. In other words, for every dollar invested in employed capital, Scott earns $1.33. Scott's return might be so high because he maintains low assets level. Companies with large cash reserves usually skew this ratio because cash is included in the employed capital computation even though it is not technically employed yet.

3.6.5 Return on Net Assets

The return on net assets (RONA) is a comparison of net income with the net assets. This is a metric of financial performance of a company that takes into account earnings of a company with regard to fixed assets and net working capital (Figure 3.8). The RONA helps the investors to determine the percentage net income the company is generating from the assets. This ratio tells how effectively and efficiently the company is using its assets to generate earnings. This is an important ratio, because in many companies the fixed assets are a single largest component of the investment.

Although there are no fixed standards or benchmarks for RONA, the higher this ratio is the better it is. Higher RONA means that the company is using its assets and working capital efficiently and effectively. An increasing RONA is an indicator of improving profitability and improving financial performance of a company. This ratio should usually be used in capital-intensive industries where major purchases are for fixed assets. It should be used in subsequent years to see how effective the investment in new fixed assets has been.

Figure 3.8 Rate of Return on Net Assets

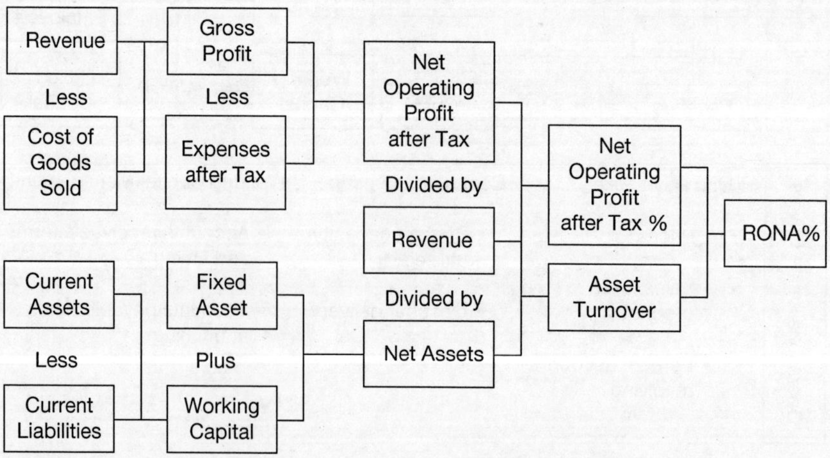

Source: Authors.

Example: To demonstrate the RONA ratio, assume that a company's financial statement shows \$100,000 in fixed assets, \$50,000 in current assets, \$30,000 in current liabilities and a net income of \$80,000. Subtracting its current liabilities of \$30,000 from its current assets of \$50,000 will yield \$20,000 in net working capital. Dividing the company's net income of \$80,000 by \$120,000 (\$100,000 fixed assets plus \$20,000 net working capital) will result in a RONA ratio of 0.67. Multiplying 0.67 by 100 will yield a ratio of 67%.

3.6.6 EVA

Probably the most widely used approach to measuring value creation is EVA. EVA is a performance measure and, when linked to management pay, provides a strong incentive for managers to select and implement value-creating investments. In the late 1980s, Joel Stern and G. Bennett Stewart III of the New York consulting firm Stern Stewart & Co. introduced the EVA performance measure. Many large American corporations have adopted EVA: Boise Cascade, Coca Cola, Whirlpool, Eli Lilly and Monsanto, to name a few. EVA, like all value-based metrices, departs from the traditional accounting model. The basic equation for calculating EVA is

$$\text{EVA} = \text{NOPAT} - \text{Cost of capital}$$

Calculation of EVA	
	Net Sales
–	Operating Expenses
=	Operating Profit (EBIT, Earnings before Interest and Tax)
–	Taxes
=	Net Operating Profit after Tax (NOPAT)
–	Capital Charges (Invested Capital × Cost of Capital)
=	EVA

NOPAT is net operating profit after tax and measures the profits the company has generated from its ongoing operations. It is similar to EBIT (a common starting point in analysts' valuation models) less taxes. EVA can be interpreted as a company's NOPAT less the capital charges. Capital charges equal the company's invested capital times the WACC. WACC equals the sum of each component of capital – short-term debt, long-term debt and shareholders' equity – weighted for its relative proportion, at market value, in the company's capital structure.

The idea behind EVA is rooted in economic income as opposed to accounting income. As economic income moves up or down, so goes the value of the business. The problem is that calculating economic income is not easy; it requires hundreds of adjustments. For example, under traditional accounting, we would expense cash disbursed for R&D, but in arriving at economic income we would capitalize R&D since it provides a future economic benefit. The list of adjustments from accounting to economic is extensive: depreciation, gains/losses, reserves, deferred taxes and so on. Since EVA is at the centre of VBM, it is important to keep the number of adjustments to those material items that significantly distort value. This is important since managers throughout the entire organization will need to understand how EVA is calculated. Keeping EVA simple will go a long way towards successful implementation.

To find out strategies for companies to increase their EVA and create shareholder value, we have to transform our formula of EVA:

$$\text{EVA} = \text{NOPAT} - (\text{Invested capital} \times \text{WACC})$$

$$\frac{\text{EVA}}{\text{Invested capital}} = \frac{\text{NOPAT}}{\text{Invested capital}} - \text{WACC}$$

$$\text{EVA} = (\text{RONA} - \text{WACC}) \times \text{Invested capital}$$

Here, $\frac{\text{NOPAT}}{\text{Invested capital}}$ is considered as RONA

EVA can also be calculated by taking the spread between the rate of RONAs and the WACC, multiplied by the invested capital. This definition shows us different strategies to increase EVA:

1. Increasing returns on existing capital (while holding WACC and invested capital constant)
2. Reductions in the cost of capital (WACC)
3. New investments that earn returns greater than the WACC (profitable growth)
4. Divestment of value-destroying activities (the reduction in invested capital will be more than compensated for by the greater spread between RONA and WACC)
5. Sustain the competitive advantage (technological or cost leadership, for example) which enables the company to generate above-normal returns (RONA > WACC), for a longer period

EVA Adjustments

When we calculate EVA, we need to calculate the cash equivalent of income (NOPAT) and the cash equivalent equity that has been invested in the business (adjusted capital). This requires that we remove many of the accounting distortions that have blurred cash flow. In his book *Quest for Value*, Bennett refers to these adjustments as 'equity equivalents', so that we can restate book values to economic values. When the market value of an organization exceeds the economic value of the organization, this is Market Value Added (MVA).

In order to calculate NOPAT, we will add back to income current year's equity equivalents that have distorted cash flows. Cumulative equity equivalents will be added back in arriving at adjusted capital. In *Quest for Value*, Bennett describes the following equity equivalent adjustments:

1. Deferred Taxes: The income statement reflects tax expenses that may or may not be paid. The difference between what has been expensed and what has paid is called deferred taxes. By adding deferred taxes back to capital, we reverse out the distortion for taxes not paid. An increase to deferred taxes in the current year would be added back to income in arriving at NOPAT.
2. LIFO Reserve: LIFO (Last in First Out) is used to price inventories on the balance sheet. Under LIFO, investments in inventory are subject to understatement. A LIFO reserve account captures the difference between LIFO and FIFO (First in First Out). This amount is added back to capital since we want to reflect the total amount of capital invested. An increase in the LIFO reserve in the current year would be added back in arriving at NOPAT.
3. Amortization of Goodwill: Non-cash expenditures such as goodwill will distort capital deployed. We are trying to measure the cash return on all cash invested into the business. Therefore, we would add back the total amount amortized for goodwill in arriving at capital and we would add back the current year's amortization in arriving at NOPAT.

4. Capitalized Intangibles: Intangibles such as R&D expenditures provide a long-term economic benefit. These transactions are capitalized under EVA, as opposed to expensing the entire amount within traditional accounting. The original R&D expense is reversed out and replaced with a net capitalized intangible (NCI). The total amount for R&D less the amount amortized is the NCI, and this represents an adjustment to capital. The amount amortized in the current year would be adjusted to earnings in arriving at NOPAT.
5. Other Reserves and Allowances: Besides the LIFO reserve, we may have material amounts related to other types of reserves and allowances. Examples include reserve for inventory obsolescence and allowance for doubtful accounts. These accounting transactions would be treated similarly to the LIFO reserve.

In summary, we are trying to arrive at earnings that are close to cash and compare this return to a capital base that is expressed in cash equivalent terms. This means that we recognize economic values, such as expenditures, that provide long-term benefits and reverse out non-cash entries as well as reserve account balances. Also, we must express the asset base (capital) in terms of replacement capital. This requires removing distortions like goodwill write offs, asset write offs and highly depreciable fixed assets that have a carrying (book) value substantially different than market or replacement values. In *Quest for Value*, Bennett summarizes the following adjustments:

Adjustments Required to Calculate NOPAT	***Adjustments Required to Calculate Capital***
+ Increase to deferred taxes	+ Deferred taxes
+ Increase to LIFO reserve	+ LIFO reserve
+ Goodwill amortized in current year	+ Total goodwill amortized to date
+ Increase to NCIs	+ NCIs
+/– Unusual loss or (gains) net of tax	+/– Cumulative loss or (gain) net of tax
+ Increase to other reserves and allowances	+ Other reserves and allowances

Example: Dwenger & Associates, a medical care practice, has a WACC of 10%. It has employed $30,000,000 of mostly long-term capital to run the practice, according to the most recent balance sheet. The most recent income statement shows the following:

Revenues	$40,000,000
–Cost of goods sold	$24,000,000
Gross profit	$16,000,000
–Operating expenses	$7,500,000
Operating profit	$8,500,000
Income tax at 40%	($3,400,000)
After tax operating profit	**$5,100,000**

The EVA for this period would be $2,100,000, calculated as follows:

EVA = NOPAT – Cost of capital
= $5,100,000 – (0.10 × $30,000,000)
= $2,100,000

3.6.7 Cash Flow Return on Investment

CFROI is another method of measuring value. Valuations are a function of looking into the future and adjusting for things that will alter value. For example, the operating cash flows we receive in the future are adjusted downward to reflect inflation. We also recognize that the marketplace is not without limitations when it comes to judging value. For example, the marketplace cannot readily comprehend the cost of capital (this is difficult enough for insiders to figure out) and thus the marketplace reacts to things like earnings to determine short-term values. We need a way of measuring value that emphasizes operating cash flows (adjusted for inflation) and compares this return to investments that are also adjusted for inflation. Such an approach to measuring value is called CFROI.

CFROI = Inflation-adjusted cash flows (cash in)/inflation-adjusted investment (cash out)

Unlike EVA, CFROI expresses cash flows and investments in current dollars. CFROI does not concern itself with the cost of capital. It looks ahead and establishes a market rate based on what investors expect over the long term. Because of this approach to valuation, CFROI tends to be more accurate than EVA in measuring value. Under CFROI, economic performance is calculated and measured by

1. identifying cash inflows and outflows over the economic life of the assets
2. adjusting both cash inflows and outflows into units of constant purchasing power
3. calculating a CFROI rate similar to how the IRR is calculated; that is, what is the rate where inflows = outflows?

Calculating CFROI

CFROI adjusts for inflation by marking up gross investments made each year, based on comparing the gross domestic product (GDP) deflator to changes in purchasing power. The useful life of assets is estimated by dividing gross investments by depreciation charges. Cash flows are determined by starting with gross cash flows or net income and making several adjustments, such as adding back interest expense. Assets that are not capitalized are separated out from capitalized investments in order to properly calculate the CFROI rate (calculated similar to IRR). CFROI, like EVA, attempts to remove accounting distortions in arriving at cash in and cash out, such as the following:

	Net income		Book value of assets
+	Rent expense (operating leases)	+	Accumulated depreciation
–	FIFO profits	+	Operating leased assets
+	Interest expense	–	Net deferred tax assets

CFROI is calculated by translating the ratio of cash in to cash out as IRR. The calculation uses the economic life of investments and considers non-capitalized assets (such as land) as residual values at the end of the valuation period. The following example will illustrate these points.

Example: Calculate CFROI

Some important points: Gross assets are the sum of non-depreciable and depreciable assets. Useful life of assets is calculated based on the relationship of gross assets to depreciation charges. We will assume this is 15 years. At the end of 15 years, non-depreciable assets are released. Gross cash flows are adjusted for monetary gains and (losses) as well as a non-LIFO inventory adjustment.

Step 1: Calculate gross cash flows and express this amount in current dollars (adjusted for inflation). Non-cash items such as depreciation are added back, interest on debt is reversed out since cost of capital is ignored and payments on operating leased assets are reversed out since off-balance sheet assets are included in capital.

Net income	$41,000
Depreciation	20,000
Interest expense	6,000
Rental expense	6,000
+/– Monetary holding gain (loss)	(3,000)
Gross cash flows in current dollars	$70,000

Step 2: Calculate gross assets (capital) and express this amount in current dollars (adjusted for inflation).

Monetary current assets	$161,000
Less: Non-interest current liabilities	84,000
Net monetary assets	77,000
Inventories	68,000
Adjust inventories to current $	49,000
Land	9,000
Adjust land to current $	3,000
Non-capitalized assets in current $	206,000
Gross plant assets	348,000
Adjust gross plant to current $	106,000
Leased property	66,000
Capitalized assets in current $	520,000
Total gross assets in current $	$726,000

Summary: Cash Inflows are $70,000 per year over 15 years + residual value of $206,000 for non-capitalized assets. Outflows are $726,000 for capital deployed (gross assets).

Step 3: Calculate CFROI like you would calculate IRR; that is, the rate where inflows ($70,000 and $206,000) equals outflows ($726,000). We can use a Microsoft Excel Spreadsheet to solve for CFROI.

Enter –726,000 in cell A1 followed by +70,000 in cells A2 through A15 and finally enter +276,000 (70,000+206,000) in cell A16. Enter the IRR function in cell A17 as = irr (a1:a16) and Excel calculates a CFROI of 6.73%.

3.6.8 Residual Cash Flow

Another approach to measuring value that we need to discuss is residual cash flow (RCF). RCF is sometimes called CVA; that is, what are the RCFs generated by investment. RCF is net cash flow less a charge for cost of capital. We can express RCF as follows:

$$RCF = \text{Adjusted operating cash flows} - (I \times \text{gross investment})$$

Here, I represents the cost of capital.

Example: Z Company owns a capital asset costing $100,000 having a useful life of 5 years with no salvage value. The asset will be depreciated over its useful life under the straight-line method. Annual cash flows from this investment are estimated to be $35,000 and the marginal tax rate applicable to the company is 35%. The WACC is 8.5%. What is the RCF per year?

Cash flow per year	$35,000
Less: Taxes (35%)	12,250
Net cash flows	22,750
Adjustment to cash flow (1)	7,000
Adjusted cash flow	29,750
Less: Cost of capital (2)	8,500
RCF per year	$21,250

1. Depreciation of $20,000 ($100,000 ÷ 5) per year × 0.35 (tax rate) = $7,000
2. Gross investment of $100,00 × 8.5% (cost of capital) = $8,500

As you can see from the previous example, RCF is much easier to calculate when compared to EVA or CFROI. However, we want RCF to be as accurate, if not more so, than EVA and CFROI. Therefore, we will need to make some additional adjustments. We can take a page out of the EVA book and apply it to RCF. For example, R&D expenses are capitalized under EVA since they provide future economic benefits. This same type of adjustment should be made to operating cash flows under RCF.

We should also remember that WACC includes the cost of debt. If operating cash flows include interest payments, then interest should be ignored in arriving at operating cash flows. Otherwise, you will double account for debt service costs, once in calculating cash flow and once in calculating a charge for cost of capital. As you might expect, in the hands of consultants RCF is subject to several other adjustments. Two notable examples are summarized in Exhibit 3.3.

RCF incorporates residual income concepts and gets back to the most important indicator—operating cash flow. By focusing on operating cash flows, RCF simplifies the valuation process and still retains high degrees of accuracy. This point was made clear when 325 companies were compared over a five-year period using EVA, CFROI and RCF. The study, published in the October 1998 issue of *Management Accounting*, concluded the following:

> EVA's creators have certainly made some incredible claims, but so far the academic testing of the measure has not shown significantly different results from residual income in most respects. Clearly the superiority of RCF is apparent over either EVA or CFROI, the recently popular measures produced by the consulting firms. (Steve 1998)

Exhibit 3.3 Adjustments in Computing RCF

The Boston Consulting Group:

a. In arriving at adjusted operating cash flows, economic depreciation is deducted. Economic depreciation refers to the sinking fund amounts required along with earned cost of capital that is required to replace the asset.
b. Similar to CFROI, adjusted operating cash flows are restated to constant dollars.
c. Weighted average cost of capital is ignored and a market driven rate is used. The market driven rate is estimated as the discount rate for equating the present value of net cash flows for an index of companies with the sum of prices for debt and equity of the same index of companies. The market driven rate is essentially the rate of return demanded in the market place.

Fredrik Weissenrieder Consulting:

a. Adjusted operating cash flows are calculated by finding the discounted cash flow that provides a net present value of zero for the economic life of the investment.
b. Gross investment excludes non-strategic assets. Investments made that have nothing to do with returns (such as furniture and fixtures) are not part of capital.

RCF does have some drawbacks, but they are few. For example, RCF is not a comparable form of measurement; that is, you cannot compare RCFs between companies. In addition, RCF is sometimes more appropriate for project evaluation rather than company valuation. However, given the fact that RCF is highly correlated to stock prices, it warrants serious consideration by all organizations concerned about measuring value.

3.6.9 Cash Value Added

CVA is an extension of RCF, which requires some discussion. CVA is an NPV model based completely on discounted cash flows. Erik Ottosson and Fredrik Weissenrieder (1996), change agents at the company, have developed the model. The CVA model distinguishes between strategic and non-strategic investments. Strategic investments are aimed at creating values and conditions for growth. The implementation of these investments is always questioned. Non-strategic investments are investments that do not add value, but aim to maintain the values of the strategic investments implemented previously. The question is when, and not whether, these investments are to be implemented. If these non-strategic investments were not carried out, it would imply that the values and the economic lives of the strategic investments would decrease. The non-strategic investments should therefore be treated as (current) costs for the continuing of operations. Outgoing from the strategic investment under consideration, a cash flow demand is calculated in absolute figures, the so-called operating cash flow demand (OCFD). When this demanded cash flow is discounted by the WACC for the economic life under consideration, the NPV of the initial investment is equal to zero. The demand is expressed in real terms year upon year, but increases are expressed in nominal terms because of inflation. An illustration of the OCFD calculation is presented in Table 3.3.

The initial investment in the above illustration is 100 and its economic life is five years. The forecast consumer price index (CPI) is used to estimate the expected level of inflation; for instance, between years 1 and 2 the CPI is expected to increase from 103 to 107, resulting in an expected level of inflation of 107/103 = 1.04, that is, 4%. In order to derive the value of

Table 3.3 Calculation of OCFD, an Example

Using Calculations Allowing for Non-constant Inflation						
		In-data Fields				
PV investment year 0	100					
WACC	10%					
The value of 1 unit of OCFD during the expected economic life	4.15					
OCFD year 1	24.07					
Year		***1***	***2***	***3***	***4***	***5***
Expected CPI		103	107	110	120	130
Inflation		3%	4%	3%	9%	8%
OCFD series		24.07	25.04	25.79	28.11	30.36
PV OCFD (=PV investment)		100				
PV OCFD – PV investment		0				

Source: Authors.

one unit of OCFD for the economic life under consideration, the NPV for the different CPIs is calculated and discounted by the WACC, in this case by 10%. The NPV is then divided by 103 to obtain the value of one unit for the first year in the economic life concerned:

$$\frac{103}{1.1}+\frac{107}{1.1^2}+\frac{110}{1.1^3}+\frac{120}{1.1^4}+\frac{130}{1.1^5}=4.15$$

In order to calculate the OCFD for the year prospectively, the initial investment is divided by the unit 4.15; in our case: 100/4.15 = 24.07, which is the OCFD for year 1. The OCFD for the first year is then adjusted for the expected inflation level for the second year in order to reach the OCFD at current (expected) prices. Thus, the OCFD for the second year is 24.07 × 1.04 = 25.04 and so on. The present value of the yearly OCFDs adds up to 100 over the economic life period and the NPV of the investment, that is, the present value of the cash flows minus the initial investment equals zero. Thus, the OCFDs show how much cash flow has to be generated to pay off the initial investment during its economic life. We follow Weissenrieder (1997) concerning the formula deduction:

+	Sales
–	Costs
=	Operating surplus
+/–	Working capital movement
–	Non-strategic investments
=	Operating cash flow
–	OCFD
=	CVA

$$\text{CVA} - \text{index} = \frac{\text{Operating cash flow}}{\text{OCFD}}$$

When the OCFDs are calculated, the management also knows the size of the OCFs needed to generate a CVA index of, for instance, 1.2; in other words the cash flow exceeds the OCFD by 20%. Furthermore, the CVA index can be split into four different margins related to sales:

1. Operating surplus margin
2. Working capital movement (WCM) margin
3. Non-strategic investment margin
4. OCFD margin

These four margins, together with sales, are five major value drivers of the CVA concept. Expressed that way, the formula is

$$\text{CVA} = \text{Sales} \times \left[\frac{\text{Operating surplus}}{\text{Sales}} - \frac{\text{WCM}}{\text{Sales}} - \frac{\text{Non} - \text{strategic investment}}{\text{Sales}} - \frac{\text{OCFD}}{\text{Sales}}\right]$$

The OCFD should not be confused with the stated, or expected, cash flow objective. If values are to be created, the investment must generate an OCF bigger than the OCFD, in other words CVA. Thus, a positive CVA indicates that the company satisfies the demands of stock markets and can be followed by an instant rise in the share price.

Multiple Choice Questions

1. Both ROI and residual income can be used for performance evaluation of ———
   a. Cost centres
   b. Profit centres
   c. Investment centres
   d. All of the above
2. Division A earns \$6,000 on an investment of \$36,000. On an investment of \$84,000, division B earns \$12,000. Which of the following is true?
   a. Division A's profits are too low.
   b. If there are further costs that are common to both divisions, the total company's ROI is probably greater than 15%.
   c. If the minimum desired ROI is 10%, division A's residual income is lower than that of division B.
   d. ROI for division B is greater than ROI for division A.
3. Which equation describes ROI? (I = investment, S = sales and N = income)
   a. S/I
   b. S/I × N
   c. S/I × S/N
   d. N/S × S/I
4. After-tax operating income minus the after-tax WACC of capital multiplied by total assets minus current liabilities equals
   a. Return on investment
   b. Residual income
   c. Economic value added
   d. WACC
5. The after-tax average cost of all the long-term funds used by a corporation equals
   a. Economic value added
   b. Return on investment
   c. Return on equity
   d. WACC

6. Using residual income as a measure of performance rather than ROI promotes goal congruence because
   a. Residual income places importance on the reduction of underperforming assets
   b. Residual income calculates a percentage return rather than an absolute return
   c. Residual income concentrates on maximizing an absolute amount of dollars
   d. Residual income concentrates on maximizing the return on sales
7. Thacker Company has two regional offices. The data for each are as follows:

	Maryland	New York
Revenues	$580,000	$596,000
Operating assets	4,800,000	9,000,000
Net operating income	2,016,000	4,860,000

   What is the ROI for the New York division?
   a. 0.42 b. 0.54 c. 0.96 d. 4.12
8. Wacker Company has two regional offices. The data for each are as follows:

	Maryland	New York
Revenues	$580,000	$596,000
Operating assets	4,800,000	9,000,000
Net operating income	2,016,000	4,860,000

   What is the Maryland Division's ROI?
   a. 0.42 b. 0.54 c. 0.96 d. 4.12
9. ROI can be increased by ____
   a. Increasing operating assets
   b. Decreasing operating assets
   c. Decreasing revenues
   d. Both (b) and (c)
10. Which of the following statements about designing an accounting-based performance measure is false?
    a. The steps may be followed in a random order.
    b. The issues considered in each step are independent.
    c. Management's beliefs are present during the analyses.
    d. Behavioural criteria are important when evaluating the steps.

Review Questions

1. Define VBM.
2. Write a brief note on evolution of VBM.
3. How does VBM maximize shareholders value?
4. Explain the criticism of traditional accounting measures with reference to shareholder value concept.
5. How does the VBM process create shareholder value?
6. Explain corporate objective function.

7. Identify different types of measures for computing shareholder value.
8. What are the differences between ROI and residual income performance measures?
9. Explain ROE as a performance measure. How the DuPont model improves the analytical power of ROE?
10. Explain ROCE as a performance measure. Differentiate it with RONA.
11. Critically evaluate the application of EVA for measuring shareholder value.
12. How to calculate cash flow ROI? What are the challenges in using CFROI in measuring value?
13. Differentiate between RCF and CVA.

Exercises

1. Alpha Company has compiled the following information for three of its divisions:

Division	*Investments (at Historical Cost), $*	*Operating Income, $*
X	560,000	66,500
Y	532,000	64,400
Z	350,000	43,120

Required:

a. Compute each division's ROI and residual income, assuming a 10% cost of capital.
b. Suppose the net book value of each division's investments is half of the historical cost. Using net book value as the measure of investment, compute each division's ROI and residual income, assuming a 10% cost of capital.
c. Comment on the division rankings in (1) and (2).
d. If the division managers are rewarded on the basis of ROI or residual income, will they find it attractive to invest in new, more costly equipment?

2. Beta Company would like to examine the sales margin and asset turnover components of ROI for three of its divisions and has accordingly assembled the following information:

Division	*Investments, $*	*Operating Income, $*	*Sales, $*
A	575,000	75,000	500,000
B	700,000	91,000	542,000
C	1,000,000	176,000	763,000

Required:

a. Compute each division's ROI, sales margin and asset turnover.
b. Comment on the divisions' relative rankings on the ratios computed in (1).

3. A business whose investors require an ROI of 8% reports an income of $1 million on an investment of $20 million. What is the residual income for this business?
4. Mark Zimmerman, manager of the components division of FedEx Corporation, is considering a new investment for his division. The division has an investment base of

$4,000,000 and an operating income of $600,000. The new investment of $500,000 supports corporate strategy and is expected to increase operating income by $50,000 next year, and acceptable level of return from corporate headquarters' point of view.

Required:

a. What is the current ROI for the Components Division?
    i. What will the ROI be if Mark undertakes the new investment?
    ii. Suppose Mark's compensation consists of a salary plus a bonus proportional to his division's ROI. Is Mark's compensation higher with or without the new investment?

5. The following information is available about the status and operations of Zamia Company, which has a minimum required ROI of 15%.

	Division A	*Division B*
Divisional investment	$500,000	$1,500,000
Divisional profit	$150,000	$540,000
Divisional sales	$1,000,000	$3,600,000

Required:

a. Compute ROI for division A.
b. Compute residual income for division B.
c. Division A could increase its profit by $40,000 by increasing its investment by $150,000. Compute its total residual income.
d. Division A could increase its return on sales by one percentage point, while keeping the same total sales and investment. Compute its ROI.
e. Division B could reduce its investment so that its asset turnover increased by one time, while holding total sales constant. Compute its ROI.

6. The following information is available about the status and operations of Timex Company, which has a minimum required ROI of 20%.

	Division A	*Division B*
Divisional investment	$400,000	$1,250,000
Divisional profit	$120,000	$580,000
Divisional sales	$800,000	$2,600,000

Required:

a. Compute ROI for division B.
b. Compute residual income for division A.
c. Division B could increase its profit by $80,000 by increasing its investment by $300,000. Compute its total residual income.
d. Division A could increase its return on sales by one percentage point, while keeping the same total sales. Compute its ROI.
e. Division A could increase its sales so that its asset turnover increased by one time, while holding total assets constant. Compute its ROI.

7. The following information relates to Toy Division of Zerox Company. Zerox's minimum cost of capital for its segments is 15%.

Sales	$4,000,000
Variable costs	1,400,000
Direct fixed costs	1,800,000
Investment	4,800,000

Required:

a. Find Zerox's ROI.
b. Find Zerox's EVA.

8. Young division has the following information for the most recent period:

Divisional Income	$11,000,000
Divisional investment	$85,000,000
Divisional sales	$100,000,000

Young has a minimum required return of 15%.

Required:

a. Compute Young's ROI.
b. Compute Young's investment turnover.
c. Compute Young's residual income.
d. Compute Young's return on sales.

9. Zamora Company is a decentralized organization with several autonomous divisions. The division managers are evaluated, in part, on the basis of the change in their return on invested assets. Operating results for the machine division for 2015 are budgeted as follows:

Sales	$5,000,000
Less variable costs	$2,500,000
Contribution margin	$2,500,000
Less fixed expenses	$1,800,000
Net operating income	$700,000

Operating assets for the division are currently $3,600,000. For 2015, the division can add a new product line for an investment of $600,000. The new product line will generate sales of $1,600,000 and will incur fixed expenses of $600,000 annually. Variable costs of the new product will average 60% of the selling price.

Required:

a. What is the effect on ROI of accepting the new product line?
b. If the company's required rate of return is 6% and residual income is used to evaluate managers, would this encourage the division to accept the new product line? Explain and show computations.

10. H is an investment group that owns a number of subsidiary companies. Each subsidiary produces a particular product, product range or service. For the purposes of management control, the subsidiary companies are organized into three sectors.

Consulting and services (CS): comprising a consultancy practice that provides advice on product design, manufacturing technique and material usage both to H group companies and to businesses outside the group. Salaries comprise about 95% of costs in the CS sector.

Heavy engineering (HE): comprising two subsidiary companies producing machinery, equipment and tools used in a variety of industrial applications. These companies require a major investment in the form of factory premises, plant and transport facilities.

Light engineering (LE): comprising four subsidiaries which produce a range of small mechanical and electrical components, many of which are designed into the products of HE sector companies. The production of these components is generally considered to be labour intensive.

At the start of 2015, the management of H decides to prepare a five-year strategic plan for the group. A team of H executives is assembled to prepare this plan. At its first meeting, the team is provided with the following summary of the group's performance in 2014.

	CS ($000)	HE ($000)	LE ($000)
Book value at 31 December 2014			
Non-current assets	80	4,970	810
Current assets	90	820	180
Current liabilities	(20)	(140)	(65)
Capital employed	150	5,650	925
Year to 31 December 2014			
Sales	860	6,320	1,918
Trading profit	220	1,073	240

All the above figures are taken from the H group's main accounting system and are prepared on a historical cost basis. The group finance charge is 12% of the capital employed in each sector at the end of the year. This figure is H Co's cost of money and is also used as the discount rate for project evaluation.

Required:

a. Calculate the ROI and residual income for each sector and comment on your calculations.
b. Discuss the relative merits of ROI and residual income as performance indicators.
c. Discuss the relevance of the information given in the question and state what additional information you would find helpful in advising H on which of its three sectors should be expanded.

11. Demena Plc has two operating divisions, the managers of which are given considerable autonomy. To assess the performance of divisional managers, the directors of the company use ROI. For this measure, the assets employed include both non-current and current assets. The company has a minimum acceptable ROI of 15% per year. The company uses straight-line depreciation. The following extract is taken from the budgets of the two divisions for 2011.

	Greenwich division	Wapping division
	£000	£000
Divisional profit	260	50
Non-current assets at cost	940	1,200
Current assets	390	180

Since the budgets were prepared, two investment opportunities have been brought before the relevant divisional managers as follows:

i. The directors of Demena would like to see the productivity of the wapping division improve. To help achieve this, they have authorized the divisional manager to buy some new equipment costing £300,000. This will have a life of five years and will lead to operating savings of £90,000 each year.
ii. A new product can be sold by the Greenwich division. This will increase sales revenue by £250,000 each year over the next five years. It will be necessary to increase marketing costs by £60,000 a year and stock held will increase by £90,000. The contribution margin ratio for the new product will be 30%.

Required:

a. Calculate the expected ROI for each division assuming first that the investment opportunities are not taken up, and then that both are.
b. How might the managers view the results of your calculations in part (1)?

12. Morgan Industries manufactures die machinery. To meet its expansion needs, it recently (2014) acquired one of its suppliers, Vienna Steel. To maintain Vienna's separate identity, Morgan reports Vienna's operations as an investment SBU. Morgan monitors all of its investment SBUs on the basis of ROI. Management bonuses are based on ROI, and all investment SBUs are expected to earn a 12% minimum before income taxes. Vienna's ROI has ranged from 14% to 18% since 2014. The company recently had the opportunity for a new investment that would have yielded 13% ROI. However, division management decided against the investment because it believed that the investment would decrease the division's overall ROI.

    The 2016 operating statement for Vienna follows. The division's operating assets were £13,000,000 at the end of 2016, a 6% increase over the 2015 year-end balance.

Vienna Division ***Operating Statement for Year Ended 31 December 2016 (Figures in '000)***		
Sales		£25,000
Cost of goods sold		£16,600
Gross profit		£8,400
Operating expense		
Administration	£2,340	
Selling	3,810	£6,150
Income before income taxes		£2,250

Required:

You are required to

a. Calculate the following performance measures for 2016 for the Vienna division:
   i. Return on average investment in operating assets employed.
   ii. Residual income calculated on the basis of average operating assets employed.
b. Which performance measure (ROI or residual income) should Morgan Industries use to provide the proper incentive for each division to act autonomously in the firm's best interests? Would Vienna's management have been more likely to accept the capital investment opportunity if residual income had been used as a performance measure instead of ROI? Explain.
c. What type of strategic performance measurement do you recommend for Vienna division? Explain.

References

Black, Fischer, Michael C. Jensen, and Myron Scholes. 1972. 'The Capital Asset Pricing Model: Some Empirical Tests', pp. 79–121 in M. Jensen ed., *Studies in the Theory of Capital Markets*. New York: Praeger Publishers.

Black, A., P. Wright, and J. Bachman. 1998. *In Search of Shareholder Value*, pp. 81–98. London: Pitman Publishing.

Boulos, F., P. Haspeslagh, and T. Noda. 2001. *Getting the Value Out of Value-based Management*, INSEAD survey, p. 54.

Copeland, T., T. Koller, and J. Murrin. 2002. *Unternehmenswert – Methoden und Strategien für eine wertorientierte Unternehmensführung*, 3rd ed. Frankfurt/New York: Campus.

Dean, J. 1951. *Capital Budgeting*. New York: Columbia University Press.

Hahn, D., and M. Hintze. 2006. Konzepte wertorientierter Unternehmensführung. In *Strategische Unternehmensplanung – Strategische Unternehmensführung*, edited by D. Hahn and B. Taylor, 9th ed., 83–114. Berlin, Heidelberg: Springer.

Hornyak, Steve. 'Budgeting Made Easy'. *Management Accounting*, October 1998: 18–23.

Ittner, C.D., and D.F. Larcker. 2001. 'Assessing Empirical Research in Managerial Accounting: A Value-based Management Perspective'. *Journal of Accounting and Economics*, 32: 349–410.

Kennedy, A. 2000. *The End of Shareholder Value – The Real Effects of the Shareholder Value Phenomenon and the Crisis It Is Bringing to Business*, 160, 207. London: Orion Business Books.

Knight, J. 1998. *Value-based Management: Developing a Systematic Approach to Creating Shareholder Value*, 173–75. New York: McGraw-Hill.

Koller, T. 1994. 'What Is Value-based Management?' *The McKinsey Quarterly*, 3: 87–101.

Leahy, T. 2000. 'Making Their Mark'. *Business of Finance*, June.

Lee, Reggie Van, Lisa Fabish, and Nancy McGaw. 2005. 'The Value of Corporate Values'. *Strategy and Business*, 39, Summer (Originally published by Booz & Company. Also available at: http://www.strategy-business.com/article/05206?gko=9c265 (retrieved on 18 December 2014).

Lewis, T.G. 1995. *Steigerung des Unternehmenswertes – Total Value Management*. Landsberg/Lech: verlag moderne industrie.

Mctaggart, James M. 1994. Value Imperative: Managing for Superior Shareholder Returns. New York: Free Press.

Ottosson, E., and F. Weissenrieder. 1996. *CVA, Cash Value Added – A New Method for Measuring Financial Performance*. Gothenburg Studies in Financial Economics, Study No 1.

Rappaport, A. 1986. *Creating Shareholder Value*. New York: The Free Press.

Rappaport, A. 1999. 'New Thinking on How to Link Executive Pay with Performance.' *Harvard Business Review*, March/April, 91–101.

Sharpe, William F. 1964. 'Capital Asset Prices: A Theory of Market Equilibrium Under Conditions of Risk'. *Journal of Finance*, 19(3): 425–442.

Simms, J. 2001. 'Marketing for Value'. *Marketing*, June 28, 34–35.

Society of Management Accountants of Canada. 1997. 'Measuring and Managing Shareholder Value Creation. Management Accounting Guideline no 44'. In *Topical Issues – Value-based Management*, edited by Scarlett Bob. Canada: Society of Management Accountants of Canada.

Stewart, G. Bennett. 1990. *The Quest for Value: The EVA Management Guide*. New York: Harper Business.

Taylor, Frederick Winslow. 1911. *The Principles of Scientific Management*. New York, London: Harper & Brothers.

Weissenrieder, F. 1997. *Value-based Management: Economic Value Added or Cash Value Added?* Department of Economics Gothenburg University, Study No 3.

Part B

Financial Management

Chapter 4

Capital Budgeting and Investment Decisions

Chapter Objectives

On completion of this chapter, you will be able to understand:

- Capital and revenue expenditure
- Classification of investment projects
- Stages of capital budgeting analysis
- Guidelines for capital budgeting
- Estimating cash flows: initial, differential and terminal
- Techniques of capital budgeting: discounted versus non-discounted
- Time value of money
- Payback period, discounted payback period and payback reciprocal
- Accounting rate of return (ARR)
- Net present value
- Profitability index/benefit–cost ratio
- Internal rate of return
- NPV profile and modified IRR (MIRR)
- NPV versus IRR: independent projects, dependant projects, differences in scale of investment, timing of cash flows and horizon problem
- Unequal life projects: replacement chain method and equivalent annual annuity
- Inflation in capital budgeting

4.1 Introduction

Capital budgeting is a sensitive managerial action. It is the investment decision that management undertakes now and then upon which the success of a business largely depends. The financial managers who are responsible for this type of investment decisions always target to choose investments with satisfactory cash flows and rates of return. Therefore, a financial manager must be able to decide whether an investment is worth undertaking and be able to choose intelligently between two or more alternatives. To do this, a sound procedure to evaluate, compare and select projects is needed. This procedure is called capital budgeting.

Irrespective of its status as debt or equity, capital is a very limited resource. There is a limit to the volume of credit that the banking system can create in the economy. Commercial banks and other lending institutions have limited deposits from which they can lend money to individuals, corporations and governments keeping a regulated portion aside. For example, the Federal Reserve System requires each bank to maintain part of its deposits as reserves. Having limited resources to lend, lending institutions are selective in extending loans to their customers. However, even if a bank was to extend unlimited loans to a company, the management of that company would need to consider the impact that increasing loans would have on the overall cost of financing, WACC. In reality, any firm has limited borrowing capacities that should be allocated among the best investment alternatives. One might argue that a company can issue an almost unlimited amount of common stock to raise capital provided that it is within the limit of authorized capital. Increasing the number of shares of company stock, however, will serve only to distribute the same amount of equity among a greater number of shareholders. In other words, as the number of shares of a company increases, the company ownership of the individual stockholder may proportionally decrease. And that is why a company cannot raise as much fund as it needs through either equity or borrowing. This necessitates a careful analysis when it evaluates long-term investment proposals. Fund constraint is an obvious limitation, but it has made the managers, dealing with funds, sophisticated in terms of critical thinking and reasoning.

The argument that capital is a limited resource is true for any form of capital irrespective of capital structure, including debt, equity, retained earnings, accounts payable or notes payable and so on. Even the best-known firm in an industry or a community can increase its borrowing up to a certain level. Once this point has been reached, the firm will either be denied for more credit or be charged a higher interest rate, making borrowing a less desirable way to raise capital. Faced with limited sources of capital, the management should carefully decide whether a particular project is an economically feasible candidate for selection. In case of more than one project, the management must identify the projects that will contribute most to profits and, consequently, to the value (or wealth) of the firm. This, in essence, is the basis of capital budgeting. Thus, capital budgeting refers to the process of selection and use of some suitable techniques by the finance managers to supplement the long-term investment decisions and to choose the best among investment alternatives that maximizes the value of the firm and wealth of the owners as well.

4.2 Capital Expenditure and Revenue Expenditure

Investment decision that is referred to here only deals with long-term decision-making. The amount of cash outlay against long-term investment decision is capital form of expenditure. Firms also have revenue type of expenditure that is a part of operating decisions. These expenditures are required for running the day-to-day activities. Capital budgeting deals only with capital expenditure. However, revenue expenditure information is used to supplement the decision-making process. Thus, it is important to separate capital expenditure from revenue expenditure. A capital investment project can be distinguished from revenue expenditures by two features:

1. Such projects are relatively large in terms of the involvement of fund and risk.
2. Significant period of time (more than one year) elapses between the investment outlay and the receipt of the benefits.

As a result, most medium- and large-sized organizations have developed special procedures and methods for dealing with these decisions. A systematic approach to capital budgeting implies:

1. formulation of long-term goals
2. creative search for and identification of new investment opportunities
3. classification of projects and recognition of economically and/or statistically dependent proposals
4. estimation and forecasting of current and future cash flows
5. suitable administrative framework capable of transferring the required information to the decision level
6. controlling of expenditures and careful monitoring of crucial aspects of project execution
7. set of decision rules that can differentiate acceptable from unacceptable alternatives is required.

4.3 The Classification of Investment Projects

Investment projects are characterized in terms of different factors. On the basis of each factor, the investment projects are typified as follows:

1. On the basis of project size: Here, projects may be small or large. Small projects may be approved by departmental managers. More careful analysis and board of directors' approval is needed for large projects of, say, half a million dollars or more. However, the definition of small and large projects depends on the policy of the firm.
2. On the basis of the type of benefits to the firm: Investment projects may bring benefits in terms of ensuring regular cash flows, decreasing risks and alike. On the basis of the nature of benefits, capital project may be categorized as follows:
   i. Projects increasing cash flows
   ii. Projects decreasing risk
   iii. Projects generating other indirect benefit (showers for workers and so on).
3. On the basis of degree of dependence: Sometimes projects under consideration are dependent. And sometimes, selection of one project does not affect the cost and benefits of other projects. Project evaluation techniques in such cases are not the same. Thus, it is important to classify the projects in terms of their degree of dependence. On the basis of degree of dependence, projects may be classified as follows:
   i. Mutually exclusive projects (can execute project A or B, but not both)
   ii. Complementary projects (taking project A increases the cash flow of project B)
   iii. Substitute projects (taking project A decreases the cash flow of project B)
   iv. Independent project (cash flows of one project are not related to other projects)
   v. Contingent projects (acceptance of one project depends on the acceptance of another)
4. On the basis of statistical dependence: Sometimes, the dependence among projects is statistically defined in terms of their directions of behaviour as follows:
   i. Positive dependence (both projects A and B have similar direction)
   ii. Negative dependence (projects A and B have inverse direction)
   iii. Statistical independence (statistically no directional relationship exists between projects)
5. On the basis of cash flows: Projects will ensure cash flows if undertaken. However, the nature of cash flow differs across the projects. Some projects require investment initially to bring regular cash inflows in the future; some others bring lump sum cash inflow

now with regular cash outflows in the future and some others maintain no such pattern. They may bring cash inflows any time and may require cash outflows anytime also. Thus, on the basis of cash flows, projects may be either of two categories:

i. Conventional cash flow (only one change in the cash flow sign)
Example: –/++++ or +/– – – –
ii. Non-conventional cash flows (more than one change in the cash flow sign)
Example: +/–/+++ or –/+/–/++++

(Note that the sign '+' refers to cash inflows and '–' refers to cash outflows.)

6. On the basis of nature of investments: A 'replacement project' is an investment that involves the replacement of existing equipment or facilities. Replacement projects include the maintenance of existing assets to continue the current level of operating activity.

An 'expansion project' is an investment in a project that broadens existing product lines and markets. Expansion projects are intended to enlarge a company's established product or market.

A 'new product or market investment' involves including a new product or entering into a new market. Investment projects that involve introducing new products or entering into new markets are riskier than the replacement and expansion projects.

A 'mandated project' is a project required by government laws or agency rules. A company is forced or coerced into a mandated project.

4.4 Three Stages of Capital Budgeting Analysis

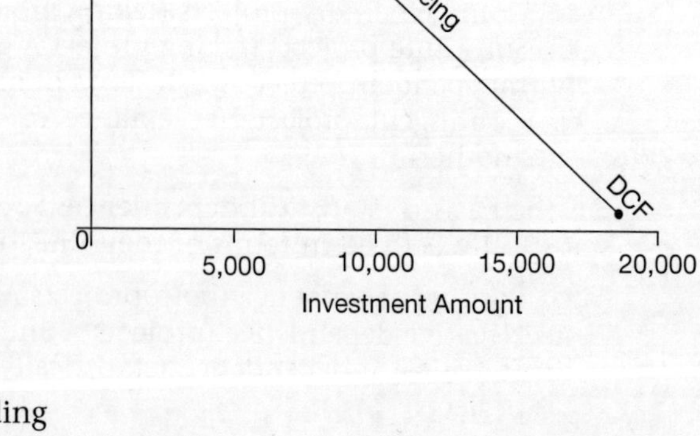

Capital budgeting analysis is a process of evaluating how investment in capital assets, assets that provide cash flow benefits for more than one year, is made. It has been said and widely believed that how you spend your money today determines what your value will be tomorrow. Therefore, we will focus much of our attention on present values so that we can understand how today's expenditures influence values in the future. A very popular approach to looking at present values of projects is discounted cash flows (DCF), although it has some limitations. However, a capital budgeting process has three sequential and logical stages to complete the final selection. These stages are detailed as follows:

1. Decision analysis for knowledge building
2. Option pricing to establish position
3. DCF for making the investment decision

4.4.1 Stage 1: Decision Analysis

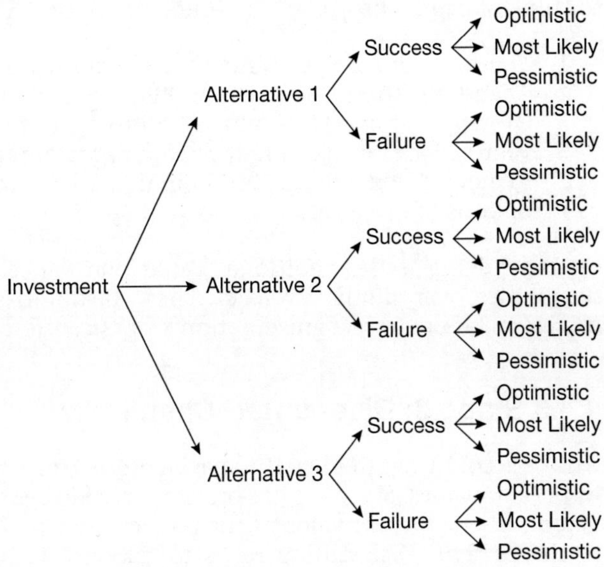

Decision making is increasingly becoming more complex today because of uncertainty. Additionally, most capital projects will involve numerous variables and possible outcomes. For example, estimating cash flows associated with a project involves working capital requirements, project risk, tax considerations, expected rates of inflation and disposal values. We have to understand existing markets to forecast project revenues, assess competitive impacts of the project and determine the life cycle of the project. If our capital project involves production, we have to understand operating costs, additional overheads, capacity utilization and start-up costs. Consequently, we cannot manage capital projects by simply looking at the numbers, that is, DCFs. We must look at the entire decision and assess all relevant variables and outcomes within an analytical hierarchy.

In financial management, we refer to this analytical hierarchy as the multiple attribute decision model (MADM). Multiple attributes are involved in capital projects and each attribute in the decision needs to be weighed differently. We will use an analytical hierarchy to structure the decision and derive the importance of attributes in relation to one another. We can think of MADM as a decision tree that breaks down a complex decision into component parts.

Therefore, our first real step in capital budgeting is to obtain knowledge about the project and organize this knowledge into a decision tree. We can use software programmes such as Expert Choice or Decision Pro to help us to build a decision tree.

4.4.2 Stage 2: Option Pricing

The uncertainty about our project is first reduced by obtaining knowledge and working the decision through a decision tree. The second stage in this process is to consider all options or choices we have or should have for the project. Therefore, before we proceed to DCFs, we need to build a set of options into our project for managing unexpected changes.

In financial management, consideration of options within capital budgeting is called contingent claims analysis or option pricing. For example, suppose you have a choice between two boiler units for your factory. Boiler A uses oil and boiler B can use either oil or natural gas. Based on traditional approaches to capital budgeting, the least costs boiler was selected for purchase, namely boiler A. However, if we consider option pricing, boiler B may be the best choice because we have a choice or option on what fuel we can use. Suppose we expect rising oil prices in the next five years. This will result in higher operating costs for boiler A, but boiler B can switch to a second fuel to better control operating costs. Consequently, we want to assess the options of capital projects.

Options can take many forms: ability to delay, defer, postpone, alter, change and so on. These options give us more opportunities for creating value within capital projects. We need to think of capital projects as a bundle of options. Three common sources of options are:

1. Timing options: The ability to delay our investment in the project.
2. Abandonment options: The ability to abandon or get out of a project that has gone bad.
3. Growth options: The ability of a project to provide long-term growth despite negative values. For example, a new research programme may appear negative, but it might lead to new product innovations and market growth. We need to consider the growth options of projects.

Option pricing is the additional value that we recognize within a project because it has flexibilities over similar projects. These flexibilities help us manage capital projects and, therefore, failure to recognize option values can result in an undervaluation of a project.

4.4.3 Stage 3: Discounted Cash Flows

Unlike accounting, financial management is concerned with the values of assets today, that is, present values. Since capital projects provide benefits into the future and since we want to determine the present value of the project, we will discount the future cash flows of a project to the present. Discounting refers to taking a future amount and finding its value today. Future values differ from present values because of the time value of money. Financial management recognizes the time value of money because:

1. 'Inflation' reduces values over time; that is, $1,000 today will have less value five years from now due to rising prices (inflation).
2. 'Uncertainty' in the future; that is, we think we will receive $1,000 five years from now, but a lot can happen over the next five years.
3. 'Opportunity costs' of money; $1,000 today is worth more to us than $1,000 five years from now because we can invest $1,000 today and earn a return.

Present values are calculated by referring to tables or we can use calculators and spreadsheets for discounting. The discount rate we will use is the opportunity costs of the investment, that is, the rate of return we require on any other project with similar risks.

4.5 Guidelines for Capital Budgeting

Capital budgeting is a technical but rational process. A finance manager deals with three basic decision criteria: financing, investment and dividend decisions. Investment decision may be short-term and long-term. Long-term investment decision is very sensitive and significant decision for a firm that involves huge capital outlay and significant risk. Thus, such decision requires careful scrutiny of every possible effect before finalizing the decision. A schematic diagram of capital budgeting process is sketched in Figure 4.1.

The figure shows the logical flow and the behaviour of the finance managers dealing with capital investment proposals. Some important guidelines at the time of evaluating capital investment proposals are as follows:

1. Proposals should be evaluated in terms of cash flows. Accounting profits should not be used due to generally accepted accounting principles (GAAP)-based adjustments. Again,

Figure 4.1 Capital Budgeting Process

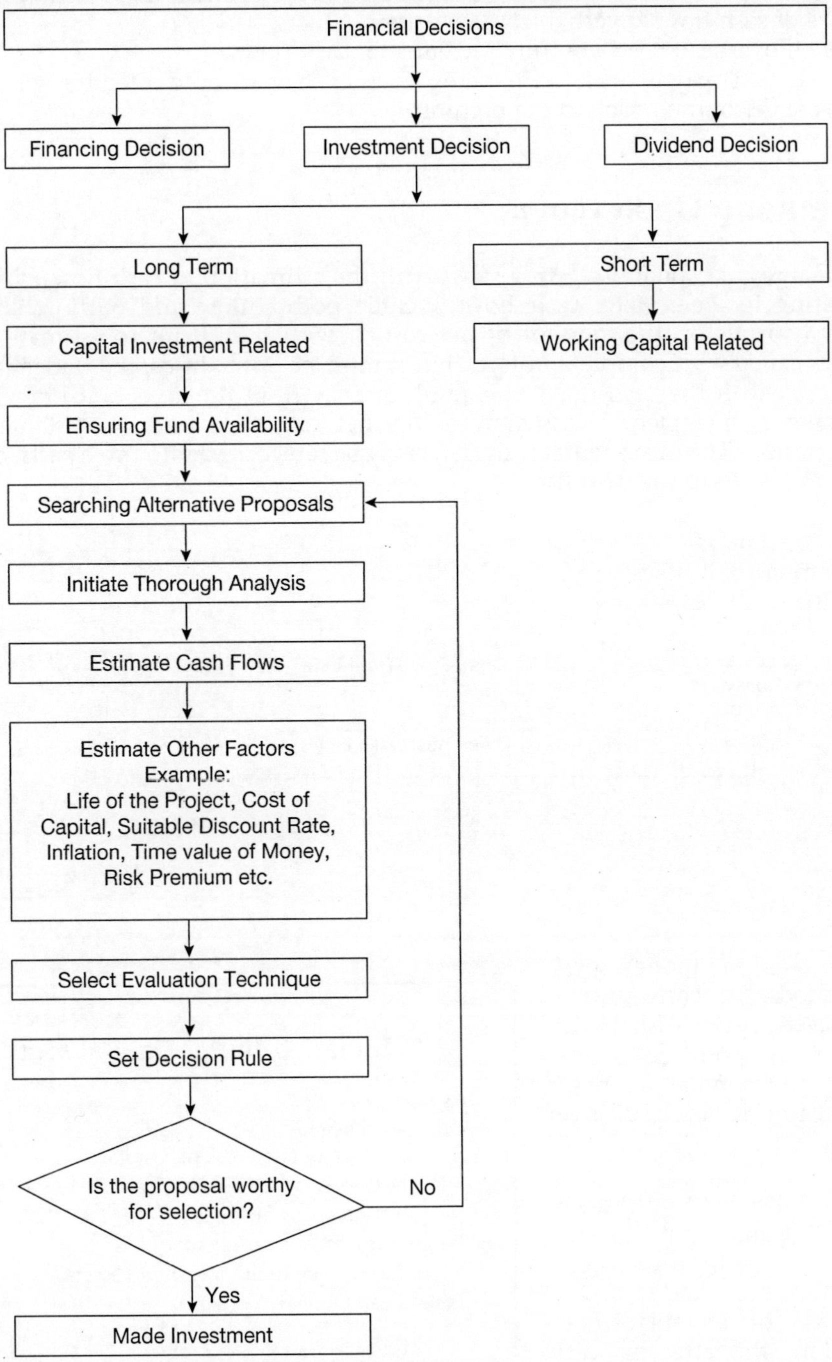

cash flows correctly reflect the timing of benefits and costs. Here, after tax, cash flows should be considered on incremental basis. Cash flows with the new project should be compared with the cash flows without the new project to take the decision.
2. Beware of cash flows diverted from existing products.
3. Decide if overhead costs are truly incremental cash flows.
4. Ignore interest payments and financing flows as they are accounted for when the cash flows are discounted back to the present.

4.6 Estimating Cash Flows

Technical analysis of capital budgeting starts with the estimation of cash flows. Cash flow is not accounting income. Here, cash flows include both inflow and outflow and project profitability depends on the amount of net cash flow. It is difficult to estimate costs and revenues associated with complex projects; but it must be done. In capital budgeting, we are concerned only with the cash flows that result directly from the acceptance of the project. This is known as incremental cash flow or the net cash flow directly attributable to an investment project. The incremental cash flows may be categorized into three parts, depending on the period related to the cash flows.

1. Initial cash outlay
2. Differential cash flows
3. Terminal cash flows

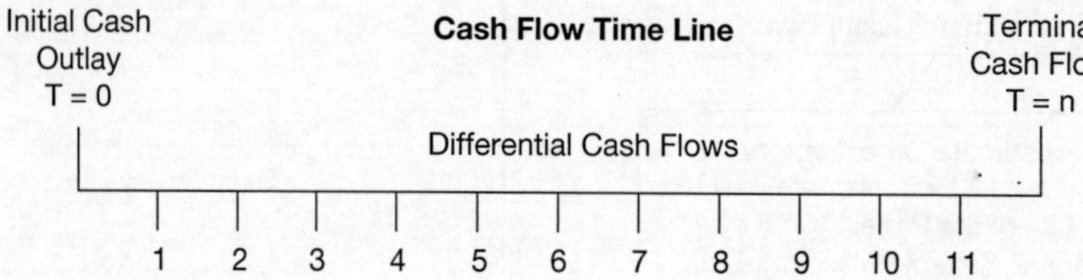

4.6.1 Initial Outlays

Initial outlays are the money spent at zero periods. In conventional type of projects, major cash outlay occurs at this point of time. However, some careful adjustments are required to calculate total cash outlay. It includes:

1. The installed cost of the asset, including amount paid to the vendor, shipping cost, accessories cost and so on.
2. In case of a replacement decision, the after-tax cash

Calculating Initial Capital Outlay

Cost of New Assets		*
(+)	Expenses Capitalized	*
(+)	Increase in Net Working Capital	*
(–)	Decrease in Net Working Capital	(*)
(+)	Net proceeds from sale of old asset, if any	*
(+)	Taxes on gain on sale of old assets	*
(–)	Savings due to the sale of old assets	(*)
Initial Cash Outlay		*

flow associated with the sale/disposal of the old machine should be deducted and any tax paid on the gain should be added.
3. Additional non-expense outlays incurred like increase/decrease of working capital investments should be adjusted.
4. Additional expenses like training costs should be considered on an after tax basis.

4.6.2 Differential Cash Flows

These are the cash flows throughout the life of the projects. Investment decisions largely depend on differential cash flows. And, thus, such cash flows are carefully calculated. Differential cash flows come from the marginal concept of economics. This is exactly the amount of cash flows generated by the proposal under consideration if chosen. It includes:

1. Incremental after-tax cash flows resulting from increased revenue from the proposal.
2. Any labour and/or material savings incurred.
3. Increases in overhead incurred.
4. Do not include any financing charges as they are implicitly taken care of in the discounting process.

Calculating Differential Cash Flows

Increase in operating revenue	
	(–) increase in operating expenses
	(–) Increase in depreciation expense
	(+) Decrease in depreciation expense
Earnings Before Interest and Taxes (EBIT)	
	(+/–) Taxes on EBIT
Net Operating Profit after Taxes (NOPAT)	
	(+) Increase in depreciation expense
	(–) Decrease in depreciation expense
Differential cash flow	

4.6.3 Terminal Cash Flows

These are the cash flows generated at the end of the life of the projects. This is in addition to differential cash flows at the time of terminating the project. At termination, due to a large number of reasons, the project may bring cash and should be considered in evaluating the project. Some reasons of terminal cash flows are as follows:

1. The project's salvage value plus any taxable gains or losses associated with the project
2. Any terminal cash flows needed, perhaps for the disposal of obsolete equipment
3. Recovery of any non-expense cash outlays associated with the project, such as recovery of increased working-capital needs associated with the proposal.

Calculating Terminal Cash Flows

Salvage value/sale proceeds of the asset		*
(–)	Taxes paid gain on sale or disposal of assets	(*)
(+)	Tax savings on sale or disposal of assets	*
(+)	Decrease in net working capital	*
(–)	Increase in net working capital	(*)
Terminal cash flow		*

Exhibit 4.1 Beware of the Four Crucial Costs

At the time of estimating cash flows, the following four problems should be handled delicately that may generate wrong estimation of cash flows.

1. Sunk costs
2. Opportunity costs
3. Externalities or effects on other parts of the firm
4. Shipping and installation costs

Sunk costs

Sunk costs are the past costs and not relevant in the decision-making process. Therefore, these are not included in the estimate of the initial outlay. These cannot be recovered regardless of the acceptance or rejection of the decision and, thus, should be discarded initially. Only the cost that is incurred in future and differs across alternatives should be considered.

Example: cost and depreciation of old asset.

Opportunity costs

Opportunity costs in capital budgeting come from the availability of alternative uses of resources owned by the firm. Here, opportunity costs refer to the cost of alternative use of resources forgone due to the project selected and must be included as costs in the estimation to make the decision worthy. When costs are used to estimate opportunity costs, current (not historic) costs are to be used.

Example: A piece of land already owned by the firm may be used for implementing different projects and must have opportunity costs across the acceptance of different projects.

Externalities

Externalities refer to the effect of the project on other part of the firm if undertaken. Thus, effects on other business lines must be included in the estimate of the operating cash flow. Because sometimes these effects are significant, that is, seriously affect the profitability of the overall business.

Example: Increase of overhead cost, labour unrests, reduction of turnover due to customer's dissatisfaction.

Shipping and installation

These costs should be considered as a part of the initial cash outlay. However, training costs that is continuous should not be a part of the initial cash outlay. However, modification costs are also included in the initial outlay for capitalization purposes. Shipping, installation and modification costs are added to the depreciable base of the project.

Example 1: Suppose Agile Manufacturer wants to replace a current machine with a newer one to ensure more sophistication in the production process. The current machine produces defective units that will not be there if the new machine is installed and used. Other comparative information under two situations is provided below. You are requested to estimate expected cash flows in case of the addition of a new machine.

Existing Situation	
Two full-time operators at $10,000 each per year	20,000
Annual cost of maintenance	5,000

Cost of defects	5,000
Original cost of the old machine	30,000
Expected old machine life in years	10
Current old machine age	5
Expected salvage value	Nil
Depreciation method: straight-line depreciation extended over 10 years	
Current salvage value	10,000
Marginal tax rate	34%
Proposed Situation	
Fully automated machine	
Cost of machine	55,000
Installation fee	5,000
Annual cost of maintenance	6,000
Annual cost of defects	2,000
Expected life in years	5
Expected salvage value	Nil
Depreciation method: straight-line depreciation extended over five years	

Solution: A careful scrutiny of the information reveals that there is no terminal value generated by the new machine. The salvage value of the new machine is zero and there is no requirement of working capital as well. The cash flows for the proposed project in two other cases (initial and differential) are calculated as follows:

Initial Outlay	
Outflows	
Cost of the machine	55,000
Installation	5,000
Inflows	
Tax savings (34% on the difference between depreciated value and salvage value)	1,700
Salvage value	10,000
Net outlay	**48,300**

Differential Outflows		
	Accounting Profit	***Cash Flows***
Savings		
Reduced salary	20,000	20,000
Reduced defects	3,000	3,000

Costs		
Increased maintenance	1,000	1,000
Increased depreciation (12,000 – 3,000)	9,000	
Net savings before taxes	13,000	22,000
Taxes at 34%	4,420	4,420
Annual net cash flows after taxes		17,580

Example 2: Assume that Apple Manufacturing is considering purchasing a new machine at $127,000, which also requires the installation cost of $20,000. The machine requires an additional inventory of $6,000, including $2,000 purchased on account. The revenue of the Apple is expected to increase by $85,000 per year, whereas operating costs are expected to increase by 35% of the increased revenue. Apple will use three-year modified accelerated cost recovery system (MACRS) depreciation and plans that the life of the machine will be four years. The salvage value of the machine at the end of four years will be $50,000. The existing cost of capital of the company is 14% and corporate tax rate is 34%. Estimate expected cash flows from the investment.

Solution: Here, the investment outlay will be calculated as under:

Cost of the asset		$127,000
Add: Installation, shipping and modification costs		20,000
Installed costs		147,000
Add: Increase in net operating working capital:		
Current assets – inventory	$6,000	
Current liabilities – accounts payable	2,000	4,000
Investment outlay		151,000

Differential cash flows for four years will be calculated as follows:

Years		***1***	***2***	***3***	***4***
1	Revenue	$85,000	$85,000	$85,000	$85,000
2	Less: Operating expenses (35% of $85,000)	29,750	29,750	29,750	29,750
3	Depreciation:				
	Year 1: 33% of $147,000	48,510			
	Year 1: 45% of $147,000		66,150		
	Year 1: 15% of $147,000			22,050	
	Year 1: 07% of $147,000				10,290
4	EBIT (1 – 2 – 3)	6,740	(10,900)	33,200	44,960
5	Less: Taxes (34%)	2,292	3,706	11,288	15,286
6	NOPAT (4 – 5)	4,448	(7,194)	21,912	29,674
7	Depreciation (3)	48,510	66,150	22,050	10,290
8	Cash Flows (6 + 7)	52,958	58,956	43,962	39,964

Finally, terminal cash flow will be calculated and added with the incremental cash flows for year 4. The terminal cash flow of this project will be:

Salvage value of the machine			$50,000
Taxes on the gain from the sale of the machine			
Salvage value		$50,000	
Cost of the machine	$147,000		
Accumulated depreciation	147,000		
Book value/written down value		0	
Gain on sale of machinery		50,000	
Taxes on gain on sale of machinery (34%)			(17,000)
Recovery of net working capital ($6,000 – $2,000)			4,000
Terminal cash flow			37,000

Thus, the estimated cash flow relating to the acquisition of the machinery can be presented as follows:

Years	***0***	***1***	***2***	***3***	***4***
Initial cash outlay	(151,000)				
Incremental cash flows		52,958	58,956	43,962	39,964
Terminal cash flows					37,000
Estimated cash flows	(151,000)	52,958	58,956	43,962	76,964

These estimated cash flows will be used to calculate DCF for finalizing capital investment decisions.

4.7 Techniques of Capital Budgeting

Capital budgeting issues are very much technical in practice. These require a lot of information. Some information comes from the internal database of the company; some comes from the market and others from feasibility studies. Capital budgeting techniques can broadly be categorized into two types:

Undiscounted	***Discounted***
Payback period	Discounted payback period
Payback reciprocal	NPV
ARR	IRR
	Net profitability index or NPV index

Undiscounted techniques do not consider time value of money and, thus, the techniques are not convincing. In economic sense, these techniques are not good at all. However, these may be used for initial screening, where the candidates for selection are voluminous. Discounted techniques are rational as all future cash flows are discounted to the current period at a certain rate that is appropriate for the company. Discounting is the common process of considering time value.

4.7.1 The Time Value of Money

Due to the current preference of time, the economic value of money changes with the passage of time. The purchasing power of money decreases due to inflationary pressure in the market. And, thus, all future cash flows should be discounted with reference to the current period of time. The rate at which the cash flows will be discounted is a critical issue. Generally, it should be the cost of capital, the rate that a firm should bear for borrowing from the market. The interaction of lenders with borrowers sets an equilibrium rate of interest. Borrowing is only worthwhile if the return on the loan exceeds the cost of the borrowed funds. Lending is only worthwhile if the return is at least equal to that which can be obtained from alternative opportunities in the same risk class. The interest rate received by the lender is made up of the following:

1. The time value of money: The receipt of money is preferred sooner rather than later. Money can be used to earn more money. The earlier the money is received, the greater the potential for increasing wealth. Thus, to forego the use of money, you must get some compensation.
2. Risk: There exists a risk of the capital sum not being repaid. This uncertainty requires a premium as a hedge against the risk; hence, the return must be commensurate with the risk being undertaken.
3. Inflation: Money may lose its purchasing power over time. The lender must be compensated for the declining spending/purchasing power of money. If the lender receives no compensation, he/she will be worse off when the loan is repaid than at the time of lending the money.

All of the above-mentioned factors are considered at the time of choosing the discounting rate at which future stream of cash flows will be converted into current period of time. Thus, the discussion has significant importance in long-term investment decisions. However, all capital budgeting techniques are discussed later, irrespective of the consideration of different factors to give a complete guide to finance professionals.

4.7.2 Payback Period

In capital investment decisions, the basic requirement in an uncertain business environment is obviously the period you need to recover at least the investment amount. 'The earlier the period is, the better the proposal is', becomes the simple decision role. If the capital investment decision is based on this philosophy, then you are following the payback period method. Thus, payback period is the period within which the selected proposal pays your investments back. The Chartered Institute of Management Accountants (CIMA) defines payback as 'the time it takes the cash inflows from a capital investment project to equalize the cash outflows', usually expressed in years. When deciding between two or more competing projects, the usual decision is to accept the one with the shortest payback.

Merits and Demerits of the Payback Period Method

Merits	It is a simple method to comprehend and easy to use.
	Requires less information and thus limited forecasting.
	Provides some information on the risk of the investment.
	Provides a crude measure of liquidity.
	Payback is often used as a 'first screening method'. When a capital investment project is being considered, the first question to ask is: 'How long will it take to payback its cost?' The company might have a target payback, and so it would reject a capital project unless its payback period was less than a certain number of years.
Demerits	To keep the method simple, it fails to consider some important macroeconomic variables that affect such decisions adversely, such as interest rate, inflation, time value of money and so on.
	Cash flows throughout the life of the project are not considered. In that case, some projects that bring significant cash flows at a later period may be rejected.
	As this is not a discounted method, the risk attached to the estimations is not considered at all. However, this limitation has been neutralized when discounted payback period is used.
	It is unable to distinguish between projects with the same payback period.
	It may lead to excessive investment in short-term projects.
	No concrete decision criteria to indicate whether an investment increases the firm's value.

Technical Presentation

The methodology of the calculation of the payback period depends on the nature of cash flows. The cash flows may be quite formal in structured form from formal investments, say, investments in banks or these may be unstructured from investments in commercial projects. Thus, the cash flows may differ in amount and pattern throughout the life. To explain both the situations, let us assume that there are two projects: Project A with five years of life being investment made in a bank, which generates equal amount of cash flows every year and project B with eight years of life being investment made in a highly sensitive commercial project with varying amount of cash flows.

	Cash Flows	
Year	***Project A***	***Project B***
0	1,000,000	1,000,000
1	250,000	50,000
2	250,000	80,000
3	250,000	100,000
4	250,000	150,000
5	250,000	250,000
6	–	300,000
7	–	200,000
8	–	400,000

Project Evaluation under the Payback Period Method

Project A: The cash flows in project A are structured. It requires an investment of $1,000,000 initially (year, t = 0) and generates cash inflows of $250,000 each year throughout the life of the project. In such cases, the payback period is simply calculated as follows:

$PP = \frac{I_o}{AVG_{inf}}$, where I_o represents initial investment and AVG_{inf} represents average of cash inflows.

Thus, for project A, the payback period will be four years ($1,000,000/$250,000). It means that project A will recover the investment in four years.

Project B: The cash flows in project B are not as structured as it was in case of project A, rather it is volatile. In such cases, the equation as used for project A is not practical for use and needs adjustments. It requires accumulated cash flows information and interpolation if the amount of accumulated cash flows does not become exactly equal to the investment at the end of any years.

Year	*Cash Flows*	*Accumulated Cash Flows*
1	50,000	50,000
2	80,000	130,000
3	100,000	230,000
4	150,000	380,000
5	250,000	630,000
6	300,000	930,000
7	200,000	1,130,000
8	400,000	1,530,000

The accumulated cash flows are not equal to exactly $1,000,000 for any year, but it should fall in between years six and seven. Now the fraction of the year should be reached through interpolation by using the equation as follows:

$$PP = t_L + \frac{I_o - ACF_L}{ACF_H - ACF_L}$$

where t_L represents the year which comes early, ACF_L represents accumulated cash flow for early year and ACF_H represents accumulated cash flow for later year. Thus, payback period for project B will be

$$PP = 6 \text{ years} + \frac{1{,}000{,}000 - 930{,}000}{1{,}130{,}000 - 930{,}000}$$

$$= 6.35 \text{ years.}$$

Thus, the payback period is calculated as 6.35 years, which can again be presented in terms of specific month and dates. What we have to do is to covert the fraction 0.35 into number of days. This can be easily done if we multiply the fraction (0.35) with the total days of the year, say, 365 (in case of leap year, 366). Here, the number of days corresponding to the fraction is 127.75 or 128 days (0.35 × 365). Once the days have been calculated, then we can use Table 4.1 to calculate the exact month and dates.

The cumulative days in the month of April amount to 120. Thus, the breakeven days in this example lie in the month of May and the exact days will be eight (128 – 120). It means that the payback period is six years, four months and eight days.

Decision: In this situation, if the decision maker wants to choose the best project on the basis of payback period, project A will be selected over project B due to lower payback period for project A (payback period of project A < payback period of project B).

Table 4.1 Fraction Conversion Table

Month	*Days*	*Cumulative Days*
January	31	31
February	28*	59
March	31	90
April	30	120
May	31	151
June	30	181
July	31	212
August	31	243
September	30	273
October	31	304
November	30	334
December	31	365

*In leap year, it will be 29.

Example 1: For a project with equal annual receipts

Years	*Cash Flows*
0	2,000,000
1	500,000
2	500,000
3	500,000
4	500,000
5	500,000

Payback period:

$$PP = \frac{I_o}{AVG_{inf}}$$
$$= \frac{\$2,000,000}{\$500,000}$$
$$= 4 \text{ years.}$$

Example 2: For a project with unequal annual receipts

Years	*Cash Flows*	*Accumulated Cash Flows*
0	1,000,000	–
1	500,000	500,000
2	250,000	750,000
3	400,000	1,150,000
4	100,000	1,250,000

Payback period:

Here, payback period lies between year two and year three. Through interpolation:

$$PP = t_L + \frac{I_o - ACF_L}{ACF_H - ACF_L}$$
$$= 2 \text{ years} + \frac{\$1,000,000 - \$750,000}{\$400,000} = 2.625 \text{ years.}$$

4.7.3 Discounted Payback Period

Discounted payback period is the revised version of the payback period where the time value of money is considered by discounting a future amount of cash to current period at a suitable discount rate. One major limitation of payback period is recovered by discounting the cash flows. Thus, the computation needs one additional step. At first, the cash flows are discounted with reference to present time period. Then, cumulative cash flows are calculated, following which interpolation is used to calculate payback period. An example is given below with two projects as before with different cash flows. Let us assume that the applicable discount rate is 10% for the company considering decision alternatives.

		Project A			Project B		
Year	**PVIF, 10%**	**Cash Flows**	**DCFs**	**Accumulated Cash Flows**	**Cash Flows**	**DCFs**	**Accumulated Cash Flows**
1	0.9091	250,000	227,275	227,275	100,000	90,910	90,910
2	0.8264	250,000	206,600	433,875	150,000	123,960	214,870
3	0.7513	250,000	187,825	621,700	250,000	187,825	402,695
4	0.6830	250,000	170,750	792,450	300,000	204,900	607,595
5	0.6209	250,000	155,225	947,675	350,000	217,315	824,910
6	0.5645				120,000	67,740	892,650
7	0.5132				100,000	51,320	943,970
8	0.4665				250,000	116,625	1,060,595

The accumulated cash flow columns for both of the projects reveal that project A is discarded with no payback period as it fails to recover even the investment amount, whereas the payback period for project B lies between years seven and eight. Through interpolation, we can calculate the exact payback period for project B as follows:

$$\text{PP} = 7 \text{ years} + \frac{1{,}000{,}000 - 943{,}970}{1{,}060{,}595 - 943{,}970}$$
$$= 7.48 \text{ years.}$$

Thus, at a 10% discount rate, project B will recover the investment in 7.48 years, which should be compared with the targeted payback period now to decide whether the company should accept the project or not. Here, project A will not be considered at all as it fails to even recover the investment. When companies use payback period, they must have some targeted payback period as selected across different categories of investment within which they like to recover investments. Thus, the calculated payback period should be compared with the targeted payback period and the project is selected only if the calculated payback period falls lower than the targeted payback period or at maximum it should be exactly equal to the targeted period.

Decision Rule:
The lower the payback period is, the worthwhile the project is.

4.7.4 Payback Reciprocal

Payback reciprocal is the reversal of payback period where results are expressed in percentages. This often gives a quick, accurate estimate of the IRR on an investment when the project life is more than twice the payback period and the cash inflows are uniform during every period, which is the case with most equipment or plant purchases. As long as the expected service life is greater than three times the calculated payback period, the reciprocal of that payback period is approximately equal to the rate of return (yield) that can be expected from the project. Used in this way, the payback reciprocal gives approximately the same answer as the more accurate rate of return (yield) method. Payback reciprocal is calculated by using the equation:

$$\text{Payback Reciprocal} = \frac{1}{\text{Payback Period}}$$

If the expected service life is of an asset is 15 years, and the calculated payback period is four years, then payback reciprocal is 0.25 (1/4), which means the expected yield from the asset will roughly be 25%.

4.7.5 Accounting Rate of Return

The ARR method (also called the ROCE or the ROI method) of appraising a capital project is used to estimate the ARR that the project should yield. If it exceeds a targeted rate of return, the project will be undertaken.

Merits and Demerits of ARR

Merits	It is a simple method to comprehend and easy to use.
	Conventional accounting system is enough to provide required information.
	Result is stated in terms of percentages, which sometimes renders better rationality to choose a project.
Demerits	It does not take account of the timing of the profits from an investment.
	It implicitly assumes stable cash receipts over time.
	It is based on accounting profits and not on cash flows. Accounting profits are subject to a number of different accounting treatments.
	It takes no account of the length of the project.
	It ignores the time value of money.

Technical Presentation

The calculation procedure of ARR is very simple and relies heavily on typical accounting information. The very limitation of ARR also generates from this advantage. As traditional accounting is based on GAAP assumptions, it results in some distorted information in the economic sense. ARR assumes all of such assumptions as no attempts are taken to reduce

GAAP assumptions at the time of calculating ARR. The following equation may be used to calculate the ARR, though it has some variants as used in different organizations:

$$\text{ARR} = \frac{\text{Net Annual Profit}}{\text{Average Investment}}$$

Note that net annual profit excludes depreciation.

Example: A project requires an investment of \$1 million and generates net receipts of \$250,000 for 10 years. Assuming that straight-line depreciation is used, the ARR of the project will be

$$\text{ARR} = \frac{\$250{,}000 - \$100{,}000}{\frac{\$1{,}000{,}000}{2}} = 30\%$$

Here, annual receipts have been reduced by annual depreciation of \$100,000 (\$1,000,000/10) and the average investment of \$500,000 is calculated by dividing the initial investment of \$1,000,000 by 2. The calculation concludes that the project will result a 30% ARR. Sometimes, annual profit is divided by initial investment as well and if this equation had been used here the ARR would be 15% (\$150,000/\$1,000,000). As already mentioned, ARR has different variants and how it will be calculated depends on the requirements of management and at times on the projects under consideration.

The Payback and ARR Methods in Practice

Despite the limitations of the payback method, it is the most widely used method in practice. There are a number of reasons for this:

1. It is a particularly useful approach for ranking projects where a firm faces liquidity constraints and requires fast repayment of investments.
2. It is appropriate in situations where risky investments are made in uncertain markets that are subject to fast design and product changes or where future cash flows are particularly difficult to predict.
3. The method is often used in conjunction with NPV or IRR method and acts as a first screening device to identify projects that are worthy of further investigation.
4. It is easily understood by all levels of management.
5. It provides an important summary method of how quickly will the initial investments be recouped.

4.7.6 Net Present Value

The NPV method is the mostly used capital budgeting decision tool, where all future cash flows are converted into present values at a suitable discount rate and then it has been compared with initial investment to calculate the net value addition or reduction if the project is undertaken. Say, for a four-year project with initial investments, the process of NPV calculation will be as follows:

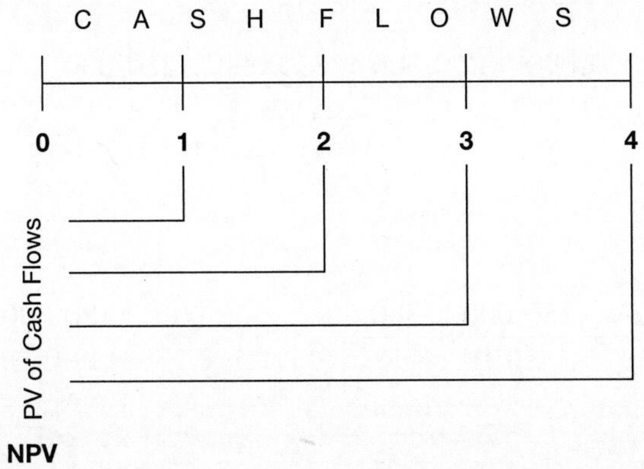

Thus, all future cash flows (t = 1, 2, 3 & 4) have been converted into present value. The present value of a sum received in a future time period will be lower due to time preference which is done here through discounting. NPV results when initial investment is deducted from total discounted value of cash inflows.

The above discussion of NPV assumes the simplest situation of investment proposal that will be presented from every possible perspective in this section later on. However, the figure can also be presented in equation form.

$$NPV = \sum_{t=0}^{n} \frac{CF_t}{(1+i)^t}$$

Where CF_t represents cash flow in period t (t = 0, 1, ..., n) and i represents the suitable discount rate.

Merits and Demerits of NPV

Merits	Decision rule gives importance to value addition.
	Considers time value of money.
	Considers all cash flows throughout the year.
	It ensures that the firm reaches an optimal scale of investment.
Demerits	Computational complexity arises when cash flows are not conventional.
	Selection of discount rate becomes difficult across different projects.
	Based on a large number of assumptions over which the decision makers have no control, say, inflation, uncertainty in cash flows and so on.
	NPV reports some absolute value that sometimes gives a very vague result.
	Expressed in terms of dollars, not in percentage.

Technical Presentation

Let us consider two projects as assumed before. Project A has five years of life, whereas project B has 8 years of life with conventional pattern of cash flow. The cash flows are discounted assuming 10% cost of capital.

Thus, NPV of project A will be

$$NPV_A = \frac{-1{,}000{,}000}{(1+0.1)^0} + \frac{250{,}000}{(1+0.1)^1} + \frac{250{,}000}{(1+0.1)^2} + \frac{250{,}000}{(1+0.1)^3} + \frac{250{,}000}{(1+0.1)^4} + \frac{250{,}000}{(1+0.1)^5}$$
$$= -52{,}325$$

And, NPV of project B will be

$$NPV_B = \frac{-1{,}000{,}000}{(1+0.1)^0} + \frac{100{,}000}{(1+0.1)^1} + \frac{150{,}000}{(1+0.1)^2} + \frac{250{,}000}{(1+0.1)^3} + \frac{300{,}000}{(1+0.1)^4} + \frac{350{,}000}{(1+0.1)^5} + \frac{120{,}000}{(1+0.1)^6} +$$
$$\frac{100{,}000}{(1+0.1)^7} + \frac{250{,}000}{(1+0.1)^8}$$
$$= 15{,}140$$

The above calculation shows that project A brings negative NPV, whereas project A results positive NPV. Negative NPV depreciates value and is, thus, rejected. Thus, if you are in comparison between these two projects, project B will be finally selected due to its capacity of adding value. Similar calculation is possible by using present value factor. For project A, present value annuity factor may be used for five years at 10% rate, that is, 3.791, assuming that the similar amount of cash inflows is generated at the end of each year. Thus, NPV for project A will be

$$NPV_A = CIF \times PVIFA_{5years,10\%} - COF$$
$$= (250{,}000 \times 3.791) - 1{,}000{,}000$$
$$= 947{,}750 - 1{,}000{,}000$$
$$= -52{,}250$$

The result of NPV for project A is very close to that one as calculated earlier and the difference is due to the fraction. However, for project B, we have to use present value interest factor for each year as the cash flow across the life is different. The equation in that case will be

$$NPV_B = \sum_{y=1}^{8} (CIF \times PVIF_{y\ years,10\%}) - COF$$

The calculation is as follows:

Year	*PVIF, y Years, 10%*	*Cash Flows*	*DCFs*
0-COF	1	1,000,000	1,000,000
1-CIF	0.9091	100,000	90,910
2-CIF	0.8264	150,000	123,960
3-CIF	0.7513	250,000	187,825
4-CIF	0.6830	300,000	204,900
5-CIF	0.6209	350,000	217,315

6-CIF	0.5645	120,000	67,740
7-CIF	0.5132	100,000	51,320
8-CIF	0.4665	250,000	116,625
NPV			60,595

Excel Tips:

Project A:
Cash flows: Cell C2–C7
Discount Rate: Cell B2
To calculate NPV, just type = NPV(B2,C2:C7) in any other cell. It will result NPV for project A.

Project B:
Cash flows: Cell C2-C10
Discount Rate: Cell B2
To calculate NPV, just type = NPV(B2,C2:C10) in any other cell. It will result NPV for Project B.

Decision Rule: NPV		
Situation	***Explanation***	***Decision***
NPV > 0	NPV is positive: It means the selection of the project is expected to increase shareholder wealth	Accept
NPV < 0	NPV is negative. It means the selection of the project is expected to decrease shareholder wealth	Reject
NPV = 0	NPV is zero. It means the selection of the project will neither increase nor decrease shareholder wealth	Indifferent

NPV Tips:

1. For a 'single' project, take it if and only if its NPV is positive.
2. For many 'independent' projects, take all those with positive NPV.
3. For 'mutually exclusive' projects, take the one with positive and highest NPV.

4.7.7 The Profitability Index

Profitability index (PI) is a variant of the NPV method. It is also known as benefit-cost ratio (B/C ratio). As a technique of capital budgeting, the application of profitability index is very straightforward. It does not use any new information. Profitability index calculates an index value as a ratio between present value of all future cash inflows and present value of cash outflows. Thus, in equation form, it can be stated as

$$PI = \frac{\sum_{t=1}^{n} \frac{CIF_t}{(1+i)^t}}{\sum_{t=0}^{n} \frac{COF_t}{(1+i)^t}}$$

where CIF_t refers to cash inflows at period t, COF_t refers to cash outflows at period t and i refers to the suitable discount rate.

Merits and Demerits of Profitability Index

Merits	Tells whether an investment increases the firm's value.
	Considers all cash flows of the project.
	Considers the time value of money.
	Considers the risk of future cash flows.
	Useful in ranking and selecting projects when capital is rationed.
Demerits	Requires an estimate of the cost of capital in order to calculate the profitability index.
	May not give the correct decision when used to compare mutually exclusive projects.

Example

Let us use the same example as used for NPV. Profitability index is calculated as follows.

	Year	PVIF, y Years, 10%	Cash Flows	DCFs
1	0-COF	1	1,000,000	1,000,000
2	1-CIF	0.9091	100,000	90,910
3	2-CIF	0.8264	150,000	123,960
4	3-CIF	0.7513	250,000	187,825
5	4-CIF	0.6830	300,000	204,900
6	5-CIF	0.6209	350,000	217,315
7	6-CIF	0.5645	120,000	67,740
8	7-CIF	0.5132	100,000	51,320
9	8-CIF	0.4665	250,000	116,625
10	Total PV of cash inflows for years 1–8			1,060,595
11	Profitability index (10/1)			1.060595

Here, profitability index of 1.06 means that the project's profitability is roughly 6%. Thus, the project is worthy for value maximization from standalone point of view. However, if there were more than one project, the project with the highest profitability index value would be selected.

Decision Rule: Profitability Index		
Situation	***Explanation***	***Decision***
PI > 1	Profitability index is more than 1. It means the selection of the project is expected to increase shareholder wealth	Accept
PI < 1	Profitability index is less than 1. It means the selection of the project is expected to decrease shareholder wealth	Reject
PI = 0	Profitability index is zero. It means the selection of the project will neither increase nor decrease shareholder wealth	Indifferent

4.7.8 The Internal Rate of Return

The IRR is the discount rate at which the NPV for a project equals zero. This rate means that the present value of the cash inflows for the project would equal the present value of its outflows. The IRR is thus the breakeven rate. Only if the rate is more than the cost of investment, is the project accepted. But finding a rate that will result in NPV being exactly zero is difficult. A trial-and-error method may be applied here to compute the breakeven discount rate that will be the IRR of the project.

Merits and Demerits of IRR

Merits	Tells whether an investment increases the firm's value.
	Considers all cash flows of the project.
	Considers the time value of money.
	Considers the risk of future cash flows
Demerits	It expresses the return in a percentage form rather than in terms of absolute dollar returns; for example, the IRR will prefer 500% of $1 to 20% return on $100. However, most companies set their goals in absolute terms and not in percentage terms, for example, target sales figure of $2.5 million.
	Requires an estimate of the cost of capital in order to make a decision.
	May not give the value-maximizing decision when used to compare mutually exclusive projects.
	May not give the value-maximizing decision when used to choose projects when there is capital rationing.
	Cannot be used in situations in which the sign of the cash flows of a project change more than once during the project's life.

Technical Presentation

The trial-and-error method to calculate IRR is a rough method and time-consuming. However, it facilitates a good start. The steps for implementing the trial-and-error method are presented as follows:

Step 1: Choose a discount rate arbitrarily and calculate NPV.

Step 2: If the NPV calculated in step 1 becomes positive, choose a higher discount rate that will generate negative NPA. And if the NPV calculated in step 1 becomes negative, choose a lower discount rate that will generate positive NPA.

Step 3: The discount rate that will produce zero NPV must lie between these two rates. The interpolation equation (as given here) may be used to calculate the discount rate that will produce zero NPV.

$$IRR = DR_L + \frac{NPA_L}{NPV_L - NPV_H} \times (DR_H - DR_L)$$

where DR_L means lower discount rate, DR_H means higher discount rate, NPV_L means NPV at lower discount rate and NPV_H means NPV at higher discount rate.

Let us try to calculate the IRR for the two projects as presented earlier with the following pattern of cash flows:

Year	*0*	*1*	*2*	*3*	*4*	*5*	*6*	*7*	*8*
A	1,000,000	250,000	250,000	250,000	250,000	250,000			
B	1,000,000	100,000	150,000	250,000	300,000	350,000	120,000	100,000	250,000

Let us assume that the cost of capital for both of the project is 10%.

Step 1: Let us use a discount rate of 5% and calculate NPV for both of the projects at 5%.

$$\text{NPV}_\text{A} = \frac{-1{,}000{,}000}{(1+0.05)^0} + \frac{250{,}000}{(1+0.05)^1} + \frac{250{,}000}{(1+0.05)^2} + \frac{250{,}000}{(1+0.05)^3} + \frac{250{,}000}{(1+0.05)^4} + \frac{250{,}000}{(1+0.05)^5}$$
$$= \$78{,}446.83.$$

$$\text{NPV}_\text{B} = \frac{-1{,}000{,}000}{(1+0.05)^0} + \frac{100{,}000}{(1+0.05)^1} + \frac{150{,}000}{(1+0.05)^2} + \frac{250{,}000}{(1+0.05)^3} + \frac{300{,}000}{(1+0.05)^4} + \frac{350{,}000}{(1+0.05)^5} +$$
$$\frac{120{,}000}{(1+0.05)^6} + \frac{100{,}000}{(1+0.05)^7} + \frac{250{,}000}{(1+0.05)^8}$$
$$= \$283{,}924.42.$$

Step 2: As the NPV calculated in step 1 is positive, let us choose a higher discount rate (15%) to generate negative NPV.

$$\text{NPV}_\text{A} = \frac{-1{,}000{,}000}{(1+0.15)^0} + \frac{250{,}000}{(1+0.15)^1} + \frac{250{,}000}{(1+0.15)^2} + \frac{250{,}000}{(1+0.15)^3} + \frac{250{,}000}{(1+0.15)^4} + \frac{250{,}000}{(1+0.15)^5}$$
$$= -\$140{,}835.85.$$

$$\text{NPV}_\text{B} = \frac{-1{,}000{,}000}{(1+0.15)^0} + \frac{100{,}000}{(1+0.15)^1} + \frac{150{,}000}{(1+0.15)^2} + \frac{250{,}000}{(1+0.15)^3} + \frac{300{,}000}{(1+0.15)^4} + \frac{350{,}000}{(1+0.15)^5} +$$
$$\frac{120{,}000}{(1+0.15)^6} + \frac{100{,}000}{(1+0.15)^7} + \frac{250{,}000}{(1+0.15)^8}$$
$$= -\$1{,}03{,}049.20.$$

Step 3: Now, we can interpolate the NPVs to compute the discount rate that will make it zero for both of the projects. In both cases, the IRR will fall between 5% and 15%.

$$\text{IRR}_\text{A} = 5\% + \frac{\$78{,}448.83}{\$78{,}448.83 - (-\$140{,}835.85)} \times (15\% - 5\%)$$
$$= 5\% + 3.577\%$$
$$= 8.58\%.$$

$$\text{IRR}_\text{B} = 5\% + \frac{\$283{,}924.42}{\$283{,}924.42 - (-\$103{,}049.20)} \times (15\% - 5\%)$$
$$= 5\% + 7.337\%$$
$$= 12.34\%.$$

In this situation, the IRR for project A is less than cost of capital and will be rejected. However, the IRR of project B is more than cost of capital and will be accepted (8.25% < 10% < 12.34%).

Alternative Way to Calculate IRR

The above discussion may not be convincing sometimes. Say, the initial discount rate is arbitrarily chosen that is supposed to be very close to the cost of capital. However, the initial rate is chosen as 5%, which produces positive NPV and in step 2 a higher rate of 15% is chosen to produce negative NPV. The chosen rates are not very close to the cost of capital, rather they far below and above the cost of capital. This is done intentionally to produce a positive and negative NPV. The chosen rate may be more close to the cost of capital, but in that case there is a possibility of more trials due to a possible chance of errors of not getting a positive and a negative NPV in first attempt. This arbitrary process may be made objective if the following steps are followed.

Step 1: Calculate average cash inflows simply by dividing the total cash inflows with the expected life of the project.

Step 2: Calculate the expected table value simply by dividing the initial cash outlay with the average cash inflows as calculated in step 1.

Step 3: Locate the expected table value in present value interest factor annuity (PVIFA) table against the life of the project. It will set the initial discounting rate.

Step 4: Compute NPV at the rate as found in step 3.

Step 5: If the NPV calculated in step 4 becomes positive, choose a higher discount rate that will generate negative NPA. And if the NPV calculated in step 4 becomes negative, choose a lower discount rate that will generate positive NPA.

Step 6: The discount rate that will produce zero NPV must lie between these two rates. Interpolation (as given here) may be used to calculate the discount rate that will produce zero NPV.

$$\text{IRR} = \text{DR}_L + \frac{\text{NPA}_L}{\text{NPV}_L - \text{NPV}_H} \times (\text{DR}_H - \text{DR}_L)$$

where DR_L means lower discount rate, DR_H means higher discount rate, NPV_L means NPV at lower discount rate and NPV_H means NPV at higher discount rate. The same example for projects A and B is solved by using this alternative way.

Project A: The average cash inflow in this project is \$250,000. Expected table value is 4.0 (\$1,000,000/\$250,000). Discount rate is selected as 8% as shown in the figure here. At an 8% discount rate, the NPV of the project is –\$1,687.49. As the NPV is negative, let us discount it at a lower rate, say, 7%. At a 7% discount rate, the NVP is \$23,410.62. By interpolating, the IRR is calculated as follows:

	6%	7%	8%	9%	10%
1					
2					
3					
4					
5	4.2124	4.1002	**3.9927**	3.8897	3.7908

$$\text{IRR}_A = 7\% + \frac{\$23,410.62}{\$23,410.62 - (-\$1,687.49)} \times (8\% - 7\%)$$
$$= 7\% + 0.93\%$$
$$= 7.93\% \cong 8\%$$

Project B: Average cash inflow in this project is $202,500. The expected table value is 4.938 ($1,000,000/$202,500). Discount rate is selected as 12% as shown in the figure. At a 12% discount rate, the NPV of the project is –$15,119.51. As the NPV is negative, let us discount it at a lower rate, say, 11%. At a 11% discount rate, the NVP is $18,705.34. By interpolating, the IRR is calculated as follows:

	10%	11%	12%	13%	14%
4					
5			↑		
6					
7					
8	5.3349	5.1461	**4.9676**	4.7988	4.6389

$$\text{IRR}_B = 11\% + \frac{\$18,705.34}{\$18,705.34 - (-\$15,119.51)} \times (12\% - 11\%)$$
$$= 11\% + 0.55\%$$
$$= 11.55\% \cong 12\%.$$

Thus, the IRR calculated under this alternative approach is very close to the IRR calculated under the trial-and-error method.

Using Excel: Excel calculates IRR for you simply by using the excel equation with reference to the cell containing cash flows. The cash flows against the two projects are provided in the cells below. At the same time, the respective equations for calculating IRRs are shown who would like to use excel for doing the job.

	B	C	D	E	F	G
11		Cash Flows				
12		Project A	Project B			
13		–1,000,000	–1,000,000			
14		250,000	100,000			
15		250,000	150,000			
16		250,000	250,000			
17		250,000	300,000			
18		250,000	350,000			=IRR(D13:D21)
19		250,000	120,000			
20	=IRR(C13:C19)		100,000			
21			250,000			
22	IRR	8%	12%			

Decision Rule: IRR		
Situation	***Explanation***	***Decision***
IRR > COC	IRR is more than cost of capital. It means the selection of the project is expected to increase shareholder wealth	Accept
IRR < COC	IRR is more than cost of capital. It means the selection of the project is expected to decrease shareholder wealth	Reject
IRR = COC	IRR is equal to cost of capital. It means the selection of the project will neither increase nor decrease shareholder wealth	Indifferent

4.7.9 NPV Profile

Figure 4.2 Graphical Presentation of the Methods

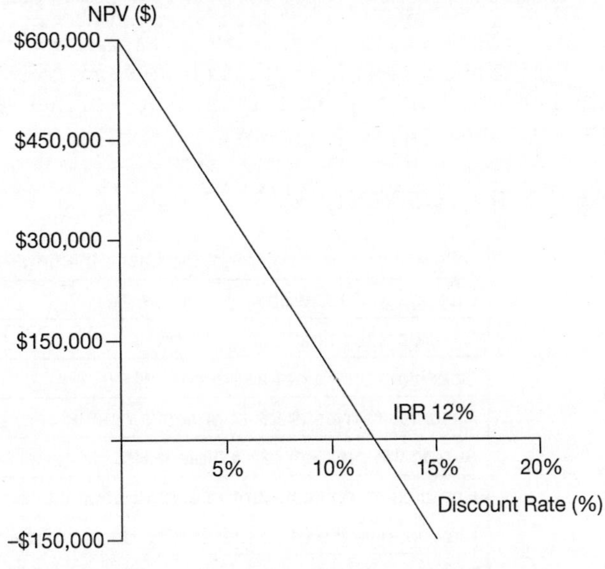

In general, the NPV and IRR methods lead to the same acceptance or rejection decision. In Figure 4.2, we illustrate graphically the two methods applied to our example project. The graph, called an NPV profile, shows the curvilinear relationship between the NPV for a project and the discount rate employed. When the discount rate is zero, NPV is simply the total cash inflows less the total cash outflows of the project. Assuming a conventional project—one where total inflows and where the initial outflow is followed by inflows—the highest NPV will occur when the discount rate is zero. As the discount rate increases, the NPV profile slopes downward to the right.

At the point where the NPV curve intersects the horizontal axis on the graph, the NPV of the project is zero. In this case, the rate is 12%. By definition, the discount rate at that point represents the IRR—the discount rate at which the project's NPV equals zero. For discount rates greater than the IRR, the NPV of the project is negative and vice versa.

4.7.10 Modified IRR

The MIRR is similar to the IRR, but is theoretically superior in that it overcomes two weaknesses of the IRR. The MIRR correctly assumes reinvestment at the project's cost of capital and avoids the problem of multiple IRRs. However, please note that MIRR is not used as widely as IRR in practice.

When cash flows are conventional, that is common practice and requires initial investment followed by regular inflows of cash, IRR can be suitably used to evaluate the profitability of the projects. Here, IRR assumes that all intermediate cash flows are reinvested at the IRR of the projects. However when cash flows are not conventional, requiring multiple investments during the lifetime of the project, there may be the existence of more than one IRRs and the use of IRR becomes impractical. MIRR is suitable in this situation which results only one rate. There are three basic steps of calculating the MIRR:

1. Estimate all cash flows as in IRR.
2. Calculate the future value of all cash inflows at the last year of the project's life.
3. Determine the discount rate that causes the future value of all cash inflows determined in step 2, to be equal to the firm's investment at time zero. This discount rate is known as the MIRR.

Thus, the equation form of calculating MIRR can be presented as follows:

$$\text{MIRR} = \sqrt[N]{\frac{\sum_{t=1}^{N} \text{CIF}_t (1+i)^{N-t}}{\sum_{t=1}^{N} \frac{\text{COF}_t}{(1+i)^t}}} - 1$$

As per the above equation, all cash inflows are converted into future values with reference to the last period of the project to calculate terminal value and then it has been divided by the present value of all cash outflows.

Merits and Demerits of MIRR

Merits	Tells whether an investment increases the firm's value.
	Considers all cash flows of the project.
	Considers the time value of money.
	Considers the risk of future cash flows.
	Assumes reinvestment at project's cost of capital.
	Avoids the problem of multiple IRRs.
Demerits	Requires an estimate of the cost of capital in order to make a decision.
	May not give the value-maximizing decision when used to compare mutually exclusive projects.
	May not give the value-maximizing decision when used to choose projects when there is capital rationing.

Example: Let us assume that a project requires an initial outlay of \$100 with three years life. The cost of capital is 10%. The cash flows are identified and terminal value of the project is calculated by using respective future value (FV) factor at 10% cost of capital.

Years	*0*	*1*	*2*	*3*
Cash flows	–100	10	60	80.00
Future value factor		1.2100	1.1000	
FV of cash inflows of year 2				66.00
FV of cash inflows of year 1				12.10
Terminal value				158.10

Now, MIRR is such a rate that makes the present value of $158.10 as exactly $100.00. Here, the rate is 16.9%.

	A	B	C	D	E	F	G
1	Years	0	1	2	3	4	5
2	Cash flows	120,000	40,000	60,000	80,000	100,000	130,000
3	Discount factor	1	0.8547	0.7305	0.6244	0.5337	0.4561
4	Present value	120,000	34,188	43,830	49,952	53370	59,293
5	NPV	120,633					
6	Reinvestment factors		1.8739	1.6016	1.3689	1.17	1
7	Future value of cash flows		74,956	96,096	109,512	117,000	130,000
8	Terminal value						527,564
9	Original investment						120,000
10	Factor (8/9)						4.396367
11	MIRR						0.344679

Decision Rule: MIRR		
Situation	***Explanation***	***Decision***
MIRR > COC	MIRR is more than cost of capital. It means the selection of the project is expected to increase shareholder wealth	Accept
MIRR < COC	MIRR is more than cost of capital. It means the selection of the project is expected to decrease shareholder wealth	Reject
MIRR = COC	MIRR is equal to cost of capital. It means the selection of the project will neither increase nor decrease shareholder wealth	Indifferent

4.8 Net Present Value Versus Internal Rate of Return

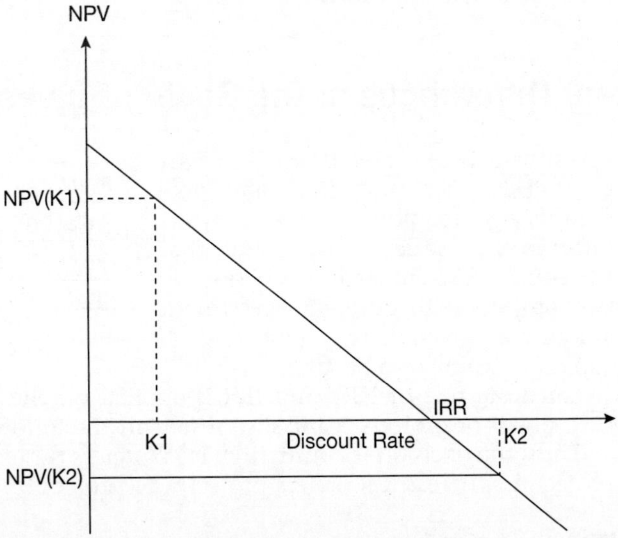

The discussion of NPV and IRR seems that any technique will result in a similar conclusion. However, in some situations, NPV and IRR produce contradictory results. This section presents the situations when NPV and IRR may result in conflicting selection.

4.8.1 Independent Projects

Independent projects are the projects where selection of one project does not preclude the choosing of the other. With conventional cash flows, no confliction in decision arises; in this case, both NPV and IRR lead to the same accept/reject decisions.

If cash flows are discounted at K1, NPV is positive and IRR > K1. Thus, the project will be accepted under both NPV and IRR rule. But if cash flows are discounted at K2, NPV is negative and IRR < K2, the project will be rejected under both NPV and IRR rule. Thus, both IRR and NPV results same conclusion when the projects are independent.

4.8.2 Dependent Projects

NPV clashes with IRR where mutually exclusive projects exist. Mutually exclusive projects are those projects that cannot be selected at a time. Say, Ajax is considering building either a one-storey (project A) or five-storey (project B) block of offices on a prime site. Both of the projects are identical in terms of life but cash flows differ. The following information is available:

	0	*1*	*NPV*	*IRR*
Project A	–9,500	11,500	$867.77	21%
Project B	–15,000	18,000	$1,239.67	20%

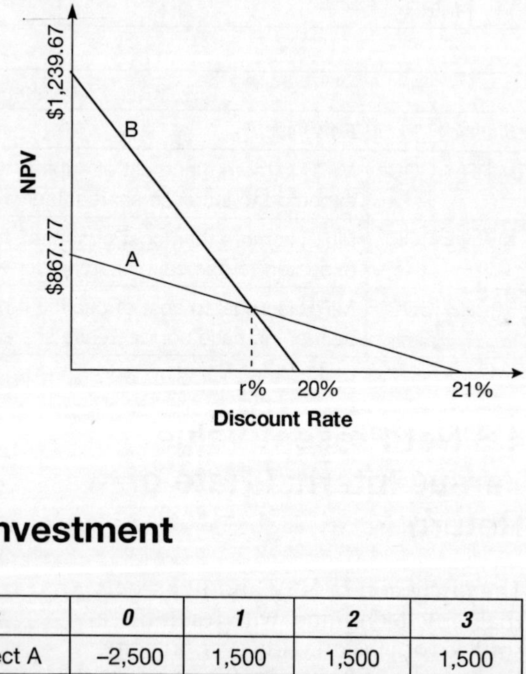

Assuming k as 10%, both projects are acceptable due to positive NPV and greater IRR. But which project will be better for Ajax. If NPV is used as a decision rule, project B will be preferable than project A. But in case of IRR, project A becomes preferable than project B. Thus, a conflicting situation arises. Up to a discount rate of r, project B is superior to project A; thereafter, project B is preferred to project A. Beyond this point, project A is superior to project B; thereafter, project A is preferred to project B. The two methods do not rank the projects as same.

4.9 Differences in the Scale of Investment

Investment is the capital outlay to start a project. NPV and IRR may give conflicting decisions where projects differ in their scale of investment, that is, require different amounts. Consider two projects with different investment amount as given here, where cost of capital is assumed to be 10%.

Years	*0*	*1*	*2*	*3*
Project A	–2,500	1,500	1,500	1,500
Project B	–14,000	7,000	7,000	7,000

Once the rule of NPV and IRR is applied on the above cash flows for projects A and B, it results in the following.

Projects	*NPV*	*IRR*
Project A	$1,118.43	36%
Project B	$3,098.15	23%

Thus, the decision is conflicting. NPV prefers project B to project A, whereas IRR prefers project A to project B.

In such a situation NPV is superior to IRR. And NPV prefers the larger project, project B, for a discount rate below 20%. The incremental cash flow approach is helpful here to explain the reason. Here, incremental approach means 'B minus A' approach. Project B is considered incremental here due to higher amount of cash flows. Thus, we will have another project, project B minus A and the calculation below shows that choosing project B is tantamount to choosing a hypothetical project 'B minus A'.

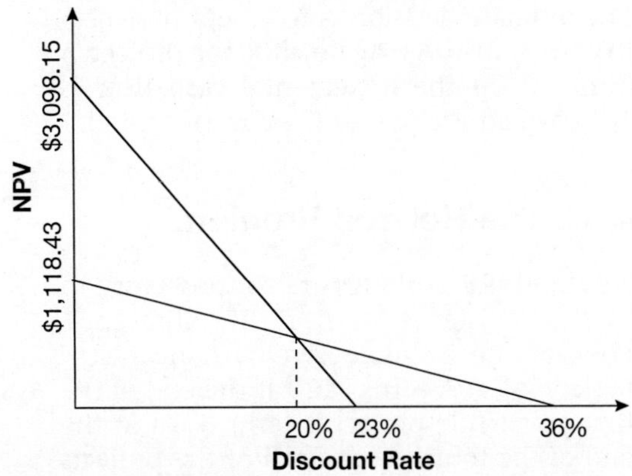

Projects	***0***	***1***	***2***	***3***
Project B	–14,000	7,000	7,000	7,000
Project A	–2,500	1,500	1,500	1,500
Project B minus A	–11,500	5,500	5,500	5,500

Here, IRR for project B minus A is 20%. The justification lies in the following points:

1. Choosing B is equivalent to choosing A along with the incremental part [A + (B – A) = B].
2. Choosing the bigger project B means choosing the smaller project A plus an additional outlay of $11,500, of which $5,500 will be realized each year for the next three years.
3. The IRR for project B minus A on the incremental cash flow is 20%.
4. Given i of 10%, this is a profitable opportunity, therefore must be accepted.
5. But, if i were greater than the IRR (20%) on the incremental cash flows, then reject the project.
6. At the point of intersection, $NPV_A = NPV_B$ or $NPV_A - NPV_B = 0$, i.e. indifferent to projects A and B.
   a. If i = 20% (IRR of 'B – A') the company should accept project A.
   b. This justifies the use of NPV criterion.

4.9.1 The Timing of the Cash Flow

NPV and IRR may give conflicting decisions in case of the same scale of investment even if there is a time difference in cash inflows. For example, look at the pattern of cash flows in the two projects with a similar scale of investment as shown here:

	0	***1***	***2***	***NPV***	***IRR***
Project A	–100	20	125.00	$19.53	22%
Project B	–100	100	31.25	$15.21	25%
A minus B	0	–80	88.15	$0.11	10%

The respective NPV and IRR for the two projects are calculated assuming cost of capital equalling 10%, which shows conflicting decisions. NPV prefers A to B, whereas IRR prefers B to A.

The ultimate decision is to accept project A [B + (A – B) = A]. Again, IRR for project A minus B on the incremental cash flow is 10%, which is equal to the cost of capital.

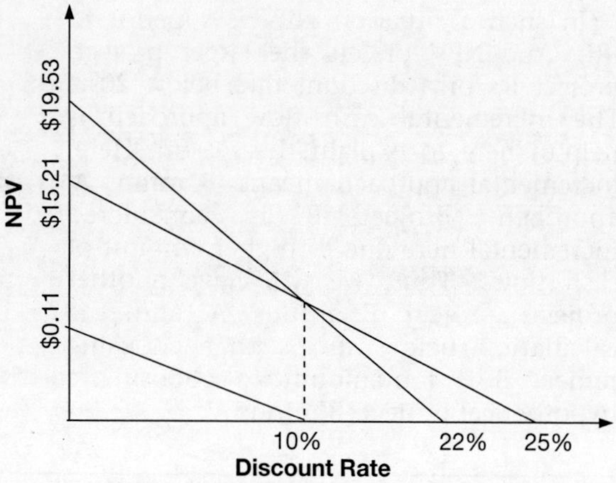

4.9.2 The Horizon Problem

NPV and IRR rankings are contradictory in case of existence of horizon differences. Look at the example given in the below table. Project A earns $120 at the end of the first year while project B earns $174 at the end of the fourth year. Each of the projects requires $100 as initial investment. Assuming 10% cost of capital, the respective NPV and IRR are calculated and given in the table.

	0	*1*	*2*	*3*	*4*	*NPV*	*IRR*
Project A	–100	120	–	–	–	$8.26	20%
Project B	–100	–	–	–	174	$17.13	15%

Thus, NPV prefers B to A, whereas IRR prefers A to B, leading to conflicting situations.

Exhibit 4.2 NPV Contradicts IRR: Summary

When comparing two projects, the use of the NPV and the IRR methods may give different results. A project selected according to the NPV may be rejected if the IRR method is used.

Suppose there are two alternative projects, X and Y. The initial investment in each project is $2,500. Project X will provide annual cash flows of $500 for the next 10 years. Project Y has annual cash flows of $100, $200, $300, $400, $500, $600, $700, $800, $900 and $1,000 in the same period. Using the trial-and-error method explained earlier, you find that the IRR of project X is 17% and the IRR of project Y is around 13%. If you use the IRR, project X should be preferred because its IRR is 4% more than the IRR of project Y. But what happens to your decision if the NPV method is used? The answer is that the decision will change depending on the discount rate you use. For instance, at a 5% discount rate, project Y has a higher NPV than X does. But at a discount rate of 8%, project X is preferred because of a higher NPV.

The purpose of this numerical example is to illustrate an important distinction: The use of the IRR always leads to the selection of the same project, whereas project selection using the NPV method depends on the discount rate chosen.

Project Size and Life

There are reasons why the NPV and the IRR are sometimes in conflict: the size and life of the project being studied are the most common ones. A 10-year project with an initial investment of $100,000 can hardly be compared with a small three-year project costing $10,000. Actually, the large project could be thought of as 10 small projects. So if you insist on using the IRR and the NPV methods to compare a big, long-term project with a small, short-term project, do not be surprised if you get different selection results. (See the equivalent annual annuity discussed later for a good way to compare projects with unequal lives.)

Different Cash Flows

Furthermore, even two projects of the same length may have different patterns of cash flow. The cash flow of one project may continuously increase over time, while the cash flows of the other project may increase, decrease, stop or become negative. These two projects have completely different forms of cash flow and if the discount rate is changed when using the NPV approach, the result will probably be different orders of ranking. For example, at 10% the NPV of project A may be higher than that of project B. As soon as you change the discount rate to 15%, project B may be more attractive.

When Are the NPV and IRR Reliable?

Generally speaking, you can use and rely on both the NPV and IRR if two conditions are met. First, if projects are compared using the NPV, a discount rate that fairly reflects the risk of each project should be chosen. There is no problem if two projects are discounted at two different rates because one project is riskier than the other. Remember that the result of the NPV is as reliable as the discount rate that is chosen. If the discount rate is unrealistic, the decision to accept or reject the project is baseless and unreliable. Second, if the IRR method is used, the project must not be accepted only because its IRR is very high. The management must ask whether such an impressive IRR is possible to maintain. In other words, the management should look into past records, and existing and future business, to see whether an opportunity to reinvest cash flows at such a high IRR really exists. If the firm is convinced that such an IRR is realistic, the project is acceptable. Otherwise, the project must be re-evaluated by the NPV method, using a more realistic discount rate.

4.10 Unequal Life Projects

NPV and IRR results contradictory conclusions when the life of projects differs significantly. To remove such problem, two methods have been presented here from the available literature. The replacement chain method equalizes the life of the project on the assumption of reinvestments producing similar cash flows and when it becomes impractical, another method called equivalent annual annuity may be used where annual cash flows are calculated to facilitate the decision-making process.

4.10.1 Replacement Chain Method

The replacement chain method takes two or more projects with lifespans that are unequal and finds the lowest common denominator and carries the projects out to that lowest common denominator or terminal year. For example, project A has a lifespan of five years and project B has a lifespan of three years. The lowest common denominator for these two projects is 15 years. So, taking the following cash flows we can illustrate how this is done.

	Years					
Projects	***0***	***1***	***2***	***3***	***4***	***5***
A	10,000	2,000	4,000	6,000	8,000	11,000
B	8,000	2,000	5,000	7,000		

Now, to carry this out to 15 years, it means that at the end of year five for project A, another negative cash flow of 10,000 (for example, a new purchase) would have to happen, therefore making year five cash flow as 1,000 (Y5 + Y0) or (11,000 – 10,000). This would also happen at year 10, but at year 15, the end of the project, the cash flow would be 11,000, because it is the end and no new purchase has to occur. The same applies to project B, but it would happen on years 3, 6, 9, 12 and 15 until the end of the project.

	Years															
Projects	***0***	***1***	***2***	***3***	***4***	***5***	***6***	***7***	***8***	***9***	***10***	***11***	***12***	***13***	***14***	***15***
A	10	2	4	6	8	1	2	4	6	8	1	2	4	6	8	1
B	8	2	5	–1	2	5	–1	2	5	–1	2	5	–1	2	5	–1

Using these extended adjusted cash flows, you would then determine the discount factors and the PV, which then could determine, the NPV. The project with the largest NPV would be the best project.

		Project A		Project B	
Year	***PVIF, 15%***	***CFs***	***PV***	***CFs***	***PV***
0	1	10,000	10,000	8,000	8,000
1	0.9091	2,000	1,818	2,000	1,818.2
2	0.8264	4,000	3,306	5,000	4,132
3	0.7513	6,000	4,508	–1,000	–751.3
4	0.683	8,000	5,464	2,000	1,366
5	0.6209	1,000	621	5,000	3,104.5
6	0.5645	2,000	1,129	–1,000	–564.5
7	0.5132	4,000	2,053	2,000	1,026.4
8	0.4665	6,000	2,799	5,000	2,332.5
9	0.4241	8,000	3,393	–1,000	–424.1
10	0.3855	1,000	386	2,000	771
11	0.3505	2,000	701	5,000	1,752.5
12	0.3186	4,000	1,274	–1,000	–318.6
13	0.2897	6,000	1,738	2,000	579.4
14	0.2633	8,000	2,106	5,000	1,316.5
15	0.2394	1,000	239	–1,000	–239.4
	PV of CIFs		31,535		15,901
	NPV		21,535		7,901

CF = cash flows.

Let us take a look at a different set of projects:

Project	***A***	***B***	***C***	***D***	***E***	***F***	***G***
Years	17	23	13	22	7	14	24

What is the lowest common factor (denominator)? You would have to factor out and then multiply by the factors for each project. (Note that if a number appears more than one time in the factor of one number you must multiply by that number as many times as it appears, if a factor appears in more than one number then you only have to multiply one time.

Project	*A*	*B*	*C*	*D*	*E*	*F*	*G*
Years	17	23	13	22	7	14	24
Factor	1 × 17	1 × 23	1 × 13	1 × 2 × 11	1 × 7	1 × 2 × 7	1 × 2 × 2 × 2 × 3
17 × 23 × 13 × 11 × 7 × 2 × 2 × 2 × 3 = 9,393,384							

Note that the 2 from project D and project F are not used because 2 has already been used in project G and it appears three times in project F; therefore, it must be multiplied three times. Also note that the 7 in project F is not used because it was already multiplied in project E.

So, in order to find the NPV for all seven projects, you would have to extend the projects out to 9,393,384 years, which is the lowest common denominator and the terminal year for all seven projects. This would take a very long time to calculate, so instead of using the replacement chain method we can use the equivalent annual annuity (EAA).

4.10.2 Equivalent Annual Annuity

An easy and intuitively appealing approach when the life of projects varies significantly is to compare the 'equivalent annual annuity' among all the projects. The equivalent annuity is the level annual payment across a project's specific life that has a present value equal to that of another cash-flow stream. Projects of equal size but different life can be ranked directly by their equivalent annuity. This approach is also known as equivalent annual cost, equivalent annual cash flow or simply equivalent annuity approach. This method finds the annual annuity that is equivalent to the NPV. To find the EAA, all you have to do is use the payment formula:

$$\text{PMT} = \text{PV} \times \frac{\text{K}}{1 - \dfrac{1}{(1+\text{K})^{\text{n}}}} \quad \text{or} \quad \text{EAA} = \text{NPV} \times \frac{\text{K}}{1 - \dfrac{1}{(1+\text{K})^{\text{n}}}}$$

where K is the discount rate and n is the life of the project. The following equation can also be used to calculate the EAA.

$$\text{EAA} = \frac{\text{NPV of Cash Flows}}{\text{PV Factor of n} - \text{year Annuity}}$$

Example: If we know that a project has a NPV of \$115.199 and a lifespan of five years with a discount rate of 10%, we can determine the EAA. The EAA would equal \$30.39.

$$90{,}000 \times \frac{1}{(1+0.30)^{1}}$$

We would calculate the EAA for all the projects and choose the project with the largest EAA. The cash flow of a project is financially equivalent to the NPV and the EAA. They are all financially equal and therefore one is not better than another.

4.11 Inflation in Capital Budgeting

So far, the effect of inflation has not been considered on the appraisal of capital investment proposals. Inflation is particularly important in developing countries as the rate of inflation tends to be rather high. As inflation rate increases, so will the minimum return required by an investor. For example, one might be happy with a return of 10% with zero inflation, but if inflation was 20%, one would expect a much greater return.

Example: Keymer Farm is considering investing in a project with the following cash flows:

Time	*Actual Cash Flows ($)*
0	(100,000)
1	90,000
2	80,000
3	70,000

Keymer Farm requires a minimum return of 40% under the present conditions. Inflation is currently running at 30% a year and is expected to continue indefinitely. Should Keymer Farm go ahead with the project?

Let us take a look at Keymer Farm's required rate of return. If it invested $10,000 for one year on 1 January, then on 31 December it would require a minimum return of $4,000. With the initial investment of $10,000, the total value of the investment by 31 December must increase to $14,000. During the year, the purchasing value of the dollar would fall due to inflation. We can restate the amount received on 31 December in terms of the purchasing power of the dollar at 1 January as follows:

Amount received on 31 December in terms of the value of the dollar at 1 January:

$$= \frac{\$14,000}{(1+0.30)^1} = \$10,769$$

In terms of the value of the dollar at 1 January, Keymer Farm would make a profit of $769, which represents a rate of return of 7.69% in 'today's money' terms. This is known as the real rate of return. The required rate of 40% is a money rate of return (sometimes known as a nominal rate of return). The money rate measures the return in terms of the dollar, which is falling in value. The real rate measures the return in constant price-level terms.

The two rates of return and the inflation rate are linked by the equation (1 + money rate) equals (1 + real rate) × (1 + inflation rate) where all the rates are expressed as proportions.

In the example above,

$$(1 + 0.40) = (1 + 0.0769) \times (1 + 0.3)$$

So, which rate is used in discounting? As a rule of thumb:

1. If the cash flows are expressed in terms of actual dollars that will be received or paid in the future, the money rate for discounting should be used.
2. If the cash flows are expressed in terms of the value of the dollar at time 0 (that is, in constant price level terms), the real rate of discounting should be used.

In Keymer Farm's case, the cash flows are expressed in terms of the actual dollars that will be received or paid at the relevant dates. Therefore, we should discount them using the money rate of return.

Time	*Cash Flow ($)*	*Discount Factor at 40%*	*PV ($)*
0	(150,000)	1.000	(100,000)
1	90,000	0.714	64,260
2	80,000	0.510	40,800
3	70,000	0.364	25,480
	NPV		30,540

The project has a positive NPV of $30,540, so Keymer Farm should go ahead with the project. The future cash flows can be re-expressed in terms of the value of the dollar at time 0 as follows, given inflation at 30% a year.

Time	*Actual Cash Flow ($)*	*Cash Flow at Time 0 Price Level ($)*	
0	(100,000)		(100,000)
1	90,000	$90{,}000 \times \frac{1}{(1+0.30)^1}$	69,231
2	80,000	$\frac{1}{(1+0.0769)^1}$	47,337
3	70,000	$70{,}000 \times \frac{1}{(1+0.30)^3}$	31,862

The cash flows expressed in terms of the value of the dollar at time 0 can now be discounted using the real value of 7.69%.

Time	*Cash Flow ($)*	*Discount Factor at 7.69%*	*PV ($)*
0	(100,000)	1.000	(100,000)
1	69,231	$\frac{1}{(1+0.0769)^1}$	64,246
2	47,337	$\frac{1}{(1+0.0769)^2}$	40,804
3	31,862	$\frac{1}{(1+0.0769)^3}$	25,490
	NPV		30,540

The NPV is the same as earlier.

4.11.1 Expectations of Inflation and the Effects of Inflation

When a manager evaluates a project or when a shareholder evaluates his/her investments, he/she can only guess what the rate of inflation will be. These guesses will probably be wrong, at least to some extent, as it is extremely difficult to forecast the rate of inflation accurately. The only way in which uncertainty about inflation can be allowed for in project evaluation is by risk and uncertainty analysis.

Inflation may be general, that is, affecting prices of all kinds, or specific to particular prices. Generalized inflation has the following effects:

1. Inflation will mean higher costs and higher selling prices. It is difficult to predict the effect of higher selling prices on demand. A company that raises its prices by 30%, because the general rate of inflation is 30%, might suffer a serious fall in demand.
2. Inflation, as it affects financing needs, is also going to affect gearing, and so the cost of capital.
3. Since fixed assets and stocks will increase in money value, the same quantities of assets must be financed by increasing amounts of capital. If the future rate of inflation can be predicted with some degree of accuracy, management can work out how much extra finance the company will need and take steps to obtain it, for example, by increasing retention of earnings, or borrowing.

However, if the future rate of inflation cannot be predicted with a certain amount of accuracy, then the management should estimate what it will be and make plans to obtain the extra finance accordingly. Provisions should also be made to have access to 'contingency funds' should the rate of inflation exceed expectations, for example, a higher bank overdraft facility might be arranged should the need arise.

Many different proposals have been made for accounting for inflation. Two systems known as 'current purchasing power' (CPP) and 'current cost accounting' (CCA) have been suggested. CPP is a system of accounting that makes adjustments to income and capital values to allow for the general rate of price inflation. CCA is a system that takes account of specific price inflation (i.e., changes in the prices of specific assets or groups of assets), but not of general price inflation. It involves adjusting accounts to reflect the current values of assets owned and used. At present, there is very little measure of agreement as to the best approach to the problem of 'accounting for inflation'. Both these approaches are still being debated by the accountancy bodies.

4.12 Comparison among the Capital Budgeting Techniques

If we are dealing with mutually exclusive projects, the NPV method leads us to invest in projects that maximize wealth, that is, capital budgeting decision is consistent with owner's wealth maximization. If we are dealing with a limit on the capital budget, the NPV and profitability index methods lead us to invest in the set of projects that maximize wealth. The DCF techniques are preferred to non-DCF techniques. The reason for such preference is that all of the DCF techniques consider all cash flows, the time value of money and the risk of future cash flows. The DCF techniques are also useful as objective decision criteria can be used to choose among the projects. But all of the DCF techniques are right in every situation. The applicability of the techniques depends on the answers of the following questions:

1. Are the projects mutually exclusive or independent?
2. Are the projects subject to capital rationing?
3. Are the projects of the same risk?
4. Are the projects of the same scale of investment?

Here, are some simple rules:

1. If the projects are independent and not subject to capital rationing, we can evaluate them and determine the ones that maximize wealth based on any of the DCF techniques.
2. If the projects are mutually exclusive, have the same investment outlay and have the same risk, we must use only the NPV or MIRR techniques to determine the projects that maximize wealth.
3. If projects are mutually exclusive and are of different risks or are of different scales, NPV is preferred over MIRR.
4. If the capital budget is limited, we can use either the NPV or the profitability index. At the same time, it should be carefully followed whether the right projects are selected to exhaust the full capital budget and total NPV is maximized.

4.13 Capital Budgeting Techniques in Practice

The discussion so far made concludes that NPV is the best in almost every situation. However, surveys and research studies in this area revealed some observations:

1. There is an increased use of more sophisticated capital budgeting techniques.
2. Most financial managers use more than one technique to evaluate the same projects with a DCF technique (NPV, IRR and profitability index) used as a primary method and payback period used as a secondary method.
3. The most commonly used technique is the IRR method, although the NPV method is gaining acceptance.
4. IRR is the popular method, most likely because it is a measure of the yield and therefore easy to understand. Financial managers, who are accustomed to deal with yields rather than dollars, as expressed in NPV, may be more comfortable dealing with IRR than the NPV.
5. Consideration of risk in capital budgeting is getting priority due to the increasing level of uncertainty in the business environment.
6. Application of different modelling like linear programming and goal programming is becoming commonplace in this area. And computerized software are highly used for different techniques such as simulation, sensitivity analysis and the like.

A careful scrutiny of Tables 4.2 and 4.3 reveals that some of the techniques are commonly used. For example, IRR as a capital budgeting technique has gained popularity across the years.

Table 4.2 Comparison of Methods Used by Large U.S. and Multinational Firms

	Large U.S. Firms	*Multinationals*	
Techniques	***Percentage Using Each Method***	***Use as Primary Method***	***Use as Secondary Method***
Payback period	80.3%	5.0%	37.6%
IRR	65.5	65.3	14.6
NPV	67.6	16.5	30.0
Other		2.5	3.2

Table 4.3 Historical Comparison of Primary use of Various Capital Budgeting Techniques

Techniques	*1959*	*1964*	*1970*	*1975*	*1977*	*1979*	*1981*
Payback period	34%	24%	12%	15%	9%	10%	5.0%
IRR	19	38	57	37	54	60	65.3
NPV				26	10	14	16.5
IRR or NPV	19	38	57	63	64	74	81.8

Source: Ross et al. (1996).

The popularity of the IRR method is troublesome since it may lead to decisions about projects that are not in the best interest of owners in certain circumstances. However, the NPV method is becoming more widely accepted and, in time, may replace the IRR as the most popular method. The payback period is generally used as a screening device, eliminating those projects that cannot even break-even. Further, payback reciprocal (1/payback) is viewed as a measure of yield. If the future cash flows are the same amount each period and if these future cash flows can be assumed to be received each period forever in perpetuity, payback reciprocal is a rough guide to a yield on the investment. Thus, if we want a 10% yield per year from an investment, it roughly tells us that the acceptable payback period should be maximum 10 years.

Problems and Solutions

Problem 1

A company wants to invest in machinery that would cost \$50,000 at the beginning of year 1. It is estimated that the net cash inflows from operations will be \$18,000 per annum for three years; if the company opts to service a part of the machine at the end of year 1 at \$10,000 and the scrap value at the end of year 3 will be \$12,500. However, if the company decides not to service the part, it will have to be replaced at the end of year 2 at \$15,400. But in this case, the machine will work for the fourth year also and get operational cash inflow of \$18,000 for the fourth year. It will have to be scrapped at the end of year four at \$9,000. Assuming cost of capital at 10% and ignoring taxes, will you recommend the purchase of this machine based on the NPV of its cash flows?

If the supplier gives a discount of \$5,000 for purchase, what would be your decision? (The present value factors at the end of years 0, 1, 2, 3, 4, 5, and 6 are respectively 1, 0.9091, 0.8264, 0.7513, 0.6830, 0.6209 and 0.5644.)

Solution

Option I: Purchase Machinery and Service Part at the End of Year 1

NPV of cash flow at 10% per annum discount rate.

$$NPV = [-50{,}000 + \{18{,}000 \div (1.1) + \{18{,}000 \div (1.1)^2\} + 18{,}000 \div (1.1)^3 + \{10{,}000 \div (1.1)\} + 12{,}500 \div (1.1)^3]$$

$= -50{,}000 + 18{,}000\ (0.9091 + 0.8264 + 0.7513) - (10{,}000 \times 0.9091) + (12{,}500 \times 0.7513)$
$= -50{,}000 + (18{,}000 \times 2.4868) - 9{,}091 + 9{,}391$
$= 50{,}000 + 44{,}762 - 9{,}091 + 9{,}391$
$\text{NPV} = -4{,}938$

Since NPV is negative, this option is not to be considered.

If the supplier gives a discount of \$5,000, then NPV = +5,000 – 4,938 = + 62.

In this case, NPV is positive but very small; therefore, this option may not be advisable.

Option II: Purchase Machinery and Replace Part at the End of Year 2

$\text{NPV} = [-50{,}000 + \{18{,}000 \div (1.1) + \{18{,}000 \div (1.1)^2\} + 18{,}000 \div (1.1)^3 + \{15{,}400 \div (1.1)^2$
$+ 27{,}000 \div (1.1)^4$
$= -50{,}000 + 18{,}000\ (0.9091 + 0.8264 + 0.7513) - (15{,}400 \times 0.8264) + (27{,}000 \times 0.6830)$
$= -50{,}000 + 44{,}762 - (15{,}400 \times 0.8264) + (27{,}000 \times 0.6830)$
$= -50{,}000 + 44{,}762 - 12{,}727 + 18{,}441$
$= 62{,}727 + 63{,}203$
$= +476$

NPV is positive, but very low as compared to the investment.

If the supplier gives a discount of ₹5,000, then NPV = 5,000 + 476 = 5,476.

Decision: Option II is worth investing in as the NPV is positive and higher as compared to option I.

(PCC November 2008)

Problem 2

A firm can make investment in either of the following two projects. The firm anticipates its cost of capital to be 10% and the net (after tax) cash flows of the projects for five years are as follows:

	0	*1*	*2*	*3*	*4*	*5*
Project A	(500,000)	85,000	200,000	240,000	220,000	70,000
Project B	(500,000)	480,000	100,000	70,000	30,000	20,000

The discount factors are as under:

	0	*1*	*2*	*3*	*4*	*5*
PVF (10%)	1	0.91	0.83	0.75	0.68	0.62
PVF (20%)	1	0.83	0.69	0.58	0.48	0.41

Required:

a. Calculate the NPV and IRR of each project.
b. State with reasons which project you would recommend.
c. Explain the inconsistency in ranking of two projects.

Solution

Computation of NPV and IRR

For project A:

Years	Cash Flows	PVF 10%	PV	PVF 20%	PV
0	–500,000	1.00	–500,000	1.00	–500,000
1	85,000	0.91	77,350	0.83	70,550
2	200,000	0.83	166,000	0.69	138,000
3	240,000	0.75	180,000	0.58	139,200
4	220,000	0.68	149,600	0.48	105,600
5	70,000	0.62	43,400	0.41	28,700
	NPV		116,350		–17,950

NPV of project A at 10% (cost of capital) is $116,350.
IRR of project A may be calculated by the interpolation method as under:
NPV at 20% is –$17,950
NPV at 10% is $116,350
∴ IRR = 10 + [{116.35 ÷ 116.35 – (–17.95)} (20–10) %] = 18.66%
For project B:

Years	Cash Flows	PVF 10%	PV	PVF 20%	PV
0	–500,000	1.00	–500,000	1.00	–500,000
1	480,000	0.91	436,800	0.83	398,400
2	100,000	0.83	83,000	0.69	69,000
3	70,000	0.75	52,500	0.58	40,600
4	30,000	0.68	20,400	0.48	14,400
5	20,000	0.62	12,400	0.41	8,200
	NPV		105,100		30,600

NPV of project B at 10% (cost of capital) is $105,100.
IRR of project B is calculated by interpolation method as under:
NPV at 10% = +105,100
NPV at 20% = +30,600
IRR = 10 + {105.10 ÷ (105.10 – 30.60)} (20 – 10) % = 24.10

Note: In the above solution, discounting factors of 10% and 20% have been used. However, instead of 20%, students may assume any rate beyond 20%, say 26%, and then NPV becomes negative. In such a case, the answers of IRR of the project may slightly vary from 24.10%.

Ranking of the Projects

The ranking of the projects will be as shown in the adjacent table.

	NPV	IRR
Project A	1	2
Project B	2	1

There is a conflict in ranking. IRR assumes that the project's cash flows are reinvested at IRR, whereas the cost of capital is 10%. The two projects are mutually exclusive. In the circumstances, the project that yields the larger NPV will earn larger cash flows. Hence, the project with larger NPV should be chosen. Thus, project A qualifies for selection.

Inconsistency in Ranking

Inconsistency in ranking arises because if NPV criterion is used, project A is preferable. If IRR criterion is used, project B is preferable. The inconsistency is due to the difference in the pattern of cash flows.

Where an inconsistency is experienced, the projects yielding larger NPV is preferred because of larger cash flows which it generates. The IRR criterion is rejected because of the following reasons:

i. IRR assumes that all cash flows are re-invested at IRR.
ii. IRR is a percentage but the magnitude of cash flow is important.
iii. Multiple IRR may arise if the projects have non-conventional cash flows.

(PE-II May 2008)

Problem 3

A company is required to choose between two machines A and B. The two machines are designed differently, but have identical capacity and do exactly the same job. Machine A costs $600,000 and will last for three years. It costs $120,000 per year to run.

Machine B is an 'economy' model costing $400,000 but will last only for two years and will cost $180,000 per year to run. These are real cash flows. The costs are forecasted in dollars of constant purchasing power. Opportunity cost of capital is 10%. Which machine the company should buy? Ignore tax.

$$PVIF_{0.10,\,1} = 0.9091,\ PVIF_{0.10,\,2} = 0.8264,\ PVIF_{0.10,\,3} = 0.7513$$

Solution

Advice to the management regarding buying of machines.

Statement Showing Evaluation of Two Machines

		Machines	
		A	***B***
i.	Purchase cost ($)	600,000	400,000
ii.	Life of machines (years)	3	2
iii.	Running cost of machine per year ($)	120,000	180,000
iv.	Cumulative present value factor for 1–3 years @ 10%	2.4868	–
v.	Cumulative present value factor for 1–2 years @ 10%	–	1.7355
vi.	Present value of running cost of machines ($)	2,98,416	3,12,390

[(iii) × (iv)]; [(iii) × (v)]			
vii.	Cash outflow of machines (₹): (i) + (vi)	8,98,416	7,12,390
viii.	Equivalent present value of annual cash outflow	3,61,273.93	4,10,481.13
[(vii) ÷ (iv)]; [(vii) ÷ (v)]			

Recommendation: The company should buy machine A since its equivalent cash outflow is less than machine B.

(PCC May 2009)

Problem 4

A company is considering the proposal of taking up a new project which requires an investment of $40,000,000 on machinery and other assets. The project is expected to yield the following earnings (before depreciation and taxes) over the next five years:

Year	Earnings
1	16,000,000
2	16,000,000
3	18,000,000
4	18,000,000
5	15,000,000

The cost of raising the additional capital is 12% and assets have to be depreciated at 20% on 'written down value' basis. The scrap value at the end of the five-year period may be taken as zero. Income tax applicable to the company is 50%.

You are required to calculate the NPV of the project and advise the management to take appropriate decision. Also, calculate the IRRs of the project.

Note: Present values of $1 at different rates of interest are as follows:

Year	*10%*	*12%*	*14%*	*16%*
1	0.91	0.89	0.88	0.86
2	0.83	0.80	0.77	0.74
3	0.75	0.71	0.67	0.64
4	0.68	0.64	0.59	0.55
5	0.62	0.57	0.52	0.48

Solution

Calculation of Net Cash Flow

Year	*Profit Before Depreciation and Tax*	*Depreciation (20% on WDV)*	*Profit Before Tax*	*Profit after tax*	*Net Cash Flow*
(1)	*(2)*	*(3)*	*(4)*	*(5)*	*(3) + (5)*
1	16,000,000	8,000,000	8,000,000	4,000,000	12,000,000
2	16,000,000	6,400,0000	9,600,000	4,800,000	11,200,000
3	18,000,000	5,120,000	12,880,000	6,440,000	11,560,000
4	18,000,000	4,096,000	13,904,000	6,952,000	11,048,000
5	15,000,000	16,384,000	–1,384,000	–692,000	15,692,000

40,000,000 × 20% = 8,000,000; (40,000,000 – 8,000,000) × 20% = 6,400,000; (32,000,000 – 6,400,000) × 20% = 5,120,000; (25,600,000 – 5,120,000) × 20% = 4,096,000; (20,480,000 – 4,096,000) = 16,384,000

Calculation of NPV

		12%		14%		16%	
Year	***Net Cash Flow***	***Factor***	***PV***	***Factor***	***PV***	***Factor***	***PV***
1	12,000,000	0.89	10,680,000	0.88	10,560,000	0.86	10,320,000
2	11,200,000	0.8	8,960,000	0.77	8,624,000	0.74	8,288,000
3	11,560,000	0.71	8,207,600	0.67	7,745,200	0.64	7,398,400
4	11,048,000	0.64	7,070,720	0.59	6,518,320	0.55	6,076,400
5	15,692,000	0.57	8,944,440	0.52	8,159,840	0.48	7,532,160
Total			43,862,760		41,607,360		39,614,960
Less: Initial investment			40,000,000		40,000,000		40,000,000
NPV			3,862,760		1,607,360		–385,040

Advice

Since NPV of the project at 12% = \$3,862,760, therefore the project should be implemented.

Calculation of IRR

$$\text{IRR} = 14\% + \frac{16.07 \times 2\%}{16.07 - (-3.86)}$$

$$= 14\% + \frac{32.14}{19.93}$$

$$= 14\% + 1.61\% = 15.61\%$$

Multiple Choice Questions

1. The capital budgeting process involves
   a. Identifying potential investments
   b. Analysing the set of investment opportunities and identifying those that will create shareholder value
   c. Implementing and monitoring the selected investment projects
   d. All of the above
2. A profitability index of 0.95 for a project means that:
   a. The present value of benefits is 95% greater than the project's costs
   b. The project's NPV is greater than zero
   c. The project returns 95 cents in present value for each current dollar invested
   d. The payback period is less than one year
3. Which of the following statements is correct?
   a. If the NPV of a project is greater than 0, its profitability index will equal 0

b. If the IRR of a project is 0%, its NPV, using a discount rate, k, greater than 0, will be 0
c. If the profitability index of a project is less than 1, its NPV should be less than 0
d. If the IRR of a project is greater than the discount rate, k, its profitability index will be less than 1 and its NPV will be greater than 0

4. Two mutually exclusive investment proposals have 'scale differences' (i.e., the cost of the projects differs). Ranking these projects on the basis of IRR, NPV, and profitability index methods ________ give contradictory results.
a. Will never b. Will always c. May d. Will generally

5. If capital is to be rationed 'for only the current period', a firm should probably first consider selecting projects by descending order of
a. NPV c. Payback period
b. IRR d. Profitability index

6. The preferred technique for evaluating most capital investments is
a. Payback period c. IRR
b. Discount payback period d. NPV

7. Suppose a particular investment project will generate an immediate cash inflow of $1,000,000 followed by cash outflows of $500,000 in each of the next three years. What is the project's IRR? Suppose a company's hurdle rate is 15%, should it accept the project?
a. 23%; reject the project c. 15%; reject the project
b. 23%; accept the project d. 15%; accept the project

8. ABC Manufacturing is evaluating a new etching tool. The equipment costs $1.0m and will generate after-tax cash inflows of $0.4m per year for six years. Assume the firm has a 15% cost of capital. What's the NPV of the investment?
a. $0.51m b. $0.45m c. $1.51m d. $1.69m

9. Should a firm invest in projects with NPV = $0?
a. Yes
b. No
c. The firm is indifferent between accepting or rejecting projects with zero NPVs
d. The firm should look at the profitability index and IRR of the projects

10. A project may have multiple IRRs when
a. The project generates an alternating series of net cash inflows and outflows
b. The project generates an immediate cash inflow followed by cash outflow
c. The project has a negative NPV
d. The project is of considerably large scale

Discussion Questions

1. What do you mean by capital budgeting? What are the basic differences between capital expenditure and revenue expenditure?
2. What are the different forms of classifying investment projects?
3. What are the different stages of capital budgeting? Critically explain the importance of each stage in capital budgeting decisions.
4. Why estimation of cash flows is so important in capital budgeting? What are the different types of cash flows in capital investment projects?
5. What are the basic differences between discounted and non-discounted techniques of capital budgeting?

6. Critically present the superiority of the application of payback period and payback reciprocal in capital investment decisions.
7. What is the basic difference between NPV and IRR? Which one is better and why?
8. What do you mean by MIRR? Is it better than IRR? Why or why not?
9. In which situations NPV and IRR result contradictory conclusions?
10. What are the techniques available to deal with unequal life projects? Make a comparative discussion.
11. How inflation is adjusted in capital budgeting decisions?

Exercises

1. Delta Corporation is considering two capital expenditure proposals. Both proposals are for similar products and both are expected to operate for four years. Only one proposal can be accepted. The following information is available:

Year	*Project A ($)*	*Project B ($)*
0 – Investment	46,000	46,000
1 – Return	6,500	4,500
2 – Return	3,500	2,500
3 – Return	13,500	4,500
4 – Return (A) and loss (B)	1,500	14,500
4 – Scrap value	4,000	4,000

Depreciation is charged on the straight line basis. Calculate the following for both projects:

a. the payback period to one decimal place
b. the average rate of return (ARR) on initial investment to one decimal place.

2. Company A is considering a new piece of equipment. It will cost $6,000 and will produce cash flows of $1,000 every year for the next 12 years (the first cash flow will be exactly one year from today).

a. What is the NPV if the appropriate discount rate is 10%?
b. What is the NPV if the appropriate discount rate is 12%?
c. What is the NPV if the appropriate discount rate is 15%?
d. Draw an NPV profile and put a comment on it.
e. Assume that the company is able to invest in an upgrade of the equipment that would cost $1,000 in year 5, but would increase the cash flows in years 6–12 to $2,000, what is the new NPV? There will be no cash inflows in year 5 and the applicable discount rate will be 15%.

3. Company X is considering a piece of equipment that costs $3,000 and will produce cash flows of $1,200 in each of the next three years. What is the IRR of the project?
4. Company Z is considering a new machine. The machine will cost $1 million and will be depreciated on a straight-line basis for five years to a zero salvage value. Revenues from the machine are expected to be $800,000 per year and all associated expenses are expected to be 50% of revenue. If the company is taxed at a rate of 34% and the appropriate discount rate is 15%, will the company invest in this new machine?

a. If the company's discount rate increases to 20%, will they invest in the machine?
b. What is the IRR of the investment?

5. Consider the following capital budgeting problem. The two machines are mutually exclusive and the firm would keep reinvesting in whatever machine it buys. Machine A would be reinvested every four years and machine B every three years. The cash flows associated with each machine are tabulated in the adjacent chart; all numbers are in thousand dollars and the relevant discount rate is 10% for both machines.

Year	*Machine A*	*Machine B*
0	–80	–100
1	50	60
2	50	60
3	50	60
4	25	–

   a. Which of the two machines is the better investment project? Analyse the question under the assumption that whatever machine the company buys has to be reinvested in perpetuity.
   b. Suppose machine A fits current technology, whereas machine B needs a one-time retooling for the company. These one-off installation costs would be $10,000 today. What is the optimal investment decision now?
   c. Suppose the firm has an old machine in place that would serve for another two years. They can postpone investing in either machine A or B and keep using this machine. When should they stop using the old machine? Cash flows for the old machine are given in the adjacent table.

Year	*1*	*2*	*3*
Cash Flow	50	20	0

   d. Suppose the investment opportunity described above lasts only for 24 years. Recalculate your decision rule for requirements (a) and (b). What is the NPV of the optimal investment policy now?

6. A corporation is considering purchasing a machine that has an expected eight-year life and will generate for the firm $11,000 per year in net operating income before taxes. The machine will be depreciated using the straight-line method to its anticipated salvage value of $12,000. The firm has a 34% marginal tax rate and the required return for this project is 12% per annum. If the machine costs $60,000, should it be purchased?
7. Another machine salesman comes by the company's office and says that he is willing to negotiate the purchase price of the machine described in the previous question. What is the maximum price the firm is willing to pay for the machine? (Hint: the price of the machine determines the level of depreciation and therefore the taxes that the firm pays.)
8. A corporation is considering purchasing a machine that has an eight-year life and will save the firm $4,500 per year in net operating costs. The machine would be depreciated on a straight-line basis to a zero salvage value. The firm has a 34% tax rate and a 12% per annum required rate of return on this project.
   a. If the machine costs $25,000, should it be purchased?
   b. If the machine can be leased for $4,000 per year payable at the end of each year, should the firm buy the machine or lease it?
   c. If the machine costs $10,000, what is the maximum lease payment the firm would be willing to pay if it was to consider a leasing alternative?

9. A company is trying to determine an optimal replacement policy for a piece of its equipment. The cost of the machine is $15,000 and the annual maintenance costs are $1,000 in the first year, $2,000 in the second year and $3,000 in the third year. Anticipated salvage values are $6,000, $3,000 and $0 at the end of years 1 through 3,

respectively. Assume that the company's revenues are unaffected by the replacement policy and that the firm has a 34% tax rate; a 12% per annum required return on this project and uses a straight-line depreciation. Should the equipment be replaced every year, every second year, or every third year? Be sure to explicitly consider the depreciation and tax effects.

10. Cement Inc. is considering an investment opportunity that requires an initial outlay equal to $575,000. In years 1 and 2 the net cash flows are expected to equal $500,000. The required rate of return is 25% per annum.

    a. Given that the Cement Inc.'s criterion whether to invest or not is the project's IRR, should the firm's managers invest in this project? Is the IRR criterion the correct decision rule in this case?
    b. After observing the managers' decision, a shrewd businessman offers the managers of Cement Inc. the following modified project. The businessman offers that the firm will pay the initial outlay $575,000 only in year 2 and receive the $500,000 in years 0 and 1. As a compensation for receiving this offer, the businessman proposes that the firm pay him $1,100,000 in year 3. Cement Inc.'s chief financial officer (CFO) argues that according to the IRR criterion the proposal is profitable since the 25% required rate of return is lower than the new IRR for this investment. Is the CFO correct in his argument that the required rate of return is lower than the IRR? Does this decision rule lead to optimal investment by the firm?

11. TA Holdings is considering whether to invest in a new product with a product life of four years. The cost of the fixed asset investment would be $3,000,000 in total, with $1,500,000 payable at once and the rest after one year. A further investment of $600,000 in working capital would be required.

    The management of TA Holdings expect all their investments to justify themselves financially within four years, after which the fixed asset is expected to be sold for $600,000.

    The new venture will incur fixed costs of $1,040,000 in the first year, including depreciation of $400,000. These costs, excluding depreciation, are expected to rise by 10% each year because of inflation. The unit selling price and unit variable cost are $24 and $12, respectively, in the first year, and expected yearly increases because of inflation are 8% and 14% respectively. Annual sales are estimated to be 175,000 units.

    TA Holdings money cost of capital is 28%.

    Is the product worth investing in?

12. SC Co is evaluating the purchase of a new machine to produce product P, which has a short product life cycle due to rapidly changing technology. The machine is expected to cost $1,000,000. Production and sales of product P are forecasted to be as follows:

Year	1	2	3	4
Production and sales (units/year)	35,000	53,000	75,000	36,000

    The selling price of product P (in current price terms) will be $20 per unit, while the variable cost of the product (in current price terms) will be $12 per unit. Selling price inflation is expected to be 4% per year and variable cost inflation is expected to be 5% per year. No increase in existing fixed costs is expected since SC Co has spare capacity in both space and labour terms.

    Producing and selling product P will call for increased investment in working capital. Analysis of historical levels of working capital within SC Co indicates that at the start of each year, investment in working capital for product P will need to be 7% of sales revenue for that year.

SC Co pays tax of 30% per year in the year in which the taxable profit occurs. Liability to tax is reduced by capital allowances on machinery (tax-allowable depreciation), which SC Co can claim on a straight-line basis over the four-year life of the proposed investment. The new machine is expected to have no scrap value at the end of the four-year period.

SC Co uses a nominal (money terms) after-tax cost of capital of 12% for investment appraisal purposes.

Required:

a. Calculate the NPV of the proposed investment in product P.
b. Calculate the IRR of the proposed investment in product P.
c. Advise on the acceptability of the proposed investment in product P and discuss the limitations of the evaluations you have carried out.

(ICMAB, April 2012)

13. A company is considering two mutually exclusive projects. Both require initial cash outlay of $10,000 each and have a life of five years. The company's required rate of return is 10% and pay tax at a 50% rate. The project will be depreciated on a straight-line basis. The before tax cash flows expected to be generated by the project are as follows:

Projects	*1*	*2*	*3*	*4*	*5*
A	4,000	4,000	4,000	4,000	4,000
B	6,000	3,000	2,000	5,000	5,000

Required:

a. Calculate for each project
   i. payback period
   ii. the ARR
   iii. the NPV and profitability index
   iv. the IRR.
b. Which project should be accepted and why?

(ICMAB, December 2010)

14. A hospital is considering to purchase a diagnostic machine costing $80,000. The projected life of the machine is eight years and has an expected salvage value of $6,000 at the end of eight years. The annual operating cost of the machine is $7,500. It is expected to generate revenues of $40,000 per year for eight years. Presently, the hospital is outsourcing the diagnostic work and is earning commission income is $12,000 per annum, net of taxes.

Required:

Whether it would be profitable for the hospital to purchase the machine? Give your recommendation under:

a. NPV method
b. Profitability index method.

Note that PV factors at 10% are given as follows:

Year 1	*Year 2*	*Year 3*	*Year 4*	*Year 5*	*Year 6*	*Year 7*	*Year 8*
0.909	0.826	0.751	0.683	0.621	0.564	0.513	0.467

(PCC Nov 2009)

15. XYZ Ltd. is planning to introduce a new product with a project life of eight years. The project is to be set up in Special Economic Zone (SEZ), qualifies for one-time (at starting) tax-free subsidy from the state government of $2,500,000 on capital investment. Initial equipment cost will be $17,500,000. Additional equipment cost of $1,250,000 will be purchased at the end of the third year from the cash inflow of this year. At the end of eight years, the original equipment will have no resale value, but additional equipment can be sold for $125,000. A working capital of $2,000,000 will be needed and it will be released at the end of the eighth year. The project will be financed with sufficient amount of equity capital.

The sales volumes over eight years have been estimated as follows:

Year	*1*	*2*	*3*	*4–5*	*6–8*
Units	72,000	108,000	260,000	270,000	180,000

The sales price of $120 per unit is expected and variable expenses will amount to 60% of sales revenue. Fixed cash operating costs will amount to $1,800,000 per year. The loss of any year will be set off from the profits of subsequent two years. The company is subject to 30% tax rate and considers 12% to be an appropriate after tax cost of capital for this project. The company follows the straight-line method of depreciation.

Required:

Calculate the NPV of the project and advise the management to take appropriate decision.

Note that the PV factors at 12% are:

Year	*1*	*2*	*3*	*4*	*5*	*6*	*7*	*8*
Factor	0.893	0.797	0.712	0.636	0.567	0.507	0.452	0.404

(PCC November 2007)

16. WX Ltd. has a machine that has been in operation for three years. Its remaining estimated useful life is eight years with no salvage value in the end. Its current market value is $200,000. The company is considering a proposal to purchase a new model of machine to replace the existing machine. The relevant information is as follows:

	Existing Machine	*New Machine*
Cost of machine	$330,000	$1,000,000
Estimated life	11 years	8 years
Salvage value	Nil	$40,000
Annual output	30,000 units	75,000 units
Selling price per unit	$15	$15
Annual operating hours	3,000	3,000
Material cost per unit	$4	$4
Labour cost per hour	$40	$70
Indirect cash cost per annum	$50,000	$65,000

The company follows the straight-line method of depreciation. The corporate tax rate is 30% and WX Ltd. does not make any investment, if it yields less than 12%.

The present value of annuity of $1 at 12% rate of discount for eight years is 4.968. The present value of $1 at 12% rate of discount, received at the end of eighth year, is 0.404. Ignore capital gains tax.

Advise WX Ltd. whether the existing machine should be replaced or not. (Hints: Decision must be taken based on NPV of the machines.)

(PE-II November 2008)

17. C Ltd. is considering investing in a project. The expected original investment in the project will be $200,000; the life of project will be five years with no salvage value. The expected net cash inflows after depreciation but before tax during the life of the project will be as follows:

Year	*1*	*2*	*3*	*4*	*5*
Cash Inflows	85,000	100,000	80,000	80,000	40,000

The project will be depreciated at the rate of 20% on original cost. The company is subjected to a 30% tax rate.

Required:

a. Calculate payback period and ARR
b. Calculate NPV and NPV index, if cost of capital is 10%.
c. Calculate IRR.

(PCC May 2008)

18. Given below are the data on a capital project 'M':

Annual cost saving	$60,000
Useful life	4 years
IRR	15%
Profitability index	1.064
Salvage value	0

You are required to calculate for this project M:

a. Cost of project
b. Payback period
c. Cost of capital
d. NPV

(PE-II June 2009)

19. Consider the following mutually exclusive projects:

	Cash Flows				
Projects	*C0*	*C1*	*C2*	*C3*	*C4*
A	–10,000	6,000	2,000	2,000	12,000
B	–10,000	2,500	2,500	5,000	7,500
C	–3,500	1,500	2,500	500	5,000
D	–3,000	0	0	3,000	6,000

Required:

a. Calculate the payback period for each project.
b. If the standard payback period is two years, which project will you select? Will your answer differ, if standard payback period is three years?
c. If the cost of capital is 10%, compute the discounted payback period for each project. Which projects will you recommend, if standard discounted payback period is (i) 2 years; (ii) 3 years?
d. Compute NPV of each project. Which project will you recommend on the NPV criterion? The cost of capital is 10%. What will be appropriate choice criteria in this case? The PV factor at 10% is:

Year	*1*	*2*	*3*	*4*
PV factor at 10% (PVF 0.10, t)	0.9091	0.8264	0.7513	0.6830

20. ZXY Company has found that after only two years of using a new machine for a semiautomatic production process, a more advanced and faster model has arrived on the market, which not only will turn out the current volume of products more efficiently but will allow an increased output of the item. The original machine had cost $32,000 and was being depreciated straight-line over a 10-year period, at the end of which it would be scrapped. The market value of this machine currently is $15,000, and a buyer is interested in acquiring it.

    The advanced model now available costs $55,000 and $500 will be spent for installation, and because of its more complex mechanism, it is expected to last eight years. A scrap value of $1,500 is considered reasonable.

    The current level of output of the old machine, now running at capacity, is 200,000 units per year, which the new machine would boost by 15%. There is no question in the minds of the sales management that this additional output could be sold. The current machine produces the product at a unit cost of $0.12 for labour, $0.48 for materials and $0.24 for allocated overhead (at the rate of 200% of direct labour). At the higher level of output, the new machine would turn out the product at a unit cost of $0.08 for labour (because one less operator is needed), $0.46 for materials (because of less spoilage) and $0.16 for allocated overhead. Differences in other operating costs, such as power, repairs and supplies, are negligible at both volume levels.

    If the new machine were run at the old 200,000-unit level, the operators would be freed for a proportionate period of time for reassignment in other operations of the company.

    The additional output is expected to be sold at the normal price of $0.95 per unit, but additional selling and promotional costs are expected to amount to $5,500 per year.

    Assume that income taxes at the rate of 36% and the company normally earns 16% after taxes on its investments.

    Required:

    a. Calculate:

        i. Payback period
        ii. ROI
        iii. NPV
        iv. Profitability index with net investment basis and without terminal value

v. Present value payback period
vi. IRR
vii. MIRR

b. Draft a brief report for presentation to the board of directors with a recommendation on the acceptability of this project and on the techniques that the board should consider when reviewing capital investment projects in the future.

(ICMAB, August 2012)

21. PR Engineering Ltd. is considering the purchase of a new machine which will carry out some operations that are at present performed by manual labour. The following information related to the two alternative models 'MX' and 'MY' is available:

	Machine 'MX'	*Machine 'MY'*
Cost of machine	$800,000	$1,020,000
Expected life	6 years	6 years
Scrap value	$20,000	$30,000

Estimated net income before depreciation and tax:

Year	*Amount ($)*	*Amount ($)*
1	250,000	270,000
2	230,000	360,000
3	180,000	380,000
4	200,000	280,000
5	180,000	260,000
6	160,000	185,000

The corporate tax rate for this company is 30% and company's required rate of ROI proposals is 10%. Depreciation will be charged on the straight-line basis.

You are required to:

a. Calculate the pay-back period of each proposal.
b. Calculate the NPV of each proposal, if the PV factor at 10% is 0.909, 0.826, 0.751, 0.683, 0.621 and 0.564.
c. Give your recommendation.

(PE-II November 2009)

Reference

Ross, S., R. Westerfield, and B. Jordon. 1996. *Essentials of Corporate Finance*. Chicago, IL: Irwin.

Chapter

5

Risk in Capital Budgeting

Chapter Objectives

On completion of this chapter, you will be able to understand:

- Nature of risk in capital budgeting
- Methods for incorporating risk in capital budgeting: certainty equivalent versus risk-adjusted discount rate method
- Time-adjusted discount rate and ascending discount rate
- Probability analysis
- Sensitivity, scenario and simulation analysis
- Decision trees, real options and portfolio risk
- Capital rationing: IRR approach versus NPV approach
- Comparison among capital budgeting techniques
- Capital budgeting techniques in practice

5.1 Introduction

Capital budgeting is a significant decision that businesses take more often, and thus it should not be based only on expected return. Rather, an optimum trade-off between risk and return should be reached before finalizing the decision to ensure value for money. Risk itself is a complex and relative issue. Further difficulties arise at the time of quantification of risk. Though some of the widely used capital budgeting techniques do not consider the risk at all, it does not necessarily mean that such consideration is secondary. Rather, due to the nature of recent business environment that is characterized by the highest level of uncertainty, the consideration of risk in capital budgeting decision becomes mandatory for making the decision more close to the reality. So far as the discussion goes, the capital budgeting decision depends on a lot of estimations in terms of return, life, discount rate and so many other parameters. Every time these estimations may go wrong. Thus, risk in capital budgeting is defined not in terms of losses that may be incurred in the future, rather it is defined in terms of the possibility of being an estimation wrong. And in most of the cases, the estimated future cash flows (returns) deviate from the actual one exerting significant amount of risk on making an earlier right decision wrong. A high-risk project may be one that gives a variation in returns between –30% and +90%, versus a lower risk project with a variation in returns of –20% to +20%. Both may lose money, but since the first one has a wide variation in returns, it is considered the more risky proposition.

Investors do not like risk and really do not like uncertainty. Therefore, they are going to demand more money (return) of higher risky projects.

Thus, it is wise to consider the risk at the time of taking such decision. Management is also risk averse like individual investors, meaning that, given the same rate of return across different investment opportunities, management would prefer an investment opportunity where risk (uncertainty) is the least. Capital budgeting decision is a strategic decision on which sometimes the existence of business depends. To address this strategic issue of considering risk in capital budgeting, a good number of techniques have already been developed and applied in real life. This section presents some of such techniques with real-life examples.

5.2 Sources and Perspectives of Risks

Risk management largely depends of the identification of the reasons of risk and its nature. Thus, the discussion of risk in capital budgeting may be related to the identification of techniques that consider risks on the basis of its sources and perspective. The finance managers dealing with long-term investment decisions are responsible to handle different types of risk that are involved in the capital budgeting process, so that the company does not face any difficulties once investment is made. Different types of risks involved in capital budgeting decision can be categorized as follows:

1. Corporate risk
2. International risk
3. Competitive risk
4. Project-specific risk
5. Industry-specific risk
6. Systematic risk

5.2.1 Corporate Risk

It is measured by a project's impact on uncertainty about the firm's future earnings. It depends on project risk and its correlation with returns on firm's other assets. If it is high, corporate risk is high unless diversification benefits are there within the firm. If the project is highly correlated with other assets, stand-alone reflects corporate risk. Let us consider a project (project X) with the pattern of profitability as shown in Figure 5.1. It reflects that project X is negatively correlated to the firm's other

Figure 5.1 Project Risk and Total Firm's Risk

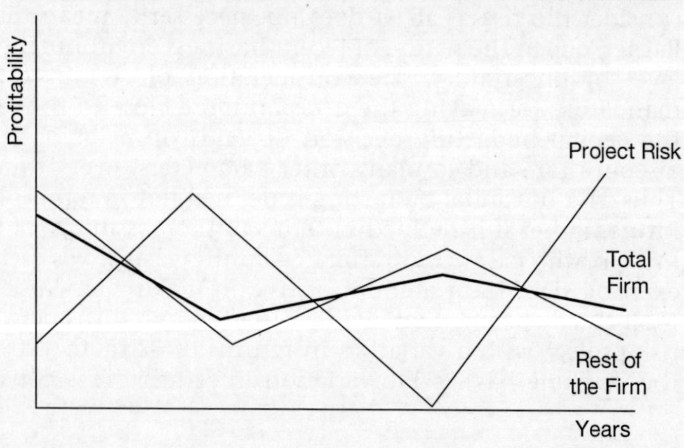

assets. If the coefficient of correlation between the profitability of firm and project is less than one, some diversification benefits exist. However, when the coefficient of correlation is exactly one, no diversification effects are there.

5.2.2 International Risk

Business has no boundary today and the same goes for risk. This type of risk may result from the rapidity of political differences and foreign exchange fluctuations, which influence the cash flows or income of an international project.

5.2.3 Competitive Risk

Business operates in a competitive environment where the pattern of competition is getting bitter each day.

Unexpected activities from competitors may result in this type of risk and this can adversely impact the project's cash flows and revenues.

5.2.4 Project-specific Risk

This type of risk may arise from decreased cash flow or income of a company in comparison with the anticipated cash flow or income due to the selection of the projects. This form of risk is thus generated from the specific project under consideration.

5.2.5 Industry-specific risk

All industries in the market do not work under similar risk exposure. Unanticipated scientific and industrial modifications and regulative amendments for a particular industry where the project originates may lead to this type of risk.

5.2.6 Systematic Risk

According to CAPM, systematic risk is the only relevant risk for capital budgeting purposes. For undiversified shareholders, including owners of small corporations, the relevant measure of risk may be the project's contribution-to-firm risk. This measure is more appropriate if there are costs associated with bankruptcy. In order to determine the risk-adjusted discount rate for a project, we need to estimate the systematic risk, that is, the project beta. Beta can be estimated using

- Accounting return data method
- Pure-play method

Firm Risk

The nature, degree and pattern of risk are dependent on the characteristics of the firm that is considering the proposals. Firm risk is also known as corporate risk, as discussed earlier. This denotes a share of all the risks of a firm contributed by a particular project.

Stand-alone Risk

This refers to the risk of a project at the time it is considered in isolation. The decision itself must have some bearing on the overall profitability of the firm. Here, the perspective is the project under consideration considered independently from others.

Market Risk

Market forces sometimes set a customized definition of risk that is true for that specific market only. This type of risk is taken into consideration from the standpoint of a diversified investor. This risk is also known as systematic risk, as defined earlier. As the principal objective of a company is the maximization of shareholder value, the ultimate important factor is the risk that is inflicted on the shareholders by the project. In case the shareholders are comprehensively diversified, the most suitable measurement method of risk is the market risk analysis. Unforeseen developments in macroeconomic elements, for example interest rate, the GDP growth rate, as well as inflation affect every type of project, though to different magnitude.

5.3 Methods for Incorporating Risk into Capital Budgeting

This section introduces different techniques used for incorporating risk into capital budgeting decisions. Risk may be incorporated through either cash flows or discount rates. Thus, two basic categories of techniques available are the certainty equivalent approach (CEA) and the risk-adjusted discount rates method.

5.3.1 Certainty Equivalent Approach

Under CEA, the financial manager substitutes the certain dollar amount that he or she feels is equivalent to the expected but risky cash flows offered by the project. In other words, adjustments are made to risky after-tax cash flows through a certainty equivalent factor (CEF) to make it certain cash flows. The greater the risk associated with a particular cash flow, the smaller is the CEF. This is the way of incorporating risk here. It can be equated as under:

$$\text{Risky Cash Flows} \times \text{Certainty Equivalent Factor} = \text{Certain Cash Flow}$$

The essence of this equation is like that \$10,000 is 90% certain, meaning that \$9,000 is 100% certain. Thus, it is better to use \$9,000 as cash flow in place of \$10,000.

Steps

The following steps can be used as a guideline to select projects under CEA.

1. Adjust all after-tax cash flows by CEFs to get certain cash flows by using the equation presented earlier.
2. Discount the certain cash flows by the risk-free rate of interest to result risk-adjusted NPV by using the following equation:

$$NPV = \sum_{t=o}^{n} \frac{CF_t \times CEF}{(1+K_{RF})^t}$$

5.3.2 Risk-adjusted Discount Rate

In the case of risk-adjusted discount rate, cash flows are not adjusted, rather the rate at which it will be discounted has been adjusted to incorporate risk. A risky cash flow is discounted at a higher rate than a less risky cash flow producing the similar effect on cash flows as done under CEA. When it becomes very difficult to set CEFs across the cash flows, it is better to use this technique. Here, discount rate is adjusted for risk premium. The rationale behind discounting a risky project at a higher rate is that investors are ready to accept a risky project if it generates return at a higher rate than a less risky project. It may seem to the students that the application is limited to the conversion of money value with reference to a specific point of time. That is right. But more often you will look that the discount rates vary across different projects in a single firm. This is due to the varying degree of risk factor attached with different projects. A project with a normal level of risk is discounted at the firm's cost of capital and projects with a greater level of risk are discounted at higher rates. For example, the following table may be a guide for selecting risk-adjusted discount rates.

Risk Class	*Project Type*	*Risk-adjusted Discount Rate*
1	Replacement, expansion	12%
2	New product development (related)	14%
3	New product development (unrelated)	16%
4	Research and development	24%

How a discount rate can be adjusted for risk?

a. Coefficient of variation: The coefficient of variation is a measure of risk. The more the value of coefficient of variation is, the riskier the project is. At a different level of coefficient of variation, a firm may use different discount rates and even that may be standardized across the firm. An example may be drawn as follows:

Coefficient of Variation	*Discount Rate*	*Coefficient of Variation*	*Discount Rate*
Up to 0.40	10%	0.71–1.00	17%
0.41–0.70	13%	Above 1.00	20%

b. The management may also develop a qualitative scale for measuring the risk. For example, the above discount rates may also come from a four-point scale that is based on different qualitative factors related to investments.

Degree of Risk	*Discount Rate*	*Degree of Risk*	*Discount Rate*
Low risk	10%	Moderate risk	17%
Normal risk	13%	High risk	20%

Example: To exemplify the situation, let us assume that a firm has two investment proposals: proposal A and proposal B. Proposal A is less risky than proposal B but requires a similar amount of investment, of $80,000. The life of proposal A is four years and that of proposal B is 5 years with the following pattern of cash flows:

Years	Cash Flows	
	Proposal A	Proposal B
0	80,000	80,000
1	40,000	20,000
2	30,000	30,000
3	20,000	20,000
4	20,000	10,000
5		40,000

The firm has selected the respective discount rates of 10% and 15% for proposals A and B due to the varying degree of risk.

Solution

	Proposal A			Proposal B		
Years	Cash Flows	PV Factor at 10%	PV	Cash Flows	PV Factor at 15%	PV
0	–80,000	1.000	–80,000	–80,000	1.000	–80,000
1	+40,000	0.909	+36,360	+20,000	0.870	+17,400
2	+30,000	0.826	+24,780	+30,000	0.756	+22,680
3	+20,000	0.751	+15,020	+20,000	0.658	+13,160
4	+20,000	0.683	+13,360	+10,000	0.572	+5,720
5				+40,000	0.497	+19,880
NPV			9,520			–1,160

Here, proposal A will be selected for ultimate investment due to positive NPA. But, proposal B may produce more NPV than proposal A if both of the proposals were discounted at a same rate. It may be said that the additional cash flows generated by proposal B are not enough to cover additional risk.

5.3.3 Certainty Equivalent Versus Risk-adjusted Discount Rate

In the CEA, the expected cash flows are adjusted downwards to incorporate risk of the project. Whereas in the risk-adjusted discount rate approach, the expected cash flows are unchanged, but the required rate of return is adjusted upwards to incorporate risk of the project. In either case, the net result is a decrease in the NPV of the investment proposal which is the justification of consideration of risk in capital budgeting. However, some other techniques are also available to do the same thing in a better and sometimes smarter way with generating other important information for the decision maker. Some of such techniques are presented here for better understanding of risk consideration in capital budgeting decisions. But the discussion is not exhaustive.

5.3.4 Time-adjusted Discount Rate

Time has a relationship with discount rate. A single proposal may be discounted at multiple rates when it covers a longer period. Cash flows in earlier years should be discounted at a lower rate and cash flows in later years should be discounted at a higher rate. The reason is that the probability of accurate estimation diminishes as the period of forecast goes longer. Obviously you can forecast tomorrow better than the day after tomorrow. This is the limitation embedded in human judgment. Say, for a project with 10 years of expected life, your discounting rate may spread as follows:

Time Period	*Discount Rate*
Year 1 to year 5	10%
Year 6 to year 8	12%
Year 9 and year 10	15%

5.3.5 Ascending Discount Rate

The ascending discount rate method takes the discount rate and adjusts it as cash flows become more uncertain over time. This is a revised version of the time-adjusted discount rate in a structured way. The scope of an arbitrary process has been reduced to a greater extent here. Over time, it becomes less and less certain what our cash flows will be. It is relatively easy to predict one year from now, but virtually impossible to know with certainty what will be 10 years from now. To build uncertainty into the NPV model, you have to adjust the discount rate. If you remember, the discount rate is made up of two parts, the cost of money and the risk premium. To build uncertainty into the model, you increase the risk premium. For example, if we know the cost of money is 10% and we have determined the risk premium to be 5%, our discount rate is 15%. But we have also determined that over time the risk premium should increase by ¾% to build in the uncertainty for each year through time. Therefore, in year 0 our discount rate would be 15%, but in year 1 our discount rate would be 15.75% or 0.1575, and in year 2 16.50% or 0.1650 and so on.

All you need to do to determine the NPV is compute your discount factors with the ascending discount rates. For example, given the following cash flow and the discount rate of 10% with an increase in risk premium of ¾% each year in time, determine the NPV.

Year	*Cash in or Out Flow*	*PVIF*	*PVIF*	*Project A*		*Project B*	
		at 10%	*Revised*	*CF*	*DCF*[3]	*CF*	*DCF*
0	COF	1	1	1,000,000	1,000,000	1,000,000	100,0000
1	CIF	0.9091	0.8639[2]	250,000	215,975	50,000	43,195
2	CIF	0.8264	0.7368	250,000	184,200	80,000	58,944
3	CIF	0.7513	0.6204	250,000	155,100	100,000	62,040
4	CIF	0.6830	0.5158	250,000	128,950	150,000	77,370
5	CIF	0.6209	0.4235	250,000	105,875	250,000	105,875
6	CIF	0.5645	0.3434			300,000	103,020

7	CIF	0.5132	0.2750			200,000	55,000
8	CIF	0.4665	0.2176			400,000	87,040
ΣCIF					790,100		592,484
NPV (ΣCIF – COF)					–209,900		–407,516

Notes:

1. COF means cash out flows; CIF means cash inflows; CF means cash flows and DCF means discounted cash flows.
2. $\frac{1}{(1+0.1575)^1} = 0.8639$, where the discount rate has been adjusted for ¾% increase each year.
3. DCF is calculated by multiplying CF with PVIF revised.

Here, both projects reveal negative NPVs and are, thus, rejected.

5.4 Probability Analysis

Probability analysis is a commonly used statistical tool whereby a probability in between 0.00 (full risk) and 1.00 (no risk) is assigned to form a probability distribution. As the value of probability gets closer to 1.00, it means the risk is getting lesser. The probability distribution may be discrete or continuous depending on the possible number of outcomes. A discrete probability distribution is formed with a limited number of outcomes by assigning probabilities to each outcome. But when, theoretically, the outcomes become unlimited, we need a continuous probability distribution. A commonly used continuous distribution is the normal distribution with a bell-shaped look. The advantages of using normal distribution are that it approximates many real-life situations and only two statistics (mean, as denoted by μ, and standard deviation, as denoted by σ) are enough to explain the situation. Here, mean represents the average value and standard deviation represents the dispersion from average value. However, normal distribution has some properties as follows:

1. The graph of the distribution is a bell-shaped curve.
2. The mean, μ, is located in the centre.
3. The distribution is symmetric about the mean.
4. The mean, median and mode are all equal.
5. The graph is an idealized (having infinite detail or resolution) representation of the data's histogram.
6. There is a fixed relationship between distance from the mean and area under the curve as follows:

Distance	*Area Coverage*
μ±1.00σ	68.3%
μ±1.64σ	90.0%
μ±1.96σ	95.0%
μ±2.00σ	95.4%
μ±2.57σ	99.0%
μ±3.00σ	99.7%

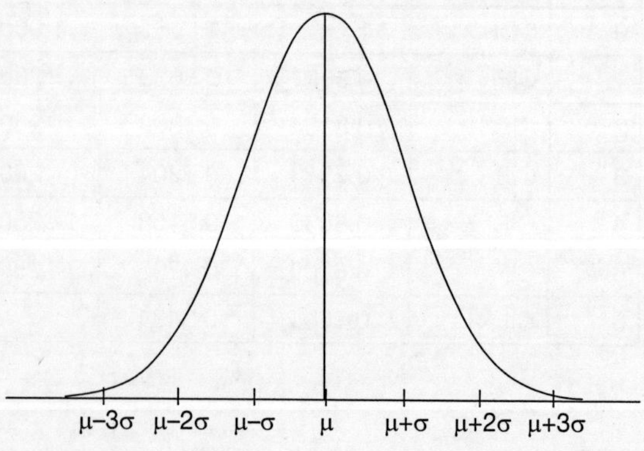

5.4.1 Steps in Probabilistic Analysis

1. Form the probability distribution with estimated cash flows and respective probability.
2. Calculate expected value (μ) and standard deviation (σ) by using the following equations:

$$\mu = \sum_{i=1}^{n} I_i P_i$$

where I_i represents expected cash inflows in period i, and P_i represents respective probability assigned to the expected cash flows for period i.

$$\sigma = \sqrt{\sum_{i=1}^{n} (I_i - \mu)^2 P_i}$$

3. When there is variation in sizes of estimated cash flows, the explanatory power of standard deviation reduces, and to explain the variations in a better way, the coefficient of variation is calculated simply by dividing standard deviation by expected return (σ/μ). The coefficient of variation provides a measure of risk that is normalized for the size of the investment. Therefore, it allows comparisons across investments of varying size.

Example: To exemplify the discussion, assume that a firm is planning to invest in a project with the expectations as given below along with the respective probabilities:

Situation	*Return in Dollar (Present Value of Future Cash Inflows)*	*Probability*
Pessimistic	200,000	0.3
Most likely	300,000	0.4
Optimistic	400,000	0.3

Compute expected return (μ), standard deviation (σ) and coefficient of variation (σ/μ).

Solution

Situation	*Return (I_i)*	*Probability (P_i)*	$I_i \times P_i$	$I_i - \mu$	$(I_i - \mu)^2 P_i$
Pessimistic	200,000	0.3	60,000	–100,000	3,000,000,000
Most likely	300,000	0.4	120,000	0	0
Optimistic	400,000	0.3	120,000	100,000	3,000,000,000
			μ = 300,000		σ = 77,459.6669

Thus, coefficient of variation (σ/μ) will be 0.2582.

5.5 Sensitivity Analysis

Most capital budgeting problems require management to make many assumptions before arriving at the investments' NPV. For example, forecasting projected cash flows may require assumptions about demand, cost of production, selling price and so on. When using sensitivity analysis, managers explore the importance of these assumptions. First, managers compute the expected (most likely) results. Then, the management allows one variable to change while holding the others constant, and NPV is recomputed. By repeating the process with all the important variables, the management can determine how sensitive the NPV is to the changes in each major assumption. Therefore, sensitivity analysis involves exploring 'what-if' situation to determine the variables to which the outcomes are particularly sensitive. The management can then challenge its assumptions about these sensitive variables. Some of such sensitive variables may be:

a. Discount rate
b. Growth rate of sales
c. Capital intensity ratio
d. Profitability ratios

Thus, sensitivity analysis demonstrates model output changes according to model input variations. A model is regarded a sensitive model with regard to an input if altering the variable input modifies the model output. A mathematical model can be outlined with the help of a number of input elements, set of equations, variable quantities and other parameters that are targeted to describe the procedure being used.

Sensitivity analysis is utilized for ascertaining the following:

a. The quality of model explanation.
b. Similarity of the model with the procedure in consideration.
c. The elements that largely contribute to the variation in output.
d. The domain in the space of input elements for which the variability of the model is the highest.
e. Unstable and optimal domains in the area of elements for application in an ensuant calibration survey.
f. Mutual or reciprocal action between elements.

Such analysis has become quite common for the following domains:

a. Risk analysis
b. Signal processing
c. Financial applications
d. Neural networks

There are various processes for carrying out sensitivity analysis and uncertainty analysis. The most fundamental method used for sensitivity analysis is based on sampling. The values are taken from the input element distributions. Usually, sensitivity analysis and uncertainty analysis are carried out in combination with help from probability distribution.

Steps

Different steps involved in sensitivity analysis are as follows:

a. Defining the target function and choosing the input of interest.
b. Allotment of distribution functions to the chosen elements.
c. Producing a matrix of inputs with the help of distribution by a suitable design.

d. Assessing the model and calculating the target function distribution.
e. Choosing a technique for evaluating the impact or comparative weight of every input element on the target function.

Implementation

Sensitivity analysis can be implemented for the following business applications:

a. Distinguishing vital presumptions or comparisons between alternative model forms.
b. Direction of data gathering in the future.
c. Determination of crucial criteria.
d. Maximization of the tolerance level of produced portions in association with the uncertainty involved in the parameters.
e. Maximization of resources apportionment.
f. Model lumping or simplification of model.

Illustration

A retailing firm is considering investing in a new store. The store will only be open for five years; thereafter the site will be redeveloped by the owner. Lease payments for the store will be $25,000 per year payable in arrears. Equipment will cost $75,000 and can be depreciated over five years to a salvage value of $20,000, and furniture and fittings will cost $75,000 and can be depreciated over five years to a salvage value of $15,000. Assume all depreciation is done on a straight-line basis. Sales from the new store are expected to be $300,000 in the first year of operations and are expected to grow at 10% per annum over the second year and at 5% per annum thereafter. The cost of sales is expected to be 60% (of sales revenue). Upfront advertising costs will be $75,000 payable immediately, and ongoing advertising and promotion costs are expected to be $15,000 in the first year, growing at the same rate of growth as sales. The firm's marginal tax rate is 33%, and the discount rate appropriate for this project is 14% per annum. Should the project be undertaken? How sensitive is the value of the project to changes in the cost of sales and the discount rate?

Solution

Information given	
Marginal corporate tax rate	33%
Discount rate	14.00%
Lease payments (yearly)	$25,000
Equipment	$75,000
Salvage value	$20,000
Furniture and fittings	$75,000
Salvage value	$15,000
First-year sales	$300,000
Initial growth period (until year)	2
Initial growth rate	10.00%
Steady-state growth rate	5.00%
Cost of sales	60.00%
Upfront advertising	$75,000
Yearly advertising and promotions	$15,000

Estimating Cash Flows

Year	*0*	*1*	*2*	*3*	*4*	*5*
Capital Flows						
Equipment	(75,000)					
Depreciation		(11,000)	(11,000)	(11,000)	(11,000)	(11,000)
Salvage value						20,000
Furniture and fittings	(75,000)					
Depreciation		(12,000)	(12,000)	(12,000)	(12,000)	(12,000)
Salvage						15,000
Revenues						
Sales growth			10%	5%	5%	5%
Sales		300,000	330,000	346,500	363,825	382,016
Expenses						
Lease payments		(25,000)	(25,000)	(25,000)	(25,000)	(25,000)
Cost of sales		(180,000)	(198,000)	(207,900)	(218,295)	(229,210)
Advertising	(75,000)	(15,000)	(16,500)	(17,325)	(18,191)	(19,101)
Tax cash flow	24,750	(18,810)	(22,275)	(24,181)	(26,182)	(28,283)
Tax carry forward	(24,750)	18,810	5,940			
Net cash flow	(225,000)	80,000	74,165	72,094	76,157	115,423
Discount factor	1.0000	0.8772	0.7695	0.6750	0.5921	0.5194
PV cash flow	(225,000)	70,175	57,068	48,662	45,091	59,947
NPV	55,943					

5.5.1 Sensitivity to Discount Rate

In Figure 5.1 at different discount rates, the NPV is given in the table and is based on values; the sensitivity is drawn in the adjacent graph. Figure 5.2 shows how sensitive the NPV is in relation to the discount rate.

5.5.2 Sensitivity to Cost of Sales

NPV may also be sensitive with regard to cost of sales. Such sensitivity of NPV with different percentages of cost of sales is shown in Figure 5.3.

5.6 Scenario Analysis

Scenario analysis is a more complex variation of sensitivity analysis. Instead of exploring the effects of a change in one variable, the management develops a scenario that might happen if a number of related variables change. As an example, if demand is lower than expected, sales

Figure 5.2 Sensitivity to Discount Rate

Discount Rate	NPV ($)
8.00	104,422
10.00	86,871
12.00	70,761
14.00	55,943
16.00	42,285
18.00	19,673
20.00	18,004
22.00	7,189
24.00	(2,853)
26.00	(12,193)
28.00	(20,893)
30.00	(29,011)
32.00	(36,596)
33.00	(40,204)

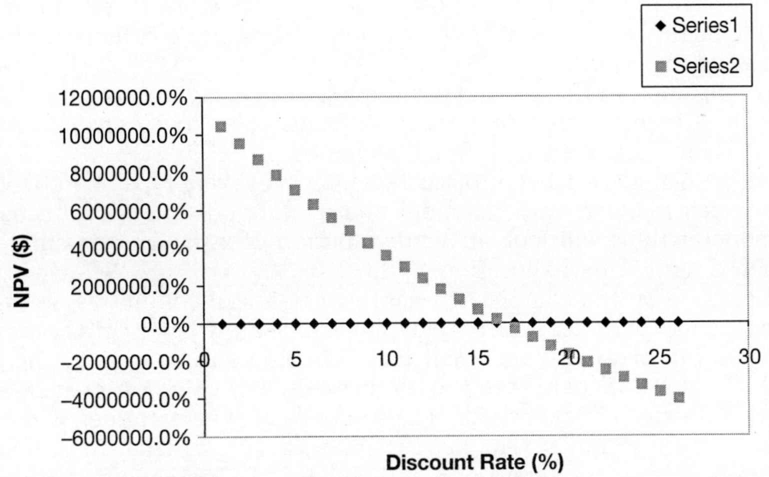

Figure 5.3 Sensitivity to Cost of Sales

Discount Rate	NPV ($)
30	293,263
35	253,710
40	214,156
45	174,603
50	135,049
55	95,496
60	55,943
65	16,389
70	(23,164)
75	(62,718)
80	(102,171)
85	(141,824)
90	(181,378)

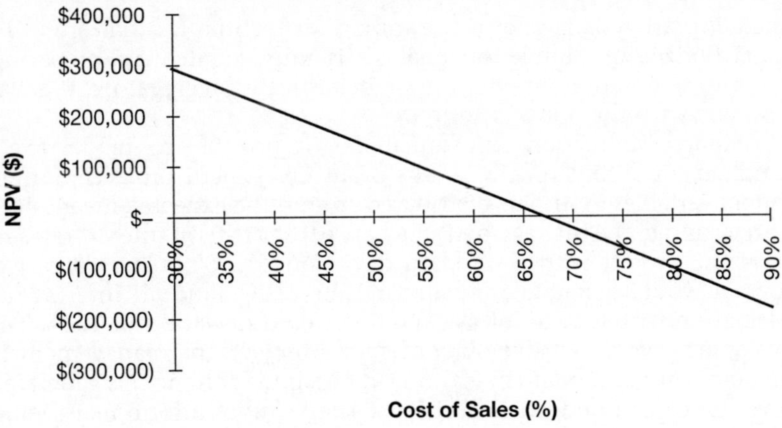

price might have to be reduced, and unit production cost might be higher. Normally, the management develops a most likely scenario and one or more pessimistic and optimistic ones. This is useful in illustrating the range of the possible NPVs and, therefore, the risk of the investments.

Scenario analysis is a method of assessing probable future occurrences by taking into account alternate probable consequences or scenarios. Scenario analysis was planned to enable quality decision-making by appropriating more comprehensive conditions of results and what they entail.

For instance, in finance and economics, a commercial enterprise may try to predict various probable outcomes regarding economy. It may also try to predict financial market yields for stocks, bonds and cash in different scenarios.

Scenario analysis takes into account subsets of every type of probability. In addition, it may also search to ascertain correlations and allocate possibilities to scenarios, as well as subsets. Scenario analysis will look at the distribution of assets among different categories of assets, which is termed asset allocation.

Counting on the complicated nature of financial conditions, scenario analysis is regarded as a popular practice. It is not easy to anticipate what is in the future, for the real future scenario can be totally unanticipated. This proves to be true for the prediction of outcomes and allocation of chances to those outcomes, and common predictions that do not pay any heed to financial market yields. The scenarios may be patterned with the help of statistical or mathematical formulae. Financial entities are able to take the scenario analysis forward by associating the asset apportionment, which the above-mentioned computations propose to the peer group, or commercial enterprise asset distribution. The financial enterprise looks to regulate its business risk, and not the portfolio risk of the customer. In geopolitics or common politics, scenario analysis includes patterning the probable optional ways of political or social ambience and potential war, and diplomatic risks. Scenario analysis has much significance in a number of sectors.

5.7 Simulation Analysis

Simulation analysis is one of the important techniques that are utilized in risk analysis in capital budgeting. Simulation analysis is implemented for preparing a probability profile regarding a criterion of merit by stochastically aggregating the variable values that are associated with the opted criterion.

Computer simulation software makes it possible to model the effects of even more economic conditions on the results of an investment project. Monte Carlo simulation uses random variables for inputs distributed around the expected means of the economic variables. As an example, the management may expect short-term interest rates to be about 4% over the life of the project with a standard deviation of 1.5%. These data would be input and the program would generate simulated results using random interest rates from a probability distribution with a mean of 4% and a standard deviation of 1.5%. Therefore, instead of just developing several possible outcomes for a project, the management can generate a range of outcomes with a standard deviation. Some simulation models generate probability acceptance curves for capital budgeting decisions. These curves inform management of the probabilities of having a positive NPV for the project.

With the help of sensitivity analysis, the sensitivity of NPV and IRR and many other types of criterion of merit to changes in fundamental elements can be ascertained. It offers data like the following: In case the quantity manufactured and sold is reduced by 1%, other factors remaining constant, the NPV also diminishes by 6%. This type of data, although helpful, cannot be sufficient with regard to decision-making. The decision-making authority also needs to have an idea about the probability of this type of events. These data may be rendered by simulation analysis.

Steps: Simulation is run in a sequential process. The process starts with patterning the project. The project pattern demonstrates the relation between the NPV with the various parameters and the external variable quantities. The parameters are regarded as variable inputs delineated by the decision-making authority and they remain unchanged in every simulation run. The external variable quantities are variable inputs that have random characteristics and are beyond the influence of the decision-making authority. The process of simulation analysis can be categorized into the following steps:

1. Assigning the probability distributions of external variable quantities and parameter values
2. Choosing a value in a stochastic manner by picking a value out of the probability distributions for every external variable quantity
3. Ascertaining the NPV matching the stochastically produced values of external variable quantities, as well as pre-assigned values of parameters
4. Performing steps 3 and 4 on several occasions for receiving a huge count of NPVs
5. Diagramming the NPV frequency distribution.

Example

Assumptions

i. Normal distribution for unit sales (mean = $1,250, standard deviation = 200)
ii. Triangular distribution for unit price (lower bound = 160, most likely = 200, upper bound = 250)

Process

Pick random variable for unit sales and price. Calculate NPV. Repeat.

Results

	Units	*Price*	*NPV*
Mean	1,260	202	95,914
Standard deviation	201	18	59,875
CV			0.62
Max	1,883	248	353,238
Min	685	163	–45,713
Probability of NPV > 0			97%

Diagramming

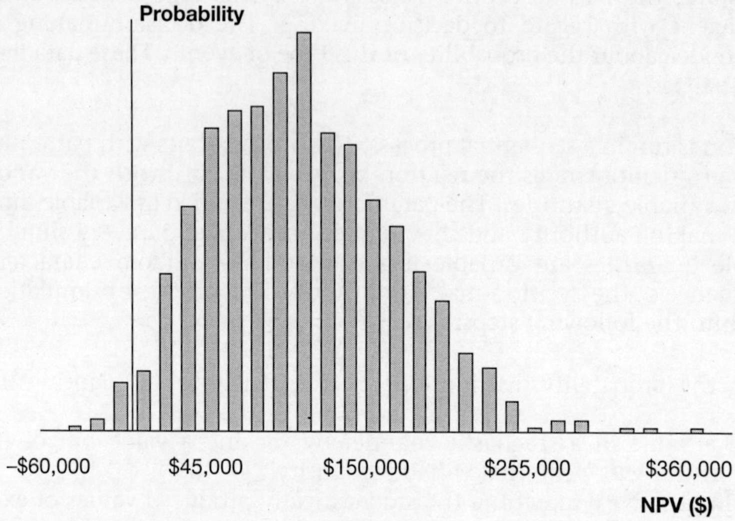

Strengths and Weaknesses of Simulation Analysis	
Strengths	Reflects probability distributions of each input
	Gives intuitive graph with ranges
Weaknesses	Still measures stand-alone risk only
	Difficult to specify distributions and correlations
	• Garbage in, garbage out
	• Looks accurate but may be a scientific wild-ass guess (SWAG)

Exhibit 5.1 Sensitivity, Scenario and Simulation: A Comparison

1. Do not provide ____________
    - Need to know if expected return is sufficient to compensate for risk
2. Only measure stand-alone risk
    - could be uncorrelated with firm's other assets or stocks in general
3. Still requires qualitative judgment
    - Example: With a 3% risk adjustment, is NPV positive?

5.8 Decision Trees

Most investment decisions are more complex than simply determining the NPV of future cash flows for a period of time and deciding to invest if the project has a positive NPV. The management often faces a series of decisions that may affect the value of the investment. Let us assume that the management is deciding whether to introduce a new product. It is evaluating whether to make an investment in the new product and test market it in a small geographical area. If the product sells well, the management will expand the test market to a larger area. Finally, if the product does well in the larger area, the management will introduce the product nationally, and there are several possible NPVs from the product depending on how well it sells nationally. The project may be abandoned based on the results of either marketing test. A decision tree provides a visual representation of these decision points and potential decisions. The value of a decision tree is that it forces the management to think through a series of 'if-then' scenarios that describe how the firm might react based on future events.

Decision-tree analysis provides a tool to study and decide on various choices available at a given point of time. It uses models of decisions that help to study the possibility of an occurrence of a particular consequence. Decision-tree analysis also studies the cost of resources, utilities and the chances of event outcomes. When there are several options to choose from, decision-tree analysis can be a wise alternative to choose and judge among the various options available. They give a structure or model that effectively investigates various probable outcomes of each option. Decision-tree analysis also helps to design a balanced and rational picture of rewards and risks that are associated with each possible optional action.

There are some rules associated with use of decision-tree analysis. For instance, when a business needs to make a decision on two courses of action, the decision is represented in a small square drawn at the left of a piece of paper. Each possible and probable solution is written on the right-hand side of the paper, along lines drawn from the square. At the end of the lines, the results are considered. It should be noted that the lines should be drawn keeping distance from one another, so that no problem arise later. The results can be either decisions or uncertain decisions. If the result considered is a decision, then another square is drawn and the same process is followed again. If the result is an uncertain decision, then it is noted by a circle in the decision tree. The decision is written above the circle or square. The possible outcomes resulting from the circle are also represented by drawing lines. The entire process is repeated until the final outcomes of the decision are reached.

Evaluation of decision-tree analysis is carried out by assigning cash value against each possible result or outcome. After working out the outcome values and assessing the probability of each result and outcome, the value in keeping a particular decision is calculated. With proper application of decision-tree analysis techniques, the best possible option that is required to develop a new service or new product can be obtained. It also gives the best decision depending on the available information and gives a framework for calculating the outcome values.

Example: Assume that a firm is considering a $1,250,000 investment in a new product. The management intends to test market the product in a small market, and if the product hits at least a moderate level of demand, the management will expand the test market area. Otherwise, it will abandon the project with no value. The management believes that the probability of meeting a moderate level of sales in the initial test market is 50%. If the product sells at least a moderate level in the expanded test area, the management will launch the product nationally. Otherwise, it will abandon the project with no value. It believes that the probability of the product performing well in the expanded market area is 75%. If the product is launched nationally, the management believes that the following three outcomes are possible:

Possible Outcome	***Probability***	***NPV of Future Cash Flows***
Pessimistic sales	25%	$2,000,000
Most likely sales	50%	$4,000,000
Optimistic sales	25%	$6,000,000

The decision tree below depicts this investment opportunity.

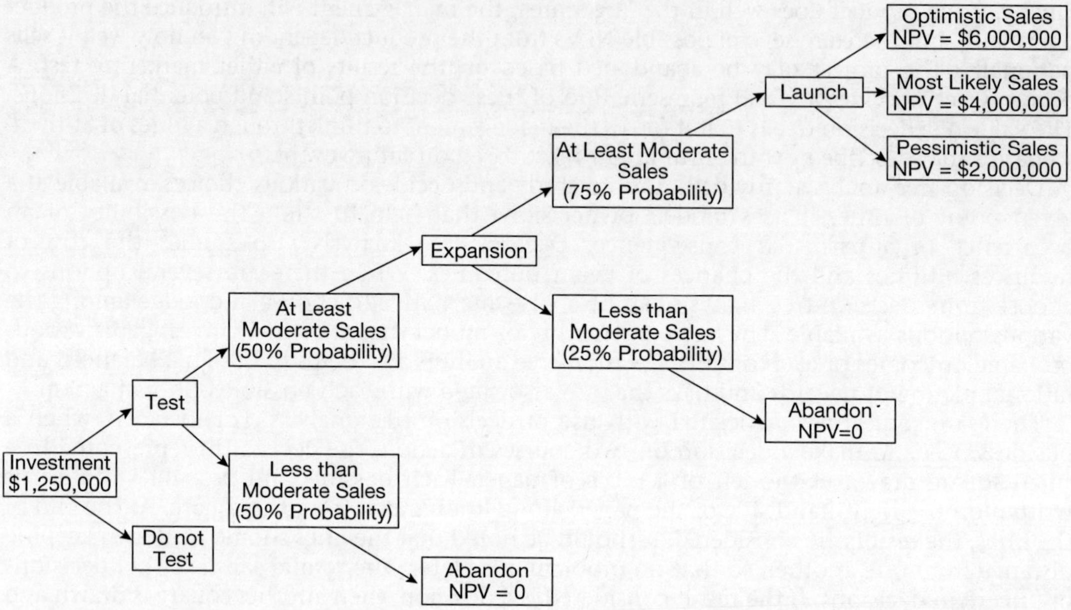

The appropriate way to calculate the expected NPV for the investment using a decision tree is to begin at the end and work backwards to the initial decision from one decision point to another.

The expected NPV of future cash flows if the product is launched:

NPV of Outcomes	***Probability***	***Expected NPV***
$2,000,000	25%	$500,000
$4,000,000	50%	2,000,000
$6,000,000	25%	1,500,000
		4,000,000

The $4,000,000 in expected NPV in the previous step is used to calculate the expected NPV of future cash flows at the point of deciding whether to expand the market test.

Outcome	***NPV of Outcomes***	***Probability***	***Expected NPV***
Moderate sales (launch)	$4,000,000	75%	$3,000,000
Less than moderate sales (abandon)	0	25%	0
			$3,000,000

The $3,000,000 in expected NPV from the previous step is used to calculate the expected NPV of future cash flows at the inception.

Outcome	*NPV of Outcomes*	*Probability*	*Expected NPV*
Moderate sales (launch)	$3,000,000	50%	$1,500,000
Less than moderate sales (abandon)	0	50%	0
			$1,500,000

The final expected NPV after considering the initial investment is calculated below:

Expected NPV of cash flows	$1,500,000
Initial investments	1,250,000
Expected NPV of the investments	250,000

Since the expected NPV is positive, the results indicate that the project should be accepted.

5.9 Real Options

Another technique that takes into account the dynamic nature of investment decision is one that views an investment as a real option. This technique assumes that once the management makes an initial investment, it has an option to take a number of future actions that will change the value of the investment. Therefore, the initial decision can be viewed as purchasing an option. Since NPV ignores the option value of an investment, it sometimes does not provide the correct answer.

Example: Assume that the management is considering bidding on the rights to extract oil from a proven site over the next five years. The extraction costs are expected to be $22 per barrel. Oil is currently selling for $21 per barrel and the management does not know whether the price will go up or down over the next five years. Using NPV with an expected price for the oil of $21, the management would clearly decide not to make the investment. The expected value of the production cost, $22 per barrel, is greater than the expected sales price of the oil, $21 per barrel.

We obtain a different answer using the real option approach. Remember that the firm is not obligated to extract the oil; it only has the option to do so. The management knows the oil prices are very volatile, and at least some time over the five year period oil will sell for more than $22 per barrel. Therefore, the investment has value and the management may reasonably bid on the rights. The NPV method understates or overstates a project's value depending on whether the investment creates or eliminates options for the firm. To correct this deficiency, the real options approach adds or subtracts an option value for the investment to get a more realistic value for the project.

$$\text{Project value} = \text{NPV} \pm \text{option value}$$

The option value is estimated much like the option value of a financial instrument is estimated. For a particular investment, the option may be a number of types, including the following:

a. *Expansion option*: The management may receive an option to expand the investment. An example of this option is a new product investment in which the management has an option to expand production after the initial investment.

b. *Abandonment options*: The management almost always has an option to abandon a project.
c. *Follow-up investment options*: The management may receive other investment opportunities when investing in the project. The expansion option is really a subset of this type of option, but follow-up investment options are more complex. As an example, investment in a particular R&D project might offer the management options for other related projects.
d. *Flexibility options*: The management may be provided with the ability to take advantages of changes in economic circumstances. As an example, an investment in machinery that can be used to produce a number of different products provides management with operating flexibility.

The analysis of real options is used to evaluate the decisions of capital budgeting. In order to maximize the value of a firm, managers need to compare the internal capacity of the firm in relation to the opportunities it is getting and then take the decisions regarding the investment of the firm accordingly. Real options are the chances given to the managers depending on the flexibility they enjoy over the timing of decisions. The real options are considered as the right to take the decision of capital investment options. An example of real option is that if the company wants to invest for the expansion of the business, then this opportunity is a real option. The concept of real options is opposite to that of financial options because the real option cannot be sold. For the case of the given example, the owner of the firm can take the decision of expanding his business but cannot sell his right of expansion to another party. The real options concept is relatively newer than that of financial options. Professor Stewart Myers was the first person to develop the term 'real options'.

With the analysis of real options, the uncertainty involved in the projects is determined and calculated by the risk-adjusting chances. Then, the decision of discounting the cash flows at a rate that is free from risk can also be taken. The approach of real options analysis actually drives the decision takers to be more rational to judge the assumptions that they are considering for their projects.

5.10 Portfolio Risk

Theoretically, the management should evaluate all possible combinations of investment projects to determine which set will provide the best trade-off between risk and return. This process is very similar to an investor's process of putting together a portfolio of financial investments. Computationally, the sets of portfolios that meet management's trade-off between risk and return can be visualized as falling on an indifference curve or risk-preference function. A risk-preference function, as shown in Figure 5.4, illustrates the efficient frontier for portfolio investments. Any portfolio of investments that falls on the line is an efficient portfolio (e.g., A, B and C); it meets management's objectives with respect to the trade-off between risk and return. Any portfolio that falls to the right is not efficient.

Figure 5.4 Risk Level (Beta Coefficient of Variation)

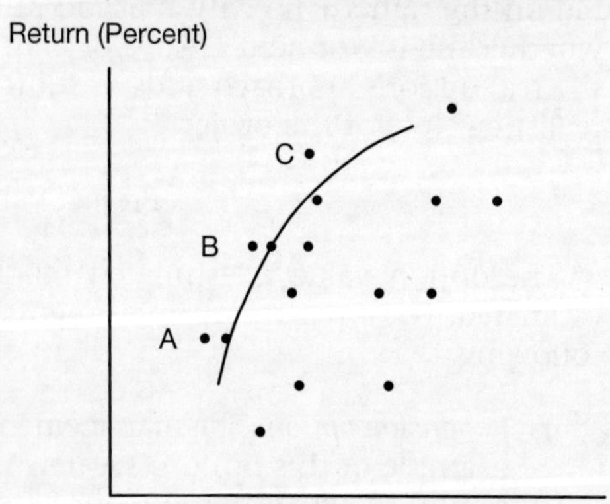

When considering a new investment to be added to an existing portfolio, the management must consider the effect of the investment on the overall risk of the portfolio. Whether or not an individual investment will change the overall risk of the firm depends on its relationship with other investments in the portfolio. If a casualty insurance company purchases the casualty insurance division of another firm, there is little risk reduction. Highly correlated investments do nothing to diversify away risk. Investments that are negatively correlated do reduce overall risk. Investments that are negatively correlated are those with performance that moves in opposite directions with changing economic conditions. Simply illustrated, if you match an investment that performs poorly during recessions with one that performs well during recessions, the risk of the two investments combined is much less than their individual risk.

A measure that is used to express the extent of the correlation between the set of investments is the coefficient of correlation from multiple regression analysis. This measure takes a value of from –1 to +1. The following table illustrates the relationship between the coefficient of correlation and the extent of risk reduction for the portfolio.

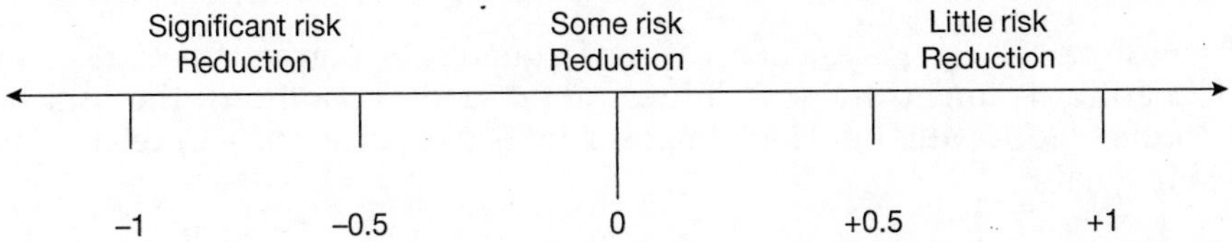

5.11 Capital Rationing

Capital rationing is a system of choosing more than one independent projects with positive values. Many companies specify an overall limit on the total budget for capital spending, which may restrict the managers to choose all value-maximizing projects. There is no conceptual justification for such budget ceiling because all projects that enhance long-run profitability should be accepted. However, it is not irrational to set such ceiling in certain situations. Some factors are identified here in favour of ceiling that requires capital rationing.

1. NPVs or IRR may strongly influence the overall budget amount.
2. Top management's philosophy toward capital spending.
3. Same managers are highly growth minded whereas others are not.
4. The outlook for future investment opportunities that may not be feasible if extensive current commitments are undertaken.
5. The funds provided by the current operations less dividends.
6. The feasibility of acquiring additional capital through borrowing or sale of additional stock.
7. Lead time and costs of financial market transactions can influence spending.
8. Period of impending change in management personnel, when the status quo is maintained.

Capital rationing occurs when a company has more amounts of capital budgeting projects with positive NPVs than it has money to invest in them. Therefore, some projects that should be accepted are excluded because financial capital is limited. This is known as artificial constraint because the management may dictate the amount to be invested for project purposes. It is also the artificial constraints because the amount is not based on the product marginal analysis in which the return for each proposal is related to the cost of capital and projects with NPVs are accepted. A company may adopt a posture of capital rationing because it is fearful of too much growth or hesitant to use external sources of financing.

5.11.1 Types of Capital Rationing

Hard Capital Rationing: This arises when constraints are externally determined. This will not occur under perfect market.

Soft Capital Rationing: This arises with internal, management-imposed limits on investment expenditure.

5.11.2 Reasons for Capital Rationing

There are basically two types of reasons of capital rationing.

External Reasons: These arise when a firm is unable to borrow from the outside. For example, if the firm is under financial distress, tight credit conditions, the firm has a new unproven product. Borrowing limits are imposed by banks particularly in relation to smaller firms and individuals.

Internal Reasons: Sometimes restrictions may come from internal management in different situations in different forms. Some of such form may be as follows:

1. Privately owned company: Owners might decide that expansion is a trouble, not worth taking. For example, there may be fear in losing control if management base has been expanded due to huge capitalized investment.
2. Divisional constraints: Sometimes the top-level management allocates a fixed amount for each division as part of the overall corporate financial management strategy just to control the capital budgeting decisions of different divisions. This is important to reduce divisional conflicts when divisions are evaluated in terms of their financial performance.
3. Human resource limitations: Companies may not have enough middle-level management to deal with new expansions and thus operations are kept within a manageable limit.
4. Dilution: There may be reluctance on part of the management to issue further equity due to the possible dilution effect leading to lower control.
5. Debt constraints: Earlier debt may contractually bind the company from increasing debt beyond a certain level. The debt–equity ratio may be fixed and new debt may not be possible due to its possible effect on debt–equity ratio.

The situations as pointed above make capital rationing rational. Within the limited fund, it is important for the management to ensure maximum value for the owners. And capital rationing makes value maximization rational.

5.11.3 Techniques of Capital Rationing

Capital rationing occurs any time when there is a budget ceiling or fund constraint in terms of taking long-term investment decisions. Such constraints are prevalent in a number of firms, particularly in those having a policy of internally financing all capital expenditures. Capital rationing also occurs when a division of a large company is allowed to make capital expenditures only up to a specified budget ceiling over which the division usually has no control. With a capital rationing constraint, the firm attempts to select the combination of investment proposals that will provide the greatest increase in the value of the firm subject to not exceeding the budget ceiling constraint. When capital is rationed over multiple periods, several alternative methods of handling constraint maximization can be applied to the capital rationing problem. These methods make use of linear, integer or goal programming. If capital is to be rationed only for the current period, the problem is reduced to selecting those projects that add the greatest increment in value per taka of investment without surpassing the budget ceiling. Assume, for example, that your firm faces the following investment opportunities:

Project	*Initial Cash Outflows ($)*	*IRR (%)*	*NPV ($)*	*PI*
A	50,000	15	12,000	1.24
B	35,000	19	15,000	1.43
C	30,000	28	42,000	2.40
D	25,000	26	1,000	1.04
E	15,000	20	10,000	1.67
F	10,000	37	11,000	2.10
G	10,000	25	13,000	2.30
H	1,000	18	100	1.10

If the budget ceiling for the initial cash outflow during the present period is $65,000 and the proposals are independent of each other, it is wise to select the combination of proposals that provides the greatest increase in firm value. Projects can be ranked in descending order of profitability according to the various DCF methods until the $65,000 budget is exhausted. Two basic approaches of such ranking are discussed here.

1. IRR approach
2. NPV approach

IRR Approach

Under this approach, projects are selected in terms of IRR of the projects. A ranking among the projects is made in terms of respective IRR and it has been graphed in descending order against total dollar investment (Figure 5.5). This graph is called investment opportunities schedule (IOS), which helps to identify the cut-off point where budgets are getting fully exhausted. Let us assume that the cost of capital is 18%. The problem with this technique is that it helps managers to identify the bundle of projects within the budget but it does not provide the guarantee that the selected projects will maximize the value of the investors. Let us draw the IOS line with the help of the following table:

Figure 5.5 Drawing IOS Line

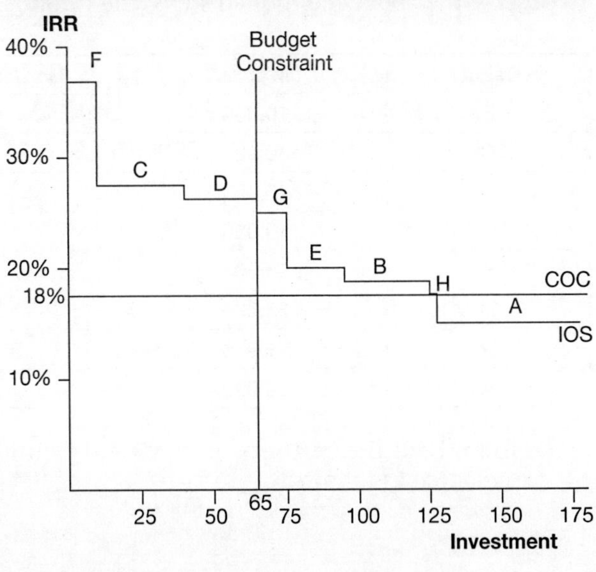

Projects	Rank (on the Basis of IRR)	Investment	Cumulative Investment
F	37	10,000	10,000
C	28	30,000	40,000
D	26	25,000	65,000
G	25	10,000	75,000
E	20	15,000	90,000
B	19	35,000	125,000
H	18	1,000	126,000
A	15	50,000	176,000

As per the calculation, only three projects (F, C and D) can be selected before exhausting the full budget. Still, three more projects (G, E and B) may be selected whose IRR is more than cost of capital. However, they will be discarded from the list of successful candidates due to the shortage of fund.

NPV Approach

This approach recovers the limitation of the IRR approach. The IRR approach provides capital rationing solution without ensuring value maximization of the owners. However, the NPV approach provides a feasible solution in rationing projects while considering value maximization as a prime goal. It is based on the present values of the projects. The following steps are followed to reach the feasible solution of rationing the projects:

1. Projects are ranked in terms of their respective IRR.
2. Then NPV with respect to each ranked projects is calculated and used.
3. Finally, projects are selected in a mix that generates the maximum value for the owners, provided that total investment have not exceeded $65,000 (budget) and projects with higher IRRs are considered initially.

To observe the above-mentioned steps, the information is suitably presented as follows:

Projects	Investment	Rank (on the Basis of IRR)	NPV ($)
F	10,000	37	11,000
C	30,000	28	42,000
D	25,000	26	1,000
G	10,000	25	13,000
E	15,000	20	10,000
B	35,000	19	15,000
H	1,000	18	100
A	50,000	15	12,000

1. To find out the best mix, it may need to initiate a trial for multiple times. The trial is presented as follows:

Trial 1

Projects	*IRR*	*Investment*	*Cumulative Investment*	*NPV*	*Cumulative NPV*
F	37	10,000	10,000	11,000	11,000
C	28	30,000	40,000	42,000	53,000
D	26	25,000	65,000	1,000	54,000

Trial 2

Projects	*IRR*	*Investment*	*Cumulative Investment*	*NPV*	*Cumulative NPV*
F	37	10,000	10,000	11,000	11,000
C	28	30,000	40,000	42,000	53,000
G	25	10,000	50,000	13,000	66,000
E	20	15,000	65,000	10,000	76,000

Only two trials reveal that the selection of four projects (F, C, G and E) is worthy to maximize the value of the owners. These four projects will maximize the value of the owners by $76,000 while earning a return more than cost of capital. It also rectifies the mistake that an investor may commit if the IRR approach is used for capital rationing.

Because of the budget constraint, you cannot necessarily invest in all proposals that increase the NPV of the firm; you invest in an acceptable proposal only if the budget constraint allows such an investment. As you can see, selecting projects by descending order of the profitability index (the ratio of the present value of future net cash flows over the initial cash outflow) allows you to select the mix of projects that gives you 'the biggest bang for the buck'—exactly what ranking projects by profitability index reveals.

Exhibit 5.2 Capital Rationing: Summary

Rationing exists whenever enterprises cannot accept all value-creating investment projects due to:

- Banks and investors say 'NO'
- Managerial conservatism

Analysis is required. One must consider sets of projects, or 'bundles', rather than individual projects. The goal should be to identify the value-maximizing bundle of projects. The danger is that the capital-rationing constraint heightens the influence of non-financial considerations, such as the followings:

- Competition among alternative strategies
- Corporate politics
- Bargaining games and psychology

The outcome could be a sub-optimal capital budget, or, worse, one that destroys value. Some remedies are the following:

- Relax and eliminate the budget constraint.
- Manage the process rather than the outcomes.
- Develop a corporate culture committed to value creation.

5.12 Making Go/No-go Project Decision

Virtually all general managers face capital budgeting decisions in the course of their careers. The most common of these is the simple 'yes' versus 'no' choice about a capital investment. The following are some general guidelines to orient the decision maker in these situations.

1. Focus on cash flows, not profits. One wants to get as close as possible to the economic reality of the project. Accounting profits contain many kinds of economic fiction. Flows of cash, on the other hand, are economic facts.
2. Focus on incremental cash flows. The point of the whole analytical exercise is to judge whether the firm will be better off or worse off if it undertakes the project. Thus, one wants to focus on the changes in cash flows effected by the project. The analysis may require some careful thought: a project decision identified as a simple go/no-go question may hide a subtle substitution or choice among alternatives. For instance, a proposal to invest in an automated machine should trigger many questions: Will the machine expand capacity (and thus permit us to exploit demand beyond our current limits)? Will the machine reduce costs (at the current level of demand) and thus permit us to operate more efficiently than before we had the machine? Will the machine create other benefits (e.g., higher quality, more operational flexibility)? The key economic question asked of project proposals should be: 'How will things change (i.e., be better or worse) if we undertake the project?'
3. Account for time. Time is money. We prefer to receive cash sooner rather than later. Use NPV as the technique to summarize the quantitative attractiveness of the project. Quite simply, NPV can be interpreted as the amount by which the market value of the firm's equity will change as a result of undertaking the project.
4. Account for risk. Not all projects present the same level of risk. One wants to be compensated with a higher return for taking more risk. The way to control for variations in risk from project to project is to use a discount rate to value a flow of cash that is consistent with the risk of that flow.

These four precepts summarize a great amount of economic theory that has stood the test of time. Organizations using these precepts make better investment decisions than organizations that do not use these precepts.

Problems and Solutions

Problem 1

You are a financial analyst hired by the Wolverine Corp., a U.S. company. It currently has no existing business in New Zealand but is considering establishing a subsidiary there. The following information has been gathered and provided to you for assessing this project:

- The initial investment required is $50 million in New Zealand dollars (NZ$). Given the existing spot rate of $0.50 per New Zealand dollar, the initial investment in U.S. dollars is $25 million. In addition to the NZ$50 million initial investment for plant and equipment, NZ$20 million is needed for working capital and will be borrowed by the subsidiary from a New Zealand bank. The New Zealand subsidiary will pay interest only on the loan each year, at an interest rate of 14%. The loan principal is to be paid in 10 years.

- The project will be terminated at the end of the third year, when the subsidiary will be sold.
- The price, demand and variable cost of the product in New Zealand are as follows:

Year	Price	Demand	Variable Cost
1	NZ$500	40,000 units	NZ$30
2	NZ$511	50,000 units	NZ$35
3	NZ$530	60,000 units	NZ$40

- The fixed costs, such as overhead expenses, are estimated to be NZ$6 million per year.
- The exchange rate of the New Zealand dollar is expected to be $0.52 at the end of year 1, $0.54 at the end of year 2 and $0.56 at the end of year 3.
- The New Zealand government will impose a tax of 30% income. In addition, it will impose a withholding tax of 10% on earnings remitted by the subsidiary. The U.S. government will allow a tax credit on the remitted earnings and will not impose any additional taxes.
- All cash flows received by the subsidiary are to be sent to the parent at the end of each year. The subsidiary will use its working capital to support ongoing operations.
- The plant and equipment are depreciated over 10 years using the straight-line depreciation method. Since the plant and equipment are initially valued at NZ$50 million, the annual depreciation expense is NZ$5 million.
- In three years, the subsidiary is to be sold. Wolverine plans to let the acquiring firm assume the existing New Zealand loan. The working capital will not be liquidated but will be used by the acquiring firm when it sells the subsidiary. Wolverine expects to receive NZ$52 million after subtracting capital gains taxes. Assume that this amount is not subject to a withholding tax.
- Wolverine requires a 20% rate of return on this project.

Required:

a. Determine the NPV of this project. Should Wolverine accept this project?
b. Assume that Wolverine is also considering an alternative financing arrangement, in which the parent would invest an additional $10 million to cover the working capital requirements so that the subsidiary would avoid the New Zealand loan. If this arrangement is used, the selling price of the subsidiary (after subtracting any capital gains taxes) is expected to be NZ$18 million higher. Is this alternative financing arrangement more feasible for the parent than the original proposal? Explain.
c. From the parent's perspective, would the NPV of this project be more sensitive to exchange rate movements if the subsidiary uses New Zealand financing to cover the working capital or if the parent invests more of its own funds to cover the working capital? Explain.
d. Assume Wolverine used the original financing proposal and that funds are blocked until the subsidiary is sold. The funds to be remitted are reinvested at a rate of 6% (after taxes) until the end of year 3. How is the project's NPV affected?
e. What is the break-even salvage value of this project if Wolverine uses the original financing proposal and funds are not blocked?
f. Assume that Wolverine decides to implement the project, using the original financing proposal. Also, assume that after one year, a New Zealand firm offers Wolverine a price of $27 million after taxes for the subsidiary and that Wolverine's original forecasts for years 2 and 3 have not changed. Compare the present value of the expected cash flows

it Wolverine keeps the subsidiary to the selling price. Should Wolverine divest the subsidiary? Explain.

(ICMAB, December 2012)

Solution

Requirement (a)

Capital budgeting analysis: Wolverine Corporation

		Year 0	*Year 1*	*Year 2*	*Year 3*
1.	Demand (units)		40,000	50,000	60,000
			NZ$	NZ$	NZ$
2.	Price per unit		500	511	530
3.	Total revenue = (1) × (2)		20,000,000	5,550,000	31,800,000
4.	Variable cost per unit		30	35	40
5.	Total variable cost = (1) × (4)		1,200,000	1,750,000	2,400,000
6.	Fixed cost		6,000,000	6,000,000	6,000,000
7.	Interest expense of New Zealand loan		2,800,000	2,800,000	2,800,000
8.	Non-cash expense (depreciation)		5,000,000	5,000,000	5,000,000
9.	Total expenses = (5) + (6) + (7) + (8)		15,000,000	15,550,000	16,200,000
10.	Before-tax earnings of subsidiary = (3) − (9)		5,00,000	10,000,000	15,600,000
11.	Host government tax (30%)		1,500,000	3,000,000	4,680,000
12.	After-tax earnings of subsidiary		3,500,000	7,000,000	10,920,000
13.	Net cash flow to subsidiary = (12) + (8)		8,500,000	12,000,000	15,920,000
14.	NZ$ remitted by subsidiary (100% of cash flow)		8,500,000	12,000,000	15,920,000
15.	Withholding tax imposed on remitted funds (10%)		850,000	1,200,000	1,592,000
16.	NZ$ remitted after withholding taxes		7,650,000	10,800,000	14,328,000
17.	Salvage value				52,000,000
18.	Exchange rate of NZ$		$52	$54	$56
19.	Cash flows to parent		$3,978,000	$5,832,000	$37,143,680
20.	PV of parent cash flows (20% of discount rate)		$3,315,000	$4,050,000	$21,495,185
21.	Initial investment by parent	–$25,000,000			
22.	Cumulative NPV of cash flows		–$21,685,000	–$17,635,000	$3,860,185

The NPV of this project is $3,860,185. Therefore, Wolverine should accept this project.

Requirement (b)

This alternative financing arrangement will have the following effects. First, it will increase the dollar amount of the initial outlay to $35 million. Second, it avoids the annual interest expense of NZ$2,800,000. Third, it will increase the salvage value from NZ$52,000,000 to NZ$70,000,000. The capital budgeting analysis is revised to incorporate these changes.

Capital Budgeting Analysis with an Alternative Financing Arrangement: Wolverine Corporation

		Year 0	*Year 1*	*Year 2*	*Year 3*
1.	Demand (units)		40,000	50,000	60,000
			NZ$	NZ$	NZ$
2.	Price per unit		500	511	530
3.	Total revenue = (1) × (2)		20,000,000	5,550,000	31,800,000
4.	Variable cost per unit		30	35	40
5.	Total variable cost = (1) × (4)		1,200,000	1,750,000	2,400,000
6.	Fixed cost		6,000,000	6,000,000	6,000,000
7.	Interest expense of New Zealand loan		0	0	0
8.	Non-cash expense (depreciation)		5,000,000	5,000,000	5,000,000
9.	Total expenses = (5) + (6) + (7) + (8)		12,200,000	12,750,000	13,400,000
10.	Before-tax earnings of subsidiary = (3) – (9)		7,800,000	12,800,000	18,400,000
11.	Host government tax (30%)		2,340,000	3,840,000	5,520,000
12.	After-tax earnings of subsidiary		5,460,000	8,960,000	12,880,000
13.	Net cash flow to subsidiary = (12) + (8)		10,460,000	13,960,000	17,880,000
14.	NZ$ remitted by subsidiary (100% of cash flow)		10,460,000	13,960,000	17,880,000
15.	Withholding tax imposed on remitted funds (10%)		1,046,000	1,396,000	1,788,000
16.	NZ$ remitted after withholding taxes		9,414,000	12,564,000	16,092,000
17.	Salvage value				70,000,000
18.	Exchange rate of NZ$		$52	$54	$56
19.	Cash flows to parent		$4,895,280	$6,784,560	$48,211,520
20.	PV of parent cash flows (20% of discount rate)		$4,079,4000	$4711,500	$27,900,185
21.	Initial investment by parent	–$35,000,000			
22.	Cumulative NPV of cash flows		–$30,920,600	–$26,209,100	$1,691,085

The analysis show that this alternative financing arrangement is expected to generate a lower net value than the original financing arrangement.

Requirement (c)

The NPV would be more sensitive to exchange rate movements if the parent uses its own financing to cover the working capital requirements. If it used New Zealand financing, a portion of NZ$ cash flows could be used to cover the interest payments on debt. Thus, there would be less NZ$ to be converted to dollars and less exposure to exchange rate movements.

Requirement (d)

The effects of the blocked funds are shown as follows:

		Year 0	Year 1	Year 2	Year 3
1.	Net cash flow to subsidiary				
	= (12) + (8)		NZ$8,500,000	NZ$12,000,000	NZ$15,920,000
				→	NZ$12,720,000
			→		NZ$9,550,600
2.	NZS remitted by subsidiary		NZ$0	NZ$0	NZ$38,190,600
3.	Withholding tax imposed on				
	Remitted funds (10%)				NZ$3,819,060
4.	NZS remitted after withholding tax				NZ$34,371,540
5.	Salvage value				NZ$52,000,000
6.	Exchange rate of NZ$				$.56
7.	Cash flows to parent				$48,368,062
8.	PV of parent cash flows				
	(20% discount rate)		NZ$0	NZ$0	
9.	Initial investment by parent	–S25,000,000			
10.	Cumulative NPV of cash flows		$0	$0	$2,990,777

Requirement (e)

First, determine the present value of cash flows excluding salvage value.

End of Year	Present Value of Cash Flows (excluding salvage value)
1	$3,315,000
2	$4,050,000
3	$4,643,333*
	$12,008,333

* This number is determined by converting the third-year NZ$ cash flows excluding salvage value (NZ$14,328,000) into dollars at the forecasted exchange rate of $.56 per New Zealand dollar.

NZ$14,328,000 × $.56 – $8,023,680

The present value of the $8,023,680 received three years from now is $4,643,333.

Then determine the break-even salvage value:

Break-even

$$\begin{aligned}\text{Salvage value} &= [\text{IO} - (\text{present value of cash flows})]\ (1 + k)^n \\ &= [\$25{,}000{,}000 - \$12{,}008{,}333]\ (1 + .20)^3 \\ &= \$22{,}449{,}601\end{aligned}$$

Since the NZ$ is expected to be $.56 in year 3, this implies that the break-even salvage value in terms of New Zealand dollars is:

$$\$22{,}449{,}601/\$.56 = \text{NZ}\$40{,}088{,}573$$

Requirement (f)

Divestiture analysis one year after the project began

	End of Year 2 (one year from now)	End of Year 3 (two years from now)
Cash flows to parent	$5,832,000	$37,143,650
PV of parent cash flows forgone if the project is divested	$4,860,000	$25,794,222

The present value of forgone cash flows is $30,654,222. Since this exceeds the $27,000,000 in proceeds from the divestiture, the project should not be divested.

Problem 2

Grameenphone, widely known as GP, is the leading telecommunications service provider in Bangladesh. It is a joint venture enterprise between Telenor and Grameen Telecom Corporation, a non-profit sister concern of the internationally acclaimed microfinance organization and community development bank Grameen Bank. Telenor, the largest telecommunications company in Norway, owns 60% shares of Grameen phone and Grameen Telecom owns the remaining 40%. This foreign subsidiary is not wholly owned by the parent, and the foreign project is partially financed with retained earnings of the parent and of the foreign subsidiary. So, Grameen phone has to balance the interest of both parties and enhance the value of the corporation side by side.

1. The parent company has invested BDT 35.8 billion in 2008 to develop the network infrastructure, including working capital. The total amount of investment in Bangladesh includes funds from both the parent and the subsidiary. We are considering only the fund from the parent company Telenor. If we imposed a fixed exchange rate of USD 1 = BDT 69.2, the U.S. dollar amount the parent's initial investment is USD 517,715,112.
2. According to the going-concern principle, the company expects to run its business for an unlimited future period. So, to prepare a capital budgeting model for the company we consider fixed revenue earned by the company, for the upcoming future period. The total revenue will be fixed at BDT 46,684,747,000. However, there are a large number of sources

of revenue like subscription revenue-postpaid BDT 448,537,000, connection revenue BDT 384,660,000, roaming revenue BDT 386,933,000, interconnection revenue – mobile operators BDT 4,605,378,000, other operating revenue BDT 1,792,891,000 and other income, net BDT 38,156,000.

3. The costs are also thought to be fixed for infinite time period. These costs and expenses include operating expenses, such as direct cost of network revenue, network operation and maintenance expenses, general and administrative expenses, selling and distribution expenses and bad debt expense. The estimated expenses based on present observation are BDT 12,792,566,000, BDT 2,442,553,000, BDT 5,627,680,000, BDT 6,660,418,000 and BDT 135,290,000, respectively.
4. The subsidiary uses the maximum rate of depreciation allowed by the Bangladesh government, which is BDT 10,395,824,000.
5. The Bangladesh government will impose a 45% tax rate on income. In addition, it will impose a 10% withholding tax on any fund remitted by the subsidiary to parent. Company submitted its tax return file to tax authorities and paid tax BDT 10,475,013,000 thereon.
6. Company's required rate of return is 17% at perpetuity basis.

Required:

a. Explain and determine, with investment appraisal techniques, whether the above investment will be worthwhile or not for parent company Telenor.
b. Exposure to exchange rate fluctuations: Grameen phone realizes that the exchange rate will typically change over time, but it does not know whether the Bangladeshi *taka* will strengthen or weaken in the future. Foreign exchange rate in these two scenarios would be (a) strong USD 1 = BDT 65 and (b) weak USD 1 = BDT 72. What will be the impact on NPV under strong and weak scenarios and also explain which scenario will be favourable for parent company Telenor?
c. Although Bangladesh does not impose any restriction on foreign subsidiary's to block funds that the subsidiary attempts to send to the parent, to narrate the impact of blocked fund on capital budgeting, we are to assume that the Bangladesh government has imposed restriction on Grameen phone on remitting cash flows for five years. Let us assume that Grameen phone invests the fund in marketable securities which are expected to yield 8% annually after taxes. What would be impact on NPV?
d. Bangladesh has a history of facing volatile inflation rate year to year and thus can influence a project's net cash flows. The inflation rate of Bangladesh for following years is given:

Year	*Inflation Rate*	*Net Profit in Million BDT*
2009	8.90%	4,750
2008	9.10%	2,900
2007	7.10%	3,060
2006	7.00%	7,848
2005	6.00%	6,913
2004	5.60%	6,183

Explain the impact of inflation on company's profitability.

(ICMAB, April 2013)

Solution (a)

Sl.	Particulars	Currency	Year 0	Year 1
1	Revenue			
	Traffic revenue	BDT		46,684,747,000
	Subscription revenue—postpaid	BDT		448,537,000
	Connection revenue	BDT		384,660,000
	Roaming revenue	BDT		386,933,000
	Interconnection revenue—mobile operators	BDT		4,605,378,000
	Other operating revenue	BDT		1,792,891,000
	Other income net	BDT		38,156,000
2	Total revenue	BDT		54,341,302,000
3	Operating expenses			
	Direct cost of network revenue	BDT		12,792,566,000
	Network operation and maintenance expenses	BDT		2,442,553,000
	General and administrative expenses	BDT		5,627,680,000
	Selling and distribution expenses	BDT		6,660,418,000
	Bad debt expense	BDT		135,290,000
4	Depreciation and amortization	BDT		10,395,424,000
5	Total operating expenses	BDT		38,054,331,000
6	Operating profit (2 – 5)	BDT		16,286,971,000
7	Finance costs, net	BDT		(966,503,000)
8	Loss on disposal of property, plant and equipment	BDT		(101,963,000)
9	Share of profit/(loss) of associate company	BDT		2,591,000
10	Profit before tax	BDT		15,219,096,000
11	Income-tax expense	BDT		10,475,013,000
12	Profit for the year (10 – 11)	BDT		4,744,083,000
13	Net cash flow to subsidiary (12 + 4)	BDT		15,139,907,000
14	BDT Remitted by subsidiary at 60% (13*0.60)	BDT		9,083,944,200
15	Withholding tax on remitted fund at 10% (14*0.10)	BDT		908,394,420
16	BDT remitted after withholding tax (14 – 15)	BDT		8,175,549,780
17	Initial investment by parent	BDT	35,800,000,000	
18	Exchange rate of BDT			0.014461316
19	Cash flow to parent	USD		118,229,209
20	PV of parent cash flows at 17%	USD		695,465,934
21	Initial investment in USD	USD	517,715,113	
22	NPV	USD		177,750,822

The NPV of this project is BDT 177,750,822,185. Therefore, Telenor should accept this project.

(b)

Sl.	Particulars	Currency	Year 0	Year 1
1	**BDT Remitted after Withholding tax (14 – 15)**	BDT		8,175,549,780
2	**Strong BDT Scenario**			
	Exchange rate of BDT ($1 = BDT 65)			0.0153846154
	Cash flow to parent	USD		125,777,689
	PV of parent cash flows at 17%	USD		739,868,758
	Initial investment in USD	USD	517,715,113	
	NPV	USD		222,153,646
3	**Weak BDT Scenario**			
	Exchange rate of BDT ($1 = BDT 72)			0.0138888889
	Cash flow to parent	USD		113,549,303
	PV of parent cash flows at 17%	USD		667,937,074
	Initial investment in USD	USD	517,715,113	
	NPV	USD		150,221,961

From the parent's point of view, appreciation of the Bangladeshi taka would be favourable since the Bangladeshi taka inflows would someday be converted to more U.S. dollars. Conversely, depreciation would be unfavourable since the weakened Bangladeshi taka would convert to fewer U.S. dollars over time.

(c)

Sl.	Particulars	Currency	Year 0	Year 5
1	FV of BDT remitted by subsidiary (FVIFA 8%, 5 years)	BDT		53,295,500,621
2	Withholding tax on remitted fund at 10% (1*0.10)	BDT		5,329,550,062
3	BDT remitted after withholding tax (1 – 2)	BDT		47,965,950,559
4	Exchange rate of BDT			0.0144613160
5	Cash flow to parent	USD		693,650,768
6	PV of parent cash flows at 17%	USD		316,304,750
7	Initial investment in USD	USD	517,715,113	
8	NPV	USD		(201,410,363)

(d) If we analyse the table, we will see the inflation rate has a negative impact on the company's profitability and thus reduces NPV. Though the reduced trend of net profit can also be influenced by other factors such as competitors, but the strong influence of inflation rate can hardly be ignored. The joint impact of inflation and exchange rate fluctuation on a subsidiary's net cash flows may produce a partial off-setting effect. Even if subsidiary earnings are inflated, they will be deflated when converted into the parent's home currency if subsidiary's currency has weakened.

Problem 3

Bengal Pharmaceuticals Ltd. needs to increase production capacity to meet increasing demand for an existing product, 'Vita Gold'. A new machine, with a useful life of four years and a maximum output of 600,000 kg of Vita Gold per year, could be bought for $800,000, payable immediately. The scrap value of the machine after four years would be $30,000. Forecast demand and production of Vita Gold over the next four years are as follows:

Year	1	2	3	4
Demand (kg)	1·4 million	1·5 million	1·6 million	1·7 million

The existing production capacity for Vita Gold is limited to 1 million kg per year and the new machine would only be used for additional demand.

The current selling price of Vita Gold is $8.00 per kilogram, and the variable cost of materials is $5.00 per kilogram. Other variable costs of production are $1.90 per kilogram. Fixed costs of production associated with the new machine would be $240,000 in the first year of production, increasing by $20,000 per year in each subsequent year of operation.

Bengal Pharmaceuticals Ltd. pays tax at a rate of 30%. Depreciation is charged on a 25% reducing balance basis. The balance of depreciation is charged in the final year of operation after deducting the scrap value.

Bengal Pharmaceuticals Ltd. uses its after-tax WACC when appraising investment projects. It has a cost of equity of 11% and a before-tax cost of debt of 8·6%. The long-term finance of the company, on a market-value basis, consists of 80% equity and 20% debt.

Required:

a. Calculate the NPV of buying the new machine and advise on the acceptability of the proposed purchase.
b. Calculate the IRR of buying the new machine and advise on the acceptability of the proposed purchase.
c. Explain the difference between risk and uncertainty in the context of investment appraisal and describe how sensitivity analysis and probability analysis can be used to incorporate risk into the investment appraisal process.

(ICMAB, December 2013)

Solution

(a) NPV Evaluation of Investment

After-tax WACC = (11 × 0·8) + (8·6 × (1 – 0·3) × 0·2) = 10%

Year	*1*	*2*	*3*	*4*
	'000	'000	'000	'000
Contribution	440	550	660	660
Less: Fixed cost	240	260	280	300
Less: Depreciation	200	150	112.5	307.5
PBT	0	140	267.5	52.5

Tax at 30%	0	42	80.25	15.75
PAT	0	98	187.25	36.75
Cash Flow after Tax (CFAT)				
PAT	0	98	187.25	36.75
Add: Depreciation	200	150	112.5	307.5
CFAT	**200**	**248**	**299.75**	**344.25**
Discount at 10%	0.9091	0.8264	0.7513	0.6830
PV of CFAT	181.82	204.96	225.21	235.13
PV of benefits	847			
Initial investment	800			
NPV	47			

The NPV is positive and therefore the investment is financially acceptable. However, demand becomes greater than production capacity in the fourth year of operation and further investment in new machinery may be needed after three years. The new machine will itself need replacing after four years if production capacity is to be maintained at an increased level. It may be necessary to include these expansion and replacement considerations for a more complete appraisal of the proposed investment.

A more complete appraisal of the investment could address issues such as the assumption of constant selling price and variable cost per kilogram and the absence of any consideration of inflation, the linear increase in fixed costs of production over time and the linear increase in demand over time. If these issues are not addressed, the appraisal of investing in the new machine is likely to possess a significant degree of uncertainty.

Workings

1. Annual contribution

Year	*1*	*2*	*3*	*4*
Excess demand (kg/yr)	400,000	500,000	600,000	700,000
New machine output (kg/yr)	400,000	500,000	600,000	600,000
Contribution ($/kg)	1.1	1.1	1.1	1.1
Contribution ($/yr)	440,000	550,000	660,000	660,000

2. Depreciation based on reducing balance method:

Depreciation, year 1	(800,000 × 0·25)	200,000
Depreciation, year 2	(600,000 × 0·25)	150,000
Depreciation, year 3	(450,000 × 0·25)	112,500
Total		462,500
Add: Scrap value		30,000
		492,500
Depreciation, year 4	(by difference)	307,500
		800,000

(b) IRR Evaluation of Investment

Year	*1*	*2*	*3*	*4*
	000	000	000	000
CFAT	**200**	**248**	**299.75**	**344.25**
Discount at 20%	0.8333	0.6944	0.5787	0.4823
PV of CFAT	166.67	172.22	173.47	166.02
PV of benefits	678			
Initial investment	800			
NPV	(122)			

IRR = 10 + [((20 – 10) × 47)/(47 + 122)] = 10 + 2.78 = 12.78%

The investment is financially acceptable since the IRR is greater than the cost of capital used for investment appraisal purposes. However, the appraisal suffers from the limitations discussed in connection with NPV appraisal in part (a).

(c) Risk refers to the situation where probabilities can be assigned to a range of expected outcomes arising from an investment project, and the likelihood of each outcome occurring can therefore be quantified. Uncertainty refers to the situation where probabilities cannot be assigned to expected outcomes. Investment project risk therefore increases with increasing variability of returns, while uncertainty increases with increasing the project life. The two terms are often used interchangeably in financial management, but the distinction between them is a useful one.

Sensitivity analysis assesses how the NPV of an investment project is affected by changes in project variables. Considering each project variable in turn, the change in the variable required to make the NPV zero is determined, or alternatively the change in NPV arising from a fixed change in the given project variable. In this way, the key or critical project variables are determined. However, sensitivity analysis does not assess the probability of changes in project variables and so is often dismissed as a way of incorporating risk into the investment appraisal process.

Probability analysis refers to the assessment of the separate probabilities of a number of specified outcomes of an investment project. For example, a range of expected market conditions could be formulated, and the probability of each market condition arising in each of several future years could be assessed. The NPVs arising from combinations of future economic conditions could then be assessed and linked to the joint probabilities of those combinations. The expected NPV (ENPV) could be calculated, together with the probability of the worst-case scenario and the probability of a negative NPV. In this way, the downside risk of the investment could be determined and incorporated into the investment decision.

Multiple Choice Questions

1. The investment proposal with the greatest relative risk would have
   a. The highest standard deviation of NPV'
   b. The highest coefficient of variation of NPV
   c. The highest expected value of NPV
   d. The lowest opportunity loss likelihood

2. Probability-tree analysis is best used when cash flows are expected to be ________
   a. Independent over time
   b. Risk-free
   c. Related to the cash flows in previous periods
   d. Known with certainty
3. You are considering two mutually exclusive investment proposals, project A and project B. B's expected value of NPV is $1,000 less than that for A, and A has less dispersion. On the basis of risk and return, you would say that
   a. Project A dominates project B
   b. Project B dominates project A
   c. Project A is more risky and should offer greater expected value
   d. Each project is high on one variable, so the two are basically equal
4. If two projects are completely independent (or unrelated), the measure of correlation between them is
   a. 0
   b. 0.5
   c. 1
   d. –1
5. Managerial options can be viewed as
   a. Methods for reducing agency risk through the use of incentives
   b. Methods for reducing total firm risk through diversification
   c. Strategies for increasing management compensation
   d. Opportunities for altering management decisions in the future
6. A managerial option, in effect,
   a. Limits the flexibility of management's decision-making
   b. Limits the downside risk of an investment project
   c. Limits the profit potential of a proposed project
   d. Applies only to new projects
7. When using a probability-tree approach, we discount the various cash flows to their present value at
   a. The firm's WACC
   b. The project's required rate of return
   c. The risk-free rate
   d. The after-tax cost of the firm's long-term debt
8. The presence of managerial, or real, options the worth of an investment project.
   a. Increases
   b. Increase or decreases
   c. Does not affect
   d. Decreases
9. Which one of the following is a measure of risk?
   a. Average
   b. Co-efficient of Variation
   c. Standard deviation
   d. Skewness
10. Time-adjusted discount rate as time period increases.
    a. Decreases
    b. Increases
    c. No change
    d. None

Discussion Questions

1. What are the different sources and perspectives of risk in capital budgeting?
2. Write a short note on different methods applied in capital budgeting to incorporate risk.
3. Compare and contrast between CEA and risk-adjusted discount rate.
4. Make a comparative discussion among sensitivity, scenario and simulation analysis.

5. What is capital rationing? When capital rationing is important? Make a comparative discussion between NPV and IRR approaches of capital rationing.
6. As a finance manager dealing with capital budgeting decision, write a critical note specifying your philosophy in real life while you are in charge of capital investment decisions.

Exercises

1. Assume today is 1 October 2011.
CIP is a manufacturing company and its board is evaluating a potential project that involves the launch of a new product that has a limited life of six years and which will require an initial investment in specialized machinery.
Project cash flows: The specialized machinery will cost $6.5 million and will be installed and paid for on 1 January 2012. The Finance Manager has forecasted that the net after-tax cash flows associated with the new product will be as follows:

Year to 31 December	*2012*	*2013*	*2014*	*2015–17*
Net after-tax cash flows	750,000	950,000	1,400,000	2,100,000

The project will have no residual value as the specialized machinery cannot be used elsewhere or sold at the end of the project. The net after-tax cash flows can be assumed to arise at the end of the year to which they relate.
Financing the project: The proposed investment is in a development region of the country and the local government is offering subsidized borrowing for 40% of the initial capital investment at an annual interest rate of 1% to encourage investment.
A further 20% of the capital required will be raised by bank borrowing, at an annual interest rate of 6%, which is the same as CIP's pre-tax cost of debt.
The duration of the borrowings will match the duration of the investment with the full amount of the borrowings repayable at the end of the six-year term. The corporate income-tax rate is 30% and tax is payable or recoverable at the end of the year to which it relates. There are sufficient taxable profits within CIP to benefit in full from the tax relief available on interest payments. CIP has sufficient cash to fund the remaining 40% of the capital expenditure.
Other information:

- CIPs current market debt: equity ratio is 1:3.
- CIP's current WACC, which is typically used for investment appraisal, is 10%. The proposed project is in a market that is expected to be riskier than its normal operations and therefore some of the board of CIP is unsure whether 10% is an appropriate rate at which to appraise the investment. The Finance Manager has suggested that either a risk-adjusted WACC should be used as a discount rate (based upon a cost of equity reflecting the business risk of the project and CIP's existing gearing) in an NPV evaluation or, alternatively, an adjusted present value (APV) approach should be adopted. He has identified PPP as a company that operates exclusively in the market of the proposed project. PPP's equity beta is 1.95 and it has a current market debt–equity ratio of 1:4. The post-tax risk-free rate of return and market rate of return are expected to be 4% and 9%, respectively, for the foreseeable future.
- Administrative costs of arranging the two borrowings are expected to be 1% of the amounts raised.

Required: Calculate, as at 1 January 2012:

a. The NPV of the project at CIP's existing WACC of 10%.
b. The NPV of the project at a risk-adjusted WACC using PPP as a proxy company in respect of business risk.
c. The APV of the project.

2. Transcend Trucking Corp. (TTC) has decided to enter into a series of five-year lease agreements with GE Corp. to provide and maintain equipment for its global transport needs. These agreements will be rolled over every five years ad infinitum. TTC has not yet decided when to initiate the first of these leasing agreements. TTC currently has a fleet of existing trucks that have three years of useful life remaining. At present, TTC's truck fleet could be sold for $3,000,000. In three-year time, the fleet salvage value will be $600,000. The current book value for the truck fleet is $2,400,000 and the fleet is being depreciated on a straight-line basis. Maintaining the truck fleet involves $150,000 worth of expenses per year. Under the leasing agreement, GE provides and maintains the equipment for a fee of $1,000,000 per annum. Regardless of the timing of the leasing decision, the firm will generate $2,100,000 in revenue and $500,000 in expenses (apart from truck fleet-related expenses) this year and each following year. The company's cost of capital is 16% (required rate of return). Assume that this project has a level of risk that is identical to the risk of the firm as a whole. Also assume that their tax rate is 34%. Should TTC immediately initiate the leasing agreement and sell their current fleet of trucks or should TTC continue using their existing fleet for three more years and then initiate the leasing agreement?
3. Gadgets, Inc. needs to allocate this year's capital expenditure budget to either construction of a new retail outlet or investment in product enhancement. The marketing department has prepared estimates of the predicted increase in sales resulting from each project. The required investment for each project is known and will be depreciated over five years. The required rate of return for both projects is identical to the firm's cost of capital of 15%. Their tax rate is 34%.

Net Retail Outlet (Figures Are in Thousand Dollars)						
Year	***0***	***1***	***2***	***3***	***4***	***5***
Investment	1,300.00	–	–	–	–	–
Revenue	–	2,000.00	2,100.00	2,205.00	2,315.25	2,431.01
Expenses	–	1,100.00	1,155.00	1,212.75	1,273.39	1,337.06
Product Enhancement (Figures Are in Thousand Dollars)						
Year	***0***	***1***	***2***	***3***	***4***	***5***
Investment	1,200.00	–	–	–	–	–
Revenue	–	1,500.00	1,575.00	1,653.75	1,736.44	1,823.26
Expenses	–	800.00	840.00	882.00	926.10	972.41

a. Calculate net cash flows for each project.
b. Calculate the NPV of each project. Which project should you choose?
c. Graph the NPV of project 1 and project 2 (y-axis) against a range of discount rates from 0% to 50% in 5% increments (x-axis).
d. Is the IRR the appropriate criterion in this case?

4. Microprocessor Inc. (MI) has decided to build a new plant in order to take advantage of overwhelming demand for their current microprocessor product. MI needs to decide whether to build the plant (a) solely to produce their current product or if they should

engineer the plant so that (b) it will also be able to produce the next generation of their product if it becomes profitable to do so. That is, there is some uncertainty about whether this type of technology will be popular in the marketplace. If it does become popular, a second generation of the product will be profitable. This uncertainty will be resolved over the next five years.

In situation (b), the plant costs more, but produces the current product more efficiently for a longer period of time. Since the firm has not used this type of plant before, there are extra training and teething costs expected in the early years of its life. Moreover, under (b), the firm will be able to produce the second generation of the product if it should be profitable to do so. Production of the second-generation product would require some minor additional capital expenditures in the plant from (b) in five years. Under situation (1), the firm will be unable to enter the market for the second generation of the product because the costs of completely reengineering the plant to enter the second-generation market will be prohibitively high.

The expected net cash flows generated by each plant option are listed below. The company's cost of capital for this type of project is 15%. Note that neither the potential investments in a plant upgrade for the second-generation product nor the potential revenues from this product have been included in the earnings estimates for plant (b). That is, for both plant options, the cash flows below relate solely to production of the current product. The competitive situation surrounding technology advances over the five-year period is highly uncertain, thereby making reliable estimation extremely difficult.

After-tax Cash Flow (Figures Are in Thousand Dollars)								
Year	*0*	*1*	*2*	*3*	*4*	*5*	*6*	*7*
Plant 1	3,322.0	1,776.5	1,397.0	996.6	554.4	145.2	42.9	13.2
Plant 2	4,286.7	772.3	1,236.4	1,762.2	1,549.9	1,217.7	666.6	236.5

Should MI prefer plant (1) or plant (2) or is it indifferent if they only pay attention to the cash flows from the first-generation product? Could your answer be affected by the fact that plant (2) may be available for future product improvements? How?

5. A retailing firm is considering investing in a new store. The cost of land is $100,000 and the cost of buildings is $200,000. For tax purposes, buildings can be depreciated over 10 years. Equipment will cost $75,000 and can be depreciated over five years, and furniture and fittings will cost $75,000 and can be depreciated over seven years. Assume that all depreciation is done on a straight-line basis. Sales from the new store are expected to be $300,000 in the first year of operations and are expected to grow at 10% per annum over the second and third years and at 5% per annum thereafter. The cost of sales is expected to be 60% (of sales revenue). Assume that the cost of sales includes a component of capital expenses. That is, although the buildings and equipment are depreciated over finite lives for tax purposes, sufficient maintenance will keep them in useable condition indefinitely. Upfront advertising costs will be $75,000 payable immediately and ongoing advertising and promotion costs are expected to be $15,000 in the first year, growing at the same rate of growth as sales. The firm's marginal tax rate is 33% and the discount rate appropriate for this project is 14.4% per annum. Should the project be undertaken? How sensitive is the value of the project to changes in the cost of sales and the risk-adjusted discount rate?

Reference

Myers, S.C. 1977. 'Determinants of Corporate Borrowing'. *Journal of Financial Economics*, 5(2): 147–75.

shares and debentures. Since preference shares and debentures have no voting rights, more funds can be raised through their issue and, at the same time, control of the company can be retained by the existing management.

j. **Long-term interest of the company:** Sometimes it happens that the type of security that seems appropriate from the viewpoint of money market conditions is not appropriate from the viewpoint of long-term interests of the company. During depression, for instance, debentures can be easily issued, but looking to nature of business, the company may not be in a position to bear the burden of interest payment. Under such circumstances, long-term interests of the company should be given more importance.
k. **Macro economic variables:** Some macro economic variables such as interest rates, inflation, price level, risk, investment behaviour and so on are very important at the time of choosing sources of funds. The management should be very careful about each variable in terms of their possible impact on defining the investors' decision criteria.

6.3 An Appropriate Capital Structure

A capital structure is a subjective issue that depends on the perspective in consideration. No short-cut rule is there to set the criteria for building an appropriate capital structure. However, every ideal capital structure should possess the following characteristics.

a. **Flexibility:** The financial requirements of the company change with circumstances. Hence, it is necessary that capital structure is flexible so that it may be adapted to changing conditions. For instance, it should be possible in times of depression when a company needs less finance to repay the debentures and redeemable preference shares. Also, there should be enough unclassified capital in the authorized capital of the company so that any expansion scheme may be easily financed. This is the reason why most of the companies fix quite a large amount of authorized capital and issue shares as and when required. For example, the authorized capital of the Indian Rayon Corporation Limited was $100 million, while its paid-up capital was $20 million. The capital structure should not be so rigid and inflexible that it becomes a burden on the management of the company.
b. **Provision against contingencies:** It should be possible to raise enough funds to meet unforeseen needs. For this purpose, generally, ordinary shares are issued first and provision is made for raising enough funds through debts in times of crisis. Keeping in view the long-term financial needs of the company, the authorized capital should also be quite large.
c. **Economy:** The capital structure should be such that it imposes less burden on the company and yet it allows enough scope for raising sufficient funds at an appropriate time. The burden of interest payment on debentures and that of dividend payments on cumulative preference shares is almost inescapable. Hence, in a business in which revenues are unstable and fluctuating, a high level of ordinary shares is most economical. However, in a business in which income is stable and regular, a large part of capital may be obtained through the issue of debentures. Thereby, enough capital can be raised, and it can be repaid when financial requirements are low. If capital is less than that required, the growth of the company is impeded and if capital is more than that required, its profitability is reduced.
d. **Consistent with the company's objectives:** The capital structure should be in conformity with the basic objectives of the company. For example, the amount of fixed

capital should be quite less than that of the short-term capital in the capital structure of a company, which is set up only for the purpose of trading. An industrial enterprise, on the other hand, needs more capital in the form of fixed assets.

e. **Profitability:** Profitability depends on the efficiency with which capital is used. If, according to the nature of business, a proper ratio is maintained between owned capital and borrowed capital, it can be efficiently utilized. Similarly, there should be a proper balance between fixed capital and working capital.
f. **Solvency:** The capital structure should not impair the solvency of the company. The amount of debts should be so fixed that interest can be paid easily and at the right time. The inflow of cash should be taken into account while fixing the proper amount of debts.
g. **Balance:** The capital structure should be kept well balanced across different sources of funds. Naturally, the debt-to-equity ratio of a firm depends on the nature of the business, although there is a general belief that the quantum of equity should be more than 50% of the total capital. For a long time, one held the view that the quantity of equities should be twice larger than the quantity of capital borrowed. In practice, however, the desirable percentage of equities to the borrowed capital is different for various companies. A balance should be established in invested capital holding account of both the cost of capital and the nature of the businesses. When the invested capital is balanced, the value of the company has been maximized through minimum cost of capital.
h. **Simplicity:** The capital structure should be kept as simple as possible from the administrative point of view to keep some option open to raise funds in the future if needed. A complex capital structure makes it difficult to come to a correct evaluation on the needs for capital and this also creates suspicion about the financial position of the company in the minds of the investors.
i. **Liquidity:** To establish and maintain the prestige of the company, it is necessary that the company always carries enough of liquid funds so that it can honour its debts anytime as they mature. If the invested capital does not envisage enough liquidity, the company will not be able to meet its engagements in time. It will face financial crises, and sometimes it will have to be liquidated, in spite of enough capital. However, the quantum of liquidity of a company depends on a certain number of factors such as the nature of the business, credit policy of the company and so on.

Although all the above factors are essential for building an appropriate capital structure, in practice, they all can hardly be combined. Hence, the management of each company should try to evolve a capital structure that suits them best in view of the nature of their business, size and duration, credit and goodwill in the market, the stages of business cycle and so on.

6.4 Patterns of Capital Structure

On the basis of the relative amounts of various types of securities issued, it is possible to differentiate among four patterns of capital structure. They are as follows:

1. Capital structure with equity shares only
2. Capital structure with equity and preference shares
3. Capital structure with equity shares and debentures
4. Capital structure with equity shares, preference shares and debentures

Three common patterns have been discussed here in some details.

6.4.1 Capital Structure with Equity Shares Only

This type of capital structure comes into being when a company issues equity shares only and does not rely on preference shares and debentures. This type of capital structure is preferred when a company's business is risky and its earnings are highly unstable. Of course, it can raise additional capital through public deposits. All companies have to raise its basic capital by issue of equity shares. Early history of raising capital always follows this pattern as initially it becomes very difficult to raise funds through issuing debt.

6.4.2 Capital Structure by Means of Equity Shares, Preferences Shares and Debentures

A company that requires a huge amount of capital will have to take on a capital structure consisting of equity shares, preferences shares and debentures. Thus, the company is able to attract all curriculums of investors. The capital structure in many of the companies in India is exactly of this nature.

Merits

1. A company following this pattern of capital structure can benefit from advantage of the entire pattern stated earlier.
2. The market of the company's securities is significantly widened; debentures can draw the most traditional investors. Preference shares can pull those investors who are prepared to face few risks if returns are little high. Equity shares can tempt those investors who are venturesome and bold enough to bear all risks of business.
3. Full reimbursement of trading on equity can be understood from this type of capital structure. Dividend rate on preference shares and rate of interest on debentures being relatively small, a high dividend rate can be offered to the equity shareholders.
4. This is a very supple model of capital structure. Supplementary capital can be raised without difficulty when required, and burden of interest expense can be abridged by reimbursement to debenture holders when possible.
5. It is the inexpensive pattern of capital structure.

Demerits

1. Throughout despair, interest payment on debentures and dividend payment on preference shares pose trouble for the company.
2. This is the most difficult prototype of capital structure and makes financial management difficult.
3. The executives are not free to contract with the earnings of the company as they hope.
4. Surprising problems cannot be met by raising added finance if the company is burdened with debt.
5. Equity shareholders earn no dividend when company's earnings are low. Whatever profit is earned, it gets distributed among preference shareholders and debenture holders.

6.4.3 Capital Structure with Equity Shares and Debentures

Most of the companies now adopt the capital structure, which includes equity shares and debentures with the aim to maintain dividend rate on equity shares by combining owners' capital with creditors' capital. This type of capital structure exists in some well-known companies.

Merits

1. It offers benefits of trading on equity. Generally, rate of interest on debentures tends to be lower than the general rate of company's earnings. Therefore, shareholders can be paid a higher rate of dividend.
2. The cost of issuing debentures is relatively low. Much publicity is not required as debentures represent safe investment.
3. Interest paid to debenture holders is deducted while assessing tax liability of the company. To that extent, tax burden on the company is reduced, making it possible to pay a higher rate of dividend to the shareholders.
4. Since debenture holders have no voting rights, interference in the management is avoided and yet additional capital can be obtained through the issue of debentures.
5. This type of capital structure can attract investors with different attitudes and likings. It can attract venture some investors as well as the conservative ones who prefer safety to high income.
6. This is a flexible capital structure. In good times, when the company has enough funds on hand, it can repay the debenture holders and get rid of the burden of interest payments.
7. Generally, the rate of interest on debentures is lower than the rate of dividend on preference shares. Hence the cost of capital is reduced if debentures are issued to obtain the required funds. In this sense, this capital structure is economical.

Demerits

1. During periods of depression, interest payment becomes a burden on the company. Because it has to pay a certain amount of interest on debentures regularly whether profits are positive or negative.
2. In case of default, debenture holders can put a company into difficulty. The company may be dragged to the law court and may be forced into liquidation.
3. The company has to bear a burden of payments of fixed interest. Also, assets of the company are charged or mortgaged to debenture holders. For these reasons, the creditworthiness of the company is reduced.
4. The directors' freedom to frame financial policy of the company is affected on account of the strict rules and regulations of the government with regard to the issue of debentures.

6.5 Planning the Initial Capital Structure

For a company who just starts the journey, it is very difficult to set the initial capital structure. As the management is totally new with the nature of the business, and the exact capital needs of the company will come out at a future time, the management should be very selective to raise funds. The following points may be considered as suggestions to guide the management for setting initial capital structure.

a. **Size of the company:** Capital structure is designed to some extent on the basis of the size of the company concerned. A small-sized company cannot easily raise funds through debts, and hence it has to accept some stringent conditions that reduce the flexibility of its capital structure. Therefore, small-sized companies generally prefer to raise most of the required capital through the issue of equity shares.

b. **Long-term interests of the company:** Sometimes the pressure of the conditions prevalent in the capital market, on the one hand, and long-term interests of the company, on the other, are found to be in conflict. For instance, in times of depression in the market it is advisable to issue debentures to raise funds for the company. However, from the viewpoint of the long-term interests of the company, the burden of fixed charges of interest may be beyond its capacity. Under such circumstances, long-term interests of the company should be given precedence over the dictates of the market conditions.
c. **Value of the assets:** In case of lower value of the assets of the company, and especially in case of the absence of mortgageable fixed assets, a company cannot issue debentures. Similarly, if the market value of company's assets is unstable, it is not advisable to issue debentures, and it is more desirable to issue equity shares to raise the required funds.
d. **Rate of interest:** Which type of securities should be issued at a definite point of time can be determined on the basis of the structure of market rates of interest. Generally, companies prefer to issue debentures when the market rate of interest is low. However, people prefer to purchase ordinary shares when the rate of interest is low.
e. **Legal restrictions:** The government may fix, by law, the maximum amount of capital which a company can raise through the issue of a particular type of security. In India, for instance, no company could raise more than $10 million of share capital without prior approval of the controller of capital issue. There are legal restrictions also on the ratio of the equity shares to debts. According to the Company's Act of 1956, the public companies in India are forbidden to issue deferred shares; thus, a company has to keep in view a number of factors while designing its capital structure. Some of these factors may be mutually inconsistent. The management has, therefore, to use its experience and expertise in evolving a balanced capital structure, taking into account the effects of all relevant factors thereof.
f. **Desire for control:** Generally, the promoters of the company and a majority of its shareholders wish to retain some control over its management. Hence, they prefer to raise funds through the issue of debentures because debenture holders have neither voting rights nor the right to participate in the company's management.
g. **Desire for flexibility:** Flexibility is also an important consideration influencing capital structure of the company. Capital structure should be adjustable to changing circumstances. It should be possible to raise additional funds easily whenever necessary. Also, it should be possible to repay the debts when there is a surplus of funds with the company. In addition, there are some other aspects of flexibility. For instance, capital structure should be such that it does not impose excessive burden of fixed charges on the company. The interest charges are fixed in respect of debentures.
h. **Nature of business:** The environment of business also exerts a sway on the capital structure of a company. If the business is such that a specific level of sales and revenue is ensured, a high level of leverage can be afforded. However, if the business is risky, sales are uncertain and demand for the product is fluctuating, leverage must be kept to a low level.
i. **Conditions of capital market:** On the basis of the conditions in the capital market, it can be judged in which types of securities the investors will prefer to invest their savings. In times of boom, they would prefer to invest in equity shares as they expect a higher rate of dividend in such situations. Also, there are good chances of capital gains due to the appreciation of shares in times of boom. Hence, companies should avoid issuing debentures in times of boom. However, if there is depression in the market, investors will not be ready to purchase equity shares. They seek security of their money along with the certainty of income. Hence, in times of depression, capital can be raised through the issue of preference shares and debentures only.

j. **Floatation costs:** The floatation cost of securities, though a less important factor, must be taken into consideration. Generally, floatation cost is high in the case of debentures and it is low in the case of equity shares. It is zero in respect of retained earnings. The other notable point is that the larger the amount of funds raised, the lower is the rate of increase in floatation cost. For this reason, floatation cost is an important consideration. At the same time, it is also necessary to remember that capital structure loses flexibility with every increase in the amount of capital raised. This disadvantage must be weighed against the gain in the form of economy in floatation cost.

k. **Cash flow analysis:** It is essential to make with an evaluation of the margin starting from the investment of the funds to the company's plans to increase it. If the funds must be increased by obligations, the company should support a burden of payment of the interests. Consequently, the margin in the future must be large enough to make it possible for the company to carry out the payment of the interests without any difficulty. If the margin is unsatisfactory, the company will not be able to pay the interest regularly and, consequently, it will have to face financial insolvency. Consequently, the invested capital should be envisaged on the basis of the evaluation of future margins.

l. **Cost of capital:** Capital structure can also be determined on the basis of an estimate of the cost of various sources of finance. Since the rate of interest on debentures is comparatively low and interest payments are tax deductible, the cost of debentures is quite low. The cost of preference share capital is also low, though not as much as that of debentures. As against this, the cost of equity share capital is relatively high. The cost of retained earnings is lower than that of equity share capital if it is used to finance business operations.

m. **Leverage effect on EPS:** To create capital structure optimum, debts should be mutual with equities in appropriate proportion. If debts are used in proper amount to finance the assets of the company, EPS would increase for two reasons. One, the interest rate on debts is usually lower than that of dividend on equity shares. Second, interest paid on debts is tax deductible. A company receiving a high level of income can raise earning per equity share through a high degree of leverage. The earning per equity share is used as a measure of the degree to which a company can depend on financial leverage.

n. **Nature of assets of the company:** If a company does not possess fixed assets of high value, and therefore it cannot mortgage its assets, it cannot issue debentures. Similarly, if the value of a company's assets is subject to wide fluctuations, it will not be advisable to issue debentures. The company will have to rely on equity shares.

o. **General level of interest rates:** The rates of interest should be taken into account while deciding the types of securities to be issued. If interest rates are high, it is better to issue ordinary shares. If the interest rates are low, it is advisable to issue debentures.

p. **Attitudes of investors:** There is a diversity of attitudes among the investors. Some investors prefer safety to high income. To meet their needs, debentures and preference shares should be issued. Some investors prefer high income to safety. To meet their needs, equity shares should be issued. Thus, it is desirable to issue securities of different kinds to obtain subscriptions from people with different attitudes and preferences. This will also ensure a wide distribution of securities.

q. **Taxation policy of the government:** When rates of tax on company's profit are very high, they prefer to issue debentures, because debenture is regarded as a debt and hence interest on it is considered as deductible expenditure in the income-tax law. Therefore, by issuing debentures, they can reduce their tax liability and pay a high rate of dividend to the shareholders. If dividends are taxed, then also the companies prefer to funds through debentures rather than shares. At present, large-scale issue of debentures by the companies in India can be attributed partly to tax relief granted on interest expenditure.

r. **Cost of financing:** The cost of financing differs from security to security. It is relatively high if financing is made through the issue of equity shares. Issue of equity shares necessitates advertisement on a large scale, payment of underwriting commission and brokerage and so on, on the other hand, issue of debentures necessitates lower expenses as debentures are regarded as safe investment. The law also requires paying comparatively low underwriting commission on debentures (the Companies Act does not allow payment of more than 5% underwriting commission on shares and more than 2.5% underwriting commission on debentures).

6.6 Risk in Firms

The risk associated with a firm can be divided into two components: (a) the risk associated with the type of business the firm operates, that is, competitive conditions, whether the industry is capital intensive or labor intensive, dangers associated with the manufacturing process and so forth is termed its business risk; and (b) the risk associated with how the firm is financed, that is, what portion of the financing is debt and what portion is equity is termed its financial risk.

a. **Business risk:** We evaluate business risk by examining the stability of a firm's operations and its ability to maintain operating income. Generally, less business risk is associated with greater stability in sales, operating expenses and the like, greater flexibility in the ability to change selling prices and less relative fixed operating costs. More often, it is measured in terms of return of asset (ROA) or ROE. When a firm is engaged in a more risky business characterized by huge investment, unstructured market, huge competition, volatility in turnover and rapid change of customer's taste/requirements, the firm is adding more business risk in its portfolio.
b. **Financial risk:** This risk is associated with the ability of a firm to meet its financial obligations, which means this form of risk arises when the firm uses the sources of financing that requires fixed payments or obligations that is, financial leverage, exists. Financial risk affects the ability of a firm to generate stable income for common stockholders, that is, financial risk affects the risk of common stock. To reduce the financial risk, an optimum capital structure is searched.

6.7 Capital Structure Theory

The motive behind capital structure is guided by some technical issues. The discussion so far made gives rationality to this. Academicians have proposed many theories regarding the capital structures of firms. The two major theories are summarized as follows:

6.7.1 Trade-off Theory

Franco Modigliani and Merton Miller, who have since won the Nobel Prize for economics, developed a theory that showed firms should favour using debt in their capital structures because the tax deductibility of interest payments is such an obvious benefit. Under a very restrictive set of assumptions, they showed that the value of a firm increases as it uses more and more debt. In fact, according to their theory, the value of the firm is maximized when it is financed with nearly 100% debt. However, the theory ignored the costs associated with bankruptcy, which can be considerably significant. When the costs of bankruptcy are considered, there is a point where the benefit of the tax deductibility of debt is more than offset by increases in the cost of debt and the cost of equity that result from the risk associated with the firm's heavy use of debt. Thus, the basic issues underlying trade-off theory can be pointed out as follows:

1. Under the assumption of no personal income taxes, no brokerage costs and no bankruptcy-related costs, a firm's value rises continuously as more debt is used due to the tax deductibility of interest on corporate debt.
2. However, there is a threshold level of debt beyond which the bankruptcy related costs become increasingly important, offsetting the tax deductibility benefit of debt.

A trade-off between bankruptcy-related costs and tax deductibility benefits should be reached according to trade-off theory.

6.7.2 Signalling Theory

Most people agree that managers and other insiders possess more information about the firm than outside investors. The fact that managers have asymmetric information, which means they have some information that outside investors do not, could mean that any action taken by a firm, including how it raises funds (capital), might provide a signal to the less-informed investors. For example, studies have shown that when firms issue new common stock to raise funds, the per share value of the stock decreases. It has been suggested that this occurs because managers would only issue new common stock if they felt that the firm's future prospects were unfavourable. Consider the fact that when new stock is issued, new stockholders join the firm's existing stockholders to share in any future changes in value. Thus, if the firm's future was extremely optimistic, managers would want to make existing stockholders happy by allowing them to receive all of the increase in value that will result from the favourable prospects, which means managers would choose to issue debt rather than equity. When debt is issued, only the contracted costs need to be paid, that is, fixed interest and the repayment of the debt, and the remaining gains from the favourable projects accrue to the stockholders. Thus, the basic issues underlying signalling theory can be pointed out as follows:

1. The status of insiders and outsiders differs in terms of the possession of information. The Modigliani–Miller (MM) assumption of symmetric information (i.e., both outside investors and inside managers have identical information about a firm's prospects) is not true. Rather, this is asymmetric, meaning that managers generally have better information than do outside investors.
2. Managers of a firm with unfavourable prospects would want to sell stock, bringing in new investors to share the losses.
3. Managers of a firm with favourable prospects would like to finance through issuing new debt to keep the gain within the old investors.
4. This type of managerial behaviour is true for matured firms having many financing options.
5. Thus, the announcement of stock offering by a matured firm gives a signal that the firm's prospect to its management is not bright.

6.8 Various Approaches to Capital Structure

There is unanimity about the fact that the capital structure should be optimum. Optimum capital structure is the combination of debt and equity that leads to the maximum value of firm. However, there is no unanimity about what capital structure is optimum. One viewpoint is that if there is a change in the nature of capital structure or in the proportion of debt to equity, it will affect EPS and the value of the firm as well. Another viewpoint is that the financing mix or combination of debt and equity has an impact on the value of the firm and on shareholders' wealth. There is nothing like optimum capital structure. There is an approach that is a middle course between the two. All these approaches are based on three factors: earnings, cost of capital and financial risk. There are five approaches of capital structure.

1. Net income approach
2. Net operating income (NOI) approach
3. Traditional approach
4. Modigliani–Miller approach
5. Pecking order theory

In the 1950s, Professor David Durand summarized prevailing thought about the debt–equity mix and identified three approaches to the issue. The first two, the 'net income approach' and the 'NOI approach', seemed illogical in both their assumptions and conclusions and were dismissed by most financial managers. The third philosophy, which Durand called the 'traditional approach', made assumptions and reached conclusions that were deemed much more reasonable and was widely accepted. The three approaches differ primarily in their assumptions about how investors react to increased levels of debt. The MM approach gives a behavioural explanation for the net operating approach. And the pecking order approach ranks different components of capital structure in a rational manner. All of the approaches are outlined in the following sections.

6.8.1 The Net Income Approach

The net income approach to an optimal capital structure states that the total value of the firm changes with a change in the financial leverage. The net income approach holds true under certain assumptions. For example, the net income approach assumes that the cost of debt is lower than the cost of equity. Therefore, an increase in the proportion of debt in the capital structure would result in a decrease in the firm's average cost of capital. A lower cost of capital would result in an increase in the value of the firm. The net income approach can be used to determine a firm's optimum capital structure where the value of the firm is highest and the cost of the capital is lowest.

Different theories of capital structure suggest that a change in financial leverage would affect the average cost of capital and market value of company's shares as well. The essence of the net income approach suggested by Durand is that when there is a change in capital structure, there takes place a change in (a) the overall cost of capital and (b) total value of the firm. To be more precise, if financial leverage is increased by raising the ratio of debts to equity, there will be a decrease in WACC and an increase in the market value of its shares. Conversely, if financial leverage is reduced by lowering the ratio of debts to equity, there will be an increase in WACC and a decrease in the market value of its shares. We try to understand this with an illustration.

Under this approach, neither creditors nor stockholders perceive that increased borrowing adds to their risks, so the firm's cost of debt and cost of equity remain constant regardless of its level of debt. Figure 6.1 summarizes this point of view. The lines for the costs of debt (K_D) and equity (K_S) are drawn horizontally to indicate that they are not changing as the financing mix goes from all equity to all debt. However, since the cost of debt is typically less than the cost of equity, the WACC declines as cheaper debt is substituted for the more expensive equity. The minimum cost of capital, corresponding to maximum value, is reached at the far right-hand side of the figure. As a result, the net income approach concludes that the best financing mix is 100% debt and no equity.

Figure 6.1 Cost of Capital Under the Net Income Approach

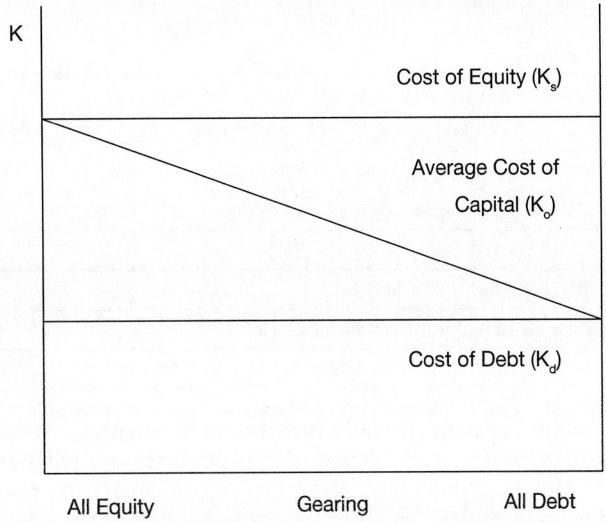

Basic Assumptions

The above discussion suggests that the net income approach is based on certain assumptions. They are as follows:

1. There are no taxes on companies.
2. The cost of debt is less than the cost of equities.
3. A change in the ratio of debts to equity does not affect the degree of risk that the investors bear. In other words, whatever may be the ratio of debts to equity, the cost of debts as well as the cost of equity capital remains constant.

The implication of these assumptions is that with the increase in debts, a less expensive source of capital increases in amount and, consequently, WACC falls, while the overall market value of the firm moves up. Conversely, when debts are reduced, a less expensive source of capital decreases in amount. Consequently, WACC rises, while the overall market value of the firm moves down.

According to this approach, the average cost of capital (K_O) declines as gearing increases. The cost of shareholders' funds (K_S) and the cost of debt (K_D) are independent. Since K_D is usually less than K_S, as debt is less risky than equity from the investor's point of view, an increase in gearing should lead to a decrease in K_O. The strict net income approach assumes that K_S and K_D remain constant.

Illustration

The latest financial statement of André Beverage plc shows that on an average it has $60,000 NOI (EBIT). The equity capitalization rate of the company is 15%. The company has outstanding 10% debenture of $200,000. Apply the net income approach of capital structure to draw a conclusion regarding the existence of debt on the overall cost of capital and value of a firm.

Solution

To show the impact of debt on cost of capital and value of the firm, let us do the calculation at three different levels of debenture: (a) $100,000, (b) $200,000 and (c) $300,000.

Particulars		*(a)*	*(b)*	*(c)*
1	NOI (EBIT)	$60,000	$60,000	$60,000
2	Less: Interest (10% of $100,000; $200,000; $300,000)	10,000	20,000	30,000
3	Earnings available to equity holders (1 – 2)	50,000	40,000	30,000
4	Equity capitalization rate (15%)	0.15	0.15	0.15
5	Market value of equity (3/4)	333,333	266,667	200,000
6	Market value of debt	100,000	200,000	300,000
7	Total value of the firm (5 + 6)	433,333	466,667	500,000
8	Overall cost of capital (1/7)	13.85%	12.86%	12%

The calculation shown in the table justifies that as the amount of debt increases in capital structure, the overall cost of capital decreases with an increase in the value of the firm.

Due to an increase of debt in capital structure, the market value of the stock also increases. Let us consider another example to show the effect of debt in setting the market price of stocks.

Illustration

Assume that a company has 5% debenture of $10,000 with EBIT of $3,000. The equity capitalization rate is 10%. Let us also assume another capital structure with $20,000 debenture to calculate the effect on the overall cost of capital, market price of stock and value of the firm. Other information relating to two situations is as follows.

Components of Capital Structure	*Situation 1*	*Situation 2*
Equity (par value $10)	25,000	15,000
5% Debenture	10,000	20,000
Total	35,000	35,000

Particulars		*Situation 1*	*Situation 2*
1	NOI (EBIT)	3,000	3,000
2	Less: Interest (5% of $10,000; $20,000)	500	1,000
3	Earnings available to equity holders (1 – 2)	2,500	2,000
4	Equity capitalization rate (10%)	.10	.10
5	Market value of equity (3/4)	25,000	20,000
6	Market value of debt	10,000	20,000
7	Total value of the firm (5 + 6)	35,000	40,000
8	Overall cost of capital (1/7)	8.57%	7.5%

9	Number of share at $10 par value	2,500	1,500
10	Market value per share:		
	$25,000/2,500 shares	10	
	$20,000/1,500 shares		13.33

Above calculation results that situation 2 is better than situation 1 in terms of cost of capital, market value of shares and value of the firm. Actually situation 2 is more levered than situation 1.

6.8.2 The NOI Approach

Figure 6.2 Cost of Capital Under NOI Approach

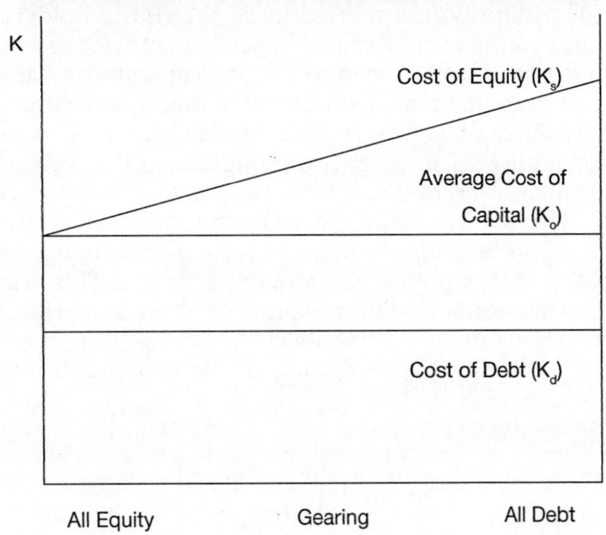

The NOI approach states that the proportion of debt and equity in the firm's structure does not have any impact on the firm's value or its cost of capital. The NOI approach assumes that while the cost of debt is constant for all levels of leverage, the cost of equity increases linearly with financial leverage. This increase is explained by the increase in the financial risk to the firm as it increases the proportion of debt in its capital structure. Cost of equity increases because the shareholders expect a higher rate of return to cover the risk of increase in leverage. Therefore, according to the NOI approach, there cannot be any optimum capital structure for a firm. Like the net income approach, this approach also assumes that creditors do not react to increased debt levels. Stockholders do find a higher debt ratio more risky, but their required rate of return increases to precisely cancel out the advantage of cheaper debt, making the firm's cost of capital constant regardless of its debt–equity mix. Figure 6.2 summarizes this point of view. The line for the cost of debt (K_D) is drawn horizontally to indicate that it does not change as the debt–equity mix goes from all equity to all debt.

The line for the cost of equity (K_S) slopes upward, capturing stockholders' increasing required rate of return. The WACC (K_O) remains constant (horizontal) as the financing mix is changed to include more debt; the cheaper debt is exactly offset by the increasing cost of the remaining equity. Since there is no low point on the cost of capital line, there is no financing mix that maximizes the firm's value. The NOI approach concludes that the debt–equity mix is irrelevant. Value comes only from the firm's operating income (EBIT) and any financing mix is as good as any other.

The NOI approach, as propounded by David Durand, examines the effects of changes in the capital structure in terms of NOI. In the net income approach discussed above, the net income available to shareholders is obtained by deducting interest on debentures from NOI.

Then, the overall value of the firm is calculated through capitalization rate of equities obtained on the basis of NOI. However, in the NOI approach, the overall value of the firm is assessed on the basis of NOI not on the basis of net income and, thus, this approach is known as the NOI approach.

The NOI approach implies that (a) whatever may be the change in the capital structure, the overall value of the firm is not affected. Thus, the overall value of the firm is independent of the degree of leverage in capital structure. (b) Similarly, the overall cost of capital is not affected by any change in the degree of leverage in capital structure. The overall cost of capital is independent of leverage.

If the cost of debt is less than that of equity capital, the overall cost of capital must decrease with the increase in debts, whereas it is assumed, under this method, that the overall cost of capital is unaffected and hence remains constant irrespective of the change in the ratio of debts to equity capital. How can this assumption be justified? The advocates of this method are of the opinion that the degree of risk of business increases with the increase in the amount of debts. Consequently, on the one hand, cost of capital decreases with the increase in the volume of debts; on the other hand, cost of equity capital increases to the same extent due to the assumption of more risks by the equity holders. Hence, the benefit of leverage is wiped out and the overall cost of capital remains at the same level as before. It follows that with the increase in debts, the rate of equity capitalization also increases and, consequently, the overall cost of capital remains constant; it does not decline. In other words, there are two parts of the cost of capital. One is the explicit cost which is expressed in terms of interest charges on debentures. The other is the implicit cost, which refers to the increase in the rate of equity capitalization resulting from the increase in risk of business due to higher level of debts.

This approach suggests that whatever may be the degree of leverage, the market value of the firm remains constant. In spite of the change in the ratio of debts to equity, the market value of its equity shares remains constant. This means that there does not exist an optimum capital structure. Every capital structure is optimum according to the NOI approach. The financing mix does not affect the average cost of capital of the company, and the total value of the firm remains unchanged with changes in the gearing.

Illustration

Latex Machining reported an NOI of $900,000 for the year just ended. The capital structure of Latex includes 7.5% ($4,000,000) debt. Its WACC is 10%. Under the NOI approach, show the effect of leverage on value of the firm and the overall cost of capital.

Solution

Particulars		***Case 1—Debt: 4 million***	***Case 2—Debt: 5 million***
Computing Value of the Firm			
1	NOI (EBIT)	900,000	900,000
2	WACC (K_o)	0.10	0.10
3	Value of the firm ($V = EBIT/K_o$) [1/2]	9,000,000	9,000,000
4	7.5% Debentures	4,000,000	5,000,000
5	Value of equity [3 – 4]	5,000,000	4,000,000
Computing Cost of Capital			
6	NOI (EBIT)	900,000	900,000
7	Less: Interest (7.5% of $4,000,000; $5,000,000)	300,000	375,000

8	Earnings available to equity holders [6 – 7]	600,000	525,000
9	Cost of equity $\left(K_S = \frac{\text{EBIT} - \text{Debt} \times K_D}{\text{Equity}}\right)$ [8/5]	12%	13.13%
10	WACC $\left(K_D \frac{D}{D+E} + K_S \frac{E}{D+E}\right)$	10%	10%

Observations

The above computation proves some observation of the NOI approach of capital structure as follows:

1. The value of a firm depends on EBIT. Capital structure is irrelevant.
2. The inclusion of more debt (case 2) in capital structure increases the cost of equity due to higher risk exposure.
3. The WACC remains constant at any level of gearing.

6.8.3 The Traditional Approach

The traditional approach assumes that both creditors and stockholders perceive that increased borrowing adds to their risks. As a firm increases its debt–equity ratio, both cost of debt and cost of equity increase. Figure 6.3 summarizes this point of view. The lines for the cost of debt (K_D) and the cost of equity (K_S) are now both drawn with an upward slope. The WACC first declines as cheaper debt is substituted for more expensive equity and then increases, swept up by the rising K_D and K_S. The cost of capital reaches the lowest point where the firm's value reaches its maximum in the middle of the graph. Accordingly, the traditional approach

Figure 6.3 Cost of Capital Under the Traditional Approach

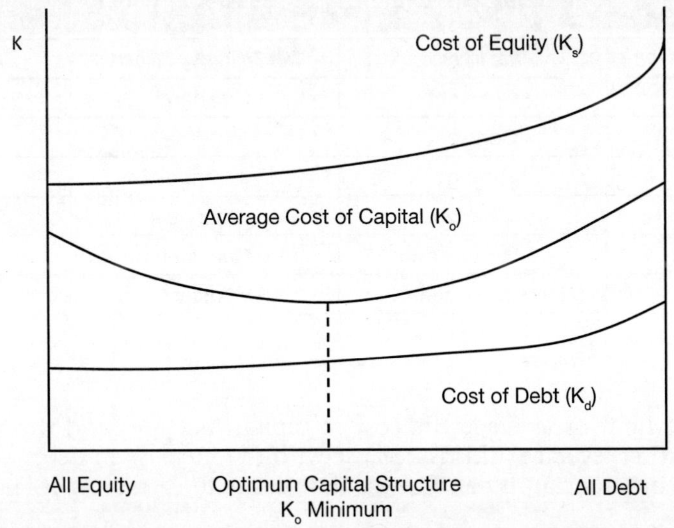

concludes that the best debt–equity mix is somewhere in the middle, a function of the rate at which the risks perceived by the investors increase.

The traditional approach is an intermediate approach between the net income approach and the NOI approach. According to this approach:

1. An optimum capital structure does exist.
2. Market value of the firm can be increased and average cost of capital can be reduced through a prudent manipulation of leverage.
3. The cost of debt capital increases if debts are increased beyond a definite limit. This is because the greater the risk of business, the higher is the rate of interest the creditors would ask for. The rate of equity capitalization will also increase with it. Thus, there remains no benefit of leverage when debts are increased beyond a certain limit. The cost of capital also goes up.

Thus, at a definite level of mixture of debts to equity capital, the average cost of capital also increases. The capital structure is optimum at this level of the mix of debts to equity capital. The effect of change in capital structure on the overall cost of capital can be divided into three stages as follows:

First Stage

In the first stage, the overall cost of capital falls and the value of the firm increases with the increase in leverage. This leverage has beneficial effect as debts are less expensive. The cost of equity remains constant or increases negligibly. The proportion of risk is less in such a firm.

Second Stage

A stage is reached when increase in leverage has no effect on the value or the cost of capital of the firm. Neither the cost of capital falls nor the value of the firm rises. This is because the increase in the cost of equity due to the assessed financial risk offsets the advantage of low-cost debt. This is the stage wherein the value of the firm is maximum and cost of capital minimum. Optimum capital structure lies in this stage.

Comparative Picture of Net Income, NOI and Traditional Approaches to Capital Structure

Capital Structures	*Net Income*	*Net Operating Income*	*Traditional*
Cost of debt (K_D)	Constant	Constant	Increase
Cost of equity (K_S)	Constant	Increase	Increase
Debt (D)	Change	Change	Change
Equity (E)	Change	Change	Change
WACC	Decrease	Constant	Decrease
Value (D + E)	Maximized	Constant	Maximized

Third Stage

Beyond a definite limit of leverage the cost of capital increases and the value of the firm decreases with further leverage. This is because with the increase in debts, investors begin to realize the degree of financial risk and hence they desire to earn a higher rate of ROE shares.

The resultant increase in the equity capitalization rate will more than offset the advantage of low-cost debt.

It follows that the cost of capital is a function of the degree of leverage. Hence, an optimum capital structure can be achieved by establishing an appropriate degree of leverage in capital structure. However, increasing leverage brings more financial risk due to the increasing amount of fixed charges (interest on debt). The traditional view follows the net income approach in that it suggests there is a benefit to be gained from increased gearing. However, increased gearing increases financial risk and K_S will, therefore, increase with gearing, but this increase is not sufficient to offset the gearing effect on K_O until a certain point is reached when the increase in K_S is such as to increase K_O. The traditional model usually incorporates an increase in K_D at a certain level of gearing due to increased risk to debt holders. This implies that there is an optimal capital structure.

Illustration

Let us consider two capital structures; one all equity and the other is geared. The information relating to these two capital structures is as follows:

	All Equity	***Geared***
EBIT	$80,000	$80,000
6% debenture	–	$500,000
Debt service costs (interest)		$30,000

Future earnings under both of these capital structures are randomly distributed with $40,000. Put a comment on potential risks assumed by the shareholders in geared capital structure under the traditional approach.

Solution

		All Equity	***Geared***
1	EBIT	$80,000	$80,000
2	Interest	–	$30,000
3	Expected earnings of shareholders [1 – 2]	$80,000	$50,000
4	Random distribution of expected earnings	$40,000	$40,000
5	Coefficient of variation [4/3]	0.5	0.8

Shareholders' earnings have greater relative dispersion for geared capital structure than for all equity one measured in terms of the coefficient of variation. The dispersion of income is the business risk but the dispersion of shareholders earnings is the financial risk assumed by the shareholders in geared capital structure.

6.8.4 The MM Approach

In the late 1950s, Professors Franco Modigliani and Merton Miller stunned the finance community by publishing a proof that, under certain circumstances, the conclusion of the NOI approach was, in fact, correct: there is no optimal financing mix. Although MM's conclusions were the same as those of the NOI approach, the way they reached their conclusions was very different.

The MM theorem is perhaps the most widely accepted capital structure theory. In 1958, they established two propositions for the relation between a firm's capital structure, its market value and cost of capital. They both won the Nobel Prize for their contribution to corporate finance. The first proposition, also referred to as the debt irrelevance theorem, states that the value of a firm is unaffected by its capital structure. The second proposition states that the required rate of ROE increases as the firm's debt–equity ratio increases. This exactly offsets the less expensive funds represented by debt.

In an article published in 1958, Modigliani and Miller (MM) propounded their view, which is known as the MM approach. Their approach is identical to the NOI approach. They have also concluded that in the absence of taxes, a firm's market value and the cost of capital remain constant to the changes in capital structure. In other words, an optimum capital structure does not exist. The NOI approach leads to the same conclusion, but MM have provided a behavioural justification in favour of this conclusion. That is, they refer to a particular behaviour of the investors in support of this conclusion.

Assumptions

MM began their analysis by making some simplifying assumptions, in particular, that the financial markets were uncomplicated and without any imperfections. Specifically, MM assumed:

1. The capital market is perfect in the sense that investors have perfect knowledge of market forces; they are free to buy and sell securities; the cost of transactions is zero; and they behave rationally.
2. Firms can be classified into different groups, consisting of firms having equal business risks. They can be divided into 'equivalent risk class'.
3. Since all investors have complete information, they all use the same figure of NOI of the firm to ascertain its market value.
4. All firms distribute the entire earning among their shareholders in the form of dividend. It means the dividend payout ratio is 100%.
5. No corporate income taxes exist initially.
6. Shareholders can obtain the same personal gearing as companies at the same cost.
7. There are no transaction costs in the arbitrage process.
8. One interest rate and it is risk less.
9. All cash flows are perpetuities, g = 0, and EPS = DPS and $K_S = \frac{DPS}{P} = \frac{EPS}{P}$

Arbitrage Process

If the price of a product is unequal in two markets, traders buy it in the market where price is low and sell it in the market where price is high. This phenomenon is known as price differential or arbitrage. As a result of this process of arbitrage, price tends to decline in the high-priced market and rise in the low-priced market unit the differential is totally removed.

MM explain their approach in terms of the same process of arbitrage. They hold that two firms, identical in all respects except leverage, cannot have different market value. If two identical firms have different market values, arbitrage will take place until the difference in the market values is removed completely.

To illustrate, let us suppose that there are two firms, X and Y, belonging to the same group of homogenous risk. The firm X is un-levered as its capital structure consists only of equity capital, while firm Y is levered as its capital structure includes 10% debentures of $100,000. In this case, according to the traditional approach, the market value of firm Y would be higher than that of firm X. However, according to the MM approach, this situation cannot persist for long. The market value of the equity share of firm Y is high but investment in it is more risky, while the market value of the equity share of firm X is low but investment in it is safe. Hence, investors will sell out equity shares of firm Y and purchase equity shares of firm X. Consequently, the market value of the equity shares of firm Y will fall, while that of firm X will rise. Through this process of arbitrage, therefore, the market values of the firms X and Y will be equalized. This is true for all firms belonging to the same group. In an equilibrium situation, the average cost of capital will be the same for all firms in the group. The opposite will happen if the market value of the firm X is higher than that of the firm Y. In this case, investors will sell equity shares of X and buy those of Y. Consequently, the market value of these two firms will be equalized. This argument is based on the assumption that investors are well informed and behave rationally, and hence they engage in personal leverage or homemade leverage as against the corporate leverage to restore equilibrium in the market.

At this stage, it is necessary to understand what personal leverage means. If the market value of a levered firm is high, investors sell its equity shares. In addition to the money received in exchange of equity shares, they borrow funds on their personal account and invest in the un-levered firm to obtain the same return for smaller investment outlay. This activity is known as personal leverage or home-made leverage.

Illustration

Two companies have identical capital requirements of $500,000. Company A is all equity financed and company B is 30% geared with 5% debt of $150,000. The calculation is as follows:

	Company A	***Company B***
NOI (EBIT)	50,000	50,000
Debt interest	–	7,500
Equity earnings	50,000	42,500
Assumed equity capitalization rate	0.10	0.11
Market value of equity	500,000	386,364
Market value of debt	–	150,000
Market value of firm	$500,000	$536,364
Cost of capital (K_O)	10%	9.3%

MM argue that the above situation is not stable. A shareholder in company B will take advantage of the better share price with the lower K_O for company B gives him, by selling shares in B and buying them in A. This process is called arbitrage and will have the effect of decreasing the market value of shares in B and increasing the market value of shares in A (supply and demand function). This process will continue until the share prices stabilize at a value that gives an equal K_O in both companies.

Illustration

Assume that a shareholder owns 10% of company B. This has a market value of $38,636 and gives him a return of $4,250 (10% of $42,500).

Note that he owns 10% of a company that is 30% geared and is presumably satisfied with the risk of a 30% gearing. He will now substitute a personal gearing of 30% for the corporate gearing and invest in company A in the following way:

He will sell his shares in company B and realize \$38,636. He will borrow \$15,000 at 5%, giving him total funds of \$53,636.

He is now geared in the same proportion as company B, that is, $\frac{\$150,000}{\$536,364} = \frac{\$15,000}{\$53,636}$

He will buy 10% of company A, which will cost \$50,000. This will give him a return of \$5,000, from which he must pay his debt interest of \$750, leaving a net return of \$4,250. This is the same as he was receiving in company B but he now has \$3,636 available for consumption. The behavioural model suggests that the arbitrage process will continue until no shareholder can make a gain from the process and at that point K_O will be identical in both companies.

Arguments Against the MM Position

These are based on reasons why the arbitrage process may not work perfectly:

1. If there is a possibility of bankruptcy and if these costs are significant, a geared firm may be less attractive.
2. The perceived risks of personal and corporate gearing may be different because of limited liability on corporate debt.
3. Personal borrowing costs are generally higher than corporate costs.
4. Transaction costs restrict arbitrage.
5. Some institutional investors may be precluded from 'personal' borrowing by the articles or by law.
6. Investors do not have access to perfect, cost-free information.

MM deny the importance of these criticisms by arguing that they are too general. They suggest that as long as there are enough market participants at the margin to behave in a manner consistent with 'homemade' gearing, the total value of the firm cannot be altered through gearing. The MM approach is most vulnerable at extreme levels of gearing.

Extreme Gearing

When gearing reaches a certain level, K_D will rise when debt investors expect the firm to pay a higher interest rate on debt. The greater the gearing, the lower the coverage of fixed charges and the riskier the loan. Even if K_D rises, MM maintain that K_O will be constant because K_S will increase at a decreasing rate to offset the increase in K_D (Figure 6.4).

Many authorities object strongly to the contention that shareholders became relatively less risk averse with extreme gearing. MM are on much weaker ground in defending their thesis for the extreme gearing case.

Moderate View

In the years since MM's contributions, finance theorists have been exploring the importance of each of MM's perfect market assumptions, how necessary each assumption is for the MM conclusions to hold. In effect, they have been searching for a compromise between the extreme results of MM and the more intuitively appealing conclusions of the traditional approach. Today, the majority opinion seems to be that there are significant 'imperfections'

Figure 6.4 Cost of Capital in Extreme Gearing

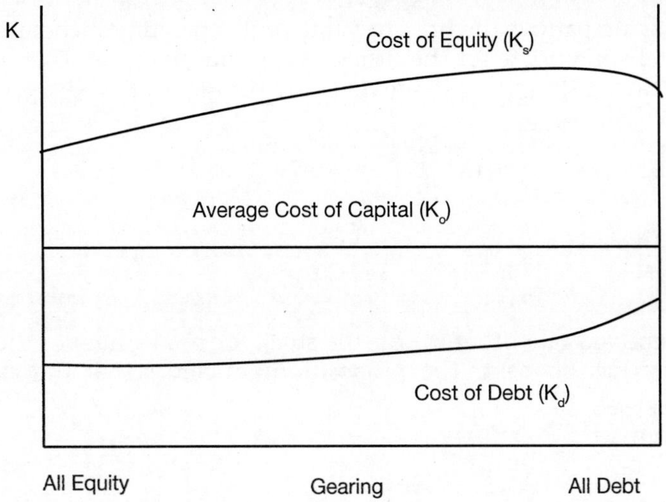

in the financial environment which tip the financing mix decision towards either equity or debt. These are:

1. Direct cost of financial distress: Legal and administrative costs of liquidation and reorganization.
2. Indirect costs of financial distress:
   a. Loss of sales due to weakened assurance of delivery.
   b. Inability to take a profitable investment.
   c. The cost of reorganizing a firm that should be liquidated.
   d. Loss of financial flexibility.
   e. Costs from conflicts among claimants.

The modern view summarizes these effects as follows:

$$V_L = V_U + T_C D - \text{Financial Distress Cost}$$

As the firm begins to take on debt, the first impact comes from the corporate tax subsidy, which lowers the cost of debt and pushes down the cost of capital. As the firm continues to borrow, both the cost of debt and cost of equity lines rise due to the increased risk perceptions from estimates of bankruptcy and agency costs pushing the cost of capital line back up. The WACC first declines and then rises. While there is a minimum cost of capital, and hence a corresponding maximum value of the firm, the WACC line is shallow at the bottom, and the precise minimum point is difficult to find. Instead, it is more useful to identify an acceptable range within which the cost of capital is at or near its minimum. Any debt–equity mix within the acceptable range is close to the optimum so that the cost of being more precise exceeds the possible added value.

MM Propositions Without Taxes

Proposition I

The total value of a company is the present value of its operating income (EBIT) discounted at the cost of capital appropriate for the firm's level of business risk. That is, when there are no taxes or transaction costs and capital markets are competitive, MM argued that

$$V_U = \frac{EBIT}{K_{SU}} \text{ or } K_{SU} = \frac{EBIT}{V_U} \tag{6.1}$$

$$V_L = V_U = \frac{EBIT}{WACC} = \frac{EBIT}{K_{SU}} \tag{6.2}$$

where K_{SU} is the expected rate of return on the stock (or total value) of the un-levered firm when the company has no debt. The proposition concludes that the value of a firm is independent of leverage.

Proposition II

The cost of equity of a levered firm (K_{SL}) equals the cost of equity of an un-levered firm (K_{SU}) plus a risk premium that depends on the firm's financial leverage. The risk premium is the product of the firm's debt–equity ratio and the difference between the firm's un-levered cost of equity (K_S) and cost of debt (K_D).

$$K_{SL} = K_{SU} + (K_S - K_D)\frac{D}{S} \tag{6.3}$$

Proposition III

The WACC is the appropriate hurdle rate for investment decisions, and the value of any investment alternative is independent of how the investment is financed. This follows directly from propositions I and II.

$$IRR > WACC \tag{6.4}$$

$$\text{where } WACC = K_S \frac{S}{V} + K_D \frac{D}{V} \tag{6.5}$$

The MM Propositions with Corporate Taxes

MM had revised their prescription for the debt–equity mix from the improbable conclusion of the NOI approach to the even more improbable conclusion of the net income approach. If corporate taxes exit, the preceding results do not hold. Given the taxes, MM re-established their propositions as follows:

Proposition I

The total value of a company is the present value of its after-tax operating income discounted at the cost of capital appropriate for the firm's level of business risk plus the present value of the tax savings from interest deductions.

$$VL = VU + D \cdot T_C \tag{6.6}$$

$$\text{where } V_U = \frac{EBIT(1-T_C)}{K_{SU}} \tag{6.7}$$

The relationship in equation (6.6) is derived by decomposing the operating cash flows between the equity and debt holders. Using the equation that CF = $CF_D + CF_S$, we can write CF = Levered CF + I where, I = $K_D \cdot D$. Substituting in equation (6.8), we have

$$CF = (EBIT - K_D \cdot D)(1 - T_C) + T_C K_D D \tag{6.8}$$

If the cash flow to shareholders is divided by its own cost of capital (K_S) and the cash flow to the debt holders by its own cost of debt (K_D), we would have

$$V_L = \frac{EBIT(1-T_C)}{K_S} + \frac{T_C K_D D}{K_D} = V_U + T_C D \tag{6.9}$$

$$V_L = \frac{EBIT(1-T_C)}{WACC} \tag{6.10}$$

$$WACC = K_D(1-T_C)\frac{D}{V} + K_{SL}\frac{S}{V}, \text{ where, } S = V_L - D \tag{6.11}$$

Thus, the proposition concludes that the value of a levered firm equals the value of an un-levered firm plus the tax savings associated with leverage (6.9).

Proposition II

The cost of equity of a levered firm (K_{SL}) equals the cost of equity of an un-levered firm (K_{SU}) plus a risk premium that depends on the firm's financial leverage and the tax rate.

$$K_{SL} = K_{SU} + (K_S - K_D)(1-T_C)\frac{D}{S} \tag{6.12}$$

Proposition III

The WACC is the appropriate 'hurdle' rate for investment decisions, but it should be calculated using the firm's target capital structure as weights for the value of any investment to be independent of how the investment is financed.

$$IRR > K_U(1-T_C)\frac{D}{V} \tag{6.13}$$

We shall consider in detail only first proposition, which states that the market value of a firm and the cost of capital are independent of the DFL in the capital structure. They explain this proposition in terms of the behaviour of investors.

Criticisms of MM Approach

1. It assumed that the capital market is perfect. However, this assumption is unrealistic. The capital market being imperfect, a discrepancy between the market values of levered and unlevelled firms is bound to persist.
2. The risk of insolvency increases with the amount of debts in a levered firm. Due to the risk of insolvency and the possibility of lower value of the assets in the event of insolvency, investment in this firm will be less attractive. Hence, its market value will persist at a low level.
3. It is assumed under this approach that investors borrow funds on personal account and invest in an unlevelled firm. This is an undesirable activity. The person indulging in personal leverage in place of corporate leverage faces a greater risk. If the un-levered company goes bankrupt, he or she loses not only own money but he or she will also lose the borrowed fund. For this reason, personal leverage is rarely resorted to. Hence, switching over of investment from levered firm to un-levered firm does not take place; arbitrage does not operate.
4. The existence of transaction costs also interferes with the working of arbitrage. Because of the costs involved in the buying and selling of securities, a smaller amount of money will be available for new investment. Hence, return on new investment will be low.
5. Institutional investors cannot engage in personal leverage. For instance, the Life Insurance Corporation (LIC) invests on a large scale in the shares and debentures of a number of companies. However, it does not resort to personal leverage by borrowing on personal account to shift its investment from the levered companies with high market value to un-levered companies with low market value. Thus, the assumption of personal leverage does not hold good.
6. If corporate taxes are introduced, it will be clear that the cost of capital is low for a levered company and its market value is high. The debts are tax deductible. Hence, cost of capital for a levered company will be relatively low. In their 1963 article, MM did recognize that the value of the firm will increase and that cost of capital will decrease with leverage due to the deductibility of interest charges for tax computation. If we accept this fact, we arrive again at the net income approach, which asserts that with the increase in the DFL the cost of capital declines and value of the firm goes up. Hence, leverage should be resorted to the maximum possible extent. The traditional approach, on the other hand, concludes that beyond a particular limit, risk increases and the cost of capital also increases with the increase in debts. As against this, the MM approach advises to fix the amount of debts in advance and suggests not crossing this limit. At this point, MM frustrate their own conclusions. When they concede that there should be a definite limit of debts, they implicitly agree with the view that an optimum capital structure does exist in reality.

Illustration: MM Propositions I and II (with No Tax)

Imagine you have discovered an investment alternative that produces an expected EBIT of \$1000.00 forever. Similar (un-levered) projects in the market have a required return of 10%. You can put up \$5,000 of your own money to invest in this project. Suppose you are considering two financing alternatives. In the un-levered alternative, you issue yourself \$5,000 in equity, S. In the levered alternative, you sell yourself \$1,000 in debt, D, and \$4,000 equity, S. The debt pays the market rate of 5% forever. In either case, you own entire expected streams of \$1,000 per year.

1. What are the cash flows under each alternative?
2. What is value of the firm under each alternative?

Cash Flows	Un-levered	Levered
EBIT	1,000	1,000
Less: Interest	–	50
Earnings before tax	1,000	950
Less: Taxes (0%)	–	–
Earnings after tax	1,000	950
Cash flow (from debt and equity)	1,000	1,000

The value of the un-levered firm is:

$$V_L = V_U = \frac{EBIT}{K_{SU}} = \frac{\$1,000}{0.10} = \$10,000$$

Cost of equity:

$$K_{SL} = K_{SU} + (K_S - K_D)\frac{D}{S}$$

$$= 10\% + (10\% - 5\%)\frac{\$1,000}{\$9,000} = 10.556\%$$

$$WACC(K_o) = 5\%\frac{\$1,000}{\$10,000} + 10.556\%\frac{\$9,000}{\$10,000} = 10\%$$

The value of the levered firm, based on value additivity, is

$$V_L = D + S = \frac{\$50}{0.05} + \frac{950}{0.10556} = \$10,000$$

The MM no tax propositions have three basic implications:

1. Capital structure is irrelevant to shareholders' wealth maximization.
2. The value of the firm (size of the pie) is determined by the firm's capital budgeting decisions. Capital structure determines how the pie is sliced up.
3. Increasing the extent to which a firm relies on debt increases both the risk and the expected return to equity but not the price per share.

Illustration: MM Propositions I and II (with Corporate Tax)

Cash Flows	Un-levered	Levered
EBIT	1,000	1,000
Less: Interest	–	50
Earnings before tax	1,000	950
Less: Taxes (34%)	340	323
Earnings after tax	660	627
Cash flow (from debt and equity)	660	677

The value of the un-levered firm is:

$$V_U = \frac{EBIT(1 - T_C)}{K_{SU}} = \frac{\$660}{0.10} = \$6,600$$

The value of the levered firm is:

$$\begin{aligned} V_L &= V_U + D.T_C \\ &= \$6,600 + \$1,000(0.34) = \$6,940 \end{aligned}$$

Cost of equity:

$$K_{SL} = \frac{(EBIT - I)(1 - T_C)}{S} = \frac{(\$1,000 - \$50)(1 - 0.34)}{\$5,940} = 10.56\%$$

$$\begin{aligned} WACC &= K_D(1 - T_C)\frac{D}{V} + K_{SL}\frac{S}{V}, \text{ where, } S = V_L - D \\ &= 5\%(1 - 0.34)\frac{1,000}{6,940} + 10.56\%\frac{5,940}{6,940} = 9.51\% \end{aligned}$$

To confirm our calculation:

$$V_L = \frac{EBIT(1 - T_C)}{WACC} = \frac{\$1,000(1 - 0.34)}{0.0951} = \$6,940$$

Test Your Understanding 1

Given below is a series of graphs. Identify those that reflect:

(a) the traditional view of capital structure
(b) MM without tax
(c) MM with tax

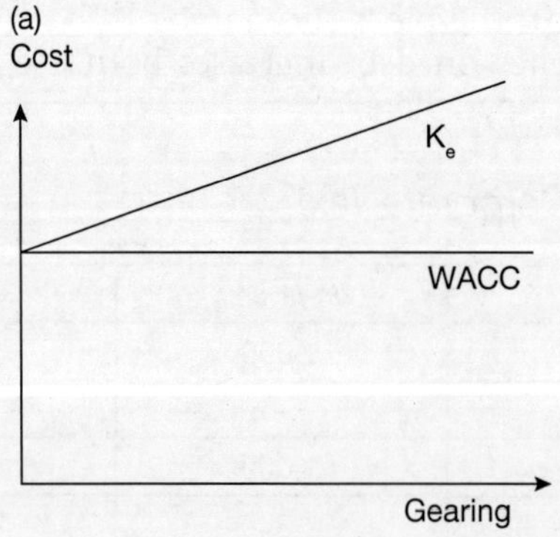

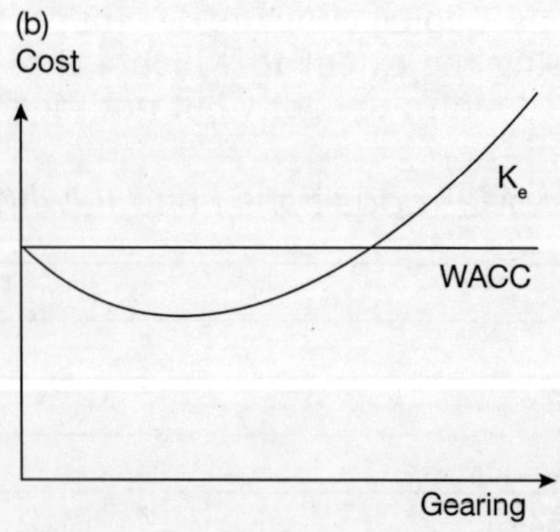

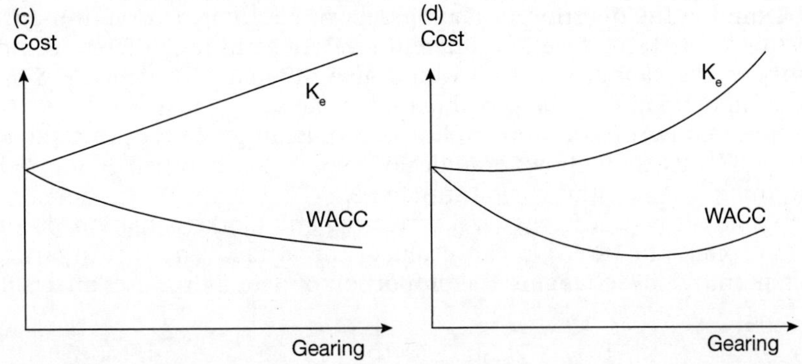

Test Your Understanding 2

Answer the following questions:

a. If a company, in a perfect capital market with no taxes, incorporates increasing amounts of debt into its capital structure without changing its operating risk, what will the impact be on its WACC?
b. According to MM, why will the cost of equity always rise as the company gears up?
c. In a perfect capital market but with taxes, two companies are identical in all respects, apart from their levels of gearing. A has only equity finance, B has 50% debt finance. Which firm would MM argue was worth more?
d. In practice, what form of finance a firm that has exhausted retained earnings is likely to select next?

6.8.5 The Pecking Order Approach

Studies of how companies raise funds in practice have shown that a large number ignore the recommendations of all the debt–equity mix theories. Instead, many seem to follow a consistent pattern year after year, financing first with retained earnings, next with the easier-to-obtain forms of borrowing such as payables and bank debt, then with more complex debt forms such as bond issues, and last with issues of common stock. Professor Stewart Meyers has labelled this pattern the pecking order approach.

6.9 Determining the Optimal Capital Structure

The optimal capital structure is such a combination of debt and equity that maximizes the value of the firm. Each firms target to reach to optimum capital structure. Though different approaches to capital structure provide contradictory results, still identifying optimum capital structure has managerial implications. This section presents the way of reaching towards a level of gearing where capital structure is optimum.

6.9.1 EBIT/EPS Analysis

One way of examining the question of issuing debt or equity is by examining the effect on the EPS of possible capital structures. At different levels of earnings, different combinations of debt and equity in the capital structure would give different EPS. Since EPS is usually an important factor in determining the actual market value of a company's shares, the financial manager should carefully consider the implications of issuing one type of capital as opposed to another. An EBIT–EPS chart shows graphically the relation between EPS and the earnings before tax and interest for various capital structures.

An EBIT/EPS analysis at a different level of gearing and market situations is a rationale to set an optimal capital structure. We can evaluate the attractiveness of a particular capital structure by examining how changing the proportion of debt a firm uses affects its EPS.

Illustration

Assume that the total capital of a hypothetical firm is $2,000,000. Other information in different economic scenarios is presented in the next table to supplement the decision-making process.

Types of Economy	***Boom***	***Normal***	***Recession***
Operating income (EBIT)	$800,000	$400,000	$100,000
Probability	0.3	0.5	0.2
Debt	$500,000	$1,000,000	$1,500,000
Debt/asset ratio	25%	50%	75%
Interest rate (I_r)	9%	11%	20%
Number of shares outstanding	300,000	200,000	100,000

If the firm only uses equity, that is, there is no debt, there will be 400,000 shares of stock outstanding. To evaluate the impact of changing the capital structure, we keep the amount of total capital the same, that is, $2,000,000. Therefore, if the firm is financed with $500,000 debt, the remaining $1,500,000 in capital will be equity and only 75% of the equity that exists. In this case, the number of shares of stock outstanding will be 300,000 = 0.75 × 400,000. The number of shares outstanding under the other alternatives is similarly computed.

Based on this information, the EPS for each situation is as follows:

When proportion of debt (D/A) = 0%

Type of Economy	***Boom***	***Normal***	***Recession***
EBIT	$800,000	$400,000	$100,000
Interest [I]	0	0	0
Earnings before taxes [EBT =EBIT – I]	$800,000	$400,000	$100,000
Taxes [T] @ 40%	$320,000	$160,000	$40,000
Earnings After Taxes [EAT = EBT – T]	$480,000	$240,000	$60,000
EPS [EAT/400,000 Shares Outstanding]	$1.20	$0.60	$.15
Probability [P_i]	0.3	0.5	0.2
Expected EPS $\left[\sum_{i=1}^{3} EPS_i \times P_i\right]$			$0.69
Standard deviation of EPS			$0.37

When proportion of debt (D/A) = 25%

Type of Economy	*Boom*	*Normal*	*Recession*
EBIT	\$800,000	\$400,000	\$100,000
Interest [I = \$500,000 @ 9%]	\$45,000	\$45,000	\$45,000
Earnings before taxes [EBT = EBIT – I]	\$755,000	\$355,000	\$55,000
Taxes [T] @ 40%	\$302,000	\$142,000	\$22,000
Earnings after taxes [EAT = EBT – T]	\$453,000	\$213,000	\$33,000
EPS [EAT/300,000 Shares Outstanding]	\$1.51	\$0.71	\$.11
Probability [P_i]	0.3	0.5	0.2
Expected EPS $\left[\sum_{i=1}^{3} EPS_i \times P_i\right]$			\$0.83
Standard deviation of EPS			\$0.50

When proportion of debt (D/A) = 50%

Type of Economy	*Boom*	*Normal*	*Recession*
EBIT	\$800,000	\$400,000	\$100,000
Interest [I = \$1,000,000 at 11%]	\$110,000	\$110,000	\$110,000
Earnings Before Taxes [EBT = EBIT – I]	\$690,000	\$290,000	(\$10,000)
Taxes [T] @ 40%	\$276,000	\$116,000	\$4,000
Earnings After Taxes [EAT = EBT – T]	\$414,000	\$174,000	(\$6,000)
EPS [EAT/200,000 Shares Outstanding]	\$2.07	\$0.87	(\$0.03)
Probability [P_i]	0.3	0.5	0.2
Expected EPS $\left[\sum_{i=1}^{3} EPS_i \times P_i\right]$			\$1.05
Standard deviation of EPS			\$0.75

When proportion of debt (D/A) = 75%

Type of Economy	*Boom*	*Normal*	*Recession*
EBIT	\$800,000	\$400,000	\$100,000
Interest [I = \$1,500,000 at 20%]	\$300,000	\$300,000	\$300,000
Earnings before taxes [EBT = EBIT – I]	\$500,000	\$100,000	(\$200,000)
Taxes [T] at 40%	\$200,000	\$40,000	\$80,000
Earnings after taxes [EAT = EBT – T]	\$300,000	\$60,000	(\$120,000)
EPS[EAT/200,000 *Shares Outstanding*]	\$3.00	\$0.60	(\$1.20)
Probability [P_i]	0.3	0.5	0.2
Expected EPS $\left[\sum_{i=1}^{3} EPS_i \times P_i\right]$			\$0.96
Standard deviation of EPS			\$1.50

Summarizing the results provided above, we have the following:

% of Debt financing	*0*	*25*	*50*	*75*
Expected EPS	\$0.69	\$0.83	\$1.05	\$0.96
Standard deviation of EPS	\$0.37	\$0.50	\$0.75	\$1.50

According to the information above, the firm's EPS peaks at a capital structure that includes 50% debt and 50% equity. However, this capital structure might not be optimal, as we will see in the sections that follow.

6.9.2 EPS Indifference Analysis

If our hypothetical firm wants to decide between two capital structures, say, all equity financing and 50% debt, then the financial manager would want to know at what levels of sales it is better to be an all-equity firm and at what levels of sales it would be better to be financed with 50% debt. This decision can be made by graphing EPS for both financing plans at various levels of sales. Figure 6.5 shows the EPS figures for our hypothetical firm at different levels of sales assuming the firm has fixed operating costs equal to \$400,000 and variable operating costs equal to 60% of sales.

The preferred financing plan is the one that produces the higher EPS. In this situation, it is imperative for the firm to finance with all equity for sales \$1.55 million; otherwise, the financing plan with 50% debt is preferred. Thus, the cut-off point is the certain level of turnover.

Figure 6.5 EPS Indifference

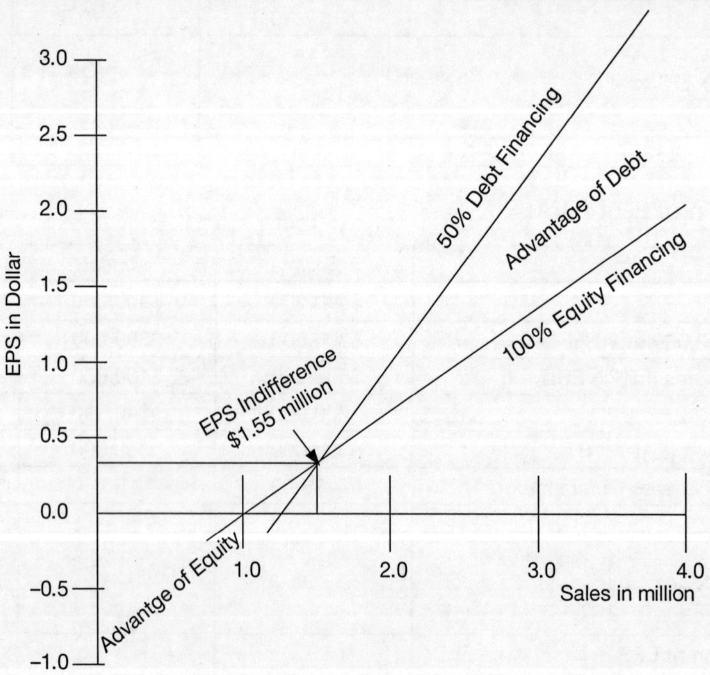

6.10 The Effect of Capital Structure on Stock Prices and the Cost of Capital

When we try to find the optimal capital structure for a firm, we want to determine the mix of debt and equity that maximizes the value of the firm that is, its stock price, not the EPS. The proportion of debt in the optimal capital structure will be less than the proportion of debt needed to maximize EPS because the market valuation of the stock considers the risk associated with the firm's operations expected well into the future and EPS is based only on the firm's operations expected for the next few years. To determine a firm's optimal capital structure, first consider the fact that the relationship of the cost of equity and the amount of debt the firm uses to finance its assets can be illustrated in Figure 6.6.

According to the figure, for a given level of operations, the required return on (cost of) equity is affected by the firm's financial risk, which is based on the amount of debt used to finance its assets. Although debt increases the cost of equity, the tax benefit associated with using debt (interest paid is tax deductible) generally requires firms to use some debt to finance assets. But, at some point, the tax benefit is overshadowed by the additional risk the firm incurs by increasing the amount of debt it uses, which causes the cost of additional debt to increase significantly. In other words, the risk of bankruptcy increases so significantly that increases in the cost of debt more than offset the benefit associated with the tax deductibility of the interest payments. Therefore, the relationship of the cost of debt, the cost of equity, and the WACC with the amount of debt used to finance assets might look like as shown in Figure 6.7.

As you can see from the figure, (a) if the firm uses only equity to finance its assets (that is, zero debt is used), then WACC is exactly equal to cost of equity; (b) as the firm begins to use some debt for financing, WACC declines, primarily because the tax benefit offered by the debt more than offsets the increased cost of equity; (c) at some point the tax benefit associated with debt is more than offset by increases in the before-tax cost of debt and the cost of equity that result from increases in the risk associated with the additional debt and, at this point, WACC begins to increase; and (d) the point where WACC is the lowest is the optimal capital structure,

Figure 6.6 Relationship of the Cost of Equity and the Amount of Debt the Firm Uses to Finance its Assets

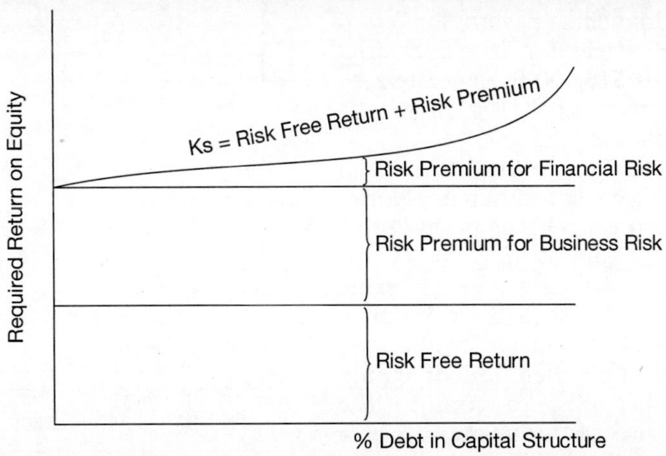

this is, the point where the value of the firm is maximized. Remember that WACC represents a cost to the firm, that is, it is the average rate of return the firm pays for the funds it uses to finance its assets, which is similar to the interest paid by an individual on a mortgage, and, rationally, the firm wants to minimize any of its costs, all else being equal.

Figure 6.7 Relationship of Cost of Debt, Cost of Equity and WACC with Amount of Debt

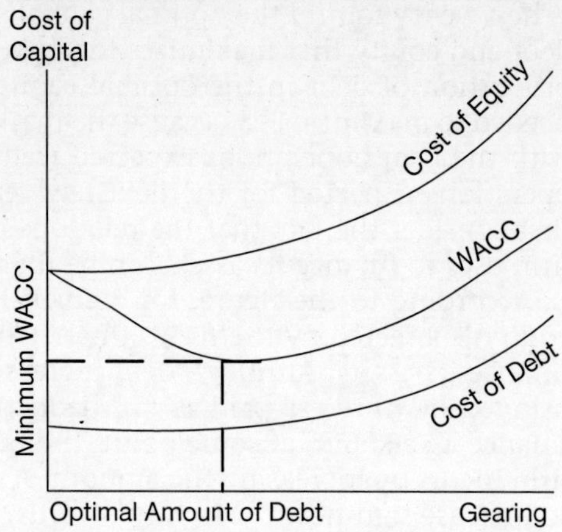

Illustration

Zaire Ltd is considering raising $200,000 for a new project. At present, the entire capital comprises equity of $800,000 in shares of $1 each. It is estimated that either debt at 8% or shares at par can be issued to raise the finance required. A likely level of earnings before tax is estimated to be $300,000 per annum and the rate of corporation tax to be used is 50%. EPS under the two alternatives would be as follows:

	Debt ($)	***Equity ($)***
EBIT	300,000	300,000
Interest at 8%	16,000	–
EBT	284,000	300,000
Tax at 50%	142,000	150,000
EAT/Net Income	142,000	150,000
Number of shares outstanding	800,000	1,000,000
EPS	0.1775	0.15

An EBIT/EPS chart can now be drawn. The 'starting point' for debt and equity can be arrived at by calculating the required EBIT under both alternatives to give a zero EPS. In case of equity financing, a zero EBIT will result zero EPS. However, for debt financing, the EBIT should be $16,000 to generate zero EPS due to the fixed charges due to the existence of 8% debt of $200,000.

The point where the two lines cross each other is the breakeven or indifference point. It can be seen that the breakeven point in this case is at an EBIT figure of $80,000. At this point, both debt and equity give the same EPS. If EBIT amounts more than $80,000, using debt will result higher EPS, while EBIT is lower than $80,000 then use of equity results in a higher EPS. To confirm the breakeven point, we can calculate EPS at a point higher than $80,000 EBIT.

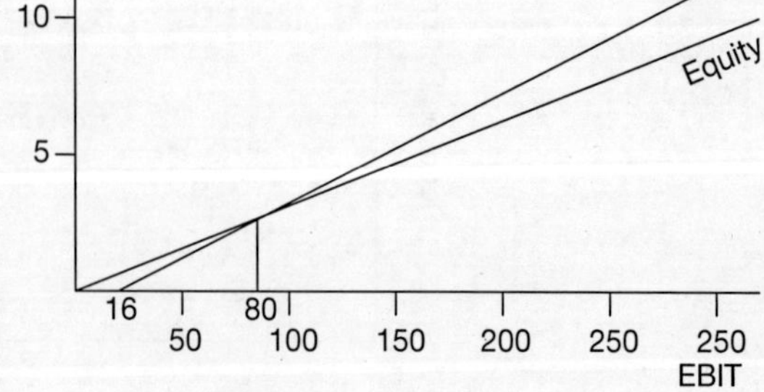

	Debt ($)	*Equity ($)*
EBIT	100,000	100,000
Interest at 8%	16,000	–
EBT	84,000	100,000
Tax at 50%	42,000	50,000
EAT/net income	42,000	50,000
Number of shares outstanding	800,000	1,000,000
EPS	0.0525	0.05

Thus at EBIT of $100,000 (higher than breakeven EBIT) EPS in the case of debt financing is higher than the EPS under equity financing. The breakeven point can be calculated algebraically as follows.

At breakeven EBIT

EPS in equity financing = EPS in debt financing

$$\frac{(\text{EBIT} - 0)50\%}{1{,}000{,}000} = \frac{(\text{EBIT} - \$16{,}000)50\%}{800{,}000}$$

EBIT = $80,000

It should be noted that EBIT/EPS analysis takes only the explicit costs of debt into account. The increase in the financial risk of the business by taking on debt should also be considered. The probability of future profits being above a breakeven point would also affect the financial manager's decision to introduce debt in the capital structure.

6.11 Degree of Leverage

The term leverage/gearing has been used throughout the chapter to mean the inclusion of debt in the capital structure. It also carries other meanings to business. Leverage literally means the benefits or advantages due for some technicalities used. Inclusion of debt in capital structure is a technique to get tax shield advantage. So a firm with debt in capital structure is termed as levered firm with the option of leverage. The leverage may also generate due to the cost structure, that is, the breakdown of total cost into fixed and variable. The lower the percentage of variable cost in cost structure, the higher is the leverage. Thus, the degree of leverage can be discussed from three different perspectives:

1. Degree of operating leverage (DOL)
2. Degree of financial leverage (DFL)
3. Degree of total leverage (DTL)

6.11.1 Degree of Operating Leverage

DOL refers to the percentage change in operating income, designated either NOI or EBIT, that results from a particular percentage change in sales. There is a good relationship between sale and income. Movements of both of the variables are unidimensional. If one increases, another increases too and vice versa. However, the degree of such relationship varies depending on the cost structure. Cost structure means the breakdown of total cost into fixed and variable. If the cost structure is highly dominated by variable cost, the DOL will be weak. However, if it is dominated by fixed costs resulting lower amount of variable cost, the DOL will be stronger. The company with strong DOL will get competitive advantage in the market in terms of pricing and profit. To calculate the DOL, the contribution format income statement will be helpful. For example, if in a certain year a company produces and sells 20,000 units at $100 per unit that costs to the company $30 each and if the company has $100,000 fixed costs, the contribution format income statement and the DOL calculation will be done as shown in the following table.

Contribution Format Income Statement		
Particulars	***Amount ($)***	***Amount ($)***
Sales (20,000 units at $100)	2,000,000	2,000,000
Less: Variable costs		
20,000 units at $30	600,000	
20,000 units at $50		1,000,000
Contribution margin	1,400,000	1,000,000
Less: Fixed costs	600,000	200,000
NOI	800,000	800,000
DOL (contribution margin/NOI)	1.75	1.25

Source: Authors.

The table shows that in an identical situation, DOL changes only due to the changes of cost structure. And it is better when variable cost is lower. Higher DOL is good due to higher possibility of maximizing income when sales increase.

6.11.2 Degree of Financial Leverage

DFL refers to the percentage change in EPS resulting from a particular percentage change in EBIT. DFL is computed as follows:

$$\text{DFL} = \frac{\text{\% change in EPS}}{\text{\% change in EBIT}} = \frac{\text{EBIT}}{\text{EBIT} - \text{I}} = \frac{\text{S} - \text{VC} - \text{F}}{\text{S} - \text{VC} - \text{FC} - \text{I}}$$

where I is the dollar interest paid on outstanding debt. The DFL equation given here applies only to firms that have no preferred stock outstanding. All else being equal, firms with riskier financial positions have higher DFLs.

6.11.3 Degree of Total Leverage

DTL refers to the percentage change in EPS resulting from a particular percentage change in sales. DTL combines DOL and DFL and is computed as follows:

$$\text{DFL} = \text{DOL} \times \text{DFL} = \frac{\text{\% change in EPS}}{\text{\% change in sale}} = \frac{\text{S} - \text{VC}}{\text{S} - \text{VC} - \text{FC} - \text{I}}$$

All else being equal, firms that have high DTLs are considered riskier in general than firms with low DTLs. To illustrate the concept of leverage, consider the following situation.

	Expected Sales	*Sales (at 10% Less than Expected)*	*% Changes*
Sales	875,000	787,500	10%
Variable operating costs (70% of sales)	612,500	551,250	10%
Gross profit	262,500	236,250	10%
Fixed operating costs	150,000	150,000	00%
EBIT	112,500	86,250	23.33%
Interest	50,000	50,000	00%
Earnings before tax	62,500	36,250	42%
Taxes at 40%	25,000	14,500	42%
Earnings after tax	37,500	21,750	42%

Source: Authors.
Notes:

- DOL = 2.33 = \$262,500/\$112,500
- DFL = 1.80 = \$112,500/(\$112,500 – \$50,000)
- DTL = 4.20 = 2.33 × 1.80 = \$262,500/(\$112,500 – \$50,000)

The table shows that when DOL is 2.33, a 10% decrease (increase) in sales will cause a 23.3% decrease (increase) in NOI. Thus, DOL represents the degree of changes in NOI due to the changes in sales. Again, when DFL is 1.80, a 23.3% decrease (increase) in EBIT will cause a 42.0% decrease (increase) in EPS (net income divided by the number of shares of common stock that are outstanding). It means that DFL represents the degree of change in EPS due to the change in EBIT. And, in combination, when DTL is 4.20, a 10% decrease (increase) in sales will cause a 42% decrease (increase) in EPS, which shows the degree of changes in EPS due to the changes in sales. The concept of leverage can be used to determine the impact that a change in capital structure will have on the riskiness, thus the WACC, of a firm.

6.12 Conclusion

A manager might not operate at the optimal capital structure because he or she might (a) find it difficult, if not impossible, to determine the optimal capital structure; (b) be reluctant to take on the amount of debt necessary to achieve the optimal capital structure (that is, have a conservative attitude towards debt financing); or (c) provide important services that prohibit him or her from endangering the ability of the firm to survive, which might be the case if the firm is financed using the optimal mix of capital. Often, firms use measures of financial liquidity, such as the times interest earned (TIE) ratio, to provide an indication of financial strength. The TIE ratio gives an indication of how many times a firm can cover the interest payments associated with its debt financing. Generally, a firm with a higher TIE ratio is said to have greater financial liquidity and lower threat of bankruptcy than a firm with a lower TIE ratio.

Capital structures vary significantly around the world. In countries where the debt is closely held so that the costs of monitoring firms are relatively low (that is, where bank loans or syndicates are used), firms have greater proportions of debt than firms in countries where debt is held by a large number of diverse investors. In countries where firms are required to regularly provide information about operations and finances to stockholders, firms have greater proportions of equity than firms in countries where such information is not required. In essence, whichever form of financing is more easily monitored by investors, to ensure that their best interests are being followed by the management, is the one that is more prevalent in capital structures. There are wide differences in capital structures among firms in the United States. Much of the difference depends on the type of operations, including the stability of sales that is associated with the firm. For example, firms in industries that have high degrees of R&D costs, such as pharmaceuticals, generally have capital structures that contain lower proportions of debt than firms in industries that have relatively stable, predictable cash flows, such as utilities. In general, non-U.S. companies have much higher debt levels than U.S. companies primarily because U.S. capital markets are relatively more developed. In addition, in most European countries and Japan, banks are more involved because they are permitted to make equity investments in non-financial corporations, a practice prohibited in the United States. It is expected that differences in capital structures will further diminish as countries rely less on banks and more on security issuance.

Decisions on the optimum level of debt will differ from firm to firm and should involve considerations of the firm's future strategies and external factors like the rate of inflation. One other factor that influences the capital mix is the attitude of company management. As employees, the management will tend to put constraints on the level of gearing as they will perceive a decrease in their job security with an increase in financial risk. However, reaching an optimum level of capital structure has significant importance in corporate finance literature and practice. So, the responsibility of finance managers in this area cannot be overlooked. Rather, around 80% of the effective time of corporate finance managers is spent on capital structure issues this way or that way.

Problems and Solutions

1. A company has $5,000 of debt at 10% interest and earns $5,000 a year before interest is paid. There are 2,250 issued shares, and the WACC is 20%.
   a. Compute market value of the company, cost of equity and market value per share.
   b. Suppose that the level of gearing is increased by issuing $5,000 more of debt at 10% interest to repurchase 562 shares (at a market value of $8.89 per share), leaving 1,688 shares in issue. Compute market value of the company, cost of equity and market value per share.

Answer:

a. The market value of the company should be as follows:

Earnings	$5,000
WACC	0.2
	$
Market value of the company ($5,000 ÷ 0.2)	25,000
Less: market value of debt	(5,000)
Market value of equity	20,000

The cost of equity is therefore $\frac{5,000-500}{20,000}=\frac{4,500}{20,000}=22.5\%$

And the market value per share is $\frac{4,500}{2,250}\times\frac{1}{0.225}=\$8.89$

b. The WACC will, according to the NOI approach, remain unchanged at 20%. The market value of the company should still therefore be $25,000.

Earnings	$5,000
WACC	0.2
	$
Market value of the company ($5,000 ÷ 0.2)	25,000
Less: market value of debt	(10,000)
Market value of equity	15,000

Annual dividends will now be $5,000 – $1,000 interest = $4,000.

The cost of equity has risen to $\frac{4,000}{15,000}=26.667\%$ and the market value per share is still: $\frac{4,000}{1,688}\times\frac{1}{0.2667}=\$8.89$

The level of gearing is a matter of indifference to an investor, because it does not affect the market value of the company, nor of an individual share. This is because as the level of gearing rises, so does the cost of equity in such a way as to keep both the WACC and the market value of the shares constant. Although, in our example, the dividend per share rises from $2 to $2.37, the increase in the cost of equity is such that the market value per share remains at $8.89.

2. Two companies are identical in every respect except for their capital structure. Their market values are in equilibrium, as follows:

	Geared	Ungeared
	$000	$000
Annual PBIT	1,000	1,000
Less: Interest (4,000 × 8%)	320	0
	680	1,000
Less: Tax at 30%	204	300
Profit after tax = dividends	476	700
Market value of equity	3,900	6,600
Market value of debt	4,180	0
Total market value of the company	8,080	6,600

The total value of the geared company is higher than the total value of the ungeared company, which is consistent with MM. All profits after tax are paid out as dividends, and so there is no dividend growth. The beta value of the ungeared firm has been calculated as 1.0. The debt capital of the geared firm can be regarded as risk free.

Calculate

a. The cost of equity in the geared company.
b. The market return R_m.
c. The beta value of the geared company.

Answer

a. Since its market value (MV) is in equilibrium, the cost of equity in the geared firm can be calculated as:

$$\frac{D}{MV} = \frac{476}{3{,}900} = 12.20\%$$

b. The beta value of the ungeared firm is 1.0, which means that the expected returns from the ungeared firm are exactly the same as the market returns, and R_m = 700/6,600 = 10.6%

c. $$\beta_g = \beta_a \times \frac{V_e + V_d(1-T)}{V_e} = 1.0 \times \frac{3{,}900 + (4{,}180 \times 0.70)}{3{,}900} = 1.75$$

The beta of the geared firm, as we would expect, is higher than the beta of the ungeared firm.

3. A company's debt–equity ratio, by market values, is 2:5. The corporate debt, which is assumed to be risk free, yields 11% before tax. The beta value of the company's equity is currently 1.1. The average return on stock market equity is 16%.

   The company is now proposing to invest in a project which would involve diversification into a new industry, and the following information is available about this industry.

   a. Average beta coefficient of equity capital = 1.59
   b. Average debt–equity ratio in the industry = 1: 2 (by market value)
   The rate of corporation tax is 30%. What would be a suitable cost of capital to apply to the project?

Answer

Step 1 The beta value for the industry is 1.59.

Step 2 (a) Convert the geared beta value for the industry to an ungeared beta for the industry.

$$\beta_a = 1.59 \times \frac{2}{2 + (1 \times 0.7)} = 1.18$$

(b) Convert this ungeared industry beta back into a geared beta, which reflects the company's own gearing level of 2:5.

$$\beta_e = 1.18 \times \frac{5 + (2 \times 0.7)}{5} = 1.51$$

Step 3 (a) This is a project-specific beta for the firm's equity capital, and so using the CAPM, we can estimate the project-specific cost of equity as follows:

$$K_{eg} = 11\% + (16\% - 11\%) \times 1.51 = 18.55\%$$

(b) The project will presumably be financed in a gearing ratio of 2:5 debt to equity, and so the project-specific cost of capital ought to be

$$[5/7 \times 18.55\%] + [2/7 \times 70\% \times 11\%] = 15.45\%$$

Multiple Choice Questions

1. A firm has a debt-to-equity ratio of 1. Its cost of equity is 16%, and its cost of debt is 8%. If the corporate tax rate is 25%, what would be its cost of equity if the debt-to-equity ratio were 0?
   a. 11.11% b. 12.57%
   c. 13.33% d. 16.00%
   e. None of the above.

2. A firm has zero debt in its capital structure. Its overall cost of capital is 9%. The firm is considering a new capital structure with 40% debt. The interest rate on the debt would be 4%. Assuming that the corporate tax rate is 34%, what would be its cost of equity capital with the new capital structure?
   a. 10.3% b. 11.0%
   c. 11.2% d. 13.9%
   e. None of the above.

3. A firm has a debt-to-equity ratio of .5. Its cost of equity is 22%, and its cost of debt is 16%. If the corporate tax rate is 0.40, what would be its cost of equity if the debt-to-equity ratio were 0?
   a. 14.00% b. 20.61%
   c. 21.07% d. 22.00%
   e. None of the above.

4. Wild Flowers Express has a debt–equity ratio of 0.60. The pre-tax cost of debt is 9% while the unlevered cost of capital is 14%. What is the cost of equity if the tax rate is 34%?
   a. 7.52% b. 8.78%
   c. 15.98% d. 16.83%
   e. 17.30%

5. Your firm has a pre-tax cost of debt of 7% and an unlevered cost of capital of 13%. Your tax rate is 35% and your cost of equity is 15.26%. What is your debt–equity ratio?
   a. 0.43 b. 0.49
   c. 0.51 d. 0.54
   e. 0.58

6. Walter's Distributors has a cost of equity of 13.84% and an unlevered cost of capital of 12%. The company has $5,000 in debt that is selling at par value. The levered value of the firm is $12,000 and the tax rate is 34%. What is the pre-tax cost of debt?
   a. 7.92% b. 8.10%
   c. 8.16% d. 8.84%
   e. 9.00%

7. The Spartan Co. has an unlevered cost of capital of 11%, a cost of debt of 8% and a tax rate of 35%. What is the target debt–equity ratio if the targeted cost of equity is 12%?
   a. 0.44 b. 0.49
   c. 0.51 d. 0.56
   e. 0.62

8. An unlevered firm has a cost of capital of 14% and EBIT of $150,000. A levered firm with the same operations and assets has both a book value and a face value of debt of $700,000 with a 7% annual coupon. The applicable tax rate is 35%. What is the value of the levered firm?

a. $696,429 b. $907,679
c. $941,429 d. $1,184,929
e. $1,396,429

9. You own 25% of Unique Vacations, Inc. You have decided to retire and want to sell your shares in this closely held, all-equity firm. The other shareholders have agreed to have the firm borrow $1.5 million to purchase your 1,000 shares of stock. What is the total value of this firm today if you ignore taxes?
a. $4.8 million b. $5.1 million
c. $5.4 million d. $5.7 million
e. $6.0 million

10. Thompson & Thomson is an all-equity firm that has 500,000 shares of stock outstanding. The company is in the process of borrowing $8 million at 9% interest to repurchase 200,000 shares of the outstanding stock. What is the value of this firm if you ignore taxes?
a. $20.0 million b. $20.8 million
c. $21.0 million d. $21.2 million
e. $21.3 million

11. In a world of no corporate taxes, if the use of leverage does not change the value of the levered firm relative to the unlevered firm this is known as
a. MM proposition III that the cost of stock is less than the cost of debt.
b. MM proposition I that leverage is invariant to market value.
c. MM proposition II that the cost of equity is always constant.
d. MM proposition I that the market value of the firm is invariant to the capital structure.
e. MM proposition III that there is no risk associated with leverage in a no-tax world.

12. The reason that MM proposition I does not hold in the presence of corporate taxation is that levered firms pay less taxes compared with identical unlevered firms.
a. Bondholders require higher rates of return compared with stockholders.
b. EPS are no longer relevant with taxes.
c. Dividends are no longer relevant with taxes.
d. All of the above.

Discussion Questions

1. What do you mean by capital structure? What are the determinants of capital structure?
2. What are the characteristics of an appropriate capital structure?
3. Which points are needed to be considered at the time of planning initial capital structure?
4. What are the different patterns of capital structure? Discuss with merits and demerits of each patterns.
5. What do you mean by 'capital structure theory'? Present a comparative discussion between trade-off and signalling theory.
6. What are the different approaches to capital structure? Present a critical presentation on

   a. net income approach
   b. NOI approach
   c. MM approach

7. How to determine an optimum capital structure? Discuss in terms of EBIT/EPS analysis.
8. What are the possible effect of capital structure on stock prices and cost of capital?
9. What do you mean by degree of leverage? Make a comparative discussion among DOL, DFL and DTL with examples.

Exercises

1. Companies A and B are identical in terms of total capital, capitalization rate, cost of debt and market risk. However, they differ in terms of capital structure. All related information is as follows:

	Company A	*Company B*
Capital structure:		
Common stock ($100 par value)	1,000,000	2,000,000
10% Debenture	2,000,000	1,000,000
Total capital	3,000,000	3,000,000
Equity capitalization rate	15%	15%

   In a latest year, EBIT of both of the companies was calculated as $50,000. Under the net income approach of capital structure, put a comment on the optimality of capital structure with reference to the cost of capital, value of the firm and the market value of shares.
2. Jaguar Leather reported annual NOI of $500,000. Its WACC is 10%. The capital structure of Jaguar includes 5% debt of $2 million. In the next year, Jaguar is planning to increase leverage by including $1 million more debt at 5%. Under the NOI approach, do you think that the revised capital structure will be an optimum one? Show the effect of the gearing on the value and cost of capital of Jaguar under the NOI approach of capital budgeting.
3. EBIT of Xian Catering is expected to be $100,000 with a random distribution of $30,000. Currently, it is evaluating two possible capital structures; one is all equity and other one is geared with 8% debt of $500,000. The decisive factor of Xian is the financial risk of its shareholders. Put a comparative comment on the degree of financial risk across two capital structures.
4. You are evaluating a proposal of investment that will generate EBIT of $20,000 forever. It requires an investment of $100,000. You have two possible sources of financing: (a) you may invest your own money and (b) you may borrow $40,000 from your banker at 5% forever with $60,000 of your own fund. Un-levered projects in the market have a required return of 10%.

   a. Under the MM proposition, compute the value from the levered and un-levered point of view.
   b. Under the MM proposition, compute the value from the levered and un-levered point of view, assuming that the tax rate is 45%.

5. Assume that a firm estimates its expected EBIT for the coming year as $500,000. Its variable cost ratio is 40% and annual fixed costs amounts to $100,000 irrespective of the volume of product. The applicable tax rate of the firm is 45%. The firm is 30% geared with 6% debt of $300,000 in its capital structure. Assuming 10% increase in sales, calculate each leverage and show the possible relationships among them.

6. The capital structure of Nesha Company Ltd. is composed of ordinary share capital of $200,000 (2,000 shares of $100 each) and 15% debt capital of $200,000. The corporate tax rate of the company is 40%. The operational data of the company for the year 2014 are as follows:

   - Sales 20,000 units at $10 each
   - Variable costs are at $4 per unit
   - Fixed cost of $70,000

   Due to increased demand for the products in the markets, the management planned to increase the production and sales of the company by phase.
   On the basis of the above data, you are required to calculate

   a. operating leverage, financial leverage and combined leverage
   b. the impact of planning to increase sales by 20% and 40%.

7. Calculate the DOL, financial leverage and combined leverage for the following firms and interpret the results, given the following data:

	P	*Q*	*R*
Output (units)	300,000	75,000	500,000
Fixed costs ($)	350,000	700,000	75,000
Unit variable cost ($)	1.00	7.50	0.10
Interest expenses ($)	25,000	40,000	Nil
Unit selling price ($)	3.00	25.00	0.50

8. Calculate the operating leverage, financial leverage and combined leverage from the following data under situations I and II and financial plans A and B:

Installed capacity		4,000 units
Actual production and sales		75% of the capacity
Selling price		$30 per unit
Variable cost		$15 per unit
Fixed cost:		
Under situation I		$15,000
Under situation II		$20,000
Capital Structure:	Financial Plan	
	A	B
Equity	$10,000	$15,000
Debt (rate of interest at 20%)	10,000	5,000
	20,000	20,000

9. Messi & Kaka Ltd. has annual EBIT of $15 million. These earnings are expected to remain constant. The market price of the company's ordinary shares is $0.86 per share cum dividend and of debentures $105.50 per debenture ex-interest. An interim dividend of six paisa per share has been declared. Income tax is at the rate of 35% and all available earnings are distributed as dividends.

Messi & Kaka Ltd.'s long-term capital structure is as follows:

	$ in '000
Ordinary shares ($0.25 per share value)	12,500
Reserve	24,300
	36,800
16% Debenture (par value $100) as on 31.12.2004	23,697
	60,497

Required:
Compute the cost of capital of the company according to the traditional theory of capital structure.

10. Vovozela Ltd. is an all-equity company with an equilibrium market value of $32.5 million and a cost of capital of 18% per annum. The company proposes to repurchase $5.0 million of equity and to replace it with 13% irredeemable loan stock.

    Vovozela earnings before tax and interest are expected to be constant for the foreseeable future. Income tax is at 13%. All profits are paid out as dividends.

    Required:

    Using the assumptions of MM explain and demonstrate how this change in capital structure will affect:

    - The market value
    - The cost of equity
    - The cost of capital of the company

11. Backwoods, a major international company with its head office in the UK, wants to raise $150 million to establish a new production plant in the eastern region of Germany. Backwoods evaluates its investments using NPV, but is not sure what cost of capital to use in the discounting process for this project evaluation.

    The company is also proposing to increase its equity finance in the near future for UK expansion, resulting overall in little change in the company's market-weighted capital gearing.

    The summarized financial data for the company before expansion are as follows:

    Income statement for the year ended 31 December 2008

	$m
Revenue	1,984
Gross profit	432
Profit after tax	81
Dividends	37
Retained earnings	44

Balance sheet as at 31 December 2008	
Non-current assets	846
Working capital	350
	1,196

Medium-term and long-term loans (see note below)	210
	986
Shareholders' funds	
Issued ordinary shares of $0.50 each nominal value	225
Reserves	761
	986

Notes on borrowings

These include $75 million 14% fixed-rate bonds due to mature in five-year time and redeemable at par. The current market price of these bonds is $120.00 and they have an after-tax cost of debt of 9%. Other medium-term and long-term loans are floating rate UK bank loans at LIBOR plus 1%, with an after-tax cost of debt of 7%.

Company rate of tax may be assumed to be at the rate of 30%. The company's ordinary shares are currently trading at $3.76.

The equity beta of Backwoods is estimated to be 1.18. The systematic risk of debt may be assumed to be zero. The risk-free rate is 7.75% and the market return is 14.5%.

The estimated equity beta of the main German competitor in the same industry as the new proposed plant in the eastern region Germany is 1.5, and the competitor's capital gearing is 35% equity and 65% debt by book values, and 60% equity and 40% debt by market values.

Required:

Estimate the cost of capital that the company should use as the discount rate for its proposed investment in the eastern company. State clearly any assumptions that you make.

12. Droxfol Co is a listed company that plans to spend $10 million on expanding its existing business. It has been suggested that the money could be raised by issuing 9% loan notes redeemable in 10 years. The current financial information on Droxfol Co is as follows:

Income statement information for the last year

	$000
PBIT	7,000
Interest	(500)
Profit before tax	6,500
Tax	(1,950)
Profit for the period	4,550

Statement of financial position for the last year	$000	$000
Non-current assets		20,000
Current assets		20,000
Total assets		40,000

Equity and liabilities		
Ordinary shares, par value $1	5,000	
Retained earnings	22,500	
Total equity		27,500
10% Loan notes	5,000	
9% Preference shares, par value $1	2,500	
Total non-current liabilities		7,500
Current liabilities		5,000
Total equity and liabilities		40,000

The current ex-dividend ordinary share price is $4.50 per share. An ordinary dividend of 35 cents per share has just been paid and dividends are expected to increase by 4% per year for the foreseeable future. The current ex-dividend preference share price is 76.2 cents. The loan notes are secured on the existing non-current assets of Droxfol and are redeemable at par in eight years. They have a current ex-interest market price of $105 per $100 loan note. Droxfol pays tax on profits at an annual rate of 30%.

The expansion of business is expected to increase PBIT by 12% in the first year. Droxfol has no overdraft.

Average sector ratios:

Financial gearing: 45% (prior charge capital divided by equity capital on a book value basis)

Interest coverage ratio: 12 times

Required:

a. Calculate the current WACC of Droxfol Co.
b. Discuss whether financial management theory suggests that Droxfol Co can reduce its WACC to a minimum level.
c. Evaluate and comment on the effects, after one year, of the loan note issue and the expansion of business on the following ratios:

    i. interest coverage ratio;
    ii. financial gearing;
    iii. EPS.

Assume that the dividend growth rate of 4% is unchanged.

13. DD Co has a dividend payout ratio of 40% and has maintained this payout ratio for several years. The current dividend per share of the company is 50 cents per share and it expects that its next dividend per share, payable in one year's time, will be 52 cents per share. The capital structure of the company is as follows:

	$ million	$ million
Equity		
Ordinary shares (per value $1 per share)	25	
Reserves	35	
		60

Debt		
Bond A (par value $100)	20	
Bond B (par value $100)	10	
		30
		90

Bond A will be redeemed at par in 10 years and pays annual interest of 9%. The current ex-interest market price of the bond is $95.08.

Bond B will be redeemed at par in four years' time and pays annual interest of 8%. The cost of debt of this bond is 7.82% per year. The current ex-interest market price of the bond is $102.01.

Bonds A and B were issued at the same time.

DD Co has an equity beta of 1.2. The risk-free rate of return is 4% per year and the average return on the market of 11% per year. Ignore taxation.

Required:

a. Calculate the cost of debt of bond A.
b. Discuss the reasons why different bonds of the same company might have different costs of debt.
c. Calculate the following values for DD Co:

   i. cost of equity, using the CAPM;
   ii. ex-dividend share price, using the dividend growth model;
   iii. capital gearing (debt divided by debt plus equity) using market values; and
   iv market value WACC.

d. Discuss whether a change in the dividend policy will affect the share price of DD Co.

14. Crastlee Inc. is evaluating two projects. The first involves a $4.725 million expenditure on new machinery to expand the company's existing operations in the textile industry. The second is a diversification into the packaging industry and will cost $9.275 million.

Crastlee's summarized balance sheet (statement of financial position) as at 31 December 2008, and those of Canall Inc and Sealalot plc, two quoted companies in the packaging industry, are shown below:

	Crestlee	Canall	Sealalot
	$m	$m	$m
Non-current assets	96	42	76
Current assets	95	82	65
	191	124	141
Ordinary shares[1]	15	10	30
Reserves	50	27	50
Medium- and long-term loans[2]	56	15	13

Current liabilities	70	72	48
Total equity and liabilities	191	124	141
Ordinary share price (cents)	380	180	230
Loan stock price ($)	104	112	–
Equity beta	1.2	1.3	1.2

a. Crestlee and Sealalot 50 cents per value, Canall 25 cents per value.
b. Crestlee 12% loan stock 2012–14, Canall 14% loan stock 2017, Sealalot medium-term bank loan.

Crestlee proposes to finance the expansion of textile operations with a $4.725 million at 11% loan stock issue, and the packaging investment with a $9.275 million rights issue at a discount of 10% on the current market price. Issue costs may be ignored.

Crestlee's managers are proposing to use a discount rate of 15% per year to evaluate each of these projects.
The risk free of interest is estimated to be 6% per year and the market return 14% per year. Corporate tax is at a rate of 33% per year.

Required:

a. Determine whether 15% per year is an appropriate discount rate to use for each of these projects. Explain your answer and state clearly any assumptions that you make.
b. Crestlee's marketing director suggests that it is incorrect to use the same discount rate each year for the investment in packaging as the early stages of the investment are more risky, and should be discounted at a higher rate. Another board member disagrees, saying that more distant cash flows are riskier and should be discounted at a higher rate. Discuss the validity of the views of each of the directors.

15. The managing director of Wemere, a medium-sized private company, wishes to improve the company's investment decision-making process by using the DCF techniques. He is disappointed to learn that estimates of a company's cost of capital usually require information on share prices which, for a private company, are not available. His deputy suggests that the cost of equity can be estimated by using data for Folten Inc, a similar sized, quoted company in the same industry, and he has produced two suggested discount rates for use in Wemere's future investment appraisal. Both of these estimates are in excess of 15% per year, which the managing director believes to be very high, especially as the company has just agreed a fixed-rate bank loan at 10% per year to finance a small expansion of existing operations. He has checked the calculations, which are numerically correct, but wonders if there are any errors of principle.

    Estimate 1: CAPM
    Data have been purchased from a leading business school:

Equity beta of Folten	1.4
Market return	14%
Treasury bill yield	6%

The cost of capital is 14% + (14% – 6%) × 1.4 = 25.2%

This rate must be adjusted to include inflation at the current level of 4%. The recommended discount rate is 29.2%

Estimate 2: Dividend valuation model

	Average share price (cents)	Dividend per share (cents)
2003	193	9.23
2004	109	10.06
2005	96	10.97
2006	116	11.95
2007	130	13.03

The cost of capital is $\frac{D_1}{P_0 - g} = \frac{14.2}{138 - 9} = 11.01\%$

where D_1 is expected dividend, P_0 is the current market price and g is the growth rate of dividend (%).

When inflation is included, the discount rate is 15.01%.

Other financial information on the two companies is as follows:

	Wemere	Folten
	\$000	\$000
Non-current assets	7,200	7,600
Current assets	7,600	7,800
Total assets	14,800	15,400
Ordinary shares (25 cents)	2,000	1,800
Reserves	6,500	5,500
Term loans	2,400	4,400
Current liabilities	3,900	3,700
	14,800	15,400

Notes:

i. The current ex-dividend share price of Folten Inc is 138 cents.
ii. Wemere's board of directors has recently rejected a takeover bid of \$10.6 million.
iii. Corporate tax is at the rate of 33%.

Required:

a. Explain any errors of principle that have been made in the two estimates of the cost of capital and produce revised estimates using both of the methods. State clearly any assumptions that you make.
b. Discuss which of your revised estimates Wemere should use as the discount rate for capital investment appraisal.
c. Discuss whether DCF techniques, including discounted payback, are useful to small unlisted companies.

Case in Action

Capital Structure Decisions: The Basics

Assume you have just been hired as business manager of PizzaPalace, a pizza restaurant located adjacent to a campus. The company's EBIT was $500,000 last year, and since the university's enrolment is capped, EBIT is expected to remain constant (in real terms) over time. Since no expansion capital will be required, PizzaPalace plans to pay out all earnings as dividends. The management group owns about 50% of the stock, and the stock is traded in the over-the-counter market.

The firm is currently financed with all equity; it has 100,000 shares outstanding; and P_0 is $25 per share. When you took your MBA Corporate Finance course, your instructor stated that most firms' owners would be financially better off if the firms used some debt. When you suggested this to your new boss, he encouraged you to pursue the idea. As a first step, assume that you obtained from the firm's investment banker the following estimated costs of debt for the firm at different capital structures:

% Financed with Debt	R_d
0%	–
20	8.0%
30	8.5
40	10.0
50	12.0

If the company were to recapitalize, debt would be issued, and the funds received would be used to repurchase stock. PizzaPalace is in the 40% state-plus-federal corporate tax bracket, its beta is 1.0, the risk-free rate is 6% and the market risk premium is 6%.

a. Provide a brief overview of capital structure effects. Be sure to identify the ways in which capital structure can affect the WACC and FCFs.

b. (1) What is business risk? What factors influence a firm's business risk?
   (2) What is operating leverage, and how does it affect a firm's business risk? Show the operating breakeven point if a company has fixed costs of $200, a sales price of $15 and variables costs of $10.

c. Now, to develop an example that can be presented to PizzaPalace's management to illustrate the effects of financial leverage, consider two hypothetical firms: firm U, which uses no debt financing, and firm L, which uses $10,000 of 12% debt. Both firms have $20,000 in assets, a 40% tax rate and an expected EBIT of $3,000.

d. (1) Construct partial income statements, which start with EBIT, for the two firms.
   (2) Now calculate ROE for both firms.
   (3) What does this example illustrate about the impact of financial leverage on ROE?

e. Explain the difference between financial risk and business risk.

f. Now consider the fact that EBIT is not known with certainty, but rather has the following probability distribution:

Economic State	*Probability*	*EBIT*
Bad	0.25	$2,000
Average	0.50	3,000
Good	0.25	4,000

Redo the part A analysis for firms U and L, but add basic earning power, ROI, [defined as (net income + interest)/(debt + equity)], and the TIE) ratio to the outcome measures. Find the values for each firm in each state of the economy, and then calculate the expected values. Finally, calculate the standard deviation and coefficient of variation of ROE. What does this example illustrate about the impact of debt financing on risk and return?

g. What does capital structure theory attempt to do? What lessons can be learned from capital structure theory? Be sure to address the MM models.

h. With the above points in mind, now consider the optimal capital structure for PizzaPalace.

i. (1) For each capital structure under consideration, calculate the levered beta, the cost of equity and the WACC.
   (2) Now calculate the corporate value, the value of the debt that will be issued and the resulting market value of equity.
   (3) Calculate the resulting price per share, the number of shares repurchased and the remaining shares.

j. Considering only the capital structures under analysis, what is PizzaPalace's optimal capital structure?

k. What other factors should managers consider when setting the target capital structure?

Source: http://www.leeds-faculty.colorado.edu (last accessed on 12 March 2013).

References

Durand, D. 1952. 'Costs of Debt and Equity Funds for Business: Trends and Problems of Measurement'. *National Bureau of Economic Research*, 215–47. Conference on Research in Business Finance, New York.

Modigliani, F. and H.M. Miller. 1963. 'Corporate Income Taxes and the Cost of Capital: A Correction'. *The American Economic Review*, 433–43.

Chapter
7

Dividend Policy

Chapter Objectives

On completion of this chapter, you will be able to understand:

- Types of dividend
- Factors affecting dividend policy
- Investors and dividend policy: Signalling, clientele and FCF hypothesis
- Payment procedure: declaration, holder of record and payment date
- Dividend policy: residual dividend policy and others
- Dividend reinvestment plans (DRIPs)
- Stock splits versus stock dividends
- Dividend irrelevance and relevance theory: MM, birds-in the-hand and tax preference

7.1 Introduction

Earnings management has become an important strategic management issue. Fund management was always a common agenda in most of the board meetings. It is considered as a constraint resource in nearly every company that requires serious management interventions. At the end of the year, when a company publishes its financial statement to the public, the financial situation becomes clear. The profit and its ultimate distribution become a serious issue to all. A wise and careful use of profit is an expectation and, at the same time, concern for all. It will represent the management philosophy that obviously exerts a considerable pressure in the market. However, with the profit, the management can undertake a lot of important actions. Some of the examples are provided in the following Figure:

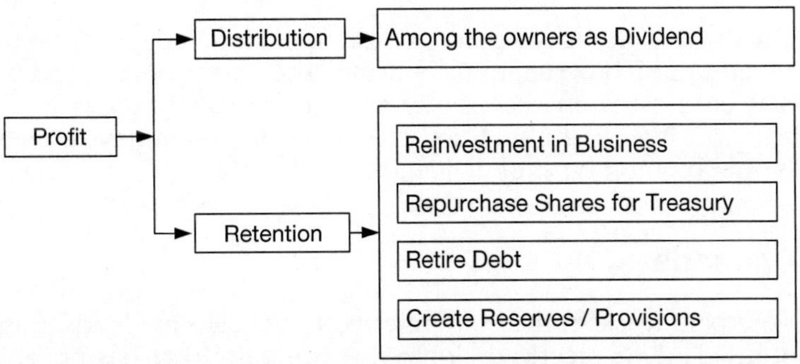

When a portion of the profit is paid out to shareholders, the payment is known as a dividend. Such payments may be in cash or in kind. Decisions about when and how much of earnings should be paid as dividends are part of the firm's dividend policy. Earnings that are paid out as dividends cannot be used by the firm to invest in projects with positive NPVs, that is, to increase the value of the firm. The dividend policy that maximizes the value of the firm is said to be the optimal dividend policy.

A dividend policy is of prime importance in any corporate set-up. How much of the earnings will be allocated as dividends and how much will be retained for investments is a critical decision on part of the management. In equation form, this relationship may be presented as:

$$\text{DIV} = \text{EAR}(1 - \text{RETR})$$

where, DIV represents the amount of dividends declared and paid, EAR represents earnings available for the declaration of dividend and RETR represents the portion of earnings retained for investment. Thus, DIV and EAR have a positive relationship, whereas DIV has a negative relationship with RETR. Therefore, an optimum level of dividend should be reached to maximize the value of the firm. Too much dividend may bring short-term gain in the image in the market but value of the firm may be depreciated through the drainage of wealth. Again, too less dividend may bring short-term agitation among the investors, although there is a scope for maximizing the value of the firm if the firm has investment opportunities. Having reinvestment opportunities have strategic importance. If the firm has investment opportunities generating return at a higher rate than the return that shareholders may earn from their own investments only then the rationality of retaining funds occurs. But, payment of dividend becomes more rationale if shareholders got the opportunity of investment at a higher rate than the firms have. However, some controversies exist in the literature on this issue, which will be addressed in later sections.

During the first part of the 20th century, dividends were the primary reason investors purchased stock. It was literally said on Wall Street, 'the purpose of a company is to pay dividends'. Today, the investor's view is a bit more refined; it could be stated, instead, as 'the purpose of a company is to increase my wealth'. Indeed, today's investor looks to dividends and capital gains as a source of increase. Microsoft, for example, did not pay a dividend until it had already become a $350 billion company, long after making the company's founders and long-term shareholders multimillionaires or billionaires.

7.2 Types of Dividends

As already mentioned, dividends may be paid in cash or in kind. It depends on the management who possesses the right of such declaration. In reality, the means of dividend payments signify something. It may be a stock market game, an equity establishment in the market, the distribution to justify the investment on the part of investors and it may also have a lot of other meanings. Here, some common types of dividends are presented for common reference and use.

7.2.1 Cash Dividends

When dividends are paid in cash, these are referred to as cash dividends. Cash dividend is a common form of dividend as practiced globally. A company that has preferred stock issued must make the dividend payment on those shares before a single penny can be paid out to the common stockholders. The preferred stock dividend is usually set, whereas the common stock dividend is determined at the sole discretion of the board of directors. It may be announced as a percentage basis or per-share basis. For example, Algae Computers have 100,000 common shares outstanding with $100 par value. If cash dividend is declared at 10%, the total amount of cash divided is $1,000,000 (100,000 shares × $100 × 0.1). And if the dividend is declared at the rate of $8 per share, then the amount of dividend will be $800,000 (100,000 shares × $8 per share).

7.2.2 Property Dividends

A property dividend is when a company distributes property to shareholders instead of cash or stock. Property dividends can literally take the form of railroad cars, cocoa beans, pencils, gold, silver, salad dressing or any other item with tangible value. Property dividends are recorded at market value on the declaration date. When the firm faces liquidity crisis and wants to keep the current stockholders base constant, it will go for property dividends.

7.2.3 Special One-time Dividends

In addition to regular dividends, there are times a company may pay a special one-time dividend. These are rare and can occur for a variety of reasons, such as a major litigation win, the sale of a business or liquidation of an investment. They can take the form of cash, stock or property dividends. Due to the temporarily lower rates of taxation on dividends, there has been an increase in special dividends paid in recent years. To add sugar to spice, there are times when these special one-time dividends are classified as a 'return of capital'. In essence, these payments are not a payout of the company's profits but, instead, returns of money shareholders have invested in the business. As a result, returns of capital dividends are tax free. Special one-time dividends sometimes offer an opportunity for arbitrage.

7.2.4 Stock Dividends

A stock dividend is a pro rata distribution of additional shares of a company's stock to owners of the common stock. A company may opt for stock dividends for a number of reasons, including inadequate cash on hand or a desire to lower the price of the stock on a per-share basis to prompt more trading and increase liquidity (i.e., how fast an investor can turn his holdings into cash). Why does lowering the price of the stock increase liquidity? On the whole, people are more likely to buy and sell a $50 stock than a $5,000 stock; this usually results in a large number of shares trading hands each day.

7.3 A Practical Example of Stock Dividends

Company ABC has 1 million shares of common stock. The company has five investors who each own 200,000 shares. The stock currently trades at $100 per share, giving the business a market capitalization of $100 million.

The management decides to issue a 20% stock dividend. It prints up an additional 200,000 shares of common stock (20% of 1 million) and sends these to the shareholders based on their current ownership. All of the investors own 200,000, or 1 of 5 of the company, so they each receive 40,000 of the new shares (1 of 5 of the 200,000 new shares issued).

Now, the company has 1.2 million shares outstanding; each investor owns 240,000 shares of common stock. The 20% dilution in value of each share, however, results in the stock price falling to $83.33. Here's the important part: the company (and our investors) are still in the exact same position. Instead of owning 200,000 shares at $100, they now own 240,000 shares at $83.33. The company's market capitalization is still $100 million.

One of the more interesting theories of corporate dividend policy is that managements should opt for stock dividends over all other kinds. This will allow investors that want their earnings retained in the business (and not taxed) to hold on to the additional stock paid out to them. Investors that want current income, on the other hand, can sell the shares they receive from the stock dividend, pay the tax and pocket the cash—in essence, creating a 'do-it-yourself' dividend.

7.4 Factors Influencing Dividend Policy

Dividend policy is not a stand-alone concept. It is commonly referred to as a financing decision. As most of the financing of a firm comes from shareholders, keeping them happy and satisfied is an important agenda for the management. And dividend policy is the weapon to do that. The policy comes from the management philosophy and thus it poses a challenge before them. However, a handful number of factors influence the nature of dividend policy. Some important factors are given below:

a. Legal, Contractual and Internal Constraints: The amount of dividends a firm pays might be limited by (a) restrictions in debt agreements that state the maximum amount of dividends that can be paid in any year; (b) the amount of retained earnings, which represents the maximum amount of dividends that can be paid at any time; (c) the liquidity position of the firm, if cash is not available, dividends cannot be paid; and (d) limits of the IRS on the amount of earnings a firm can retain for non-specific reasons. However, some more specific constraints under each category are identified as follows:

Legal Constraints

1. Most states' securities regulations prevent firms from paying out dividends from any portion of the company's 'legal capital' which is measured by the par value of common stock or par value plus paid-in-capital.
2. Dividends are also sometimes limited to the sum of the firm's most recent and past retained earnings, although payment in excess of current earnings is usually permitted.
3. Most states also prohibit dividends when firms have overdue liabilities or are legally insolvent or bankrupt.
4. Even the IRS has ruled in the area of dividend policy.
5. Specifically, the IRS prohibits firms from acquiring earnings to reduce stockholders' taxes.
6. The IRS can determine that a firm has accumulated an excess of earnings to allow owners to delay paying ordinary income taxes (on dividends), it may levy an excess earnings accumulation tax on any retained earnings above $250,000.
7. It should be noted, however, that this ruling is seldom applied.

Contractual Constraints

1. In many cases, companies are constrained in the extent to which they can pay dividends by restrictive provisions in loan agreements and bond indentures.

2. Generally, these constraints prohibit the payment of cash dividends until a certain level of earnings is achieved or to a certain dollar amount or percentage of earnings.
3. Any violation of these constraints generally triggers the demand for immediate payment.

Internal Constraints

1. A company's ability to pay dividends is usually constrained by the amount of available cash rather than by the level of retained earnings against which to charge them.
2. Although it is possible to borrow to pay dividends, lenders are usually reluctant to grant them because using the funds for this purpose produces no operating benefits that help to repay them.

b. Investment opportunities: Firms that need great amounts of funds for positive NPV investments usually pay relatively lower amounts of dividends than firms with few positive NPV investments. Thus, the availability of reinvestment opportunities is an important factor.

c. Alternative sources of capital: The higher the costs of issuing new common stock, generally the lower the relative amount of dividends paid by a firm; firms that are concerned about diluting current ownership through new issues of common stock are likely to pay relatively low dividends.

d. Effects of dividend policy on cost of equity (K_S): In an effort to minimize WACC through the cost of equity (K_S), a firm will examine the effect a dividend policy has on its required rate of return. Factors such as risk perception, information content (signalling) and preference for current returns versus future returns (that is, dividend yield or capital gains) are considered when the dividend policy is established.

e. Shareholders' considerations: Declaration and payment of dividend is a form of direct interaction by the management with the shareholders of the company. Thus, they should consider the possible effect of dividend on shareholders in terms of, say, tax matters, investment opportunities of shareholders, dilution of ownership, possibility of gain in the market and so on.

f. Capital market considerations: Sometimes, the capital market as a regulator can play a vital role in framing the dividend policy of firms. Say, for example, in Bangladesh, the Dhaka Stock Exchange (DSE) carefully observes the dividend declared (both time and percentages) by listed companies and goes for different restrictions if anything unexpected happens.

g. Macro economic variables: Some macro economic variables like inflation, market interest rates, market risks, money value and foreign exchange fluctuations also affect the dividend policy of a firm. If investors can earn higher return from some other sources, they withdraw their investment in stocks. At the time of inflation, firms depend on retained earnings for possible investment and it results a low payout ratio. If the market interest rate becomes high, investors' required rate of return also increases. Sometimes, the monetary policy and fiscal policy of a government also affect the long-term dividend policy of a firm due to its capacity to control different macro economic variables.

7.5 Investors and Dividend Policy

The relationship between dividend policy and investors is multifaceted. Investors are the first party to be affected due to the dividend policy of a firm. Investors' reactions to changes in dividend policies can be summarized as follows.

7.5.1 Signalling Effect

There is a belief that managers change dividends (increase or decrease) only when it is necessary, decreases occur only when the firm is facing financial difficulty, while increases occur only when it is expected that the firm can continue to pay higher dividends long into the future. If this is true, then changes in a firm's dividend policy provide information to investors, who will react accordingly. For example, investors would consider an increase (decrease) in dividends to be good (bad) news, and thus increase (decrease) the price of the firm's stock.

The basic issue underlying signalling hypothesis is that changes in the dividend policy give signals regarding the firm's financial condition. A dividend increase may signal good future earnings. A dividend decrease may signal poor future earnings. The theories so far have assumed that investors and managers have the same information set. When it comes to prospect for the company, managers may have better information than investors. Therefore, unexpected changes in dividends may relay information to the market that it did not know before. Managers do not cut dividends unless the firm is in financial distress. It is therefore believed that firms do not increase dividends beyond Wall Street's expectations unless managers anticipate stronger earnings than expectations. Unexpected changes in dividends relay information to the market.

7.5.2 Clientele Effect

Different groups of investors or clienteles prefer different dividend policies. Firms past dividend policies determine their current clientele of investors. Clientele effects impede changing dividend policy. Taxes and brokerage costs hurt investors who have to switch companies. Investors needing current income will be drawn to firms with high payout ratios. Investors preferring to avoid taxes will be drawn to firms with lower payout ratios (i.e., firms draw a given clientele, given their stated dividend policy). Firms should avoid making drastic changes in their dividend policy. Each firm, therefore, attracts the type of investor that likes its dividend policy. Tax-free foundations and retirees at lower marginal tax rates prefer cash now and on a predictable basis. Investors at higher marginal tax rates might prefer capital gains to dividends. With capital gains, they can better time their tax liabilities.

7.5.3 FCF Hypothesis

If investors truly want managers to maximize the value of the firm, then dividends should be paid only when the firm has no investment opportunities with positive NPVs. In other words, a firm should pay dividends only when it has funds that are not needed to invest in positive NPV projects, that is, only FCFs should be paid as dividends. If this theory is correct, then we might expect a firm's stock price to increase when it decreases dividends to invest in positive NPV projects, and we might expect the stock price to decrease when the firm increases dividends because it no longer has as many positive NPV projects as it did in prior years.

7.6 Payment Procedures

Payment of dividend involves some predefined processes and requires some time. Generally, board of directors in a meeting proposes a certain percentage of dividends for the period, and it has been finalized in annual general meeting (AGM) through voting of shareholders. Thus, the rate is finalized and the process of the payment of dividend starts. A record date is fixed and dividends are paid at a later date to the listed shareholders on the record date. Dividends may be paid once a year, or interim dividends may also be paid that depends of the profitability and dividend policy. A vast majority of dividends are paid four times a year on a quarterly basis. This means that when an investor sees that Coca-Cola pays a $0.88 dividend, he will actually receive $0.22 per share four times a year. Some companies, such as McDonald's, pay dividends on an annual basis. However, some dates are very much important in the dividend payment procedure.

7.6.1 Declaration Date

The declaration date is the day the board of director announces their intention to pay a dividend. On this day, the company creates a liability on its books; it now owes the money to the stockholders. On the declaration date, the board will also announce a date of record and a payment date.

7.6.2 Holder-of-record Date

This is the date when the firm opens its ownership books to determine who will receive dividends. Persons whose names appear in the ownership books after the holder-of-record date, which is also termed as the date of record, but prior to the date the dividend is paid will not receive a dividend payment. An investor must be listed as a holder of record to ensure the right of a dividend payout.

7.6.3 Ex-dividend Date

Once the company sets the record date, the stock exchanges or the National Association of Securities Dealers, Inc. fixes the ex-dividend date. After the record date has been determined, then the ex-dividend date is assigned. The ex-dividend date for stocks is typically two business days prior to the record date. If an investor buys a stock before the ex-dividend date, then he or she will receive the dividend payment. If an investor purchases the stock on or after the ex-dividend date, then he or she is not entitled to receive the dividend. Two working days before the holder-of-record date is termed as ex-dividend date. Ex-dividend means without dividend; so, on the ex-dividend date, the stock begins to sell without the right to receive the next dividend payment. In essence, the stock sells without the right to receive the dividend payment because there is not enough time for the names of new stockholders to be registered before the holder-of-record date. Shares listed on the New York Stock Exchange (NYSE) go ex-dividend four business days before the record date. This NYSE rule is generally followed by the other exchanges.

Example

Declaration Date	Ex-dividend Date	Record Date	Payable Date
27 July 2004	6 Aug 2004	10 Oct 2004	10 Sep 2004

On 27 July 2004, Company XYZ declares a dividend payable on 10 September 2004 to its shareholders. XYZ also announces that shareholders on record of the company's books on or before 10 August 2004 are entitled to the dividend. The stock would then go ex-dividend two

business days before the record date. In this example, the record date falls on a Tuesday. Excluding weekends and holidays, the ex-dividend is set two business days before the record date or the opening of the market—in this case on the preceding Friday. This means that anyone who bought the stock on Friday or thereafter would not get the dividend. At the same time, those who purchased before the ex-dividend date received the dividend. With a significant dividend, the price of a stock may move up by the dollar amount of the dividend as the ex-dividend date approaches and then fall by that amount after the ex-dividend date. A stock that has gone ex-dividend is marked with an 'x' in newspapers on that day.

7.6.4 Payment Date

It is the date the firm mails the dividend checks to the holder of record. This date is generally a week or more after the date of record so that the company has sufficient time to ensure that it accurately pays all those who are entitled.

7.7 Dividend Policy

Dividend policy is the philosophy of the management. The management chooses the right dividend policy from a large number of alternatives available in the literature and practice. Selecting a dividend policy does not necessarily mean that the same policy will be existed for an unlimited period of time. The management may change it if they feel that the policy is not well accepted by the market. They may also change it with the changing nature of business and pattern of stockholding. However, it is not good, in any cases, to change the dividend policy more frequently. Some of the common types of dividend policy are discussed here.

7.7.1 Residual Dividend Policy

As an investor, you should want the firm to retain any earnings it can invest at a rate of return that is at least as high as your opportunity cost. Firms that agree with this concept might follow a residual dividend policy where dividends are paid only if earnings are greater than what is needed to finance the equity portion of the firm's optimal capital budget for the year. Therefore, if the residual dividend policy is followed, the firm should not pay dividends when it is necessary to issue new common stock to provide equity financing for the current capital budgeting needs.

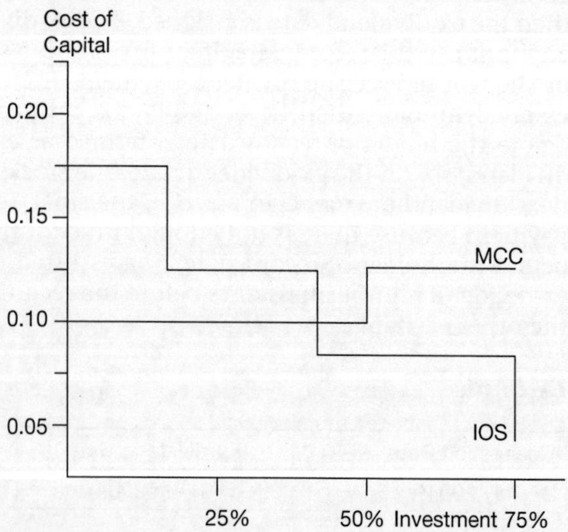

Thus, the basic principle underlying the residual dividend policy is to retain and reinvest earnings as long as returns on the investments exceed the returns stockholders could obtain on other investments of comparable risk. This concept is also illustrated graphically. A corporation should retain all necessary earnings to invest up to the level indicated by the intersection of the marginal cost of capital and investment opportunity schedule functions. Residual earnings are distributed to shareholders. A residual dividend policy suggests that dividends should be that part of earnings that cannot be invested at a rate at least equal to the WACC.

Residual Dividend Policy Steps

Residual dividends are calculated as per the following steps:

1. Determine the optimal capital budget.
2. Determine the retained earnings that can be used to finance the capital budget.
3. Use retained earnings to supply as much of the equity investment in the capital budget as necessary.
4. Pay dividends only if there are leftover earnings.

Illustration

Lead International has a requirement of $1,000,000 for its capital budgeting purpose. Lead has a 40:60 debt–equity ratio. The current income statement of Lead reveals $600,000 net income. Compute the amount of dividend payment under residual dividend policy.

1.	Capital requirements	$1,000,000
2.	Financing through debt (1 × 0.4)	$400,000
3.	Financing through equity (1 × 0.6)	$600,000
4.	Net income	$800,000
5.	Residual income (4 – 3)	$200,000
6.	Dividend paid (5)	$200,000
7.	Dividend payout (6/4)	25%

At any level of net income, the dividend payout can be calculated similarly.

7.7.2 Stable, Predictable Dividend Policy

Some managers believe that dividends should never be decreased unless it is absolutely necessary to do so. These managers probably follow a stable, predictable dividend policy that requires that the firm pays a dividend that is the same every year or is constant for some period and is then increased at particular intervals, that is, dividend payments are fairly predictable. Greater predictability is associated with greater certainty and less risk, which implies a lower overall WACC and a higher firm value. In practice, more firms actually follow some form of this dividend policy.

Due to the possibility of a negative signal to investors, many CFOs have set the policy of never reducing their dividends. Dividends are increased only if the management is certain that future earnings will support such a high dividend. A variation of this policy is one in which dividends exhibit a stable, predictable growth rate. In that instance, the company has to set the policy in such a way that the growth rate can be sustained for the foreseeable future.

Stable, Predictable Dividend Policy Steps

1. Pay a predictable dividend every year.
2. Base optimal capital budget on residual retained earnings (after dividend).

7.7.3 Constant Payout Ratio Policy

It is possible that a company could set a policy to payout a certain percentage of earnings as dividends. The problem is that such a policy would not fit the needs of the firms' stockholders, since it would cause a great deal of volatility in dividends paid.

A firm's dividend payout ratio is defined as the proportion of EPS that is paid out as dividends (dividend per share, DPS), that is, payout ratio (DPS/EPS). Firms that follow a constant payout ratio dividend policy pay the same percentage of earnings as dividends each year. For example, a firm might pay 60% of its earnings as dividends. If so, then dividends will fluctuate as earnings fluctuate.

Constant Payout Ratio Policy Steps

1. Pay a constant proportion of earnings (if positive).
2. Base optimal capital budget on residual retained earnings.

7.7.4 Low Regular Dividend plus Extras

This policy requires a firm to pay some minimum dollar dividend each year and then to pay an extra dividend when the firm's performance is above normal (or above some minimum standard). This policy is a hybrid of the last two policies. It is meant to keep expectations low for dividends, and supplement those dividends with bonuses in good years. The problem is the potential for negative signalling.

Low Regular Dividend plus Extras Steps

1. Pay a predictable dividend every year.
2. In years with good earnings pay a bonus dividend.
3. Base optimal capital budget on residual of regular dividend and compromising with bonus for capital budgeting projects.

7.8 Selecting High Dividend Stocks

An investor desiring to put together a portfolio that generates high dividend income should place great scrutiny on a company's dividend payment history. Only those corporations with a continuous record of steadily increasing dividends over the past 20 years or longer should be considered for inclusion. Furthermore, the investor should be convinced the company can continue to generate the cash flow necessary to make the dividend payments; a handgun manufacturer, for example, may have a long history of high dividend payments while generating strong cash flow from operations yet not make a good investment because it faces litigation which, if successful, will bankrupt the business. The following points regarding dividends should be considered carefully before investment is made in shares.

7.8.1 Dividends Related to Cash Flow, Not Reported Earnings

This brings up an important point: Dividends are dependent upon cash flow, not reported earnings. Almost any board of directors would still declare and pay a dividend if cash flow was strong, but the company reported a net loss on a GAAP basis. The reason is simple: investors that prefer high dividend stocks look for stability. A company that lowers its dividend is probably going to experience a decline in stock price as jittery investors take their money elsewhere. Companies will not raise the dividend rate because of one successful year; so afraid are they of lowering the dividend they will wait until the business is capable of generating the cash to maintain the higher dividend payment forever. Likewise, they will not lower the dividend if they think the company is facing a temporary problem.

7.8.2 Dividend Payout Ratio

The percentage of net income that is paid out in the form of dividend is known as the dividend payout ratio. This ratio is important in projecting the growth of the company, because, its inverse, the retention ratio (the amount not paid out to shareholders in the form of dividends), can help project a company's growth. Calculation of the dividend payout ratio is very simple. The ratio results when the total amount of dividend paid is divided by the amount of income available to common stockholders. For example, Coca-Cola's 2003 cash flow statement shows that the company paid \$2.166 billion in dividends to shareholders. The income statement for the same year shows that the business had reported a net income of \$4.347 billion. To calculate the dividend payout ratio, the investor would do the following:

$$\text{Dividend Payout Ratio} = \frac{\text{Dividend}}{\text{Earnings}} = \frac{\$2.166}{\$4.347} = 49.8\%$$

The answer, 49.8%, reports that Coca-Cola paid out nearly 50% of its profit to shareholders over the course of the year.

Exhibit 7.1 Dividend Policies Followed by Leading Companies in India

Dividend is a payment made by a company out of its profit. For investors, dividend is a source of earning apart from the capital appreciation that share of a company provides. It becomes important for an investor to investigate the dividend policy followed by the companies. Dividend policy is a part of the corporate governance policy of a company. Many investor-friendly companies have their dividend policy documented in some form or the other. The following details give an insight into dividend policies followed by some of the leading companies in India.

Company	***Dividend Policy***	***Dividend Paid***	
		Year	***Amount (₹)***
Larsen and Toubro	The boards of directors review the dividend policy periodically. L&T pays a dividend because the company's investors in India and abroad view this as an important market signal of the management's confidence in the future.	2010–11	14.50
		2009–10	12.50
		2008–09	10.50
		2007–08	17.00

CRISIL	CRISIL believes in maintaining a fair balance between cash retention and dividend distribution. Cash retention is required to finance acquisitions and future growth, and also as a means to meet any unforeseen contingency. CRISIL has also been conscious of the need to maintain stability in its dividend payout over the years. From 2008, CRISIL has commenced the practice of paying dividend on a quarterly basis.	2011–12 2010–11 2009–10 2008–09	60 200 100 70
HDFC Bank	HDFC Bank has had a consistent dividend policy that balances the dual objectives of appropriately rewarding shareholders through dividends and retaining capital, in order to maintain a healthy capital adequacy ratio to support future growth. It has had a consistent track record of moderate but steady increases in dividend declarations over its history with the dividend payout ratio ranging between 20% and 25%.	2010–11 2009–10 2008–09 2007–08	16.5 12.00 10.00 8.50
Infosys	Currently, Infosys pays dividends to its shareholders. The current dividend policy is to distribute not more than 30% of the PAT (unconsolidated Indian GAAP) as dividend. The board of directors reviews the dividend policy periodically and on 15 April 2008 decided to hike the dividend policy to up to 30% of post-tax profits from 20% of post-tax profits earlier	2011–12 2010–11 2009–10 2008–09	37 30 25 23.50
ONGC	As per the guideline dated 11 February 1998 from the Government of India, all profit-making PSUs which are essentially commercial enterprises should declare the higher of a minimum dividend of 20% on equity or a minimum dividend payout of 20% of post-tax profit. The minimum dividend payout in respect of enterprises in the oil, petroleum, chemical and other infrastructure sectors such as us should be 30% of post-tax profits.	2010–11 2009–10 2008–09 2007–08	8.75 33 32 32

Source: http://healthofmywealth.com/dividend-policies-followed-by-leading-companies-in-india/

7.8.3 Dividend Yield

The dividend yield tells the investor how much he is earning on a common stock from the dividend alone based on the current market price. Dividend yield is calculated by dividing the actual or indicated annual dividend by the current price per share.

For example, the *Washington Post* pays an annual dividend of $7 and trades at $910 per share; Altria Group (formerly Philip Morris) pays an annual dividend of $2.72 and trades at $49.75 per share. By calculating dividend yield, the investor can compare the amount he would earn in cash income annually from each security.

$$\text{Dividend Yield}_{\text{Washington}} = \frac{\text{Dividend Per Share}}{\text{Market Price Per Share}} = \frac{\$7}{\$910} = 0.0077 \text{ or } 0.77\%$$

$$\text{Dividend Yield}_{\text{Altria}} = \frac{\text{Dividend Per Share}}{\text{Market Price Per Share}} = \frac{\$2.72}{\$49.75} = 0.0548 \text{ or } 5.48\%$$

In other words, despite the fact that the *Washington Post* pays a higher per-share dividend, \$100,000 invested in its common stock would yield only \$770 in annual income as opposed to the same amount invested in Altria Group, which would yield \$5,500. An investor interested in dividend income and not capital gains should opt for the latter, all else being equal.

7.8.4 Double Taxation

Dividends, like interest, are taxed at a person's individual tax rate. Capital gains taxes, on the other hand, are assessed according to the length of time an investor held his investment and can be as low as half the rate levied on dividends income. This difference in tax treatment is another reason many investors opt for long-term equity holdings that reinvest capital into the business instead of paying it out in the form of a dividend; by avoiding the double-taxation, they can compound their wealth at a faster rate.

There is a significant political controversy over the fact that profits paid out as dividends are subject to double taxation. The corporation paid income taxes on the profit it earned (original tax). The owners of the business then take that profit out for their personal use in the form of a dividend and are taxed at personal income tax rates (second tax). In effect, they have paid the government twice.

The proponents of the dividend tax argue that the wealthy, by definition, own significantly more investments than the poor. Therefore, it would be possible for someone to earn billions of dollars in dividend income and not pay a dime in federal taxes. This, they say, is inherently unfair. The gap between the rich and the poor would explode overnight.

7.8.5 Debt Restrictions

Many companies are not able to pay dividends because bank loans, lines of credit or other debt financing place strict limitations on the payment of common stock dividends. This type of covenant restriction is disclosed in a company's 10K filing with the Securities and Exchange Commission (SEC). Unless you need the money for living expenses or you are an experienced investor that regularly allocates capital, the first thing you should do when you acquire a stock that pays a dividend is enrol it in a dividend reinvestment plan, or DRIP for short.

7.9 Dividend Reinvestment Plans

DRIPs permit stockholders to have dividend payments automatically reinvested in the firm's stock. DRIPs allow stockholders to buy additional shares of a firm's stock on a pro rata basis using the cash dividend paid by the firm. Often there are little or no brokerage fees involved with DRIPs. When an investor enrols in a DRIP, he will no longer receive dividends in the mail or directly deposited into his brokerage account. Instead, those dividends will be used to purchase additional shares of stock in the company that paid the dividend. Some variations of DRIPs are commonly observed in the market like:

1. With bank-directed DRIPs, banks purchase additional shares on the open market in huge blocks, which substantially reduces per-share commissions.
2. With company-directed DRIPs, the company itself issues new shares in exchange for the cash dividend, completely eliminating commissions.
3. With brokerage-directed DRIPs, brokerage firms such as Charles Schwab will reinvest dividends for shareholders who hold stocks in street name at no charge.

7.9.1 Benefits of Enrolling in a DRIP

1. Enrolling in a DRIP is easy. The paperwork (both online and in print) can normally be filled out in less than a minute.
2. Dividends are automatically reinvested. Once the investor has enrolled in a DRIP, the process becomes entirely automated and requires no more attention or monitoring.
3. Many DRIPs are often part of a direct stock purchase plan. If the investor holds at least one of his shares directly, he can have his checking or savings account automatically debited on a regular basis to purchase additional shares of stock.
4. Purchases through dividend reinvestment programmes are normally subject to little or no commission.
5. DRIPs allow the investor to purchase fractional shares. Over decades, this can result in significantly more wealth in the investors' hands.
6. An investor can enrol only a limited number of shares in the DRIP and continue to receive cash dividends on the remaining shares.

7.9.2 DRIPs in Action

Full Enrolment in a DRIP

Jane Smith owns 1,000 shares of Coca-Cola. The stock currently trades at $50 per share and the annual dividend is $0.88 per share. The quarterly dividend has just been paid ($0.88 divided by 4 times a year = $0.22 per share quarterly dividend). Before she enrolled in Coca-Cola's DRIP, Jane would normally receive a cash deposit of $220 in her brokerage account. This quarter, however, she logs into her brokerage account and finds she now has 1,004.40 shares of Coca-Cola. The $220 dividend that was normally paid to her was reinvested in whole and fractional shares of the company at $50 per share.

Partial Enrolment in a DRIP

William Jones owns 500,000 shares of the Altria group. The stock currently trades at $49.75 and pays an indicated annual dividend of $2.72 per share ($0.68 per quarter). William would like to receive some cash for living expenses but would like to enrol some of the shares in a DRIP. He calls his broker and has 300,000 shares enrolled in Altria's DRIP. When the quarterly dividend is paid, William will receive cash dividends of $136,000. He will also receive 4,100.50 additional shares of the Altria Group, giving him holdings of 304,100.50 shares (300,000 shares × $0.68 dividend = $204,000 divided by $49.75 per share price = 4,100.50 new shares of the Altria Group).

Notice that William now has 4,100.50 additional shares of Altria stock. When the next quarterly dividend is paid, he will receive $0.68 for each of those shares. That additional income works out to $2,788.34. Those dividends will be partially reinvested in the stock, buying more shares which will pay more dividends.

In even the smallest portfolio, DRIPs can result in substantial increases in value over extended periods of time. To demonstrate the power of dividend reinvestment through DRIPs, consider the example given in Jerry Edgerton and Jim Frederick's 1 August 1997 *Money* magazine article, 'Build Your Wealth Drip by Drip': if you had put $10,000 in Standard & Poor's 500 stock index at the end of 1985 and not bothered to reinvest your dividends, you would have had $29,150 by the end of 1995. Had you reinvested the dividends, however, your total would have been more than $40,000. In other words, reinvesting those seemingly small dividends resulted in an extra $10,850 over 10 years. Assuming you continued to add to your principal investment and held those stocks for 30 or 40 years, the difference could be hundreds of thousands of dollars or more.

7.10 Stock Splits and Stock Dividends

To this point, we have examined the dividend policy that relates to cash payments. Some firms pay dividends in the form of stock or change the number of shares of stock that is outstanding through a stock split. As you will discover in the discussion that follows, neither of these actions by themselves has economic value in the sense that each does nothing to change stockholders' wealth.

7.10.1 Stock Splits

A stock split is, in essence, a very large stock dividend. In cases of stock splits, a company may double, triple or quadruple the number of shares outstanding. The value of each share is merely lowered; economic reality does not change at all. It is, therefore, completely irrational for investors to get excited over stock splits. Many firms believe their stock has an optimal price range within which their stock should trade. If the price of the stock exceeds the price range, then the firm will execute a stock split. If a firm initiates a 2-for-1 stock split, each existing stockholder will receive two shares of stock for each one share he or she now owns. This action should cut the market price of the stock exactly in half. But, there is evidence that shows the price of the stock actually settles above one half the pre-split price. Perhaps the reason this occurs is that investors believe the split provides positive information; specifically, that the firm expects the price of the stock to increase further above the optimal range in the future. In any event, there really is no specific economic value associated with a stock split. As an investor, unless the market reacts positively or negatively to the split, the only effect the split has is to increase the number of shares of stock you own, with each share valued at a lower relative price such that your wealth position has not changed. Sometimes, 'reverse stock split' practices are also found in the market where more shares have been merged into one. In that case, the number of shares outstanding reduces and par value per share increases, but the total of stockholders equity remains unchanged.

7.10.2 Stock Dividends

This is a situation when dividends are paid in the form of stock rather than cash. Like stock splits, a stock dividend does not have specific economic value; rather, it increases the total number of shares of stock each stockholder owns. At the same time, the stock price per share decreases because investors have not provided any funds for the additional shares of stock. A firm might use a stock dividend to keep the price of its stock within a particular range.

Balance Sheet Presentation of Stock Split and Stock Dividend	
Situation: Original Data (Before Stock Split and Stock Dividend)	
Common stock (80,000 shares authorized, 30,000 shares issued and outstanding at a par value of $10)	$300,000
Additional paid-in capital	$100,000
Retained earnings	$100,000
Total stockholders' equity	$500,000
Book value per share ($500,000/30,000 shares)	$16.67
Situation: After 2-to-1 Stock Split	
Common stock (80,000 shares authorized, 60,000 shares issued and outstanding at a par value of $5)	$300,000
Additional paid-in capital	$100,000
Retained earnings	$100,000
Total stockholders' equity	$500,000
Book value per share ($500,000/30,000 shares)	$8.33
Situation: After a 10% Stock Dividend	
Common stock (80,000 shares authorized, 33,000 shares (30,000 × 1.1) issued and outstanding at a par value of $10)	$330,000
Additional paid-in capital ($100,000 + 3000 shares at $20 each)	$160,000
Retained earnings	$10,000
Total stockholders' equity	$500,000
Book value per share ($500,000/33,000 shares)	$15.15

Note: market value per share at the time of dividend announcement was $30.

7.10.3 Balance Sheet Effects

For stock splits, the only effect on the balance sheet is that the number of shares outstanding changes relative to the split, which also changes the stated par value of the stock (if there is one). If a firm executes a 2-for-1 split, for example, it would double the number of shares outstanding and halve the par value of the stock reported on the balance sheet. The total dollar values in each common equity account would not change. When a stock dividend is paid, on the other hand, the firm must transfer capital from retained earnings to the 'Common stock' account and the 'Additional paid-in capital' account to reflect the fact that a dividend was paid. The dollar value of stock dividend is calculated by using the following equation and the same amount will be transferred from retained earnings to capital or paid-in capital account.

$$\text{Amount of Stock Dividend} = (\text{Number of Shares Outstanding} \times \text{\% of Stock Dividend}) \times \text{Market Value Per Share}$$

To illustrate, consider a firm decides to pay a 5% stock dividend. The market price of the firm's stock is $80 and it has 20 million shares of $2 par stock outstanding before the declaration of stock dividend. Thus, the dollar value of stock dividend will be [$80,000,000 (20 million × 5%) × $80]. A total of $80 million will be transferred from retained earnings and the allocation between capital and paid up capital will be as follows:

1.	Market value per share	$80
2.	Par value per share	$2
3.	Number of shares outstanding	20,000,000
4.	Stock dividend declared	5%
5.	Number of new shares (3 × 4)	1,000,000
6.	Dollar value of stock dividend (1 × 5)	$80,000,000
7.	Amount transferred from retained earnings	$80,000,000
8.	Amount transferred to common stock (2 × 5)	$2,000,000
9.	Amount transferred to additional paid in capital (7 – 8)	$78,000,000

After the stock dividend, the firm would show $80 million less in retained earnings. In the common equity portion of the balance sheet, there would now be 21 million shares of stock outstanding (20 million existing shares plus 1 million shares associated with the stock dividend), the 'Common equity' account would increase by $2 million (1 million shares $2 par), and the 'Additional paid-in capital' would increase by $78 million ($80 million less than $2 million increase in 'Common equity').

7.10.4 Price Effects

Even though both stock splits and stock dividends only increase the number of outstanding shares of the stock, studies have shown that the market price of the stock affected by such actions might change, if investors expect future earnings and cash dividends to increase (decrease), then the price will increase (decrease) above the relative price associated with the stock split or the stock dividend. For example, if investors believe a firm initiated a 2-for-1 stock split because its future earnings will cause the price of the stock to increase well above its optimal range, then their reaction to the split will cause the post-split price of the stock to be greater than one half the pre-split prices. If the future expectations do not pan out, however, the price of the stock will eventually settle at about one half the pre-split prices.

7.11 Dividend Theory

Researchers argue whether there exists an optimal dividend policy. Some academicians argue that a firm's dividend policy does not affect the value of a firm (dividend irrelevance theory), while others argue that the dividend policy is an important factor in the determination of a firm's value (dividend relevance theory). The theories also consider investors attitude towards the return: Are they happy with dividends or prefer capital gains? This issue is highly debated and thus different theories address these issues differently.

Dividends or Capital Gains: Dividends are the current (revenue gains) from the investment in stock, whereas capital gains arise when a particular stock is traded at a higher price than the cost. As there are tax differences; that is, the tax rate for capital gain is lower than tax on regular income, investors may prefer lower amount of dividend if there is a guarantee that it will result higher market price and thus higher capital gains. Suppose all shareholders are in the 28% tax bracket and have a choice between investing in firm G which pays no dividend or firm D that does pay a dividend. Firm G's stock is currently \$100 and has a 20% ROE. Assume that the investor does not sell the shares and the capital gain is untaxed. Therefore, the value of the share one year from now should be \$120. On the other hand, firm D pays a \$20 dividend. What's the value of each of these shares?

If markets are efficient, then firms that are equally risky must have the same after-tax value. Assume that firm D's stock will be \$100 next year after the \$20 dividend is paid.

$$P_0 = \frac{100 + 20(1 - 0.28)}{(1 + 0.2)^1} = \$95.33$$

The difference between the price of firm D's stock and firm G's stock is simply the present value of the taxes that must be paid by the investor. Thus, due to the tax differences, customers' preferences may vary between dividends and capital gains. The firm should take care of these issues at the time of selecting its dividend policy. The ultimate goal of financial managers should be the maximization of shareholder wealth. And shareholder wealth can be maximized by maximizing the price of the stock. The price of the stock is the expected present value of future cash flows. Future cash flows may be generated through dividends and capital gains. The dividend theories concerning the analysis of future cash flows and its possible effect on stock prices have broadly been classified into two types.

Dividend Irrelevance Theory	***Dividend Relevance Theory***
MM Theorem	Bird-in-the-hand theory Gordon model Walter model Linter model
	Tax preference theory
	Agency theory
	Signalling theory
	Transaction cost theory

7.11.1 Dividend Irrelevance Theory

Dividend policy is irrelevant. Investors do not care about payout. If dividends are too high, investors may use some of the funds to buy more of the firm's stock. If dividends are too low, investors may sell off some of the stock to generate additional funds. Miller and Modigliani showed algebraically that dividend policy did not matter:

1. They showed that as long as the firm was realizing the returns expected by the market, it did not matter whether that return came back to the shareholder as dividends now, or reinvested.
2. They would see it in dividend or price appreciation.
3. The shareholder can create their own dividend by selling the stock when cash is needed.
4. Miller and Modigliani argued that dividend policy should be irrelevant to stock price.

5. Dividends are irrelevant to value as in the final equation of value (V) dividend is non-existed.
6. Value of the firm:

$$V_t = \frac{1}{1+r_t}[D_t + V_{t+1} - m_{t+1}P_{t+1}]$$
$$= \frac{1}{1+r_t}[D_t + V_{t+1} - I_t + X_t - D_t]$$
$$= \frac{1}{1+r_t}[V_{t+1} - I_t + X_t]$$

where r_t represents discount rate, D_t represents total dividend paid, V_{t+1} represents the firm value at period t + 1 calculated as n_tP_{t+1} (number of shares at period t multiplied by price per share at period t + 1) and $m_{t+1}P_{t+1}$ represents the amount raised through equity that is calculated as $I_t - [X_t - D_t]$, where I_t represents capital investment at period t and X_t represents income at period t.

Assumptions

To reach to their conclusion, MM made some unrealistic assumptions. They made these assumptions to simplify the analysis. Some assumptions of MM are:

1. No transactions costs to buy and sell securities
2. No flotation costs on new issues
3. No taxes
4. Perfect information
5. Dividend policy does not affect K_e

7.11.2 Bird-in-the-hand Theory

High dividends increase stock value. Dividends are less risky than potential future capital gains; hence, investors like dividends. Therefore, high dividend payout ratios will lower K_e (reducing the cost of capital) and increase stock price. The bird-in-the-hand theory relies on the premise that a bird in hand is better than two in the bush, meaning what is available at present is preferable to what may be available in the future. The theory is advocated by different researchers in different ways. Some of such variants are presented here.

7.11.3 Gordon Model

Gordon model is the basic model under bird-in-the-hand theory which makes dividend policy relevant with reference to the valuation of a firm. The model is based on the following assumptions:

1. The firm is an all-equity firm. All investment plans are financed with retained earnings
2. r and k_e are constant
3. The firm has perpetual life
4. The retention ratio (b) and growth rate (g) are constant
5. $k_e > br$

The Gordon dividend model derives the cost of equity from the following deceptively simple statement: The value of a share is the present value of the future anticipated dividend stream from the share, where the future anticipated dividends are discounted at the appropriate risk-adjusted cost of equity.

$$P_0 = \frac{D_1}{1+K_e} + \frac{D_1(1+g)}{(1+K_e)^2} + \frac{D_1(1+g)^2}{(1+K_e)^3} + \frac{D_1(1+g)^3}{(1+K_e)^4}$$

$$= \sum_{t=1}^{\infty} \frac{D_1(1+g)^{t-1}}{(1+K_e)^t} = \frac{D_1}{K_e - g}$$

Provided $|g| < K_e$

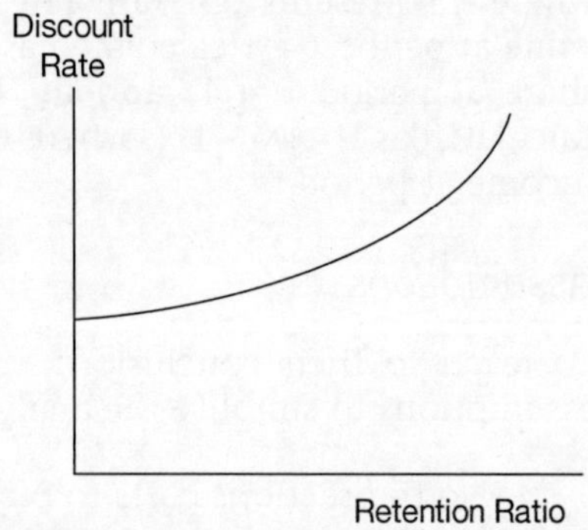

Notice that if the condition $|g| < K_e$ is violated, the formula $P_0 = \frac{D_1}{K_e - g}$ gives a negative answer. However, this does not mean that the value of the share is negative; rather, it means that the basic condition has been violated. In finance examples, violations of $|g| < K_e$ usually occur for very fast growing firms, in which, at least for short periods of time, we anticipate very high growth rates, so that $|g| < K_e$. In this case, the original dividend discount formula shows that P_0 will have an infinite value. Since this result is clearly unreasonable (remember that we are valuing a security), it probably means either (a) that the long-term growth rate is less than the discount rate K_e, or (b) that the discount rate K_e is too low.

The Gordon model is quite similar to the Walter model with one extension. Walter assumed that when expected return from investment is equal to cost of capital, the decision maker will be indifferent. However, Gordon argues that dividend policy affects the value of share in such a situation as well. The investors are rational in terms of risk avoidance. The future dividend is uncertain both with respect to the amount and the timing and thus the shareholders prefer current dividend. The retained earnings are evaluated as a risky promise that affects stock prices adversely. Thus, the discount rate would vary with the level of retained earnings as shown in Table 7.1. The omission of dividends would lower the value of the shares. For a dummy firm, the application of the Gordon model is presented below. It shows how g and K_e are calculated.

Table 7.1 Computations under Gordon Model

	A	*B*	*C*	*D*	*E*
1					
2					
3	1988	0.15			
4	1989	0.17	13.33%		
5	1990	0.21	23.53%		
6	1991	0.25	19.05%		
7	1992	0.30	20.00%		

	A	B	C	D	E
8	1993	0.34	13.33%		
9	1994	0.38	11.76%		
10	1995	0.42	10.53%		
11	1996	0.48	14.29%		
12	1997	0.54	12.50%		
13	1998	0.60	11.11%		
14	Compound growth, 10 yr		14.87%	= (B13/B3)^(1/10) – 1	
15	Compound growth, 5 yr		12.03%	= (B13/B8)^(1/5) – 1	
16					
17	Gordon model				
18	P_0		49.00	(1998 share price)	
19	D_0		0.60	(1998 dividend)	
20	K_e				
21	At 10-year growth		16.28%	= B19 * (1 + C14)/B18 + C14	
22	At 5-year growth		13.40%	= B19 * (1 + C15)/B18 + C15	

Source: Authors.

7.11.4 Walter Model

The Water model makes dividend relevant for maximizing the value of the shareholders. Investment policy of a firm is interlinked with dividend policy. According to Walter, firms will decide whether to pay dividend or not on the basis of available investment opportunities. If the firm has investment opportunities generating a return (r) more than that of the cost of capital (k, expected return of shareholders), the firm should retain earning. However, if it is believed that the available investment opportunities cannot earn at least the cost of capital, then it should pay dividend. In such a situation, shareholders themselves will invest their funds in some projects to maximize their wealth in a better way than the firm. Thus, the Walter model suggests making a comparison between the rates and concludes:

$r > k$	Retain earnings for investing in profitable business to maximize wealth of shareholders
$r = k$	Pay dividends to maximize the wealth of shareholders by themselves
$r < k$	Indifferent

Assumptions

The critical assumptions of the Walter model are as follows:

1. All financing is done through retained earnings
2. Business risk of the firm remains constant. Additional investment adds no risk to r and k
3. Firm has perpetual life
4. Beginning EPS and DPS remain unchanged

Interpretation

The formula derived by Professor Walter shows how the dividend policy can be used to maximize the wealth of the equity holders. He argues that in the long run, the share prices reflect only the present value of the expected dividends. Retentions influence share price through their effect on further dividends. According to him, the relationship between dividends and share prices can be shown on the basis of the following formula:

$$P = \frac{D + \frac{r}{k}(EPS - DPS)}{k}$$

Here, P represents market value of the ordinary shares of the company, r represents return on internal retention (the rate company earns on retained profits), k represents capitalization rate (the rate expected by the investors by way of return from the particular category of shares), EPS represents earnings per share and DPS represents dividend per share.

A close study of the formula would indicate that Professor Walter emphasizes two factors that influence the market price of a share. The first is the DPS and the second is the relationship between internal return on retained earnings and the market expectation from that company as reflected in the capitalization rate. In other words, if the internal return of retained earnings is higher than the market capitalization rate, the value of the ordinary shares would be high even if the dividends are low. However, if the internal return within the business is lower than what the market expects, the value of the share would be low. In such a case, the shareholders would prefer that a higher dividend is declared so that they can utilize the funds so obtained elsewhere in more profitable opportunities.

The formula by Professor Walter explains to a great extent the dividend practices of companies. The formula explains that the growth companies may even pay low dividends, still the prices of their shares will not come down, rather they will go up. It also explains why the market price of shares of certain companies who pay higher dividends and retain very low profits is also high. In fact, the market price of shares is dependent upon two factors.

First, the quantum of dividend and second, the profitable opportunities available to the company in investing the monies retained. When a company retains a part of its profits, it has to think in terms of the cost of such retention. The retention of profits depends upon whether it is cheaper and more profitable for the shareholders of the company to have the corporate earnings retained in the business or get the same in the form of cash dividend. This involves a comparison between the cost of retained earnings and the cost of distributing them. The cost of retained earnings, therefore, involves an opportunity cost, that is, the benefits which the shareholders forgo in terms of the leaving funds in the business. These considerations help the companies shape their dividend policies.

7.11.5 Lintner Model

In the 1950s, Lintner conducted a classic series of interviews with corporate managers about their dividend policy. He then proceeded to formulate a seemingly logical model of how companies decide on dividend payments. The findings of Lintner's survey can be summarized in four 'stylized facts' as interpreted by Marsh and Merton:

1. Firms have long-term target dividend payout ratios.
2. Managers focus more on dividend changes than on absolute levels.

3. Dividend changes follow shifts in long-term, sustainable earnings. This trend implies that managers tend to 'smooth' dividends so that changes in transitory earnings are unlikely to affect dividend payments over the short term.
4. Managers are reluctant to make changes to dividends that might have to be reversed. They are particularly concerned about having to rescind a dividend increase.

Lintner's model is consistent with these facts and provides a good intuitive explanation of dividend payments. The essence of Lintner's dividend model is that, if a firm persisted with its target payout ratio, then the dividend payment in the ensuing year (DIV1) would equal a constant proportion of EPS (EPS1), or

$$\text{DIV1} = \text{target ratio} \times \text{EPS1}$$

If a firm is adhered to its target payout ratio, it would change its dividend whenever its earnings changed. However, the managers in Lintner's survey were reluctant to do this. They believed that shareholders prefer a steady progression in dividends. If, for instance, circumstances appeared to warrant a large increase in their company's dividend, they would move only partially towards their target dividend. Their dividend changes appear to conform to the following model:

$$\begin{aligned} \text{DIV1} - \text{DIV0} &= \text{adjustment rate} \times \text{target change} \\ &= [\text{adjustment rate} \times (\text{target ratio} \times \text{EPS1}) - \text{DIV0}] \end{aligned}$$

This equation can be rewritten in a summarized form as

$$\text{D1} - \text{D0} = \text{a} \times (\text{TE1} - \text{D0}) = \text{aTE1} - \text{aD0}$$

Here, a represents adjustment rate, T represents target rate, D1 represents current dividend, D_0 represents previous dividend and E1 represents current earnings. The equation states Lintner's model as it is discussed by Brealey and Myers. The next question to be addressed is: How this equation can be fitted to empirical data, preferably by least squares estimates, in order to estimate values for the adjustment rate (a) and the target rate (T) of dividend payments for any specific company.

7.11.6 Tax Preference Theory

Low dividends increase stock value. Dividends received are taxable in the current period. Taxes on capital gains, however, are deferred into the future when the stock is actually sold. In addition, the maximum tax rate on capital gains is usually lower than the tax rate on ordinary income. Therefore, low dividend payout ratios will lower K_e (reducing the cost of capital), raise g, and increase stock price.

Retained earnings lead to capital gains, which are taxed at lower rates than dividends—28% maximum versus 39.6%. Capital gains taxes are also deferred. This could cause investors to prefer firms with low payouts, that is, a high payout results in a low Po.

There are three ways in which taxes affect the dividend preferences of shareholders.

1. For individual investors, tax rates differ for capital gains and dividends.
2. Taxes on capital gains are not due until the stock is sold.
3. If the stock is held until the shareholder expires, no tax is due at all.

For years the capital gains rate was significantly below the dividend income rate, prompting many companies to retain more income, and declare smaller dividends. However, if there is no difference between taxes paid on regular income and capital gains, tax preference theory will not work. With the Jobs and Growth Tax Relief Reconciliation Act of 2003, the dividend tax rate has fallen sharply. In some countries, tax rate on dividend have even been reduced to encourage investments in the stock market. In such situations, the preference of dividends will be more than capital gain due to tax preference.

Exhibit 7.2 Tax Preference Theory

Jumping on the Dividend Bandwagon

The tax cut makes equity attractive in more ways than one:

The dividend tax cut signed into law by President Bush in late May already is leading some publicly traded companies to boost the dividends they pay shareholders, hoping it will help the share price. And even those that can't afford to offer much in the way of dividends may find a way to benefit from other parts of the tax law changes.

Last week Goldman Sachs and Bank of America joined the companies that have jumped on the dividend bandwagon. Goldman last week more than doubled its dividend to $0.25 per share, and BofA raised its quarterly dividend 25% to $0.80, from $0.64.

One of the first companies to anticipate the dividend tax cut was Microsoft Corp., which announced its first-ever annual dividend, of $0.16, in January....

Still, it's equity dividends that have suddenly become more attractive to investors. That has many publicly traded companies suddenly revisiting how they use their free cash. Many now are favoring dividends over their previous stock-boosting efforts, such as tax-advantaged share buybacks.

Source: Britt Erica Tunick, from *Investment Dealers' Digest*, June 30, 2003.

7.11.7 Agency Theory

Agency theory supports payment of dividend due to reduced agency costs. The argument in favour of generous dividend payments is to make the owners active in the reinvestment decision by them to maximize their wealth. Agency problem originates from the sense that managers may not necessarily always act to maximize shareholders' wealth. The problem here is the separation of ownership and control, which gives rise to agency conflicts. When the levels of retained earnings are high, managers may channel funds into bad projects either in order to advance their own interests or due to incompetency. Hence, generous dividend policy enhances the firm's value because it can be used to reduce the amount of FCFs in the discretion of the management and thus controls the overinvestment problem.

Transaction cost theory proposes that generous dividend policy reduces FCFs and reduces the value of the firm due to the rise of costly external financing. However, agency theory believes that this extra cost of rising external financing is mediated by reducing agency conflicts. The idea is that the payment of dividends is one possible solution to the problem of collective action that tends to lead to monitoring of the firm and its management. The payment of dividends and the subsequent raising of external finance induce investigation by financial intermediaries such as investment banks, regulators of the securities exchange where the firm's stock is traded and potential investors. Again, the concept of agency costs should be considered from both shareholders' and debt holders' point of view. Agency costs from the viewpoint of debt holders come from potential wealth transfer from bond to equity holders through assets' substitutions. Agency theory also addresses this problem through giving dividends to the shareholders and raising debt for reinvestment on new debt contracts to reduce the potential for wealth transfer.

7.11.8 The Signalling Theory

Signalling theory is based on the idea of information asymmetries between different participants in the market and in particular between managers and investors. Under such conditions, managers use the costly payment of dividend as to signal the market on its prospect. The firm may be temporarily undervalued when investors have to meet their liquidity needs. If investors sell their holdings when the firm is undervalued, then there is a wealth transfer from old to new shareholders. However, the firm can save losses to existing shareholders by paying dividends. Although investors pay taxes on the dividends, the benefits from holding on to the undervalued firm more than offset these extra tax costs. A poor-quality firm would not mimic the dividend behaviour of an undervalued firm because holding on to overvalued shares does not increase wealth.

The signalling hypothesis can explain the preference for dividends over stock repurchases in spite of the tax advantage of the latter. Particularly, the regular dividend signals an ongoing commitment to pay out cash. This signal is consistent with Linter's observation that managers are typically reluctant to decrease dividend levels. However, unlike regular dividends, repurchases and special dividends can be used to signal prospects without long-term commitment to higher payouts. Therefore, announcements of increases in regular dividends signal permanent improvements in performance and should be interpreted as confidence in the firm on behalf of managers, thus triggering a price rise. Conversely, announcements of dividend decreases should be interpreted as signalling poor performance and lack of managerial confidence and should therefore trigger drops in prices.

If changes in the levels of dividend release information to the market, then firms can reduce price volatility and influence share prices by paying dividends. However, it is only unexpected changes that have an informative value and that can thus impact prices. Therefore, the value of the signal depends on the level of information asymmetries in the market. For example, in developing countries where capital markets are typically less efficient and where information is not as reliable as in more sophisticated markets, the signalling function of dividend may be more important. However, the dividend impact on prices is only temporary as information will eventually be revealed whether or not the dividend signal is sent.

7.11.9 The Transaction Cost Theory

Transaction cost theory puts emphasis on transaction costs incurred by both investors and company relating to dividend. Firms may incur costs in distributing dividends while investors may also incur costs in collecting and reinvesting these payments. Moreover, both firms and investors may incur costs when, due to paying dividends, the firm has to raise external finance in order to meet investment needs. Indeed, the transaction costs incurred in having to resort to external financing is the cost of dividend. In contrast, dividends are beneficial as they save the transaction costs associated with selling stocks for consumption purposes. Either way, if there are additional transaction costs that are associated with paying or not paying dividends, then dividend policy should impact earnings expectations and hence share price and firm value.

Alternatively, dividends may influence value if dividend policy has an impact on the management's investment decisions. For example, managers may decide to forgo positive NPV investments because dividend payments exhausted internal finance and raising external funds involves transaction or other costs. Thus, cost of dividend may also arise from managers' decision of cutting investment proposals with positive NPVs. In such a situation, if the management pays dividend and still wants to avail positive NPV projects, they have to go for external financing with the incurrence of transaction costs that decreases shareholders wealth. Transaction costs include flotation costs to the firm by raising additional external finance such as underwriter fees, administration costs, management time and legal expenses. Further, when the firm pays dividend and then has to raise additional external finance, existing shareholders suffer dilution of control. Thus, to maintain control or for other reasons, existing shareholders may subscribe to the new issue, incurring trading costs such as stamp duty and stockbrokers' commissions. Ultimately, all these transaction costs are reflected in the share price and firm value.

In addition to explicit transaction costs, there are also less obvious costs that are associated with paying dividend and resorting to external finance, and which are due to information asymmetries and pecking order considerations. Particularly, raising new equity can be costly if it comes at a time when the shares are temporarily undervalued or due to the signals this action sends to the market regarding the value of the firm. Similarly, debt issues are also problematic because the announcement of the issue may be associated with increased probability of default and with managers trying to issue debt before such bad news is revealed. Like explicit transaction costs, these less obvious costs should also impact earnings expectations and be reflected in the firm's share price and value.

Due to the transaction costs associated with external finance, the transaction cost theory suggests that firms should utilize retained earnings to the extent possible. Dividend should only be paid when this does not require any external financing for investment. Again, small firms are likely to find the payment of dividends more costly as compared with larger firms due to their difficulties of rising external financing from the market. The growth firms who are small have a lot of reinvestment proposals and thus have low payout ratio due to the avoidance of transaction costs. Thus, transaction cost theory implies the following:

1. Give generous dividend when there are no positive NPV projects under consideration and thus no requirements of external financing that may incur additional transaction costs.
2. Have a low payout ratio when transaction costs on external financing for investment in positive NPV projects are high.

7.12 Implications of Three Theories

The three theories presented earlier have sharp distinction. Their implications are also remarkable. Dividend irrelevance theory votes for any or no dividend as it has no effect on value of the firm. Because dividend decision is a financing decision and only investment decision affects the value, bird-in-the-hand theory votes for higher dividend as capital gains are riskier. Higher dividend in the current period reduces K_e and thus increases value. On the other hand, tax preference theory brings tax issue on dividend and capital gain and votes for lower dividend that will increase the value of the firm. Possible effects of these theories on stock price and cost of equity are presented in Figure 7.1.

Theory	*Implication*
Irrelevance	Any payout is OK
Bird in the hand	Set high payout
Tax preference	Set low payout

Figure 7.1 Possible Effects of Dividend Irrelevance Theory, Bird-in-the-hand Theory and Tax Preference Theory on Stock Price and Cost of Equity

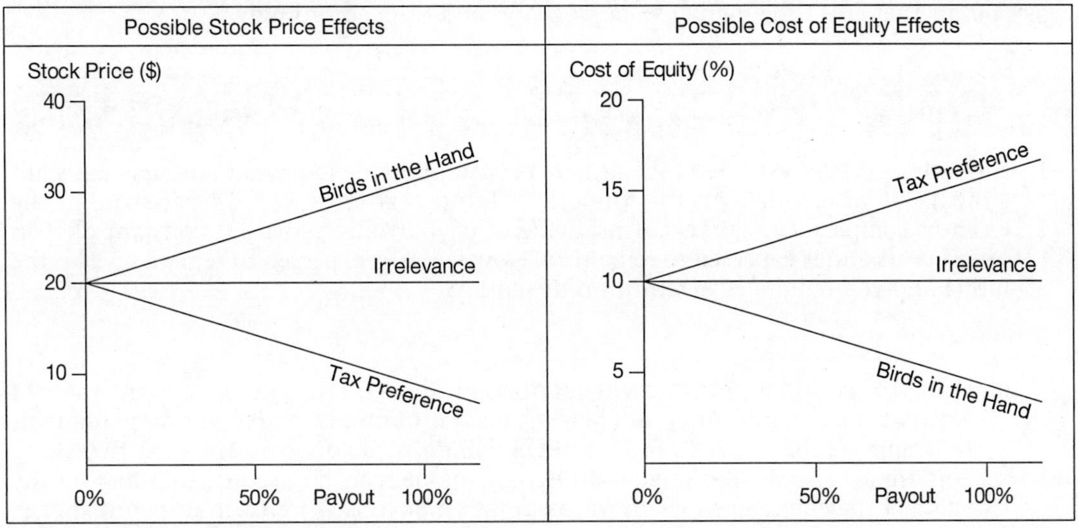

7.13 Stock Repurchases

Stock repurchases refers to the purchasing and retiring of stock by the issuing corporation. A repurchase is a partial liquidation since it decreases the number of shares outstanding. It may also be thought of as an alternative to cash dividends. There may be a large number of reasons that support the behaviour of the management at the time of stock repurchases:

1. Investment in treasury, giving the signal in the market that stock is undervalued.
2. Increase debt–equity ratio.
3. Eliminate certain stockholders (targeted).
4. Tax benefits.
5. Using the shares for some other purposes.
6. To increase EPS and ROE resulting in a higher market price.
7. To reduce the chance of a hostile takeover.

In some countries like Bangladesh, stock repurchases are restricted to save the capital market from unscrupulous investors. Stock exchanges carefully observe this sort of transaction to control the unexpected game in the market.

7.14 Conclusion

There is great variation in dividend policies of firms in different parts of the world. In most parts of the world, dividend policies are based on local tax laws. For example, in countries where the tax on capital gains is less than the tax on dividends, firms tend to retain greater amounts of earnings than in countries where the tax on dividends is relatively small. Also, in countries that have few regulations to protect small stockholders, companies tend to pay greater amounts of earnings as divided.

Dividend may not be a compulsory payment, but shareholders always expect to have a good amount of dividend. And, obviously, the amount of dividend declared by a firm affects the market price of a firm and thereby the value. The degree may vary from market to market due to other factors that actively affect market price. Thus, managers should understand the trigger points that affect the market value of shares and react accordingly.

Problems and Solutions

1. Novex Industrial is expected to maintain a constant dividend payout ratio and constant growth rate of earnings for the foreseeable future. Earnings were \$4 per share in the recently completed fiscal year. The dividend payout ratio has been constant 50% in recent years and is expected to remain so. Novex ROE is expected to remain 15% in the future and you require 12% return on the equity.

Required:

a. Using the constant growth dividend discount model, calculate the current value of Novex equity shares. After an aggressive acquisition and marketing programme, it now appears that Novex's EPS and ROE will grow rapidly over the next two years. You are aware that the dividend discount model can be useful in estimating the value of the equity even when the assumption of constant growth does not apply.
b. Calculate the current value of Novex's equity using the dividend discount model, assuming that the Novex dividend will grow at a 20% rate for the next two years, returning in the third year to the historical growth rate for the foreseeable future.

Answer:

NOVEX Industries

a. Constant growth (single-stage) dividend discount model:-

$Vo = D_1\ (k - g)$
Vo = Value at the beginning.
D_1 = Next-year dividend.
K = Required rate of return.
G = Constant growth rate.
D_1 = [EPS] (1 + g) D/P ratio
= (\$4.00) (1 + 0.06) (0.50)
= \$2.12
K = given 12% or 0.12
G = (ROE) (1 – 0.50)
= (0.15)(0.50) = 0.075
Vo = \$2.12/(0.12 – 0.015)
= \$47.11.

b. Multistage dividend discount model (where g_1 = 20% and $g_2 = V_1$

$V_1 = D_1/(1 + k) + D_2/(1+k)^2 + D_3/(k - g_2)/(1 + k)^2$
D_1 = [EPS] (1 + g) D/P ratio
= \$4.00 (1.20) (0.50)
= \$2.40
$D_2 = D_1\ (1 + g_1)$
= \$2.40 (1.20)
= \$2.88

$K = \text{given } 12\% \text{ or } 0.12$
$G_2 = 0.075$
$D_3 = D_2\,(1 + g_2)$
$= \$2.88\,(1.075)$
$= \$3.096$
$Vo = \$2.40/1.12 + (\$2.88)/(1.12)^2 + [\$3.096/0.12 - 0.075)/(1 + k)^2$
$= \$2.143 + \$2.296 + \$54.847$
$= \$59.29$

2. X Limited earns $6 per share having a capitalization rate of 10% and has an ROI at the rate of 20%. According to Walter's model, what should be the price per share at 30% dividend payout ratio? Is this the optimal payout ratio as per Walter?

Answer:

Walter model is $V_c = \dfrac{D + \dfrac{R_a}{R_c}(E - D)}{R_c}$

Market value of the share $= \dfrac{1.80 + \dfrac{0.20}{0.10}(6 - 1.80)}{0.10}$

$$P = \frac{1.80 + \frac{0.20}{0.10}(4.20)}{0.10}$$

$$P = \frac{1.80 + 8.40}{0.10}$$

$P = \$102$

This is not the optimum payout ratio because $R_a > R_c$ and therefore V_c can further go up if the payout ratio is reduced.

3. The following numbers in dollars are collected from the annual report of XYZ Limited:

	Amount ($)
Net profit	3,000,000
Outstanding 12% preferred stocks	10,000,000
Number of equity shares	300,000
Return on investments	20%

What should be the approximate dividend payout ratio so as to keep the share price at $42 by using the Walter model?

Answer:

	Amount ($)
Net profit	3,000,000
Less: Preferred dividend	1,200,000
Earnings available to equity shareholders	1,800,000
Number of equity shares	300,000
EPS	6

Cost of capital (K_e) is assumed to be 16%.
Let the dividend payout ratio be X and so the share price will be

$$P = \frac{D}{K_e} + \frac{\frac{r(E-D)}{K_e}}{K_e}$$

Here, D = 6x; E = \$6; r = 0.20 and K_e = 0.16 and P = \$42.
Hence,

$$42 = \frac{6}{0.16} + \frac{0.2(6-6)}{0.16 \times 6.16}$$

Or

$$42 = 37.50X + 46.875\ (1 - x)$$
$$= 9.375x = 4.875$$
$$X = 0.52$$

So the required dividend payout rate will be = 52%.
Note: Students can assume any percentage other than 16%.

4. The following information pertains to Y Company Limited:

	Amount (\$)
Earnings of the company	500,000
Dividend payout ratio	60%
Number of equity shares	100,000
Return on investments	20%
Rate of return on investment	15%

a. What would be the market value per share as per Walter's model?
b. What is the optimum dividend payout ratio according to Walter's model and the market value of the company's share at that payout ratio?

Answer:

Walter's model is given by

$$P = \frac{D + (E-D)\left(\frac{r}{K_e}\right)}{K_e}$$

where P is the market price per share, E is the EPS = \$5, D is the DPS = \$3, r is the return earned on investment = 15%, K_e is the cost of equity capital = 12% and

$$P = \frac{3 + (5-3)\left(\frac{0.15}{0.012}\right)}{0.12} = \frac{3 + (2)\left(\frac{0.15}{0.012}\right)}{0.12} = \$45.83$$

a. According to Walter's model when the ROI is more than the cost of equity capital, the price per share increases as the dividend payout ratio decreases. Hence, the optimum dividend payout ratio in this case is nil.

b. So, at a payout ratio of zero, the market value of the company's share will be:

$$\frac{0+(5-0)(0.15/0.012)}{0.12}=\$52.08$$

5. A company has a book value per share of $137.80. Its ROE is 15% and follows a policy of retaining 60% of its annual earnings. If the opportunity cost of capital is 18%, what is the price of its share? (Adopt the perpetual growth model to arrive at your solution.)

   Answer: EPS = $137.8 × 0.15 = $20.67
   Dividend = 0.40 × 20.67 = $8.27
   The growth in dividend would be:
   g = 0.6 × 0.15 = 0.09
   Perpetual growth model formula: $P_0 = \frac{\text{Dividend}}{K_e - g}$

   $$P_0 = \frac{8.27}{0.18-0.09}$$

   P_0 = $91.89

Multiple Choice Questions

1. If a firm adopts a residual distribution policy, distributions are determined as a residual after funding the capital budget. Therefore, the better the firm's investment opportunities, the lower should be its payout ratio.
   a. True
   b. False
2. Even if a stock split has no information content, and even if the DPS adjusted for the split is not increased, there can still be a real benefit (i.e., a higher value for shareholders) from such a split, but any such benefit is probably small.
   a. True
   b. False
3. Which of the following should not influence a firm's dividend policy decision?
   a. The firm's ability to accelerate or delay investment projects.
   b. A strong preference by most shareholders for current cash income versus capital gains.
   c. Constraints imposed by the firm's bond indenture.
   d. The fact that much of the firm's equipment has been leased rather than bought and owned.
   e. The fact that Congress is considering changes in the tax law regarding the taxation of dividends versus capital gains.
4. Which of the following would be most likely to lead to a 'decrease' in a firm's dividend payout ratio?
   a. Its earnings become more stable.
   b. Its access to the capital markets increases.
   c. Its R&D efforts pay off, and it now has more high-return investment opportunities.
   d. Its accounts receivable decrease due to a change in its credit policy.
   e. Its stock price has increased over the last year by a greater percentage than the increase in the broad stock market averages.

5. If a firm adheres strictly to the residual dividend policy, then if its optimal capital budget requires the use of all earnings for a given year (along with new debt according to the optimal debt/total assets ratio), then the firm should pay
   a. No dividends except out of past retained earnings.
   b. No dividends to common stockholders.
   c. Dividends only out of funds raised by the sale of new common stock.
   d. Dividends only out of funds raised by borrowing money (i.e., issue debt).
   e. Dividends only out of funds raised by selling off fixed assets.
6. Which of the following statements is correct?
   a. The tax code encourages companies to pay dividends rather than retain earnings.
   b. If a company uses the residual dividend model to determine its dividend payments, dividends payout will tend to increase whenever its profitable investment opportunities increase.
   c. The stronger management thinks the clientele effect is, the more likely is the firm to adopt a strict version of the residual dividend model.
   d. Large stock repurchases financed by debt tend to increase EPS, but they also increase the firm's financial risk.
   e. A dollar paid out to repurchase stock is taxed at the same rate as a dollar paid out in dividends. Thus, both companies and investors are indifferent between distributing cash through dividends and stock repurchases programmes.
7. P&D Co. has a capital budget of $1,000,000. The company wants to maintain a target capital structure which is 30% debt and 70% equity. The company forecasts that its net income this year will be $800,000. If the company follows a residual dividend policy, what will be its total dividend payment?
   a. $100,000 b. $200,000 c. $300,000 d. $400,000
   e. $500,000
8. Ting Technology has a capital budget of $850,000. It wants to maintain a target capital structure of 35% debt and 65% equity, and it also wants to pay a dividend of $400,000. If the company follows a residual dividend policy, how much net income must it earn to meet its capital budgeting requirements and pay the dividend, all while keeping its capital structure in balance?
   a. $904,875 b. $952,500 c. $1,000,125 d. $1,050,131
   e. $1,102,638
9. Brooks Corp.'s projected capital budget is $2,000,000, its target capital structure is 60% debt and 40% equity, and its forecasted net income is $600,000. If the company follows a residual dividend policy, what total dividends, if any, will it pay out?
   a. $240,000 b. $228,000 c. $216,600 d. $205,770
   e. $0
10. D. Paul Inc. forecasts a capital budget of $725,000. The CFO wants to maintain a target capital structure of 45% debt and 55% equity, and it also wants to pay dividends of $500,000. If the company follows the residual dividend policy, how much income must it earn, and what will its dividend payout ratio be?

	Net Income	Payout
a.	$898,750	55.63%
b.	$943,688	58.41%
c.	$990,872	61.34%
d.	$1,040,415	64.40%
e.	$1,092,436	67.62%

11. Dentaltech Inc. projects the following data for the coming year. If the firm follows the residual dividend policy and also maintains its target capital structure, what will its payout ratio be?

EBIT	$2,000,000	Capital budget	$850,000
Interest rate	10%	% Debt	40%
Debt outstanding	$5,000,000	% Equity	60%
Shares outstanding	$5,000,000	Tax rate	40%

a. 37.2% b. 39.1% c. 41.2% d. 43.3%
e. 45.5%

12. Keys Financial has done extremely well in recent years, and its stock now sells for $175 per share. The management wants to get the price down to a more typical level, which it thinks is $25 per share. What stock split would be required to get to this price, assuming the transaction has no effect on the total market value? Put another way, how many new shares should be given per one old share?
a. 6.65 b. 6.98 c. 7.00 d. 7.35
e. 7.72

Discussion Questions

1. What is the scope of dividend policy? What are the different types of dividends?
2. What are the factors that influence dividend policy?
3. How investors are affected due to dividend policy? Discuss in terms of signalling effect, clientele effect and FCF hypothesis.
4. What are the different types of dividend policies? How the amount of dividend is calculated under residual dividend policy?
5. Which factors you will consider at the time of selecting high dividend stock?
6. What are DRIPs? How DRIPs are operated? What are the benefits of DRIPs?
7. Make a comparative discussion between stock dividend and stock split with its possible effects.
8. What are the different types of dividend theories? Make a comparative discussion between dividend relevance and dividend irrelevance theory.
9. What are the basic issues underlying bird-in-the-hand theory and tax preference theory of dividend?
10. How does the Gordon model differ from the Walter model of dividend?
11. Make a comparative presentation among birds in the hand, tax preference and dividend irrelevance theory on stock prices and cost of capital.

Exercises

1. Agile Manufacturer has a capital budget of $1,000,000, but it wants to maintain a target capital structure of 60% debt and 40% equity. The company forecasts this year's net income to be $600,000. If the company follows a residual dividend policy, what will be its dividend paid?
2. If Consolidated Power is priced at $50.00 with dividend, and its price falls to $46.50 when a dividend of $5.00 is paid, what is the implied marginal rate of personal taxes

for its stockholders? Assume that the tax on capital gains is 40% of the personal income tax.

3. You are comparing the dividend policies of three dividend-paying utilities. You have collected the following information on the ex-dividend behaviour of these firms.

	NE Gas	*SE Bell*	*Western Electric*
Price before	50	70	100
Price after	48	67	95
Dividends/share	4	4	5

If you were a tax-exempt investor, which company would you use to make 'dividend arbitrage' profits? How would you go about doing so?

4. Southern Rail has just declared a dividend of $1. The average investor in Southern Rail faces an ordinary tax rate of 50%. Although the capital gains rate is also 50%, it is believed that the investor gets the advantage of deferring this tax until future years (the effective capital gains rate will therefore be 50% discounted back to the present). If the price of the stock before the ex-dividend day is $10 and it drops to $9.20 by the end of the ex-dividend day, how many years is the average investor deferring capital gains taxes? (Assume that the opportunity cost used by the investor in evaluating future cash flows is 10%.)
5. LMN Corporation, a real-estate company, is planning to pay a dividend of $0.50 per share. Most of the investors in LMN are other corporations that pay 40% of their ordinary income and 28% of their capital gains as taxes. However, they are allowed to exempt 85% of the dividends they receive from taxes. If the shares are selling at $10 per share, how much would you expect the stock price to drop on the ex-dividend day?
6. UJ Gas is a utility that has followed a policy of increasing dividends every quarter by 5% over dividends in the prior year. The company announces that it will increase quarterly dividends from $1.00 to $1.02 next quarter. What price reaction would you expect to the announcement? Why?
7. Microsoft, which has had a history of high growth and pays no dividends, announces that it will start paying dividends next quarter. How would you expect its stock price to react to the announcement? Why?
8. JC Automobiles is a small auto parts manufacturing firm. It has paid $1.00 in annual dividends each year for the past five years. It announces that dividends will increase to $1.25 next year. What would you expect the price reaction to be? Why? If your answer is different from the previous problem, explain the reasons for the difference.
9. Would your answer be different for the previous problem if JC Automobiles were a large firm followed by 35 analysts? Why or why not?
10. Wee Mart, a retailer of children's clothes, announces a cut in dividends following a year in which both revenues and earnings dropped significantly. How would you expect its stock price to react? Explain.
11. RJR Nabisco, in response to stockholder pressure in 1996, announced a significant increase in dividends paid to stockholders financed by the sale of some of its assets. What would you expect the stock price to do? Why?
12. RJR Nabisco also had $10 billion in bonds outstanding at the time of the dividend increase in problem 11. How would you expect the bonds to react to the announcement? Why?
13. When firms increase dividends, stock prices tend to increase. One reason given for this price reaction is that dividends operate as a positive signal. What is the increase in dividends signalling to markets? Will markets always believe the signal? Why or why not?

Case in Action

Dividend Policy: Microsoft vs. Berkshire Hathaway

Years ago, a financial media expert on CNBC, Mary Richards, said that 'the big question weighing heavily on everyone's minds was whether Bill Gates at Microsoft and Warren Buffett at Berkshire Hathaway (the two richest CEOs in the World) would ever initiate a pay out of dividends at their respective companies'. Ms Richards disagreed with the expectation of many shareholders who were waiting for a dividend payout'. Ms. Richards went on further to say, 'If it isn't broke don't fix it. Microsoft and Berkshire should continue to retain all earnings and hold large sums of cash for future investments'.

The second guest on the show, Alice Morgan, was an expert in Modigliani and Miller's 'dividend irrelevancy' proposition and said to Ms. Richards, 'I think that we are wasting our time about whether or not Microsoft and Berkshire should pay dividends. It doesn't impact stock prices. Moreover, those shareholders who don't like Microsoft's and Berkshire's dividend policy can create 'homemade dividends'. There are options to pursue such as the 'residual dividend' policy. Finally, I believe Gates and Buffett should maintain their current capital structure as being optimal'.

1. Comment on Ms. Richards's suggestion of not paying any dividend. What are the pros and cons of such a policy at Microsoft and Berkshire?
   Answer. Ms. Richards made it clear that she does not believe a dividend should be paid by either company. She must believe that these companies can internally invest the capital to grow their business because it is not a good financial move to sit on this amount of cash. It either should be working to grow the business, or being paid to investors in the form of a dividend.
   Some of the pros of dividends are that they are attractive to investors because they receive a cash return, stock price usually increases with the announcement of a dividend increase, dividends can absorb excess cash flows, cash cow companies who do not have a need to internally reinvest this capital can pay it out to the investors and investors can opt to automatically reinvest the dividend to increase their position in the stock. Cons involve double taxation (taxed as earnings and taxed at the capital gain rate for investors), dividends can reduce internal sources of financing, companies are expected to keep increasing dividends (even in lean years where they may have to borrow to pay the dividend), if the dividend is ever cut it harms the stock price (even if it is for a strategic internal growth project) and starting to pay a dividend is a negative sign to Wall Street because they could believe the stock is done growing. All of these pros and cons apply to both Microsoft and Berkshire.
2. What did Ms. Morgan mean when she said that shareholders who do not like Microsoft's or Berkshire's dividend policy can create 'homemade dividends?'
   Answer. A homemade dividend can occur from the investor that owns a stock that does not pay a dividend. If they want a 2% dividend, they can sell 2% of their holdings. This works well for investors of companies that do not pay a dividend, and whose investors like taking their dividend in cash. This does not work if the investor wants to reinvest the dividend, since that would be equal to not selling the stock in the first place.
   Here is an example of the homemade dividend:
   An investor owns 500 shares of EBAY at $30. The investor wants a 1% dividend; they can sell five shares for $150 in cash. In year 2 they will likely also sell five shares (rounding 4.95 up to 5).
3. Ms. Morgan referred to a residual dividend policy. How would a residual policy work for both Microsoft and Berkshire in terms of the DPS the companies could afford to pay, referring to the most recent financial information you have access to?

Answer. The residual dividend policy is used to finance new projects through equity that is internally generated. Dividend payments are made from the equity that remains after all the project capital needs are accounted for. This remaining equity on the balance sheet is known as residual equity. It is advisable that companies that follow the policy of residual dividend should maintain a balanced debt–equity ratio. This does not exist at Microsoft because it has no debt, but does apply to Berkshire. This policy is feasible for Berkshire to follow, but not advised because Berkshire should not pay a dividend. If Berkshire was to follow this policy, it would keep a 28% ratio of debt to equity.

4. Comment on whether Microsoft's or Berkshire's respective share price will suffer if dividends are not paid at Berkshire, or not continued to be paid at Microsoft, while the companies continue to hold such high amounts of cash and short-term marketable securities.

   Answer. Berkshire's share price will not suffer because their stock has not paid a dividend in the past. They have reinvested the capital internally and have seen great returns that have beat the market. Berkshire investors are not looking for a dividend either, or they would not have tied up a minimum of $130,000 in the stock.

   Microsoft's share price will likely suffer due to the fact that the street has been expecting them to increase dividends. They sat on very large amounts of cash for so long, not reinvesting it, nor paying it out to investors that the investment community grew tired of Microsoft.

   Microsoft regained interest in their stock by paying a dividend, including a one-time 9% dividend. If Microsoft stopped paying a dividend, and did not have internal projects lined up, their stock will likely decrease in value upon news of the dividend cut.

5. In your opinion should either Microsoft or Berkshire pay a dividend?

   Answer. Microsoft should pay a dividend, but Berkshire should not. Microsoft has proven that they cannot find projects to invest their capital into, and in that case, I believe they should pay a dividend. I also believe if Microsoft pays a dividend, it will be more attractive to a larger pool of investors. Berkshire has been very successful in finding new companies to acquire, and have always had a good return on their investments. Berkshire should continue to be aggressive in purchasing new companies and earning their investors a better return than the market.

Source: http://www.mbacasestudysolutions.com/Blog/Dividend_Policy_MSFT_Berkshire_Hathaway.html

Case in Action

Info Edge (India) Limited

Dividend Policy

This policy will regulate the process of dividend declaration and its pay-out by the company in accordance with the provisions of the Companies Act, read with the applicable Rules framed thereunder, as may be in force for the time being ('Companies Act').

Preamble

Dividend is the payment made by a company to its shareholders, usually in the form of distribution of its profits. The profits earned by the company can either be retained in business or used for acquisitions, expansion or diversification, or it can be distributed to the shareholders. The company may choose to retain a part of its profits and distribute the balance among its shareholders as dividend. This policy aims to reconcile between all these needs.

The dividend payout of a company is driven by several factors. Some companies pay a lower dividend. The idea is to retain profits and invest it for further expansion and modernization of the business. On the other hand, there are companies which prefer to pay higher dividend. These companies may not necessarily be growth-oriented companies with greater emphasis on retaining their shareholder base.

The objective of this policy is to ensure a regular dividend income for the shareholders and long-term capital appreciation for all stakeholders of the company. The company would ensure to strike the right balance between the quantum of dividend paid and amount of profits retained in the business for various purposes. The board of directors will refer to the policy while declaring/recommending dividends on behalf of the company. Through this policy, the company would endeavour to maintain a consistent approach to dividend payout plans.

The company believes that it operates in the high potential and fast growing internet segment. This offers huge investment opportunities. Therefore, the retention of surplus funds for future growth will override considerations of returning cash to the shareholders. However, considering the consistent and impressive generation of profits year on year, there is a need to provide greater clarity on the dividend payout philosophy of the company.

Category of Dividends

The Companies Act provides for two forms of dividends—final and interim. The board of directors shall have the power to recommend final dividend to the shareholders for their approval in the general meeting of the company. The board of directors shall have the absolute power to declare interim dividend during the financial year, as and when they consider it fit.

a. Final Dividend

The final dividend is paid once for the financial year after the annual accounts are prepared. The board of directors of the company has the power to recommend the payment of final dividend to the shareholders in a general meeting. The declaration of the final dividend shall be included in the ordinary business items that are required to be transacted at the AGM.

Process for Approval of Payment of Final Dividend

1. Board to recommend quantum of final dividend payable to shareholders in its meeting in line with this policy;
2. Based on the profits arrived at as per the audited financial statements;
3. Shareholders to approve in AGM;
4. Once in a financial year.

b. Interim Dividend

This form of dividend can be declared by the board of directors one or more times in a financial year as may be deemed fit by it. The board of directors of the company would declare an interim dividend, as and when considered appropriate, in line with this policy. Normally, the board could consider declaring an interim dividend after finalization of quarterly (or half yearly) financial accounts. This would be in order to supplement the annual dividend or in exceptional circumstances.

Process for Approval of Payment of Interim Dividend

1. Board may declare interim dividend at its complete discretion in line with this policy;
2. Based on profits arrived at as per quarterly (or half-yearly) financial statements including exceptional items;
3. One or more times in a financial year.

Declaration of Dividend

Subject to the provisions of the Companies Act, dividend shall be declared or paid only out of

i. Current financial year's profit:
   a. after providing for depreciation in accordance with law;
   b. after transferring to reserves such amount as may be prescribed or as may be otherwise considered appropriate by the board at its discretion.
ii. The profits for any previous financial year(s):
   a. after providing for depreciation in accordance with law;
   b. remaining undistributed; or
iii. out of (i) and (ii) both.

Factors to Be Considered While Declaring Dividend

The decision regarding dividend payout is a crucial decision as it determines the amount of profit to be distributed among shareholders and amount of profit to be retained in business. The board of directors will endeavour to take a decision with an objective to enhance shareholders wealth and market value of the shares. However, the decision regarding payout is subject to several factors and, hence, any optimal policy in this regard may be far from obvious. The dividend payout decision of any company depends upon certain external and internal factors as identified below.

External Factors

1. State of Economy: In case of uncertain or recessionary economic and business conditions, the board will endeavour to retain larger part of profits to build up reserves to absorb future shocks.
2. Capital Markets: When the markets are favourable, dividend payout can be liberal. However, in case of unfavourable market conditions, the board may resort to a conservative dividend payout in order to conserve cash outflows.
3. Statutory Restrictions: The board will keep in mind the restrictions imposed by the Companies Act with regard to declaration of dividend.

Internal Factors

Apart from the various external factors aforementioned, the board will take into account various internal factors while declaring dividend, which inter alia will include

1. Profits earned during the year;
2. Present and future capital requirements of the existing businesses;
3. Brand/business acquisitions;
4. Expansion/modernization of existing businesses;
5. Additional investments in subsidiaries/associates of the company;
6. Fresh investments into external businesses;
7. Any other factor as deemed fit by the board.

Dividend Range

The company stands committed to deliver sustainable value to all its stakeholders. The company will strive to distribute an optimal and appropriate level of the profits earned by it in its business and investing activity, with the shareholders, in the form of dividend. As explained in the earlier part of this policy, determining the dividend payout is dependent upon several factors, both internal to a business and external to it. Taking into consideration the aforementioned factors, the board will endeavour to maintain a dividend payout in the range of 15%–25% of profits after tax (PAT) on standalone financials.

However, the board may amend the payout range, whenever considered appropriate by it, keeping in mind the aforesaid factors having a bearing on the dividend payout decision.

Review

This policy will be reviewed periodically by the board.

Source: http://www.infoedge.in/pdfs/Dividend-Policy.pdf

References

Brealey, R.A., and S.C. Myers. 1984. *Principles of Corporate Finance, 2nd Edition.* New York: McGraw Hill.

Gordon, M.J. 1962. *The Investment, Financing and Valuation of the Corporation.* Homewood, IL: Richard D. Irwin, Inc.

Lintner, J. 1956. 'Distribution of Incomes of Corporations among Dividends, Retained Earnings and Taxes'. *American Economic Review*, May, 97–113.

Marsh, Terry, and Robert C. Merton. 1986. *Dividend Variability and Variance Bounds Tests for the Rationality of Stock Market Prices. American Economic Review,* 76: 483–98.

Modigliani, F., and M.H. Miller. 1961. 'Dividend Policy, Growth and the Valuation of Shares'. *Journal of Business*. 34: 411–33

Walter, J.E. 1966. 'Dividend Policies and Common Stock Prices'. *Journal of Finance*. 11: 29–41.

Part C

Corporate Restructuring

Chapter 8

Corporate Restructuring: An Overview

Chapter Objectives

On completion of this chapter, you will be able to understand:

- Basics of corporate restructuring
- Meaning, definitions and a brief history of restructuring
- Motives behind corporate restructuring
  - Motives behind expansion
  - Motives behind corporate control
  - Motives behind contraction
  - Motives behind change in ownership structure of restructuring
- Significance of corporate restructuring
- Kinds/forms of corporate restructuring
  - Portfolio restructuring
  - Financial restructuring
  - Organizational restructuring
  - Technological restructuring
- Choice of corporate restructuring
  - Expansion
  - Contraction
  - Corporate control
  - Changes in ownership structure
- Present scenario of corporate restructuring
- Limitations of corporate restructuring

In this changed business paradigm, only those organizations rule who visualize the possibilities before they appear as plausible. The present business environment, characterized by globalization and liberalization, accommodates organizations that are coming up with innovative strategies to survive and flourish. In this punishing global economic climate, companies are thriving to reach the pinnacle of success seeking competitive edge over their rivals. While the waves of liberalization and deregulation have been shaking the corporate shore around the globe, the domestic organizations are falling prey to the fierce competition and unprecedented challenges carried by this emerging business scenario. The recessionary trend consequent to the Wall Street tsunami has made for the organizations a maze with no exit. Drowning in the luxury of producing goods only to keep life simple is suicidal, rather an unquenched thirst must always prevail that makes the quest for value sustainable. Falling Sensex, squeezed employment market and growing number of discerning consumer abash the managers to put a single step forward. An incessant quest with inventing intelligence alone can unfold the way to deliver superior performance and value for all the stakeholders. Existence of keen competition with its number and volume also made the texture of the competitors stronger and shock absorber both financially and strategically, creating a wide exposure for the business enterprises to build armour for protecting themselves from the threats lying in and forthcoming from the environment. Thus, organizations are left with no choice except becoming excellent in all respects, be it product or process, staff or shareholders, customers or creditors.

The aspiration for all the business concerns now is 'how to become world class'. So, corporate restructuring that brings excellence is inevitable to re-establish an organization's competitive advantage and respond more quickly and effectively to new opportunities and challenges. Business excellence, as the terminal station of all strategies, holds great promise for organizations that desire to transform themselves proactively to shape their destiny and the future of their stakeholders. Corporations all over the world are striving hard to achieve excellence that helps them navigate from their present condition to world class and, in turn, to satisfy their stakeholders. The resonating phrase 'business excellence', in its true sense, is the systematic and continuous improvement of business performance to get enlightened customers, efficient process management and increased shareholders' value. By improving an organization's culture, business excellence through strategic tools broadly channels and encourages the use of best practices into areas where its effect will be most beneficial to performance. Achieving business excellence and thereby creating value for a company are considered to be the most vital as well as significant objectives of today's business enterprises with an aim to ensure long-run survival and sustainable growth over time. Keeping this objective in mind, the concept of corporate restructuring has emerged. Corporate restructuring usually implies restructuring the corporate sector from multidimensional angles with a view to obtain competitive edge and thereby ensuring business success.

8.1 Meaning and Definitions

The word 'structure' used in an economic context implies a specific, stable relationship among the key elements of a particular function or process. To 'restructure' means the (hopefully) purposeful process of changing the structure of an institution: a company, an industry, a market, a country, the world economy and so on. This structure defines the constraints under which institutions function in their day-to-day operations and their pursuit of better economic performance.

a. The term 'restructuring' as per *Oxford dictionary,* means 'to give a new structure to rebuilt or rearrange'.
b. According to Sander et al., 'restructuring is an attempt to change the structure of an institution in order to relax some or all of the short-run constraints. It is concerned with changing structures in pursuit of a long run strategy'.
c. Crum and Goldberg define restructuring of a company as 'a set of discrete decisive measures taken in order to increase the competitiveness of the enterprise and thereby to enhance its value'.

We define corporate restructuring as a change in the operational structures, investment structures, financing structures and governance structure of a company. The objective of restructuring is to transform the company into an enterprise that is of high value to its owners. Exhibit 8.1 tries to provide an exclusive definition of corporate restructuring.

Simply stated, corporate restructuring is a comprehensive process by which a company can consolidate/split up its business operations and strengthen its positions for achieving its short-term as well as long-term corporate objectives, synergistic, dynamic and continuing as a competitive and successful entity.

Exhibit 8.1 In Search of an Exclusive Definition

'Corporate Restructuring' is a very wide and varied term having no legal definition. It has neither a clear and precise meaning nor it can be defined with precision. However, it indicates to:

a. Any change in the business capacity or portfolio that is carried out by an inorganic route; or
b. Any change in the capital structure of a company that is not a part of its ordinary course of business; or
c. Any change in the ownership of or control over the management of the company or a combination thereof.

Let us discuss the above points in detail below to have a clear meaning of corporate restructuring:

a. 1) Any change in the business capacity or portfolio carried out by inorganic route.
    - Tata Motors launched Sumo and later, Indica, leading to an expansion of its business portfolio. However, these products were launched from Tata Motor's own manufacturing capacity in through an organic route. Hence, it would not qualify as 'corporate restructuring'.
    - Tata Motors acquisition of Jaguar Land Rover from Ford, through Jaguar Land Rover Limited is 'corporate restructuring'.
    - Grasim's acquisition of Larsen & Toubro's (L&T) cement division through UltraTech Cement Limited is an example of 'corporate restructuring'.

   2) Change in the business portfolio could also be in the nature of reduction of business handled by a company.
    - In the case of Grasim and L&T, the demerger of L&T's cement business into UltraTech Cement Limited was reduction of its business portfolio and thus, amounted to 'corporate restructuring' of L&T.

b. Any change in the capital structure of a company that is not in the ordinary course of its business. This can be further explained with the help of the following:
    - Car finance loan
    - Scheduled repayment of a term loan, etc. keeps on changing the debt-equity ratio within planned or targeted range. Such changes do not qualify as 'corporate restructuring'. However,
        - An initial public issue
        - Follow-on public issue
        - Buy-back of equity shares may alter the capital structure of a Company permanently. Such activities are not in the ordinary course of business of company—amounts to 'corporate restructuring'.
    - Borrowing of a significant amount as term loan
    - Issue of five-year nonconvertible debentures, etc. Such changes may alter the debt-equity ratio significantly but still these do not qualify as leading to 'corporate restructuring.'

Capital structure refers to the debt equity ratio, that is, the proportion of debt and equity in the total capital of a company. This capital structure is never static and changes almost daily.

- If the debt/equity ratio fluctuates within a targeted or planned range, such changes in the capital structure do not amount to 'capital restructuring'.
- Borrowing of a significant amount of term loan or an issue of five year non-convertible debenture does not qualify to be called 'corporate restructuring'.
- An initial public issue, or a follow-on public issue or buy-back of equity shares would permanently alter the capital structure of a company and thus, would amount to 'corporate restructuring'

c. Any change in the ownership of a company or control over its management
   - Merger of two or more companies belonging to different promoters
   - Demerger of a company into two or more with control of the resulting company passing on to other promoters
   - Acquisition of a company
   - Sell-off of a company or its substantial assets
   - Delisting of a company

All these would qualify to be called exercises in 'corporate restructuring'.

8.2 Corporate Restructuring in India: A Historical Background

The financial crisis of the late 1990s devastated emerging market economies and presented considerable obstacles to achieve a sustainable recovery. The rises in unemployment, sharp jumps in interest rates, double-digit decline in output and plummeting exchange rates engendered considerable sufferings: enormous shifts in the profitability of business activities and a massive overhang of bankrupt corporations and bad loans on the balance sheets of banks.

Since the announcement of the new economic policy in July 1991, the Indian corporate sector has witnessed several changes and new challenges in the Indian economy. The tide of liberalizations, privatizations and globalization (LPG) has been speeded around the globe. In order to keep pace with the global rhythm of LPG, restructuring the corporate sector from multidimensional angles has acquired due importance in the Indian economy. The major policy changes introduced since July 1991 include: (a) abolition of industrial licensing; (b) lifting of restrictions on the size of firms; (c) drastic reduction in the areas reserved for the public sector; (d) disinvestments of government equity in public sector undertakings; (e) liberalization of foreign investment regulations; (f) liberalization of import tariffs; (g) removal of all quantitative restrictions on imports; (h) abolition of the office of the controller of capital issues and freedom to companies to set premium on their share issues; (i) freedom granted to the corporate sector to raise capital from abroad; (j) reducing the central excise and customs duties and (k) reducing income tax rates both for corporate and individual assessees.

Due to these policy changes, the corporate restructuring wave started in India from 1994. Of course, it was started by Suaraj Paul when he tried to take over Escorts. The other major restructuring were that of Ashok Leyland by the Hinduja's Shaw Wallace, Dunlop own Falcon Tyres by the Chabbaria group, Ceat Tyres by the Goenkas and Consolidated Coffee by Tata Tea, RIL and RPL merger, Tata Tea's leveraged buyout of Tetley and restructuring of Dabur India Ltd and so on.

While presenting the budget for the financial year 1999–2000, the then finance minister of India stressed

> [the need for corporate restructuring] with growing liberalizations of the economy has brought the need for corporate restructuring so that companies can focus better on their core activities. The corporate sector has been voicing the need for a flexible fiscal policy for regulating business reorganizations. In response to this need, I propose a comprehensive set of amendments in the Income Tax Act to make such business re-organizations fully tax neutral.

In paragraph 87 of the same budget, the finance minister focused on de-merger. The de-merger wave started in India from 2000–01 for availing huge amount of tax benefits, increasing corporate control and enhancing shareholders' value. So shareholders' value creation is of utmost importance in the present backdrop of corporate restructuring.

The former chairman and the CEO of Coca-Cola, Roberto C. Goizueta, made a lengthy statement in favour of value creation through corporate restructuring, which is reproduced below:

> At the Coca Cola Company, our publicly stated mission is to create value over time for the owners of our business. In fact, in our society, that is the mission of any business: to create value for its owners. We live in a democratic capitalist society, and here, people create specific institutions to help meet specific needs. Governments are created to help meet civic needs. Philanthropies are created to help meet social needs and companies are created to help meet economic needs. Business distributes the lifeblood that flows through economic system, not only in the form of goods and services, but also in the form of taxes, salaries and philanthropies. Creating value is a core principal on which our economic system is based; it is the job we owe to those who have entrusted us with their assets. We work for our shareowners. That is – literally – what they have put us in business to do. Saying that we work for our share owners may sound simplistic- but we frequently see companies that have forgotten the reason they exist. They may even try in vain to be all things to all people and serve many masters in many different ways. In any event, they miss their primary calling, which is to stick to the business of creating value for their owners.

Therefore, corporate restructuring is one of the means that can be employed to meet the challenges that confront business and also enhanced value for shareholders.

8.3 Motives Behind Corporate Restructuring

If we look at the motives behind corporate restructuring, we will find four separate sets of reasons for different choice of corporate structuring, namely, expansion, corporate control, contraction and change in ownership structure. The details of the reasons are presented here.

8.3.1 Motives Behind Expansion

Any single reason for expansion can be found irrelevant as it differs with situations and company's strategy. Important reasons for expansion can be subdivided as follows:

a. *Growth:* Every company wants to grow and corporate restructuring provides ways for the companies to throw off cash flows beyond its internal needs. At present, globalization demands an absolute level of size simply to be able to carry out the operations of the company.

b. *Technology:* Technology plays an important role as a driver in expansion strategy. Generally, a firm with improved and superior technology wants to engineer its technological superiority by acquiring firms of inferior technology. The reverse is also true as the firm with inferior technology may prefer to acquire technologically superior firm to sharpen its competitive edge.
c. *Product Advantage and Product Differentiation:* This reason gets more relevance in expansion internationally when a firm finds acceptance for its product abroad.
d. *Government Policy:* Different regulations, tax burden and other restrictions imposed by the government also induce companies to increase size. To enjoy specific advantage in different zone and in different economies company's first choice goes for acquiring a firm with existing facilities in that place.
e. *Exchange Rates:* This reason is specially identified with expansion leading to international mergers. Comparative strength or weakness of the domestic versus foreign currency makes a difference in price paid for acquisition, production costs and the value-repatriated profit to the parent.
f. *Political/Economic Stability:* Political stability, that is, the frequency with which a government changes, the order of transferring power and the change in the policy and outlook due to change in the administration becomes a decisive factor in expansion. Economic stability demands a low and predictable inflation rate, controlled industrial relations and so on.
g. *Differential Labour Costs, Productivity:* Difference in labour costs in different geographic region with its associated productivity certainly creates an impact in monitoring companies to expand.
h. *Diversification:* One of the important drivers for expansion is the diversification both geographically and by product line. It may come in the form of vertical integration, both forward and backward, which also helps in reducing risk.

Motives Behind Corporate Control

An important motive for corporate control is to ensure that a programme for the successful performance of the firm can be carried through without interruption. However, several other motives to gain corporate control remain, such as

a. *Improving Leverage Ratio*: To reinforce effective control, capital structure of the firm is changed. Adopting buyback mechanism, debt–equity ratio or leverage ratio is attempted to improve. This is because even if the amount of debt is not changed, the amount of common stock is reduced so the leverage ratio is increased.
b. *Utilization of Surplus Cash*: In order to increase shareholders' return and finally the wealth of shareholders, the firm may undertake the strategy of distributing surplus cash and thereby the firm is able to enhance the EPS. Thus, the company can maintain shareholders' value in a situation of poor state of the secondary market by a return of surplus cash to shareholders.
c. *Enhancement of Voting Power*: Another important motive of corporate control is to enhance the voting or controlling power of the promoters without spending own money.
d. *Preventing Undervaluation*: If the management believes that the common stock of the company is undervalued by the market, it can enhance control on the valuation of shares by buyback of the shares with a view to recognize true value of those shares as the announced buyback price is invariably higher than the prevailing market price.

e. *Anti-takeover Defence*: If the insiders judge the firm to be undervalued, they may have concerns that the firm is subject to a takeover bid at a relatively small premium. The large premium involved in the repurchase tender offer may convey information to the non-insiders that the value of the shares is at least as high as conveyed by the premium and may be perhaps even higher in the future.

Motives Behind Contraction

The company, trimming its size through demerger, anticipates the benefits of restructuring by outperforming the market indexes. A different mechanism shedding the business off through demerger takes place with a number of motivations such as the following:

a. *Improving Performance*: The accountability created by restructuring through demerger often improves performance, and investors also benefit from the greater visibility of the demerged entities to analysts and the public.
b. *Booming Independence*: Demerger is intended to promote independence as the separated company can operate freely at its own discretion. Often the function of this kind of restructuring is to move assets to owners who can utilize them more effectively. This helps the economic system move assets to their highest valued uses.
c. *Effort to Unlearn*: Some demerger effort is undoubtedly an attempt to correct previous investment decisions materialized through mergers and acquisitions. The firms' inability to effectively exploit the possible opportunities through consolidation motivate them to salvage a portion of their investments by separating where the opportunities could be exploited more effectively.
d. *Strategic Adjustment*: Sometimes, divestiture involves selling to a value-increasing buyer, which is planned before mergers and acquisitions activity. Such type of divestiture is pre-planned because they may represent a poor fit to the acquiring firm.
e. *Increasing Value:* Demerger represents harvesting value by unlocking the hidden value. By making financial and managerial resources available and concentrating on the core competency, the firm is able to enhance shareholders' value as well as value of the firm.

Motives Behind Change in Ownership Structure

Various motives act as drivers in restructuring activities that result in a change in the ownership structure. Some of them can be summarized as follows:

a. *Manoeuvring Leverage:* The most important reason for changes in ownership structure, whether debt-preferred stock is exchanged for common stock or, conversely, common stock for more senior claims, is to manoeuvre leverage of the firm.
b. *Alternation in the Control Structure:* Restructuring of this kind is aimed at changing the control structure of the firm. By repurchasing substantial percentage of shares or by initial public offerings, the firms want to reshuffle the voting rights of the shareholders to change the control pattern of the firm.
c. *Providing Fairness to Minority Shareholders:* A critical element in restructuring activities through going private transactions is fairness to minority or outside shareholders to avoid accusations of security fraud against controlling shareholders.
d. *Changing the Nature of Firm:* If a firm wants to come out from the regulations of the security and exchange board of respective country, it may prefer that a small group of investors will buy the entire equity interest in previous public corporations.

8.4 Significance of Corporate Restructuring

Corporate restructuring is a strategic decision leading to the maximization of the company's growth by enhancing its production and marketing operations, reduced competition, free flow of capital, globalization of business and so on. Sections 391 and 394 of the Companies Act constitute a legislative tool that facilitates corporate restructuring in a variety of ways. Underlining the significance of corporate restructuring, justice Chandrachud said:

> Corporate enterprise must be armed with the ability to be efficient and to meet the requirements of a rapidly evolving business reality. Corporate Restructuring is one of the means that can be employed to meet the challenges and problems which confront business. The law should be slow to retard or impede the discretion of corporate enterprise to adapt itself to the needs of changing times and to meet the demands of increasing competition.

Some of the most common reasons of corporate restructuring are briefly discussed here:

a. *Economics of Scale:* Economies of scale arise when increase in the volume of production leads to a reduction in the cost of production per unit. For instance, overhead costs can be substantially reduced on account of sharing central services such as accounting and finance, personnel and legal, sales promotion and advertisement, top-level management and so on. So when two or more companies combine, certain economies are realized due to the larger volume of operations of the combined entity. These economies arise due to increased production capacity, strong distribution networks, effective engineering services, R&D facilities, data processing system and others.
b. *Operating Economies:* Apart from economies of scale, a combination of two or more firms may result in reduction of costs due to operating economics. A merged firm may avoid overlapping. Various functions may be consolidated and duplicate channels may be eliminated by implementing a proper planning and control system.
c. *Synergy:* Synergy refers to a situation where the combined firm is more valuable than the sum of the individual combining firms. It refers to benefits other than those related to economies of scale. Apart from operating economies, synergy may also arise from enhanced managerial capabilities, creativity, innovativeness, R&D, productivity improvements, improved procurement and the elimination of duplication.
d. *Reduction in Tax Liability:* In India, a profitable company is allowed to merge with a sick company to set off against its profits, the accumulated losses and unabsorbed depreciation. A large number of companies in India have merged to take advantage of this provision. The conditions to claim this tax benefit have been further relaxed by amendments in Section 72A of the Income-tax Act.
e. *Managerial Effectiveness:* One of the potential benefits of merger is an increase in managerial effectiveness. This may occur if the existing management team, which is performing poorly, is replaced by a more efficient one.
f. *Other reasons* of corporate restructuring are appended as follows:
    i. To return to the shareholders of the surplus cash which is not required in the near foreseeable future.
    ii. To enhance the EPS of the company.
    iii. To provide to shareholders/investors that the market is presently undervaluing the share of the company in relation to its intrinsic value and the proposed buyback will facilitate recognition of the true value.

iv. To increase the promoters' voting power.
v. To maintain shareholders' value in a situation of poor state of the secondary market by a return of surplus cash to the shareholders.
vi. Eliminating the takeover threats.
vii. An opportunity to grow faster, with a ready-made market share.
viii. To eliminate a competition by buying it out.
ix. Diversification with minimum cost and immediate profit.
x. To forestall the company's own takeover by a third party.

8.5 Kinds/Forms of Corporate Restructuring

It is argued that managers should restructure companies to improve value; otherwise, external raiders will get an opportunity to take over the company. Therefore, they claim that it is in the best interest of both managers and shareholders to keep the gap between potential and actual value as close as possible. The management can improve operations by increasing revenue or reducing cost, acquiring or disposing of assets and improving the financial structure of the company.

Executives often restructure their companies for enhancing productivity, reducing costs or increasing shareholder's wealth. They classify restructuring activities into four categories: portfolio restructuring, financial restructuring, organizational restructuring and technological restructuring. These are discussed here briefly:

a. *Portfolio Restructuring:* It includes significant changes in the mix of assets owned by a firm or the lines of business in which a firm operates, including liquidation, divestitures, asset sales and spin-offs. The management may restructure its business in order to sharpen focus by disposing of a unit that is peripheral to their core business and in order to raise capital or rid itself of a languishing operation by selling off a division. Moreover, a company can involve on an aggressive combination of acquisitions and divestitures to restructure its portfolio.
b. *Financial Restructuring*: Financial structure refers to the allocation of the corporate flow of funds—cash or credit—and to the strategic or contractual decision rules that direct the flow and determine the value added and its distribution among the various corporate constituencies. It includes significant changes in the capital structure of a firm, including leveraged buyouts, leveraged recapitalizations and debt for equity swaps, mergers, acquisitions, joint ventures, strategic alliances and so on. According to Donaldson (1994):

> The elements of the corporate financial structure include the scale of the investment base, the mix between active investment and defensive reserves, the focus of investment (choice of revenue source), the rate at which earnings are reinvested, the mix of debt and equity contracts, the nature, degree and cost of corporate oversight (overhead), the distribution of expenditures between current and future revenue potential, and the nature and duration of wage and benefit contracts.

Financial restructuring generates economic value.
c. *Organizational Restructuring:* Organizational restructuring includes significant changes in the organizational structure of a firm, including redrawing of divisional

Table 8.1 Average Impact of Restructuring on a Company's Performance

Type of Restructuring	Mean Percentage Performance Improvement	Median Percentage Performance	Percentage Positive Means	Number of Studies Size	Average Sample
Portfolio	5.6	2.9	86*	21	154
Financial	37.5	24.5	86*	27	35
Organizational	–0.21	0.1	50	4	207
*Significantly different from 50% (base case) at $p < 0.01$.					

Source: Bowman and Singh (1999).

boundaries, flattening of hierarchic levels, spreading of the span of control, reducing product diversification, revising compensation, streamlining processes, reforming governance and downsizing employment. The findings of Bowman, et al. (1999) indicated that lay-offs unaccompanied by other organizational changes tend to have a negative impact on performance. Downsizing announcements combined with organizational restructuring are likely to have a positive, though small, effect on performance.

Studies reveal that, generally, there is a statistically significant improvement in the organizational performance after a restructuring event. However, it may not be the case always. It is cited that the average percentage change in performance is positive for financial and portfolio restructuring, while it is negligible or sometimes negative in the case of organizational restructuring (Table 8.1).

The portfolio and financial restructuring displays a higher percentage of positive returns than organizational restructuring. In five out of six cases (i.e., 86%) of financial and portfolio restructuring, the impact on performance was positive, while for organizational restructuring, the impact was positive for 50% of the cases.

d. *Technological Restructuring:* An alliance with other companies to exploit technological expertise is termed as technological restructuring.

8.6 Choice of Corporate Restructuring

The term 'corporate restructuring' is quite wide, covering various aspects. It may be chosen from among four broad groups (Figure 8.1):

a. Expansion
b. Contraction
c. Corporate control
d. Changes in ownership structures.

The various components under each and every group of corporate restructuring are discussed here in brief:

Figure 8.1 Types of Corporate Restructuring

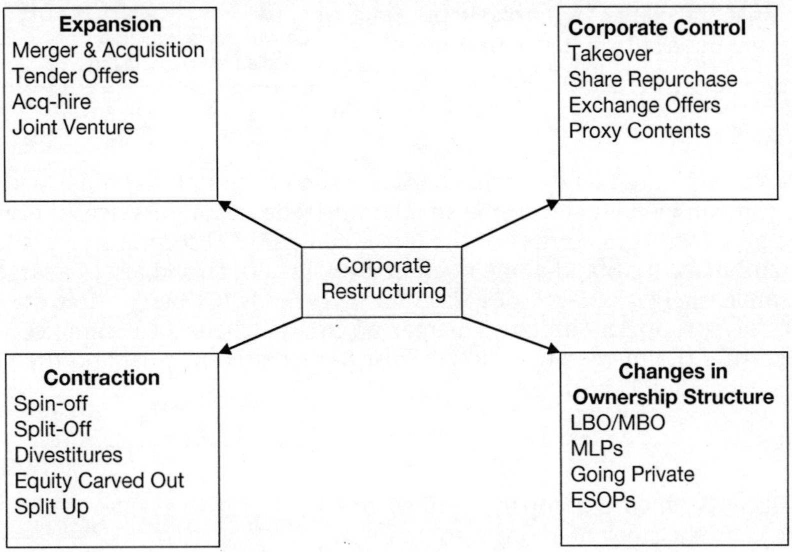

Source: Adapted from Mallik and Rakshit (2006).

8.6.1 Expansion

Expansion basically implies expanding or increasing the size and volume of business of the firm. There are a variety of reasons for companies to expand in an inorganic way, rather than naturally or organically. First of all, growth happens much faster, virtually overnight in some cases, whereas natural organic growth takes time as its sales grow. A company may want to eliminate competitors, enter a new geographic market, introduce a new product line, or bring on the talent and management team that results from an expansion transaction.

Expansion can be accomplished through mergers, asset acquisitions, tender offers or joint ventures. The following methods can be used to help a company grow without having to create a whole other business entity.

Mergers

A transaction where two firms agree to integrate their operations on a relatively on co-equal basis is called merger. It is defined as the fusion of two or more companies through direct acquisition of the net assets of the other(s). It results when the shareholders of more than one company, usually two, decide to pool the resources of the companies under a common entity. Accordingly, in a merger, two or more companies combine into a single unit and lose their individual identities. A merger can take place through an amalgamation or absorption.

Amalgamation

An amalgamation is when two or more companies enter into the merger agreement to form a completely new entity. In this type of merger, both companies lose their identity and a new company is formed to manage the consolidated assets. Amalgamation tends to occur when both companies are of equal size.

For example, the merger of Brooke Bond India Ltd with Lipton India Ltd resulted in the formation of a new company Brooke Bond Lipton India Ltd.

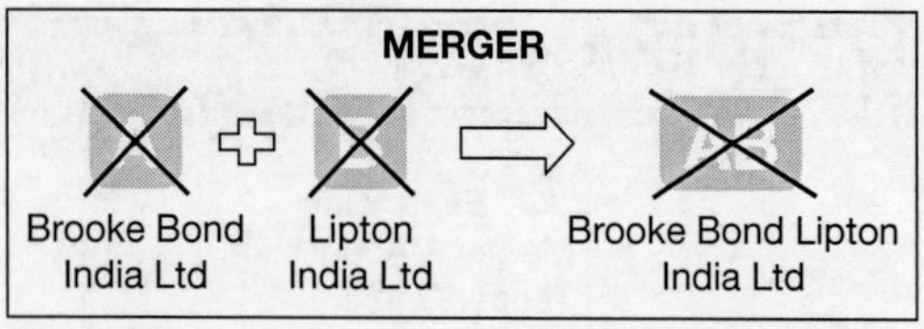

Absorption

Absorption is when the merger occurs between two entities of dissimilar size. In such a case, the larger company would absorb the smaller one. The fusion dissolves the smaller company and places all its assets in control of the larger company. Absorption may also take a smaller company and make it a stand-alone operating division or subsidiary of a larger company.

For example, merger of Bank of Rajasthan with the ICICI Bank. After the merger Bank of Rajasthan ceases to exist. Similarly, merger of Oriental Bank of commerce with the Global Trust Bank. After the merger, the Global Trust Bank ceased to exist and the Oriental Bank of Commerce expanded its business.

Acquisition

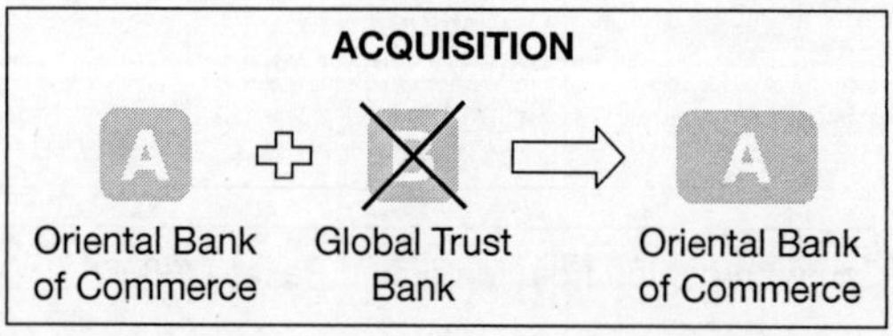

An acquisition is when a company (public or private) buys up the stock of another company. An acquisition may also take the form of an 'asset acquisition', where rather than buying the stock, the buyer simply buys the entirety or a portion of the assets of another company. The assets may be tangible, such as plants and machinery, or intangible assets, such as patents and trademarks. The target company may then continue as a smaller company or dissolve.

For example, the acquisition of the cement division of Tata Steel by Lafarge of France, where Lafarge acquired only the 1.7 million tone cement plant and its related assets from Tata Steel. The assets being purchased may also be intangible in nature. For example, Coca-Cola purchased soft drinks brands like Thumps Up, Limca, and Gold Spot from Parle by paying ₹1.7 billion to Parle.

Acq-hire

An 'Acq-hire' (i.e. acquisition-by-hire) may occur especially when the target company is quite small or is in the start-up phase. In this case, the acquiring company simply hires the staff of the target company, thereby acquiring its talent (if that is its main asset and demand). The target company simply dissolves and little legal issues are involved.

Tender Offer

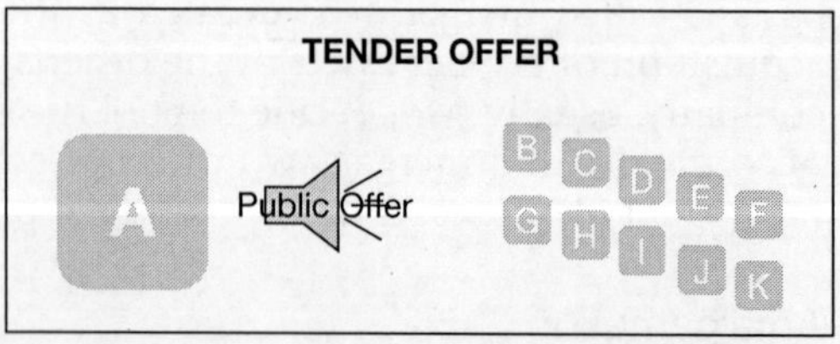

A tender offer is an offer or invitation (usually announced in a newspaper advertisement) by an acquiring company to the general shareholders of a target company to purchase a majority of the equity at a premium to market value at a specified price during a specified time, subject to the tendering of a minimum and maximum number of shares. For example, if a target corporation's stock were trading at ₹10 per share, an acquirer might offer ₹11.50 per share to shareholders on the condition that 51% of shareholders agree. Cash or securities may be offered to the target company's shareholders, although a tender offer in which securities are offered as consideration is generally referred to as an 'exchange offer'.

For instance, takeover by Tata Tea of Consolidated Coffee Ltd is an example of tender offer where more than 50% of shareholders of Consolidated Coffee Ltd sold their holding to Tata Tea at the offered price which was more than the investment price.

In a tender offer, the bidder contacts shareholders directly; the directors of the company may or may not have endorsed the tender offer proposal.

Joint Venture

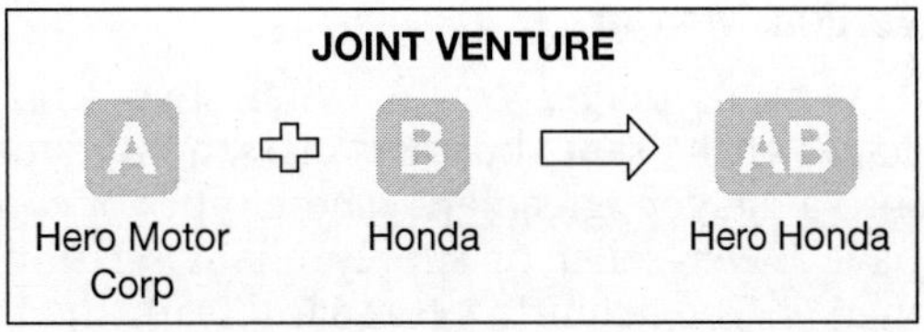

In a joint venture, two or more companies come together and carry on operations in both or at a single place of their origin. The profit and losses are shared as per their agreement. Synergies occur when businesses capitalize on joint opportunities or other combined efforts to obtain an effect greater than working alone, whether it is increased revenue or decreased costs. The venture can be for one specific project only or for a continuing business relationship. For example, Tata Teleservices (74%) and NTT DoCoMo (26%) merged and started a company called Tata Docomo.

'Sony-Ericsson' is a joint venture by the Japanese consumer electronics company 'Sony Corporation' and the Swedish telecommunications company 'Ericsson' to make mobile phones. The stated reason for this venture is to combine Sony's consumer electronics expertise with Ericsson's technological leadership in the communications sector. Both companies have stopped operations.

Key Differences Between Mergers and Acquisitions

Although often very similar, mergers and acquisitions are two distinctly separate types of transactions. In the purest sense, a 'merger' refers to a merger of equals: two companies of the same size come together, surrender their shares and issue new shares for a new, combined company. In a merger, the merging organizations surrender their shares and issue new shares for a new, combined company.

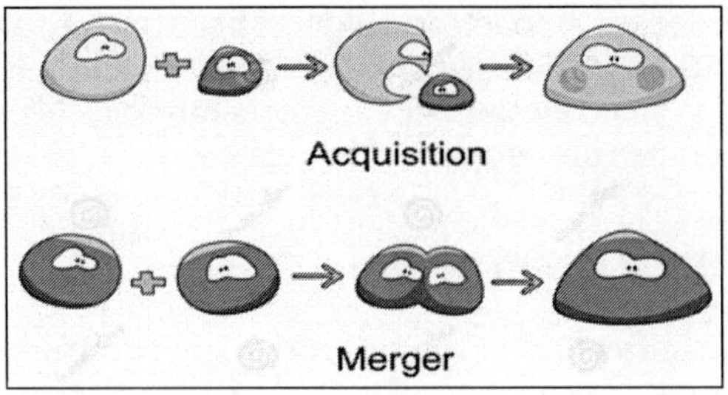

A merger of equals is actually quite rare since most deals that are reported as a merger are actually acquisitions, where one firm actually purchases and assumes ownership of the other. Acquisitions are often publicized as mergers because they are easier for the target firm and public relation (PR) teams to swallow and are believed to help promote a more successful integration of the firms' operations.

Types of Mergers

Horizontal Merger

A horizontal merger is when two companies from the same business class or market enter into a merger agreement. In a horizontal merger, the merged companies benefit from economies of scale and increase total market share by consolidating facilities, combining operations, increasing working capital, reducing competition, or reducing advertisement costs and so on.

A merger between Coca-Cola and the Pepsi beverage division, for example, would be horizontal in nature. The goal of a horizontal merger is to create a new, larger organization with more market share. Because the merging companies' business operations may be very similar, there may be opportunities to join certain operations, such as manufacturing, and reduce costs.

Vertical Merger

A vertical merger occurs when two firms from different stages of the same business class, activity or operation enter into a merger agreement. These types of companies typically have buyer–seller or supply chain relationships before the merger. The acquiring company reaps the benefits of a reduced inventory and more efficient allocation working capital. An example of a vertical merger is a car manufacturer purchasing a tyre company. Vertical mergers can be in the form of forward integration of business (e.g., a manufacturing company entering in the direct marketing function, which was not its foray in the erstwhile times) or in the form of backward integration of business [e.g., a manufacturing company also focusing on the producing the required raw materials and managing its supply chain activities on its own, which was not its foray earlier).

Example: Tata Motors Ltd acquired TrilixSrl, an Italian design and engineering firm, to enhance its styling and design capabilities to global standards.

Conglomerate Merger

A conglomerate merger arises when two or more firms in different markets producing unrelated goods join together to form a single firm. An example of a conglomerate merger is that between an athletic shoe company and a soft drink company. The firms are not competitors producing similar products (which would make it a horizontal merger) nor do they have an input–output relation (which would make it a vertical merger). The resulting company is faced with the same competition in each of its two markets after the merger as the individual firms were before the merger. On a general analysis, it can be concluded that horizontal mergers eliminate sellers and hence reshape the market structure, that is, they have a direct impact on seller concentration, whereas vertical and conglomerate mergers do not affect market structures, for example, the seller concentration directly.

The conglomerate mergers rarely result in immediate financial benefits for either company and so are seldom seen today.

8.6.2 Contraction

Contraction is the second form of restructuring. In the case of contraction, generally the size of the firm gets reduced. Contraction may take place in the form of divestitures (which includes spin-off, split-off, and split-ups), equity-carved out and asset sale.

Divestiture

The word 'divestiture' may not be as popular as the word 'merger or acquisition' since there is only a few definitions mentioned in the accounting textbooks. As the word merger or acquisition refers to the combination of independent business units into a single entity, divestiture is the other way around. While mergers are based on the principle of synergy, which says 2 + 2 = 5!, divestiture, on the other hand, is based on the principle of 'energy', which says 5 – 3 = 3!

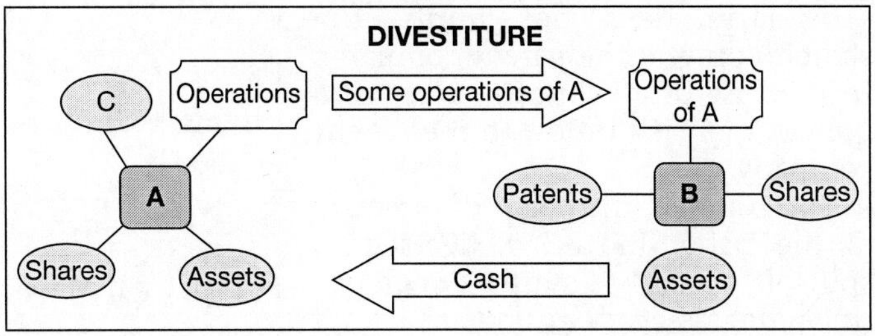

Divesture is a transaction through which a firm sells a portion of its assets or a division to another company. It involves selling some of the assets or division for cash or securities to a third party which is an outsider. From the seller's perspective, it is a form of contraction from the buyer's point of view, it represents expansion.

For example, when Coromandal Fertilizers Limited sold its cement division to India Cements Limited, the size of Coromandal Fertilizers Limited contracted, whereas the size of India Cements Limited expanded. Hence, a divestiture is the obverse of a purchase.

Among the various methods of divestiture, the most important ones are partial sell-off, demerger (spin-off and split off), and equity carve out. Some scholars define divestiture rather narrowly as partial sell off and some scholars define divestiture more broadly to include partial sell offs, demergers and so on.

Sell-off

It is the sale of a division or subsidiary of a parent company to a third party for cash or other assets or through initial public. Usually, companies sell underperforming segments to reallocate resources to higher valued uses. Another reason is if the parent company is experiencing financial difficulties and needs resources, but has exhausted debt or equity sources, selling a division or subsidiary may be its only resource option.

Spin-offs

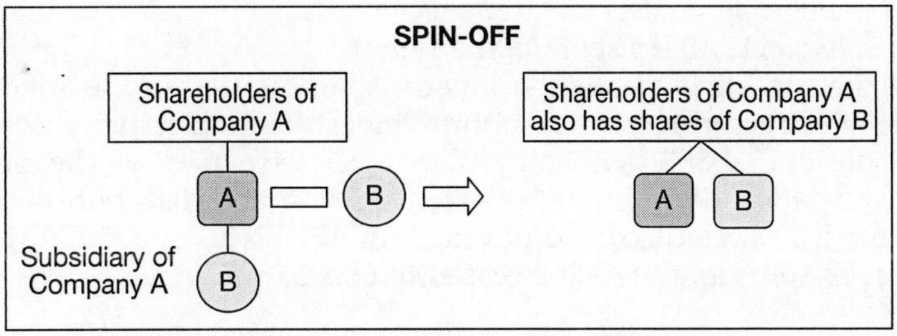

It is an event through which a new company is created and separated from its parent company. After the event there are two separate companies, each with their own outstanding share capital. Shareholders of the parent company are distributed shares in the spun-off company on a pro rata basis (for example, each shareholder in parent 'company A' will receive five shares in the spun-off 'company B'). Both the entities have their own management and run individually after the spin-off without the interventions of the parent company. A spin-off generally does not result in an infusion of cash to the parent firm.

For example, by spinning off its investment division, Kotak Mahindra Capital Finance Ltd. formed a subsidiary known as Kotak Mahindra Capital Corporation.

Split-offs

In the case of split-off, a new company is created in order to take over the operations of an existing division or unit of a company. A portion of the existing shareholders of the company obtains stocks in the subsidiary (i.e., the new company) in exchange for stocks of the parent company. As a result, the equity base of the parent company is reduced representing the downsizing of the firm. Thus, shareholding of the new entity (i.e., subsidiary) does not imply the shareholding of the parent company. In the case of a split-off, there is no question of cash inflow to the parent company.

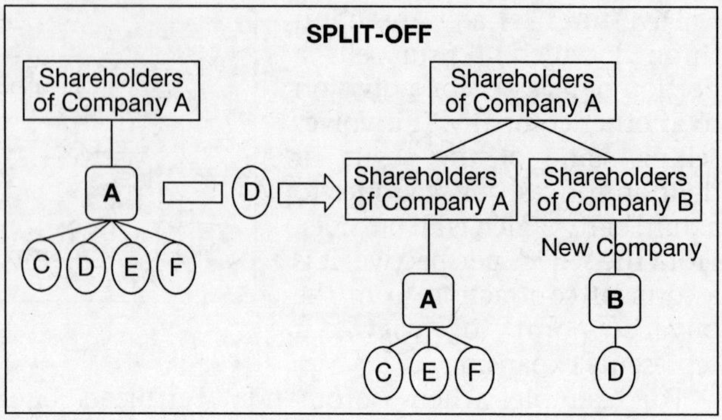

For example, the board of directors of the Dabur India Ltd. decided to split-off their Pharma segment (including assets) and transfer it to a new company from the year 2002–03. The de-merger proposal was a significant strategic decision reflecting corporate restructuring initiative and was expected to provide greater focus on independence to the company's two main segments. The fast-moving consumer goods (FMCG) business remained within Dabur India Ltd., which concentrated on its core competencies in personal care, health care and Ayurvedic specialties. The new pharmaceutical company Dabur pharma Ltd. focused on its expertise in allopathic, oncology, formulations and bulk drugs.

Split-ups

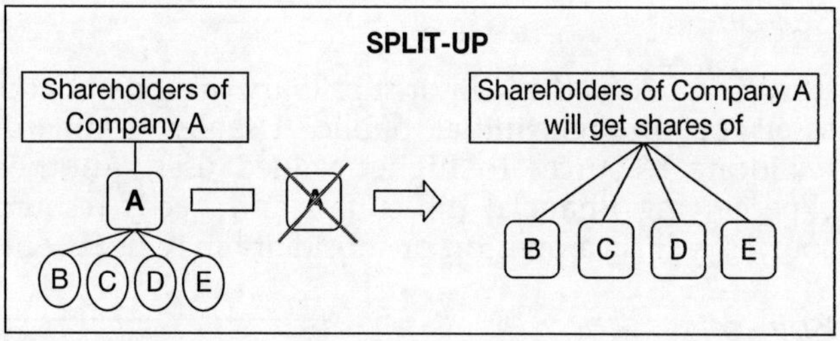

A split-up involves transfer of property from a parent company to its existing or newly created subsidiary companies and then liquidation of the parent company through a distribution of the subsidiary companies' stock to the parent shareholders in exchange for all its stock. After a split-up, the parent company no longer exists, only the spun-off units of the original company survive.

Restructuring of the Andhra Pradesh State Electricity Board (APSEB) is a good example of split-up. APSEB was split-up in 1999 as a part of the power sector reforms. The power generation division and the transmission and distribution division of APSEB was transferred to two different companies namely APGENCo and APTRANACo, respectively. As a result of such split-up, the APSEB ceased to exist.

Equity Carve-out

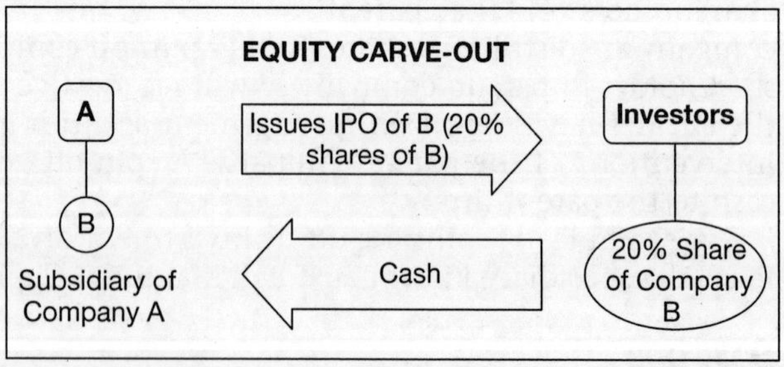

With a carve-out, a new independent company is created by detaching part of the parent's businesses and selling the shares of the new company in a public offering. In general, the parent remains in possession of a substantial fraction of the equity (usually greater than 50%) of the carved-out company. With ownership of over 50%, the parent company still retains the right to undertake spin-offs and split-offs on a tax-free basis.

The parent undertakes a carve-out explicitly in order to raise funds in the capital market: these funds can be retained within the firm or used to pay creditors or shareholders. Carved-out divisions tend to be high-value assets and often, after some time, the parent re-acquires the carved-out division or divests it into another mode.

Asset Sale

An asset sale involves the sale of tangible or intangible assets of the company to generate cash. This cash can be used to pay out a dividend, adjust capital structure, or purchase other assets or investments. In an extreme case, an asset sale may be part of a liquidation plan where a company ceases all business operations and sells all its assets.

8.6.3 Corporate Control

Changes in control of a company often occur as a result of a change of ownership transaction as discussed earlier. However, change in control of a company can also occur without an acquisition or divestiture. Corporate control is the control over the management of the firm.

Corporate control is another type of restructuring that involves obtaining control over the management of a firm. As ownership and control are not always separated, the top managers and promoter group who stand to lose from competition in the market may use the democratic rules to benefit themselves for corporate control. A large block of shares may give effective control even when there are no majority owners.

A change of control can result from the following.

Share Repurchase/Buyback of Shares

Stock repurchase, also known as buyback of shares in India, is buying of its own shares by the company. This leads to reduction in the equity capital of the company and, in turn, strengthens the promoters' controlling position by increasing their stake. There are three methods of share repurchase:

- *Repurchase tender offer:* Here, the firm specifies the number of shares it proposes to buyback, the fixed price it would pay and the time period for the offer would be open for the shareholders to tender their shares.

For example, in the year 2000, Bajaj Auto made tender offer to buy its shares at ₹400 per share, when the shares were trading at around ₹300 per share.

- *Open market repurchase*: Here, the firm buys from the market at the prevailing market price.

For example in March 2008, Madras Cements completed its buyback offer, amounting to ₹670 million, within two months of making the open offer.

- *Targeted repurchase:* Here, the firm buys shares from a select group of investors.
  For example, the Great Eastern Shipping Company bought shares from select investors to protect itself from a hostile takeover bid led by the Abhishek Dalmia group.

Exchange Offers

It is an offer by a firm to give one type/class of security (such as a debenture or preference share), in exchange for another type of security (such as equity share) in either the same firm or another firm. For example, a company may redeem its own debentures with other debentures of equivalent value. This offer occurs when the firm has poor cash flow. Similarly a firm may redeem shares in itself for other stocks, either of its own or of another firm. It is very commonly found in mergers and acquisitions.

Proxy Contest

By definition, a proxy contest is a strategy that involves using shareholders' proxy votes to replace the existing members of a company's board of directors. By removing existing board members, the person or company launching the proxy contest can establish a new board of directors that is better aligned with their objectives.

For example, in February of 2008, Microsoft Corporation made an unsolicited offer to buy Yahoo for $31 per share. At that time, this offer represented a 62% premium to Yahoo's stock price. With the potential to realize a large capital gain on their investment, many shareholders would have liked to see the merger with Microsoft become a reality. Unfortunately, the board of directors at Yahoo felt the offer by Microsoft undervalued the company. Negotiations between the executives at Microsoft and Yahoo eventually stalled, and Microsoft withdrew their offer on 3 May 2008. Less than two weeks later, billionaire Carl Icahn launched an effort aimed at replacing the board of directors at Yahoo via a proxy contest.

Takeover

A takeover generally refers to transfer of control of a firm from one group of shareholders to another group of shareholders. In short, in takeover the controlling interest of a firm changes from hands of one group to another. In theory, the acquirer must buy more than 50% of the paid-up capital of the target company to enjoy complete control. However, in practice, effective control can be exercised by holding in between 20% and 40%, because the remaining shareholders are small and scattered.

For example, United Breweries acquired a majority stake in Deccan aviation Ltd. Mahindra Telecom takeover of Satyam. Other examples are Indal by Hindalco, IPCL by Reliance Industries, VSNL by Tatas and BALCO by Sterlite.

Takeover can be either hostile or friendly.

Hostile Takeover

It is a takeover of a company against the wishes of current management and the board of directors. This takeover may be attempted by another company or by HNI. If the price offered is high enough, shareholders may vote to accept the offer even if the management resists and claims that the company is actually worth even more. If the acquirer raises the price high enough, the management may change its attitude, converting the hostile takeover into a friendly one.

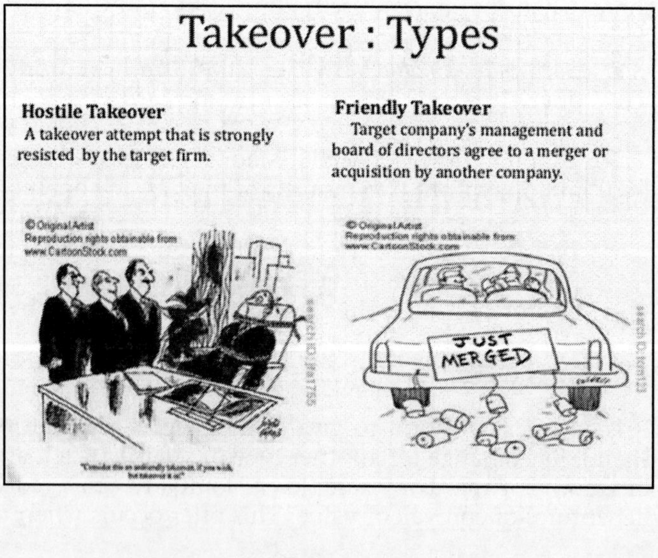

For example, the recently completed Arcelor Mittal deal is an example of hostile takeover, where the LN Mittal group acquired management control of Arcelor against the wishes of the Arcelor management. Other examples are India Cements' takeover of Rassi Cements in 1998 and ITC Ltd takeover of East India Hotels Ltd in 2000.

Friendly Takeover

It is a takeover effected with the consent of the taken over company. In this case, there is an agreement between the managements of the two companies through negotiations, and the takeover bid may be with the consent of majority shareholders of the target company. It is also known as negotiated takeover.

For example, the merger of Brooke Bond and Lipton has formed a new entity Broke Bond Lipton with permission of its board; it is termed as friendly takeover

8.6.4 Changes in Ownership Structure

A company can also go for restructuring without purchasing new company or selling existing company or part of it. It is by obtaining corporate control over the management of other company. Control is the process by which managers influence other members of a company to implement the organizational strategies. The following are various techniques of obtaining corporate control.

Leveraged Buyout (LBO)

A leveraged buyout, or LBO, is an acquisition of a company or division of another company financed with a substantial portion of borrowed funds. In an LBO, the company acquiring the target company will finance the acquisition with a combination of debt and equity, much like an individual buying a house with a mortgage. Just as a mortgage is secured by the value of the house being purchased, some portion of the debt incurred in an LBO is secured by the assets of the acquired business. Unlike a house, however, the bought-out business generates cash flows that are used to service the debt incurred in its buyout—in essence, the acquired company helps pay for itself.

For example, Tata Steel's acquisition of Corus is a classic example of leveraged buyout. Typically, in such a buyout, as much as 90% of the funds required for the takeover are mobilized through borrowings principally through junk bonds carrying high interest.

Another, Tata Tea acquisition of UK heavyweight brand Tetley for an astounding 271 million pounds was the first-ever LBO by any Indian company. Tetley's price tag of 271 million pounds (US$450 million) was more than four times the net worth of Tata Tea, which stood at US$114 million. What made it possible was the financing mechanism of LBO. This mechanism allowed the acquirer (Tata Tea) to minimize its cash outlay in making the purchase.

Management Buyout (MBO)

MBOs, or the management buyouts, are a special case of a leveraged acquisition. As the name very well suggests, it occurs when a company's managers buy or acquire a large part of the company. Similar to an MBO is a management buy-in (MBI), in which an external management team acquires the shares. An MBO can occur for a number of reasons, as given here:

- The owners of the business want to retire and want to sell the company to the management team they trust (and with whom they have worked for years).

- The owners of the business have lost faith in the business and are willing to sell it to the management (who believes in the future of the business) in order to get some value for the business.
- The managers see a value in the business that the current owners do not see and do not want to pursue.

In most situations, the management team does not have enough money to fund the equity needed for the acquisition (to be combined with bank debt to constitute the purchase price) so that management teams work together with financial sponsors to part-finance the acquisition.

For example, Company XYZ is a publicly traded company where the management controls 30% the company's stock and the remaining 70% is stock floated to the public. Under the terms of an MBO, the management will arrange to purchase enough shares of the outstanding stock from the public so that they end up with a controlling interest of at least 51% of the company's total shares. In order to finance their venture, the management group may look to a bank or venture capitalists to assist them in financing the acquisition.

Master Limited Partnerships

Master limited partnerships (MLPs) are limited to apply to enterprises that engage in certain businesses, mostly pertaining to the use of natural resources, such as petroleum and natural gas extraction and transportation. They combine the tax advantages of a partnership and higher dividend yields with the day-to-day tradability of common stocks.

MLPs consist of a general partner who manages the operations and limited partners, who own the rest of the units for the partnership. Unlike corporations, MLPs are not subject to double taxation. Their stocks are called units, while their dividends are called distributions. The units are very easy to buy and sell, as they trade just like any other stock.

Going Private

'Going private' is a transaction or a series of transactions that convert a publicly traded company into a private entity. Once a company goes private, its shareholders are no longer able to trade their shares in the open market. As a result of such an initiative, the company is delisted from the stock exchange and stopped being publicly traded.

The problem with public company can be the public interest. Public companies have complicated relationships with their shareholders. Shareholders are needy, despite the efforts of executives to keep stock prices and returns consistently on the rise. By going private, executives can clear their minds and focus on the business with fewer stakeholders to please. No more quarter-by-quarter management and managers can work with long-term goals, which in the end will be better for business. Again, by going private, companies no longer have to worry about the reports of analysts and the media, or public scrutiny about salaries and benefits.

For example, after eight months of manoeuvring, Dell CEO and founder Michael Dell has finally taken the company private on 29 October 2013. Under the terms of the agreement, Dell stockholders will receive $13.75 in cash for each share of Dell common stock they hold, plus payment of a special cash dividend of $0.13 per share to stockholders of record as of the close of business on 28 October 2013, for a total consideration of $13.88 per share in cash. The total transaction is valued at approximately $24.9 billion.

Employee Stock Option Plan

ESOPs are 'employee stock option plans' under which employees receive the right to purchase a certain number of shares in the company at a predetermined price, as a reward for their performance and also as motivation for employees to keep increasing their performance. Employees typically have to wait for a certain duration known as 'vesting period' before they can exercise the right to purchase the shares.

Interestingly, many companies abroad use ESOPs as a technique of corporate finance for a variety of purposes—to finance expansion, to make an acquisition, to spin off a division, to take a company private and so on. This has yet to catch on in India, perhaps because the scale of ESOP so far is too small for many of these uses.

Infosys grew very fast; many employees who got ESOPs of Infosys in the early days and preferred to keep these shares have today turned millionaires. Infosys used to even award drivers, office assistants and secretaries with ESOPs and many of them have also turned millionaires.

8.7 Restructuring Process

The methodology of enterprise restructuring is based on a strategic planning process consisting of three important phases (Figure 8.2).

- Diagnostic phase: Diagnosis of the company through 'strategic appraisal'.
- Planning phase: Preparation of the 'strategic improvement plan'.
- Implementation phase: Restructuring, including monitoring of progress and revisions of the previous phases.

The process and methodology of diagnostic review and strategic planning is summarized in Figure 8.2. The diagnostic phase analyses the internal and external environment of the company, its relative position on the market and its position relative to the competition. Thus, in-depth studies are conducted into the operations of the company, in particular its marketing, production, organization and finance functions, problems encountered, their causes and possible solutions. The local and export market is extensively investigated, as is the competition. Based on this information, the SWOT analysis is completed: the relative strengths and weaknesses (internal) and the opportunities and threats in the external environment. Through this analysis, the company's competitive advantages on the market can be determined.

With a thorough and detailed diagnostic, the development of the restructuring plan is not very difficult. Based on the SWOT, the corporate objectives, mission statement and subsequently corporate and business unit strategies are developed—strategic planning. Having

Figure 8.2 Restructuring Process

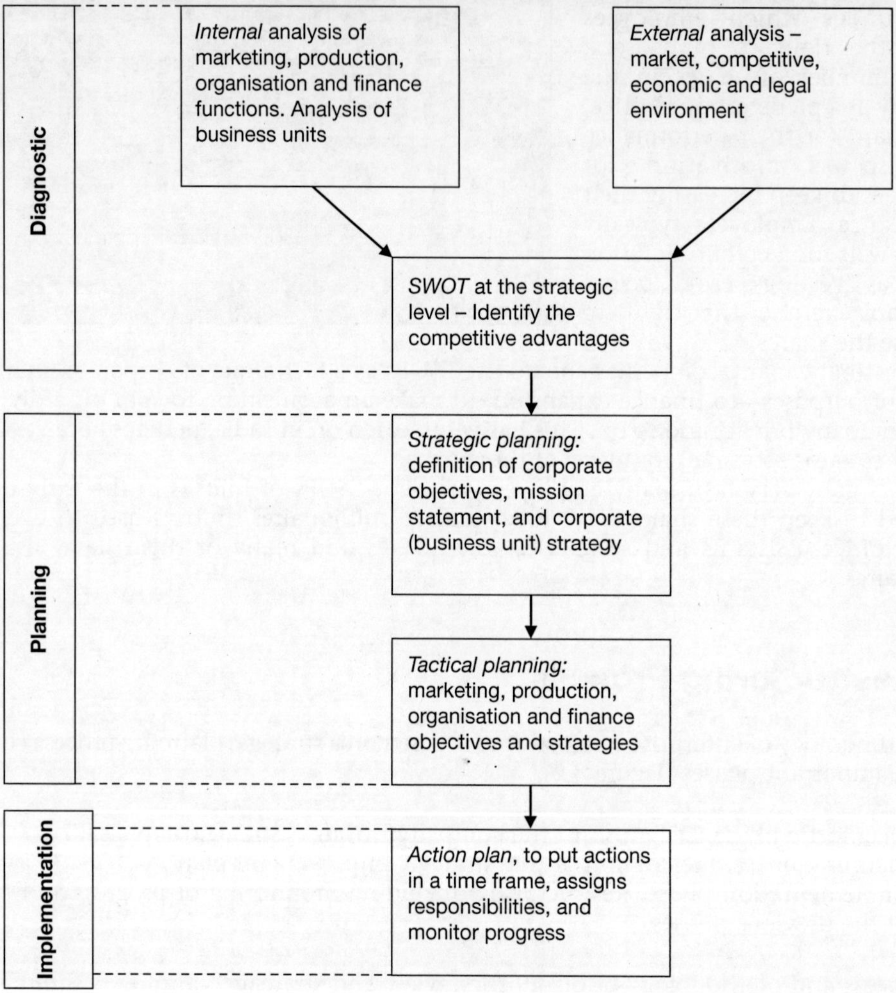

completed this important step, the corresponding objectives and actions at the functional level (marketing, production, organization, and finance) logically follow. Accordingly, financial projections (scenarios) are developed, as is an action plan clearly outlining what is to be done to implement the restructuring plan, when and by whom.

The Company Diagnostic

The company diagnostic, or the 'strategic appraisal' of the enterprise, consists of five consecutive steps (Table 8.2). This leads to a diagnostic report by the fourth month of project implementation. Apart from technical studies, the diagnostic phase includes a number of participatory planning sessions with middle and higher management staff, aiming to uncover

Table 8.2 An Example of Diagnostic Table

Problems Observed	***Consequences***	***Solutions***
Marketing		
Clients do not trust local products, prefer imported ones	No sales, loss of market to imports	Produce foreign products under license
....		
Production		
All installations and buildings are greatly overdimensioned to current and expected needs	High-energy, maintenance and depreciation expenses	Downscaling of existing facilities. If replacement is considered, lower but more flexible capacities
....		
Organization/HRM		
Company structure is production and technology orientated, with excessive vertical integration (all support functions in house)	Company is not market orientated/organized. Many support units not feasible to keep 'in-house'. The same for by-products	Profit centre approach, lease out or sell unprofitable support units, buy outside support if cheaper, divest some by-product units
....		
Finance		
No provision of accurate and timely financial information to management	Management cannot make well-informed decisions	Monthly management accounts
....		

strategic bottlenecks for the company's development, assessing the options and defining new strategic directions.

1. *Identification of 'stakeholders'* in the company—who will be affected. These are the management, shareholders, workers (some of whom may be shareholders as well), clients, suppliers, distributors, creditors, banks, government and others. Are they willing to collaborate in the restructuring exercise? Are there any conflicting interests among the stakeholders?
2. *Pre-assessment* of the current situation. What are the present product/market combinations? How has the company performed in recent years? What would be the outcome of a strategy 'continue business as usual'? Would the company be able to secure its continuity without restructuring?
3. *Internal analysis* aims at identification of strengths and weaknesses in the company's structure, culture and resources. The internal analysis includes a review of sales, costs, profits, organizational structure, management style, technology, financial results and other factors. For the main functional areas of marketing, production, organization and finance diagnostic tables are made, demonstrating the problems found, their consequences and possible solutions. The internal analysis also identifies SBUs that could be operated independently from the rest of the enterprise. Core businesses and

core competencies are identified, that is SBUs that are considered crucial to the company's existence and survival. Determine the competitive strengths and weaknesses of SBUs, starting with the 'core businesses'.

4. *External analysis* of the economic environment, markets and competition. This implies a critical analysis of elements/developments outside the company that are (potentially) relevant to the performance of the company, and most of which cannot be directly influenced by the company. This includes an assessment of macroeconomic, legal and political developments in the country, market analysis (prospective product/market combinations), customers, competitors, distribution channels, logistics and the environment.
5. *SWOT analysis* at the strategic level: Relative strengths, weaknesses, opportunities and threats (SWOT). This helps the enterprise identify its competitive advantages on the market. Competitive advantages may be found at the level of manufacturing (enabling a company to produce a product cheaper), product design and/or quality (enabling a company to reach higher levels of customer satisfaction), marketing (enabling the company to exploit market opportunities), distribution (aiming to better reach the client) and many others.

The SWOT (Figure 8.3) summarizes the findings from the diagnostic and places this information in a strategic framework for company improvement. Through the SWOT, we match strengths with opportunities (take advantage), aim to convert weaknesses into strengths (improve) and determine how threats can be avoided by specific actions (upgrade). Thus, the SWOT helps determine what the company already does well, how it can use these skills to grab opportunities, and where it needs to make improvements to counter threats and overcome weaknesses. The SWOT, which is the outcome of the diagnostic study, is an extremely important step in establishing the priorities for the restructuring plan. In fact, having completed the diagnostic tables and SWOT, the outline for the restructuring plan is shown in Figure 8.4.

Figure 8.3 SWOT Analysis

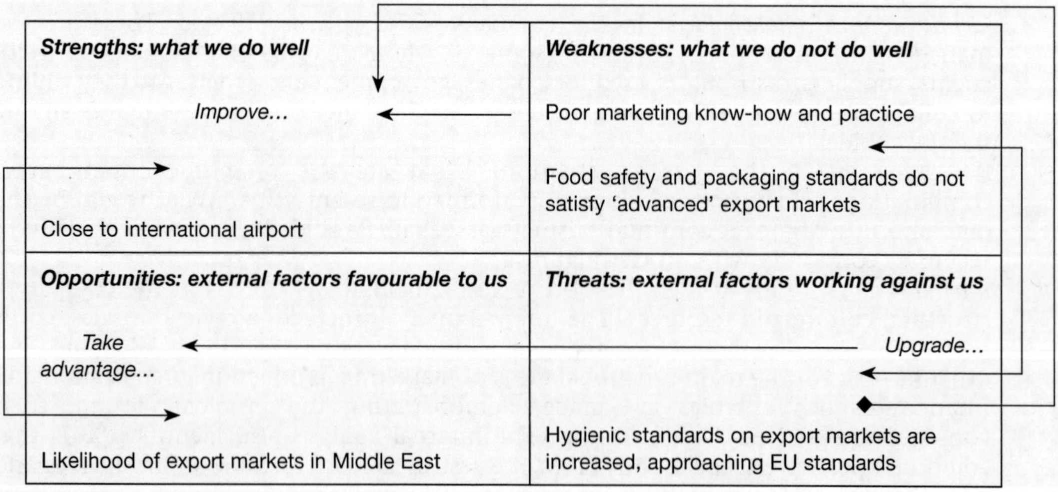

Figure 8.4 Contents of Restructuring Plan

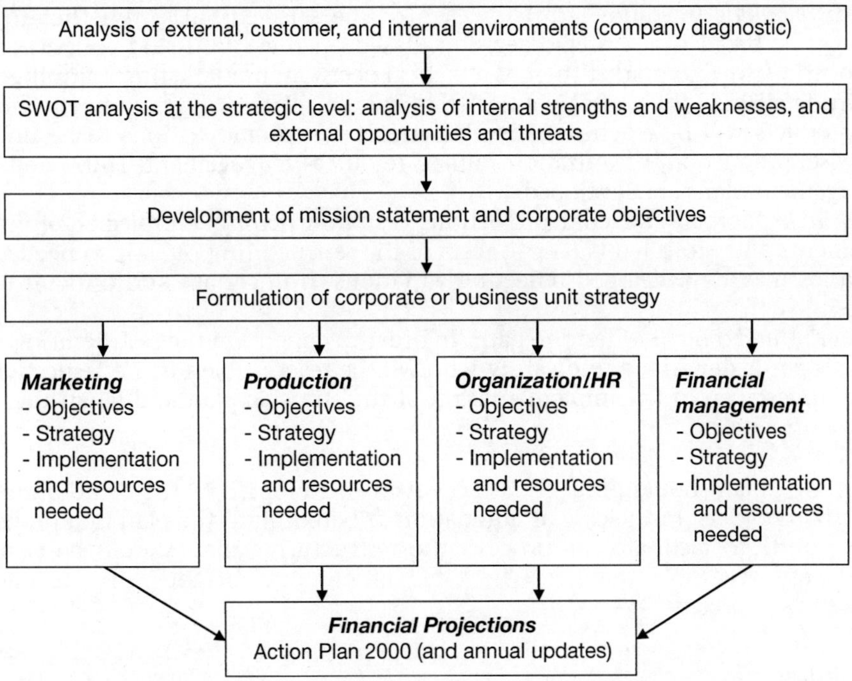

The Restructuring Plan

The 'strategic planning' process consists of another four steps (step six to nine), during which concrete restructuring actions are formulated. Step 10 aims to put in place a framework to monitor to what extent the restructuring plan is being implemented and its goals are being realized ('strategy implementation').

6. *Strategic planning*: Define global objectives. Based on the SWOT, the enterprise's objectives, its strategic vision and business philosophy are formulated. What do we want to achieve in terms of profit, market penetration, client satisfaction and other objectives at the corporate level. Which business are we in, or do we want to be in, and in which we no longer operate. Define a new mission statement, showing what the company is, what it stands for, and what it does for others. Strategic planning aims to lay down the strategic directions that the company will follow in the medium and long terms. This is not very detailed. Strategic planning deals with 'trends' rather than details.
7. *Corporate planning*: Making the strategic choices (long term), affirming the commitment to undertake corporate restructuring. It includes a decision as to which of the current SBUs to drop (divest), which ones to develop further and which new ones to start with. These decisions are obviously based on the internal strengths, external opportunities and corporate objectives identified before. They include an assessment of the 'attractiveness of the market', on the one hand, and 'the ability of the company to

compete successfully on that market', on the other hand. The strategic choices to be made, set priorities for possible investment decisions at the corporate and SBU levels and require an analysis of their financial and operational feasibility.

8. *Tactical planning* (medium term) for each of the selected SBUs. Whether to produce sausages or bread is a strategic decision, based on the SWOT and conclusions of the diagnostic. 'How' to market them is a tactical decision: in marketing planning, we work out in detail how the strategic objectives that are related to the commercialization of the products will be reached. This plan indicates 'specific' actions to be undertaken. Likewise, production, organization/human resources management (HRM) and financial management plans are developed.
9. *Financial implications*: Revenue projections/cash flow planning, projected profit and loss statements and projected balance sheets of the restructuring plan. If so needed, several scenarios may be developed reflecting variations in uncertain and difficult to predict factors.
10. *Monitoring and control*: Milestone path. In order to concretize the restructuring effort, an action plan is developed, indicating who will be responsible for the respective actions to be undertaken in the implementation of the strategic plan and when these actions will be undertaken.

The restructuring plan should probably be approved and adopted by the board of directors or meeting of shareholders. In the case of liquidation or bankruptcy, the plan is approved by the bankruptcy court. To facilitate the process, the restructuring plan should be written in a logical and easy accessible manner. The table of contents of the restructuring plan is graphically shown in Figure 8.4.

Implementation

During the implementation of the restructuring plan, the action plan plays a key role. As this plan indicates what is to be done, when and by whom, it guides day-to-day actions of the management. The plan is adapted regularly as the market conditions change. However, the global objectives and strategies should not normally be changed, unless there is really a significant shift in the company's external and internal environment. Changes in company strategy probably require a decision of the board of directors or shareholders.

It is noted that, apart from the above-mentioned strategic and tactical planning, the company will also engage in some micro planning at the department and even personnel levels. The action plan forms the basis for the subsequent development of department plans and, eventually, personal performance and development plans.

8.8 Present Scenario of Corporate Restructuring

Today, a restructuring wave is sweeping the corporate sector all over the world, taking within its fold both big and small entities, comprising old economy business conglomerates and new economy companies and even the infrastructure and service sectors. Mergers, acquisitions and takeovers have become an integral part of the new economic paradigm. Conglomerates are being formed to combine businesses, and where synergies are not achieved, demergers have become the order of the day. With the increasing competition and the economy, heading towards globalization, the corporate restructuring activities are expected to occur at a much larger scale than at any time in the past, and are stated to pay a major role in achieving the competitive edge for India in international market place.

The process of restructuring through mergers and acquisitions has been a regular feature in the developed and free economies such as Japan, the United States and European countries with special reference to the UK, where hundreds of mergers take place every year. The mergers and takeovers of multinational corporate houses across the borders have become a normal phenomenon.

Corporate restructuring being a matter of business convenience, the role of legislation, executive and judiciary, is that of a facilitator for restructuring on healthy lines. The stand of the government is that monopoly is not necessarily bad provided market dominance is not abused. In this era of hyper-competitive capitalism and technological change, industrialists have realized that corporate restructurings are perhaps the best route to reach a size comparable to global companies so as to effectively compete with them. The harsh reality of globalization has dawned that companies which cannot compete globally must sell out as an inevitable alternative.

8.8.1 Global Scenario

During the past decade, corporate restructuring has increasingly become a staple of management life and a common phenomenon around the world. An unprecedented number of companies across the world have reorganized their divisions, restructured their assets, streamlined their operations and spun off their divisions in a bid to spur the company's performance. It has enabled numerous organizations to respond quickly and more effectively to new opportunities and unexpected pressures so as to re-establish their competitive advantage. The suppliers, customers and competitors also have an equally profound impact while working with a restructured company.

Globalization gives the consumer many choices—technologies are changing, established brands are being challenged by value—for money products, the movement of goods across countries is on the rise and entry barriers are being reduced. As markets consolidate into fewer and larger entities, economies become more concentrated. In this international scenario, there is a heavy pronunciation on the quality, range, cost and reliability of product and services. Companies all over the world have been reshaping and repositioning themselves to meet the challenges and grab the opportunities thrown open by globalization. The management strategy in turbulent times is to focus on core competencies—selling loss-making companies and acquiring those, which can contribute to profit and growth of the group. The underlying objective is to achieve and sustain superior performance. In fact, most companies in the world are merging to achieve an economic size as a means of survival and growth in the competitive economy. There has been a substantial increase in the quantum of funds flowing across nations in search of restructuring and takeover candidates. The UK has been the most important foreign investor in the United States in recent years with British companies. In telecom, the biggest deals include AT&T–TCI, SBC–Ameritech and so on. There have been huge oil sector mergers, the biggest being Exxon–Mobile, BP–Amoco and Total–Petrofina. It is estimated that one in four U.S. workers has been affected by the wave of mergers and acquisition activity. In the Japanese context, mergers and acquisitions are less relevant as they believe in alliances and joint ventures than mergers and acquisitions. Also, research has shown that Japanese are the least-preferred merger partner/acquirer. The reason being incompatible on language.

Exhibit 8.2 Japanese Firms Are Responding Quickly to the Recession, but Are They Doing Enough?

Illustration by *Claudio Munoz*

In recent months, Toyota has replaced its bosses, halted pet projects and temporarily cut production in Japan almost in half. Toshiba took control of affiliates and said it would shut down unprofitable businesses. Sony plans to halve the number of its suppliers to save ¥500 billion ($5.2 billion) this year alone. All have cut back their part-time and temporary workers, who had only ever been promised a paycheque, not a job for life. The actions of these prominent Japanese companies have encouraged others to follow suit.

During the 'lost decade' of 1991–02, Japanese firms dithered rather than adopting the hard measures that might have prevented a long stagnation. But this time the response has been much faster and deeper. After all, if any country ought to know how to respond to a low- or no-growth environment it is Japan: it has had plenty of practice. The press has done its part, continually reminding the public of the 'once in a century' nature of the crisis and thus providing support for the lay-offs. And banks have played a more constructive role than they did in the 1990s, by refusing to extend credit to some needy firms that cannot meet their obligations—to the dismay of politicians and bureaucrats. It helps that unlike during the bursting of the country's bubble economy in 1991, the crisis originated outside Japan and all unpleasant measures could be blamed on the American bankers whom many Japanese held responsible for it. And the sudden collapse of export sales, which happened in tandem with a spike in commodity prices and an appreciation of the yen (which makes Japan's exports more expensive), meant that corporate Japan had no choice but to act.

All this is quite a turnaround. During the lost decade, Japan regarded its problems as a private, domestic matter: it resented outside pressure to sort out errant banks, speculative property developers, excessively ambitious conglomerates and so on. Corporate reforms were introduced, though slowly and imperfectly. Jobs, sacrosanct in Japan, were eventually shed. The reaction this time is notable because it capitalizes on the changes introduced back then and provides an opportunity to push for even more restructuring. It is sorely needed. The drop-off in demand from the West has clobbered Japan's export economy. Foreign trade is down one-third. Japan's economy is expected to contract by 6% this year, making it the worst-hit among rich countries. Industrial overcapacity is thought to be much higher than in America or Europe. Indeed, things are so bad that it is generally assumed that they cannot get any worse, and will instead improve over the next six months as the inventory cycle turns and firms restock. This has helped push the Nikkei 225 share index up by around 40% since March, when it hit a 26-year-low. Many firms failed to restructure seriously during the lost decade, especially after 2002 when record profits poured in from exports. Companies refused to streamline their sprawling operations and spin off non-core units (it is common for firms to own their own holiday resorts, for instance). But the recession has strengthened the hand of reformers.

The most widespread form of restructuring is the easiest: cutting staff. Since the 'lost decade', Japan's labour force has become more flexible, as the post-war tradition of lifetime employment has waned. 'Non-regular' workers, as temps and part-timers are known, have increased from one-fifth to one-third of the workforce. Labour represents around 70% of Japanese business costs: though hard on individuals who are sacked, the rise of non-regular workers has let firms cut costs fast. It is still difficult and expensive to lay off 'regular' workers. Firms typically provide the main pensions to staff they jettison, as well as lump-sum severance packages. This explains why companies such as Toshiba must raise huge sums to cover restructuring costs.

But is the restructuring going far enough? The emphasis has been on cost-cutting, rather than overhauling business models. And most of the big moves have been made by Japan's big export-focused firms, which were the first to be affected by the downturn. There has been much less reform among Japan's huge swathe of inefficient, domestically oriented companies. Moreover, even those firms that are trying to cut costs have tried to spread the pain among their suppliers, which may actually make things worse in the long run. The advantage of commercial camaraderie is that firms can count on at least a little business to keep them alive. But propping up ailing ones ultimately harms their healthier rivals, by depriving them of resources they could more fruitfully deploy, including capital and qualified staff. An executive at a medium-sized supplier to a big electronics firm explains how. The electronics firm continues to do business with weak suppliers offering inferior technology, depressing prices and profits for stronger ones. This has forced him to cut his research budget. 'How can we keep up with the technology cycles if we lack the profits to invest?' he asks.

Source: Corporate restructuring in Japan, *The Economist*, 18 June 2009.

8.8.2 Indian Scenario

In the last few years, India has followed the worldwide trends in consolidation amongst companies through mergers and acquisitions. Companies are being taken over, units are being hived off, joint ventures tantamount to acquisitions are being made and so on. It may be reasonably stated that the quantum of corporate restructurings in the last few years must be more than the corresponding quantum in the four and a half decades after independence. Today, the Indian economy is passing through recession. In such a situation, corporates which are capable of restructuring can contribute towards economic revival and growth. Despite the sluggish economic scenario in India, merger and amalgamation deals have been on the increase. The obvious reason is—as the size of the market shrinks, it becomes extremely difficult for all the companies to survive, unless they cut costs and maintain prices. In such a situation, merger eliminates duplication of administrative and marketing expenses. The other important reason is that it prevents price war in a shrinking market. Companies, by merging, reduce the number of competitors and increase their market share.

Tata's pioneering acquisition of Corus, coupled with Hindalco's acquisition of Novelis and other acquisitions, exemplifies the arrival of India Inc in the global arena. The event is path breaking and displays a level of confidence and values, which places the Indian industry at an altogether new level.

During the year 2006, India Inc acquired several other foreign companies, namely, Arcelor (by Mittal Steel) Betapharm (by Dr Reddy's lab), Terapia (by Ranbaxy), Sabah Forest Industries (by BILT), Eight O'Clock Coffee (by Tata Tea), Hansen (by Suzlan Energy Ltd), and Ritz-CarlonBostan (by Indian Hotels). The other major takeover making waves has been the acquisition of majority interest of Hutch–Essar by Vodafone.

The Supreme Court of India (October 1994) in the landmark judgment of the HLL–TOMCO merger has states as follows:

> In this era of hypercompetitive capitalism and technological change, industrialists have realised that corporate restructurings are perhaps the best route to reach a size comparable to global companies so as to effectively compete with them. The harsh reality of globalisation has dawned that companies which cannot compete globally must sell out as an inevitable alternative.

Corporate India is facing new flexibility requirements due to restructuring, some of which are discussed here:

a. *Employment:* Companies are moving away from relying on workers on open-ended, full-time contracts and, increasingly, use part-time, temporary, 'contingent' and contract workers.
b. *Jobs:* The content of jobs is being expanded to encompass a greater variety of tasks.
c. *Skills:* New work practices are raising skill levels and requirements, and workers are thus required to continuously upgrade their skills so as to be able to cope.
d. *Workplace:* Home- and tele-working is growing, thanks to new information and communication technologies.
e. *Working time:* Increases in demand are met by overtime work or by 'a more flexible approach as to when and how to work', so as to extend operating hours without having to pay overtime rates.
f. *Remuneration:* Profit-sharing, ESOPs and various types of bonuses are becoming more and more common.
g. *Management:* Indians are beginning to understand that a more flexible world is demanding a different kind of management philosophy.
h. *Organization:* There is a trend towards flatter organizational structures. It is clear that corporate restructuring is a deep and pervasive phenomenon across India. The increasing trend of mergers and acquisitions is one of the clearest and most readily measurable manifestations of restructuring.

8.9 Limitations of Corporate Restructuring

Corporate restructuring is the buzzword for those companies which are in dire straits. The best thing that may be done by these companies is to restructure operations so that things may improve. But how practicable are the corporate restructuring activities? Is it the panacea for all corporate ills? A number of limitations can be associated with corporate restructuring, these are as follows:

a. *Work assurance:* Before the announcement of corporate restructuring, especially during integration, the employees of the ailing firm feel relief, but in most cases the reality becomes bitter than the employees used to experience before integration. The management of the acquiring firm takes policy for performance improvement, resulting in the closure of certain divisions or departments tolling a number of jobs.
b. *Retention of best management:* Retaining the best management combination is always an uphill task, with differing pay scales, responsibility levels, product and service portfolios, and organizational vision. Companies pay more attention to the financial figures and benefit is weighed only numerically but they remain very unprofessional in handling the transition process, since corporate restructuring is still a new phenomenon. Joint committees to determine new management provisions are rare and often ineffective.
c. *Delay in deal finalization:* New structures are announced after long delays, and communication is woefully lacking. A gag order is a knee-jerk reaction when corporate senses that things are going wrong. After the initial announcement of corporate restructuring, it takes to finalize the deal as it involves so many issues like board-room tussles, labour trouble and queries from shareholders.
d. *Executive stress:* In most cases, the divisions and products get closure after corporate restructuring. After restructuring, the control of the companies goes to a separate set of management, creating a stress on the executives. While the restructuring takes place through contraction by way of separation the distribution of management brings a large number of denials from the management.
e. *Workers' woes:* At union levels, there is outright opposition to restructuring activities. A number of mergers await legal clearance months after announcement. This is because unions protest pay changes, proposed lay-offs, outsourcing and asset liquidation.
f. *Cultural mismatch:* The situation mostly arises in merger and takeovers when the organizational culture of one firm gets mismatched with other firms. This results in the destroying efficiency of the worker as well as management of both the firms.
g. *Inability to create value:* Corporate restructuring is aimed at generating value for the firm and finally for the shareholders. But very frequently it is observed that the organizations could not create value instead they have destroyed it. Sudden change in the management and organizational vision creates a gap, leaving certain capacity idle and promoting inefficiency in utilization of resources.

For understanding corporate restructuring from strategic perspective, you are requested to follow the companion website (https://study.sagepub.in/shil_FMSP) of the book to download 'Chapter 22: Corporate Restructuring: A Strategic Perspective' free.

Problems and Solutions

1. Amtrak is considering splitting itself up into two parts—the railroad business and the station management business. The split would be done by making a tax-free distribution of shares in a new company, Amstation, to all Amtrak shareholders. This would save Amtrak $50 million next year in administrative costs. Before bringing this proposal to the board, the management would like to demonstrate that shareholders will be better off after the split. Evaluate the proposal, based on the following estimates:

	Existing Amtrak	Estimated Amrak Sans Stations	Estimated Amstation
EBITDA	$475.00	$375.00	$100.00
Tax rate	30%	30%	32%
Beta	0.8	0.85	0.7
Growth rate	3.50%	2.50%	4.5%
Equity	€6,500	€5,500	€1,000
Debt	€6,000	€5,000	€1,000
Risk free	4%	4%	4%
Market risk premium	5.5%	5.5%	5.5%
Debt spread	2.5%	2%	4%

Answer:

Breaking up is hard

	Existing Amtrak	Estimated Amrak Sans Stations	Estimated Amstation
EBITDA	$475.00	$375.00	$100.00
Tax rate	30%	30%	32%
Beta	0.8	0.85	0.7
Growth rate	3.50%	2.50%	4.5%
Equity	€6,500	€5,500	€1,000
Debt	€6,000	€5,000	€1,000
Risk free	4%	4%	4%
Market risk premium	5.5%	5.5%	5.5%
Debt spread	2.5%	2%	4%
Re	8.40%	8.68%	7.85%
Rd	6.50%	6.00%	8.00%
WACC	6.55%	6.54%	6.65%
Enterprise PV	€16,108	€9,505	€4,872
Equity PV	€10,108	€4,505	€3,872
Additional gains/losses		€1,267	€0
Choice	€10,108		€9,644

2. Zombie Inc, a manufacturer of Voodoo dolls for medicinal purposes, is being forced into involuntary liquidation. Ernst & Young is brought in to handle the sale of assets and distribution of proceeds. Ernst & Young estimates that accounts receivable can be collected for 80% of amounts due, inventory can be sold at 50% of book, and the market value of Zombie is about 75% of its depreciated value.

The liquidators' fees are 500,000 and other bankruptcy-related cost amount to $700,000. Federal taxes due are $2 million, and a wrongful death lawsuit is being brought against the company in Haiti. How much can the banks expect to get?

Assets		***Liabilities***	
Cash	100,000	Accounts payable	1,000,000
Accounts receivable	900,000	Short-term secured debt	100,000
Other short-term assets	5,100,000	Long-term bank debt	9,000,000
Property, plant and equipment	8,000,000	Shareholders' equity	4,000,000
Total	14,100,000	Total	14,100,000

Answer:

Assets	***Book***	***Liquidation***	***Liabilities***	***Book***
Cash	100,000	100,000	Accounts payable	1,000,000
Accounts receivable	900,000	720,000	Short-term secured debt	100,000
Other short-term assets	5,100,000	2,550,000	Long-term bank debt	9,000,000
Property, plant and equipment	8,000,000	6,000,000	Shareholders' equity	4,000,000
Total	14,100,000	9,370,000	Total	14,100,000

	Claim	***Get***	***Balance***
Total available			9,370,000
Secured creditors	100,000	100,000	9,270,000
Bankruptcy costs	1,200,000	1,200,000	8,070,000
Taxes	2,000,000	2,000,000	6,070,000
Unsecured creditors	10,000,000	6,070,000	
A/P	1,000,000	607,000	10%
Banks	9,000,000	5,463,000	90%

Multiple Choice Questions

1. Which one of the following is not a motive behind corporate restructuring?
   a. Growth b. Diversification c. Defence d. None
2. Which one of the following kind of corporate restructuring is initiated to exploit the technological expertise of other companies?
   a. Technological b. Financial c. Organizational d. Portfolio
3. If a company wants corporate restructuring due to the pressure of big volume of transactions crossing the border, what form of corporate restructuring should be a right choice?
   a. Changes in ownership structure c. Expansion
   b. Corporate control d. Contraction

4. Which one of the following is a contraction form of corporate restructuring?
   a. Spin-off b. Leveraged buyout c. Split-off d. Split-up
5. Which one of the following is not an expansion form of corporate restructuring?
   a. Acq-hire b. Merger and acquisition c. Joint venture d. Takeover
6. When the merger occurs between two entities of dissimilar size, it is called ________
   a. Absorption b. Acquisition c. Amalgamation d. Acq-hire
7. In which form of merger, two companies from the same business class or market enter into a merger agreement.
   a. Conglomerate b. Horizontal c. Vertical d. None
8. It is a takeover of a company against the wishes of current management and the board of directors.
   a. Friendly b. Proxy contest c. Hostile d. None
9. Which one of the following is an important limitation of corporate restructuring?
   a. Executive stress b. Workers' woes c. Cultural mismatch d. All
10. In a restructuring process, 'action plan' should be implemented in which of the following phases.
    a. Diagnostic b. Planning c. Implementation d. Any

Review Questions

1. What is corporate restructuring? Discuss the significance of corporate restructuring.
2. 'Corporate restructuring is a new concept of shareholders' value generation'. Do you agree? Why?
3. Trace the historical background of corporate restructuring.
4. List and explain the most common reasons of corporate restructuring.
5. Briefly explain the various elements of corporate restructuring.
6. Write a critical note on the present scenario of corporate restructuring, both from global viewpoint and Indian viewpoint.
7. Write short notes on the following topics:
   a. Mergers and acquisitions
   b. Absorption
   c. Tender offers
   d. Assets acquisitions
   e. Joint venture
   f. De-merged company
   g. Resulting company
   h. Spin-offs
   i. Spilt offset
   j. Divestitures
   k. Equity carved out
   l. Split-up
   m. Anti-takeover defences
   n. Share repurchases
   o. Exchange offers
   p. LBO
   q. ESOP
8. What are the limitations of corporate restructuring? Discuss.

Case in Action

Dabur's Growth Strategy in India

Dabur India Ltd. (Dabur), a leading Indian FMCG company, was established in 1884 as a small pharmacy based in Calcutta (now Kolkata). Since then, it had gone on to become a ₹22 billion company (as of 2007). Its product range included toothpastes and toothpowder (Dabur Red and Lal Dant Manjan), hair oils (Vatika), shampoos (Vatika), digestives (Hajmola), fruit juices (Real), nature care isabgol, medicated oils, Ayurvedic products (such as Churnas, Asav Arishtas, Ras Rasaynas, and Chyawanprash) and Honey. It had two major SBUs—Consumer Care Division and Consumer Health Division. Its products were produced in 13 manufacturing locations in Nepal, Nigeria, Egypt, Dubai, and Bangladesh and its products were sold in more than 50 countries. The company had adopted a combination of the organic and inorganic routes in fuelling its growth. Organically, the company started serving the southern region of the country in 2002, which was neglected earlier, to increase its sales. Further, it enhanced its product portfolio in the various product categories. For instances, homemade cooking pastes like ginger, garlic, tomato *puree* and were added to the food business.

On the inorganic growth front, the company acquired the Balsara group of companies in 2005. This acquisition gave Dabur new brands in toothpaste (Promise, Babool and Meswak), mosquito repellents (Odomos), toilet cleaners (Sani Fresh) and air fresheners (Odonil). The acquired toothpaste business balanced the oral care products portfolio as Dabur's sales came from the northern and the eastern parts of the country while Balsara's were from the southern and the western parts of the country. Analysts felt that the combined manufacturing facilities were also likely to yield synergistic effects for Dabur. Besides, the acquisition was expected to result in exploiting economies of scale in marketing, sales and distribution. Dabur was a market leader in herbal digestives, branded honey and Chyawanprash and had a significant share of 26% in baby oil in 2007. The company had more than 30 brands in its portfolio. Some analysts saw this as a cause for concern. They said that the company should focus on a few champion brands. Otherwise, its efforts to sustain so many products and brands would be dissipated. This line of thought was substantiated by the fact that Dabur was not a category leader in any of the consumer products category where it was present. For instance, in the toothpaste market, as of 2007, the company's market share was just 8% against Colgate Palmolive India's nearly 48%, though it had four brands.

Analysts were of the opinion that Dabur should discard products whose volumes were not growing fast enough to deliver margins. In the shampoos market, the company's brand Vatika had a market share of just 5% as of 2007 with a turnover of approximately ₹1.2 billion, though it had been in existence for 10 years. The company intended to double its turnover by focusing on sachets. However, analysts felt that it would not be easy for the company to do so in light of the growing competition from FMCG giants Hindustan Unilever Ltd. and Procter and Gamble Co. Ltd. Due to its small market share, analysts believed that Vatika would not be able to negotiate with the big retailers and consequently its profit margins would suffer. The management at Dabur, however, contended that it had two umbrella brands—Dabur and Vatika—which were being promoted aggressively and consolidated. Further, the company's focus was to be present in as many categories as possible, as long as they offered a herbal platform, even if the company's relative market share in those categories is small.

Source: http://www.icmrindia.org/Short Case Studies/Business Strategy/CLBS109.htm

Questions for Discussion

1. What are your views on the growth strategy adopted by Dabur? Give reasons in support of your answer.
2. Dabur has been following a strategy of creating multiple brands to pursue growth. Do you agree with this statement?
3. What are your views on the resource utilization of Dabur as per the adopted growth strategy? Give reasons in support of your answer.

References

Bowman E.H., H. Singh, M. Useem et al. 1999. 'When Does Restructuring Improve Economic Performance?' *California Management Review*, 41(2): 36.

Bowman, E.H., and H. Singh. 1999. 'When Does Restructuring Improve Performance?' *California Management Review,* Winter, 34–54.

Crum, B. and J. Goldberg. 1998. 'National Oil and Gas Policy Reforms'. *Journal of Financial Economics*, 2: 261–300.

Donaldson, Gordon. 1994. 'Corporate Restructuring: Managing the Change Process from Within'. Boston, US: Harvard Business School Press.

Goizueta, Roberto C. 1997. 'Coca-Cola Chairman Noted for Company Turnaround'. *The New York Times*.

Mallik, A.K., and D. Rakshit. 2006. 'Corporate Restructuring through Demerger: A Case Study'. *Finance India*, 20(4): 1321–38.

Sander et al. 2001. 'Two- and Three-year Achievement Results from the Memphis Restructuring Initiative'. *School Effectiveness and School Improvement*, 12(3): 323–46.

Supreme Court of India, Hindustan Lever Employees Union vs Hindustan Lever Limited and Ors on 24 October, 1994, Bench: A.M. Ahmadi, Cj, R.M. Sahai, S.C. Sen, Case No: Special Leave Petition (civil) 11006 of 1994.

Further Readings

Allen, D. 1997. *An Introduction to Strategic Financial Management*. London: CIMA/Kogan Page.

Arthur, R., and H. Waya. 1963. *A Critical Study of Accounting for Business Combinations, Accounting Research Study,* p. 7. New York: American Institute of Certified Public Accountants.

Bhattacharyya, H.K. 1988. 'Amalgamation and Takeovers'. *Company News and Notes,* 1–11.

Chandra, P. 2004. *Financial Management: Theory and Practice*. New Delhi: Tata McGraw Hill.

Cooper, Donald R., and Pamel S. Schindler. 2003. *Business Research Methods*, 8th ed. Tata Mcgraw Hill Publication.

Copeland, T., T. Koller, and J. Murrin. 1994. *Valuation: Measuring and Managing the Value of Companies*. New York: John Wiley (International Edition).

Copeland, T.E., and J.F. Weston. 1988. *Financial Theory and Corporate Policy*. New York: Addison-Wesley.

Cusatis, P., J. Miles, and J.R. Woolridge. 1993. 'Restructuring through Spin-offs: The Stock Market Evidence'. *Journal of Financial Economics*, 33: 293–311.

Godbole Prasad, G. 2013. *Mergers, Acquisitions and Corporate Restructuring,* 2nd ed. New Delhi: Vikas Publishing House.

Hampton, J.J. 2003. *Financial Decision Making: Concepts, Problems, and Cases*. New Delhi: Prentice Hall of India.

Mergers & Acquisitions in India, May 2015, Nishith Desai Associates. Available at http://articles.economictimes.indiatimes.com/2013-12-30/news/45675580_1_ma-transactions-deals-harish-hv (last accessed on 25 May 2016).

Focus on Financial Sector Development, TNN Apr 24, 2007. Available at http://articles.economictimes.indiatimes.com/keyword/financial-sector (last accessed on 25 May 2016).

Chetan, K.S. 2012. 'A Study of the Stock Market's Reaction to Announcements of Acquisitions by Mid Cap Indian IT Companies'. *Indian Journal of Finance*, 6.

ICAI, Statements of Accounting Standards (AS 14): Accounting for Amalgamation. New Delhi: ICAI. Also available at http://www.icai.org/resource/as14_defin.html

Khan, A.Q., and D.R. Mehta. 1996. 'Voluntary Divestitures and the Choice between Sell-offs and Spin-offs'. *Financial Review*, 4: 885.

Jain, P.K. 2013. 'Impact of Corporate Governance Index on Post-M&A Performance of Indian Acquiring Companies'. *Research Bulletin*, 37, Institute of Cost Accountants of India.

Pandey, I. M. 2010. *Financial Management*, 10th ed. New Delhi: Vikas Publishing.

Shah, Anup P. 2014. Cited in his article 'Corporate Restructuring—Position Under the Companies Bill, 2012' in India Tax Hub on May 13.

Sudarsanam, P.S. 1997. *Essence of Mergers and Acquisitions*. New Delhi: Prentice Hall of India.

Verma, J.C. 2002. *Corporate Mergers, Amalgamations, and Takeovers*. New Delhi: Bharat Publishing House.

Chapter 9
Merger and Acquisition

Chapter Objectives

On completion of this chapter, you will be able to understand:

- The concept of mergers and acquisitions (M&As)
- Types of merger
  - Horizontal mergers, vertical mergers, conglomerate mergers, triangular merger
  - Purchase mergers and consolidation mergers
- History of merger waves
  - Merger waves in the United States: First, second, third, fourth and fifth merger waves
  - Merger waves in the UK
  - Merger waves: The Indian experience
- Why do firms merge?
- Theories of merger: internalization, technological competence, transaction cost and other theories
- Synergies in M&As
- Impact of M&As on stakeholders
- Why do M&As quite often fail?
- Strategic issues in M&A
- Integration in post-merger period
- Managing risk in M&A, causes and preventive measures
- Procedure for merger
- Valuation process in the case of M&A

I stepped out of my car in the parking lot of Google's Mountain View headquarters and, not having a clue which way to go, started following the man ambling down the sidewalk wearing a very odd backpack. A giant spherical camera stuck up behind his shoulders, bouncing above his head like a floating eyeball, capturing everything around us, slurping up oceans of data. We turned the corner and I did a double take as a driverless car slowly cruised by. It was a pair of first impressions that reminded me just how wide ranging and intellectually ambitious Google has become.

Since its early days, Google has looked outside itself for inspiration on new directions its business could take. The search giant's mergers and acquisitions team set new records in 2010 and 2011 for the sheer number of companies it acquired. Last year alone it bought up 25 companies, one every two weeks. If you count the firms acquired for patents and intellectual property, the total number is a whopping 79. Taking a look at Google's peers, it becomes clear just how astonishing these numbers are. Facebook bought just ten companies in 2011; Apple, Amazon, and Microsoft only three apiece.

The pace of acquisition has certainly slowed a little in 2012, with only eleven so far, counting the acquisition of Snapseed-creator Nik Software we reported on this morning. But one of the deals which closed this year was the $12 billion purchase of Motorola Mobility, by far the most money Google has ever spent on an acquisition and the largest number of new employees. It's also a purchase far outside its comfort zone of software.

Google has taken plenty of flack for its extremely broad—some would say lack—of focus. But by and large it's been the most successful among the massive tech firms when it comes to incorporating new companies. Doubleclick and AdSense, both acquired, are major drivers of Google's revenue. YouTube dominates online video. Android goes head-to-head with Apple in mobile. And it's not just companies that are bolted on whole cloth. Premier products like Google Maps, Docs, Analytics, and Voice were also crafted in large part by teams brought in from outside.

Perhaps the most striking fact touted by the Google? In Silicon Valley, the natural order for founders who are acquired is to work in a company for a short period of time while their stock options vest, then leave to start something new. 'Holding onto a founder for a year is considered an accomplishment,' says venture capitalist David Packman. Yet according to David Lawee, who runs the company's M&A department, founders from nearly two thirds of the startups acquired by Google are still with the company.

Is there something special about Google's DNA that makes it particularly adept at buying and integrating other companies? And has this aggressive M&A been key to Google's success? That was the question I had come to answer.

Source: Popper (2012).[1]

M&A is the most popular form of corporate restructuring for expanding or increasing the size and volume of business. The corporate world today is witnessing a sudden surge in this form of corporate restructuring, sweeping across all the industries that have totally restructured the market place. It has been a prominent trend in the advanced capitalist countries since the late 19th century. However, it has become a regular phenomenon only recently in developing countries. The total number of M&As worldwide increased almost four-fold during 1990 to 2001. This trend is different from an earlier scenario wherein the M&As was looked upon as a threat and had evoked images of dark shadows and backdoor entries to the corporate world. However, at present, it has assumed an international dimension due to global economic integration and dismantling of barriers to trade and investment. Back to home, M&As is not new to the Indian economy. In the past, companies have also used this form of restructuring strategies to grow. Having spread their wings haphazardly during the days of the controlled regime, Indian corporate houses are now refocusing on the lines of core competence, market share and global competitiveness. This process of refocusing has been accelerated by the arrival of foreign competitors. Naturally, this requires companies to grow and expand in businesses that they understand well. M&A is one of the most effective methods of corporate restructuring and has, therefore, become an integral part of the long-term business strategy of corporate enterprises. Under this background, the present chapter attempts to discuss trends, historical evolution, reasons, different forms and aspects of M&As.

[1] http://www.theverge.com/2012/9/17/3322854/google-startup-mergers-acquisitions-failure-is-a-feature

9.1 The Concept of M&As

Mergers result in the combination of two or more companies into one, wherein the merging entities lose their identities. Generally, the company that survives is the buyer, which retains its identity, and the seller companies are extinguished. No fresh investment is made through this process. However, an exchange of shares takes place between the entities involved in such a process.

In India, a merger is called 'amalgamation'. Merging companies are called 'amalgamating companies'. The new company is called 'amalgamated company'.

Merger is of two types:

a. *Merger through Absorption:* Absorption is the combination of two or more companies into an existing company and all companies except one lose their identity.

Examples: Western Union Bank Merged With IDBI, New Bank of India Merged With PNB and Bank of New York Merged With Mellon Financial.

b. *Merger through Consolidation:* A consolidation is a combination of two or more companies into a new company. All companies are dissolved to form a new company.

Examples: Hindustan Computers Ltd, Hindustan Instruments Ltd,
Indian Software Co. Ltd, Indian Reprographic Ltd and HCL Ltd.

9.2 Varieties of Mergers

From the perspective of business structures, there is a whole host of different mergers. Here are a few types, distinguished by the relationship between the two companies that are merging:

a. *Horizontal merger:* Two companies that are in direct competition and share the same product lines and markets.
b. *Vertical merger*: A customer and company or a supplier and company. Think of a cone supplier merging with an ice cream maker.
c. *Market-extension merger*: Two companies that sell the same products in different markets.
d. *Product-extension merger:* Two companies selling different but related products in the same market.
e. *Conglomeration*: Two companies that have no common business areas.

9.2.1 Horizontal Merger

A horizontal merger is a merger occurring between companies producing similar goods or offering similar services. Such companies are in direct competition and share the same product lines and markets. This type of merger occurs frequently as a result of larger companies attempting to create more efficient economies of scale. The amalgamation of Daimler-Benz and Chrysler is a popular example of a horizontal merger.

Horizontal mergers permit the surviving company to control a greater share of the market and, it is hoped, gain economies of scale.

This type of merger can have either a very large effect or little to no effect on the market. When two extremely small companies combine, or horizontally merge, the results of the merger are less noticeable. These smaller horizontal mergers are very common. If a small local drug store were to horizontally merge with another local drugstore, the effect of this merger on the drugstore market would be minimal. In a large horizontal merger, however, the resulting ripple effects can be felt throughout the market sector and sometimes throughout the whole economy.

Large horizontal mergers are often perceived as anticompetitive. If one company holding 20% of the market share combines with another company also holding 20% of the market share, their combined shareholding will then increase to 40%. This large horizontal merger has now given the new company an unfair market advantage over its competitors.

9.2.2 Vertical Merger

A vertical merger is a merger between two firms involved in the same business but on different levels. For example, a merger between two companies producing different goods or services for one specific finished product where one firm acquires another firm that is in the same industry but at another stage in the production cycle. The merger permits the firm to gain more control of another level of the manufacturing or selling process within that single industry. This type of merger involves a customer and a company or a supplier and a company merging. Imagine a baseball bat company merging with a wood production company. This would be an example of the supplier merging with the producer and is the essence of vertical mergers.

Firms vertically integrate for many reasons. Some of the most common are to reduce uncertainty over the availability or quality of supplies or the demand for output, to take advantage of available economies of integration, to protect against monopolistic practices of either suppliers or buyers with which the firm must otherwise deal, and to reduce transactions costs such as sales taxes and marketing expenses. Through a vertical merger, the acquiring firm may lower its cost of production and distribution and make more productive use of its resources.

9.2.3 Conglomerate Merger

A conglomerate merger is a merger between firms that are involved in totally unrelated business activities. There are two types of conglomerate mergers: pure and mixed. Pure conglomerate mergers involve companies with nothing in common, while mixed conglomerate mergers involve companies that are looking for product extensions or market extensions. A conglomerate merger occurs when the companies are not competitors and do not have a buyer–seller relationship and is made up of a number of different, seemingly unconnected businesses. In a conglomerate, one company owns a controlling stake in a number of smaller companies, which conduct business separately. Each of a conglomerate's subsidiary businesses runs independently of the other business divisions, but the subsidiaries' management reports to senior management at the parent company. The largest conglomerates diversify business risk by participating in a number of different markets, although some conglomerates elect to participate in a single industry, for example, mining. These are the two philosophies guiding many conglomerates:

a. By participating in a number of unrelated businesses, the parent corporation is able to reduce costs by using fewer resources.
b. By diversifying business interests, the risks inherent in operating in a single market are mitigated.

History has shown that conglomerates can become so diversified and complicated that they are too difficult to manage efficiently. Since the height of their popularity in the period between the 1960s and the 1980s, many conglomerates have reduced the number of businesses under their management to a few choice subsidiaries through divestiture and spin-offs.

There are many reasons for companies to want to merge, which include increasing market share, synergy and cross-selling. Companies also merge to diversify and reduce their risk exposure. However, if a conglomerate becomes too large as a result of acquisitions, the performance of the entire company can suffer.

One example of conglomerate merger would be Phillip Morris, a tobacco company, which acquired General Foods in 1985.

9.2.4 Triangular Merger

In a triangular merger, the acquiring corporation could acquire control of the target corporation without being a constituent corporation. The acquiring corporation forms a new subsidiary into which the target corporation is merged. The stockholders of the acquiring corporation do not have the right to vote on the merger since they are not a constituent corporation. The stockholders of the target corporation will have the same rights as in a two-party merger. A triangular merger refers to the acquisition of a local company through a share swap with a local subsidiary that is wholly owned by a foreign buyer.

9.2.5 Forward Triangular Merger

Forward triangular merger (Figure 9.1) is a type of merger that occurs when the subsidiary of the acquiring corporation merges with the target firm. In a forward triangular merger, the subsidiary's equity merges with the target firm's stock. As a result of the merger, the target becomes a part of the original subsidiary of the acquirer. This form of acquisition is often used for regulatory reasons.

The stock of the acquiring parent corporation is issued in the transaction. No stock of the subsidiary may be issued and the subsidiary must be at least 80% owned by the acquirer.

Figure 9.1 Forward Triangular Merger Structure

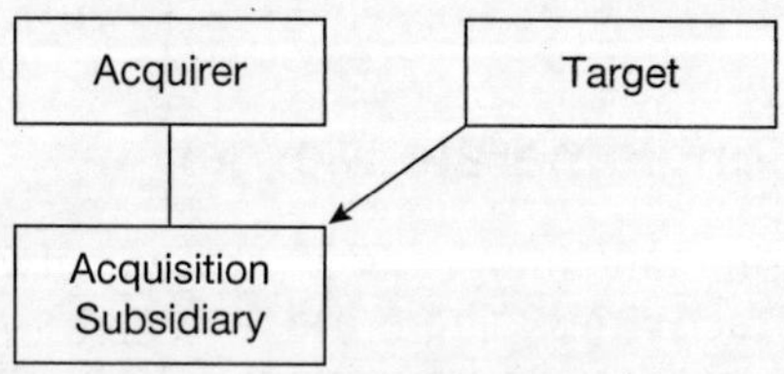

Source: Orlanski, Leib, Tom Petrides and Craig M. Carpente, 'Basic Legal Structures for Selling a Business'. Available at www.financialpoise.com (last accessed on 27 May 2015).

9.2.6 Reverse Triangular Merger

When the subsidiary of the acquiring corporation merges with the target firm, it is referred to as the reverse triangular merger. In this case, the subsidiary's equity merges with the target firm's stock. As a result of the merger, the target would become a wholly-owned subsidiary of the acquirer and shareholders of the target would get shares of the acquirer. In a reverse triangular merger, the merger proceeds in the same manner as a triangular merger, except that the subsidiary is merged into the target corporation. The outstanding shares of stock of the subsidiary, all of which are owned by the acquiring corporation, are converted into shares of stock of the target corporation. The shares of stock of the target corporation are converted into securities of the acquiring corporation. The advantage of this merger is that the target corporation will become a wholly-owned subsidiary of the acquiring corporation without any change in its corporate existence.

The reverse triangular merger, in fact, is a subsidiary of the acquiring corporation merging with the target firm stock (Figure 9.2). The initiator of the merger obtains the target stock as a wholly-owned subsidiary of the acquirer and shareholders of the target and gets shares of the acquirer.

Additionally, there are two types of mergers that are distinguished by how the merger is financed. Each has certain implications for the companies involved and for investors.

Figure 9.2 Reverse Triangular Merger Structure

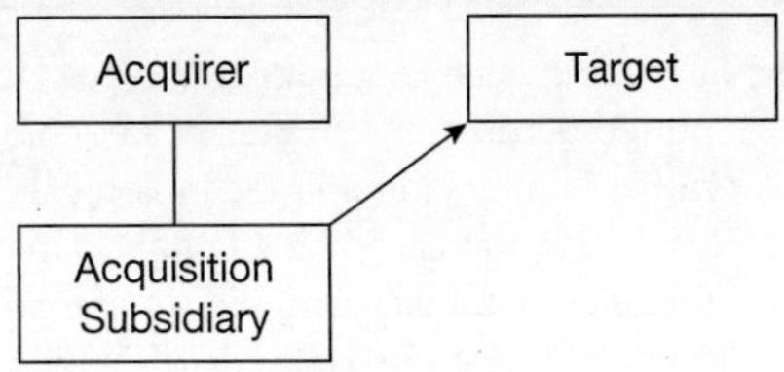

Source: Royse, Roger. 'Negotiating Reverse and Forward Triangular Mergers'. Available at http://www.slideshare.net, (last accessed on 22 June 2014).

9.2.7 Purchase Mergers

As the name suggests, this kind of merger occurs when one company purchases another company. The purchase is made with cash or through the issue of some kind of debt instrument; the sale is taxable.

Acquiring companies often prefer this type of merger because it can provide them with a tax benefit. Acquired assets can be written-up to the actual purchase price, and the difference between the book value and the purchase price of the assets can depreciate annually, reducing taxes payable by the acquiring company.

9.2.8 Consolidation Mergers

With this merger, a brand new company is formed, and both companies are bought and combined under the new entity. The tax terms are the same as those of a purchase merger.

9.3 Historical Perspective of M&As/M&As Waves

M&As can be classified as strategies or quasi-strategies adapted by businesses to achieve growth, expand, disseminate value and basically become better equipped to face competition. These are first started in the 1890s, and the United States recorded the most important M&A activity during this period.

9.3.1 The Merger Movements of the United States

Several countries have experienced high levels of M&A activity in the past. The United States has the longest history of substantial takeover activity going back to the 1890s. Several merger movements have occurred in the United States, and each was more or less dominated by a particular type of merger. All of the merger movements occurred when the economy experienced sustained high rates of growth and coincided with particular developments in business environments.

The different merger waves in the United States have been characterized as follows (Exhibit 9.1):

Exhibit 9.1 A Glimpse on Merger Wave

a. The First Wave: Horizontal Merger Wave (1897–1904)
   - Spurred by drive for efficiency, lax enforcement of anti-trust laws (Sherman Anti- Trust Act) and westward migration and technological changes
   - Resulted in increased concentration in primary metals, transportation, and mining
   - Fraudulent financing and the stock market crash of 1904 ended this boom.
   - 1911: Anti-trust Case (Standard Oil, US Steel)
   - 1914: Federal Trade Commission established

b. The Second Wave: Vertical Merger Wave (1920–29)
   - Driven by entry of the United States into the First World War and the post-war boom.
   - Passage of Clayton Act, which further defined what constituted monopolistic practices, along with the stock market crash of 1929 ended this wave.
   - 1930: investigations, scandals, prosecutions
   - 1936: Clayton Act heavily amended to eliminate loopholes

c. The Third Wave: Conglomerate Merger Wave (1960–69)
   - Emergence of Financial Engineering
   - 1968: Recession/Stagflation/off Gold Standard, oil recessions
   - 1970: AT&T, Xerox, IBM, Investigations cut off by Nixon Administration

d. The Fourth Wave: The Retrenchment Era (1981–89)
   - Strategic U.S. buyers and foreign multinationals dominated the first half of the decade
   - Second half dominated by financial buyers (Growth of junk bond market and the emergence of Drexel Burnham as a market maker created liquidity.)
   - Wave ended with the bankruptcy of several LBOs and demise of Drexel Burnham.

e. The Fifth Wave: Age of the Strategic Megamerger (1992–2000)
   - Dollar volume of transactions reached record levels in each year between 1995 and 2000.
   - Purchase prices reached record levels due to a soaring stock market, trend toward consolidation in many industries, technological innovation, and benign antitrust policies.
   - Wave ended with the collapse in global stock markets and worldwide recession.

f. The Sixth Wave: Age of Cross-border Transactions and Horizontal Megamergers (2004 onwards)
   - Propelled by low interest rates, buoyant equity markets, increasing synchronization among world's economies, globalization, and high commodity prices.

The First Wave (1897–1904)

This wave mainly consisted of horizontal mergers, which resulted in high concentration of many industries, including heavy manufacturing industries. The period was one of rapid economic expansion. In this wave, the industrial production grew by 100%. This wave involved an estimated 15% of all manufacturing assets and employees. An important characteristic of this merger wave was the simultaneous consolidation of producers within industries, thus qualifying for the description 'horizontal consolidation'. Many of the giants of the U.S. corporate world, such as General Electric, Eastman Kodak, American Tobacco and DuPont, were formed during the first wave through such consolidation. Approximately 71 important oligopolistic or near-competitive industries were converted into near monopolies by merger. More than 1800 firms disappeared into consolidations. Of the approximately 93 consolidations, 72 controlled as least 40% market share and 42 controlled at least 70% of their industries.

Although the Sherman Act[2] to control and prevent monopolies had come into effect in the year 1890, it had little immediate effect on the progress or the ferocity of the first wave. This movement peaked in the year 1899 and almost ended in the year 1903 when a severe economic depression set in. The year 1904 decision of the Supreme Court in the Northern Securities case might have contributed to ending the merger wave.

The Second Wave (1920–29)

This wave was a much smaller one than the first wave in terms of its relative impact. In total, it involved less than 10% of the economy's assets. Many combinations in this period occurred outside the previously consolidated heavy manufacturing industries. The public utilities and banking industries were among the most active. About 60% of the mergers occurred in the food processing, chemicals and mining sectors. A large portion of mergers in the 1920s represented product extension mergers, as in the cases of IBM, General Foods and Allied Chemicals, market extension mergers in food retailing, department stores, motion picture theatres and vertical mergers in the mining and metals industries. Since the Sherman Act had proved to be ineffective, the Clayton Act[3] was passed, which basically labelled monopolies as illegal. The second wave accompanied economic growth and stock market boom in the United States. The second wave gave rise to many oligopolistic industrial structures. It, however, collapsed in the year 1929, with the stock market crash of that year and in the following four years of worldwide depression, many of the utility holding companies formed collapsed into bankruptcy.

The Merger Movement Between 1940 and 1947

The Second World War and the early post-war years were accompanied by rapid growth of the economy and an upsurge in merger activity. Being lacking any significant changes in technological and business environments, however, the merger movement was much smaller than the earlier ones.

The Third Wave (1960–69)

The mergers that took place during this period (1960–69) were mainly conglomerate mergers. Mergers were inspired by high stock prices, interest rates and strict enforcement of antitrust laws. The bidder firms in the third wave merger were smaller than the target firms. Mergers

[2] The Sherman Act was passed in 1890 and was named after its author, Senator John Sherman, an Ohio Republican, the chairman of the Senate Finance Committee, who was also Rockefeller's colleague. The purpose of the Act was to oppose the combination of entities that could potentially harm competition, such as monopolies or cartels and today still forms the basis for most antitrust litigation by the U.S. federal government.

[3] A federal law enacted in 1914 as an amendment to the Sherman Anti-Trust Act. Substantively, the Act seeks to capture anticompetitive practices in their incipiency by prohibiting particular types of conduct, not deemed in the best interest of a competitive market.

were financed from equities; the investment banks no longer played an important role. The major industries that saw the merger movement during this phase were aerospace, industrial machinery, railway equipment, auto parts, textiles and tobacco. These kinds of mergers were sponsored by equities, thereby eliminating the roles of banks which they actively played in investment activities earlier. In the year 1968, the attorney general decided to break the multinationals, which resulted in the end of merging activities after that. The decision was triggered by the inefficient performance of the multinationals. But the 1970s saw the emergence of mergers that made their mark by performing effectively. Some mergers in the 1970s which have set precedence were the International Nickel Company (INCO)–ESB merger; United Technologies and OTIS Elevator Merger and the merger between Colt Industries and Garlock Industries.

The Fourth Wave (1981–89)

The late 1970s witnessed a small revival of takeover activity but this did not last long owing to the second oil crisis in the year 1979 and the deep recession of the early 1980s. It was in the middle of the 1980s that there was a fresh surge of takeover activity leading to the fourth merger wave in U.S. history. This wave actually consisted of two waves—acquisitions and divestitures. These two types of corporate restructuring activities are highly correlated with a correlation coefficient of 0.95 (Sudarsanam 2009). Divestitures generally constituted 20%–40% of the M&A activity during this period. Thus, many U.S. corporations engaged in simultaneous expansion and downsizing of their businesses, expanding those that offered scope for greater competitive advantage and exiting those in which their historic competitive advantage had been eroded. Many U.S. companies not only made numerous acquisitions but also sold off some of their component businesses in a move towards increasing the focus of their business portfolio and restricting it to what they deemed were core businesses in which they judged themselves to have competitive advantage. The fourth wave subsided after the year 1989 and the fifth wave enveloped the U.S. economy from 1993 to 2000.

The Fifth Wave (1992–2000)

The fifth wave of the 1990s, to some extent, continued the theme of focus on core competencies as the source of competitive advantage. The fifth wave can be called the mother of all the previous waves as the deals sizes in terms of values and numbers assumed gigantic proportions. In the year 2000, the value of M&A deals was U.S.$1.8 trillion as compared to the previous peak of U.S.$324 billion in the year 1989. In this phase, the firms started making acquisitions on the basis of the need to augment their resources and capabilities in order to enhance their competitive advantage. The 1990s saw the emergence of new technologies such as the Internet, cable television and satellite communication, which spawned new industries and firms with new technological capabilities. Starting in the fourth merger wave (1992–98) and continuing today, companies are more likely to acquire in the same business, or close to it, firms that complement and strengthen an acquirer's capacity to serve customers. Buyers are not necessarily hungry for the target companies' physical assets. Now they are going after entirely different prizes. The hot prizes are not things—they are thoughts, methodologies, people and relationships. Many companies are being bought for their patents, licenses, market share, brand name, research staffs, methods, customer base or culture. Soft capital, like this, is very perishable, fragile and fluid. Integrating it usually takes more finesse and expertise than integrating machinery, real estate, inventory and other tangibles. Hence, it may be said that the evolution of M&As has been long drawn. Many economic factors have contributed to its development. There are several other factors that have impeded their growth. As long as economic units of production exist, M&As would continue for an ever-expanding economy.

The Sixth Wave (Year 2004 Onwards)

The last wave of the mergers and restructuring activities can be said to have started from the year 2003 and is still continuing. This wave is characterized by deals in which corporate governance and shareholder activism are of primary importance. Deals have now reached such humongous proportions that LBOs have become the dominant method for acquisitions. Private equity deals are also on the increase.

9.3.2 Merger Waves in the EU

The European Union (EU) member countries have experienced increasing levels of takeover activity since the year 1984. Two waves can be identified for this region; a small one during the years 1987–92 and a vastly bigger one between the years 1995 and 2001. The late 1980s and the 1990s, which accompanied the two merger waves in the EU, have been epochal and turbulent times in the history of the continent. This was a period of continual changes with newer and ever more audacious initiatives being taken in the spheres of politics, economics and the social institutions to further European integration. Among them is the Single-Market initiative, which came into effect in the year 1992, and the European Economic and Monetary Union project[4], which has ushered in monetary union among 12 out of 15 member states with the introduction of a single currency, euro, from the year 1999. This was also the period when the Cold War[5] ended, the Berlin Wall collapsed and the countries of Eastern and Central Europe started dismantling state controls of their economies and adopting free markets and private enterprise with enthusiasm and passion.

These historic events were also accompanied by the spread of deregulation and privatization by member states to improve the competitiveness of the EU economies. Although stock markets have traditionally been less important as a source of funding for EU firms, apart from UK firms, than in the United States, the stock markets experienced prolonged bull phases. The technological changes in IT, telecommunications, biotechnology and so on provided new growth opportunities which the EU firms sought to exploit through M&As.

9.3.3 Merger Waves in the UK

Active merger movement in the UK can be traced to the 1960s, although two mini merger booms happened in the 1890s and 1920s. The 1960s and 1980s merger waves in the United States have a striking parallel to the merger waves in the United States during the same period.

[4] The Economic and Monetary Union (EMU) is an umbrella term for the group of policies aimed at converging the economies of members of the European Union in three stages so as to allow them to adopt a single currency, the euro. As such, it is largely synonymous with the euro zone.

[5] Cold War was the conflict between the Communist nations led by the erstwhile Soviet Union and the democratic nations led by the United States. It was fought by all means—propaganda, economic war, diplomatic haggling and occasional military clashes. There were deep-rooted ideological, economic and political differences between the United States and the Soviet Union before the Second World War. These differences were intensified as a result of their mutual suspicions immediately after the Second World War, which led to a situation of cold war between them.

The first wave peaking in the year 1968 was largely fuelled by horizontal mergers. This characteristic differentiates the UK wave from the U.S. wave of the same period. The latter represented a shift from monopolistic and oligopolistic mergers of the first two waves to conglomerate mergers. Under the Labour government of the year 1964, a new industrial policy was adopted to strengthen the UK companies into 'national champions' that could take on competitors on world markets. The Industrial Reorganization Corporation was the newly created instrument for bringing about this transformation. During the years 1965–69, Industrial Reorganization Corporation sponsored approximately 50 horizontal mergers. The mergers sponsored by the Industrial Reorganization Corporation generally escaped antitrust scrutiny by the Monopolies and Mergers Commission.

The second wave, which peaked in the year 1972, was also characterized by horizontal mergers but on a slightly smaller scale. There was also greater incidence of conglomerate mergers. While horizontal mergers accounted for 82% of number and 89% of assets involved in mergers considered by the Mergers Panel of the Monopolies and Mergers Commission during the years 1965–69, in the following wave, in the years 1970–74, the corresponding figures are 73% and 65%, respectively.

The third wave was of tidal proportions as compared to the previous two. As in the United States, this wave coincided with a stock market bull run from the recession of the years 1980–81 to the market crash of the 1987. Massive restructuring was seen in the manufacturing industries and in the financial services sector in the 1980s. The 'Big Bang Deregulation'[6] of the financial services sector in the City of London heralded the arrival of the U.S. investment banks, which brought not only their huge capital-raising capabilities but also their investment banking expertise and techniques in the areas of M&As advisory work, corporate restructuring, risk management, securities trading and stock broking. The effect of the Big Bang on the financial sector in the UK can be termed as cataclysmic as most of the British merchant banks, brokerage houses and securities firms were systematically swallowed up, initially by American and subsequently by continental European companies.

The fourth wave happened in the 1990s when UK experienced a series of privatizations. Sectors such as water, electricity and gas were privatized. Further deregulation of the telecom industry took place, increasing pressure on British Telecom—a monopoly—to restructure. Many firms undertook divestitures.

9.3.4 Global Scenario of M&As

The global M&A scenario from the years 1992 to 2006 has been shown in Figure 9.3. The year 2000 was a very prominent year for M&As globally. Deals worth around €4,000 billion (approximately U.S.$5785.68 billion) were struck in the year 2000. The year 2006 followed suit with around €3,700 billion (U.S.$5351 billion).

Table 9.1 shows some of the biggest M&A deals globally between 2000 and 2010.

[6] The phrase 'Big Bang', used in reference to the sudden deregulation of financial markets, was coined to describe measures, including abolition of fixed commission charges and of the distinction between stock-jobbers and stock-brokers on the London Stock Exchange and change from open outcry to electronic, screen-based trading, enacted by the UK government in 1986. In the UK, Big Bang became one of the cornerstones of the Thatcher government's reform programme. Prior to these reforms, the once-dominant financial institutions of the City of London were failing to compete with foreign banking. The effects of Big Bang were dramatic, with London's place as a financial capital decisively strengthened, to the point where it arguably became the world's most important financial centre.

Figure 9.3 Global M&A Scenario

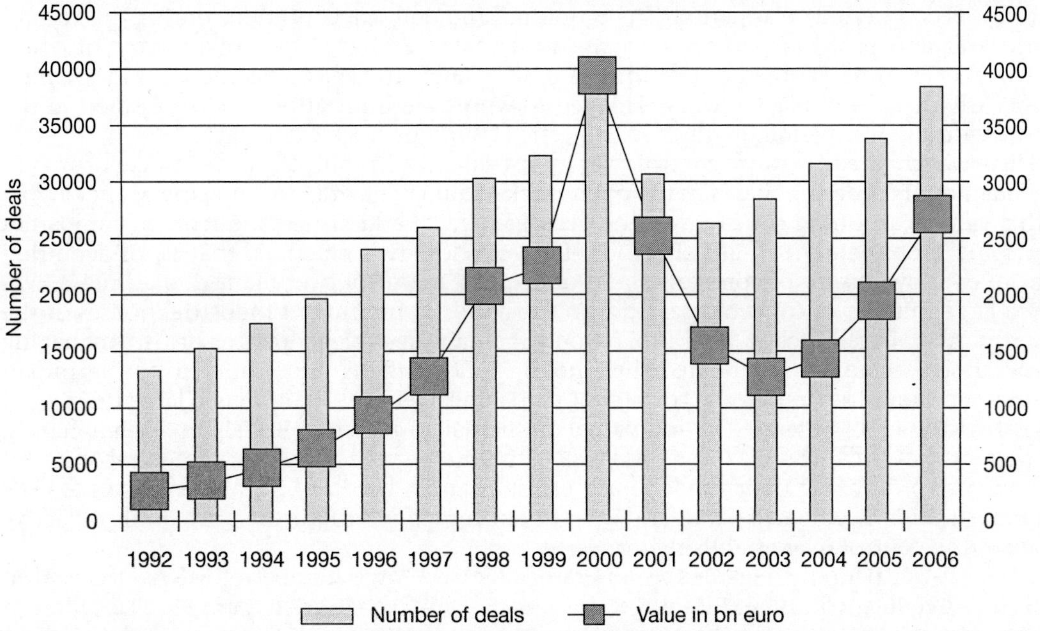

Source: www.worksproject.be/documents/Buelens.ppt (last accessed on 26 July 2016).

Table 9.1 Top 10 Global M&As (2000–10)

Rank	***Year***	***Purchaser***	***Target***	***Transaction Value (U.S.$ millions)***
1	2000	America Online Inc. (AOL)	Time Warner	164,747
2	2000	Glaxo Wellcome Plc.	SmithKline Beecham Plc.	75,961
3	2004	Royal Dutch Petroleum Co	Shell Transport & Trading	74,559
4	2006	AT&T Inc.	BellSouth Corporation	72,671
5	2001	Comcast Corporation	AT&T Broadband & Internet	72,041
6	2009	Pfizer Inc.	Wyeth	68,000
7	2000	Nortel Networks Corporation: Spin-off		59,974
8	2002	Pfizer Inc.	Pharmacia Corporation	59,515
9	2004	JP Morgan Chase & Co	Banc One Corp	58,761
10	2008	Inbev Inc.	Anheuser-Busch Companies, Inc	52,000

Source: http://en.wikipedia.org/wiki/Mergers_and_acquisitions#Major_M.26A

9.3.5 Historical Perspective of M&A in India

M&As have played an important role in the transformation of the industrial sector of India since the Second World War period. The economic and political conditions during the Second World War and post-war periods gave rise to a spate of M&As. The inflationary situation during the wartime enabled many Indian businessmen to amass income by way of high profits, dividends and black money. This led to wholesale infiltration of businessmen in the industry during war period, giving rise to hectic activity in stock exchanges.

There was a craze to acquire control over industrial units in spite of swollen prices of shares. The practice of cornering shares in the open market and trafficking of managing agency rights with a view to acquiring control over the management of established and reputed companies had come prominently to light. The net effect of these two practices, that is, of acquiring control over ownership of companies and of acquiring control over managing agencies, was that a large number of concerns passed into the hands of prominent industrial houses of the country. As it became clear that India would be gaining independence, British managing agency houses gradually liquidated their holdings at fabulous prices offered by the Indian business community. Besides the transfer of managing agencies, there were a large number of cases of transfer of interests in individual industrial units from British to Indian hands. Further, at that time, it used to be the fashion to obtain control of insurance companies for the purpose of utilizing their funds to acquire substantial holdings in other companies. The big industrialists also floated banks and investment companies for furtherance of the objective of acquiring control over established concerns.

The post-war period is regarded as an era of M&As. A large number of M&As occurred in industries like jute, cotton textiles, sugar, insurance, banking, electricity and tea plantation. It has been found that, although there was a large number of M&As in the early post independence period[7], the anti-big government policies and regulations of the 1960s and 1970s seriously deterred M&As. This does not mean that M&As were uncommon during the controlled regime. The deterrent was mostly to horizontal combinations which result in concentration of economic power to the common detriment. However, there were many conglomerate combinations. In some cases, even the government encouraged M&As, especially for sick units. Certain historic mergers/amalgamations did take place which are worthy of mention.

Mergers/Amalgamations before liberalization in India

Bank of Hindustan, set up in the year 1870, was the earliest Indian Bank. Banking in India on modern lines started with the establishment of three presidency banks under Presidency Bank's Act of the year 1876, that is, Bank of Calcutta, Bank of Bombay and Bank of Madras. In the year 1921, all presidency banks were amalgamated to form the Imperial Bank of India.

LIC of India was incorporated in the year 1956 with the amalgamation of over 200 insurance companies and provident societies. Previously, it was known as Oriental Life Insurance Company. The company was the first to offer life coverage in India. There was a similar development in the general insurance business.

The National Textiles Corporation (NTC) took over a large number of sick textile units.

[7] Post independence, for about 10 years, India was receptive towards foreign investment due to various reasons. Thereafter, due to change in policies, India became a closed economy. Hence, it became nearly impossible for an Indian business firm to think of inviting foreign investment, leave alone investing abroad. The concept of M&As gained popularity in India, after the government introduced the new economic policy in 1991, thereby paving the way for economic reforms and opening up a whole lot of challenges in both the domestic and international spheres.

In the year 1950, the Goenka group acquired two British trading houses, namely the Duncan Brothers and Octavius Steel. They also had some successful acquisitions in the areas of tea, automobiles, tyres, jute, electric cables and cotton textiles.

Mergers/Amalgamations after Liberalization in India

The functional importance of M&As is undergoing a sea change since liberalization in India. The Monopolies and Restrictive Trade Practices (MRTP) Act and other legislations have been amended paving way for large business groups and foreign companies to resort to the M&A route for growth. Further, the SEBI (Substantial Acquisition of Shares and Takeover) Regulations, of the years 1994 and 1997, have been notified. The decision of the government to allow companies to buy back their shares through the promulgation of a buyback ordinance, and other such developments, have influenced the market for corporate control in India. M&As as strategies were employed by several corporate groups such as R.P. Goenka, Vijay Mallya and Manu Chhabria for growth and expansion of their empires in India in the 1980s. Some of the companies taken over by the RPG group included Dunlop, Ceat, Phillips Carbon Black and Gramophone India. The first of the acquisitions was Ceat Tyres of India in the year 1981.

The group then went on to acquire KEC (1982), Searle India (now RPG Life Sciences, 1983), Dunlop (1984), Gramophone Company of India Ltd (now Saregama India, 1986) and finally CESC, Harrisons Malayalam, Spencer & Co. and ICIL, all in 1989.

Vijay Mallya's United Breweries (UB) group was straddled mostly by M&As. Further, in the post-liberalization period, the giant Hindustan Lever Limited has employed M&A as an important growth strategy. The Ajay Piramal group has almost entirely been built up by M&As. The south-based Murugappa group built an empire by employing M&A as a strategy. Some of the companies acquired by the Murugappa group include EID Parry, Coromondol Fertilizers, Bharat Pulverising Mills, Sterling Abrasives, Cut Fast Abrasives and so on. Other companies and groups whose growth has been contributed by M&As include Ranbaxy Laboratories Limited and Sun Pharmaceuticals Industries, particularly during the latter half of the 1990s.

During this decade, there had been a plethora of M&As happening in every sector of the Indian economy. Even the known and big industrial houses of India, like the Reliance group, Tata group and Birla group, have engaged in several big deals.

The Recent Trends in the Indian M&As Scenario (2001–11)

Indian activities in the arena of M&As have indeed increased manifold over the last one decade. According to the India Brand Equity Foundation, the trust run by the Union Ministry of Commerce and Confederation of Indian Industry (CII), outward investment to the tune of $80 billion has been made between 2000 and 2010; the UK and the United States have emerged as the favoured destinations.

A CII survey report shows that Indian companies actually helped save and create thousands of jobs in the United States through acquisitions of local firms there. It reports that since the year 2005, nearly 65% of the Indian companies operating in the United States have added jobs to their operations; more than 80% of the hiring was local.

Some of the Significant M&A Deals Involving Indian Companies

The Tata Group

In February 2000, the Tetley group, the world's second largest producer and distributor of tea, was purchased by India's Tata group for British £271 million. In the year 2004, Tata Motors acquired Daewoo's truck manufacturing unit in South Korea. In the year 2005, Tata Motors

Table 9.2 A Snapshot of the Major Merger Deals Involving Indian Companies (2007–10)

Rank	Year	M&A Deals	Deal Value (U.S.$ Billions)	Sector
1	2007	CORUS–Tata Steel	12.2	Steel
2	2010	Reliance Natural–Reliance Power	11.0	Oil and gas
3	2007	HUTCHISON–Vodafone	10.8	Telecom
4	2010	ZAIN–Bharti	10.7	2010
5	2007	NOVELIS–Hindalco	6.0	Aluminium
6	2007	NOVELIS–Hindalco	6.0	Aluminium
7	2010	PIRAMAL–Abbott	3.7	Pharmaceuticals
8	2008	IMPERIAL–ONGC Videsh	2.8	Oil and gas
9	2008	TATA TELE–NTT Docoma	2.7	Telecom
10	2008	Centurion Bank–HDFC Bank	2.4	Banking and financial services

Source: Grant Thornton Deal Tracker 2010.

acquired 21% of Aragonese Hispano Carrocera, giving it controlling rights of the company. In January 2007, Tata Steel purchased a 100% stake in the Corus group at 608 pence per share in an all cash deal, cumulatively valued at U.S.$12.04 billion, fending off a serious challenge from CSN, the Brazilian steel maker. The deal marked the largest Indian takeover of a foreign company and made Tata Steel, the world's fifth-largest steel group. In June 2008, Tata Motors acquired British Jaguar Land Rover (JLR), which includes the Daimler and Lanchester brand names, from Ford for U.S.$2.3 billion. In April 2011, Tata Chemicals acquired a 25.1% stake in an ammonia-urea fertilizer complex in Gabon for U.S.$290 million in which Singapore-based agro-product processor and supplier Olam International owns a 63% stake and the Republic of Gabon holds 12%. The company acquired the stake as a strategic investor and is likely to invest another U.S.$170 million in the second phase of expansion of the fertilizer complex (Table 9.2).

Aditya Birla Group

In February 2007, the Aditya Birla group's Hindalco entered into an agreement to acquire Canadian company Novelis for U.S.$6 billion, making the combined entity the world's largest rolled aluminium producer. The group also owns copper mines in the Great Sandy Desert, Western Australia and the Mt. Isa Block in Queensland.

UB Group

United Spirits Ltd (USL), the flagship of the UB group and the world's third largest spirits producer, purchased the Scottish distiller Whyte and Mackay in May 2007 for British £595 million. This included brands like The Dalmore, Isle of Jura, Glayva, Fettercairn, Vladivar Vodka and Whyte & Mackay Scotch. In the year 2006, Asian Opportunities and Investments Limited, UB's wholly-owned subsidiary in Mauritius, announced the acquisition of French wine maker Bouvet Ladubay for €14.75 million.

Bharti Group

The U.S.$10.7 billion acquisition of Zain's African business by Bharti Airtel in the year 2010 was the second largest ever involving an Indian company.

ONGC

In January 2009, ONGC Videsh Limited (OVL) completed the acquisition of Imperial Energy Corporation Plc, a UK-based company having exploration and production assets in the Tomsk region of Western Siberia, Russia, with an investment of over U.S.$2.1 billion.

Suzlon Energy

In March 2006, Hansen Transmissions, the Belgian gearbox maker for wind turbines, was acquired by the Tulsi Tanti-led wind turbine major, Suzlon Energy, through its subsidiary, AE-Rotor Holding BV, for €465 million in cash. In May 2007, a series of protracted bidding resulted in Suzlon Energy acquiring the majority shareholding in Repower, the German wind turbine manufacturer, for €1.3 billion. Suzlon subsequently strengthened its position by buying another 30% stake in June 2008, for more than €350 million. In 2009, Suzlon raised its share to 92% of Repower.

Mahindra & Mahindra

In January 2007, Mahindra and Mahindra Limited, through its Mauritius-based subsidiary Mahindra Forgings Global Limited, acquired a 90.47% stake in Schoneweiss & Co. GmbH, a leading company in the forgings sector in Germany and valued at €90 million then. The value of the deal was not disclosed.

Meanwhile, foreign companies were also busy in snapping up Indian companies as and when they smelt opportunities. Here are a few most notable ones.

Vodafone

In the year 2007, the Vodafone group bought out the 33% stake of the Essar group for U.S.$5 billion in Hutchison Essar. Earlier on 11 February 2007, Vodafone had agreed to acquire the controlling interest of 67% held by Li KaShing Holdings in Hutchison-Essar for U.S.$11.1 billion.

Daiichi-Sankyo

In June 2008, Daiichi-Sankyo of Japan acquired a 34.8% stake in Ranbaxy for U.S.$2.4 billion. In November 2008, the Japanese drugs major completed the takeover in a deal worth U.S.$4.6 billion by acquiring a 63.92% stake in Ranbaxy.

Holcim

A 67% stake in Ambuja Cement India Limited was acquired by Holcim, the Swiss-based cement and construction materials giant, for U.S.$634.9 million.

IBM

The year 2004 deal involving the acquisition of business process outsourcing service provider Daksh e-Services by technology behemoth IBM was valued between U.S.$130 and 170 million. M&As have become the accepted way to grow business in today's world. It is less time consuming than green-field projects and a higher cost is compensated by technology transfer and instant market access.

9.4 Why Do Firms Merge?/Reasons for Merger/Theories of Merger

M&As are strategic decisions leading to the maximization of a company's growth by enhancing its production and marketing operations. They have become popular in the recent times because of the enhanced competition, breaking of trade barriers, free flow of capital across countries and globalization of business as a number of economies are being deregulated and integrated with other economies. A number of motives are attributed for the occurrence of mergers. Again, the variety of these reasons for M&As and the diversity of their consequences have given rise to a series of theories/hypotheses, each of which attempts to explain part of this phenomenon known as 'theories of merger'. These theories/hypotheses can be subsumed into the following.

9.4.1 Synergy/Efficiency Theory

Synergy implies a situation where the combined firm is more valuable than the sum of the individual combining firms. It is defined as 'two plus two equal to five' $(2+2=5)$ phenomenon. Synergy refers to benefits other than those related to economies of scale. Operating economies are one form of synergy benefits. However, apart from operating economies, synergy may also arise from enhanced managerial capabilities, creativity, innovativeness, R&D and market coverage capacity due to the complementarily of resources and skills and a widened horizon of opportunities.

An undervalued firm will be a target for acquisition by other firms. However, the fundamental motive for the acquiring firm to take over a target firm may be the desire to increase the wealth of the shareholders of the acquiring firm. This is possible only if the value of the new firm is expected to be more than the sum of individual value of the target firm and the acquiring firm. For example, if A Ltd and B Ltd decide to merge into AB Ltd then the merger is beneficial if

$$V(AB) > V(A) + V(B)$$

where V (AB) is the value of the merged entity, V (A) is the independent value of company A and V (B) is the independent value of company B.

A merger that results in meeting the test of increasing the wealth of the shareholders is said to contain synergistic properties. Synergy is the increase in the value of the firm combining two firms into one entity, that is, it is the difference value between the combined firm and the sum of the value of the individual firms. Igor Ansoff (1987) classified four different types of synergies. These are as follows.

Operating Synergy

The key to the existence of synergy is that the target firm controls a specialized resource that becomes more valuable when combined with the bidding firm's resources. The sources of synergy of specialized resources will vary depending upon the merger. In case of horizontal merger, the synergy comes from some form of economies of scale which reduce the cost or from increase market power which increases profit margins and sales. There are several ways in which the merger may generate operating economies. The firm might be able to reduce the cost of production by eliminating some fixed costs. The R&D expenditures will also be substantially reduced in the new set-up by eliminating similar research efforts and repetition of work already done by the target firm.

The management expenses may also come down substantially as a result of corporate reconstruction. The selling, marketing and advertisement department can be streamlined. The marketing economies may be produced through savings in advertising (by reducing the need to attract each other's customers), and also from the advantage of offering a more complete product line (if the merged firms produce different but complementary goods), since a wider product line may provide larger sales per unit of sales efforts and per sales person. When a firm having strength in one functional area acquires another firm with strength in a different functional area, synergy may be gained by exploiting the strength in these areas. A firm with a good distribution network may acquire a firm with a promising product line and thereby can gain by combining strength of these two. The argument is that both firms will be better off after the merger. A major saving may arise from the consolidation of departments involved with financial activities, for example, accounting, credit monitoring, billing, purchasing and so on. Thus, when two firms combine their resources and efforts, they will be able to produce better results than they were producing as separate entities because of savings various types of operating costs. These resultant economies are known as synergistic operating economies.

In a vertical merger, a firm may combine either with its supplier of input (backward integration) and/or with its customers (forward integration). Such merger facilitates better coordination and administration of the different stages of business stages of business operations—purchasing, manufacturing and marketing—eliminates the need for bargaining (with suppliers and/or customers) and minimizes uncertainty of supply of inputs and demand for product and saves costs of communication.

An example of a merger resulting in operating economies is the merger of Sundaram Clayton Ltd (SCL) with TVS-Suzuki Ltd (TSL). By this merger, TSL became the second largest producer of two-wheelers after Bajaj. The main objective motivation for the takeover was TSL's need to tide over its different market situation through increased volume of production. It needed a large manufacturing to reduce its production costs. A large amount of funds would have been required for creating additional production capacity. SCL also needed to upgrade its technology and increase its production. SCL's and TCL's plants were closely located which added to their advantages. The combined company has also been able to share the common R&D facilities.

Financial Synergy

Financial synergy refers to increase in the value of the firm that accrues to the combined firm from financial factors. There are many ways in which a merger can result into financial synergy and benefit. A merger may help in:

- eliminating financial constraint
- deployment surplus cash
- enhancing debt capacity
- lowering the financial costs
- better credit worthiness

Financial constraint: A company may be constrained to grow through internal development due to shortage of funds. The company can grow externally by acquiring another company by the exchange of shares and thus releasing the financing constraint.

Deployment of surplus cash: A different situation may be faced by a cash-rich company. It may not have enough internal opportunities to invest its surplus cash. It may either distribute its surplus cash to its shareholders or use it to acquire some other company. The shareholders may not really benefit much if surplus cash is returned to them since they would have to pay tax at an ordinary income tax rate. Their wealth may increase through an increase in the market value of their shares if surplus cash is used to acquire another company. If they sell their shares, they would pay tax at a lower, capital gains tax rate. The company would also be enabled to keep surplus funds and grow through acquisition.

Debt capacity: A merger of two companies, with fluctuating, but negatively correlated, cash flows, can bring stability of cash flows of the combined company. The stability of cash flows reduces the risk of insolvency and enhances the capacity of the new entity to service a larger amount of debt. The increased borrowing allows a higher interest tax shield which adds to the shareholders wealth.

Financing cost: The enhanced debt capacity of a merged firm reduces its cost of capital, and as the probability of insolvency is reduced due to financial stability and increased protection to lenders, the merged firm should be able to borrow at a lower rate of interest. This advantage may, however, be taken off partially or completely by increase in the shareholders risk on account of providing better protection to lenders. Another aspect of the financing costs is issue costs. A merged firm is able to realize economies of scale in flotation and transaction costs related to an issue of capital. Issue costs are saved when the merged firm makes a larger security issue.

Better creditworthiness: This helps the company to purchase the goods on credit, obtain bank loan and raise capital in the market easily. RP Goenka's Ceat tyres sold off its tyre cord division to Shriram Fibers Ltd in 1996 and also transferred its fibre glass division to FGL Ltd, another group company to achieve financial synergies.

Managerial Synergy

One of the potential gains of merger is an increase in managerial effectiveness. This may occur if the existing management team, which is performing poorly, is replaced by a more effective management team. Often a firm, plagued with managerial inadequacies, can gain immensely from the superior management that is likely to emerge as a sequel to the merger. Another allied benefit of a merger may be in the form of greater congruence between the interests of the managers and the shareholders.

A common argument for creating a favourable environment for mergers is that it imposes a certain discipline on the management. If lacklustre performance renders a firm more vulnerable to potential acquisition, existing managers will strive continually to improve their performance.

Sales Synergy

These synergies occur when a merged organization can benefit from common distribution channels, sales administration, advertising, sales promotion and warehousing. The Industrial

Credit and Investment Corporation of India Ltd (ICICI) acquired Tobaco Company, ITC, Classic and Anagram Finance to obtain quick access to a well-dispersed distribution network.

9.4.2 Diversification

A commonly stated motive for mergers is to achieve risk reduction through diversification. The extent to which risk is reduced depends upon on the correlation between the earnings of the merging entities. While negative correlation brings greater reduction in risk, positive correlation brings lesser reduction in risk. If investors can diversify on their own by buying stocks of companies which propose to merge, they do not derive any benefits from the proposed merger. Any investor who wants to reduce risk by diversifying between two companies, say, ABC Company and PQR Company, may simply buy the stocks of these two companies and merge them into a portfolio. The merger of these companies is not necessary for him to enjoy the benefits of diversification. As a matter of fact, his 'homemade' diversification gives him far greater flexibility. He can contribute the stocks of ABC Company and PQR Company in any proportion he likes as he is not confronted with a 'fixed' proportion that result from the merger.

Thus, diversification into new areas and new products can also be a motive for a firm to merge another with it. A firm operating in North India, merging with another firm operating primarily in South India, can definitely cover broader economic areas. Individually, these firms could serve only a limited area. Moreover, products diversification resulting from merger can also help the new firm fighting the cyclical/seasonal fluctuations. For example, firm A has a product line with a particular cyclical variations and firm B deals in product line with counter-cyclical variations. Individually, the earnings of the two firms may fluctuate in line with the cyclical variations. However, if they merge, the cyclically prone earnings of firm A would be set off by the counter-cyclically prone earnings of firm B. Smoothing out the earnings of a firm over the different phases of a cycle tends to reduce the risk associated with the firm. Through the diversification effects, merger can produce benefits to all firms by reducing the variability of firm's earnings. If firm A's income generally rises when B's income generally falls, and vice-a-versa, the fluctuation of one will tend to set off the fluctuations of the other, thus producing a relatively level pattern of combined earnings. Indeed, there will be some diversification effect as long as the two firms' earnings are not perfectly correlated (both rising and falling together). This reduction in overall risk is particularly likely if the merged firms are in different lines of business.

The diversification motive is based on the proposition that if two risky projects are combined, then the risk of combination will be less than the weighted average of the risk of these two projects. The greatest benefit from diversification can be obtained by continuing firms from different industries, that is, conglomerate mergers, where two firms with poorly correlated cash flows merged to create a portfolio of firms. However, the portfolio of firms in a conglomerate merger is costly as the acquisition of firms is a costly exercise. On the other hand, a shareholder can easily create a diversified portfolio of firms merely by holding the shares of diversified companies. This is much easier and cheaper than creating a portfolio of firms in conglomerate merger.

Thus, firms diversify to achieve

- sales and growth stability
- favourable growth developments
- favourable competition shifts
- technological changes.

9.4.3 Accelerated Growth/Growth Theory

Growth is essential for sustaining the viability, dynamism and value-enhancing capability of company. A growth-oriented company is not only able to attract the most talented executives but it would also be able to retain them. Growing operations provide challenges and excitement to the executives as well as opportunities for their job enrichment and rapid career development. This helps to increase managerial efficiency. Other things remaining the same, growth leads to higher profits and increasing shareholders' value. A company can achieve its growth objective by

- expanding its existing markets
- entering in new markets.

A company may expand and/or diversify its markets internally or externally. If the company cannot grow internally due to lack of physical and managerial resources, it can grow externally by combining its operations with other companies through M&As. M&As may help to accelerate the pace of a company's growth in a convenient and inexpensive manner.

Internal growth requires that the company should develop its operating facilities including manufacturing, research, marketing and so on. Internal development of facilities for growth also requires time. Thus, lack or inadequacy of resources and time needed for internal development constrains a company's pace of growth. The company can acquire production facilities as well as other resources from outside through M&As. Specially, for entering in new products/markets, the company may lack technical skills and may require special marketing skills and/or a wide distribution network to access different segments of markets. The company can acquire existing company or companies with requisite infrastructure and skills and grow quickly.

M&As, however, involve cost. External growth could be expensive if the company pays an excessive price for merger. Benefits should exceed the cost of acquisition for realizing a growth that adds value to shareholders. In practice, it has been found that the management of a number of acquiring companies paid an excessive price for acquisition to satisfy their urge for high growth and large size of their companies. It is necessary that price may be carefully determined and negotiated so that merger enhances the value of shareholders.

For example, the RPG group had a turnover of only ₹800 million in 1979. This has increased to about ₹56000 million in 1996. This phenomenal growth was due to the acquisitions of a several companies by the RPG group. Some of the companies acquired are Asian Cables, CEAT, Calcutta Electricity Supply and Company, SAE and so on.

9.4.4 Increased Market Power/Monopoly Theory

A merger can increase the market share of the merged firm. The increased concentration or market share improves the profitability of the firm due to economies of scale. The bargaining power of the firm with labour, suppliers and buyers is also enhanced. The merged firm can also exploit technological breakthroughs against obsolescence and price wars. Thus, by limiting competition, the merged firm can earn supernormal profit and strategically employ the surplus funds to further consolidate its position and improve its market power.

The acquisition of Universal Luggage by Blow Plast is an example of limiting competition to increase market power. Before the merger, the two companies were competing fiercely with each other leading to a severe price war and increased marketing costs. As a result of the merger, Blow Plast has obtained a strong hold on the market and now operates under near-monopoly situation. Yet, another example is the acquisition of Tomco by Hindustan Lever. Hindustan

Lever at the time of merger was expected to control one third of three million tonne soaps and detergents markets and, thus, substantially reduce the threat of competition.

Merger is not the only route to obtain market power. A firm can increase its market share through internal growth or ventures or strategic alliances. Also, it is not necessary that the increased market power of the merged firm will lead to efficiency and optimum allocation of resources. Market power means undue concentration which could limit the choice of buyers as well as exploit suppliers and labour.

9.4.5 Purchase of Assets at Bargain Price/Bargaining Power Theory

Mergers may be explained by the opportunity to acquire assets, particularly land, mine rights, plant and equipment at lower cost than would be incurred if they were purchased or constructed at current market prices. If market prices of many stocks have been considerably below the replacement cost of the assets they represent, expanding firm considering constructing plants, developing mines or buying equipment. Often it has found that the desired asset could be obtained cheaper by acquiring a firm that already owned and operated the asset. Risk could be reduced because the assets were already in place and an organization of people knew how to operate them and market their products. Many of mergers can be financed by cash tender offers to the acquired firm's shareholders at price substantially above the current market. Even so, the assets can be acquired for less than their current cost of construction. The basic factor underlying this is that inflation in construction costs not fully reflected in stock prices because of high interest rates and limited optimism (or downright pessimism) by stock investors regarding future economic conditions.

9.4.6 Increased External Financial Capability/Theory of Financial Stability

Many mergers, particularly those of relatively small firms into large ones, occur when the acquired firm simply cannot finance its operations. This situation is typical in a small growing firm with expanding financial requirements. The firm has exhausted its bank credit and has virtually no access to long-term debt or equity markets. Sometimes the small firms have encountered operating difficulty and the bank has served notice that its loans will not be renewed. In this type of situation, a large firm with sufficient cash and credit to finance the requirements of the smaller one probably can obtain a good situation by making a merger proposal to the small firm. The only alternative the small firm may have is to try to interest two or more larger firms in proposing merger to introduce completion into their bidding for the acquisition.

The smaller firm's situation might not be so bleak. It may not be threatened by non-renewable of a maturing loan. However, its management may recognize that continued growth to capitalize on its markets will require financing beyond its means. Although its bargaining position will be better, the financial synergy of the acquiring firm's strong financial capability may provide the impetus for the merger.

Sometimes the financing capability is possessed by the acquired firm. The acquisition of a cash-rich firm whose operations have matured may provide additional financing to facilitate growth of the acquiring firm. In some cases, the acquiring firm may be able to recover all or part of the cost of acquiring the cash-rich firm when the merger is consummated and the cash then belongs to it. A merger may also be based upon the simple fact that the combination will make two small firms with limited access to capital markets large enough to achieve that access on a reasonable basis. The improved financing capability provides the financial synergy.

9.4.7 Increased Managerial Skills

The internalization theory is based on the idea of intangible assets: in order for corporations to attract mergers or acquisitions, they must have intangible assets that make them profitable. These assets can include knowledge of a particular market, know-how in a particular technology or an enviable reputation for product quality. Usually, these assets have two major characteristics: they must have the attributes of a public good (that is, their running costs within the corporation must be zero) and they must have high transaction costs, so the most profitable way of acquiring them is through mergers or acquisitions rather than purchase or rental. The internalization theory assumes that the purchasers of the targeted corporations want to obtain their intangible assets. These assets will produce a competitive advantage that should eventually find expression in increased profit. When intangible assets are recognized, it is usually by competitors. As a result, the internalization theory best explains horizontal mergers.

9.4.8 Reduction in Tax Liability/Theory of Tax Synergy

Under Income Tax Act, there is a provision for set-off and carry forward of losses against its future earnings for calculating its tax liability. A loss-making or sick-company may not be in a position to earn sufficient profits in future to take advantage of the carry forward provision. If it combines with a profitable company, the combined company can utilize the carry forward loss and save taxes with the approval of the government. In India, a profitable company is allowed to merge with a sick company to set-off against its profits the accumulated loss and unutilized depreciation of that company. A number of companies in India have merged to take advantage of this provision. The following is the list of some companies along with the amount of tax benefits enjoyed:

- Orissa synthesis merged with Straw product Ltd (₹160 million)
- Ahmadabad cotton Mills merged with Arvind Mils (₹33.4 million)
- Sidhpur Mills merged with Reliance Industries Ltd (₹33.4 million)
- Alwyn Missan merged with Mahinder and Mahindra Ltd (₹24.7 million)
- Hyderabad Alwyn merged with Voltas Ltd (₹16000 million).

When two companies merge through an exchange of shares, the shareholders of selling company can save tax. The profits arising from the exchange of shares are not taxable until the shares are actually sold. When the shares are sold, they are subject to capital gain tax rate which is much lower than the ordinary income tax rate.

A strong urge to reduce tax liability, particularly when the marginal tax rate is high is a strong motivation for the combination of companies. For example, the high tax rate was the main reason for the post-war merger activity in the United States. Also, tax benefits are responsible for one third of mergers in the United States.

9.4.9 Economies of Scale

Economies of scale arise when increase in the volume of production leads to a reduction in the cost of production per unit. Merger may help to expand volume of production without a corresponding increase in fixed costs. Thus, fixed costs are distributed over a large volume of production, causing the unit cost of production to decline. Economies of scale may also arise from other indivisibilities such as production facilities, management functions and management resources and systems. This happens because a given function, facility or resource is utilized for a large scale of operation. For example, a given mix of plant and machinery can produce scale economies when its capacity utilization is increased.

Economies will be maximized when it is optimally utilized. Similarly, economies in the use of the marketing function can be achieved by covering wider markets and customers using a given sales force and promotion and advertising efforts. Economies of scale may also be obtained from the optimum utilization of management resource and systems of planning, budgeting, reporting and control. A company establishes management systems by employing enough qualified professionals irrespective of its size. A combined firm with a large size can make the optimum use of the management resource and systems resulting in economies of scale.

9.4.10 Vertical Integration/Transaction Cost Theory

Vertical integration is a combination businesses of companies with the business of a supplier or customer generally motivated by a pure desire:

a. To secure a source of supply for key materials or sources.
b. To secure a distribution outlet or a major customer for the company's products.
c. To improve profitability by expanding into high margin activities of suppliers and customers.

Thus, vertical merger may take place to integrate forward or backward. Forward integration is where company merges to come close to its customers. A holiday tour operator might acquire chain of travel agents and use them to promote his own holiday rather than those of rival tour operators. So both forward and downstream vertical integration involve takeover of customer business.

Backward integration occurs when a company comes close to its raw materials or suppliers. The real gain can be achieved by integrating backward if the raw material market is not perfectly competitive and the firm has to buy raw materials at monopolistic prices, hence merge to obtain control of supplies. There are many reasons why firms want to be integrated vertically at different stages. Some of these reasons are technological economies like avoidance of reheating and transportation cost, as in the case of iron and steel producer. Transactions within a firm might eliminate costs of searching for prices, contracting, advertising and costs of communicating and coordination. Proper planning for production and inventory management may improve due to more efficient information flow within a single firm. Further, these merger help avoid inefficient market transactions and result in reduced exchange inefficiencies.

Tata Tea's acquisition of consolidated coffee which produces coffee beans and Asian Coffee, which possesses coffee beans, was also backward integration that helped reduce exchange inefficiencies by eliminating market transactions. The recent merger of Samtel Electron services (SED) with Samtel Color Ltd (SCL) entailed backward integration of SED, which manufactures electronic components required to make picture tubes with SCL, a leading maker of colour picture tube. Thus, when companies engaged at different stages of production or value chain merge, economies of vertical integration may be realized. For example, the merger of a company engaged in oil exploration and production (like ONGC) with a company engaged in refining and marketing (like HPCL) may improve coordination and control.

Vertical integration, however, is not always a good idea. If a company does everything in-house, it may not get the benefit of outsourcing from independent suppliers who may be more efficient in their segments of the value chain.

9.4.11 Technological Competence Theory

The mounting importance of technology has given rise to a new theory that is an extension of the internalization theory, namely, the technological competence theory recently developed by John Cantwell and based on the internalization of intangible technological assets. It assumes that technology consists of two factors: one that can be codified (e.g., written information about the technology, plans and so on) and another that cannot be codified (e.g., certain abilities needed to operate it, particular knowledge, the ways in which it operates and so on). It is this latter factor that constitutes technological competence, that is to say, an intangible asset. Technological competence is thought, moreover, to be of cardinal importance for corporate success. This theory has certain consequences. First, when targeted corporations are in industries with high technological coefficients, potential purchasers will be more inclined to install R&D capacity there, thus enhancing local innovation. Second, when local corporations have low technological capacities, M&As may increase the technological content of production. Third, in intermediary cases when corporations engage in research but are not on the cutting edge of technology, M&As may result in the complete absorption of the targeted industry.

9.4.12 Early Entry and Market Penetration

An early mover strategy can reduce the lead time taken in establishing the facilities and distribution channels. So, acquiring companies with good manufacturing and distribution network or few brands of a company gives the advantage of rapid market share. The ICICI, a leading financial institution, secured a foothold in retail network through acquisition of Anagram Finance Company and ITC Classic. Anagram had a strong retail franchise, distribution network of over 50 branches in Gujarat, Rajasthan and Maharashtra and a depositor base of over 0.2 million depositors. ICICI was, therefore, attracted by the retail portfolio of Anagram, which was active in lease and hire purchase, car purchase, truck finance and customer finance. These acquisitions thus helped ICICI to obtain quick access to a well-dispersed distribution network.

Further, market penetration means developing new and large markets for a company's existing products. Market penetration strategy is generally pursued within markets that are becoming more global. Cross-border mergers are a means of becoming or remaining major players in such markets. Hence, this strategy is mainly adopted by multinational companies (MNCs) to gain to new markets. They prefer to merge with a local established company which knows behaviour of the market and has established customer base. One such example is the Indian market. Few instances of MNC-related mergers are:

- Whirlpool Corporation's entry into India by acquiring Kelvinator India.
- Coca–Cola, while re-entering the Indian market in 1993, acquired Parle, the largest player in market with several established brands and nationwide bottling and marketing network.
- H.J. Heinz entered into India through acquisition of Glato Industries.
- HLL acquired Dollops, Kwality, Milk Food to gain an entry into ice cream market with the help of their marketing networks, production facilities, brands and so on.

9.4.13 Revival of Sick Companies

An important motive for merger is to turn around a financially sick company through the process of merger. Amalgamations, taking place under the aegis of the Board for Industrial and Financial Reconstruction (BIFR) fall under this category.

BIFR found revival of ailing companies by means of a healthy company as the most successful route for revival of their financial wealth. First, the purpose is to revive a group of sick companies by merging it with groups of healthy company by obtaining concessions from financial institutions and government agencies and obtaining benefits of tax concessions under section 72A of the Income Tax Act, 1961. Second, it also helps to preserve group reputation. Some of the group companies that have amalgamated through the BIFR include Mahindra Missan Allwyn with Mahindra and Mahindra, Hyderabad, Allwyn with Voltas and so on.

BIFR Motivated Rehabilitation Merger

Year	*Transferor Sick Company*	*Taken Over by Transferee Company*
April 95	Tata Keltron Ltd	Tata Telecom Ltd
April 95	Titagarh Papers Mills Ltd	Titagarh Steels Ltd
April 95	Pentasia Chemicals Ltd	Asian Paints Ltd
April 96	Biax Ltd	Cimmco Birla Ltd
April 97	Universal Steel Alloys Ltd	Bharat Gears Ltd

Consolidation at the Group Level

Group company mergers are generally initiated with a view to affect consolidation to derive critical mass to cut costs in order to achieve focus and eliminate competition. Such mergers within group are also aimed at restructuring their diverse units to create a more viable unit, to revive sickness, improve borrowed capital. There are few other micro-economic reasons to decide on mergers with group consideration as their sole consideration:

- To achieve economies of scale
- To reduce cost of administration and management expenses in companies within the same group
- To bifurcate business by floating separate products this is referred to as demerger.

An example of restructuring and consolidation within the group companies is the case of Nirma Ltd merging with it its group companies Nirma detergents, Nirma soaps and detergents, Shina soaps and detergents and Nirma chemicals. The objective was to make Nirma a strong and resilient corporate entity capable of facing global competition by restructuring management, sizable reduction in management costs and increased professionalism. Merger of Videocon groups Videocon Narmada Electronics with its flagship company Videocon International led to operating efficiencies by controlling costs under one head.

9.4.14 Following Parent's Footsteps

Some of mergers in India belonging to multinational giants take place as a result of direct fallout of mergers of their parent companies taking place in their home countries. Some instances of such mergers are listed below:

a. As per the dictates of their parent companies, their two Indian counterparts, namely, The General Electric Company of India Ltd and The English Electric Company of India

Ltd, were merged from 1 April 1992 and changed their name to GEC. Alsthen India Ltd (just like the GEC, Alsthen N.V. Ltd formed by merger of two largest industrial groups, The General Electric company plc. UK and Alcatel Alsthen, France).

b. Novartis India (51% of Novartis AG) was formed in India by the merger of Hindustan Ciba Giegy and Sandoz India Ltd in 1996 following the merger of their global parents.

9.4.15 Increase Promoter's Stake/Promoters' Theory

Another motive for merger could be to increase the stake of promoters. Thus, company 'A', which is family owned, could be merged with company 'B', which is a listed company with family stake in it. By the process of merger, the family stake could be consolidated without going through the complications of SEBI guidelines of 4 August 1994. Therefore, mergers could be motivated by the need to enhance promoter's holdings in post-merger company. For instance, Nanda family's holding in escorts Ltd was 20% before merger. Its merger with Escorts Tractors Ltd increased their holding by another 20%. Similarly, the merger of Reliance Polythylene and Reliance Polypropylene into Reliance Industries swap ratio of 100:30 and 100:25, respectively, resulted in an increase in Ambani's stake from 23% to 37%. The higher stakes helps to ward off takeover bids.

9.4.16 Defensive Manoeuvre/Raider Theory

Merger can be used as shields for protection from raiders. A merger or acquisition can be used by a company as defensive manoeuvre to resist takeover by another company. If a firm feels that it could be acquired by another firm, it may consider getting involved in a merger game. In doing so, it is able to expand its size, making its acquisition very expensive. Also, by increasing market capitalization of the merged company's threat of takeover can be tackled. For instance, the merger of Jindal Ferro Alloys with Jindal Strips helped Jindal Ferro Alloys improve its share price from ₹65 to ₹170 and market capitalization of ₹1.6 billion to ₹5.5 billion with the help of swap ratio of 45 Jindal strips for every 100 Jindal Ferro alloy shares.

9.4.17 Acquire Global Competitive Strength/Internalization Theory

With competitive forces resulting from globalization and deregulation, many industries have forced most corporate to consolidate. European and Asian markets have become more receptive to merger and acquisitions. On the one hand, European countries face competitive pressures from creation of single euro currency; on the other hand, the Asian crisis has forced most Asian nations to look to the West for technological and capital support. Hence, mergers are planned to acquire global competitive strength.

After the pitched battle against MNCs in the domestic arena, Indian companies have also felt the need of becoming global. The globalized business environment thus demands that Indian industries restructure themselves. Its size and capacities are small as compared to MNCs. Industries have to increase their capacity, induct new technology and development markets. Globalization has thus resulted in major implications for industrial competitiveness by lowering the cost of labour and opening markets to a great number of producing firms. To meet the opportunities thrown open by the fast growing world, generic market and to acquire global competitive strength, cross-border M&As are being resorted to such mergers provide opportunities for taking up larger projects. Also, the merged company is able to compete more effectively with increased size.

The recent acquisition of Tetley, the world's largest tea brand, by Tata Tea, the world's largest integrated tea company, has been driven by the fact that Tetley fits perfectly into Tata Tea's globalization drive and could be a perfect launch vehicle to achieve greater synergies in the global arena. The acquisition has brought with it greater market penetration, helped improve operating efficiencies and resulted in instant expansion of product lines of Tata Tea–Tetley combines.

The process of globalization and increasing integration of the Indian economy with the international market will have its impact sooner or later. Ansoff (1965) suggested a number of reasons that are attributed to the occurrence of M&As. For example, it suggested that M&A are intended to:

a. limit competition
b. utilize underutilization market power
c. overcome the problem of slow growth and profitability in one's own industry
d. achieve diversification
e. gain economies of scale and increase income with proportionately less investment establish a transnational bridgehead without excessive start-up costs to gain access to a foreign market
f. utilize underutilized resources—human and physical and managerial skills
g. displace existing management
h. circumvent government regulations
i. reap speculative gains attendant upon new security issue or change in P/E ratio
j. create an image of aggressiveness and strategic opportunism empire building and to amass vast economic powers of the economy.

9.4.18 Economic Disturbances/Disturbance Theory

This approach holds that the motives of acquisitions occur as a result of economic disturbances. Economic disturbances cause changes in individuals' expectation and increase the general degree of uncertainty. Thus, they alter the array of individual expectations.

These theories show the variation in reasons for a merger or acquisition. Khemani (1990) expressed this very well:

> There are multiple reasons, motives, economic forces and institutional factors that can be taken together or in isolation, influence corporate decisions to engage in mergers or acquisitions. Over the last few years, the pressures originating from international competition, financial innovation, economic growth and expansion, heightened political and economic integration, and technological change have all contributed to the increased pace of mergers and acquisitions. Of course, mergers and acquisitions can still be motivated by such classic commercial and economic considerations as broadening the range of related products and the geographic market, diversification, and the risks and benefits of vertical integration. Finally, new or modified tax regimes, the cost of capital, and policy on such things as foreign property, economic regulations and privatization also have an effect on the inter-sectoral/international variations in the number of mergers and acquisitions.

9.5 Impact of M&As on Stakeholders

There are many parties who have interest, either direct or indirect, in the success of an organization. The M&As of organizations will have significant impact not only on the direct owners, that is, shareholders, but also on various other groups like employees, consumers, government, general public and so on. The impact of M&As on different stakeholders is discussed as follows:

1. **Impact on Shareholders:** Increasing the shareholders' value is generally a prime objective of most of M&As today. The value to shareholders through M&As could be increased either by cutting the costs by combining similar assets in the merging concerns or by enhancing the revenue by focusing on enhancing capabilities and revenues, and combining complementary competencies. However, most of the studies on the impact of M&As on shareholders wealth reveal that on an average, M&As consistently benefit the target company's shareholders, but not the acquirers' shareholders. Various consulting firms have also estimated that from one-half to two-thirds of M&As do not come up to the expectations of those transacting them, and many resulted in divestitures.
2. **Impact on Employees:** Human resource is another sensitive issue on the road to consolidation. M&As have a profound impact on employment in all sectors of the economy. M&As invariably result in decline in the number of branches and thus lead to staff retrenchments. Consequently, mergers often lead to higher workloads being placed on remaining staff, with companies requiring flexibility in terms of working hours, mobility and skills, excellent and highly motivated employees of the merged entity may feel frustrated and may resign or they may not give their best to the organization. So the retention of best talent and also motivation of the staff in the M&As game has become a major challenge for the companies. Mergers have also brought about a change in the nature and quality of employment in the different sector.
3. **Impact on Customers:** In the changed economic scenario, the companies are providing a number of products to the customers at reduced prices. This is because the new market entrants are seeking to compete on the basis of the price. They are able to do this because new information and communication technology allows them to save cost by operating with fewer branches or without a traditional branch network (e.g., ICICI Bank and HDFC Bank). Customers are provided with new products and services with time flexibility. Customers need not to stick on to bank working hours to conduct their business. Public sector banks have also initiated these steps in order to meet consumer needs.
4. **Impact on Government:** The M&As to be successful should be created by market-driven forces of synergy and other motives. However, the some of the recent M&As are not market driven and created for mutual benefit of both acquirer and the target companies (mergers of Times Bank with HDFC Bank in 2000, Centurion Bank with Bank of Punjab in 2005 and so on). In this context, the government and supervisory authorities have to provide an environment conducive for consolidation and convergence through appropriate fiscal and monetary policies supported by sound regulatory and supervisory framework. Otherwise, a few large institutions may create an oligopolistic structure of the market. Thus, the government should remain alert to in M&As for a sound and balanced economy.
5. **Impact on Organization Culture:** Every organization has its own culture and some traditional activities. As organizational culture is the part of employees' identity, if the cultural issues are not effectively addressed, it may lead to loss of commitment among employees resulting in lost opportunities to retain qualified personnel and motivate individuals. A merger deal, which may appear to be perfectly sound from financial point of view, may fail miserably if cultural and human issues are not properly addressed in

the newly created entity. Merger of New Bank of India with Punjab National Bank is a classic case of cultural differences on account of which the merged entity suffered a lot immediately following the merger.

6. **Impact on Public:** The local character of some of the organization is another concern arising on account of M&As. It is learnt that SBI never thought of merging its associates with itself because each of the associate banks has its own regional flavour, a clientele with which it is more comfortable after having nurtured it over many years and therefore enjoys a niche presence. If the regional banks, for instance, State Bank of Travancore, State Bank of Indore or State Bank of Mysore, is merged into a single giant entity, it may affect the regional subsidiary and also the parent bank. Some of these banks have strong local or regional flavour to their operations that could get eroded if they were to merge with the parent.

9.6 Why Do M&As Quite Often Fail?

Although the M&As basically aim at enhancing the shareholders' value or wealth, the results of several empirical studies reveal that M&As consistently benefit the target company's shareholders but not the acquirer company shareholders. A majority of corporate mergers fail. Failure occurs on average, in every sense, acquiring firm stock prices likely to reduce when mergers are announced, many acquired companies sell off, and profitability of the acquired company is lower after the merger relative to comparable non-merged firms. Consulting firms have also estimated that from one-half to two-thirds of M&As do not come up to the expectations of those transacting them, and many resulted in divestitures. Statistics show that roughly half of acquisitions are not successful. M&As fail quite often and fail to create value or wealth for shareholders of the acquirers. A definite answer as to why mergers fail to generate value for acquiring shareholders cannot be provided because mergers fail for a host of reasons. Some of the important reasons for failures of mergers are discussed as follows:

i. *Excessive premium:* In a competitive bidding situation, a company may tend to pay more. Often, the highest bidder is one who overestimates value out of ignorance. Though he emerges as the winner, he happens to be in a way the unfortunate winner. This is called the winner's curse hypothesis. When the acquirer fails to achieve the synergies required compensating the price, the M&A fails. The more you pay for a company, the harder you will have to work to make it worthwhile for your shareholders. When the price paid is too much, how well the deal may be executed, the deal may not create value.

ii. *Size issues:* A mismatch in the size between acquirer and target has been found to lead to poor acquisition performance. Many acquisitions fail either because of 'acquisition indigestion' through buying too big targets or failed to give the smaller acquisitions the time and attention it required.

iii. *Lack of research:* Acquisition requires gathering a lot of data and information and analysing them. It requires extensive research. A carelessly carried out research about the acquisition causes the destruction of the acquirer's wealth.

iv. *Diversification:* Very few firms have the ability to successfully manage the diversified businesses. Unrelated diversification has been associated with lower financial performance, lower capital productivity and a higher degree of variance in performance for a variety of reasons, including a lack of industry or geographic knowledge, a lack of focus as well as perceived inability to gain meaningful synergies. Unrelated acquisitions, which may appear to be very promising, may turn out to be big disappointment in reality.

v. *Previous acquisition experience:* While previous acquisition experience is not necessarily a requirement for future acquisition success, many unsuccessful acquirers usually have little previous acquisition experience. Previous experience will help the acquirers to learn from the previous acquisition mistakes and help them to make successful acquisitions in the future. It may also help them by taking advice in order to maximize chances of acquisition success. Those serial acquirers, who possess the in-house skills necessary to promote acquisition success as well-trained and competent implementation team, are more likely to make successful acquisitions.

vi. *Unwieldy and inefficient:* Conglomerate mergers proliferated in the 1960s and 1970. Many conglomerates proved unwieldy and inefficient and were wound up in the 1980s and 1990s. The unmanageable conglomerates contributed to the rise of various types of divestitures in the 1980s and 1990s.

vii. *Poor cultural fits:* Cultural fit between an acquirer and a target is one of the most neglected areas of analysis prior to the closing of a deal. However, cultural due diligence is every bit as important as careful financial analysis. Without it, the chances are great that M&As will quickly amount to misunderstanding, confusion and conflict. Cultural due diligence involve steps like determining the importance of culture, assessing the culture of both target and acquirer. It is useful to know the target management behaviour with respect to dimensions such as centralized versus decentralized decision making, speed in decision making, time horizon for decisions, level of teamwork, management of conflict, risk orientation, openness to change and so on. It is necessary to assess the cultural fit between the acquirer and target based on cultural profile. Potential sources of clash must be managed. It is necessary to identify the impact of cultural gap, and develop and execute strategies to use the information in the cultural profile to assess the impact that the differences have.

viii. *Poor organizational fit:* Organizational fit is described as the match between administrative practices, cultural practices and personnel characteristics of the target and acquirer. It influences the ease with which two organizations can be integrated during implementation. Mismatch of organizational fit leads to failure of mergers.

ix. *Poor strategic fit:* A merger will yield the desired result only if there is strategic fit between the merging companies. Mergers with strategic fit can improve profitability through reduction in overheads, effective utilization of facilities, the ability to raise funds at a lower cost and deployment of surplus cash for expanding business with higher returns. But many a time, lack of strategic fit between two merging companies, especially lack of synergies, results in merger failure. Strategic fit can also include the business philosophies of the two entities (ROI versus market share), the time frame for achieving these goals (short term versus long term) and the way in which assets are utilized. For example, the P&G–Gillette merger in the consumer goods industry is a unique case of acquisition by an innovative company to expand its product line by acquiring another innovative company, which was described by analysts as a perfect merger.

x. *Striving for bigness:* Size no doubt is an important element for success in business. Therefore, there is a strong tendency among managers whose compensation is significantly influenced by size to build big empires. Size-maximizing firms may engage in activities, which have negative NPV. Therefore, when evaluating an acquisition it is necessary to keep the attention focused on how it will create value for shareholders and not on how it will increase the size of the company.

xi. *Faulty evaluation:* At times acquirers do not carry out the detailed diligence of the target company. They make a wrong assessment of the benefits from the acquisition and land up paying a higher price.

xii. *Poorly managed integration:* Integration of the companies requires a high quality management. Integration is very often poorly managed with little planning and design. As a result, implementation fails. The key variable for success is managing the company better after the acquisition than it was managed before. Even good deals fail if they are poorly managed after the merger.

xiii. *Failure to take immediate control:* Control of the new unit should be taken immediately after signing of the agreement. ITC did so when they took over the BILT unit, even though the consideration was to be paid in five yearly instalments. ABB put new management in place on day one and reporting systems in place by three weeks.

xiv. *Failure to set the pace for integration:* The important task in the merger is to integrate the target with acquiring company in every respect. All functions such as marketing, commercial; finance, production, design and personnel should be put in place. In addition to the prominent persons of acquiring company, the key persons from the acquired company should be retained and given sufficient prominent opportunities in the combined organization. Delay in integration leads to delay in product shipment, development and slowdown in the company's road map. Acquisition of Scientific Data Corporation by Xerox in 1969 and AT&T's acquisition of computer maker NCR Corporation in 1991 were troubled deals, which resulted in large write offs. The speed of integration is extremely important because uncertainty and ambiguity for longer periods destabilizes the normal organizational life.

xv. *Incomplete and inadequate due diligence:* Lack of due diligence is lack of detailed analysis of all important features like finance, management, capability, physical assets as well as intangible assets results in failure. ISPAT Steel is a corporate acquirer that conducts M&A activities after elaborate due diligence.

xvi. *Ego clash:* Ego clash between the top management and subsequently lack of coordination may lead to collapse of company after the merger. The problem is more prominent in cases of mergers between equals.

xvii. *Merger between equals:* A merger between two equals may not work. The Dunlop Pirelli merger in 1964, which created the world's second largest tier company, ended in an expensive divorce. Manufacturing plants can be integrated easily, but human beings cannot. Merger of equals may also create ego clash.

xviii. *Over leverage:* Cash acquisitions result in the acquirer assuming too much debt. Future interest cost consumes too great a portion of the acquired company's earnings (Business India 2005).

xix. *Incompatibility of partners:* An alliance between two strong companies is a safer bet than between two weak partners. Frequently many strong companies actually seek small partners in order to gain control while weak companies look for stronger companies to bail them out. But experience shows that the weak link becomes a drag and causes friction between partners. A strong company taking over a sick company in the hope of rehabilitation may itself end up in liquidation.

xx. *Limited focus:* If merging companies have entirely different products, markets systems and cultures, the merger is doomed to failure. Added to that as core competencies are weakened and the focus gets blurred the fallout on bourses can be dangerous. Purely financially motivated mergers such as tax-driven mergers on the advice of accountant can be hit by adverse business consequences. The Tatas, for example, sold their soaps business to Hindustan Lever.

xxi. *Failure to get figures audited:* It would be a serious mistake if the takeovers were concluded without a proper audit of financial affairs of the target company. Although the company pays for the assets of the target company, it also assumes responsibility to pay all the liabilities. Areas to look for are stocks, saleability of finished products, receivables and their collectibles, details and location of fixed assets, unsecured loans, claims under litigation, loans from the promoters and so on. When ITC took over the paperboard making unit of BILT near Coimbatore, it arranged for comprehensive audit of financial affairs of the unit. Many a time, the acquirer is misled by window-dressed accounts of the target.

xxii. *Failure to get an objective evaluation of the target company' condition:* Risk of failure will be minimized if there is a detailed evaluation of the target company's business conditions carried out by the professionals in the line of business. Detailed examination of the manufacturing facilities, product design features, rejection rates, and distribution systems, profile of key people and productivity of the workers is done. Acquirer should not be carried away by the state-of-the-art physical facilities like a good headquarters building, guest house on a beach, plenty of land for expansion and so on.

xxiii. *Failure of top management to follow-up:* After signing the M&A agreement, the top management should not sit back and let things happen. First 100 days after the takeover, determine the speed with which the process of tackling the problems can be achieved. Top management follow-up is essential to go with a clear roadmap of actions to be taken and set the pace for implementing once the control is assumed.

xxiv. *Mergers between lame ducks:* Merger between two weak companies does not succeed either. The example is the Studbacker–Packard merger of 1955 when two ailing carmakers joined hands. By 1964, both companies were closed down.

xxv. *Lack of proper communication:* Lack of proper communication after the announcement of M&As will create a lot of uncertainties. Apart from getting down to business quickly companies have to necessarily talk to employees and constantly. Regardless of how well executives communicate during a merger or an acquisition, uncertainty will never be completely eliminated. Failure to manage communication results in inaccurate perceptions, lost trust in management, morale and productivity problems, safety problems, poor customer service, and defection of key people and customers. It may lead to the loss of the support of key stakeholders at a time when that support is needed the most.

xxvi. *Failure of leadership role:* Some of the role leadership should take seriously are modelling, quantifying strategic benefits and building a case for M&A activity and articulating and establishing high standard for value creation. Walking the talk also becomes very important during M&As.

xxvii. *Inadequate attention to people issues:* Not giving sufficient attention to people issues during due diligence process may prove costly later on. While a lot of focus is placed on the financial and customer capital aspects, not enough attention is given to aspects of human capital and cultural audit. Well-conducted HR due diligence can provide very accurate estimates and can be very critical to strategy formulation and implementation.

xxviii. *Strategic alliance as an alternative strategy:* Another feature of the 1990s is the growth in strategic alliances as a cheaper, less risky route to a strategic goal than takeovers.

xxix. *Loss of identity:* Merger should not result in loss of identity, which is a major strength for the acquiring company. Jaguar's car image dropped drastically after its merger with British Leyland.

xxx. *Diverging from core activity:* In some cases, a merger reduces buyers' efficiency by diverting it from its core activity and too much time is spent on new activity neglecting the core activity.

xxxi. *Expecting results too quickly:* Immediate results can never be expected except those recorded in red ink. Whirlpool ran up a loss $100 million in its Philips white goods purchase. R.P. Goenk's takeovers of Gramophone Company and Manu Chhabria's takeover of Gordon Woodroffe and Dunlops fall under this category.

Making the mergers work successfully is not that easy as here we are not only just putting the two organizations together but also integrating people of two organizations with different cultures, attitudes and mindsets. Meticulous pre-merger planning, including conducting proper due diligence, effective communication during the integration, committed and competent leadership, speed with which the integration plan is integrated all this pave for the success of mergers. While making the merger deals, it is necessary not only to make analysis of the financial aspects of the acquiring firm but also the cultural and people issues of both the concerns for proper post-acquisition integration.

9.7 Procedure for Merger

The procedure for merger and amalgamation is different from takeover. Mergers and amalgamations are regulated under the provisions of the Companies Act, 1913, whereas takeovers are regulated under the SEBI (Substantial Acquisition of Shares and Takeovers) Regulations.

The beginning to amalgamation may be made through common agreements between the transferor and the transferee but mere agreement does not provide a legal cover to the transaction unless it carries the sanction of the company court for which the procedure laid down under section 391 of the Companies Act should be followed for giving effect to amalgamation through the statutory instrument of the court's sanction.

Although chapter V of the Companies Act, 1956, comprising sections 389 to 396A, deals with the issue and related aspects covering arbitration, compromises, arrangements and reconstructions but at different times and under different circumstances in each case of merger and amalgamation application of other provisions of the Companies Act, 1956, and ruled made thereunder may necessarily be attracted. So, the procedure does not remain simple or literally confined to chapter V.

The procedure is complex, involving not only the compromises or arrangements between the company and its creditors or any class of them or between the company and its members or any class of them but it involves safeguard of public interest and adherence to public policy. These aspects are looked after by the central government through official liquidator on the Company Law Board, Department of Company Affairs and the court has to be satisfied of the same.

9.7.1 Top Management's Commitments

The top management defines the organization's goal and outlines the policy framework to achieve these objectives. The organization's goal for business expansion could be accomplished, inter alia, through business combinations assimilating a target corporate that can remove the present deficiencies in the organization and can contribute in the required direction to accomplish the goal of business expansion through enhanced commercial activity, that is, supply of inputs and market for output product diversification, adding up new products and improved technological process, providing new distribution channels and market segments, making available technical personnel and experienced skilled manpower, R&D establishments and so on. These depend upon the specific need and cost advantage with reference to creating a new set-up or acquiring a well-established set-up firm.

9.7.2 Search for a Merger Partner

The top management may use their own contacts with competitors in the same line of economic activity or in the other diversified field which could be identified as better merger partners or may use the contacts of merchant bankers, financial consultants and other agencies in locating suitable merger partners. A number of corporate candidates may be short listed and identified. Such identification should be based on the detailed information of the merger partners collected from published and private sources. Such information should reveal the following aspects:

a. Organizational history of business and promoters and capital structure
b. Organizational goals
c. Product, market and competitors
d. Organizational set-up and management pattern
e. Assets profile: Movable and immovable assets, land and building
f. Manpower: Skilled, unskilled, technical personnel and detailed particulars of management employees.

9.7.3 Negotiations

The top management can negotiate at a time with several identified short-listed companies suited to be merger partners for settling terms of merger and pick up one of them that offer most favourable terms. Negotiations can be had with target companies before making any acquisitional attempt. The same drill of negotiations could be followed in the cases of merger and amalgamation. The following section provides activity schedule for planning merger, covering different aspects like preliminary consultations with the perspective merger partner and seeking its willingness to cooperate in investigations. There are other aspects, too, in the activity schedule, covering quantification action plan, purpose, shape, and date of merger, profitability and valuation, taxation aspects legal aspects and development plan of the company after the merger.

The actual procedure to be adopted during the merger process is as follows.

9.7.4 Steps in Merger Process

Once the merger partner has been identified and terms of merger are settled, the following procedure is followed (Figure 9.4).

1. Scheme of Amalgamation: The scheme of amalgamation should be prepared by the companies that have arrived at a consensus to merge. There is no specific form prescribed for a scheme of amalgamation but the scheme should generally contain the following information:

a. Particulars about transferee and transferor companies.
b. Appointed date.

Figure 9.4 Steps in Merger Process

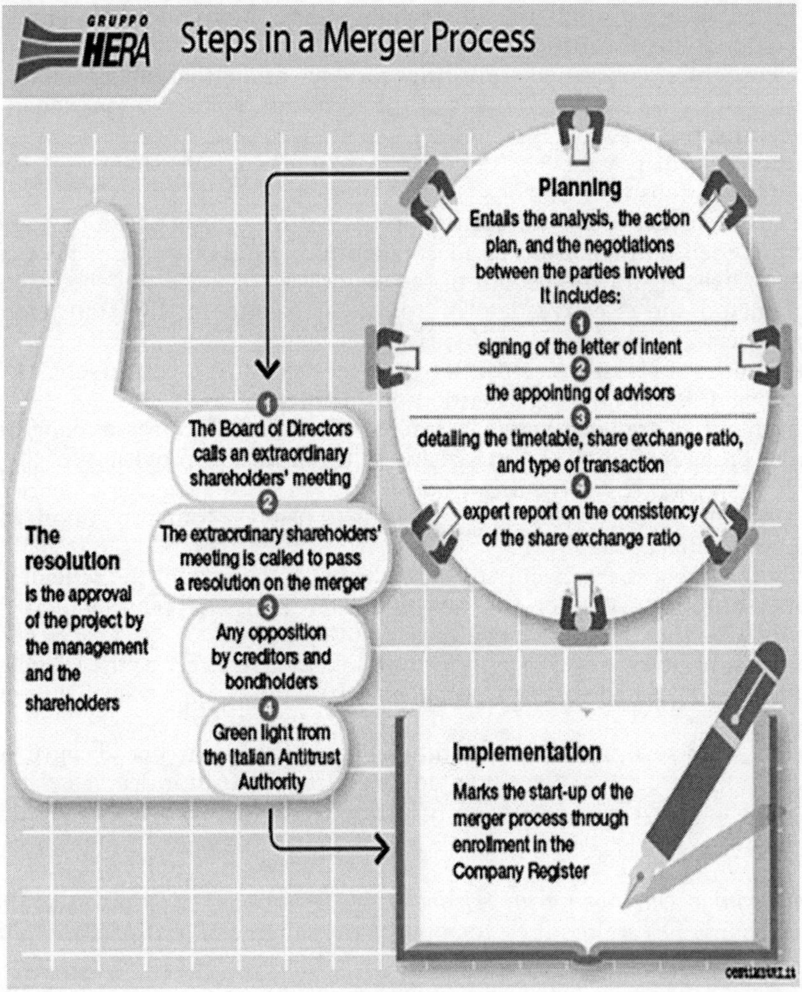

Source: http://eng.gruppohera.it/group/corporate_governance/words_understand/page25.html (last accessed on 12 January 2014).

c. Main terms of transfer of assets from transferor to transferee with power to execute on behalf or for transferee the deed or documents being given to transferee.
d. Main terms of transfer liabilities from transferor to transferee covering any conditions attached to loans/debentures/bonds/other liabilities from bank/financial institution/trustees and listing conditions attached thereto.
e. Effective date when the scheme will come into effect.
f. Conditions as to carrying on the business activities by the transferor between the 'appointed date' and the 'effective date'.
g. Description of happenings and consequences of the scheme coming into effect on the effective date.

h. Share capital of the transferor company specifying authorized capital, issued capital and subscribed and paid-up capital.
i. Share capital of the transferee company covering above heads.
j. Description of the proposed share exchange ratio, any conditions attached thereto, any fractional share certificates to be issued, transferee company's responsibility to obtain consent of concerned authorities for issue and allotment of shares and listing.
k. Surrender of shares by shareholders of the transferor company for exchange into new share certificates.
l. Conditions about payment of dividend, ranking of equity shares, pro rata dividend declaration and distribution.
m. Status of employees of the transferor companies from the effective date and the status of the provident fund, gratuity fund, superannuity fund or any special scheme or funds created or existing for the benefit of the employees.
n. Treatment on the effective date of any debit balance of the transferor company's balance sheet.
o. Miscellaneous provisions covering income-tax dues, contingencies and other accounting entries deserving attention or treatment.
p. Commitment of transferor and transferee companies towards making applications/ petitions under sections 391 and 394 and other applicable provisions of the Companies Act, 1956, to their respective High Courts.
q. Enhancement of borrowing limits of the transferee company upon the scheme's coming into effect.
r. Transferor and transferee companies give assent to change in the scheme by the court or other authorities under the law and exercising the powers on behalf of the companies by their respective boards.
s. Description of powers of delegate of transferee to give effect to the scheme.
t. Qualification attached to the scheme, which requires approval of different agencies and so on.
u. Description of revocation/cancellation of the scheme in the absence of approvals qualified in clause t above not granted by concerned authorities.
v. Statement to bear costs and so on in connection with the scheme by the transferee company.

2. Approval of Board of Directors for the Scheme: Respective board of directors of the transferor and transferee companies are required to approve the scheme of amalgamation.

3. Approval of the Scheme by Specialized Financial Institutions/Banks/Trustees: The board of directors should in fact approve the scheme only after it has been cleared by the financial institutions/banks, which have granted loans to these companies or the debenture trustees to avoid any major change in the meeting of creditors to be convened at the instance of the Company Court's under section 391 of the Companies Act, 1956. Approval of the Reserve Bank of India (RBI) is also needed where the scheme of amalgamation contemplates issue of share/payment of cash to non-resident Indians or foreign nationals under the provisions of the Foreign Exchange Management (Transfer or Issue of Security by a Person Resident Outside India) Regulations, 2000. In particular, regulation 7 of the these regulations provides for compliance of certain conditions in the case of scheme of merger or amalgamation as approved by the court.

4. Intimation to Stock Exchange: Listing agreements entered into between company and stock exchange require the company to communicate price-sensitive information to the stock exchange immediately and simultaneously when released to press and other electronic media on the conclusion of board meeting according approval to the scheme.

5. *Application to the Court:* The next step is to make an application under section 39(1) to the High Court having jurisdiction over the Registered Office of the company, and the transferee company should make separate applications to the High Court. The application shall be made by a judge's summons in Form No. 33 supported by an affidavit in Form No. 34 [see rule 82 of the Companies (Court) Rules, 1959]. The following documents should be submitted with the judge's summons:

a. A true copy of the company's memorandum and articles
b. A true copy of the company's latest audited balance sheet
c. A copy of the board resolution that authorises the director to make the application to the High Court.

6. *High Court Directions:* Upon the hearing of the summons, the High Court shall give directions fixing the date, time and venue and quorum for the members' meeting and appoint an advocate chairman to preside over the meeting and submit a report to the court. Similar directions are issued by the court for calling the meeting of creditors in case such a request has been made in the application.

7. *Approval of Registrar of High Court for Calling the Meeting of Members/Creditors:* Pursuant to the directions of the court, the transferor and the transferee companies shall submit for approval to the registrar of the respective High Courts the draft notices calling the meetings of the members in Form No. 36 together with a scheme of arrangements and explanations, statement under section 393 of the Companies Act and form of proxy in Form No. 37 of the Companies (Court) Rules to be sent to members along with the said notice. Once the registrar has accorded approval to the notice, it should be signed by the chairman appointed for meeting by the High Court who shall preside over the proposed meeting of members.

8. *Despatch of Notices to Members/Shareholders:* Once the notice has been signed by the chairman of the forthcoming meeting as aforesaid, it could be despatched to the members under certificate of posting at least 21 days before the date of the meeting.

9. *Advertisement of the Notice of Members' Meetings:* The court may direct the issuance of notice of the meeting of these shareholders by an advertisement. In such case, rule 74 of the Companies (Court) Rules provides that the notice of the meeting should be advertised in such a newspaper and in such a manner as the court might direct not less than 21 clear days before the date fixed for the meeting. The advertisement shall be in Form No. 38 appended to the Companies (Court) Rules. The companies should submit the draft for the notice to be published in Form No. 38 in an English daily together with a translation thereof in the regional language to the registrar of the High Court for his approval. The advertisement should be released in the newspapers after the registrar approves the draft.

10. *Confirmation about Service of the Notice:* Ensure that at least one week before the date of the meeting, the chairman appointed for the meeting files an affidavit to the court about the service of notices to the shareholders that the directions regarding the issue of notices and advertisement have been duly complied with.

11. *Holding the Shareholders' General Meeting and Passing the Resolutions:* The general meeting should be held on the appointed date. Rule 77 of the Companies (Court) Rules prescribes that

the decisions of the meeting held pursuant to the court order should be ascertained only by taking a poll. The amalgamation scheme should be approved by the members, by a majority in number of members present in person or on proxy and voting on the resolution and this majority must represent at least three-fourths this in value of the shares held by the members who vote in the poll.

12. Filing of Resolutions of General Meeting: Once the shareholders' general meeting approves the amalgamation scheme by a majority in number of members holding not less than three-fourths in value of the equity shares, the scheme is binding on all the members of the company. A copy of the resolution passed by the shareholders approving the scheme of amalgamation should be filed with the Registrar of Companies (ROC) in Form No. 23 appended to the Companies (Central Government's) General Rules and Forms, 1956, within 30 days from the date of passing the resolution.

13. Submission of Chairman's Report to Court: The chairman of the general meeting of the shareholders is required to submit to the court within seven days from the date of the meeting a report in Form No. 39 of the Companies (Court) Rules, 1959, setting out therein the number of persons who attend either personally or by proxy, and the percentage of shareholders who voted in favour of the scheme as well as the resolution passed by the meeting.

14. Submission of Joint Petition: Within seven days from the date on which the chairman has submitted his report about the result of the meeting to the court, both the companies should make a joint petition to the High Court for approving the scheme of amalgamation. This petition is to be made in Form No. 40 of the Companies (Court) Rules. The court will fix a date of hearing of the petition. The notice of the hearing should be advertised in the same papers in which the notice of the meeting was advertised or in such other newspapers as the court may direct, not less than 10 days before the date fixed for the hearing (rule 80 of Companies (Court) Rules.

15. Issue of Notice to the Company Law Board: On receipt of the petition for amalgamation under section 391 of the Companies Act, 1956, the court will give a notice of the petition to the Regional Director, Company Law Board, and will take into consideration the representations, if any, made by him.

16. Hearing of Petition and Confirmation of Scheme: Having taken up the petition by the court for hearing, it will hear the objections first and if there is no objection to the amalgamation scheme from the regional director or from any other person who is entitled to oppose the scheme, the court may pass an order approving the scheme of amalgamation in Form No. 41 or Form No. 42 of the Companies (Court) Rules. The court may also pass order directing that all the property, rights and powers of the transferor company specified in the schedules annexed to the order be transferred without further act or deed to the transferee company and that all the liabilities and duties of the transferor company be transferred without further act or deed.

17. Filing of Court Order with ROC by Both the Companies: Both the transferor and transferee companies should obtain the court's order sanctioning the scheme of amalgamation and file the same with ROC with their respective jurisdiction as required vide section 394(3) of the Companies Act, 1956, within 30 days after the date of the court's order in Form No. 21 prescribed under the (Central Government's) General Rules and Forms, 1956. The amalgamation will be given effect to from the date on which the High Court's order is filed with the registrar.

18. *Transfer of Assets and Liabilities:* Section 394(2) vests power in the High Court to order for the transfer of any property or liabilities from the transferor company to the transferee company. In pursuance of and by virtue of such order such properties and liabilities of the transferor shall automatically stand transferred to transferee company without any further act or deed from the date the court's order is filed with the ROC.

19. *Allotment of Shares:* Pursuant to the sanctioned scheme of amalgamation, the shareholders of the transferor company are entitled to get shares in the transferee company in the exchange ratio provided under the said scheme. There are three different situations in which allotment could be given effect.

a. Where the transferor company is not a listed company, the formalities prescribed under the listing agreement do not exist and the allotment could take place without setting the record date or giving any advance notice to shareholders except asking them to surrender their old share certificates for exchange by the new ones.
b. The second situation will emerge different where the transferor company is a listed company. In this case, the stock exchange is to be intimated of the record date by giving at least 42 days' notice or such notice as provided in the listing agreement.
c. The third situation is where allotment to non-resident Indians is involved and permission of the RBI is necessary. The allotment will take place only on receipt of RBI permission. In this connection, refer to regulations 7, 9 and 10B of the Foreign Exchange Management (Transfer or Issue of Security by a Person Resident Outside India) Regulations, 2000, as and where applicable.

Having made the allotment, the transferee company is required to file with the ROC with return of allotment in Form No. 2 appended to the Companies (Central Government's) General Rules and Forms within 30 days from the date of allotment in terms of section 75 of the Act. The transferee company shall, having issued the new share certificates in lieu of and in exchange of old ones, surrender by transferor's shareholders should make necessary entries in the register of members and index of members for the shares so allotted in terms of sections 150 and 151, respectively, of the Companies Act, 1956.

20. *Listing of the Shares at Stock Exchange:* After the amalgamation is effected, the company that takes over the assets and liabilities of the transferor company should apply to the stock exchanges where its securities are listed for listing the new shares allotted to the shareholders of the transferor company.

21. *Court Order to Be Annexed to Memorandum of Transferee Company:* It is the mandatory requirement vide section 391(4) of the Companies Act, 1956, that after the certified copy of the court's order sanctioning the scheme of amalgamation is filed with the registrar, it should be annexed to every copy of the memorandum issued by the transferee company. Failure to comply with this requirement renders the company and its officers liable to punishment.

22. *Preservation of Books and Papers of Amalgamated Company:* Section 396A of the Act requires that the books and papers of the amalgamated company should be preserved and not be disposed of without prior permission of the central government.

23. *The Post-merger Secretarial Obligations:* There are various formalities to be complied with after amalgamation of the companies is given effect to and allotment of shares to the shareholders of the transferor company is over. These formalities include filing of returns with

the ROC, transfer of investments of the transferor company in the name of the transferee, intimating banks and financial institutions, creditors and debtors about the transfer of the transferor company's assets and liabilities in the name of the transferee company and so on.

24. Withdrawal of the Scheme Not Permissible: Once the scheme for merger has been approved by the requisite majority of shareholders and creditors, the scheme cannot be withdrawn by subsequent meeting of shareholders by passing resolution for withdrawal of the petition submitted to the court under section 391 for sanctioning the scheme.

25. Cancellation of the Scheme and Order of Winding-up: It was held by the Supreme Court in *J.K. (Bombay) (P) Ltd* v. *New Kaiser-I-Hind* that the effect of a winding-up order is that except for certain preferential payments provided in the Act, the property of the company is applied in satisfaction of its liabilities *pari passu*. *Pari passu* distribution is to be made in satisfaction of its liabilities as they exist at the commencement of the winding-up.

So long as the scheme is in operation and is binding on the company and its creditors, the rights and obligations of those on whom it is binding are undoubtedly governed by its provisions. But once the scheme is cancelled under section 392(2) on the ground that it cannot be satisfactorily worked and a winding-up order is passed, such an order is deemed to be for all purposes to be one made under section 433. It is not because as if the scheme has been sanctioned under section 391 that a winding-up order under section 392(2) cannot be made.

9.8 Valuation

In a merger deal, it is very important to calculate the value of the target. This valuation carries a significant importance in the whole merger process, which requires a careful analysis of the target from every respect. It requires expertise on different business valuation models, although valuation of a target is different than valuation of an existing firm on going-concern basis. We need to assign a value or more specifically a range of values to the target company so that we can guide the M&A process. We need answers to several questions: How much should we pay for the target company, how much is the target worth, how does this compare to the current market value of the target company and so on? It should be noted that the valuation process is not intended to establish a selling price for the target company. In the end, the price paid is whatever the buyer and the seller agree to. Different valuation models available are as follows:

a. *Public comps*: In this analysis, comparable publicly traded companies are identified and replicated to find a suitable value of the target. This analysis indicates how the stock markets are valuing companies that are similar to the target which is used as a reference value for the target.
b. *Transaction comps*: In this case, a comparable previous transaction is identified and replicated to find a suitable value of the target. This analysis indicates the valuations at which prior M&A transactions have been done in the same industry as that of the target.
c. *DCF analysis*: DCF is one of the most important valuation techniques which is widely used due to high acceptability and objectivity. The valuation decision is treated as a capital budgeting decision using the DCF model. The reason why the DCF model is used widely for valuation is the followings:

    - DCF captures all of the elements important to valuation.
    - DCF is based on the concept that investments add value when returns exceed the cost of capital.
    - DCF has support from both research and within the marketplace.

d. *Sum-of-the-parts analysis*: This method is applied when a potential target has more than one line of business that can be separately traced. Each part might have its own public comps, transaction comps and DCF (with different WACCs for each part). The total value is the sum of the parts.
e. *Other methods*: Depending on the unique characteristics of the transaction, a number of other analyses may be performed to arrive at fair value like LBO analysis, historical exchange ratio analyses and so on.

This following sections present a very brief discussion on different valuation models as identified earlier.

9.8.1 Public Comps

Compare the current trading level of a company to its peer group of companies.

The peer group is a set of 5 to 10 companies that are most similar to the target in terms of business mix and strategy, geographic risks (same country), margins and size (that is, processed meats and raw meats are different).

To find a good peer group, start broad and then narrow the list to the most comparable peers. Also refer to equity research reports, industry reports, the company's 10K where it discusses competitors and Bloomberg (Quote 2) to identify the most comparable peers (look at filing 8K prospectuses when they do a filing for new debt or equity in, say, freeedgar).

The goal of the analysis is to understand how the market is valuing the peer group in terms of price to earnings, price to book value, price to cash flow to equity, what the price/earnings to growth (PEG) ratio is, enterprise value to revenues, EBITDA, net assets and so on. Also understand if merger premium is already built into price, industry groups should know this.

There are always some industry-specific comps (telecom—enterprise value to POPs and SUBs, electric utilities—$/Mw and so on). Make sure you capture these in your analysis.

Using these, one can try to value the target bearing in mind that public comps do not reflect the 'control premium' that an acquirer will pay for buying control of the target. The control premium is generally around 30% for U.S. transactions. Also, some companies that are widely perceived to be acquisition targets may have some premium built into their stock price.

The most common multiples are:

a. Equity multiples: P/E (price/last 12-month (LTM) EPS, Price/1-Year forward EPS; note that the earnings need to be after preferred dividends so that they are earnings that are available to common shareholders), price to book (price/book value of equity per share).
b. Enterprise value multiples: EV/revenues, EV/EBITDA, EV/EBIT. (Note that the revenues, EBITDA and EBIT multiples could be computed for LTM and 1-year forward projected numbers.)

9.8.2 Transaction Comps

The goal here is to understand the multiples at which transactions in the target's industry sector have been announced or completed. The important difference with public comps is that in this case a control premium is built into the offer price and therefore the multiples.

Specifically, determine the pricing of past deals as compared to the target's financial performance and unaffected (pre-announcement) market value.

The transactions selected should be as comparable to proposed transaction as possible, so one should look for recent deals, where a company with highly similar business was acquired, in the same country as the target and so on.

The most common ones are the same as in the case of public comps but, additionally, transaction comps also cover premium paid (offer price premium as a percentage of 1-day, 1-week and 4-week trading prices).

9.8.3 Discounted Cash Flows (DCF)

Discount unleveraged projected FCFs (or in some cases dividend-able income) at the company's cost of capital to obtain an economic present value of assets. Subtract the market value of outstanding net debt and preferred capital from the present value of assets to get the present value of equity. FCF is after-tax operating earnings plus non-cash charges less increases in working capital less capital expenditures. (On leveraged DCF analysis, FCF is reduced by after-tax interest expense.)

Sensitivities on discount rates, terminal value assumptions and operating scenarios are frequently used to estimate the uncertainty in the values obtained.

9.8.4 Leveraged Buyout (LBO)

The goal here is to understand for how much value a financial buyer (with no operating synergies) could buy the target.

To understand the economics of an LBO, let us do an example: Company A's equity market capitalization is $100MM and it has a debt of $75MM. This year, it reported an EBITDA of $50MM. A financial sponsor realizes that the even if it bought the stock at a 30% premium to market for $130MM, it could generate attractive returns. So, the sponsor approaches the management and structures a deal where the firm borrows an additional $100MM to buy back stock. The sponsor supplies the remaining $30MM required to buy the public float and ends up owning a 100% of the equity of the firm. The new firm has $75MM of old and $100MM of new debt outstanding, which is sustained by the $50MM of annual EBITDA and an equity cushion of $30MM.

To finance an LBO, the restructured company has to have a debt to total capitalization (debt + equity) not exceeding 80% and a debt to EBITDA ratio that does not exceed five times. Note that these could vary based on the nature of the industry.

Assume current market scenarios for pricing the new debt.

The exit mechanism is an important element since it defines what the sponsor will do in, say, five years to exit the investment. In other words, is the sponsor planning an IPO or sale to strategic players? The sponsor's returns will be driven by EBITDA growth rate, margins improvements, Capex and exit multiples.

In an LBO, the entire equity is privately held, while in a leveraged recapitalization, there is usually a small percentage owned by the public.

9.9 DCF Techniques

To value the target, this section presents the use of DCF techniques in detail considering its importance and too much calculative as compared to other techniques. This discussion assumes that the learners have enough capturing on the topics discussed in the capital budgeting chapter (Chapter 4). The valuation computation under DCF techniques includes the following steps:

a. Discounting the future expected cash flows over a forecast period.
b. Adding a terminal value to cover the period beyond the forecast period.

c. Adding investment income, excess cash and other non-operating assets at their present values.
d. Subtracting out the fair market values of debt so that we can arrive at the value of equity.

Before we get into the valuation computation, we need to ask: What are we trying to value? Do we want to assign value to the equity of the target? Do we value the target company on a long-term basis or a short-term basis? For example, the valuation of a company expected to be liquidated is different from the valuation of a going concern. Some situations are highlighted here:

a. M&As through acquiring the equity plus outstanding liability of the target. For example, assume that company A has agreed to acquire 100% ownership (equity) of company B for \$200 million. Company B has \$50 million of liabilities outstanding. Thus, the purchase price would be \$250 million summing both equity and liability together. Here, company A acquired company B assuming that B's business will generate an NPV of \$250 million.
b. For publicly traded companies, the market value of the stock is easily determined assuming an efficient market in operation. The value of the equity plus the value of the debt is the total market value of the target company. Referring back to the example of companies A and B, assume that company B has 3,500,000 shares of stock outstanding. Company B's stock is selling for \$60 per share and the fair market value of B's debt is \$60 million. The total market value of company B will be as follows.

Market value of stock (3,500,000 × \$60)	\$210 million
Market value of debt	\$60 million
Total market value of company B	\$270 million

A word of caution about relying on market values within the stock market is that stocks rarely trade in large blocks similar to M&A transactions. Consequently, if the publicly traded target has low trading volumes, then prevailing market prices are not a reliable indicator of value.

9.9.1 Income Streams

One of the dilemmas within the M&A process is the selection of income streams for discounting. Income streams include earnings, EBIT, EBITDA, operating cash flow, FCF, EVA and so on.

In financial management, we recognize that value occurs when there is a positive gap between return on invested capital and cost of capital. Additionally, we recognize that earnings can be judgmental, subject to accounting rules and distortions. Valuations need to be rooted in 'hard numbers'. Therefore, valuations tend to focus on cash flows, such as operating cash flows and FCFs over a projected forecast period.

9.9.2 Free Cash Flow

One of the more reliable cash flows for valuations is FCF. FCF accounts for future investments that must be made to sustain cash flow. Compare this to EBITDA, which ignores any and all future required investments. Consequently, FCF is considerably more reliable than EBITDA and other earnings-based income streams. The basic formula for calculating FCF is:

$$\text{FCF} = \text{EBIT}\ (1 - t) + \text{Depreciation} - \text{Capital Expenditures} \pm \text{Net Working Capital}$$

Here, (1 – t) is the after tax percentage, used to convert EBIT to after taxes. Depreciation is added back since this is a non-cash flow item within EBIT. Capital expenditures represent investments that must be made to replenish assets and generate future revenues and cash flows.

Net working capital requirements may be involved when we make capital investments. At the end of a capital project, the change to working capital may get reversed. An example of computing FCF is as follows:

a. EBIT		$400
b. Less: Taxes		130
c. Operating profit after tax	a – b	270
d. Add: Depreciation		75
e. Gross cash flow	c + d	345
f. Change in working capital		42
g. Capital expenditures		270
h. Operating FCF	e – f – g	117
i. Cash from non-operating assets*		10
j. FCF	H + i	127

*Investments in marketable securities.

In addition to paying out cash for capital investments, we may find that we have some fixed obligations. A different approach to calculating FCF is:

$$\text{FCF} = \text{Cash flow from operating activities (after tax)} - \text{Interest}\ (1 - t) - \text{PD} - \text{RP} - \text{RD} - \text{E}$$

where PD is preferred stock dividends, RP is expected redemption of preferred stock, RD is expected redemption of debt and E is expenditures required to sustain cash flows.

To compute FCF under the new approach, follow the example below:

The following projections have been made for the year 2010:

- Operating CFATs are estimated as $190,000
- Interest payments on debt are expected to be $10,000
- Redemption payments on debt are expected to be $40,000
- New investments are expected to be $20,000
- The marginal tax rate is expected to be 30%

Compute FCF based on the above data.

After tax operating cash flow	$190,000
Less: After-tax interest ($10,000 × (1 – 0.30))	7,000
Debt Redemption Payment	40,000
New Investments	20,000
FCF	$123,000

9.9.3 Discount Rate

Now that we have some idea of our income stream for valuing the target company, we need to determine the discount rate for calculating present values. The discount rate used should match the risk associated with the FCFs. If the expected FCFs are highly uncertain, this increases risk and increases the discount rate. The riskier the investment, the higher is the discount rate and vice versa. Another way of looking at this is to ask you—what rate of return do investors require for a similar type of investment?

Since valuation of the target's equity is often the objective within the valuation process, it is useful to focus our attention on the 'targeted' capital structure of the target company. A review of comparable firms in the marketplace can help ascertain targeted capital structures. Based on this capital structure, we can calculate an overall WACC. The WACC will serve as our base for discounting the FCFs of the target company.

9.9.4 Application of DCF Techniques for Valuation

Valuing a target company is more or less an extension of what we know from capital budgeting. If the NPV of the investment is positive, we add value through an M&A. Follow the examples below to review NPV technique.

Example 1: Calculate the NPV.

Company A is considering acquiring company B for \$100,000 in cash. B's cost of capital is 16%. Based on market analysis, a targeted cost of capital for B is selected as 12%. A has estimated that B can generate \$9,000 of FCFs over the next 12 years. Using NPV, should A acquire B?

Present value of the initial cash outlay (t = 0)	(\$100,000)
Present value of FCF (\$9,000 × 6.1944*)	55,750
NPV	(\$44,250)

*Present value factor of annuity at 12%, 12 years.

Based on NPV, A should not acquire B since there is a negative NPV for this investment.

We also need to remember that some acquisitions are related to physical assets and some assets may be sold after the merger. Follow the example below:

Example 2: Calculate the NPV.

Agora Company has decided to sell its business for a sales price of \$50,000. Agora's balance sheet discloses the following:

Balance Sheet			
Assets	***Amount (\$)***	***Liabilities and Equity***	***Amount (\$)***
Cash	3,000	Liabilities	80,000
Accounts receivable	7,000	Equity	122,000
Inventory	12,000		

Equipment: Dye	115,000		
Equipment: Cutting	35,000		
Equipment: Packing	30,000		
Total assets	202,000	Total Liabilities and equity	202,000

PQS Company is interested in acquiring two assets—dye and cutting equipment. PQS intends to sell all remaining assets for $35,000. PQS estimates that total future FCFs from the dye and cutting equipment will be $26,000 per year over the next eight years. The cost of capital is 10% for the associated FCFs. Ignoring taxes, should PQS acquire Agora for $50,000?

Amount paid to Agora	$ (50,000)
Amount due to creditors	(80,000)
Less: Cash on hand	3,000
Less: Cash from sale of assets	35,000
Total initial cash outlay	(92,000)
Present value of FCF for 8 years at 10%: $26,000 × 5.3349	138,707
NPV	$46,707

Based on NPV, PQS should acquire Agora for $50,000 since there is a positive NPV of $46,707.

A solid estimation of incremental changes to cash flow is critical to the valuation process. Because of the variability of what can happen in the future, it is useful to run cash flow estimates through sensitivity analysis, using different variables to assess 'what-if' type analysis. Probability distributions are used to assign values to various variables. Simulation analysis can be used to evaluate estimates that are more complicated.

9.9.5 The Valuation Process

We have set the stage for valuing the target company. The overall process is centred on FCFs and the DCF model. We will now focus on the finer points in calculating the valuation. In valuation of the target, the following steps may be applied with some minor customizations in line with the situation:

1. *Historical Financial Analysis:* A detail analysis of past performance, including a determination of what drives performance. Several financial calculations need to be made, such as FCFs, return on capital and so on. Ratio analysis and benchmarking (for understanding benchmarking in detail, please follow the companion website of the book. You can download 'Chapter 23: Benchmarking' free) are also used to identify trends that will carry forward into the future.
2. *Forecast based on the Analysis*: It will be necessary to estimate the future financial performance of the target company. This requires a clear understanding of what drives performance and what synergies are expected from the merger.
3. *Estimate Cost of Capital*: We need to determine a WACC for discounting the FCFs.

4. *Estimate Terminal Value*: We will add a terminal value to our forecast period to account for the time beyond the forecast period.
5. *Test and Interpret Results*: Finally, once the valuation is calculated, the results should be tested against independent sources, revised, finalized, and presented to senior management.

9.9.6 Historical Financial Analysis

We start the valuation process with a complete analysis of historical performance. The valuation process must be rooted in factual evidence. This historical evidence includes at least the last five years (preferably the last 10 years) of financial statements for the target company. By analysing past performance, we can develop a synopsis or conclusion about the target company's future expected performance. It is also important to gain an understanding of how the target company generates and invests its cash flows.

One obvious place to start is to assess how the merger will affect earnings. P/E ratios (price to EPS) can be used as a rough indicator for assessing the impact on earnings. The higher the P/E ratio of the acquiring firm compared to the target company, the greater is the increase in EPS to the acquiring firm. Dilution of EPS occurs when the P/E ratio paid for the target exceed the P/E ratio of the acquiring company. The size of the target's earnings is also important; the larger the target's earnings are relative to the acquirer, the greater is the increase to EPS for the combined company. The following examples will illustrate these points.

Example 3: Calculate combined EPS.

Company G has plans to acquire company H by exchanging stock. G will issue 1.5 shares of its stock for each share of H. The financial information for the two companies is as follows:

	G	*H*
Net income	$400,000	$100,000
Shares outstanding	200,000	25,000
EPS	$2.00	$4.00
Market price of stocks	$40.00	$48.00

G expects the P/E ratio for the combined company to be 15.

Particular	*G*	*H*	*Combined*
Net income	$400,000	$100,000	$500,000
Number of shares (25,000×1.5)	200,000	37,500	237,500
EPS			$2.11
Expected P/E ratio			×15
Expected price of stock			$31.65

Before we move on to our next example, we should explain exchange ratios. The exchange ratio is the number of shares offered by the acquiring company in relation to each share of the target company. We can calculate the exchange ratio as:

Price Offered by Acquiring Firm/Market Price of Acquiring Firm

Example 4: Determine dilution of EPS.

ABC Company will acquire all of the outstanding stocks of XYZ Company through an exchange of stock. ABC is offering $65.00 per share for XYZ. The financial information for the two companies is as follows:

	ABC Company	***XYZ Company***
Net income ($)	50,000	10,000
Shares outstanding	5,000	2,000
EPS ($)	10.00	5.00
Market price of stock ($)	150.00	
P/E ratio	15	

a. Calculate shares to be issued by ABC: $65/$150 × 2,000 shares = 867 shares to be issued.
b. Calculate combined EPS: ($50,000 + $10,000)/(5,000 + 867) = $10.23
c. Calculate P/E ratio paid: Price offered/EPS of target or $65.00/$5.00 = 13
d. Compare P/E ratio paid to current P/E ratio: Since 13 is less than the current ratio of 15, there should be no dilution of EPS for the combined company.
e. Calculate maximum price before dilution of EPS: 15 = price/$5.00 or $75.00 per share. $75.00 is the maximum price that ABC should pay before EPS are diluted.

It is important to note that we do not want to get overly preoccupied with earnings when it comes to financial analysis. Most of our attention should be directed at drivers of value, such as return on capital. For example, FCF and EVA are much more important drivers of value than EPS and P/E ratios. Therefore, our financial analysis should determine how does the target company create value: Does it come from equity, what capital structure is used and so on? In order to answer these questions, we need to:

a. Calculate value drivers, such as FCF.
b. Analyse the results, looking for trends and comparing the results to other companies.
c. Looking back historically in order to ascertain a 'normal' level of performance.
d. Analysing the details to uncover how the target company creates value and noting what changes have taken place.

9.9.7 Value Drivers

Three core financial drivers of value are:

a. Return on invested capital (NOPAT/invested capital)
b. FCFs
c. EVA (NOPAT – cost of capital)

A value driver can represent any variable that affects the value of the company, ranging from great customer service to innovative products. Once we have identified these value drivers, we gain a solid understanding about how the company functions. The key is to have these value drivers fit between the target company and the acquiring company. When we have a good fit or alignment, the management will have the ability to influence these drivers and generate higher values.

In the book *Valuation: Measuring and Managing the Value of Companies* (McKinsey et al., 2010), the authors break down value drivers into three categories:

Type of Value Driver	*Management's Ability to Influence*
Level 1. Generic	Low
Level 2. Business units	Moderate
Level 3. Operating	High

For example, sales revenue is a generic value driver (level 1), customer mix would be a business unit value driver (level 2) and customers retained would be an operating value driver (level 3). Since value drivers are inter-related and since management will have more influence over level 3 drivers, the key is to ascertain if the merger will give the management more or less influence over the operating value driver. If yes, then an M&A could lead to revenue or expense synergies. Be advised that you should not work in reverse order, that is from level 1 down to level 3. For example, an increase in sales pricing will add more value to level 1, but in the long run you will hurt customers retained (level 3) and thus you may end up destroying value.

Once we have identified value drivers, we can develop a strategic view of the target company. This strategic view along with drivers of value must be considered in making a performance forecast of the target company. We want to know how the target company will perform in the future. In order to answer this question, we must have a clear understanding of the advantages that the target company has in relation to the competition. These competitive advantages can include things like customer mix, brand names, market share, business processes, barriers to competition and so on. An understanding of competitive advantages will give us insights into future expected growth for the target company.

9.9.8 Forecasting Performance

Now that we have gained some insights into future growth, we can develop a set of performance scenarios. Since no one can accurately predict the future, we should develop at least three performance scenarios:

a. Conservative Scenario: Future growth will be slow and decline over time.
b. General Industry Scenario: Continued moderate growth similar to the overall industry.
c. Improved Growth Scenario: Management has the ability to influence level 1 value drivers and we can expect above-average growth.

Keep in mind that performance scenarios have a lot of assumptions, and many of these assumptions are based on things like future competition, new technologies, changes in the economy, changes in consumer behaviour and so on. The end result is to arrive at a 'most likely' value between the different scenarios.

Example 5: Overall value per three scenarios.

You have calculated three NPVs over a 12-year forecast period. Based on your analysis of value drivers, strategies, competition and other variables, you have assigned the following values to each scenario:

Scenario	*Probability*	×	*NPV*	=	*Expected Value*
Conservative	20%		$180,000		36,000
Normal	65%		460,000		299,000
M&A growth	15%		590,000		88,500
Overall value of target company					423,500

The valuation model should include a complete set of forecasted financial statements. Usually, a set of forecasted financial statements will start with the sales forecast since sales is a driver behind many account balances. A good sales forecast will reflect future expected changes in sales prices, volumes and other variables.

Two important points when preparing your forecast are:

1. Historical Perspective: Make sure the pieces of your forecast fit together and flow from historical performance. Historical values are very important for predicting the future. You can gain a historical perspective by simply plotting financial trends (see Example 6).
2. Forecast Period: Your forecast period should cover a long enough period for the target company to reach a stable and consistent performance level. For example, a company has reached a stable point when it can earn a constant rate of return on capital for an indefinite period and the company has the ability to reinvest a constant proportion of earnings back into the business.

Rarely is the forecast period less than seven years. When in doubt, use a longer forecast than a shorter forecast.

The final step in forecasting the financials is to estimate the value drivers and verify the value drivers against historical facts. As we indicated, three core drivers are return on capital, FCF and EVA. Make sure you test your results; are key drivers consistent with what has happened in the past, what are the trends for future growth, what are the competitive trends, how will this impact performance and so on?

Example 6: Plotting historical trends to help with preparing forecasted financial statements.

	2006	*2007*	*2008*	*2009*	*2010*
Operations:					
Growth in revenues	14%	12%	11%	11%	10%
Growth in margins	7%	7%	6%	5%	5%
Working capital:					
Cash	2%	2%	2%	3%	3%
Accounts receivable	12%	13%	13%	13%	14%
Accounts payable	4%	4%	5%	5%	5%
Investments:					
Assets to sales	30%	31%	28%	29%	28%
Return on capital	14%	12%	13%	13%	12%

When we have completed the valuation model, we will have a set of forecasted financial statements supporting each of our scenarios:

- Forecasted income statement: Three scenarios
- Forecasted balance sheet: Three scenarios
- Forecasted FCFs: Three scenarios
- Forecasted return on capital: Three scenarios
- Forecasted performance ratios: Three scenarios

Example 7: Forecasted income statement for scenario 2: Moderate ($ millions).

	2011	*2012*	*2013*	*2014*	*2015*	*2016*	*2017*
Revenues	$6.50	$6.70	$6.85	$6.95	$7.05	$7.09	$7.12
Less: Operating exp.	3.20	3.30	3.41	3.53	3.65	3.72	3.78
Less: Depreciation	0.56	0.54	0.52	0.85	0.80	0.77	0.72
EBIT	2.74	2.86	2.92	2.57	2.60	2.60	2.62
Less: Interest	0.405	0.380	0.365	0.450	0.440	0.410	0.390
Earnings before tax	2.335	2.480	2.555	2.12	2.16	2.19	2.23
Less: Taxes	0.780	0.810	0.870	0.650	0.660	0.71	0.73
Net income	1.555	1.670	1.685	1.470	1.500	1.48	1.50

9.9.9 Terminal Values

It is quite possible that FCFs will be generated well beyond our forecast period. Therefore, many valuations will add a terminal value to the valuation forecast. The terminal value represents the total present value that we will receive after the forecast period.

Example 8: Adding terminal value to valuation forecast.

NPV for forecast period (Example 5)	$423,500
Terminal value for beyond forecast period	183,600
Total NPV of the target company	$607,100

There are several approaches to calculating the terminal value:

Dividend Growth: Simply take the FCF in the final year of the forecast, add a nominal growth rate to this flow and discount the FCF as perpetuity. The terminal value is calculated as follows:

$$\text{Terminal Value} = \frac{\text{FCF}(t+1)}{\text{WACC} - g}$$

Here, (t + 1) refers to the first year beyond the forecast period, is the weighted average cost of capital and is the growth rate, usually a very nominal rate similar to the overall economy.

It should be noted that FCF used for calculating terminal values is a normalized FCF representative of the forecast period.

Example 9: Calculate terminal value using dividend growth.

You have prepared a forecast for 10 years, and the normalized FCF is $45,000. The growth rate expected after the forecast period is 3%. The WACC for the target company is 12%.

$$(\$45{,}000 \times 1.03)/(0.12 - 0.03) = \$46{,}350/0.09 = \$515{,}000$$

If we wanted to exclude the growth rate in Example 9, we would calculate terminal value as $46,350/0.12 = $386,250. This gives us a much more conservative estimate.

Adjusted Growth: Growth is included to the extent that we can generate returns higher than our cost of capital. As a company grows, you must reinvest back into the business and thus FCFs will fall. Therefore, the adjusted growth approach is one of the more appropriate models for calculating terminal values.

$$\text{Terminal Value} = \frac{\text{EBIT}(1-\text{T})(1-\text{g/r})}{\text{WACC}-\text{g}}$$

Here, T is the tax rate, g is the growth rate and r is the rate of return on new investment.

Example 10: Calculate terminal value using adjusted growth.

Normalized EBIT is $60,000 and the expected normal tax rate is 30%. The overall long-term growth rate is 3% and the WACC is 12%. We expect to obtain a rate of return on new investments of 15%.

$$\text{Here, terminal value} = \frac{\$61{,}800(1-0.30)(1-0.03/0.15)}{0.12-0.03} = \frac{\$43{,}260 \times 0.80}{0.09} = \$384{,}533$$

If we use FCFs, we would have the following type of calculation:

EBIT	$60,000
Remove taxes (1 – T)	×0.70
Operating income after taxes	42,000
Depreciation (non-cash item)	12,000
Less: Capital expenditures	(9,000)
Less: Changes to working capital	(1,000)
FCF	44,000
Growth rate at 3%	×1.03
FCF (t + 1)	45,320
Adjust growth > return on capital	×0.80
Adjusted FCF (t + 1)	36,256
Divided by WACC – g or 0.12 – 0.03	0.09
Terminal value	$402,844

EVA Approach: If your valuation is based on EVA, then you should extend this concept to your terminal value calculation:

$$\text{Terminal Value} = \text{NOPAT}(t+1) \times (1 - g/rc)/\text{WACC} - g$$

Here, rc is the return on invested capital.

Terminal values should be calculated using the same basic model you used within the forecast period. You should not use P/E multiples to calculate terminal values since the price paid for a target company is not derived from earnings, but from FCFs or EVA. Finally, terminal values are appropriate when two conditions exist:

a. The target company has consistent profitability and turnover of capital for generating a constant return on capital.
b. The target company is able to reinvest a constant level of cash flow because of consistency in growth.

If these two criteria do not exist, you may need to consider a more conservative approach to calculating terminal value or simply exclude the terminal value altogether.

Example 11: Summarize valuation calculation based on expected values under three scenarios:

Present value of FCFs for 10-year forecast period	$62,500
Terminal value-based on Perpetuity	87,200
Present value of non-operating assets	8,600
Total value of target company	158,300
Less: Outstanding debt at fair market value:	
Short-term notes payable	(6,850)
Long-term bonds (25-year grade BB)	(26,450)
Long-term bonds (10-year grade AAA)	(31,900)
Long-term bonds (5-year grade BBB)	(22,700)
Present value of lease obligations	(17,880)
Total value assigned to equity	52,520
Outstanding shares of stock	7,000
Value per share ($52,520/7,000)	$7.50

Example 12: Calculate value per share.

You have completed the following forecast of FCFs for an eight-year period, capturing the normal business cycle of Gemini Company:

Year	*FCF*	*Year*	*FCF*
2016	$1,550	2020	$1,656
2017	1,573	2021	1,680
2018	1,598	2022	1,703
2019	1,626	2023	1,725

Gemini has non-operating assets of $150. These assets have an estimated present value of $500. Based on the present value of future payments, the present value of debt is $2,800. Terminal value is calculated using the dividend growth model. A nominal growth rate of 2%

will be used. Gemini's targeted cost of capital is 14%. Gemini has 3,000 shares of stock outstanding. What is Gemini 's value per share?

Year	FCF	×	PV at 14%	=	Present Value
2016	$1,550		0.8772		$1,360
2017	1,573		0.7695		1,210
2018	1,598		0.6750		1,079
2019	1,626		0.5921		963
2020	1,656		0.5194		860
2021	1,680		0.4556		765
2022	1,703		0.3996		681
2023	1,725		0.3506		605
Total present value for forecast period					$7,523
Terminal value = ($1,725 × 1.02)/(0.14 – 0.02)					14,663
Value of non-operating assets					500
Total value of Gemini					22,686
Less value of debt					(2,800)
Value of equity					19,886
Shares outstanding					3,000
Value per share					$6.63

Multiple Choice Questions

1. A merger is a combination of businesses in which
   a. Two businesses combine to form a new business
   b. The participants are necessarily comparable in size, competitive position, profitability and market capitalization
   c. One of the two firms becomes a wholly owned subsidiary of the other firm
   d. None of the above

2. Assuming we are valuing a going concern, which of the following types of income streams would be most appropriate for valuing the company?
   a. Earnings Before Interest and Taxes
   b. Free Cash Flows
   c. Operating income after taxes
   d. Price to earnings ratio

3. The following estimates have been made for the year 2015:

Operating income (EBIT)	$6,000
Depreciation	500
Cash taxes to be paid	950
Income from non-operating assets	60

No capital investments or changes to working capital are expected. Based on this information, the projected FCFs for 2015 are:
a. $5,610 b. $4,550 c. $4,490 d. $6,550

4. Marshall Company is considering acquiring Lincoln Associates for $600,000. Lincoln has total outstanding liabilities valued at $200,000. The total purchase price for Marshall to acquire Lincoln is
a. $200,000 b. $400,000 c. $600,000 d. $800,000

5. Which of the following are commonly cited reasons for M&As?
a. Synergy
b. Market power
c. Strategic realignment
d. All of the above

6. You have been asked to calculate a terminal value for a valuation forecast. The normalized FCF within the forecast is $11,400. A nominal growth rate of 3% will be applied along with a WACC of 15%. Using the dividend growth model, the terminal value that should be added to the forecast is
a. $78,280 b. $86,200 c. $95,000 d. $97,850

7. Information from a valuation model for Gemini Corporation is summarized below:

Total present value of forecasted FCFs	$150,000
Terminal value added	450,000
Total present value of non-operating assets	20,000
Total present value of outstanding debts	120,000

If Gemini has 20,000 shares of outstanding stock, the value per share of Gemini is
a. $15.00 b. $25.00 c. $30.00 d. $35.00

8. All of the following are common motives for a merger or acquisition except for
a. Operating synergy
b. Financial synergy
c. Raising the cost of capital
d. Buying undervalued assets.

9. Once a merger has been finalized, one of the primary responsibilities of senior executive management as it relates to post merger integration is to
a. Facilitate functional integration
b. Develop personnel retention programmes
c. Lead change through communication
d. Manage all of the integration projects

10. One of the challenges within post-merger integration is to retain key (essential) personnel. Which of the following might help retain key personnel?
a. Assign personnel to new locations
b. Invite personnel to management meetings
c. Offer personnel severance packages
d. Recruit personnel differently than normal

Review Questions

1. What do you mean by mergers? Give a detailed classification of mergers.
2. Distinguish between vertical and horizontal merger, using suitable examples.
3. Explain historical evolution and trends of merger waves in the United States.
4. Write a short note on merger waves in the Indian scenario.

5. List and explain the various motives of mergers.
6. Critically examine the various theories of mergers.
7. List and explain the different sources of financial synergy in M&As.
8. Discuss the impact of M&As on various groups of stakeholders.
9. Why do M&As quite often fail? List the important reasons for failures of mergers.
10. What are the prime reasons that make M&A risky?
11. Identify and explain the strategic issues in M&A.
12. Discuss the guidelines for managing the integration process in M&A.
13. Write short notes on:
    a. Identifying synergies in M&A
    b. Method of financing the M&A deal
14. Briefly discuss the causes of risk in M&As.
15. What are the methods of preventing risk in M&A?

Exercises

1. Essex wants to acquire 100% stock of Xavier for $500 million. However, Xavier's most recent balance sheet reports $100 million of liabilities outstanding. Compute the cost of acquisition.
2. Consider the example of Essex and Xavier above. Now assume that Xavier is a publicly traded company with a total of 30 million of common stock outstanding with $10 par value. However, the market value is $60 per share. The fair value of Xavier's outstanding liability is $90 million. Compute the cost of acquisition.
3. Consider the following information, which has been extracted from the financial statements of Xavier:

EBIT	$600 million
Taxes	at 30%
Depreciation	$50 million
Change in working capital	–$40 million
Capital expenditures	180 million
Cash flow from non-operating assets	20 million

   Compute FCF of Xavier based on the above information.
4. Consider the following information which has been extracted from the financial statements of Essex:
   - Operating CFATs are estimated as $500 million
   - Interest payments on debt are expected to be $10 million
   - Redemption payments on debt are expected to be $40 million
   - New investments are expected to be $15 million
   - The marginal tax rate is expected to be 30%
5. Company X is considering acquiring company Y for $250,000 in cash. Y's cost of capital is 14%. Based on market analysis, a targeted cost of capital for Y is selected as 10%. X has estimated that Y can generate $10,000 of FCFs over the next 10 years. Using NPV, should X acquire Y?

6. Mini Company has decided to sell its business for a sales price of $100,000. Mini's balance sheet discloses the following:

Balance Sheet			
Assets	***Amount ($)***	***Liabilities and Equity***	***Amount ($)***
Cash	10,000	Liabilities	120,000
Accounts receivable	20,000	Equity	180,000
Inventory	30,000		
Equipment: Dye	120,000		
Equipment: Cutting	80,000		
Equipment: Packing	40,000		
Total assets	300,000	Total Liabilities and Equity	300,000

Maxi Company is interested in acquiring two assets: dye and cutting equipment. Mini intends to sell all remaining assets for $50,000. Maxi estimates that total future FCFs from the dye and cutting equipment will be $50,000 per year over the next eight years. The cost of capital is 12% for the associated FCFs. Ignoring taxes, should Maxi acquire Mini for $80,000?

7. Company M has plans to acquire company N by exchanging stock. M will issue two shares of its stock for each share of N. Financial information for the two companies is as follows:

	M	***N***
Net income	$50 million	$20 million
Shares outstanding	200,000	50,000
EPS	$4.00	$6.00
Market price of stocks	$30.00	$45.00

M expects the P/E ratio for the combined company to be 15. Compute the expected price of stock after the exchange.

8. ABC will acquire all of the outstanding stock of XYZ through an exchange of stock. ABC is offering $80.00 per share for XYZ. Financial information for the two companies is as follows:

	ABC Company	***XYZ Company***
Net income ($)	100,000	70,000
Shares outstanding	8,000	4,000
EPS ($)	20.00	10.00
Market price of stock ($)	180.00	
P/E ratio	18	

a. Calculate shares to be issued by ABC.
b. Calculate combined EPS.
c. Calculate P/E ratio paid.
d. Compare P/E ratio paid to current P/E ratio.
e. Calculate maximum price before dilution of EPS.

9. You have prepared a forecast for 10 years and the normalized FCF is $50,000. The growth rate expected after the forecast period is 5%. The WACC for the target company is 10%. Compute the terminal value.
10. Compute terminal value based on the following data:
    - Normalized EBIT, $80,000
    - Expected normal tax rate, 30%
    - Overall long-term growth rate, 4%
    - WACC, 13%
    - Expected rate of return on new investments, 15%
11. You have completed the following forecast of FCFs for a 10-year period, capturing the normal business cycle of Exit company:

Year	*FCF*	*Year*	*FCF*
2016	$1,820	2021	$1,730
2017	1,930	2022	1,970
2018	1,780	2023	1,635
2019	1,690	2024	1,290
2020	1,850	2025	1,980

Exit has non-operating assets of $200. These assets have an estimated present value of $600. Based on the present value of future payments, the present value of debt is $2,500. Terminal value is calculated using the dividend growth model. A nominal growth rate of 3% will be used. Exit 's targeted cost of capital is 15%. Exit has 3,500 shares of stock outstanding. What is Exit 's value per share?

Case in Action

Centurion Bank and Bank of Punjab: A Merger in Private Banking

Introduction

In the last two decades, private banks have taken to the consolidation route in a big way for growth. Most of the private sector banks are profitable and have adequate capital and technology edge. Due to intensifying competition, the access to low-cost deposits is critical for growth. Therefore, size and geographical reach becomes the key for smaller banks. The choice before smaller private banks is to merge and form bigger and viable entities or merge into a big private sector bank. Analysts are quite upbeat about the development. According to them 'There is a need for consolidation in the private banking space, although it will finally depend on the fundamentals of each case. Smaller banks will have to consolidate to survive'. When Government of India and the RBI had been talking about the need for consolidation in the banking sector, one bank that had set a scorching pace for M&A was Centurion Bank. According to bankers 'There is now a compelling reason for banks to merge because a lot of the old crutches have gone. Competition has increased, margins are squeezed, products have become more complex and the customer has become more discerning. In this scenario, a national footprint is a must'. At that time Centurion Bank expanded its footprints substantially by the merger with Bank of Punjab.

Centurion Bank Limited

Centurion Bank had a cheque red history. It was set up by former Citibanker Dev Ahuja, core promoter of 20th Century Finance Corporation Limited when the RBI gave out private banking license. Centurion Bank was incorporated on 30 June 1994 and it got the certificate of Commencement of Business on 20 July 1994. The main equity of the bank was provided by the promoters. In 1995, 20th Century Finance Corporation Limited had been amalgamated with Centurion Bank Limited when a rating agency downgraded it with knee jerk reaction. In December 2002, Sabre Capital Worldwide conducted an exclusive due diligence of Centurion Bank for a possible capital infusion. Sabre Capital Worldwide was a private equity fund established by a team of bankers to invest in and to help in managing financial service businesses in emerging markets. At that time Centurion Bank was in trouble. It was with less capital adequacy ratio. It had posted a net loss of ₹161.8 crore for the year ended 31 March 2002. It also incurred a net loss of ₹3.6 crore for the first quarter ended 30 June 2002. In 2003, Sabre Capital Worldwide submitted the proposal to revive the Centurion Bank. The proposal was approved by RBI and Bombay High Court. The scheme consisted of three major proposals: restructuring of capital by reducing the face value of the bank's share from ₹10 to ₹1, infusion of fresh capital of ₹319 crore in two phases, and takeover of management control by Sabre Capital Worldwide and merger of Bank of Muscat with Centurion Bank. On 8 May 2003 Bank of Muscat merged its Bangalore branch with Centurion Bank. Bank of Muscat had invested around ₹75 crore in Centurion Bank. Other main shareholders of Centurion Bank were International Finance Corporation (IFC), Asian Development Bank (ADB), and Keppel Group of Singapore.

The Centurion Bank was set up in a fully computerised environment with ATM facility at every branch. Computer networking between branches could indeed claim to be a 'Bank with a difference'. The Bank had introduced, for the first time in the country, the concept of 'Anywhere Banking' which enabled to operate the account from any other branch of the bank. The main feature of the bank was that it was a professionally managed bank with a globally experienced management team. Centurion Bank Limited constantly endeavored to offer customized services that were driven by customer requirements rather than just exhibiting technological prowess.

Bank of Punjab

Bank of Punjab was promoted by Darshanjit Singh, Harpreet Singh, Tejinder Singh, Indudeep Kaur and Tejbir Singh. The bank stared its operation from April 1995. Its first branch was in Chandigarh, Punjab. By March 1996, its deposit base was ₹2,342.17 crore. In 4 years, the annual growth raised to ₹3,244.76 which was 200%.The lending policy of the bank was not cautious and constructive but based on principles of prudent lending with maximum emphasis on security. As agriculture is considered as backbone of the country, the Bank of Punjab had introduced 'Kissan Dost Agriculture Finance Scheme' to small farmers. Bank of Punjab was the first bank to focus on retail banking and to introduce fax banking and tele banking for its customers. It had a tie up with Master Card.

About the Deal

The board of directors and the shareholders of Centurion Bank and Bank of Punjab had approved the merger on 3 August 2005. The new entity named as 'Centurion Bank of Punjab'. RBI had approved merger of Centurion Bank and Bank of Punjab effective from 1 October 2005. It had been decided that in the Board, Centurion Bank's Chairman Rana Talwar, and Managing director Shailendra Bhandari would be the chairman, and managing director of the merged entity while Tejbir Singh, executive director,

Bank of Punjab would be the whole time executive director of the merged entity. KPMG India Private Ltd and NM Raiji & Co were the independent valuers and Ambit Corporate Finance was the sole investment banker to the transaction. Regarding Swap ratio it had been fixed at 4:9, that was, for every four shares of ₹10 of Bank of Punjab, its shareholders would receive nine shares of ₹1 of Centurion Bank. It had been decided that there would be no cash transaction in the course of the merger; it would be settled through the swap of shares. After the merger, the shareholding of Bank of Punjab promoters would shrink to 5%. The family of Darshanjit Singh who promoted Bank of Punjab held 15.62%, while associates held another 11.40% before merger. After the merger the promoter stake would fall down to around 5% and for associate that would be7-8%. The major stakeholder's stake in the Centurion Bank would fall after merger. Bank of Muscat's stake would fall to 25% from 31%, Keppel's stake would be at 9% from current level of 11.33% and Rana Talwar's Saber Capital would have a stake of 4.4% as against 5.61%. The promoters of the Bank of Punjab and major stakeholders of Centurion bank would have a combine stake of around 42% in the merged entity—Centurion Bank of the Punjab.

Positive Side

After the merger, combined entity the Centurion Bank of Punjab would be among the top ten private sector banks in the country. According to Mr Talwar 'The merger is a win-win for the shareholders, customers and staff of the two banks. The reason for the merger is the fantastic fit in terms of achieving scale and geographical presence. After the regulatory approvals, there would be crossover of products and services,' Bank of Punjab was a great fit with Centurion Bank. The latter was strong in retail and had a solid management made up mainly by former Citi banker who had turned it around and recapitalized it. It had also lots of capital after restructuring and recapitalization by Sabre Capital Worldwide. On the other hand Bank of Punjab lacked capital and had high Non Performing Assets (NPA) levels. It was not very good at retail, but had good Small and Medium Enterprise Credit. After the merger with Bank of Muscat, Centurion Bank was with enough cash at its disposal to absorb the business of Bank of Punjab and was confident enough to lend succour to the blockade bank. Bank of Punjab needed the merger more than Centurion Bank. The former had to contend with a rapid increase in the proportion of its bad loans in 2005. Before merger, Bank of Punjab was with 9% capital adequacy ratio near the regulatory, the merger had come in handy for Centurion Bank to ward off regulatory intervention. It was not even a year since the combine of Mr Rana Talwar and Bank of Muscat bailed out Centurion Bank from the brink of disaster. Centurion Bank's net worth had almost turned negligible and only substantial cash infusion saved it. The merger, however, bring some value to Centurion Bank shareholders. At about 4.24%, Bank of Punjab boasts of one of the lowest cost of deposits in the banking industry. Bank of Punjab's network of 136 branches was also almost entirely complementary to that of Centurion Bank. The acquisition cost is also attractive for Centurion Bank. The price-to-book multiple for the acquisition works out to 1.85. The Centurion Bank stock trades at a price-to-book of 2.9 times. The acquisition would, thus, be cost-effective for Centurion Bank shareholders.

Rana Talwar, Chairman, Centurion Bank Limited said, 'We are delighted at the opportunity the merger of Centurion Bank and Bank of Punjab creates. Both Banks have excellent franchises, which will complement each other. The combined entity will be a powerful private sector bank with a nationwide reach. The merged entity will be well capitalized, have strong management team, and will be able to achieve considerable revenue and cost synergy. The combined bank will be full-service commercial bank with a strong presence in the retail and SME segments. Both the banks had strong brand names in their respective markets and the new bank will build upon these powerful brands'. According to Ms Kanan Shah, research analyst with Net worth Stock Broking, 'Consolidation is good for the banking industry. Now banking has become like a commodity business. For instance, people can bargain on interest rates. In such a scenario, scale is important for survival. Every bank in India is now ready for consolidation. The merger between Centurion Bank and Bank of Punjab will help Centurion more, as it will be able to expand faster. Bank of Punjab would not have done well on its own. It would have had to be acquired either by a private sector bank or by a foreign bank in order to have sustained'. About Centurion's prospects, post-merger, she said, 'Centurion is a relatively new bank and its growth has been slow. It takes time to expand and increase the reach. That is why this merger will help'.

The merger of the banks would have a presence of 240 branches and extension counters, 386 ATMs, with about 2.2 million customers. The combined entity as at March 2005 stood at ₹696 crore with Centurion's net worth at ₹511 crore and Bank of Punjab's net worth at ₹181 crore. The total assets of combined entity (Centurion Bank of Punjab) will have ₹9,395 crore, deposit ₹7,837 crore and operating profit ₹43 crore. The merged entity would have a paid up share capital of ₹130 crore. The combined entity would have net non-performing Assets (NPAs) of about 3.6% as on March 2005. Centurion Banks net non-performing assets (NPAs) as on 31 March 2005 stood at 2.49% while for Bank of Punjab the figure stood at 4.6%. The combined entity would have adequate capital adequacy of 16.1% to provide for its growth plans. Centurion Banks capital adequacy on a standalone basis stood at 23.1% while for Bank of Punjab the figure stood at 9.21%. According to Mr Singh 'The growth momentum of both banks will now combine and the resulting multiplier effect will produce electrifying results. The two banks represent a perfect fit in all respect with virtually negligible overlaps'.

Branch network of the two banks would complement each other. The combined entity will have a nationwide reach. Centurion Bank was strong in South India, Maharashtra and Goa whereas Bank of Punjab was strong in Punjab, Haryana and Delhi. In Punjab, it had fabulous franchise. It had more branches than any other private sector bank. Centurion Bank had 82% of business coming from retail, while Bank of Punjab was strong in the small and medium enterprises (SMEs) segment and agricultural sector. The combined bank would be full-service commercial bank with a strong presence in the Retail, Small and Medium Enterprises and Agricultural segments. The two Banks had a few things in common. Both were new generation private sectors banks, neither had trade unions, both had core banking system, although the platform were different. Centurion Bank of Punjab merger was just a starting. It surely encourages other private banks to go for the M&A road for consolidation.

Source: www.banknetindia.com

Questions for Discussion

1. Discuss the historical background and operational activities of Centurion Bank Limited and Bank of Punjab.
2. Briefly elaborate on the positive aspects of the merger of Centurion Bank and Bank of Punjab.

References

Ansoff, H.I. 1965. *Corporate Strategy: An Analytic Approach to Business Policy for Growth and Expansion.* New York: McGraw-Hill.

———. 1987. 'The Emerging Paradigm of Strategic Behavior'. *Strategic Management Journal*, 8, 501–15.

Business India. 2005. 'Biggest deal?' *Business India*, March, 162–63.

Cantwell, J.A. 1986. 'Technological Innovation and International Production in the Industrial World. A Study of the Accumulation of Capital in International Networks'. PhD thesis, University of Reading.

Chellasamy, P., and J. Udhaya Kumar. 2007. 'A Case Study on Financial Performance of Centurion Bank and Bank of Punjab-in Pre and Post Merger Period'. *Journal of Global Economy*, 3(3): 77–86, www.rcssindia.org (last accessed on 12 January 2015).

Khemani, R.S. 1990. 'Recent Trends in Merger and Acquisition Activity in Canada and Selected Countries', Paper presented at the Investment Canada Conference, Corporate Globalization through Mergers and Acquisitions, Toronto, November.

McKinsey, Tim Koller, Marc Goedhart, and David Wessel. 2010. *Valuation: Measuring and Managing the Value of Companies*, University Edition. New York: Wiley.

Popper, B. 2012. 'Failure Is a Feature: How Google Stays Sharp Gobbling up Startups'. *The Verge*.

Sudarsanam, S. 2009. *Creating Value from Mergers and Acquisitions: The Challenges*. Harlow, UK: Prentice Hall.

Further Readings

Northern Securities Co. v. United States, 193 U.S. (1904), was a case heard by the U.S. Supreme Court in 1903. The Court ruled 5 to 4 against the stockholders of the Great Northern and Northern Pacific railroad companies, who had essentially formed a monopoly, and to dissolve the Northern Securities Company. Wikipedia. Available at https://en.wikipedia.org/wiki/Northern_Securities_Co._v._United_States (last accessed on 12 July 2012).

Supreme Court of India. *J.K. (Bombay) (P) Ltd vs New Kaiser-I-Hind Spg. & Wvg. Co.* On 22 November 1968. Available at www.indiankanoon.org/doc/96082 (last accessed on 5 March 2013).

Chapter 10

Takeover

Chapter Objectives

On completion of this chapter, you will be able to understand:

- The concept of takeover
- Types of takeover
  - Friendly takeover, hostile takeover, bailout takeover, reverse takeovers, horizontal takeover, vertical takeover, conglomerate takeover
- Takeover vs. merger
- Motives behind takeovers
- Defences to hostile takeovers
  - Shark repellent, golden parachute, bankmail, crown jewel defence, flip-in, greenmail, Jonestown defence, killer bees (business), leveraged recapitalization, lobster trap, poison pill, Nancy Reagan defence, Pac-Man defence, pension parachute, safe harbour, scorched earth, targeted repurchase, white knight, whitemail
- Legal regime for takeover code in India
- Economic aspects of takeover
- Accounting aspects of takcover
- Impact of takeover on stakeholders
- Special issues from SEBI

A Bavarian Botch-up

In July 1997, the two Bavarian banks, BayerischeVereinsbank and Hypobank merged to form Hypo Vereinsbank (HVB). The move seemed to make sense in the context of Germany's inefficient and fragmented banking market. The two banks were long-time rivals, located close to each other. With a similar branch network and a similar mix of businesses, they identified several opportunities to cut costs. HVB also hoped the merger would enable it to become a major player in the German mortgage banking market.

However, the merger was more a reaction to the prevailing circumstances than a proactive, well-thought-out strategy. Vereinsbank was on the verge of a hostile takeover by Deutsche Bank. It had approached Commerzbank for support in warding off this takeover attempt but later resigned itself to a deal with Hypobank. On its part, Hypobank even though it was making decent profits was worried about being taken over by Dresdner Bank. Bavarian politicians actively supported the merger as they wanted to create a national champion. This was a part of their grandiose plan to convert Munich into a financial centre that could rival Frankfurt. The government offered a one-off tax waiver on the exchange of shares involved in the transaction. Without this concession, the merger might not have gone ahead.

It was quite clear that several issues had been left unresolved at the time of the merger. Moreover, there was tension in the air due to rumors that Vereinsbank's ultimate goal was a takeover of Hypobank. Albrecht Schmidt, the head of Vereinsbank, took charge of the merged entity. Vereinsbank took nine of the 14 seats on the Board of Management and also gained control over many key departments. Ebenhard Martini, the Chief of Hypobank decided to move on to the more ornamental Supervisory Board. (Under German laws, limited companies typically have two boards, a Board of Management, vested with executive powers and a Supervisory Board which oversees the functioning of the Board of Management).

These moves were however, consistent with Martini's delegating philosophy and Schmidt's hands on management style. Martini's hands-off-approach could also have been due to Hypobank's non-performing assets (NPA) in the property business. These assets had resulted from Hypobank's aggressive lending in East Germany during the construction boom following German unification.

Only a year after the merger, did the seriousness of the bad loans problem become evident? In October 1998, Schmidt announced that loan provisions of $2.1 billion would have to be made. He also hinted that these losses had been covered up by Hypobank. This led to a serious clash with Martini. The merged entity's reputation was damaged. People felt that a backroom struggle was going on between the chief executives of the pre-merger entities.

Only in October 1999, after an auditor submitted his report, was Schmidt's assessment vindicated. Martini and the four remaining members on the Board of Management, from Hypobank resigned. Later, Schmidt signalled peace by putting ex-Hypobankers in charge of the property division and giving them many of the top jobs in accounting and controlling.

Meanwhile, the integration proceeded smoothly. 500 overlapping branches were closed. Much of the systems integration was also completed in less than three years, well ahead of schedule. In May 2000, encouraged by the performance of HVB, Schmidt announced he was acquiring Bank Austria, the biggest bank in Austria.

Source: A summary of BayerischeVereinsbank–Hypobank merger based on 'A Bavarian Botch-up', *The Economist*.[1]

Takeovers are taking place all over the world. Those companies whose shares are under-quoted on the stock market are under a constant threat of takeover. In fact, every company is vulnerable to a takeover threat. The takeover strategy has been conceived to improve corporate value, achieve better productivity and profitability by making optimum use of the available resources in the form of men, materials and machines.

Earlier in India, well-performing companies were not allowed to utilize their surplus funds and managerial competence to takeover suitable and promising companies and 'build on them' with their own funds and technical, administrative, financial and marketing expertise. They had to wait for companies to go sick, be referred to BIFR, and be taken over under a rehabilitation scheme prepared by a nominated operating agency and sanctioned by BIFR. In India, the process of economic liberalization and globalization ushered in the early 1990s created a highly competitive business environment, which motivated many companies to

[1] Available at http://www.economist.com/node/28755

restructure their corporate strategies. The restructuring process led to an unprecedented rise in strategies like amalgamations, mergers, including reverse mergers, demergers, takeovers, reverse takeovers and other strategic alliances.

10.1 The Concept of Takeover

A takeover takes place when one company acquires control of another company, usually a smaller company than the first company. It may be defined as a transaction or series of transactions whereby a person (individual, a group of individuals or a company) acquires control over the assets of another company, either directly by becoming the owner of those assets or indirectly by obtaining the control of the management of the company (Weinberg and Blank 1999). The company that acquires control of another company is called the 'acquirer' (offeror), whereas the company that is acquired is called the 'target' (offeree). In a case where shares are closely held (i.e., held by a small number of persons) a takeover will generally be effected by agreement with the holders of the majority of the share capital of the company being acquired. Where the shares are held by the public generally, the takeover may be effected:

a. by an agreement between the acquirer and the controllers of the acquired company;
b. by purchases of shares on the stock exchange; or
c. by means of a 'takeover bid'.

A takeover bid is a technique for effecting a takeover or a merger[2]: in the case of a takeover, the bid is frequently against the wishes of the management of the target company; in the case of a merger, the bid is generally by consent of the management of both companies. It may be defined as an offer to acquire shares of a company whose shares are not closely held (dispersed shareholding), addressed to the general body of shareholders with a view to obtaining at least sufficient shares to give the offeror voting control of the company.

A takeover bid may be undertaken in the form of an offer to purchase shares for cash or of a share-for-share exchange or of a combination of those two forms. In other words, the consideration part in a takeover bid may be cash, or shares/debentures of the acquiring company, or the shares of a third company that has nothing to do with the takeover.

10.2 Kinds of Takeover

There are several different types of takeover. The main types are as follows:

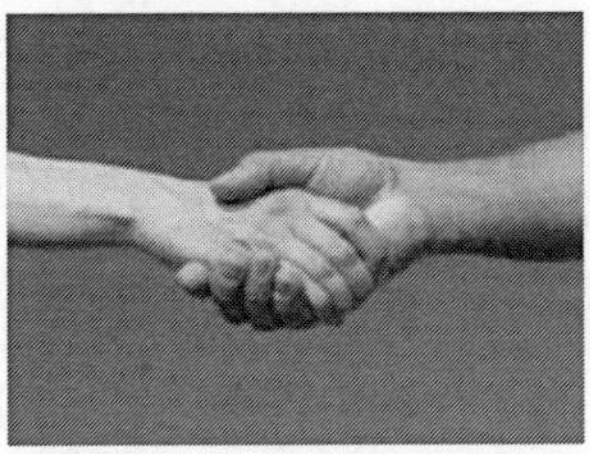

1. **Agreed/Negotiated Takeover/Friendly Takeover:** Where the board of directors of the target agree to the takeover, accept the offer in respect of their own shareholdings (which might range from nil or negligible to controlling stake) and recommend other shareholders to

[2] The distinction between a 'takeover' and a 'merger' is that in a takeover the direct/indirect control over the assets of the acquired company passes to the acquirer, in a merger the shareholding in the combined company will be spread between the shareholders of the two companies. Often the distinction is a question of degree.

accept the offer. The directors of the target may agree to do so right from the start after early negotiations or even after public opposition to the bid (which may or may not have resulted in an improvement in the terms of the proposed offer); or the directors of the target may actually have approached the offeror to suggest the acquisition. In a friendly takeover, the controlling group sells its controlling shares to another group of its own accord. However, as we shall see later, because of regulation 12 read with regulation 3(1)(c) of the SEBI Takeover Regulations, 1997, there is no compulsion to make an open offer in a friendly takeover. A friendly takeover is resorted to promote some common objectives of both the parties.

2. **Defended/Hostile Takeover:** A takeover would be considered 'hostile' if the board rejects the offer, but the bidder continues to pursue it, or if the bidder makes the offer without informing the board beforehand.

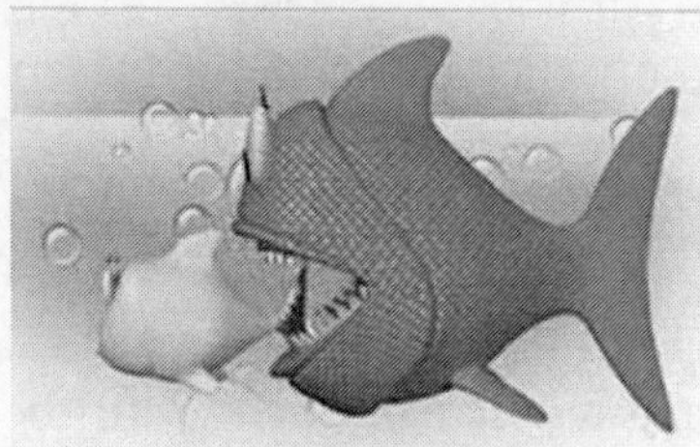

   It is sometimes also called 'unsolicited or unwelcome bid' because it is offered by the acquirer without any solicitation or approach by the target company.

   In a hostile takeover, the directors of the target company decide to oppose the acquiring company's offer, recommend shareholders to reject the offer and take further defensive measures to thwart the bid. The decision to defend may be influenced by a number of factors but more often than not it is with the intention of (a) stopping the takeover (which, in turn, may be prompted by the genuine belief of the directors that it is in interests of the company to remain independent or by a desire of the directors to protect their own personal positions or interests); or (b) persuading the bidder to improve the terms of its offer.

Types of Hostile Takeover

Tender offer: The acquirer makes a public offer at a fixed price above the current market price.

Creeping tender offer: Slowly buying enough shares from the open market to effect a change in management.

Proxy fight: The acquirer tries to persuade enough shareholders, usually a simple majority, to replace the management with a new one which will approve the takeover.

   The best-known recent example is Mittal's bid for Arcelor, where the existing management is opposing the bid. In such a case, the shareholders get to decide whether the incumbent management stays or the new owner gets to run the company. In India, hostile takeovers are very few in comparison to what one sees abroad. It is mainly because promoter shareholding in India is quite high and the likelihood of financial institutions supporting the current management is also high.

3. **Bail Out Takeover:** Takeover of a financially sick company by a financially rich company as per the provisions of the Sick Industrial Companies (Special Provisions) Repeal Act, 2003, to bail out the former from losses.

4. **Reverse Takeover:** This happens when a private (not traded on the stock market) company buys a publicly traded company as a means of acquiring public status without having to list itself.

   A takeover usually takes place when a smaller company folds into a larger one through exchange of shares or cash. However, when the tables are turned and the acquiring company is weaker or smaller than the one being gobbled up, this is termed a reverse takeover. Typically, reverse takeovers take place through a parent company merging into a subsidiary, or a profit-making firm merging into a loss-making one.

In the case of Cairn India and Vedanta, the latter is the larger parent company, making this a simple takeover.

Reverse takeovers are quite commonplace in the United States, but are few and far between in India. One example of a reverse takeover was when ICICI merged with its arm ICICI Bank in 2002. The parent company's balance sheet was more than three times the size of its subsidiary at the time. The rationale for the reverse takeover was to create a universal bank that would lend to both industry and retail borrowers. When reverse takeovers happen, the resulting entity may either take on the name of the smaller firm or the larger one.

The ICICI group retained ICICI Bank as the brand name for the new entity. However, when Godrej Soaps—profitable and with a turnover of ₹4.37 billion—did a reverse takeover with loss-making Gujarat Godrej Innovative Chemicals (turnover of ₹0.6 billion), the resulting firm was named Godrej Soaps.

In the context of business, takeover is of three types:

1. **Horizontal Takeover:** It is the takeover of one company by another company in the same industry. The main purpose behind this kind of takeover is achieving the economies of scale or increasing the market share, For instance, the takeover of Hutch by Vodafone.
2. **Vertical Takeover:** It is takeover by one company with its suppliers or customers. The former is known as backward integration and the latter is known as forward integration. For instance, the takeover of Sona Steerings Ltd by Maruti Udhyog Ltd is backward takeover. The main purpose of this takeover is reduction of costs.
3. **Conglomerate Takeover:** It is the takeover of one company by another company operating in totally different industries. The main purpose of this kind of takeover is diversification.

10.3 Takeover Versus Merger

A merger involves the mutual decision of two companies to combine and become one entity; it can be seen as a decision made by two 'equals'. The combined business, through structural and operational advantages secured by the merger, can cut costs and increase profits, boosting shareholder values for both groups of shareholders. A typical merger, in other words, involves two relatively equal companies, which combine to become one legal entity with the goal of producing a company that is worth more than the sum of its parts. In a merger of two corporations, the shareholders usually have their shares in the old company exchanged for an equal number of shares in the merged entity. For example, back in 1998, American automaker Chrysler Corp merged with German automaker Daimler Benz to form DaimlerChrysler. This has all the makings of a merger of equals as the chairmen in both organizations became joint leaders in the new organization. The merger was thought to be quite beneficial to both companies as it gave Chrysler an opportunity to reach more European markets and Daimler Benz would gain a greater presence in North America.

A takeover, on the other hand, is characterized by the purchase of a smaller company by a much larger one. This combination of 'unequals' can produce the same benefits as a merger, but it does not necessarily have to be a mutual decision. A larger company can initiate a hostile takeover of a smaller firm, which essentially amounts to buying the company in the face of resistance from the smaller company's management. Unlike in a merger, in a takeover, the acquiring firm usually offers a cash price per share to the target firm's shareholders or the acquiring firm's shares to the shareholders of the target firm according to a specified conversion ratio. Either way, the purchasing company essentially finances the purchase of the target company, buying it outright for its shareholders. An example of an acquisition would be how the Walt Disney Corporation bought Pixar Animation Studios in 2006. In this case, this takeover was friendly, as Pixar's shareholders all approved the decision to be acquired.

10.4 Motives Behind Takeovers

There may be different motives/causes behind launching a takeover bid and it is not necessary, as widely believed, that only poorly performing firms are the potential targets of a hostile bid. Bidders seem to pursue companies with strong operating managements as often as they pursue companies that have been clearly mismanaged. In fact, bidders seldom seem to be interested in a firm where a turnaround is unlikely. For instance, truly sick companies—or at least those whose problems do not appear to be easily remedied—become indigestible and survive, immune from takeover, precisely because of their inefficiency. A bidder offers a premium, often very high, to acquire a target and a rational bidder will offer such a premium over the market price (and incur notoriously high transaction costs as well) only if it believes that the future value of the target's stock under different management will exceed the price it offered the target's shareholders within a relatively brief period. There may be a number of objectives behind mounting a hostile bid. It may be a strategic objective like consolidation/expansion of the raider/acquirer. It may be aimed at achieving 'economies of scale'/critical mass/reducing costs in a particular product/service market. It may also be aimed at acquiring substantial market share or creating a sort of a monopoly.

The following are the primary motives/causes of a takeover:

1. **Assets at a Discount:** This refers to a situation where the offeror can acquire the assets/shares of a target at less than the value, which the offeror or its shareholders place upon them: a process commonly referred to by financial journalists as 'acquiring assets at a discount'. The situations in which assets may be available at a discount are the following:

    a. Where the target has not put its assets to their most efficient use;
    b. Where its directors are unaware of the true value of its assets;
    c. When it has an inefficient capital structure;
    d. Where it has followed a policy of limited distribution of dividends;
    e. Where the shares have a poor market rating relative to its real prospects; or
    f. Where due to any other non-economic reasons, the shares of the target are trading at low prices.

2. **Earnings at a Discount:** It is because the offeror can, by taking over the target, acquire the right to its earnings at a lower multiple than the market places on the offeror's own profits, a process that can be described as acquiring 'earnings at a discount'.
3. **Synergy:** Synergy is the most cited motive for takeovers. Its basic assumption is that the value of the combination of the offeror and the offeree is greater than the sum of the individual values of the two corporations. The source of such gains in a takeover is the

potential cost savings realized from the integration of the production and investment infrastructure of the offeror and the offeree, especially economies of scale, enhanced organizational efficiencies and increased market power.

4. **Diversification:** Takeovers are frequently inspired by the offeror's desire to avoid 'putting all its eggs in one basket'. Instead, a corporation may wish to 'hedge its bets'. The coinsurance theory suggests that by acquiring another corporation having imperfectly correlated earnings (irrespective of whether the offeree is inside or outside of the offeror's industry), such an offeror corporation will be able to derive a combined earnings stream that is less volatile than either of the individual companies' earnings stream.
5. **Economics:** In addition to the synergy benefit of economies of scale, two other economic motives that stimulate takeovers are horizontal and vertical integration. In theory, horizontal integration, or the acquisition of competitors, provides the offeror corporation with an increase in market share and market power and, in turn, allows the corporation to set and maintain prices above previously competitive levels. Furthermore, vertical integration, or the acquisition of potential buyer or seller firms, offers a variety of possible benefits to the offeror corporation, including a more dependable source of supplies, and lower inventory costs.
6. **Tax:** A variety of tax savings may result from a takeover. To illustrate, the offeror obtains a valuable savings if the offeree possesses transferable tax losses that the offeror is able to offset against its own income. Another potential tax benefit arises where the market value of the offeree's depreciable assets is greater than their book value.
7. **Inefficient Management Hypothesis:** The inefficient management hypothesis suggests that where a corporation has inefficient management, there exists an incentive for an offeror company to acquire it and install new leaders who are better able to harness the full potential of the offeree's assets. If more effective and efficient management of the offeree's assets is ultimately achieved, then the resulting gains accrue directly to the offeror.
8. **Undervaluation Theory:** The undervaluation theory is based on the assumption that the offeree firm is undervalued by the market, and that the offeror is in possession of such special or inside information that will not become available to the market generally, until after the takeover. Thus, the offeror is motivated to acquire the offeree with the expectation of reaping the gain that will result once the market valuation adjusts upward.
9. **Hubris Hypothesis:** The hubris hypothesis of takeovers, proposed by Richard Roll, implies that managers of an offeror corporation may pay a premium to acquire an offeree that the market has already correctly valued for their own personal motives rather than for pure economic gains. Roll suggests that the pride of the offeror's managers may cause them to place greater significance on their own valuation of the offeree than on that of the market's valuation.

10.5 Steps in a Takeover

There are four basic and not necessarily sequential steps, in acquiring a target firm. The first is the development of a rationale and a strategy for doing takeovers, and the understanding of what the strategy requires in terms of resources. The second is the choice of a target for the takeover and the valuation of the target firm, with premiums for the value of control and any synergy. The third is the determination of how much to pay on the takeover, how best to raise funds to do it and whether to use stock or cash. This decision has significant implications for the choice of accounting treatment for the takeover. The final step in the takeover, and perhaps the most challenging one, is to make the takeover work after the deal is complete.

10.5.1 Developing a Takeover Strategy

Not all firms that make takeovers have takeover strategies, and not all firms that have takeover strategies stick with them. In this section, we consider a number of different motives for takeovers and suggest that a coherent takeover strategy has to be based on one or another of these motives. These motives were studied in detail in the last chapter, as the motives behind mergers and takeovers are the same.

Firms that are undervalued by financial markets can be targeted for takeover by those who recognize this mis-pricing. The acquirer can then gain the difference between the value and the purchase price as surplus. For this strategy to work, however, three basic components need to come together.

1. *A capacity to find firms that trade at less than their true value*: This capacity would require either access to better information than is available to other investors in the market, or better analytical tools than those used by other market participants.
2. *Access to the funds that will be needed to complete the takeover*: Knowing a firm is undervalued does not necessarily imply having capital easily available to carry out the takeover. Access to capital depends upon the size of the acquirer—large firms will have more access to capital markets and internal funds than smaller firms or individuals—and upon the acquirer's track record—a history of success at identifying and acquiring undervalued firms will make subsequent takeovers easier.
3. *Skill in execution*: If the acquirer, in the process of the takeover drives the stock price up to and beyond the estimated value, there will be no value gain from the takeover. To illustrate, assume that the estimated value for a firm is $100 million and that the current market price is $75 million. In acquiring this firm, the acquirer will have to pay a premium. If that premium exceeds 33% of the market price, the price exceeds the estimated value, and the takeover will not create any value for the acquirer.

While the strategy of buying undervalued firms has a great deal of intuitive appeal, it is daunting, especially when acquiring publicly traded firms in reasonably efficient markets, where the premiums paid on market prices can very quickly eliminate the valuation surplus. The odds are better in less efficient markets or when acquiring private businesses.

Acquire poorly managed firms and change management. Some firms are not managed optimally and others often believe they can run them better than the current managers. Acquiring poorly managed firms and removing incumbent management, or at least changing existing management policy or practices, should make these firms more valuable, allowing the acquirer to claim the increase in value. This value increase is often termed the 'value of control'.

Prerequisites for Success

While this corporate control story can be used to justify large premiums over the market price, the potential for its success rests on the following:

a. The poor performance of the firm being acquired should be attributable to the incumbent management of the firm, rather than to market or industry factors that are not under management control.

b. The takeover has to be followed by a change in management practices, and the change has to increase value. As noted in the last chapter, actions that enhance value increase cash flows from existing assets, increase expected growth rates, increase the length of the growth period, or reduce the cost of capital.
c. The market price of the takeover should reflect the status quo, that is, the current management of the firm and their poor business practices. If the market price already has the control premium built into it, there is little potential for the acquirer to earn the premium. In the last two decades, corporate control has been increasingly cited as a reason for hostile takeovers.

10.5.2 Choosing a Target Firm and Valuing Control/Synergy

Once a firm has a takeover motive, there are two key questions that need to be answered. The first relates to how to best identify a potential target firm for a takeover, given the motives. The second is the more concrete question of how to value a target firm.

Choosing a Target Firm

Once a firm has identified the reason for its takeover programme, it has to find the appropriate target firm.

a. If the motive for takeovers is undervaluation, the target firm must be undervalued. How such a firm will be identified depends upon the valuation approach and model used. With relative valuation, an undervalued stock is one that trades at a multiple (of earnings, book value or sales) well below that of the rest of the industry, after controlling for significant differences on fundamentals. Thus, a bank with a price to book value ratio of 1.2 would be an undervalued bank, if other banks have similar fundamentals (ROE, growth and risk) but trade at much higher price to book value ratios. In DCF valuation approaches, an undervalued stock is one that trades at a price well below the estimated DCF value.
b. If the motive for takeovers is diversification, the most likely target firms will be in businesses that are unrelated to and uncorrelated with the business of the acquiring firm. Thus, a cyclical firm should try to acquire countercyclical or, at least, non-cyclical firms to get the fullest benefit from diversification.
c. If the motive for takeovers is operating synergy, the typical target firm will vary depending upon the source of the synergy. For economies of scale, the target firm should be in the same business as the acquiring firm. Thus, the takeover of Security Pacific by Bank of America was motivated by potential cost savings from economies of scale. For functional synergy, the target firm should be strongest in those functional areas where the acquiring firm is weak. For financial synergy, the target firm will be chosen to reflect the likely source of the synergy—a risky firm with limited or no standalone capacity for borrowing, if the motive is increased debt capacity, or a firm with significant net operating losses carried forward, if the motive is tax benefits.
d. If the motive for the merger is control, the target firm will be a poorly managed firm in an industry where there is potential for excess returns. In addition, its stock holdings will be widely dispersed (making it easier to carry out the hostile takeover) and the current market price will be based on the presumption that incumbent management will continue to run the firm.
e. If the motive is managerial self-interest, the choice of a target firm will reflect managerial interests rather than economic reasons.

10.5.3 Valuing the Target Firm

The valuation of a takeover is not fundamentally different from the valuation of any firm, although the existence of control and synergy premiums introduces some complexity into the valuation process. Given the inter-relationship between synergy and control, the safest way to value a target firm is in steps, starting with a status quo valuation of the firm, and following up with a value for control and a value for synergy.

Status Quo Valuation

We start our valuation of the target firm by estimating the firm value with existing investing, financing and dividend policies. This valuation, which we term the 'status quo valuation', provides a base from which we can estimate control and synergy premiums. In particular, the value of the firm is a function of its cash flows from existing assets, the expected growth in these cash flows during a high growth period, the length of the high growth period and the firm's cost of capital.

The Value of Corporate Control

Many hostile takeovers are justified on the basis of the existence of a market for corporate control. Investors and firms are willing to pay large premiums over the market price to control the management of firms, especially those that they perceive to be poorly run. This section explores the determinants of the value of corporate control and attempts to value it in the context of a takeover.

Determinants of the Value of Corporate Control

The value of wresting control of a firm from incumbent management is inversely proportional to the perceived quality of that management and its capacity to maximize firm value. In general, the value of control will be much greater for a poorly managed firm that operates at below optimum capacity than for a well-managed firm. The value of controlling a firm comes from changes made to existing management policy that can increase the firm value. Assets can be acquired or liquidated, the financing mix can be changed and the dividend policy re-evaluated, and the firm can be restructured to maximize value. If we can identify the changes that we would make to the target firm, we can value control. The value of control can then be written as:

Value of control = [Value of firm, optimally managed – Value of firm with current management]

The value of control is negligible for firms that are operating at or close to their optimal value, since a restructuring will yield little additional value. It can be substantial for firms operating at well below optimal, since a restructuring can lead to a significant increase in value.

Valuing Operating Synergy

There is a potential for operating synergy, in one form or the other, in many takeovers. Some disagreement exists, however, over whether synergy can be valued and, if so, what that value should be. One school of thought argues that synergy is too nebulous to be valued and that any systematic attempt to do so requires so many assumptions that it is pointless. If this is true, a firm should not be willing to pay large premiums for synergy if it cannot attach a value to it.

While valuing synergy requires us to make assumptions about future cash flows and growth, the lack of precision in the process does not mean we cannot obtain an unbiased estimate of value. Thus, we maintain that synergy can be valued by answering two fundamental questions.

1. *What form is the synergy expected to take?* Will it reduce costs as a percentage of sales and increase profit margins (e.g., when there are economies of scale)? Will it increase future growth (e.g., when there is increased market power) or the length of the growth period? Synergy, to have an effect on value, has to influence one of the four inputs into the valuation process—cash flows from existing assets, higher expected growth rates (market power, higher growth potential), a longer growth period (from increased competitive advantages), or a lower cost of capital (higher debt capacity).
2. *When will the synergy start affecting cash flows?* Synergies can show up instantaneously, but they are more likely to show up over time. Since the value of synergy is the present value of the cash flows created by it, the longer it takes for it to show up, the lesser its value.

Once we answer these questions, we can estimate the value of synergy using an extension of DCF techniques. First, we value the firms involved in the merger independently, by discounting expected cash flows to each firm at the WACC for that firm. Second, we estimate the value of the combined firm, with no synergy, by adding the values obtained for each firm in the first step. Third, we build in the effects of synergy into expected growth rates and cash flows and we value the combined firm with synergy. The difference between the value of the combined firm with synergy and the value of the combined firm without synergy provides a value for synergy.

Valuing Financial Synergy

Synergy can also be created from purely financial factors. We will consider three legitimate sources of financial synergy—a greater 'tax benefit' from accumulated losses or tax deductions, an increase in debt capacity and therefore firm value and better use for 'excess' cash or cash slack. We will begin the discussion, however, with diversification, which though a widely used rationale for mergers is not a source of increased value by itself.

Structuring the Takeover

Once the target firm has been identified and valued, the takeover moves forward into the structuring phase. There are three interrelated steps in this phase. The first is the decision on how much to pay for the target firm, synergy and control built into the valuation. The second is the determination of how to pay for the deal, that is, whether to use stock, cash or some combination of the two, and whether to borrow any of the funds needed. The final step is the choice of the accounting treatment of the deal because it can affect both taxes paid by stockholders in the target firm and how the purchase is accounted for in the acquiring firm's income statement and balance sheets.

Deciding on a Takeover Price

The value determined in consideration of synergy and control represents a ceiling on the price that the acquirer can pay on the takeover rather than a floor. If the acquirer pays the full value, there is no surplus value to claim for the acquirer's stockholders and the target firm's stockholders get the entire value of the synergy and control premiums. This division of value is unfair, if the acquiring firm plays an indispensable role in creating the synergy and control premiums.

Consequently, the acquiring firm should try to keep as much of the premium as it can for its stockholders. Several factors, however, will act as constraints. They include:

1. *The market price of the target firm, if it is publicly traded, prior to the takeover*: Since takeovers have to based on the current market price, the greater the current market value of equity, the lower is the potential for gain to the acquiring firm's stockholders. For instance, if the market price of a poorly managed firm already reflects a high probability that the management of the firm will be changed, there is likely to be little or no value gained from control.
2. *The relative scarcity of the specialized resources that the target and the acquiring firms bring to the merger:* Since the bidding firm and the target firm are both contributors to the creation of synergy, the sharing of the benefits of synergy among the two parties will depend in large part on whether the bidding firm's contribution to the creation of the synergy is unique or easily replaced. If it can be easily replaced, the bulk of the synergy benefits will accrue to the target firm. If it is unique, the benefits will be shared much more equitably. Thus, when a firm with cash slack acquires a firm with many high-return projects, value is created. If there are a large number of firms with cash slack and relatively few firms with high-return projects, the bulk of the value of the synergy will accrue to the latter.
3. *The presence of other bidders for the target firm:* When there is more than one bidder for a firm, the odds are likely to favour the target firm's stockholders. Bradley et al. (1988) examined an extensive sample of 236 tender offers made between 1963 and 1984 and concluded that the benefits of synergy accrue primarily to the target firms when multiple bidders are involved in the takeover. They estimated the market-adjusted stock returns around the announcement of the takeover for the successful bidder to be 2% in single bidder takeovers and –1.33% in contested takeovers.

Payment for the Target Firm

Once a firm has decided to pay a given price for a target firm, it has to follow up by deciding how it is going to pay for this takeover. In particular, a decision has to be made about the following aspects of the deal.

1. *Debt versus equity*: A firm can raise the funds for a takeover from either debt or equity. The mix will generally depend upon both the excess debt capacities of the acquiring and the target firm. Thus, the takeover of a target firm that is significantly under levered may be carried out with a larger proportion of debt than the takeover of one that is already at its optimal debt ratio. This, of course, is reflected in the value of the firm through the cost of capital. It is also possible that the acquiring firm has excess debt capacity and that it uses its ability to borrow money to carry out the takeover. Although the mechanics of raising the money may look the same in this case, it is important that the value of the target firm does not reflect this additional debt. The additional debt has nothing to do with the target firm, and building it into the value will only result in the acquiring firm paying a premium for a value enhancement that rightfully belongs to its own stockholders.
2. *Cash versus stock*: There are three ways in which a firm can use equity in a transaction. The first is to use cash balances that have been built up over time to finance the takeover. The second is to issue stock to the public, raise cash and use the cash to pay for the takeover. The third is to offer stock as payment for the target firm, where the

payment is structured in terms of a stock swap—shares in the acquiring firm in exchange for shares in the target firm. The question of which of these approaches is best utilized by a firm cannot be answered without looking at the following factors.

1. *The availability of cash on hand*: Clearly, the option of using cash on hand is available only to those firms that have accumulated substantial amounts of cash.
2. *The perceived value of the stock*: When stock is issued to the public to raise new funds or when it is offered as payment on takeovers, the acquiring firm's managers are making a judgment about what the perceived value of the stock is. In other words, managers who believe that their stock is trading at a price significantly below value should not use stock as currency on takeovers, since what they gain on the takeovers can be more than what they lost in the stock issue. On the other hand, firms that believe their stocks are overvalued are much more likely to use stock as currency in transactions. The stockholders in the target firm are also aware of this and may demand a larger premium when the payment is made entirely in the form of the acquiring firm's stock.
3. *Tax factors:* When a takeover is a stock swap, the stockholders in the target firm may be able to defer capital gains taxes on the exchanged shares. Since this benefit can be significant in a takeover, the potential tax gains from a stock swap may be large enough to offset any perceived disadvantages.

The final aspect of a stock swap is the setting of the terms of the stock swap, that is, the number of shares of the acquired firm that will be offered per share of the acquiring firm. While this amount is generally based upon the market price at the time of the takeover, the ratio that results may be skewed by the relative mispricing of the two firms' securities, with the more overpriced firm gaining at the expense of the more under-priced (or at least, less overpriced) firm. A fairer ratio would be based upon the relative values of the two firms' shares.

10.6 Defences to Hostile Takeovers

In a takeover battle if the board/management chooses to reject a bid, it may have to take effective defensive measures in order to stall the raider from carrying out the takeover operation. These defence mechanisms may be put in place after the bid has been made or may have been there prior to the bid having been made.[3] The most obvious case for defence is that

[3] Apart from purely defensive strategies that may have been built into the company's by-laws, there are certain other barriers to takeover, which may not exactly be in the league of defences to hostile takeovers. Nonetheless, they do pose considerable difficulties to the potential acquirer. These barriers may be categorized into structural and technical barriers. The structural barriers basically result from underlying structure of the economy, including such diverse factors as the distribution of wealth, market size, role of financial institutions, the political and legal system and sociocultural environment found in different countries. The tendency of companies to remain private constitutes by far the greatest structural barrier to a hostile bid. Moreover, even in the case of listed companies, if the substantial shareholding is concentrated in a few hands/families and dispersed among public, mounting a hostile bid may prove difficult. State ownership often presents an additional source of structural barriers. Financial institutions commanding substantial voting rights either through direct equity holding or through proxies can often thwart a hostile bid if they decide to support the incumbent management.

On the other hand, technical barriers are the brainchild of the companies themselves. Through internal regulations such as restricting voting rights, issuing shares with weighted voting rights, giving more powers to incumbent management and so on, companies seek to limit the ability of a potential predator to mount a successful hostile bid for a company, or to increase the cost of making such a bid.

by rejecting an initial bid, the board may be seeking to receive a higher offer or inviting a competitive bidder. By mounting a vigorous defence, the board may be able to fetch a better price for surrendering its stake in the target. Defence may also be raised on the ground that the company's net worth is much more than the bidder had calculated. This may be the case when the management of the target company has some privileged and commercially sensitive information, which, if released, would increase the market value of the firm. By mounting such a defence, management may be able to increase the market value of the target firm to such an extent that the bid fails, or, even if the bid succeeds, secure a higher price for their shareholders. Another reason for mounting a defence may be the management's genuine belief that the company is better off by remaining an independent entity.

Finally, the acceptability or rejection of a takeover bid and the extent of its regulation also depends upon the social and political philosophy of a country. For example, in the UK the accountability of management to the shareholders is paramount. The companies are expected to pay out a large proportion of their earnings as dividend payments in order to avert the threat of a hostile bid and they frequently cite the takeover threat as a serious impediment to investing, particularly, in R&D-related projects.

On the other hand, companies in other European Union countries are not so shareholder centric. Shareholders are clearly one interest group, but many others exist: workers, the existing management, suppliers, providers of finance other than shareholders (like banks and financial institutions) and other related companies. Such groups are often referred to as stakeholders in a company—those who are involved in the day-to-day operations and who in most EU countries have a right to play a part in the process of running and controlling the company.

Of course, in a country like India, where an active market for corporate control is still to develop, the question of corporate accountability either to shareholders or to other stakeholders has hardly received any significance worth mentioning. In the pre-liberalization era, India's giant industrial houses, most of them family controlled, enjoyed the government-conferred monopoly status upon them and they hardly bothered to increase shareholder value. Equally guilty have been Indian banks and financial institutions, which held substantial stake in large public companies but they largely remained passive onlookers and never questioned management's/board's decision even if the decision went against their own interests as a shareholder in the company. Post-liberalization era, due to increasing competition from foreign and some new aggressive domestic players, has brought about some welcome changes in the area of corporate accountability. A healthy return to shareholders is increasingly being recognized as an important benchmark of corporate success. Therefore, in India it is highly desirable that a healthy market for corporate control is allowed to develop.

The anti-takeover defences can be broadly categorized into two types as follows:

a. Pre-offer defences like staggered board, Poison pills, super-majority clause, golden parachute, dual class recapitalization and
b. Post-offer defences like Pac-Man defence, Greenmail, asset restructuring and litigation liability restructuring.

Some of the significant takeover defences are discussed here.

Staggered Board

This defence involves an amendment of the by-laws of the company to create a staggered board of directors. A staggered board is a board whose members are elected in different years or, in other words, only part of the board comes up for election each year. Implementation of a staggered board may cause an acquirer to have to wait for several years or at least until the next annual general meeting before it controls the board of directors. Because the acquirer would not control the board initially, the acquirer would not have the power to change management or the corporation's business plan. As with the other pre-tender offer defences, courts will allow amendment of the charter to create a staggered board of directors provided the amendment is allowed under the governing corporation law and the amendment was made for a valid business reason.

Buyback of Shares

- Open market repurchases
- Self-tenders

Critics of the buyback strategies argue that the discriminatory effects on target shareholders will defeat value-increasing bids. Open market purchases tend to distort shareholder preference and defeat value-increasing bids. In a model given by Bradley and Rozenweig (1986) the result of open market purchases is that it amounts to a special dividend payout to selling shareholders that distorts shareholder choice. However self-tenders can be defended on the ground that buyback creates an auction for the companies' resources among competing management teams. Proponents argue that they tend to defeat value-decreasing offers and not value increasing ones. The critics, however, argue that if the target finances the self-tender through the sale of special synergy assets, the bidder may simply withdraw its bid. Self-tender is not like an auction process. Target management is spending the shareholders' money and not its own funds.

Shark Repellent

A shark repellent is any method of driving sharks away from an area, object, person or animal. Also known as 'porcupine provision', this is a slang term for any one of a number of measures taken by a company to defend an unwanted or hostile takeover attempt. In many cases, a company will make special amendments to its charter or by-laws that become active only when a takeover attempt is announced or presented to shareholders with the goal of making the takeover less attractive or profitable to the acquisitive firm.

Most companies want to decide their own fates in the marketplace, so when the sharks attack, shark repellent can send the predator off to look for a less feisty target. While the concept is a noble one, many shark repellent measures are not in the best interests of shareholders, as the actions may damage the company's financial position and interfere with the management's ability to focus on critical business objectives.

Some examples of shark repellents are golden parachutes, poison pills, scorched earth policies and safe harbour strategies

For example:

a. Fair price provision requiring a bidder to pay the same price to all shareholders. This raises the stakes and discourages tender offers designed to attract only those shareholders most eager to replace management.
b. Golden parachute contract with top executives that makes it prohibitively expensive to get rid of existing management.
c. Defensive merger, in which a target company combines with another organization that would create antitrust or other regulatory problems if the original, unwanted takeover proposal was consummated.

d. Staggered board of directors, a way to make it more difficult for a corporate raider to install a majority of directors sympathetic to his or her views.
e. Supermajority provision, which might increase from a simple majority to two-thirds or three-fourths the shareholder vote required to ratify a takeover by an outsider.

Golden Parachute

This defence requires management to arrange employment contracts between the management and key employees to increase their post-employment compensation in the event of a hostile takeover. When golden parachutes are created for management and key employees, a corporation becomes less attractive to the acquirer because generous payments to departing management and employees could financially deplete the corporation.

Golden parachutes have been justified on three grounds. First, they may enable corporations that are prime takeover targets to hire and retain high-quality executives who would otherwise be reluctant to work for them. Second, since the parachutes add to the cost of acquiring a corporation, they may discourage takeover bids. Finally, if a takeover bid does occur, executives with a golden parachute are more likely to respond in a manner that will benefit the shareholders. Without a golden parachute, executives might resist a takeover that would be in the interests of the shareholders, in order to save their own job.

As golden parachutes have grown increasingly lucrative, they have come under criticism from shareholders who argue that they are a waste of corporate assets. These shareholders point out those managers already have a fiduciary duty to act in the best interests of their shareholders and should not require golden parachutes as an incentive. Especially suspect are large parachutes that are awarded once a takeover bid has been announced. Critics charge that these last-minute parachutes are little more than going-away presents for the executives and may encourage them to work for the takeover at the expense of the shareholders.

Bankmail

Bankmail is an agreement between a bank and a firm pondering a takeover, or a firm which is about to experience a hostile takeover. Under the terms of the agreement, the bank refuses to provide financing to rival firms. This practice is used as leverage in takeover negotiations, and as an anti-hostile takeover tactic. While bankmail does not eliminate the competition or the risk of a takeover, it will create some breathing room and leverage.

When a firm is considering a takeover with another firm, financing is usually a major issue. If the firm feels threatened by an opponent, it may enter into a bankmail agreement, thus forcing the opponent to seek financing elsewhere or abandon the deal. While the opponent considers its options, the original firm may be able to quickly move in and finish the deal.

In the instance of a hostile takeover, bankmail can prevent a hostile takeover by restricting the funds available to the rival firm. In addition, it allows the vulnerable firm to pursue other avenues, hopefully resolving the situation to satisfaction. This time may give the firm a chance to come up with a working strategy to prevent the takeover and, more importantly, it allows the target firm to attempt to muster some resources of its own.

Crown Jewels

These are precious assets of the target, often termed as crown jewels, which attract the raider to bid for the company's control. On facing a hostile bid, the company sells these assets at its own initiative, leaving the rest of the company intact and hence removes the incentive for which the bid was offered. Instead of selling the assets, the company may also lease them or mortgage them so that the attraction of free assets to the predator is suppressed. By selling these jewels, the company removes the inducement that may have caused the bid.

An example from Japan: In 2005, Japan's Livedoor warned the Nippon Broadcasting System Inc against the adoption of a 'crown jewel' takeover defence. Livedoor called upon the target company to retain the key assets of the radio broadcast station while it battled Fuji Television for takeover bids; the assets included major stakes in Fuji TV, Japan's top television network, and music label Pony Canyon.

Flip-in

It is a provision in the target company's corporate charter or bylaws, which gives current shareholders of a targeted company, other than the hostile acquirer, rights to purchase additional stocks in the targeted company at a discount rate. These rights to purchase occur only (a) before a potential takeover and (b) when the acquirer surpasses the 'kick-in' or threshold point of obtaining outstanding shares (usually 20%–50%). No potential acquirer or other shareholder will risk triggering a poison pill by accumulating more than the threshold level of shares because of the threat of massive discriminatory dilution. The threshold level therefore effectively sets a ceiling on the amount of stock that any shareholder can accumulate before launching a proxy contest. In 2004, Peoplesoft was employing the flip-in model against Oracle Corporation's multibillion hostile takeover bid. Andrew Bartels, a research analyst for Forrester Research, said 'The poison pill is designed to make it more difficult for Oracle to take over the organization. The customer assurance program is designed to compensate customers should there be a takeover. It's a financial liability for Oracle'. Oracle attempted to pursue the court's dissolution of this programme, and in December of 2004 succeeded with a final bid of approximately $10.3 billion.

Greenmail

A targeted share repurchase, or greenmail, is the buyback of the shares owned by a particular shareholder of the target who has made or threatened a takeover bid. The greenmail payment is typically at a premium over the prevailing market price. A large block of shares is held by an unfriendly company, which forces the target company to repurchase the stock at a substantial premium to prevent the takeover. The critique of this theory is that the management, which has mismanaged the target's assets, pays greenmail in order to perpetuate its ability to exploit the targets. According to this view, greenmail should be prohibited because it decreases shareholders' wealth and discriminates unfairly.

This term originated in 1983, during the height of the hostile takeover boom in the United States. In the 1980s, numerous companies swallowed each other up, taking advantage of increased liquidity to hold up a variety of new assets. Some companies were naturally displeased with this state of affairs, and they attempted to fight such takeovers. Green mailers saw a potential for making substantial amounts of money and seized upon it.

A greenmail attempt requires a lot of accessible funds, because the green mailer must be able to purchase enough shares in a company to legitimately threaten a takeover. Once the shares are acquired, the green mailer can alert the company to the situation, if the company has not already realized, and the company is invited to make an offer to buy the shares back. The company will typically pay a premium above the actual value of the stock to regain control of the shares, allowing the green mailer to profit, sometimes substantially.

When a company pays greenmail, it may also attempt to negotiate an agreement with the green mailer, usually to the effect that the attempt will not be repeated. Many companies also try to keep greenmail attempts a secret, to discourage any further attempts, and because capitulating to what is really just blackmail can be a bad public relations move. However, greenmailers may go public in the hopes of forcing a high settlement, an attempt that sometimes backfires.

This practice is perfectly legal: there is nothing to stop someone from buying a controlling share in a company, and nothing to stop a company from buying that share back. However, some people believe that it is a rather slimy business practice, and these individuals would prefer to see regulations that could prevent greenmail. At the very least, greenmail attempts could potentially be prosecuted by savvy attorneys if the greenmailer slipped up and crossed the line into blackmail, because blackmail is most certainly illegal.

Jonestown Defence/Suicide Pill

In general sense, a suicide pill is a pill, capsule, ampoule or tablet containing a fatally poisonous substance that a person ingests deliberately in order to quickly cause his/her own death. This is done in order to avoid an imminent and far more unpleasant death (such as through torture).

In a similar manner, the Jonestown defence/suicide pill is an extreme corporation defence against hostile takeovers. In this strategy, the target firm engages in tactics that might threaten the firm's existence to thwart an imposing acquirer's bids.

Killer Bees (Business)

Killer bees are firms or individuals that are employed by a target company to fend off a takeover bid; these include investment bankers (primary), accountants, attorneys, tax specialists and so on. They aid by utilizing various anti-takeover strategies, thereby making the target company economically unattractive and acquisition more costly.

Leveraged Recapitalization

Under this strategy, a company incurs significant additional debt to repurchase stocks through a buyback programme or distributes a large dividend among the current shareholders. This will cause the share price to increase significantly, making the company a less attractive takeover target. Following a leveraged recapitalization, a raider would pay more, thus minimizing any gains and acting as a deterrent. This strategy, a popular form of poison pill, serves two purposes: (a) increase debt to make the acquisition price more costly and (b) to maintain shareholder interest in takeover attempts.

Lobster Trap (Finance)

A lobster trap is an anti-takeover strategy used by target firms. In a lobster trap, the target firm issues a charter that prevents individuals with more than 10% ownership of convertible securities (includes convertible bonds, convertible preferred stock and warrants) from transferring these securities to voting stock.

Poison Pill

A defensive tactic, which was originated and mainly employed in the United States, a poison pill is a shareholder rights plan that encourages a would-be acquiring company to talk to target's directors before seeking to acquire more than a certain percentage of the target's stock, because not doing so will result in substantial economic harm to the acquirer as the rights held by it will become void, and all other shareholders will be able to buy shares of the target at half price (Wingerson and Dorn 1992). A rights plan can be adopted without shareholder approval and the directors authorize the rights to be distributed as a dividend to the target's shareholders. These rights can be redeemed by the board of directors or exercised. If they are exercised, the resultant preferred stock might be convertible into ordinary shares at an extremely attractive price—essentially raising the cost of the bid. Such pills are referred to as 'flip-overs'. Alternatively, the rights might be purchased by the issuing firm at a large premium over the issue price, with the large shareholder excluded from the repurchase. These are known as 'flip-ins'.

Nancy Reagan Defence

The Nancy Reagan Defence is a tactic used to counter a takeover bidder who has made a formal bid to shareholders to buy their shares. When the board of directors of the target company meet to consider the bid, they 'just say no'.

Legal/Political Defences

Here the target firms seek the intervention of the regulatory bodies or indulge in political lobbying to repel the hostile bidder. This might be in the form of an appeal to the competition regulatory bodies that the resultant entity would violate the anti-trust norms. However, these strategies rarely succeed, often resulting in delays and increase in the costs of the bid to both the bidder and the target. However, in countries like India, political/legal interventions can cause considerable delays, which can either frustrate the initial bidder leading it to withdraw or costs may escalate so much due to delay that the bidder may be forced to withdraw on prudent economic considerations.

Joint Holding/Joint Voting Agreement

Two or more major shareholders may enter into an agreement for block voting or block sale of shares rather than separate voting. This agreement is entered into with the cooperation and blessings of target company's management who likes to have a control.

Interlocking Shareholdings or Cross Shareholdings

Two or more group companies acquire shares of each other in large quantity or one company may distribute shares to the shareholders of its group company to avoid threats of takeover bids. If the interlocking of shareholdings is accompanied by a joint voting agreement, then the joint system of defence is termed as 'Pyramiding', which is the safest device or defence.

Pac-Man Defence

Most people who grew up with video games remember the classic Pac-Man game, in which the player controls Pac-Man trying to consume various rewards while evading the ghosts in pursuit. Pac-Man is utterly defenceless and must run away from the ghosts until he consumes an 'energizer' which allows Pac-Man to turn around and chase his pursuers for a period of time.

The basic idea of the Pac-Man defence is that the company being acquired attempts to purchase the would-be buyer. The Pac-Man defence follows the video game's concept because the once-vulnerable company (i.e., Pac-Man) stops trying to avoid its enemy (i.e., acquirer) and strikes back with a hostile takeover of its own. This tactic has been employed by companies that do not wish to be purchased and so try to scare off buyers. The takeover target uses whatever resources available (even taking from its war chest) to defeat the acquisition, most often by purchasing a large amount of shares in the other company. The most quoted example in U.S. corporate history is the attempted hostile takeover of Martin Marietta by Bendix Corporation in 1982. Bendix purchased a controlling stake in Martin Marietta, and essentially owned the company. However, in the brief period between Bendix owning and controlling the company, Martin Marietta's management sold off all non-essential assets to finance its own hostile takeover against Bendix. The Pac-Man defence was supported by United Technologies and Bendix was placed in the difficult position of fending off the counter-takeover. When the dust settled, Bendix was acquired, but not by Martin Marietta; instead, by the Allied Corporation.

Pension Parachute

It is a device to prevent surplus pension assets from being obtained by an acquirer in a hostile takeover. A pension parachute prevents the raiding firm of a hostile takeover from utilizing the pension assets to finance the acquisition. When the target firm is threatened by an acquirer, the pension plan assets are only available to benefit the pension plan participants.

Safe Harbor

It is a tactic in which the target of an unfriendly takeover makes itself less attractive by taking a specific action. Under implementation of this provision, a target company will acquire a troublesome firm in order to raise the acquisition price and make acquisition by other parties economically unattractive.

Scorched Earth

A scorched earth policy is a military tactic that involves destroying anything that might be useful to the enemy while advancing through or withdrawing from an area. In business, the scorched-earth defence is a form of risk arbitrage and anti-takeover strategy. When a target firm implements this provision, it will make an effort to make it unattractive to the hostile bidder. For example, a company may agree to liquidate or destroy all valuable assets, also called 'crown jewels', or schedule debt repayment to be due immediately following a hostile takeover.

Targeted Repurchase

A targeted repurchase is a technique used to spoil a hostile takeover in which the target firm purchases back its own stock from an unfriendly bidder, usually at a price well above market value. For an example, on 20 August 2002, KBF Pollution Management, Inc, a recycling services provider, reported that it would repurchase stock from its current shareholders. KFB planned to fund its share repurchase programme through initiation of service for many new generators, some of which are Fortune 500 companies, and expectations of third-quarter revenues exceeding second-quarter revenues by 30%. Under KBF's share repurchase plan, KBF stock can be purchased by block purchase from time to time as long as it is in compliance with SEC's rule 10b-18, subject to market conditions, meets legal requirements, and other factors. The repurchased shares are held in KBF's treasury where they are either inactive or applied to corporate use.

White Knight (Business)

The white knight strategy involves the target firm finding a more suitable acquirer (the 'white knight') and prompting it to compete with the initial hostile acquire to takeover the firm. The basic premise of this strategy is that if being taken over is nearly certain; the target firm ought to attempt to be taken over by the firm that is deemed most acceptable to its management.

In business, a white knight may be a corporation, a private company or a person that intends to help another firm. There are many types of white knights. Alternatively, a grey knight is an acquiring company that enters a bid for a hostile takeover in addition to the target firm and first bidder, perceived as more favourable than the black knight (unfriendly bidder), but less favourable than the white knight (friendly bidder).

The first type refers to the friendly acquirer of a target firm in a hostile takeover attempt by another firm. The intention of the acquisition is to circumvent the takeover of the object of interest by a third, unfriendly entity, which is perceived to be less favourable. The knight might defeat the undesirable entity by offering a higher and more enticing bid, or strike a favourable deal with the management of the object of acquisition.

In short, if company T (target) is going to be acquired by company H (hostile firm), but company A (acquirer) can acquire ownership of company T, then company A would be acting as the white knight. The second type refers to the acquirer of a struggling firm that may not necessarily be under threat by a hostile firm. The financial standing of the struggling firm could prevent any other entity being interested in an acquisition. The firm may already have huge debts to pay to its creditors, or worse, may already be bankrupt. In such a case, the knight, under huge risk, acquires the firm that is in crisis. After acquisition, the knight then rebuilds the firm, or integrates it into itself.

Whitemail

Whitemail, coined as an opposite to blackmail, is an anti-takeover arrangement in which the target company will sell significantly discounted stock to a friendly third party. In return, the target company helps thwart takeover attempts, by (a) raising the acquisition price of the raider, (b) diluting the hostile bidder's number of shares, and (c) increasing the aggregate stock holdings of the company.

The majority of American companies utilize minimum one anti-takeover defence. The two most common anti-takeover defences are the poison pill and the staggered board. The staggered board is implemented by approximately 60% of the big corporations for forbidding a bidder from altering the total board according to its choice. The poison pill is utilized by approximately 50% of the important institutions and this causes a firm to become a target costly to a prohibitive degree.

In India, the companies are able to access lesser anti-takeover defences in comparison to the American companies. For the purpose of preventing a takeover effort, the Indian companies currently adopt the following anti-takeover defences:

- Effecting creeping enhancement
- Making preferential allotment
- Selling the crown jewels
- Amalgamating group companies
- Searching for a white knight

10.7 Legal Regime for Takeover Code in India

The 20th century began with the process of transformation of the entire business scenario. The economy of India, which was hitherto controlled and regulated by the government, was set free to seize new opportunities available in the world. With the announcement of the policy of globalization, the doors of the Indian economy were opened for the overseas investors. However, to compete at the world platform, the scale of business was needed to be increased. In this changed scenario, mergers and acquisitions were the best option available for the corporates considering the time factor involved in capturing the opportunities made available by the globalization.

This new weapon in the armoury of corporates though proved to be beneficial, but soon the predators with huge disposable wealth started exploiting this opportunity to the prejudice of retail investor. This created a need for some regulation to protect the interest of investors so that the process of takeover and mergers is used to develop the securities market and not to sabotage it. In the year 1992, with the enactment of the SEBI Act, SEBI was established as a regulatory body to promote the development of the securities market and protect the interest of investors in the securities market. Further, it obtained the power to make regulations for the above objectives. Thus, SEBI appointed a committee headed by P.N. Bhagwati to study the effect of takeovers and mergers on securities market and suggest the provisions to regulate takeovers and mergers.

In its report, the committee stated the necessity of a Takeover Code on the following grounds:

a. The confidence of retail investors in the capital market is a crucial factor for its development. Therefore, their interest needs to be protected.
b. An exit opportunity shall be given to the investors if they do not want to continue with the new management.
c. Full and truthful disclosure shall be made of all material information relating to the open offer so as to take an informed decision.
d. The acquirer shall ensure the sufficiency of financial resources for the payment of acquisition price to the investors.
e. The process of acquisition and mergers shall be completed in a time-bound manner.
f. Disclosures shall be made of all material transactions at earliest opportunity.

10.7.1 Procedure for Takeover

The takeover may take place through different methods. A company may acquire the shares of an unlisted company through what is called acquisition under the Companies Act, 2013. However, where the shares of the company are widely held by the general public, it involves the process as set out in the SEBI (Substantial Acquisition of Shares and Takeover) Regulations, 2011.

The term 'takeover' has not been defined under the SEBI (Substantial Acquisition of Shares and Takeover) Regulations, 2011; the term basically envisages the concept of an acquirer taking over the control or management of the target company. When an acquirer acquires substantial quantity of shares or voting rights of the target company, it results in the substantial acquisition of shares.

For the purposes of understanding the implications arising from the aforementioned paragraph, it is necessary for us to dwell into what is the actual meaning of:

i. ***Acquirer:*** An acquirer means (includes persons acting in concert (PAC) with him) any individual/company/any other legal entity that intends to acquire or acquires substantial quantity of shares or voting rights of the target company or acquires or agrees to acquire control over the target company.
ii. ***Target company:*** A target company is a listed company, that is, whose shares are listed on any stock exchange and whose shares or voting rights are acquired/being acquired or whose control is taken over/being taken over by an acquirer.
iii. ***Control:*** Control includes the right to appoint directly or indirectly or by virtue of agreements or in any other manner majority of directors on the board of the target company or to control management or policy decisions affecting the target company. However, in case there are two or more persons in control over the target company the successor of any one of such persons from such control will not be deemed to be a change in control of management nor shall any change in the nature and quantum of control amongst them constitute change in control of management provided this transfer is done in terms of regulation 3(1)(e). Also, if consequent upon change in control of the target company in accordance with regulation 3, the control acquired is equal to or less than the control exercised by person(s) prior to such acquisition of control, such control will not be deemed to be a change in control.
iv. ***Promoter:*** The definition of promoter includes 'any person who is in control of the target company' or 'named as promoter in an offer document or shareholding pattern filed by the target company with the stock exchanges according to the listing

agreement, whichever is later'. The clauses that formed part of the earlier definition but now stand deleted are: 'any persons who is directly or indirectly in control of the company' and 'any person named as person acting in concert with the promoter in any disclosure made in terms of the listing agreement with the stock exchange or any other regulations or guidelines made or issued by the board under the Act'.

The takeover code has also modified the definition of individual. The new definition of individual includes:

a. spouse, parents, sisters, brothers and children of the promoter;
b. a company in which 10% or more of the share capital is held by the promoter or his immediate relative or a firm/Hindu undivided family in which the promoter or his immediate relative is a member holding an aggregate share capital of 10% or more; and
c. any company in which the company specified in sub-clause above holds 10% or more of the share capital (the earlier threshold was 26%).

v. ***Persons acting in concert (PAC):*** PACs are individuals/companies/any other legal entities who are acting together for a common objective or for a purpose of substantial acquisition of shares or voting rights or gaining control over the target company pursuant to an agreement or understanding whether formal or informal. Acting in concert would imply cooperation, coordination for acquisition of voting rights or control. This cooperation/coordinated approach may either be direct or indirect.

The concept of PAC assumes significance in the context of substantial acquisition of shares since it is possible for an acquirer to acquire shares or voting rights in a company 'in concert' with any other person in such a manner that the acquisition made by them may remain individually below the threshold limit but may collectively exceed the threshold limit.

Unless the contrary is established, certain entities are deemed to be PAC like companies with its holding company or subsidiary company, mutual funds with its sponsor/trustee/asset management company and the likes.

vi. ***Substantial quantity of shares or voting rights:*** The said regulations have discussed this aspect of 'substantial quantity of shares or voting rights' separately for two different purposes:

(I) For the purpose of disclosures to be made by acquirer(s):

a. *5% or more shares or voting rights:* A person who, along with 'PAC, if any, acquires shares or voting rights (which when taken together with his existing holding) would entitle him to more than 5% or 10% or 14% shares or voting rights of target company, is required to disclose the aggregate of his shareholding or voting rights to the target company and the stock exchanges where the shares of the target company are traded within two days of receipt of intimation of allotment of shares or acquisition of shares.
b. *More than 15% shares or voting rights:* An acquirer, who holds more than 15% shares or voting rights of the target company, shall within 21 days from the financial year ending March 31 make yearly disclosures to the company in respect of his holdings as on the mentioned date.

The target company is, in turn, required to pass on such information to all stock exchanges where the shares of 'target company' are listed, within 30 days from the financial year ending March 31 as well as the record date fixed for the purpose of dividend declaration.

(II) For the purpose of making an open offer by the acquirer

a. 15% shares or voting rights: An acquirer who intends to acquire shares that along with his existing shareholding would entitle him to more than 15% voting rights can acquire such additional shares only after making a public announcement to acquire at least additional 20% of the voting capital of the target company from the shareholders through an open offer.
b. Creeping limit of 5%: An acquirer who is having 15% or more but less than 75% of shares or voting rights of a target company can consolidate his holding up to 5% of the voting rights in any financial year ending 31st March. However, any additional acquisition over and above 5% can be made only after making a public announcement. However, in pursuance of regulation 7(1A) any purchase or sale aggregating to 2% or more of the share capital of the target company are to be disclosed to the target company and the stock exchange where the shares of the target company are listed within two days of such purchase or sale along with the aggregate shareholding after such acquisition/sale. An acquirer who has made a public offer and seeks to acquire further shares under regulation 11(1) shall not acquire such shares during the period of six months from the date of closure of the public offer at a price higher than the offer price.
c. Consolidation of holding: An acquirer who is having 75% shares or voting rights of the target company can acquire further shares or voting rights only after making a public announcement specifying the number of shares to be acquired through open offer from the shareholders of a target company.

In order to appreciate the implications arising here from, it is pertinent for us to consider the meaning of the term 'public announcement'.

10.7.2 Public Announcement

A public announcement is generally an announcement given in the newspapers by the acquirer, primarily to disclose his intention to acquire a minimum of 20% of the voting capital of the target company from the existing shareholders by means of an open offer. However, an acquirer may also make an offer for less than 20% of shares of target company in case the acquirer is already holding 75% or more of voting rights/shareholding in the target company and has deposited in the escrow account in cash a sum of 50% of the consideration payable under the public offer.

The acquirer is required to appoint a merchant banker registered with SEBI before making a public announcement and is also required to make the public announcement within four working days of the entering into an agreement to acquire shares, which has led to the triggering of the takeover, through such merchant banker.

The other disclosures in this announcement would, *inter alia,* include:

a. the offer price,
b. the number of shares to be acquired from the public,
c. the identity of the acquirer,
d. the purposes of acquisition,
e. the future plans of the acquirer, if any, regarding the target company,
f. the change in control over the target company, if any,

g. the procedure to be followed by acquirer in accepting the shares tendered by the shareholders and the period within which all the formalities pertaining to the offer would be completed.

The basic objective behind the public announcement being made is to ensure that the shareholders of the target company are aware of the exit opportunity available to them in case of a takeover/substantial acquisition of shares of the target company. They may, on the basis of the disclosures contained therein and in the letter of offer, either continue with the target company or decide to exit from it.

10.7.3 Procedure to Be Followed after the Public Announcement

In pursuance of the provisions of regulation 18 of the said regulations, the acquirer is required to file a draft offer document with SEBI within 14 days of the public announcement through its merchant banker, along with filing fees of ₹50,000 per offer document (payable by banker's cheque/demand draft). Along with the draft offer document, the merchant banker also has to submit a due diligence certificate as well as certain registration details.

The filing of the draft offer document is a joint responsibility of both the acquirer and the merchant banker. Thereafter, the acquirer through its merchant banker sends the offer document as well as the blank acceptance form within 45 days from the date of public announcement to all the shareholders whose names appear in the register of the company on a particular date. The offer remains open for 30 days. The shareholders are required to send their share certificate(s)/related documents to the registrar or merchant banker as specified in the public announcement and offer document.

The acquirer is obligated to offer a minimum offer price as is required to be paid by him to all those shareholders whose shares are accepted under the offer, within 30 days from the closure of offer.

10.7.4 Exemptions

The following transactions are, however, exempted from making an offer and are not required to be reported to SEBI:

i. Allotment to underwriter pursuant to any underwriting agreement;
ii. Acquisition of shares in ordinary course of business by;

   a. registered stock brokers on behalf of clients;
   b. registered market makers;
   c. public financial institutions on their own account;
   d. banks and financial institutions as pledges;

iii. Acquisition of shares by way of transmission on succession or by inheritance;
iv. Acquisition of shares by government companies;
v. Acquisition pursuant to a scheme framed under section 18 of the Sick Industrial Companies (Special Provisions) Act, 1985, of arrangement/restructuring including amalgamation or merger or demerger under any law or regulation, Indian or foreign;
vi. Acquisition of shares in companies whose shares are not listed.

However, if by virtue of acquisition of shares of unlisted company, the acquirer acquires shares or voting rights (over the limits specified) in the listed company, the acquirer is required to make an open offer in accordance with the regulations.

10.7.5 Minimum Offer Price and Payments Made

It is not the duty of SEBI to approve the offer price; however, it ensures that all the relevant parameters are taken into consideration for fixing the offer price and that the justification for the same is disclosed in the offer document. The offer price shall be the highest of

- Negotiated price under the agreement, which triggered the open offer.
- Price paid by the acquirer or PAC with him for acquisition if any, including by way of public rights/preferential issue during the 26-week period prior to the date of the public announcement.
- Average of weekly high and low of the closing prices of shares as quoted on the stock exchanges, where shares of the target company are most frequently traded during 26 weeks prior to the date of the public announcement.

In case the shares of the target company are not frequently traded, then the offer price shall be determined by reliance on the following parameters: the negotiated price under the agreement, highest price paid by the acquirer or PAC with him for acquisition, if any, including by way of public rights/preferential issue during the 26-week period prior to the date of the public announcement and other parameters, including return on net worth, book value of the shares of the target company, EPS, price earning multiple vis-à-vis the industry average.

Acquirers are required to complete the payment of consideration to shareholders who have accepted the offer within 30 days from the date of closure of the offer. In case the delay in payment is on account of the non-receipt of statutory approvals and if the same is not due to wilful default or neglect on part of the acquirer, the acquirers would be liable to pay interest to the shareholders for the delayed period in accordance with regulations. Acquirers are, however, not to be made accountable for postal delays.

If the delay in payment of consideration is not due to the above reasons, it would be treated as a violation of the regulations.

10.7.6 Safeguards Incorporated so as to Ensure That the Shareholders Get Their Payments

Before making the public announcement, the acquirer has to create an escrow account having 25% of total consideration payable under the offer of size ₹1 billion (additional 10% if offer size is more than ₹1 billion). The escrow could be in the form of cash deposited with a scheduled commercial bank, bank guarantee in favour of the merchant banker or deposit of acceptable securities with appropriate margin with the merchant banker. The merchant banker is also required to confirm that firm financial arrangements are in place for fulfilling the offer obligations. In case, the acquirer fails to make payment, merchant banker has a right to forfeit the escrow account and distribute the proceeds in the following way.

a. One-third of amount to the target company.
b. One-third to regional stock exchanges, for credit to investor protection fund and so on.
c. One-third to be distributed on pro rata basis among the shareholders who have accepted the offer.

The merchant banker advised by SEBI is required to ensure that the rejected documents, which are kept in the custody of the registrar/merchant banker, are sent back to the shareholder through registered post.

Besides forfeiture of escrow account, SEBI can take separate action against the acquirer, which may include prosecution/barring the acquirer from entering the capital market for a period and so on.

10.7.7 Penalties

The regulations have laid down the general obligations of the acquirer, target company and the merchant banker. For failure to carry out these obligations as well as for failure/non-compliance of other provisions of the regulations, regulation 45 provides for penalties. Any person violating any provisions of the regulations shall be liable for action in terms of the regulations and the SEBI Act.

If the acquirer or any PAC with him fails to carry out the obligations under the regulations, the entire or part of the sum in the escrow amount shall be liable to be forfeited and the acquirer or such a person shall also be liable for action in terms of the regulations and the Act.

The board of directors of the target company failing to carry out the obligations under the regulations shall be liable for action in terms of the regulations and SEBI Act.

The board may, for failure to carry out the requirements of the regulations by an intermediary, initiate action for suspension or cancellation of registration of an intermediary holding a certificate of registration under section 12 of the Act. Provided that no such certificate of registration shall be suspended or cancelled unless the procedure specified in the regulations applicable to such intermediary is complied with.

For any misstatement to the shareholders or for concealment of material information required to be disclosed to the shareholders, the acquirers or the directors where he (acquirer) is a body corporate, the directors of the target company, the merchant banker to the public offer and the merchant banker engaged by the target company for independent advice would be liable for action in terms of the regulations and the SEBI Act.

The penalties referred to in sub-regulations (1) to (5) may include:

a. criminal prosecution under section 24 of the SEBI Act;
b. monetary penalties under section 15H of the SEBI Act;
c. directions under the provisions of section 11B of the SEBI Act.

Regulations have laid down the penalties for non-compliance. These penalties may include forfeiture of the escrow account, directing the person concerned to sell the shares acquired in violation of the regulations, directing the person concerned not to further deal in securities, monetary penalties, prosecution and so on which may even extend to the barring of the acquirer from entering and participating in the capital market. Action can also be initiated for suspension, cancellation of registration against an intermediary such as the merchant banker to the offer.

The provisions dealt with in this section are some of the important provisions that are required to be complied with when dealing with the procedure to be complied with in order to take over a company.

10.8 Economic Aspects of Takeover

In a takeover, the management of the acquirer may maintain the legal identify of both the companies and operate them under the direction of separate boards of directors (having common directors) or the management may decide that both the companies should merge or amalgamate in a new company or one may amalgamate or merge with the other so that there is only one company, either the new company or the merged or the amalgamated company functioning under a unified command of one board of directors. In either case, the object of a successful takeover should be the overall economic betterment of the shareholders, the management, staff and all other employees, suppliers of raw materials and other consumables, personnel engaged in the marketing network, the ultimate consumer, the public at large and the government. By virtue of better management of the business and affairs of the company, with the active and dedicated association of qualified and experienced technical, managerial, financial and marketing personnel, the value of the shares should increase, employees should feel assured of timely payment of their salaries and other dues, suppliers should get timely payments for their supplies, end products of the company are freely available, government dues are paid on time and the company contributes to the society in which it operates and the areas whereof it serves. Socially conscious management of such a unified company is supposed to look after the surroundings and the environment of the place where it works.

Besides being beneficial to the concerned companies, takeovers are also beneficial to the economy in the following manner:

a. *Disciplining the capital market:* Takeovers help in disciplining the market as inefficient and errant companies get taken over due to their low book value and share prices. This process also helps in discovering the potential of the acquired companies, if any.
b. *Consolidation of efforts and capacities:* In the yesteryears, government authorities had issued licenses to units with capacities much below the minimum economic size. Due to increased competition in markets, many of these are either incurring losses or earning marginal profits. Also, in the light of stringent control standards and emergence of multinationals, small units have realized the importance of conservation of resources and reduction of costs. However, due to lack of proper infrastructure and sufficient capacity, they are unable to implement their schemes efficiently. In such circumstances, takeovers can be an effective mode of consolidating splintered capacities to reach the minimum economic size. This will be a means of not only revival of sick units but also prevention of sickness (to understand the corporate sickness in detail, please follow the companion website of the book and download Chapter 21: Corporate Sickness for free). Consolidation of capacities enables the industries to gain competitive strength in domestic and international markets.
c. *Concentrating on core competencies:* Due to the restrictive licensing policies followed by the government, in the past, large companies were not allowed to grow and diversify easily. Rigorous provisions of MRTP posed serious obstacles. The companies were required to diversify into totally unrelated areas. However, due to recent developments like liberalization and increasing pressure of competition, they are realizing the need to focus on core competition, for which mergers and takeovers offer green pastures. This is because these strategies enable the companies to rationalize their portfolios, enhance entity value and increase leveraging capability.

The unified command of the company in a takeover transaction should ensure creation of more wealth through optimum competence, improved productivity and higher profitability. All initiatives to enhance productivity, performance and market capitalization should be supported. Thus, the takeover strategy has been conceived to improve general economic well-being of all those who are, directly or indirectly, connected with the corporate sector. It is adopted to increase the corporate value, achieve better productivity and profitability by making optimum use of the available resources in the form of men, materials and machines.

10.9 Accounting Aspects of Takeover

Accounting considerations are vital in planning a takeover. While many such transactions are based upon industrial or other operation considerations, others depend upon the financial impact of transactions on the financial position of the parties. In a takeover, if the acquirer is an individual, he has to write in his personal books of account the amounts invested in the shares of the company, whose majority shares or control has been taken over by him. This investment in the shares of the target company shall be reflected in his personal return of income at the end of the financial year.

a. Holding Company's Books of Account: The books of account of the holding company will be accordingly written as under:

If consideration for the acquired shares has been paid in cash only:

Investments account	Debit
Cash account	Credit

If only fully paid shares have been allotted by the acquiring company to the shareholders of the target company, whose shares have been acquired, in exchange for their shares:

Investments account	Debit
Share capital account	Credit

If the consideration has been paid partly in cash and partly in the form of fully paid shares:

Investments account	Debit
Cash account (for the cash portion)	Credit
Share capital account (for the fully paid shares portion)	Credit

Besides the books of account, the acquiring or the holding company shall also maintain a register of investments in accordance with the provisions of the Companies Act, 2013.

b. Subsidiary companies books of account: There will be no accounting entry in the books of account of the target company or the subsidiary company. However, in the register of members of the subsidiary company, the transfer of shares of the shareholders, whose shares have been acquired by the holding company, shall be registered as soon as the relevant instruments of transfer along with the relevant share certificates have been received and the registration of their transfer. The share certificates shall be sent to the holding company after making due endorsement of the transfer under the authentication of the authorized signatory of the subsidiary company.

10.10 Impact of Takeover on Stakeholders

Takeovers have the potential to fundamentally affect a number of stakeholders, the most notable of which are the offeror and offeree corporations, the employees of both firms, and the management and shareholders of the offeree. While it is understood that the fallout from takeovers will vary according to the facts of a particular case, studies have revealed certain patterns or trends in how each group is affected.

1. Offeror and Offeree Corporations

Involvement in a takeover scenario is prima facie a risky venture for both the offeror and the offeree. Although the extensive varieties and complexities of the takeovers that have occurred in Canada and the United States have served as a barrier to an all-encompassing, and generally applicable, research project on the consequences of takeovers on the companies involved, a number of more limited studies have been conducted. Many of these have revealed ambivalent conclusions. For example, research conducted revealed that the number of acquired firms that report an increase in their profits three to five years after the takeover is virtually equivalent to the number that report a decrease. As well, a study of takeovers based on firm-specific accounting data in the United States revealed that the profitability of acquired assets in their sample deteriorated significantly after being acquired.

In addition to the effects on profitability, takeovers can also cause more fundamental changes in the merging firms, such as divestitures of portions of the offeror or offeree (or both), dramatic shifts in corporate culture and, in certain cases, the collapse of one or both of the merged corporations.

2. Employees

The employees of the offeror and offeree are probably the most vulnerable stakeholders throughout a takeover. Economists have recognized that takeovers threaten the two most important pillars of an employee›s career: job security and job satisfaction. First of all, consolidations are frequently accompanied by a loss of jobs. An increase in economies of scale may result in the closure of certain sections of the merged companies and, in turn, corresponding layoffs. As well, takeovers are often accompanied by the divestiture of divisions or departments of the acquired company for a quick profit, again resulting in considerable loss of jobs. With respect to job satisfaction, takeovers may result in a deterioration of employee morale due to problems such as uncertainty of job description, shifts in corporate culture or separation anxiety. Again, there may be job separation anxiety, or the fear by employees that relationships will be severed as a result of dismissals, transfers, or restructuring, skyrockets during a takeover. Furthermore, on the basis of a study of 150 large mergers and acquisitions in the United States, Harlow Unger reported in 1986 that the turnover of senior executives of acquired companies is almost 50% within the first year after the merger, and nearly 75% by the end of three years.

3. Management and Shareholders of Offeree

An offeree's management and shareholders are the two most integral groups in the determination of whether a takeover is successful. The offeree's directors may, or may not, choose to recommend to the shareholders to accept the offeror's bid. As well, corporate management may choose to deploy a strategic defensive tactic to fend off the predator company. The shareholders, on the other hand, as owners, must make the ultimate decision as to whether to acquiesce to or to fight the offeror. Thus, the participation of and the interaction between these two stakeholders during a takeover is essential to the ultimate result.

However, the balance within this relationship is constantly threatened by the reality that an offeree's management and shareholders fundamentally possess conflicting objectives. For example, studies indicate that there is a high managerial turnover following takeovers, thus making management naturally adverse to successful changes in ownership. As well, corporate managers typically possess keen competitive and possessive instincts, which propel directors to fight for their companies' independence and survival.

In contrast, the motivations of the shareholders of an offeree are generally based on share wealth maximization. The key consideration in deciding whether to accept or reject a takeover bid is the share price being offered. A study of the takeovers of 10 Canadian firms revealed that the target's shareholders tend to do very well, averaging a gain of 35.6% over their estimated market value. As well, a study by Professor EspinEckbo of the 1,930 mergers and takeovers of Canadian public companies between 1964 and 1983 found that the offerees' shares averaged an 11.87% increase in share value over the 12 months preceding and four months following the first public announcement of a possible pending reconsolidation. Thus, an offeree's shareholders generally benefit from a takeover.

While it would be misleading to suggest that all directors and shareholders of target companies behave in the stereotyped manner suggested above, on a theoretical plane these two stakeholders do have fundamentally adverse ambitions which create the potential for serious problems such as conflicts of interest and breaches of fiduciary duties.

10.11 Special Issues from SEBI

Volume-weighted Average Market Price: Volume-weighted average market price means the product of the number of equity shares traded on a stock exchange and the price of each equity share divided by the total number of equity shares traded on the stock exchange.

Example 1: Volume-weighted average market price.

Sl. No.	*Number of Shares Traded [A]*	*Market Price per Share [B]*	*Total [A × B]*
1	200	500	100,000
2	300	667	200,100
3	500	898	449,000
4	700	450	315,000
5	600	999	599,400
	2,300		1,663,500

Volume-weighted average market price = Total [A × B]/number of shares traded [A]
= 1,663,500/2,300
= 723.26

Weighted Average Number of Total Shares: Weighted average number of total shares means the number of shares at the beginning of a period, adjusted for shares cancelled, bought back or issued during the aforesaid period, multiplied by a time-weighing factor.

Example 2: Weighted average number of shares.

200,000 shares of A Limited were outstanding as on 1 April 2011. The company issued 100,000 equity shares on 1 October 2011.

Weighted average number of shares outstanding during the year:
= {[12 × 200,000] + [100,000 × 6]}/12 = 250,000

Direct Acquisition of Shares and Control: While an acquirer himself or with PAC engages with the acquisition of shares, initial trigger limits have been revised at 25%. Creeping acquisition limit has been retained at 5%, which can be done at the rate of 5% every year till the holdings reach 75%. However, open offer has been made mandatory when there is change in control. Gross acquisitions alone shall be taken into account regardless of any intermittent fall in shareholding or voting rights whether owing to disposal of shares held or dilution of voting rights owing to fresh issue of shares by the target company.

Example 3: Mr A holds 20% and his wife holds 10% of equity share capital of ABC Ltd as on 31 March 2014. Mr A acquires additional 2% on 1 September 2014 and another 3% on 31 December 2014. He sold 4% of his shares on 31 January 2015 in the open market. He wants to acquire another 2% on 1 March 2015. Can he do the same?

Yes, but he will have to make an open offer.

In the case of acquisition of shares by way of issue of new shares by the target company or where the target company has made an issue of new shares in any given financial year, the difference between the pre-allotment and the post-allotment percentage voting rights shall be regarded as the quantum of additional acquisition.

Example 4: XYZ Ltd has 100,000 shares outstanding in the market. Mr A holds 30,000 shares. The company makes a further issue of 10,000 shares. Mr A is allotted 5,000 shares and remaining 5,000 shares are allotted to a foreign institutional investor. Calculate the percentage of additional acquisition by Mr A.

Pre-allotment holding: 30% [(30,000/100,000) × 100]
Post-allotment holding: 31.81% [(35,000/110,000) × 100]
Additional acquisition: 1.81%

Example 5: Suppose in Example 4 above, Mr A acquires 3,000 shares prior to above allotment. Calculate the percentage of additional acquisition by A.

Pre-allotment holding: 33% [(33,000/100,000) × 100]
Post-allotment holding: 34.54% [(38,000/110,000) × 100]
Additional acquisition: 1.54%

So total additional acquisition during the year is 3% [(3,000/100,000) × 100] +1.54% = 4.54%

It has been further stated in regulation 3(3) that for the purposes of sub-regulations (1) and (2), acquisition of shares by any person, such that the individual shareholding of such person acquiring shares exceeds the stipulated thresholds, shall also be attracting the obligation to make an open offer for acquiring shares of the target company irrespective of whether there is a change in the aggregate shareholding with PAC.

Example 6: Mrs A holds 10% and Mr A holds 22% of equity share capital of ABC Ltd as on 31 March 2014. He acquires additional 4% from Mrs A. Whether he will have to make an open offer?

Mr A will have to make a public announcement as his individual holding increases beyond 25%.

Example 7: Suppose A has 18% shares of ABC Ltd instead of 22% as mentioned in Example 6 above. He acquires additional 5.1% from Mrs A. Whether he will have to make an open offer?

Mr A will have to make a public announcement as his individual holding increases beyond 5% creeping acquisition limit during the year.

Indirect Acquisition of Shares or Control: For the purposes of regulations 3 and 4, acquisition of shares or voting rights in, or control over, any company or other entity, that would enable any person and PAC with him to exercise or direct the exercise of such percentage of voting rights in, or control over, a target company, the acquisition of which would otherwise attract the obligation to make a public announcement of an open offer for acquiring shares under these regulations, shall be considered as an indirect acquisition of shares or voting rights in or control over the target company.

Example 8: H Ltd owns 60% of equity shares of T Ltd. Mr A owns 5% and Mrs A holds 10% equity shares in T Ltd. Mr A acquires 20% stake in H Ltd. Whether he will have to make an open offer?

No, he will not have to make an open offer. As 20% stake is a minority stake, which does not enable the holder to influence the decisions of H Ltd, it does not enable him to exercise voting rights over T Ltd.

Example 9: Mr A owns 5% and Mrs A holds 10% equity shares in T Ltd. Mr A acquires 60% of shareholding in Z Ltd which owns 12% in T Ltd. Will he be required to make an open offer?

Yes, he will have to make an open offer. As 60% stake is a majority stake which enables the holder to influence the decisions of Z Ltd. It enables him to exercise voting rights of 27% over T Ltd.

In case of an indirect acquisition, where

a. the proportionate 'net asset value' of the target company as a percentage of the consolidated net asset value of the entity or business being acquired; or
b. the proportionate 'sales turnover' of the target company as a percentage of the consolidated sales turnover of the entity or business being acquired; or
c. the proportionate 'market capitalization' of the target company as a percentage of the 'enterprise value' for the entity or business being acquired

is more than 80% on the basis of the most recent audited annual financial statements, such indirect acquisition shall be regarded as a direct acquisition.

Example 10: XYZ is an unlisted company. It owns 51% in A Ltd, a listed company (target). The consolidated turnover of XYZ Ltd is ₹30 billion and the consolidated NAV is ₹10 billion. The standalone sales turnover of A Ltd is ₹25 billion and its standalone NAV is ₹8.5 billion.

Proportionate NAV of A Ltd as a percentage of the consolidated NAV of XYZ Ltd is 85.00% (850/1,000 × 100).

Proportionate sales of A Ltd as a percentage of the consolidated sales of XYZ Ltd is 83.33% (2,500/3,000 × 100).

Hence, this acquisition shall be deemed as direct acquisition of A Ltd and hence all the requirements for direct acquisition shall be applicable.

Voluntary Offer: The acquirer together with PAC must hold 25% or more equity shares or voting rights for voluntary offer. The acquirer or PAC should not have acquired any shares by creeping acquisition or by any mode, which is exempted during the 52 weeks preceding the public announcement. However, he can acquire shares by way of bonus or stock split or an open offer. The open offer shall be for minimum of 10% of outstanding shares. If a voluntary open offer is made, the followings should be complied with:

a. The acquirer shall not acquire any shares during the open offer otherwise than under the open offer.
b. The acquirer cannot acquire any shares for a period of six months after completion of open offer. However, he can make another voluntary offer or make a competing offer during the said period.

Disclosure Requirements: Initial disclosure shall be made when aggregate shareholding of the acquirer along with PACs reaches 5%. Once the holding crosses 5%, every purchase and sale aggregating to 2% shall have to be disclosed. Disclosure is to be made within two working days to the stock exchange and the target company. Creation of pledge or any other encumbrance shall be treated as acquisition and release of such pledge or encumbrance shall be treated as disposal and disclosures shall have to be made accordingly. However, scheduled commercial banks and public financial institutions are exempted from disclosure requirements if they act as a pledgee in connection with a pledge of shares for securing indebtedness in the ordinary course of business.

Example 11: Mr A acquires 2% shares or voting rights of T Ltd on 1November 2014, which taken together with 4% shares or voting rights already held by him, or in association with Mr P, aggregates to more than 5% shares of T Ltd.

Then A and P need to disclose their aggregate shareholding and voting rights to T Ltd and the Bombay Stock Exchange (BSE; where it is listed) on or before 3November 2014 in the format in Annexure A given by SEBI in Circular no. SEBI/CFD/DCR/SAST/2/2011/10/20, dated 20 October 2011.

Example 12: Mr A along with Mr P holds 6% (5% or more) shares or voting rights of T Ltd. On 1November 2014, A acquires 2% shares or voting rights of T Ltd.

Then, Mr A shall disclose such acquisition of 2% shares to T Ltd and BSE (where it is listed) on or before 3 November 2014 in the format in Annexure B given by SEBI in Circular no. SEBI/CFD/DCR/SAST/2/2011/10/20, dated 20 October 2011.

Example 13: On 1 November 2014, X holding 10% shares in T Ltd pledges 3% of his shares (shares taken by way of encumbrance shall be treated as an acquisition) to Mr A already holding 6% shares in T Ltd.

Then, A shall disclose such acquisition and Mr X such disposal (by way of encumbrance) of 3% shares to T Ltd and BSE (where it is listed) on or before 3 November 2014 in the format in Annexure B given by SEBI in Circular No. SEBI/CFD/DCR/SAST/2/2011/10/20 dated 20 October 2011.

Continual Disclosures: These disclosures should be made by every person which together with PACs hold more than 25% of shares or voting rights in the target company and also the promoters of the target company. They have to disclose their aggregate shareholding and voting rights as of the 31 day of March in the target company. Disclosure should be made within seven working days from the end of the financial year to every stock exchange where the shares of the company are listed and to the company.

Example 14: As on 31 March 2014, Mr A together with Mr P holds shares of T Limited, which entitles them to exercise more than 25% voting right in T Limited.

They shall disclose their aggregate shareholding and voting rights within seven working days from 31 March 2014 to BSE and T Limited.

Offer Size: The offer size under regulations 3 and 4 shall be for at least 26% of total shares of the target company, as of 10th working day from the closure of the tendering period. Obligation has been placed on the acquirer to take into account all potential increases in the number of outstanding shares during the offer period contemplated as of the date of the public announcement. If there is an increase in the total number of shares, after the public announcement, which is not contemplated on the date of the public announcement then the offer size shall be proportionately increased.

Example 15: Mr A wants to acquire 25% of the equity share capital of T Ltd. He has made a public announcement on 1 October 2014. The tendering period is from 1 November to 16 November 2014. T Ltd has 100,000 equity shares outstanding as on 1 October 2014. The company also has 10,000 compulsorily convertible debentures outstanding, against which 5,000 equity shares will have to be issued. They are due for conversion on 17 November 2014 and shares will have to be issued immediately.

Mr A will have to make an open offer. The minimum size of the open offer shall be 26% total shares of the target company. The 26% shall be calculated on the enhanced number of shares, that is, 105,000. Hence, he will have to make an open offer for 27,300 shares.

Minimum Price

The minimum offer price for direct acquisition shall be the highest of the following:

a. the highest negotiated price per share of the target company for any acquisition under the agreement attracting the obligation to make a public announcement of an open offer;
b. the volume weighted average price paid or payable for acquisitions, whether by the acquirer or by any PAC with him, during the 52 weeks immediately preceding the date of the public announcement;
c. the highest price paid or payable for any acquisition, whether by the acquirer or by any PAC with him, during the 26 weeks immediately preceding the date of the public announcement;
d. the volume-weighted average market price of such shares for a period of 60 trading days immediately preceding the date of the public announcement as traded on the stock exchange where the maximum volume of trading in the shares of the target company are recorded during such period, provided such shares are frequently traded;
e. where the shares are not frequently traded, the price determined by the acquirer and the manager to the open offer taking into account valuation parameters, including book value, comparable trading multiples and such other parameters as are customary for valuation of shares of such companies; and
f. the per-share value computed under sub-regulation (5), if applicable.

Example 16: Mr A wants to take over CBB Ltd, a listed company. CBB Ltd has 100,000,000 shares outstanding. He purchased shares of CBB Ltd on as per details presented in the table given below. Some purchases were made on stock exchange and some of them were made on privately from other shareholders.

Date of Acquisition	Price Paid per Share	No of Shares Acquired
15 Mar 2014	500	1,500,000
15 Apr 2014	550	500,000
15 May 2014	650	1,000,000
15 Jun 2014	450	2,500,000
15 Jul 2014	700	500,000
17 Aug 2014	750	1,000,000
12 Sep 2014	470	500,000
06 Oct 2014	590	500,000
09 Nov 2014	640	1,000,000
09 Dec 2014	900	1,000,000
Total		10,000,000

He enters into an agreement with Mr H, who holds 16% shares of CBB Ltd on 15 March 2015 to purchase his entire shareholding at the rate of 850 per share. The shares of CBB Ltd are frequently traded. The public announcement was made on 1 April 2015. Calculate the minimum price payable in the open offer.

The minimum open offer price shall be the highest of the following:

a. ₹850 agreed to be paid to Mr H.
b. ₹900 being the highest price paid for any acquisition during the 26 weeks immediately preceding the date of the public announcement (since 1 October 2014).
c. ₹750 being the volume-weighted average market price of such shares for a period of 60 trading days immediately preceding the date of the public announcement.
d. ₹764 being the volume-weighted average price paid for acquisitions during 52 weeks preceding the date of public announcement.

Date of Acquisition	Price Paid per Share [A]	No of Shares Acquired [B]	Total [A × B]
15 Apr 2014	550	500,000	275,000,000
15 May 2014	650	1,000,000	650,000,000
15 Jun 2014	450	2,500,000	1,125,000,000
15 Jul 2014	700	500,000	350,000,000
17 Aug 2014	750	1,000,000	750,000,000
12 Sep 2014	470	500,000	235,000,000
06 Oct 2014	590	500,000	295,000,000
09 Nov 2014	640	1,000,000	640,000,000
09 Dec 2014	900	1,000,000	900,000,000
15 Mar 2015	850	1,60,00,000	13,600,000,000
Total		2,45,00,000	18,820,000,000

VWAP = 18,820,000,000/24,500,000 = ₹764.
So, the minimum price will be ₹900 per share.

The conditions for minimum price in case of indirect acquisitions are also the same. However, one additional criterion has been prescribed, which is as follows:

a. The highest price paid or payable for any acquisition, whether by the acquirer or by any PAC with him, between the earlier of, the date on which the primary acquisition is contracted, and the date on which the intention or the decision to make the primary acquisition is announced in the public domain, and the date of the public announcement of the open offer for shares of the target company made under these regulations.
b. Also, the cutoff date is the date of contract or the date on which the intention or the decision to make the primary acquisition is announced in the public domain instead of the date of the public announcement.

In the case of an indirect acquisition and open offers under sub-regulation (2) of regulation 5 where:

a. the proportionate net asset value of the target company as a percentage of the consolidated net asset value of the entity or business being acquired;
b. the proportionate sales turnover of the target company as a percentage of the consolidated sales turnover of the entity or business being acquired; or
c. the proportionate market capitalization of the target company as a percentage of the enterprise value for the entity or business being acquired; is in excess of 15%, on the basis of the most recent audited annual financial statements, the acquirer shall, notwithstanding anything contained in sub-regulation (2) or (3), be required to compute and disclose, in the letter of offer, the per-share value of the target company taken into account for the acquisition, along with a detailed description of the methodology adopted for such computation.

Example 17: Astra Inc is a company incorporated in the United States. It has a subsidiary in India by the name of Astra India Limited, which is listed on BSE and the National Stock Exchange (NSE). Vertigo Inc acquires 51% in Astra Inc for $6,000. The consolidated NAV of Astra Inc is $40 billion, consolidated sales is $80 billion and market capitalization is $100 billion. NAV of Astra India is $10 billion, sales are $30 billion and market capitalization is $30 billion.

Since there is an indirect acquisition of Astra India, Vertigo will have to make an open offer in India. Since the proportionate NAV, sales and market cap of Astra India as a percentage of the consolidated NAV, sales and market cap of Astra INC is 25%, 37.5%, and 30%, respectively, the provisions of this sub-regulation are attracted. Hence, Vertigo Inc is required to compute and disclose, in the letter of offer, the per-share value ascribed to Astra India when determining the price for the acquisition of Astra Inc, along with a detailed description of the methodology adopted for such computation.

Multiple Choice Questions

1. While calculating the enterprise value, which one of the following should be deducted from the market capitalization of a company?
   a. Debt
   b. Cash and cash equivalents
   c. Minority interest
   d. Preferred shares

2. Immediate relative excludes which one of the following:
   a. Spouse b. Parent c. Child d. Son-in-law
3. Initial trigger limit for direct acquisition of shares and control is
   a. 10% b. 15% c. 25% d. 20%
4. Creeping acquisition limit is
   a. 5% b. 10% c. 15% d. 20%
5. For voluntary offer, the acquirer together with PAC must hold ________ or more equity shares or voting rights.
   a. 10% b. 15% c. 25% d. 20%
6. Disclosure of stockholding is to be made within ________ working days from the end of financial year to every stock exchange where the shares of the company are listed and to the company.
   a. 7 b. 10 c. 22 d. 31
7. Letter of offer is to be filed with SEBI within ________ working days from the date of detailed public announcement through manager to the open offer.
   a. 5 b. 10 c. 15 d. 20
8. In case of voluntary offer, the minimum offer size should be
   a. 5% b. 10% c. 15% d. 20%
9. In case of mandatory offer, the minimum offer size should be
   a. 15% b. 20% c. 25% d. 26%

Review Questions

1. Define the term 'takeover'. How is takeover different from merger?
2. List and explain the various definitions of a takeover.
3. Briefly explain the various types of takeovers, by proving suitable examples.
4. Briefly highlight the different modes of takeovers.
5. List the important motives for effecting a takeover.
6. Write a short note on takeover theories.
7. What is a takeover bid? What are the two types of takeover bids?
8. 'Takeovers are beneficial to the economy'. Do you agree? Justify your answer in the light of the economic aspects of takeovers.
9. Identify the three main strategies to consider when investing in takeover.
10. What do you understand by 'golden parachute' as a takeover strategy?
11. Define the term 'greenmail', and give an example.
12. How is poison pill used as a takeover strategy?
13. Write short notes on:
    a. shark repellent
    b. crown jewel defence
    c. leveraged recapitalization
    d. Pac-Man defence
14. Write a critical note on the takeover code in the Indian context.
15. Briefly explain the various procedures in involved in takeovers.
16. What are the economic considerations in a takeover?
17. Explain the accounting aspects of a takeover, using a suitable example.

18. What are the methods of financing a takeover?
19. List and explain the major advantages of takeovers.
20. Briefly explain the issues in the areas of public policy in the process of takeovers.

Exercises

1. Consider the following information relating to the purchase of shares:

Number of Shares Purchased	300	700	400	500	800
Market Price per Share	150	180	120	360	420

Based on the above information, compute volume-weighted average market price.

2. Company X follows English calendar year for reporting and disclosure purpose. On 1 January 2015, the company has 150,000 shares outstanding. The company issued another 50,000 shares on 30 April 20015. Compute the weighted average number of shares.
3. Anil holds 15% and his wife holds another 15% of equity share capital of Baraka Ltd as on 31 March 2015. Anil acquires additional 5% on 1 September 2015 and another 4% on 31 December 2015. He sold 3% of his shares on 31 January 2016 in the open market. He wants to acquire another 3% on 1 March 2016. Can he do the same?
4. XYZ Ltd has 200,000 shares outstanding in the market. Zeeman holds 50,000 shares. The company makes a further issue of 20,000 shares. Zeeman is allotted 10,000 shares and remaining 10,000 are allotted to a JVI Inc. Calculate the percentage of additional acquisition by Zeeman.
5. Mrs Chowdhury holds 22% and Mr Chowdhury holds 10% of equity share capital of ABC Ltd as on 31 March 2015. He acquires additional 4% from Mrs Chowdhury. Whether he will have to make an open offer?
6. XYZ is an unlisted company. It owns 60% in A Ltd, a listed company (target). The consolidated turnover of XYZ Ltd is ₹50 billion and the consolidated NAV is ₹30 billion. The standalone sales turnover of A Ltd is 35 billion and its standalone NAV is 10 billion.
7. Jack wants to acquire 25% of equity share capital of P Ltd. He has made a public announcement on 1 October 2014. The tendering period is from 1 November to 16 November 2014. P Ltd has 120,000 equity shares outstanding as on 1 October 2014. The company also has 15,000 compulsorily convertible debentures outstanding, against which 10,000 equity shares will have to be issued. They are due for conversion on 17 November 2014 and shares will have to be issued immediately. What will be the offer size?
8. Roghu wants to take over Primex Ltd, a listed company. Primex Ltd has 100,000,000 shares outstanding. He purchased shares of Primex Ltd on as per details presented in the table given below. Some purchases were made on the stock exchange and some of them were made on privately from other shareholders.

Date of Acquisition	*Price Paid per Share*	*No of Shares Acquired*
25 Mar 2014	200	1,000,000
25 Apr 2014	300	800,000
25 May 2014	400	900,000
25 Jun 2014	450	1,500,000

25 Jul 2014	600	800,000
20 Aug 2014	350	1,200,000
15 Sep 2014	480	600,000
10 Oct 2014	590	700,000
10 Nov 2014	600	1,300,000
10 Dec 2014	800	1,100,000

He enters into an agreement with Mr Ajex who holds 16% shares of Primex Ltd on 15 March 2015 to purchase his entire shareholding at the rate of 850 per share. The shares of Primex Ltd are frequently traded. The public announcement was made on 1 April 2015. Calculate the minimum price payable in the open offer.

9. Zamini Inc is a company incorporated in the United States. It has a subsidiary in India by the name of Zamini India Limited, which is listed on BSE and NSE. Zelco Inc acquires 51% in ZaminiInc for $50 billion. The consolidated NAV of Zamini Inc is $45 billion, consolidated sales is $90 billion and market capitalization is $120 billion. NAV of Zamini India is $12 billion, sales are $32 billion and market capitalization is $25 billion. Put a critical note on minimum price and offer in line with SEBI guidelines for Zamini.

Case in Action

Takeover of Raasi Cements by India Cements

Introduction

In January 1998 there was an unusual press conference at Hyderabad's Hotel Viceroy. Seventy-seven-year-old B.V. Raju (Raju), vice-chairman of the Hyderabad (India)-based Raasi Cements (Raasi), mobilized all his daughters, sons-in-law and grandchildren in a display of family unity. 'We are one united family and will ward off any takeover threats. I am a humble, simple man who has always maintained a low profile. But when it comes to fighting, I shall not be found wanting', he declared. Raju's comments came in response to reports that N. Srinivasan (Srinivasan) was buying Raasi's share in the market. The Raasi scrip, which hovered around ₹50 until November 1997, tripled in value to ₹158 in January 1998. Srinivasan had acquired 18.03% of Raasi shares by January 1998. While he was responding to the takeover reports, Raju recalled, 'I made an offer to Srinivasan to buy the shares with a 10% profit margin and 20% interest from the date of purchase. Though he told me he had no ulterior motives, it appears as if he is still on a buying spree'. In January 1998, *Business India* reported, 'Rubbing salt into his wound is the fact that when India Cements was passing through difficult times in 1987–89, the then IDBI chairman, S. S. Nadkarni, had requested Raju to take over the ailing company. However, he had refused saying 'one should not close in on a weak colleague'. Analysts pointed out that India Cements Limited (ICL) had strategic advantages in taking over Raasi. In 1997, ICL added 2.2 million tonnes per annum (mtpa) new capacity through acquisitions and expansions. The addition of Raasi's 2 mtpa capacity would make it the undisputed leader in the south of the country. Again, a Raasi takeover meant automatically acquiring 39.5% equity in the 1 mtpa Sri Vishnu Cement Ltd. (SVCL), another group company.

Background

ICL was one of the largest cement producers in south India. The company had a strong presence in the states of Tamil Nadu, Kerala and Andhra Pradesh. Cement constituted approximately 97% of ICL's total revenues. Besides cement, the company had a presence in wind energy and real estate. In early 1998, ICL had six cement plants, three each in Tamil Nadu and Andhra Pradesh and its capacity had increased to 5.2 mtpa. ICL entered Andhra Pradesh by acquiring the Chilamakur plant from Coromandel Fertilizers in 1990. In September 1997, ICL took a 100% stake in Visaka Industries Ltd through its subsidiaries and associate companies. Also in 1998, ICL acquired the Yerranguntla plant from the Cement Corporation of India (CCI). Raasi was promoted by Raju and his son-in-law, N.P.K. Raju in 1978. Other than cement, the group also had interests in ceramics and paper. Raasi's cement division had a capacity of 1.60 mtpa. Raasi seemed to be an attractive target for ICL as it was a relatively low cost producer. Analysts felt that Raasi failed to capitalize on its low production cost, because of its weak marketing set-up, particularly in Kerala and Tamil Nadu. As a result, Raasi tended to dump the cement in its weak markets thereby putting pressure on other players in the region. SVCL was promoted in 1985 by Raju and the Andhra Pradesh Industrial Development Corporation (APIDC). It became a sick unit in 1990. A rehabilitation package was worked out by the BIFR in 1995, under which Raasi was permitted to bring in nearly ₹50 million as share capital. At that time it was stated that the shares allotted to the promoters would be locked in for a period of three years from the date of allotment. To that effect, the promoters had also given non-disposal undertakings to the Financial Institutions. With this share allotment, Raasi held 39.5% in the equity capital of SVCL.

The takeover of Raasi also would help in rationalization of various markets between ICL and Raasi, and interchangeable use of Sankar, Coromandel and Raasi brand names. Analysts felt that if ICL was indeed interested in Raasi and was buying its stock, then it was probably doing so in the belief that the family, despite Raju's assertion, would sell out. Raju had no sons, but his three sons-in-law were involved with the running of the company, and at least one of them seemed to be interested in selling out. ICL was no stranger to Raasi. In 1995, one of Raju's sons-in-law sold the 0.68 million shares in his possession (roughly 4% of the company's equity) to Srinivasan, on the understanding that the shares would be bought back in more favourable times. According to Raju this was done without his knowledge. Since then, ICL had been quietly increasing this stake. The company bought an additional 0.13 million shares in 1996–97 at an average price of ₹90, taking its stake to around 5%. When the share dipped to ₹50 in October 1997, it was an opportune moment for ICL to increase its holdings in Raasi and by late 1997, ICL increased its stake in Raasi to 8%.

Industry Profile

In the late 1990s, the Indian cement industry was a highly fragmented one. There were 117 plants belonging to 59 companies spread across the length and breadth of the country, with an installed capacity of 109.97 mtpa. In the early 1990s, the industry expanded considerably as new plants with large capacities came up. The success of the economic reforms of the early 1990s was a boost to the expansion plans of the cement companies. However, in the mid and late 1990s, as demand for cement declined, the share prices of most companies fell. In the late 1990s, acquisitions triggered off consolidation in the cement industry. The process of consolidation started in 1998 with ICL taking over Visaka Cement and CCI's plant at Yerraguntla (Andhra Pradesh) and Grasim taking over Dharani Cement and Shri Digvijay Cements. Also, in 1998, Lafarge, a French building material multinational, took over Tata Iron and Steel Co's (Tisco) 1.7 mtpa plant. The main reason for the sudden spate of acquisitions was that overcapacity had squeezed margins, making it impossible for the smaller, inefficient players, especially in the north and west, to carry on with their operations.

The Takeover of Raasi

By January 1998, Srinivasan had accumulated 18.03% of Raasi's equity, both through open market purchases as well as by buying out the stake of an estranged faction of the Raju family. In February 1998, Srinivasan announced an open offer to acquire an additional 20% of Raasi's equity. He offered ₹300 per share, 72.41% above the stock market price of ₹174 on 26 February 1998. Raasi's shareholders seemed to find it hard to turn down his offer. On 1 March 1998, the state-owned APIDC sold its 2.13% stake in Raasi to ICL. Subsequently, a Chennai-based stockbroker, Valampuri & Co., cornered 1.40% of Raasi's equity from the market for Srinivasan, taking ICL's stake in Raasi to 21.56%. Srinivasan was also negotiating with V.P. Babaria, a transporter for both ICL and Raasi, to pick up his 7% stake in the latter. If Babaria sold his stake, ICL's stake in Raasi would go up to 28.56%. With more than 25% of Raasi's equity in his kitty, Srinivasan would be in a position to veto any special resolution put up for the approval of Raasi's shareholders. A confident Srinivasan told *Business Today* in Chennai: 'Raju cannot wish me away and that's irrespective of the response ICL will elicit for its public offer, which will be open between April 15 and May 15, 1998'.

Unwilling to take any chances, Raju planned to execute a series of defensive manoeuvres to stall Srinivasan. Raasi could get its shareholders to approve the hiving-off of the 39.5% stake it owned in SVCL. But this could be opposed by the financial institutions as Raasi had promised BIFR, while taking over the sick company, which it would not dispose of the shares. Raju also had the option of making a counter offer to his shareholders, and weaning away potential sellers from Srinivasan. But this was an expensive option (Raju needed approximately ₹1 billion to make a counter bid) and he did not seem to have the funds to pull it off. Raju's efforts to find a 'white knight' didn't succeed either. R. Kunjitapadam, technical adviser and vice chairman, Raasi, said, 'Some companies did try to help us out of the crisis. We were looking for assistance in the form of a white knight, or joint participation in developing the company further, and parting at a later date'.

Raasi approached three sources: Kumar Mangalam Birla (Chairman, A.V. Birla Group), GACL and Switzerland's Holder Bank. Birla wanted a 51% stake while GACL seemed to prefer a takeover. Raju then made a final attempt by talking to Holder bank, but the latter wanted to merge Raasi with its Indian enterprise, Kalyanpur Cements. Raju expected help from the Andhra Pradesh government and other state industrialists who were against ICL's takeover bid. However, Mr Chandra Babu Naidu, the Chief Minister of Andhra Pradesh, refused to meet a delegation of state industrialists who wanted to present Raju's case. His only comment to the sale of APIDC's stake in Raasi was, 'The old man will be unhappy. In March 1998, realizing his predicament, Raju began to negotiate with Srinivasan to sell his 33% shares in the company. In an exclusive interview to Business India Raju said, 'Though I had 33% of the shares and associates held 10%, I needed another ₹1 billion for 51%. I did not want to incur further debts. It will take me ten births to repay them. Let this child of mine be happy, even if it's with a new owner'.

After protracted negotiations with an ICL team which flew down from Chennai to Hyderabad, Raasi decided to let ICL buy its shares at ₹286 a share. In April 1998, Business World reported, 'On paper Raju has reaped a harvest of ₹1.49 billion on this deal. But after deduction of all dues and shares for friends and relatives from the promoters' stake of 33%, Raju will net only ₹30 million in his personal account'. Commenting on the sell-out, Srinivasan said, 'We are happy that Dr. B.V. Raju and his associates have agreed to sell their stake in Raasi Cement. The consolidation process will be beneficial to both companies as it would result in production, marketing and distribution synergies'. 'At a later date, we plan to merge both the companies', he added. The takeover of Raasi by ICL led to a new controversy over the ownership of SVCL. SVCL was of strategic importance to both ICL and Raju. In early 1998, when ICL made known its intention to take over Raasi, it was believed that SVCL, in which Raasi had a 39.5% stake, would be part of the deal. However, when ICL came up with its open offer for Raasi, it discovered that the latter's entire stake in SVCL had been sold to some of the promoter's group companies.

In late 1997, Raasi had convened a couple of board meetings and its shares in SVCL were divested at ₹10 each, allegedly to Raju's friends and relations. Till the eventual takeover was complete no one questioned this deal. After the takeover of Raasi, ICL examined Raasi's books and found that it had violated the SEBI takeover guidelines which prohibited the target management from disposing off any asset during the open offer period. ICL complained to SEBI that Raasi had divested its 39.5% holding in SVCL in favour of nine firms controlled by Raju, in violation of the SEBI takeover code and the Companies Act. SEBI ordered an investigation into the legality of this share transfer and the Hyderabad City Civil Court was to judge how fair the transfer was to the shareholder of Raasi. Company sources said that Srinivasan would try to convince the courts that the shares were sold at a throwaway price of ₹10. This would make the deal detrimental to shareholders' interests under Section 397 of the Companies Act, 1956, which dealt with 'prevention of oppression,' and defined oppression as 'lack of probity and fair dealing in the affairs of a company to the prejudice of its members'.

In August 1998, Raju and his associates announced an open offer for a 20% stake in SVCL at ₹25 per share to increase their share from 39.5% to around 60%. On September 4, 1998, SEBI allowed Raju to go ahead with his open offer. Confident of the success of the open offer Raju increased the original offer price of ₹25 per share to ₹100 in September 1998. Meanwhile, in August 1998, Raju also picked up a 26.21% stake in SVCL, buying the shares of Industrial Development Bank of India (13.16%), Industrial Credit and Investment Corporation of India (6.53%), and the Industrial Finance Corporation of India (6.52%).With this acquisition he increased his holdings in SVCL to 65.71%. Raju then tried to raise his stake in SVCL to over 90%. If all went well, Raju could delist the company by making another open offer to the remaining shareholders. Even if he had to return the 39.5% stake to Raasi, he would still hold a controlling stake of over 50%. If SEBI was convinced that the share transfer was detrimental to the interests of Raasi's shareholders, it had two options.

One, the transfer could be reversed: Raju could be legally forced to return the 39.5% stake to Raasi. Or, SEBI could direct Raju to pay the difference of ₹90 per share to Raasi. In mid-1999, almost a year after SEBI started its investigations; it was yet to make a public statement on what its investigations had revealed. In October 1999 Raju sold his disputed 39.5% stake in SVCL to ICL. In a compromise reached in Hyderabad, Raju sold his shares for ₹1.15 billion, at ₹120 a share. Commenting on the surrender, Raju said, 'I have had a long and successful innings, but the younger generation of the family is more interested in high technology areas like software. In view of my age and keeping in mind the interest of the stakeholders in SVCL, we decided to divest in favour of ICL'. With this, ICL acquired 88.55% of SVCL's paid up capital. All cases relating to the matter, pending before SEBI were dropped. In December 1999, ICL Securities Ltd. (ICLSL), along with ICL and Raasi made an offer for the purchase of the remaining shares of SVCL (constituting 11.45% of the equity share capital) at ₹98.25 per share. By the end of 2000, SVCL became a subsidiary of ICL.

Source: http://www.icmrindia.org/free resources/case studies/raasi-cements-takeover1.htm

Questions for Discussion

1. Explain the rationale behind the takeover of Rassi Cements by ICL.
2. Trace the developments and major events that led to ICL taking over control of Rassi Cements.

References

Bradley, M., A. Desai, and E.H. Kim. 1988. 'Synergistic Gains from Corporate Acquisitions and Their Division Between the Stockholders of Target and Acquiring Firms'. *Journal of Financial Economics*, 21(1): 3–40.

Bradley, M., and Michael Rosenzweig. 1986. 'Defensive Stock Repurchases'. *Harvard Law Review*, 99(7): 1377–1430.

Roll, Richard. 1986. 'The Hubris Hypothesis of Corporate Takeovers'. *Journal of Business*, 59(2): 197–216.

Unger, Harlow. 1986. 'The People Trauma of Major Mergers'. *Journal of Industrial Management*, 10(17).

Weinberg, M.A., and M.V. Blank. 1999. *Takeovers and Mergers*, vol. 1, p. 1005. London: Sweet and Maxwell.

Wingerson, Mark R., and Christopher H. Dorn. 1992. 'Institutional Investors in the U.S. and the Repeal of Poison Pills: A Practitioner's Perspective'. *Columbia Business Law Review*, 223.

Further Readings

Our Milestones: Acquisition of Raasi Cement (Andhra Pradesh) with an Installed Capacity of 1.8 Million Tonnes in 1998. Available at http://www.indiacements.co.in (last accessed on 28 May 2016).

Takeover of Raasi Cements by India Cements, Icmrindia Case Studies. Available at http://books.google.co.in/booksid/nCcmGBwyyEC&pg/PA89&lpg/PA89&dq (last accessed on 25 May 2014).

Chapter 11

Demerger

Chapter Objectives

On completion of this chapter, you will be able to understand:

- The basics of demerger
- Conceptualization of demerger
- Procedural aspects of demerger under the Companies Act, 2013
- Effects of demerger
- Applicability of demerger
- Legal aspects
- Taxation aspects
  - Taxation of shareholders in demerged company
  - Tax benefits to resulting company
  - Amortization of expenditure in case of demerger (section 35DD)
  - Cost of shares acquired in the scheme of demerger (section 49)
- Demerger versus reconstruction
- Demerger versus hiving-off
- Advantages of demerger
- Disadvantages of demerger

A Demerger Cure for the Ills at Barclays

Having been asked to do three impossible things before breakfast—recreate a culture of integrity and ethics within his bank; pull out of some of the more profitable but contentious areas of investment banking such as, for example, speculating on movements in the price of food, and to do this while ensuring that the group grew its profits at least as fast as the competition—Barclays Bank chief executive Anthony Jenkins was always likely to stumble.

His failure to please all the people all of the time led to an 8% drop in Barclays' shares following the publication of his results last week.

This week he faces many of his key shareholders and analysts in a series of meetings. If they are as rude to him to his face as they have been in talking behind his back, it will be uncomfortable.

If any good is going to come out of this, it might just be the recognition that his job is indeed impossible.

One of the features of the last year has been how morale in the UK High Street business of Barclays has soared. Decent people who had worked for the bank for years, and had become ever more uneasy sacrificing clients for the sake of profits as demanded by the investment banking side, felt the tide was once again flowing their way.

Regional managers up and down the country have seized every business platform available to them to explain the Jenkins reforms and throw their weight behind them. There is a long way to go but he has made a good beginning. Where Jenkins came unstuck last week was on the payment of bonuses to his investment bankers, coupled with the fact that the cost of these was greater than the amount the bank proposed to pay in dividends.

The charge was that these favored employees were getting more out of the bank than the owners were, so the bank was still being run for the benefit of its employees rather than its shareholders. If Jenkins' reforms had made any difference to the culture of the investment bank, it was not obviously visible.

That is a pretty harsh judgment, but what it highlights is how the two businesses—the commercial bank and the investment bank—have different needs and incompatible cultures and should not be part of the same organization.

The combination only worked in the past under Bob Diamond because the commercial bank was willing to play second fiddle for the benefit of the group as a whole.

It does not work the other way, with ethical High Street banking the priority, because having once been top dogs; investment bankers will never accept the subordinate role.

The business models are quite different too. In banking, you can make money by being an extremely efficient provider of a commodity service—hence the relentless focus in costs in the strategy being pursued by Antonio Horta-Osorio at Lloyds Banking Group and presumably by TSB; or you can provide high-value services at high cost which is what investment banks try to do. It rarely works to try to do both.

The solution surely is to separate the two organizations, to demerge what was Barclays Capital—and allow it to develop as an independent, separately run investment bank.

It might well be that it will function better with its headquarters in North America, where it has a major business largely derived from the New York-based business of Lehman Brothers, given that the American political and cultural establishment is more tolerant of the prevailing investment banking morethan are Europeans.

The converse is that Barclays could focus on getting its domestic operations right and rehabilitating itself with UK public and politicians.

Source: 'A Demerger Cure for the Ills at Barclays', Analysis & Features, *Evening Standard*.[1]

11.1 Introduction

The trend of demergers has gained momentum as several of the businesses of companies have become bigger and their true value is not reflected in the stock price of these companies. Moreover, these companies want to focus on one business and help other

[1] Published on 18 February 2014. Available at http://www.standard.co.uk/business/markets/a-demerger-cure-for-the-ills-at-barclays-9136665.html

businesses to raise their own capital and attract investors. In this context, the remarks of Mr T.V. Raghunath, Executive Director, Kotak Mahindra Investment Banking, is worth to be mentioned, 'Companies which have more than one business and the smaller business is not recognised in valuations of these companies are going for demergers'.

The other reason for the demerger is the split among family members. Most of the experts state that demerger creates more value for the shareholders in the long run than mergers since the re-rating of shares begins immediately after the demerger announcement. If a company hives off a division and lists it as a new company, the combined valuation of the demerged entities is often greater than the market price of the parent company before the split. After the parting, one plus one is not two but almost three. That's because though there is no addition to the assets of the two companies, the new company is usually more focused. As a result, the market re-rates the parent company and assigns a value to the newborn entity.

11.2 Conceptualization of Demerger

A demerger is the opposite of a merger (the practice of combining several companies under one corporate roof). In other words, demerger is a technique of corporate restructuring in which an independent company is created from a parent company. A demerger hives off parts of a company into separate operations in a belief that they will perform better that way. For instance, Rolls-Royce Motors was created from the demerger of the Rolls-Royce car business from Rolls-Royce Limited in 1973. Presently, many Indian companies are also looking at this form of restructuring for lucrative business opportunities.

The main objective behind a demerger is to provide for a clear, precise and undistracted focus on a core business for the parent company. The new company does not depend on or compete for resources allocation with the parent company. Demerger motivates the management to perform better and experiment with new opportunities available. The process of a demerger is more or less the same as that of a merger, with the difference being that merger takes place to integrate the companies, while demerger takes place to disintegrate the segments of a company. Some examples of demergers in India are the demerger of Aptech Computers from Apple Computers Ltd and the demerger of Sandoz India Ltd from the parent company, Sandoz. The following example will clarify the concept of demerger further.

When one company, say, X Ltd having 10 undertakings, transfers one or more of its undertakings to a new company, say, Y Ltd, it is a case of demerger. X Ltd is the demerged company and Y Ltd is the resulting company. A hypothetical example is given in Figure 11.1 where pre-demerger and post-demerger situations are presented in a simple situation.

11.3 Definitions

Different authors and authorities have defined demerger in different ways:

a. *Srinivas R. Kandula* (2001) opines that 'the demerger relates to conversion of a business or division, in a diversified company into a separate new company accompanied by free distribution of its shares to the existing shareholders, i.e. shareholders of the original company'.
b. *Ravi M. Kishore* (2003) states that demerger or spin-off is done for strategic reasons and in this, a corporate body splits into two or more corporate bodies and the assets are transferred to each of these bodies and is characterized with the separation of management and accountability.

Figure 11.1 Pre- and Post-demerger Compared

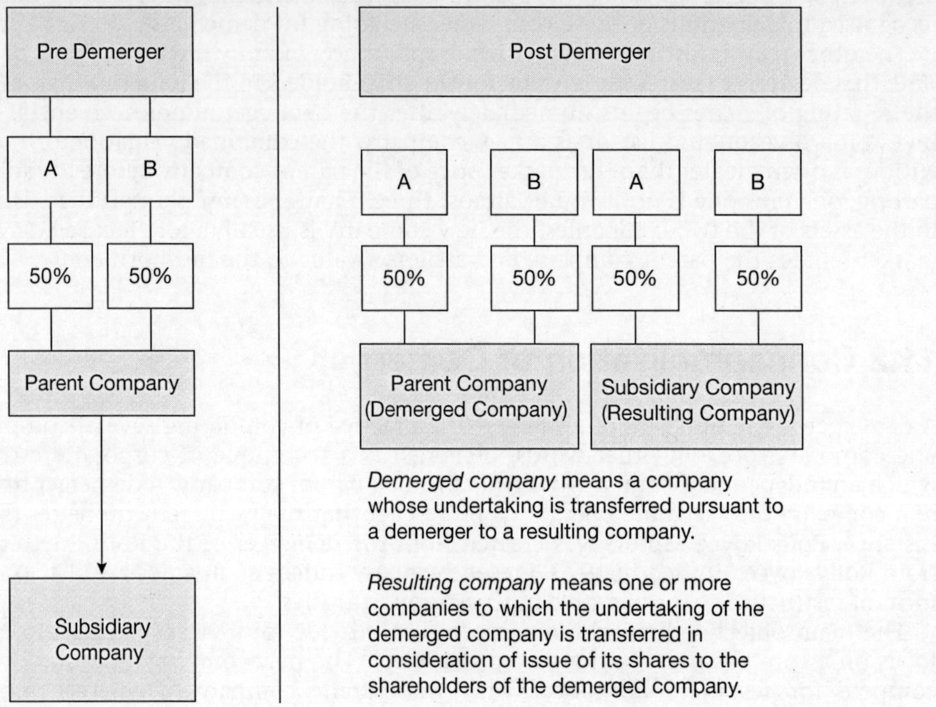

Source: Author's own.

c. *Wikipedia.org* defines demerger in the financial context as a specialized form of spin-out which is used to create a new public company as it simplifies the process of listing the shares on a public stock exchange.
d. According to *Victoria Strong* (2005), 'Broadly, a demerger refers to a situation where an entity undertakes a re-organisation of its operations and structure, leaving its members in the same economic position as they were immediately before the re-organisation. It is a form of structural readjustment for corporations in which a corporate or trust group splits into two more entities or groups. In such cases, the underlying owners of the head entity will directly control each of the demerged entities or groups. Effectively, ownership of the demerged entity is passed from an indirect ownership by the shareholders of the head entity to a direct ownership of the demerged entity'.
e. In the words of *Agawam*, 'a demerger is a form of restructure in which investors in the head entity (for example, shareholders or unit-holders) gain direct ownership in an entity that they formerly owned indirectly (the "demerged entity"). Underlying ownership of the companies and/or trusts that formed part of the group does not change. The company or trust that ceases to own the entity is known as the "demerging entity". The entity that emerges has its own board of directors and, if listed on a stock exchange, have separate listings. The purpose of demerger is to revive a company's flagging commercial fortunes, or simply to lift its share price'.

f. A corporate strategy to sell off subsidiaries or divisions of a company is called demerger.
g. The Companies Act, 2013: It defines a demerger in relation to companies and includes transfers, pursuant to the scheme of arrangement by a 'demerged company' of one or more undertakings to any resulting company in such a manner as provided in section 2(19AA) of the Income-tax Act, 1961, subject to it fulfilling the conditions stipulated therein and shares allotted by the 'resulting company' to the shareholders of the demerged company against transfer of its assets and liabilities.
h. The Income-tax Act: The definition of 'demerger' as given under section 2(19AA) of the Income-tax Act is unduly restrictive and subject to various conditions. Some of the conditions mentioned are:

   i. The first condition is that all the property of the undertaking should become the property of the resulting company.
   ii. Conditions of sections 391 to 394 should be satisfied.
   iii. Similarly, all the liabilities relating to the undertaking immediately before the demerger should become the liabilities of the resulting company.
   iv. Explanation 2 provides that not only identified liabilities should be transferred to the resulting company, but also general borrowings in the ratio of the value of the assets transferred to the total value of the assets of the demerged company.
   v. Assets and liabilities have to be transferred at book value.

Thus, demergers are meant to do away with subsidiaries, sub-units, sub-divisions and so on. A new company is formed and, as a consequence, the assets and liabilities (at the book value) of the parent company are transferred to the newly formed company as decided. The new company has its separate and legal existence. The shareholders of the demerged company are issued shares of this new company. Neither purchase nor a sale transaction takes place in a demerger.

11.4 Procedural Aspects of Demerger

It is necessary that the articles of association should have the provision of reduction of its share capital in any way, and its memorandum of association should provide for demerger, division or split of the company in any way. Under the Companies Act, demerger is to be included within the compromise or arrangement and its procedure is as follows:

i. First of all, the division/unit to be 'demerged is identified'.
ii. Then, the decision regarding the 'appointed date for demerger' is taken.
iii. Separate balance sheets for the division to be demerged and rest of the company as on appointed date is prepared.
iv. The market valuation report of tangible and intangible assets being transferred is sought after, if necessary.
v. The balance sheets for both the divisions, to be demerged and rest of the company, are audited by the statutory auditors.
vi. The proposed reduction in the share capital/reserves of the demerged company is worked out. A ratio of shares of the resulting company to be issued for number of shares that are reduced by the demerged company is also fixed.
vii. Subsequently, application for availability of name of the resulting company, which will acquire the unit to be spun off, and clearance of the name is obtained.
viii. A scheme of rearrangement is prepared next.

ix. The approval of scheme of demerger is finished at the board meeting of the demerged company. The company is required to pass a special resolution here, which is subject to the confirmation by the court by making an application.

x. After that an application to the High Court, where the registered office of the demerged company is situated, is made for an order convening separate meetings of the creditors, shareholders, or any class of them. The notice to the shareholders/creditors convening the meeting for the approval will usually consist of the following detail:

   a. Full details of the scheme
   b. Effect of the scheme on shareholders, creditors and employee
   c. Details of the valuation report

Notice of the meeting must be given to the creditors and/or members and sent individually to each shareholder/creditor. Each notice must be accompanied by a copy of the scheme, explanatory statement and a proxy form. The notice of the meeting must be advertised in such newspapers and in such manner as the judge may direct. The chairman of the meeting or other person directed to issue the advertisement and notices must file an affidavit within the prescribed time before the date of the meeting showing that the directions regarding issue of notices and advertisements have been duly complied with. On the date of the meeting, the decisions of the meetings must be ascertained only be taking a poll.

xi. Afterwards, the scheme obtains the approval of the court to convene general body meeting.

xii. Also, the scheme gets its approval at the creditors' meeting.

xiii. *Filing chairman's report on the outcome of the meetings with the high court:* The Chairman of each meeting must file a report in the court within that time fixed by the judge or where no time has been fixed, within 7 days after the conclusion of the meeting. The report must state accurately the number of creditors or class of creditors or number of members or class of members, as the case may be, who were present and who voted at the meeting either in person or by proxy, their individual values and the way they voted. The report shall be in Form 39 annexed to the Companies (Court) Rules, 1959.

xiv. *Filing petition in the high courts:* Where the proposed demerger is approved by the various meetings with or without modification, the company must present the petition to the court, for confirmation of the demerger within prescribed days of the filing of the chairman's report.

xv. The court shall fix a date for hearing of the petition and direct advertising in the same newspapers in which the notices of the meetings were advertised or in such other papers as the court might direct.

xvi. If the court sanctions the demerger, it may give such directions as it considers necessary for the proper working of the demerger. The certified copy of the order must be filed within prescribed days from the date of the order or such other time as may be fixed by the court.

xvii. Applications for orders in connection with the demerger or for any variation and so on shall be made by Judges Summons supported by an affidavit for directions as to the proceedings to be taken. Notice of the summons shall be given in such manner and to such person as the court may direct. On hearing the summons, the court may make such order or directions as may be necessary.

xviii. Incorporate the company that will be the resulting company.

xix. Carry out the transfer of assets and liabilities.

xx. Intimate about the demerger to all the concerned parties and authorities.

xxi. Obtain/endorse licenses.

11.5 Effects of Demerger

a. Tax neutrality of the assets transferred to the resulting company.
b. To extend the benefit of carry forward of loss or depreciation relating to the transferred undertaking to the resulting company.
c. To extend the benefits like sections 80IA, 80IB and so on to the split-off unit.
d. To allow the expenditure incurred for demerger.
e. Tax neutrality of the demerger for the shareholders of the demerged company.

11.6 Applicability

A demerger in India is applicable in the following cases:

a. Companies incorporated under the Companies Act, 2013.
b. Any authority or a body constituted or established under a central, state or provincial act
c. A local authority
d. A public sector company
e. A foreign company
f. Any institution, association or body assessed as a company or declared by the Central Board of Direct Taxes (CBDT) as a company.

11.7 Legal Aspects of Demerger

According to sub-section (19AA) of section 2 of the Income-tax Act, 1961:

> "demerger" in relation to companies, means transfer, pursuant to a scheme of arrangement under sections 230 to 234 of the Companies Act, 2013, by a demerged company of its one or more undertakings to any resulting company in such a manner that:
>
> i. all the property of the undertaking, being transferred by the demerged company, immediately before the demerger, becomes the property of the resulting company by virtue of the demerger;
> ii. all the liabilities relatable to the undertaking, being transferred by the demerged company, immediately before the demerger, become the liabilities of the resulting company by virtue of the demerger;
> iii. the property and the liabilities of the undertaking or undertakings being transferred by the demerged company are transferred at values appearing in its books of account immediately before the demerger;
> iv. the resulting company issues, in consideration of the demerger, its shares to the shareholders of the demerged company on a proportionate basis;
> v. the shareholders holding not less than three-fourths in value of the shares in the demerged company (other than shares already held therein immediately before the demerger, or by a nominee for, the resulting company or, its subsidiary) become shareholders of the resulting company or companies by virtue of the demerger, otherwise than as a result of the acquisition of the property or assets of the demerged company or any undertaking thereof by the resulting company;
> vi. the transfer of the undertaking is on a going concern basis;

the demerger is in accordance with the conditions, if any, notified under sub-section (5) of section 72A by the Central Government in this behalf.

Explanation 1: For the purposes of this clause, "undertaking" shall include any part of an undertaking, or a unit or division of an undertaking or a business activity taken as a whole, but does not include individual assets or liabilities or any combination thereof not constituting a business activity.

Explanation 2: For the purposes of this clause, the liabilities referred to in sub-clause (ii), shall include:

a. the liabilities which arise out of the activities or operations of the undertaking;
b. the specific loans or borrowings (including debentures) raised, incurred and utilized solely for the activities or operations of the undertaking; and
c. in cases, other than those referred to in clause (a) or clause (b), so much of the amounts of general or multipurpose borrowings, if any, of the demerged company as stand in the same proportion which the value of the assets transferred in a demerger bears to the total value of the assets of such demerged company immediately before the demerger.

Explanation 3: For determining the value of the property referred to in sub-clause (iii), any change in the value of assets consequent to their revaluation shall be ignored.

Explanation 4: For the purposes of this clause, the splitting up or the reconstruction of any authority or a body constituted or established under a Central, State or Provincial Act, or a local authority or a public sector company, into separate authorities or bodies or local authorities or companies, as the case may be, shall be deemed to be a demerger if such split up or reconstruction fulfils such conditions as may be notified in the Official Gazette, by the Central Government.

From the above definition, the following points emerge about demergers:

i. Demerger is essentially a scheme of arrangement under sections 230 to 234 of the Companies Act, 2013, requiring approval by:
   - a majority of shareholders holding shares representing three-fourths value in meeting convened for the purpose; and
   - sanction of the high court.
ii. Demerger involves 'transfer' of one or more 'undertakings'.
iii. The transfer of 'undertakings' is by the demerged company, which is otherwise known as the transferor company. The company to which the undertaking is transferred is known as the resulting company, which is otherwise known as the 'transferee company'.

11.8 Taxation Aspects of Demerger

a. Taxation of shareholders in demerged company

i. Dividend*:* Section 2(22) has been amended by inserting a new clause (v) to provide that no dividend income shall arise in the hands of shareholders of the demerged company on demerger.
ii. Capital gains*:* A new clause (vid) in section 47 has been inserted to provide that no capital gains shall arise to shareholders of the demerged company on account of receipt of any shares from the resulting company.

b. Tax benefits to resulting company

i. Expenses incurred for the purpose of demerger shall be allowed at 20% every year from the year in which the demerger takes place.
ii. Depreciation shall be apportioned between the demerged company and the resulting company in the ratio of the number of days for which the assets were used by them.
iii. The accumulated losses and unabsorbed depreciation in a demerger shall be allowed to be carried forward by the resulting company.
iv. Benefits available for demerger are also extended to authorities or boards set up by the central or state government.

Note that there is no lock in period for demergers like in case of amalgamation.

Comments: Clause (iv) in section 2(19AA) provides that the consideration should consist only of shares in the sub-resulting company and composite consideration in the form of shares and cash or shares and debentures and so on are not covered for availing of the exemption.

Courts' View:

i. The Gujarat High Court, in *CIT* v. *Gautam Sarabhani Trust,* (1988) 173 ITR 216, held that exemption under section 47 will not be available if there is composite consideration.
ii. The Madras High Court, in *CIT* v. *MCTM Corporation Pvt. Ltd.*, (1996) 221 ITR 524, held that exemption under section 47 shall be available even if composite consideration is given.

Suggestions:

i. It is suggested that suitable amendments may be made to ensure that even if the resulting company issues composite consideration it would come within the scope of the definition of demerger. The difficulties arising in the case of odd lots should also be taken care of.
ii. Further, it is suggested that the consideration received in the form of cash may be required to be invested in approved securities with a suitable lock in period.

c. Amortization of expenditure in case of demerger (section 35DD)

Expenses by an Indian company incurred after 1 April 1999 for the demerger of an undertaking shall be amortised at 20% each year starting from the year in which amalgamation or demerger takes place.

d. Cost of shares acquired in the scheme of demerger (section 49)

Cost of acquisition of shares in the resulting company shall be the amount which bears to the cost of acquisition of shares held in the demerged company the same proportion as the net book value of assets transferred in a demerger bears to the net worth of the demerged company immediately before such merger (section 49(2C)). The cost of acquisition of shares in the demerged company shall be reduced by the proportion being the ratio which the net book value of the assets transferred bears to the net worth of the demerged company (section 49(2D)).

11.9 Demerger Versus Reconstruction

As already discussed, 'demerger' means transfer, pursuant to a scheme of arrangement under respective sections of the Companies Act by the demerged company of its one or more undertakings to a new company formed for the purpose, known as the resulting company, in such a manner that all the property of the undertaking, being transferred by the demerged company becomes the property of the resulting company by virtue of the demerger; all the liabilities relatable to the undertaking, being transferred by the demerged company, become the liabilities of the resulting company by virtue of the demerger; the property and the liabilities of the undertaking or undertakings being transferred by the demerged company are transferred at values appearing in its books of account immediately before the demerger.

In the case of reconstruction, a new company (hereinafter referred to as 'transferee company') is formed, the existing company (hereinafter referred to as 'transferor company') is dissolved by passing a special resolution for members voluntary winding up and authorizing the liquidator to transfer the undertaking, business, assets and liabilities of the transferor company to the transferee company. The transferee company pays the consideration by issue and allotment of its shares to the shareholders of the transferor company in accordance with the predetermined share exchange ratio. In this process, the old company exists with substantially the same shareholders, same undertaking and business.

The difference between the two terms comes to the fore only when a scheme of arrangement is framed for sanction by the court. Demerger forms part of a scheme of compromise or arrangement within the ambit of sections 230 to 234 of the Companies Act, 2013. In addition, demergers that envisage the reduction of share capital will attract other provisions of the Companies Act, 2013, including sections 235 and 236.

One of the methods for achieving a demerger is through a scheme of reconstruction. A demerger represents a milestone and is not the final step in the process of corporate restructuring. After the demerger, companies can pursue their separate strategies to enhance shareholder value and further streamline their respective portfolios.

11.10 Demerger Versus Hiving-off

There is a common misconception in the corporate world that demerger and hiving-off are similar as far as the Indian corporate scenario is concerned and, hence, undertaking corporate restructuring using any one of the two modes for investment purposes, for raising capital or for increasing profits through cost reduction, does not make any difference. However, it is fallacious. The major divergences between these two are as follows:

i. *Consideration:* In the case of hiving-off, the payment of a lump sum sale consideration is required in respect of transfer of an undertaking by slump sale. However, in demerger the resulting company issues, in consideration of the demerger, its shares to the shareholder of the demerged company on a proportionate basis.
ii. *Valuation of Asset:* In hiving-off, values are not assigned to individual assets and liabilities of the undertaking, whereas in case of demerger, the assets and liabilities of the demerged company are transferred at the value appearing at the books of accounts immediately before the demerger to the resulting company.
iii. *Carry Forward of Depreciation:* In hiving-off, unabsorbed depreciation/loss can be carried forward only by a transferor company, whereas in the case of demerger, the resulting company avails the benefit of such depreciation/loss.

iv. *Cost of Assets in Hands of the Transferee:* In a slump sale, to determine the actual cost of assets transferred, the lump sum consideration received is apportioned in a fair and reasonable manner among the assets, whereas in the case of demerger the assets are valued at the book value as appearing in the books of the transferor.

11.11 Advantages of Demerger

The rationale behind a demerger, tracking stock or carve-out is that 'the parts are greater than the whole'.

i. *Help a company raise additional equity funds*: This corporate restructuring technique, which involves the separation of a business unit or subsidiary from the parent, can help a company raise additional equity funds.
ii. *Shareholders get better information*: Most importantly, shareholders get better information about the business unit because it issues separate financial statements. This is particularly useful when a company's traditional line of business differs from the separated business unit.
iii. *Investors are better equipped*: With separate financial disclosure, investors are better equipped to gauge the value of the parent corporation. The parent company might attract more investors and, ultimately, more capital.
iv. *Reduce internal competition*: Also, separating a subsidiary from its parent can reduce internal competition for corporate funds. For investors, that's great news: it curbs the kind of negative internal wrangling that can compromise the unity and productivity of a company.
v. *Motivates employees:* For employees of the new separate entity, there is a publicly traded stock to motivate and reward them. Stock options in the parent often provide little incentive to subsidiary managers, especially because their efforts are buried in the firm's overall performance.
vi. *Enhancing responsibility and accountability:* As each division has its separate heads, their progress can be monitored more effectively. This triggers performance pressure and eventually brings out positive returns, better accountability and enhanced responsibility.
vii. *De-cluttering management processes*: Spin-offs provide an opportunity to cut out unnecessary and redundant activities out of business processes, techniques and methods. It helps streamline the processes and de-clutter. This induces efficiency at various levels and proper utilization of resources in the organizations, both the parent company and the divisions.
viii. *Defence against hostile takeover:* Demerger is also a valuable defensive strategy. It helps safeguard the 'crown jewel' (most lucrative segment of business) from the predator (acquirer). It makes the company look like risky and non-attractive to the acquirer so as to save the most important unit.
ix. *Concentrate on core competencies and activities:* Demerger helps in reducing the diversion of resources and help in integrating the resources. This facilitates the business leaders to identify the core area where the company can have a competitive edge in case of product, service or processes. Further, resources are dedicated in one direction and the core competencies are developed.
x. *Reduction of excessive government intervention:* In the case of over-diversified and inflated business organizations, the government intervenes to ensure that the company does not have monopoly capacity or intention. This calls for complicated compliances, which may reduce the profitability of the firm.

xi. *Specific corporate bodies for specialized business:* The division helps in dividing inputs according to specialized activities that may build efficiency in the organization.
xii. *Family business segregation:* At times, the ancestral family businesses are split. In that case, to justify the partition among the family members, a demerger of segments may seem an optimal solution.
xiii. *Offsetting diseconomies of large scale:* Sometimes, the companies outgrow themselves and the cost of production also rises due to large amounts of production, and the overall profitability starts to decline. In this case, demerger may help in controlling production activities and costs. This helps to counter diseconomies of scale.

Therefore, a demerger may not always have negative reasons or pessimistic basis. A demerger may take place to safeguard the interest of the company, to grow, to avoid losses, or to increase profitability also.

11.12 Disadvantages of Demerger

i. *Harder to tap credit markets*: Demerged firms are likely to be substantially smaller than their parents, possibly making it harder to tap credit markets resulting costlier finance that may be affordable only for larger companies.
ii. *Difficult to attract interest of institutional investors*: The smaller size of the firm may mean that it has less representation on major indexes, making it more difficult to attract interest from institutional investors.
iii. *Losing the synergy*: Meanwhile, there are the extra costs that the parts of the business face if separated. When a firm divides itself into smaller units, it may be losing the synergy that it had as a larger entity. For instance, the division of expenses, such as marketing, administration and R&D, into different business units may cause redundant costs without increasing overall revenues.
iv. *Loss of economies of scale:* If a company is not already experiencing diseconomies of scale and a demerger is done, the cost of production may get affected and profitability may suffer in this case.
v. *Increased costs and overheads:* By creating a separate entity, a number of costs may increase that can affect profitability. This may require duplication of resource inputs or equipment, which may add to the costs. The viability of additional expenditure should be cautiously evaluated.
vi. *Lower turnover and profits:* Due to the possibility of increasing costs, limited funds and challenge to establish the firm as a new identity, there may be teething problems for the new segment that may yield lesser profits than expected.
vii. *Company's new identity:* This is a challenge for business leaders to position and perform above expectations of stakeholders as a new identity as the company as a new identity is prone to be judged and scrutinized critically.
viii. *The new public issue appeal:* The temptation of selling shares of the new company by its shareholders may depress the market value of its shares. This is counter to the objective for formulating a spin-off. If this phenomenon is not controlled, it can negatively affect the valuation of the new divisions.

Thus, the decision of a demerger has to be taken with due diligence, and any frivolous moves by any of the related companies may be detrimental to the value of the firm in the market.

11.13 Types of Demerger

There are following types of demergers:

a. *Divestitures*: In this case, an undertaking is being sold to an outside party.
b. *Spin-off*: Where the holding company distributes its shares in a subsidiary company to its shareholders, this type of demerger is known as spin-off.
c. *Equity carved out*: In this case, the parent company allows some small part of its shareholding in its subsidiary to be sold out to public and enjoys control by holding controlling interest.
d. *Split up*: In this case, the parent company splits into two or more parts and ceases to exist.
e. *Split off*: It is the case of reorganization of controlling interest. Shareholders of the parent company get shares in the subsidiary company in exchange of their shares in the parent company.

11.14 Practical Scenarios to Understand Demerger

Scenario 1

The scenario presented below identified two companies where one company wants to separate a division and another company wants to invest in that division, making the demerger process more logical.

a. Company A, a listed company, has an integrated complex of chemical plants. It also has division A1, which does not have synergy with the rest of integrated plants. Company A considers this a bad investment and wants to sell.
b. Company B, also a listed company, has an integrated complex of chemical plants. The company is interested in buying the division A1 as it considers the division having better synergy with its other divisions.
c. Both companies and their plants are located in the same state at a distance of 200 km from each other.
d. Company A has incurred ₹900 million on putting up division A1, including the working capital requirements. Shareholders are ready to sell the division at book value. Company A has incurred this amount in the following manner:
   - ₹200 million through promoters' loan.
   - ₹200 million through internal accruals.
   - ₹200 million by way of working capital loan from the consortium of two banks.
   - ₹300 million by way of term loan from the same consortium.

Planning Payment of Purchase Consideration and Legal and Commercial Matters

a. Company A is having cash crunch and wants early solution to the same. The company requires some amount of purchase consideration in cash and some amount in the form of share in Company B as investment. The payment of purchase consideration can be planned as follows:

i. ₹20 million will be paid as cash. This amount of ₹200 million can be paid by company B through internal accruals or it can be raised through right issue of shares or preferential allotments or through loans.
ii. Preferential allotment of shares from company B equivalent to ₹200 million to company A. Valuation of shares of company B shall be calculated as prescribed in preferential issue guidelines.
iii. Term loans and working capital loans can be swapped, that is, company B banker or some other consortium of two or more banks can swap the loan.
iv. Company B and its promoters can give their guarantee to the loan with the existing consortium, thus relieving company A and its promoters from any liability in this regard.

b. While raising ₹200 million by company B, the following provisions of different regulations should be kept in mind:

i. In case it is raised through right issue or preferential allotment, then provisions of continuous listing should be kept in mind. These provisions provide that public shareholding in the company should not be in any case less than 25%. In case it falls below 25%, company B requires bringing it back to 25% in such period as may be prescribed by rule 19A of the Securities Contracts (Regulation) Rules, 1956. At present, this rule provides a period of 12 months from the date of such fall.
ii. In case the acquirer acquires shares or voting rights in company B through preferential allotment which taken together with shares or voting rights already held by him and persons in acting with concert with him entitles him to exercise 25% or more of the voting rights in company B, then public announcement under the provisions of SEBI (Substantial Acquisition of Shares and Takeovers) Regulations, 2011 (hereinafter Takeover Regulations) is required to be made. Section 13(2)(g) of the Takeover Regulations provide that public announcement pursuant to an acquirer acquiring shares or voting rights in or control over the target company, under preferential issue, shall be made on the date on which the board of directors of the target company authorises such preferential issue.
iii. In case it is raised through loans, then the provisions of the Companies (Acceptance of Deposits) Rules, 2014, become applicable except where financial institution or bank stipulates that the promoters can bring loans to such extent while approving swapping of loans.

c. Apparently this method of payment of purchase consideration does not come in the definition of demerger as defined in section 2(19AA) of the Income-tax Act, 1961. Section 2(19AA) of the Income-tax Act provides as follows:

i. All the property of the undertaking, being transferred by the demerged company, immediately before the demerger, becomes the property of the resulting company by the virtue of demerger.
ii. All the liabilities relatable to the undertaking, being transferred by the demerged company, immediately before the demerger, become the liabilities of the resulting company by virtue of the demerger.
iii. The property and the liabilities of the undertaking or undertakings being transferred by the demerged company are transferred at values appearing in its books of account immediately before the demerger.
iv. The resulting company issues, in consideration of the demerger, its shares to the shareholders of the demerged company on a proportionate basis.

v. The shareholders holding not less than three-fourths in value of the shares in the demerged company (other than shares already held therein immediately before the demerger, or by a nominee for, the resulting company or its subsidiary) become the shareholders of the resulting company or companies by virtue of the demerger, otherwise than as a result of the acquisition of the property or assets of the demerged company or any undertaking thereof by the resulting company.
vi. The transfer of the undertaking is on a going concern basis.
vii. The demerger is in accordance with the conditions, if any, notified under sub-section (5) of section 72A by the central government in this behalf.

d. In such scenario, it is better to follow the slump sale method as mentioned in section 50B of the Income-tax Act, 1961. A business transfer agreement can be executed between the demerged company and the resulting company clearly defining the overall scope of such transfer.
e. The slump sale method is a faster method and takes around 3 to 6 months' time for completion.
f. Under the slump sale method, stamp duty on transfer of land will also become applicable and capital gain tax will also become leviable.

Scenario 2

In this scenario, all the terms are same as of scenario 1 except that company A has incurred the amount of ₹900 million in the following manner:

- ₹400 million through further issue of equity shares.
- ₹200 million by way of working capital loan from the consortium of two banks.
- ₹300 million by way of term loan from the same consortium.

Planning Payment of Purchase Consideration and Legal and Commercial Matters

a. Company A is not under cash pressure. The payment of purchase consideration can take following form:

    - Equity shares to be issued by company B (resulting company) to the shareholders of the company A (demerged company). The number of shares and nominal value of shares shall be such as calculated by the chartered accountant as prescribed. In listed companies' case, the price prevailing on the valuation date is the value of the shares provided shares are regularly traded.
    - Term loans and working capital loans can be swapped in the following manner: (a) company B banker or some other consortium of two or more banks can swap the loan; (b) company B and its promoters can give their guarantee to the loan with the existing consortium, thus relieving company A and its promoters from any liability.

b. This method of payment of purchase consideration comes in the definition of demerger as defined in section 2(19AA) of the Income-tax Act. Other conditions of this section also need to be complied.
c. This method under sections 230 to 233 of the Companies Act, 2013, takes around 12 to 18 months' time for completion.
d. Under this method, stamp duty on transfer of land (generally states exempt these type of schemes from stamp duty; however, few states have started taxing such

transactions) and capital gain tax under the Income-tax Act are not applicable on these transactions.

e. As per provisions of Section 10(1)(d)(ii) and (iii) of the SEBI (Substantial Acquisition of Shares and Takeovers) Regulations, 2011, these regulations are not applicable to the schemes as envisaged in this scenario.
f. However, provisions regarding continuous listing should be taken care of.

In both scenarios, while making planning the provisions of the Competition Act also need to be taken care of.

11.15 Valuation Aspects

a. One of the most important part of the demerger scheme is the process of valuation and it involves:
   - Evaluating the value of the merging company or its business and/or of its shares
   - Evaluating the securities of the issuing company on a standalone basis
   - Determining the exchange ratio for the securities so as to ensure fair consideration.
b. The report is subject to scrutiny by the lending and investment institutions, regional director and official liquidator.
c. Approval of the scheme and the valuation report by a majority of the shareholders and creditors does not mean that the court is bound to treat the same as final. The court can view it from the test of fairness.
d. On some occasions, the court does appoint independent valuers where dissenting shareholders or creditors make a strong case for such an action.
e. Valuation not required in the case of merger of a wholly owned subsidiary.

11.16 Methods of Valuation Used in Corporate Restructuring

a. Earnings-based methods
b. Asset-based methods
c. Market value of shares (stock market quotations)

Methods of Accounting:

a. The pooling of interest method
b. Purchase method

Changes in Shareholders Wealth after Demerger

Case 1: Television Eighteen India Limited

Demerged Company	:	Television Eighteen India Limited
Resulting Company	:	Network 18 Fincap Limited
Effective Date	:	27 September 2006

Scheme of Demerger : The shareholders will get the equity shares of the resulting company, that is, Network 18 Fincap Limited in the ratio of 12 equity shares of ₹5.00 each for every 10 shares of ₹10.00 each held by them in the company. Subsequently, 14 equity shares of ₹5.00 each of Television Eighteen India Limited will be issued in lieu of every 10 equity shares of ₹10.00 each held by the members of the company.

Eligibility Date : 24 November 2006

Shareholders' Wealth:

Table 1A Pre-demerger Shareholders' Wealth in Television Eighteen India Limited

Company	*Equity Shares*	*Average Pre-demerger Share Price*	*Shareholders' Wealth*
Television Eighteen India Limited	100	₹616.61	₹61,661.00

Table 1B Post-demerger Shareholders' Wealth in Television Eighteen India Limited

Company	*Equity Shares*	*Average Post-demerger Share Price*	*Shareholders' Wealth*
Television Eighteen India Limited	140	₹639.20	₹89,488.00
Network 18 Fincap Limited	120	432.97	51,956.40
Total Shareholders' Wealth After Demerger			**₹141,444.40**

From Tables 1A and 1B, it is seen that there has been an increase in the shareholders wealth of Television Eighteen India Limited after demerger by 129.39%.

Case 2: Great Eastern Shipping Company Limited

Demerged Company : Great Eastern Shipping Company Limited

Resulting Company : Great Offshore Limited

Effective Date : 16 October 2006

Scheme of Demerger : The shareholders will get the Equity shares of the resulting company, that is, Great Offshore Ltd in the ratio of 1 equity share of ₹10.00 each credited as fully paid-up in cash for every five equity shares of ₹10.00 each held by the members of the company. Subsequently, five equity shares of the company shall be reduced to 4 equity shares of ₹10.00 each.

Eligibility Date : 8 November 2006

Shareholders' Wealth:

Table 2A Pre-demerger Shareholders' Wealth in Great Eastern Shipping Company Limited

Company	*Equity Shares*	*Average Pre-demerger Share Price*	*Shareholders' Wealth*
Great Eastern Shipping Company Limited	100	₹256.36	₹25,636.00

Table 2B Post-demerger Shareholders' Wealth in Great Eastern Shipping Company Limited

Company	*Equity Shares*	*Average Post-demerger Share Price*	*Shareholders' Wealth*
Great Eastern Shipping Company Limited	80	₹209.41	₹16,752.50
Great Offshore Limited	20	703.81	14,076.50
Total Shareholders' Wealth after Demerger			**₹30,829.00**

From Tables 2A and 2B, it is seen that there has been an increase in the shareholders' wealth of Great Eastern Shipping Company after demerger by 20.26%.

Case 3: Zee Entertainment Enterprise Limited

Demerged Company : Zee Entertainment Enterprise Limited

Resulting Company : Zee News Limited and Wire and Wireless India Limited

Effective Date : 22 November 2006

Scheme of Demerger : Shareholders of the company received 45 shares of Zee News Limited and 50 shares of Wire and Wireless India Limited for every 100 shares held in the company.

Eligibility Date : 16 December 2006

Shareholders' Wealth:

Table 3A Pre-demerger Shareholders' Wealth in Zee Entertainment Enterprise Limited

Company	*Equity Shares*	*Average Pre-demerger Share Price*	*Shareholders' Wealth*
Zee Entertainment Enterprise Limited	100	₹291.72	₹29,172.00

Table 3B Post-demerger Shareholders' Wealth in Zee Entertainment Enterprise Limited

Company	*Equity Shares*	*Average Post-demerger Share Price*	*Shareholders' Wealth*
Zee Entertainment Enterprise Limited	100	₹277.09	₹27,709.00
Wire and Wireless India Limited	50	89.11	4,455.50
Zee News Limited	45	40.32	1,814.40
Total Shareholders' Wealth after Demerger			**₹33,978.90**

From Tables 3A and 3B, it is seen that there has been an increase in the shareholders' wealth of Zee Entertainment Enterprise Limited after demerger by 16.48%.

Case 4: Camlin Limited

Demerged Company : Camlin Limited
Resulting Company : Camlin Fine Chemical Limited
Effective Date : 17 December 2006
Scheme of Demerger : The shareholders will get the equity shares of the resulting company, that is, Camlin Fine Chemicals Limited in the ratio of 1 equity share each credited as fully paid-up in cash for every 1 equity share each held by the members of the company.
Eligibility Date : 19 February 2007

Shareholders' Wealth:

Table 4A Pre-demerger Shareholders' Wealth in Camlin Limited

Company	*Equity Shares*	*Average Pre-demerger Share Price*	*Shareholders' Wealth*
Camlin Limited	100	₹186.91	₹18,691.00

Table 4B Post-demerger Shareholders' Wealth in Camlin Limited

Company	*Equity Shares*	*Average Post-demerger Share Price*	*Shareholders' Wealth*
Camlin Limited	100	₹135.09	₹13,509.00
Camlin Fine Chemical Limited	100	53.95	5,395.00
Total Shareholders' Wealth after Demerger			**₹18,905.00**

From Tables 4A and 4B, it is seen that there has not been any significant difference in shareholders' wealth of Camlin Limited before and after the demerger as there has been increase in earnings of shareholders' wealth by 1.14%.

Observation: From the above studies, it is observed that, the samples under study excluding Camlin Limited have shown significant difference in the shareholders' wealth before and after demerger. In other words, shareholders' wealth has appreciated corresponding to the demerger. In 80% of the sample, there was negative synergy in their diversified business. Thus, due to demergers or spin-offs, the companies were successful in getting proper valuation of their various diversified businesses.

11.17 Some Important Considerations in Demerger

Demerged vs. Resulting Company: A demerger results in the transfer by a company of one or more of its undertakings to another company. The company whose undertaking is transferred is called the demerged company.

The company (or the companies) to which the undertaking is transferred is referred to as the resulting company.

According to sub-section (19AAA) of section 2 of the Income-tax Act, 1961, 'demerged company' means the company whose undertaking is transferred, pursuant to a demerger, to a resulting company.

According to sub-section (41A) of section 2 of the Income-tax Act, 'resulting company' means one or more companies (including a wholly owned subsidiary thereof) to which the undertaking of the demerged company is transferred in a demerger, and the resulting company in consideration of such transfer of undertaking issues shares to the shareholders of the demerged company and includes any authority or body or local authority or public sector company or a company established, constituted or formed as a result of demerger.

Appointed Date: It is the date on which assets and liabilities of the transferor company vest in and stand transferred to the transferee company.

a. Accounts on the appointed date form the basis for valuation of shares and determination of the share exchange ratio.
b. Appointed date is relevant for the purpose of assessment of income of the transferor and transferee companies.

The appointed date signifies the basic condition to be satisfied before a restructuring exercise is recognized as demerger for the purposes of tax laws.

The other way of looking at the appointed date is to consider the date as the demarking line to rearrange the affairs of the companies before the date so that, thereafter, there arises no need to revisit as to which of the assets have to be kept with the demerged company and that with the resulting company. This will cover tangible, intangible assets as well as HR, their retirement dues and so on. The assets will also include assets held on lease, hire purchase, assets used by the executives and key personnel in their residences and so on. If the demerger is followed by any infusion of fresh capital by foreign partners in the resulting company, then every single item of asset, liability, key personnel and so on will become very important and assume a lot of significance, and lack of proper planning in the initial days will create unavoidable issues arising at a later date. In the case of liabilities, it is better to record all the liabilities in the books of accounts so that the split is done in the proper way. This is especially true for contingent liabilities.

Effective Date: It is the date on which scheme is complete and effective, that is, a certified copy of the high court order is filed with registrar of company or the last of the approvals obtained.

From the effective date, the demerger becomes effective and the transferor company stands changed/dissolved.

Record Date: It is the cut-off date on which details of owners or shareholders for the companies are taken for the purpose of corporate action.

Exchange Ratio: The valuer determines the value of the demerged undertaking and original company, and in the process, after considering all the relevant data, fixes the exchange ratio, which later is incorporated in the scheme of arrangement placed before the high court for its approval.

Multiple Choice Questions

1. X Ltd. having 10 undertakings transfers two of its undertakings to a new company, Y Ltd. Here the status of Y Ltd is
   a. Demerged company
   b. Acquiring company
   c. Resulting company
   d. Acquired company

2. Demerger in India is applicable to
   a. Companies incorporated under the Companies Act, 2013
   b. A public sector company
   c. A foreign company
   d. All of the above

3. As per Income-tax Act, no _______ income shall arise in the hands of shareholders of the demerged company on demerger.
   a. Capital gain
   b. Dividend
   c. Interest
   d. None

4. As per the Income-tax Act, no _______ shall arise to shareholders of the demerged company on account of receipt of any shares from the resulting company.
   a. Capital gain
   b. Dividend
   c. Interest
   d. None

5. Expenses by an Indian company incurred after 1 April 1999 for demerger of an undertaking shall be amortized at _______ each year starting from the year in which amalgamation or demerger takes place.
   a. 10%
   b. 20%
   c. 30%
   d. None

6. Which one of the following is not an advantage of demerger?
   a. Help a company raise additional equity funds
   b. Company's new identity
   c. Shareholders get better information
   d. Reduce internal competition

7. In which of the following type of demerger an undertaking is being sold to outside party?
   a. Divestitures
   b. Spin-off
   c. Equity carved out
   d. Split up

8. In which of the following methods stock market quotation is used for valuation in corporate restructuring?
   a. Earnings-based method
   b. Asset-based method
   c. Market value of shares
   d. None

9. It is the date on which assets and liabilities of the transferor company vest in and stand transferred to the transferee company.
   a. Appointed date
   b. Effective date
   c. Record date
   d. None

10. It is the cut-off date on which details of owners or shareholders for the companies are taken for the purpose of corporate action.
    a. Appointed date
    b. Effective date
    c. Record date
    d. None

Review Questions

1. State the concept of demerger. How is it different from a merger? Identify the salient features of a demerger.
2. List and explain the procedure for demerger under the Indian Companies Act, 1956.
3. What are the legal aspects of demerger? Provide suitable examples.
4. List the tax benefits of demergers to the resulting company.
5. What is a demerger? What are the various reasons for a firm to opt for a demerger?
6. How are demergers beneficial for a company?
7. 'Demergers may have their advantages and constraints'. Discuss the statement.
8. Enumerate the various constraints associated with demerger decisions.
9. Briefly highlight the major advantages and disadvantages of demergers.
10. Discuss the tax reliefs for the resulting company arising out of demerger.
11. Distinguish between:
    a. Demerger and reconstruction
    b. Demerger and hiving-off

Case in Action

Wockhardt: A Case of Demerger

Introduction

At a time when mergers and acquisitions seem to be the prescription of choice for most of the pharmaceutical companies worldwide, demerger was the kind of prescription the domestic pharmaceutical conglomerate Wockhardt had been looking desperately for long. The company, which had traditionally been a conglomerate operating in as diverse businesses as pharmaceuticals, agri-sciences, parentals and hospitals, had been losing focus and was not commanding the kind of valuations its peers like Ranbaxy and Dr. Reddy's were accorded; while Dr. Reddy's Lab and Ranbaxy enjoyed P/E multiple of more than 80, Wockhardt could manage just 50. Further, the company's woes stemmed from the fact that the core requirement of each of these businesses—capital, technology, and distribution strength—were diverse and hence required total focus. Also, while its peers like Dr. Reddy's and Ranbaxy have been pure pharma plays, Wockhardt's business portfolio comprised a mix of high-growth and low-growth businesses.

Demerger Dosages

To have focused businesses and improve shareholder wealth, the company engaged the services of McKinsey, a global management consultancy firm in 2000. The consultancy firm's major recommendations included splitting the company into two separate business entities to improve valuation. The vertical split was suggested so as to remove the drag of the large asset base of the non-pharma business or the life sciences business, which had been impacting the returns on net worth. Around 80% of the earnings (before interest and depreciation) of the company were from the pharma division, which had less than 35% of the total assets. Given this, a split made a lot of sense. The company believed that ROCE from the current levels of around 11% would move up to more than 30% for their pharma division while for life sciences division the same would go down to 6%. Further, the company's poor RONW (Return on Net Worth) of 11% then was also attributed to the life sciences business. The reason for such a large variation in the company's ROCE was the massive amounts of real estate assets in the books of the life sciences division. These assets were proving to be a drag on the group's overall profitability. The life sciences businesses, which accounted for only 25% of the overall revenues of the group, of this, agri-sciences, contributed 10%, parentals 10%, and hospital business 5%. However, according to industry experts and growth estimates life sciences division was expected to grow significantly at more than 25 to 30% for the next 3–4 years while pharma division was expected to grow at a lower rate of around 20%. To reap the benefits in these two areas it became clear that the company needed to be more focused on each of these businesses, which would have been not possible otherwise.

The rationale behind the demerger was to unlock the full potential of Wockhardt businesses by creating two separate companies. While Wockhardt Ltd. was planned to be totally focused on the knowledge-based pharmaceutical business at the same time concentrating on being globally competitive and creating large brands, Wockhardt Life Sciences Ltd. was decided to include IV fluids, agri-sciences and hospital business and leverage on the opportunity to realize its full growth potential in the next decade. It was also decided that each company would leverage the strength of the other's core services through outsourcing of various facilities like R&D in order to achieve optimization of resources and costs. The demerger came into effect from 1 January 2000. As a process of demerger, the existing company Wockhardt Ltd was renamed Wockhardt Life Sciences while the demerged entity, which comprises pharmaceutical business, was named Wockhardt Ltd. The agri-sciences business, parentals and hospital business were transferred to Wockhardt life sciences division. It is decided that common functions like projects division to be handled by life sciences while finance and R&D divisions will be under the control of Wockhardt and life sciences would outsource these functions from Wockhardt. As a result of the demerger, Wockhardt has become a focused pharmaceutical company, concentrating on developing knowledge-based businesses. The company's primary focus involves the manufacture and marketing of pharmaceutical formulations and bulk drugs, supported by strong research capabilities. As part of the other recommendations made by the consultancy firm, Wockhardt acquired Merind for ₹1 billion from the Tatas as part of the consolidation in the pharma business. This made sense as the product profiles of both the merging companies complemented each other well.

Growth Diagnosis: Post-demerger

Wockhardt registered a healthy growth rate in both the top line as well as bottom line during the first half of FY02. The company's sales grew by 15.6%, while its profit after tax increased by 39%. The company's operating profit during the period grew by an impressive 36%; this helped Operating Profit Margin (OPM) to improve by 280 basis points (bps) to 18.4% from 15.6% YoY. Net profit margin (NPM) too witnessed an improvement of 230 bps from 11.1% to 13.4%, during the period understudy. Another major positive aspect about the financial performance of the company is the fall in interest outgo. The interest expenditure declined by a substantial 42% during the first half of the current financial year. The company's ROCE also improved remarkably by 450 bps from 21.3% recorded in the last fiscal year ending 31 December 2000 to 25.8% in the 1HFY02, ending 30 June 2001. However, a hundred percent jump in tax outgo is a cause of concern. Nevertheless, on the whole, the performance of the company is an encouraging one.

Wockhardt Limited Financial & Operating Review Period ended 31 December, 2003 (in million ₹)						
	Wockhardt Ltd. (Q4)			***Wockhardt Ltd. (FY 2003)***		
Particulars	***2003***	***2002***	***Growth %***	***2003***	***2002***	***Growth %***
Revenue from Operations	1,995	1,773	12.5	7,658	7,416	3.3
Operating Expenditure	1,376	1,411	–2.5	5,634	5,626	0.1
R&D Expenditure	136	137	–0.7	444	404	9.9
Operating Profit	483	225	114.7	1,580	1,386	14.0
Operating Margin %	24.2%	12.7%	–	20.6%	18.7%	–
Interest	–44	17	–	–28	73	–
Depreciation	41	36	13.9	161	136	18.4
Profit from Operations	486	172	182.6	1,447	1,177	22.9
Other Income	4	8	–	13	17	–
Pre-tax profits	490	180	172.2	1,460	1,194	22.3
Provision for Tax: Current	35	1	3,400	103	80	28.8
Deferred	32	–4	–	23	26	–11.5
Profits after Tax	423	183	131.1	1,334	1,088	22.6
Paid-up Equity share capital	363	363	–	363	363	–

Business-wise Performance (in million ₹)

Business	***Q4 ended Dec 2003***	***Q4 ended Dec 2002***	***Growth %***	***Jan–Dec 2003***	***Jan–Dec 2002***	***Growth %***
Formulations	1,069	922	16	4390	4530	–3.1
Exports	837	758	10.4	2941	2419	21.6
Bulk drug: Domestic	90	94	–4.3	327	467	–29.9
Total	1,995	1773	12.5	7658	7416	3.3

Source: www.envestindia.com

Questions for Discussion

1. Explain the rationale behind the demerger of Wockhardt Ltd.
2. Critically examine the financial and operation performance of Wockhardt Ltd. in the post-demerger phase.

Case in Action

JK Industries: A Case Demerger

Introduction

JK Industries (JKI), the flagship company of the Hari Shankar Singhania Group is one of the leading automotive tyre manufacturers in India. The company which had diversified presence with business interest in Pharma, Sugar, Agriseeds and Tyres has decided to exit from non-tyre businesses and has undertaken a restructuring programme in this regard. By this restructuring exercise, the company has divested its Pharma business to JK Drugs & Pharmaceuticals Ltd (JKDPL) and is also in the process of spinning off its Sugar and Agribusiness to JK Sugar Ltd and JK Agri Genetics Ltd. respectively. Later JKI has divested its stake in JKPDL to TEVA Pharma of Israel thus existing from pharma sector. Post demerger and also the completion of capital restructuring at JK Industries pushed the company to 16th largest tyre manufacturer in the world. The merger of JK Tyre and Vikrant Tyres made JKI to cross turnover of over ₹20 billion in the year 2003.

Further, the company, which made a 51% strategic acquisition of Vikrant tyres in 1997 from the Karnataka government, has completed the modernization and expansion of Vikrant tyres. JKI manufactures tyres and tubes, and steel-belted radial tyres, under the brand name JK Tyres. For the manufacture of tyres, JKI has technical collaboration with General Tire International, United States. JKI will become the second largest player in the four-wheeler tyres segment on combined capacity basis (JK tyres + Vikrant tyres). The 'Rubber and Plastic New, USA' lists JK Industries as the 16th largest tyre manufacturer in the world.

JK Tyres introduced the dual-contact high-traction and high-performance 'Aquasonic' Steel Radial Car Tyre. It also developed India's first and only H-rated 'Ultima-XS' especially for Mercedes Benz. During the year 2000, in the truck and bus tyre segments—'Tanker Lug' and 'Jet Haul'—have been introduced as specific application products. In the LCV category, 'WL 407' tyre has been developed and 'Ultima-XP' car radial tyre has been developed with value-added features.

As part of its efforts towards enhancing export volumes of tyres, JKI through a wholly owned foreign subsidiary tied up with a Chinese company for sourcing light commercial vehicle (LCV) bias tyres for the export markets. It has opened a new office at Singapore through its subsidiary in exploring the possibility of opening up more offices abroad as part of its added thrust towards enhancing the company's export volumes and sales of truck and LCV tyres in the coming years.

The company has diversified into hybrid and high-yielding seeds by setting up JK Agri-genetics to produce cereals, seeds, pulses and so on. The company's sugar operation (JK Sugars) is located in UP and it has set up a 3,120 tonnes of cane per day (TCD) sugar project at Meerganj, UP.

JKI has also diversified into pharma business and set up facility to produce of 7-ADCA and semi-synthetic cephalosporins at Gajraula, UP. The plant that started commercial production of February 1995. Later, the company has hived off its pharma business to JK Drugs & Pharmaceuticals (JKDPL). Subsequently, JKI has divested its stake in JKPDL to TEVA Pharma of Israel, thus exiting from the pharma sector.

The company has four subsidiary investment companies, namely Hansdeep Investment, Hidrive Finance, Panchanan Investment, and Radial Finance. It also has three fully owned subsidiaries abroad—JK International, UK, JK Asia Pacific, Hong Kong and JK Asia Pacific(S) Pet Limited. The company, along with TIDCO, has promoted JK Pharma Chem. for the manufacture of penicillin-G.

Evaluating Financial Performance of the Company

Aimed at creating separate business with greater focus on their core competencies, JK Industries embarked on a demerger drive. The tremendous possibilities anticipated in this strategic restructuring resulted in strengthening market leadership, one step forward to achieve excellence. An idle look on certain key ratios, that indicate both operating and financial performance of the demerged company, will make the anticipation's realistic base more candid. Though the company's long-term debt–equity ratio remained higher than the industry average both during pre and post demerger period which has further increased after demerger, the tendency of company's increasing dependence on debt after hiving-off exposes its enhanced risk taking capability. This can be further fortified by the increased interest paying ability of the company during post demerger period. The other two ratios, fixed-asset turnover and inventory turnover, have also been improved after demerger showing a positive impact of the company's separation strategy on their operating performance. However, a different picture is visualized in case of current ratio and debtors turnover ratio where remarkable change after demerger is absent, rather a reverse situation calls for a sound receivables management of the company.

During comparison, one should not lose sight of the fact that the company's position with respect to industry was not better during the pre-demerger period, which also remained lower than the industry benchmark during the post-demerger period. However, compared to its pre-separation period, it bettered afterwards recognizing a hopeful impact of demerger.

Financial Performance Indicators Both During Pre- and Post-demerger Period

	Long-term Debt Equity		**Current**		**Fixed asset Turn over**		**Inventory Turn Over**		**Debtors Turnover**		**Interest Coverage**	
Ratio State	**JK**	**Ind**	**JK**	**Ind**	**JK**	**Ind**	**JK**	**Ind**	**JK**	**Ind**	**JK**	**Ind**
Pre Demerger	0.75	0.73	0.87	1.31	1.25	2.14	7.57	7.95	6.45	6.80	1.20	1.53
Post Demerger	1.37	0.67	0.87	1.13	1.63	2.31	9.94	8.63	6.09	8.44	1.36	2.48

Pre-demerger State

Year	**ROCE**	**RONW**	**EPS**
2001–02	7.69	1.76	3.51
2000–01	8.77	2.69	4.57
1999–00	10.40	5.20	9.12
1998–99	9.88	3.41	6.04
Total	36.74	13.06	23.24
Average	9.19	3.27	5.81

Post-demerger State

Year	**ROCE**	**RONW**	**EPS**
2006–07	14.71	17.38	21.21
2005–06	7.54	3.10	5.19
2004–05	5.34	2.21	4.19
2003–04	8.42	2.83	2.99
Total	36.01	25.52	33.58
Average	9.00	6.38	8.40

Depending on certain measuring tools, the analysis can be carried further to scan the impact of demerger on the financial performance of the company. Apparently, the company's average ROCE position looks worse in the post-demerger period than its pre-demerger counterpart but this is due to its earlier years' lower value. At the initial years of demerger, the company could not get the pace as desired which came in the later years showing almost twice ROCE in the year 2006–07 than the average ROCE of initial years. A similar trend is also observed in case of RONW and EPS of the company during the post-demerger period, implying the company's ability to utilize capital more efficiently towards increasing shareholder value. Though the average RONW of 6.38% during the post-demerger period is losing its comparability with the industry position but its remarkable improvement after hiving-off justifies separation, a timely taken strategy towards achieving excellence. Thus, the financial performance of the company is witnessing an elevated result, which can be more explicit if EPS of the company during the pre-demerger period is weighed with that of its post-separation counterpart. And the excessive high EPS, coupled with high RONW and ROCE in the year 2006–07, propagates the company's capability to hold the pace of growth it desired. Hence, the company's aim to pave the way for unlocking shareholders' value to excel in performance gets daylight through demerger by and large the indicators say so.

Evaluating Demerger as a Value-generating Strategy

Having gone through the analysis based on traditional measures, the success of strategic decision taken to hive-off has been established. Now, the desired view that demerger drives business to achieve excellence can further be tested and proved if the value-generating strength using shareholders value added (SVA), the measuring tool that considers both realized and unrealized value added is juxtaposed to its financial performance. SVA, that is, MVA plus dividend paid by the company during the period has been attempted to measure whether demerger generates value, both realized and unrealized, with a view to trace the rationality of the management's decision to hive-off. MVA, the spread between company's market capitalization and book value of capital as recommended by Stern Stewart, also forms the part of the present analysis to portray the company's value-creating capacity in terms of unrealized gain. Due to more volatility present in the Indian market the MVA, as recommended by Stern Stewart, has been altered as the excess of company's closing market capitalization over its opening counterpart after adjusting issue of bonus share or right share or any conversion into equity of preference shares or debentures so that the number of outstanding equity shares of the company remains the same between the two periods. MVA, which shows company's unrealized capital gain during the post-demerger period, leaves its pre-demerger counterpart far away to compare. This was possible due to increase in share price after the demerger takes place. Thus, the market's responsiveness to demerger is remarkable that fortifies demerger's ability to create value towards achieving excellence. The indication given by SVA showed a landmark increase waving a hope to keep its steadiness in the forthcoming years. As the shareholders expect competitive return on their investment through dividend and value appreciation, increase in SVA ensures them about the company's journey in a continuous growth path. One can easily find average SVA of ₹733.4 million during the post-demerger period compared with average SVA of ₹42.30 million during the pre-demerger period a justifiable evidence adopting demerger. Thus, focusing on their core business JK Industries was able to create value for its shareholders that smoothens the path to excel.

Average at a Glance

	Pre-demerger	***Post-demerger***
MVA	–3.77	65.59
SVA	4.23	73.34

Value Creation during Pre- and Post-demerger

Year	*SVA*	*MVA*
2006–07	20.97	12.65
2005–06	–27.98	–35.68
2004–05	204.42	196.93
2003–04	95.93	88.44
Total	293.34	262.34
Average	73.34	65.59

Year	*SVA*	*MVA*
2001–02	–8.07	–15.85
2000–01	–41.49	–48.40
1999–00	60.71	52.07
1998–99	5.75	–2.89
Total	16.90	–15.07
Average	4.23	–3.77

Source: Das et al. (2012).

Questions for Discussion

1. Critically examine the financial performance of JK Industries during its pre- and post-demerger periods and give your comments on it.
2. Is JK Industries demerger a value-generating strategy? Provide reasons in support of your answer.

Annexure I Balance Sheet

	2007	*2006*	*2005*	*2004*	*2003*	*2002*	*2001*	*2000*	*1999*	*1998*
SOURCES OF FUNDS:										
Share Capital	30.79	30.79	37.46	37.46	37.46	37.46	34.54	36.54	36.54	36.54
Reserves Total	503.13	560.93	745.14	818.76	856.53	875.45	573.07	585.07	594.78	616.29
Total Shareholders' Funds	533.92	591.72	782.60	856.22	893.99	912.91	607.61	621.61	631.32	652.83
Secured Loans	686.82	724.77	671.28	656.51	738.19	728.18	638.19	635.65	706.48	748.91
Unsecured Loans	228.13	219.10	159.22	94.16	99.87	130.86	91.62	36.19	25.19	33.50
Total Debt	914.95	943.87	830.50	750.67	838.06	859.04	729.81	671.84	731.67	782.41
Total Liabilities	1,448.87	1,535.59	1,613.10	1,606.89	1,732.05	1,771.95	1,337.42	1,293.45	1,362.99	1,435.24
APPLICATION OF FUNDS:										
Gross Block	2,156.07	2,084.22	1,938.72	1,884.26	1,855.63	1,809.81	1,118.81	1,049.16	982.03	902.35
Less: Accumulated Depreciation	957.27	860.03	764.74	677.15	590.80	507.51	433.55	382.75	333.76	288.49
Less: Impairment of Assets	0.00	0.00	0.00	0.00	0.00	0.00	0.00	0.00	0.00	0.00
Net Block	1,198.80	1,224.19	1,173.98	1,207.11	1,264.83	1,302.30	685.26	666.41	648.27	613.86
Lease Adjustment	0.00	0.00	0.00	0.00	0.00	0.00	0.00	0.00	0.00	0.00
Capital Work in Progress	20.34	22.51	61.63	16.43	7.02	11.63	7.79	11.16	67.80	113.26
Investments	62.60	61.46	250.04	252.26	252.02	252.63	498.27	498.35	486.26	403.20

(continued)

(continued)

	2007	**2006**	**2005**	**2004**	**2003**	**2002**	**2001**	**2000**	**1999**	**1998**
Current Assets, Loans and Advances										
Inventories	502.85	368.59	244.03	178.17	211.31	187.07	176.91	191.15	153.83	226.08
Sundry Debtors	435.52	477.89	411.79	449.52	412.59	342.49	198.49	197.53	181.25	230.35
Cash and Bank	29.22	39.32	36.11	38.23	25.32	39.86	55.17	18.88	41.01	26.63
Loans and Advances	132.59	127.72	120.90	110.38	137.14	148.13	108.84	94.70	122.76	202.41
Total Current Assets	1,100.18	1,013.52	812.83	776.30	786.36	717.55	539.41	502.26	498.85	685.47
Less: Current Liabilities and Provisions										
Current Liabilities	800.05	766.34	675.13	627.74	564.45	527.02	387.48	378.38	334.14	369.88
Provisions	35.90	30.52	26.24	21.42	20.96	9.96	13.35	14.47	10.75	19.44
Total Current Liabilities	835.95	796.86	701.37	649.16	585.41	536.98	400.83	392.85	344.89	389.32
Net Current Assets	264.23	216.66	111.46	127.14	200.95	180.57	138.58	109.41	153.96	296.15
Miscellaneous Expenses not written off	8.22	9.16	12.94	15.42	14.41	15.94	7.52	8.12	6.70	8.77
Deferred Tax Assets	22.41	16.42	14.36	2.39	6.01	18.10	0.00	0.00	0.00	0.00
Deferred Tax Liability	127.73	14.81	11.31	13.86	13.19	9.22	0.00	0.00	0.00	0.00
Net Deferred Tax	–105.32	1.61	3.05	–11.47	–7.18	8.88	0.00	0.00	0.00	0.00
Total Assets	1,448.87	1,535.59	1,613.10	1,606.89	1,732.05	1,771.95	1,337.42	1,293.45	1,362.99	1,435.24
Contingent Liabilities	74.36	87.84	57.15	87.53	95.92	123.79	109.95	74.14	121.72	75.45

Annexure II Profit and Loss

JK Tyre & Industries Ltd (₹ in Cr.)

	2007	2006	2005	2004	2003	2002	2001	2000	1999	1998
INCOME:										
Sales Turnover	3,195.71	2,952.69	2,383.82	2,237.5	2,018.53	2,321.89	1,332.55	1,338.27	1,288.79	1,553.24
Excise Duty	400.64	362.92	305.27	317.63	345.19	451.29	240.56	257.12	216.68	265.4
Net Sales	2,795.07	2,589.77	2,078.55	1,919.87	1,673.34	1,870.6	1,091.99	1,081.15	1,072.11	1,287.84
Other Income	12.56	20.52	19.32	27.69	61.53	28.38	11.84	9.91	9.26	17.46
Stock Adjustments	127.51	110.33	28.86	–71.92	39.42	43.31	1.91	19.05	–71.43	31.68
Total Income	2,935.14	2,720.62	2,126.73	1,875.64	1,774.29	1,942.29	1,105.74	1,110.11	1,009.94	1,336.98
EXPENDITURE:										
Raw Materials	1,981.35	1,912.08	1,424.89	1,186.54	1,068.25	1,149.78	665.14	649.39	595.59	839.37
Power and Fuel Cost	139.79	139	111.08	97.52	94.46	93.58	43.33	41.31	39.18	52.29
Employee Cost	166.97	153.43	140.67	136.51	123.34	140.73	71.3	67.54	59.82	62.47
Other Manufacturing Expenses	94.69	97.97	81.34	64.19	60.95	71.87	39.98	41.57	31.24	78.05
Selling and Admin Expenses	221.63	195.14	184.45	180.31	178.43	181.51	97.64	106.5	88.43	89.05
Miscellaneous Expenses	63.42	51.21	49.88	47.24	49.26	58.44	40.6	35.43	32.89	3.01
Less: Pre-operative Expenses Capitalized	0	0	0	0	0	0	0	0	0	0
Total Expenditure	2,667.85	2,548.83	1,992.31	1,712.31	1,574.69	1,695.91	957.99	941.74	847.15	1,124.24
Operating Profit	267.29	171.79	134.42	163.33	199.6	246.38	147.75	168.37	162.79	212.74
Interest	91.1	79.06	67.33	85.51	101.42	158.09	98.12	103.85	115.32	150.67

(continued)

(continued)

	2007	***2006***	***2005***	***2004***	***2003***	***2002***	***2001***	***2000***	***1999***	***1998***
Gross Profit	176.19	92.73	67.09	77.82	98.18	88.29	49.63	64.52	47.47	62.07
Depreciation	75.44	70.93	63.65	61.34	59.13	68.38	33.04	31.07	25.39	30.55
Profit Before Tax	100.75	21.8	3.44	16.48	39.05	19.91	16.59	33.45	22.08	31.52
Tax	0	0	0	0	0.9	1.75	0	0.7	0	5.45
Fringe Benefit tax	2.87	3.31	1.2	0	0	0	0	0	0	0
Deferred Tax	31.15	1.44	–14.52	4.29	16.06	–1.94	0	0	0	0
Reported Net Profit	66.73	17.05	16.76	12.19	22.09	20.1	16.59	32.75	22.08	26.07
Extraordinary Items	–0.23	4.97	7.87	–0.07	–0.21	–0.56	–0.21	0.78	0.27	1.1
Adjusted Net Profit	66.96	12.08	8.89	12.26	22.3	20.66	16.8	31.97	21.81	24.97
Adjusted below Net Profit	0	0	–36.98	0	1.25	0.83	0	0	0	0
P&L Balance brought forward	27.88	41.53	40.32	43.01	33.21	0	31.71	17.68	15.46	18.65
Statutory Appropriations	0	0	0	0	0	0	0	0	0	0
Appropriations	69.5	30.7	–21.43	14.88	13.54	–12.28	23.34	18.71	19.86	29.26
P&L Balance carried down	25.11	27.88	41.53	40.32	43.01	33.21	24.96	31.72	17.68	15.46
Dividend	8.32	7.7	7.49	7.49	7.49	7.78	6.91	8.64	8.64	12.96
Preference Dividend	0	0	0	0	0	0	0.08	0.28	0.28	1.11
Equity Dividend %	27	25	20	20	20	22.5	20	25	25	37.5
EPS-Unit Currency	21.21	5.19	4.19	2.99	5.64	3.51	4.57	9.12	6.04	5.46
Book Value-Unit Currency	119.51	129.87	101.22	113.72	116.65	243.7	175.91	179.39	182.2	188.43

References

Corporate Spin Off. Available at https://en.wikipedia.org/wiki/Corporate_spin-off (last accessed on 5 May 2015).

Daş, B., Sathya Swaroop Debasish, and Debdas Rakshit. 2012. *Corporate Restructuring: Merger, Acquisition and Other Forms*. Mumbai: Himalaya Publishing House.

Kandula, Srinivas R. 2001. *Strategic Human Resource Development*. New Delhi: Prentice Hall.

Kishore, Ravi M. 2003. *Financial Management* (4th ed.). New Delhi: Taxman Allied Services.

Victoria Strong. 2005. 'Demerger Duty Relief'. Available at https://www.liv.asn.au/getattachment/f2466b51-c4ac-437e-86a1-137d76435f90/Demerger-Duty-Relief.aspx (last accessed on 5 June 2015).

Further Readings

Chakravarty, S.M. 1993. *Growth Prospects for Cement Industry in India*. New Delhi: Aashish Publications.

Cimenterie Nationale. 2007. History of Cement. Available at www.cimnat.com.lb (last accessed on 11 November 2007).

Gokarn, Subir, and Rajendra Vaidya. 1993. 'Deregulation and Industrial Performance: The Indian Cement Industry'. *Economic and Political Weekly*, 28(8–9): 33–41.

Krishnan, A. 'Demergers: Dividing to Multiply'. Available at www.thehindubusinessline.com (last accessed on 25 July 2016).

Lafarge. 2004. All about Cement. Available at http://www.lafarge.com (last accessed on 26 March 2006)

Sanjiv Shankaran. 'Wockhardt: The Demerger Tonic'. Available at http://www.hinduonnet.com/businessline/2000/03/26/stories/202618lb.htm

Srikanth, B.L. 'Corporate Restructuring: Incentives A'. Srikanth, BL Research Bureau. Available at http://www.hinduonnet.com/businessline/2000/03/05/stories/200542a4.htm

www.wockhardt.com/ (last accessed on 21 August 2016).

Chapter 12

Joint Venture

Chapter Objectives

On completion of this chapter, you will be able to understand:

- The concept of joint venture
- Basic elements of a joint venture
- Differentiate between joint venture vs. strategic alliance
- Equity variations:
    - Majority joint ventures
    - The 50–50 joint venture
- The reasons to form a joint venture
- Some examples of joint venture
    - IBM (U.S.) and Lenovo Group (China) (2004)
    - Pontiac Land Group (Singapore) and West Paces Hotel Group (U.S.) (2006)
    - Siemens AG (Germany) and Nokia Corp. (Finland) (2006)
    - Hit Company (Republic of Slovenia) and Harrah's Entertainment (U.S.) (2007)
    - Posco (South Korea), SeAH Corp. (South Korea) and U.S. Steel (U.S.) (2007)
- Structuring the joint venture
    - Company
    - Limited liability partnerships (LLPs)
    - Strategic alliance
- Managing a joint venture
    - Dominant parent enterprises
    - Shared management ventures
- Factors to be considered to form a joint venture
- Advantages of a joint venture
- Disadvantages of a joint venture
- Setting up a joint venture in India
    - Government approvals for joint ventures
    - Types of joint ventures
    - Incorporation
    - Inter-corporate investment under section 372A of the Companies Act
    - Termination of joint ventures
- Documents for establishing a joint venture
    - Memorandum of understanding (MoU)
    - Joint venture or shareholders' agreement
    - Constitutional documents and others

KBA-NotaSys and Lumenco Launch LenSys Joint Venture

KBA-NotaSys S.A. of Lausanne, Switzerland and Lumenco Inc. of Englewood, CO, United States of America are pleased to announce that they are combining their technologies and expertise through the formation of a joint venture, LenSys Sarl, which will focus on the development, sales and marketing, of a new range of novel level-one security features.

The family of features proposed by LenSys combines Lumenco's patented micro lens optics with KBA-NotaSys' precise multicolor offset elements produced on the Super Simultan press. The strength of the feature is the easy recognition by the general public with stunning color and shape changing effects. The offset element and its associated lens structure are designed and originated in combination to ensure both functionality and security. The combination of elements – the lenses themselves and the offset print enhance the security of the feature through the layered construction and at the same time provide unrivalled flexibility in banknote design even allowing the integration of the feature in an existing note design.

Eric Boissonnas, CEO of KBA-NotaSys, describes KBA-NotaSys' motivation to create this joint venture as: Another step in positioning our Super Simultan technology as the most cost-efficient way of creating highly-secure level-one security features. The combination of Lumenco's expertise in micro lens technology and the improved Simultan technology will create very striking security features. We are thrilled to now be able to present this to the market and develop the features even further.

Mark Raymond and Hector Porras, founders of Lumenco, comment: 'Lumenco's goal was to find a respected development and commercialization partner that understood the technical aspects of its technology and the potential of printed micro lenses integrated into banknotes.

KBA-NotaSys represents a solid partner that will allow Lumenco to commercialize its micro lens technologies at the highest level and we are very excited to have the best possible partner in the banknote industry'.

The new company, LenSys Sarl, is registered in Switzerland and will be managed by a board composed of representatives from both KBA-NotaSys and Lumenco. The day-to-day operation of the company will be headed by Michael Blesovsky who has a long established track-record in the industry.

Source: Press release published at http://www.kba-notasys.com/news-and-events/press-releases/kba-notasys-and-lumenco-launch-lensys-joint-venture/

12.1 Introduction

In increasing numbers, businesses have been reaching beyond national boundaries in an effort to locate new opportunities for growth, new markets and new venture capital. As business projects get larger, technology becomes more expensive, and the costs of failure become too large to be borne alone, businesses feel the need to work with joint venture. Each foreign market offers unique opportunities and risks, and many firms naturally look to joint ventures with one or more partners for assistance in entering new markets. Joint ventures have become a major feature of the international business landscape due to increased global competitiveness and technological innovation.

Joint ventures are common and successful in several industries. For example, in the land development and construction industries, joint ventures are often used to obtain sufficient financing to acquire large land tracts or to undertake major building projects. Joint ventures are also common in the manufacturing, mining and service industries. A joint venture may be formed to conduct R&D work on a new product or technical application, to manufacture or produce various products, to market and distribute products and services in a specified geographic area or to perform a combination of these functions.

In general, a joint venture is an association of two or more entities (whether corporate, government, individual or otherwise) combining property and expertise to carry out a single business enterprise and having a joint proprietary interest, a joint right to control and sharing of profits and losses.

12.2 Definition

Some definitions of joint venture are given as follows:

a. *Wikipedia* defines a joint venture as 'an entity formed between two or more parties to undertake economic activity together. The parties agree to create a new entity by both contributing equity, and they then share in the revenues, expenses, and control of the enterprise. The venture can be for one specific project only, or a continuing business relationship. This is in contrast to a strategic alliance, which involves no equity stake by the participants, and is a much less rigid arrangement'.
b. In the words of Levins and Lawor (1988): 'A joint venture is a contractual agreement joining together two or more parties for the purpose of executing a particular business undertaking. All parties agree to share in the profits and losses of the enterprise'.
c. Levins opines a joint venture as 'a new firm formed to achieve specific objectives of a partnership like temporary arrangement between two or more firms (Kelshikar and Shah 2015). JVs are advantageous as a risk reducing mechanism in new-market penetration, and in pooling of resource for large projects. They, however, present unique problems in equity ownership, operational control, and distribution of profits (or losses). Research indicates that two out of five JV arrangements last less than four years, and are dissolved in acrimony'.

12.3 Basic Elements of a Joint Venture

A joint venture possesses the following basic elements:

a. *Contractual Agreement:* Joint ventures are established by express contracts that consist of one or more agreements involving two or more individuals or organizations and that are entered into for a specific business purpose.
b. *Specific Limited Purpose and Duration:* Joint ventures are formed for a specific business objective and can have a limited lifespan or be long term. Joint ventures are frequently established for a limited duration because of the fact that (a) the complementary activities involve a limited amount of assets; (a) the complementary assets have only a limited service life; and/or (b) the complementary production activities will be of only limited efficacy.

c. *Joint Property Interest:* Each joint venture participant contributes property, cash, or other assets and organizational capital for the pursuit of a common and specific business purpose. Thus, a joint venture is not merely a contractual relationship, but rather the contributions are made to a newly formed business enterprise, usually a corporation, limited-liability company, or partnership. As such, the participants acquire a joint property interest in the assets and subject matter of the joint venture.
d. *Common Financial and Intangible Goals and Objectives:* The joint venture participants share a common expectation regarding the nature and amount of the expected financial and intangible goals and objectives of the joint venture. The goals and objectives of a joint venture tend to be narrowly focused, recognizing that the assets deployed by each participant represent only a portion of the overall resource base.
e. *Shared Profits, Losses, Management and Control*: The joint venture participants share in the specific and identifiable financial and intangible profits and losses, as well as in certain elements of the management and control of the joint venture.

12.4 Joint Venture Versus Strategic Alliance

The points of distinction between joint venture and strategic alliance are presented as follows:

Joint Venture	Strategic Alliance
1. In a joint venture, two or more organizations set up a separate, 'independent' organization for a 'specific purpose'.	1. A strategic alliance is simply a business-to-business 'collaboration' where two or more corporates share resources and capabilities to 'achieve some business purpose'.
2. In joint venture, some formalities are made. A formal contract or agreement is written.	2. Strategic alliances are less formal than joint ventures. A new entity need not be created.
3. In case of joint venture, it has clear and legal boundaries.	3. In strategic alliance, the boundaries are defined by partnering firms.
4. Joint ventures are formed to capitalize on knowledge in parent firms and to generate knowledge.	4. Strategic alliances are formed in to order to learn from the partner. Knowledge is located in partners.

12.5 Equity Variations

Majority Joint Ventures: A majority ownership whereby the 'foreign' company has the controlling share. It has the advantages of great control and confidence towards the joint venture company, as well as it is more committed.

The 50–50 Joint Venture: The best known and probably the ideal type of joint venture is where a completely new entity is created 'from scratch' and each partner has an equal contribution in the form of a 50–50 shareholding. It has the advantages of providing maximum incentive for both parties to make the relationship work and focusing the activities of the joint venture towards clearly defined goals that complement the independent activities of each company.

Minority Joint Ventures: The 50–50 joint venture may not be appropriate in every situation, nor will it be possible in countries with strict foreign investment rules that require majority control to remain in local hands.

The minority ownership of a joint venture, however, should not automatically be regarded as a disincentive since there are other ways to protect the interests of the minority partner. Regardless of shareholding, it is usually possible to build into any agreement a formal provision relating to the management and control of the joint venture, as well as clauses covering other potential areas of difficulty. This could include when and how profits should be distributed, how the product is to be marketed, financing of the joint venture, how arbitration will be managed and so on.

a. One way of maintaining more control in a 50–50 or minority joint venture is to keep control over supply of a key component.
b. If a joint venture is formed as a company, it is possible to appoint other directors to the board who can also bring other levels of skill or influence to the venture. This includes the option of appointing a neutral, independent chairperson who has the respect of all parties.

12.6 Why to Form a Joint Venture?

There are many motivations that lead to the formation of a joint venture. Some of such motivations are discussed here:

a. *Risk Sharing:* Risk sharing is a common reason to form a joint venture, particularly, in highly capital-intensive industries and in industries where the high costs of product development equal a high likelihood of failure of any particular product.
b. *Economies of Scale:* If an industry has high fixed costs, a joint venture with a larger company can provide the economies of scale necessary to compete globally and can be an effective way by which two companies can pool resources and achieve critical mass.
c. *Market Access:* For companies that lack a basic understanding of customers and the relationship/infrastructure to distribute their products to customers, forming a joint venture with the right partner can provide instant access to established, efficient and effective distribution channels and receptive customer bases. This is important to a company because creating new distribution channels and identifying new customer bases can be extremely difficult, time-consuming and expensive activities.
d. *Geographical Constraints:* When there is an attractive business opportunity in a foreign market, partnering with a local company is attractive to a foreign company because penetrating a foreign market can be difficult both because of a lack of experience in such market and because of local barriers to foreign-owned or foreign-controlled companies.
e. *Funding Constraints:* When a company is confronted with high up-front development costs, finding the right joint venture partner can provide necessary financing and credibility with third parties.
f. *Prelude to Acquisition:* When a company wants to acquire another, but cannot due to cost, size or geographical restrictions or legal barriers, teaming up with a joint venture partner (JVP) is an attractive option. The joint venture is substantially less costly and

thus less risky than complete acquisitions, and is sometimes used as a first step to a complete acquisition with the JVP. Such an arrangement allows the purchaser the flexibility to cut its losses if the investment proves less fruitful than anticipated or to acquire the remainder of the company under certain circumstances.

12.7 Some Examples of Recent Joint Ventures

Some examples of recent joint ventures are as follows:

Parties to Joint Venture:	***IBM (U.S.) and Lenovo Group (China) (2004)***
Per cent participation:	18.9/81.1
Dollar value:	$1.75 billion
Subject:	IBM sold its PC division to China-based Lenovo Group. Companies entered into a joint venture that would make Lenovo the third largest PC maker in the world, behind Dell and Hewlett Packard, and give IBM an 18.9% stake in Lenovo.
Parties to Joint Venture:	***Pontiac Land Group (Singapore) and West Paces Hotel Group (U.S.) (2006)***
Per cent participation:	50:50
Subject:	Pontiac and West Paces formed a joint venture known as the West Paces Hotel Group Asia. Headquartered in Singapore, this hotel management company will introduce new luxury hotels across Asia. Pontiac Land will focus on business development and securing strategic partnerships in Asia with leading high net-worth families and institutions. West Paces Hotel Group, headquartered in Atlanta, Georgia (U.S.), will contribute management and operations expertise in designing properties geared toward affluent travellers.
Parties to Joint Venture:	***Siemens AG (Germany) and Nokia Corp. (Finland) (2006)***
Per cent Participation:	50:50
Dollar Value:	$19.9 billion
Subject:	Siemens AG and Nokia Corp. combined their fixed and mobile network infrastructure businesses in a joint venture known as Nokia Siemens Networks. The joint venture formation was a reaction to recent mergers in the industry, such as Alcatel with Lucent, and the rise of low-cost Chinese competitors such as Huawei Technologies Co Ltd and ZTE Corp Nokia Siemens Networks became the second largest company, behind Ericsson, in wireless networks and third in fixed-line, behind Alcatel and Cisco Systems and is headquartered in Finland.
Parties to Joint Venture:	***Hit Company (Rep. of Slovenia) and Harrah's Entertainment (U.S.) (2007)***
Per cent Participation:	50:50
Dollar Value:	$700 million

Subject:	Slovenian gaming company Hit and U.S. casino operator Harrah's Entertainment formed a joint venture to build a major new gaming and entertainment centre in Slovenia, completed in 2009, provided that the Slovenian government loosens gaming legislation. The project rests on the Slovenia government's willingness to tweak legislation: currently, foreigners can hold no more than 20% in a gaming venture, and the gaming tax is set at a high 30%. Harrah's was in talks with the government on changes to the gaming law that would allow foreigners to hold a 50% stake. Harrah's would also like the government to lower the gaming tax.
Parties to Joint Venture:	***Posco (South Korea), SeAH Corp. (South Korea) and U.S. Steel (U.S.) (2007)***
Per cent Participation:	35:30:35
Dollar Value:	$93 million
Subject:	U.S. Steel partnered with Posco, South Korea's leading steel producer, and SeAH, a tubular steel maker, in the venture to be called United Spiral Pipe LLC, to build a new U.S. facility that will produce spiral-welded pipe for the natural gas industry.

12.8 Types of Joint Venture

Structuring any joint venture may pose a challenge. This is especially true where parties from different jurisdictions and various cultural backgrounds are involved. After parties have decided on fundamental issues, such as the commercial nature, scope and mutual objectives of the joint venture, the JVPs must determine the geographic location of the venture and what form or legal structure the joint venture will take.

Generally, the structure chosen will be between different types of partnerships, corporations, or some form of a limited-liability company, depending on the tax and tort liability each JVP wants to be exposed to. The precise tax and legal features of vehicles of the same general type will vary from one country to another, but forms of businesses can be broadly classified as follows:

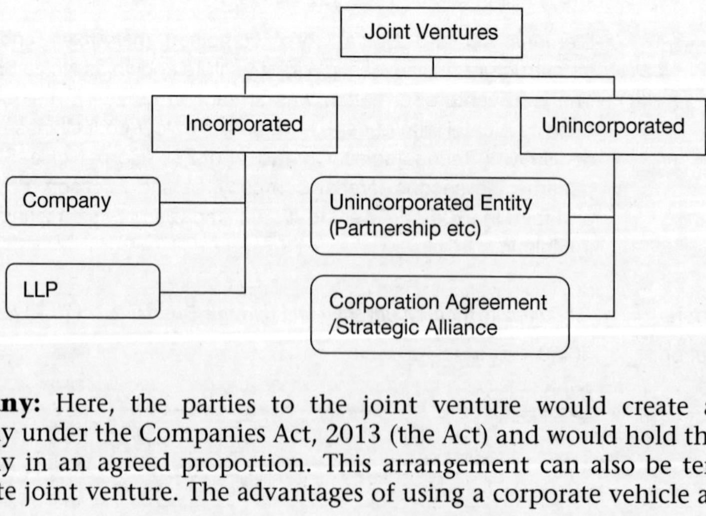

a. **Company:** Here, the parties to the joint venture would create a joint venture company under the Companies Act, 2013 (the Act) and would hold the shares of such company in an agreed proportion. This arrangement can also be termed as equity/ corporate joint venture. The advantages of using a corporate vehicle are as follows:

- It is a universally recognized medium which gives an independent legal identity to the joint venture;
- It puts in place a better management and employee structure;
- Participants have the benefit of limited liability and the flexibility to raise finance; and
- The company will survive as the same entity despite a change in its ownership.

b. **LLPs:** In 2008, the Limited Liability Partnership Act, 2008 (the LLP Act) introduced LLPs in India. An LLP is a beneficial business vehicle as it provides the benefits of limited liability to its partners and allows its members the flexibility of organizing their internal structure as a partnership based on an agreement. Under an LLP, there may be two distinct types of partners: general and limited. The general partner carries responsibilities similar to the one that carries in a general partnership, including the ability to legally bind the whole partnership and being personally liable for debts and obligations of the partnership. The limited partner, on the other hand, mainly contributes capital and receives a specified share of the profits. The limited partner is excluded from the active management of the partnership, but is exempt from personal liability for debts and obligations of the partnership.

c. **Partnerships:** A partnership firm created under the Partnership Act, 1932, is in many respects simpler than a company, and may perhaps be regarded as a halfway house between a corporate joint venture and a purely contractual arrangement. All partners in a partnership have personal liability for debts and other obligations incurred by the partnership. One advantage of a partnership in the United States and many other countries is that normally no income or franchise tax is imposed on it. Also, all partners can act on behalf of, and legally bind, the partnership via third parties.

d. **Un-incorporated Joint Ventures: Cooperation Agreements/Strategic Alliances:** The most basic form of association is to conclude a purely contractual arrangement like a cooperation agreement or a strategic alliance wherein the parties agree to collaborate as independent contractors rather than shareholders in a company or partners in a legal partnership. What qualifies such business relationships as an unincorporated joint venture is when such business relationship between two or more parties is in furtherance of a common purpose or action for a profitable venture, proceeds of which are to be shared in an agreed ratio. This type of agreement is ideal where the parties intend not to be bound by the formality and permanence of a corporate vehicle. Such alliances are highly functional constructs that allow companies to acquire products, technology and working capital to increase production capacity and improve productivity. Strategic alliances provide companies an opportunity to establish a de facto geographical presence and aid in accessing new markets, increase market penetration and sales and market share.

12.9 Managing the Joint Venture

In the management of a joint venture, the following issues are considered:

a. *Dominant Parent Enterprises:* Some joint ventures are dominant parent enterprises—projects are managed by one parent like wholly owned subsidiaries. The dominant parent selects all the functional managers for the enterprise. The board of directors, although made up of executives from each parent, plays a largely ceremonial role as the dominant parent executives and make all the venture's operating and strategic decisions. Having managers from only one parent can lead to frustrations for the managers as well as parent company executives.

A dominant parent enterprise is appropriate where a JVP is chosen for reasons other than managerial input, that is, financial backing, access to resources, patents, or because it consumes a large amount of the product to be made. Dominant parent joint ventures are also appropriate when a company takes on a partner solely in response to pressures from a host government. In such situations, a foreign company often prefers to find a passive local company that (a) has no knowledge of the product, (b) is willing to be a passive investor and (c) is neither a government agency nor controlled by the government. The passive partner, who may be supplying technology or money, must trust the competence and honesty of the dominant parent. If the local partner never learns the business of the joint venture, the dominant parent's bargaining position with the host government will remain strong.

b. *Shared Management Ventures*: Other joint ventures are shared management ventures, where both parents manage the enterprise. Each parent supplies both functional managers and executives to serve on the board of directors. Here, the board of directors has a real decision-making function.

One type of shared management venture is the 50:50 joint venture, in which each partner contributes 50% of the equity in return for 50% participating control. Under such participation, each JVP is equally at risk and is not subservient to the other JVP, as would be the case where majority control is vested in one party. This sharing of interest and control also raises the possibility of deadlock during disputes and early termination of the joint venture.

It is important to note that not all shared management ventures own equal shares. Joint ventures are flexible so that they can be structured in such a way that one JVP has more than a co-equal role in the joint venture (e.g., 40/60). Shared management is critical in ventures where both JVPs are needed for managerial input, as in manufacturing situations where one parent is supplying technology and the other knowledge of the local market. However, deteriorating performance in a shared management venture obliges each parent to become more involved in the operation of the venture. Unless either parent is willing to defer to the other's knowledge or expertise, the decision-making process can become slow and can confuse and trigger a series of events that can lead to the destruction of the venture.

Because the amount and type of help needed from a partner may change over time, some companies opt to begin their venture under a shared management that they can later convert to a dominant venture. However, once both parents have become accustomed to operating the venture, such transitions become difficult to make.

The high failure rate of shared management ventures suggests that dominant ventures outperform shared management ventures. Since shared management ventures are not consistently used for riskier business tasks, their high failure rate is a strong indication that they are more difficult to operate than dominant parent ventures. Parents of the venture may, and often do, disagree over strategic and organizational decisions. Differences in the parent venture's priorities, direction, and perhaps values result in confusion, frustration and slowness in the decision-making process and may place a joint venture at a distinct competitive disadvantage. As a result, if a partner is chosen for reasons other than managerial input, a dominant parent structure will usually be best.

12.10 Factors to Be Considered to Form a Joint Venture

The various factors that are usually considered before formation of a joint venture are as follows:

a. Screening of prospective partners.
b. Joint development of a detailed business plan and shortlisting a set of prospective partners based on their contribution to developing a business plan.

c. Due diligence: Checking the credentials of the other party ('trust and verify'—trust the information you receive from the prospective partner, but it is a good business practice to verify the facts through interviews with third parties).
d. Development of an exit strategy and terms of dissolution of the joint venture.
e. Most appropriate structure (e.g., most joint ventures involving fast growing companies are structured as strategic corporate partnerships).
f. Availability of appreciated or depreciated property being contributed to the joint venture; by misunderstanding the significance of appreciated property, companies can fundamentally weaken the economics of the deal for themselves and their partners.
g. Special allocations of income, gain, loss or deduction to be made among the partners.
h. Compensation to the members that provide services.

12.11 Advantages of a Joint Venture

Businesses of any size can use joint ventures to strengthen long-term relationships or to collaborate on short-term projects. A successful joint venture gives rise to the following benefits:

a. Combines complementary R&D or technology.
b. Provides companies with the opportunity to obtain new capacity and expertise.
c. Allows efficient commercialization of a technology or business concept.
d. Develops or acquires marketing or distribution expertise.
e. Helps in sharing of scientists or professionals with unique skills. The complexity of the knowledge to be transferred is a key factor in determining the contractual relationship between the partners. One or more participants may seek to learn more about a relatively new product market activity. This might concern all aspects of the activity or a limited segment like R&D, production, marketing or product servicing.
f. Allows companies to enter into related businesses or new geographic markets or obtain new technological knowledge.
g. Because of a relatively short lifespan (five to seven years), it does not represent a long-term commitment.
h. Improves access to financial resources for both partners. Financial resources increase because when two parties undertake economic activity together, then they share expenses. This leads to more access to each other's financial sources.
i. Financial support or sharing of economic risk. It reduces the risks in a number of ways as the activities can be expanded with smaller investment outlays than if financed independently. A small firm with a new product idea that involves high risk and requires relatively large amounts of investment capital may form a joint venture with a large firm. The larger firm might be able to carry the financial risks and be interested in becoming involved in a new business activity that promises growth and profitability. In addition, the larger firm might thereby gain experience in the new area of activity that may represent the opportunity for a major new business thrust in the future.
j. Proper utilization of resources. Resources are inputs into a firm's production process, such as capital, equipment, the skills of individual employees, patents, finance and talented managers. Resources are either tangible or intangible in nature. With increasing effectiveness, the set of resources available to the firm tend to become larger. Individual resources may not yield to a competitive advantage. It is through the synergistic combination and integration of sets of resources that competitive advantages are formed.

k. Accelerates revenue growth
l. It has the ability to increase profit margins
m. Expansion to new domestic markets and international markets. It also helps in expanding the firm's operations into foreign countries. The local partners contribute in the form of specialized knowledge about local conditions, which are essential to the success of the venture.
n. New product development.
o. Higher rate of profit and more control over the operations.
p. Sharing of risk and ability to combine the local in-depth knowledge with a foreign partner with know how in technology or process.
q. Tax advantages are a significant factor in many joint ventures.
r. A joint venture can also be very flexible. For example, a joint venture can have a limited lifespan and only cover part of what company needs, thus limiting the commitment for both parties and the business' exposure.
s. Market conditions require initial long-term build-up of contacts or creation of demand, for example, China.

12.12 Disadvantages of a Joint Venture

Partnering with another business can be complex. It takes time and effort to build the right relationship. Problems are likely to arise if

a. the objectives of the venture are not 100% clear and communicated to everyone involved;
b. the partners have different objectives for the joint venture;
c. varied organizational structures may lead to less efficient decision-making;
d. there is an imbalance in levels of expertise, investment or assets brought into the venture by the different partners;
e. cultural difference: different cultures and management styles result in poor integration and cooperation;
f. the partners do not provide sufficient leadership and support in the early stages;
g. high level of commitment of staff and management may not exist;
h. time consuming (especially where a new venture is involved);
i. political risks in the country where the joint venture is based and
j. working in a different legal and commercial system.

Success in a joint venture depends on thorough research and analysis of aims and objectives. This should be followed up with effective communication of the business plan to everyone involved.

12.13 Setting up a Joint Venture in India

Joint venture companies are the most preferred form of corporate entities for doing business in India. There are no separate laws for joint ventures in India. The companies incorporated in India, even with up to 100% foreign equity, are treated the same as domestic companies. A joint venture may be any of the business entities available in India.

12.13.1 Government Approvals for Joint Ventures

All the joint ventures in India require governmental approvals, if a foreign partner or a non-resident Indian or person of Indian origin partner is involved. The approval can be obtained from either RBI or Foreign Investment Promotion Board (FIPB). In case, a joint venture is covered under automatic route, then the approval of RBI is required. In other special cases, not covered under the automatic route, a special approval of FIPB is required.

The government has outlined 37 high-priority areas covering most of the industrial sectors. Investment proposals involving up to 74% foreign equity in these areas receive automatic approval within two weeks. An application to the RBI is required. Besides the 37 high-priority areas, automatic approval is available for 74% foreign equity holdings setting up international trading companies engaged primarily in export activities.

The approval of a foreign equity is not limited to 74% and to high-priority industries. Greater than 74% of equity and areas outside the high-priority list are open to investment, but government approval is required. For these greater equity investments or for areas of investment outside of high priority, an application in the form FC (SIA) has to be filed with the secretariat for industrial approvals. A response is given within six weeks. Full foreign ownership (100% equity) is readily allowed in power generation, coal washeries, electronics, export-oriented unit (EOU) or a unit in one of the export processing zones).

For major investment proposals or for those that do not fit within the existing policy parameters, there is the high-powered FIPB. The FIPB is located in the office of the prime minister and can provide single-window clearance to proposals in their totality without being restricted by any predetermined parameters.

Foreign investment is also welcomed in many of infrastructure areas, such as power, steel, coal washeries, luxury railways and telecommunications. The entire hydrocarbon sector, including exploration, producing, refining and marketing of petroleum products, has now been opened to foreign participation. The government had recently allowed foreign investment up to 51% in mining for commercial purposes and up to 49% in the telecommunication sector. The government is also examining a proposal to do away with the stipulation that foreign equity should cover the foreign exchange needs for import of capital goods. In view of the country's improved balance of payments position, this requirement may be eliminated.

This section sets forth some important steps for forming a joint venture company in India.

1. Types of Joint Ventures: Three most common types of joint venture companies may be described as follows:

a. Two parties, who/which may be individuals or companies, one of them non-resident or both residents, incorporate a company in India. Business of one party is transferred to the company, and as consideration for such transfer, shares are issued by the company and subscribed by that party. The other party subscribes for the shares in cash.
b. Alternately, the above two parties subscribe to the shares of the joint venture company in agreed proportion, in cash, and start a new business.
c. Promoter shareholder of an existing Indian company and a third party, who/which may be individual/company, one of them non-resident or both residents, collaborate to jointly carry on the business of that company and its shares are taken by the said third party through payment in cash.

2. Incorporation: In case a new joint venture company has to be formed in India, the following are pertinent issues need to be decided:

a. Formalities

i. Whether the joint venture company will be a public or a private limited company;
ii. The place of registered office of the joint venture company;
iii. Propose a name of the joint venture company and check its availability from the ROC where the registered office of the company is to be situated and the company is to be incorporated;
iv. Choose the subscribers to the memorandum of association (MoA) which will obviously include the partners to the joint venture and their nominees;
v. Prepare the memorandum and articles of association (AoA) in consultation with the joint venture partners, get them printed and suitably stamped, and submitting the same with required documents to ROC along with fees payable;
vi. On receipt of certificate of incorporation, the new company may start business:
   a. in case of private company, immediately.
   b. in case of public company, after obtaining certificate of commencement of business for which the company has to file with the ROC prospectus/statement in lieu of prospectus, and the statutory declaration, duly stamped.

b. Articles: To avoid contradictions, the AoA should contain the stipulations mentioned in the joint venture agreement (JVA) and clearly delineate the rights and obligations of the partners.

c. Non-resident partner: In case one of the partners of the joint venture company is a non-resident, the approval of RBI will be required for acquiring shares of the company and establishing place of business in India as per the Foreign Exchange Management Act, 1999 (FEMA). Presently, persons resident outside India are permitted to invest into securities of Indian companies depending on the sectoral caps and as per the provisions of the FEMA and the delegated legislation thereunder. The FEMA (Transfer or Issue of Security by a Person Resident outside India) Regulations, 2000 (TISPRO Regulations), more specifically Schedule I of TISPRO Regulations, provide for investments into Indian companies under the foreign direct investment (FDI) route. Investments can be made by persons resident outside India in the shares/compulsorily convertible debentures/preference shares of an Indian company, through two routes: the automatic route and the government route. Under the automatic route (requiring no prior approval), the foreign investor or the Indian company does not require any prior government approval. The categories of investments that do not qualify to come under the automatic route would be carried out via the non-automatic route, where special approval of the FIPB, and/or other specified government department(s) is required.

3. 50:50 Joint Venture Entities to Be Considered Foreign Entities

In the event a 50:50 joint venture company is categorized as a foreign-owned Indian entity, then the downstream investments and sectors in which investments are made by the joint venture entity will be subject to foreign investment restrictions. The threshold (to establish foreign ownership) of 50% is inconsistent with Press Notes 2, 3 and 4 of 2009, which placed the relevant threshold at 51%.

4. Foreign Institutional Investment

Schedule II of the TISPRO Regulations provides for purchase/sale of shares or convertible bonds of an Indian company by a registered FII/sub-account under the 'portfolio investment scheme' (PIS) route. It is pertinent to note that a foreign investor cannot acquire listed shares of Indian companies on a recognized stock exchange in India through a registered broker, unless such foreign investors are registered as a FII/sub-account and the investments are made under the PIS route as per the provisions of Schedule II of the TISPRO Regulations. FII/sub-accounts are registered with the SEBI under its SEBI (Foreign Institutional Investors) Regulations, 1995 (SEBI FII Regulations).

However, compliance requirement for transferring shares varies depending upon the residency of the transferor and transferee of the shares as mentioned as follows:

Transferor	Transferee	Compliance, if any
Indian resident	Indian resident	None, record of transfer on share certificate
Indian resident	Non-resident	Filing of Form FC-TRS with the RBI
Non-resident	Indian resident	Reporting requirements with the authorized dealer, subject to the restriction that the Indian resident should not have any previous tie-up or venture in the same field
Non-resident	Non-resident	None, intimation to RBI recommended

5. Competition Law Issues

Section 6 of the Competition Act, 2002, makes void any combination that causes or is likely to cause an appreciable adverse effect on competition within India and requires every acquirer to notify the Competition Commission of India of a combination and seek its approval prior to effectuating the same unless such combination has been specifically exempted.

Applicability of the *De Minimis* Exemption

The Government of India has notified certain thresholds (assets of 250 crores and turnover of 750 crores), whereby all transactions which do not meet such thresholds need not be notified to the CCI. Therefore, if the joint venture partners were to set up a fresh joint venture, which has nil or negligible assets and no value attributable to its turnover at the time that the partners to the joint venture subscribe to the shares of such joint venture company, it may be argued that such acquisition may not need to be notified.

6. Termination of Joint Ventures

Any number of events may lead to the termination of a joint venture. Many termination events are anticipated and provided for in the JVA. For example, a breach of the JVA may trigger termination, as will other events, such as failure to meet R&D deadlines. A joint venture may terminate upon achieving its objectives. Alternatively, a joint venture may terminate upon failing to meet its objectives. The agreement could provide that one JVP buy the other out or sell its shares, or vice versa.

Excessive costs, failure to achieve projected income or unforeseen capital requirements may make the continuation of a joint venture unattractive. In addition, a change in the joint venture's objectives or those of a shareholder may also lead to the early termination of the joint venture. Changes in objectives may result from a JVP's internal strategic redirection, competitive advances, or market changes beyond the control of the joint venture or its shareholders. Disagreement by JVPs on fundamental management issues may also lead to termination.

An obvious disadvantage of sharing capital obligations is the need to share profits generated from the actual operation of the joint venture. Issues can arise in this area not so much because of the cash contributed, but because of the fact that the parties will also be contributing intangible assets to the business, such as intellectual property rights and technical expertise. Technology and management sharing can potentially create significant problems among the parties. In particular, one party's mastery of the other's technology can lead to improvements on that technology beyond the intended services of the joint venture, a factor that tends to discourage companies from disclosing their technologies for fear of losing the competitive edge to their JVP.

Many commentators argue that joint ventures offer a structure for reducing the 'free riding' of the local joint venture partner because both partners contribute to the costs associated with the exploitation of the technology in proportion to their expected benefits. The theory is that a joint venture partner will have an incentive to focus on protecting the results of the joint venture activities rather than trying to replicate independently the results for its own account.

12.14 Documents for Establishing a Joint Venture

The documentation that usually has to be put in place when establishing a joint venture company in India includes:

1. Memorandum of understanding: The foreign investor and the Indian partner need to establish a clear understanding of each other's objectives for the venture and ensure that they are compatible. The MOU (sometimes called the letter of intent or heads of agreement) can help to achieve this. It should be prepared carefully, with thorough discussion and mediation between the parties. The MOU should usually address:

    i. the parties' intentions and likely progression of the venture;
    ii. commercial terms (such as contributions to the joint venture) in enough detail to ensure that any differences can be identified early in the process;
    iii. management, control and safeguards; division of early costs;
    iv. exclusivity arrangements;
    v. the extent to which the MOU is to be legally binding.

2. *Joint venture or shareholders' agreement:* The JVA establishes the relationship between joint venture partners and the way in which the company will be run. It usually includes clauses on

    i. shares
    ii. management structure
    iii. withdrawal rights
    iv. competition issues
    v. dispute resolution
    vi. IPR
    vii. any warranties or indemnities.

As an example, a JVA often includes an arbitration clause. This normally addresses, among other things:

i. the place of arbitration;
ii. the language in which the arbitration will be conducted;
iii. the number of arbitrators;
iv. the procedure to be followed by the arbitrator or arbitrators.

3. *Constitutional documents:* These are the memorandum and AoA. The article of association is a binding legal document that formalises the constitution of the new company. It should replicate as far as commercially and technically appropriate the terms of the JVA. Consistency between the two documents is important. In the event of any dispute between the AoA and the JVA, the articles prevail.
4. Registered user agreement.
5. Technology licence and know-how agreement (if there is a technology and know-how transfer involved).
6. Directors' service agreements.
7. Corporate governance and policy manual.
8. Other agreements commonly negotiated include those relating to supply, distribution, secondments and confidentiality.

A potential list applicable to different forms of joint venture is given here for an easy checklist.

Nature of Joint Venture Entity	***Documentation***
Incorporated joint venture entity	***Company***
	• JVA/shareholders' agreement (JVA/SHA)
	• MoA and AoA of the joint venture entity
	• Other agreements such as trademark licenses and technology transfers.
	LLP
	• LLP agreement
	• Other agreements such as trade mark licenses and technology transfers.
Unincorporated joint venture entity	***Partnership***
	• Partnership agreement
	• Other agreements such as trademark licenses and technology transfers.
	Cooperation/Strategic Alliance/Consortium
	• Cooperation agreement
	• Other agreements such as trademark licenses and technology transfers.

12.15 Joint Venture Agreement

A JVA is a contract between two or more parties, which can be made up of individuals, sole proprietors, corporations or other types of businesses to assume a project or business activity together. The operations of a joint venture depend on the terms and conditions mentioned in the agreement. Thus, a careful attention is required before finalizing the JVA. The following points demand extra attention from strategic point of view:

a. **Capital contribution:** The capital to be contributed by each party in the agreement should be clearly specified in the JVA. The agreement should specify the initial capital contributions to be made by each party and how future capital contributions will be allocated, which should usually be equal to its respective ownership percentage.

b. **Control:** All the parties in the joint venture should have control in proportion to their ownership interest and proportionate control of the governance of the joint venture. Each joint venture partner should assume full responsibility for executing each element of the work assigned to it. Usually, a joint venture will have a management committee (referred to by various names, including 'executive committee' or 'board'), that controls the overall business. If a partner owns less than 50% of ownership, it is usually referred to as a minority participant, and can be outvoted on most of the business decisions made by the committee. This really means that for the most part, the joint venture is controlled by the party owning 51% or more of the business. However, the agreement should specify the provision of control of the activities by all the participants. There should be some major decisions requiring a unanimous vote to substantiate some level of control attributable to all the parties, including minority participants (e.g., items related to expansion, borrowing, lending money and so on).
c. **Management:** The participants must share in the management of the joint venture. The agreement should address the issue of the overall management or governance of the business of the joint venture and the day-to-day management of the joint venture's operation. The participants should participate in the overall management, decision-making, and day-to-day operations, including decisions on the hiring and firing of management personnel (and, if appropriate, non-management personnel) for the joint venture. This can be accomplished through a management committee, as described under 'control,' though this is not the only acceptable mechanism. Under a management committee structure, the committee is responsible for managing and directing the business of the joint venture. Each participant is represented on the management committee and votes according to its ownership interest in the venture. Each participant on the management committee not only has a right, but an obligation, to receive and consider the views of the minority participant. The agreement should specify the frequency of the management committee meetings, and formal agendas and meeting minutes should be prepared. In addition, the agreement should provide for the day-to-day management of the joint venture and specify the roles and responsibilities of each participant.
d. **Risks:** Each of the participants in the joint venture must share the risks of the business in proportion to their ownership interest. These risks include financial, legal, operational and so on. The agreement should include provisions for proportional sharing in profits as well as losses. However, a monthly distribution of actual profits or monthly payment of a management fee, as defined in the agreement, consistent with industry standards, is permissible.
e. **Profits:** Each of the participants must also share in the profits and losses in proportion to the ownership interest. Accounting methods and the timing of distribution should be included in the agreement and reviewed for reasonableness. There should be no provisions in the agreement have the effect of creating separate profit centres to siphon profits before each participant's share is calculated. For example, requirements to purchase goods and/or services from one of the participants that result in controlling profits remaining for distribution to the joint venture participants are not acceptable. However, purchasing goods and/or services from one of the participants may be acceptable if the terms are spelled out and the cost of the goods reflects the actual cost of the product plus any processing/handling costs and reasonable overhead expenses.

A minority participant in a JVA should be very careful with reference to the points identified above. Otherwise, the joint venture may not be viable financially and may fail as well. Some examples are given here to understand the scenarios from a real-life perspective. These examples are presented from a minority partner's point of view intentionally to generate more wisdom to finance students who may work at strategic level.

Example 1: Suppose a partner (company A) holds 20% ownership in a retail joint venture. The partner shares in the capital contribution, control, overall management (through participation in the management committee), risks and profits of the joint venture that rightly commensurate with its stated ownership interest. The partner is assigned some roles in the business to play, including 'participation in' and 'assistance with' various activities which routinely occur in the day-to-day operation of the business. These roles may be valued as part of the overall management of the business, but should not be valued in terms of performing a distinct, clearly defined portion of the work, since the extent of this participation is unknown and is neither distinct nor clearly defined.

Now, let us assume that the partner is also assigned the role of finding vendors to be utilized by the business and recruiting minority employees for the business.

The major day-to-day activities performed by the business are determined to be approximately:

Operations ***(1/3 of the business effort)***	***Product*** ***(1/3 of the business effort)***	***Administration/Corporate Support*** ***(1/3 of the business effort)***
HR (supervise on-site operations staff, hire/fire staff, scheduling, training, etc.)	Negotiation of special programmes, rebates, display allowances, etc.	Business development/landlord relations
Loss prevention	Inventory management	Legal services
Safety/security	Pricing	Accounting/payroll/taxes
Cash management	Décor/display	Policies/procedures
Day-to-day landlord relations	Product assortment (retail) /menu development (food)	HR/training programmes
Maintenance/cleaning	Purchasing	Other corporate support
Budgeting/monitoring performance	Budgeting/monitoring performance	Budgeting/monitoring performance

The partner's roles of recruiting minority employees and finding vendors are activities included under broader categories: HR (under the 'Operations' category of the business) and purchasing (under the 'Product' category of the business). There are numerous daily activities involved in the subcategories of 'HR' and 'purchasing'. All of 'operations' is about one-third of the business effort in this example and all of 'Product' is also about one-third of the business effort. HR is the only one task within the 'operations' category and purchasing is the only task within the 'Product' category. Recruiting minority employees and finding minority vendors are small tasks within the broader subcategories. In addition, it is difficult, if not impossible, to quantify the value of these tasks in terms of their impact on gross receipts. In fact, it is likely that this portion of the work is negligible since neither of these activities actually involves management of a function or control of a result (i.e., vendors may be located; however, the level of purchasing to be accomplished from these vendors, their product placement within the facility, prices to be paid for merchandise and so on are outside of the control of the partner. Minority employees may be recruited; however, their hiring, training, management and retention are outside of the partner's control). In this instance, the partner's management would not have sufficient data to approve the joint venture for counting towards its participation because the portion of the work to be performed by the partner is very difficult to quantify. In this instance, the management of company A should request that the joint venture participants clarify the role of company A in order to understand the nature and extent of the role that it could play.

Conversely, assume that all other factors are the same as described above (i.e., the ownership is stated as 20% and capital contributions, management and so on are commensurate), except that the partner independently performs all functions in the operations category. In this case, it could reasonably be determined that the partner performs at least 33% of the work for its 20% ownership share. However, because the definition states that the partner shares in the capital contribution, control, management, risks and profits of the joint venture commensurate with its ownership interest, a joint venture where the partner's contributions are not proportionate does not meet the definition of a joint venture. In this instance, the participation could be counted at 20%, not a greater percentage, which might be indicated by the portion of the work performed by the partner.

Example 2: In this example, a joint venture between company A and company B operates a news/gift concession at an airport. Company A (minority) is reported to have a 15% share in the ownership of the joint venture. The minority has contributed capital from its own funds in proportion to its stated ownership. The minority participates on the management committee and there are a number of business decisions requiring unanimous consent. The minority's share of the profits and risks of the joint venture are proportionate to its stated ownership interest. There are management fees paid to company B; however, they are calculated as a reimbursement of costs incurred to perform support functions and are not a profit centre. The minority is assigned the following activities:

a. Supervise the manager in developing the annual budget of the joint venture;
b. Evaluate day-to-day operations and make recommendations to improve efficiencies;
c. Sourcing and recruitment of personnel;
d. Supervise employee training and development;
e. Develop marketing and promotional concepts;
f. Assist and advise regarding the needs of the local community;
g. Identify potential vendors and
h. Monitor store compliance with other income programmes.

Given the description of the various activities above, it is not possible to ascertain exactly what portion of the work will be performed by the minority. In order to assign any credit for the minority's role, additional information is needed for each of the assigned roles as follows:

a. *Supervise the manager in developing the annual budget of the joint venture:* Who does the manager report to for other functions? What control does the minority have over the budget? While budgeting is important, it is only an annual budget and the description does not really indicate a very active role. How much time will be spent on this? Exactly what will the minority do?
b. *Evaluate day-to-day operations and make recommendations to improve efficiencies:* Without further explanation, this appears to be a relatively meaningless role. What happens to the evaluations and recommendations once they are made? How often does this occur? Who actually does it? This seems to apply more to the overall management of the business. There is no supporting evidence to indicate that it is a distinct, clearly defined role.
c. *Sourcing and recruitment of personnel:* What exactly does this activity entail? Is the minority actually responsible for hiring? How often does this occur and what is the level of effort expended to accomplish this? Does on-site staff participate? If so, to what extent?

d. *Supervise employee training and development:* Who will the minority supervise? What level of effort is required for this activity? How much time is involved? Describe the nature of the training and development to be supervised.
e. *Develop marketing and promotional concepts:* Is the minority solely responsible for marketing? What level of effort is required? How much time is involved? What is the budget for this? Are employees involved? If so, to whom do they report?
f. *Assist and advise regarding the needs of the local community:* An 'assist' role does not appear to represent a 'distinct, clearly defined' portion of the work. What is meant by the 'needs of the local community?' Describe what the needs of the community might be. This seems to be a minor role in the overall scope of the operations.
g. *Identify potential vendors:* What happens after the vendors are identified? Who has control over determining if they are used? Who negotiates with them and determines if goods or services will be purchased? What does this represent in dollars compared to the total purchases made?
h. *Monitor store compliance with other income programmes:* This is, again, very unclear. What happens after monitoring? Who determines what compliance is necessary? What happens in the event of non-compliance? How often is this monitoring done? How long does it take? How is it accomplished in other operations? How important is this in the scope of the operation?

As you can see, before any credit is assigned for minority's participation, there are a number of questions to be answered and issues to be resolved. Until the minority is assigned a 'distinct, clearly defined' portion of the work to perform, no credit can be given.

Example 3: A joint venture between company A and company B operates a food/beverage concession consisting of eight locations at a metropolitan city. Company A is reported to have a 35% share in the ownership of the joint venture. Company A has contributed its proportionate share of the capital obtained through a combination of its own funds (15% of the required investment) and a loan from company B (85% of the required investment). A loan agreement has not been supplied. Company A participates on a management committee and certain business decisions require unanimous consent. It shares in the profits and risks of the joint venture in proportion to its stated ownership interest. There are no management fees paid to either party. The following is the description of company A's role in the operation of the business as supplied in the JVA:

a. The company will have primary responsibility for the operation of gourmet coffee locations in locations 1, 2 and 3.
b. The company will employ staff to manage and operate said locations in accordance with the lease agreement and direction provided by the management committee.
c. The company will attend and participate in weekly manager's meetings.
d. The company will attend and participate in monthly meetings of the management committee.

Given the above situation, the minority should request the following information in order to assess the credit to be counted towards its participation for this joint venture:

a. A copy of the proposed loan agreement in order to ensure that the loan provides required information of the joint venture guidance.
b. A clear explanation of what 'primary responsibility' actually means.
c. An estimate of gross receipts to be earned by company A-operated locations compared to total gross receipts.

While there are questions to be answered in order to determine the credit to be counted for this joint venture, the fact that the minority will be assigned specific units to operate will provide a more objective basis for establishing credit.

12.16 Some Important Considerations in Joint Venture Operation

Equity shares	Ownership/voting shares of the parties will be vital: • will it be a 50:50 deadlock joint venture—or will one of the parties have a majority interest? • will economic ownership and voting rights be the same?
Funding	It is crucial to establish the legal obligations of the parties in respect of capital contributions, both at the outset and in the future: • will initial capital be provided in cash/non-cash assets? • initial debt–equity ratio? • obligations to contribute further capital, perhaps up to a maximum limit and/or in defined tranches? or no obligation to commit future finance? • shareholder loans? • obligation to provide guarantees or counter-indemnities to support finance raised by the joint venture? • by what authority/procedure are new issues of shares to be made, by mutual agreement or by majority decision of the shareholders/board of directors? pro rata offerings? • outside finance? project finance to be secured on, and serviced from, the income stream of the venture? • venture capital funding? Many start-up ventures now seek funding in part from a venture capital or similar equity provider. Such finance providers will have particular objectives, including negotiation of exit routes to ensure an ability to sell their investment, hopefully at a profit, within a relatively short period (routes may include: a put option; redemption or buy back of shares; a right to initiate a trade sale or public offering; rights of 'drag along' or 'tag along'). Techniques may also be used to incentivise management or founders of the JVC.

Corporate governance	Management structure and corporate governance rights will usually be closely related to equity ownership. The key issues include
	• rights to appoint directors;
	• who will appoint the executive management team?
	• what authority is to be given to individual managers (e.g., CEO)? what matters must be dealt with at board level?
	• what are to be 'reserved matters' for decision by the shareholders themselves and/or will any 'super-majority' vote be required for particular decisions at shareholder or board level? Matters which might be considered include:
	    • changes in the JVC's AoA;
	    • new issues of share capital (including grant of share options);
	    • significant changes in nature of the business of the JVC;
	    • major acquisitions or disposals;

(continued)

(continued)

<table>
<tr><td></td><td><ul>
<li>capital expenditure or contract commitments in excess of pre-agreed limits;</li>
<li>borrowing limits;</li>
<li>dividend policy;</li>
<li>appointment and dismissal of key management;</li>
<li>material dealings with intellectual property; and</li>
<li>dealings between the JVC and its shareholders (except arms' length dealings in the ordinary course of business).</li>
</ul></td></tr>
<tr><td>Minority protection</td><td>If a minority interest is involved, such a participant will wish to protect its interests in a number of areas. The objectives may include:
<ul>
<li>to participate in management through board representation;</li>
<li>to be involved in major decisions (including, possibly, a right of veto);</li>
<li>to protect against its equity stake being improperly diluted;</li>
<li>to ensure proper distribution of profits;</li>
<li>to establish adequate access to information regarding the joint venture's affairs;</li>
<li>to establish 'exit' routes (including, possibly, put option rights or 'tag along' rights).</li>
</ul>
The interests of the minority participants will, of course, need to be reconciled with those of the majority participant. The latter will often have different objectives, such as to control management appointments, to minimize minority veto rights and, frequently, to establish 'drag along' or other rights to enable it to deliver a sale of the joint venture as a whole to a third party. A balance will have to be struck.</td></tr>
<tr><td>Exit</td><td>When, and how, should a party be able to exit or terminate its interest in the joint venture? Parties are often reluctant at the start of their joint venture to discuss the possibility of its break-up or termination. A well-prepared joint venture should, nevertheless, provide for that possibility. Basic exit or termination scenarios include the following:
<ul>
<li>Unilateral exit or termination (i.e., the wish of one party to terminate and/or exit by notice): This will usually involve a right to sell to a third party purchaser subject to a right of pre-emption in favour of the continuing parties. Sometimes, it will not be feasible to permit transfer without consent of the other shareholder(s) (this simple formula at least reduces the length of the agreement!); the question then is whether a party should have a right to compel liquidation in certain circumstances;</li>
<li>Termination for cause or as a result of a 'trigger event'. If the parties agree that a particular event should trigger the right of another party to institute a call option or other termination procedure, the 'trigger event' needs to be carefully defined, for example:
<ul>
<li>insolvency of a party;</li>
<li>change of control? (inclusion of a change of control provision can be material and contentious, particularly if the joint venture comprises a significant part of a party's business);</li>
<li>material breach? (this is often more relevant for a venture where funding commitments are significant);</li>
<li>deadlock.</li>
</ul></li>
</ul></td></tr>
<tr><td>Put/call options</td><td>Sometimes the parties will agree at the outset that one party will have a right, at a specified time and usually at a specified price or at a third party valuation, to 'put' its shares (i.e., an option to require the other party to buy that party's shares) or a right to 'call' for the other party's shares (i.e., an option to acquire that other party's shares in the JVC).</td></tr>
</table>

(Continued)

(Continued)

<table>
<tr><td>Pre-emption rights</td><td>It is common for joint ventures to include contractual provisions, whereby prior to a proposed transfer of shares to a third party, the other shareholders are given a pre-emption right. Points that arise include the following:<ul><li>The price may be set by reference to a price which an identified third party purchaser is prepared to pay (the continuing party having a right to match that pricea right of first refusal); or a price proposed by the transferor before it finds a third party purchaser (the continuing party having a right of first offer at that price); or a price determined by a third party valuer (if the latter, it will be important to establish the valuation criteria to be applied—including whether or not a discount/premium is to apply to reflect the size of the shareholding being sold);</li><li>If a majority party wishes to sell, should it be entitled to 'drag along' the minority party (i.e. require the minority party to sell its shares at the same price per share as that offered by the third party) so that it can deliver the whole JVC to the third party?;</li><li>Should the minority party have the right to 'tag along' or 'piggy-back' by requiring that a third party purchaser must extend to the minority party the same offer price per share as it is offering to the majority party?</li></ul></td></tr>
<tr><td>Deadlock resolution</td><td>Joint ventures carry with them an inherent prospect of management deadlock. Schools of thought differ as to the desirability of formal deadlock resolution mechanisms. Some parties require the certainty of outcome, leading to mechanisms such as a casting vote or a role for a third-party non-executive 'swing' vote.<ul><li>A common formula is for any deadlock/dispute to be escalated to the chairmen/chief executives of the joint venture participants or, perhaps, an intermediate panel of executives or, sometimes, to be subject to a formal mediation procedure.</li><li>If there is a prolonged and fundamental dispute, do the parties wish to include a specific 'divorce' mechanism such as a right to terminate and initiate liquidation; or to commence a 'shoot-out' procedure (e.g., a 'Russian roulette' or 'Texas shootout' procedure) between the parties as a result of which one party will buy out the other:<ul><li>a 'Russian roulette' procedure is basically one which allows one party to offer to buy out the shares of the other party at a certain price but with the other party having the right to decide either to accept and sell its shares or, instead, to buy out the first party's shares at the same price;</li><li>a 'Texas shoot-out' (at least in some variants) is where both parties wish to buy, and a sealed bid procedure takes place to determine who is the higher bidder.</li></ul></li></ul>These mechanisms can be contentious. Their most significant advantage is that the uncertain outcome may act as an incentive to persuade the parties to reach a commercial solution before they are implemented. Another school of thought dislikes such formal deadlock resolution mechanisms and believes that the inherent continuing damage to a joint venture of a prolonged deadlock will create, for all parties, a commercial need to reach an agreed solution.</td></tr>
</table>

Multiple Choice Questions

1. A ________ is a contractual agreement joining together two or more parties for the purpose of executing a particular business undertaking.
   a. Strategic alliance b. Joint venture c. LBO d. Merger

2. The best known and probably the ideal type of joint venture is where a completely new entity is created 'from scratch' and each partner has an equal contribution.
   a. Majority joint venture
   b. Minority joint venture
   c. 50:50 joint venture
   d. None
3. Which one of the following is a reason for forming a joint venture?
   a. Sharing risk
   b. Managing geographical constraints
   c. Enjoying economies of scale
   d. All of the above
4. Which one of the following joint venture is not an example of 50:50 joint venture?
   a. Hit Company (Republic of Slovenia) and Harrah's Entertainment (U.S.) (2007)
   b. IBM (U.S.) and Lenovo Group (China) (2004)
   c. Pontiac Land Group (Singapore) and West Paces Hotel Group (U.S.) (2006)
   d. Siemens AG (Germany) and Nokia Corp. (Finland) (2006)
5. What may be a preferred form of joint venture?
   a. Company
   b. Strategic alliance
   c. Partnership
   d. Any
6. Which one of the following is not an advantage of joint venture?
   a. Acceleration of revenue growth
   b. New product development
   c. Time consuming
   d. Ability to increase profit margins
7. Which one of the following is not a disadvantage of joint venture?
   a. Partners may have different objectives for the joint venture
   b. Varied organizational structures
   c. Acceleration of revenue growth
   d. Working in a different legal and commercial system
8. The government had recently allowed foreign investment up to _______ in mining for commercial purposes.
   a. 49% b. 50% c. 51% d. None
9. In case one of the partners of the joint venture company is a non-resident, approval will be required for acquiring shares of the company from _______
   a. RBI b. FIPB c. SEBI d. None of the above
10. Which one of the following is an important document for incorporated company joint venture entity?
    a. JVA/shareholders' agreement
    b. MoA and AoA of the joint venture entity
    c. Trademark licenses
    d. Partnership agreement

Review Questions

1. Explain the meaning and nature of joint ventures.
2. What are the basic elements of a joint venture?
3. How are joint ventures different from strategic alliance?
4. List and explain the various equity variations in a joint venture.
5. Elaborate on the different motivations that lead formation of a joint venture.
6. How are joint ventures managed?
7. List the various factors that are usually considered before formation of a joint venture.
8. Briefly discuss the advantages and disadvantages associated with joint ventures.
9. Explain the important steps for forming a joint venture company in India.
10. Write a critical note on the documentations required for establishing a joint venture.

Case in Action

Bharti–Walmart Retail

Introduction

On 27 November 2006, Walmart Stores, Inc (Walmart), the world's largest retailer, and Bharti Enterprises Ltd. (Bharti), a leading business group in India, signed a MoU to explore business opportunities in the Indian retail industry. This joint venture marked the entry of Walmart into the Indian retailing industry. According to Sunil B. Mittal (Mittal), chairman and managing director, Bharti, 'The joint venture with equal stakes will operate in areas where the government allows foreign investment in retail like cash-and-carry and logistics. The retail shops will be owned by Bharti Enterprises under the Walmart franchise. The idea is to give Indians the lowest price every day'. Many analysts opined that both the parties in the venture had their own strengths and would complement each other. Viswanathan Vasudevan, an equity analyst at the Singapore-based Aquarius Investment Advisors Pte, said, 'It's a great fit for Walmart as Bharti knows the rules of the game and will save Walmart a lot of time and energy to overcome the system. For Bharti, you can't get a better partner than Walmart in retail'. Gajendra Nagpal, director, Unicorn Investments, said, 'This joint venture is a winning combination. Walmart's logistics skill and Bharti's execution capability will create a potent force in the Indian market'. This franchise strategy with Bharti was a deviation from Walmart's usual way of entering countries. This was because the policy restrictions on FDI in the Indian retail sector. As part of the agreement, Bharti was expected to pay a royalty between 2% and 3% of sales to Walmart for using the latter's brand name. The Bharti–Walmart joint venture was expected to open its stores in India from August 2007. Though the parties did not disclose the financials of the deal, according to retail industry sources, the Bharti–Walmart venture would make an initial investment of US$100 million, which could further increase to US$1.46 billion. Walmart had reportedly brought in two veteran executives, Andy Guttery and Lance Rettig, to implement its operations in India under the joint venture. Walmart had also roped in Raj Jain, emerging markets president and CEO, Walmart, to head the cash-and-carry business in India.

The retail industry in India is estimated at about US$300 billion and was expected to grow to US$427 billion in 2010 and US$637 billion in 2015. Moreover, only 3% of the Indian retail industry was in the organized sector. Foreign retailers were keen to enter India's rapidly growing retail market. However, the government had permitted retailers of single brand products to own a majority stake in a joint venture with a local partner (with prior government permission). Retailers of multibrands were only permitted to operate through franchisees and licensees, or a cash-and-carry wholesale model. The biggest competitor for Bharti–Walmart was expected to be Reliance Retail, the retail wing of Reliance, which had planned to establish 10,000 stores by 2010. It had already opened 11 pilot stores under the 'Reliance Fresh' format in Hyderabad. Even Pantaloon Retail, the retail arm of the Future Group was expected to give stiff competition as it had a first-mover advantage. Kishore Biyani, CEO, Future Group, said, 'Our strength is that we understand the Indian consumer better than Walmart and we also have a window of opportunity and the first-mover advantage. For instance, we will have 100 Big Bazaars across India by the time the first store (of Bharati–Walmart) opens its doors here'.

A few other Indian retailers felt that the entry of foreign retail giants like Walmart, Carrefour SA and Tesco Plc (Tesco) would result in Indian retailers learning some of the best international practices in retailing. However, analysts noted that the success of the joint venture would depend on how successful Walmart is in building a cost-efficient supply chain and sourcing network so that the cost savings are passed on the end consumer through its trademark 'everyday low price' strategy. Some experts felt that Walmart may find it difficult to achieve economies of scale in items such as personal consumer products and may be able to achieve more success in fruits and vegetables as there was still scope for disintermediation. Some also cited the fact that Walmart's business model was not successful in all foreign markets. For example, Walmart had withdrawn its retail operations in Germany and South Korea.

However, in the short term, the Bharti–Walmart joint venture was confronted with problems due to the opposition by the Left parties as they insisted that the government should look into the matter to stop the 'backdoor entry' of Walmart into India. These parties opposed the joint venture stating that FDI in retail trade was not allowed under the existing policy and that it would impact the vast number of unorganized retailers, domestic manufacturers and farmers in India.

Source: http://www.icmrindia.org/Short Case Studies/Business Strategy/CLBS078.htm

Questions for Discussion

1. Discuss the rationale that led to the joint venture between Bharati and Walmart in the Indian retail sector.
2. What mutual benefits and strategic synergies are expected from the Bharati and Walmart joint venture?
3. Do you foresee any future challenges that would be confronted by Bharati and Walmart venture? If yes, identify the specific challenges and suggest methods to overcome these.

Case in Action

Sony Ericsson

Introduction

Sony Ericsson is a joint venture established on 3 October 2001 by the Japanese consumer electronics company Sony Corporation and the Swedish telecommunications company Ericsson to make mobile phones. The stated reason for this venture is to combine Sony's consumer electronics expertise with Ericsson's technological leadership in the communications sector. Both companies have stopped making their own mobile phones. The company's global management is based in Hammersmith, London, and it has R&D teams in Sweden, Japan, China, Germany, the United States, India, Pakistan and the United Kingdom. By 2007, it was the fourth-largest cell phone manufacturer in the world after Nokia, Motorola and Samsung. The sales of products largely increased due to the launch of the Walkman and Cyber-shot series.

Performance of Sony Ericsson

While Sony Ericsson has been enjoying strong growth recently, its South Korean rival LG Electronics overtook it in Q1 2008 due to the company's profits falling significantly by 43% to €133 million (approximately US$193.6746 million), sales falling by 8% and market share dropping from 9.4% to 7.9%, despite favourable conditions that the handset market is expected to grow by 10% in 2008. Sony Ericsson announced another profit warning in June 2008 and saw net profit crash by 97% in Q2 2008, announcing that it would cut 2,000 jobs, leading to wide fear that Sony Ericsson is on the verge of decline along with its struggling rival, Motorola. In Q3, the profits were much on the same level; however, November and December saw increased profits along with new models being released such as the C905 being one of the top sellers across the United Kingdom. Sony Ericsson has, as of 18 July 2008, approximately 9,400 employees and 2,500 contractors worldwide. Hideki Komiyama is the president of the company and has been since 1 November 2007, when he replaced Miles Flint. The corporate executive vice president is Anders Runevad.

Troubles in Ericsson's Mobile Phone Business

In the United States, Ericsson partnered with General Electric in the early nineties, primarily to establish a U.S. presence and brand recognition. Ericsson had decided to source pon chips for its phones from a single source, a Philips facility in New Mexico. In March 2000, a fire at the Philips factory contaminated the sterile facility. Philips assured Ericsson and Nokia (the other major customer of the facility) that production would be delayed by less than a week. When it became clear that production would actually be compromised for months, Ericsson was faced with a serious shortage. Nokia had already begun to obtain parts from alternative sources, but Ericsson's position was much worse as both production of current models and the launch of new ones was held up. Ericsson, which had been in the cellular phone market for decades and was the world no. 3 cellular telephone handset maker, was struggling with huge losses in spite of booming sales since 2000 due to this fire and its inability to produce cheaper phones like its competitor Nokia. To curtail the losses, it was thinking of outsourcing production to Asian companies that can produce the handset for lower costs. Speculation had begun about a possible sale by Ericsson of its mobile phone division but the company's president said that it had no plans to do that. 'Mobile phones is really a core business for Ericsson. We wouldn't be as successful (in networks) if we didn't have phones,' he said.

Background of the Joint Venture

Sony was a marginal player in the worldwide cell phone market with a share of less than 1% in 2000. It was also struggling in this area with losses but wanted to focus more in this area. In April 2001, Sony confirmed that it was in talks with Ericsson for a possible collaboration in the handset business. This was soon after Toshiba and Siemens had announced plans in November 2000 to work together on handsets for 3G mobile networks. By August 2001, the two companies had finalized the terms of the merger announced in April. The company was to have an initial workforce of 3,500 employees.

Early Troubles

In spite of having aimed to be profitable in its very first year, Ericsson's market share actually fell and in August 2002, Ericsson said it would stop making mobile phones and end its partnership with Sony if the business continues to disappoint even as Sony said it was fully committed to the joint venture and wanted to make it a success. However, in January 2003, both companies said they would inject more money into the joint venture in a bid to stem the losses. Sony Ericsson's strategy was to release new models capable of digital photography as well as other multimedia capabilities such as downloading and viewing video clips and personal information management capabilities. To this end, it released several new models which had built-in digital camera and colour screen which were novelties at that time. The high-end P800, which featured a built-in camera and PDA attributes, was successful and helped in turning around. The joint venture, however, continued to make bigger losses in spite of booming sales. Thus, it kept postponing its target date for making a profit from its first year to 2002 to 2003 to second half of 2003. It even failed in its mission of becoming the top seller of multimedia handsets and was in fifth place and struggling in 2003.

Beginning of the Turnaround

In June 2003, Sony Ericsson said it would stop making CDMA cell phones for the U.S. market and would focus on GSM, which was and remains the dominant technology. It also slashed jobs in R&D in the United States and Germany. In October 2003, it posted its first quarterly profit but warned that falling prices on phones and competition would make it difficult to stay in black. Sony Ericsson's recovery is credited to the success of the T610 model. Following the success of its P800 phone, Sony Ericsson introduced the P900 at simultaneous events in Las Vegas and Beijing in October 2003. It was pegged as smaller, faster, simpler and more flexible than its predecessor. In March 2004, Ericsson said it would try to block its rival Nokia from gaining control of Symbian, an industry consortium that makes operating software for phones. In 2004, Sony Ericsson's market share increased from 5.6% in the first quarter to 7% in the second quarter. In July 2004, Sony Ericsson unveiled the P910 communicator with its integrated thumb board, broad e-mail support, quadruple memory and improved screen. In February 2005, Sony Ericsson president Miles Flint announced at the 3GSM World Congress that Sony Ericsson will unveil a mobile phone-cum-digital music player in the next month. It would be called the Walkman phone and would play music file formats such as MP3 and AAC.

Success with Walkman Phones and Beyond

On 1 March 2005, Sony Ericsson introduced the K750i with a 2 megapixel camera, the W800i, the first of the highly successful Walkman phones capable of doing 30 hours of music playback and two low-end phones. On 1 May 2005, Sony Ericsson agreed to become the global title sponsor for the WTA Tour in a deal worth 88 million U.S. dollars over 6 years. The women's pro-tennis circuit was renamed the Sony Ericsson WTA Tour. Just over a month later on June 7, it announced sponsorship of West Indian batsmen Chris Gayle and Ramnaresh Sarwan. In October 2005, Sony Ericsson presented the first mobile phone based on UIQ 3, the P990. On 2 January 2007, Sony Ericsson announced in Stockholm that it will be having some of its mobile phones produced in India. It announced that its two outsourcing partners, Lextronic and Foxconn, would produce 10 million cell phones per year by 2009. CEO Miles Flint announced at a press conference held with India's communications minister Dayanidhi Maran in Chennai that India was one of the fastest-growing markets in the world and a priority market for Sony Ericsson with 105 million users of GSM mobile telephones. On 2 February 2007, Sony Ericsson acquired UIQ Technology, a Swedish software company from Symbian Ltd. UIQ will remain an independent company, Miles Flint announced. On 15 October 2007, Sony Ericsson announced on Symbian Smartphone Show that they will be selling half of its UIQ share to Motorola, thus making UIQ technology owned by two large mobile phone companies.

Success with Cyber-shot

Sony Ericsson has also had great success with their Cyber-shot brand. It was launched in 2005 by the K750, which was one of the most popular Sony Ericsson phones. The reasons were it had memory card capability, which was very novel then. The Cyber-shot became very popular very quickly, because unlike Walkman, which had a very good media package and a poor camera, it had a decent media viewing and good cameras. In 2007, their first 5-megapixel camera phone, the K850 was announced. It was very successful. They also announced the C905 in 2008, which was very important because it was the world's first announced 8-megapixel phone. Indian operations are headed by Mr Sudhin Mathur from the Gurgaon office. Regional offices are in west, south and east. The western region office is in Mumbai, headed by Mr S. Perincherry and Mr Chauhan. South operations are controlled by Mr Madhoo Ramaswamy from the Banglore office. Eastern India office is in Saltlake, Kolkata, headed by marketing manager Mr Sudipta Pakrashi. Currently, India has been announced as a region headed by Mr Anil Sethi.

Main Areas of Interest

The Sony Ericsson K750i is one of the most successful Sony Ericsson products.

Sony Ericsson currently concentrates on the categories of: music, camera, business (web and email), design, all-rounder and budget-focused phones. Its four largest categories are:

a. The Walkman-branded W-series music phones, launched in 2005. The Sony Ericsson W-series music phones are notable for being the first music-centric series mobile phones, prompting a whole new market for portable music that was developing at the time. Sony Ericsson's Walkman phones have previously been commercially endorsed by pop stars Christina Aguilera and Jason Kay across Europe.
b. The Cyber-shot-branded line of phones, launched in 2006 in newer models of the K series phones.
c. This range of phones is focused on the quality of the camera included with the phone. Cyber-shot phones always include a flash, some with a xenon flash, and also include auto-focus cameras. Sony Ericsson kicked off its global marketing campaign for Cyber-shot phones with the launch of 'Never Miss a Shot'. The campaign featured top female tennis players Ana Ivanović and Daniela Hantuchová. On 10 February 2008, the series has been expanded with the announcement of C702 and C902 phones.
d. The BRAVIA-branded line of phones, launched in 2007 Japan market only. Now, two mobile phones (FOMA SO903iTV and FOMA SO906i) use BRAVIA brand. BRAVIA-branded phones are able to watch 1seg terrestrial television.
e. The UIQ smartphone range of mobiles, introduced with the P series in 2003 with the introduction of P800.
f. They are notable for their touchscreens, QWERTY keypads (on most models) and use of the UIQ interface platform from Symbian OS. This has since expanded into the M series and G series phones.
g. The Xperia range of mobile phones, heralded by the Sony Ericsson XPERIA X1 on February 2008 at the Mobile World Congress (formerly 3GSM) held in Barcelona Spain, had opened the door

for integration of Windows Mobile Operating System into Sony Ericsson powerhouse smartphones. XPERIA was the first trademark promoted by the Sony Ericsson as its own and is designated to provide technological convergence among its target user base.

Source: www.essays.se

Questions for Discussion

1. Briefly sketch the background to formation of joint venture of Sony Ericsson.
2. Discuss the troubles with mobile phone business of Erricson and with Sony Ericsson joint venture.
3. How Walkman phones changed the business fortune of Sony Ericsson?
4. List and explain the product range of Sony Ericsson.

References

Kelshikar, S.D., and M. Shah. 2015. 'Corporate Restructuring: A Conceptual Framework'. *International Journal of Research in Computer Application & Management*, 5(7): 38.

Levins, Cary, and James S. Lawlor. 1988. "Legal Considerations of Joint Ventures". In *The Handbook of Joint Venturing*. Edited by John D. Carter, Robert F. Cushman, and C. Scott Hartz. Homewood, IL: Dow Jones–Irwin.

Further Readings

Arun, T.K. 2006. 'It's Advantage Bharti in Deal with Wal-Mart'. *The Economic Times*, 29 November.

'Bharti Ties-up with Wal-Mart'. *The Financial Express*, 27 November 2006.

'Bharti Retail Foray with Wal-Mart'. 2006. Available at http://in.biz.yahoo.com/061117/203/69hfc.html

Bhattacharya, Sindhu. 2006. 'You Can Shop at Wal-Mart in 2007'. Available at http://www.dnaindia.com/report.asp?NewsID=1066554 (last accessed on 1 September 2016).

http://www.akamai.com/html/customers/case_study_sonyericsson.html (last accessed on 18 May 2014).

Ramesh, R. 2006. 'Wal-Mart Moves into India'. Available at http://business.guardian.co.uk/story/0,,1958228,00.html#article_continue (last accessed on 14 July 2016).

'Reliance Retail Eyes Pan-India Footprint in 5-yrs'. *Business Standard*, 4 November 2006.

Sony and Ericsson in Joint-venture Talks. Available at http://www.itworldcanada.com (last accessed on 11 May 2014).

Sony in Memory Chip Joint Venture. Available at http://news.bbc.co.uk/2/hi/business/.stm (last accessed on 17 May 2014).

Thakur, Rajeshwari Adappa, and Kala Vijayraghavan. 2006. 'Bharti May Pay 2–3% for WalMart Brand Name'. *The Economic Times*, 27 November.

Venkatesh, P., and S.K. Chaudhuri. 2004. 'Sony Ericsson's Alliance: The Synergies'. Available at http://www.ibscdc.org/Case_Studies/Strategy/Mergers,Acquisitions,Alliances and Synergies/MAA0005.htm (last accessed on 20 August 2016).

'Wal-Mart Deal Runs into a Big Red Wall'. 2006. Available at http://www.tribuneindia.com/2006/20061129/main7.htm (last accessed on 21 August 2016).

Chapter 13

Strategic Alliance

Chapter Objectives

On completion of this chapter, you will be able to understand:

- Basics of strategic alliance
- Meaning, definitions and a brief history of strategic alliance
- Characteristics of strategic alliance
- Reasons for forming strategic alliance
    - Types of strategic alliances
    - Franchising
    - Licensing
    - Management contract
    - Turnkey project
- Tasks for the start-up phase of an alliance
    - Analyse history of inter-institutional relationships
    - Review organizational mandates and cultures
    - Define roles within the individual organizations
    - Address potential operational challenges
    - Implement a monitoring framework to assess alliance performance
- Benefits of strategic alliances
    - Few examples
    - Bank of India (BOI) and Small Industries Development Bank of India (SIDBI)
    - Motorola and In-Focus Joint Systems
    - General Motors and Daewoo
- Risks in strategic alliances
- Measuring strategic alliance success
    - Drivers of strategic alliance
    - Strategic alliance formation
    - Strategic alliance relationship attributes
- Model of successful strategic alliances

One of the fastest-growing trends for businesses today is the increasing number of strategic alliances. According to Booz-Allen & Hamilton (1997), the number of alliances is growing by 20% a year, with 10,000 new alliances reported in 1998 alone. Companies participating in alliances report that at much as 18% of their revenues come from their alliances. The most active area for alliances is Europe where, according to a Booz-Allen survey, many companies report as much as 42% of their revenues coming from alliances with ROIs from their alliances of over 23%. Many companies reported a higher ROI on their alliances than on their core businesses. The 25 companies most active in alliances achieved a 17.2% ROE—40% more than the average of the Fortune 500 companies. Alliances clearly pay off for the participants.

In the new economy, strategic alliances enable businesses to gain competitive advantage through access to a partner's resources, including markets, technologies, capital and people. Teaming up with others adds complementary resources and capabilities, enabling participants to grow and expand more quickly and efficiently. Especially, fast-growing companies rely heavily on alliances to extend their technical and operational resources. In the process, they save time and boost productivity by not having to develop their own, from scratch. They are thus freed to concentrate on innovation and their core business. Many fast-growing companies use strategic alliances to benefit from more established channels of distribution, marketing or brand reputation of bigger, better-known players. However, more traditional businesses tend to enter alliances for reasons such as geographic expansion, cost reduction, manufacturing and other supply-chain synergies.

As global markets open up and competition grows, midsize companies need to be increasingly creative about how and with whom they align themselves to go to the market. For example, strategic alliances form a key element of Toshiba's corporate strategy. They helped the company to become one of the leading players in the global electronics industry. In the early 1990s, Toshiba signed a co-production agreement for light bulb filaments with GE. Jack Welch, the legendary former CEO of GE, was a Toshiba's admirer. According to him, a phone call to Japan was enough to sort out problems if and when they arise, in no time. Since then, Toshiba formed various partnerships, technology licensing agreements and joint ventures. Toshiba's alliance partners include Apple Computers, Ericsson, GE, IBM, Microsoft, Motorola, National Semi Conductor, Samsung, Siemens, Sun Microsystems and Thomson.

Toshiba formed an alliance with Apple Computer to develop multimedia computer products. Apple's strength lay in software technology, while Toshiba contributed its manufacturing expertise. Toshiba created a similar tie-up with Microsoft for hand-held computer systems. In semiconductors, Toshiba, IBM and Siemens came together to pool different types of skills. Toshiba was strong in etching, IBM in lithography and Siemens in engineering. The understanding among the partners was limited to research. For commercial production and marketing, the partners decided to be on their own. In flash memory, Toshiba formed alliances with IBM and National Semi Conductor. Toshiba's alliance with Motorola has helped it become a world leader in the production of memory chips. The tie-up with IBM has enabled Toshiba to become a world's largest supplier of colour flat panel displays for notebooks.

13.1 Strategic Alliance Defined

It is difficult to find a definition of strategic alliance as most writers remain flexible and imply strategic alliance to be any kind of inter-firm links, including mergers and licensing.

Merriam-Webster's Collegiate Dictionary (3rd ed) defines alliance as 'an association or union formed for the furtherance of 'the common interests and aims of the members'.

A strategic alliance associates two or more firms, each desiring to gain manifestedly as well as un-manitestedly by linking specific aspects of their businesses.

The most comprehensive definition has been provided by Yoshino and Rangan (1995), which has the following three necessary and sufficient characteristics.

- The two or more firms that unite to pursue a set of agreed-upon goals remain independent subsequent to the formation of the alliance.

- The partner firms share the benefits of the alliance and control over the performance of assigned tasks—perhaps the most distinctive characteristic of alliances and the one that makes them so difficult to manage.
- The partner firms contribute on a continuing basis in one or more key strategic areas, for example, technology, product and so forth.

By this definition, Yoshino and Rangan (1995) exclude the following from the term strategic alliance: mergers, takeovers and acquisitions, joint ventures of overseas subsidiaries of multinational corporations undertaken for the purpose of entering new geographic markets, licensing and cross-licensing agreements and franchising deals and include inter-firm links established through contractual agreements like joint R&D, joint product development, long-term sourcing agreements, joint manufacturing/marketing, and shared distribution/service; equity arrangements without creation of any new entity like minority equity investments, and equity swaps and with creation of new entity of non-subsidiary joint ventures with or without equal equity holding.

In brief, an alliance may be defined as cooperation between two or more independent firms involving shared control and continuing contributions by all partners for mutual benefit.

13.2 Characteristics of Strategic Alliance

Generally, strategic alliances are arrangements between two or more entities that are created to achieve mutual goals through collaboration. Compared to other types of company-to-company relationship, strategic alliances often have the following characteristics:

a. The two or more firms (partner) that unite to pursue a set of agreed-upon goals.
b. Each partner retains its business independence.
c. The partner firms share the benefits of the alliance and control over the performance of assigned tasks.
d. Usually a non-equity, loosely structured relationship
e. One company will take a lead role in any contract or marketing and the others will be 'partners' in the work. They could work as sub-contractors or suppliers to the main company.
f. The alliance can be struck between companies which would normally be considered competitors.
g. The relative size of the partners is not a significant factor.
h. Each partner must contribute distinctive 'core strengths', for example, technology, manufacturing capacity and access to distribution.

In order to demonstrate the potential of an alliance approach, institutions seeking to form an alliance will need to actively manage and monitor the alliance to ensure that it extends beyond collaboration on individual projects. Institutions will want, in particular, to avoid the worst-case scenario—that they simply work separately on issues of common interest and meet occasionally to discuss their findings. As the institutes begin to work together, they should seek to foster incremental levels of shared functions and actions, such as:

a. Corporate management
    - real vested interest of the CEOs: each hopes to gain strategically from the relationship;
    - joint ownership and co-management of the relationship and
    - risks and benefits identified, recognized and shared by all parties.

b. Financial management
   - mechanisms put in place for managing and reporting on the shared investments and costs of the work.

c. Project management
   - greater scope and scale of projects carried out in collaboration by the parties and
   - planned interaction leading to greater depth and intensity of knowledge exchange and actions.

d. Communications management
   - common language to describe the relationship and
   - protocols for managing delivery of knowledge products and services of the alliance.

e. Staff management
   - incentives and reward systems for staff making the alliance work (ensuring that alliance activities are a priority among all parties).

f. Results management
   - ensuring common understanding and ownership of the alliance's goals and objectives and
   - planning and monitoring the full range of projects and actions to determine whether outcomes from the alliance activities have broader reach and impact.

13.3 Reasons for Forming Strategic Alliances

To understand a firm's competitive strategy, it is necessary to understand the value chain of its business (Porter 1985). Every firm performs a set of discrete tasks related to designing, producing, marketing, delivering and supporting its products. Value activities are normally physically and technologically distinct. In essence, a value chain disaggregates a firm into its component activities. While firms in the same industry tend to have similar value chains, the value chains of competitors often differ in emphasis. Identifying these differences is the first step towards understanding companies' competitive strategies. A firm's value chain and the way it performs individual activities are a reflection of its history, its strategy, its approach to implementing its strategy and the underlying economics of the activities themselves.

Herein lies the strategic logic of alliances—that advantages traditionally gained through internal development may now be secured through external networks. Multinational and national firms alike can strive to compete globally through coalitions or strategic alliances with other independent firms. Coalitions or alliances are, according to Porter (1990), a 'way of broadening scope without broadening the firm by contracting with an independent firm to share activities'. Firms usually enter into alliances in an ad hoc fashion, driven by immediate, tactical reasons.

The major reasons for alliances may include the following:

a. Entering New Markets: Often, a company that has a successful product or service has a desire to introduce it into a new market. Yet, perhaps the company recognizes that it lacks the necessary marketing expertise because it does not fully understand customer needs, does not know how to promote the product or service effectively or does not understand or have access to the proper distribution channels. Rather than painstakingly trying to develop this expertise internally, the company may identify another organization that possesses those desired marketing skills. Then, by capitalizing on the product development skills of one company and the marketing skills of the other, the resulting alliance can serve the market quickly and effectively. Alliances may be particularly helpful when entering a foreign market for the first time because of the extensive cultural differences that may abound. They may also be effective domestically when entering regional or ethnic markets.

b. Reducing Manufacturing Costs: Strategic alliances may allow companies to pool capital or existing facilities to gain economies of scale or increase the use of facilities, thereby reducing manufacturing costs. In the increasingly competitive European automobile market, when the Japanese are seeking to gain market share as they did in the United States during the 1980s, many European companies have formed joint ventures to reduce manufacturing costs. Ford and Volkswagen are jointly planning to make four-wheel-drive vehicles in Portugal, and Nissan and Ford intent to build a plant in Spain to produce vans. These companies will benefit from cost sharing and will reduce expenses by building and operating facilities in relatively low-cost countries, at least by West European standards.

Companies may also reduce costs through strategic alliances with suppliers or customers, reaching agreements to supply products or services for longer periods and working together, meet customers' needs, each partner may apply its expertise, and benefits may be shared in the form of lower costs or new products.

c. Developing and Diffusing Technology: Alliances may also be used to build jointly on the technical expertise of two or more companies in developing products technologically beyond the capability of the companies acting independently. For example, Compaq Computer Corporation, a leading hardware manufacturer, and Microsoft Corporation, the leading software developer, entered into a broad alliance in which they plan to focus on ways to make personal computers easier to install and use. One of their goals is to develop 'plug-and-play' computer systems that would allow consumers to buy a computer and use it immediately rather than having to load software or install extra parts. In addition, users would be able to add capabilities or capacity for more powerful software programs without tinkering with the inner workings of the machine. The partnership will also focus on developing pen-based computers and mobile PCs, promising areas of technology that have been slow to evolve into commercial products. By pooling resources to develop combination hardware–software products built upon the expertise of each company, Compaq and Microsoft intend to create a new market and reap the associated benefits.

The other reasons for alliances could be to:

i. *Satisfy customer demands:* Customer demands in many markets are changing. For example, in office automation, customers now prefer a 'systems solution' and want to rely on a single company to service all equipment.
ii. *Share R&D costs:* High financial stakes and a cut-throat global market have fuelled a spate of competitive alliances in a number of industries.
iii. *Capture new developments:* Companies that are leaders in their fields can maintain that position by using alliances to capture new developments, and keep their technological resource base ahead of the competition.
iv. *Make economies:* Alliances can enlarge dramatically the scope of a company's operations. Alliances focusing on scope help counter the ever-shorter product cycle of modern technology.
v. *Jump market barriers:* However potent the producer company's name may be in its 'home' markets, that company may not market even its mature products best in international markets. Alliance marketing, franchising, distribution and licensing deals can leave a development focused company free to concentrate on new products.
vi. *Speed product introduction:* The narrowing of the development-to-market lead time has been a crucial feature of the past decade. In many sectors, the first company to

introduce a new product enjoys a dominant market position and stands the best chance of recouping costs before the competition arrives to drive prices down or before patent protection expires.

vii. *Pre-empt competitive threats:* In industries in which a few large players increasingly dominate markets, some companies resort to an 'if you can't beat them, join them' approach.

viii. *Use excess capacity:* A large number of companies have used the restructuring effect of manufacturing alliances to soak up excess capacity.

13.4 Types of Strategic Alliances

Corporate strategic objectives are multidimensional and often contradictory. Actions dictated by one strategic objective frequently impede another, equally important objective, requiring managers to prioritize, often with limited success. An alliance-seeking firm may take into account two managerial dimensions such as cooperation and competition/conflict. The task of managing alliances is to optimize along these two dimensions.

The strategic goals of partner firms fall into four broad categories. Two are positive and relate to enhancing firm effectiveness, two defensive, aimed at preventing loss of effectiveness. The first strategic goal is to add value to an activity. The second goal of a partner is to augment its strategic competencies through learning from its opposite. On the defensive side, a partnering firm may maintain strategic flexibility by keeping the options open and creating new options when feasible. Finally, a firm may guard against its core competencies or strategic advantages being appropriated by a partner.

In any joint work, firms are likely to be concerned with sharing the pie, but another, more serious, aspect to conflict is that the firms may be, or anticipate being, rivals in the marketplace. The extent of organizational interaction in the cooperative approach to a joint activity is not merely the frequency of interaction between the collaborating firms but a proxy for a number of related issues.

Taking the extreme values, high and low of conflict potential and cooperative interaction, Yoshino and Rangan (1995) have classified strategic alliances into four distinct types, pro-competitive, non-competitive, competitive and pre-competitive as shown in Figure 13.1.

Figure 13.1 Typology of Alliance

Conflict potential	Extent of Organizational Interaction: Low	Extent of Organizational Interaction: High
High	Pre-competitive alliances	Competitive alliances
Low	Pro-competitive alliances	Non-competitive alliances

Source: Yoshino, Michael Y. and S. Rangan (1995).

The extent of organizational interactions is high among competitive and non-competitive alliances and low among pre-competitive and pro-competitive alliances. The conflict potential among partners is high among pre-competitive and competitive alliances and low among pro-competitive and non-competitive alliances.

a. *Pro-competitive alliances* are generally inter-industry vertical value-chain relationships, as between manufacturers and their suppliers or distributors. Once managed at arm's length, they are now accorded much more attention as the strategic nature of these links is widely recognized.

General Motors' and Hitachi's working together to develop electronic car is representative of pro-competitive alliances. In such links, although firms work closely to develop or improve products and processes, this type of cooperation requires low levels of organizational interaction. Moreover, the firms tend not to be rivals. Indeed, some firms, such as Toyota, rely on a federation of pro-competitive alliances to compete against their market rivals at low levels, the strategic objectives of protecting core competencies and learning take a back seat to those of maintaining strategic flexibility and adding value. Hence, firms like General Motors tend to maintain more than one link for the same activity. Cases of strategic alliances in the Indian industry include a representative of pro-competitive alliance between Telco Ltd and Cummins Engine Company Incorporated (CECI) where the joint venture is set to manufacture diesel engines for Telco vehicles in Jamshedpur.

b. Non-competitive alliances tend to be intra-industry links among non-competitive firms, for example, General Motors and Isuzu, which are jointly developing a small car that both will sell. The level of interaction in this cooperative effort is high. Joint development of a new car calls for close contacts at different levels and in multiple functions (e.g., design, engineering, manufacturing and marketing, to name a few). The firms' competitive universes meet, but only occasionally, and neither views the other as a major rival. Given the partners' significant commitments of time and effort, neither is likely to seek to duplicate its efforts in another alliance. The firms are therefore unlikely to rank flexibility, maintenance and protecting core competencies as high priorities. Learning, on the other hand, is likely to be high on the agendas of the partner firms' managers. Although in the same industry, the partners are sufficiently dissimilar to render an alliance worth considering.

The Indian industry includes a representative of a non-competitive alliance between Ranbaxy Laboratories Limited and Eli Lilly of the United States, where the joint venture is to manufacture and market Lilly brands in the Indian market.

c. Competitive alliances are similar to non-competitive alliances in terms of the joint activity (and hence in the level of organizational interaction) but differ in that the partners are apt to be direct competitors in the final product market. Examples include the ties between General Motors and Toyota, which are jointly manufacturing cars in California, between Siemens and Philips, which are jointly developing a one-megabyte chip, between Motorola and Toshiba, which jointly plan to manufacture microprocessors in Japan, and between Ford and Nissan, which are jointly to manufacture vans in the United States. Such cooperation calls for intense interaction between the paired firms, even though they are direct rivals, with an implicit high potential for conflict. Here, as in the case of non-competitive alliances, maintaining strategic flexibility is unlikely to be uppermost in the minds of managers. Adding value is likely to be important, but not the highest strategic priority.

In the face of competitive rivalry, leakage of information is apt to be detrimental; hence, protection of core strategic competencies is critical. Learning, given the opportunity for it, is also apt to be ranked high by managers.

The Indian industry includes representatives of a competitive alliance between Tata Tea Ltd (TTL) and Hitachi of Japan, where the joint venture will largely function as a marketing and trading company with an aim to market TTL's products in Japan and international market, between Videocon and Sansui, where the Videocon shall use for five years the technology as well as the brand name of Sansui to enter the European market, between Doordarshan and CNN of the United States for CNN to telecast for two years on the Doordarshan network, between Ansal Group and Daewoo Corporation of South Korea and other such joint ventures to develop roads and expressways, between Raymond Industries and Clarity Denim Industries of Italy and other such joint ventures to manufacture denim fabric.

d. Pre-competitive alliances typically bring together firms from different, often unrelated, industries to work on well-defined activities, such as new technology development. DuPont and Sony's cooperative development of optical memory-storage products is an example. Working together, the two firms, neither of which possesses the technological or market know-how to succeed alone, expect to develop a product they will subsequently manufacture and market independently. The joint activity is well defined, involving only limited interaction between the firms, largely confined to researchers from the respective companies.

However, being potential rivals in the memory-storage market adds another dimension to the relationship. Because a technology explored by partners in a precompetitive alliance is liable to be just one of many possibilities, the cooperating firms tend to maintain strategic flexibility by not confining themselves to one relationship. That is, flexibility is a key management concern. Moreover, as product development proceeds and commercialization nears, the competitive element may begin to colour the relationship, with each firm trying to gain insight into the core competencies of the other, rendering protection of core strengths another critical strategic management objective in precompetitive alliances.

An important characteristic of these types of alliances is their capacity to transform an inter-firm relationship from one type to another.

Cases of strategic alliances in the Indian industry, as discussed in detail later, include a representative of precompetitive alliance between Tata Industries Limited and IBM World Trade Corporation of the United States in the field of electronics to make the joint venture India's top information and technology company.

The managers involved in strategic alliances may attend to all the four objectives—maintaining flexibility, protecting core competencies, enhancing learning and maximizing value—recognizing that their relative priority or order of importance tends to vary among the different types of alliances. The relative priority or descending order of importance generally for managers of precompetitive strategic alliances would be flexibility, core protection, learning and value adding. The same for competitive strategic alliances would be core protection, learning, value adding and flexibility. For non-competitive strategic alliances, they would be learning, value adding, flexibility and core protection, and for pro-competitive strategic alliances they would be value adding, flexibility, core protection and learning.

Strategic alliances can be considered on a spectrum ranging from informal collaboration (which hardly merits the term strategic alliance) to group structures and finally merger. Alliances at the left-hand end of the spectrum allow organizations to maintain a great deal of autonomy. Moving across the different types (to the right) requires greater commitment and leads to greater integration.

However, the type of alliance chosen for a particular venture needs to suit the circumstances. A few of them are explained here:

a. Franchising: Franchising is a business strategy for getting and keeping customers. It is a business strategy centred on a strategic alliance between groups of people who share specific relationships and responsibilities in addition to being licensed to use a franchiser's brand name and proprietary way of doing business. It is a marketing system for creating an image in the minds of current and future customers about how the company's products and services can help them.

The parties involved typically enter into a franchise agreement, which binds the parties together through contractual provisions. This is an arrangement whereby someone with a good idea for a business (the franchisor) sells the rights to use the businesses name and sell a product or service to someone else (the franchisee). A franchise agreement will usually specify the given territory the franchisee can use as well as the extent to which the franchisee will be supported by the franchisor (e.g., training and marketing campaigns).

To be successful in franchising, one must understand the business and legal ramifications of the relationship with the franchisers and all the franchisees. The focus must be on working with other franchisees and company managers to market the brand, and fully use the operating system to get and keep customers.

b. Licensing: It is a form of strategic alliance that involves the sale of a right to use certain proprietary knowledge, that is, intellectual property. The intellectual property may be either registered publicly or retained within the firm, which is referred to as know-how. It may include commercial and administrative knowledge as well as technical knowledge. The licensing agreement is the legal agreement setting out what is to be transferred from licensor to licensee and under what conditions. It also includes cross-licensing, which is an agreement between two parties to grant a license to each other for the exploitation of the subject-matter claimed in patents. It is the mutual sharing of patents between companies without exchange of a license fee if both patent portfolios are about equal in value. The importance of licensing is as follows:

i. It multiplies the resources available to the developers of intellectual property.
ii. It creates teams of willing professionals to work on, develop, produce and market the intellectual property.
iii. It provides access to new streams of money that are otherwise unattainable.

c. Management Contract: A management contract is an arrangement under which the operational control of an enterprise is vested by contract in a separate enterprise that performs the necessary managerial functions in return for a fee. Management contracts involve not just selling a method of doing things (as with franchising or licensing) but involve actually doing them. A management contract can involve a wide range of functions such as technical operation of a production facility, management of personnel, accounting, marketing services and training.

Management contracts have been used to a wide extent in the airline industry and when foreign government action restricts other entry methods. Management contracts are often formed where there is a lack of local skills to run a project. It is an alternative to FDI as it does not involve as high risk and can yield higher returns for the company.

d. Turnkey Projects: A turnkey or a turnkey project is a form of strategic alliance in which a separate entity is responsible for setting up a plant or equipment (e.g., trains/infrastructure) and putting it into operations. It can include contractual actions at least through the system, subsystem or equipment installation phase and may include follow-on contractual actions, such as testing, training, logistical and operational support. It is often given to the best bidder in a procurement process. A system is an assemblage of inter-related elements comprising a unified whole. Phase, from the Greek phasis, meaning appearance, has a number of related meanings in English. Procurement is the acquisition of goods or services at the best possible total cost of ownership, in the right quantity, at the right time, in the right place for the direct benefit or use of the governments, corporations or individuals generally, but not limited to a contract.

Turnkey projects can also be extended, known as turnkey plus, where there is perhaps a small equity interest by the supplier and it will later on continue its operation through a management contract or licensing. A management contract is an arrangement under which operational control of an enterprise is vested by contract in a separate enterprise which performs the necessary managerial functions in return for a fee.

Turnkey projects are usually very complex and involve a mix of technical, financial, political and social factors. It is also special in that there is a definite start/end date and it consists of a bundle that is unique to each client.

Some of the key elements of a typical turnkey project are as follows:

- Preparation of equipment specifications for the desired system.
- Preparation of the bid documents.
- Selection of the appropriate equipment vendors and contractors.
- Review and approval of the design drawings.
- Obtaining necessary permits and approvals.
- Construction/installation of the equipment.
- System start-up.
- Performance testing.
- Operator training.
- Demonstration of regulatory compliance.
- System operation and maintenance.

13.5 Tasks for the Start-up Phase of an Alliance

Starting an alliance is not an easy task. It involves many steps, which are discussed here:

1. Analyse History of Inter-institutional Relationships: Relationship analysis is an important component in exploring how an alliance will work. It may be useful to review some of the successes and challenges the institutions have encountered in working together in the past. They will need to map the history of interaction across the organizations involved, with an assessment focus: what worked? What were the challenges?

2. Review Organizational Mandates and Cultures: A critical success factor in making an alliance work is the mutual understanding of organizational mandates and cultures. The institutions will have each emerged out of different circumstances, with many changes in leadership, management, funding levels and strategic priorities over their histories. As a result, each institute has its own unique organizational culture—mandates, constituencies, business models, management structures and communications practices. While the institutions may have known each other and worked together on many different projects, there may not yet be a shared understanding of exactly how and why each institution functions the way it does. Working together will help build a shared understanding of mandates and cultures, but a more formal articulation of these will also be necessary.

3. Define Roles Within the Individual Organizations: An alliance will need to cross-functional boundaries of each organization. The institutions will need to identify the key personnel and articulate their roles. For example, the researchers will need to review their work plans. Financial personnel will need to meet to discuss models for sharing and reporting on funds raised to support activities, including a common format for reporting on in-kind contributions. Communications staff will need to interact on a regular basis to establish a common communications strategy for the alliance.

4. Address Potential Operational Challenges:

a. *Consistency of commitment and timeliness of actions:* A common challenge in collaborative work is the clash of individual institutional priorities and the priorities of the collaboration. Institutions will need to set principles, incentives and performance criteria for all personnel involved in the work of the alliance.

b. *Recognition of boundary relationships:* Each organization in the prospective alliance will belong to many other networks and partnerships. In effect, there are concentric rings of relationships spreading out from the alliance. Institutes will need to plan how to inform and engage other networks and organizations in the various activities of the alliance.

c. *Funding the costs of alliance management:* A common factor in the failure of alliances is the lack of funding available to actually manage the relationship. Institutes will need to determine what the realistic costs are for staff, time and communications necessary to ensure that the relationship does in fact lead to a real added value and better outcomes. In addition, they will need to determine how to make the case for donor support for these costs.

d. *Financial planning and management:* The institutes will need to consider how to manage the funds that are raised to support the alliance. Options may include:

   i. Each institute raises and manages its own funds to participate in the alliance.
   ii. One institute raises funds from several donors and distributes resources to the other institutes in the alliance.
   iii. Each institute raises funds but combines those funds in a common trust fund with trustees drawn from each institute.

Some thoughts on each option are as follows:

   i. If each organization raises and manages its own funds, then some consideration should be given to a financial reporting framework that aggregates the funds raised and spent by each institute in order to demonstrate the overall financial value of the collaboration.
   ii. A common agreement on how the funds will be distributed will need to be secured. Openness on daily rates and overheads will be necessary in order to understand any apparent inequities in amounts distributed to individual alliance members.
   iii. As above, one of the challenges for a common trust fund will be recognizing that each organization has its own daily rates and overheads, and mechanisms for tracking time to projects. If donors are investing in a central fund, will they expect to see comparable fees and overheads paid out to each organization?
   iv. Regardless of which option is adopted, it would be highly beneficial to negotiate with all the donors a common reporting format and schedule to reduce the transactional costs of multiple formats required by different donors.
   v. Also, some thought should be given to how to show the in-kind contributions of each organization.

e. *Developing a common communications strategy:* Some consideration should be given to having the communications staff of each institute work together to identify audiences, messages, vehicles and tactics for alliance work. Branding issues need to be agreed upon. Joint publishing protocols need to be reviewed. Opportunities for sharing media contacts and so forth should be explored.

5. Implement a Monitoring Framework to Assess Alliance Performance: In order to determine whether the partners in the alliance are learning what they need to learn to function as an alliance, they will need to monitor performance on two key points:

a. *Effectiveness of the pilot venture:* Is this alliance really leading to new knowledge and greater impact? An outcome map with progress markers should be established, that will allow the institutes to demonstrate whether and how the objectives of the alliance are being achieved.
b. *Efficiency of the pilot venture:* Are the management issues being addressed? Each institute should develop a few measures to evaluate its own performance, as well as what they might expect from the other parties. These metrics can then be integrated into a shared alliance scorecard that all institutes can use to monitor the pilot alliance's performance.

13.6 Benefits of Strategic Alliances

'If you think that you can go it alone in today's global economy, you are highly mistaken', Jack Welch, chief executive of General Electric, one of the most powerful companies in the world and one of the most active in the area of strategic networking, observed in an interview (Harbison and Pekar 1998: 11).

A business strategic alliance is also means to an end, not just an end in itself. Strategic alliances often take place between firms of different industries and of varied sizes, for vertical or horizontal links, consolidation of positions or any of the following:

a. *Gain a means of distribution in international market:* It may be beneficial for an exporter to ally with an international partner to understand the functioning and the international market network.
b. *Overcome legal or regulatory barriers:* In some countries, it is mandatory to have local partners in order to conduct business. Thus, alliances offer suitable options.
c. *Diversification:* It may be advantageous to enter into an alliance, as a business guide to minimize pitfalls in a new business territory.
d. *Avoiding competition:* An alliance may be entered into with a market leader or a major competitor to avoid competition.
e. *Focus on new products and restructuring:* An alliance in the form of an R&D alliance may focus at the development of new products. Apart from this, an alliance may also enable the firm to adapt to a more effective organizational structure.
f. *Informal and flexibility:* Alliances are less formal than joint ventures. A formal contract may not be written.
g. *Innovation:* It increases the capital for research and product development at lower risk.
h. *Time pressure:* It reduced the product lead times and life cycles.
i. *Skill:* It brings together the complementary skills that cannot be possible for a company to develop on its own.
j. *Technology transfer:* It increases the access to knowledge and expertise beyond company boarders.
k. *Economies of scale:* It rapidly achieves the scale of operation, that is, bigger is better.
l. *Foreign market:* It develops a habit to enter into international market by expansion of channels.

In addition to the above, strategic alliances often bring partners the following benefits:

a. Access to their partner's distribution channels and international market presence
b. Access to their partner's products, technology and intellectual property
c. Access to partner's capital
d. New markets for their products and services or new products for their customers
e. Increased brand awareness through partner's channels
f. Reduced product development time and faster-to-market products
g. Reduced R&D costs and risks
h. Rapidly achieve scale, critical mass and momentum (economies of scale, bigger is better)
i. Establish technological standards for the industry and early products that meet the standards by-product utilization
j. Management skills

13.7 Challenges of the Strategic Alliance

The enterprises enter strategic alliances with other enterprises in order to improve their own competitive position using the resources that others possess and/or which can be developed in cooperation with other business subjects. The cooperation between the enterprises creates the new outlook towards the world because it substitutes the enterprise as a basic source of the economic strength. The examples of cooperation in the global economy are numerous.

If the cooperation is executed with clear strategy and goals on the long-term basis and is connected with the strategic activities of the partner enterprises that remain legally independent, we talk about the strategic partnership. The strategic partnerships represent today one of the fastest-growing trends in the world industry. The recent research of Booz-Allen & Hamilton (1997) showed that, in the last two years, almost 20,000 different strategic alliances have been established. From 1990 until 1996, almost 36,000 strategic alliances have been established between the industries involved in information technology (Booz-Allen and Hamilton Surveys 1997).

The strategic alliance implies the mutual effort of two or more enterprises in realization of the previously agreed goals (Harroch 2000). It represents the connection with the competitor, supplier or customer in whom, by combining the advantages and strengths of the partner, a better competitive position on the global world market is achieved (Anand and Khanna 2000). They are specific organizational forms between the market and the hierarchies. As Gomes-Casseres (1996: 59) pointed out, 'alliances fill the wide gap between these two extremes – they are a unique way to govern incomplete contracts between separate parties'.

The strategic alliances can be simple, with two partner enterprises which share the technological and/or marketing resources, but also very complex and include numerous enterprises from various countries. The enterprises can belong to different strategic alliances according to the same or different strategic businesses or dimensions.

The alliances are not exclusively reserved for global business giants only. The strategy of completely independent market activities is today the most risky and at least prospective for long-term success. It is more difficult for firms to remain self-sufficient in an international business environment that demands both focus and flexibility (Morrison and Mezentseff 1997: 351). The difficulties in realization of the approach to the international market, in realization of sufficient economy of scale and scope as well as the major progress in production and technology lead the enterprises to cooperation.

The partnership between the enterprises becomes, in itself, the effective strategy for the overcoming of the gaps in the know-how, resources and abilities in order to realize the competitiveness on global markets. It all leads to the present-day appearance of economy: the intertwining and interconnection of the enterprises exists together with ever-growing giants of the competitiveness in the struggle for 'future markets'.

Different interpretations and definitions of the strategic alliances contain several common elements.

Primarily, all alliances are made by at least two partners who cooperate in order to realize the common goals. The strategic alliance thus implies the mutual effort of two or more enterprises in realization of the previously agreed goals. That is why the syntagma, 'the marriage between two enterprises', is often used for the strategic alliances. This analogy emotionally represents the purpose of the alliance for the partners: 'together in good and evil, till death do us part' (Doz and Hamel 1998: 30).

The alliances are based on the reciprocity: the partners take over, change or integrate the specific business resources for their own benefit (Cauley de la Sierra 1994: 4). The earlier competitors on the market become often partners in the alliance. Over half of the total number of the alliances established in the past few years are made between the competitors. The situations occur when the enterprises are the partners in one business activity and competitors in another one.

The industries and markets change their structures by increasing the importance of strategic alliances. The alliances between enterprises are established in order to achieve mutual goals of partner enterprises. We can say that the enterprises as well as the strategic alliances are, in fact, different forms (organizational and inter-organizational) with the same purpose: to form and supervise the competence in order to achieve the competitive abilities that enable the maximization of economic results.

The specific motives for joining the strategic alliance can be different for each enterprise: synergic impacts, conquering the new markets, sharing of the risk, technology transfer, education, better usage of the resources, pressure on competition and so on. All those motives can find their source either in 'competitive race for the future' or in 'competitive race for the world market'. Which out of these two motives will the enterprise choose as the reason for joining the strategic alliance depends on the manner in which the alliance creates the value. The process of cooperation in the alliance can bring to the identification of the unrecognized opportunities on the market.

13.8 Strategic Alliance in the Indian Industry

The emerging globalization due to liberalization is opening up yet another major dimension in the field of strategic management—the strategic alliance. The concept of strategic alliance is causing far more impact than that of a mere business management practice. Apart from creating transnational corporations, it is fading the boundaries of identity of not only corporations, but even that of nations. Some cases of strategic alliances of Indian companies are discussed here:

According to Ratan Tata, very few Indian businessmen have the capability of competing on their own in the emerging environment of globalization. The businessmen are concerned about their individual sovereignty, whereas they should be looking at alliances and aggregation of companies as it so often happens abroad (Karmali and Ravi 1995). In the Tata–IBM joint venture in the field of electronics, Tata has accepted five IBM members in the eight-member management committee. Ratan Tata says that his group has no fetish about control.

IBM World Trade Corporation and Tata Industries Limited have entered into a joint venture to form Tata Information Systems Limited (TISL) to make it the country's top information and technology company in terms of market share, customer satisfaction and in being viewed as a national asset.

TTL, the world's largest integrated tea company, will control a 51% majority equity stake in its Japanese joint venture with Hitachi, one of the largest conglomerates in Japan. Hitachi will have a 49% stake. The TTL–Hitachi joint venture will largely function as a marketing and trading company with an aim to market TTL's products in the growing Japanese market and also enter the field of international business, including commodities trading. Once the tea and coffee exports gets underway on a major scale, the joint venture will target the arena of international business, including spices and other commodities and third-country trading. A Japanese base will give TTL a competitive advantage not only in terms of servicing other countries but also in assessing one of the world's most demanding markets: Japan.

CECI, the U.S.$5 billion company of the United States, and pioneers in the manufacture of diesel engines, is all set to make a big sway in the Indian diesel engine market with its joint venture with Telco Ltd to manufacture Telco engines. CECI is setting up a new line of smaller engines for Telco vehicles in Jamshedpur. Significantly, this plant would have 20% to 30% of CECI's current worldwide capacity. CECI has also tied up with the Tatas to expand its turbocharger capacity in India.

The telecom sector has seen a series of strategic alliances between the Indian partners and foreign companies, as the Indian government has laid down a condition that no foreign company can enter the Indian telecom sector without its having a joint venture with an Indian company.

A series of joint ventures thus ventured into overnight are the following: Reliance Industries Ltd and Nynex Corporation; Aditya Birla Group and AT&T; Tata Industries and Bell Canada; Essar Group and Bell Atlantic; Ashok Leylands (Hindujas)–HCL and Singapore Telecom; BPL Systems and US West; RPG Telecom (Basic) and NTT Corporation; RPG Telecom (GSM) and Air Touch; SPIC Group and Telstra; B.K. Modi Group (Basic) and Telecom Asia (Thailand); B.K. Modi Group (GSM) and Vanguard; Max (GSM) and British Telecom; Arvind Mills Ltd. and France Telecom; Crompton Greaves and Millicom; Y.K. Modi Group (Basic) and Korea Telecom, Qualcomm; Bharti Telecom & Stet; Ispat Group (Mittals) and British Columbia, Hughes Network; Indchem and Jasmine/Telia; and Usha Martin and Telekom Malaysia.

Videocon has also entered into a technology transfer arrangement with Sansui's range of audio systems. The products will be sold under the brand name 'Sansui by Videocon'. Realizing that it would be difficult for it to enter the European market with its brand name, it decided to initially use Sansui's brand name for five years and later sell its products under the Videocon brand name.

Doordarshan went in for a two-year strategic alliance with CNN for 24 hours news channel accepting U.S.$1.5 million (₹4.65 crore) a year as the minimum charge and a 50% share in the advertisements. Doordarshan could thus avoid competition with global competitors initially. After two years, even if CNN is not agreeable to renew the contract, Doordarshan will be in a better position to face global competition.

Ranbaxy Laboratories Limited (Ranbaxy), a leading pharmaceutical company in India, is driven by a mission 'to become a research-based international pharmaceutical company'. Its strengths lie in R&D and world-class manufacturing facilities. Its commitment to brand building and internationalization is spearheaded through strategic alliances and creation of subsidiaries and affiliates in major pharmaceutical markets of the world. Ranbaxy has a strong distribution network in India, being able to reach customers through more than 1,400 stockists. Its aggressive marketing strategies have enabled it to carve out a unique niche and leadership position in the Indian market for antibiotics and antibacterial and, more recently, in select overseas markets. In 1993, the company formed a joint venture with Eli Lilly—one of the largest pharmaceutical companies in the United States—to manufacture and market Lilly brands in the Indian market. Ranbaxy Genpharm was incorporated in 1993. This joint venture has acquired an existing manufacturing facility for oral Cephalosporin dosage forms, which is approved by the Health Protection Branch, Canada. Its expansion and upgradation is planned to meet the standards of the FDA in the United States. The process of internationalization has been based on the twin pillars of world-class manufacturing and the company's applied research capability. Accordingly, the thrust is on forming strategic alliances in order to gain entry into the developed countries, and subsidiaries and joint ventures in the emerging markets and making continued efforts to export worldwide. The company is also reportedly negotiating with several international pharmaceutical companies to forge strategic alliances in the UK, the United States, Germany and South Africa. Ranbaxy is of the view that a big market exists for generic drugs in the United States as well as in Europe and it plans to enter this market with drugs carrying a distinct brand identity.

Ansal group of Delhi and the U.S.$34 billion Daewoo Corporation of South Korea have tied up for a 50:50 equity joint venture to develop roads and expressways. They have already been pre-qualified by the government for these Asian Development Bank- and World Bank-funded projects. Some of the other joint ventures for the five projects each are estimated to cost between ₹2.5 and 3 billion are Hyundai Engineering & Construction in tie-up with Unitech, Tralfagar House International together with THC India, Samsung and Tarmat, CCI China, Orient Structural, Walter Bau Aktiengesellschaft, Germany, and Simplex Concrete 26 Piles, L&T and Colas, France, Gruppo Dipenta Construction of Italy, who have jointly bid with Lanco Construction and Graham of the UK, who would be the main engineering partner of Satyam & Sankaranarayana.

Arvind Mills Limited has entered into a marketing and technology transfer agreement with Alamac Knit Fabrics, the wholly owned $425 million subsidiary of West Point Stevens, America's leading knitwear fabric manufacturer. Under the agreement, the U.S. company will transfer its marketing and technical know-how to manufacture high-quality cotton knitwear to Arvind Mills. Alamac will also assist Arvind Mills in the construction of a knitting plant in India. While Alamac will continue to concentrate its efforts in the Western hemisphere, Arvind Mills will market its quality cotton knitwear under the 'Arvind Alamac' brand name in the Indian sub-continent, Asia and Africa. This strategic alliance is expected to enhance the potential of both the partners to participate in the widening world market. The other recent moves of Arvind Mills (world's fifth-largest denim producer with a capacity to produce 70 million metres) include the acquisition of 'Big Lauffenmuhle' in Germany and a technical and marketing alliance with Spinnerei and Weberei Dietfurt AG, which is a part of the Swiss conglomerate Oerlikon Buhrle, for Swiss voiles. The international brand names 'Arrow' and 'Lee' too have been brought to India by Arvind Mills. Arvind Fashions, a 100% subsidiary of Arvind Mills, has a technical tie-up with VF Corporation of the United States, which owns Lee label. VF Corporation brands (Lee, Wrangler and Hustler) taken together command the largest share in the U.S. jeans market (30%). Arvind Mills and FM Hammerle Verm Ogensverwaltungs, GesmbH (FM Hammerle), Europe's pre-eminent shirting fabric producer, have forged a strategic cooperation pact to become an 'unbeatable combination' for manufacturing and marketing high-quality shirting fabric for the global market. Under this, the advantages of Arvind Mills are combined with FM Hammerle's brand name, design innovativeness and extremely high standards of quality. The manufacturing facility of this alliance was expected to go on stream in 1996. This strategic alliance reinforced Arvind Mills' ambition to become a member of the world's big league of players in the international market for textile products. This strategic alliance envisages three significant steps: (a) FM Hammerle will make an investment of Vikalpa $60 million (about ₹190 crore) to assist Arvind Mills in setting up a modern manufacturing facility. (b) The partners will float a joint venture marketing company for exporting to the NAFTA countries of the United States, Canada and Mexico. (c) The product manufactured will be sold under the brand name 'Arvind Hammerle'.

In manufacturing, the European partner will assist in product mix, technology selection, access to designs, collections and new product development. In marketing, Hammerle will continue to focus its efforts in Europe while Arvind Mills will concentrate on the Indian subcontinent, certain parts of Asia and Africa.

In the denim fabric segment, there have been many strategic alliances. Mafatlal Industries Ltd. has tied up this year with Burlington Industries of the UK in a 50:50 joint venture, to manufacture 10 million meters of denim fabric per annum. Seventy-five per cent of its products will be bought back by Burlingtons. Raymond Industries has also entered into collaboration with Italy's Clarity Denim Industries to manufacture 15 million metres of denim fabric per annum. Seventy-five per cent of the production is earmarked for exports. Modern has tied up with the Ireland-based Atlantic Mills, owned by the Tencate group of Holland, said to be one of the best denim plants in Europe. This tie-up has strengthened Modern's rope dyeing technology for heavy-weight denims.

13.9 Few Examples of Strategic Alliances

13.9.1 BOI and SIDBI

BOI and SIDBI have entered into a strategic alliance and signed an MOU, which formalizes a comprehensive arrangement to boost credit flow to the small and medium enterprises (SME) sector. BOI expects to leverage the 'term loan' assessment skills of SIDBI in meeting the requirements of the SME sector. Under the mutually agreed arrangement, BOI and SIDBI would jointly identify projects for financing and those found viable and acceptable as per norms of SIDBI/BOI would be taken up for comprehensive financing. The finance would also be in foreign currency for export units. SIDBI/BOI would either take-up co-financing or exclusive financing of term loans (at 9.5% fixed rate interest), while working capital requirements (at 10.75% floating rate of interest) would be met exclusively by BOI. Along with SIDBI, BOI will also widen the extension of micro credit through the vast network of rural and semi-urban branches. N. Balasubramanian, chairman, SIDBI, said that its BOI alliance was the first of its kind and would be initially be implemented at 11 centres (Pune, Aurangabad, Ahmedabad, Surat, Indore, Faridabad, Ludhiana, Tirupur, Coimbatore, Bangalore and Visakhapatnam), covering 58 identified clusters. Financing under this alliance would encompass the small-scale industries sector, medium sector, services and infrastructure sector. According to M. Balachandran, chairman and managing director, BOI, this alliance assumes particular significance in the context of the finance minister's recent exhortation to chairmen of public sector banks to step up credit flow to the SME sector, which is a growth engine contributing significantly to the country's economy in terms of production, exports as well as employment generation

13.9.2 Motorola and In-Focus Joint Systems

Motorola and In-Focus Systems saw an opportunity to gain a share in the burgeoning worldwide market for high-performance video display panels. In-Focus developed a new technology that lets it make passive matrix displays that are almost as good as active matrix displays but cost much less. Motorola purchased a 20% interest in In-Focus for $20 million.

They then formed an equally owned joint venture to build display panels incorporating In-Focus's technology into Motorola's integrated circuits. In-Focus obtained the capital it needed, a key customer, and access to Motorola's international distribution manufacturing capabilities. Motorola locked in a strategic technology that it was unable to develop internally. The technology permits Motorola to leapfrog past rival Japanese competitors. It also created a captive customer for its integrated chips while getting equity that could rocket in value.

13.9.3 General Motors and Daewoo: An Unsuccessful Alliance

Not all international alliances are success stories. In 1986, General Motors coveted South Korea's low labour costs and Daewoo Motor Company wanted to produce automobiles, so they joined forces to build the Pontiac LeMans. However, the plans failed. Sales of the car plummeted 39% between 1988 and 1990 and had subsequently experienced further erosion. After the first cars produced experienced quality problems, General Motors sent engineers to Korea for corrective action. Korea's cheap labour failed to materialize: the economy improved, the dollar declined and the demands of newly formed labour unions intensified. Perhaps the most serious problem was the two companies' conflicting goals. Whereas Daewoo wanted to upgrade the models to penetrate its domestic market, General Motors wanted to keep costs down. Clearly, this alliance was doomed from the beginning. Key problems included limited understanding of each other's goals and insufficient effort to re-evaluate plans when problems surfaced.

In 1988, Mitsubishi and Daimler-Benz launched their strategic alliance with much fanfare. The capabilities of these giants seemed well-matched and global competition drove them into each other's arms. The leaders of the companies signed a deal in principle to collaborate in various areas. But no concrete projects were launched then, and no major ones were forthcoming later. The alliance was stillborn. It has faded away quietly.

IBM and Apple launched another much-touted strategic alliance in 1990. A multi-party agreement outlined areas of collaboration, including investments in joint ventures and collaborative labs. Together, they would take on Intel and Microsoft. It didn't happen. Eight years later, this strategic alliance, too, is fading away, though not so quietly.

13.10 Benefits in Developing Strategic Alliances Derived from above Examples

The reasons for strategic alliances become apparent when one understands the benefits. This applies to businesses and organizations of all sizes. The same holds true, regardless of whether one enters into strategic alliances as an individual or organization. Many of the benefits create high value for different segments of the distribution chain rather than all the segments. In developing your strategic alliances, there are several general areas in which profit can be made from building alliances.

i. *Technological Sophistication*

   a. An exchange of technology to complement your core strengths shores up your core weakness and improves production capabilities to better serve customers. An example of this type of alliance is the alliance of Kinko's Service Corp. of Ventura (copy centres) and Xerox Engineering Systems to establish a nationwide network for faxing large-format documents. This service is especially valuable to architects, contractors and advertising agencies. Kinko's gets a revenue boost and Xerox gets additional placement and unit sales.

b. To receive a technological contribution or possibly a technological edge in your industry like the alliance between IBM and Apple to develop a new computer operating system that allows both hardware formats to communicate, or like Nynex Corp and Philips Electronics who joined to develop screen telephones for residential use.

ii. *Increase Market Share*

a. Co-branding, such as snack manufacturers who are now mixing two nationally known names and logos on a single product. Examples of this are Betty Crockers' Soda-Licious, soda pop fruit snacks, made with 7UP and 7UP Cherry. Also popular is milk chocolate-covered Pretzel Flipz by Nestlé featuring Rold Gold pretzels.
b. Access to new markets, both domestic and international. Copeland Corporation joined with the largest compressor manufacturer in India, Kirloskar, to bring air conditioning to a growing middle class.
c. Reduce direct competition as the Sun/IBM alliance has attempted in creating the Java operating system to keep Microsoft at bay.
d. To gain market share, Lexus and Coach, the New York-headquartered manufacturer of fine leather products teamed up in an exclusive partnership to produce the Limited Lexus ES 300 Coach Edition.

iii. *Improved Customer Service:* Improved product offering becomes possible through an alliance buying cooperatives. Additional product lines become available to the members because of the cooperative's buying strength. Improved customer loyalty was developed by United Airlines through their alliance with Starbucks. United now serves Starbucks gourmet coffee to their passengers at 30,000 feet. In addition, they do it in cups bearing the logos of both companies. Through alliance relationships, many businesses have found strategies to provide better and quicker customer service while keeping their costs manageable. Look for companies that have a similar customer base to yours and enter into a discussion about how to work together.

iv. *Innovation*

a. The computer and electronics industries have profited greatly from alliance relationships. Innovation has become commonplace for firms that have chosen to work together. The University of Toronto's Innovations Foundation signed an agreement with Northway Explorations Ltd and Polyphalt, a private Ontario, Canada company, to deliver polymer-modified asphalt materials technology for longer lasting roads to the commercial market.
b. *To differentiate oneself from the competition.* Steelcase's alliance with Peerless Lighting, located in Berkeley, California, offers state-of-the-art office lighting. The relationship has brought Steelcase an additional $15 to $35 million in annual furniture sales. Also, they received additional dollars from the light fixture billings.

v. *Cost Savings*

a. In manufacturing elements of your product or entire product that could be built in plants (owned by others or in joint venture) with up-to-date technology, cost savings can be great. Sharing resources, or outsourcing, rather than owning and operating a manufacturing plant, will allow a synergistic partnering agreement to concentrate on your core strengths. This is the idea behind the Donnelly Corporation and their venture with Applied Films Laboratory, Inc. for manufacturing and supplying the world market in display-coated glass for liquid crystal displays (LCDs). In distribution, access to orders that can be economically and efficiently produced also generates reasonable profit through alliance relationships.

b. Shared locations such as Bank of America and many other banks across the country are that are locating branch offices in suburban supermarkets. They are saving resources while simplifying the lives of their consumers by reducing the amount of their consumers—daily running around.

vi. *Financial Stability*: Partnering in a poor economy or recession makes good sense, especially when sales are flat and prices are deflating. Continental Airlines accessed optical industry consumers by partnering with Swan Optical, Inc, an industry supplier, to increase business through an air travel discount certificate programme for purchasers of optical frames supplied by Swan. Achieving economies of scale is possible in alliance relationships when partners share facilities, equipment and employees. Alliance relationships allow partners to share the financial risks associated with developing new products and entering into new markets.

13.11 Risks in Strategic Alliances

Strategic alliances have their own risks, particularly if the parties are not financially equals. These risks include the loss of operational control and confidentiality of proprietary information and technology. Some alliances can involve a clash of corporate cultures or the perceived diminution of independence. In addition, the parties may deprive themselves of future business opportunities with competitors of their strategic partner.

Strategic alliances can lead to competition rather than cooperation, to loss of competitive knowledge, to conflicts resulting from incompatible cultures and objectives and to reduced management control. An alliance can fail, if there is:

a. failure to understand and adapt to a new style of management
b. failure to learn and understand cultural differences between the organizations
c. lack of commitment to succeed
d. strategic goal divergence
e. insufficient trust
f. operational and geographical overlap
g. unrealistic expectations

13.12 Measuring Strategic Alliance Success

This section identifies the key drivers of success in strategic alliances and proposes an integrated conceptual framework.

1. Drivers of Strategic Alliances: Much attention has recently been devoted to issues surrounding strategic alliances as organizations are increasingly turning to alliances to help them successfully compete in the marketplace. Literature suggests that the most common types of drivers that influence the propensity of firms to enter into strategic alliances are turbulence in markets, resource constraints, market uncertainty, globalization of the industry, fast technological change, economies of scale, prior involvement in strategic alliances, risk sharing and consolidation of market position. Competitive forces also play a critical role in strategy formulation in organizations. All these factors can be grouped into two broad categories—environmental characteristics and firm characteristics—that mostly influence the propensity of firms to enter into strategic alliances.

a. *Environmental Characteristics:* In a conventional sense, an organization's environment consists of actors and forces outside the firm, which affect the company's attitudes, actions and outcomes. Today, organizations operate in a global environment that is characterized as diverse, knowledge-rich and unstable. The relentless challenges of globalization mandate alliances, making it absolutely essential to strategy. Organizations are increasingly recognizing that an individual firm is insufficient to deal with rapid changes in the environment. Uncertainties concerning product markets, changing barriers to foreign trade and investment, technological volatility, market turbulence and rapidly changing economies of scale have all been proposed as contributors to environmental uncertainty and linked to increased cooperative behaviour between firms.
b. *Firm Characteristics:* Competition plays an important role in determining strategic position undertaken by firms. Alliances improve the strategic position of firms in competitive markets by providing resources from other firms that enable them to share costs and risks in product design, production, marketing or distribution. Forging an alliance enables a firm to focus resources on its core skills and competencies while acquiring other components or capabilities it lacks from the marketplace. Such resources give firms to weather business downturns and other setbacks, and ensure more even and predictable resource flows. Alliances can often improve the market power of a firm because either the alliance partner is a customer for the product or because the distribution channels and buying power of the partners can be combined. Also, the close inter-firm relationships within alliances can provide customer information. Further, organizational culture affects strategic options that are perceived and chosen and establishes consistent management style and marketing practices. It has been observed that in an information-rich environment an organizational culture that fosters learning has become an important contributory factor for forming strategic alliances.

2. Strategic Alliance Formation: The two key determinants identified in the literature on strategic alliance formation are partner match and strategic orientation of the partnering firm.

a. *Partner Match:* Partner match calls for the creation of alliances in which the chosen partners are similar in management style and company culture. Considerations such as domain similarity and goal compatibility have been found to enhance the effectiveness of inter-organizational dyads. The findings of the study undertaken by Bucklin and Sengupta (1993) indicate that compatibility of the partners is critical to an alliance's success.
b. *Strategic Orientation:* The strategic orientation of a firm reflects the willingness of the firm to enter into strategic alliances and to adopt innovative strategies. Firms select strategies to improve their competitive postures and to gain an advantage over one or more competitors. Strategic alliances are formed based on strategies of how to manage

environmental uncertainties, how to overcome lack of resources and, in particular, how to manage the firm's range of inter-organizational relations.

3. Strategic Alliance Relationship Attributes: Present studies have focused on commitment, collaboration, communication, trust and conflict resolution as the important attributes of alliance relationships. The existence of these attributes implies that both partners acknowledge their mutual dependence and their willingness to work for the survival and prosperity of the relationship.

a. *Trust:* The centrality of trust in developing long-term organizational relationships has been emphasized in the alliance literature. The existence of trust in a relationship reduces the perception of risk associated with opportunistic behaviour. Partners that trust each other generate greater profits, serve customers better and are more adaptable.

   Indeed, it has been argued that trust is so important to alliances that it is considered the 'cornerstone of the strategic partnership success'. This discussion leads to the following proposition:
b. *Communication:* Communication between partners is critical for building a successful relationship. In order to achieve the benefits of collaboration, effective communication between partners is essential (Cummings 1984). Communication allows the partners to understand the alliance goals, roles and responsibilities of all the actors. It also helps with the sharing and dissemination of individual experiences (Inkpen 1996). In sum, more successful alliance relationships are expected to exhibit higher levels of communication quality, more information sharing between partners, and more participation in planning and goal setting than less successful alliances. Stated more formally, we propose the following:
c. *Commitment:* Commitment suggests a future orientation in which partners attempt to build a relationship that can weather unanticipated problems. A high level of commitment provides the context in which both parties can achieve individual and joint goals without raising the spectre of opportunistic behaviour (Cummings 1984). Indications of commitment include investment by the participating organizations, exclusive agreements between the organizations and the absence of major conflicts between the organizations. Committed partners are likely to be more cooperative, communicative and flexible in accommodating conflict issues. Commitment development between partners within an alliance would act as a counterbalance against failure of the strategic alliance. The following proposition is derived from this discussion:
d. *Collaboration:* Collaboration is the key dimension of the strategic alliance relationship. The alliance partners must collaborate to achieve their strategic objectives. The collaborative associations are interactive and adaptive in nature. Understanding the nature and scope of collaboration is essential in analysing the operation and success of an alliance. A highly collaborative relationship provides the flexibility and adaptability necessary to overcome uncertainties, resolve conflicts and achieve mutually beneficial outcomes.

   In sum, it can be said that more successful alliance relationships are expected to be characterized by higher levels of commitment, collaboration, communication and trust than are less successful alliances. Thus, the proposition:
e. *Conflict Resolution:* Conflict often exists in inter-organizational relationships due to the inherent interdependencies between partners that posited that firms in strategic alliances are motivated to engage in joint problem solving because they are, by definition, linked together to manage an environment that was more uncertain and

turbulent than each one could control. Conflict may be distinguished as functional or dysfunctional. Functional conflict would enhance an alliance's performance, while dysfunctional conflict within the alliance would affect the effectiveness of alliance performance. Dysfunctional conflicts are counterproductive and are likely to strain the fabric of the partnership.

13.13 Model of Successful Strategic Alliances

In view of the preceding discussion, the following model (Figure 13.2) and features are proposed by Zaman and Mavondo (2001) for a success in strategic alliance.

a. **Values:** To be successful in an alliance, the organizations need to hold a shared set of values about the cause they are championing and about ways of working together. These values will influence the way the parties approach the alliance and how they work together.
b. **Leadership:** Partnerships require champions in each of the participating organizations, and these individuals need to take direct responsibility for achieving the partnership goals. Partnerships also require the unequivocal support of the leaders of the participating organizations.
c. **Clarity of mission and strategy:** Strategic alliances need a compelling mission, realistic objectives and a clear strategy for achieving them. Each partnership needs to have great clarity over its goals, achievable objectives with win-win opportunities for both organizations.
d. **Board commitment:** The boards of all participating organizations need to be strongly committed to the partnership and willing to support it through the good times and the difficult times.
e. **Resources:** Strategic alliances need to be properly resourced and there needs to be great honesty and realism about the time and financial commitments each organization

Figure 13.2 Features of Successful Strategic Alliances

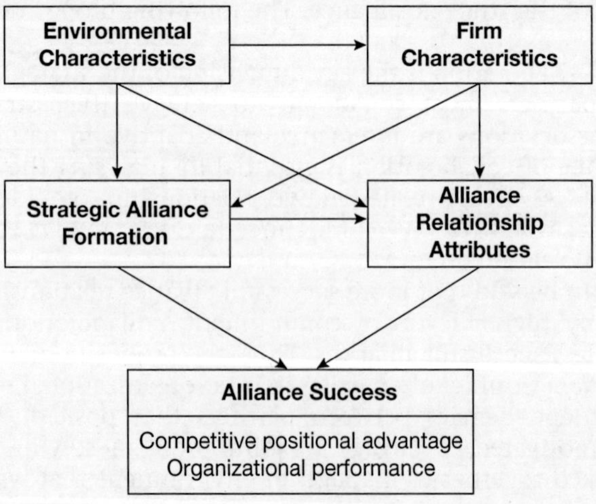

will have to make to the partnership. When it comes to reporting on how the resources have been applied, the financial reports need to be tailored to the needs of the partnership and not to necessarily follow the standard reporting formats of the participating organizations.

f. **Open and honest communications:** Managers need to recognize that many different stakeholders, such as funders, board and committee members, staff, chapters and volunteers, may be affected by a strategic alliance. Each requires regular and thorough communication. Formal communications should be supported by plenty of informal communication, ideally at board, senior management and staff levels.
g. **Commitment to good faith negotiations:** When the alliance is being established, there should be three ground rules. Without prior agreement of all partners:
    i. There should be no material changes in the partnership proposition
    ii. Negotiators must be named and there should be no changes during negotiations
    iii. There must be no negotiations with other external parties.

13.14 Conclusion

One of the fastest-growing trends for business today is the increasing number of strategic alliances. Strategic alliances can be one of the most cost-effective growth strategies for any company to employ as long as they are aware that the most important skill needed to succeed in strategic alliances is not marketing, managing, financing or even negotiating. A strategic alliance is less involved than a joint venture where two companies typically pool resources in creating a separate entity. Strategic alliances can be tricky. Partnerships foster mutual benefits, but the alliances exist only as long as they are advantageous to both parties. Even so, the concept of gaining a marketplace advantage by teaming up with another company whose products or services fit well with one's own is not only seductive, it is also critical for an increasing number of businesses.

Strategic alliances are sweeping through nearly every industry and are becoming an essential driver of superior growth. Alliances range in scope from an informal business relationship based on a simple contract to a joint venture agreement in which for legal and tax purposes either a corporation or partnership is set up to manage the alliance. Alliances are a way of reaping the rewards of team effort—and the gains from forming strategic alliances appear to be substantial. If managed wisely, a strategic alliance can help companies develop and exploit their unique strengths.

Multiple Choice Questions

1. What is a strategic alliance?
    a. Any form of partnership between one firm and another
    b. Formal agreement committing two or more firms to exchange resources to produce products or services
    c. Formal agreement to share profits from a shared investment
    d. Formal agreement to share knowledge
2. Currently, alliances account for ________% of the revenue of the largest 1,000 firms in the United States.
    a. 15 b. 25 c. 35 d. 45

3. A(n) ________ exists whenever two or more independent organizations cooperate in the development, manufacture or sale of products or services.
   a. Vertical market
   b. Strategic alliance
   c. Initial public offering
   d. Market transaction

4. What is the most frequent internal motive for a strategic alliance?
   a. Resource need
   b. Risk limitation
   c. Cost minimization
   d. Current poor performance

5. In a situation when potential confliction is high and extent of organizational interaction is low, what type of alliance is usually formed?
   a. Pre-competitive alliances
   b. Pro-competitive alliances
   c. Competitive alliances
   d. Non-competitive alliances

6. Which one of the following collaboration encourages greater integration?
   a. Strategic partnership
   b. Merger
   c. Joint venture
   d. None

7. Which one of the following is a risk of strategic alliance?
   a. Failure to understand and adapt to a new style of management.
   b. Failure to learn and understand cultural differences between the organizations.
   c. Lack of commitment to succeed.
   d. All.

8. A ________ is a form of non-equity alliance that exists when one firm allows another to use its brand name to sell its products.
   a. Supply agreement
   b. Licensing agreement
   c. Distribution agreement
   d. Joint venture

9. Which of the following is not part of the strategic focus when a company is pursuing a build objective?
   a. Exploitable corporate strengths
   b. Product innovation
   c. Distribution innovation
   d. Competitor confrontation

10. When both parties to an alliance are seeking to learn something from that alliance, a ________ can evolve.
    a. Learning race
    b. Dynamic race
    c. Learning dynamic
    d. Learning curve.

Review Questions

1. Define the term 'strategic alliance'. Discuss the nature of strategic alliances in modern-day business.
2. List and explain the salient characteristics of strategic alliance.
3. What are the major reasons for forming strategic alliances?
4. List and briefly discuss the various types of strategic alliances.
5. Write short notes on (a) licensing and (b) franchising.
6. Briefly discuss the different tasks for the start-up phase of an alliance.
7. Elaborate on the benefits of strategic alliance. Provide a few suitable examples.
8. List the risks associated with strategic alliance.
9. Identify and briefly explain the key drivers of strategic alliances.
10. Elaborate on the detailed process of forming a strategic alliance.
11. Does strategic alliance provide tangible benefits of corporate enterprises? Give examples in support of your answer.
12. Discuss the Zaman and Mavondo model of successful in strategic alliance.

Case in Action

Strategic Alliances: A Key Element of the Toshiba's Corporate Strategy

Toshiba firmly believes that a single company cannot dominate any technology or business by itself. Toshiba's approach is to develop synergistic relationships with different partners for different technologies. Strategic alliances form a key element of Toshiba's corporate strategy. They helped the company to become one of the leading players in the global electronics industry.

Developing Relationships

Toshiba believes in a flexible approach because some tension is natural in business partnerships, some of which may also sour over time. Toshiba executives believe that the relationship between the company and its partner should be like friends, not like that of a married couple. Toshiba senior management is often directly involved in the management of strategic alliances. This helps in building personal equations and resolving conflicts.

Source: http://ventures.powweb.com/business_guide/cs_alliances_toshiba.html

Case in Action

Strategic Alliance of Yahoo! and eBay's

Introduction

Yahoo! and eBay entered into a strategic alliance to pool their resources in an effort to boost their revenues and consolidate their position in the competitive Internet industry. On 25 May 2006, Yahoo! Inc. (Yahoo!), the world's largest online media company, announced its plans to form a strategic alliance with eBay Inc (eBay), the world's largest online auction company. Under their partnership, Yahoo! would exclusively provide online banners and graphic advertisements at eBay's site. In return, Yahoo! would promote PayPal, eBay's online payment service, as a preferred payment provider for purchases made online on the Yahoo! website. PayPal would provide an array of payment options to Yahoo!'s users navigating the web for shopping, auctions, and subscription services. Commenting on the alliance, Chief Executive of Yahoo!, Terry Semel, said, 'The deal offers great opportunities for both companies to share great assets with each other. It's all about creating more value and a better experience for users as well as for advertisers'.

Yahoo! and eBay also planned to form a co-branded toolbar, which could be downloaded onto the user's web browser, which in turn would direct the users to eBay's auction site and Yahoo!'s search engine. On eBay's site, the toolbar would provide links to the Yahoo! home page, Yahoo! Mail, and My Yahoo! options on the Yahoo! website. Yahoo! and eBay further planned to collaborate on a click-to-call functionality, which would allow users navigating the web to contact advertisers directly through the phone instead of their websites. To make the click-to-call functionality operational, eBay's Skype or Yahoo's Messenger service would likely be used. The partnership between Yahoo! and eBay was expected to be completely implemented by 2007. eBay sought to increase its advertising revenues through this alliance as Yahoo! had experience in search advertising. Catherine England, spokesperson for eBay, said, 'We [currently] manage ads in-house and through a few affiliates. It was a variety of sources and its' just not an area that we focused on. Through this partnership with Yahoo, we'll be able to leverage their expertise in that area'. Analysts opined that Yahoo! and eBay had joined forces to consolidate their respective positions in the Internet industry.

Rick Aristotle Munarriz, senior analyst at Motley Fool, said, 'This is a great move for both of them. These are two companies that were great and their performance on the market in the past few years has been a little disappointing so it's their way of saying "Hey, we can matter again"'. The deal also highlighted the intense competitive environment in the Internet industry. Experts opined that the alliance would help Yahoo! counter the market threat from Google Inc. (Google). Google had emerged as the biggest competitor to Yahoo!, especially in the growing search-based advertising market. Google was the most popular search engine and held a 43.1% share in the online search market in the United States compared to Yahoo!'s market share of 28% in April 2006. Google was also rumoured to be making effort to build its own merchant service that could rival eBay. Andy Beal, CEO of Fortune Interactive, a search marketing consulting firm, said, 'While I don't think you can point your finger to one specific product offered by Google that is causing fear to Yahoo! and eBay, the combination of all Google's recent initiatives is causing both Yahoo! and eBay to reach out to each other for support'.

However, some analysts termed the deal as 'being too late'. Allen Weiner, a Gartner Inc. analyst, said, 'There's no question that this is a significant partnership, but it seems reactive. It's anti-climactic, because we've been waiting for years. If they had done this two or three years ago, they would have done it from a position of strength'.

Source: http://www.icmrindia.org/Short Case Studies/Business Strategy/CLBS076.htm

Questions for Discussion

1. Do you feel that the deal between Yahoo! and eBay is a 'strategic alliance'? Support you answer.
2. Identify and explain the benefits of the strategic alliance between Yahoo! and eBay.
3. 'This strategic alliance would help Yahoo! counter the market threat from Google Inc.'. Explain this statement in the light of hostile takeovers by big market players.

References

Anand, Bharat N., and Tarun Khanna. 2000. 'Do Firms Learn to Create Value? The Case of Alliances'. *Strategic Management Journal*, 21: 295–315.

Booz-Allen and Hamilton Surveys. 1997. Available at http://www.amiltd.com/allianceportfolio.html (last accessed on 12 February 2000).

Bucklin, L., and S. Sengtupa. 1993. 'Organising Successful Co-Marketing Alliances'. *Journal of Marketing*, 57(4): 32–46.

Cauley de la Sierra, Margaret. 1994. *Managing Global Alliances. Key Steps for Successful Collaboration*. EIU Series. Wokingham: Addison-Wesley.

Cummings, T. 1984. 'Transorganizational Development'. *Research in Organizational Behaviour*, 6: 367–422.

Doz, Yves L., and Gary Hamel. 1998. *Alliance Advantage: The Art of Creating Value Through Partnering*. Boston, MA: Harvard Business School Press.

Gomes-Casseres, Benjamin. 1996. *The Alliance Revolution*. Cambridge, MA: Harvard University Press.

Harbison, J.R., and P. Pekar. 1998. *Smart Alliances: A Practical Guide to Repeatable Success*. San Francisco, CA: Jossey-Bass.

Harroch, R.D. 2000. *Strategic Alliances Monograph*. Available at http:/www.orrickemerging.com

Inkpen, A. 1996. 'Creating Knowledge through Collaboration'. *California Management Review*, 39(1): 123–40.

Karmali, Naazneen, and A.B. Ravi. 1995. 'Living in Today's World'. *Business India*, June 19–July 2, 54–62.

Morrison, Michael, and Larissa Mezentseff. 1997. 'Learning Alliances: A New Dimension of Strategic Alliances'. *Management Decision*, 35(5): 351–57.

Porter, M.E. 1985. *Competitive Advantage: Creating and Sustaining Superior Performance*, 321. New York: The Free Press.

Porter, M.E. 1990. *Competitive Advantage of Nations*, 612–13. New York: Free Press.

Yoshino, Michael Y, and S. Rangan. 1995. *Strategic Alliances: An Entrepreneurial Approach to Globalization*. Boston, MA: Harvard Business School Press.

Zaman, M., and F. Mavondo. 2001. 'Measuring Strategic Alliance Success: A Conceptual Framework'. Available at http://WWW/ANZMAC2001/anzmac/AUTHORS/pdfs/Zaman.pdf (last accessed on 26 November 2003).

Further Readings

Ando, Ritsuko. 'Yahoo, eBay Pact Seen a Step to Global Partnership'. Available at www.today.reuters.com

Charny, Ben. 'What the eBay-Yahoo Deal Means to Google'. Available at www.oraclewatch.eweek.com.

Del Conte, Natali T. 'Yahoo, eBay Strike Multi-Year Ad, Transactions Deal'. Available at www.pcmag.com (last accessed on 22 August 2016).

Liedtke, Michael. Ap, *Yahoo, eBay Join in Partnership to Challenge Google*. Available at www.abcnews.com (last accessed on 1 September 2016).

Yahoo, eBay Ally on Ads. Available at www.redherring.com (last accessed on 16 August 2016).

Yahoo–EBay Deal. Available at www.chron.com (last accessed on 25 May 2006).

Google sees closer ties to eBay despite Yahoo deal. Available at www.moneycontrol.com (last accessed on 21 August 2016).

http://icmrindia.org/business%20Updates/micro%20casestudies/Business%20Strategy/MCBS0032.htm

Chapter 14

Leveraged Buyout

Chapter Objectives

On completion of this chapter, you will be able to understand:

- The meaning and definition of leveraged buyout (LBO)
- The history of LBO
- Difference between LBO and management buyout
- Objectives of LBO
- Essential characteristics of an ideal LBO candidate
- Different sources of LBO financing
    - Senior debt
    - Subordinated debt
    - Mezzanine finance
    - Loan stock
    - Preference shares
    - Ordinary shares
- The process of building an LBO model
- Different stages of LBO operation
    - First stage: Arrangement of finance
    - Second stage: Going private
    - Third stage: Restructuring
    - Fourth stage: Reverse LBO
- The advantages of LBO
- The limitations of LBO
- Value generation through LBO

The leveraged buyout—a deal structure made popular during the Wall Street boom of the 1980s and again in the wake of the tech bubble—could become much more common soon, according to a report from BofA Merrill Lynch. BofA credit strategists Hans Mikkelsen and Yuriy Shchuchinov write that current market conditions have become 'unusually conductive for leveraging transactions for this stage in the typical cycle,' and that as a result, 'credit investors should be concerned about more extreme re-leveraging in the form of leveraged buyouts'.

A leveraged buyout typically involves a relatively small equity investment into a takeover target, with loans that are usually multiples of the size of the equity in terms of dollar value making up the difference.

In the aftermath, companies often have to resort to stringent cost-cutting measures to service the debts that were used to execute the buyout. The bigger the deal, the more the debt. And the BofA strategists say they even envision deals up to $20 billion:

> Clearly at this stage in the cycle we are nowhere near once again talking about Home Depot as an LBO candidate. In fact, most LBOs will likely initially be rather small—less than $5 bn with a few up to $10 bn in transaction enterprise value, consistent with deals seen post-Lehman.
>
> However, in an area of historically low yields and abundant liquidity in the public markets, with banks having finally rebuilt capital, we think we have the ingredients in place for even larger deals, up to $20 bn.

Markets have QE3 to thank in part for the return of the LBO, according to the report. As the Federal Reserve continues to buy mortgage-backed securities, yields grind lower, and banks no longer see most fixed-income assets as attractive investments. Now, Mikkelson and Shchuchinov think banks will instead be forced to lend in order to make money, and that 'they will also be willing to expand lending for highly leveraged transactions (as long as leverage stays below 6× per guidance from the regulators)'.

The BofA strategists expand on this by noting that finding sufficient equity to put into the LBO investments will be the real limiter on deal size:

> The most constraining factor for deal size appears to be equity, not debt. During the pre-Lehman environment large LBO deals were possible as private equity firms pooled resources in so-called 'club deals'. Subsequent litigation makes it less likely that enough firms are willing to pool enough resources any time soon for such mega deals, in our view.
>
> However, the example of Synthes, discussed below, highlights that we could still potentially see a three-firm club deal for a $20 bn LBO—such a deal would likely require perhaps $2 bn of equity from each private equity firm. Furthermore, nothing prevents private equity from pooling resources with alternative investors such as pension funds.

Mikkelson and Shchuchinov explain that last year, when Johnson and Johnson acquired Synthes, a post-transaction SEC filing revealed that three private equity firms came together and submitted a $20 billion bid to buy out the company.

Although the consortium of PE firms ultimately didn't win the deal, the BofA strategists write that 'it also makes the clear point that a $20 bn LBO was feasible at the time'. Since bond yields – and thus the cost of financing a big buyout with mostly debt—have only continued to fall since the Synthes deal, Mikkelson and Shchuchinov figure the current environment has only gotten better for LBOs.

Source: Boesler (2012).

14.1 Introduction

In the realm of increased globalized economy, M&As have assumed significant importance both within the country and across the borders. Such acquisitions need huge amount of finance to be provided. In search of an ideal mechanism to finance an acquisition, the concept of LBO has emerged. Dependency on venture capital funding may be subject to expensive in nature, because in such a case the acquiring firm may have to transfer a considerable (as much as 70%) quantum of the ownership of the acquired firm to the venture capitalists. On the other hand, the excess cash over and above the normal working capital requirements may also be considered as an alternative to finance an acquisition. But the availability of huge amount of liquid cash is a major constraint. The option of the use of stock may be another route for such financing. But here also the availability of such option is very much insignificant in a buyout programme by privately held firms. Due to such reasons, the asset-based financing or LBO has become important in the world of finance.

14.2 History of the LBO

While it is unclear when the first LBO was carried out, it is generally agreed that the first early LBOs were carried out in the years following the Second World War. Prior to the 1980s, the LBO (previously known as a 'bootstrap' acquisition) was, for years, little more than an obscure financing technique.

In the years following the end of the Second World War, the Great Depression was still relatively fresh in the minds of America's corporate leaders, who considered it wise to keep corporate debt ratios low. As a result, for the first three decades following the Second World War, very few American companies relied on debt as a significant source of funding. At the same time, American business became caught up in a wave of conglomerate building that began in the early 1960s. In some cases, corporate governance guidelines were inconsistently implemented. The ranks of middle management swelled and corporate profitability began to slide. It was in this environment that the modern LBO was born.

In the late 1970s and early 1980s, newly formed firms such as Kohlberg Kravis Roberts and Thomas H. Lee Company saw an opportunity to profit from inefficient and undervalued corporate assets. Many public companies were trading at a discount to net asset value, and many early LBOs were motivated by profits available from buying entire companies, breaking them up and selling off the pieces. This 'bust-up' approach was largely responsible for the eventual media backlash against the greed of so-called 'corporate raiders', illustrated by books such as *The Rain on Macy's Parade* and films such as *Wall Street* and *Barbarians at the Gate*, based on the book by the same name.

As a new generation of managers began to take over American companies in the late 1970s, many were willing to consider debt financing as a viable alternative for financing operations. Soon LBO firms' constant pitching began to convince some of the merits of debt-financed buyouts of their businesses. From a manager's perspective, LBOs had a number of appealing characteristics:

a. Tax advantages associated with debt financing,
b. Freedom from the scrutiny of being a public company or a captive division of a larger parent,
c. The ability of founders to take advantage of a liquidity event without ceding operational influence or sacrificing continued day-to-day involvement, and
d. The opportunity for managers to become owners of a significant percentage of a firm's equity.

14.3 Meaning and Definition

Basically, the term 'leveraged buyout' signifies the acquisition of a business mostly with the help of debt capital or borrowed capital. The term 'leveraged' signifies the most significant and major use of debt or loan capital for financing the acquisition. The term 'buyout', on the other hand, signifies the gain of control of a majority of the equity of the target company. A typical LBO transaction involves the set-up of an acquisition vehicle, termed special-purpose vehicle (SPV), jointly funded by financial investors and the management of the target company. The LBO may be defined in different ways, some of which are as follows:

a. In the opinion of James C. Van Horne, an LBO represents 'an ownership transfer consummated importantly with debt'.
b. According to I.M. Pandey, LBO 'is a kind of acquisition of a company which is financed through debt. LBO generally involves debt from 70–90% of purchase price, usually accompanied by low credit rating'.
c. According to Brealey et al., LBOs are 'diet deals', a kind of acquisition where a large fraction of the purchase price is financed by debt and the company goes private and its shares are no longer traded on the open markets.
d. Prasad G. Godbole provides an elaborate definition of LBO. He opines that LBO mobilizes the borrowed or debt funds considering the level of assets and cash flows of the target company and utilizing these raised debt funds to acquire the target company. He states that practically LBOs take place as follows:
    - A private company is incorporated (totally or partially owned) to act as SPV.
    - Then, borrowed funds are deployed into SPV considering the target company's asset and cash-flow base.
    - Acquires the whole or partial share capital of the target company. Further, merging the target company with the SPV. At this stage, loans of the SPV and assets of the target company come together in one balance sheet. Also, it makes the target company go private and gets unlisted from stock exchanges.
e. According to Miller, the LBO is 'a financing technique of purchasing a private company with the help of borrowed or debt capital'.
f. Weston et al. (1990) define LBO as 'the acquisition, financed largely by borrowings of all the stocks or assets, of a hither to public company by a small group of investors'
g. The Center for Private Equity and Entrepreneurship, United States, describes an LBO as 'the acquisition of a company or division of a company with a substantial portion of borrowed funds'.

The LBOs are basically cash transaction in nature, where cash is borrowed by the acquiring firm and the debt financing represents 50% or more of the purchase price. Generally, the tangible assets of the target company are used as the collateral security for the loans borrowed by acquiring firm in order to finance the acquisition. Sometimes, a proportionate amount of the long-term financing is secured with the fixed assets of the firm and in order to raise the balance amount of the total purchase price, unrated or low-rated debt known as junk bond financing is utilized.

An LBO is very similar to buying a house using a combination of a down payment and a mortgage—in both transactions, you save money by putting down a small amount in cash and then borrowing the rest. In an LBO, the 'down payment' is called equity (cash) and the 'mortgage' is called debt. The private equity (PE) firm uses debt to boost its returns. All else being equal, using more leverage (debt) means that the PE firm will earn a higher return on its investment.

To see why this is true, consider the following scenario: you buy a company for $100 using 100% cash and then sell it five years later for $200. Let us compare that to what happens when you buy the same company for $100, but use only 50% cash and sell it five years later, still for $200 (shown as $150 here because the $50 in debt must be repaid):

Company value:	$100
Sale value:	200

Scenario 1: 100% cash acquisition					
Cash used: 100%	$100				
Debt used: 0.0%	-				
Purchase	*Year 1*	*Year 2*	*Year 3*	*Year 4*	*Exit*
	$(100)	$-	$-	$-	$200
Return multiple:					2.0×
IRR					15%

Scenario 2: 50% cash acquisition					
Cash used: 50%	$50				
Debt used: 50%	50				
Purchase	*Year 1*	*Year 2*	*Year 3*	*Year 4*	*Exit*
	$(50)	$-	$-	$-	$150
Return multiple:					3.0×
IRR					25%

You can see the massive difference—the multiple jumps from 2× to 3×, a 50% increase, and the IRR jumps from 15% to 25%. And this analysis assumes that the $50 of debt we use in the beginning to purchase the company stays on its balance sheet until year 5 and that nothing is repaid.

14.4 Characteristics and Features of LBOs

Different features of LBOs have been mentioned here, which will help to understand LBO more closely.

a. *A kind of acquisition:* LBOs can be characterized as a kind of acquisition that turns a public company into a private company. This process is done by a group of institutional investors and funding it through debt financing.
b. *Company goes private:* The company goes private and the shares of this company are not traded on the stock exchange after the LBO process. This is a process designed for a strategic change.
c. *Greater proportion of debt in capital structure:* In the capital structure of an LBO firm, debt is the major constituent. The point to remember is that the debt incorporated into capital structure is not permanent. The objective behind LBO is to reduce wasteful investment and force improvement in operational efficiencies LBO and high debt

financing is compatible with the companies having abundant cash and fewer investment avenues.

d. *No separation of ownership and control:* The management becomes the owner and their interest vests in optimizing the efficiency in profits. LBO forms a concentrated ownership and there is no separation of ownership and control.
e. *Incentives to employees:* As the structure of a company changes and it goes private, there falls a greater pressure on the employees and managers to work harder and efficiently because they are given a stake in the business, like stock options or ownership of shares directly. This triggers employee commitment. The profitable interest of the employees generates greater profitability and added responsibility towards organizational progress and sustenance.
f. *Private equity:* In LBO, the stock, that is, collection of shares, is held by not the individual investors out of the public, but by few partners who are generally institutional investors, and this stock is known as private equity.
g. *Potentially stable cash flows:* The LBO firm should have the stability of cash flows, both historical and operational, at present. The target company must have adequate potential for generating greater cash flows that can optimally balance the debt burden.
h. *Management expertise is critical:* The company's success after the acquisition critically depends on the management expertise, skills and knowledge.
i. *Difficult in re-financing:* The debt re-financing for an LBO firm is generally difficult as it already has debts to pay back.
j. *Risky venture:* LBO is a high-risk and high-return opportunity. Large stake of all the stakeholders is there. If the LBO is not a successful venture, it can lead to bankruptcy. Besides this, it promises greater future returns.
k. *Prompt decision-making:* The decision-making process is prompt, spontaneous and centralized as it is now a private company.
l. *Superior profits:* The shareholders' future profits depend upon the management's expertise to generate superior operating profits such that there are adequate funds available to be disbursed after servicing the debt.
m. *Greater incentives to management and employees:* LBO offers greater incentives for management. It offers profit sharing as a private company.
n. *Time-specific partnership:* LBO is a time-specific partnership, and after a stipulated time, the private company again becomes a public limited company. Further, it is necessary to identify the salient features of the target company in order to make the LBO a success.

14.5 Leveraged Buyout and Management Buyout

In a typical LBO programme, the acquiring group consists of a small number of persons or organizations sponsored by buyout specialists or investment bankers. This group, with the help of certain financial instruments like high-yield high-risk debt instruments (junk bonds), deferred payment instruments, private placement instruments, bridge finance, loans from venture capitalists, merchant bankers and so on, acquires all or nearly all the outstanding shares of the target firm and takes the target firm private. The buyout group may or may not include current management of the target firm. If the group so does, the buyout may be regarded as 'MBO'. Except this functional difference, an MBO is also regarded as an LBO in the sense that for an MBO operation, the buying group puts up only a small part of the purchase price and borrows the amount through private sources.

14.6 Objectives of an LBO

The primary objective of an LBO is to ensure that the balance sheet of the acquiring firm does not suffer due to the additional funding costs of such acquisition. At the same time, the acquiring firm would be benefited from the acquisition of the brand of the target company. Moreover, the acquiring company can expand its business horizon in the international market without making any huge outlay of wealth from the internal resources. Rather, the major part of the acquisition is financed by borrowed capital. To be very specific, the entire (almost) buyout is made on the basis of leveraged capital and that is why it is known as LBOs. Things will be much clearer from the following example.

In 2000, Tata Tea acquired the world's second largest tea brand Tetley at a price of £271 million. Out of which £235 million was raised in the form of borrowed capital. For such acquisition, Tata Tea has created an SPV, Tata Tea (Great Britain), which is the 100% subsidiary of Tata Tea, in order to acquire the assets of the target company Tetley. The company raised the amount of debt capital against the tangible assets of Tetley. Here, TTL created the SPV with an aim to ensure that the balance sheet of Tata Tea is not affected by the additional funding costs, while the company can enjoy the benefits of such acquisition.

14.7 Process of a Typical LBO Transaction

In a LBO transaction, the first step is looking for deal source, so the PE fund manager is going to find out some LBO candidate companies. In order to choose a suitable candidate for LBO, fund managers play an important role. For example, they would observe whether the target firm is legally correct, and then they would figure out the candidate's current tax payment and financial position and performance through financial statements. Because high debt financing could reduce company's tax payment, which is the most attractive reason to adopt LBO, the fund manager must calculate whether this tax shield could really help target firm's development. However, when they consider about tax shield benefit, they must observe company's debt capability, which could be traced by the candidate's financial performance. Choosing a target firm is crucial to determine whether LBO transaction would be successful or not, so one should be sure that there are no information asymmetries in research.

After the fund manager determines candidate for LBO transaction, they would make a plan for improving company's business, and forecast the future financial performance in order to determine the potential expiration date for exit. When fund manager selects target firm for LBO transaction, they should construct an initial exit strategy in terms of current financial situation. Then, the PE fund manager would figure out how much financing will be required in this transaction, and they must determine new capital structure in this candidate company.

As mentioned above, fund providers are formed by a wealthy individual, bank, pension fund, insurance, hedge fund and other public institution. When a fund manager figures out the budget for LBO transaction, they would negotiate with fund providers in order to acquire financial support. Bank loan is the primary source of acquisition financing which could follow fixed interest payment. And, then, mezzanine debt would be the secondary financing source for LBO, which is required for higher-than-expected return from bank loan. According to characteristic of mezzanine debt, it is often repaid when company is sold. Thus, mezzanine debt bears much higher risk, and the risk premium would be comparatively higher than bank loan. In negotiation, the fund manager must determine the final loan agreement which is flexible in expiration date. The loan agreement would be negotiable to extend the date for financial support in case LBO transaction could not achieve target performance within the initial period.

Figure 14.1 Structure of a Typical LBO

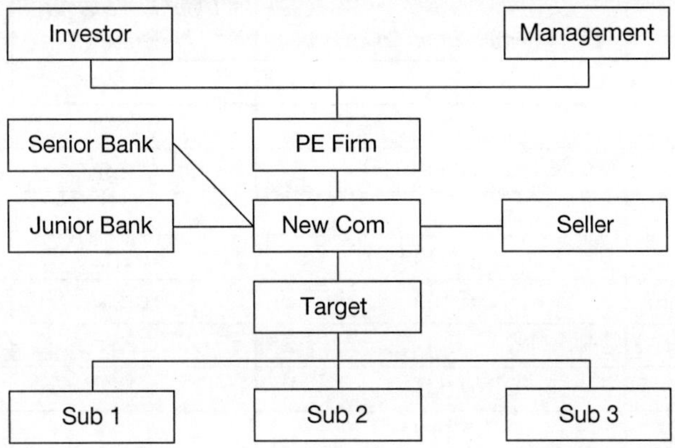

Source: Adapted from Andersen (2008).

However, the fund manager should often report their performance during transaction; this can help investors to follow up their investment, and will be easier for the second financing. In Figure 14.1, a typical LBO structure is presented for easy understanding. A PE firm consists of general partners and limited partners. LBO is one of private equity investment techniques in the financial market, which is described by New Com. Responsibility of the LBO fund manager is to look for target for LBO transaction, and their financing is mainly from bank loan, mezzanine debt and other sources. Banks will be senior loan in New Com, thus bank loan would be ranked before the PE firm. Mezzanine debt and other sources are belonging to junior loan, which is ranked after senior loan. Normally, the PE firm and LBO fund may provide security for loans, but their assets are only the shares in the LBO fund and target firm, respectively. If something goes wrong in an LBO transaction, the bank will get its money first.

The fund manager would adjust the capital structure of target after they have sufficient capital for LBO transaction, and they would process the investment plan to create value addition. If the company achieves the final target performance in a certain period, the fund manager would push the company exiting from LBO transaction. Otherwise, the expiration date of this transaction has to be extended. As mentioned above, the fund manager should construct an initial exit strategy when they determine the target firm. This exit strategy would change due to variable economic environment, thus the fund manager should trace internal environment and external environment in order to find out the most beneficial exit strategy.

14.8 Success Factors of LBO/Essential Characteristics of an Ideal LBO Candidate

In order to make an LBO programme successful, certain characteristics should be fulfilled. Fulfilment of these characteristics is not always mandatory, but the existence of such features may be expected to help make the programme fruitful as well as effective. For example, a study identified the differences between buyout firms and non-buyout firms in terms of free cash flow and capital expenditures parameter which is summarized in Table 14.1. Some important characteristics are pointed out here:

Table 14.1 Buyout Firms have Higher FCF and Lower Capital Expenditures

	Buyout Firms/Firms Going Public	Other Non-buyout Firms	Difference
1980–89			
FCF	0.081	0.029	0.052***
Capital expenditure ratio	0.096	0.155	−0.059***
1990–99			
FCF	0.049	−0.018	0.067***
Capital expenditure ratio	0.103	0.133	-0.030***
2000–12			
FCF	0.041	−0.017	0.058***
Capital expenditure ratio	0.272	0.462	−0.190***

Source: Mehran and Peristiani (2013).
Notes: FCF ratio – After tax net cash flow minus dividends and interest payments divided by net sales;
Capital expenditure ratio – Capital expenditure divided by net sales
***Significant at the 1% level.

a. *Efficient and experienced management team*: In order to motivate the lenders as well as investors for providing borrowed or loan capital to a considerable extent and with a view to make the LBO programme successful, a strong management body comprising of experienced as well as professionally highly qualified chief financial executives, CEOs, directors, senior managers and so on is quite essential. The management team should have long track record in the industry and should also have a desirable experience of handling large projections effectively and efficiently. The existence of such an efficient and experienced management team will help to create confidence in the minds of the lenders in lending huge amount of fund, to the LBO candidate.
b. *Assurance of sufficient and stable cash flow*: With a view to service the debt borrowed for the acquisition and in order to ensure the smooth ongoing operations of the firm, the existence of sufficient, strong and secure cash flow is considered indispensable for a successful LBO programme. An LBO candidate having strong and stable cash flow can easily impress the lenders to provide huge amount of loan capital required for the purpose of acquisition under the LBO programme and also to produce the highest borrowing capacity of the firm. To be very much specific, future cash flows based on strong and stable track record of past performance can easily be used for maximizing the lender's belief and for generating due impression, which, in turn, will help to make the LBO programme successful.
c. *Lower degree of operating risk*: In an LBO programme, the financial risk is very high since it is mostly based on leveraged capital or debt capital. Thus, in order to sustain in the market, the degree of operating risk arising out of normal business activities should be as less as possible. Companies with strong market positions, diversified products portfolio, strong customer base and new innovative power to cope with the changing business world and so on usually have lower operating risk since their cash flows are less dependent on a single source of income and they are not subject to the risk arising out of loss of customers, obsolescence of any existing product, change in the economy

of a particular geographical region and so on. Companies with high operating risk may not be able to afford any adverse year because its financial risk is already high under the LBO programme.

d. *Limited amount of debt:* There should have been limited amount of debt in the firm's balance sheet compared to the value of the tangible assets of the firm that can be used as collateral securities for raising the loan capital required to finance the LBO programme. The lower the amount of existing debt relative to the collateral value of such assets, the greater will be the borrowing capacity of the firm. On the other side of the coin, if the balance sheet of the acquiring company (i.e., the LBO candidate) is already overburdened by debt capital, the acquiring company may have to face difficulties in financing the acquisition through the option of LBO.
e. *Flexibility for cost cutting:* As there is an increase in debt burdens of the company, it is necessary to make additional payments for added quantity of debt. There should be some reduction of costs possible in various areas of business internally. The management must take a strategic view, but at the same time look into reducing redundant costs so as to keep operating profits flowing in. The challenge here is balancing reduction of costs and maintaining the quality standards of the organization simultaneously.
f. *Attractiveness of target company in the industry*: The company fundamentals should be consistent with the potential growth. It should be a mature and stable company with not an abrupt change in technology. It is necessary to look for abundance in cash flows and fewer investment avenues.
g. *Diversified business portfolio*: In case of large conglomerate giants, it is of advantage to focus on the underperforming companies of a conglomerate. The underperforming segment should not be considered critical to the overall conglomerate success. This makes it a win-win situation to go for LBO in the purview of both seller and buyer.
h. *Limited time for LBO partnerships*: The stipulated time for going private puts the management under pressure to perform and generate profitability in a medium term. In this, the overall performance can be improved by paying comparatively more attention to strategies and factors rather than focusing on long-term perspectives. Therefore, a focused approach is necessary and proper cost-cutting tactics should be used.
i. *Borrowing capacity*: In an LBO, it is necessary to assimilate the debt properly in the organization. A balanced approach should be there in which the asset base of the company should suffice the amount of debt and interest payments. It is necessary to understand that available assets should be seen as those that are not used as collateral. Therefore, it is mandatory to maintain lower debt in comparison to the collateral value of the firm's asset. This provides the company with greater borrowing capacity. In case this aspect is neglected, it becomes difficult to borrow further.
j. *LBO and the stakeholders' interest*: Amongst the stakeholders, it is necessary to look at the interest of the equity holders and debt holders. It can be well balanced if the manager's equity can be increased to cushion for future, so as to motivate them to perform better and stay committed to the organization. A major risk that lurks for the bond holders is that the secured debt gets converted into junk and then gets converted from secured to risky. This aspect needs a managerial balancing act.
k. *Other factors*: Apart from the above-mentioned factors, lenders or investors may look for some other important factors depending upon the nature of the business of the LBO candidate. Such factors may be tangible or intangible in nature. For instance, the existence of a strong asset base in the balance sheet of the company is one of the most important tangible factors because such assets are used as collateral for financing the LBO programme. An LBO candidate having strong asset base can easily raise capital to

finance the LBO. On the other hand, timing is another important factor to make an LBO programme successful. Proper timing is very much important to maximize the probability of making the LBO transaction successful.

LBO Candidate Criteria

Specific criteria for a good LBO candidate include:

- Steady and predictable cash flow
- Clean balance sheet with little debt
- Strong, defensible market position
- Limited working capital requirements
- Minimal future capital requirements
- Heavy asset base for loan collateral
- Divestible assets
- Strong management team
- Viable exit strategy
- Synergy opportunities
- Potential for expense reduction

14.9 Sources of LBO Financing

In a leveraged transaction, the majority of a company's capitalization is debt financed, which enables financial sponsors to achieve their IRR targets and corporates to acquire larger companies. The equity is provided by the buyer and is frequently 30% to 40% of the total capitalizations. There are a number of types of financing which can be used in an LBO. These include, for example, the following (in order of their risk):

a. **Senior debt:** This debt ranks ahead of all other debt and equity capital in the business. Bank loans are typically structured in up to three trenches: 'A', 'B' and 'C'. The debt is usually secured on specific assets of the company, which means the lender can automatically acquire these assets if the company breaches its obligations under the relevant loan agreement; therefore, it has the lowest cost of debt. These obligations are usually quite stringent, though senior debt is often not subject to reporting requirements as they are usually unrated. The bank loans are usually held by a syndicate of banks and specialized funds. Typically, the terms of senior debt in an LBO will require repayment of the debt in equal annual instalments over a period of approximately seven years. Senior debt is pre-payable and has a floating rate of interest. From the lender's perspective, this is the most secure form of financing. A financial buyer will usually want the LBO to be financed by as much senior debt as possible as it provides the 'platform' for the debt financing, since it is the lowest-cost form of financing.

   However, the providers of senior debt will be reluctant to accept very high levels of senior debt (which may affect their security) or may impose conditions which are unacceptable to the equity investor. As a result, senior debt will often only form about 50% of the total financing.

b. **Subordinated debt:** This debt ranks behind senior debt in order of priority on any liquidation. The terms of the subordinated debt are usually less stringent than those of senior debt. Repayment is usually required in one 'bullet' payment at the end of the term. Since subordinated debt gives the lender less security than senior debt, lending costs are typically higher. An increasingly important form of subordinated debt is the high yield bond, often listed on Indian markets. High-yield bonds can be either senior or subordinated securities that are publicly placed with institutional investors. They are fixed-rate, publicly traded, long-term securities with a looser covenant package than senior debt, though they are subject to stringent reporting requirements. High-yield bonds are not pre-payable for the first five years and after that, they are pre-payable at a premium.

c. **Mezzanine finance:** This is usually high-risk subordinated debt (pre-payable at a premium), and is regarded as a type of intermediate financing between debt and equity and an alternative to high-yield bonds. An enhanced return is made available to lenders by the grant of an 'equity kicker' (e.g., warrants, options and shares), which crystallizes upon an exit. A form of this is called a PIK, which reflects interest 'paid in kind', or rolled up into the principal, and generally includes an attached equity warrant (for larger financings).

d. **Loan stock:** This can be a form of equity financing if it is convertible into equity capital. The question of whether loan stock is tax deductible should be investigated thoroughly with the company's advisers.

e. **Preference shares:** This forms part of a company's share capital and usually gives preference shareholders a fixed dividend and fixed share of the company's equity (subject to there being sufficient available profits).

f. **Ordinary shares:** This is the riskiest part of an LBO's capital structure. However, ordinary shareholders will enjoy the majority of the upside if the company is successful. Only some of these forms of financing will be used in a transaction, unless the transaction is extremely complex.

Furthermore, this list is a very general summary, and many of these categories comprise a number of different products. There are also certain types of financing which do not fall within these categories. Generally, the following typical financial instruments are used for financing an LBO.

Elements of Capital	*% of Total Capital*	*Tenure (in Years)*	*Traditional Suppliers of Capital*
Senior debt: Revolving term	30%–60%	5–8	Investment banks and commercial banks
Subordinated debt: Senior/ subordinated notes, discount notes, traditional mezzanine etc.	10%–25%	7–10	Investment banks, commercial banks and mezzanine funds
Preferred stock/mezzanine securities: preferred stock, PIK debt warrants	0%–35%	7–10+	Investment banks, commercial banks, mezzanine funds
Common equity: Common equity vender loan notes (deeply subordinated)	25%–40%	3–7, 10–12	Private equity fund, vendor loan notes

14.10 Building an LBO Model

A basic LBO model is similar in many respects to a standalone DCF model in that exactly the same methodology is used to derive the company's financial statements. The major difference is that an LBO analysis, unlike a DCF, takes account of interest charges and debt repayments. As a result, the financial statements need to be adjusted to include these payments. Different patterns of LBO models is presented in Exhibit 14.1 with reference to different time periods. The key steps in completing an LBO model are as follows:

Exhibit 14.1 Different Patterns of LBO Models

Classic LBO Models: Late 1970s and Early 1980s

- Debt is normally four to five times of equity. Debt amortized over no more than 10 years.
- Existing corporate management is encouraged to participate.
- Complex capital structure: As a percentage of total funds raised
  - Senior debt (60%)
  - Subordinated debt (26%)
  - Preferred stock (9%)
  - Common equity (5%)
- Firm frequently takes public within seven years as tax benefits diminish.

Break-up LBO Model (Late 1980s)

- Same as classic LBO but debt serviced from operating cash flow and asset sales
- Changes in tax laws reduced popularity of this approach
  - Asset sales immediately upon closing of the transaction no longer deemed tax-free.
  - Previously, could buy stock in a company and sell the assets. Any gain on asset sales was offset by a mirrored reduction in the value of the stock.

Strategic LBO Model (1990s)

- Exit strategy is via IPO
- Lower D/E ratios so as not to depress EPS.
- Financial buyers provide the expertise to grow earnings.
  - Previously, their expertise focused on capital structure
- Structured deals so that debt repayment is not required until 10 years after the transaction to reduce pressure on immediate performance improvement
- Buyout firms often purchase a firm as a platform for leveraged buyouts of other firms in the same industry.

LBOs in the New Millennium

- Explosion in frequency and average size of LBOs in the United States during the 2005–07 period ($5–$10 billion range)
- Tendency for buyout firms to bid for targets as a group ('Club Deals')
- Increased effort to 'cash out' earlier than in past to boost returns due to increased competition for investors
- LBO 'boom' fuelled by
  - Global savings glut resulting in cheap financing
  - Fed 'easy' money policies
  - Excess capacity in many industries encouraging consolidation
  - Attempt to avoid onerous reporting requirements of Sarbanes-Oxley
- LBOs increasingly common in the European Union due to liberalization and 'catch-up' to the United States.

1. *Forecast cash flows:* Projected cash flows should be modelled in exactly the same manner as for a DCF valuation. The forecast period should end no earlier than the latest date on which an exit is expected or the latest date on which the debt is expected to be repaid in full (whichever is later). While a DCF valuation requires the unlevered FCFs to be discounted to provide enterprise value, an LBO uses FCFs to derive IRRs.
2. *Estimate debt capacity:* The next step is to estimate the amount of debt that the company can take on. The financial statements should make provisions for interest and debt costs. The company can only bear debt to the extent that it has available cash flows. Note that all existing debt will need to be refinanced. When modelling, consult your team about the financing assumptions to be used. These will vary according to market conditions, industry characteristic and company-specific issues. Consultation with the leveraged finance team or the financial sponsors group is advisable, since they have more day-to-day experience about the current parameters in the marketplace. Set out below are some parameters that will influence financing considerations for the model:

    - Minimum interest cover (times)
    - Total debt/EBITDA (times)
    - Senior debt repayment (in years)
    - Mezzanine debt repayment (in years)
    - Senior debt interest rate
    - Subordinated interest rate
    - Mezzanine finance exit IRR

    It may also be appropriate to model the potential sale of non-core assets in order to ensure maximum leverage. Note that, when modelling interest charges, a circular reference is likely to be encountered resulting from calculating interest payable as the average of the debt at the start and end of the relevant period. This is to be expected and iterations can be used to resolve the circular reference. The best way to avoid this is to copy the formula to another cell and delete the cells generating the circular reference before making any amendments to the model. When all changes have been made, you can copy the formula back into the relevant cells.
3. *Estimate equity required:* The equity required is, in simplistic terms, the cost of acquiring the company (including existing debt) less its debt capacity. The total cost of the company comprises both the purchase price and transaction expenses. The level of transaction costs should not be underestimated—these can often amount to approximately 3% of the purchase price, particularly for smaller transactions.
4. *Estimate the exit price:* A financial buyer will typically wish to exit within three to five years. The expected value of the company at that time is critically important to the buyer. Therefore, an estimate of the value of the business should be made, usually as a multiple of EBIT or EBITDA, at the end of that period. As a base case, the multiple should normally be no more than the multiple paid for the business by the financial buyer. Furthermore, a discount of 10% to 15% should be included if an initial public offering is the most likely exit route. For different exit strategies, see Table 14.2.
5. *Calculate the IRR:* There is an Excel function that can be used to estimate the IRR.

14.11 Stages of LBO Operation

Four distinct but related stages are envisaged for the proper implementation of an LBO programme, which are described next.

14.11.1 First Stage: Arrangement of Finance

The first stage of the operation consists of raising the cash required for the buyouts and working out a management incentive system. The equity base of the new firm consists of around 10% of cash put up by the company's top management or buyout specialists. Outside investors like merchant bankers, venture capitalists and commercial banks then arrange to provide the remaining equity. Usually 50% of the cash is raised by borrowings against the company's assets in secured bank acquisition loans from commercial banks. The remaining cash is obtained by issuing certain debts in a private placement, usually with pension funds, insurance companies, venture capital firms or public offerings through high-risk high-yield junk bonds. Private placement and junk bonds are subordinated forms of debts (often referred to as mezzanine money') and they secure a place in between the secured debts from banks and risky residual claims of shareholders.

14.11.2 Second Stage: Going Private

In this stage, the organizing or sponsoring group purchases all the outstanding shares of the target company and takes it private through stock purchase format or purchases all assets through asset purchasing format. For the latter case, the purchasing group forms another new, privately held corporation. To reduce the debt by paying off a part of bank loans, the new owners sometimes sell off part of the corporation and may begin disposing of the inventory.

14.11.3 Third Stage: Restructuring

In this stage, the new management would try to enhance the generation of profit and cash flows by reducing certain operating costs and changing the marketing strategy. For this operation, it may adopt any or all of the below given policies:

i. Consolidation and reorganization of existing production facilities;
ii. Changing the product mix (thereby changing the quality of the product) and changing the policy relating to customer services and pricing;
iii. Trimming employment through attrition;
iv. Phasing out employees in turn and reduction on spending on R&D, new plants and equipments and so on, so long as there is a need to redeem the fresh acquired debts;
v. Extraction and implementation of better terms from various suppliers.

However, while undertaking the above-stated restructuring activities, due attention should be given for the approval of genuine capital expenditure programmes for the growth of the firm; otherwise, the long-term growth of the firm would hamper.

14.11.4 Fourth Stage: Reverse LBO

In this stage, the investor group may take the company to public again, if the already restructured company emerges stronger and the goals set by the LBO groups have already been achieved. This is known as the process of 'reverse LBO' or the process of 'going public', where the process is effected through public equity offerings. The sole purpose of this exercise is to create liquidity for existing shareholders. This type of reverse LBO is executed mostly by ex-post successful LBO companies.

Table 14.2 Potential Investment Exit Strategies for an LBO Fund

Exit Strategy	*Comments*
Sale	Often the equity holders will seek an outright sale to a strategic buyer, or even another financial buyer.
Initial public offering	While an initial public offering is not likely to result in the sale of the entire entity, it does allow the buyer to realize a gain on its investment.
Recapitalization	The equity holders may recapitalize by re-leveraging the entity, replacing equity with more debt, in order to extract cash from the company.

Source: Author's own.

14.12 The Advantages of LBO

Certain important advantages can be obtained from an LBO programme. The major advantages of the LBO are as follows:

a. With the help of an LBO strategy, the acquiring company can be benefited from the acquisition of international brand without having significant impact of the additional funding costs on the balance sheet of the firm. In other words, the acquiring company can expand its business network in the international market based on leveraged capital, that is, without occurring huge amount of outlay from the internal resources of the firm.
b. Since in the LBO system, a new company is created to procure the debt capital as well as other sources of finance required for the acquisition, the volatility of earnings of that new created company, popularly known as SPV, does not affect the business of the acquiring company. After the passage of certain years, when debts are fully repaid, the parent acquiring company is merged with its SPV that was created purposefully. As a result, the parent acquiring company can enjoy the benefits of entire acquisition without confronting the adverse business as well as financial risk arising out of such acquisition.
c. Moreover, the newly created company can enjoy tax benefits in operating the business for a considerable time period of five to six years. Due to the existence of high amount of leveraged or debt capital, in the capital structure of the company, tax benefits can be achieved in respect of payment of interests. Moreover, higher amount of assets set-up will provide greater amount of tax savings in the form of depreciation expense.
d. The LBO system helps in stimulating the cross-border acquisition since this system ensures the supply of required amount of capital needed for large acquisitions. As a result, a firm can enlarge its business network not only in the domestic market but also in the international market.
e. High gearing tends to be a discipline on management, since a company's cash flow is usually quite tight due to the necessary pay-down of interest and debt. The management is therefore likely to focus on driving down costs and controlling capital expenditure.
f. In a highly leveraged company, a relatively small increase in the company's enterprise value can lead to a substantial increase in the value of its equity. In a bull market, the

attractiveness of an LBO will therefore increase. Of course, the gearing effect also means that high gearing increases an equity investor's risk, since a relatively small decline in enterprise value could severely impact the value of the equity investment. Moreover, high interest charges increase the risk of default by the company.

14.13 The Limitations of LBO

Even though the value is created through an LBO exercise, it cannot be claimed to be free from criticisms. The most important drawbacks of the LBO system are stated as follows:

a. The LBO programme is subject to high degree of financial risk since it is mostly based on borrowed capital. On the other hand, if the degree of operating risk of the LBO candidate is also high, it may be difficult for the firm to service the debt properly which, in turn, may lead to the firm into bankruptcy in the near future. In addition to that, the fluctuation in interest rate is another important point to be considered here. The rise in interest rate may create genuine problems for a firm that has more variable debt rate. In order to meet all these categories of risk, a strong and stable cash flow is quintessential. The lack of such secure and stable cash flows may raise meaningful questions about the existence of the concerned firm.
b. In order to implement the LBO programme, an LBO candidate should have strong asset base that can be used as collateral for financing the acquisition. Moreover, an experienced as well as efficient team of management is also important. Thus, a firm that lacks these requirements may not be able to finance its acquisition plan.

Finally, if the firm cannot afford the interest burden to be boned by it due to any reason, the ultimate liability of repayment of the huge amount of loans will be on the shoulder of that firm. Naturally, the acquiring firm should always remain aware regarding the fact that the LBO programme is subject to high degree of risk.

14.14 Value Generation Through LBO

Every restructuring programme must generate some additional values for the business, owners, shareholders and so on. Therefore, an LBO exercise also creates certain additional values for various groups involved in such an operation. In order to identify the basic sources of value generation in an LBO, one must consider its underlying assumptions:

a. that the current price of the target firm understates the original value of the firm;
b. so some values are created by taking the firm private;
c. the values so created are transferred to the shareholders and buyout groups from other parties involved in such an operation.

Since the assumptions clearly reflect the position of value creation through an LBO operation, one must identify the sources of value so generated. The sources are as follows:

a. 'Reduction in agency cost' is the most important source of value in an LBO. An LBO refers to take a public corporation to private. In case of a public corporation, the management is different from its owners. In practice, however, the management sometimes takes some suboptimal decisions without the prior approval of its owners, which are proved to be costly and detrimental to the growth of the firm and beneficial to the management. On the contrary, when a public corporation goes private, the owners and the management are the same and, in all cases, the management takes decisions that are not only cost-effective, but also for the growth of the organization. Agency cost refers to the difference of the firm value when the management and owners are the same than that of the firm value when different groups function as owners and managers. By taking a public corporation to private, an LBO exercise tries to eliminate such an agency cost that is considered as a value gain for a restructured firm.

b. The second source of value gain is associated with 'efficiency'. It is argued that a private firm is much more efficient in taking decisions in relation to a changing environment than that of a public corporation, where every decision is not required to be ratified by the general body before implementation. Thus, action can be taken more speedily since major new programmes do not have to be justified by detailed studies and reports to the board of directors. It is this efficiency in decision-making that creates value for an LBO. Again, production and portfolio efficiencies are perceived with an LBO operation because of the involvement of specialized LBO firms. Such efficiencies create 'synergistic' benefits, which ultimately generate value.
c. Another source of value gain in case of an LBO is 'tax benefits' as in such an operation, the interest obligation of the private firm is expected to certain tax benefits. Again, the concept of stepping up of assets for depreciation as an ingredient of LBO calls for additional tax advantages.
d. Finally, it is understood that management or investors in an LBO deal have more 'information' on the value of the firm than the ordinary shareholders. Because of this information, a buyout proposal gives indication to the market that the post-buyout scenario would certainly provide more operating incomes than previously expected or that the firm is less risky than perceived by the public at present. It is this asymmetric information that adds value to an LBO, and because of this value, the buyout investors do not mind paying large premiums on such deals.

The value so created through an LBO exercise is exclusively meant for the shareholders of the restructured firm and partly for the specialists engaged in such an operation. Basically, this is considered as a 'wealth transfer' mechanism in a sense that because of the financial leverage, the gain achieved by the shareholders came at the expense of the firm's debt holders. Thus, it can be inferred that 'the value gains to shareholders are partly the result of efficiency gains, tax benefits, better information and a reduction in agency cost' (Bansal and Yuyuenyongwatana 1996).

14.15 Valuation

An LBO can be evaluated from the perspective of common equity investors or of all investors and lenders

a. From common equity investors' perspective:

$$NPV = PV_{FCFE} - I_{EQ} \geq 0$$

where PV_{FCFE} is the present value of FCFs to common equity investors and I_{EQ} is the value of common equity.

b. From investors' and lenders' perspective:

$$NPV = PV_{FCFF} - I_{TC} \geq 0NPV$$

where present value of FCFs to the firm and is the total investment or the value of total capital, including common and preferred stock and all debt.

The valuation of established companies that are the usual acquisition targets of LBO funds can be done using two primary methods:

- **Market comparisons:** These are metrics such as multiples of revenue, net earnings and EBITDA that can be compared among public and private companies. Usually, a discount of 10% to 40% is applied to private companies due to the lack of liquidity of their shares.
- **DCF analysis:** This is based on the concept that the value of a company is based on the cash flows it can produce in the future. An appropriate discount rate is used to calculate a NPV of projected cash flows.

14.16 LBO: A Simple Example

This example presents an idea on how an LBO operation may generate values from a very simple and easy-to-understand scenario. Without going for buying a business, we may have a look at the injection of more debt on any purchase scenario to visualize the beauty of leveraged operation. This example is intended to demonstrate the effect of leverage when making an acquisition. Suppose you bought building on 31 December 2010 as an investment for $750,000 with a down payment of $75,000. The remaining $675,000 of the purchase price was financed through a bank loan with an interest rate of 7.5%. Your annual rental income from the house is $250,000 and your annual expenses are $50,000 in maintenance charges and $10,000 in property taxes. For simplicity, you may consider the following assumptions:

a. no income taxes,
b. all cash flows occur at the end of each year,
c. the value of the rental property remains fixed.

You have projected income for the next five years as given here:

Income Statement ***Year Ending December 31,***	***2011***	***2012***	***2013***	***2014***	***2015***
Rental income	$250,000	$250,000	$250,000	$250,000	$250,000
Maintenance charges	50,000	50,000	50,000	50,000	50,000
Property taxes	10,000	10,000	10,000	10,000	10,000
Rental income	190,000	190,000	190,000	190,000	190,000
Interest payments	50,625	40,172	28,935	16,855	3,869
FCF used to repay debt	139,375	149,828	161,065	173,145	186,131

Assuming that all FCF each year is used to repay debt and the value of the property remains fixed, your equity ownership in the house should steadily increase over the period as you pay down your mortgage:

Year Ending December 31,	*2010*	*2011*	*2012*	*2013*	*2014*	*2015*
Mortgage						
Beginning balance	$675,000	$675,000	$535,625	$385,797	$224,732	$51,587
(Payments)/borrowings	0	(139,375)	(149,828)	(161,065)	(173,145)	(51,587)
Ending balance	675,000	535,625	385,797	224,732	51,587	0
Interest expense at		50,625	40,172	28,935	16,855	3,869
Capitalization						
Debt	$675,000	$535,625	$385,797	$224,732	$51,587	$0
Equity	75,000	214,375	364,203	525,268	525,268	750,000
Total capitalization	750,000	750,000	750,000	750,000	750,000	750,000
Ownership						
Debt	90.0%	71.4%	51.4%	30.0%	6.9%	0.0%
Equity	10.0%	28.6%	48.6%	70.0%	93.1%	100.0%
Total capitalization	100.0%	100.0%	100.0%	100.0%	100.0%	100.0%

The above table indicates that at the end of five years in 2015, your equity ownership as a percentage of total capitalization increases from 10% to 100%, resulting a handsome amount of ROE as follows:

Return on Investment	
Equity value	$884,544
Compound annual ROE	63.81%

Taking into account the value of the building at the end of 2015, your initial $75,000 investment is worth nearly $900,000, representing a compounded annual return of 64%. Because you were able to take advantage of leverage in financing the purchase, you now own an asset of relatively significant equity value relative to the amount of your initial equity investment.

Financing the purchase of the building with significant amounts of debt will dramatically influence your return on the investment. To further illustrate this, consider the effect of varying combinations of debt and equity to make the original purchase. Furthermore, assume that the real estate market takes a turn for the worse and that you can only rent the house for $125,000 a year while still having to pay the same expenses in maintenance and property taxes. Assuming that you are stuck with this investment for the next five years, your income stream can be summarized as follows:

Income Statement *Year Ending December 31,*	*2011*	*2012*	*2013*	*2014*	*2015*
Rental income	$125,000	$125,000	$125,000	$125,000	$125,000
Maintenance charges	50,000	50,000	50,000	50,000	50,000
Property taxes	10,000	10,000	10,000	10,000	10,000
Rental income	65,000	65,000	65,000	65,000	65,000
Interest payments	50,065	48,901	47,647	46,295	44,837
FCF used to repay debt	14,935	16,099	17,353	18,705	20,163

If you eventually sell the house in 2015 for $500,000, $750,000 or $1 million, your compounded annual ROI in each financing scenario can be summarized as follows:

	100% Equity		50% Debt/50% Equity		75% Debt/25% Equity	
Sale Price	Proceeds to Equity Holders	Return to Equity Holders	Proceeds to Equity Holders	Return to Equity Holders	Proceeds to Equity Holders	Return to Equity Holders
$500,000	$825,000	1.92%	$348,830	(1.44%)	$75,971	(16.53%)
750,000	1,075,000	7.47%	598,830	9.81%	325,971	11.70%
1,000,000	1,325,000	12.05%	848,830	17.75%	575,971	25.16%

The proceeds to you at exit include the repayment of the outstanding mortgage balance and the proceeds from your exiting sale price. Note how increasing financing leverage magnifies your IRR, either positively or negatively. While this example is rather simple, we see that levering up to make an investment in any asset increases financial risk and significantly influence one's gain or loss on the investment.

14.17 LBO: A Complex Example

Let us assume that the purchase price of a target amount of $200 and it requires additional transaction costs of $5. Financing will be done through debt and equity as follows:

Use of Funds		Sources of Funds	
Purchase price	$200	Senior debt (at 9.0%)	$45
Transaction costs	5	Junior debt (at 13.0%)	100
		Equity	60
Total	$205	Total	$205

An analysis of the target company results the following assumption for a five-year period, which is helpful for financial projections.

Assumptions	Year 1	Year 2	Year 3	Year 4	Year 5
Sales growth	5.00%	5.00%	5.00%	5.00%	5.00%
Cost of goods sold (COGS) as a percentage of Sales	60.00%	60.00%	60.00%	60.00%	60.00%
Selling, general and administrative (S,G&A) expenses as a percentage of Sales	15.00%	15.00%	15.00%	15.00%	15.00%
Depreciation as a percentage of Sales	5.50%	5.50%	5.50%	5.50%	5.50%
Transaction cost amortization (in 5 years)	$1.00	$1.00	$1.00	$1.00	$1.00
Tax rate	35%	35%	35%	35%	35%
Capital expenditure as a percentage of sales	5.50%	5.50%	5.50%	5.50%	5.50%
Increase in working capital as a percentage of increase in sales	7.00%	7.00%	7.00%	7.00%	7.00%

Based on the assumptions made above, the targeted projection is made as follows:

Target Projections	*Year 0*	*Year 1*	*Year 2*	*Year 3*	*Year 4*	*Year 5*
Net sales	170	178.5	187.4	196.8	206.6	217
COGS	102	107.1	112.5	118.1	124	130.2
S,G&A	25.5	26.8	28.1	29.5	31	32.5
Depreciation	9.4	9.8	10.3	10.8	11.4	11.9
Operating income	33.1	34.8	36.5	38.4	40.3	42.3
Transaction fee amortization	–	1	1	1	1	1
EBIT	33.1	33.8	35.5	37.4	39.3	41.3
Interest expense:						
Senior debt: 9.0%		4.1	3	1.9	0.5	–
Junior debt: 13.0%		13	13	13	13	11.5
Total interest expense		17.1	16	14.9	13.5	11.5
Pre-tax income		16.8	19.5	22.5	25.8	29.8
Income taxes		5.9	6.8	7.9	9	10.4
Net income		10.9	12.7	14.6	16.8	19.4
FCF calculation:						
Net income		10.9	12.7	14.6	16.8	19.4
Plus: Depreciation		9.8	10.3	10.8	11.4	11.9
Plus: Transaction fee amortization		1	1	1	1	1
Less: Capital expenditures		(9.8)	(10.3)	(10.8)	(11.4)	(11.9)
Less: increase in working capital		(0.6)	(0.6)	(0.7)	(0.7)	(0.7)
FCF		11.3	13.1	15	17.1	19.6

Capitalization over the five years has been shown below, which ends up with 66% financing from equity and 34% from junior debt.

Capitalization	*Year 0*	*Year 1*	*Year 2*	*Year 3*	*Year 4*	*Year 5*
Senior debt—beginning balance		45.0	33.7	20.6	5.7	–
Mandatory amortization—$1.0		1.0	1.0	1.0	1.0	–
Cash sweep		10.3	12.1	14	4.7	–
Senior debt—ending balance	45	33.7	20.6	5.7	–	–
Junior debt—Beginning balance		100	100	100	100	88.6
Mandatory amortization – $0.0		–	–	–	–	–
Cash sweep		–	–	–	11.4	19.6
Junior debt—ending balance	100.0	100.0	100.0	100.0	88.6	68.9
Senior debt—ending balance	45.0	33.7	20.6	5.7	–	–
Junior debt—ending balance	100.0	100.0	100.0	100.0	88.6	68.9

Equity (including net income)	60.0	70.9	83.6	98.2	115.0	134.3
Total capitalization	205.0	204.6	204.2	203.9	203.6	203.3
Senior debt	22.0%	16.5%	10.1%	2.8%	0.0%	0.0%
Junior debt	48.8%	48.9%	49.0%	49.0%	43.5%	33.9%
Equity	29.3%	34.7%	40.9%	48.2%	56.5%	66.1%

It is important to calculate the returns to investors and determine whether the deal is attractive. To do that, IRR may be used as a decisive tool and a sensitivity table may be generated to provide a clear picture of volatility of return to the investors. The following table presents the return and sensitivity analysis considering three exit multiples hypothetically at different years.

LBO Return Calculations

Cash Flows to Common Equity			***Year 0***	***Year 1***	***Year 2***	***Year 3***	***Year 4***	***Year 5***
EBITDA			42.5	43.6	45.9	48.2	50.7	53.2
Total debt			145	133.7	120.6	105.7	88.6	68.9
Exit Multiple			***Outflow***			***Inflows***		
	5.5×		–60	106.2	131.6	159.4	190	223.9
	6.5×		–60	149.9	177.4	207.6	240.7	277.1
	7.5×		–60	193.5	223.3	255.8	291.4	330.4
Exit In:		***IRR***			[(43.6 × 5.5) −133.7]			
Year 1	5.5×	77.10%	–60	106.2				
	6.5×	149.80%	–60	149.9				
	7.5×	222.50%	–60	193.5				
Year 2	5.5×	48.10%	–60	–	131.6			
	6.5×	72.00%	–60	–	177.4			
	7.5×	92.90%	–60	–	223.3			
Year 3	5.5×	38.50%	–60	–	–	159.4		
	6.5×	51.30%	–60	–	–	207.6		
	7.5×	62.20%	–60	–	–	255.8		
Year 4	5.5×	33.40%	–60	–	–	–	190	
	6.5×	41.50%	–60	–	–	–	240.7	
	7.5×	48.40%	–60	–	–	–	291.4	
Year 5	5.5×	30.10%	–60	–	–	–	–	223.9
	6.5×	35.80%	–60	–	–	–	–	277.1
	7.5×	40.70%	–60	–	–	–	–	330.4

This table shows that IRR reduces as exit years have been extended. The rate is increasing as exit multiple is increasing. Based on this, a decision can be easily made whether the LBO deal is lucrative or not. For example, here the least IRR is 30%, which is handsome. If it is the case that in the worst scenario, the deal will generate 30% IRR, the deal can be finalized.

Multiple Choice Questions

1. LBO was previously known as _______
   a. Bootstrap acquisition b. Merger
   c. Acquisition d. Absorption
2. _______ is a kind of acquisition of a company which is financed through debt.
   a. Merger b. LBO c. Acquisition d. Absorption
3. When the buyout group includes current management of the target firm, it is usually _______
   a. Management buyout b. LBO
   c. Any d. None
4. Which one of the following is the required criterion for LBO candidate?
   a. Steady and predictable cash flow
   b. Clean balance sheet with little debt
   c. Strong management team
   d. All of the above
5. Which one of the following sources of financing is significantly used in case of LBO?
   a. Senior debt b. Subordinated debt
   c. Preferred stock d. Common equity
6. Tendency for buyout firms to bid for targets as a group is called _______
   a. Anti-takeover defence b. Spin off
   c. Club deals d. None
7. Which one of the following is not an exit strategy for an LBO fund?
   a. Initial public offering b. Recapitalization
   c. Sale d. Transfer
8. Which one of the following is not an advantage of LBO?
   a. Discipline on management b. High degree of financial risk
   c. Tax benefits d. Acquisition of international brand
9. If the present value of FCFs to common equity investors becomes greater than the value of common equity in an LBO, it results in positive NPV to _______
   a. Common equity holder b. Lenders
   c. Preferred equity holder d. All
10. Which one of the following valuation methods in case of LBO does not fall within market-based valuation methods?
    a. Multiples of revenue b. Net earnings
    c. DCF analysis d. EBITDA

Review Questions

1. Define LBO and state how it is undertaken.
2. Sketch the historical developments of LBO.
3. What can be inferred by the term 'leveraged buyout'? Discuss the characteristics of this strategy.
4. LBOs are popular in the United States and are gaining momentum in the Indian economy. What, according to you, are the advantages offered by LBO that have made them popular?
5. 'The LBO can be successful if the critical factors are taken care of'. Comment.
6. 'LBO is lucrative when the target company has certain critical characteristics'. Discuss. Elaborate on the process followed for an LBO.
7. 'The LBO can be a double-edged sword'. Comment on the statement.
8. Briefly explain the various sources of LBO financing.
9. Discuss the key steps involved in an LBO model.
10. Elaborate on the different stages of LBO operation.
11. Write short notes on
    (a) Objectives of a LBO
    (b) Management buyout
12. Write a critical note on the value generated through LBO.

Case in Action

The LBO of AGI

Overview

In October of 2003, Kirkland Partners, a private equity fund based in Chicago, was considering the leveraged acquisition of a small chain of fitness centres in New England. Such an acquisition would complement Kirkland's investments in private medical companies targeted to older, wealthier individuals. The question was whether the seller's asking price of $31 million was worth paying, and if so, how the acquisition could be financed.

The New England company, Active Generation, Inc (AGI), was considered a good opportunity because its layout, equipment and target client group were very similar to Kirkland's previous, successful, LBO and its owners, based in Rhode Island, had been interested in selling Active Generation so that they could create liquid estates for their heirs. In recent years, AGI had refocused their equipment and staff to target middle-aged and retired health-conscious clients. The fitness centres offered dietary supplements, natural foods, and chiropractic services as well as equipment rooms and exercise classes. AGI's management had been interested in expanding through an acquisition, but the owners were not willing to come up with the additional capital needed.

Kirkland's chief investment officer had to develop an offering price for Active Generation that was low enough to make the acquisition's value positive in the future. She was also concerned with possible exit strategies in five to seven years, although at its present size a public offering was out of the question. With the right incentives for management, it was reasonable to assume that under Kirkland's ownership, AGI's operating margin could be increased from 7.0% to 7.8%, principally from the outsourcing of billing facilities and improved loyalty incentives that would secure long-term contracts with affinity groups. AGI's owner-CEO had been considering retirement for some time and, unfortunately, had not been aggressive with respect to expansion. Kirkland believed that AGI's historical sales growth of 8% could easily be increased to 11%. After four years, however, Kirkland did not consider that growth would continue above the growth rate of the U.S. economy without further significant investment in the AGI operation. Kirkland was not prepared to consider such a commitment in formulating its offer.

In order to improve operating performance and growth for at Active Generation, Kirkland Partners realized that some incremental investment in working capital, estimated to be 12% of each incremental dollar of sales, would be necessary, given Active Generation's anticipated 2003 sales level of $44 million. The cost of maintaining plant and equipment was assumed to have been matched by depreciation charges.

Health centre shares were trading in the public market at 12.6 times expected 2004 EPS and 1.3 times recent book value per share. Stock market analysts at First Chicago Securities had calculated a Beta factor of only 0.9 for such companies, which on average had a 20:80 debt–equity ratio. Long-term government securities were trading on a yield basis of 5.2%. Market analysts believed that the inherent investment risk in investing in large company stocks required a 5.5% market premium over long-term, risk-free securities. Similarly, analysts believed that the risk in investing in small private company stocks required a 12.0% market premium over long-term, risk-free securities. AGI's corporate tax rate was 28%.

Kirkland Partners had been discussing the potential acquisition with several bankers. Initial calculations suggested that the acquisition might be financed with a leveraged capital structure such as the follows:

Assets		***Liabilities***	
Purchase price	85%	Senior debt (at 10%)	65%
New capex	10%	Subordinated debt (at 15%)	10%
Other	5%	Equity	25%
	100%		100%

In considering their options for estate planning, the owners of Active Generation had appointed a Boston-based appraisal firm to provide a valuation of their fixed property, plant and equipment and other long-term assets under two scenarios: one, if Active Generation were to commence its operation all over again, what would it cost to replace all of its long-term assets at current market prices; two, if they were to halt all operations immediately, what cash proceeds could they expect from a liquidation of those assets.

The appraisal stated that the replacement value of the fixed assets (the fitness centres and the exercise equipment) was $15,658,600, and the company's unused land was appraised at $11.3 million. If Active Generation were to simply go out of business, the fitness centres could be liquidated for about $9,649,800. Active Generation's present balance sheet discloses net working capital of $9,246,000. Active Generation's management had always been fearful of financing with debt, so their only capital was represented by equity, which had a book value of $23,646,000.

Source: www.stern.nyu.edu/~igiddy/cases/agi_lbo.doc

Questions for Discussion

1. What is the company's WACC?
2. Use DCF valuation to estimate the company's stand-alone value.
3. Estimate a range of post-acquisition values for the company, taking into account the debt used for the LBO, possible corporate restructurings, and other effects.
4. Can the deal be financed in a way that satisfies all investors?

Case in Action

Tata Tea–Tetley: Acquisition Through LBO

History of TTL

Incorporated in 1962 and controlled by the House of Tatas, TTL commenced operations in 1964 with the manufacture of packaged tea. The instant tea plant started in 1965. It acquired the business of James Finlay, UK, and its seven associated tea companies in India, with effect from 1976. The technical and financial collaboration with James Finlay expired in 1971. Today, the company along with its subsidiaries has a significant presence in over 40 countries worldwide. The tea industry is cyclical in nature. India is the largest producer and consumer of tea in the world and Tata Tea is one of the largest selling brands in India, which is the largest black tea market in the world. TTL acquired the shareholding of the Tetley group, UK, through a new subsidiary company, Tata Tea (GB). Tetley is the second largest branded tea company in the world and is the market leader in tea products in Canada, the UK and a number of other European countries. In September 2000, the company exited from the loss-making mushroom company, Saptarishi Agro Industries (65% stake), by selling it to a LM Thapar group company for a consideration of ₹50 lakhs. In December 2000, the bulk tea segment launched one of its superfine, premium dust teas under the brand name of Kanniamallay Tea. The brand is produced from the Kanniamallay estate of Tata Tea. Bambio Investment & Trading Co Ltd was merged with TTL in October 2001 with prior approval from the board of directors. TTL has started production of organic green tea at Chanduvare estate near Munnar. The green tea is cultivated in a 500-hectare estate. The cost of production of green tea is higher than that of ordinary tea, with labour costs 60% higher. The organic tea will be marketed mainly in Europe and will use the Tetley network to market the same. During 2002–03, the Tetley group outsourced its entire manufacturing operations to a joint venture and formed another joint venture company to retain its presence in the food service sector.

The subsidiaries of Tata tea are Tata Coffee Ltd, Tata Tea Inc, and Tata Tea (GB) Ltd. As a part of restructuring of South India Plantation operations, the company has transferred its business and undertakings of 16 tea estates in Munnar to Kanan Devan Hills Plantations Company Pvt Ltd (KDHP) with effect from 1 April 2005.

The Honourable High Court at Calcutta approved the merger of Tata Tetley with the company with effect from 1 April 2005 and hence Tata Tetley has become a unit of the company. During 2006–07, the company acquired 25% shareholding in Energy Brands Inc, USA (EBI) through its overseas subsidiaries. EBI, commonly known as Glaceau, is the maker of Vitaminwater, Smartwater and Fruitwater and is the pioneer and leader in the Enhanced Water market in the United States. Along with the company, the main promoter of the company, Tata Sons Ltd, also acquired a 5% stake in SEBI. The company has identified a domestic acquisition opportunity in the Water segment and the company's board decided at its meeting held on 1 June 2007 to acquire a 15% stake in Mount Everest Mineral Water Ltd (MEMW) by subscribing to a Preferential issue at a negotiated price of ₹140 per share, which will be followed by purchasing another 9.15% stake from the current promoters of MEMW at the same price of ₹140 per share. The company is waiting for approval from the Calcutta High Court on the scheme of reconstruction of its North India Plantation operations.

Financing Pattern of Tetley Acquisition

As mentioned earlier, apart from the size of deal, the interesting point of this case is the financing pattern adopted by TTL for acquisition of Tetley. It actually pursued the strategy of LBO for that purpose. LBO is basically defined as the 'acquisition of a company, financed by the borrowing of all the stocks or assets of a public limited company by a small group of investors. This buying may be sponsored by buyout specialists or investment bankers that arrange such deals and usually includes representation by incumbent management'. Figure 1 provides a detailed explanation of the LBO strategy adopted by TTL. The acquisition has been structured in such a way that although Tata Tea retains full control over the venture, the debt portion of the deal does not affect its balance sheet. The deal has been tied up through an LBO based on Tetley's assets so that Tata Tea's gearing is not impaired as a result of it. Tata Tea has created a SPV, Tata Tea (Great Britain), to acquire all the assets of Tetley. The SPV was capitalized at £70 million, of which Tata Tea contributed £60 million (Tata Tea raised £45 million through a global depository receipts issue). The U.S. subsidiary of the company, Tata Tea Inc, contributed the balance £10 million. More specifically, such deal has been financed 77% by debt capital and the rest 23% by equity capital. Rabobank provided the most significant portion (£185 million) of such debt. The debt was actually raised against Tetley's brands and physical assets. Tetley's assets were pledged with the lending institutions and banks and after the redemption of the debt; TTL will have the option to merge with Tata Tea (GB) (i.e., SPV).

It is evident from Figure 1 that the actual cost incurred by TTL for Tetley acquisition was £271 million, Tata Tea has spent £9 million on legal service and bank charges. Due to this strong, balanced and structured deal, the debt portion of the deal did not affect the capital structure of TTL. It would be clearer if we deeply study the capital structure of TTL as presented in Table 1.

From Table 1, it is evident that the equity share capital of TTL was increased by ₹7.60 crore in the financial year 1999–2000 due to Tetley's acquisition. Moreover, the reserve total of the company was enhanced by ₹339.84 crore in the same financial year, representing 74.52% of the reserve total of its immediately preceding financial year (i.e., 1998–99). This enhancement in reserve total was actually the consequence of issuance equity shares at a high rate of premium. More precisely, the amount of share premium was increased by ₹304.68 crore in the financial year 1999–2000, that is, the year in which equity shares were issued by TTL. Due to the enhancement of the value of reserve total, the capital employed of the company got affected from the financial year 1999–2000 and onwards. However, there is no significant increase in the secured as well as unsecured loans due to that acquisition. Actually, the debt of £235 million procured in order to finance Tata Tea (GB) is not incorporated here. Hence, it reveals that the debt portion of the deal did not affect the capital structure of the company. Tata Tea's capital structure was affected only due to its contribution in equity finance of its SPV. In addition, due to this strategy, the revenue and earnings of the acquiring company were not affected substantially.

Figure 1 Structure of Tata Tea's LBO Deal

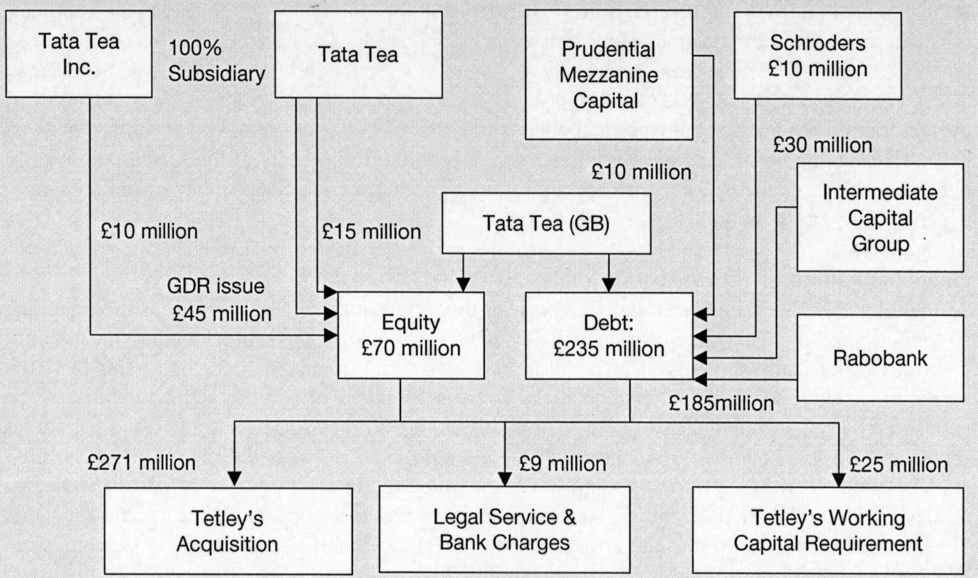

Major Findings

From Table 2, it is found that the average ROI of the company corresponding to the post-acquisition period (13.06%) is almost half of that the pre-acquisition period (24.50%). It simply indicates the ability of the company to earn profit on its investment. However, this argument is very much thin and apparent in nature. If we observe the year-wise percentage of ROI, then we shall find that there is a continuous increasing trend in ROI from the financial year 2001–02 (i.e., just after the year of acquisition). This implies that the company has started increasing its return on its investment gradually after the cross-border acquisition. Initially after the acquisition, the ROI had been significantly affected due to increase in investment (Tata Tea's contribution of £60 million to its SPV with a view to finance this newly created company) without any immediate revenues and profits.

In this context, the most worth mentioning point is that the acquirer (i.e., TTL) issued equity share capital at a high rate of premium to meet the capital need of its SPV. If, however, the acquisition did not taken place, there would have been no need of issuing such equity shares. Now, if we exclude the impact of equity issue at a high rate of premium, the amount of capital employed will be changed from the financial year 1999–2000 onwards and we can get the revised ROI, as shown in Table 2. Such revised values of ROI would help us to examine the performance of the company by excluding the impact of this acquisition. Bearing the same logic in mind, we have also computed the revised values of EVA and the revised percentages of RONW. So far as the revised ROI is concerned, then it is also found that the average ROI of the post-acquisition period (18.22%) is far lower than that of pre-acquisition period (26.51%). Here also, from the year-wise percentage of ROI, we can observe an increasing trend from the financial year 2001–02, implying thereby that the company has now started performing well and in the near future, the positive expectation regarding company's performance may be anticipated.

Table 1 Capital Structure of TTL from 1 April 1995 to 31 March 2006.

	2005–06	*2004–05*	*2003–04*	*2002–03*	*2001–02*	*2000–01*	*1999–00*	*1998–99*	*1997–98*	*1996–97*	*1995–96*
Share capital	56.22	56.22	56.22	56.22	56.22	56.22	56.22	48.62	48.62	48.62	48.62
Reserves total	1,105	992.75	919.03	922.41	911.77	840.76	795.88	456.04	330.4	282.25	258.4
Total shareholders' funds	1,161.3	1,049	975.25	978.63	967.99	896.98	852.1	504.66	379.02	330.87	307.02
Less miscellaneous expenses	33.66	34.52	0	40.99	1.34	0	0	0	0	0	0
Net shareholders' funds	1,127.6	1,014.5	975.25	937.64	966.65	896.98	852.1	504.66	379.02	330.87	307.02
Secured loans	234.51	179.38	180.86	168.36	114.05	123.16	137.23	124.65	157.5	115.47	110.15
Unsecured loans	6.84	11.99	16.5	57.03	100.18	115.87	132.51	114.21	129.24	175.79	110.59
Total debt	241.35	191.37	197.36	225.39	214.23	239.03	269.74	238.86	286.74	291.26	220.74
Capital employed	1,368.95	1,205.8	1,172.6	1,163	1,180.9	1,136	1,121.8	743.52	665.76	622.13	527.76

Table 2 Computation of ROI, Revised ROI, EPS, EVA and Revised EVA

Year	*ROI (%)*	*Revised ROI (%)*	*EPS (₹)*	*EVA (₹ in crores)*	*Revised EVA (₹ in crores)*
1995–96	19.77	19.77	9.48	17.45	17.45
1996–97	20.68	20.68	11.40	30.21	30.21
1997–98	27.69	27.69	20.00	67.02	67.02
1998–99	32.13	32.13	25.27	77.46	77.46
1999–2000	22.09	32.29	21.19	29.94	75.88
2000–01	14.81	21.52	16.91	1.45	47.39
2001–02	9.55	13.63	12.88	–37.03	8.74
2002–03	11.12	15.75	11.66	–36.25	4.59
2003–04	12.06	17.28	15.19	–23.43	22.51
2004–05	15.07	21.08	21.53	7.62	49.26
2005–06	17.48	23.36	31.57	52.41	94.16

Here, the most worth mentioning point is that this evaluation of performance of TTL is based only on the data of TTL. The financial data of Tetley are not included here at all. Hence, this performance evaluation is not based on the consequence of acquisition; rather, it is the appraisal of performance of the acquirer only. The values of EVA also reflect the same picture. The average value of EVA of the post-acquisition period (₹7.34 crores) is almost seven times lower than that of the pre-acquisition period (₹44.42 crores). Apparently, it may be viewed as the indication of deterioration of corporate surplus. However, from a very close look, it can be seen that the company has started generating corporate surplus (denoted by positive EVA) from the financial year 2004–05, and it would not be unwise to expect that in the near future, the company would be able to create value. So far as the revised EVA is concerned, the performance of the company corresponding to the post-acquisition period is far better than the performance of the same period examined on the basis of EVA that have been computed without excluding the impact of equity capital issue on the amount of capital employed. This simply implies that the increase in capital employed due to the issuance of equity shares at a high rate of premium was to some extent responsible for reduction in the values of EVA. However, the performance of the company is quite poor in the post-acquisition period in comparison with that of the pre-acquisition period since the average of the revised EVA of the post-acquisition period (₹35.85 crore) is 49.51% lower than that of the pre-acquisition period (₹53.60 crore). However, here also an increasing trend in the values of EVA is evident from the financial year 2003–04 onwards, which may be viewed as the indication of the performance of the company regarding its value creation.

From the perspective of shareholders' earnings, the position of the company is quite better since the average EPS corresponding to the post-acquisition period (₹18.57) is higher than that of the pre-acquisition period (₹17.47). Moreover, except the financial year 2002–03, there is an increasing trend in EPS also from the year 2001–02 and onwards. This is also the reflection of improvement of corporate performance of the company from the viewpoint of its shareholders. In the present context, another important point to be mentioned is that there is no adverse impact on the share prices of TTL in India even if its ROI has been declined, and it reported negative EVA in three consecutive years after the acquisition.

There was a continuous upward trend in share prices of the company in the post-acquisition period in comparison with the pre-acquisition period. This is a good sign. However, the volatility of the post-acquisition period is much higher than that of the pre-acquisition period. However, the risks of these two

Table 3 Basic Parameters in Pre- and Post-acquisition

	Pre-acquisition Period	*Post-acquisition Period*
Beta (β) values	0.1146	0.1164
Standard deviation	96.7052	12.6474
Mean	354.00413	40.3763
Coefficient of Variance	27.32	62.47

periods as measured by beta (β) are almost the same. This is the real picture as well as the reflection of the argument that in spite of the declining average values of ROI and reporting of corporate value deterioration in few years pertaining to the post-acquisition period, the sentiment of the market as well as investors remained intact, nay, have reported positive response about the future prospect of the company.

It is evident from Tables 4 and 5 that the RONW of the concerned company is far better compared to industry average during the entire study period. However, the RONW of the company corresponding to the post-acquisition period (10.50%) is lower by more than 50% of that of the pre-acquisition period (22.65%), which reflects the company's inability regarding earnings on net worth. However, here also a continuous increasing trend of RONW from the financial year 2001–02 is evident, which conveys the same message like ROI. If we look at the revised percentages of RONW, we can find that the average of revised RONW of the post-acquisition period (15.90%) is also far lower than that of the pre-acquisition period (24.45%) and an upward trend in the revised RONW is also prevalent from the financial year 2001–02, which represents the same picture as mentioned earlier in the case of simple RONW (i.e., non-revised). The interest coverage ratio actually measures the company's ability to pay interest on its long-term debts. The higher this ratio, the higher is the ability of the company to pay interests on debts. This ability of the company is better than the industry in the entire study period. More specifically, this particular ability of the company has amazingly been enhanced in the post-acquisition period (8.31) from the pre-acquisition period (4.94), which conveys the message of security to the long-term debt providers regarding the recovery of their debts.

If we look at the working capital management of the company, we may analyse inventory turnover ratio and debtors' turnover ratio for that purpose. Inventory turnover position of the company is slightly unsatisfactory compared to industry average, as reported by lower average values of inventory turnover of the company in comparison with industry average in both the periods. The debt collection ability of the company is quite unsatisfactory in the pre-acquisition period compared to the industry average, but such ability of the company has significantly been improved in the post-acquisition period in comparison with the industry average. Moreover, the debtors' turnover ratio of the company corresponding to the post-acquisition period is higher by more than 50% of that of the pre-acquisition period. This is actually the indication of improvement in debtors' management of the company, which is claimed to be a significant component of working capital management.

Moreover, regarding the management of working capital, we may analyse Table 6.

It is observed from Table 6 that the average value of net current asset of the post-acquisition period (₹93.90 crores) is almost 55% lower than that of the pre-acquisition period (₹209.44 crores). This implies that the company is reducing its holdings of net current assets gradually over the period. On the other side, it is also clear that the company is increasing the value of its investments over the period under study. The average investment of the company in the post-acquisition period (₹797.05 crores) is four times higher than that in the pre-acquisition period (₹193.71 crores). That means the company is following the strategy of reducing its holding on net current assets and increasing its investment gradually. Moreover, due to this strategy, the company will not suffer from liquidity problem. This is so because the company will be in a position to collect liquid funds when required with the help of the

Table 4 Percentages of RONW, Interest Coverage Ratio, Inventory Turnover and Debtors' Turnover

	RONW (%)			Interest Coverage Ratio (%)		Inventory Turnover		Debtors' Turnover	
Year	*Tata Tea*	*Industry Avg*	*Revised RONW (%)*	*Tata Tea*	*Industry Avg*	*Tata Tea*	*Industry. Avg*	*Tata Tea*	*Industry. Avg*
1995–96	15.47	10.54	10.47	3.55	2.8	7.42	6.96	6.07	8.54
1996–97	18.38	23.88	18.38	3.26	4.95	6.71	8.47	6.52	10.82
1997–98	28.78	20.76	28.78	5.19	4.90	7.39	7.78	8.54	12.48
1998–99	31.12	12.76	31.12	6.63	3.63	6.49	6.66	10.50	11.91
1999–00	19.48	7.56	33.50	6.07	3.15	5.21	6.26	11.02	11.05
2000–01	**11.75**	**3.15**	**19.49**	**4.48**	**1.84**	**4.95**	**7.67**	**11.46**	**12.58**
2001–02	7.07	4.22	11.17	3.37	2.29	6.03	7.57	12.42	12.17
2002–03	7.42	7.00	11.65	4.56	3.45	6.67	7.46	13.06	12.85
2003–04	9.58	11.76	15.07	7.60	6.19	6.98	7.21	17.48	15.75
2004–05	13.02	10.49	19.68	12.58	5.54	6.49	6.57	27.14	14.73
2005–06	15.23	9.49	21.91	13.46	3.74	6.35	7.75	24.96	17.07

modern e-banking system. That means the concerned company is definitely taking the advantage of modernization as well as automation of modern e-infrastructure for operating its business successfully.

Table 5 Average Values

	TTL		***Industry Average***	
	Pre-acquisition	***Post-acquisition***	***Pre-acquisition***	***Post-acquisition***
RONW	22.65	10.50	15.10	8.31
Revised RONW	24.45	15.90		
Interest coverage ratio	4.94	8.31	3.90	4.24
Inventory T.O.	6.64	6.50	7.23	7.31
Debtors T.O.	8.53	19.00	10.96	14.51

Table 6 Values of Net Current Assets and Investments

Year	***Net Current Assets (₹ in crores)***	***Investments (₹ in crores)***
1995–96	162.11	181.58
1996–97	213.64	184.30
1997–98	235.11	177.84
1998–99	226.89	231.12
1999–2000	608.55	199.56
2000–01	**180.88**	**621.91**
2001–02	134.48	738.40
2002–03	119.81	748.47
2003–04	61.28	835.45
2004–05	60.04	865.86
2005–06	34.24	1,106.83

From the entire analysis, it is observed that LBO is an important as well as interesting technique used for financing in the arena of cross-border acquisition around the globe. With the help of this pattern of financing, TTL financed its SPV [i.e., Tata Tea (GB)] in relation to the acquisition of Tetley in a balanced way without having any impact of long-term debt on its capital structure. Moreover, such deal did not adversely affect the earnings of the company substantially. However, as far as the financial performance of the acquiring company is concerned, it may be argued that the performance of the company in the post-acquisition period is quite poor compared to that in the pre-acquisition period. However, the share price movement of the company reflects the something different picture. However, since the Indian stock market is not efficient enough, it would not be the sign of wisdom to conclude anything about the performance of the company on the basis of its share price movement. Nevertheless, from the in-depth analysis of the financial performance of the company, it may be argued that the company has now started performing well and began to report positive corporate surplus from the financial year 2004–05. However, if we want to evaluate the ultimate effectiveness of such acquisition, we have to wait for the near future. After the final repayment of the entire debt of Tata Tea (GB), if TTL gets merge along with its SPV, that is, Tata Tea (GB), then it would be possible to evaluate the ultimate success of such strategy of corporate restructuring as well as the performance of the merged entity.

Source: Das et al. (2009).

Questions for Discussion

1. Briefly discuss the historical background and operational activities of TTL.
2. Comment on the financing pattern of the acquisition of Tetley by the LBO route.
3. Elaborate on the financial performance of TTL after its acquisition of Tetley.

References

Andersen, T.K. 2008. 'Buyout Transaction'. Merc. Private Equity and Hedge Fund. Copenhagen University. 25 May.

Bansal, Vipul K., J.F. Marshall, and R.P. Yuyuenyongwatana. 1995. 'Macroeconomic Derivatives: More Viable than First Thought!'. *Global Finance Journal*, 6(2): 101–10. Available at http://www.sciencedirect.com/science/article/pii/1044028395900144/part/first-page-pdf (last accessed on 3 August 2016).

Boesler, Matthew. 2012. 'Leveraged Buyouts Are about to Make a Big Comeback on Wall Street, and We Could See a $20B Deal'. *Business Insider*, 6 November. Available at http://www.businessinsider.com/bofa-leveraged-buyout-risk-returns-2012-11. (last accessed on 28 August 2016).

Center for Private Equity and Entrepreneurship. 2003. 'Note on Leveraged Buyouts'. New Hampshire, USA: Tuck School of Business at Dartmouth College. Available at wenku.baidu.com/view/c8be0f0c844769eae009ed6b.html (last accessed on 14 May 2015).

Das, Bhagaban, Debdas Raskhit, and Sathya Swaroop Debasish. 2009. *Corporate Restructuring: Mergers, Acquisitions and Other Forms*. Mumbai: Himalaya Publishers House.

Mehran, Hamid, and Stavros Peristiani. 2013. 'U.S. Leveraged Buyouts: The Importance of Financial Visibility'. *Liberty Street Economics*, 28 August.

Miller, Merton H. 1988. 'The Modigliani-Miller Propositions after Thirty Years'. *Journal of Economic Perspectives*, 2(4): 99–120.

Olsen, Jonathan. 2002. 'Note on Leveraged Buyouts'. New Hampshire, USA: Tuck School of Business at Dartmouth College. Available at http://pages.stern.nyu.edu/~igiddy/LBO_Note.pdf (last accessed on 17 April 2015).

Weston, J.F., K.S. Chung, and S.E. Hoag, 1990. *Mergers, Restructuring, and Corporate Control*. New Jersey: Prentice Hall.

Further Readings

Halpern, P., R. Kieschnick, and W. Rotenberg. 1999. 'An Examination of Agency Costs in Firms Which Subsequently Engage in an LBO'. University of Toronto Working Paper.

Kaplan, S. 1989. 'The Effects of Management Buyouts on Operating Performance and Value.' *Journal of Financial Economics*, 24: 217–54.

Kaplan, S. 1992. 'The Staying Power of Leveraged Buyouts'. University of Chicago Working Paper, 1992.

EVCA. 2004. 'Benchmarking European Tax and Legal Environments'. EVCA Benchmark Paper.

www.evca.com, website of the European Private Equity and Venture Capital

www.nottingham.ac.uk/business/cmbor, The Centre for Management Buyout Research's website.

www.icmrindia.org/casestudies & www.asiacase.com (last accessed on 2 September 2016).

Chapter 15

Employee Stock Ownership Plans

Chapter Objectives

On completion of this chapter, you will be able to understand:

- The concept of ESOP
- The need for employee share ownership
  - Macro principles
  - Micro principles
- Different types of employee share ownership plans
  - Non-leveraged ESOP
  - Leveraged-issuance ESOP
  - Leveraged-buyout ESOP
- The legal framework of ESOP in India
  - The Companies Act, 1956
  - The Income-tax Act, 1961
- The accounting aspect of ESOP
- Impact of tax on employees and companies due to ESOP
- A comparison between MBO and ESOP
- Advantages and disadvantages of ESOP
- The achievement of ESOP
  - In industrialized countries
  - In developing countries

The First ESOP

The first ESOP—implemented by Peninsula Newspapers Inc. in the United States in 1956—arose when ESOP inventor Louis O. Kelso restructured the firm's profit-sharing plans to produce a financing mechanism to purchase 72% of the shares of a newspaper chain. The shares were acquired from three major shareholders and paid for from future company profits. The selling shareholders also acted as lenders by accepting interest-bearing notes from the company-sponsored profit-sharing plans; the company guaranteed the note. Each year during the term of the note, the company made a tax-deductible contribution to its profit-sharing plans. Those funds, in turn, were used to repay the notes. The key characteristics that distinguished the ESOP from a conventional profit-sharing plan were that:

1. It enabled employees to use leveraged financing to acquire a block of shares at the current price and have those shares paid for with the company's future pre-tax earnings.
2. The ESOP's share acquisition debt was based on a corporate guarantee, so that individual employees bore on personal liability for that debt.

15.1 Introduction

Until a few years back, the general idea amongst employees was to get a good job, preferably in an MNC, stay around until retirement and lead a happy life. It was a situation like 'employment for life' (or imprisonment for life, depending on how one views it!). Employees were loyal to the company they served and companies; by and large, did not retrench employees.

Suddenly, in the last few years, a large number of things have changed. No longer are employees willing to stay in the same company for life unless they are satisfied with the returns they get from their jobs. This could range from better remuneration to growth prospects to a better working environment. Employers too do not want to be stuck with inefficient employees but would like to have the best people around. They have been forced to find innovative ways to attract and retain good people. Companies, particularly new economy companies have been forced to reform their work culture to become more employee friendly. One of the most common employee motivation and retention methods is through ESOPs or employee stock ownership plans.

Though relatively new in India, ESOPs, having come at a fairly 'right' time, have seen wide growth. While the major beneficiaries are employees of software and Internet companies, who get the shares of a company at a comparatively lower rate, other sectors are gradually becoming aware of the benefits of ESOPs. In fact, even companies like ICICI and Hindustan Lever have ESOPs.

15.2 The Concept of ESOP

An ESOP is a programme that allows employees to purchase stock in the companies they work for. It confers on employees the right to share in the wealth of the company and the right to exercise some degree of control over company affairs. ESOPs can improve employees' work efforts, provide an incentive for employees to stay at a company, and allow retiring owners to transfer shares of stock to employees. This is a new financing technique that is experiencing phenomenal growth in the United States and the world.

An ESOP allows companies to share ownership with employees without requiring the employees to invest their own money. With an ESOP, shares of company stock are contributed to the ESOP on behalf of the employees. Although other employment-based plans, such as stock bonus and profit-sharing plans, may contain company stock, an ESOP is required to invest primarily in company stock.

It offers extraordinary benefits to companies and their shareholders and employees. ESOPs provide a market for the shares of closely held businesses, motivate greater employee productivity and provide tax advantages in the financing of acquisitions, capital improvements, charitable giving and stock purchases from retiring owners.

15.2.1 ESOP: The Basic Features

Conventional stock option plans give an employee the right (but not obligation) to buy, that is, option to buy a fixed number of shares of the company at a stated price during a specified period, often at a discount from the market price at the date of grant. The options under a plan vests over a period to an employee subject to fulfilment of certain employment-related conditions, for example, continued employment for a specified period. In the case of a performance-based plan, the employees have to meet specified goals in addition before vesting can occur. The options may vest on one date ('cliff' vesting) or in stages over time ('gradual' vesting). After the vesting date, an employee may exercise his right to buy the share during a predefined period called exercise period. The options are forfeited for the non-fulfilment of certain conditions (e.g., staying with the company). The key dates in a simple cliff-vesting share option plan are shown in the following diagram (Sutton 2000).

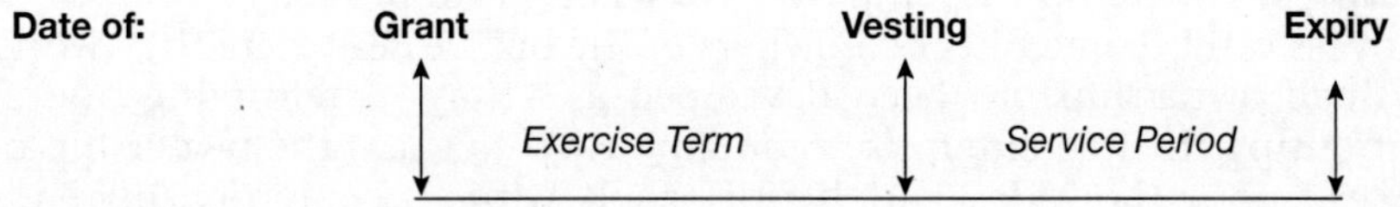

Grant Date is the date at which the enterprise and its employees agree to the terms of an employee share-based payment plan. At grant date, the enterprise confers on the employees the right to cash or shares of the enterprise, provided the specified vesting conditions, if any, is met.

Vesting Period is the period between the grant date and the date on which all the specified vesting conditions of an employee share-based payment plan are to be satisfied.

Exercise Period is the time period after vesting within which the employee should exercise his right to apply for shares against the option vested in him in pursuance of the employee stock option scheme. If the employee does not exercise his rights during this period, the option lapses. The amount, if any, paid by the employee at the time of grant of option is forfeited by the company.

Clearly, employees hope that the share price will be above the exercise price at some point during the exercise term.

15.3 A Brief History

The ESOP concept was developed in the 1950s by lawyer and investment banker Louis Kelso, who argued that the capitalist system would be stronger if all workers, not just a few stockholders, could share in owning capital-producing assets. He believed that the capitalist system would function more efficiently if all workers shared in owning capital-producing assets. In 1956, Kelso implemented for a San Francisco newspaper the first ownership transfer to employees by means of what later became known as 'The Kelso Plan'. In 1958, he collaborated with the philosopher Mortimer Adler to write *The Capitalist Manifesto* outlining the economic, social and political benefits that would ensue from broad-based employee ownership.

In the early 1970s, Kelso and Russell Long (cited in Freeman 2007) claimed that employee ownership builds commitment, which leads to productivity and profits, and argued that legislation facilitating broader-based ownership would not only increase corporate performance, but also ease workplace tensions, reduce disparities of wealth and help build a better society. ESOP never lost its importance as a mechanism to give employees the ownership of the company, rather, it led to loyalty and increased productivity.

Moreover, in the mid- to late 1980s, as hostile takeovers became common, due in part to the ease of obtaining financing, companies began to understand that ESOPs had a collateral benefit: a large number of shares in presumably friendly hands. Even if the plan passed the voting or tender decisions through to participants, employee shareholders could largely be expected to vote against a hostile takeover that might mean a loss of jobs for a large number of employees. ESOPs are found in publicly traded and closely held companies of every size; however, most such companies have over 15 or so employees due to the costs of setting up and administering an ESOP.

15.4 Employee Share Ownership: Why Needed?

Macro Principles: The purpose of employee ownership is to provide a means by which the mass of employees can become direct co-owners of the businesses where they work.

Employee share ownership has been developed as a way of reforming one of the key problems confronting the free enterprise economy: How to share the ownership of society's capital resources among the widest number of people without compromising either private ownership or economic freedom. Employee share ownership preserves both of these principles. It does so by providing employees with the means to purchase a personal stake in the enterprise that employs them. In sum, employee ownership aims to assist employees to become genuine 'capitalists'.

Without the kind of widespread joint ownership offered by employee share plans, there is no sure ground upon which to reconcile the old hostility between capital and labour. This is because the basis of that antagonism has been precisely the ownership—and (or) control—of capital on one side and the lack of capital on the other. For this reason, Employee Share Ownership Plans (ESOPs) offer a historical opportunity to address a source of major social and economic dislocation and conflict and to strengthen, in a fundamental way, the free enterprise system.

Micro Principles: There are certain implications that flow from employee ownership, and the structure of employee share plans, which provide additional incentives for strong, pro-ESOP policies.

i. **Productivity:** Employee share ownership is identified as a means of enhancing enterprise performance through promoting worker productivity. The theoretical basis for this rationale is generally located in agency theory. In the corporate governance context, agency theory has highlighted the 'corporate governance problem' arising out of the separation between 'ownership' and 'control'. Shareholders and managers may have divergent interests and shareholders may find it difficult and expensive to monitor management, particularly where they hold small stakes in many different firms. Agency theory has also been used as a theoretical framework in studies of financial participation. It is argued that agency costs arise as a result of the divergent interests between employees and other stakeholders in the company (principally managers and owners). Managers may seek to ameliorate these agency costs through directly monitoring employees and/or through adopting incentive-based forms of remuneration. Employee share ownership is one such incentive mechanism by which to reduce costs to the company through more closely aligning the interests of employees with those of other stakeholders in the company.
ii. **Savings:** The long-term shortage of savings in an ageing community, identified in the Intergenerational Report 2002–03, seems to require the development of a more sophisticated approach to national savings policy. In addition to superannuation, a serious national savings policy would seem to demand a range of savings instruments designed to meet a spectrum of different savings objectives. In this, ESOPs would have

a vital role to play. ESOP savings can clearly be distinguished, on the one hand, from obligatory, managed, indirect investments in a super fund and, on the other, from discretionary, personal share investment in businesses over whose fate the investor has no control.

ESOP savings offer both the directness of a personal share investment and a measure of influence over the performance of the investment.

iii. **Investment tool:** ESOPs also serve as a venture capital vehicle. They provide employees with a way of participating in a buy-ins and buyouts and of financing, in return for equity, the capital expansion of a business.

iv. **HRM:** There is a range of industrial relations or HRM rationales for employee share ownership. Employee share ownership is viewed by some as a potential means of enhancing industrial democracy or of bringing the employee into corporate governance. For some, employee share ownership is a means of increasing employee understanding of how the company for which they work operates and, more broadly, of 'absorbing the principles on which the economy of the country is run'. For others, employee share ownership is seen as a means of facilitating labour–management cooperation through breaking down the 'them' and 'us' mentality. Some identify ESOPs as a substitute for salary or wages when business is not performing well. More recently, employee share ownership, as a means of financial participation, is identified by HRM scholars as one practice within a 'bundle' of HR practices that together constitute a high-performance work system. Employee share ownership also intersects with the discourse on labour–management 'partnerships'.

v. **Defence against hostile takeover:** Finally, in relation to corporate governance, ESOPs are identified as a potential defence against hostile takeover bids or as a means of rescuing companies in financial difficulties. ESOPs may also be a mechanism through which employees can 'buy out' a company or a government can privatise a government enterprise.

15.5 Types of Employee Share Ownership Plans

Companies can present different kinds of share ownership plans, depending on what they are trying to get out of the offering. The various plans offer different tax advantages and disadvantages, both to the company issuing the options and to the employees receiving them. In general, most options fall into one of three categories:

15.5.1 Non-leveraged ESOP

This type of ESOP is one which does not involve borrowing any funds to acquire stock of the sponsoring employer. It is funded by contributions of cash or stock directly from the employer sponsor. Shares of stock contributed by the corporation are 'newly issued shares'. New shares are issued to the ESOP and a deduction is taken by the corporation for their appraised fair market value as of the date of contribution. Alternatively, cash can be contributed to the plan in annual discretionary amounts as cash flow permits, to purchase shares at a later date, or simultaneously, from either the corporation or another shareholder (see Figure 15.1).

Generally, a non-leveraged ESOP is established to promote growth of the company sponsor by creating tax deductions with newly issued shares, thus improving cash flow and reducing taxes. It is also one of the best plans for gradual accumulation of retirement benefits tied to the value of employer stock and for promoting participatory management structures. The purpose of the ESOP can be to purchase shares from a shareholder on a cash flow basis where the tax incentives attributable to leveraged ESOPs are either not important or do not require borrowing funds. Using a non-leveraged ESOP will also avoid the impact of debt on the corporation's value and balance sheet. Also, funding an ESOP on a cash flow basis suggests that the company's obligation to repurchase shares from departing participants may be easier to manage than with the leveraged variety. This corporate obligation is called 'repurchase liability'. The following table shows a brief comparative example of the ESOP's cash flow advantage over non-ESOP plans.

Figure 15.1 Non-leveraged ESOP

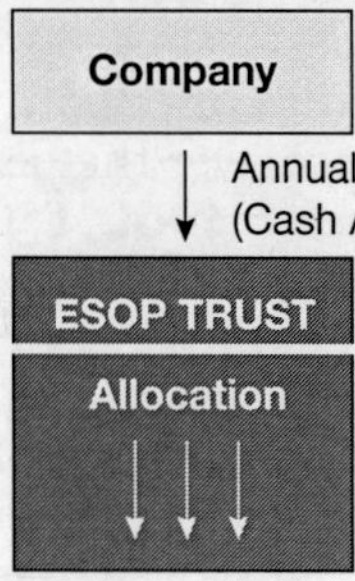

	No Employee Benefits Plan	*Employee Benefits Plan*	*ESOP*
Pre-tax income	₹150,000	₹150,000 (cash)	₹150,000 (stock)
Contributions/deductions	0	₹50,000	₹50,000
Taxable income	₹150,000	₹100,000	₹100,000
Income tax (say, 40%)	₹60,000	₹40,000	₹40,000
Net income	₹90,000	₹60,000	₹60,000
Cash flow	₹90,000	₹60,000	₹110,000

15.5.2 Leveraged-issuance ESOP

An 'issuance ESOP' uses financing to acquire newly issued shares from the employer sponsor. The shares are allocated to the participants' accounts as the loan is repaid. During this repayment, the shares are released from a special ESOP account, called a 'suspense account,' to the ESOP participants' accounts according to formulas developed by the IRS (see Figure 15.2).

Figure 15.2 Leveraged-issuance ESOP

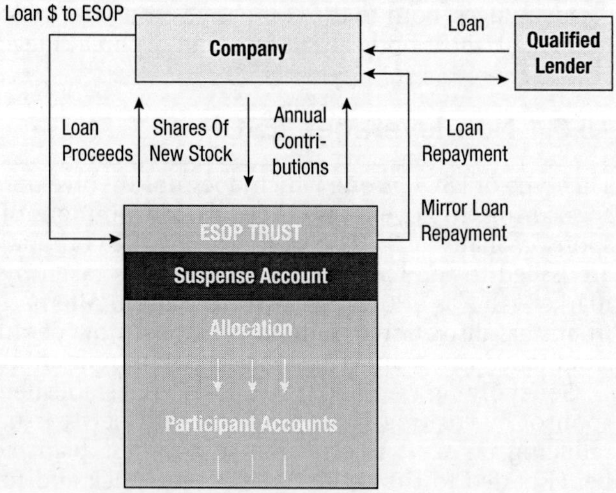

The corporate advantages of an issuance ESOP are that it creates tax-advantaged financing for purchasing capital goods, for expanding by merger or acquisition, or simply by increasing capital formation. For whatever purpose, the principal borrowed to buy the stock effectively becomes tax deductible by virtue of it being repaid via plan expense/ contributions. The company is therefore able to borrow money this way on a fully deductible basis.

Several side effects of issuance ESOPs must be considered. First, they have a dilutive effect on existing shareholders if the company value does not grow faster than the value of the percentage of the stock sold to the ESOP. Second, there is repurchase liability for the future retirement benefits in the plan. The company will someday have to repurchase shares distributed from the ESOP to participants. For whatever purpose, therefore, the ESOP is effectively permitting the company to 'borrow from its retirement plan' by permitting current deductions for contributions that are used as capital in the company, until benefits need to be paid. This improves the corporation's cash flow, pending a required retirement or other future plan distribution when shares are distributed and repurchased.

15.5.3 Leveraged-buyout ESOP

Figure 15.3 Leveraged-buyout ESOP

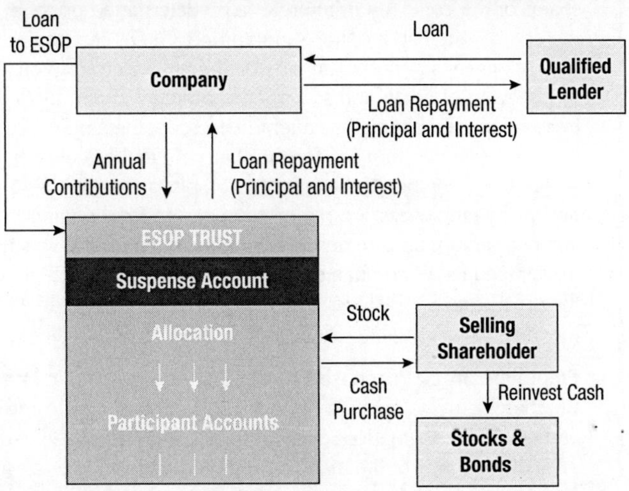

This form of leveraged ESOP is a lot like the issuance ESOP, except the financing is used to buy stock from a selling (and usually retiring) shareholder (see Figure 15.3).

These transactions have gained notoriety as a succession planning tool for closely held businesses. The tax incentives that accompany these types of transactions include tax-deferred capital gains and tax-favoured financing. They can be very compelling from an estate planning or succession planning viewpoint. A seller who properly structures his transaction may sell his stock to an ESOP and not pay any immediate capital gains tax on the sale. The seller may reinvest the sale proceeds within 12 months of the stock sale to the ESOP and defer the capital gains tax liability indefinitely (known as a '1042 Rollover Transaction'). This is much like the election available to reinvest the proceeds from the sale of your house. As a result, the seller will have all of the deferred taxes at work in his reinvestment portfolio. The company, in turn, will have paid the purchase price entirely in pre-tax dollars.

As in the issuance ESOP, the debt principal is repaid with pre-tax dollars. Another consequence is that the corporation's future repurchase liability will be equal to the fair market value of the stock purchased by the plan. In contrast to the issuance ESOP, no dilution is suffered by existing shareholders. Shareholders who do not sell their shares to the ESOP may find themselves competing with the corporation for assets with which to sell their stock in the future, if repurchase liability or growth in the stock value, or a combination of both, create a significant drain on corporate cash flow. It may also not be prudent to overburden a company with ESOP debt.

In order to fully understand whether some type of ESOP or ESOP transaction can be good for a company and its employees, it is critical to first identify the objectives of all those involved. Often, there are overlapping and conflicting objectives. For example, the company's expansion objectives, or other shareholders objectives, may compete with the objectives of the potential selling shareholders. Furthermore, the impact of an ESOP on the employees and the ability to motivate employees must be seriously considered. With regard to employee questionnaires, feasibility studies and further information and assistance from organizations, the ESOP association can go a long way towards helping you answer these questions.

Apart from stock option plans, other stock-based compensation plans exists. Such plans include employee stock purchase plans (ESPPs), restricted stock units (RSUs), stock appreciation rights (SAR)/phantom shares. Choice of such plans depends on various factors such as industry practice, tax implications, share market condition, growth expectation of the company and so on. Exhibit 15.1 depicts the nature of different stock option plans.

Exhibit 15.1 Different Stock-based Compensation Plans

Employee Stock Option Plan: ESOP is a stock option plan that gives employees the right to acquire shares of the company in future at a predetermined price, even if the fair market value of the stock has increased from that of option's grant price. Often, companies will require the employee to hold the allotted options for a period of time before being exercised. Typically, the options are non-transferable, except in the event of death and so on. The company either allots fresh shares or buys them in the market by treasury operation. Any time after the exercise, the employee can sell the stock. In case of cashless option, the employee does not pay for the share but realizes the net gain on the date of exercise.

Starting as employee benefit pension plans, now ESOPs are used in different ways. Under compensation plan, employees are partly compensated by issuance of shares, whereas the objective of a non-compensatory plan is to raise additional capital or to diversify share ownership to include employees. In a leveraged ESOP, companies borrow capital (through ESOP trust) from financial institution and often use the process as a vehicle for LBOs. For external ESOPs, an external trust or association is created to hold the 'ownership'. Internal ESOP runs with an internal workers' trust.

Employee Stock Purchase Plans: ESPPs are systematic investment plans where the employee acquires the shares after a specified period, upon contribution to the share price in monthly instalments. At the end of the offering period, contributions are accumulated and used to purchase shares at a discount, say, 10% of the lower of the market price on the opening or closing date of the offer period as per the plan. If the employee does not remain with the company till the date of allotment, he loses his right to acquire the shares and is eligible for refund of her contribution. The employee can sell the shares acquired under ESPP at any time after expiry of the lock-in-period.

Restricted Stock Units

Under this scheme, the employer company makes an unsecured promise to the employees to transfer shares free of cost at the end of a designated period and after fulfilment of certain conditions like, achieving the targets, continuation of employment and so on. After allotment, the employee can sell the shares in the market.

Stock Appreciation Rights/Phantom Shares

In the SAR scheme, compensation is made in cash, based on the price increase of the share during a certain period. Actually, under SAR, appreciation in stock price between the date of grant and the date of exercise is delivered to the employee in cash.

There are some other less frequently used programmes like performance share plan, performance unit plan, deferred compensation system and so on.

Source: Dhar and De (February 2008).

15.6 The Legal Framework of ESOP India

15.6.1 The Companies Act, 2013

The Companies Act defines 'employees' stock option' as the option given to the directors, officers or employees of a company or of its holding company or subsidiary company or companies, if any, which gives such directors, officers or employees the benefit or right to purchase, or to subscribe for, the shares of the company at a future date at a predetermined price. A company is required to disclose by way of notes additional information regarding aggregate expenditure on the employee stock option scheme and ESPPs.

As per Section 2(37) of the Companies Act, 2013, 'employee' means:

a. a permanent employee of the company who has been working in India or outside India; or
b. a director of the company, whether a whole-time director or not, but excluding an independent director; or
c. an employee as defined in clauses (a) or (b) of:
    - a subsidiary, in India or outside India,
    - or of a holding company of the company or
    - of an associate company.

But does not include:

i. an employee who is a promoter or a person belonging to the promoter group; or
ii. a director who either himself or through his relative or through any body corporate, directly or indirectly, holds more than 10% of the outstanding equity shares of the company.

As per Section 53 of the Companies Act, 2013, a company is not allowed to issue share at a discount. If it issues such shares, these will be void and the company will be punished. However, Section 54 offers situations when a company may issue sweat equity shares of a class of shares already issued, if the following conditions are fulfilled, namely:

a. the issue is authorized by a special resolution passed by the company;
b. the resolution specifies the number of shares, the current market price, consideration, if any, and the class or classes of directors or employees to whom such equity shares are to be issued;
c. not less than one year has, at the date of such issue, elapsed since the date on which the company had commenced business; and
d. where the equity shares of the company are listed on a recognized stock exchange, the sweat equity shares are issued in accordance with the regulations made by the SEBI in this behalf and if they are not so listed, the sweat equity shares are issued in accordance with such rules as may be prescribed.

15.6.2 SEBI Guidelines, 1999 (Updated up to September 2009)

SEBI defines 'employee stock option' as the option given to the whole-time directors, officers or employees of a company that gives such directors, officers or employees the benefit or right to purchase or subscribe at a future date, the securities offered by the company at a predetermined price.

SEBI also defines 'employee stock option scheme (ESOS)' as a scheme under which a company grants employee stock option and 'employee stock purchase scheme (ESPS)' as a scheme under which the company offers shares to employees as part of a public issue or otherwise.

Any company whose securities are listed on any stock exchange may offer equity to its employees under the Employee Stock Option Scheme subject to the following conditions:

1. An employee shall be eligible to participate in ESOS of the company.
2. An employee who is a promoter or belongs to the promoter group shall not be eligible to participate in the ESOS.
3. A director who either by himself or through his relative or through any body corporate, directly or indirectly, holds more than 10% of the outstanding equity shares of the company shall not be eligible to participate in the ESOS.
4. No ESOS can be offered to employees of a company unless the shareholders of the company approve ESOS by passing a special resolution in the general meeting.
5. The issue of shares/convertible instruments under an ESOP shall not exceed 5% of the paid-up capital of the company in any one year.
6. Clause 4 of the guidelines on preferential issues providing for pricing shall also be applicable to the ESOPs.
7. Shareholders' permission must be taken after providing them with complete details.
8. A company introducing ESOPs shall submit a certificate to the concerned stock exchange at the time of the listing of the securities issued through the scheme certifying as to whether the securities has been issued as per the scheme to the permanent employees.
9. The companies would be free to devise the ESOPs for the issue of shares/warrants or debt instruments/bonds with warrants including the terms of payment.
10. Companies are free to determine the exercise price of the stock options they offer.
11. If the exercise price is at a discount to the market price, the discount will be treated as a cost.
12. A minimum lock-in period of one year from the date of grant will be applicable.

15.6.3 The Income-tax Act, 1961

The relevant sections of the Income-tax Act relating to ESOP are 17(2), 47(iii), 48 and 49(2AA).

1. Salary and perquisite: Section 17(1) of the Income-tax Act, 1961, contains an inclusive definition of 'Salary', which includes, inter alia, 'any fees, commissions, perquisites or profits in lieu of or in addition to any salary or wages'.

The ESOP availed by an employee would not amount to salary, fee, commission or profit in lieu of salary. At the maximum, it can be argued to be a 'perquisite'.

Section 17(2) contains an inclusive definition of the term 'perquisite', and sub-clause (iii) thereof states that the term includes the value of any benefit or amenity granted or provided free of cost or at a concessional rate by an employer (including a company) to an employee to whom the provisions of paragraphs (a) and (b) of this sub-clause do not apply and whose income under the head 'Salaries' (whether due from, or paid or allowed by, one or more employers), exclusive of the value of all benefits or amenities not provided for by way of monetary payment, exceeds ₹50,000.

Sub-clause (vi) of the same section states that perquisites include the value of any specified security or sweat equity shares allotted or transferred, directly or indirectly, by the employer, or former employer, free of cost or at concessional rate to the assessee. For the purposes of this sub-clause,

> 'specified security' means the securities as defined in clause (h) of Section 2 of the Securities Contracts (Regulation) Act, 1956 (42 of 1956) and, where employees' stock option has been granted under any plan or scheme therefore, includes the securities offered under such plan or scheme;
>
> 'sweat equity shares' means equity shares issued by a company to its employees or directors at a discount or for consideration other than cash for providing know-how or making available rights in the nature of intellectual property rights or value additions, by whatever name called;
>
> the value of any specified security or sweat equity shares shall be the fair market value of the specified security or sweat equity shares, as the case may be, on the date on which the option is exercised by the assessee as reduced by the amount actually paid by, or recovered from, the assessee in respect of such security or shares;
>
> 'fair market value' means the value determined in accordance with the method as may be prescribed;
>
> 'option' means a right but not an obligation granted to an employee to apply for the specified security or sweat equity shares at a predetermined price.

The provision below the above clause reads as under:

> Provided that nothing in this sub-clause shall apply to the value of any benefit provided by a company free of cost or at a concessional rate to its employees by way of allotment of shares, debentures or warrants directly or indirectly under any Employees Stock Option Plan or Scheme of the company offered to such employees in accordance with the guidelines issued in this behalf by the Central Government.

The Central Government issued the 'guidelines' referred to in the proviso above by Notification No. 323/2001 (R.No. 142/48/2001-TPL) dated 11 October 2001, effective from 1 April 2000, which enumerates the various aspects that ought to be included in any employees stock option plan or scheme. The guidelines, inter alia, provide for the following:

Para 2 of the 'guidelines' specifies the conditions that are to be incorporated in the option plan or scheme, and the proviso that follows the said Para, reads as follows:

> Provided that the conditions contained in the written document shall not be changed after the date the scheme or plan comes into effect.

Para 2 of the guidelines states that the plan or scheme shall be as per the SEBI guidelines.

Para 4 of the guidelines states that it applies to both listed and unlisted companies which are defined in Section 2(17) of the Act.

Para 5 of the guidelines states that a person holding more than 10% of the shares in a company would not be eligible to participate in employee stock option plan or scheme of the company.

Further, para 6 of the guidelines read as follows:

> Every company issuing shares directly or through its parent under an Employees Stock Option Plan or Scheme to its employees shall furnish a copy of the document describing the particulars as specified in clause (2) above to the Chief Commissioner of Income Tax having jurisdiction over it

within a period of 6 months from the date of issue of these guidelines or within 6 months of the effective date of the scheme or plan, whichever is later. If the Plan or Scheme is incorporated in any language other than English, an English translation of the same should also be enclosed.

The foregoing is summarized as follows:
The perquisite value that arises out of issuance of stocks under an employee's stock option plan or scheme shall not be taxed, if:

a. the plan or scheme conforms to the 'guidelines'.
b. a copy of the plan or scheme is furnished to the commissioner of income tax having jurisdiction over the assessee.
c. the conditions contained in the plan or scheme are not 'changed'.

Note that the ESOP plan or scheme needs no 'approval' of the authority. Mere 'furnishing' of the plan or scheme is sufficient compliance with the guidelines.

2. Section 47 lists transactions not regarded as transfer, but the proviso to clause (iii) of the section specifies that the transfer of a capital asset in the form of ESOP, when transferred under a gift or will, shall attract capital gain. Such transfers are excluded from the exemption granted by the substantive portion of the clause. Additionally, the fourth proviso to Section 48, read with the proviso to Section 47(iii), specifies that if ESOPs are gifted, the market value on the date of the gift would be considered as the sale price on which the transfer of the ESOP would be taxed.

3. Section 49(2AA) specifies that where the capital gain arises from the transfer of the shares, the value of which has been taken into account while computing the value of perquisite under clause (2) of Section 17, the cost of acquisition of such shares shall be the value under that clause.

15.7 The Accounting Aspect of ESOP: The Indian GAAP

The regulatory framework of accounting of ESOPs in India is at its infancy. There is no standard on the issue by the Institute of Chartered Accountants of India (ICAI). At present, ESOP accounting in India is governed by the SEBI guidelines issued in 1999 and the Guidance Note issued by the ICAI in 2003. As per the professional ethics requirement of the ICAI, requirements of a guidance note are not mandatory for compliance, and such a guidance note only provides guidance on any accounting matter to the preparers and auditors of financial statement. As such, Indian companies rarely follow the requirements of the guidance note.

Thus, the source of regulation is the SEBI guidelines that were issued in 1999 (SEBI 1999). The Employee Stock Option Scheme and Employee Stock Purchase Guidelines, 1999 (SEBI guidelines hereinafter) originally issued in 1999 by the SEBI require mandatory disclosure of impact on profits for not following a fair value approach. However, to compute fair value, the companies are permitted to adopt the option value calculated by applying the difference between market price on grant date or by applying Black–Scholes or similar valuation methods. In effect, the position is akin to that of the APB Opinion 25 of the United States. Thus, compensation cost implicit in an option may be based on the intrinsic value method of APB 25, although the term 'fair value method' is used. SEBI guidelines provide for detailed disclosure rules for directors' report and the financial statement. The important requirements are amortization of compensation cost over the vesting period on straight-line basis and detailed disclosure of option statistics regarding grant, vesting and exercise. An illustration is also provided in the guidelines showing the required journal entries to be made for a fixed plan.

Moreover, the requirements of the guidelines being applicable in all stock option schemes established on or after June 1999, the prior schemes are out of the purview of the guidelines. SEBI guidelines were amended in 2002 and 2003 and the amended guidelines now provide for a detailed disclosure, including disclosure of stock option compensation expenses computed by applying the fair value method and impact of non-recognition of fair value compensation cost on basic and diluted EPS.

In view of this, the accounting for ESOP is discussed below in different scenarios:

a. When issued at par (at face value), that is, the face value of the share is fully received in cash from the employee. In this case, the accounting is simple.

	Debit	Credit
Bank/cash A/c	Debit	
Share capital A/c		Credit

b. When issued at premium, that is, the share is issued at a price above the face value, and the premium and face value of share is paid in cash by the employee. Again, in this case the accounting is simple.

	Debit	Credit
Bank/cash A/c	Debit	
Share premium A/c		Credit
Share capital A/c		Credit

c. When Issued at a discount, that is, under ESOP, the share is issued to the employee below the face value.

As per the Companies Act, the shares cannot be issued at a discount and thus the controversy would start about the accounting of amount between face value and the amount received from the employee. To explain it in a simple language, when a share of face value of ₹100 is issued to an employee at ₹10, how the difference of ₹90 would be accounted in the books of account of the company in the absence of any accounting standard or guidance note published by ICAI. As explained above, basically ESOP given to an employee is an incentive to the employee, that is, the employee would stand to benefit by getting a share at a discounted price. In the case of a quoted company, when a share is quoted above par, say, if a share of ₹100 is quoting at ₹500 and ESOP is granted at ₹200 (subject to SEBI regulations), the employee gets a share worth ₹500 at ₹200 and such ESOP works as an incentive to him. By such ESOP, even the company stands benefited, that is, the employee remains with the company for longer period and thus becomes a valuable asset in the organization. However, the controversy starts when a quoted share, say, of a face value of ₹100 and quoting at, say, ₹150 is issued as ESOP to an employee at ₹50 by way of incentive, how the 50 rupees, that is, difference between face value and issue price of ESOP, is to be accounted. An argument can be advanced that since the company has received an amount lesser than that face value of equity share for giving benefit to its employees, it should be treated as a revenue expenditure under any name called, say, 'employee benefit account' and, accordingly, it is suggested that the accounting be made as follows:

	Debit	Credit
Bank/cash A/c	Debit	
Employee benefit A/c	Debit	
Share capital A/c		Credit

However, Mr Hargovind, retired member of the Income-tax Appellate Tribunal, in one of his article on the subject opined that as per the SEBI guidelines, the amount discounted is to be accounted as employee compensation. It has to be amortized over a period of time. However, the learned author further opined that the issue of amortization can be finally resolved by a specific provision in the Act; thus, the issue is debatable and not free from doubt.[1] A comparative discussion on accounting for ESOP under SEBI guidelines and U.S. GAAP is discussed in Exhibit 15.2.

Exhibit 15.2 Accounting for ESOP

SEBI guidelines

In case of employee stock option plans, the difference between the price at which your employees can exercise their options and the market price—on the date on which the option is granted—must be taken as an expenditure on your profit and loss account, although there is no actual cash outflow. However, this can be spread out over the entire period during which the scheme is in play, instead of taking the blow in one year.

A guideline issued by the SEBI for stock options requires companies to show expenses in either of the following ways:

- Show in the form of option discount [difference between market price of the share at the date of grant of the option under ESOP over the exercise price of the option (including upfront payment, if any)]; or
- The fair value of the option measured by the Black and Scholes model.

But, this model understates the value of the option as it gives the liberty of choosing the variables to the corporate. If variables like standard deviation of the scrip and interest rate are changed, the value of option will also change.

Variations in option value using the Black and Scholes model

There are five variables that could change the option value. These are:

a. Fall in the share price at the time of announcement of ESOP.
b. Increase of the exercise price.
c. Use of lower interest rate.
d. Use of lower standard deviation.
e. Use of shorter vesting period.

The accounting value as measured above should be accounted as employee compensation (aggregate of accounting value of the options so granted under ESOS during the accounting period) and has to be amortized on a straight-line basis over the vesting period.

[1] ESOP and SWEAT Equity—Treatment under Companies Act, Income-tax Act and Accounting of the Same. Available at http://ganesh007.pbworks.com/w/file/fetch/.../10_esop_and_sweat_equity.doc (accessed on 4 March 2015).

Market experts raise questions about this form of accounting, as it does not use the time value of money in measuring the cost of the stock option. This borrowed framework has the same lapses as the U.S. GAAP.

U.S. GAAP

The FASB (Financial Accounting Standard Board) has given two choices for accounting of ESOP:

a. To take the cost of stock options to the financial statements directly.
b. To make pro forma disclosures of cost by way of notes to accounts.

Almost all companies chose the second option, as it did not reduce the profit figures.

FASB's accounting regulations for stock-based compensation also have some loopholes.

Instance: INFOSYS uses both U.S. GAAP and Indian Accounting Standards (IAS) for accounting the ESOP.

As per U.S. GAAP, Infosys uses the intrinsic value-based method for stock issued to employees, to account for employee stock-based compensation plan. The company has therefore adopted the pro forma disclosure provisions of U.S. GAAP.

As per Indian accounting procedures, INFOSYS has valued its ESOP in the form of option discount and accounted the expenses.

15.8 ESOP: Tax Issues for Employees and Companies

Share premium account: As per SEBI guidelines, the difference between the market value of the share on the date of grant and the face value of the option shares should be credited to the share premium account. As per Section 78 of the Act, the value of the premium, whether in cash or otherwise, can be utilized, inter alia, for issuing bonus shares.

However, listed companies are also covered by the SEBI guidelines on issue of bonus shares. As per the guidelines, bonus shares can be issued only out of free reserves built out of genuine profits or share premium collected in cash. Accordingly, any premium that is received otherwise in cash cannot be utilized for issue of bonus shares by a listed company.

15.8.1 Trust Route

Companies can structure ESOS via a trust route, that is, a company would set up a trust which would purchase shares of the company and the trust would give ESOS to the employees of the company. In view of the SEBI guidelines being silent on the matter, an issue that arises is the position of issues of shares to a trust for employees vis-à-vis the SEBI guidelines. A view can be taken that the trust route is covered by the SEBI guidelines since:

i. The issue of shares to such a trust is in effect issue of shares to employees and therefore the SEBI guidelines should apply. Should the intention be of not permitting the trust route, the SEBI guidelines would have specified the same. (However, equally the reference in the SEBI guidelines is only to employees and not to a trust.)
ii. The second provision to Section 77(2) provides that a firm can give loan to a trust for purchase of shares of the company if shares are held by or for the benefit of the

employees. If trust route were to be discouraged, the said proviso would have been deleted, which is not done. Incidentally, in the absence of clarity on the subject, a contrary view may be taken that the SEBI guidelines do not apply in case a listed company desires to issue shares under ESOP to a trust and the company would be free to determine the terms and conditions of ESOP.

15.8.2 ESOP for Private Unlisted Companies

It is possible that even an unlisted private company offers ESOP to its employees. Such private company may or may not have an intention to make an IPO and list its securities on the stock exchanges. In such a scenario, the company could face several issues in introducing the ESOP scheme such as:

- Valuation
- Exit mechanism

It would appear that such companies would have to provide for a suitable mechanism to induce the employees to subscribe to the ESOP by providing reasonable exit options along with a fair chance to share the wealth which he would create and is reflected in the form of enhanced earnings and net worth of the company. In such cases, valuations that are based on future earning capacity could greatly help. In most cases, an impending IPO is the ideal exit mechanism.

Another issue may arise in case of the unlisted company, which has an existing ESOP scheme, merges with a listed company and the shares of the listed companies are issued to the employees of the unlisted company in lieu of their existing holding under ESOP. Under such circumstances, an issue may arise as to whether SEBI guidelines are applicable to such ESOP post-merger scenario. Since no shares are being issued under ESOP by the listed firm, SEBI guidelines should not apply.

15.8.3 Tax Implications in the Hands of the Employees

In case where options are exercised and the employee acquires shares, the differential of the fair market value of the shares on the date of exercise and the option price would be taxable as perquisites in the hands of the employee. Since the perquisite would form part of the salary, the employer would be required to deduct appropriate taxes on such perquisite according to the provisions of Section 192 of the Act.

The employer would have to adopt an appropriate mechanism to deduct tax as no amount is being paid by the employer to the employee at the time of options being exercised. An ESOP can also be with a cashless option, wherein the employees do not have to pay for the options granted or exercised by them. Upon exercise of the option, the shares are sold immediately and the difference between the sale price and the exercise price is paid to the employee. As per the recent amendments in the Act, the difference between the market value of the shares on the date of exercise of the option and the exercise price would be taxable as perquisites in the hands of the employee.

As the shares are immediately sold upon the exercise of the option, there would be almost no capital gains accruing of the result of the sale and, therefore, it is likely that the entire amount is received by the employee would be taxed as perquisite in his hands.

Incidentally, the Authority for Advance Ruling in case of PNo 15 of 1998 (102 Taxman 74) has held that the money received on exercise of stock option by the employees of Indian subsidiary of a foreign company is to be regarded as 'income from salaries'. In this regard, an issue arises as to whether the said ratio would still apply even after the amendment to the Act (insertion of clause (iiia) to Section 17(2)).

15.8.4 Tax Implications in the Hands of the Company

An issue is whether the amount debited to employee compensation expense in the profit and loss account (₹4 million) can be claimed as revenue expenditure under Section 37(1) of the Act. Currently, there is no specific provision under the Act that provides for such a deduction, which is debited to the profit and loss account on a notional basis. Summing up, in spite of a genuine attempt by SEBI/revenue authorities to prescribe guidelines, certain issues have remained unanswered.

15.9 MBO Versus ESOP: Which One Is Better?

ESOPs gained popularity beginning in the 1970s and were portrayed as a tax-advantaged way to sell a significant stake in a company to its existing employees, thus motivating them to truly behave like 'owners'. In theory, the idea makes a lot of sense—in practice, it could be argued that selling the company to a sponsored management team (management buyout or MBO) is more effective. Let us take a look.

15.9.1 ESOP Benefits

a. Ability for the owners to defer taxes on proceeds in specific circumstances.
b. Allows an owner to gain liquidity when the company has a limited buyer market.
c. Opportunity for owners to reward employees on a tax-deferred basis as the contribution is made entirely by the company and is not taxed to employees personally as it is allocated.

15.9.2 MBO Benefits Versus ESOP

a. MBO will, in most circumstances, yield a higher valuation for the owners.
b. The senior management team will achieve a greater ownership stake.
c. No continuing obligation by the current owners—in ESOPs, the owners may be obligated to make a personal guarantee or pledge collateral to satisfy bank loan requirements.
d. Private equity sponsors make better operational partners than commercial banks.
e. The tax benefits of an ESOP, in the current period of 15% long-term capital gains tax rate, may be less than the higher after-tax valuation that could potentially be obtained in an MBO.
f. Less annual paperwork than an ESOP.
g. Due to the tax-deferred nature of ESOPs, they are subject to intense regulatory scrutiny, annual valuations and potential tax audits.

15.9.3 ESOP Requirements

Leveraged ESOPs (the customary form) require a significant asset base and a current balance sheet with limited operational debt or consistent cash flow. Debt financing for the ESOP is typically obtained from commercial banks to fund the trust that is created to purchase the shares of the company, which are subsequently disbursed to employees. ESOPs were created by the government to indent employee ownership in companies, and government regulation requires that 30% of the ownership must be sold to the ESOP for the owner to defer the capital gains on the proceeds (gains are deferred if reinvested in the stocks or bonds of domestic public companies until such investments are liquidated).

Annual, independent valuations are required for ESOPs by the department of labour, and an excise tax is levied if the company (post-ESOP) is resold within three years.

Even with the numerous requirements, an ESOP makes sense for a company in the following situation:

a. A company that has a limited buyer market due to either industry or company specific issues.
b. A company with an inexperienced or shallow management team.
c. A company that wants to offer stock ownership to all employees.

15.9.4 MBO Benefits

Today, there are more than 1,000 private equity and venture funds with an estimated $300 billion in collective funds to invest. These funds specialize in buying companies, recapitalizing companies and sponsoring management teams that wish to buy their company from a majority owner (MBOs). In most circumstances, higher valuations can be obtained through MBOs than would be experienced through ESOPs, through competitive markets established by investment bankers for their clients and through the equity sponsor's ability to borrow more aggressively (in conjunction with their own equity contribution) than a standalone ESOP candidate. More importantly, the percentage of ownership that can be achieved by an experienced management team in an MBO (through the use of equity contributions and performance options) is greater than the ownership stake typically achieved by a management team in an ESOP.

For these and other reasons, it is recommended that companies considering ESOPs investigate the other M&A-related options available to them, including a sponsored MBO, as discussed here.

15.10 Advantages of ESOPs

ESOPs can provide employees with substantial financial benefits through stock ownership while providing companies with attractive tax advantages and a powerful corporate finance tool. By making employees partial owners of the business, a company may also realize productivity improvements, since workers benefit directly from corporate profitability and are thus working in their own interest.

Although the advantages of ESOPs are attracting growing numbers of companies, there is also some risk to consider. Because the ESOP is invested primarily in employer securities, its success depends on the long-term performance of the company and its stock. There is, therefore, a greater degree of risk involved because of the concentration of employee capital.

An ESOP is not appropriate in every circumstance, but the many benefits of employee ownership and ESOP financing merit close consideration of this concept:

i. *Capital appreciation:* Companies sell some or all of their equity to employees and by doing so convert corporate and personal taxes into tax-free capital appreciation. This allows the owner to sell 100% of his or her company, get money out tax-free and still maintain control of the company.
ii. *Incentive-based retirement:* ESOP provides a cost-effective plan to motivate employees. After all, who works harder, owners or employees?
iii. *Tax advantages:* Enables tax-advantaged purchasing of stock of a retiring company owner. With this purpose, a company owner may sell their shares to the ESOP and incur no taxable gain on the sale. A company owner can sell all or some of the company to the employees cost free. Owners who sell 30% or more of their company to an ESOP are allowed to 'roll-over' the proceeds into other securities and defer taxation on the gain.
iv. *Company reduces its tax liability*. A company can reduce its corporate income taxes and increase its cash flow and net worth by simply issuing treasury stock or newly issued stock to its ESOP.
v. ESOPs can *recover taxes paid* in prior years.
vi. ESOPs *infuse working capital* and cash flow to the corporation unlike pension or profit sharing plans that reduce corporate cash.
vii. ESOPs give the corporate tax deductions with no cash expenditure. The corporation can use the tax savings to reduce prices and increase market share.
viii. ESOPs *reduce the cost of employee benefits* significantly.
ix. ESOPs allow the corporation to give *loyal employees* a piece of the action to reduce pressures for a raise in salary.

15.11 Disadvantages of ESOPs

As attractive as these tax benefits are, however, there are limits and drawbacks. ESOPs can be used in corporations, but do not qualify for the rollover treatment discussed above and have lower contribution limits.

i. *Dilution:* If the ESOP is used to finance the company's growth, the cash flow benefits must be weighed against the rate of dilution.
ii. *Fiduciary liability:* The plan committee members who administer the plan are deemed to be fiduciaries and can be held liable if they knowingly participate in improper transactions.
iii. *Liquidity:* If the value of the stock appreciates substantially, the ESOP and/or the company may not have sufficient funds to repurchase stock, upon employees' retirement.
iv. *Stock performance:* If the value of the company does not increase, the employees may feel that the ESOP is less attractive than a profit-sharing plan. In an extreme case, if the company fails, the employees will lose their benefits to the extent that the ESOP is not diversified in other investments.
v. *Complex:* There is a lot to learn when setting up an ESOP and this can be a deterrent for some. However, SES advisors can assist in getting over the learning curve (SES

Advisors, Inc. is a national ESOP consulting firm that assists private business owners and their companies in planning their internal succession strategies using ESOPs).

vi. *Expensive to implement:* Legal fees, stock valuation and lender costs will depend on the size of the transaction, but can mount quickly.

vii. *Need annual upkeep:* A valuation of your company must be performed on a yearly basis to appraise the value of your business. Annual ESOP recordkeeping is also necessary. Finally, as legislation changes, so will your ESOP plan document need to change and there can be some legal costs associated with these amendments.

viii. *Excessive leverage:* To initially implement an ESOP, the company may borrow money from an institutional lender. In order to do so, a company will need to have sufficient cash flow and unencumbered assets.

ix. *Complicated accounting:* ESOP debt is recorded as employer debt and this can be tricky for accountants to grasp. As always, we are happy to work with your advisors to get past such road bumps.

As with any business decision, the benefits must be weighed against the disadvantages and we would be happy to assist you in seeing if an ESOP will be the most advantageous way to transition ownership in your company. The law does not allow ESOPs to be used in partnerships and most professional corporations. Private companies must repurchase shares of departing employees, and this can become a major expense. The cost of setting up an ESOP is also substantial—perhaps $30,000 for the simplest of plans in small companies and on up from there. Any time new shares are issued, the stock of existing owners is diluted. That dilution must be weighed against the tax and motivation benefits an ESOP can provide. Finally, ESOPs will improve corporate performance only if combined with opportunities for employees to participate in decisions affecting their works.

15.12 Overview of ESOP Incentives

Many companies that have implemented employee ownership programmes have developed some means of facilitating employee acquisition of shares. The following sections present a selection of various employee ownership incentives that have been adopted in different countries. They illustrate the broad flexibility and range of choices available to policymakers in crafting an employee ownership strategy. However, a recommended guideline for ESOPs is presented in Exhibit 15.3 for companies who are planning to adopt ESOP programme soon.

15.12.1 Incentives for Companies

- Tax deduction for contributions made to the ESOP by the sponsoring corporation within certain limits, including contributions to repay ESOP debt.
- Allow company to apply profits to buy shares for employees up to specified limits.
- Permit tax deduction for corporate matching contribution of employee savings deferrals to employee trust to purchase shares.
- Tax deduction on dividends used to repay debt that was used to acquire employee shares or paid in cash to employees based on their shareholdings.
- Tax deferral and/or reduction on the value of stock distributed to plan participants.
- Lower tax rates for meeting or exceeding minimum ownership levels by employees.
- Corporate tax reduction based on the percentage of company owned by employees.

Exhibit 15.3 ESOP Limitations: How Small Is Too Small?

Companies of any size can sponsor ESOPs, but in practice ESOPs do not usually make sense for very small companies. There are few ESOP companies with fewer than 20 employees. To find whether an ESOP is financially practical for your company, you need to estimate how much an ESOP would cost. To get an accurate picture, your estimate should include fees associated with plan document preparation, required government filings, professional valuation and plan administration. You also need to assess if you have adequate cash flow to buy shares.

If you are considering a leveraged ESOP, your estimate should also include loan commitment and document fees, lender's legal counsel fees and possibly services of a financial consultant to structure the transaction. Some of these fees are transaction based, such as documentation or filing fees; and others will be ongoing, such as yearly valuation (usually about half the cost of the transaction valuation) and administration.

Due to the cost associated with the set-up and maintenance of an ESOP, it is a good idea to consider additional things to see if the cost of the ESOP is justifiable for your business. Some of these include the cost associated with alternative sale options, the value of the ESOP tax incentives based on your current tax bracket, a comparison of annual ESOP costs to annual contributions, and the size of your eligible payroll. Generally, businesses with the following characteristics are good ESOP candidates:

- Minimum of $500,000 in eligible payroll.
- Reasonable levels of debt.
- Company is currently profitable or has the potential for profitability in the near term.
- Successor management is in place.

If this initial analysis indicates you might be a good candidate for an ESOP, the next step is conducting a more detailed pre-feasibility study. It is important to work with knowledgeable professionals and get multiple cost estimates to ensure your company is getting the best deal.

Source: ESOP Facts, NCEO. For a further discussion on calculating and assessing the cost of setting up and maintaining an ESOP, please see the NCEO publication: 'How Small Is Too Small for an ESOP?' Available at www.nceo.org/articles/too-small-for-esop.

15.12.2 Incentives for Employees

- Defer taxes on voluntary employee savings (and any interest earned) that are held in trust to purchase shares on option.
- Tax exemption on shares held in trust for employees (or subject to restrictions) until distributed to the employee.
- Tax exemption on dividends paid on shares held in employee trust.
- Employee discounts on stock purchased under an approved employee share scheme.
- Allow employees to defer income on pre-tax basis to purchase shares.
- Exempt employee shareholdings from social security taxes.
- Lower tax rates on distributions of employee shares held in trust for longer periods of time (typically three to six years).
- Tax credit up to 25% of salary for share purchases or investments in employee venture capital companies.

- Permit employees to purchase shares at asset valuation or book value prior to a competitive bidding process by strategic investors.
- Tax deduction for voluntary employee contributions used to repay ESOP debt.

15.12.3 Incentives for Selling Shareholders

- The government provides credit for an estate to pay taxes over an extended period if the estate sells stock to an ESOP.
- Allow deferral of capital gains taxes for stock sold to employee trust and reinvested in domestic securities.

Exhibit 15.4 Recommended Guidelines for ESOPs

Guidelines for the operation of ESOPs help ensure that they will achieve their intended goal of promoting broad-based employee participation in ownership and could also encourage the use of ESOPs in private companies. ESOP laws typically require participation by all eligible employees. The allocation of the assets within the ESOP is subject to anti-discrimination requirements to ensure that ESOP benefits are not limited to a small minority of employees. The following are typical ESOP guidelines:

Shares must be held in an ESOP trust: A trust must be established to hold employee shares, share equivalents or share options ('shares').

Eligibility requirements: All full-time employees who have worked at the enterprise for a minimum period of time, for example, one year must be eligible to receive offers of shares.

Allocation standards to ensure broad-based participation: The allocation of shares must be determined according to a written formula in the trust document. Such formula could provide for any combination of the following:

- equal allocation of shares for all eligible employees;
- allocation based on an equal percentage of annual salary, or on a combination of salary and years of service or a similar formula;
- allocation based on the discretion of company management and/or the ESOP trustees according to an assessment of individual employee performance, subject to anti-discrimination standards.

Vesting requirements: Shares may be subject to vesting schedules to defer the time in which employees obtain full rights to the shares allocated to them. One example would be five-year vesting in equal annual percentages so that an employee would be 20% vested after one year, 40% after two years and so on.

Valuation of shares: Companies whose shares are not listed on an established stock exchange must have their shares valued by an independent valuator at least annually. The valuator must be independent of the company to ensure an arm's-length analysis.

Record-keeping, communications and information disclosure: The compliance officer is, among other things, responsible for maintaining accurate records of plan transactions and the status of individual employee accounts, as well as providing employees with timely information about their assets in the trust.

Sale of shares: The trust document must clearly state the means s by which employees may sell their shares. Such provisions shall specify that upon termination of employment employees shall have the right to transact for all vested shares. Upon termination of employment, shares will be deemed to have been sold.

Source: Binns and Gilbert (2004).

15.12.4 Credit Support for Companies

- Tax deduction for companies that make loans available to employees to purchase shares.
- Reduce taxes for financial institutions on interest income from loans to ESOPs or other employee trusts.
- Reduce corporate income tax for lenders that commit a minimum percentage of their loan portfolio to ESOP loans.
- Allow employee-owned companies long-term leases of SOEs with a 20% down payment.

15.12.5 Credit Support for Employees

- Extended repayment terms for employee loans.
- Allow employees to use government pensions or severance pay benefits as collateral for loans to acquire shares in privatization transactions.
- Provide subsidized interest rates for employee loans to acquire shares.

15.13 Achievements of ESOP

15.13.1 In Industrialized Countries

ESOPs became a significant movement in the United States since 1974, when the Employee Retirement Income and Security Act (ERISA) gave the ESOP legal recognition and fiscal advantages. Since 1974, over 11,000 ESOPs have been established in the United States. This includes most airlines, most petroleum companies, most major money lender banks and household names like Xerox and Polaroid. The employees' share in ESOP companies typically ranges from 15% to 100%, and the trend is towards majority ownership by the employees. Avis, the world's second-largest car rental company, was 100% purchased for U.S.$1.75 billion by its 20,000 employees. After the employee buyout, Avis changed its motto from 'we try harder' to 'owners try harder', and has become more successful than ever.

Over 20 acts promulgated by the U.S. Congress since 1974, and many more acts passed by state legislatures, contain provisions that promote ESOPs. The net effect of this legislation is that at present, in the United States, the cheapest way for a corporation to finance expansion is to borrow through an ESOP trust by selling shares on credit to its employees, and the most advantageous way for an owner who wants to sell for any reason, is to sell his shares to his employees.

It has been shown by comparative studies that companies that have introduced significant employee ownership perform better than comparable companies which have not. In very general terms, it can be said that the percentage of added profitability is of the same order of magnitude as the percentage of employee ownership: for example, if a company becomes 50% employee owned, it can expect to become 50% more profitable.

While headlines have been made by employee buyouts which turned failing companies around and saved them from liquidation, employee buyouts of troubled companies comprise only about 2% of all U.S. ESOPs. Some 98% of ESOPs have been established in going concerns and usually helped to make them more successful than before. Of particular significance to Sri Lanka is the fact that ESOPs have been quite successful in factories with a large immigrant labour force whose educational level was lower than the average in Sri Lanka. Ownership is something that even illiterate workers can understand.

These economic effects were paralleled by the beneficial social effect of ESOPs. Where employee ownership was introduced, strikes stopped, petty theft disappeared and labour–management confrontations were replaced by mutual search for increased profitability.

ESOPs enjoy support by management (which usually initiates the ESOP), present owners, organized labour, the government and naturally the employees. Politically, the ESOP concept cuts across the traditional division between right and left and enjoys support across the political spectrum—from both Democrats and Republicans in the United States, from both the Conservative and the Labour Party in the UK.

In the UK, the ESOP movement has become significant since 1987. ESOP legislation was enacted in 1989 and again in 1990. Some 300 ESOPs have been established so far, and the number is rapidly growing. The UK ESOP closely resembles the U.S. model.

15.13.2 In Developing Countries

Two countries, for their own social and political reasons, have applied on a large scale the principles of ownership economics, through mechanisms different from the U.S. ESOP model.

In Mexico, after the general failure of cooperatives and collectives in the land reform sector, the farmers were reorganized in 'smallholder agricultural corporations'. This is a private sector corporation in which each farmer has a double role: as worker and as shareowner. His shareholding corresponds to the land area that he voluntarily puts at the disposal of the corporation (while retaining the title). Over 10,000 such smallholder corporations were established in Mexico (notably for sugar, cotton and oilseeds), and they have been quite economically successful.

In Malaysia, the government's 'bumiputera' initiative aims to give more economic power to the Malay majority. To this end, state-owned estates have been divested to their (predominantly Malay) labour force, with private sector management. In this case as well, the results are reported to be quite favourable.

The first developing country to apply the U.S. ESOP model was Egypt, where a pilot enterprise, the Alexandria Tyre Company, was initiated in 1988. The ESOP concept, adapted to Egyptian legal and social conditions, was actively embraced by the Egyptian government. The government regards ESOP as a way to divest itself of troubled state-owned enterprises without the political liability attached to sale to already wealthy persons or to foreign corporations. Three such divestitures are now being studied, with The U.S. Agency for International Development (USAID) and the International Bank for Reconstruction and Development (IBRD) support. The ESOP receives wide coverage in the government press, and favourable treatment in both right and left opposition newspapers. At the same time, several Egyptian private sector leaders started installing ESOPs in their own enterprises.

Argentina passed in July 1989 an economic reform law containing many expanded-ownership provisions. The national carrier, Aerolineas Argentinas, is presently being privatized, and one of the criteria for choice of purchaser is the percentage of ownership he will provide to the employees.

Guatemala, Costa Rica, Mexico and South Africa are actively studying the application of ESOP.

In the Philippines, President Aquino sold through an ESOP shares to all workers in her family estate, Hacienda Luisita (a sugar plantation). In the former East Block, ESOP-like set-ups were promoted in Poland, Czechoslovakia, Hungary and even in the Soviet Union.

In India, many feel ESOPs make sense only to software companies. This is more because the practice is widely seen in this sector. The picture is, however, changing. More and more non-software companies are beginning to implement the plans. To name a few are Reliance, ACC, UTI Bank and Ranbaxy. Most companies often use ESOPs either to retain talent or plug an employee from its competitor. However, ESOP has far more potential than these. According to the CFO, ESOPs are relevant where an employee plays an important role in the ongoing growth of a company. During the boom period, the attrition rate of employees is heavy and, hence, ESOP is clubbed as a part of pay package. In the changed scenario caused by the post-September 11 events and slowdown, the attrition rate is less of a concern for corporates. The sluggishness is not seen to last indefinitely, says the CFO of Polaris, N. Vaidhyanathan. Employees will, therefore, be bound to derive more benefit from exercising stock option, if offered currently.

Multiple Choice Questions

1. ESOP has been implemented first in ________
   a. India b. The United States c. The UK d. Middle East
2. The period between the grant date and the date on which all the specified vesting conditions of an employee share-based payment plan are to be satisfied is called ________
   a. Vesting period b. Exercise period c. Gradual vesting d. Cliff vesting
3. The option that vests in stages over time is called ________
   a. Vesting period b. Exercise period c. Gradual vesting d. Cliff vesting
4. The type of ESOP that does not involve borrowing is ________
   a. Leveraged ESOP b. Non-leveraged ESOP
   c. LBO d. None
5. As per the Income-tax Act 1961, ESOP can be argued to be as ________
   a. Profit in lieu of salary b. Salary
   c. Perquisites d. Commission
6. A person would not be eligible to participate in employee stock option plan if he holds more than ________ of the shares in the respective company.
   a. 10% b. 20% c. 30% d. 40%
7. ESOP inventor Louis O. Kelso was a/an ________
   a. Investment banker b. Economist c. Doctor d. Poet
8. An ESOP allows companies to share ________ with employees without requiring the employees to invest their own money.
   a. Profit b. Ownership c. Asset d. Liability
9. Under which of the following schemes the employee acquires the shares after a specified period, upon contribution to the share price in monthly instalments?
   a. ESOP b. RSU c. ESPP d. SAR
10. As per Section 53 of the Companies Act 2013, a company is not allowed to issue share at ________
    a. Par b. Discount c. Premium d. None

Review Questions

1. What do you understand by employee share ownership plans (ESOPs)? Briefly explain the nature of employees' stock options.
2. Distinguish between stock options plan and stock ownership plans.
3. Trace the evolution and historical growth of ESOPs.
4. Briefly elaborate on the micro and macro principles of employee shares ownership.
5. List the reasons of using ESOPs and the possible benefits thereof.
6. Discuss the various types of ESOPs.
7. Distinguish between leverage and non-leveraged ESOPs.
8. Write a note on the mechanism of a leveraged ESOP.
9. Write a critical note on the legal framework of ESOPs in the Indian scenario.
10. Discuss the various tax issues of ESOPs for employees and companies.
11. Distinguish between ESOPs and MBO.
12. List and explain the advantages and disadvantages of ESOPs.
13. Write short notes on:
    a. accounting aspect of ESOP
    b. non-leveraged ESOP
14. Write a critical note on the achievement of ESOPs in both industrialized and developing countries.

Case in Action

ESOPs by Infosys Technologies Ltd

Introduction

Infosys Technologies (Infosys) Ltd, one of India's best-known computer software companies, provided consulting and IT services to clients globally. With over 19,000 employees worldwide, Infosys was the second-largest exporter of software from India, after Tata Consultancy Services (TCS). Based in India's 'Silicon City' of Bangalore, Infosys offered a range of customized software services, including development, maintenance, reengineering and consulting. The company had also set up several dedicated offshore software development centres for large clients. Infosys was widely considered to be one of India's most respected and admired companies. The company was well known for its excellent governance and financial reporting practices.

Infosys had been one of the first companies in India to issue ESOP to its employees. In recent times, accounting for stock options had become a controversial subject in the United States. With its American Depository Receipts listed on the NASDAQ, Infosys was not insulated from the debate in the United States. By 2003, the debate on expensing stock options in the income statements had become intense. Analysts speculated that the main regulatory body in the United States, the SEC might make it mandatory for tech companies to expense stock options. In India, the SEBI had also issued accounting guidelines or stock options. Infosys had first issued ESOPs before SEBI guidelines were issued. It was therefore not bound to follow the SEBI guidelines in its accounting treatment for expensing ESOPs up to 2002. However, according to a report published by CRISIL, India's leading credit rating agency, had the company expensed ESOPS, there would have been a drastic decline in the reported profits and therefore a decline in the EPS. The Infosys management realized the need for a suitable methodology that would present a fair and accurate picture of stock options to investors.

Corporate compensation policies had evolved over time as companies looked for innovative ways of motivating employees. Employees were compensated in various ways, such as cash wages bonuses, perquisites and stock options. IT companies primarily used stock options to motivate and retain talent. In the simplest and most common form, a company granted options that gave an employee the right but not an obligation to buy the company's stock at some point in the future at a predetermined price. For instance, a company might issue options on 1 January 2003 to an employee to purchase 1,000 shares of its common stock at a price of ₹100 per share. If the share price exceeded ₹100, then the employee could exercise his/her option and make a profit. For example, if the share price reached ₹200, the employee could book a profit of (200 –100) × ₹(1,000) = ₹0.1 million. Most stock options came with a 'vesting period'. Employees could not exercise their options until the vesting period was over. Typical vesting periods ranged from three to five years. In the above example, the company could specify that the 1,000 options had a vesting period of, say, four years. At the end of every year, 250 options might vest. Typically, if the options were not exercised at the end of a vesting period, they could be accumulated and carried forward.

Two of the stock options plans offered by Infosys Ltd. are presented in Table 1.

Table 1 Infosys ESOPs

Description	***Stocks Options under 1998 Plan***	***Stocks Options under 1998 Plan***
Total number of shares	3.2 million ADS representing 1.6 million shares	6.6 million shares
The pricing formula	Not less than 90% of the fair market value as on date of grant	At the fair market value as on date of grant
Ratio of ADS to equity shares	One share represents two ADSs	N.A.
Options granted during the year	580,200 options representing 290,100 equity shares	616,850 options representing 616,850 equity shares
Weighted average price per option granted	$61.85 (₹2,988); 100% of fair market value on the date of grant during the year	₹3,754 (100% of fair market value on the date of grant during the year
Option vested (as on 31 March 2003)	630,004 options representing 3,15,002 equity shares	1,222,639 options representing 1,222,178 equity shares
Options exercised during the year	89,540 options representing 44,770 equity shares	12,178 options representing 12,178 equity shares
Money raised on exercise of options	$2,114,348 (₹102.2 million)	₹33 million

Options forfeited during the year	249,748 options representing 124,874 equity shares	212,316 options representing 212,316 equity shares
Total number of options in force at the end of the year	2,503,406 options representing 1,251,703 equity shares	5,061,171 options representing 5,061,171 equity shares
Grant to senior management and independent directors	Nil	Claude Smadja
Employees receiving 5% or more of the total number of options granted during the year	Nil	Nil

Source: Infosys, Annual Report 2003.

To summarize, it can be said that proper use of an ESOP can provide employees with a substantial capital stake in their company, improve corporate performance, provide a tax-favoured market for the shares of a departing owner in a family or closely held firm, and increase the motivation and commitment of employees in the company.

Source: www.sesadvisors.com (last accessed on 1 September 2016).

Questions for Discussion

1. Why are ESOPs issued by a corporate?
2. Explain the rationale behind the ESOP offering by Infosys Technologies Ltd.
3. Briefly discuss the salient features of ESOPs offered by Infosys Technologies Ltd.

Case in Action

Royal Bank of Trinidad and Tobago

The Royal Bank of Trinidad and Tobago (RBTT) was established in 1971 when the Royal Bank of Canada (RBC) decided to divest itself of its bank holdings in Trinidad and Tobago. Though not a privatization in the formal sense, RBTT was nevertheless created as a result of a divestiture that was similar in many respects to what would have occurred if the bank had been sold by the government.

As part of the buyout of RBC, the employee pension fund was frozen and the plan's excess assets (funds left over after purchasing annuities for participating employees) were transferred to a newly created ESOP in 1976. The ESOP became a major equity investor in the new RBTT by purchasing a block of stock at the offering price of $1.55 per share. All full-time RBTT employees were assigned an individual account within the ESOP and RBTT stock acquired with the pension assets was allocated on a pro rata basis to employees' accounts based on their respective assets in the frozen pension plan. Employees were also given an opportunity to invest their own funds to purchase additional RBTT shares for their ESOP accounts.

As a result the ESOP became the bank's largest single shareholder and it has remained one of the largest shareholders up to the present time. The ESOP's ownership of RBTT has been as high as 20% of total shares outstanding, which was the legal limit for a single shareholder under Trinidad and Tobago law without triggering a requirement to bid for the whole company.

The ESOP is administered by RBTT's trust company. Three trustees have the fiduciary responsibility to ensure that the ESOP's assets are managed in the best interests of the employees. Two of the trustees are appointed by RBTT management and one trustee is elected by employees every five years. Under the laws of Trinidad and Tobago, trustees are required to act in unanimity on all official activities, including the voting of the ESOP's stock.

RBTT employees are eligible to receive year-end bonuses, subject to the bank's earning net profits. Bonuses over the years have typically amounted to an average 8% of annual pay. Employees are legally required to invest 40% of their net bonus into the ESOP but may invest the entire bonus. Any money invested into the ESOP is exempt from taxation. (RBTT permits employees to access the value of their ESOP accounts for current liquidity by taking out loans backed by their ESOP shares.)

When no additional shares are available (as when the ESOP held the legal limit of 20% of RBTT's shares) employees were able to invest their bonus payments into phantom shares or options that provided equivalent value to actual RBTT shares.

RBTT also pays an annual dividend to all shareholders of record. Over the years, the average value of share dividends has been about 6% of the per share value. Dividends on ESOP shares are also exempt from taxation.

Employees must stay with RBTT for at least five years to become fully vested in the shares in their ESOP account. When they leave the company, they are required to sell their shares back to the ESOP at the then-current market value. Employees receive a lump-sum distribution in cash for the entire value of their ESOP account. Employees leaving the bank prior to attaining qualified retirement age are taxed at an average of 15% (which is lower than the standard tax rate). Employees who attain retirement age (60 or 65, depending on their position within the bank) receive their ESOP distribution tax free.

RBTT stock has performed quite well over the years. With the ESOP purchasing at $1.55 per share in 1976, the value of RBTT shares has increased to $45 per share in 2004. As a result, many employees have received handsome ESOP distributions, which have enabled them to enjoy a happy and secure retirement. A typical employee leaving prior to retirement with at least five years with the bank could qualify for an ESOP distribution of about two to three times his/her annual salary.

Source: Hubert Alleyne, Executive Officer (retired), Royal Bank of Trinidad and Tobago.

Questions for Discussion

1. How RBTT has been created?
2. How the pension fund of RBC has been managed?
3. How ESOP of RBTT is administered?
4. Write a critical note on employees' right from ESOP trust.

References

Binns, David M., and Ronald J. Gilbert. 2004. 'The Role of Employee Stock Ownership Plans in the Restructuring and Privatization of State-Owned Financial Institutions'. Paper presented at the 6th Annual Financial Markets and Development Conference on 'The Role of State-Owned Financial Institutions: Policy and Practice', 26–27 April, Washington, DC.

Dhar, Satyajit, and De, Subhabrata. 2008. 'ESOP Administration: An Insight'. *Chartered Secretary*, 186–192.

Freeman, Steven F. 2007. 'Effects of ESOP Adoption and Employee Ownership: Thirty years of Research and Experience'. Working Paper no. 07-01, Graduate Division, School of Arts and Sciences, Center for Organizational Dynamics, University of Pennsylvania.

Sutton, T. 2000. *Corporate Financial Accounting and Reporting,* p. 508. London: FT/Prentice Hall.

Further Readings

ESOPs: An Introduction. Available at www.iupindia.org/1005/PO_BookReview_70.html (last accessed on 1 September 2016).

ESOP Practices in India: An Overview. Available at www.globalequity.org/ (last accessed on 1 September 2016).

http://www.infosys.com/investors/reports-filings/quarterly-results/2008-2009/Q4/Q4-2008-AD.pdf (last accessed on 22 August 2016).

www.icmrindia.org/casestudies (last accessed on 23 August 2016).

Part D

Strategic Finance

Chapter

16

Financial Engineering

Chapter Objectives

On completion of this chapter, you will be able to understand:

- The definitions and scope of financial engineering
- Systematic versus unsystematic financial risk
- Principles of managing risk
- Gap analysis: Dollar gap, incremental and cumulative gaps
- Duration gap analysis
- Risk management strategy
- Hedging and financial engineering: Cash market instruments and derivatives
- Application of financial engineering
- Application of the building-block approach
- Reasons for rapid growth in financial engineering

Financial Engineering to Athens's Rescue

Athens has struggled to get its Eurozone creditors to talk about debt relief. This is because it's not urgent. But if the negotiators resolve the immediate crisis, which could lead to bankruptcy in a few weeks, debt relief should come onto the table.

Debt relief isn't front and center in the current talks because Greece's borrowings have already been restructured once, in 2012. The debt is still huge, 313 billion euros, or about $353 billion, 175% of the Greek gross domestic product. But the bulk, about €184 billion, is now owed to Eurozone governments and pays low interest. What is more, Greece doesn't have to start repaying it until 2020 and then has over 30 years to finish. The so-called present value of this debt, what it is worth today, is therefore much lower than its official face value.

Unfortunately, this isn't the full story. Greece has four other sources of borrowing: €27 billion owed to the European Central Bank; €20 billion owed to the International Monetary Fund; debt owed to private investors; and short-term treasury bills. The private debt isn't an immediate problem, because most of it has also been stretched out over a long period. Nor are the treasury bills, as Athens is still able to roll them over as they come due. But the E.C.B. and I.M.F. debt is problematic because most of it comes due in the next five years. In fact, there is a crunch in the next few months, with over €10 billion in repayments due by the end of September.

The snag is that I.M.F. and E.C.B. debt cannot be rescheduled without breaching rules and treaties. This is why the focus of the current talks is about lending Greece more money, so that it can meet these obligations. Both Greece and its creditors agree that this is the immediate need. Where they disagree is over what strings should be attached to the additional loans. That's why there is now a serious risk of Greece's going bust. If that possibility is avoided, the issue of longer-term debt relief will come onto the table. Not only does Greece want it; the I.M.F. thinks it is necessary to make the country's debt sustainable.

The Eurozone will also be under pressure to provide yet more loans to Athens because the money left in the current bailout program won't be sufficient to cover all the repayments due to the E.C.B. and I.M.F. What is more, the country has other needs, such as paying overdue bills to suppliers, recapitalizing Greek banks and repaying the loans it has forcibly extracted from local authorities within Greece. Since the Eurozone won't agree to a write-down of its loans, the obvious solution is to give Athens an even longer holiday before it needs to start repaying this debt and to stretch out the period in which it has to finish doing so. The present value of the debt would shrink again. Some observers complain that such a move would do nothing to cut the overall size of Greece's debt. Although this wouldn't matter if everybody were rational and focused on present value, it might still undermine confidence and so prevent a proper economic recovery.

This is where some financial engineering may be useful. The Greek government has proposed splitting most of the Eurozone debt into two parts: one would carry a higher interest rate; the other wouldn't pay interest at all. Athens then wants this 'zero coupon' debt to be gradually written off. While the Eurozone won't accept the write-off, the debt-splitting program could be modified to make it workable. The key insight is that the zero-coupon debt will have a much lower present value than its face value. If Greece could find some organizations to take on this liability for a payment equivalent to its present value, it would cut substantially the face value of its debt.

Companies and infrastructure projects might be interested. They would be essentially receiving long-term loans, which they would repay in one chunk with all the interest rolled up. That's the sort of financing Europe's economy could do with, as it needs to bolster investment. The twist is that the companies or projects would receive the upfront cash from Greece but repay the loans to Athens's creditors. These would have to agree to a change in the counterparty, but they wouldn't have to write off any loans. Such a program could square Greece's demand for lower headline debt with the unwillingness of Eurozone governments to acknowledge to their taxpayers that they had lost money on lending to Athens.

Some creditor countries will, of course, ask why they should offer yet more help to Greece. The answer is partly that the collapse of a country so close to home is not in their interest. But it is also ethical. Other Eurozone countries prevented Greece's defaulting on its debts at the start of the crisis because they were afraid that doing so would bankrupt their own banks, which had lent Athens most of the money. They, therefore, bear some of the blame for Greece's predicament and some of the responsibility for sorting it out.

Source: Dixon (2015).

16.1 Introduction

Financial engineering is perhaps the latest terminological addition to the world of finance and this is a new example of invasion of social thinking by technology. Many of the most innovative new products traded in the capital markets and derivative instrument markets today originated as the financial engineering solution to fit a specific client needs and situation. The term 'financial engineering' came into use after the discovery of the Black–Scholes option pricing model in 1973. Their scientific discovery led to a new methodology to solve practical financial problems. Regardless of how today's environment came about, two things are certain. First, the volatility of market rates has created ever-increasing demand for clever financial products to manage financial risk. Second, current technology has made it possible for financial institutions to create, price and hedge products specifically designed to neutralize these financial risks. From these foundations, financial engineering was born.

The financial risk faced by companies has increased tremendously over the last few decades and the payoffs of managing risk successfully are very high. In response to this increased risk and the incentive to manage it, older instruments of risk management such as forwards and futures have been expanded in scope, and many new instruments are devised. Financial engineering is the process of adaptation of existing financial instruments and processes to develop new ones in order that financial market participants can effectively cope with the changing situation. Financial engineering is well on the way to becoming an independent discipline with its own professional bodies. An example is the American Association of Financial Engineers, set up in 1991.

16.2 Financial Engineering: Definitions and Scope

Financial engineering has been defined from different perspectives. Some of such definitions have been presented here. In the words of Marshal and Bansal (1992), financial engineering is the lifeblood of financial innovation—the process that seeks to adapt existing financial instruments and processes and develop the new ones so as to enable financial market participants to cope more effectively with the changing world in which we live. The process of financial engineering can be viewed as the 'fine tuning' of an existing financial product to improve its return or risk characteristics in light of changing market conditions. It can be considered as a process that allows existing financial products to overhaul and restructure to take advantage of changed taxation, legal or general economic climate (Eales 2000). It involves the designing, the development and implementation of innovative financial instruments and processes, and formulation of creative solutions to problems in finance (Finnerty 1988). Financial engineering is continuously focusing on the risk–reward trade-off by developing the high-yield investment avenues for the investors. These definitions together build an idea on financial engineering that covers mostly sophisticated products and processes in the field of highly volatile financial markets.

The scope of financial engineering is not limited to corporate finance and its institutional applications. Most of the financial innovations that have taken place in the recent time have been directed towards retail (consumer) level. In addition to corporate finance, nowadays, financial engineering has been extended to investment and money management, risk management, personal financial planning and relationship marketing too. In the investment and money management, financial engineering is continuously focusing on the risk–reward trade-off by developing the high-yield investment avenues for the investors. By applying the concept of repackaging and overcollateralization, a financial engineer tries to transform the high-risk investment instruments to low-risk investment instruments.

In today's deregulated market with the severe competition, financial institutions are constantly introducing new products and services to gain the market share. The factors contributing to the growth of financial product and process innovations through financial engineering are intensified international competition, tax asymmetries and tax advantage, reduction in the transaction cost due to increased operational efficiency, increase in the price and interest rate volatility, advances in the financial theories, reduction in agency cost, regulatory and legislative changes, increased liquidity, increased competition due to globalization, liberalization and deregulation, the explosive growth in IT, accounting benefits and increased customer involvement to choose the right instrument among the myriad of products.

Figure 16.1 Maslow's Needs Hierarchy and Financial Need Hierarchy

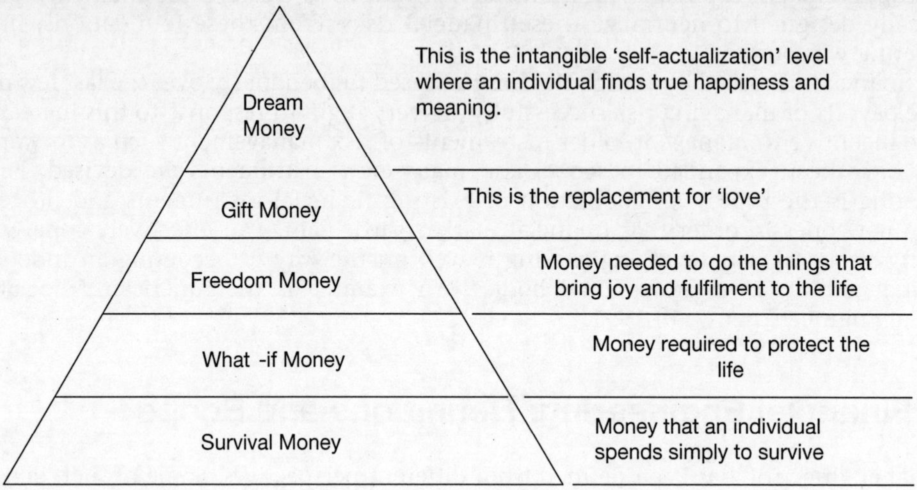

Many financial institutions are successful in satisfying the basic financial needs of the customers in terms of saving and/or investment objectives or motives. However, today's conservative investments do not allow the investors to bring the expected rate of return and to cope up with the inflation. The demographic and socio-economic variables play an important role while deciding the hierarchical needs of saving motives. In order to understand the market needs, it is crucial to understand the hierarchy of financial needs for the innovation and delivery of the financial products. Figure 16.1 shows that financial need hierarchy is similar to Maslow's need hierarchy theory, which defines that the lower, basic needs pertaining to human survival must be met before the higher needs can be addressed, which are not directly related to the survival but relate to the life enhancement and quality of life. The theory is also applicable while defining the hierarchy structure of saving motives in financial behaviour of an individual.

16.3 Financial Risk

Financial risk is an umbrella term for multiple types of risk associated with financing, including financial transactions that include company loans in risk of default. Risk is a term often used to imply downside risk, meaning the uncertainty of a return and the potential for financial loss. The term financial risk covers the range of risks affecting financial outcomes faced by a firm. It is essentially of two kinds: systematic and unsystematic.

16.3.1 Systematic Risk

Systematic risk is risk associated with market returns. This risk can be attributed to broad factors. It is risk to your investment portfolio that cannot be attributed to the specific risk of individual investments. It is like a surprise that affects a large number of assets, although at varying degrees. It is sometimes called market risk or non-diversifiable risk. Sources of systematic risk could be macroeconomic factors, such as inflation, changes in interest rates, fluctuations in currencies, recessions, wars and so on. Macro factors that influence the direction and volatility of the entire market would be systematic risk. An individual company cannot control systematic risk. Some of its components are as follows:

a. **Business risk** is the risk of fluctuations in sales revenue. It arises from macroeconomic factors such as economic swings and deregulation, and demand factors such as seasonality of demand. This risk is not totally systematic, however, and some of it can be reduced by diversification of the firm's operations. The risk of property loss, and product liability suits, can be insured against.
b. **Financing risk** arises from leverage. It is possible to minimize it by restricting the amount of debt in the firm, even though there may be tax advantages to borrowing.
c. **Inflation risk** arises from unanticipated inflation. In international trade, it arises from the movement away from purchasing power parity (PPP).
d. **Default or credit risk** is the risk of default of payment by debtors of the firm. Large banks use credit rating agencies, such as Moody's Investor Services and Standard and Poor's Corporation, to rate borrowers. Though this risk is mostly systematic, it can be diversified in some cases (e.g., by banks holding a large portfolio). Some forms of credit risk can be insured against, for example, export credit.
e. When it is difficult to buy or sell a financial instrument at its market price, then there is marketability, **or liquidity risk** associated with it. This risk is un-diversifiable and is completely systematic. Some insurance companies insure this risk to some extent.
f. **Operating risk** is generated from operating leverage which is the commitment of the firm to fixed production charges (fixed costs). The greater the operating leverage, the greater is the risk to the firm. Reducing operating leverage wherever possible helps.
g. **Political risk** can be both domestic and foreign; it is particularly high when operating in some politically unstable Third World countries. This risk is highly systematic and un-diversifiable.

16.3.2 Unsystematic Risk

Unsystematic risk is a company-specific or industry-specific risk. This risk is attributable or specific to the individual investment or small group of investments. It is uncorrelated with stock market returns. Other names used to describe unsystematic risk are specific risk, diversifiable risk, idiosyncratic risk and residual risk. Strikes, accidents and takeovers are examples of unsystematic risk. Unsystematic risks are considered governable by the company or industry. Proper diversification can nearly eliminate unsystematic risk. If an investor owns just one stock or bond and something negative happens to that company, the investor suffers great harm. However, if an investor owns a diversified portfolio of 20, 30 or 40 individual investments, the damage done to the portfolio is minimized. The important concept of unsystematic risk is that it is not correlated to market risk and can be nearly eliminated by diversification. Unsystematic risk comprises primarily of price risks.

a. **Interest rate risk** arises both from fixed- and floating-rate debt. Unanticipated changes in floating interest rates can cause costs to rise. However, Putnam (1986) shows that the real interest rate on floating-rate debt is more or less fixed, while it is floating in case of fixed-rate debt. Thus, the real interest costs are known with certainty in case of floating-rate debt. Effectively, therefore, floating-rate debt offers a long-run hedge against inflation risk. It is clear that inflation and interest rate risks are closely related. At the same time, a fixed-rate debt can cause financial difficulties in case interest rates drop. This is therefore a major risk faced by almost all companies.

b. **Currency (or foreign exchange) risk** arises when cash inflows or outflows take place in foreign currency. This risk can be either diversified or hedged.

c. **Commodity price risk** arises from unanticipated changes in commodity prices and can be hedged.

16.4 Principles of Managing Risk

In managing risk, it is important to identify the risk profile of the company. Unsystematic risk, which can also be called specific risk, is the risk that applies only to one specific company. Poor performance, product returns or recalls, employee strikes or office calamities are all examples of unsystematic risk. Unsystematic risk is significant if an investor has a large portion of his portfolio invested in one specific company or industry. The need to balance the effects of unsystematic risk, so that a portfolio is not completely wiped out by a single event, is why advisors usually suggest investors diversify their portfolio. Diversification prevents a portfolio from suffering too greatly when one company or industry suffers a significant loss of market share or confidence, or some other financial calamity.

Systematic risk is the risk that is inherent in being involved in the stock market. It is the effect on a portfolio that comes from whatever affects the stock market as a whole, such as wars, inflation, interest rates, political changes and global economic matters. Those events affect not just a single company or industry but the entire financial world. Balancing systematic risk is difficult, because no company or industry can avoid the losses that come from major news in the financial or political world. There are ways to hedge the losses that might occur.

Financial literature has concerned itself mainly with the systematic risk of a firm, measured through its beta. In fact, as per the CAPM, not managing unsystematic risk does not increase the rate of return required by investors. However, by significantly lowering the level of the firm's expected cash flows, it can and does, in practice, reduce the value of the firm. It is necessary therefore to manage unsystematic risk in cases where it could adversely impact on a firm's existence. Total risk is the sum of the systematic and unsystematic risks. Shapiro and Titman (1986) advocate a total risk approach to risk management. Total risk, being the sum of systematic and unsystematic risks, should be considered by the firm. The objective of the shareholders would then be to search for an optimal risk profile, where the marginal cost of bearing risk equals the marginal cost of managing it.

Risk management requires the identification of the risks to which the firm is exposed, quantification of these exposures wherever possible, determination of the desired outcomes and engineering a strategy to achieve these outcomes. A look at the coverage ratios is a good first step. However, for detailed identification of risk, a series of cash budgets must be prepared using different economic variables and considering the use of different risk-reducing mechanisms. Each time, the risk must be identified/evaluated in terms of the probability of not being able to meet essential payments/obligations.

Wherever possible, risk should be quantified. Non-financial companies can carry out a sensitivity analysis by making a computer model that determines the relationship of inputs/outputs/sales and so on to different prices, such as interest rates. By varying prices, their effect on pre-tax income can be determined. Alternatively, the historical sensitivity of the company's equity value to changes in prices can be measured. The coefficients of a simple linear regression are used to estimate the sensitivity of the value of the firm to changes in the respective variables. This approach is similar in some ways to determining the beta under CAPM.

Table 16.1 A Summary of Interest Rate Risk Analysis

Impact on	*Measured through*	*Formula*	*Method*
Profitability	Net interest income	Interest income – interest expense	Gap analysis
Value of equity	Market value of equity	Market value of assets – market value of debt	Duration analysis

Source: Authors.

Financial companies can measure the degree of interest rate risk on the profitability and market value of equity. Profitability is measured in terms of net interest income (NII), which is the difference between interest income and interest expense. Impact of interest rate risk on NII is measured through gap analysis. On the other hand, market value of equity is computed by deducting the market value of debt from the market value of assets. The impact of interest rate risk on the market value of equity is measured through duration analysis. A summary of interest rate risk analysis is presented in Table 16.1.

Gap analysis is based on the difference between the value of rate-sensitive assets (RSA) and the value of the rate-sensitive liabilities (RSL). Using gap, the impact on the firm of changes in the interest rate is given by $\Delta NII = GAP \times \Delta r$, where NII is the net interest income and Δr represents the change in interest rate. The measure, duration, which was developed in 1938 by Frederick Macaulay, is the most widely used measure of interest-rate sensitivity of an asset, and is the effective maturity of an asset/liability expressed in units of time. The Macaulay duration is given by

$$D = \frac{\Delta(dS/S)}{(dR/R)}$$

where S is the instrument's spot price and R equals 1 plus the asset's yield (for example, yield to maturity). Thus, D measures the response of price to a proportional change in the interest rate. If V is the value of the firm and Δ represents the change operator, then

$$\frac{\Delta V}{V} = \frac{\Delta(1+r)}{(1+r)} \times D$$

In this process of risk measurement, it is essential to understand the underlying determinants of the risk. In case of interest rate risk, the underlying factor would largely comprise of inflation. Therefore, the management of interest rate risk and inflation risk will have to go together. As emphasized earlier, it is more important to place the risk in perspective. If the company is not threatened by bankruptcy if prices move, then a more passive strategy, involving perhaps a periodic monitoring of overall corporate exposure, is probably sufficient. These considerations will help the firm to determine the desired outcomes of risk management.

16.5 Gap Analysis

The gap analysis is probably the most widely used technique for assessing interest rate risk. It compares the value of assets that either mature or are re-priced within a given time interval to the value of liabilities that either mature or are re-priced during the same time period. In a typical gap management process, bank management divides all assets and liabilities on the balance sheet according to their interest rate sensitivity. An asset or a liability with an interest rate subject to change within a year is considered rate sensitive. One whose interest rate cannot change for more than a year is considered fixed. The gap between RSA and RSL is defined as:

$$GAP = RSA - RSL$$

The gap can be expressed either as dollars or as a percentage of total earning assets. If RSA is greater than RSL, the gap is positive; if RSA is less than RSL, the gap is negative; and if RSA is equal to RSL, the gap is zero. A zero dollar gap would protect bank profits from changes in interest rates.

To compare two or more banks, or make track a bank over time, use the

i. Relative gap ratio = GAP$/total assets or
ii. Interest rate sensitivity ratio = RSA$/RSL$.

Controlling the size of the gap is an important decision that depends both on the degree of risk that a bank's management is willing to accept and on its forecast of future interest rate movements. For example, assume that we are at the bottom of a business cycle and that interest rates are low and expected to rise. Under such circumstances, the bank management would want a large positive gap. The reason is that given expected higher interest rates in the future, the bank wants to hold rate-sensitive assets in order to take advantage of future higher interest rates and to hold fixed-rate liabilities in order to lock in the current low interest rates, thus a positive gap. However, at the top of the business cycle when interest rates are high and expected to decline, a negative gap is desirable. In this case, the desired balance sheet portfolio consists of fixed-rate assets and rate-sensitive liabilities. Finally, if the bank's management wishes to minimize interest rate risk, a zero gap is the portfolio strategy. In sum, the greater the gap, either positive or negative, the greater is the bank's exposure to interest rate risk.

16.5.1 Dollar Gap

It is the absolute measure of gap between respective assets and liabilities without considering the incremental or cumulative effects. Interest rate forecasts can be important in earning bank profit. If interest rates are expected to increase in the near future, the bank could use a positive dollar gap as an aggressive approach to gap management. If interest rates are expected to decrease in the near future, the bank could use a negative dollar gap (so as rate fell, bank deposit costs would fall more than bank revenues, causing profit to rise).

16.5.2 Incremental and Cumulative Gaps

Incremental gaps measure the gaps for different maturity buckets (e.g., 0–30 days, 30–90 days, 90–180 days and 180–365 days). Cumulative gaps add up the incremental gaps from maturity bucket to bucket.

16.5.3 Measuring Interest Rate Sensitivity and the Dollar Gap

a. Gap, interest rates, and profitability: The change in the dollar amount of ΔNII is

$$\Delta NII = RSA\$(\Delta i) - RSL\$(\Delta i) = GAP\$(\Delta i)$$

b. Defensive versus aggressive asset/liability management:

   i. Defensively guard against changes in NII (e.g., near-zero gap).
   ii. Aggressively seek to increase NII in conjunction with interest rate forecasts (e.g., positive or negative gaps).
   iii. Many times some gaps are driven by market demands (e.g., borrowers want long-term loans and depositors want short-term maturities.

c. Three problems with dollar gap management:

   i. Time horizon problems related to when assets and liabilities are re-priced. Dollar gap assumes they are all re-priced on the same day, which is not true.

      For example, a bank could have a zero 30-day gap, but with daily liabilities and 30-day assets, NII would react to changes in interest rates over time. A solution is to divide the assets and liabilities into maturity buckets (i.e., incremental gap).
   ii. We assume that the correlation between the movement in market interest rates and in the interest income and interest expense is one.

      Many variable rate assets do not adjust quickly and fully to changes in market interest rates, for example, residential real estate loans. A solution is the standardized gap, for example, a variable rate asset whose interest rate has been shown to be rather insensitive to market interest rate movement might be considered as a fixed rate.

      For example, assume GAP\$ = RSA\$ – RSL\$ = \$200 (commercial paper) – \$500 (certificates of deposit, CDs) = –\$300. Assume the CD rate is 105% as volatile as 90-day T-bills, while the commercial paper rate is 30% as volatile. Now, we calculate the standardized gap = 0.30(\$200) – 1.05(\$500) = \$60 – \$525 = –\$460, which is much more negative!
   iii. Focus on NII rather than on shareholder wealth. Dollar gap may be set to increase Net Interest Margin (NIM) if interest rates increase, but equity values may decrease; if successful, aggressive gap management may increase the level of NII, but it is also likely to add to the volatility of that income. Even defensive gap management may produce a decline in shareholder wealth, because of the less-than-perfect correlation between asset earnings, liability costs and general market interest rate movements.

16.5.4 A Closer Look at Gap Analysis

RSA and RSL are re-priced within a period of time called a maturity bucket. Re-pricing occurs whenever either maturity or a roll date is reached. The roll date is the reset date specified in floating-rate instruments that determines the new market benchmark rate used to set cash flows (e.g., coupon payments). The Federal Reserve set the six maturity buckets: 1 day; 1 day–3 months; 3–6 months; 6–12 months; 1–5 years; >5 years. Different formulations in gap analysis are restated next followed by an example.

Re-pricing Gap = RSA – RSL
ΔR = interest rate shock
$\Delta NII = GAP \times \Delta R$ for each maturity bucket i
Cumulative Gap (CGAP) = $\Sigma_i \, GAP_i$
$\Delta NII = GAP \times \Delta R_i$, where ΔR_i is the average interest rate change on RSA and RSL
Gap ratio = CGAP/assets

Example 1: Conduct a gap analysis based on the following information:

Assets	*$ million*	*Liabilities and Net Worth*	*$ million*
Short-term (1-year fixed-rate) consumer loans	50	Equity capital (fixed)	20
Long-term (2-year fixed-rate) consumer loans	25	Demand deposits	40
3-month T-bills	30	Passbook savings	30
6-month T-bills	35	3-month CDs	40
3-year T-bonds	70	3-months bankers' acceptances	20
10-year, fixed-rate mortgages	20	6-month commercial paper	60
30-year floating-rate mortgages (9 months adjustment period)	40	1-year time deposits	20
		2-year time deposits	40
Total	270	Total	270

Solution 1:

Maturity Buckets	*RSA*	*RSL*	*GAP*	*CGAP*	*GAP Ratio*
1 day	0	0	0		
1 day–3 months	30	40 + 20	–30		
3 months–6 months	35	60	–25		
6 months–12 months	50 + 40	20	70		
1 year				0 – 30 – 25 + 70 = 15	15/270 = 5.6%
1 year–5 years	25 + 70	40	55		
5 years				0 – 30 – 25 + 70 + 55 = 70	70/270 = 25.9%
>5 years	20	20 + 40 + 30	–70		

Assume an across-the-board 1% increase in interest rates.

Maturity Buckets	*RSA*	*RSL*	*GAP*	*ΔR*	*ΔNII = GAP×DR*
1 day	0	0	0	0.01	0
1 day–3 months	30	40 + 20	–30	0.01	–$300,000
3–6 months	35	60	–25	0.01	–$250,000
6–12 months	50 + 40	20	70	0.01	$700,000
1–5 years	25 + 70	40	55	0.01	$550,000
>5 years	20	20 + 40 + 30	–70	0.01	–$700,000
1 year CΔNII			15	0.01	$150,000
5 years CΔNII			70	0.01	$700,000

16.6 Duration Gap Analysis

While GAP$ can adjust NIM for changes in interest rates, it does not consider effects of such changes on asset, liability and equity values. An alternative method for measuring interest rate risk, called duration gap analysis, examines the sensitivity of the market value of the financial institution's net worth to changes in interest rates (Exhibit 16.1). Duration gap analysis is based on Macaulay's concept of duration, which measures the average lifetime of a security's stream of payments. Recall that duration is a useful concept, because it provides a good approximation, particularly when interest rate changes are small, of the sensitivity of a security's market value to a change in its interest rate using the following formula:

$$\%\Delta P \approx -DUR \times \frac{\Delta i}{1+i}$$

where

$\%\Delta P = \frac{P_{t+1} - P_t}{P_t}$ = percentage change in the market value of the security

DUR = duration

i = interest

After having determined the duration of all assets and liabilities on the bank's balance sheet, the bank manager could use this formula to calculate how the market value of each asset and liability changes when there is a change in interest rates and then calculate the effect on net worth. In duration gap analysis, the following assumptions are made:

a. The duration of assets and liabilities must be known precisely
b. The market value of assets must be known
c. The change in interest rates can only be a parallel shift
d. Convexity is not expected to influence valuation
e. Term structure of interest rate is flat

Under duration gap analysis, duration gap is computed by using the following formula:

$$\text{Duration Gap} = \text{asset duration} - (\text{liabilities duration} \times \text{weight})$$

$$\text{Duration Gap} = D_A - (D_L \times W_L)$$

where D_A is the average duration of assets, D_L is the average duration of liabilities and W_L is the ratio of total liabilities to total assets. Duration gap can be positive, negative or zero. The change in net worth or equity value (or ΔE) here is different from the market value of a bank's stock (which is based on future expectations of dividends). This new value is based on changes in the market values of assets and liabilities on the bank's balance sheet.

Example 2: Based on the information given in the following balance sheet, show the changes in the value of equity.

Assets	***$***	***Duration (Years)***	***Liabilities***	***$***	***Duration (Years)***
Cash	100	0	CD, 1 year	600	1.0
Business loans	400	1.25	CD, 5 years	300	5.0
Mortgage loans	500	7.0	Total liabilities	$900	2.33
			Equity	100	
Total	$1,000	4.0	Total	$1,000	

Solution 2

$$\text{Duration Gap} = 4.0 - (0.9)(2.33) = 1.90 \text{ years}$$

Suppose interest rates increase from 11% to 12%. Now, $\%\Delta E = (-1.90)(1/1.11) = -1.7\%$

$$\$\Delta E = -1.7\% \times \text{total assets} = 1.7\% \times \$1{,}000 = -\$17$$

Example 3: The bank manager wants to know what happens when interest rates rise from 10% to 11%. The total asset value is $100 million (average duration 2.70 years), and the total liability value is $95 million (average duration 1.03 years). Calculate the change in the market value of the assets and liabilities.

Solution 3: With a total asset value of $100 million, the market value of assets falls by $2.5 million ($100 million × 0.025 = $2.5 million):

$$\%\Delta P \approx -\text{DUR} \times \frac{\Delta i}{1+i}$$

where

DUR = Duration = 2.70
Δi = Change in interest rate (0.11 – 0.10) = 0.01
i = interest rate = 0.10

Thus,

$$\%\Delta P \approx -2.70 \times \frac{0.01}{1+0.1} = -0.025 = -2.5\%$$

With total liabilities of $95 million, the market value of liabilities falls by $0.9 million ($95 million × 0.009 = –$0.9 million):

$$\%\Delta P \approx -\text{DUR} \times \frac{\Delta i}{1+i}$$

where

DUR = Duration = 1.03
Δi = Change in interest rate (0.11 – 0.10) = 0.01
i = interest rate = 0.10

Thus,

$$\%\Delta P \approx -1.03 \times \frac{0.01}{1+0.1} = -0.009 = -0.9\%$$

The result is that the net worth of the bank would decline by $1.6 million (–$2.5 million – (–$0.9 million) = –$2.5 million + $0.9 million = –$1.6 million).

The bank manager could have obtained the answer even more quickly by calculating what is called a duration gap, which is defined as follows:

$$\text{Duration Gap} = D_A - (D_L \times W_L) = 2.70 - \left(1.03 \times \frac{95}{100}\right) = 1.72 \text{ years}$$

To estimate what will happen if interest rates change, the bank manager uses the duration gap calculation to obtain the change in the market value of net worth as a percentage of total assets. In other words, the change in the market value of net worth as a percentage of assets is calculated as

$$\frac{\Delta NW}{A} \approx -\text{Duration Gap} \times \frac{\Delta i}{1+i}$$

By using the above formula, it is easy to calculate any change in the market value of net worth as a percentage of assets if interest rate changes. Assuming interest rate increase from 10% to 11, let us compute the change in net worth.

A rise in interest rates from 10% to 11% would lead to a change in the market value of net worth as a percentage of assets of –1.6%:

$$\frac{\Delta NW}{A} \approx -\text{Duration Gap} \times \frac{\Delta i}{1+i}$$

where,

Duration Gap = 1.72
Δi = Change in interest rate (0.11 – 0.10) = 0.01
i = interest rate = 0.10

$$\frac{\Delta NW}{A} = -1.72 \times \frac{0.01}{1+0.10} = -0.016 = -1.6\%$$

With assets totalling $100 million, it indicates a fall in the market value of net worth of $1.6 million, which is the same figure as computed before.

Exhibit 16.1 Defensive and Aggressive Duration Gap Management

- If you think interest rates will decrease in the future, a positive duration gap is desirable—as rates decline, asset values will increase more than liability values increase (a positive equity effect).
- If you predict an increase in interest rates, a negative duration gap is desirable—as rates rise, asset values will decline less than the decline in liability values (a positive equity effect).
- Of course, zero gap protects equity from the valuation effects of interest rate changes—defensive management.
- Aggressive management adjusts duration gap in anticipation of interest rate movements.

16.6.1 Problems with Duration Gap

Duration gap management is overly aggressive management that 'bets the bank'. This happened to First Pennsylvania Corp. in the late 1970s. With rates high at the end of an expansion, it bought long-term securities with short-term borrowed funds (negative dollar gap, positive duration gap). However, instead of rates falling, they shot up further, causing both negative NIMs and losses on equity leading to bankruptcy. Moral: don't bet the bank on interest rates!

Any duration analysis assumes that the yield curve is flat, and shifts in the level of interest rates imply parallel shifts of the yield curve. In reality, the yield curve is seldom flat, and short-term and long-term interest rates have different volatilities or shifts over time.

Average durations of assets and liabilities drift or change over time and not at the same rates. At one point, the duration gap may be 2.0, but one year later it may be only 0.5. Some experts advise rebalancing to keep the duration gap in a target range over time.

16.7 Risk Management Strategy

There are three fundamental ways of managing risk: insurance, asset/liability management and hedging. We discuss these here.

a. *Insurance* is available against some risks (but not, generally, against price risks). However, other cheaper alternatives to insurance are usually available. This is because insurance companies have to return a profit after taking into account things like moral hazard and adverse selection, which steeply raise their costs.
b. *On-balance sheet asset/liability management:* In this method, the firm has to hold the right combination of on-balance sheet assets and on-balance sheet liabilities, based on the principle of immunization. Immunization was proposed by F.M. Redington in the early 1950s. To immunize risk, one has to select assets so that not only the present value, but also their duration equals those of the liabilities, such that:

$$\text{Duration of assets} \times \text{Market value of assets} = \text{Duration of liabilities} \times \text{Market value of liabilities}$$

There is a problem associated with immunization. As prices change, the same process of asset/liability adjustment has again to be carried out, which can prove extremely expensive, especially during periods of extremely volatile interest rates. Further, hedges often do much better. Apart from immunization, some price risks, such as foreign exchange exposure resulting from overseas competition, can also be managed by directly borrowing in the competitor's currency or by moving production abroad. These are also on-balance sheet, but, in general, these are costly solutions.
c. *Off-balance sheet hedging:* In hedging, ideally, there have to be two investments (say, A and B) that are perfectly correlated; one takes a temporary position by buying one and selling the other, so that the net position is absolutely safe. Though similar in some ways to asset/liability management, hedging is primarily off-balance sheet. Sometimes, however, a hedge can take the form of an on-balance sheet position (Marshall and Bansal 1992b). The following equation holds:

$$\text{Expected change in value of A} = a + \Delta \text{ Change in value of B}$$

Here, Δ measures the sensitivity of changes in A to changes in the value of B, and is called the hedge ratio. The view that states that ideally Δ should equal 1 is now viewed unfavourably and is called the naive view. However, Johnson (1960) and Stein (1961) took a portfolio approach to hedging. In the case of futures, for example, the goal of hedging, they felt, should be to minimize the variance of the profit associated with the combined cash and futures position. Ederington extended this approach further in

1979. In the Johnson/Stein/Ederington (JSE) method, the spot price is regressed against the futures price using an ordinary least-squares regression. The risk minimizing or the minimum variance hedge ratio is then given by the slope of the regression line (Marshall and Bansal 1992b).

Example 4: Consider a bank with the following balance sheet:

Assets	*Value*	*Duration of the Asset*	*Liabilities*	*Value*	*Duration of the Liability*
Cash	200	0	5-year loan (LIBOR + 0.1%)	750	1.5
3-year loan (7%)	1,000	2.20	5-year loan (6%)	150	3
7-year loan (8%)	800	4	7-year loan (8%)	300	6

Solution 4

Asset side:

The total value of assets, as you can see, is \$200 + \$1,000 + \$800 = \$2,000.

- Duration of a financial security is the extent of its exposure to interest rate risk. For example, the duration of the 3-year loan at 7% in this example is 2.20. This means that if interest rates go up by 1%, the value of this loan, which is \$1,000 now, will go down by 2.20%. Of course, if interest rates go down by 1%, then the value of this loan will go up by 1%.
- Duration of the total assets is just the weighted average of the component durations on the asset side.
- Duration of assets = D_A= (200/2,000) × 0 + (1,000/2000) × 2.20 + (800/2,000) × 4 = 2.7.
- This means that the total value of the assets will go 'down' by 2.7% if interest rates go 'up' by 1%. Remember again that duration is a measure of interest rate risk. It tells us the sensitivity of the value of an asset or portfolio to changes in interest rates. Also, note that cash always has zero duration.

Liability side:

- Total value of liabilities, as you can see, is \$750 + \$150 + \$300 = \$1,200.
- Duration of the total liabilities is again just the weighted average of the component durations on the liability side.
- Duration of total liabilities = D_L = (750/1,200) × 1.5 + (150/1,200) × 3 + (300/1,200) × 6 = 2.8125.
- This means that the total value of the liabilities will go 'down' by 2.8125% if interest rates go 'up' by 1%.

Now, what is the 'complete' situation here in terms of interest rate risk? Recall that D_A= 2.7; therefore, the total value of the assets will go down by 2.7% if interest rates go down by 1%. However, D_L = 2.8125; therefore, the total value of the liabilities will down by 2.8125% if interest rates go up by 1%. In other words, the bank's net worth (assets minus liabilities) may be exposed to a loss in case interest rates go up, because if that happens, value of assets may decrease more than the value of liabilities. To check whether this is the case in our example, we quantify this interest rate risk exposure as follows:

Duration Gap = D_A – (total liabilities/total assets) × D_L
= 2.7 – (1,200/2,000) × 2.8125
=1.0125

Since duration gap is positive, this means the bank's net worth (assets minus liabilities) will suffer if interest rates go up. In our case, duration gap is 1.0125. This says that if interest rates go up by 1%, then the net worth of the bank's balance sheet (which is now \$2,000 – \$1,200 = \$800) will go down by 1.0125%.

Immunization

Now, we will discuss how we can immunize this interest rate risk. This practice of interest rate risk management is called duration matching. The purpose of duration matching, which is a hedging method, is to decrease the duration gap to zero, because if the duration gap is zero, then this means that the net worth of the balance sheet is immune to changes in interest rate, that is, the net worth (value of assets minus the value of liabilities) do not change if interest rate changes. (It becomes immune.) To see how one can achieve this, consider the duration gap equation again:

$$\text{Duration Gap} = D_A - (\text{total liabilities/total assets}) \times D_L$$

At the moment, this is positive, it is equal to 1.0125 and we want to decrease it to zero. We can concentrate on the liability side and increase the duration of liability side just enough to make the duration gap zero.

Now, look at the floating-rate loan on the liability side, that is a five-year loan at Libor +0.1%. The face value of this loan is \$750. Suppose you swap part of this loan in exchange of paying a fixed interest rate of 7.25%. Since this is a liability, you are at the moment paying Libor +0.1% on a value of \$750 over the course of next five years. Say, you swap \$x out of this \$750, that is, the other party pays you Libor +0.1% over the notional principal of \$x (i.e., she assumes your liability) and you pay her a fixed rate of 7.25% over the next five years. After this swap, your liability side will look as follows:

Liabilities	***Value***	***Duration of the Liability***
5-year loan (LIBOR + 0.1%)	750 – X	1.5
5-year loan (7.25%)	X	4.3
7-year loan (8%)	300	6
5-year loan (6%)	150	3

All we have to decide now is the value of X such that duration gap is zero with a target D_L of 4.5 so that 60% (1,200/2,000) of this become 2.7, resulting a zero duration gap. Now, it can be easily computed by solving the following equation for X:

$$\left[\frac{750-X}{1{,}200}\times 1.5\right]+\left[\frac{X}{1{,}200}\times 4.3\right]+\left[\frac{300}{1{,}200}\times 6\right]+\left[\frac{150}{1{,}200}\times 3\right]=4.5$$

16.8 Hedging and Financial Engineering

Financial engineering has been defined as 'the design, the development, and the implementation of innovative financial instruments and processes, and the formulation of creative solutions to problems in finance'. This is a very broad definition, but the primary objective of financial engineering is to meet the needs of risk management. Financial engineering takes a building-block approach to the building of new instruments. This approach was first demonstrated by Black and Scholes (1973) in considering a call option as a continuously adjusting portfolio of two securities:

1. Forward contracts on the underlying asset
2. Riskless securities

Most of the hedges can be constructed from futures, forwards, options and swaps, which are now known as the building-blocks of financial engineering. By combining forwards, options, futures and swaps, with the underlying cash position, a firm's risk exposure can be manipulated in a practically infinite variety of ways.

16.9 Building-blocks of Financial Engineering

The building-block approach first was suggested by Smithson (1987) for financial engineering and products. According to this approach, the instruments are less different than first they meet the eye, and complicated-looking instruments can be broken down into just a few simpler instruments, while even the simpler instruments can be broken down into small basic components. The building-block includes some physical tools that are used for engineering purpose. The physical tools of financial engineering include the instruments and the processes that can be pieced together to accomplish some specific purposes. The processes include different trading mechanisms and techniques, such things as electronic securities trading, public offering, private placements of securities, self-registration, electronic fund transfer and any other innovative methods or different requirements to reduce the cost of transaction or risks or any other problems existing in the trade processes. At a very broad level, the basic instruments are cash market instruments and derivatives.

16.9.1 Cash Market Instruments

Cash market instruments include debt market instruments like fixed income securities and equity and equity-related securities. Cash market is characterized by the delivering of traded asset, either immediately or shortly thereafter. Payment is usually made immediately, although credit arrangements are sometimes used.

16.9.2 Derivatives

Derivatives are financial contracts whose values depend on the value of some underlying assets or references. They serve valuable purposes in providing a mean of risk management, speculation, arbitrage and efficient portfolio adjustment. Derivatives can be in different forms varying from plain vanilla to exotics. The four most basic types of derivatives stand out: forward contracts, futures contracts, swaps and options. Typical forward, futures and swap contracts are self-financing or zero-cost instruments.

Futures Contracts

In futures contracts, the sale and purchase of a specified asset at some specified future date is contractually agreed to at a price determined now. The buyer places a small initial margin, usually tendered in T-bills or other forms of security, with the broker. Essentially, therefore, a position can be taken without investment in the futures market, and they are therefore off-balance sheet transactions. Changes in the contract price are settled daily, with each trader marking his position to market. If the margin falls below a point, a margin call is made on the buyer. This process by and large eliminates credit risk. Whereas a few major instances of default have occurred, for example, the default of silver contracts by Hunt Brothers, it is true that, in general, there is an extremely low default rate in futures. Finally, at the time of delivery, the buyer receives (wherever feasible) the asset that was purchased, by paying the contract price.

Futures can be used to hedge against commodity price risk, interest rate risk and exchange rate risk. The main types of futures are commodities futures, financial futures and futures on indices. The first organized commodity futures market was the Chicago Board of Trade (CBT), established in 1848. The first financial futures contract was introduced on 20 October 1975, by the CBT. Financial futures markets are now much larger than traditional commodity futures markets.

Financial futures are used primarily to trade interest rate risk. The markets for financial futures are very liquid, and, of course, there is no cost of storage. Most financial futures contracts fall into three categories:

a. *Interest rate futures:* These include futures on interest-bearing instruments such as T-bills, T-notes, T-bonds, certificates of deposit, Eurodollars and so on. These are a popular and useful method of hedging interest rate risk. These contracts enable borrowers to lock in interest rates for some future period.

b. *Foreign currency futures:* These are available in all major currencies and are used for hedging foreign exchange risk.

c. *Share price index futures:* The first of these was introduced in the United States only in 1982. They are traded on the Standard and Poor's 500 Index, the New York Stock Exchange Composite Index and the Value Line Index. These are obviously non-deliverable. Instead, these are settled in cash by marking to the market 'at the closing value of the respective underlying spot stock market index on the last trading day'.

Forward Contracts

These are similar to futures. Here, the owner of the forward contract is obliged to buy a specified asset on a specified date at the exercise price specified in the contract. No payment is made at any time at the commencement or during the term of the contract, making it an off-balance sheet instrument. Forwards seem to have a flaw. 'Whichever way the price of the deliverable instrument moves, one party has an incentive to default. There are many cases where defaults have occurred in the real world'. Therefore, forward contracts usually involve counterparties who have prior knowledge of each other.

Though the oldest among financial instruments hedging risk, forward markets continue to thrive in spite of the subsequent emergence of futures markets, which are very similar to futures in many ways, because of different clienteles and other reasons. First, forward contracts are tailored to fit the needs of the customer. Second, futures do not exist for all commodities and on all financials. Third, there is a difference in accounting treatment between futures and forwards in some countries. And, lastly, there is the likelihood of a possible mismatch between the length of the hedger's hedging horizon and the maturity date of the futures. Forwards take care of this.

The forward markets in currencies are the most highly developed of all the forwards markets. Large banks buy and sell forward currency, usually for periods up to one year ahead. In the case of the major currencies, forward contracts of up to five years or more are now common.

Swaps

The term 'swap agreement' covers a range of transactions 'where two or more entities exchange or swap cash flows in the same or in two or several different currencies and/or interest rate bases for a predetermined length of time'. Swaps are used primarily to hedge against interest rate and foreign exchange risks. The first currency swap was introduced in 1976, and interest rate swap only in 1981. However, in spite of this, swap markets now overwhelm any other financial innovation by the sheer volume of transactions. A survey undertaken by the Federal Reserve Bank of the United States in 1989 showed that 64% of all interbank foreign exchange transactions were spot transactions, a massive 27% were swap transactions and only 4.2% were forward transactions. Interest rate swaps now dominate the market for swaps. In this type of swap, the two different interest rates determine the cash flows.

Swap financing transactions can be classified into four. The first category is the parallel or back-to-back loans. The second is swap transactions, comprising, inter alia, of currency swaps, currency coupon swaps, interest rate swaps, basis rate swaps, commodity swaps, swaps with timing mismatches, swaps with option-like payoffs (swaptions, also called contingent swaps or option swaps), deferred swaps, forward swaps, circus swaps, principal-only swaps, amortizing swaps, zero coupon swaps and long-dated or long-term foreign exchange contracts. The third category is the forward rate agreements (FRAs), and lastly we have the caps, collars and floors.

Options

In an options contract, 'one party has the right, but not the obligation, to do something—usually to buy or sell some underlying asset'. Of course, the seller of the options contract has an absolute obligation. When the buyer has a right to buy, then it is a call option, and when the right is to sell, it is a put. The price paid for the option is in the form of a flat upfront sum called premium. Options that can be exercised only on the maturity date are called European options, and those that can be exercised at any time are called American options. Most of the traded options are American options.

Trading in call options began on the Chicago Board Options Exchange (CBEO) in April 1973. The paper by Black and Scholes (1973) appeared at about the same time. Thereafter, there has been a phenomenal growth in option trading. Much of this has been fuelled by the standardization of contracts and the consequent lowering in transaction costs. The fundamental use of options is in trading risk in an asymmetric manner.

Apart from single-period options such as calls and puts, there are many others. Multiperiod options—which include interest rate caps, interest rate floors and interest rate collars—are important because they are easily combined with other instruments, such as swaps, to achieve very specialized solutions to some problems of hedging. Additionally, there are options on caps, called captions, and options on swaps, called swaptions (which are also classified sometimes under swaps). Further, multiperiod currency options have been introduced and multiperiod commodity options are about to be introduced. There are also compound options that are options on options; for example, debt is a compound option to equity holders. Similarly, risky bonds, common stock, leases and life insurance policies can be visualized as compound options.

16.10 Application of Financial Engineering

As mentioned earlier, financial engineering can be applied in a wide varieties of financial operations and strategies, for instance, asset/liability management, tax-driven deals, risk management, arbitrage and speculation, leverage buyout and restructuring, structured finance, portfolio management and so many other cases. But, in general financial engineering may be applied in three major areas:

a. Hedging and risk management
b. Arbitrage and speculation
c. Structured finance

16.10.1 Hedging and Risk Management

In the face of risk, financial engineering can offer two extreme alternatives: First, risk can be replaced with certainty in which adverse and beneficial part are both removed. The second alternative can be replacing adverse risk and leaving the beneficial part alone. In many cases, the eradication of risks is just what is needed, but it is easy to imagine the desire to eliminate only the adverse risk and leaving the beneficial one in place. The second alternative illustrates a perfect hedge that is impossible in practice. Between these two extremes, financial engineering offers an almost unlimited range of possibilities, allowing deals and hedges to be tailored precisely to match individual requirements.

Hedging may be defined as a position taken as a temporary substitute for a later cash position. That is, taking a derivative position opposite to the existing exposure. A hedge is a financial instrument whose sensitivity to a particular financial price offsets the sensitivity of the firm's core business to that price. In the financial markets in recent years, derivatives are playing an important role in the process of decision-making of investors, corporations, and investment funds. The critical importance of using derivatives properly has created a new activity called risk management. Risk management can be considered as the practice of defining the desired level of risk, identifying the firm's current level of risk, and using derivatives or other financial instruments to adjust the actual level of risk to the desired level of risk. Risk management has also started an entirely new industry of financial institutions that offers to take positions in derivatives opposite the end users, which are corporations or investment funds.

16.10.2 Speculation and Arbitrage

The efficient market hypothesis (Fama 1965) maintains that market pressures brought about by intense competition among speculators and arbitragers to exploit information and price discrepancies will ensure that competitive markets are informationally efficient at all times. The question of market efficiency or lack of that in the market is critically important to financial engineers. Much of financial engineering over the last decades has sought to develop new and innovative instruments and strategies to exploit price discrepancy opportunities.

Speculation involves contemplation of the future, formulation of expectation and taking of position in order to profit. Speculators are basically forecasters acting upon their forecasts in where prices are determined by the transaction of supply and demand. Successful speculation depends on the acquisition of superior information and/or the ability to interpret information and its implications better than others. Arbitrage is an activity with a long history and involves two or more simultaneous transactions in different markets in order to take advantage of price discrepancies between them. Unlike speculation, arbitrage profit arises from discrepancy in price relationship.

16.10.3 Structured Finance

Structured finance relates to a group of complex financial instruments and mechanisms that defers a simple universal definition, but, broadly defined, it could be described as referring to the repackaging of cash flows that can transform the risk, return and liquidity characteristics of financial portfolios.

A more straightforward interpretation is provided in BIS (2005), where structured finance is defined as a form of financial intermediation which is based on securitization technology: Structured finance '... involves the pooling of assets and the subsequent sale to investors of claims on the cash flows backed by these pools. Typically, several classes (or tranches) of securities are issued, each with distinct risk-return profiles'. Structured finance denotes the art and science of designing financial products to satisfy the different needs of investors and borrowers as closely as possible. Structured finance encompasses all advanced private and public financial arrangements that serve to efficiently refinance and hedge any profitable economic activity beyond the scope of conventional forms of on-balance sheet securities (debt, bonds and equity) at lower capital cost and agency costs from market impediments and liquidity constraints.

16.11 Application of the Building-block Approach

There are three major methods of actually working on the building-block approach: (a) to look at the risk and payoff profiles, (b) to look at time-line cash flow diagrams and (c) there is the arithmetic approach recently introduced by Donald J. Smith. The boxed cash flow diagrams approach is also sometimes used.

In each of these approaches, the process is essentially the same. First of all, a graphical or mathematical view of the current risk exposure is projected. This picture is overlaid with the cash flows associated with the hedging instruments under consideration. Then, the residual or net cash flows are examined. Ultimately, by varying the delivery months and the strike prices and so on, the risk exposure is manipulated in the desired manner. To facilitate the calculations and analysis, spreadsheets and special software packages are put to use. It is usually possible to achieve the objective using different combinations of hedging instruments. The combination or strategy that is least costly is accepted. The securities resulting from this process are often given special names, or simply called synthetic securities. We look below at some examples of synthetic securities. This list is only illustrative; the actual range of products, as can well be imagined, is almost infinite.

16.11.1 Payoff Profiles Method

In this method, the risk and payoff profiles of the instrument are drawn, and the combinations of some of the simpler instruments can be seen in this way.

i. Synthetic future: A forward/future can be synthesized by 'snapping together' a European call and a European put with the same time to maturity and exercise price.
ii. Swaps with option-like characteristics: Swaps can be constructed to have option-like provisions, which limit the range of outcomes. These include the floating floor-ceiling and the fixed floor-ceiling swaps.

16.11.2 Time-line Cash Flow Method

The time-line cash flow diagrams are very intuitive and easy to grasp. Usually, the direction of the arrows represents the direction of the cash flows; the long arrow denotes the principal and short arrows the exchange of other cash flows. The following examples illustrate this approach:

i. Reverse floater: In a reverse or inverse floater, the coupon payment on an inverse floater decreases as LIBOR increases. It can be synthesized in many ways.
ii. Synthesis of a deep-discount dollar bond.

iii. Synthetic dual currency bond.
iv. A forward swap: This instrument is also called a delayed start swap, and combines forwards with a swap, or two swaps.
v. Foreign-pay zero.

16.11.3 Arithmetic Approach

The notation of the arithmetic approach is illustrated by A = B + C, where A, B and C represent expected cash flows from these securities. The '='sign represents identical cash flows in terms of amount, currency and timing. A '+' indicates a long position and a '–' indicates a short position. The following examples are based on this approach.

i. Synthetic fixed-rate debt: This is given by the following combination. Here, FRN stands for fixed-rate note.

– FRN	=	– Typical FRN	+	Interest Rate Swap	+	Floor
Swap fixed rate + 0.25%		LIBOR + 0.25% (Minimum 5%)		pay fixed, receive LIBOR		4.75%

ii. Asset swaps: In asset swaps, the cash flow characteristics of the underlying asset are changed. If the usual FRN is taken as the asset, then an asset swap could look like this:

+ FRN	=	+ Typical FRN	–	Interest Rate Swap	–	Floor
Swap fixed rate + 0.25%		LIBOR + 0.25% (Minimum 5%)		receive fixed, pay LIBOR		4.75%

iii. Mini–max or 'collared' floater: This is basically a typical FRN with the addition of a maximum coupon rate and is synthesized as follows:

+ Mini–max FRN	=	+ Unrestricted FRN	+	Annuity	–	Cap	+	Floor
LIBOR + 0.5% Minimum 5% Maximum 9%		LIBOR		0.5%		8.5%		4.5%

iv. Inverse floater: Discussed earlier as a reverse floater, this can be synthesized in many ways, one of which is illustrated here:

– Inverse floater	=	– Two FRNs	+	Unrestricted FRN	–	Cap
16%-LIBOR		8%		LIBOR		16%

v. Participation agreement: The outcome of a participation agreement is that the buyer 'has the benefit of a ceiling on LIBOR but makes settlement payments at a constant fraction of the rate differential when LIBOR is below the ceiling'. It is synthesized as follows (where NP is the notional principal, NP* is the given amount of interest rate protection and PR, or the participation rate, is 62.5%):

+	Participation Agreement	=	+	Cap	–	Floor
	10% ceiling (NP = NP*)			10% (NP = NP*)		10% (NP = 0.375 NP*)

16.11.4 Other Examples of Financial Engineering

Some other common examples of the building-block approach to financial engineering are as follows:

i. Synthetic options: Black and Scholes (1973) showed that a call option can be synthesized from forward contracts and riskless securities.
ii. Bonds with embedded options: Bonds with warrants/convertible bonds/callable bonds have options embedded in them. In a convertible bond, the bondholder has the right (but not the obligation) to convert the bond into some specified asset of the issuer. In a callable bond, the issuer has the right (but not the obligation) to call the bond for redemption prior to maturity. Varieties of other types of bonds have also been synthesized, which has given the bondholder an option.
iii. Synthetic futures: These can be built from forward contracts. We can also use an appropriate combination of single-period options to synthesize a futures contract.
iv. Synthetic swaps: Since the payoff profile of swaps is similar to that of a forward contract, they can easily be synthesized from forwards. A swap can also be synthesized from an appropriate strip of futures or from a strip of futures-like option combinations.

16.12 Reasons for Rapid Growth in Financial Engineering

Since the 1950s and 1960s, and particularly in the last decade, the global and financial environment has changed rapidly. In particular, the breakdown of the Bretton Woods agreement in 1972, which ultimately led to floating exchange rates, has led to major increases in volatility and competition. Technology has improved dramatically in this period. Government debt has also increased in most countries. Marshall and Bansal (1992a) has classified the causes of increasing risk into two: environmental and intra-firm. We use this classification here to analyse the reasons why the increase in risk and major developments in finance, taken together, created the right environment for rapid growth in financial engineering.

16.12.1 Environmental Factors

Increase in Price Volatility

Price volatility has three dimensions, including the speed of price change, the frequency of price change and the magnitude of price change. Most markets have experienced increases in the speed, frequency and magnitude of price changes since the mid-1970s. The term 'price' here includes the price of money, foreign exchange, stocks and commodities. The currency floats have meant that the stability of exchange rates is a thing of the past. Interest rates have been very volatile too; for example, in June 1982, AA bonds were yielding 15.3%. In May 1986, the same bonds yielded 8.9% and in April 1989, 10.2% (Brigham and Gapenski 1990). Oil prices are the best example of dramatic commodity price volatility, and the October 1987 stock crash illustrates the volatility in stock prices. There was also a major volatility in overall prices, that is, inflation, over the past three decades. This all-round increase in volatility has led to tremendous increases in the risks that companies face and enhanced the need for hedging the risks.

Globalization of the World Economy and Competition

Globalization has increased the size of markets and competition exposing the modern corporations to significant risks and, in many cases, cutting profit margins. Increased size of markets has led to more use of debt in capital structures and increasing reliance on leverage to enhance returns. Commerce has grown very rapidly in the past two decades.

Deregulation and Increase in Competition

Much of financial engineering activity has been fostered by an atmosphere of deregulation of the industry and encouragement of entrepreneurial experimentation. Deregulation fed competition forced once protected industries to become more efficient or to close down, and thus release their resources to more productive ends. Initially, investment banks were the only ones which could offer various services regarding risk management. Deregulation of the financial markets has brought in new entrants into the financial markets, particularly non-banking financial institutions (NBFIs), who have aggressively competed with the traditional banking sector, by introducing new products and services. In return, banks were forced to come out with innovative ways to compete with NBFIs by taking recourse to off-balance sheet transactions.

Advances in Technology and Communication

Technological advances have motivated a great deal of financial engineering. Many of technological breakthroughs involve the computer, high-speed processors, powerful desktop units, network systems, enhanced methods of data entry and so on. Funds can be transferred from ATMs and telephones now. Computers have entered the field of finance in a big way.

Development of New Markets and Market Linkages

There has been an explosive growth of futures and options exchanges worldwide. Twenty-four-hour trading has become possible on futures and options exchanges across the globe. The Chicago Exchange has developed a computer system on which trade can now be carried out at any time, replacing human activity on the floor.

Dramatic Decline in Information and Transaction Costs

There has been a tremendous decline in transaction costs and spreads, for example, the cost of transacting a share of $100 has declined from $1 in the 1970s to under two cents in the 1990s (Marshall and Bansal 1992b). Computerized databases of financial transactions are available to subscribers. Information asymmetry has considerably declined.

Advances in Financial Theory

Finance, as a formal discipline, is concerned with value and risk, and financial engineering cannot be used effectively without a solid foundation in financial theory. Developments in finance theory have contributed immensely to the development of new hedging techniques.

Perhaps most notable of these are evidenced by the work of Markowitz (1952), who laid the basis for modern portfolio theory, Sharpe (1964), whose CAPM provided a deeper insight into risk, Black and Scholes (1973), whose seminal work on option pricing revolutionized the way in which contingent claims could be valued, and some adopted models to multiperiod interest rate and exchange rate options, introduced in the late 1980s.

Tax Asymmetries

Tax asymmetries exist if two firms are subject to different tax rates, and these are often exploitable by financial engineers. Much financial engineering is inspired by tax asymmetries. Taxes differ across industries and countries, over time. Also, some firms have sufficient tax credits/write-offs, which give them an advantage over other firms. For example, zero-coupon yen bonds were treated liberally in Japan. In the United States, the abolition, in 1984, of the withholdings tax on interest payments to overseas investors in the domestic securities of the United States influenced the growth of interest rate swaps (Das 1989).

Arbitrage Opportunities

The globalization of the financial markets has meant that arbitrage opportunities across different capital markets could be identified and exploited. In theory, exploiting these differentials through arbitrage should eventually lead to their disappearance.

Completing Markets

Often there have been gaps in the financial markets which have been identified and filled up with new kinds of instruments. For example, at one time there were no interest rate forward contracts; interest rate swaps were then designed to fill this gap. Thus, swaps complete markets.

Standardization

There has been an increasing standardization of financial instruments, for example, in futures, options and swaps. This has expanded the market.

Low Documentation Costs

Many of the new financial instruments require little documentation, no prospectus and so on. This has made them attractive to companies.

16.12.2 Intra-firm Factors

Liquidity Needs

Liquidity has many faces and meaning in finance. It is often used to refer to the ease with which an asset can be converted to cash or ability to raise cash in hurry, or the degree to which a security's value will deviate from par as economic conditions change, the degree to which a market can absorb and sales of securities without imposing excessive transaction costs. Companies need liquidity of their 'FCFs'. To make use of funds temporarily not needed, money markets and sweep markets have developed rapidly. The same purpose in the longer term is served by floating-rate notes, adjustable rate preferred stock and so on.

Risk Aversion

Risk aversion is considered a fundamental tenet of financial theory that rational individuals have an aversion to financial risk, meaning that individuals are only willing to bear risk if they are adequately compensated for doing so. Nowadays, there are a wide varieties of innovative instruments capable to limit the risk (e.g., adjustable rate debt, adjustable preferred stock, collateralized mortgage obligation bonds and so on). These products expose their holders to considerably less risks. Besides all these instruments, there has been introduction of very efficient risk management instruments like interest rate futures, interest rate options, stock index futures and so many other instruments. The risk aversion of firms to the increasing risks has been an important driving force in motivating innovations.

Agency Costs

Agency cost is another motivating force behind much financial engineering. Many of financial innovations during the 1980s were due, at least in part, to their ability to reduce agency costs. LBOs are a clear example. Securing the capital to make LBOs possible required new forms of financing, inspiring still other innovations, for example, junk bond market. Marshall and Bansal (1992) show how LBOs were motivated by the desire to reduce agency costs. The financing of such activity required new forms of financing, including junk bonds.

Quantitative Sophistication of Management Training

The increase in the quantitative skills possessed by managers has led to a demand for better tools of financial management.

Accounting Objectives

At times, financial innovation has been fuelled by the desire to improve accounting figures.

Many forms of financial innovation, including Eurobonds, Eurodollars, electronic funds transfer and so on, have arisen from these factors. The development of financial engineering is perhaps the most important of the outcomes of the changes discussed above.

16.13 Conclusion

Financial engineering has proved extremely effective in managing the increased financial risk witnessed over the past few decades, and particularly in the last decade. 'It's rare that a day goes by in the financial markets without hearing of at least one new or hybrid product' (Smith 1990). Using a building-block approach, it appears that almost all requirements of risk management can be met by a suitable product. These instruments and their ever-expanding markets also seem to be playing a role in increasing efficiency in capital markets. Cox (1976) has suggested that 'futures trading increases market information and thereby increases the efficiency of spot prices'. By 'efficiency' he meant that spot prices provide more accurate signals for resource allocation when the given commodity has a futures market. In summation, we note that financial engineering as a major discipline within finance is playing an important role and has come to stay.

Multiple Choice Questions

1. Which one of the following risk is attributable or specific to the individual investment or small group of investments?
   a. Systematic   b. Unsystematic   c. Both   d. None

2. Systematic risk is not caused by _______
   a. Currency fluctuation
   b. Changes in interest rates
   c. Accidents
   d. Inflation

3. Which one of the following is a type of unsystematic risk?
   a. Currency   b. Political   c. Liquidity   d. Credit

4. To understand the impact of interest rate risk on the market value of equity, which one of the following analysis is conducted?
   a. Gap analysis
   b. Duration analysis
   c. Net interest income
   d. None

5. To understand the impact of interest rate risk on profitability, which one of the following analysis is conducted?
   a. Gap analysis
   b. Duration analysis
   c. Net interest income
   d. None

6. Duration analysis is based on the formula _______
   a. Interest income – Interest expense
   b. Market value of assets – Market value of liabilities
   c. Market value of assets – Market value of equity
   d. None

7. Which one of the following scenario would protect bank profits from changes in interest rates?
   a. RSA > RSL   b. RSA = RSL   c. RSA < RSL   d. None

8. Which one of the following formula results gap ratio?
   a. GAP × DR   b GAP × DRi   d. CGAP/assets   d. None

9. Which one of the following is not an assumption of duration gap analysis?
   a. The duration of assets and liabilities must be known precisely.
   b. Convexity is not expected to influence valuation.
   c. The change in interest rates can only be a parallel shift.
   d. Term structure of interest rate is volatile.

10. Financial engineering may be applied in _______
    a. Hedging and risk management
    b. Structured finance
    c. Arbitrage and speculation
    d. All of the above

Review Questions

1. Define financial engineering. What is the scope of financial engineering?
2. What is financial risk? Identify different types of systematic and unsystematic risks a firm is exposed to.
3. Write a critical note on principles of risk management.
4. Define gap analysis. How gap analysis is used to reduce firm's exposure to interest rate risk?
5. What is duration gap analysis? How the effect of interest rate change on market value of equity is being computed under duration gap analysis?
6. What are the different types of risk management strategy? How immunization is used as a strategy to manage risk?
7. Explain the building-blocks of financial engineering with reference to cash market instruments and derivatives.
8. What are the areas of applying financial engineering?
9. Identify the areas of applying building-block approach. Explain the arithmetic approach in detail.
10. What are the reasons for rapid growth in financial engineering?
11. Which of the following assets or liabilities fit the one-year rate or re-pricing sensitivity test?

    a. 91-day U.S. Treasury bills
    b. 1-year U.S. Treasury notes
    c. 20-year U.S. Treasury bonds
    d. 20-year floating-rate corporate bonds with annual re-pricing
    e. 30-year floating-rate mortgages with re-pricing every two years
    f. 30-year floating-rate mortgages with re-pricing every six months
    g. Overnight fed funds
    h. 9-month fixed-rate CDs
    i. 1-year fixed-rate CDs
    j. 5-year floating-rate CDs with annual re-pricing
    k. Common stock

Exercises

1. Consider a bank with the following balance sheet:

Assets	***Value***	***Duration of the Asset***	***Liabilities***	***Value***	***Duration of the Liability***
Cash	$1,500	0	5yr loan at Libor	$2,000	2
3-year loan at 6%	$3,000	3	4yr loan at 6%	$1,000	3
5-year loan at 8%	$3,000	4	5yr loan at 6%	$2,000	4.9

   a. Find the duration of the asset side. If interest rate goes up by 1%, what will happen to the total value of the assets? Find the duration of the liability side. If interest rate goes up by 1%, what will happen to the total value of the liabilities?
   b. Find the duration gap. If interest rate goes up by 1%, what will happen to the net worth of the bank's balance sheet?

c. Suppose the portfolio manager wants to reduce the duration gap to zero and thus immunize all interest rate risk. For that purpose he wants to swap $X of the 5-year loan at Libor with a 5-year loan at 8% fixed rate. The duration of the fixed-rate 5-year loan at 8% is 4.5. What is the size $X of the swap such that duration gap becomes zero?

2. Consider a bank with the following balance sheet:

Assets	***Value***	***Duration of the Asset***	***Liabilities***	***Value***	***Duration of the Liability***
Cash	$3,000	0	4yr loan at Libor	$1,000	1
6-year loan at 5%	$1,500	5.3	4yr loan at 5%	$1,000	3
5-year loan at 6%	$1,500	4.2	5yr loan at 6%	$2,000	4

a. Find the duration gap. If interest rate goes up by 1%, what will happen to the net worth of the bank's balance sheet?
b. Suppose the portfolio manager wants to reduce the duration gap to zero and thus immunize all interest rate risk. For that purpose, he wants to swap $X of the 4-year loan at Libor with a 4-year loan at 7% fixed rate. The duration of the fixed-rate 4-year loan at 7% is 3.5. What is the size of the swap $X so that duration gap becomes 0?

3. Nearby Bank has the following balance sheet (in millions):

Assets		***Liabilities and Equity***	
Cash	$60	Demand deposits	$140
5-year treasury notes	60	1-year certificates of deposit	160
30-year mortgages	200	Equity	20
Total assets	$320	Total liabilities and equity	$320

What is the maturity gap for Nearby Bank? Is Nearby Bank more exposed to an increase or decrease in interest rates? Explain why?

4. Prime Bank has the following market value balance sheet (in millions, annual rates):

Assets		***Liabilities and Equity***	
Cash	$20	Demand deposits	$100
15-year commercial loan at 10% interest, balloon payment	160	5-year CDs at 6% interest, balloon payment	210
30-year mortgages at 8%		20-year debentures at 7% interest	120
interest, monthly amortizing	300	Equity	50
Total assets	$480	Total liabilities and equity	$480

a. What is the maturity gap for Prime Bank?
b. What will be the maturity gap if the interest rates on all assets and liabilities increase by 1%?
c. What will happen to the market value of the equity?
d. If interest rates increased by 2%, would the bank be solvent?

5. NRB Commercial Bank has $20 million in cash and a $180 million loan portfolio. The assets are funded with demand deposits of $18 million, a $162 million CD and $20 million in equity. The loan portfolio has a maturity of two years, earns interest at the annual rate of 7%, and is amortized monthly. The bank pays 7% annual interest on the CD, but the interest will not be paid until the CD matures at the end of two years.
   a. What is the maturity gap for NRB Commercial Bank?
   b. Is NRB Commercial Bank immunized or protected against changes in interest rates? Why or why not?
   c. Does NRB Commercial Bank face interest rate risk? That is, if market interest rates increase or decrease 1%, what happens to the value of the equity?
   d. How can a decrease in interest rates create interest rate risk?
6. Phoenix Insurance has reported the following balance sheet (in thousands):

Assets		***Liabilities and Equity***	
2-year Treasury note	$175	1-year commercial paper	$135
15-year munis	165	5-year note	160
		Equity	45
Total assets	$340	Total liabilities and equity	$340

   All securities are selling at par equal to book value. The two-year notes are yielding 5%, and the 15-year munis are yielding 9%. The one-year commercial paper pays 4.5%, and the five-year notes pay 8%. All instruments pay interest annually.
   a. What is the weighted-average maturity of the assets for Phoenix?
   b. What is the weighted-average maturity of the liabilities for Phoenix?
   c. What is the maturity gap for Phoenix?
   d. What does your answer to part (c) imply about the interest rate exposure of Phoenix Insurance?
   e. Calculate the values of all four securities of Phoenix Insurance's balance sheet assuming that all interest rates increase 2%. What is the dollar change in the total asset and total liability values? What is the percentage change in these values?
   f. What is the dollar impact on the market value of equity for Phoenix? What is the percentage change in the value of the equity?
   g. What would be the impact on Phoenix's market value of equity if the liabilities paid interest semi-annually instead of annually?
7. Farmers Bank has a very simple balance sheet. Assets consist of a two-year, $1 million loan that pays an interest rate of LIBOR plus 4% annually. The loan is funded with a two-year deposit on which the bank pays LIBOR plus 3.5% interest annually. LIBOR currently is 4%, and both the loan and deposit principal will be paid at maturity.
   a. What is the maturity gap of this balance sheet?
   b. What is the expected NII in years 1 and 2?
   c. Immediately prior to the beginning of year 2, LIBOR rates increased to 6%. What is the expected NII in year 2? What would be the effect on NII of a 2% decrease in LIBOR?
   d. How would your results be affected if the interest payments on the loan were received semi-annually?
   e. What implications do these results have on the effectiveness of the maturity model as an immunization strategy?

References

BIS (Bank for International Settlements). 2005. 'The Role of Ratings in Structured Finance: Issues and Implications'. Report submitted by a working group established by the Committee on the Global Financial System.

Black, F., and M. Scholes. 1973. 'The Pricing of Options and Corporate Liabilities'. *The Journal of Political Economy*, 81(3): 637–654.

Brigham, E.F, and L.C. Gapenski. 1990. *Intermediate Financial Management.* 3rd ed. Chicago, IL: The Dryden Press.

Cox, C.C. 1976. 'Futures Trading and Market Information'. *Journal of Political Economy*, 84: 1215–37.

Das, Satyajit. 1989. *Swap Financing.* Melbourne: The Law Book Company Ltd.

Dixon, Hugo. 2015. 'Financial Engineering to Athens's Rescue'. *The New York Times*, 14 June. Available at http://www.nytimes.com/2015/06/15/business/international/financial-engineering-to-athenss-rescue.html?_r=0

Eales, B. 2000. *Financial Engineering.* New York: St. Martin's Press.

Ederington, L. 1979. 'The Hedging Performance of the New Futures Markets'. *Journal of Finance, 34*: 157–170.

Fama, E.F. 1965. 'The Behavior of Stock-Market Prices'. *The Journal of Business*, 38(1): 34–105.

Finnerty, J. 1988. 'Financial Engineering in Corporate Finance: An Overview'. *Financial Management*, 17, 14–33.

Johnson, L. 1960. 'The Theory of Hedging and Speculation in Commodity Futures'. *Review of Economic Studies, 27*, 139–151.

Macaulay, F. 1938. *Some Theoretical Problems Suggested by the Movement of Interest*

Rates, Bond Yields, and Stock Prices in the United States since 1856. New York: National Bureau of Economic Research.

Markowitz, H. 1952. 'Portfolio Selection'. *The Journal of Finance*, 7(1): 77–91.

Marshall, John F., and Vipul K. Bansal. 1992a. *Financial Engineering: A Complete Guide to Financial Innovation.* New York: New York Institute of Finance.

———. 1992b. *Financial Engineering.* Needham Heights, MA: Allyn and Bacon.

Putnam, B. 1986. 'Managing Interest Rate Risk: An Introduction to Financial Futures and Options' in J.M. Stern and D.H. Chew, Jr. (eds.) *The Revolution in Corporate Finance.* Oxford: Basil Blackwell.

Shapiro, A. and S. Titman. 1986. 'An Integrated Approach to Corporate Risk Management' in J.M. Stern, and D.H. Chew Jr. (eds.) *The Revolution in Corporate Finance.* Oxford: Basil Blackwell.

Sharpe, W. 1964. 'Capital Asset Prices: A Theory of Market Equilibrium under Conditions of Risk', *Journal of Finance, 19*: 425–442.

Smith, Donald J. 1989. 'The Arithmetic of Financial Engineering'. *Journal of Applied Corporate Finance*, 1(4): 49–58.

Smithson, C.W. 1987. 'The LEGO Approach to Financial Engineering'. *Midland Corporate Finance Journal*, 4(4): 16–28.

Stein, J. 1961. 'The Simultaneous Determination of Spot and Futures Prices'. *American Economic Review, 51*: 1012–1025.

Smith, Clifford W., Jr., Charles W. Smithson, and D.S. Wilford. 1990. 'Managing Financial Risk' in *The Handbook of Financial Engineering.* New York: Harper Business Books.

Chapter

17

Option Pricing

Chapter Objectives

On completion of this chapter, you will be able to understand:

- Call and put options
- Payoffs at expiration
- Options pricing: The basics of pricing
- Determinants of option value
- American versus European options
- Intrinsic value and time value
- Option premiums and theoretical value
- Option pricing models
- Binomial model
- Black–Scholes model
- Put–call parity
- Profit and loss diagrams
- Options pricing: The Greeks

Black–Scholes: Robert Merton on the Options Pricing Model

Scholes's and Black's insight, which was a critical insight, was that hedging an option removes its systematic risk. At first I said, 'That's impossible.' But I looked into it. I went back to them and said, 'You guys are absolutely right, but for the wrong reason.' The hedge removes *all* risk. There are two derivations of the formula: theirs and mine. They were nice enough to include mine in their paper. They put in a single footnote that said basically, 'Bob Merton gave this to us.' Black, to the end of his life, thought their solution was more elegant. But the replication system, the one I came up with, has caught on. Later I named the model the Black–Scholes model, in an appendix to a Samuelson paper. It seems a little pretentious to name something in your own name.

An option is essentially financial insurance. It's the right but not the obligation to take some kind of action in the future, like to buy or sell an asset. Holding an option can be very valuable. The theory describes not just the price of an option but what a low-cost intermediary or institution could manufacture the options for. It's kind of a production theory for finance instruments. I can come up with a completely new instrument and calculate what it should be worth. That had an important effect on the speed of innovation. Black–Scholes filled a need. In the 1970s we had stagflation; we had Bretton Woods coming apart, currencies bouncing around, OPEC. It was, 'Oh, my God!' The stock market fell 50% in real [inflation-adjusted] terms in 18 months.

In the old options market, dealers ran ads in the newspaper with teasers, with posted prices for something that should change value by the minute. Can you imagine posting prices in the newspaper? It's just bizarre. There were the damnedest kinds of things being used to price options—cube-root rules and stuff that came out of thin air.

Source: Merton (2014).

17.1 Introduction

Options are derivative contracts that give the holder the right, but not the obligation, to buy or sell the underlying asset at a specified price (called a strike price or an exercise price) on or before a specified future date. Although the holder (also called the buyer) of the option is not obligated to exercise the option, the option writer (known as the seller) has an obligation to buy or sell the underlying asset if the option is exercised. Options are side bets between investors concerning the future price level of an underlying asset relative to a fixed benchmark. As they are created when two investors take opposite sides of the 'bet,' they are in zero net supply. There are two types of options—call options and put options.

17.2 Call and Put Options

A call option gives the buyer of the option the right to buy the underlying asset at a fixed price, called the strike or the exercise price, any time prior to the expiration date of the option: The buyer pays a price for this right. If at expiration, the value of the asset is less than the strike price, the option is not exercised and expires worthless. If, on the other hand, the value of the asset is greater than the strike price, the option is exercised—the buyer of the option buys the stock at the exercise price and the difference between the asset value and the exercise price comprises the gross profit on the investment. The net profit on the investment is the difference between the gross profit and the price paid for the call initially. A payoff diagram illustrates the cash payoff on an option at expiration. For a call, the net payoff is negative (and equal to the price paid for the call) if the value of the underlying asset is less than the strike price. If the price of the underlying asset exceeds the strike price, the gross payoff is the difference between the value of the underlying asset and the strike price, and the net payoff is the difference between the gross payoff and the price of the call. This is illustrated in Figure 17.1.

Figure 17.1 Payoff on Call Option

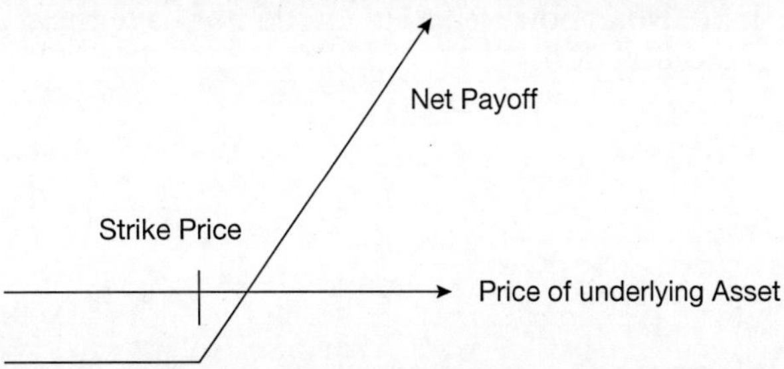

A put option gives the buyer of the option the right to sell the underlying asset at a fixed price, again called the strike or exercise price, at any time prior to the expiration date of the option. The buyer pays a price for this right. If the price of the underlying asset is greater than the strike price, the option will not be exercised and will expire worthless. If, on the other hand, the price of the underlying asset is less than the strike price, the owner of the put option will exercise the option and sell the stock at the strike price, claiming the difference between the strike price and the market value of the asset as the gross profit—again, netting out the initial cost paid for the put yields the net profit from the transaction. A put has a negative net payoff if the value of the underlying asset exceeds the strike price, and has a gross payoff equal to the difference between the strike price and the value of the underlying asset if the asset value is less than the strike price. This is summarized in Figure 17.2.

Figure 17.2 Payoff on Put Option

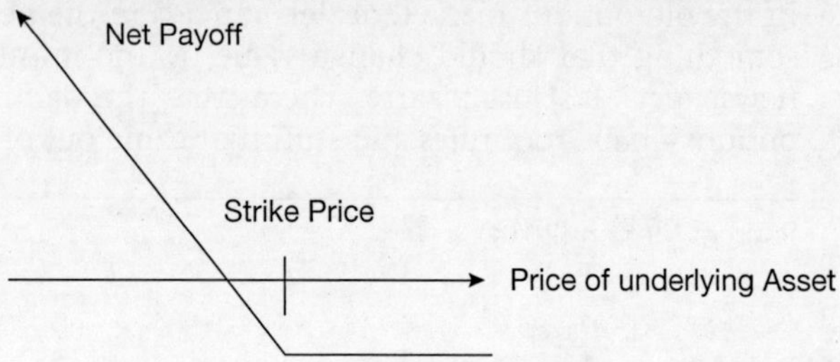

17.3 Payoffs at Expiration

A call option has value to its owner at expiration (T) only if the price of the underlying asset (S_T) is above the strike price (k). Thus, buying a call is a bet on price and will end up above this benchmark. If it is, the payoff on the call is $S_T - k$; if not, the payoff is not $S_T - k$ (which is negative if $S_T < k$) but rather 0 (because the owner has a choice, an option). The owner of the option simply lets it expire unexercised when the exercise value would be negative. Note that the buyer of an option purchases a choice (right), the seller of an option incurs an obligation. We write the payoff of the call option as:

$$c_T = \begin{cases} s_T - k & \text{if} \quad s_T \geq k \quad \text{(in the money)} \\ 0 & \text{if} \quad s_T < k \quad \text{(out of the money)} \end{cases}$$

or

$$c_T = \text{Max}(S_T - k, 0)$$

Once again, the owner of a call option benefits if the price of the underlying asset ends up above the strike price at the expiration of the option.

Graphically, on the expiration date (Figure 17.3).

The dotted line is the 'profit' of the position which was commonly but incorrectly examined. A put option works in the 'opposite' way (Figure 17.4). It allows you to sell for. So, you (the owner) are interested in (are betting on) states in which the true price is low (lower than). Note, however, that you do not have the same interest in a low price as does the seller of a call option.

$$p_T = \begin{cases} k - s_T & \text{if} \quad s_T \leq k \\ 0 & \text{if} \quad s_T > k \end{cases}$$

Or

$$p_T = \text{Max}(k - S_T, 0)$$

Figure 17.3 Payoff Diagrams: Call Option

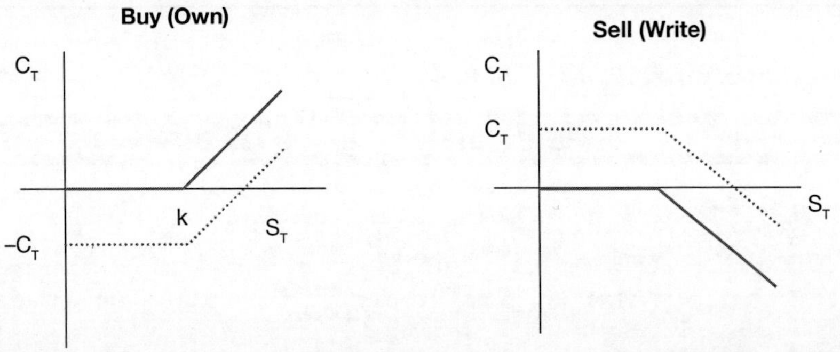

Figure 17.4 Payoff Diagrams: Put Option

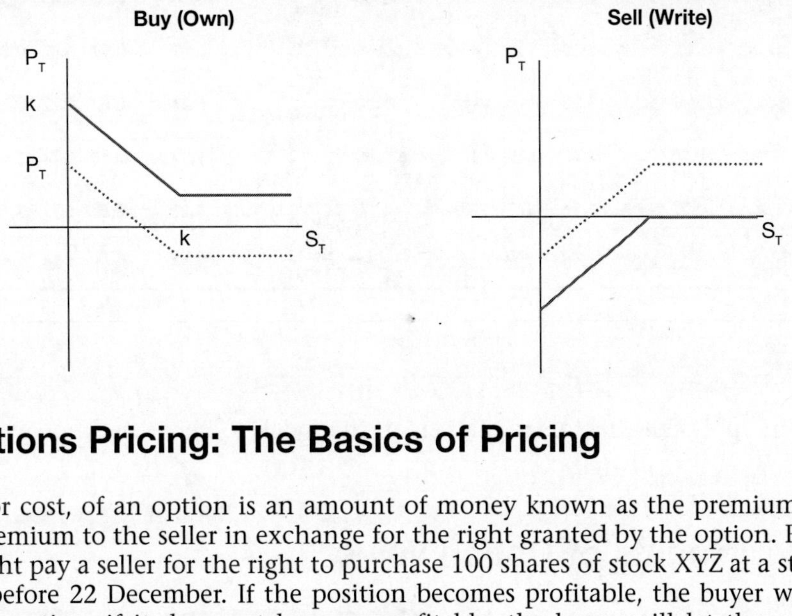

17.4 Options Pricing: The Basics of Pricing

The price, or cost, of an option is an amount of money known as the premium. The buyer pays this premium to the seller in exchange for the right granted by the option. For example, a buyer might pay a seller for the right to purchase 100 shares of stock XYZ at a strike price of \$60 on or before 22 December. If the position becomes profitable, the buyer will decide to exercise the option; if it does not become profitable, the buyer will let the option expire worthless. The buyer pays the premium so that he or she has the 'option' or the choice to exercise or allow the option to expire worthless.

Premiums are priced per share. For example, the premium on an IBM option with a strike price of \$205 might be quoted as \$5.50, as shown in Figure 17.5. Since equity option contracts are based on 100 stock shares, this particular contract would cost the buyer \$5.50 × 100, or \$550. The buyer pays the premium whether or not the option is exercised and the premium is non-refundable. The seller gets to keep the premium whether or not the option is exercised.

An option premium is its cost—how much the particular option is worth to the buyer and seller. While supply and demand ultimately determine price, other factors also play a role.

Figure 17.5 Option Chain for the October 2012 IBM Contract

Name	Last	Change		
(IBM) INTERNATIONAL BUSINESS MA	$210.59	0.20(0.10%)	Options Chain	Add to Portfolio

Chain Type: Calls and Puts | Chain Type: All | Expiration: Oct 2012 | View Chain

Calls								Puts						
Contract Name	Last Trade	Change	Bid	Ask	Volume	Interest	Strike Price	Contract Name	Last Trade	Change	Bid	Ask	Volume	Interest
IBM\12J20 \190.0	21.15	0.12	20.55	20.90	15	5,038	190.00	IBM\12V20 \190.0	0.18	-0.03	0.17	0.21	445	8,351
IBM\12J12 \195.0	16.10	0.00	15.25	15.65	5	5	195.00	IBM\12V12 \195.0	0.04	-0.03	0.06	0.05	23	33
IBM\12J20 \195.0	16.50	0.54	15.80	16.05	6	4,11[illegible]	195.00	IBM\12V20 \195.0	0.41	-0.05	0.39	0.42	456	6,514
IBM\12J12 \200.0	10.29	-0.08	10.50	10.70	24	24	200.00	IBM\12V12 \200.0	0.06	-0.05	0.05	0.10	66	123
IBM\12J20 \200.0	11.40	0.10	11.35	11.55	139	4,993	200.00	IBM\12V20 \200.0	0.87	-0.07	0.83	0.88	1,217	6,978
IBM\12J12 \205.0	5.50	-0.57	5.70	5.90	91	118	205.00	IBM\12V12 \205.0	0.28	-0.07	0.22	0.27	313	656
IBM\12J20 \205.0	7.18	-0.15	7.25	7.40	515	7,548	205.00	IBM\12V20 \205.0	1.77	-0.13	1.74	1.80	680	6,524
IBM\12J12 \210.0	1.90	-0.22	1.89	1.99	470	709	210.00	IBM\12V12 \210.0	1.35	-0.30	1.32	1.40	660	630
IBM\12J20 \210.0	4.00	-0.05	4.00	4.10	1,324	14,249	210.00	IBM\12V20 \210.0	3.54	-0.09	3.45	3.55	524	5,373

Source: CBOE.com

Option traders apply these factors to mathematical models to help determine what an option should be worth.

17.5 Determinants of Option Value

The value of an option is determined by a number of variables relating to the underlying asset and financial markets (Table 17.1).

Table 17.1 Six Factors that Affect Option Prices

Sl	*Factors*	*Affects*
1	Underlying price	Intrinsic value
2	Strike price	
3	Time until expiration	Probability of a profitable move
4	Volatility	
5	Interest rates	Cost of money
6	Dividends	Share price adjustment

1. **Price of the Underlying Asset:** Options are assets that derive value from an underlying asset. Consequently, changes in the value of the underlying asset affect the value of the options on that asset. Since calls provide the right

to buy the underlying asset at a fixed price, an increase in the value of the asset will increase the value of the calls. Puts, on the other hand, become less valuable as the value of the asset increase.

2. **Strike Price of Option:** A key characteristic used to describe an option is the strike price. In the case of calls, where the holder acquires the right to buy at a fixed price, the value of the call will decline as the strike price increases. In the case of puts, where the holder has the right to sell at a fixed price, the value will increase as the strike price increases.
3. **Time to Expiration on Option:** Both calls and puts become more valuable as the time to expiration increases. This is because the longer time to expiration provides more time for the value of the underlying asset to move, increasing the value of both types of options. Additionally, in the case of a call, where the buyer has to pay a fixed price at expiration, the present value of this fixed price decreases as the life of the option increases, further increasing the value of the call.
4. **Variance in Value of the Underlying Asset:** The buyer of an option acquires the right to buy or sell the underlying asset at a fixed price. The higher the variance in the value of the underlying asset, the greater the value of the option. This is true for both calls and puts. While it may seem counter-intuitive that an increase in a risk measure (variance) should increase value, options are different from other securities since buyers of options can never lose more than the price they pay for them; in fact, they have the potential to earn significant returns from large price movements.
5. **Riskless Interest Rate Corresponding to Life of Option:** Since the buyer of an option pays the price of the option up front, an opportunity cost is involved. This cost depends upon the level of interest rates and the time to expiration on the option. The riskless interest rate also enters into the valuation of options when the present value of the exercise price is calculated, since the exercise price does not have to be paid (received) until expiration on calls (puts). Increases in the interest rate will increase the value of calls and reduce the value of puts. Table 17.2 summarizes the variables and their predicted effects on call and put prices.
6. **Dividends Paid on the Underlying Asset:** The value of the underlying asset can be expected to decrease if dividend payments are made on the asset during the life of the option. Consequently, the value of a call on the asset is a decreasing function of the size of expected dividend payments, and the value of a put is an increasing function of expected dividend payments. A more intuitive way of thinking about dividend payments, for call options, is as a cost of delaying exercise on in-the-money options. To see why, consider an option on a traded stock. Once a call option is in the money,

Table 17.2 Summary of Variables Affecting Call and Put Prices

Factors	*Effect on*	
	Call Value	*Put Value*
Increase in an underlying asset's value	Increases	Decreases
Increase in strike price	Decreases	Increases
Increase in variance of an underlying asset	Increases	Increases
Increase in time to expiration	Increases	Increases
Increase in interest rates	Increases	Decreases
Increase in dividends paid	Decreases	Increases

exercising the call option will provide the holder with the stock, and entitle him or her to the dividends on the stock in subsequent periods. Failing to exercise the option will mean that these dividends are foregone.

17.6 American Versus European Options

A primary distinction between American and European options is that American options can be exercised at any time prior to their expiration, while European options can be exercised only at expiration. The possibility of early exercise makes American options more valuable than otherwise similar European options; it also makes them more difficult to value. There is one compensating factor that enables the former to be valued using models designed for the latter. In most cases, the time premium associated with the remaining life of an option and transactions costs makes early exercise suboptimal. In other words, the holders of in-the-money options generally gets much more by selling the option to someone else than by exercising the options.

While early exercise is not optimal generally, there are at least two exceptions to this rule. One is a case where the underlying asset pays large dividends, thus reducing the value of the asset, and any call options on that asset. In this case, call options may be exercised just before an ex-dividend date, if the time premium on the options is less than the expected decline in asset value as a consequence of the dividend payment. The other exception arises when an investor holds both the underlying asset and deep in the money puts on that asset at a time when interest rates are high. In this case, the time premium on the put may be less than the potential gain from exercising the put early and earning interest on the exercise price.

17.7 Intrinsic Value and Time Value

The two components of an option premium are the intrinsic value and the time value. The intrinsic value is the difference between the underlying price and the strike price. Specifically, the intrinsic value for a call option is equal to the underlying price minus the strike price; for a put option, the intrinsic value is the strike price minus the underlying price:

$$\text{Intrinsic value (call)} = \text{underlying price} - \text{strike price}$$

$$\text{Intrinsic value (put)} = \text{strike price} - \text{underlying price}$$

By definition, the only options that have intrinsic value are those that are in the money. For calls, in the money refers to options where the exercise (or strike) price is less than the current underlying price. A put option is in the money if its strike price is greater than the current underlying price.

$$\text{In the money (call)} = \text{strike price} < \text{underlying price}$$

$$\text{In the money (put)} = \text{strike price} > \text{underlying price}$$

Any premium that is in excess of the option's intrinsic value is referred to as time value. For example, assume a call option has a total premium of \$9.00 (this means that the buyer pays, and the seller receives, \$9.00 for each share of stock or \$900 for the contract, which is equal to 100 shares). If the option has an intrinsic value of $7.00, its time value would be $2.00 ($9.00 – $7.00 = $2.00).

Time value = premium – intrinsic value

In general, the more time to expiration, the greater will be the time value of the option. It represents the amount of time that the option position has to become more profitable due to a favourable move in the underlying price. In general, investors are willing to pay a higher premium for more time (assuming the different options have the same exercise price), since time increases the likelihood that the position can become profitable. Time value decreases over time and decays to zero at expiration. This phenomenon is known as time decay. An option premium, therefore, is equal to its intrinsic value plus its time value.

Option premium = intrinsic value + time value

17.8 Option Premiums and Theoretical Value

It is important to differentiate between an option premium and its theoretical value. As discussed previously, the option premium is the price the option buyer pays to the seller in order to have the right granted by the option, and it is the money the seller receives in exchange for writing the option.

The theoretical value of an option, on the other hand, is the estimated value of an option—a price generated by means of a model. It is what an option should currently be worth using all the known inputs, such as the underlying price, strike and days until expiration. These factors often change during an option's lifetime, and some fluctuate in value on a continuing basis throughout any trading session.

A pricing model will create theoretical values, but they are just that—theoretical. Specific values for each factor can be used to predict an option contract's theoretical value at a given point in the future.

When options are first listed on a stock, for example, the market makers will not know what sort of implied volatility to use, so they must make educated guesses (theoretical values). The implied volatility will then change based upon the supply and demand for the options.

17.9 Option Pricing Models

Option traders utilize various option pricing models to attempt to set a current theoretical value. Models use certain fixed knowns in the present—factors such as underlying price, strike and days till expiration—along with forecasts (or assumptions) for factors like implied volatility, to compute the theoretical value for a specific option at a certain point in time. Variables will fluctuate over the life of the option, and the option position's theoretical value will adapt to reflect these changes. Option pricing theory has made vast strides since 1972, when Black and Scholes published their path-breaking paper providing a model for valuing dividend-protected European options. They used a 'replicating portfolio', a portfolio composed of the underlying asset and the risk-free asset that had the same cash flows as the option being valued, to come up with their final formulation. While their derivation is mathematically complicated, there is a simpler binomial model for valuing options that draws on the same logic.

Figure 17.6 Options Calculator from Options Industry Council Website

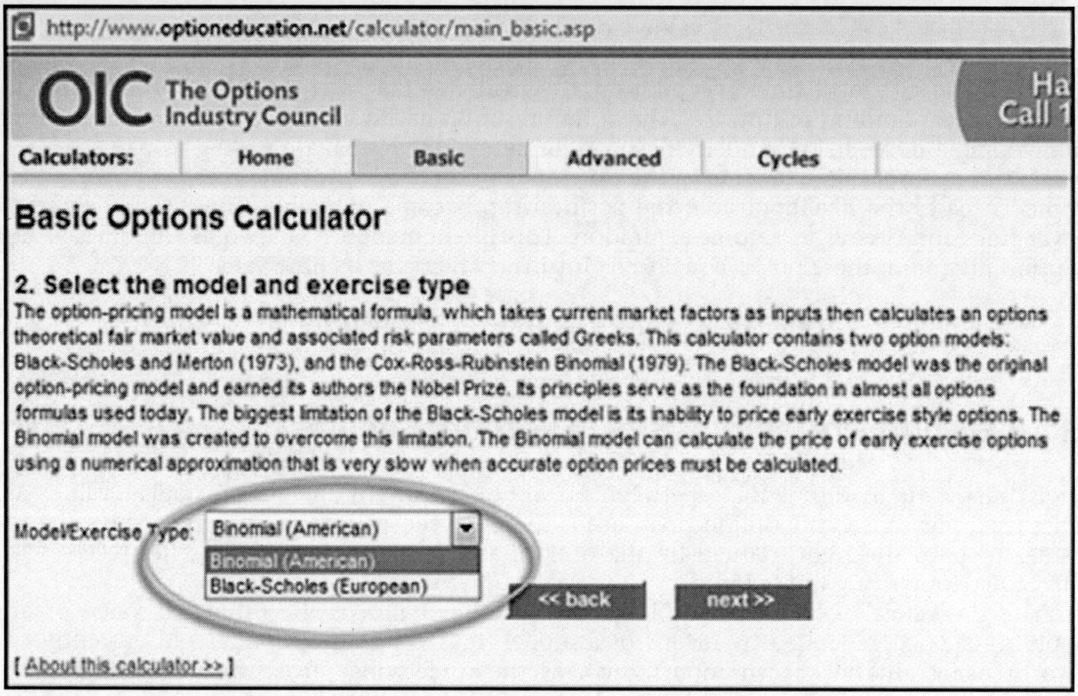

Most professional traders and investors who trade significant option positions rely on theoretical value updates to monitor the changing risk and value of option positions and to assist with trading decisions. Many options trading platforms provide up-to-the-minute option price modelling values, and option pricing calculators can be found online at various Web sites, including the Options Industry Council (http://www.optioneducation.net/calculator/main_calculator.asp). This particular calculator allows users to select by model/exercise type, as shown in Figure 17.6.

17.9.1 The Binomial Model

The Cox–Rubenstein (or Cox–Ross–Rubenstein) binomial option pricing model is a variation of the original Black–Scholes option pricing model. It was first proposed in 1979 by financial economists/engineers John Carrington Cox, Stephen Ross and Mark Edward Rubenstein. The model is popular because it considers the underlying instrument over a period of time, instead of just at one point in time, by using a lattice-based model. A lattice model takes into account expected changes in various parameters over an option's life, thereby producing a more accurate estimate of option prices than created by models that consider only one point in time. Because of this, the Cox–Ross–Rubenstein model is especially useful for analysing American-style options, which can be exercised at any time up to expiration (European-style options can only be exercised upon expiration). The Cox–Ross–Rubenstein model uses a risk-neutral valuation method. Its underlying principal purports that when determining option prices, it can be assumed that the world is risk neutral and that all individuals (and investors) are indifferent to risk. In a risk-neutral environment, expected returns are equal to the risk-free rate of interest. The Cox–Ross–Rubenstein model makes certain assumptions, including:

- No possibility of arbitrage; a perfectly efficient market.
- At each time node, the underlying price can only take an up or a down move and never both simultaneously.

The Cox–Ross–Rubenstein model employs an iterative structure that allows for the specification of nodes (points in time) between the current date and the option's expiration date. The model is able to provide a mathematical valuation of the option at each specified time, thereby creating a 'binomial tree'—a graphical representation of possible values at different nodes.

The Cox–Ross–Rubenstein model is a two-state (or two-step) model in that it assumes the underlying price can only either increase (up) or decrease (down) with time until expiration. Valuation begins at each of the final nodes (at expiration) and iterations are performed backwards through the binomial tree up to the first node (date of valuation). In very basic terms, the model involves three steps:

1. The creation of the binomial price tree.
2. Option value calculated at each final node.
3. Option value calculated at each preceding node.

While the math behind the Cox–Ross–Rubenstein model is considered less complicated than the Black–Scholes model, traders can again make use of online calculators and trading platform-based analysis tools to determine option pricing values. Figure 17.7 shows an

Figure 17.7 The Cox–Ross–Rubenstein Model Applied to an American-style Options Contract, Using the Options Industry Council's Online Pricing Calculator

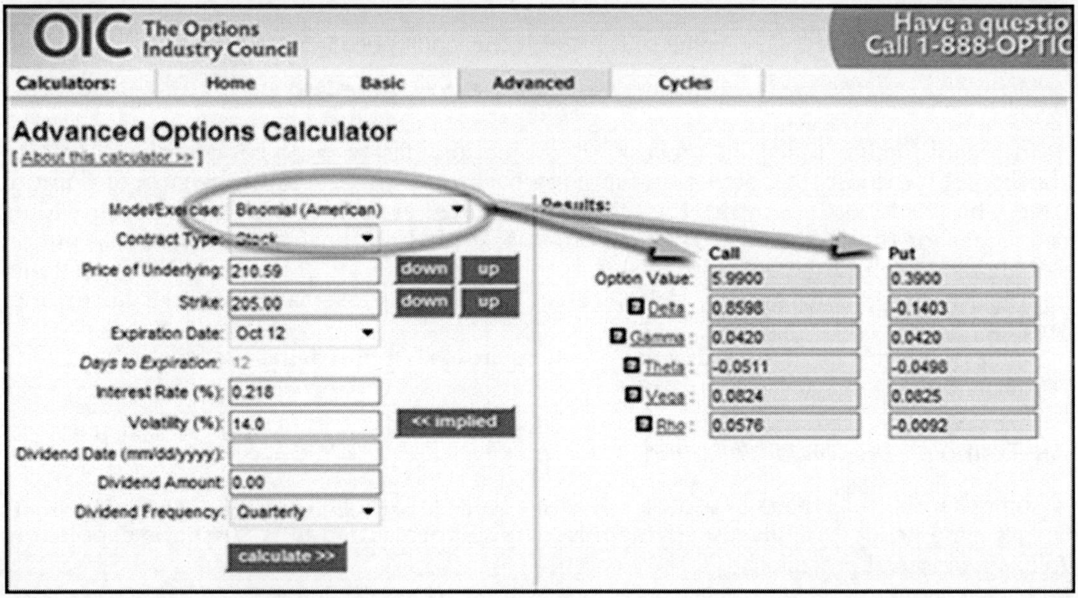

example of the Cox–Ross–Rubenstein model applied to an American-style options contract. The calculator produces both put and call values based on variables input by the user.

The binomial option pricing model is based upon a simple formulation for the asset price process, in which the asset, at any time period, can move to one of two possible prices. The general formulation of a stock price process that follows the binomial is shown in Figure 17.8 for a two-period process.

In this figure, S is the current stock price; the price moves up to S_u with probability p and down to S_d with probability 1 – p at any time period.

Figure 17.8 General Formulation for a Binomial Price Path

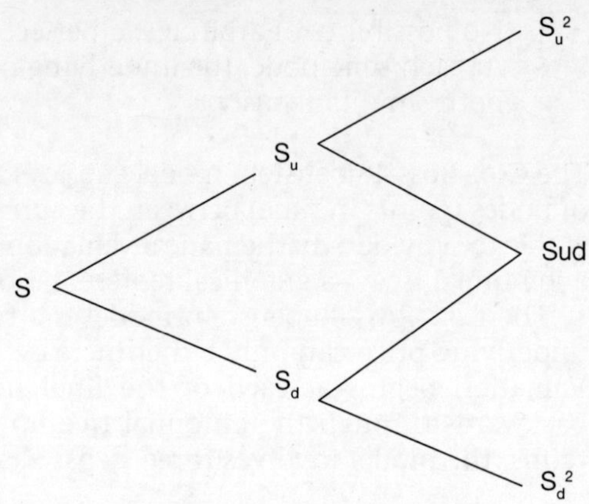

Creating a Replicating Portfolio

The objective of creating a replicating portfolio is to use a combination of risk-free borrowing/lending and the underlying asset to create the same cash flows as the option being valued. The principles of arbitrage apply here, and the value of the option must be equal to the value of the replicating portfolio. In the case of the general formulation above, where stock prices can either move up to S_u or down to S_d in any time period, the replicating portfolio for a call with strike price k will involve borrowing $B and acquiring Δ of the underlying asset, where

$$\Delta = \text{Number of units of the underlying asset bought} = (C_u - C_d)/(S_u - S_d)$$

where

$$C_u = \text{Value of the call if the stock price is } S_u$$

$$C_d = \text{Value of the call if the stock price is } S_d$$

In a multiperiod binomial process, the valuation has to proceed iteratively; that is, starting with the last time period and moving backwards in time until the current point in time. The portfolios replicating the option are created at each step and valued, providing the values for the option in that time period. The final output from the binomial option pricing model is a statement of the value of the option in terms of the replicating portfolio, composed of Δ shares (option delta) of the underlying asset and risk-free borrowing/lending.

Value of the call = Current value of underlying asset × Option delta – Borrowing needed to replicate the option.

An Example of Binomial Valuation

Assume that the objective is to value a call with a strike price of 50, which is expected to expire in two time periods, on an underlying asset whose price currently is 50 and is expected to follow a binomial process:

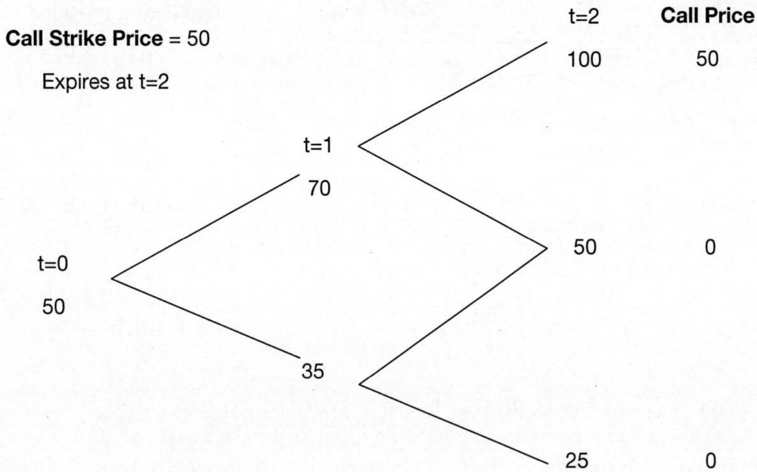

Now assume that the interest rate is 11%. In addition, define

a. Δ = Number of shares in the replicating portfolio
b. B = Dollars of borrowing in replicating portfolio

The objective is to combine Δ shares of stock and B dollars of borrowing to replicate the cash flows from the call with a strike price of $50. This can be done starting with the last period and working back through the binomial tree.

Step 1: Start with the end nodes and work backward.

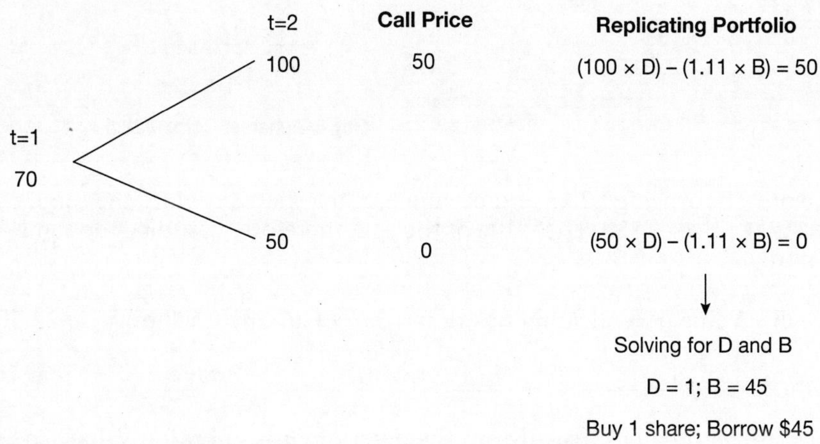

Thus, if the stock price is $70 at t = 1, borrowing $45 and buying one share of the stock will yield the same cash flows as buying the call. The value of the call at t = 1, if the stock price is $70, is therefore

Value of call = Value of replicating position = 70Δ – B = 70 – 45 = 25.
Considering the other leg of the binomial tree at t = 1,

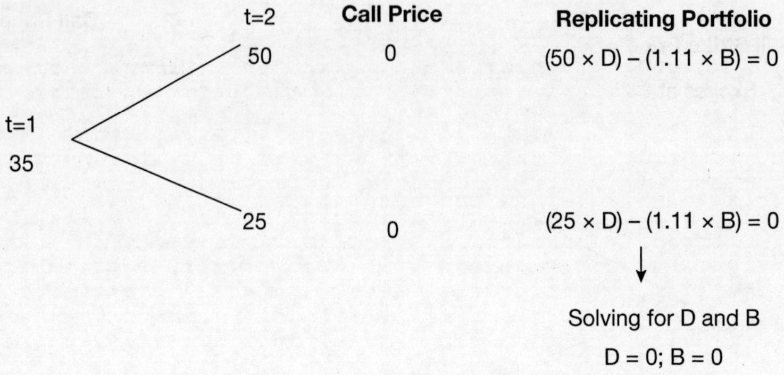

If the stock price is 35 at t = 1, then the call is worth nothing.

Step 2: Move backward to the earlier time period and create a replicating portfolio that provides the cash flows the option provides.

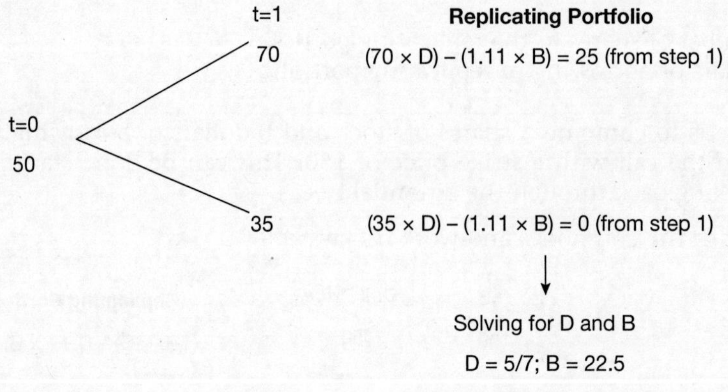

In other words, borrowing \$22.5 and buying 5/7 of a share provides the same cash flows as a call with a strike price of \$50. The value of the call, therefore, has to be the same as the value of this position.

Value of call = Value of replicating position = 5/7 × Current stock price – \$22.5 = \$13.20.

The Determinants of Value

The binomial model provides insight into the determinants of option value. The value of an option is not determined by the expected price of the asset but by its current price, which, of course, reflects expectations about the future. This is a direct consequence of arbitrage. If the option value deviates from the value of the replicating portfolio, investors can create an arbitrage position, that is, one that requires no investment, involves no risk and delivers positive returns. To illustrate, if the portfolio that replicates the call costs more than the call does in the market, an investor could buy the call, sell the replicating portfolio and be guaranteed the difference as a profit. The cash flows on the two positions offset each other, leading to no cash flows in subsequent periods. The option value also increases as the time to expiration is extended, as the price movements (u and d) increase, with increases in the interest rate.

17.9.2 The Black–Scholes Model

The Black–Scholes model for calculating the premium of an option was introduced in 1973 (Black and Scholes 1973). The formula, developed by three economists—Fischer Black, Myron Scholes and Robert Merton—is perhaps the world's most well-known options pricing model. Black passed away two years before Scholes and Merton were awarded the 1997 Nobel Prize in Economics for their work in finding a new method to determine the value of derivatives (the Nobel Prize is not given posthumously; however, the Nobel committee acknowledged Black's role in the Black–Scholes model).

While the binomial model provides an intuitive feel for the determinants of option value, it requires a large number of inputs, in terms of expected future prices at each node. The Black–Scholes model is not an alternative to the binomial model; rather, it is one limiting case of the binomial. The binomial model is a discrete-time model for asset price movements, including a time interval (t) between price movements. As the time interval is shortened, the limiting distribution, as t approaches 0, can take one of two forms. If t approaches 0, price changes become smaller, the limiting distribution is the normal distribution and the price process is a continuous one. If t approaches 0, price changes remain large, the limiting distribution is the Poisson distribution, that is, a distribution that allows for price jumps. The Black–Scholes model applies when the limiting distribution is the normal distribution[1] and it explicitly assumes that the price process is continuous and that there are no jumps in asset prices.

The Model

The Black–Scholes model is used to calculate the theoretical price of European put and call options, ignoring any dividends paid during the option's lifetime. While the original Black–Scholes model did not take into consideration the effects of dividends paid during the life of the option, the model can be adapted to account for dividends by determining the ex-dividend date value of the underlying stock. The model makes certain assumptions, including:

- The options are European and can only be exercised at expiration.
- No dividends are paid out during the life of the option.
- Efficient markets (i.e., market movements cannot be predicted)
- No commissions.
- The risk-free rate and volatility of the underlying are known and constant.
- Follows a lognormal distribution; that is, returns on the underlying are normally distributed.

[1] Stock prices cannot drop below zero, because of the limited liability of stockholders in publicly listed firms. Hence, stock prices, by themselves, cannot be normally distributed, since a normal distribution requires some probability of infinitely negative values. The distribution of the natural logs of stock prices is assumed to be log normal in the Black–Scholes model. This is why the variance used in this model is the variance in the log of stock prices.

The version of the model presented by Black and Scholes was designed to value European options, which were dividend protected. Thus, neither the possibility of early exercise nor the payment of dividends affects the value of options in this model. The value of a call option in the Black–Scholes model can be written as a function of the following variables:

S = Current value of the underlying asset
K = Strike price of the option
t = Life to expiration of the option
r = Riskless interest rate corresponding to the life of the option
σ^2 = Variance in the ln(value of the underlying asset

The model itself can be written as

$$\text{Value of call} = SN(d_1) - Ke^{-rt}N(d_2)$$

where

$$d_1 = \frac{\ln\left(\frac{S}{K}\right) + \left(r + \frac{\sigma^2}{2}\right)t}{\sigma\sqrt{t}}$$

$$d_2 = d_1 - \sigma\sqrt{t}$$

The model is essentially divided into two parts: the first part, SN(d1), multiplies the price by the change in the call premium in relation to a change in the underlying price. This part of the formula shows the expected benefit of purchasing the underlying outright. The second part, N(d2)Ke^(-rt), provides the current value of paying the exercise price upon expiration (remember, the Black–Scholes model applies to European options that are exercisable only on expiration day). The value of the option is calculated by taking the difference between the two parts, as shown in the equation. The process of valuation of options using the Black–Scholes model involves the following steps:

Step 1: The inputs to the Black–Scholes are used to estimate d_1 and d_2.

Step 2: The cumulative normal distribution functions, $N(d_1)$ and $N(d_2)$, corresponding to these standardized normal variables are estimated.

Step 3: The present value of the exercise price is estimated, using the continuous time version of the present value formulation:

$$\text{Present value of exercise price} = Ke^{-rt}$$

Step 4: The value of the call is estimated from the Black–Scholes model.

The mathematics involved in the formula is complicated and can be intimidating. Fortunately, however, traders and investors do not need to know or even understand the math to apply Black–Scholes modelling in their own strategies. As mentioned previously, options traders have access to a variety of online options calculators and many of today's trading platforms boast robust options analysis tools, including indicators and spreadsheets that perform the calculations and output the options pricing values. An example of an online Black–Scholes calculator is shown in Figure 17.9; the user must input all five variables (strike price, stock price, time (days), volatility and risk-free interest rate).

Figure 17.9 An Online Black–Scholes Calculator

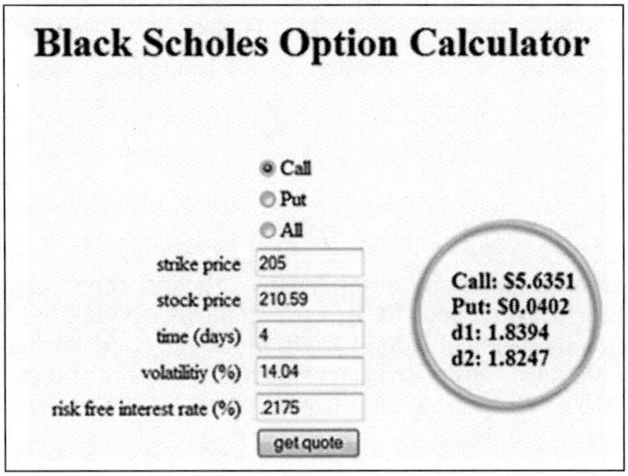

Source: www.tradingtoday.com

The Replicating Portfolio in the Black–Scholes

The determinants of value in the Black–Scholes are the same as those in the binomial—the current value of the stock price, the variability in stock prices, the time to expiration on the option, the strike price and the riskless interest rate. The principle of replicating portfolios that is used in binomial valuation also underlies the Black–Scholes model. In fact, embedded in the Black–Scholes model is the replicating portfolio.

$$\text{Value of Call} = \underbrace{SN(d_1)}_{\text{Buy } N(d_1) \text{ shares}} \quad \underbrace{-Ke^{-rt}N(d_2)}_{\text{Borrow } Ke^{-rt}N(d_2)}$$

$N(d_1)$, which is the number of shares that are needed to create the replicating portfolio, is called the 'option delta'. This replicating portfolio is self-financing and has the same value as the call at every stage of the option's life.

Model Limitations and Fixes

The version of the Black–Scholes model presented above does not take into account the possibility of early exercise or the payment of dividends, both of which impact the value of options. Adjustments exist, which, while not perfect, provide partial corrections to value.

1. Dividends

The payment of dividends reduces the stock price. Consequently, call options become less valuable and put options more valuable as dividend payments increase. One approach to dealing with dividends to estimate the present value of expected dividends paid by the underlying asset during the option life and subtracts it from the current value of the asset to use as 'S' in the model. Since this becomes impractical as the option life becomes longer, an alternate approach can be used. If the dividend yield (y = dividends/current value of the asset) of the underlying asset is expected to remain unchanged during the life of the option, the Black–Scholes model can be modified to take dividends into account.

$$C = Se^{-yt}N(d_1) - Ke^{-rt}N(d_2)$$

where

$$d_1 = \frac{\ln\left(\frac{S}{K}\right) + \left(r - y + \frac{\sigma^2}{2}\right)t}{\sigma\sqrt{t}}$$

$$d_2 = d_1 - \sigma\sqrt{t}$$

From an intuitive standpoint, the adjustments have two effects. First, the value of the asset is discounted back to the present at the dividend yield to take into account the expected drop in value from dividend payments. Second, the interest rate is offset by the dividend yield to reflect the lower carrying cost from holding the stock (in the replicating portfolio). The net effect will be a reduction in the value of calls, with the adjustment, and an increase in the value of puts.

2. Early Exercise

The Black–Scholes model is designed to value European options, that is, options that cannot be exercised until the expiration day. Most of the options analysed are American options, which can be exercised any time before expiration. Without working through the mechanics of valuation models, an American option should always be worth at least as much and generally more than a European option because of the early exercise option. There are three basic approaches for dealing with the possibility of early exercise. The first is to continue to use the unadjusted Black–Scholes and regard the resulting value as a floor or conservative estimate of the true value. The second approach is to value the option to each potential exercise date. With options on stocks, this basically requires that you value options to each ex-dividend day and choose the maximum of the estimated call values. The third approach is to use a modified version of the binomial model to consider the possibility of early exercise.

While it is difficult to estimate the prices for each node of a binomial, there is a way in which variances estimated from historical data can be used to compute the expected up and down movements in the binomial. To illustrate, if σ^2 is the variance in ln (stockprices), the up and down movements in the binomial can be estimated as follows:

$$u = \text{Exp}\left[\left(r - \frac{\sigma^2}{2}\right)\left(\frac{T}{m}\right) + \sqrt{\sigma^2 \frac{T}{m}}\right]$$

$$d = \text{Exp}\left[\left(r - \frac{\sigma^2}{2}\right)\left(\frac{T}{m}\right) - \sqrt{\sigma^2 \frac{T}{m}}\right]$$

where u and d are the up and down movements per unit time for the binomial, T is the life of the option and m is the number of periods within that lifetime. Multiplying the stock price at each stage by u and d will yield the up and down prices. These can then be used to value the asset.

3. The Impact of Exercise on the Value of the Underlying Asset

The derivation of the Black–Scholes model is based upon the assumption that exercising an option does not affect the value of the underlying asset. This may be true for listed options on stocks, but it is not true for other types of options. For instance, the exercise of warrants increases the number of shares outstanding and brings fresh cash into the firm, both of which will affect the stock price.[2] The expected negative impact (dilution) of exercise decreases the value of warrants compared to otherwise similar call options. The adjustment for dilution in the Black–Scholes to the stock price is fairly simple. The stock price is adjusted for the expected dilution from the exercise of the options. In the case of warrants, for instance

$$\text{Dilution-adjusted } S = \frac{S\,n_s + W n_w}{n_s + n_w}$$

where

S = Current value of the stock
n_w = Number of warrants outstanding
W = Market value of warrants outstanding
n_s = Number of shares outstanding

When the warrants are exercised, the number of shares outstanding increases, reducing the stock price. The numerator reflects the market value of equity, including both stocks and warrants outstanding. The reduction in S will reduce the value of the call option.

There is an element of circularity in this analysis, since the value of the warrant is needed to estimate the dilution-adjusted S and the dilution-adjusted S is needed to estimate the value of the warrant. This problem can be resolved by starting the process off with an estimated value of the warrant (say, the exercise value), and then iterating with the new estimated value for the warrant until there is convergence.

Valuing Puts

The value of a put can be derived from the value of a call with the same strike price and the same expiration date through an arbitrage relationship that specifies that

$$C - P = S - Ke^{-rt}$$

where C is the value of the call and P is the value of the put (with the same life and exercise price). This arbitrage relationship can be derived fairly easily and is called put–call parity. To see why put–call parity holds, consider creating the following portfolio:

a. Sell a call and buy a put with exercise price K and the same expiration date 't'.
b. Buy the stock at current stock price S.

The payoff from this position is riskless and always yields K at expiration (t). To see this, assume that the stock price at expiration is S^*:

[2] Warrants are call options issued by firms, either as part of management compensation contracts or to raise equity.

Position	Payoffs at t if S* > k	Payoffs at t if S* < k
Sell call	–(S* – k)	0
Buy put	0	k – S*
Buy stock	S*	S*
Total	k	k

Since this position yields k with certainty, its value must be equal to the present value of k at the riskless rate(ke^{-rt}).

$$S + P - C = ke^{-rt}$$

$$C - P = S - ke^{-rt}$$

This relationship can be used to value puts. Substituting the Black–Scholes formulation, with the dividend adjustment, for the value of an equivalent call,

$$\text{Value of put} = Se^{-yt}(N(d_1)-1)-ke^{-rt}(N(d_2)-1$$

where

$$d_1 = \frac{\ln\left(\frac{S}{K}\right)+\left(r-y+\frac{\sigma^2}{2}\right)t}{\sigma\sqrt{t}}$$

$$d_2 = d_1 - \sigma\sqrt{t}$$

17.10 Put–Call Parity

Put–call parity is an options pricing concept first identified by economist Hans Stoll (1969). It defines the relationship that must exist between European put and call options with the same expiration and strike price (it does not apply to American-style options because they can be exercised any time up to expiration). The principle states that the value of a call option, at one strike price, implies a fair value for the corresponding put and vice versa. The relationship arises from the fact that combinations of options can create positions that are identical to holding the underlying itself (a stock, for example). The option and stock positions must have the same return or an arbitrage opportunity would arise. Arbitrageurs would be able to make profitable trades, free of risk, until put/call parity returned. Arbitrage is the opportunity to profit from price variances on one security in different markets. For example, arbitrage would exist if an investor could buy stock ABC in one market for \$45 while simultaneously selling stock ABC in a different market for \$50. The synchronized trades would offer the opportunity to profit with little to no risk.

Put options, call options and the underlying stock are related in that the combination of any two yields the same profit/loss profile as the remaining component. For example, to replicate the gain/loss features of a long stock position, an investor could simultaneously hold a long call and a short put (the call and put would have the same strike price and same expiration). Similarly, a short stock position could be replicated with a short call plus a long put and so on. If put–call parity did not exist, investors would be able to take advantage of arbitrage opportunities.

Options traders use put–call parity as a simple test for their European-style options pricing models. If a pricing model results in put and call prices that do not satisfy put–call parity, it implies that an arbitrage opportunity exists and, in general, should be rejected as an unsound strategy.

There are several formulas to express put–call parity for European options. The following provides an example of a formula that can be used for non-dividend-paying securities:

$$c = S + p - X_e - r(T - t)$$

$$p = c - S + X_e - r(T - t)$$

where
c = call value
S = current stock price
p = put price
X = exercise price
e = Euler's constant (exponential function on a financial calculator equal to approximately 2.71828
r = continuously compounded risk free rate of interest
T = Expiration date
t = Current value date

Many trading platforms that offer options analysis provide visual representations of put–call parity. Figure 17.10 shows an example of the relationship between a long stock/long put position (shown in red) and a long call (in blue) with the same expiration and strike price. The

Figure 17.10 An Example of a Put–Call Parity Chart Created with an Analysis Platform

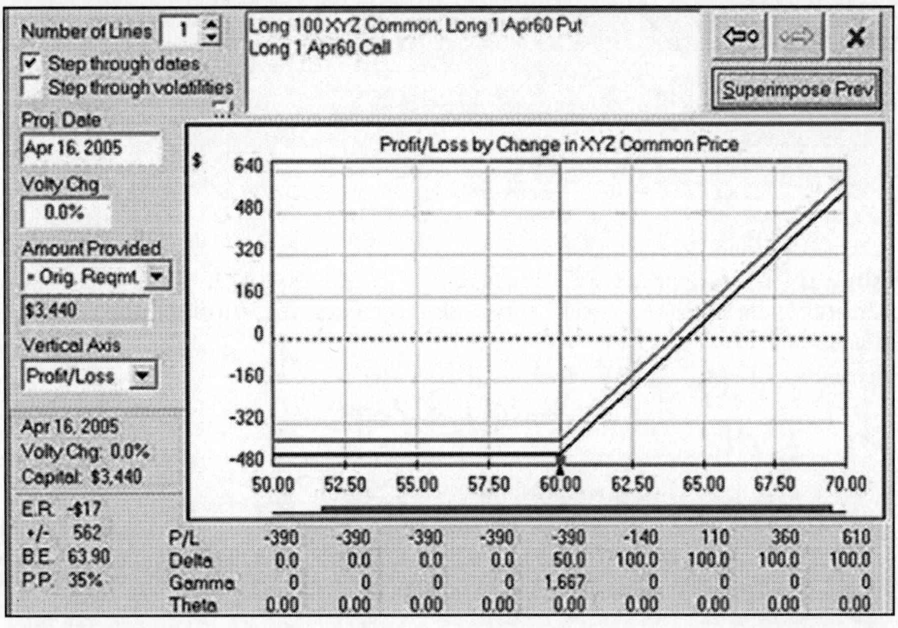

difference in the lines is the result of the assumed dividend that would be paid during the option's life. If no dividend was assumed, the lines would overlap.

By using the put/call parity, the law of one price allows us to find a particular relation between the current value of a put, the current value of a call, the current value of the underlying stock, and a risk-free bond's value. Consider the following two strategies:

a. Buy a call and write (sell) a put on the same underlying, with the same strike price k, and the same expiration date T;
b. Buy the underlying stock and borrow so you must payback k at time T.

The time T payoffs of these two strategies as a function of the price of the underlying are:

Strategy 1

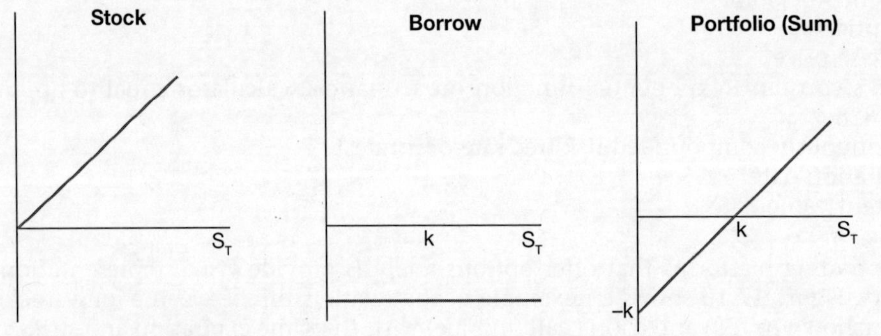

Strategy 2

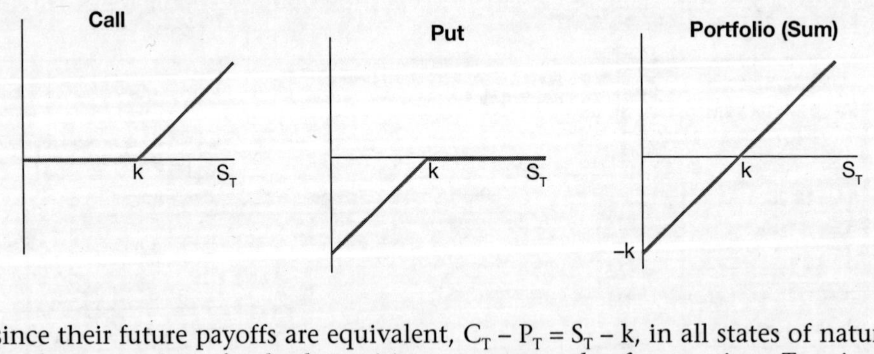

Now, since their future payoffs are equivalent, $C_T - P_T = S_T - k$, in all states of nature (note that the only uncertainty for both positions concerns the future, time T, price of the underlying stock), their current prices must also be equal.

$$\text{So, } c_t - p_t = s_t - k/R_f$$

$$\text{Thus, } p_t = c_t - s_t + k/R_f$$

so we can find P_T if we know C_T; hence, our concentration, as is traditional, is on call options.

17.11 Profit and Loss Diagrams

A profit and loss diagram, or risk graph, is a visual representation of the possible profit and loss of an option strategy at a given point in time. Option traders use profit and loss diagrams to evaluate how a strategy may perform over a range of prices, thereby gaining an understanding of potential outcomes. Because of the visual nature of a diagram, traders can evaluate the potential profit and loss, and the risk and reward of the position, at a glance.

To create a profit and loss diagram, values are plotted along the x and y axes. The horizontal axis (the x-axis) shows the underlying prices, labelled in order with lower prices on the left and rising prices towards the right. The current underlying price is usually centred along this axis. The vertical axis (the y-axis) represents the potential profit and loss values for the position. The breakeven point (that indicates no profit and no loss) is usually centred on the y-axis, with profits shown above this point (higher along the y-axis) and losses below this point (lower on the axis). Figure 17.11 shows the basic structure of a profit and loss diagram.

The graph line represents the potential profit and loss across the range of underlying prices. For simplicity, we will begin by taking a look at a long stock position of 100 shares. Assume an investor has bought 100 shares of stock for $25 each, or a total cost of $2,500. Figure 17.12 shows the potential profit and loss for this position. When the graph line is on $25 (the cost per share), note that the profit and loss value is $0.00 (breakeven). As the stock price moves higher, so does the profit; conversely, as the price moves lower, the losses increase. The figure shows the position breaks even at $25 (our purchase price) and as the stock's price increases (moving right along the x-axis) the profits correspondingly increase. Since there is, in theory, no upper limit to the stock's price, the graph line shows an arrow on one end.

Figure 17.11 Profit and Loss Diagram

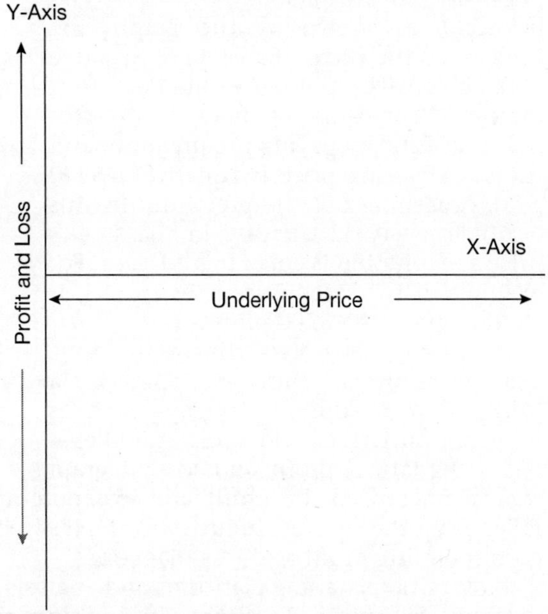

Figure 17.12 A Profit and Loss Diagram for a Hypothetical Stock

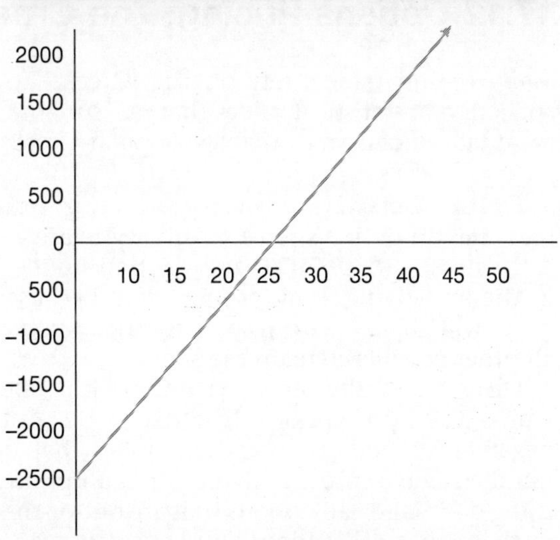

In this example, shown in Figure 17.13, a call option has a strike price of $50 and a $200 cost (for the contract). The downside risk is $200—the premium paid. If the option expires worthless (for example, the stock price was $50 at expiration), the loss would be $200, as shown by the graph line intersected the y-axis at a value of negative 200. The breakeven point would be a stock price of $52 at expiration; here, the investor has 'lost' $200 by paying the premium and the stock's rising price is equal to a $200 gain, cancelling out the premium. In this example, every $1 increase in the stock's price at expiration is equal to a $1 gain. For example, if the stock price rises to $54, it would represent a $200 profit.

Figure 17.13 A Profit and Loss Diagram for a Long Option Position

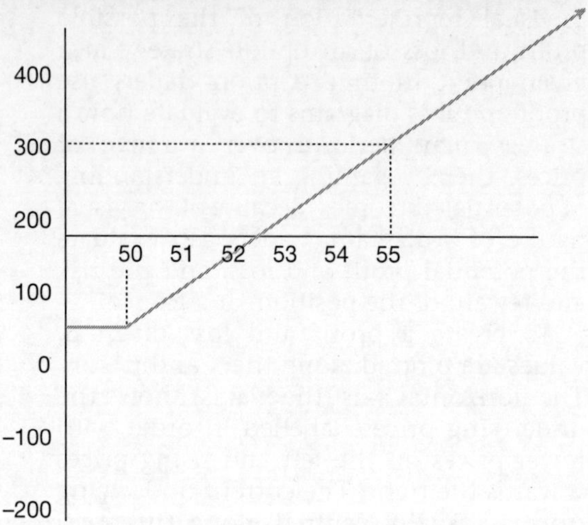

It should be noted that the above example shows a typical graph line for a long call; each option strategy—such as long call butterflies and short straddles—has a 'signature' profit and loss diagram that characterized the profit and loss potential for that particular strategy. Figure 17.14, taken from the Options Industry Council's website, shows various options strategies and the corresponding profit and loss diagrams.

Most options trading platforms and analysis software allow traders to create profit and loss diagrams for specified options. In addition, the charts can be created by hand, by using spreadsheet software such as Microsoft Excel, or by purchasing commercially available analysis tools.

17.12 Options Pricing: The Greeks

Many option traders rely on the 'Greeks' to evaluate option positions. The Greeks are a collection of statistical values that measure the risk involved in an options contract in relation to certain underlying variables. Popular Greeks include Delta, Vega, Gamma and Theta.

Δ **Delta: Sensitivity to underlying price:** Delta, the most popular options Greek, measures an option's price sensitivity relative to changes in the price of the underlying, and is the number of points that an option's price is expected to move for each one-point change in the underlying. Delta is important because it provides an indication of how the option's value will change with respect to price fluctuations in the underlying instrument, assuming all other variables remain the same.

Delta is typically shown as a numerical value between 0.0 and 1.0 for call options and 0.0 and −1.0 for put options. In other words, option delta will always be positive for calls and negative for puts. It should be noted that delta values can also be represented as whole numbers between 0.0 and 100 for call options and 0.0 to −100 for put options, rather than using decimals. Call options that are out-of-the-money will have delta values approaching 0.0; in-the-money call options will have delta values that are close to 1.0.

Figure 17.14 Various Profit and Loss Diagrams for Different Options Strategies from the Options Industry Council Website

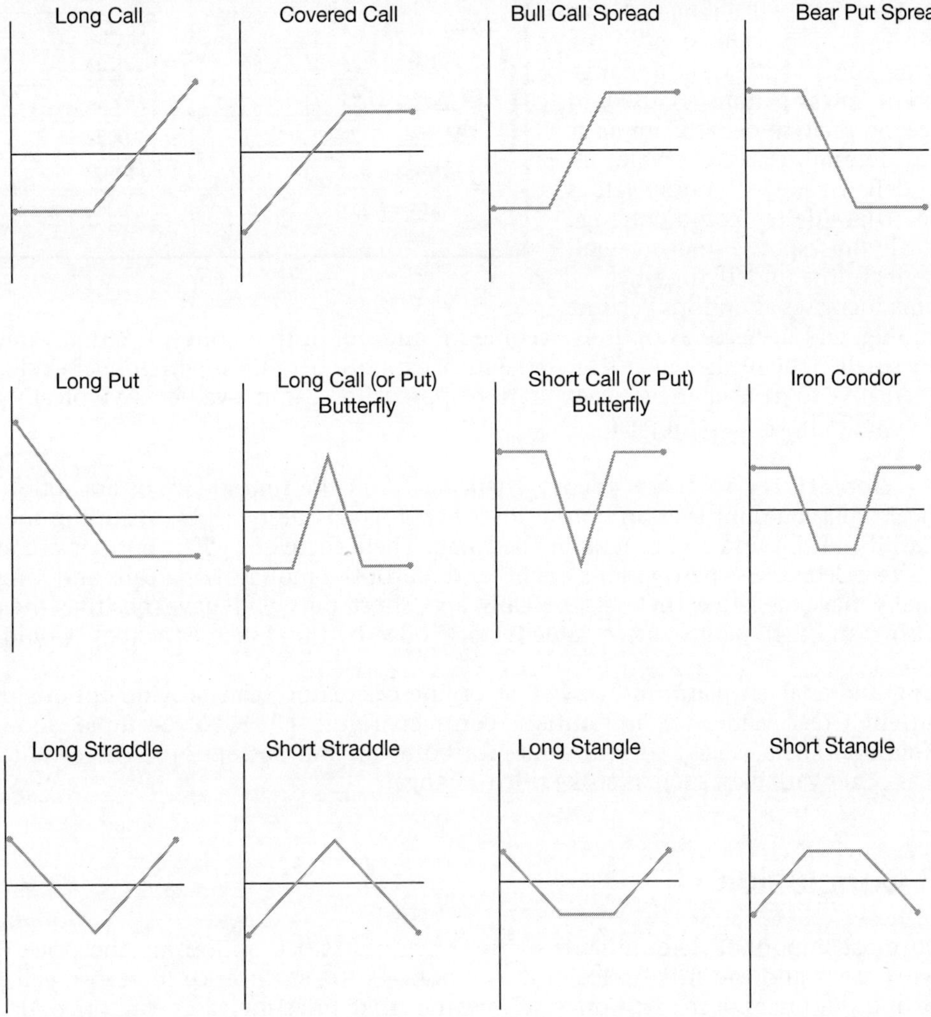

ν Vega: Sensitivity to underlying volatility: Vega measures an option's sensitivity to changes in the volatility of the underlying. Vega represents the amount that an option's price changes in response to a 1% change in volatility of the underlying market. The more time there exists until expiration, the more impact increased volatility will have on the option's price.

Because increased volatility implies that the underlying instrument is more likely to experience extreme values, a rise in volatility will correspondingly increase the value of an option and, conversely, a decrease in volatility will negatively affect the value of the option.

Γ Gamma: Sensitivity to delta: Gamma measures the sensitivity of delta in response to price changes in the underlying instrument. Gamma indicates how delta will change relative to each one-point price change in the underlying. Since delta values change at different rates, gamma is used to measure and analyse delta. Gamma is used to determine how stable an option's delta is; higher gamma values indicate that delta could change dramatically in response to even small movements in the underlying price.

Figure 17.15 The Greeks

	Call	Put
Option Value:	5.0300	0.0200
Delta :	0.9797	-0.0203
Gamma :	0.0193	0.0193
Theta :	-0.0057	-0.0052
Vega :	0.0093	0.0093
Rho :	0.0306	-0.0006

Gamma increases as options become at-the-money and decrease as options become in- and out-of-the-money. Gamma values are generally smaller, the further away from the date of expiration; options with longer expirations are less sensitive to delta changes. As expiration approaches, gamma values are typically larger as delta changes have more impact.

Θ Theta: Sensitivity to time decay: Theta measures the time decay of an option—the theoretical dollar amount that an option loses every day as time passes, assuming the price and volatility of the underlying remain the same. Theta increases when options are at-the-money; theta decreases when options are in- and out-of-the money. Long calls and long puts will usually have negative theta; short calls and short puts will have positive theta. By comparison, an instrument's whose value is not eroded by time, such as a stock, would have zero theta.

Trading and analysis platforms, as well as online calculators, can provide options traders with current Greek values for any options contract. Figure 17.15, for example, shows the Delta, Gamma, Theta, Vega and Rho values for both call and put options. These values will change as other variables, such as strike price, change.

17.13 Conclusion

The two most important determinants of the price of a stock option are the price of the underlying stock and the strike price of the option. As the stock price increases, call prices increase and put prices decrease. Conversely, as the strike price increases, call prices decrease and put prices increase. Time remaining until option expiration is an important determinant of option value. As time remaining until option expiration lengthens, both call and put option prices normally increase. Stock price volatility also plays an important role in determining option value. As stock price volatility increases, both call and put option prices increase.

Put–call parity states that the difference between a call price and a put price for European-style options with the same strike price and expiration date is equal to the difference between the stock price less a dividend adjustment and the discounted strike price. Put–call parity is based on the fundamental principle that two securities with the same riskless payoff on the same future date must have the same price today. The Black–Scholes–Merton option pricing formula states that the value of a stock option is a function of the current stock price, stock dividend yield, the option strike price, the risk-free interest rate, the time remaining until option expiration and the stock price volatility. The model assumes constant stock price volatility and yields option prices that may differ from stochastic volatility option prices. Nevertheless, even when volatility is stochastic, the model yields accurate option prices for options with strike prices close to a current stock price. Therefore, when using implied volatility to estimate underlying stock price volatility, it is best to use at-the-money options.

Multiple Choice Questions

1. Before expiration, the time value of an in-the-money call option is always _______
   a. Zero b. Positive c. Negative d. None
2. At expiration, the time value of an in-the-money put option is always _______
   a. Zero b. Positive c. Negative d. None
3. Prior to expiration _______
   a. The intrinsic value of a call option is greater than its actual value
   b. The intrinsic value of a call option is always positive
   c. The actual value of a call option is greater than the intrinsic value
   d. The intrinsic value of a call option is always greater than its time value
4. If the stock price increases, the price of a put option on that stock _______ and that of a call option _______
   a. Decreases, increases b. Increases, decreases
   c. Decreases, decreases d. Increases, increases
5. Other things being equal, the price of a stock call option is positively correlated with the following factors except _______
   a. The stock price b. The stock volatility
   c. The time to expiration d. The exercise price
6. Delta is defined as _______
   a. The change in the value of an option for a dollar change in the price of the underlying asset
   b. The change in the value of the underlying asset for a dollar change in the call price
   c. The percentage change in the value of an option for a 1% change in the value of the underlying asset
   d. The change in the volatility of the underlying stock price
7. The gamma of an option is _______
   a. The volatility level for the stock that the option price implies
   b. The continued updating of the hedge ratio as time passes
   c. The percentage change in the stock call option price divided by the percentage change in the stock price
   d. The sensitivity of the delta to the stock price
8. A one-dollar decrease in a call option's exercise price would result in a(n) _______ in the call option's value of _______ one dollar.
   a. Increase, more than b. Decrease, more than
   c. Decrease, less than d. Increase, less than

9. Use the Black–Scholes option pricing model for the following problem. Given: S_o = $70; X = $70; T = 70 days; r = 0.06 annually (0.0001648 daily); σ = 0.020506 (daily). No dividends will be paid before the option expires. The value of the call option is ________
   a. $10.16 b. $5.16 c. $0.00 d. $2.16
10. An American-style call option with six months to maturity has a strike price of $35. The underlying stock now sells for $43. The call premium is $12. What is the intrinsic value of the call?
    a. $12 b. $8 c. $0 d. $23

Review Questions

1. Differentiate between put option and call option.
2. How the payoffs from put and call option can be worked out?
3. Write a short note on option pricing.
4. What are the factors that affect option prices?
5. Differentiate between American and European options.
6. What are the uses of intrinsic value and time value in option valuation?
7. Option pricing models are used to calculate the theoretical value of option. Evaluate.
8. What is the use of replicating portfolio in the binomial model?
9. Explain Black–Scholes model in detail.
10. What is the use of replicating portfolio in the Black–Scholes model?
11. Define put–call parity with examples.
12. What is a profit–loss diagram? Explain graphically.
13. Explain Delta, Vega, Gamma and Theta.

Exercises

1. Assume the stock price of 100 and the strike price of 100 with time to expiration of one year. Further, assume that the risk-free rate is 4% and the stock volatility is 30%. What is the call option price? (Hint: use the Black–Scholes model.)
2. Using the assumption of the above question but the stock volatility has dropped to 20%, what is the change in the call option price? Show that the result is consistent with using a sensitivity measure.
3. An interest rate model is arbitrage free if the pricing of a zero coupon bond by the backward substitution approach is the same as the discounted value for any interest rate volatilities and spot curves. Show that the Ho–Lee model is arbitrage free. (Hint: use the Ho–Lee model to show that the pricing of a five-year zero coupon bond using the interest rate model is equal to discounting the $1 payment at the five-year rate.)
4. Let us consider a European call option with five-year time to expiration to buy a three-year bond at a strike 75. Assuming a flat yield curve of 6% and term structure of spot volatility of 20%, what is the option price? (Hint: use the bond option model.)
5. Consider a call option on the yield spread between a 10-year zero coupon bond and the two-year zero coupon bond. The strike is 5 basis points. The yield curve is assumed to be flat and the term structure of spot volatilities is linearly declining at 0.1% annually, starting 10% for the first year. What is the price of the spread option? (Hint: use the spread option model.)
6. What is the price of a European call option on the exchange rate with strike 1.2, expiring in one year, assuming that the exchange rate volatility is 14.1%?

References

Black, Fischer, and Myron S. Scholes. 1973. 'The Pricing of Options and Corporate Liabilities'. *Journal of Political Economy*, 81(3): 637–54.

Cox, J.C., S.A. Ross, and M. Rubinstein. 1979. 'Option Pricing: A Simplified Approach'. *Journal of Financial Economics,* 7(3): 229.

Hans R. Stoll. 1969. 'The Relation Between Put and Call Prices'. *The Journal of Finance*, 24(5): 801–824.

Merton, Robert. 2014. 'Black–Scholes: Robert Merton on the Options Pricing Model'. *Bloomberg Business*, 4 December. Available at http://www.bloomberg.com/bw/articles/2014-12-04/black-scholes-robert-merton-on-the-options-pricing-model

Chapter

18

Swap

Chapter Objectives

On completion of this chapter, you will be able to understand:

- Uses of swaps
- Types of swaps
- Interest rate swaps
- Using swaps to transform liabilities
- Using swaps to transform assets
- Financial intermediaries
- Comparative advantage
- LIBOR/swap zero rates
- Valuation of interest rate swaps
- Currency swaps
- Valuation of currency swaps
- Credit risk issues

Interest Rate Risk

The Group contracts fixed rate currency swaps and uses simple floating to fixed rate interest rate swaps to meet its objective of protecting borrowing costs and differentials between borrowing and deposit rates within parameters set by the Board. Interest rate swaps and the fixed interest element of currency swaps are accounted for as hedges and, as such, changes in fair values resulting from changes to market rates are not recognised in the Group balance sheet nor in reported profits. The cash flow effects of interest rate swaps match cash flows on the underlying instruments such that there is no net cash flow effect from movements in market interest rates. As at 31 December 2004, the majority of interest costs and differentials had been protected through to December 2005.

If the Group had not transacted interest rate swaps or fixed interest rate cross currency swaps to hedge its interest rate risk, based upon the net debt position at 31 December 2004, an increase in short-term interest rates across all currencies by one percentage point would increase the Group's annual net interest payable by £1.1m (2003 — increase by £1.3m). The Group's financial assets and liabilities, excluding fixed interest rate currency swaps, were principally at floating interest rates and thus their fair values are not directly affected by movements in market rates of interest.

Source: This excerpt is taken from the SNN (Smith and Nephew SNATS)_20-F filed 25 November 2005.[1]

18.1 Introduction

A swap is an agreement between two or more parties to exchange a set of cash flows over a period of time. Sometimes, a swap is also defined as a derivative in which two or more parties agree to exchange cash flows of one party's financial instrument for those of the other party's financial instrument. The related benefits depend on the type of financial instruments involved in the agreement. For example, in the case of a swap involving two bonds, the benefits can be the periodic interest (coupon) payments associated with such bonds. Specifically, two counterparties agree to exchange one stream of cash flows against another stream. These streams are called the legs of the swap. The swap agreement defines the dates when the cash flows are to be paid and the way they are accrued and calculated. Usually, at the time when the contract is initiated, at least one of these series of cash flows is determined by an uncertain variable such as a floating interest rate, foreign exchange rate, equity price or commodity price.

The cash flows are calculated over a notional principal amount. Contrary to a future, a forward or an option, the notional amount is usually not exchanged between counterparties. Consequently, swaps can be in cash or collateral. Swaps can be used to hedge certain risks, such as interest rate risk, or to speculate on changes in the expected direction of underlying prices. Swaps were first introduced to the public in 1981 when IBM and the World Bank entered into a swap agreement. Today, swaps are among the most heavily traded financial contracts in the world: the total amount of interest rates and currency swaps outstanding is more than $348 trillion in 2010, according to the Bank for International Settlements (BIS, 2010).

18.2 Uses of Swaps

Swaps allow companies to convert all or part of their fixed-rate debt to floating or vice versa. For example, in Figure 18.1, counterparty A starts with a variable-rate debt obligation, requiring periodic interest payments based on LIBOR plus a spread. We make the assumption that counterparty A would rather not have this variable-rate exposure, preferring instead to pay a fixed interest amount over the remaining term of the debt. Counterparty B, on the other hand, is in exactly the opposite situation. B has issued fixed-rate debt and would rather pay on a variable-rate basis.

When the two enter into the swap agreement, they maintain their original interest expense obligations, but the additional cash flows of the swap effectively transform their exposures from floating to fixed for counterparty A and from fixed to floating for counterparty B.

[1] Available at http://www.wikinvest.com/stock/Smith_&_Nephew_SNATS_%28SNN%29/Interest_Rate_Risk

Figure 18.1 Plain Vanilla Interest Rate Swap

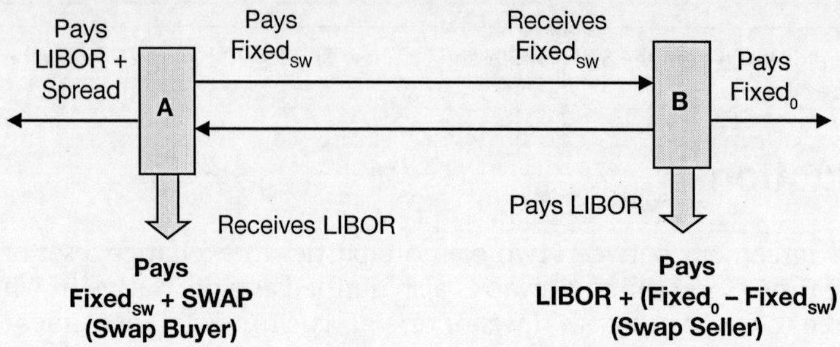

Counterparty A still bears the cost of the original spread over LIBOR and counterparty B ends up with an exposure to LIBOR. Counterparty B is also responsible for paying (or receiving) the difference between the fixed rate on the original debt and the swap's fixed rate.

The advantages of swaps are as follows:

1. Swap is generally cheaper. There is no up-front premium and it reduces transactions costs.
2. Swap can be used to hedge risk, and long time period hedge is possible.
3. It provides flexible and maintains informational advantages.
4. It has longer term than futures or options. Swaps will run for years, whereas forwards and futures are for the relatively short term.
5. Using swaps can give companies a better match between their liabilities and revenues.

Swaps are not free of disadvantages, some of which are as follows:

1. Early termination of swap before maturity may incur a breakage cost.
2. Lack of liquidity.
3. It is subject to default risk.

18.3 Types of Swaps

Swaps are specifically tailored to the needs of all the parties entering into them. As such, they are not traded on an exchange, but instead are traded 'over the counter' (OTC). Brokers—either independent or divisions of investment banks—provide live, tradable price quotes for a wide range of swaps. Additionally, brokers provide liquidity to the market by acting as intermediaries between investors wanting to take different positions. Swaps are extremely flexible instruments. Unlike a bond, where the details are set in stone at the time of issuance, the various details of a swap can be amended, upon mutual agreement, at any time. However, even with this flexibility, each swap remains eminently liquid and easily valued. In the most basic (usually called 'plain vanilla') of swap contracts, the interest rate swap, one party to the contract pays a fixed rate of interest, and the other pays a floating rate of interest. Amidst of different categories of swaps in the literature, the following classification is commonly referred and used:

1. Interest rate swaps
2. Currency swaps
3. Commodity swaps
4. Equity swaps

1. Interest Rate Swaps: An interest rate swap is an exchange between two counterparties of interest obligations (payments of interest) or receipts (investment income), in the same currency on an agreed amount of notional principal for an agreed period of time. The agreed amount is called 'notional principal' because it is not a loan or investment. The principal amount is neither exchanged at the outset nor repaid at maturity. The most common interest rate swaps involve the exchange of interest from a fixed to a floating basis or vice versa.

2. Currency Swaps: A currency swap is an agreement to exchange interest obligations or interest receipts between two different currencies. The market standard is to quote a fixed rate of interest in one currency against a floating rate of interest (generally in the U.S. dollars). A rate of exchange between the two currencies must be established at the outset. This will produce principal amounts in the two currencies upon which payments of interest will be made. At the final maturity of the transaction, along with the final periodic payment of interest, the swap counterparties must exchange the principal amounts of the two currencies which were fixed at the outset. The exchange of two principal amounts at the beginning of the swap is not necessary, but it can take place if required. The exchange of principal at the end of the transaction must take place. It is this exchange that offsets interest rate differentials between the two currencies.

3. Commodity Swaps: This is a swap where payments are based on the prices of commodities. One party pays a fixed price for the good over life of the swap while the other pays a floating price for the good, depending on current market prices.

4. Equity Swaps: With an equity swap, payments are made based on a notional principal which is an equity portfolio. The payments are fixed and floating. The floating-rate sum is based on the return on the relevant index for the period while the fixed rate sum is agreed in advance.

18.4 Interest Rate Swaps

Interest rate swaps are derivative instruments commonly used by sophisticated investors to allow cash flows on interest-earning securities or loans to be exchanged. One of the most common examples of an interest rate swap is when two parties have different terms on loan agreements (e.g. fixed vs. variable interest rates), and one party undertakes payments linked to short-term floating interest rates (such as LIBOR) in order to receive fixed payments. The counterparty to this transaction then undertakes the fixed payments. According to the Bank for International Settlements, the notional amounts outstanding for interest rate swaps were upwards of $364 trillion at the end of 2010, dwarfing the OTC markets for other types of derivative contracts.

A 'plain vanilla' interest rate swap involves two parties exchanging interest rate payments based on a notional principal for a set period of time. One party pays a fixed rate and the other pays a floating rate. Let us consider that two parties, A and B, have entered into an agreement. The agreement involves 'A' paying fixed interest payments to 'B', and 'B' paying floating interest payments to 'A' every m months. LIBOR is usually the floating rate. The coupon of a floating-rate bond is set at the beginning of the coupon period. As an example, consider a bond that pays LIBOR + 1%, with coupons occurring every six months. Assume that the bond just paid a coupon and that the six-month LIBOR equals 2.5%. The next coupon payment will be set at 2.5% + 1% = 3.5% of par (i.e., 3.5% × 0.5 × 100 = $17.5 on a $100 par bond).

Example 1: A simple three-year interest rate swap agreement has been initiated on 5 March 2004 between MSFT and INTC. Amount of notional capital is $100 million. MSFT pays fixed interest at the rate of 5% annually, compounded semi-annually, whereas INTC pays floating at six-month LIBOR. Payments are made semi-annually.

Solution 1:

Table 18.1 Computing the Cash Flows to be Exchanged

Date	Six-month LIBOR Rate (%)	Paid by	
		MSFT	INTC
5-Mar-04	4.2		
5-Sep-04	4.8	(0.05/2) × $100 = $2.50	(0.042/2 × $100 = $2.10
5-Mar-05	5.3	(0.05/2) × $100 = $2.50	(0.048/2 × $100 = $2.40
5-Sep-05	5.5	(0.05/2) × $100 = $2.50	(0.053/2 × $100 = $2.65
5-Mar-06	5.6	(0.05/2) × $100 = $2.50	(0.055/2 × $100 = $2.75
5-Sep-06	5.9	(0.05/2) × $100 = $2.50	(0.056/2 × $100 = $2.80
5-Mar-07	6.4	(0.05/2) × $100 = $2.50	(0.059/2 × $100 = $2.95

However, MSFT and INTC will not exchange the whole amount as computed in Table 18.1, rather the net cash flow will be paid as shown in Table 18.2. Such arrangement reduces credit risk.

Table 18.2 Computing the Net Cash Flows to be Exchanged

Date	Six-month LIBOR Rate (%)	Floating CF Received	Fixed CF Paid	Net CF
5-Mar-04	4.2			
5-Sep-04	4.8	2.10	–2.50	–0.40
5-Mar-05	5.3	2.40	–2.50	–0.10
5-Sep-05	5.5	2.65	–2.50	0.15
5-Mar-06	5.6	2.75	–2.50	0.25
5-Sep-06	5.9	2.80	–2.50	0.30
5-Mar-07	6.4	2.95	–2.50	0.45

The computation above reflects that the principal amounts are never exchanged. That is why it is called notional principal. Even if principal amounts were exchanged, the nature of the deal would not be changed in any way as shown in Table 18.3.

Table 18.3 Computing the Net Cash Flows to be Exchanged Including Principal

Date	Six-month LIBOR Rate (%)	Floating CF Received	Fixed CF Paid	Net CF
5-Mar-04	4.2			
5-Sep-04	4.8	2.10	–2.50	–0.40
5-Mar-05	5.3	2.40	–2.50	–0.10
5-Sep-05	5.5	2.65	–2.50	0.15
5-Mar-06	5.6	2.75	–2.50	0.25
5-Sep-06	5.9	2.80	–2.50	0.30
5-Mar-07	6.4	102.95	–102.50	0.45

18.5 Using Swaps to Transform Liabilities

Swaps can be used to transform liabilities from one state to another. Specifically, a floating-rate loan can be transformed to a fixed-rate loan and vice versa.

18.5.1 Floating-rate Loan to Fixed-rate Loan

In the previous example, MSFT could use a swap to transform a floating-rate loan into a fixed-rate loan. Assume that MSFT has borrowed $100 million at Libor + 10 basis points. To understand basis points, follow Exhibit 18.1.

This is a floating-rate loan. If MSFT enters into the swap, it will face three sets of cash flows:

a. Payment of LIBOR + 10 basis points to outside lenders.
b. Inflow of LIBOR under the terms of the swap.
c. Payment of 5% under the terms of the swap.

Net CF = 5.1% Fixed!

Exhibit 18.1 Meaning of 'Basis Point (bp)'

A basis point, or bp, is a common unit of measure for interest rates and other percentages in finance. One basis point is equal to 1/100th of 1%, or 0.01% (0.0001), and is used to denote the percentage change in a financial instrument. The relationship between percentage changes and basis points can be summarized as follows: 1% change = 100 basis points and 0.01% = 1 basis point.

Basis Points	Percentage Terms
1	0.01%
10	0.1%
50	0.5%
100	1%
1,000	10%
10,000	100%

Thus, MSFT has been able to switch from a LIBOR + 10 basis points floating loan to a 5.1% fixed loan on $100 million.

18.5.2 Fixed-rate Loan to Floating-rate Loan

On the other hand, INTC could transform a fixed-rate loan into a floating-rate loan. Assume that INTC has borrowed $100 million at 5.2%. This is a fixed-rate loan. If INTC enters into the swap, it will face three sets of cash flows:

a. Payment of 5.2% to outside lenders.
b. Inflow of 5% under the terms of the swap.
c. Payment of LIBOR under the terms of the swap.

Net CF = LIBOR + 0.2%.

Thus, INTC has been able to switch from a 5.2% fixed loan to a LIBOR + 0.2% floating loan on $100 million (Figure 18.2).

Figure 18.2 Using Swaps to Transform Liabilities

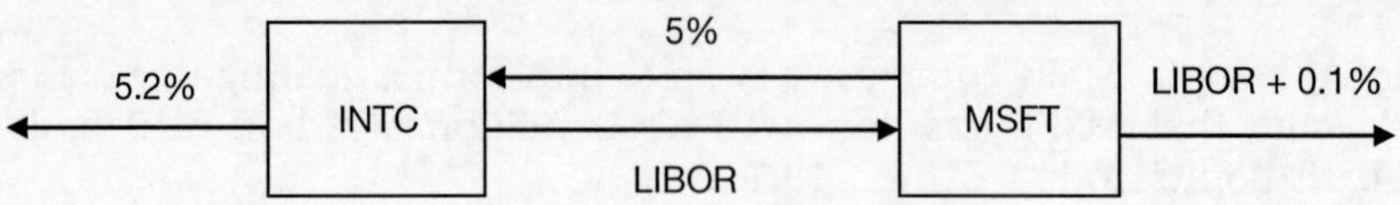

18.6 Using Swaps to Transform Assets

As discussed above, swap can also be used to transform assets from one state to another. This may be done by transforming a fixed-rate asset to floating-rate asset and vice versa.

18.6.1 Fixed-rate Asset to Floating-rate Asset

Let us follow the same example with some modifications. Now assume that MSFT owns $100 million in bonds paying 4.7% per annum over the next three years. If MSFT enters into the swap to make it a floating-rate asset, it will face three sets of cash flows:

a. Inflow of 4.7% from the bonds.
b. Inflow of LIBOR under the terms of the swap.
c. Payment of 5% under the terms of the swap.

Net CF = LIBOR – 0.3%.

18.6.2 Floating-rate Asset to Fixed-rate Asset

On the other hand, INTC can change the floating-rate asset to fixed-rate asset if it wants so (Figure 18.3). Assume that INTC owns $100 million in bonds paying LIBOR – 0.2% over the

Figure 18.3 Using Swaps to Transform Assets

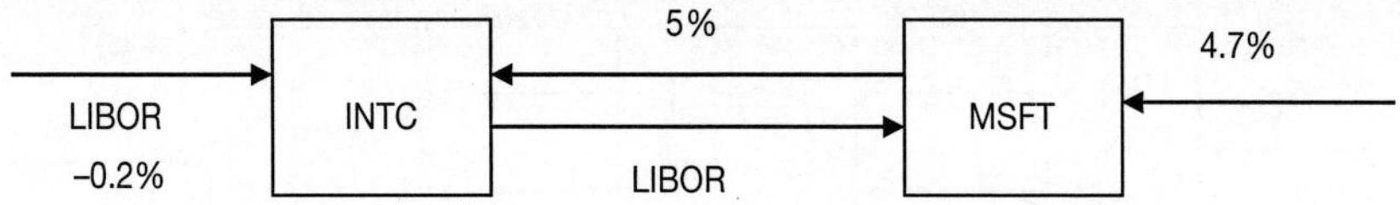

next three years. If INTC enters into the swap to transform it into fixed-rate asset, it will face three sets of cash flows:

a. Inflow of LIBOR – 0.2% from the bonds.
b. Inflow of 5% under the terms of the swap.
c. Payment of LIBOR under the terms of the swap.

Net CF = 4.8%.

18.7 Financial Intermediaries

Usually companies do not enter into swap agreements directly. Instead, they deal with a financial intermediary (e.g., a bank). Swaps are set up so that the financial intermediary earns three to four basis points on offsetting transactions. It is important to understand the role of financial intermediaries in swap transactions. Thus, the role of financial intermediaries is shown below in two of the transactions as already discussed, transforming liabilities and transforming assets.

18.7.1 Transforming Liabilities

As mentioned in Figure 18.4, MSFT ends up borrowing at 5.115% in place of 5.1%. This extra 0.015% is for the inclusion of financial institution as intermediary. Similarly, NTC ends up borrowing at LIBOR + 0.215%, which is also higher by 0.015% (previously, it was LIBOR + 0.2%) for the same reason. Thus, the financial intermediary makes 0.3% (5.015% – 4.985%) if neither INTC nor MSFT defaults.

Figure 18.4 Transforming Liabilities via Financial Institution

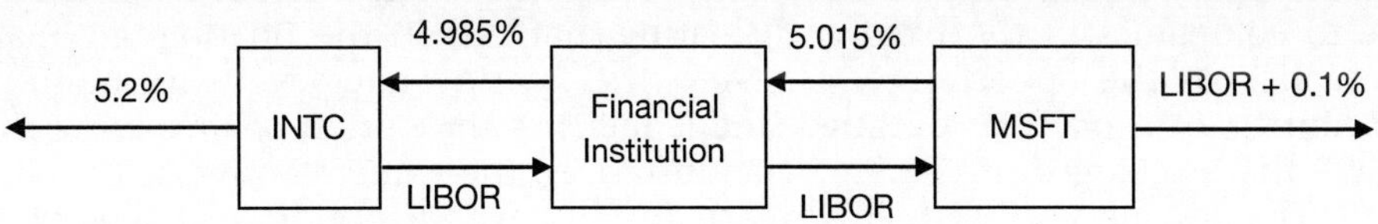

18.7.2 Transforming Assets

In this case, MSFT ends up earning at LIBOR – 0.315% (5.015% – 4.7%), which was LIBOR – 0.3% before. This 0.015% reduction in earning is for the inclusion of financial institution as

Figure 18.5 Transforming Assets via Financial Institution

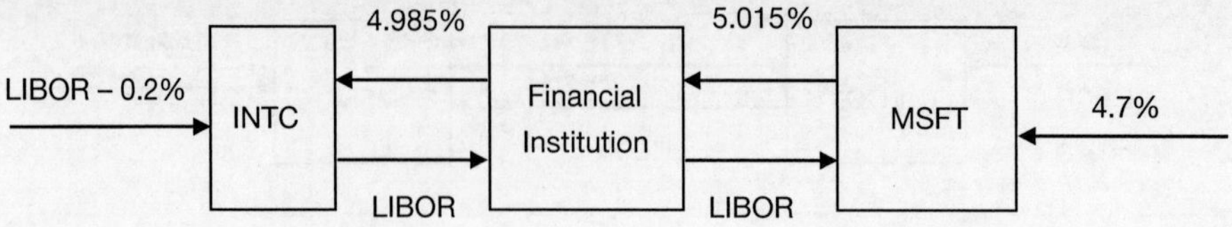

intermediary. At the same time, INTC ends up earning at 4.785% (4.985% – 0.2%), which is also 0.015% less than the previous 4.8%. The financial intermediary makes 0.3% (5.015% – 4.985%) if neither INTC nor MSFT defaults (Figure 18.5).

Major financial institutions act as market makers in the swap market. They need to hedge their positions by decomposing the swap into FRAs or bonds, and then they take the opposite position in the 'synthetic swap'. Quotes should be read as the 'fixed rate' that is paid to receive LIBOR. If you want to receive (buy) LIBOR, you pay the offer rate. If you want to receive fixed (i.e., sell LIBOR) you will get the bid rate.

18.8 Comparative Advantage

An explanation commonly put forward to explain the popularity of swaps concerns comparative advantages. Consider the use of an interest rate swap to transform a liability. Some companies, it is argued, have a comparative advantage when borrowing in fixed-rate markets, while others have a comparative advantage in floating-rate markets. When obtaining a new loan, it makes sense for a company to go to the market where it has a comparative advantage. This may lead to a company borrowing fixed when it wants floating, or vice versa. The swap is used to transform the different types of liabilities.

The total apparent gain from an interest rate swap agreement is always, where is the difference between the interest rates facing the two companies in fixed-rate markets, and is the difference between the interest rates facing the two companies in floating-rate markets.

18.8.1 Criticism of the Comparative Advantage Argument

Why should the spreads between the rates offered to A and B be different in fixed and floating markets? Now that the swap market has been in existence for some time, we might reasonably expect these types of differences to have been arbitraged away. The reason why spread differentials appear to continue to exist may be due in part to the nature of the contracts available to companies in the fixed and floating markets. In the floating-rate market, the lender usually has the opportunity to review the floating rates every six months. If the creditworthiness of A or B has declined, the lender has the option of increasing the spread over LIBOR that is charged. In extreme circumstances, the lender can refuse to roll over the loan at all. The providers of fixed-rate finance do not have the option to change the terms of the loan in this way.

The spreads between the rates offered to A and B are a reflection of the extent to which B is more likely to default than A. During the next six months, there is very little chance that either A or B will default. As we look further ahead, default statistics show that the probability of a default by a company with a low credit rating (such as B) increases faster than the probability of a default by a company with a high credit rating (such as A). This is why the spread between the five-year rates is greater than the spread between the six-month rates.

Example 2: Consider two companies, one with an AAA rating and one with a BBB rating. Rates available to both companies in the fixed and floating markets are as follows:

	Fixed	*Floating*
AAA Corp	10.00%	Libor + 0.30%
BBB Corp	11.20%	Libor + 1.00%
Difference	1.20%	0.700%

Clearly, BBB Corp has a comparative advantage in floating-rate markets and AAA Corp has a comparative advantage in fixed markets. If they enter into a swap, the expected gain is 0.5% (1.20% – 0.7%). If AAA Corp wants to borrow floating, and BBB Corp wants to borrow fixed, then the relationship is shown below in Figure 18.6.

Figure 18.6 Comparative Advantage

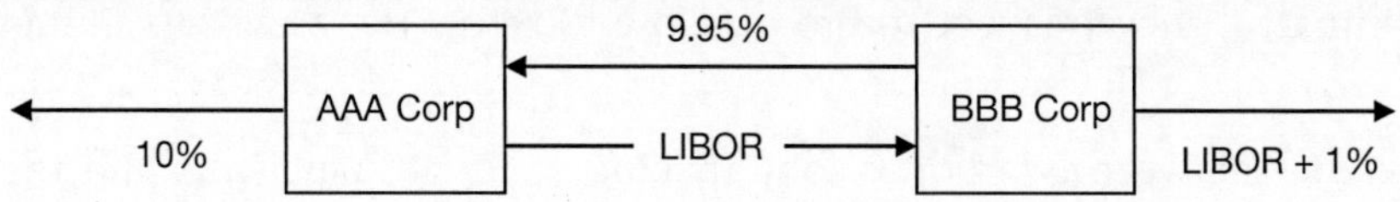

Net effect:

AAA Corp pays LIBOR + 0.05%. This is 0.25% cheaper than borrowing directly in the floating-rate market. BBB Corp pays 10.95%. This is 0.25% cheaper than borrowing directly in the floating-rate market. Total gains = 0.25% + 0.25% = 0.5%

Figure 18.7 Comparative Advantage via Financial Institution

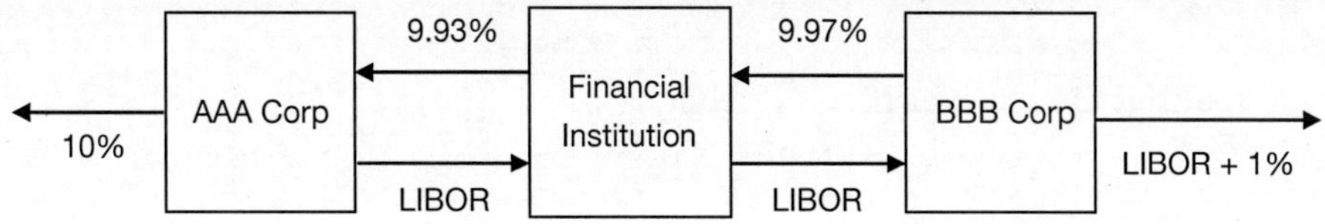

Net effect:

AAA Corp pays LIBOR + 0.07%. This is 0.23% cheaper than borrowing directly in the floating-rate market. BBB Corp pays 10.97%. This is 0.23% cheaper than borrowing directly in the floating-rate market. Financial institution makes 0.04% if there is no default. Total gain = 0.23% + 0.23% +0.04% = 0.5% (Figure 18.7).

18.9 LIBOR/Swap Zero Rates

LIBOR is only observable for maturities of up to one year. Thus, swap rates need to be used for longer maturities. The value of a newly issued floating-rate bond that pays six-month LIBOR is always equal to PAR when the LIBOR/swap zero curve is used for discounting. (If the bond pays LIBOR and it is discounted at LIBOR, then it sells at PAR.) Thus, for a newly issued swap:

$$B_{fix} = B_{fl} = PAR$$

Thus, swap rates can be seen as the rate applicable to PAR yield bonds.

Example 3: Let the 6-month, 12-month and 18-month LIBOR/swap zero rates are 4%, 4.5% and 4.8%, respectively. The two-year swap rate is 5%, then the two-year zero rate can found by solving for R in:

$$2.5e^{-0.04*0.5} + 2.5e^{-0.045*1} + 2.5e^{-0.048*1.5} + 102.5e^{-2R} = 100$$
$$R = 4.953\%R$$

18.10 Valuation of Interest Rate Swaps

When it is initiated, a swap is worth zero (or close to zero). Two ways of valuing an interest rate swap:

a. Difference between two bonds (one making fixed-rate payments and the other one making floating-rate payments).
b. A portfolio of FRAs.

18.10.1 Valuation in Terms of Bond Prices

Remember that swaps only involve the exchange of net CFs. However, we could assume that full bond and principal payments are exchanged without changing the dynamics and value of the swap.

- For a fixed-rate receiver (floating-rate payer):

$$V_{swap} = B_{fix} - B_{float}$$

- For a floating-rate receiver (fixed-rate payer):

$$V_{swap} = B_{float} - B_{fix}$$

Therefore, swap values are symmetrical.

When we covered interest rates, we saw how to value a fixed-rate bond. B_{fl} is worth the PAR value (L) right after a coupon payment (because the next coupon is set exactly equal to the observed floating rate on that date).

- The value of B_{fl} is given by

$$(L + K^*)e^{-(r^*)(t^*)}$$

where
t^* is the time at which the next exchange of payments is made (i.e., the next coupon is paid).
K^* is the floating payment that will be made at t^*
r^* is the LIBOR/swap zero rate for a maturity t^*

Example 4:
Swap agreement:
Pay six-month LIBOR
Receive 8% per annum (with semi-annual compounding).
Notional $100 million
Time to maturity: 1.25 years.
Three-, 9- and 15-month LIBOR rates: 10%, 10.5% and 11%, respectively.
The LIBOR rate at the last payment was 10.2% (with semi-annual compounding).

$$K^* = \frac{1}{2} \times 0.102 \times 100 = 5.1$$

$$t^* = 0.25$$

Time	B(fix) CF	B(fl) CF	Discount Factor	PV of B(fix) CF	PV of B(fl) CF
0.25	4	105.1	0.9753	3.901	102.505
0.75	4		0.9243	3.697	
1.25	104		0.8715	90.64	
Total				98.238	102.505

$V_{swap} = B_{fix} - B_{float} = 98.238 - 102.505 = -4.267.$

18.10.2 Valuation in Terms of FRAs

A swap can be seen as a portfolio of FRAs. The first payment in a swap is known today (or at inception), the remaining payments can be seen as FRAs. Remember, FRAs are valued assuming that forward interest rates are realized.

Steps:

1. Use the LIBOR/swap zero curve to calculate forward rates for each of the LIBOR rates that will determine swap CFs.
2. Calculate swap CFs on the assumption that LIBOR rates will equal the forward rates (i.e., assuming that forward rates are realized).
3. Discount these swap CFs (using the LIBOR/swap zero curve) to obtain the swap value.

Example 5:
Swap agreement:
Pay six-month LIBOR
Receive 8% per annum (with semi-annual compounding).
Notional: $100 million
Time to maturity: 1.25 years.
Three-, 9- and 15-month LIBOR rates: 10%, 10.5% and 11%, respectively.
LIBOR rate at the last payment was 10.2% (with semi-annual compounding).

Time	B(fix) CF	B(fl) CF	Net CF	Disc. Factor	PV of Net CF	
0.25	4.0	–5.100	–1.100	0.9753	–1.073	Known
0.75	4.0	–5.522	–1.522	0.9243	–1.407	FRA 1
1.25	4.0	–6.051	–2.051	0.8715	–1.787	FRA 2
Total					–4.267	

Row 1: The CFs that will be exchanged in three months are known today (we know the fixed payments and the floating coupon is set at the beginning of the coupon period, which occurred six months ago).

Row 2: CFs in nine months assuming that the fwd rates are realized. Remember,

$$R_F = \frac{R_2T_2 - R_1T_1}{T_2 - T_1}$$

So the fwd rate (with cont. comp.) between three and nine months is:

$$R_F = \frac{(0.105)(0.75) - (0.1)(0.25)}{0.75 - 0.25} = 0.1075$$

Or 11.044% with semi-annual comp. Thus, the cash outflow in nine months is 100 × 0.11044 × ½ = 5.522.

18.11 Currency Swaps

Another popular type of swap is known as a currency swap. In its simplest form, this involves exchanging principal and fixed-rate interest payments on a loan in one currency for principal and fixed-rate interest payments on an approximately equivalent loan in another currency. It requires the principal to be specified in each of the two currencies. Usually, the principal amounts are exchanged at the beginning and at the end of the life of the swap. The principal values are initially equivalent (using the exchange rate) so that the swap is worth zero at inception.

18.11.1 Reasons for Currency Swaps

A currency swap can be used to transform a loan in one currency into a loan in another currency. To illustrate how a currency swap works, we suppose that company A and company B are offered the fixed five-year rates of interest in U.S. dollars and Sterling shown as follows:

Borrowing Rates Motivating Currency SWAP		
Quoted rates have been adjusted to reflect tax advantages/disadvantages		
	Dollars	**Sterling**
Company A	8.00%	11.6%
Company B	10.00%	12.0%

Company A has a comparative advantage in the U.S. dollar market, while company B has a comparative advantage in the sterling market. In Section 18.2, we argued that comparative advantages were largely illusory when fixed and floating rates are compared. Here, we are comparing the rates offered in two different currencies, and it is more likely that the comparative advantages are genuine. We suppose that A wants to borrow sterling while B wants to borrow dollars. This creates a perfect situation for a currency swap.

Companies A and B each borrow in the market where they have a comparative advantage; that is, company A borrows dollars while company B borrows sterling. They then use a currency swap to transform A's loan into a sterling loan and B's loan into a dollar loan.

As already mentioned, the difference between the dollar interest rates minus the difference between the sterling interest rates will be the total expected gain to all parties. There are many ways in which the swap can be organized. Figure 18.8 shows one possible arrangement. Company A borrows dollar while company B borrows sterling. The effect of the swap is to transform the U.S. dollar interest rate of 8% per annum to a sterling interest rate of 11% per annum for company A. This makes company A 0.6% per annum better off than it would be if it went directly to sterling markets. Similarly, company B exchanges a sterling loan at 12% for a dollar loan at 9.4% and ends up 0.6% better off than it would be if it went directly to dollar markets. The financial intermediary gains 1.4% per annum on its dollar cash flows and loses 1% per annum on its sterling cash flows. Ignoring the difference between the two currencies, it makes a net gain of 0.4% per annum. As predicted, the total gain to all parties is 1.6% per annum.

A currency swap agreement requires the principal to be specified in each of the two currencies. The principal amounts are usually exchanged at the beginning and at the end of the life of the swap. They are chosen so that they are approximately equal at the exchange rate at the beginning of the swap's life.

The reader may feel that the swap in Figure 18.8 is unsatisfactory because the financial institution is exposed to foreign exchange risk. However, the financial institution can avoid this risk by buying the sterling it needs per annum in the forward market for each year of the life of the swap. This will lock in a net gain in U.S. dollars. If we tried to redesign the swap so that the financial institution makes a 0.4% spread in dollars and a zero spread in sterling, we might come up with the arrangement in Figure 18.9 or Figure 18.10. In Figure 18.9, company B bears some foreign exchange risk because it pays 1% per annum in sterling and 8.4% in dollars.

In Figure 18.10, company A bears some foreign exchange risk because it receives 1% per annum in dollars and pays 12% in sterling. In general, it makes sense for the financial institution to bear the foreign exchange risk because it is in the best position to hedge it. Like interest rate swaps, currency swaps are frequently warehoused by financial institutions. The financial institution then carefully monitors its exposure to various currencies so that it can hedge its risk.

Figure 18.8 Currency Swap

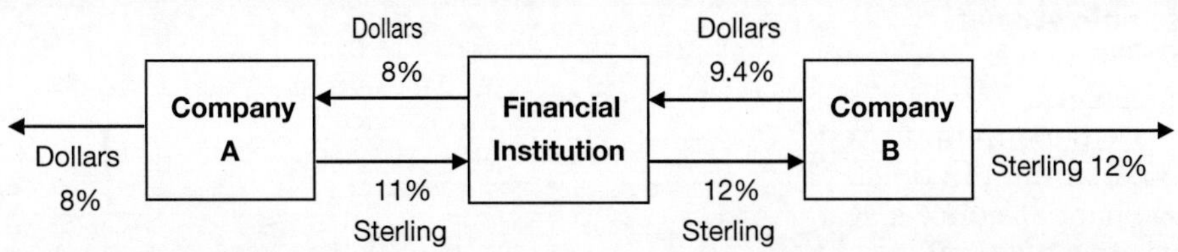

Figure 18.9 Alternative Arrangement for Currency Swap; Company B Bears Some Foreign Currency Risk

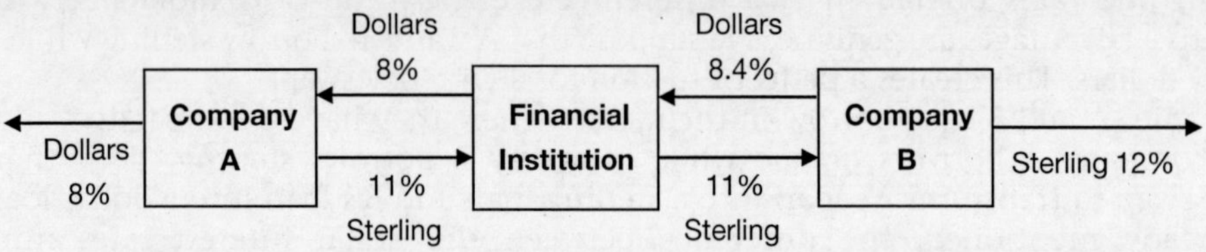

Figure 18.10 Alternative Arrangement for Currency Swap; Company A Bears Some Foreign Currency Risk

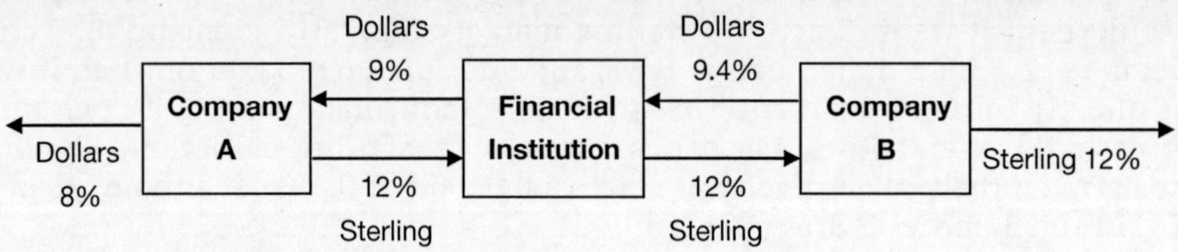

18.11.2 Valuation of Currency Swaps

There are two ways of valuing a fixed-for-fixed currency swap:

a. Difference between two bonds (one foreign bond and one local bond)
b. A portfolio of forward contracts

Valuation in Terms of Bond Prices

- When dollars are received (foreign currency is paid):

$$V_{swap} = B_D - S_O B_F$$

- When dollars are paid (foreign currency is received):

$$V_{swap} = S_O B_F - B_D$$

Remember, the exchange rate is defined as the cost of one unit of foreign currency. In this case, dollars/foreign.

Example 6:
Assume:
Japanese rate: 4% flat.
U.S. rate: 9% flat.
Swap agreement:
Receive: 5% per annum in yen.
Pay: 8% per annum in dollars.
Exchange happens once a year.
Notional yen: 1,200 million

Notional dollar: $10 million
S_o = 1/110 (in $/yen)
Time to maturity: 3 years

Solution 6

Time	CF on Dollar Bond ($)	PV ($)	CF fwd on Yen Bond (Yen)	PV(yen)
1	0.8	0.7311	60	57.65
2	0.8	0.6682	60	55.39
3	0.8	0.6107	60	53.22
3	10	7.6338	1,200	1,064.30
		9.6439		**1,230.55**

$$V_{swap} = S_O B_F - B_D$$

$$V_{swap} = \frac{1}{110} 1{,}230.55 - 9.6439 = 1.5430$$

Valuation in Terms of Forward Contracts

You can value the swap as a portfolio of forward contracts. Remember, forward foreign exchange contracts can be valued by assuming that forward exchange rates are realized. Also remember that forward exchange rates are given by

$$F_o = S_O e^{(r-r_f)T}$$

Example 7:
Assume:
Japanese rate: 4% flat.
U.S. rate: 9% flat.
Swap agreement:
Receive: 5% per annum in yen.
Pay: 8% per annum in dollars.
Exchange happens once a year.
Notional yen: 1,200 million
Notional dollar: $10 million
= 1/110 (in $/yen)
Time to maturity: 3 years

Time	CF on Dollar Bond ($)	CF fwd on Yen Bond (Yen)	Fwd Rate	Dollar Value of Yen CF	Net CF ($)	PV ($)
1	−0.8	60	0.009557	0.5734	−0.2266	−0.2071
2	−0.8	60	0.010047	0.6028	−0.1972	−0.1647
3	−0.8	60	0.010562	0.6337	−0.1663	−0.1269
3	−10	1,200	0.010562	12.6743	2.6746	2.0417
Total						**1.5430**

CF on dollar bond ($) = 0.08 × 10 = 0.8
CF fwd on yen bond (yen) = 0.05 × 1,200 = 60

$$F_o = S_o e^{(r-r_f)T} = \frac{1}{100} e^{(0.09-0.04)^1} = 0.009557$$

18.12 Credit Risk Issues

Consider a financial institution that has entered into offsetting contracts with two companies. If neither party defaults, the financial institution remains fully hedged. Suppose that sometime after the initiation of the contracts, the contract with company B has a positive value to the financial institution while the contract with company A has a negative value. If company B defaults, the financial institution is liable to lose the whole of the positive value it has in this contract. To maintain a hedged position, it would have to find a third party willing to take company's B position. To induce the third party to take the position, it would have to pay the third party an amount roughly equal to the value of its contract with B prior to the default.

A financial institution has credit risk exposure from a swap only when the value of the swap to the financial institution is positive. What happens when this value is negative and the counterparty gets into financial difficulties? In theory, the financial institution could realize a windfall gain since a default would lead to it getting rid of a liability. In practice, it is likely that the counterparty would choose to sell the contract to a third party or rearrange its affairs in some way so that its positive value in the contract is not lost. The most realistic assumption for the financial institution is therefore as follows. If the counterparty goes bankrupt, there will be a loss if the value of the swap to the financial institution is positive, and there will be no effect on the financial institution's position if the value of the swap is negative.

In general, the expected loss from a default on a currency swap is greater than the expected loss from a default on an interest rate swap. This is because, in the case of a currency swap, principal amounts in different currencies are exchanged. It is important to distinguish between the credit risk and market risk to a financial institution in any contract. As discussed earlier, the credit risk arises from the possibility of a default by the counterparty when the value of the contract to the financial institution is positive. The market risk arises from the possibility that market variables such as interest rates and exchanged rates will move in such a way that the value of a contract to the financial institution becomes negative. Market risks can be hedged by entering into offsetting contracts; credit risks cannot be hedged.

18.13 Conclusion

An interest rate swap can help protect the issuer of bonds, Treasuries, or loans against interest rate risk by transferring the risk to another party in exchange for a variable payment. A swap contract is an agreement to exchange future cash flows. Swaps can remove market risk but not credit risk. The most common type of swap agreement is the fixed-floating interest rate swap, otherwise known as a plain-vanilla swap, and is the most common type of interest rate derivative. The payment is calculated by multiplying the interest rate times a notional principal, which is not exchanged, but is simply a number used to calculate both interest payments. The counterparty paying the fixed amount is the fixed-rate payer and the counterparty paying the floating rate is the floating-rate payer. The fixed payment of a swap is known as the fixed leg while the floating payment is referred to as the floating leg. However, only the net difference between these obligations is paid, and who pays whom depends on whom the change in interest rates favours. For instance, if the float rate rises above the fixed rate, then the floating-rate payer pays the fixed-rate payer the difference between the floating rate and the fixed rate, but if the floating rate falls below the fixed rate, then the fixed-rate payer pays the floating-rate payer the difference in interest rates. It is possible for one counterparty to receive all of the payments without paying anything, or it could go back and forth, depending on how interest rates fluctuate.

The frequency of the payment is the tenor or coupon frequency. Common tenors are one month, three months, six months and annually. Sometimes, the two legs of a swap have different tenors.

Other interest rate derivatives include the basis swap, which has two floating legs but no fixed leg. Thus, it is exchanging payments based on a floating interest rate on one index to that of another, such as the prime interest rate and the LIBOR. Basis, as used here, is the difference between two rates, such as the difference between spot prices and futures prices of a given commodity, so risk can arise when basis changes.

Another type of interest rate derivative is the cross-currency interest rate swap, or just currency swap, in which both legs of the swap are denominated in different currencies. Most of the swaps are set up to exchange a fixed interest rate in one currency with a floating rate in the other currency. To remove exchange rate risk, the notional amount of the swaps is generally exchanged. Therefore, if the exchange rate at the signing of the swap agreement is $1.25 to €1, and a company wants to exchange a fixed rate based on €1,000,000 for a floating rate in USD, then the euro party will give €1,000,000 to the other party and receive $1.25 million in U.S. dollars. This removes the exchange rate risk, and the swap agreement itself removes interest rate risk, which was its purpose. If a company wanted to remove foreign exchange risk without exchanging currencies, then that risk can be hedged with a forward agreement—specifically, an FX forward—or with interest rate futures or options to mitigate its risk.

Multiple Choice Questions

1. In a swap motivated by credit differentials, a firm should borrow in the market where
   a. It can borrow at the cheapest rate
   b. It can borrow for the longest period
   c. It has an absolute advantage
   d. It has a comparative advantage

2. The swap floating rate usually is based on
   a. The prime rate
   b. Libor
   c. The T-bill rate
   d. The call money rate

3. A type of risk inherent in swaps that is not inherent in listed options is
   a. Market risk
   b. Counterparty risk
   c. The risk of a price decline
   d. The risk of a price rise

4. Regarding interest rate swaps, all of the following are true except
   a. You may either pay or receive the floating rate
   b. You may either pay or receive the fixed rate
   c. The principal changes hands at the beginning of the swap
   d. Interest may be determined in advance or in arrears

5. Which of the following is true regarding foreign currency swaps?
   a. Principal changes hands at the beginning of the swap only
   b. Principal changes hands at the end of the swap only
   c. Principal changes hands at the beginning and end of the swap
   d. Principal does not change hands
6. An option on a swap is a ________
   a. Swaption b. Caplet c. Floorlet d. Swaplet
7. A swaption involves a ________
   a. Good faith deposit b. Down payment c. Premium d. Short sale
8. Interest rate swaps are usually possible because international financial markets in different countries are ________
   a. Efficient b. Perfect c. Imperfect d. None
9. The basic motivations for swaps are shown below.
   a. To provide protection against future changes in exchange rates
   b. To eliminate interest rate risks arising from normal commercial operations
   c. To reduce financing costs
   d. All of the above
10. Currency swaps involve ________
    a. One currency b. Two currencies c. Foreign stocks d. None

Discussion Questions

1. Define swap. What are the uses of swap?
2. What are the advantages and disadvantages of swap?
3. What are the different types of swap?
4. Explain interest rate swap with an example.
5. How swap is used to transform liabilities?
6. How swap is used to transform assets?
7. What are the uses of financial intermediaries to transform assets and liabilities?
8. Critically explain the criticisms of comparative advantage.
9. Explain LIBOR/swap zero rates.
10. Explain valuation of interest rate swaps in terms of bond prices and FRAs.
11. Define currency swap and the reasons of currency swap.
12. Explain valuation of currency swaps in terms of bond prices and forward contracts.
13. Explain the similarity between a swap and a forward contract.
14. Forward, futures and option contracts had been used by financial institutions to hedge risk for many years before swaps were invented. If financial institutions already had these hedging instruments, why do they need swaps?
15. Distinguish between a swap buyer and a swap seller? In which markets does each have the comparative advantage?

Exercises

1. An insurance company owns $50 million of floating-rate bonds yielding LIBOR plus 1%. These loans are financed by $50 million of fixed-rate guaranteed investment contracts

costing 10%. A finance company has $50 million of auto loans with a fixed rate of 14%. The loans are financed by $50 million of CDs at a variable rate of LIBOR plus 4%.

a. What is the risk exposure of the insurance company?
b. What is the risk exposure of the finance company?
c. What would be the cash flow goals of each company if they were to enter into a swap arrangement?
d. Which company would be the buyer and which company would be the seller in the swap?
e. Diagram the direction of the relevant cash flows for the swap arrangement.
f. What are reasonable cash flow amounts, or relative interest rates, for each of the payment streams?

2. In a swap arrangement, the variable-rate swap cash flow streams often do not fully hedge the variable-rate cash flow streams from the balance sheet due to basis risk.

a. What are the possible sources of basis risk in an interest rate swap?
b. How could the failure to achieve a perfect hedge be realized by the swap buyer?
c. How could the failure to achieve a perfect hedge be realized by the swap seller?

3. A commercial bank has $200 million of floating-rate loans yielding the T-bill rate plus 2%. These loans are financed by $200 million of fixed-rate deposits costing 9%. A savings bank has $200 million of mortgages with a fixed rate of 13%. They are financed by $200 million of CDs with a variable rate of the T-bill rate plus 3%.

a. Discuss the type of interest rate risk each financial institution faces.
b. Propose a swap that would result in each financial institution having the same type of asset and liability cash flows.
c. Show that this swap would be acceptable to both parties.
d. What are some of the practical difficulties in arranging this swap?

4. Bank 1 can issue five-year CDs at an annual rate of 11% fixed or at a variable rate of LIBOR plus 2%. Bank 2 can issue five-year CDs at an annual rate of 13% fixed or at a variable rate of LIBOR plus 3%.

a. Is a mutually beneficial swap possible between the two banks?
b. Where is the comparative advantage of the two banks?
c. What is the net quality spread?
d. What is an example of a feasible swap?

5. The first bank can issue one-year, floating-rate CDs at prime plus 1% or fixed-rate CDs at 12.5%. The second bank can issue one-year, floating-rate CDs at prime plus 0.5% or fixed-rate at 11%.

a. What is a feasible swap with all of the benefits going to the first bank?
b. What is a feasible swap with all of the benefits going to the second bank?
c. Draw a diagram for each situation.
d. What factors will determine the final swap arrangement?

6. Two multinational corporations enter their respective debt markets to issue $100 million of two-year notes. Firm A can borrow at a fixed annual rate of 11% or a floating rate of LIBOR plus 50-basis points, re-priced at the end of the year. Firm B can borrow at a fixed annual rate of 10% or a floating rate of LIBOR, re-priced at the end of the year.

a. If firm A is a positive duration gap insurance company and firm B is a money market mutual fund, in what market(s) should each firm borrow so as to reduce their interest rate risk exposures?

b. In which debt market does firm A have a comparative advantage over firm B?
c. Although firm A is riskier than firm B, and therefore must pay a higher rate in both the fixed-rate and floating-rate markets, there are possible gains to trade. Set up a swap to exploit firm A's comparative advantage over firm B. What are the total gains from the swap trade? Assume a swap intermediary fee of 10 basis points.
d. The gains from the swap trade can be apportioned between firms A and B through negotiation. What terms of trade would give all the gains to firm A? What terms of trade would give all the gains to firm B?
e. Assume swap pricing that allocates all the gains from the swap to firm A. If A buys the swap from B and pays the swap intermediary's fee, what are the end-of-year net cash flows if LIBOR is 8.25%?
f. If A buys the swap in part (e) from B and pays the swap intermediary's fee, what are the end-of-year net cash flows if LIBOR is 11%? Be sure to net swap payments against cash market payments for both firms.
g. If all barriers to entry and pricing inefficiencies between firm A's debt markets and firm B's debt markets were eliminated, how would that affect the swap transaction?

7. Describe how an inverse floater works to the advantage of an investor who receives coupon payments of 10% minus LIBOR if LIBOR is currently at 4%? When is it a disadvantage to the investor? Does the issuing party bear any risk?
8. A financial institution has $500 million of assets with a duration of nine years and $450 million of liabilities with a duration of three years. The financial institution wants to hedge its duration gap with a swap that has fixed-rate payments with a duration of six years and floating-rate payments with a duration of two years. What is the optimal amount of the swap to effectively macro-hedge against the adverse effect of a change in interest rates on the value of the financial institution's equity?
9. A Swiss bank issues a $100 million, three-year Eurodollar CD at a fixed annual rate of 7%. The proceeds of the CD are lent to a Swiss company for three years at a fixed rate of 9%. The spot exchange rate is SF1.50/$.

a. Is this expected to be a profitable transaction?
b. What are the cash flows if exchange rates are unchanged over the next three years?
c. What is the risk exposure of the bank's underlying cash position?
d. How can the Swiss bank reduce that risk exposure?
e. If the U.S. dollar is expected to appreciate against the Swiss franc (SF) to SF1.65/$, SF1.815/$ and SF2.00/$ over the next three years, what will be the cash flows on this transaction?
f. If the Swiss bank swaps U.S.$ payments for SF payments at the current spot exchange rate, what are the cash flows on the swap? What are the cash flows on the entire hedged position? Assume that the U.S.$ appreciates at the rates in part (e).
g. What are the cash flows on the swap and the hedged position if actual spot exchange rates are as follows:
   End of year 1: SF 1.55/U.S.$
   End of year 2: SF 1.47/U.S.$
   End of year 3: SF 1.48/U.S.$
h. What would be the bank's risk exposure if the fixed-rate Swiss loan was financed with a floating rate U.S. $100 million, three-year Eurodollar CD?
i. What type of hedge is appropriate if the Swiss bank in part (h) wants to reduce its risk exposure?
j. If the annual Eurodollar CD rate is set at LIBOR and LIBOR at the end of years 1, 2 and 3 is expected to be 7%, 8% and 9%, respectively, what will be the cash flows on the bank's un-hedged cash position? Assume no change in exchange rates.

k. What are the cash flows on the bank's un-hedged cash position if exchange rates are as follows:
   End of year 1: SF 1.55/U.S.$
   End of year 2: SF 1.47/U.S.$
   End of year 3: SF 1.48/U.S.$
l. What are both the swap and total hedged position cash flows if the bank swaps out its floating rate U.S.$ CD payments in exchange for 7.75% fixed-rate, SF payments at the current spot exchange rate of SF1.50/$?
m. Use the following spot rates for par value coupon bonds to forecast expected future spot rates. (Hint: Forecast expected future spot rates using implied forward rates.)
   one-year 7.0%
   two-year 8.5%
   three-year 9.2%
n. Use the rate forecasts in part (m) to calculate the cash flows on an 8.75% fixed to floating-rate swap of U.S. dollars to Swiss francs at SF1.50/$.

10. Use the following balance sheet information (in millions) to construct a swap hedge against interest rate risk exposure.

Assets		***Liabilities and Equity***	
Rate sensitive assets	$50	Rates sensitive liabilities	$75
Fixed rate assets	150	Fixed-rate liabilities	100
		Net worth	25
Total assets	$200	Total liabilities and equity	$200

Rate-sensitive assets are re-priced quarterly at the 91-day Treasury bill rate plus 150 basis points. Fixed-rate assets have five years until maturity and are paying 9% annually. Rate-sensitive liabilities are re-priced quarterly at the 91-day Treasury bill rate plus 100 basis points. Fixed-rate liabilities have two years until maturity and are paying 7% annually. Currently, the 91-day Treasury bill rate is 6.25%.

a. What is the bank's current NII? If Treasury bill rates increase 150 basis points, what will be the change in the bank's NII?
b. What is the bank's re-pricing or funding gap? Use the re-pricing model to calculate the change in the bank's NII if interest rates increase 150 basis points.
c. How can swaps be used as an interest rate hedge in this example?

11. Use the following information to construct a swap of asset cash flows for the bank in problem 14. The bank is a price taker in both the fixed-rate market at 9% and the rate-sensitive market at the T-bill rate plus 1.5%. A securities dealer has a large portfolio of rate-sensitive assets funded with fixed-rate liabilities. The dealer is a price taker in a fixed-rate asset market, paying 8.5% and a floating-rate asset market paying the 91-day T-bill rate plus 1.25%. All interest is paid annually.

a. What is the interest rate risk exposure to the securities dealer?
b. How can the bank and the securities dealer use a swap to hedge their respective interest rate risk exposures?
c. What are the total potential gains to the swap trade?
d. Consider the following two-year swap of asset cash flows: An annual fixed-rate asset cash flow of 8.6% in exchange for a floating-rate asset cash flow of T-bill plus 125 basis points. The total swap intermediary fee is five basis points. How are the swap

gains apportioned between the bank and the securities dealer if they each hedge their interest rate risk exposures using this swap?

e. What are the swap net cash flows if T-bill rates at the end of the first year are 7.75% and at the end of the second year are 5.5%? Assume that the notional value is $107.14 million.

f. What are the sources of the swap gains to trade?

g. What are the implications for the efficiency of cash markets?

12. Consider the following currency swap of coupon interest on the following assets:

- 5% (annual coupon) fixed-rate U.S. $1 million bond
- 5% (annual coupon) fixed-rate bond denominated in Swiss francs

Spot exchange rates: SF1.5/$

a. What is the face value of the SF bond if the investments are equivalent at spot rates?

b. What are the end-of-year cash flows, assuming no change in spot exchange rates? What are the net cash flows on the swap?

c. What are the cash flows if spot exchange rates fall to SF0.50/$? What are the net cash flows on the swap?

d. What are the cash flows if spot exchange rates rise to SF 2.25/$? What are the net cash flows on the swap?

e. Describe the underlying cash position that would prompt the FI to hedge by swapping dollars in exchange for Swiss francs.

13. Consider the following fixed floating-rate currency swap of assets:
5% (annual coupon) fixed-rate U.S. $1 million bond. Floating-rate SF1.5 million bond set at LIBOR annually. Currently, LIBOR is 4%. Face value of swap is SF1.5 million. Spot exchange rates: SF1.5/$.

a. What are the end-of-year cash flows assuming no change in the spot exchange rates? What are the net cash flows on the swap at the spot exchange rates?

b. If the one-year forward rate is SF1.538 per U.S.$, what are the end-of-year net cash flows on the swap? Assume LIBOR is unchanged.

c. If LIBOR increases to 6%, what are the end-of-year net cash flows on the swap? Evaluate at the forward rate.

14. A U.S. thrift has most of its assets in the form of French franc-denominated floating-rate loans. Its liabilities consist mostly of fixed-rate dollar-denominated CDs. What type of currency risk and interest rate risk does this FI face? How might it use a swap to eliminate some of these risks?

15. Companies X and Y have been offered the following rates per annum on a $5 million 10-year investment:

	Fixed Rate	*Floating Rate*
Company X	8.0%	LIBOR
Company Y	8.8%	LIBOR

Company X requires a fixed-rate investment; company Y requires a floating-rate investment. Design a swap that will net a bank, acting as intermediary, 0.2% per annum and will appear equally attractive to X and Y.

16. A financial institution has entered into an interest rate swap with company X. Under the terms of the swap, it receives 10% per annum and pays six-month LIBOR on a

principal of $10 million for five years. Payments are made every six months. Suppose that company X defaults on the sixth payment date (end of year 3) when the LIBOR/swap interest rate (with semi-annual compounding) is 8% per annum for all maturities. What is the loss to the financial institution? Assume that six-month LIBOR was 9% per annum halfway through year 3. Use LIBOR discounting.

17. A financial institution has entered into a 10-year currency swap with company Y. Under the terms of the swap, the financial institution receives interest at 3% per annum in Swiss francs and pays interest at 8% per annum in U.S. dollars. Interest payments are exchanged once a year. The principal amounts are 7 million dollars and 10 million francs. Suppose that company Y declares bankruptcy at the end of year 6, when the exchange rate is $0.80 per franc. What is the cost to the financial institution? Assume that, at the end of year 6, the interest rate is 3% per annum in Swiss francs and 8% per annum in U.S. dollars for all maturities. All interest rates are quoted with annual compounding.
18. Companies A and B face the following interest rates (adjusted for the differential impact of taxes):

	A	*B*
U.S. dollars (floating rate)	LIBOR + 0.5%	LIBOR + 1.0%
Canadian dollars (fixed rate)	5.0%	6.5%

Assume that A wants to borrow U.S. dollars at a floating rate of interest and B wants to borrow Canadian dollars at a fixed rate of interest. A financial institution is planning to arrange a swap and requires a 50-basis-point spread. If the swap is equally attractive to A and B, what rates of interest will A and B end up paying?

19. The LIBOR zero curve is flat at 5% (continuously compounded) out to 1.5 years. Swap rates for 2- and 3-year semi-annual pay swaps are 5.4% and 5.6%, respectively. Estimate the LIBOR zero rates for maturities of 2.0, 2.5 and 3.0 years. (Assume that the 2.5-year swap rate is the average of the 2- and 3-year swap rates and use LIBOR discounting.)
20. Overnight Indexed Swap (OIS) rates have been estimated as 3.4% for all maturities. The three-month LIBOR rate is 3.5%. For a six-month swap where payments are exchanged every three months, the swap rate is 3.6%. All rates are expressed with quarterly compounding. What is the LIBOR forward rate for the three-month to six-month period if OIS discounting is used?

Reference

Bank for International Settlements (BIS). 2010. 'Triennial and Semi-annual Surveys: Positions in Global Over-the-Counter (OTC) Derivatives Markets at end-June 2010'. Bank for International Settlements, November.

Chapter

19

Forwards and Futures

Chapter Objectives

On completion of this chapter, you will be able to understand:

- Forward contracts
- Futures contracts
- Types of futures contracts
- Features of futures contracts
- Differences between forward contracts and futures contracts
- Underlying asset and contract size
- Price
- Trading arrangements
- Conversion factor
- Invoice price
- Cheapest-to-deliver security
- Forward and futures prices
- Spreads
- Hedging with forwards and futures
- Short hedge or hedging a sales price
- Long hedge or hedging a purchase price

A World with No Futures

To fully appreciate the benefits of liquid futures (and forward) markets, it's easiest to first imagine an economy without them. For example, suppose that the owner of an oil field is trying to decide how many barrels to produce this year. Being a good capitalist, he wants to maximize the present discounted value of his operation throughout its lifetime. If he sells more barrels this year, he naturally earns more revenues now, but at the cost of fewer barrels that he can sell in the future. In order to rationally approach this problem, therefore, the oil tycoon needs to compare the spot price of oil today with the expected price he can fetch in the future.

Even at this stage we can see the fallacy in typical environmentalist condemnations of 'shortsighted' big business. It would be sheer lunacy for the Big Oil companies to exhaust their reserves in a few years. Better than anyone else (for it's their money on the line), the people running the oil companies would have expert forecasts of available supplies and world prices at various points in the future.

If the alarmists really were correct, and humans really were using up a particular resource (such as oil) too quickly, then the impending scarcity (and hence high prices) would signal the owners to restrict current output in order to sell at the higher prices in the future. The reduction in present supply would raise spot prices today, causing consumers of oil to ration their usage. In short, the market would voluntarily do just what the conservationists want.

Unfortunately, there is a snag in this benign process. The people who are experts in pumping, storing, and distributing oil might not be exactly the same people who have the best forecasts concerning the future price of oil. Thus the owner of an oil field might think that next year's spot price could be \$50 or \$60 or even \$70 a barrel, and not be sure how many barrels to produce this year accordingly.

On the other hand, an analyst armed with excellent data sources and supercomputers might be quite certain that next year's spot price of oil will be at least 18 percent higher than today's, yet he might be reluctant to buy thousands of barrels of oil and store them for a year.

An organized futures market in crude oil eliminates these types of problems. The oil producer needn't speculate (literally) on what the price of oil may or may not be in twelve or eighteen months' time; he can simply sell oil futures at a guaranteed futures price. On the other hand, the speculator who believes 'the market' is improperly pricing oil futures can stake out a position accordingly, by buying futures if he thinks they are underpriced or selling them if he thinks the futures price is too high.

The speculator needn't know the slightest thing about actually handling physical barrels of oil; as the delivery date nears, he can unload his futures contracts to another party at their market price. If his predictions were accurate, then his contracts will have appreciated in value from the time he acquired them.

Source: Murphy (2006).

19.1 Forward Contracts

A forward contract is an agreement in which the seller is obliged to deliver an underlying asset or to make cash settlement at a future maturity (expiration) date at a forward price agreed at the start of the contract. The buyer agrees to pay for the underlying asset or to make settlement at a future date. Cash-settled forward contracts are called non-delivery forwards (NDFs). NDFs are settled at maturity and no delivery of primary assets is assumed. The future delivery date or settlement date is usually the same as the expiration date. The value of the forward contract is equal to zero at the initiation and no money changes hands.

The global market for forward contracts is a network of financial institutions, mostly banks that make market in these transactions. Forward contracts are not traded on exchanges. They are OTC contracts. Forward contracts are privately negotiated between two parties—at least one of which is usually a financial intermediary (market maker, dealer), a commercial or an investment bank. The other party of a forward contract may be one of two types: end user or other dealer. An end user is typically a corporation, government or a private person. Forward contracts are widely used in foreign exchange markets. The profit or loss from a forward contract depends on the difference between the forward price and the spot price of the asset on the day the forward contract matures. Forward contracts are settled only at maturity. As per the following time line, a forward contract is a commitment to purchase at a future date a given amount of a commodity or an asset at a price agreed on today. The price fixed now for future exchange is the forward price. The buyer obtains a 'long position' in the asset/commodity.

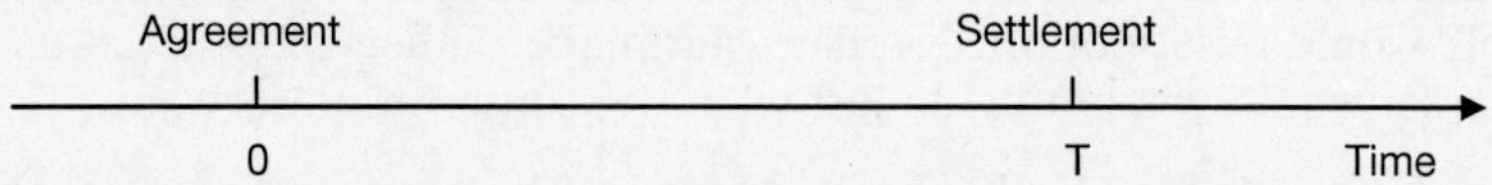

The dealer quotes a bid and asks price or rate. The bid is the price at which the dealer is willing to pay and the ask price is the price at which the dealer is willing to sell. The competition makes bid–ask spreads low. Dealers make a profit from the market-making activity. They do not hold the exposure. They offset the exposure with other derivative or spot transactions. The terms of the contract, such as identity and amount of the underlying asset, expiration date and settlements, are directly negotiated between two parties.

A forward contract can be either purchased or sold. The buyer is called the long and the seller is called the short. The negotiated forward price for future delivery of the asset is different from the current cash price (spot price). The forward price is fixed. It is possible to terminate the position prior to expiration by entering a new forward contract expiring at the same time as the original contract. To completely offset the original forward position, the second transaction must be with the same counterparty. The termination of the original forward position with the other counterparty does not eliminate credit risk. With the sophisticated terms of forward contract, it may be difficult or more costly to terminate the contract before it matures. Illiquidity is a by-product of the contract's flexibility. Features of forward contracts may be identified as follows:

a. Traded OTC (not on exchanges)
b. Custom tailored
c. No money changes hands until maturity
d. Non-trivial counterparty risk

Example: Consider a three-month forward contract for 10,000 bushels of soybean at a forward price of $3.5/bushel. The long side is committed to buy 10,000 bushels of soybean from the short side three months from now at the price of $3.50/bushel.

Date of Agreement: December 10

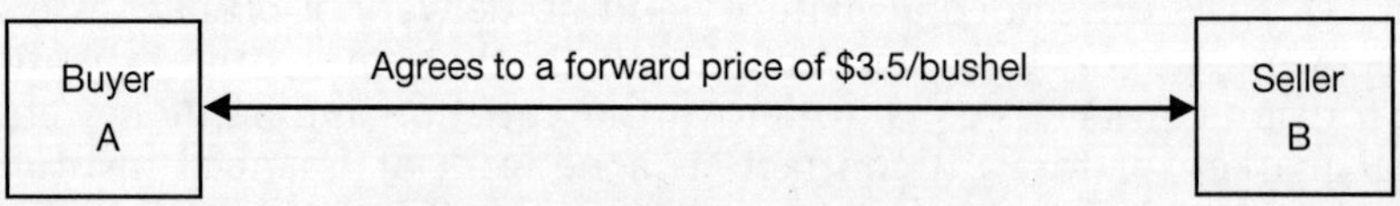

Date of Settlement: December 20

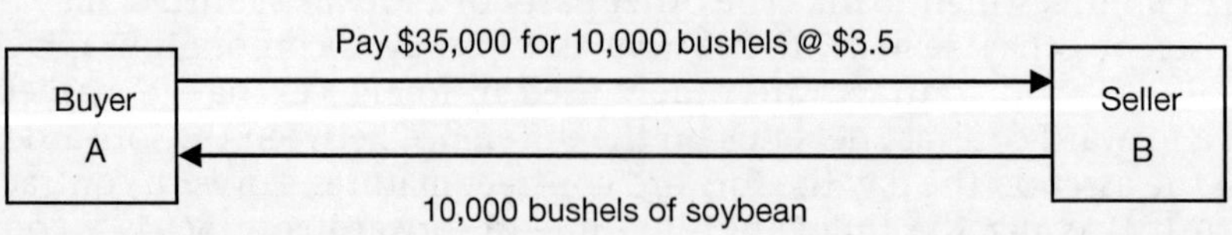

19.1.1 Forward Pricing Scenario

Consider at date t an investor who wants to hold at a future date T one unit of a bond with coupon rate c and time t price P_t. He enjoys the following alternatives:

a. Either he buys at date t a forward contract from a seller who will deliver at date T one unit of this bond at a fixed price F_t, or
b. He borrows money at a rate r to buy this bond at date t.

Given that both trades have a cost equal to zero at date t, in the absence of arbitrage opportunities, the cash flows generated by the two operations at date T must be equal. From this we obtain

$$F_t = P_t \times \left[1 + r\left(\frac{T-t}{360}\right)\right] - 100 \times c \times \left(\frac{T-t}{365}\right)$$

Example: On 5 January 2001, we consider a forward contract maturing in six months, written on a bond whose coupon rate and price are 10% and \$115, respectively. Assuming a 7% interest rate, the forward price $F_{05-01-01}$ is equal to

$$F_{05-01-01} = 115 \times \left[1 + 7\%\left(\frac{184}{360}\right)\right] - 100 \times 10\% \times \left(\frac{184}{365}\right) = 114.07$$

19.2 Futures Contracts

A futures contract is a contract between two parties to exchange assets or services at a specified time in the future at a price agreed upon at the time of the contract. In most conventionally traded futures contracts, one party agrees to deliver a commodity or security at some time in the future, in return for an agreement from the other party to pay an agreed-upon price on delivery. The former is the seller of the futures contract, while the latter is the buyer.

Futures contracts are created and traded on organized futures exchanges (Table 19.1). Contracts are highly standardized in terms of the amount and type of the underlying asset involved and the available dates in which it can be delivered. The exchanges themselves provide assurances that contracts will be honoured through clearing houses. One of the primary roles of the clearing house is to be the opposite party to all trades. Buyers and sellers of futures contracts do not deal directly with each other but with a clearing house. The exchange clearing house is responsible for settling daily gains and losses (marking to market), guaranteeing the transactions and deliveries. A major advantage of organized exchanges is their ability to manage credit risk. Credit risk is the risk that a holder of an unprofitable futures contract will default.

An investor wishing to buy or sell in the futures market is required to post an initial margin in the form of cash or government securities, a portion of the full price. In marking-to-market, the contract is revalued at the end of each day's trading, and gains or losses are computed. Gains increase the value of the margin account and may be withdrawn. If the margin account drops below a certain level, called the maintenance margin, the holder of the futures contract receives a margin call and is required to restore the account to its initial level. If the holder fails to do so, the contract is closed by the broker.

A futures contract obliges its purchaser to buy a given amount of a specified asset at some stated time in the future (known as the delivery date) at the futures price. Similarly, the seller of the contract is obliged to deliver the asset at the futures price. In the futures market, less than 2% of the contracts traded involve the actual delivery of the underlying asset. Rather, the buyers of futures contracts usually sell their contracts before the delivery date, thus offsetting (unwinding) their positions. Like most assets, the profit or loss on a futures contract is determined by the difference between the selling and buying price. Profits and losses on futures contracts are realized daily. Futures contracts are designed to address the limitations of forward contracts particularly illiquidity and counterparty risk.

A futures contract is an exchange-traded, standardized, forward-like contract that is marked to the market daily. Futures contract can be used to establish a long (or short) position in the underlying commodity/asset. Forward and futures contracts are derivative securities because of the following two important reasons:

- payoffs determined by prices of the underlying asset
- zero net supply

Table 19.1 Future Exchanges and Instruments

CME	*CBOT*	*LIFFE*
Eurodollar Futures	30-Year U.S. Treasury Bonds	Long Gilt Contract
13-Week Treasury Bill Futures	10-Year U.S. Treasury Notes	German Government Bond Contract
Libor Futures	5-Year U.S. Treasury Notes	Japanese Government Bond Contract
Fed Funds Turn Futures	2-Year U.S. Treasury Notes	3-Month Euribor Future
10-Year Agency Futures	10-Year Agency Notes	3-Month Euro Libor Future
Argentine 2X FRB Brady Bond Futures	5-Year Agency Notes	3-Month Sterling Future
Argentine Par Bond Futures	Long-term Municipal Bond Index	3-Month Euro Swiss Franc Future
Brazilian 2 × C Brady Bond Futures	30-Day Federal Funds Mortgage	3-Month Euroyen (TIBOR) Future
Brazilian 2 × EI Brady Bond Futures		3-Month Euroyen (LIBOR) Future
Mexican 2 × Brady Bond Futures		2-Year Euro Swapnote
Euro Yen Futures		5-Year Euro Swapnote
Japanese Government Bond Futures		10-Year Euro Swapnote
Euro Yen Libor Futures		
Mexican TIIE Futures		
Mexican CETES Futures		

Note: CBOT = The Chicago Board of Trade; CME = The Chicago Mercantile Exchange; LIFFE = The London International Financial Futures Exchange.

19.3 Types of Futures Contracts

There are four broad types of futures contracts:

a. Futures on commodities (grains, metals and food)
b. Futures on currencies
c. Futures on interest bearing instruments (Eurodollar deposits, treasury bonds, notes and bills)
d. Futures on stock indexes

19.3.1 FX Futures

FX futures are standardized exchange-traded contracts calling for delivery of a specified quantity of a foreign currency at a fixed date in the future. Investors must post margin, which is marked to market daily. All FX futures contracts are settled in cash.

19.3.2 IR Futures

Interest rate futures contracts are traded on organized exchanges. In the world, interest rate futures (eurodollar, T-bills, T-note, T-bond, municipal bond) contracts represent more than one-half of the entire futures market.

19.3.3 Stock Index Futures

Stock index futures specify an equity index as the underlying asset. Stock index futures can only be settled in cash.

19.3.4 Stock Futures

Stock futures are futures contracts on individual stocks. Futures on stocks are very popular among small individual investors.

19.4 Features of Futures Contracts

Futures contracts usually have the following features:

a. Standardized contracts with underlying commodity or asset, quantity (contract size) and maturity
b. Traded on exchanges
c. Guaranteed by the clearing house—little counterparty risk
d. Gains/losses settled daily—marked to market
e. Margin account required as collateral to cover losses
f. Clearing house warrants performance

19.5 Differences Between Forward Contracts and Futures Contracts

Important differences between forward and futures contracts are presented in Table 19.2.

Table 19.2 Difference Between Forward and Futures Contract

Forward Contracts	*Futures Contracts*
Unregulated market	Regulated and highly controlled market.
Customized sizes and maturities. It creates a 'perfect' hedge that exactly matches underlying exposure.	Standardized sizes and expiration periods. Hedge position may not provide an exact dollar-for-dollar offset to underlying exposure.
Participants must negotiate rates and prices.	Pricing is extremely efficient. No negotiations
Prices depend on credit risk and relationship.	Prices are the same for all.
Custom made product may be difficult to exit.	Liquidity and flexibility. Hedge position may be entered and exited when needed.
One delivery date.	Delivery is realized several days after maturity.
Credit risk of the counterparty may be huge.	There is no credit risk.
There is no margin system.	Margin system may be expensive.

19.6 Underlying Asset and Contract Size

The underlying asset that the seller delivers to the buyer at the end of the contract may exist (interest rate) or may not exist (bond). The underlying asset of the CBOT 30-Year U.S. Treasury bond future is a fictive 30-year maturity U.S. Treasury bond with 6% coupon rate. The contract size specifies the notional principal or principal value of the asset that has to be delivered. The notional principal of the CBOT 30-Year U.S. Treasury bond future is $100,000. The principal value of the Matif 3-month Euribor Future to be delivered is €1,000,000.

19.7 Price

The futures price is quoted differently depending on the nature of the underlying asset. When the underlying asset is an interest rate, the future price is quoted to the third decimal point as 100 minus this interest rate. When the underlying asset is a bond, it is quoted in the same way as a bond, that is, as a percentage of the nominal value of the underlying. The tick is the minimum price fluctuation that can occur in trading. Sometimes daily price movement limits as well as position limits are specified by the exchange.

19.8 Trading Arrangements

A clearing house (an example is given in Exhibit 19.1) is a financial institution that provides clearing and settlement services for financial and commodities derivatives and securities transactions. These transactions may be executed on a futures exchange or securities exchange,

Exhibit 19.1 BMF—Bolsa de Mercadorias & Futuros*

Key Features

a. Demutualized, recently reorganized as a corporation.
b. Offers pit trading as well as electronic trading.
c. It has the status of self-regulatory organization.
d. Contracts: foreign exchange, interest rates, equity index, commodities

- Futures, options on futures and flex options on U.S. dollar exchange rate
- Futures and swap on ID × U.S. Dollar spread (DDI or cupom cambial)
- Futures and options on futures on overnight interest rate (DI)
- Futures, options on futures and flex options on stock indices (Bovespa Index)
- Futures and options on futures for gold and other commodities
- Futures on Global Bonds and US Treasury notes
- Futures on inflation indices

e. Acts as a clearing house for derivatives, foreign exchange and bonds.
f. Provides registration of OTC derivatives.

Source: Author's own.
*The BMF uses the English name of Brazilian Mercantile and Futures Exchange.

as well as off-exchange in the OTC market. A clearing house stands between two clearing firms (also known as member firms or clearing participants) and its purpose is to reduce the risk of one (or more) clearing firm failing to honour its trade settlement obligations. A clearing house reduces the settlement risks by netting offsetting transactions between multiple counterparties, by requiring collateral deposits (also called 'margin deposits'), by providing independent valuation of trades and collateral, by monitoring the credit worthiness of the clearing firms and, in many cases, by providing a guarantee fund that can be used to cover losses that exceed a defaulting clearing firm's collateral on deposit. Also, it acts as a clearing firm. Some special trading arrangements in case of trading futures contracts are as follows:

a. Clearing house acts as a party to all buyers and sellers: Obligated to deliver or supply delivery
b. Initial margin: Funds deposited to provide capital to absorb losses
c. Marking to market: Each day profits or losses from new prices are reflected in the account
d. Maintenance or variation margin: An established margin below which a trader's margin may not fall
e. Margin call: When the maintenance margin is reached, broker will ask for additional margin funds

19.9 Conversion Factor

When the underlying asset of a futures contract does not exist, the seller of the contract has to deliver a real asset that may differ from the fictitious asset in terms of coupon rate or maturity. Conversion factor tells you how many units of the actual asset are worth as much as one unit of the fictive underlying asset. Given a futures contract and an actual asset to deliver, it is a constant factor that is known in advance. Conversion factors for next contracts to mature are available on web sites of futures markets. Expressed as a percentage of the nominal value, the conversion factor denoted 'CF' is the present value at maturity date of the futures contract of the actual asset discounted at rate r.

Consider a futures contract whose fictitious underlying asset is a 'm' year maturity bond with a coupon rate equal to r. Suppose that the actual asset delivered by the seller of the futures contract is a x-year maturity bond with a coupon rate equal to c.

Example: Consider a one-year futures contract whose underlying asset is a fictitious 10-year maturity bond with a 6% annual coupon rate. Suppose that the asset to be delivered is at date 1 a 10-year maturity bond with a 5% annual coupon rate. The conversion factor is computed as

$$CF = \sum_{i=1}^{10} \frac{50}{(1+6\%)^i} + \frac{1{,}000}{(1+6\%)^{10}} = \$926.3991$$

19.10 Invoice Price

The conversion factor is used to calculate the invoice price. It is the price that the buyer of the futures contract must pay the seller when a bond is delivered. It is computed as

$$\text{Invoice price} = \text{size of the contract} \times [\text{futures price} \times \text{CF}]$$

Example: Suppose a futures contract whose contract size is $100,000, the future price is 98. The conversion factor is equal to 106.459 and the accrued interest is 3.5. The invoice price is equal to

$$\text{Invoice price} = \$100{,}000 \times [98\% \times 106.459\% + 3.5\%] = \$104{,}329.82$$

19.11 Cheapest-to-deliver

In a futures contract, it is the cheapest security that can be delivered to the long position to satisfy the contract specifications. The cheapest-to-deliver security is relevant only for contracts that provide a variety of slightly different securities that may be delivered. This is common in Treasury bond futures contracts, which typically specify that any treasury bond can be delivered, so long as it is within a certain maturity range and has a certain coupon rate. Determining the cheapest-to-deliver security is important for the short position, because there is often a disparity between the market price of a security and the conversion factor used to determine the value of the security being delivered. This makes it advantageous for the seller to pick a specific security to deliver over another. Since it is assumed that the short position will provide the cheapest to deliver security, the market pricing of futures contracts is generally based on the cheapest to delivery security.

At the repartition date, there are, in general, many bonds that may be delivered by the seller of the futures contract. These bonds vary in terms of maturity and coupon rate. The seller may choose from the available bonds that are the cheapest to deliver. The seller of the contract delivers a bond with price (CP) and receives the invoice price (IP) from the buyer. The objective of the seller is to find the bond that achieves:

$$\text{Max (IP – CP) = Max (futures price} \times \text{CF – quoted price).}$$

Suppose a futures contract with a contract size of $100,000 and price of 97. Three bonds (A, B and C) are identified with the following details:

Bond	***Quoted Price***	***Conversion Factor***	***IP-CP***
Bond A	103.90	107.145%	3,065$
Bond B	118.90	122.512%	–6,336$
Bond C	131.25	135.355%	4,435$

Now search for the bond that maximizes the quantity IP-CP. Cheapest to deliver is bond C.

Example: Yesterday, you bought 10 December live-cattle contracts at CME, at the closing price of $0.7455/lb. The contract has following specifications:

- Contract size 40,000 lbs.
- Agreed to buy 400,000 pounds of live cattle in December.
- Value of position yesterday: (0.7455) (10) (40,000) = $298,200.
- No money changed hands.
- Initial margin required (5% – 20% of contract value).

Today, the futures price closes at $0.7435/lb, 0.20 cents lower.

The value of your position is (0.7435) (10) (40,000) = $297,400, a loss of $800.

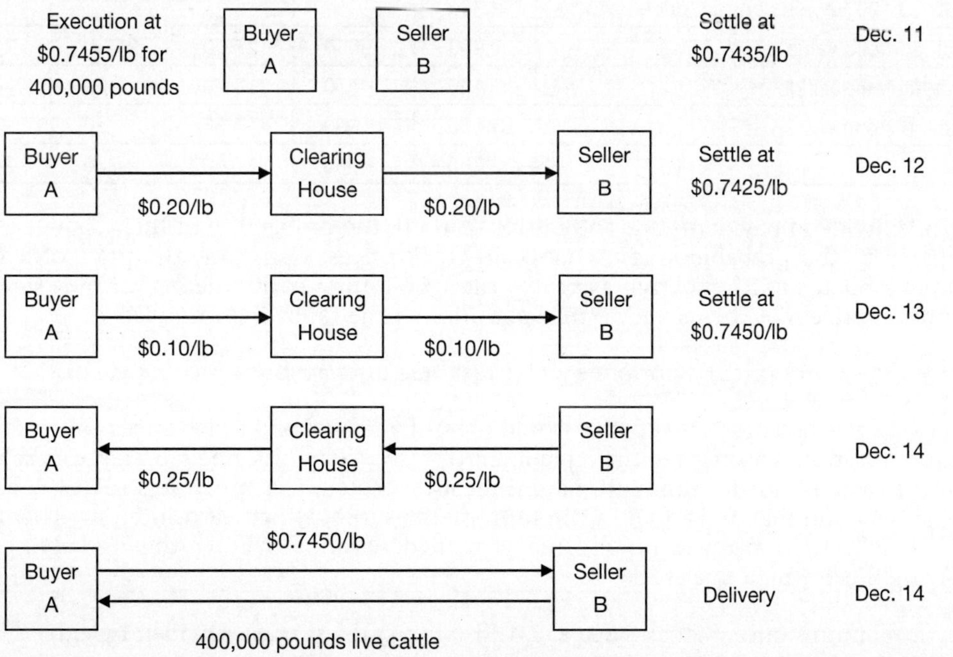

19.12 Forward and Futures Prices

A futures contract is nothing more than a standard forward contract. Therefore, the determinants of the value of either type of contract are the same. On the date of agreement, the price of a futures contract is determined by the spot price of the underlying asset, adjusted for time plus benefits and carrying costs accrued during the time until settlement. Even if the contract is closed out before the delivery date, these costs and benefits are taken into account in determining the price of the contract, since there may be a delivery. Benefits that accrue with ownership include dividends and interest that is paid by the underlying asset. Costs associated with ownership include storage costs, such as with oil, and the interest rate used to determine the present value of a transaction, which represents the opportunity cost of delaying the transaction. To simplify the following discussion, benefits and costs will be restricted to present value and income yield.

When a futures contract is initially agreed to, the NPV of the transaction must be equal for both parties; otherwise, there would be no agreement. The delivery price is the price agreed to in the contract. However, with time, the position of the parties will change as a spot price of the underling changes, with the gains by one party equal to loss of the other party. As the settlement date approaches, the prices of the futures contract and its underlying asset must necessarily converge, so that on the delivery or settlement date, the futures price will equal the spot price of the underlying asset. Because futures contracts can be used to hedge positions in the underlying asset, a perfectly hedged position must necessarily yield the risk-free rate of return; otherwise, arbitrage opportunities would arise that would conform the rate of return to the risk-free rate of return.

For instance, suppose that you invest \$2,600 in an exchange-traded fund (ETF) that tracks the NASDAQ 100 and you enter into a short position for a hypothetical futures contract for the NASDAQ 100 for a price of \$2,700.

NASDAQ 100 futures contract price	2,700				
Stock portfolio value	2,600	2,650	2,700	2,750	2,800
Short futures position payoff	100	50	0	–50	–100
Dividend income	50	50	50	50	50
Total	2,750	2,750	2,750	2,750	2,750

While dividend payments are not entirely certain, the probability of their change is small compared to the probability of a change in stock prices. Generally, the price of a futures contract is related to its underlying asset by the spot–futures parity theorem, which states that the futures price must be related to the spot price by the following formula:

$$\text{Futures price} = \text{Spot price} \times (1 + \text{Risk-free interest rate} - \text{Income yield}).$$

Otherwise, the deviation from parity would present a risk-free arbitrage opportunity. Entering a futures position does not require a payment of cash, so the risk-free rate that can be earned from the cash is added. (Although margin must be posted, it is much less than the value of the contract and margin can be in the form of Treasuries, which earn interest.) The income yield is subtracted because no income is earned without owning the underlying asset. Applying this formula to a stock:

$$\text{Futures price} = \text{Stock price} \times (1 + \text{Risk-free interest rate} - \text{Dividend yield}).$$

Example: Futures market arbitrage opportunity if spot-futures parity violated

Suppose that you pay $2,600 for one share of a stock index ETF that tracks the NASDAQ 100 at the beginning of the year and that it pays $52 in dividends during the year. At the same time, you sell a futures contract short for the NASDAQ 100 that is cash settled, requiring you to pay $2,700 at the end of the year. (Note this futures contract is hypothetical since there is no contract for just one share of an ETF or stock, but it simplifies the math while still illustrating the principle.) Suppose further that:

- Risk-free rate = 5%
- Dividend yield = 2%

Therefore, the futures settlement price should be = ETF price × (1 + 0.05 – 0.02) = $2,600 × 1.03 = $2,678, but if it is $2,700 instead, here is what you can do:

Cash Flow If Futures Contract Is Mispriced According to Spot–Futures Parity				
	Initial Cash Flow		***Cash Flow in 1 Year***	
Borrow at 5% interest	$2,600		–$2,730	= 2,600 * 1.05
Buy stock index ETF	–$2,600	S_t +	$52	Dividend payment
Sell stock index futures short	0	$-S_t$ +	$2,700	Mispriced
Total	$0		$22	Risk-free profit
Cash Flow If Futures Contract Is Priced According to Parity				
Borrow at 5% interest	$2,600		–$2,730	= 2600 * 1.05
Buy stock index ETF	–$2,600	S_t +	$52	Dividend payment
Sell stock index futures short	0	$-S_t$ +	$2,678	Correctly priced
Total	$0		$0	No profit

At the end of the year, the trader with a long position pays you the settlement price of the futures contract in exchange for your ETF; therefore, if the futures contract was overpriced, then you can earn a riskless profit by the amount of the overpricing. Although the net initial investment is zero, the futures cash flow in one year is a riskless positive number that is exactly equal to the mispricing of the futures contract compared to what it would be at parity. Because of this riskless arbitrage, traders would bid up the price of the stock or ETF and bid down the price of the futures contract until parity was satisfied. If the futures contract was less than the corresponding stock price, then a reversal of the arbitrage could be done to earn riskless profits, thereby bidding up the futures price and bidding down the stock price. To summarize:

$$F_o = S_o(1 + r_f - d)$$

where

F_o = initial futures price
S_o = initial stock price
r_f = risk-free interest rate
d = dividend yield

The parity relationship is also known as the cost-of-carry relationship because it asserts that the futures price is determined by the relative costs of buying a stock with deferred delivery in the futures market versus buying it in the spot market with immediate delivery and carrying it as inventory. When buying the stock, the interest that could be earned with the money used to buy the stock is forfeited for the duration of the stock ownership. However, dividend payments may be received. Thus, the net carrying cost advantage of deferring delivery of the stock is the risk-free interest rate minus the dividend per period, which is why the futures price differs from the spot price by the amount of the future-parity equation.

The parity relation must also hold for longer contract periods. Because money has time value, there must be a larger difference between the price of a longer term futures contract and the current spot price compared to a short-term contract; therefore, for a contract maturity of t periods, the spot–futures parity equation is modified:

$$F_o (1 + r_f - d)^t$$

This is equivalent to the formula for calculating this future value of an investment, where the spot price is the initial value, the term $(1 + r_f - d)$ is the interest rate, and t represents the number of compounding periods. The spot–futures parity equation can also be applied to other futures contracts with different underlying assets by making the appropriate modifications. For instance, for bonds, the coupon payment would be equal to the dividend payment. If the underlying asset pays no dividends, such as a commodity like silver, then the dividend is simply set equal to zero; therefore, the price of the futures contract would be equal to asset price multiplied by the risk-free interest rate. By taking the long position in the futures contract, the trader can earn the risk-free rate of interest with the money that would otherwise be used to buy the asset; ergo, the long position must agree to a higher price to compensate the short position for holding an asset that pays no interest or dividends.

19.12.1 Spreads

Because the price of a futures contract is fixed relative to its underlying asset for any maturity, there must also be a relationship between futures contracts of the same underlying asset but with different maturities. If this relationship does not hold, then arbitrage opportunities will arise that will cause prices to conform to parity. If the risk-free interest rate is greater than the dividend yield, then futures prices will be higher for contracts with a longer maturity. This is usually the case, but there are times when the risk-free interest rate is actually lower than the dividend yield, in which case futures contracts with longer maturities will be cheaper than futures contracts with shorter terms. The price relationship between futures contracts of different maturities can be used by finding the relationship between the equations for each individual contract:

$$F_{t_1} = S_o(1 + r_f - d)^{t_1}$$

$$F_{t_2} = S_o(1 + r_f - d)^{t_2}$$

$$\frac{F_{t_2}}{F_{t_1}} = (1 + r_f - d)^{(t_2 - t_1)}$$

$$F_{t_2} = F_{t_1}(1 + r_f - d)^{(t_2 - t_1)}$$

Note that this equation is similar to the spot–futures parity equation, except that the price of the futures contract of shorter maturity is substituted for the current spot price. Delaying delivery from t_1 to t_2 allows the earning of risk-free interest during that time interval, but it also entails the loss of the dividend yield during that time period, hence the equation. Since both the dividend yield and the interest rate are annual yields, the time difference between two contracts is generally calculated as the number of months between the delivery dates divided by the 12 months of the year.

Example: Spread pricing

Consider a hypothetical futures contract that is priced at \$100 for January delivery. The risk-free rate is 3% and the dividend yield is 1%. Therefore, the futures price for April delivery, which is three months later, should be

$$\$100\ (1 + 0.03 - 0.01)^{((4-1)/12)} = \$100\ (1.02)^{(3/12)} = \$100\ (1.02)^{(1/4)} = \$100.50$$

The above arguments make it apparent that futures contracts of different maturities based on the same underlying asset move in unison. In the spot–future parity theorem, an assumption is made that the futures contract would only pay on delivery. However, futures are marked to market daily, which causes the futures price to deviate from parity and to deviate from the forward price. If interest rates are high, then marking to market will give an advantage to the long position, causing the price of futures contracts to be greater than the corresponding forward contracts. If interest rates are low, then the advantage accrues to the short positions, so that futures prices will be less than parity. Because higher interest rate favours the long position, futures traders are willing to accept a higher price on the futures contract, while a negative correlation between futures prices and interest rates will favour the short position, causing the futures price to be less than the corresponding forward price.

However, since the covariance between futures prices and interest rates is low, the price differential between forwards and futures is negligible, except for futures contracts on long-term fixed income securities, since their value is highly dependent on interest rates, thus causing a substantial spread between forwards and futures prices.

19.12.2 Forward and Futures Prices: Some Other Factors

How the prices of forward and futures contracts are affected when the underlying asset pays a known income, has a cost of carry, such as storage costs, or offers any convenience yield, which is the additional benefit of holding the asset rather than holding a forward or futures contract on the asset, such as being able to take advantage of shortages.

When calculating present or future values of contracts, it is conventional to use the continuously compounded risk-free interest rate, which is e^{rT}, where r is the interest rate and T refers to years. Hereafter, e^{rT} will be referred to as the growth factor. Thus, the future price can easily be computed by considering the growth factor and spot price, assuming that there is not cost of carry and holding gain by using the following formula:

$$F_o = S_o e^{rT}$$

If an asset provides a known income, then the value of a forward contract on the asset is modified by subtracting the present value (PV) of the income from the spot price, then finding the future value of that result as given in the following formula:

$$F_o = (S_o - I)e^{rT}$$

Here, $I = PV(I_1) + PV(I_2) + \cdots = I_1 e^{-rt_1} + I_2 e^{-rt_2} \ldots$

Example: Calculating the forward price for a forward contract with known income

Current stock price	: \$100
Continuously compounded risk-free interest rate per year	: 0.06
Contract duration	: 10 months
Quarterly dividends	: \$0.50
Present value of dividend payment 1	: \$0.49
Present value of dividend payment 2	: \$0.49
Present value of dividend payment 3	: \$0.48
Present value of dividend payment 4	: \$0.47
Total present value of dividends (income)	: \$1.93
Forward price $[(100 - 1.93) \times e^{(0.06 \times 10/12)}]$	: \$103.10

When the amount of income earned by holding an asset is a fixed percentage of the asset's value rather than a specified sum, then the yield is subtracted from the interest rate used to calculate the future value of the forward contract:

$$F_o = S_o e^{(r-y)T}$$

Example: Forward contract on an asset paying a known yield

S&P 500 index	: 800.00
Time remaining until delivery (fraction of year = 3 months)	: 0.25
Risk-free interest rate	: 6%
Dividend yield	: 1%
Forward contract value $[800 \times e^{(0.06 - 0.01) \times 0.25}]$	: \$810.06

Note that if the yield of the asset is greater than the risk-free interest rate, then the forward price will be less than the spot price, since the holder of the asset is earning a greater yield than the risk-free interest rate. Similarly, for forward contracts on currencies, the interest rate that can be earned on the foreign currency is subtracted from the domestic interest rate:

$$F_o = S_o e^{(r_d - r_f)T}$$

Example: Calculating the forward rate on a currency contract:

Foreign exchange rate	: \$0.95
Foreign interest rate	: 5%
Domestic interest rate	: 3%
Time (in years)	: 10.0
Forward price $[\$0.95 \times e^{(0.03 - 0.05) \times 10}]$	: \$1.16

19.12.3 Mark-to-market Value of Forward and Futures Contracts

When a forward or futures contract is first agreed upon, the value of the contract must be zero; otherwise, there would be no agreement. As time passes, the spot price of the underlying will vary, but the delivery price will remain fixed, in which case the value of the contract will vary with the value of the underlying. Oftentimes, banks or other financial institutions will need to know the value of forward contracts, so their value must be marked to market, to determine their value before the delivery date. Futures contracts are always marked to market daily.

The present value of a forward or futures contract can be calculated by subtracting the present value of the spot price minus the present value of the delivery price for the long party. The value of the contract to the short party is the present value of the delivery price minus the present value of the spot price:

$$\text{Value of contract to long party} = \text{PV (spot price)} - \text{PV (delivery price)} = (F_0 - K)e^{-rT}.$$

$$\text{Value of contract to short party} = \text{PV (delivery price)} - \text{PV (spot price)} = (K - F_0)e^{-rT}.$$

(Noting that since the value of the futures or forward contract is equal and opposite for the long and short party, the remaining equations will apply to the long party.) If the asset pays a set income, then the value of the contract is equal to the following:

$$\text{Contract value} = \text{PV (spot price)} - \text{PV (income)} - \text{PV (delivery price)} = S_0 - I - Ke^{-rT}.$$

By combining the above equations, the value of a forward contract with a given yield, y, is

$$\text{Contract value of asset with known yield} = S_0e^{-yT} - Ke^{-rT}.$$

Note that in the above equations, the present value of the spot price is, of course, just the spot price.

19.13 Hedging with Forwards and Futures

Hedging in the futures market can be an important component in a producer's price risk management toolbox. However, even for producers who never hedge directly in the futures market, understanding the mechanics behind a futures hedge, and how to calculate the expected net selling or buying price resulting from a hedge, can be important information in analysing the quality of any cash market selling or buying opportunity.

A futures market hedge involves taking a position in the futures market as a temporary substitute for a transaction that will occur in the cash market at a later date. As long as the futures and cash markets move together, any loss in one market will be offset by a gain in the other market, and the net transaction price incurred at the end of the hedge period will equal the price that was expected when the hedge was set.

The key element in arriving at an accurate cash price expectation resulting from a futures market hedge is having an accurate basis forecast. Hedging is essentially the trading of price risk for basis risk. The more accurately the basis is forecast, the closer will be the final transactions price to the price anticipated when the hedge was placed.

19.13.1 Short Hedge or Hedging a Sales Price

A producer who expects to sell something in the cash market later can protect the futures cash market price by selling a futures contract for the identical commodity now. This is also called as a short hedge. When the initial trade is the sale of a futures contract, the seller is said to be 'short' in the market. The seller has sold a commitment to make delivery of a commodity.

Once a futures hedge has been initiated, the producer has exchanged market price risk for basis risk. Basis risk is the risk that the futures and cash prices do not end up with the same relationship that was initially anticipated. If the basis ends up weaker than expected (i.e., the cash price is lower relative to futures than anticipated), the producer's actual net selling price will be lower than thought when the hedge was initiated. If the basis is stronger than expected (cash price higher relative to futures than initially anticipated), the net selling price will be higher than originally thought. The only thing that can affect the final outcome of a hedged position is a change in basis relative to expected basis.

Assume it is 1 May, and a grain producer is considering hedging 15,000 bushels of soybeans for the October delivery; that is, the producer wants to deliver soybeans into the cash market at harvest, but wants to lock in the harvest price in May (recall that 5,000 bushels is equal to one futures contract). To calculate the expected price from the hedged position, the producer must note the current futures price for the November soybean futures contract. This futures price must then be 'localized', or translated into an expected local cash price. This is done by adjusting the futures price by the basis. The relevant basis is the one the producer thinks will exist in October (i.e., the October cash soybean price minus the November soybean futures contract price), not the basis that exists on 1 May. If the producer has paid close attention to previous years' basis relationships in the October delivery period, he/she will be in a position to derive an accurate estimate of the expected price resulting from a hedge for the October delivery of soybeans.

Basis = **Spot Price** of asset being hedged – **Future Price** of contract used for hedging

Suppose on 1 May the November soybean futures contract is trading for $6.50 per bushel. Based on previous experience, the producer expects basis in October to be minus $0.40. In other words, the producer's cash soybean price in October is expected to be $0.40 below the November soybean futures price in October. The producer would expect to receive a selling price of $6.10 per bushel soybeans in October if a hedge were initiated on 1 May. This comes from a 1 May futures price for November soybeans of $6.50 localized by the negative $0.40 basis. However, to initiate a hedge, the producer must work with a futures broker. The producer will have to pay the broker a commission to initiate the futures position and deposit the initial margin required for the position in a futures trading account (recall the discussion of futures margins from Chapter 1). Assume the commission is $50 per contract, or $0.01 per bushel for a 5,000-bushel contract. Then, the net price the producer expects to receive for cash soybeans in October is $6.09 per bushel. This comes from adjusting the expected cash price of $6.10 per bushel for the 1 cent per bushel broker's commission. As long as the basis forecast is accurate, the producer can be confident he/she will receive $6.09 per bushel regardless of what happens to soybean prices between May and October.

Example 1 illustrates the hedge described above. Note the producer nets $6.09 per bushel for soybeans in October regardless of whether prices rise or fall over the hedge period. This is based on the assumption that the basis expectation is realized at the end of the hedge period. In other words, there is no change in basis, that is, the basis remained constant from the time the hedge was initiated to the time that the hedge was lifted.

Example 1: Short Hedge or Hedging a Sales Price

Assume it is 1 May, and a grain farmer wants to protect the price received for October harvested soybeans. November soybean futures contracts are trading for $6.50 per bushel. The farmer would hedge harvest soybean prices by selling November futures on 1 May. Adjusting the 1 May futures price for the expected basis in October, and the futures broker's commission derive the expected cash price in October.

Date: 1 May	
Futures price (grain farmer sells 3 November soybean futures contracts)	$6.50
+ Expected basis	–$0.40
– Brokers commission	$0.01
= Expected net selling price	$6.09

Scenario 1: Perfect hedge (declining prices)

Assume the November futures contract is $5.50 when the cash sale is made in October, and basis turns out as expected. The producer sells the cash soybeans for $5.10 per bushel (futures is $5.50 and the basis is –$0.40). He then buys the November futures contract he sold on 1 May back for $5.50 per bushel. The basis was accurately forecast, and his net selling price is as expected.

Date: October		
Futures price (grain farmer buys 3 November soybean futures contracts)		$5.50
+ Expected basis		–$0.40
– Brokers commission		$0.01
+ Future's profit ($6.50-$5.50)		$1.00
= Net selling price		$6.09
Reconcile:		
Cash price ($5.50 – $0.40)	$5.10	
Net future's profit ($1.00 – $0.01)	$0.99	$6.09

The combination of a cash price of $5.10/bushel plus a futures profit of $0.99/bushel nets the grain producer an effective soybean price of $6.09/bushel, which is what was expected. This is a perfect hedge because the expected basis is same as the final basis. The basis remained constant. Observe that the hedge gave protection from downside price risk.

Scenario 2: Perfect hedge (raising prices)

Assume the November futures contract is $7.50 when the cash sale is made in October, and basis turns out as expected. The producer sells the cash soybeans for $7.10 per bushel (futures is $7.50 and the basis is –$0.40). He then buys the November futures contract he sold on 1 May back for $7.50/bushel. The basis was accurately forecast, and his net selling price is as expected.

Date: October	
Futures price (grain farmer buys 3 November soybean futures contracts)	$7.50
+ Expected basis	–$0.40

– Brokers commission		$0.01
– Future's loss ($7.50 – $6.50)		$1.00
= Net selling price		$6.09
Reconcile:		
Cash price ($7.50 – $0.40)	$7.10	
Net future's loss ($1.00 + $0.01)	$1.01	$6.09

The combination of a cash price of $7.50/bushel minus a futures loss of $1.00 nets the grain producer an effective soybean price of $6.09/bushel, which is what was expected. Observe that there is no change in the basis estimated and the final basis. Also, realize that in the case of rising prices the hedge prevented the farmer from taking advantage of rising prices.

Scenario 3: Imperfect hedge (basis risk – weakening basis)

This is the same as scenario 1, except in this case the basis turns out to be weaker than expected by $0.10/bushel. A weaker basis means that the cash price is lower relative to futures than had been expected. The expected basis is minus $0.40, whereas the actual basis is minus $0.50. If the basis is weaker by 10 cents, the cash price is 10 cents lower than would have been the case if the basis forecast had been correct.

Date: October		
Futures price (grain farmer buys 3 November soybean futures contracts)		$5.50
+ Expected basis		–$0.50
– Brokers commission		$0.01
+ Future's profit ($6.50 – $5.50)		$1.00
= Net selling price		$5.99
Reconcile:		
Cash price ($5.50 – $0.50)	$5.00	
Net future's profit ($1.00 – $0.01)	$0.99	$5.99

While the futures hedge did protect the cash position from most of the price decline, the unexpected weakening of the basis did result in a lower net sales price than originally anticipated. Observe that even though this hedge was able to prevent the price risk, there was basis risk. For a short hedger, weakening basis results in lower net selling price. Different methods are observed in future market, which is guided by the wisdom and intuition of the particular investor. One of such methods is Elliot Wave Principle which is briefed in Exhibit 19.2.

Scenario 4: Imperfect hedge (basis risk – strengthening basis)

This is similar to scenario 3, except that the basis ends up stronger than expected. A stronger than expected basis means that the cash price is higher relative to the soybean futures price than had been originally anticipated.

Exhibit 19.2 The Elliot Wave Principle

A method used in futures trading, as well as many other derivatives is known as the Elliott wave principle. Used as tool for technical analysis tool, its primary usages is to analyse and forecast current market trends.

The Elliot wave principle is used to identify investor psychology, collective facets as well as the high and low prices. The tool helps a trader discover the impact of social principles and events, and how prices are affected by social events. The tool creates patterns that are known to traders as Elliott waves (also known as just waves).

The basic theory behind this principle is the investor psychology will move between optimism and pessimism. The actual swift changes in moods will in actuality create patterns that are confirmed in the markets price movements. These happen throughout the trend as well as on a specific time scale.

Market prices will switch to one of these three phases: impulsive, motive and or corrective. These are shown throughout all times of the trend. These 'impulsive' waves will always be sub-divided into sets of five lower degree waves. They will alternate between motives and corrective, showing that waves 1, 3 and 5 are impulses, and waves 2 and 4 are lesser re-traces of 1 as well as 3.

The corrective wave chart will subdivide into three lesser waves, which will start with the 5 wave reverse trend impulse, a re-trace, and an additional impulse.

During a bear market, the major trend is going to be downward; therefore, the pattern will be in reverse (five waves downwards and three waves upwards). Motive waves continually will move along with the trend, whilst the corrective waves are going to move in opposition to it.

Source: Author's own.

Date: October		
Futures price (grain farmer buys 3 November soybean futures contracts)		$5.50
+ Expected basis		–$0.30
– Brokers commission		$0.01
+ Future's profit ($6.50 – $5.50)		$1.00
= Net selling price		$6.19
Reconcile:		
Cash price ($5.50 – $0.30)	$5.20	
Net future's profit ($1.00 – $0.01)	$0.99	$6.19

This time the producer ends up better off than expected as a result of a stronger basis. Futures prices over the hedge period fell by more than cash prices resulting in a stronger than expected cash market. In the case of rising prices (such as in scenario 2), cash price would have to raise more than futures prices for the basis to strengthen. For a short hedger, strengthening basis results in higher net selling price.

19.13.2 Long Hedge or Hedging a Purchase Price

The mechanics of hedging a commodity to be purchased in the cash market at a later date are similar to the sales hedge described above. The one difference is that a purchase hedge is initiated by buying a futures contract. This is also called as a long hedge. When the initial trade is the purchase of a futures contract, the seller is said to be 'long', in the market. The seller has sold a commitment to take delivery of a commodity.

As prices rise, the cash commodity to be purchased later is becoming more expensive, but futures prices are also rising, generating a profit in the futures position. This profit is used to offset the increased price of the cash commodity, and, if basis has been forecast accurately, the net purchase price originally established by the hedge becomes the effective price paid for the cash commodity.

Assume it is 1 November and a dairy producer would like to lock in a purchase price for 15,000 bushels of corn to be bought in June and used as feed next summer. By hedging in a specific corn futures contract month, a dairy farmer effectively locks in the price he/she will pay for corn for the summer feeding period. In the example here, the farmer can hedge 15,000 bushels of corn to be bought in the cash market in June by buying 3 July corn futures contracts (i.e., contracts for the delivery of corn next July). The important information for the farmer is the current futures price for the July delivery, and the expected basis in June (i.e., the difference between the June cash corn price July futures price in June). The purchase price hedge is illustrated in example below. It considers the four scenarios covered in the selling hedge. Again, as long as the producer has accurately forecast the June basis, the hedged purchase price will be realized whether corn prices move up or down over the hedge period. The only thing that will affect the actual purchase price relative to the expected price established by the hedge is a basis that differs from the expected basis.

Example 2: Long Hedge or Hedging a Purchase Price

Assume it is 1 November and a dairy farmer wants to lock in the purchase price for 15,000 bushels of corn to be bought in June. The farmer would need to purchase 3 July corn contracts to hedge June corn purchases. The expected basis in June is \$0.15 under July contract. The expected June purchase price is derived by adjusting the July futures price traded on 1 November for the expected basis in June and the futures broker's commission.

Date: 1 November	
Futures price (dairy farmer buys July corn contracts)	\$2.50
+ Expected basis	–\$0.15
+ Brokers commission	\$0.01
= Expected net purchase price	\$2.36

Scenario 1: Perfect hedge (raising prices)

Assume the July futures corn futures price is \$3.50 per bushel when cash corn is purchased in June, and the basis turns out as expected. The producer buys cash soybeans for \$3.35 per bushel (futures is \$3.50 and the basis is –\$0.15). He then sells the July futures contract he bought on 1 November for \$2.50 per bushel. The basis was accurately forecast and his net purchase price was as expected.

Date: June	
Futures price (dairy farmer buys July corn contracts)	\$3.50
+ Expected basis	–\$0.15
+ Brokers commission	\$0.01

– Future's profit ($3.50 – $2.50)		$1.00
= Net purchase price		$2.36
Reconcile:		
Cash price ($3.50 – $0.15)	$3.35	
– Net future's profit ($1.00 – $0.01)	$0.99	$2.36

Note that the futures profit is subtracted from, and the broker's commission added to, the net buying price E of the dairy farmer. These items affect the farmer's net corn purchase price. The combination of a cash price of $3.35/bushel minus a futures profit of $0.99 nets the dairy producer an effective corn price of $2.36/bushel, which is what was expected.

Scenario 2: Perfect hedge (declining prices)

Assume the July futures corn futures price is $1.50 per bushel when cash corn is purchased in June, and the basis turns out as expected. The producer buys cash soybeans for $1.35 per bushel (futures is $1.50 and the basis is –$0.15). He then sells the July futures contract he bought on 1 November for $2.50 per bushel. The basis was accurately forecast and his net purchase price was as expected.

Date: June		
Futures price (dairy farmer buys July corn contracts)		$1.50
+ Expected basis		–$0.15
+ Brokers commission		$0.01
+ Future's loss ($2.50 – $1.50)		$1.00
= Net purchase price		$2.36
Reconcile:		
Cash price ($1.50 – $0.15)	$1.35	
+ Net future's loss ($1.00 + $0.01)	$1.01	$$2.36

The combination of a cash price of $1.50/bushel plus a futures loss of $1.01 nets the dairy farmer an effective corn purchase price of $2.36 /bushel, which is what was expected.

Scenario 3: Imperfect hedge (basis risk – weakening basis)

This is the same as scenario 1, except in this case the basis turns out to be weaker than expected by $0.10/bushel. A weaker basis means that the cash price is lower relative to futures than had been expected. If the basis is weaker by 10 cents, the cash price is 10 cents lower than would have been the case if the basis forecast had been correct.

Date: June	
Futures price (dairy farmer buys July corn contracts)	$3.50
+ Expected basis	–$0.25
+ Brokers commission	$0.01
– Future's profit ($3.50 – $2.50)	$1.00
= Net purchase price	$2.26

Reconcile:		
Cash price ($3.50 – $0.25)	$3.25	
– Net future's profit ($1.00 – $0.01)	$0.99	$2.26

While the futures hedge offset the increase in cash prices, the unexpected weakening of the basis did result in a lower net purchase price than originally anticipated. For a long hedger, weakening basis gives a better net buying or purchase price.

Scenario 4: Imperfect hedge (basis risk: strengthening basis)

This is similar to scenario 3, except that the basis ends up stronger than expected by $0.10/bushel. A stronger than expected basis means that the cash price is higher relative to futures than had been originally anticipated.

Date: June		
Futures price (dairy farmer buys July corn contracts)		$3.50
+ Expected basis		–$0.05
+ Brokers commission		$0.01
– Future's profit ($3.50 – $2.50)		$1.00
= Net purchase price		$2.46
Reconcile:		
Cash price ($3.50 – $0.05)	$3.45	
– Net future's profit ($1.00 – $0.01)	$0.99	$2.46

This time the dairy farmer ends up worse off than expected as a result of a stronger basis. Futures prices over the hedge period rose by less than cash prices, resulting in a stronger than expected cash market. This leads to a higher net purchase price than originally anticipated. For a long hedger, strengthening basis gives a worse net buying price. Exhibit 19.3 provides some hands on tips for the trader in hedging market.

Exhibit 19.3 Ten Don'ts in Hedging

1. Don't enter the futures market until you understand how to use it.
2. Don't ask your broker to make management decisions for you.
3. Don't combine hedging and speculating.
4. Don't hedge unless you 'know' your 'basis'.
5. Don't hedge if you can't meet additional margin calls.
6. Don't view futures markets as an outlet for delivery of your crop.
7. Don't think of futures markets as a way to get higher prices.
8. Don't lift your hedge before you buy or sell your commodity in the cash market.
9. Don't forget that hedging insulates you from subsequent major price changes—both downward and upward.
10. Don't expect hedging to be panacea for poor management.

Source: https://cdp.wisc.edu/agGrains/07-Hedging.doc

19.14 Conclusion

Forward and futures markets are yet another refinement in the growing complexity of a modern financial economy. By distilling the purely speculative aspect out of inter-temporal transactions and placing this risk on those who want to bear it, forward and futures contracts foster a greater specialization in the division of labour. Even though the vast majority will never own such contracts, all consumers benefit from the more efficient allocation of resources and production decisions over time.

The basic relationship between the futures/forward prices, which mature at time T, and spot prices is

$$F_t = S_o e^{rf-T}$$

This is derived from the no arbitrage condition that using a futures contract is the same as a strategy that involves borrowing, buying, holding and repaying. We can use this condition to derive a no arbitrage relationship between futures/forward prices and spot price for any financial asset.

For commodities, we can do the same thing but we need to include the effects of actually holding the physical asset. This means that we must include the storage costs and potential spoilage. By incorporating these additional factors, we can derive a no arbitrage pricing relationship for commodities. However, for commodities, the price cycle and the value of actually holding the underlying asset are also important factors that cause the no arbitrage condition to be consistently violated when we examine actual futures/forward prices in the market.

Multiple Choice Questions

1. Which is the most active group of futures?
   a. Energy
   b. Agriculture
   c. Currency
   d. Financials
2. The trading procedure on the floor of the futures exchange is referred to as _______
   a. Against actual
   b. Open interest
   c. Open outcry
   d. Index participation
3. The number of long or short futures positions outstanding is called the _______
   a. Reportable position
   b. Minimum volume
   c. Open interest
   d. Spread position
4. The risk of unexpected change in the relationship between currency futures prices and currency spot prices is called _______
   a. Basis risk
   b. Currency risk

c. Exchange rate risk
d. Interest rate risk

5. The advantage of using forward contracts to hedge versus a naked position is the
a. Ability to liquidate the contract when needed
b. Ability to eliminate currency risk
c. Ability to take advantage of favourable currency movements
d. Two or more of the above

6. What is the chief risk to firms when hedging with futures?
a. Futures prices will increase
b. Futures prices will decrease
c. Insufficient cash to maintain the futures position
d. A change in basis

7. A speculator that has a _______ futures contract has taken a _______ position.
a. Sold; long
b. Purchased; short
c. Sold; short
d. Purchased; sold

8. A foreign currency _______ contract calls for the future delivery of a standard amount of foreign exchange at a fixed time, place, and price.
a. Futures
b. Forward
c. Option
d. Swap

9. Futures contracts require that the purchaser deposit an initial sum as collateral. This deposit is called a _______
a. Collateralized deposit
b. Marked market sum
c. Margin
d. Settlement

10. Which of the following statements regarding currency futures contracts and forward contracts is not true?
a. A futures contract is a standardized amount per currency whereas the forward contact is for any size desired.
b. A futures contract is for a fixed maturity whereas the forward contract is for any maturity you like up to one year.
c. Futures contracts trade on organized exchanges, whereas forwards take place between individuals and banks with other banks via telecom linkages.
d. All of the above are true.

Discussion Questions

1. Define forward contracts? Differentiate between short and long position.
2. What do you mean by futures contracts? Differentiate between forward and futures contracts.
3. What are different types of futures contracts? Explain them briefly.

4. Identify different features of futures contracts.
5. What is the use of cheapest-to-deliver?
6. Write a short note of forward and future prices.
7. What is the use of mark-to-market value in case of forward and futures contracts?
8. How forward and futures contracts are used for hedging purpose?
9. Differentiate between short hedge and long hedge.
10. Develop an understanding of the mechanics of futures contracts.

Exercises

1. The futures price for March T-bonds is 96–27. The manager of a $100 million bond portfolio, the duration of which will be 6.7 years in March, wishes to use these futures for hedging this portfolio. This manager thinks one of two T-bonds will be cheapest to deliver; some data for these two bonds are as follows:

Bond	*Quoted Price ($)*	*Conversion Factor*	*Duration in March*
A	111–22	1.1462	9.3 years
B	106–26	1.0987	10.2 years

   a. Which bond is the cheapest to deliver? Explain why by showing calculations.
   b. How should the portfolio manager use March T-bond futures to produce a new portfolio having an overall duration of zero? How many contracts? Long or short?

2. The current spot rate for the British pound is $1.5540, and the current three-month forward rate is $1.5459. The U.S. interest rate is currently 2.5%.

   a. What is the current interest rate in Great Britain?
   b. What is the theoretical price of March futures for the British pound? Assume the March contract expires in exactly five months.

3. During March 2002, you sell a December futures contract for soybeans at $5.10. You close out the contract in December and sell cash beans at the Grainville Elevator in the same month. The CBOT price at the time is $4.80. The local December basis is $0.30. Calculate your net price on the soybeans. Recalculate the net price received for the beans if the CBOT price is $5.40 at the time you close the contract and sell the beans.
4. Assume that in August when his crop looks quite favourable, a farmer observes that the futures market is offering $3.25 per bushel for December delivery of corn. He knows from the historical basis records that he kept the basis is 10 cents under the December futures contract. He lifts the hedge November when the December futures are trading at $3.10.

   a. By hedging in the December futures at what price he can lock in if there is no basis risk?
   b. What is the final net selling price if the basis at the time of actual sale is minus 20 cents?

5. You have 3,000 bushels of soybeans to market. You sell a futures contract for March beans (see CBOT price data sheet). You close the contract and sell cash beans in late February at Grainville Elevator. The CBOT price at the time is $5.41.Using the

Grainville basis calculated in Exercise 3, what price did you net on the beans? The market looks very strong in February when you close out your futures position ($5.41). You decide to hold onto the beans. You end up selling them to Grainville Elevator in June when the CBOT price is $5.02. What price did you net on your beans?

References

Hedging Agventures. Available at https://cdp.wisc.edu/agGrains/07-Hedging.doc (last accessed on 5 June, 2015).

Murphy, Robert P. 2006. 'The Social Function of Futures Markets'. *Mises Daily*, 29 November. Available at https://mises.org/library/social-function-futures-markets (last accessed on 19 June, 2016).

Chapter

20

Stock Market Index

Chapter Objectives

On completion of this chapter, you will be able to understand:

- Types of indexes
- Index versions
- Weighting
- Determinants of a stock index
- Market indices based on concept of average or price pondered market indices
- Standard or value pondered market indices
- Purposes of indices
- The U.S. markets indices
- Indices of fast-growing markets
- Signals from the stock index

How to Invest Based on Stock Market Indexes

With investments based on indexes, you can invest in the general market or a particular industry. Say that you want to invest in the Dow Jones Industrial Average (DJIA). After all, why try to 'beat the market' if just matching it is sufficient to grow your wealth?

Why not have a portfolio that directly mirrors the DJIA? Well, it's too impractical and expensive to invest in all 30 stocks that are in the DJIA. Fortunately, there are alternatives that can accomplish the act of 'investing in indexes.' Here are a couple of the better ways:

- Index mutual funds: An index mutual fund is much like a regular mutual fund except that it will only invest in securities (in this case, stocks) that match as closely as possible the basket of stocks that are in that particular index. There are index mutual funds, for example, that track the DJIA and the Standard & Poor's 500.
- Exchange Traded Funds (ETFs): ETFs have similar characteristics to a mutual fund except for a few key differences. An ETF can reflect a basket of stocks that mirror a particular index, but the ETF can be traded like a stock itself.

You can transact ETFs like stocks in that you can buy, sell, or go short. You can put stop losses on them and you can even purchase them on margin. ETFs can give you the diversification of mutual funds coupled with the versatility of stocks. Examples of ETFs that track indexes are the DJIA ETF (symbol DIA) and the ETF for NASDAQ (QQQ).

Source: http://www.dummies.com/how-to/content/how-to-invest-based-on-stock-market-indexes.html

20.1 Introduction

Stock market is a place where the stocks of a listed company are traded. A single figure that sums up the overall performance of the market on a daily basis is the stock index. A good stock index captures the movement of the well-diversified and highly liquid stocks. For a layman, it is the pulse rate of the economy. Index movements reflect the changing expectations of the stock market about future dividends of the corporate sector. The index is calculated by finding the weighted average of the prices of the most actively traded companies in the market, where the weights are generally in proportion to the market capitalization of the company. Indices are relative numbers that, if they lined up, show tendency, volume and velocity of some economy and social occurrences. Basic market volatility is often measured by market averages or indices consisting of a group of securities, whose mission is to reflect the whole market. A large number of averages and indices are fabricated in order to reflect volatility of whole markets. The most known market indices are certainly Dow Jones Averages and Standard & Poor's Index.

Stock exchanges as a centre for trading were established as early as the 16th century. In Antwerp, a major financial hub in Belgium, traders gathered together in 1531 to speculate in shares and commodities. This was the world's first stock exchange. London and Paris set up exchanges sometime near the end of the 17th century. Close to 100 years later, in 1792, the NYSE was established, which is still one of the world's most powerful exchanges.

In India, the Stock Exchange, Mumbai, was established in 1875 as 'The Native Share and Stockbrokers Association' (a voluntary non-profit-making association) and is now popularly known as the Bombay Stock Exchange (BSE). The other major exchange is the National Stock Exchange of India Limited (NSE) and was incorporated in November 1992. These two trading zones are responsible for 99.9% of the trading done in India.

20.2 Types of Indexes

A 'world' or 'global' stock market index includes (typically large) companies without regard for where they are domiciled or traded. Two examples are MSCI World and S&P Global 100.

A 'national' index represents the performance of the stock market of a given nation—and by proxy, reflects investor sentiment on the state of its economy. The most regularly quoted market indices are national indices composed of the stocks of large companies listed on a nation's largest stock exchanges, such as the American S&P 500, the Japanese Nikkei 225 and the British FTSE 100.

a. Broad market index: This consists of all the large, liquid stocks of the country and becomes the benchmark for the entire capital market of the country. An example for this is the S&P CNX 500.
b. Specialized index: We can have either industry or sector-specific index for any particular sector of the economy, which then serves as the benchmark for that particular industry, or we can have an index for the highly liquid stocks. Taking an example for an industry-specific index, we have the S&P Banking Index, which is a capitalization-weighted index of 26 domestic equities traded on the NYSE and National Association of Securities Dealers' Automated Quotation (NASDAQ). The stocks in the index are high-capitalization stocks representing a sector of the S&P 500. Similarly, the S&P CNX Nifty is a relevant example for an index composed of highly liquid stocks.

20.3 Index Versions

Some indices, such as the S&P 500, have multiple versions (Arnott et al. 2005). These versions can differ based on how the index components are weighted and on how dividends are accounted for. For example, there are three versions of the S&P 500 index: price return, which only considers the price of the components, total return, which accounts for dividend reinvestment and net total return, which accounts for dividend reinvestment after the deduction of a withholding tax (Broby 2007). As another example, the Wilshire 4500 and Wilshire 5000 indices have five versions each: full capitalization total return, full capitalization price, float-adjusted total return, float-adjusted price and equal weight. The difference between the full capitalization, float-adjusted and equal weight versions is in how index components are weighted (Fernholz et al. 1998; Haugen and Baker 1991).

20.4 Weighting

An index may also be classified according to the method used to determine its price (Table 20.1). In a price-weighted index, such as the Dow Jones Industrial Average (DJIA), Amex Major Market Index and the NYSE ARCA Tech 100 Index, the price of each component stock is the only consideration when determining the value of the index. Thus, price movement of even a single security will heavily influence the value of the index even though the dollar shift is less significant in a relatively highly valued issue, and moreover ignoring the relative size of the company as a whole. In contrast, a market-value-weighted or capitalization-weighted index, such as the Hang Seng Index, factors in the size of the company. Thus, a relatively small shift

Table 20.1 Summary on Computation of Index

Index	***Price-weighted index***	***Market capitalization-weighted***	***Equal-weighted index***
Description	Average price of companies included in the index	Total market value of the companies included in the index is taken into consideration	All stock returns are given the same weight
How it is calculated	(Add the market price of all stocks in the index) ÷ (number of stocks in the index)	(The sum of the current stock prices) × (number of shares outstanding of all stocks in the index)	Index is calculated with equal dollar investment in each stock in the index
Characteristics	Sensitive to large stock price movement regardless of the size of the company	A small shift in the price of a big company will heavily impact the value of the index	Tends to have higher stock turnover than market capitalization-weighted index funds and, as a result, they usually have higher trading costs
Example(s)	DJIA and Japanese Nikkei 225	Bursa Malaysia	U.S. Value Line Composite Average

Source: Author's own.

in the price of a large company will heavily influence the value of the index. In a market-share-weighted index, price is weighted relative to the number of shares, rather than their total value.

Traditionally, capitalization- or share-weighted indices all had a full weighting, that is, all outstanding shares were included. Recently, many of them have changed to a float-adjusted weighting that helps indexing.

A modified capitalization-weighted index is a hybrid between capitalization weighting and equal weighting. It is similar to a capitalization weighting with one main difference: The largest stocks are capped to a percentage of the weight of the total stock index, and the excess weight will be redistributed equally amongst the stocks under that cap. Moreover, in 2005, Standard & Poor's introduced the S&P Pure Growth Style Index and S&P Pure Value Style Index which were attribute-weighted. That is, a stock's weight in the index is decided by the score it gets relative to the value attributes that define the criteria of a specific index, the same measure used to select the stocks in the first place. For these two stocks, a score is calculated for every stock, whether it is their growth score or the value score (a stock cannot be both), and accordingly they are weighted for the index.

20.5 Determinants of a Stock Index

Following parameters should be taken into picture before one constructs a stock index:

1. Liquidity: Liquidity of stocks is measured by the 'impact cost' criterion which determines the cost faced when actually trading the index. For example, if the current market price of a stock is ₹200 and a trader purchases it at ₹202 (due to involved transaction costs), then the market impact cost is 1% and the stock is considered highly liquid for lower impact cost.
2. Diversification: Diversification, by putting stocks of various sectors that reflect the economy, is used to cancel out stock noise which is essentially the individual stock fluctuations and to reduce investor's risks. An index must thus have a balanced representation of all sectors.
3. Optimum size: More stocks lead to greater diversification, but the limiting factor is the size of the index. Increasing number of stocks in an index from 10 to say 30 gives a sharp reduction in risks, but increasing the number beyond a point does very little in risk reduction. Further, it might lead to addition of illiquid stocks. For example, the optimal size for BSE is 30.
4. Market capitalization: The index should include primarily the stocks of companies that have significant market capitalization with respect to the index such that any major change in the price of the stock is reflected in the index. For example in BSE 30 Index, the scrip must have a minimum of 0.5% of the market capitalization of the index.
5. Averaging: Every stock primarily moves for two reasons: the news about the company and the news about the country. An ideal index is affected only by the latter, that is, the news of the economy, and the effect of the former is knocked out by proper averaging. The various methods of averaging employed are:
   - Price-weighted: The weights assigned are proportional to the stock prices.
   - Market capitalization-weighted: The equity price is weighted by the market capitalization of the company. Hence, each constituent stock in the index affects the index value in proportion to the market value of all outstanding shares.

$$\text{Index} = \frac{\text{Current market capitalization}}{\text{Base market capitalization}} \times \text{Base value}$$

where

CMS = Sum of (current market price × outstanding shares) of all securities in the index
BMS = Sum of (market price × issue size) of all securities as on base date.

- Equal-weighted: The weights are equal and assigned irrespective of both market capitalization and price.

Index revision is done periodically taking into consideration the factors mentioned above. The relevant index body makes clear, researched and publicly documented rules for this purpose. These rules are applied regularly, to obtain changes to the index set. However, it is ensured that the value of the index does not change significantly after the revision of the index set.

20.6 Market Indices Based on Concept of Average or Price Pondered Market Indices

Market indices based on concept of average or price pondered market indices are calculated by adding shares price of chosen companies and dividing their sum by a number defined as 'divisor' in that moment. The most famous index in this group is certainly Dow Jones Averages. The base for calculation is portfolio consisting of one share of each company included in the index. Ponder of some company is defined by company share price. The base algebraic definition of average is

$$\text{Average} = \frac{\sum_{i=0}^{n} P_{it}}{d}$$

where P_{it} means the price of stock i in period t, n is the number of shares included in the average and d means the divisor.

A very important characteristic of average is that stock split, or excluding some share from index and replacing it with another company share, requires divisor adjustment, in order to eliminate its influence on average value. The most known indices in this group are Dow Jones Averages and particular DJIA, Value Line Composite Averages consist of 1,600 shares from NYSE and OTC, Nikkei Average consists of 225 of the biggest Japanese companies and so on.

20.7 Standard or Value Pondered Market Indices

Standard or value pondered market indices are obtained by putting in relation total market value of chosen companies in present time, with total market value of chosen companies in base period. The base algebraic definition is

$$\text{Indices} = \frac{\sum P_i Q_i}{\sum P_o Q_o} \times n$$

where

P_i represents the present market price,
Q_i represents the present number of shares,
P_o represents the market price in base period,
Q_o represents the number of shares in base period and
n is the base value established for base period.

Market value of shares is obtained by multiplying number of shares with its price. Base value is the value set for base period. Index value and ponder value depend on two factors: price and number of shares. Other activities of companies that change their value (like issue of new shares, fusion, stock split and so on) require adjustment of divisor in order not to change index value. The most known indices in this group are Standard & Poor's 500 composite index, NYSE indices, NASDAQ indices, Amex index, Wilshire 5000, Russell 2000 and so on.

20.8 Purposes of Indices

The main purposes of indices are:

1. Description of what happens at market, which means to establish whether market is in expansion or contraction.
2. Forecasting.
3. Focus on securities, which service is to follow trends of securities, continuously, which enable investors react on time if price of some securities goes up or down.

Market indices such as DJIA and S&P provide some useful indicators about stock market performances.

The second purpose of market indices is index derivatives generating. Those derivatives are index option and index futures, and base instrument of this contract is stock market index.

20.9 The U.S. Market Indices

The most known indices at the U.S. markets are Dow Jones Averages, including industry, transportation and utilities; Standard & Poor's 500 composite indices and separate indices including industrial companies (S&P Industrials), transportation companies (Transportation Index), utility companies (Utility Index) and financial companies (Financial Index); further, there are NYSE indices: industrial, transportation, utility and financial; indices announced by the National Association of Securities Dealers using NASDAQ system: composite, industrial, insurance and banks; American Stock Exchange (Amex) Market Value Index, which includes almost all 800 shares in demand at this stock market. For smaller companies, there is Russell 2000.

20.9.1 S&P 500 Composite Stock Price Index

In 1923, Standard & Poor's Corporation has declared market index based on 233 shares with 26 sub-indices. In 1957, it has been decided to increase number of shares at 500.

S&P index is a base index that is quotient of total market value of 500 chosen companies at exact day, with total market value of chosen companies in base period (1941–43). Total market value in base period has been replaced by 10, in other words 1941–43 = 10.

In practice, for daily calculating, S&P index value is being obtained by dividing of total market value of 500 chosen companies by divisor. Divisor replaces value in base period and enables index value comparing during the time.

$$\text{Index value} = \frac{\text{Market value of 500 companies}}{\text{Last index divisor}}$$

Index and index's divisor are calculated in the following way:

First, total market value of 500 chosen companies is to be calculated for base period: Number of issued shares is to be multiplied by its price, and all 500 values are to be added.

In addition, the obtained market value in base period is to be indexed so that if market value is, for example, \$100,000,000 and if it is considered that worth 10 index's points, it is obtained \$100,000,000 = 10.

Next step is to calculate index's divisor for base period. It is obtained from next equation:

$$\text{Index value} = \frac{\text{Market value}}{\text{Index's divisor}}$$

where

$$\text{Index's divisor} = \frac{\text{Market value}}{\text{Index value}}$$

which means

$$\frac{100{,}000{,}000}{10} = 10{,}000{,}000$$

The index's divisor obtained in this way enables index value calculation for next day by dividing market value for that day by index's divisor. For example, if total market value of 500 chosen companies in next day has grown at \$110,000,000, then

$$\text{S\&P Index} = \frac{110{,}000{,}000}{10{,}000{,}000} = 11$$

20.9.2 Dow Jones Average

All the Dow Jones Averages are calculated in the same way, so that Dow Jones Averages calculation will be explained on DJIA example. All the Dow Jones Averages are calculated in the same way. Follow the example as given in Dow Jones Industrial Average (DJIA) section to understand the method of computing such averages. The base value for DJIA is calculated considering shares of the most representative companies in the USA market.

$$\text{DJIA} = \frac{\sum_{i=1}^{30} P_{it}}{d}$$

where P_{it} is the price of share i in the time t, and d is the divisor.

Defining divisor value is dictated by requirement that taking measures by companies, that do reflect on shares' price, like for example, stock split, are allowed to exert influence on index value. The new divisor's equation is:

$$\text{New divisor} = \text{Current divisor} \cdot \frac{\text{Total adapted market value}}{\text{Total not adapted market value}}$$

The total not adapted market value is obtained by adding the final price of 30 shares. The total adapted market value is obtained when the final price of a share has been replaced by new price.

20.10 Indices of Fast-growing Markets

In the less-developed markets, there are fewer companies. Therefore, the index envelops all or the most of shares. Under such circumstances, the index serves for trends at share market identification and for following dynamics of shares market development.

20.10.1 Dow Jones Industrial Average

To show how the DJIA is calculated, let us use a snapshot of the stock values for 30 companies used to calculate the DJIA. After closing hours on Friday, 11 April 2008, the DJIA is calculated as 12325.42. Summing all the stock values at the same moment results the following:

$$80.35 + 36.11 + 45.06 + 45.56 + 38.20 + 37.69 + 78.43 + 75.71 + 89.60 + 23.71 + 61.33 + 49.64 + 89.55 + 36.75 + 20.17 + 46.57 + 28.38 + 22.08 + 118.78 + 66.33 + 43.86 + 55.85 + 41.71 + 29.11 + 20.92 + 70.18 + 71.85 + 35.83 + 54.66 + 31.35 = 1{,}545.32$$

So how do you get from 1,545 to 12,325? The answer comes by using the official industrial averages divisor. As of this very moment, the divisor is 0.122834016. Now we can calculate things, though the result might surprise you:

$$1{,}545.32/0.122834016 = 12{,}580.55$$

So why is there a difference? Because of what is called after-hours trading. The stock values we used for this math were the closing values of those stocks, but after the stock exchange was closed, the stocks continue to be traded. The result was that the market went down 256.56 points. Now, let us try this math again:

$$(1{,}545.32/0.122834016) - 256.56 = 12{,}323.99$$

Truth be told, at this point, I do not really understand why this is not an exact calculation, but it is pretty darn close so it will certainly illustrate what you are trying to calculate. The key is that the general calculation for the DJIA is:

Sum of all stock values in the index/official DJ divisor.

20.10.2 Australia Stock Exchange Price Index

Australia Stock Exchange (ASX) Price Index envelops about 300 companies that are in demand at ASX. The chosen companies' represent 29 economic sectors that are 2/3 market capitalization at ASX.

$$\text{Current index value} = \text{Yesterday's index value} \cdot \frac{\text{Sum of current closing price}}{\text{Adapted sum of yesterday's closing price}}$$

20.10.3 Korea Composite Stock Price Index

The Korea Composite Stock Price Index (KCSPI) envelops all 683 companies that are in demand at Korea Stock Exchange. The KCSPI computing formula is

$$\text{KCSPI} = \frac{\text{Current total market value}}{\text{Base total market value}} \times 100$$

20.10.4 India

SENSEX: SENSEX is associated with BSE and has been calculated since 1986. Initially, it was calculated based on total market capitalization methodology, and the methodology was changed in 2003 to free-float market capitalization. Hence, these days, the SENSEX is based on the free-float market cap of 30 SENSEX stocks traded on the BSE relative to the base value which is 100 (1978–79), and it is calculated for every 15 seconds.

Free-float market capitalization is defined as the value of all the shares available for public trading excluding the promoter equity, holdings through FDI route, holdings by private corporate, and holdings by employee welfare funds.

Why is Free Float Market Cap?

1. It depicts the market more rationally.
2. It removes undue influence of government or promoter shareholding, thereby giving the equal opportunity for companies to be in SENSEX.
3. Almost all the indices all over the world are calculated by this methodology.
4. It gives fund managers more authentic information for benchmark comparisons.

How the SENSEX 30 stocks are selected?

1. Listing history
2. Trading frequency
3. Rank based on the market cap (should be among top 100)
4. Market capitalization weight
5. Industry/sector they belong
6. Historical record

How SENSEX is calculated?

The formula used to calculate the value of SENSEX is

$$\text{SENSEX} = \sum_{i=1}^{30} \text{Free float market cap}_i \times \text{Index factor}$$

where $$\text{Index factor} = \frac{100}{\text{Market cap value in 1978–79}}$$

For example, assume that SENSEX has only two stocks, namely, SBI and Reliance. Total shares in SBI are 500, out of which 200 are held by government and only 300 are available for public trading. Reliance has 1,000 shares, out of which 500 are held by promoters and 500 are available for public trading. Assume that price of SBI stock is ₹100 and Reliance is ₹200. Then free-floating market cap of these two companies will be

300 shares @ ₹100 + 500 shares @ ₹200 = ₹130,000

Assume that market cap during the year 1978–79 was ₹25,000.

Then, $\text{SENSEX} = 130{,}000 \times \dfrac{100}{25{,}000} = 130{,}000 \times 0.004 = 520.$

The methodology in the example is exactly followed to calculate the value of SENSEX, only difference being the inclusion of 30 stocks.

NIFTY: NIFTY is associated with NSE, and it is also calculated by the same methodology with two key differences:

1. Base year is 1995, and base value is 1,000.
2. NIFTY is calculated based on 50 stocks.

SENSEX EPS: We all know that EPS is calculated for all the companies to show how much net profit a company generates for every outstanding share. Likewise, EPS is calculated for SENSEX as well so that we can have a better understanding about the market.

Let us see how it is calculated. All you need for this calculation is EPS of all the 30 SENSEX stocks along with their free-float adjustment factor.

Take the HDFC Bank for the example. The present EPS for HDFC Bank is ₹44. The free-float adjustment factor is 0.85, which just means that 85% of total outstanding shares are held by non-promoters and are available in the market for trade.

Multiply the EPS with the adjustment factor, which is ₹37.4 (₹44 × 0.85). This ₹37.4 is the contribution of HDFC Bank towards SENSEX EPS. Likewise, we need to calculate for all 30 stocks and add these together to get the final value of SENSEX EPS, which should be somewhere around ₹900 these days. We can calculate NIFTY EPS in the same manner.

SENSEX PE: PE ratio is calculated for companies that show what the investors are ready to pay for every rupee of earnings. If we calculate the same thing by taking into account all the 30 SENSEX stocks, then we will end up with SENSEX PE.

How to calculate? Consider the same HDFC Bank. Multiply the market price of HDFC Bank with the number of shares outstanding, which should be equal to market capitalization.

$$\text{Market capitalization} = \text{Share price} \times \text{Total shares.}$$

Then, calculate the net profit by multiplying the EPS with total shares. Do this for all the 30 SENSEX stocks:

$$\text{SENSEX PE} = \frac{\text{Sum of market capitalization of 30 SENSEX stocks}}{\text{Sum of net profit of all the SENSEX 30 stocks}}$$

At present, SENSEX PE is around 12 and it provides useful information about SENSEX. Analysts predict the level of SENSEX using this number only. Suppose SENSEX PE is 12 and SENSEX EPS is 900, then the index is 10,800. For example, if you believe, earnings of the companies would grow at 10% this year, then apply the same growth rate to both SENSEX PE and SENSEX EPS to predict the SENSEX next year which would be 13 × 1,000 = 13,000.

20.11 Signals from the Stock Index

The Index finds uses in various fields, starting from economic research to helping investors choose appropriate portfolio for investment. For example, the index funds are funds that passively invest in the market, that is, the portfolio returns of the index funds is same as that of the Index.

Since the Index is an indicator of the overall mood of the investors in the secondary market, it helps a company answer questions like: Is it the right time to take out an IPO, how to price the issue and so on.

It acts as a signal to the government of the 'feel-good' factor prevailing in the economy. As much as the finance ministry may want to ignore it, the performance of the stock market right after the introduction of the budget gives an immediate feedback to the finance minister about the acceptability of the budget.

However, the market index is a double-edged sword. Because the index is influenced by expectations of the future performance of the stocks, it leads to a self-fulfilling prophecy. Suppose an investor thinks that the stock of the company is going to go down and this feeling prevails across the market, then everyone would want to get out of the company's stock. This will automatically lead to the stock prices crashing.

The stock index can often also act as a trigger to herd mentality. Any downturn in the market would be reinforced by the collective action of the investors to hedge against any losses and get out of the market. This would further depress the market.

This herd mentality is often used to the advantage of speculators. The speculator buys long, thus creating waves in the market that the stock he is investing in is 'hot'. Thus, everyone would follow suit, giving the speculator a good short-term profit margin.

The stock index is often more a representation of investors' perceptions (noise element) rather than real news. The dot-com bubble of 2000 is a case in point. There was a rush of investment in anything even remotely connected with IT, driving up the stock prices way above what they should have been according to their P/E ratios.

Thus, it can be seen that though the index is a popular investor's guide, it is riddled with imperfections that can often confuse rather than help.

The index popularly used in India is the NSE CNX Nifty. There are processes afoot to reduce the pure noise element and speculative margin of the index. The basic problem arises due to imperfect information reflected by the inclusion of illiquid stocks in the calculation of the index. Illiquid stock is one which is not actively traded in the market or has been lying dormant for a long time. Inclusion of such stocks leads to problems of stale prices, bid–ask bounce and ease in manipulation.

Bid–ask bounce: Illiquid stocks have a wide bid–ask spread. Thus, even when no news is breaking, when a stock price is not changing, the 'bid–ask bounce' is about prices bouncing up and down between bid and ask. Such changes are spurious in nature.

Stale prices: A stock index is supposed to represent the state of the stock market at the closing time (3:30 pm in NSE) on a particular day. However, the last traded price of an illiquid stock (if included in the index) may be even a week old, thus distorting the index.

Hence, to make an index useful, there has to be continuous evaluation of the stocks listed, and any stock that remains inactive for a period of time should be de-listed or removed from the index. A prudent investor is one who exercises caution while interpreting the market index, taking into account all its inconsistencies.

Multiple Choice Questions

1. A single figure that sums up the overall performance of the market on a daily basis is the ______
   a. Stock index b. Price index c. Commodity index d. None
2. The world's first Stock Exchange was in ______
   a. Antwerp, Belgium b. London c. Paris d. New York
3. A ______ stock market index includes companies without regard for where they are domiciled or traded.
   a. National b. Global c. Regional d. None
4. An ______ index represents the performance of the stock market of a given nation and by proxy, reflects investor sentiment on the state of its economy.
   a. National b. Global c. Regional d. None
5. Which one of the following is an example of global stock market index?
   a. American S&P 500
   b. British FTSE 100
   b. Japanese Nikkei 225
   d. S&P Global 100
6. In which type of weight, the price of each component stock is the only consideration when determining the value of the index?
   a. Price-weighted index
   b. Market-value weighted or capitalization-weighted index
   c. Modified capitalization-weighted index
   d. Float-adjusted weighting
7. Which one of the following is not an example of price-weighted index?
   a. Dow Jones Industrial Average
   b. NYSE ARCA Tech 100 Index
   c. Amex Major Market Index
   d. Hang Seng Index
8. Which one of the following is not an active determinant of stock index?
   a. Market capitalization
   b. Diversification
   c. Optimum size
   d. Capital and dividend gain
9. NIFTY is calculated based on how many stocks?
   a. 100 b. 50 c. 150 d. 200
10. Which one of the following does not fall within the group of standard or value pondered market indices?
    a. Standard & Poor's 500 composite index
    b. NYSE indices
    c. SENSEX
    d. NASDAQ indices

Discussion Questions

1. What are the different types of indices?
2. What do you understand by index versions?
3. What are different styles of weighing? Make a comparative discussion.
4. Make a listing of determinants of stock index.
5. What are the purposes of market indices?
6. Write a short note on:
    a. U.S. market indices.
    b. Indices of fast-growing markets.
7. Write a short note on signals from the stock index.

References

Arnott, R.D., J. Hsu, and P. Moore. 2005. 'Fundamental Indexation'. *Financial Analysts Journal,* 60(2): 83–99.

Broby, D.P. 2007. *A Guide to Equity Index Construction.* London: Risk Books.

Fernholz, R., R. Garvy, and J. Hannon. 1998. 'Diversity-weighted Indexing'. *Journal of Portfolio Management,* 24(2): 74–82.

Haugen, R.A., and N.L. Baker. 1991. 'The Efficient Market Inefficiency of Capitalization-weighted Stock Portfolios'. *Journal of Portfolio Management,* 17(3): 35–40.

Time Value Tables

Future Value Interest Factor of $1 per Period at i% for n Periods, FVIF(i,n)

Period	*1%*	*2%*	*3%*	*4%*	*5%*	*6%*	*7%*	*8%*	*9%*	*10%*	*11%*	*12%*	*13%*	*14%*	*15%*	*16%*	*17%*	*18%*	*19%*	*20%*
1	1.010	1.020	1.030	1.040	1.050	1.060	1.070	1.080	1.090	1.100	1.110	1.120	1.130	1.140	1.150	1.160	1.170	1.180	1.190	1.200
2	1.020	1.040	1.061	1.082	1.103	1.124	1.145	1.166	1.188	1.210	1.232	1.254	1.277	1.300	1.323	1.346	1.369	1.392	1.416	1.440
3	1.030	1.061	1.093	1.125	1.158	1.191	1.225	1.260	1.295	1.331	1.368	1.405	1.443	1.482	1.521	1.561	1.602	1.643	1.685	1.728
4	1.041	1.082	1.126	1.170	1.216	1.262	1.311	1.360	1.412	1.464	1.518	1.574	1.630	1.689	1.749	1.811	1.874	1.939	2.005	2.074
5	1.051	1.104	1.159	1.217	1.276	1.338	1.403	1.469	1.539	1.611	1.685	1.762	1.842	1.925	2.011	2.100	2.192	2.288	2.386	2.488
6	1.062	1.126	1.194	1.265	1.340	1.419	1.501	1.587	1.677	1.772	1.870	1.974	2.082	2.195	2.313	2.436	2.565	2.700	2.840	2.986
7	1.072	1.149	1.230	1.316	1.407	1.504	1.606	1.714	1.828	1.949	2.076	2.211	2.353	2.502	2.660	2.826	3.001	3.185	3.379	3.583
8	1.083	1.172	1.267	1.369	1.477	1.594	1.718	1.851	1.993	2.144	2.305	2.476	2.658	2.853	3.059	3.278	3.511	3.759	4.021	4.300
9	1.094	1.195	1.305	1.423	1.551	1.689	1.838	1.999	2.172	2.358	2.558	2.773	3.004	3.252	3.518	3.803	4.108	4.435	4.785	5.160
10	1.105	1.219	1.344	1.480	1.629	1.791	1.967	2.159	2.367	2.594	2.839	3.106	3.395	3.707	4.046	4.411	4.807	5.234	5.695	6.192
11	1.116	1.243	1.384	1.539	1.710	1.898	2.105	2.332	2.580	2.853	3.152	3.479	3.836	4.226	4.652	5.117	5.624	6.176	6.777	7.430
12	1.127	1.268	1.426	1.601	1.796	2.012	2.252	2.518	2.813	3.138	3.498	3.896	4.335	4.818	5.350	5.936	6.580	7.288	8.064	8.916
13	1.138	1.294	1.469	1.665	1.886	2.133	2.410	2.720	3.066	3.452	3.883	4.363	4.898	5.492	6.153	6.886	7.699	8.599	9.596	10.699
14	1.149	1.319	1.513	1.732	1.980	2.261	2.579	2.937	3.342	3.797	4.310	4.887	5.535	6.261	7.076	7.988	9.007	10.147	11.420	12.839
15	1.161	1.346	1.558	1.801	2.079	2.397	2.759	3.172	3.642	4.177	4.785	5.474	6.254	7.138	8.137	9.266	10.539	11.974	13.590	15.407
16	1.173	1.373	1.605	1.873	2.183	2.540	2.952	3.426	3.970	4.595	5.311	6.130	7.067	8.137	9.358	10.748	12.330	14.129	16.172	18.488
17	1.184	1.400	1.653	1.948	2.292	2.693	3.159	3.700	4.328	5.054	5.895	6.866	7.986	9.276	10.761	12.468	14.426	16.672	19.244	22.186
18	1.196	1.428	1.702	2.026	2.407	2.854	3.380	3.996	4.717	5.560	6.544	7.690	9.024	10.575	12.375	14.463	16.879	19.673	22.901	26.623
19	1.208	1.457	1.754	2.107	2.527	3.026	3.617	4.316	5.142	6.116	7.263	8.613	10.197	12.056	14.232	16.777	19.748	23.214	27.252	31.948
20	1.220	1.486	1.806	2.191	2.653	3.207	3.870	4.661	5.604	6.727	8.062	9.646	11.523	13.743	16.367	19.461	23.106	27.393	32.429	38.338
25	1.282	1.641	2.094	2.666	3.386	4.292	5.427	6.848	8.623	10.835	13.585	17.000	21.231	26.462	32.919	40.874	50.658	62.669	77.388	95.396
30	1.348	1.811	2.427	3.243	4.322	5.743	7.612	10.063	13.268	17.449	22.892	29.960	39.116	50.950	66.212	85.850	111.065	143.371	184.675	237.376
35	1.417	2.000	2.814	3.946	5.516	7.686	10.677	14.785	20.414	28.102	38.575	52.800	72.069	98.100	133.176	180.314	243.503	327.997	440.701	590.668
40	1.489	2.208	3.262	4.801	7.040	10.286	14.974	21.725	31.409	45.259	65.001	93.051	132.782	188.884	267.864	378.721	533.869	750.378	1,051.668	1,469.772
50	1.645	2.692	4.384	7.107	11.467	18.420	29.457	46.902	74.358	117.391	184.565	289.002	450.736	700.233	1,083.657	1,670.704	2,566.215	3,927.357	5,988.914	9,100.438

Present Value Interest Factor of $1 per Period at i% for n Periods, PVIF(i,n)

Period	1%	2%	3%	4%	5%	6%	7%	8%	9%	10%	11%	12%	13%	14%	15%	16%	17%	18%	19%	20%
1	0.990	0.980	0.971	0.962	0.952	0.943	0.935	0.926	0.917	0.909	0.901	0.893	0.885	0.877	0.870	0.862	0.855	0.847	0.840	0.833
2	0.980	0.961	0.943	0.925	0.907	0.890	0.873	0.857	0.842	0.826	0.812	0.797	0.783	0.769	0.756	0.743	0.731	0.718	0.706	0.694
3	0.971	0.942	0.915	0.889	0.864	0.840	0.816	0.794	0.772	0.751	0.731	0.712	0.693	0.675	0.658	0.641	0.624	0.609	0.593	0.579
4	0.961	0.924	0.888	0.855	0.823	0.792	0.763	0.735	0.708	0.683	0.659	0.636	0.613	0.592	0.572	0.552	0.534	0.516	0.499	0.482
5	0.951	0.906	0.863	0.822	0.784	0.747	0.713	0.681	0.650	0.621	0.593	0.567	0.543	0.519	0.497	0.476	0.456	0.437	0.419	0.402
6	0.942	0.888	0.837	0.790	0.746	0.705	0.666	0.630	0.596	0.564	0.535	0.507	0.480	0.456	0.432	0.410	0.390	0.370	0.352	0.335
7	0.933	0.871	0.813	0.760	0.711	0.665	0.623	0.583	0.547	0.513	0.482	0.452	0.425	0.400	0.376	0.354	0.333	0.314	0.296	0.279
8	0.923	0.853	0.789	0.731	0.677	0.627	0.582	0.540	0.502	0.467	0.434	0.404	0.376	0.351	0.327	0.305	0.285	0.266	0.249	0.233
9	0.914	0.837	0.766	0.703	0.645	0.592	0.544	0.500	0.460	0.424	0.391	0.361	0.333	0.308	0.284	0.263	0.243	0.225	0.209	0.194
10	0.905	0.820	0.744	0.676	0.614	0.558	0.508	0.463	0.422	0.386	0.352	0.322	0.295	0.270	0.247	0.227	0.208	0.191	0.176	0.162
11	0.896	0.804	0.722	0.650	0.585	0.527	0.475	0.429	0.388	0.350	0.317	0.287	0.261	0.237	0.215	0.195	0.178	0.162	0.148	0.135
12	0.887	0.788	0.701	0.625	0.557	0.497	0.444	0.397	0.356	0.319	0.286	0.257	0.231	0.208	0.187	0.168	0.152	0.137	0.124	0.112
13	0.879	0.773	0.681	0.601	0.530	0.469	0.415	0.368	0.326	0.290	0.258	0.229	0.204	0.182	0.163	0.145	0.130	0.116	0.104	0.093
14	0.870	0.758	0.661	0.577	0.505	0.442	0.388	0.340	0.299	0.263	0.232	0.205	0.181	0.160	0.141	0.125	0.111	0.099	0.088	0.078
15	0.861	0.743	0.642	0.555	0.481	0.417	0.362	0.315	0.275	0.239	0.209	0.183	0.160	0.140	0.123	0.108	0.095	0.084	0.074	0.065
16	0.853	0.728	0.623	0.534	0.458	0.394	0.339	0.292	0.252	0.218	0.188	0.163	0.141	0.123	0.107	0.093	0.081	0.071	0.062	0.054
17	0.844	0.714	0.605	0.513	0.436	0.371	0.317	0.270	0.231	0.198	0.170	0.146	0.125	0.108	0.093	0.080	0.069	0.060	0.052	0.045
18	0.836	0.700	0.587	0.494	0.416	0.350	0.296	0.250	0.212	0.180	0.153	0.130	0.111	0.095	0.081	0.069	0.059	0.051	0.044	0.038
19	0.828	0.686	0.570	0.475	0.396	0.331	0.277	0.232	0.194	0.164	0.138	0.116	0.098	0.083	0.070	0.060	0.051	0.043	0.037	0.031
20	0.820	0.673	0.554	0.456	0.377	0.312	0.258	0.215	0.178	0.149	0.124	0.104	0.087	0.073	0.061	0.051	0.043	0.037	0.031	0.026
25	0.780	0.610	0.478	0.375	0.295	0.233	0.184	0.146	0.116	0.092	0.074	0.059	0.047	0.038	0.030	0.024	0.020	0.016	0.013	0.010
30	0.742	0.552	0.412	0.308	0.231	0.174	0.131	0.099	0.075	0.057	0.044	0.033	0.026	0.020	0.015	0.012	0.009	0.007	0.005	0.004
35	0.706	0.500	0.355	0.253	0.181	0.130	0.094	0.068	0.049	0.036	0.026	0.019	0.014	0.010	0.008	0.006	0.004	0.003	0.002	0.002
40	0.672	0.453	0.307	0.208	0.142	0.097	0.067	0.046	0.032	0.022	0.015	0.011	0.008	0.005	0.004	0.003	0.002	0.001	0.001	0.001
50	0.608	0.372	0.228	0.141	0.087	0.054	0.034	0.021	0.013	0.009	0.005	0.003	0.002	0.001	0.001	0.001	0.000	0.000	0.000	0.000

Future Value Interest Factor of an Ordinary Annuity of $1 per Period at i% for n Periods, FVIFA(i,n)

Period	1%	2%	3%	4%	5%	6%	7%	8%	9%	10%	11%	12%	13%	14%	15%	16%	17%	18%	19%	20%
1	1.000	1.000	1.000	1.000	1.000	1.000	1.000	1.000	1.000	1.000	1.000	1.000	1.000	1.000	1.000	1.000	1.000	1.000	1.000	1.000
2	2.010	2.020	2.030	2.040	2.050	2.060	2.070	2.080	2.090	2.100	2.110	2.120	2.130	2.140	2.150	2.160	2.170	2.180	2.190	2.200
3	3.030	3.060	3.091	3.122	3.153	3.184	3.215	3.246	3.278	3.310	3.342	3.374	3.407	3.440	3.473	3.506	3.539	3.572	3.606	3.640
4	4.060	4.122	4.184	4.246	4.310	4.375	4.440	4.506	4.573	4.641	4.710	4.779	4.850	4.921	4.993	5.066	5.141	5.215	5.291	5.368
5	5.101	5.204	5.309	5.416	5.526	5.637	5.751	5.867	5.985	6.105	6.228	6.353	6.480	6.610	6.742	6.877	7.014	7.154	7.297	7.442
6	6.152	6.308	6.468	6.633	6.802	6.975	7.153	7.336	7.523	7.716	7.913	8.115	8.323	8.536	8.754	8.977	9.207	9.442	9.683	9.930
7	7.214	7.434	7.662	7.898	8.142	8.394	8.654	8.923	9.200	9.487	9.783	10.089	10.405	10.730	11.067	11.414	11.772	12.142	12.523	12.916
8	8.286	8.583	8.892	9.214	9.549	9.897	10.260	10.637	11.028	11.436	11.859	12.300	12.757	13.233	13.727	14.240	14.773	15.327	15.902	16.499
9	9.369	9.755	10.159	10.583	11.027	11.491	11.978	12.488	13.021	13.579	14.164	14.776	15.416	16.085	16.786	17.519	18.285	19.086	19.923	20.799
10	10.462	10.950	11.464	12.006	12.578	13.181	13.816	14.487	15.193	15.937	16.722	17.549	18.420	19.337	20.304	21.321	22.393	23.521	24.709	25.959
11	11.567	12.169	12.808	13.486	14.207	14.972	15.784	16.645	17.560	18.531	19.561	20.655	21.814	23.045	24.349	25.733	27.200	28.755	30.404	32.150
12	12.683	13.412	14.192	15.026	15.917	16.870	17.888	18.977	20.141	21.384	22.713	24.133	25.650	27.271	29.002	30.850	32.824	34.931	37.180	39.581
13	13.809	14.680	15.618	16.627	17.713	18.882	20.141	21.495	22.953	24.523	26.212	28.029	29.985	32.089	34.352	36.786	39.404	42.219	45.244	48.497
14	14.947	15.974	17.086	18.292	19.599	21.015	22.550	24.215	26.019	27.975	30.095	32.393	34.883	37.581	40.505	43.672	47.103	50.818	54.841	59.196
15	16.097	17.293	18.599	20.024	21.579	23.276	25.129	27.152	29.361	31.772	34.405	37.280	40.417	43.842	47.580	51.660	56.110	60.965	66.261	72.035
16	17.258	18.639	20.157	21.825	23.657	25.673	27.888	30.324	33.003	35.950	39.190	42.753	46.672	50.980	55.717	60.925	66.649	72.939	79.850	87.442
17	18.430	20.012	21.762	23.698	25.840	28.213	30.840	33.750	36.974	40.545	44.501	48.884	53.739	59.118	65.075	71.673	78.979	87.068	96.022	105.93
18	19.615	21.412	23.414	25.645	28.132	30.906	33.999	37.450	41.301	45.599	50.396	55.750	61.725	68.394	75.836	84.141	93.406	103.74	115.27	128.12
19	20.811	22.841	25.117	27.671	30.539	33.760	37.379	41.446	46.018	51.159	56.939	63.440	70.749	78.969	88.212	98.603	110.28	123.41	138.17	154.74
20	22.019	24.297	26.870	29.778	33.066	36.786	40.995	45.762	51.160	57.275	64.203	72.052	80.947	91.025	102.44	115.38	130.03	146.63	165.42	186.69
25	28.243	32.030	36.459	41.646	47.727	54.865	63.249	73.106	84.701	98.347	114.41	133.33	155.62	181.87	212.79	249.21	292.10	342.60	402.04	471.98
30	34.785	40.568	47.575	56.085	66.439	79.058	94.461	113.28	136.31	164.49	199.02	241.33	293.20	356.79	434.75	530.31	647.44	790.95	966.71	1,181.9
35	41.660	49.994	60.462	73.652	90.320	111.43	138.24	172.32	215.71	271.02	341.59	431.66	546.68	693.57	881.17	1,120.7	1,426.5	1,816.7	2,314.2	2,948.3
40	48.886	60.402	75.401	95.026	120.80	154.76	199.64	259.06	337.88	442.59	581.83	767.09	1,013.7	1,342.0	1,779.1	2,360.8	3,134.5	4,163.2	5,529.8	7,343.9
50	64.463	84.579	112.80	152.67	209.35	290.34	406.53	573.77	815.08	1,163.9	1,668.8	2,400.0	3,459.5	4,994.5	7,217.7	10,436	15,090	21,813	31,515	45,497

Present Value Interest Factor of an (Ordinary) Annuity of $1 per Period at i% for n Periods, PVIFA(i,n)

Period	1%	2%	3%	4%	5%	6%	7%	8%	9%	10%	11%	12%	13%	14%	15%	16%	17%	18%	19%	20%
1	0.990	0.980	0.971	0.962	0.952	0.943	0.935	0.926	0.917	0.909	0.901	0.893	0.885	0.877	0.870	0.862	0.855	0.847	0.840	0.833
2	1.970	1.942	1.913	1.886	1.859	1.833	1.808	1.783	1.759	1.736	1.713	1.690	1.668	1.647	1.626	1.605	1.585	1.566	1.547	1.528
3	2.941	2.884	2.829	2.775	2.723	2.673	2.624	2.577	2.531	2.487	2.444	2.402	2.361	2.322	2.283	2.246	2.210	2.174	2.140	2.106
4	3.902	3.808	3.717	3.630	3.546	3.465	3.387	3.312	3.240	3.170	3.102	3.037	2.974	2.914	2.855	2.798	2.743	2.690	2.639	2.589
5	4.853	4.713	4.580	4.452	4.329	4.212	4.100	3.993	3.890	3.791	3.696	3.605	3.517	3.433	3.352	3.274	3.199	3.127	3.058	2.991
6	5.795	5.601	5.417	5.242	5.076	4.917	4.767	4.623	4.486	4.355	4.231	4.111	3.998	3.889	3.784	3.685	3.589	3.498	3.410	3.326
7	6.728	6.472	6.230	6.002	5.786	5.582	5.389	5.206	5.033	4.868	4.712	4.564	4.423	4.288	4.160	4.039	3.922	3.812	3.706	3.605
8	7.652	7.325	7.020	6.733	6.463	6.210	5.971	5.747	5.535	5.335	5.146	4.968	4.799	4.639	4.487	4.344	4.207	4.078	3.954	3.837
9	8.566	8.162	7.786	7.435	7.108	6.802	6.515	6.247	5.995	5.759	5.537	5.328	5.132	4.946	4.772	4.607	4.451	4.303	4.163	4.031
10	9.471	8.983	8.530	8.111	7.722	7.360	7.024	6.710	6.418	6.145	5.889	5.650	5.426	5.216	5.019	4.833	4.659	4.494	4.339	4.192
11	10.368	9.787	9.253	8.760	8.306	7.887	7.499	7.139	6.805	6.495	6.207	5.938	5.687	5.453	5.234	5.029	4.836	4.656	4.486	4.327
12	11.255	10.575	9.954	9.385	8.863	8.384	7.943	7.536	7.161	6.814	6.492	6.194	5.918	5.660	5.421	5.197	4.988	4.793	4.611	4.439
13	12.134	11.348	10.635	9.986	9.394	8.853	8.358	7.904	7.487	7.103	6.750	6.424	6.122	5.842	5.583	5.342	5.118	4.910	4.715	4.533
14	13.004	12.106	11.296	10.563	9.899	9.295	8.745	8.244	7.786	7.367	6.982	6.628	6.302	6.002	5.724	5.468	5.229	5.008	4.802	4.611
15	13.865	12.849	11.938	11.118	10.380	9.712	9.108	8.559	8.061	7.606	7.191	6.811	6.462	6.142	5.847	5.575	5.324	5.092	4.876	4.675
16	14.718	13.578	12.561	11.652	10.838	10.106	9.447	8.851	8.313	7.824	7.379	6.974	6.604	6.265	5.954	5.668	5.405	5.162	4.938	4.730
17	15.562	14.292	13.166	12.166	11.274	10.477	9.763	9.122	8.544	8.022	7.549	7.120	6.729	6.373	6.047	5.749	5.475	5.222	4.990	4.775
18	16.398	14.992	13.754	12.659	11.690	10.828	10.059	9.372	8.756	8.201	7.702	7.250	6.840	6.467	6.128	5.818	5.534	5.273	5.033	4.812
19	17.226	15.678	14.324	13.134	12.085	11.158	10.336	9.604	8.950	8.365	7.839	7.366	6.938	6.550	6.198	5.877	5.584	5.316	5.070	4.843
20	18.046	16.351	14.877	13.590	12.462	11.470	10.594	9.818	9.129	8.514	7.963	7.469	7.025	6.623	6.259	5.929	5.628	5.353	5.101	4.870
25	22.023	19.523	17.413	15.622	14.094	12.783	11.654	10.675	9.823	9.077	8.422	7.843	7.330	6.873	6.464	6.097	5.766	5.467	5.195	4.948
30	25.808	22.396	19.600	17.292	15.372	13.765	12.409	11.258	10.274	9.427	8.694	8.055	7.496	7.003	6.566	6.177	5.829	5.517	5.235	4.979
35	29.409	24.999	21.487	18.665	16.374	14.498	12.948	11.655	10.567	9.644	8.855	8.176	7.586	7.070	6.617	6.215	5.858	5.539	5.251	4.992
40	32.835	27.355	23.115	19.793	17.159	15.046	13.332	11.925	10.757	9.779	8.951	8.244	7.634	7.105	6.642	6.233	5.871	5.548	5.258	4.997
50	39.196	31.424	25.730	21.482	18.256	15.762	13.801	12.233	10.962	9.915	9.042	8.304	7.675	7.133	6.661	6.246	5.880	5.554	5.262	4.999

Index

Answer Key to Multiple Choice Questions

Chapter 1									
1. c	2. a	3. d	4. b	5. a	6. c	7. b	8. d	9. c	10. d
Chapter 2									
1. d	2. d	3. a	4. c	5. c	6. b	7. a	8. d	9. c	10. b
Chapter 3									
1. c	2. c	3. d	4. b	5. d	6. c	7. b	8. a	9. b	10. a
Chapter 4									
1. d	2. c	3. c	4. c	5. d	6. d	7. a	8. a	9. c	10. a
Chapter 5									
1. b	2. b	3. a	4. a	5. d	6. b	7. c	8. a	9. b	10. b
Chapter 6									
1. b	2. c	3. b	4. c	5. e	6. b	7. c	8. c	9. e	10. a
11. d	12. a								
Chapter 7									
1. a	2. a	3. d	4. c	5. b	6. d	7. a	8. b	9. e	10. a
11. d	12. c								
Chapter 8									
1. d	2. a	3. c	4. b	5. d	6. a	7. b	8. c	9. d	10. c
Chapter 9									
1. a	2. c	3. a	4. d	5. d	6. d	7. b	8. c	9. d	10. b
Chapter 10									
1. b	2. d	3. c	4. a	5. c	6. a	7. a	8. b	9. d	
Chapter 11									
1. c	2. d	3. b	4. a	5. b	6. b	7. a	8. c	9. a	10. c
Chapter 12									
1. b	2. c	3. d	4. b	5. d	6. c	7. c	8. c	9. a	10. d
Chapter 13									
1. a	2. c	3. b	4. a	5. a	6. b	7. d	8. c	9. d	10. a
Chapter 14									
1. a	2. b	3. a	4. d	5. a	6. c	7. d	8. b	9. a	10. c
Chapter 15									
1. b	2. a	3. c	4. b	5. c	6. a	7. a	8. b	9. c	10. b

Chapter 16									
1. b	2. c	3. a	4. b	5. a	6. b	7. b	8. c	9. d	10. d
Chapter 17									
1. b	2. a	3. c	4. a	5. d	6. a	7. d	8. d	9. b	10. b
Chapter 18									
1. d	2. b	3. b	4. c	5. c	6. a	7. c	8. c	9. d	10. b
Chapter 19									
1. b	2. c	3. c	4. a	5. b	6. c	7. c	8. a	9. c	10. d
Chapter 20									
1. a	2. a	3. b	4. a	5. d	6. a	7. d	8. d	9. b	10. c